5th International Workshop on Semantic Evaluation 2010

(SemEval 2010)

Held at ACL 2010

Uppsala, Sweden
15-16 July 2010

ISBN: 978-1-61738-821-7

Printed from e-media with permission by:

Curran Associates, Inc.
57 Morehouse Lane
Red Hook, NY 12571

proceedings.com

Some format issues inherent in the e-media version may also appear in this print version.

Printed by Curran Associates, Inc. (2010)

Association for Computational Linguistics
209 N. Eighth Street
Stroudsburg, Pennsylvania 18360

Phone: 1-570-476-8006
Fax: 1-570-476-0860

acl@aclweb.org

Additional copies of this publication are available from:

Curran Associates, Inc.
57 Morehouse Lane
Red Hook, NY 12571 USA
Phone: 845-758-0400
Fax: 845-758-2634
Email: curran@proceedings.com
Web: www.proceedings.com

Preface

Welcome to SemEval 2010!

Thank you for offering so many different and intriguing semantic analysis tasks, and for creating so many great systems to solve them. We are very much looking forward to this workshop, and are curious to hear about your work.

– Katrin and Carlo.

Organizers:

Katrin Erk, University of Texas at Austin
Carlo Strapparava, ITC IRST

Program Committee:

Eneko Agirre	Timothy Baldwin	Marco Baroni
Chris Biemann	Chris Brew	Nicoletta Calzolari
Dmitriy Dligach	Phil Edmonds	Dan Gildea
Iris Hendrickx	Veronique Hoste	Nancy Ide
Elisabetta Jezek	Peng Jin	Adam Kilgarriff
Su Nam Kim	Ioannis Klapaftis	Dimitrios Kokkinakis
Anna Korhonen	Zornitsa Kozareva	Sadao Kurohashi
Els Lefever	Ken Litkowski	Oier Lopez de Lacalle
Suresh Manandha	Katja Markert	Lluis Marquez
Diana McCarthy	Saif Mohammad	Roser Morante
Preslav Nakov	Vivi Nastase	Hwee Tou Ng
Manabu Okumura	Martha Palmer	Ted Pedersen
Marco Pennacchiotti	Massimo Poesio	Valeria Quochi
German Rigau	Lorenza Romano	Anna Rumshisky
Josef Ruppenhofer	Emili Sapena	Kiyoaki Shirai
Ravi Sinha	Caroline Sporleder	Mark Stevenson
Stan Szpakowicz	Mariona Taule	Dan Tufis
Tony Veale	Marc Verhagen	Yannick Versley
Richard Wicentowski	Yunfang Wu	Dekai Wu
Nianwen Xue	Deniz Yuret	Diarmuid O Seaghdha

Table of Contents

Conference Program

Thursday, July 15, 2010

09:00–10:40 Task description papers

09:00–09:20 *SemEval-2010 Task 1: Coreference Resolution in Multiple Languages*
Marta Recasens, Lluís Màrquez, Emili Sapena, M. Antònia Martí, Mariona Taulé, Véronique Hoste, Massimo Poesio and Yannick Versley

09:20–09:40 *SemEval-2010 Task 2: Cross-Lingual Lexical Substitution*
Rada Mihalcea, Ravi Sinha and Diana McCarthy

09:40–10:00 *SemEval-2010 Task 3: Cross-Lingual Word Sense Disambiguation*
Els Lefever and Véronique Hoste

10:00–10:20 *SemEval-2010 Task 5 : Automatic Keyphrase Extraction from Scientific Articles*
Su Nam Kim, Olena Medelyan, Min-Yen Kan and Timothy Baldwin

10:20–10:40 *SemEval-2010 Task 7: Argument Selection and Coercion*
James Pustejovsky, Anna Rumshisky, Alex Plotnick, Elisabetta Jezek, Olga Batiukova and Valeria Quochi

11:00–12:40 Task description papers

11:00–11:20 *SemEval-2010 Task 8: Multi-Way Classification of Semantic Relations between Pairs of Nominals*
Iris Hendrickx, Su Nam Kim, Zornitsa Kozareva, Preslav Nakov, Diarmuid Ó Séaghdha, Sebastian Padó, Marco Pennacchiotti, Lorenza Romano and Stan Szpakowicz

11:20–11:40 *SemEval-2 Task 9: The Interpretation of Noun Compounds Using Paraphrasing Verbs and Prepositions*
Cristina Butnariu, Su Nam Kim, Preslav Nakov, Diarmuid Ó Séaghdha, Stan Szpakowicz and Tony Veale

11:40–12:00 *SemEval-2010 Task 10: Linking Events and Their Participants in Discourse*
Josef Ruppenhofer, Caroline Sporleder, Roser Morante, Collin Baker and Martha Palmer

12:00–12:20 *SemEval-2010 Task 12: Parser Evaluation Using Textual Entailments*
Deniz Yuret, Aydin Han and Zehra Turgut

12:20–12:40 *SemEval-2010 Task 13: TempEval-2*
Marc Verhagen, Roser Sauri, Tommaso Caselli and James Pustejovsky

Thursday, July 15, 2010 (continued)

14:00–15:20 Task description papers

14:00–14:20 *SemEval-2010 Task 14: Word Sense Induction & Disambiguation*
Suresh Manandhar, Ioannis Klapaftis, Dmitriy Dligach and Sameer Pradhan

14:20–14:40 *SemEval-2010 Task: Japanese WSD*
Manabu Okumura, Kiyoaki Shirai, Kanako Komiya and Hikaru Yokono

14:40–15:00 *SemEval-2010 Task 17: All-Words Word Sense Disambiguation on a Specific Domain*
Eneko Agirre, Oier Lopez de Lacalle, Christiane Fellbaum, Shu-Kai Hsieh, Maurizio Tesconi, Monica Monachini, Piek Vossen and Roxanne Segers

15:00–15:20 *SemEval-2010 Task 18: Disambiguating Sentiment Ambiguous Adjectives*
Yunfang Wu and Peng Jin

16:00–17:30 Task description posters

SemEval-2010 Task 11: Event Detection in Chinese News Sentences
Qiang Zhou

SemEval-2 Task 15: Infrequent Sense Identification for Mandarin Text to Speech Systems
Peng Jin and Yunfang Wu

16:00-17:30 Posters

RelaxCor: A Global Relaxation Labeling Approach to Coreference Resolution
Emili Sapena, Lluís Padró and Jordi Turmo

SUCRE: A Modular System for Coreference Resolution
Hamidreza Kobdani and Hinrich Schütze

UBIU: A Language-Independent System for Coreference Resolution
Desislava Zhekova and Sandra Kübler

Corry: A System for Coreference Resolution
Olga Uryupina

Thursday, July 15, 2010 (continued)

Thursday, July 15, 2010 (continued)

SJTULTLAB: Chunk Based Method for Keyphrase Extraction
Letian Wang and Fang Li

Likey: Unsupervised Language-Independent Keyphrase Extraction
Mari-Sanna Paukkeri and Timo Honkela

WINGNUS: Keyphrase Extraction Utilizing Document Logical Structure
Thuy Dung Nguyen and Minh-Thang Luong

KX: A Flexible System for Keyphrase eXtraction
Emanuele Pianta and Sara Tonelli

BUAP: An Unsupervised Approach to Automatic Keyphrase Extraction from Scientific Articles
Roberto Ortiz, David Pinto, Mireya Tovar and Héctor Jiménez-Salazar

UNPMC: Naive Approach to Extract Keyphrases from Scientific Articles
Jungyeul Park, Jong Gun Lee and Béatrice Daille

SEERLAB: A System for Extracting Keyphrases from Scholarly Documents
Pucktada Treeratpituk, Pradeep Teregowda, Jian Huang and C. Lee Giles

SZTERGAK : Feature Engineering for Keyphrase Extraction
Gábor Berend and Richárd Farkas

KP-Miner: Participation in SemEval-2
Samhaa R. El-Beltagy and Ahmed Rafea

UvT: The UvT Term Extraction System in the Keyphrase Extraction Task
Kalliopi Zervanou

UNITN: Part-Of-Speech Counting in Relation Extraction
Fabio Celli

FBK_NK: A WordNet-Based System for Multi-Way Classification of Semantic Relations
Matteo Negri and Milen Kouylekov

Thursday, July 15, 2010 (continued)

JU: A Supervised Approach to Identify Semantic Relations from Paired Nominals
Santanu Pal, Partha Pakray, Dipankar Das and Sivaji Bandyopadhyay

TUD: Semantic Relatedness for Relation Classification
György Szarvas and Iryna Gurevych

FBK-IRST: Semantic Relation Extraction Using Cyc
Kateryna Tymoshenko and Claudio Giuliano

ISTI@SemEval-2 Task 8: Boosting-Based Multiway Relation Classification
Andrea Esuli, Diego Marcheggiani and Fabrizio Sebastiani

ISI: Automatic Classification of Relations Between Nominals Using a Maximum Entropy Classifier
Stephen Tratz and Eduard Hovy

ECNU: Effective Semantic Relations Classification without Complicated Features or Multiple External Corpora
Yuan Chen, Man Lan, Jian Su, Zhi Min Zhou and Yu Xu

UCD-Goggle: A Hybrid System for Noun Compound Paraphrasing
Guofu Li, Alejandra Lopez-Fernandez and Tony Veale

UCD-PN: Selecting General Paraphrases Using Conditional Probability
Paul Nulty and Fintan Costello

Friday, July 16, 2010

09:00–10:30 System papers

09:00–09:15 *UvT-WSD1: A Cross-Lingual Word Sense Disambiguation System*
Maarten van Gompel

09:15–09:30 *UBA: Using Automatic Translation and Wikipedia for Cross-Lingual Lexical Substitution*
Pierpaolo Basile and Giovanni Semeraro

09:30–09:45 *HUMB: Automatic Key Term Extraction from Scientific Articles in GROBID*
Patrice Lopez and Laurent Romary

Friday, July 16, 2010 (continued)

09:45–10:00 *UTDMet: Combining WordNet and Corpus Data for Argument Coercion Detection*
Kirk Roberts and Sanda Harabagiu

10:00–10:15 *UTD: Classifying Semantic Relations by Combining Lexical and Semantic Resources*
Bryan Rink and Sanda Harabagiu

10:15–10:30 *UvT: Memory-Based Pairwise Ranking of Paraphrasing Verbs*
Sander Wubben

11:00–12:30 System papers

11:00–11:15 *SEMAFOR: Frame Argument Resolution with Log-Linear Models*
Desai Chen, Nathan Schneider, Dipanjan Das and Noah A. Smith

11:15–11:30 *Cambridge: Parser Evaluation Using Textual Entailment by Grammatical Relation Comparison*
Laura Rimell and Stephen Clark

11:30–11:45 *MARS: A Specialized RTE System for Parser Evaluation*
Rui Wang and Yi Zhang

11:45–12:00 *TRIPS and TRIOS System for TempEval-2: Extracting Temporal Information from Text*
Naushad UzZaman and James Allen

12:00–12:15 *TIPSem (English and Spanish): Evaluating CRFs and Semantic Roles in TempEval-2*
Hector Llorens, Estela Saquete and Borja Navarro

12:15–12:30 *CityU-DAC: Disambiguating Sentiment-Ambiguous Adjectives within Context*
Bin LU and Benjamin K. Tsou

14:00–15:30 PANEL

16:00–17:30 Posters

VENSES++: Adapting a deep semantic processing system to the identification of null instantiations
Sara Tonelli and Rodolfo Delmonte

Friday, July 16, 2010 (continued)

SemEval-2010 Task 1: Coreference Resolution in Multiple Languages

Marta Recasens[⋆] **Lluís Màrquez**[†] **Emili Sapena**[†] **M. Antònia Martí**[⋆]
Mariona Taulé[⋆] **Véronique Hoste**[‡] **Massimo Poesio**[◇] **Yannick Versley**[⋆⋆]

⋆: CLiC, University of Barcelona, {mrecasens,amarti,mtaule}@ub.edu
†: TALP, Technical University of Catalonia, {lluism,esapena}@lsi.upc.edu
‡: University College Ghent, veronique.hoste@hogent.be
◇: University of Essex/University of Trento, poesio@essex.ac.uk
⋆⋆: University of Tübingen, versley@sfs.uni-tuebingen.de

Abstract

This paper presents the SemEval-2010 task on *Coreference Resolution in Multiple Languages*. The goal was to evaluate and compare automatic coreference resolution systems for six different languages (Catalan, Dutch, English, German, Italian, and Spanish) in four evaluation settings and using four different metrics. Such a rich scenario had the potential to provide insight into key issues concerning coreference resolution: (i) the portability of systems across languages, (ii) the relevance of different levels of linguistic information, and (iii) the behavior of scoring metrics.

1 Introduction

The task of coreference resolution, defined as the identification of the expressions in a text that refer to the same discourse entity (1), has attracted considerable attention within the NLP community.

(1) *Major League Baseball* sent *its* head of security to Chicago to review the second incident of an on-field fan attack in the last seven months. *The league* is reviewing security at all ballparks to crack down on spectator violence.

Using coreference information has been shown to be beneficial in a number of NLP applications including Information Extraction (McCarthy and Lehnert, 1995), Text Summarization (Steinberger et al., 2007), Question Answering (Morton, 1999), and Machine Translation. There have been a few evaluation campaigns on coreference resolution in the past, namely MUC (Hirschman and Chinchor, 1997), ACE (Doddington et al., 2004), and ARE (Orasan et al., 2008), yet many questions remain open:

- To what extent is it possible to implement a general coreference resolution system portable to different languages? How much language-specific tuning is necessary?
- How helpful are morphology, syntax and semantics for solving coreference relations? How much preprocessing is needed? Does its quality (perfect linguistic input versus noisy automatic input) really matter?
- How (dis)similar are different coreference evaluation metrics—MUC, B-CUBED, CEAF and BLANC? Do they all provide the same ranking? Are they correlated?

Our goal was to address these questions in a shared task. Given six datasets in Catalan, Dutch, English, German, Italian, and Spanish, the task we present involved automatically detecting full coreference chains—composed of named entities (NEs), pronouns, and full noun phrases—in four different scenarios. For more information, the reader is referred to the task website.[1]

The rest of the paper is organized as follows. Section 2 presents the corpora from which the task datasets were extracted, and the automatic tools used to preprocess them. In Section 3, we describe the task by providing information about the data format, evaluation settings, and evaluation metrics. Participating systems are described in Section 4, and their results are analyzed and compared in Section 5. Finally, Section 6 concludes.

2 Linguistic Resources

In this section, we first present the sources of the data used in the task. We then describe the automatic tools that predicted input annotations for the coreference resolution systems.

[1] http://stel.ub.edu/semeval2010-coref

Proceedings of the 5th International Workshop on Semantic Evaluation, ACL 2010, pages 1–8,
Uppsala, Sweden, 15-16 July 2010.

	Training			Development			Test		
	#docs	#sents	#tokens	#docs	#sents	#tokens	#docs	#sents	#tokens
Catalan	829	8,709	253,513	142	1,445	42,072	167	1,698	49,260
Dutch	145	2,544	46,894	23	496	9,165	72	2,410	48,007
English	229	3,648	79,060	39	741	17,044	85	1,141	24,206
German	900	19,233	331,614	199	4,129	73,145	136	2,736	50,287
Italian	80	2,951	81,400	17	551	16,904	46	1,494	41,586
Spanish	875	9,022	284,179	140	1,419	44,460	168	1,705	51,040

Table 1: Size of the task datasets.

2.1 Source Corpora

Catalan and Spanish The AnCora corpora (Recasens and Martí, 2009) consist of a Catalan and a Spanish treebank of 500k words each, mainly from newspapers and news agencies (El Periódico, EFE, ACN). Manual annotation exists for arguments and thematic roles, predicate semantic classes, NEs, WordNet nominal senses, and coreference relations. AnCora are freely available for research purposes.

Dutch The KNACK-2002 corpus (Hoste and De Pauw, 2006) contains 267 documents from the Flemish weekly magazine Knack. They were manually annotated with coreference information on top of semi-automatically annotated PoS tags, phrase chunks, and NEs.

English The OntoNotes Release 2.0 corpus (Pradhan et al., 2007) covers newswire and broadcast news data: 300k words from The Wall Street Journal, and 200k words from the TDT-4 collection, respectively. OntoNotes builds on the Penn Treebank for syntactic annotation and on the Penn PropBank for predicate argument structures. Semantic annotations include NEs, words senses (linked to an ontology), and coreference information. The OntoNotes corpus is distributed by the Linguistic Data Consortium.[2]

German The TüBa-D/Z corpus (Hinrichs et al., 2005) is a newspaper treebank based on data taken from the daily issues of "die tageszeitung" (taz). It currently comprises 794k words manually annotated with semantic and coreference information. Due to licensing restrictions of the original texts, a taz-DVD must be purchased to obtain a license.[2]

Italian The LiveMemories corpus (Rodríguez et al., 2010) will include texts from the Italian Wikipedia, blogs, news articles, and dialogues (MapTask). They are being annotated according to the ARRAU annotation scheme with coreference, agreement, and NE information on top of automatically parsed data. The task dataset included Wikipedia texts already annotated.

The datasets that were used in the task were extracted from the above-mentioned corpora. Table 1 summarizes the number of documents (docs), sentences (sents), and tokens in the training, development and test sets.[3]

2.2 Preprocessing Systems

Catalan, Spanish, English Predicted lemmas and PoS were generated using FreeLing[4] for Catalan/Spanish and SVMTagger[5] for English. Dependency information and predicate semantic roles were generated with JointParser, a syntactic-semantic parser.[6]

Dutch Lemmas, PoS and NEs were automatically provided by the memory-based shallow parser for Dutch (Daelemans et al., 1999), and dependency information by the Alpino parser (van Noord et al., 2006).

German Lemmas were predicted by TreeTagger (Schmid, 1995), PoS and morphology by RFTagger (Schmid and Laws, 2008), and dependency information by MaltParser (Hall and Nivre, 2008).

Italian Lemmas and PoS were provided by TextPro,[7] and dependency information by MaltParser.[8]

[2]Free user license agreements for the English and German task datasets were issued to the task participants.

[3]The German and Dutch training datasets were not completely stable during the competition period due to a few errors. Revised versions were released on March 2 and 20, respectively. As to the test datasets, the Dutch and Italian documents with formatting errors were corrected after the evaluation period, with no variations in the ranking order of systems.

[4]http://www.lsi.upc.es/ nlp/freeling

[5]http://www.lsi.upc.edu/ nlp/SVMTool

[6]http://www.lsi.upc.edu// xlluis/?x=cat:5

[7]http://textpro.fbk.eu

[8]http://maltparser.org

3 Task Description

Participants were asked to develop an automatic system capable of assigning a discourse entity to every mention,[9] thus identifying all the NP mentions of every discourse entity. As there is no standard annotation scheme for coreference and the source corpora differed in certain aspects, the coreference information of the task datasets was produced according to three criteria:

- Only NP constituents and possessive determiners can be mentions.
- Mentions must be referential expressions, thus ruling out nominal predicates, appositives, expletive NPs, attributive NPs, NPs within idioms, etc.
- Singletons are also considered as entities (i.e., entities with a single mention).

To help participants build their systems, the task datasets also contained both gold-standard and automatically predicted linguistic annotations at the morphological, syntactic and semantic levels. Considerable effort was devoted to provide participants with a common and relatively simple data representation for the six languages.

3.1 Data Format

The task datasets as well as the participants' answers were displayed in a uniform column-based format, similar to the style used in previous CoNLL shared tasks on syntactic and semantic dependencies (2008/2009).[10] Each dataset was provided as a single file per language. Since coreference is a linguistic relation at the discourse level, documents constitute the basic unit, and are delimited by "#begin document ID" and "#end document ID" comment lines. Within a document, the information of each sentence is organized vertically with one token per line, and a blank line after the last token of each sentence. The information associated with each token is described in several columns (separated by "\t" characters) representing the following layers of linguistic annotation.

ID (column 1). Token identifiers in the sentence.

Token (column 2). Word forms.

[9]Following the terminology of the ACE program, a *mention* is defined as an instance of reference to an object, and an *entity* is the collection of mentions referring to the same object in a document.

[10]http://www.cnts.ua.ac.be/conll2008

ID	Token	Intermediate columns	Coref
1	Major	...	(1
2	League	...	_
3	Baseball	...	1)
4	sent	...	_
5	its	...	(1)|(2
6	head	...	_
7	of	...	_
8	security	...	(3)|2)
9	to	...	_
...	...	...	...
27	The	...	(1
28	league	...	1)
29	is	...	_

Table 2: Format of the coreference annotations (corresponding to example (1) in Section 1).

Lemma (column 3). Token lemmas.

PoS (column 5). Coarse PoS.

Feat (column 7). Morphological features (PoS type, number, gender, case, tense, aspect, etc.) separated by a pipe character.

Head (column 9). ID of the syntactic head ("0" if the token is the tree root).

DepRel (column 11). Dependency relations corresponding to the dependencies described in the Head column ("sentence" if the token is the tree root).

NE (column 13). NE types in open-close notation.

Pred (column 15). Predicate semantic class.

APreds (column 17 and subsequent ones). For each predicate in the Pred column, its semantic roles/dependencies.

Coref (last column). Coreference relations in open-close notation.

The above-mentioned columns are "gold-standard columns," whereas columns 4, 6, 8, 10, 12, 14, 16 and the penultimate contain the same information as the respective previous column but automatically predicted—using the preprocessing systems listed in Section 2.2. Neither all layers of linguistic annotation nor all gold-standard and predicted columns were available for all six languages (underscore characters indicate missing information).

The coreference column follows an open-close notation with an entity number in parentheses (see Table 2). Every entity has an ID number, and every mention is marked with the ID of the entity it refers to: an opening parenthesis shows the beginning of the mention (first token), while a closing parenthesis shows the end of the mention (last token). For tokens belonging to more than one mention, a pipe character is used to separate multiple entity IDs. The resulting annotation is a well-formed nested structure (CF language).

3.2 Evaluation Settings

In order to address our goal of studying the effect of different levels of linguistic information (preprocessing) on solving coreference relations, the test was divided into four evaluation settings that differed along two dimensions.

Gold-standard versus **Regular setting.** Only in the gold-standard setting were participants allowed to use the gold-standard columns, including the last one (of the test dataset) with true mention boundaries. In the regular setting, they were allowed to use only the automatically predicted columns. Obtaining better results in the gold setting would provide evidence for the relevance of using high-quality preprocessing information. Since not all columns were available for all six languages, the gold setting was only possible for Catalan, English, German, and Spanish.

Closed versus **Open setting.** In the closed setting, systems had to be built strictly with the information provided in the task datasets. In contrast, there was no restriction on the resources that participants could utilize in the open setting: systems could be developed using any external tools and resources to predict the preprocessing information, e.g., WordNet, Wikipedia, etc. The only requirement was to use tools that had not been developed with the annotations of the test set. This setting provided an open door into tools or resources that improve performance.

3.3 Evaluation Metrics

Since there is no agreement at present on a standard measure for coreference resolution evaluation, one of our goals was to compare the rankings produced by four different measures. The task scorer provides results in the two mention-based metrics B^3 (Bagga and Baldwin, 1998) and CEAF-ϕ_3 (Luo, 2005), and the two link-based metrics MUC (Vilain et al., 1995) and BLANC (Recasens and Hovy, in prep). The first three measures have been widely used, while BLANC is a proposal of a new measure interesting to test.

The mention detection subtask is measured with recall, precision, and F_1. Mentions are rewarded with 1 point if their boundaries coincide with those of the gold NP, with 0.5 points if their boundaries are within the gold NP including its head, and with 0 otherwise.

4 Participating Systems

A total of twenty-two participants registered for the task and downloaded the training materials. From these, sixteen downloaded the test set but only six (out of which two task organizers) submitted valid results (corresponding to nine system runs or variants). These numbers show that the task raised considerable interest but that the final participation rate was comparatively low (slightly below 30%).

The participating systems differed in terms of architecture, machine learning method, etc. Table 3 summarizes their main properties. Systems like BART and Corry support several machine learners, but Table 3 indicates the one used for the SemEval run. The last column indicates the external resources that were employed in the open setting, thus it is empty for systems that participated only in the closed setting. For more specific details we address the reader to the system description papers in Erk and Strapparava (2010).

5 Results and Evaluation

Table 4 shows the results obtained by two naive baseline systems: (i) SINGLETONS considers each mention as a separate entity, and (ii) ALL-IN-ONE groups all the mentions in a document into a single entity. These simple baselines reveal limitations of the evaluation metrics, like the high scores of CEAF and B^3 for SINGLETONS. Interestingly enough, the naive baseline scores turn out to be hard to beat by the participating systems, as Table 5 shows. Similarly, ALL-IN-ONE obtains high scores in terms of MUC. Table 4 also reveals differences between the distribution of entities in the datasets. Dutch is clearly the most divergent corpus mainly due to the fact that it only contains singletons for NEs.

Table 5 displays the results of all systems for all languages and settings in the four evaluation metrics (the best scores in each setting are highlighted in bold). Results are presented sequentially by language and setting, and participating systems are ordered alphabetically. The participation of systems across languages and settings is rather irregular,[11] thus making it difficult to draw firm conclu-

[11]Only 45 entries in Table 5 from 192 potential cases.

	System Architecture	ML Methods	External Resources
BART (Broscheit et al., 2010)	Closest-first with entity-mention model (English), Closest-first model (German, Italian)	MaxEnt (English, German), Decision trees (Italian)	GermaNet & gazetteers (German), I-Cab gazetteers (Italian), Berkeley parser, Stanford NER, WordNet, Wikipedia name list, U.S. census data (English)
Corry (Uryupina, 2010)	ILP, Pairwise model	SVM	Stanford parser & NER, WordNet, U.S. census data
RelaxCor (Sapena et al., 2010)	Graph partitioning (solved by relaxation labeling)	Decision trees, Rules	WordNet
SUCRE (Kobdani and Schütze, 2010)	Best-first clustering, Relational database model, Regular feature definition language	Decision trees, Naive Bayes, SVM, MaxEnt	—
TANL-1 (Attardi et al., 2010)	Highest entity-mention similarity	MaxEnt	PoS tagger (Italian)
UBIU (Zhekova and Kübler, 2010)	Pairwise model	MBL	—

Table 3: Main characteristics of the participating systems.

sions about the aims initially pursued by the task. In the following, we summarize the most relevant outcomes of the evaluation.

Regarding languages, English concentrates the most participants (fifteen entries), followed by German (eight), Catalan and Spanish (seven each), Italian (five), and Dutch (three). The number of languages addressed by each system ranges from one (Corry) to six (UBIU and SUCRE); BART and RelaxCor addressed three languages, and TANL-1 five. The best overall results are obtained for English followed by German, then Catalan, Spanish and Italian, and finally Dutch. Apart from differences between corpora, there are other factors that might explain this ranking: (i) the fact that most of the systems were originally developed for English, and (ii) differences in corpus size (German having the largest corpus, and Dutch the smallest).

Regarding systems, there are no clear "winners." Note that no language-setting was addressed by all six systems. The BART system, for instance, is either on its own or competing against a single system. It emerges from partial comparisons that SUCRE performs the best in *closed*×*regular* for English, German, and Italian, although it never outperforms the CEAF or B^3 singleton baseline. While SUCRE always obtains the best scores according to MUC and BLANC, RelaxCor and TANL-1 usually win based on CEAF and B^3. The Corry system presents three variants optimized for CEAF (Corry-C), MUC (Corry-M), and BLANC (Corry-B). Their results are consistent with the bias introduced in the optimization (see English:*open*×*gold*).

Depending on the evaluation metric then, the rankings of systems vary with considerable score differences. There is a significant positive correlation between CEAF and B^3 (Pearson's $r = 0.91$, $p < 0.01$), and a significant lack of correlation between CEAF and MUC in terms of recall (Pearson's $r = 0.44$, $p < 0.01$). This fact stresses the importance of defining appropriate metrics (or a combination of them) for coreference evaluation.

Finally, regarding evaluation settings, the results in the *gold* setting are significantly better than those in the *regular*. However, this might be a direct effect of the mention recognition task. Mention recognition in the regular setting falls more than 20 F_1 points with respect to the gold setting (where correct mention boundaries were given). As for the *open* versus *closed* setting, there is only one system, RelaxCor for English, that addressed the two. As expected, results show a slight improvement from *closed*×*gold* to *open*×*gold*.

6 Conclusions

This paper has introduced the main features of the SemEval-2010 task on coreference resolution.

	CEAF			MUC			B^3			BLANC		
	R	P	F_1	R	P	F_1	R	P	F_1	R	P	Blanc
SINGLETONS: Each mention forms a separate entity.												
Catalan	61.2	61.2	61.2	0.0	0.0	0.0	61.2	100	75.9	50.0	48.7	49.3
Dutch	34.5	34.5	34.5	0.0	0.0	0.0	34.5	100	51.3	50.0	46.7	48.3
English	71.2	71.2	71.2	0.0	0.0	0.0	71.2	100	83.2	50.0	49.2	49.6
German	75.5	75.5	75.5	0.0	0.0	0.0	75.5	100	86.0	50.0	49.4	49.7
Italian	71.1	71.1	71.1	0.0	0.0	0.0	71.1	100	83.1	50.0	49.2	49.6
Spanish	62.2	62.2	62.2	0.0	0.0	0.0	62.2	100	76.7	50.0	48.8	49.4
ALL-IN-ONE: All mentions are grouped into a single entity.												
Catalan	11.8	11.8	11.8	100	39.3	56.4	100	4.0	7.7	50.0	1.3	2.6
Dutch	19.7	19.7	19.7	100	66.3	79.8	100	8.0	14.9	50.0	3.2	6.2
English	10.5	10.5	10.5	100	29.2	45.2	100	3.5	6.7	50.0	0.8	1.6
German	8.2	8.2	8.2	100	24.8	39.7	100	2.4	4.7	50.0	0.6	1.1
Italian	11.4	11.4	11.4	100	29.0	45.0	100	2.1	4.1	50.0	0.8	1.5
Spanish	11.9	11.9	11.9	100	38.3	55.4	100	3.9	7.6	50.0	1.2	2.4

Table 4: Baseline scores.

The goal of the task was to evaluate and compare automatic coreference resolution systems for six different languages in four evaluation settings and using four different metrics. This complex scenario aimed at providing insight into several aspects of coreference resolution, including portability across languages, relevance of linguistic information at different levels, and behavior of alternative scoring metrics.

The task attracted considerable attention from a number of researchers, but only six teams submitted their final results. Participating systems did not run their systems for all the languages and evaluation settings, thus making direct comparisons between them very difficult. Nonetheless, we were able to observe some interesting aspects from the empirical evaluation.

An important conclusion was the confirmation that different evaluation metrics provide different system rankings and the scores are not commensurate. Attention thus needs to be paid to coreference evaluation. The behavior and applicability of the scoring metrics requires further investigation in order to guarantee a fair evaluation when comparing systems in the future. We hope to have the opportunity to thoroughly discuss this and the rest of interesting questions raised by the task during the SemEval workshop at ACL 2010.

An additional valuable benefit is the set of resources developed throughout the task. As task organizers, we intend to facilitate the sharing of datasets, scorers, and documentation by keeping them available for future research use. We believe that these resources will help to set future benchmarks for the research community and will contribute positively to the progress of the state of the art in coreference resolution. We will maintain and update the task website with post-SemEval contributions.

Acknowledgments

We would like to thank the following people who contributed to the preparation of the task datasets: Manuel Bertran (UB), Oriol Borrega (UB), Orphée De Clercq (U. Ghent), Francesca Delogu (U. Trento), Jesús Giménez (UPC), Eduard Hovy (ISI-USC), Richard Johansson (U. Trento), Xavier Lluís (UPC), Montse Nofre (UB), Lluís Padró (UPC), Kepa Joseba Rodríguez (U. Trento), Mihai Surdeanu (Stanford), Olga Uryupina (U. Trento), Lente Van Leuven (UB), and Rita Zaragoza (UB). We would also like to thank LDC and die tageszeitung for distributing freely the English and German datasets.

This work was funded in part by the Spanish Ministry of Science and Innovation through the projects TEXT-MESS 2.0 (TIN2009-13391-C04-04), OpenMT-2 (TIN2009-14675-C03), and KNOW2 (TIN2009-14715-C04-04), and an FPU doctoral scholarship (AP2006-00994) held by M. Recasens. It also received financial support from the Seventh Framework Programme of the EU (FP7/2007-2013) under GA 247762 (FAUST), from the STEVIN program of the Nederlandse Taalunie through the COREA and SoNaR projects, and from the Provincia Autonoma di Trento through the LiveMemories project.

	Mention detection			CEAF			MUC			B^3			BLANC		
	R	P	F_1	R	P	F_1	R	P	F_1	R	P	F_1	R	P	Blanc
Catalan															
closed×gold															
RelaxCor	100	100	100	70.5	70.5	**70.5**	29.3	77.3	42.5	68.6	95.8	**79.9**	56.0	81.8	59.7
SUCRE	100	100	100	68.7	68.7	68.7	54.1	58.4	**56.2**	76.6	77.4	77.0	72.4	60.2	**63.6**
TANL-1	100	96.8	98.4	66.0	63.9	64.9	17.2	57.7	26.5	64.4	93.3	76.2	52.8	79.8	54.4
UBIU	75.1	96.3	84.4	46.6	59.6	52.3	8.8	17.1	11.7	47.8	76.3	58.8	51.6	57.9	52.2
closed×regular															
SUCRE	75.9	64.5	69.7	51.3	43.6	47.2	44.1	32.3	**37.3**	59.6	44.7	51.1	53.9	55.2	**54.2**
TANL-1	83.3	82.0	82.7	57.5	56.6	**57.1**	15.2	46.9	22.9	55.8	76.6	**64.6**	51.3	76.2	51.0
UBIU	51.4	70.9	59.6	33.2	45.7	38.4	6.5	12.6	8.6	32.4	55.7	40.9	50.2	53.7	47.8
open×gold															
open×regular															
Dutch															
closed×gold															
SUCRE	100	100	100	58.8	58.8	**58.8**	65.7	74.4	**69.8**	65.0	69.2	**67.0**	69.5	62.9	**65.3**
closed×regular															
SUCRE	78.0	29.0	42.3	29.4	10.9	15.9	62.0	19.5	**29.7**	59.1	6.5	11.7	46.9	46.9	**46.9**
UBIU	41.5	29.9	34.7	20.5	14.6	**17.0**	6.7	11.0	8.3	13.3	23.4	**17.0**	50.0	52.4	32.3
open×gold															
open×regular															
English															
closed×gold															
RelaxCor	100	100	100	75.6	75.6	**75.6**	21.9	72.4	33.7	74.8	97.0	**84.5**	57.0	83.4	61.3
SUCRE	100	100	100	74.3	74.3	74.3	68.1	54.9	**60.8**	86.7	78.5	82.4	77.3	67.0	**70.8**
TANL-1	99.8	81.7	89.8	75.0	61.4	67.6	23.7	24.4	24.0	74.6	72.1	73.4	51.8	68.8	52.1
UBIU	92.5	99.5	95.9	63.4	68.2	65.7	17.2	25.5	20.5	67.8	83.5	74.8	52.6	60.8	54.0
closed×regular															
SUCRE	78.4	83.0	80.7	61.0	64.5	**62.7**	57.7	48.1	**52.5**	68.3	65.9	**67.1**	58.9	65.7	**61.2**
TANL-1	79.6	68.9	73.9	61.7	53.4	57.3	23.8	25.5	24.6	62.1	60.5	61.3	50.9	68.0	49.3
UBIU	66.7	83.6	74.2	48.2	60.4	53.6	11.6	18.4	14.2	50.9	69.2	58.7	50.9	56.3	51.0
open×gold															
Corry-B	100	100	100	77.5	77.5	77.5	56.1	57.5	56.8	82.6	85.7	84.1	69.3	75.3	**71.8**
Corry-C	100	100	100	77.7	77.7	**77.7**	57.4	58.3	57.9	83.1	84.7	83.9	71.3	71.6	71.5
Corry-M	100	100	100	73.8	73.8	73.8	62.5	56.2	**59.2**	85.5	78.6	81.9	76.2	58.8	62.7
RelaxCor	100	100	100	75.8	75.8	75.8	22.6	70.5	34.2	75.2	96.7	**84.6**	58.0	83.8	62.7
open×regular															
BART	76.1	69.8	72.8	70.1	64.3	67.1	62.8	52.4	57.1	74.9	67.7	71.1	55.3	73.2	57.7
Corry-B	79.8	76.4	78.1	70.4	67.4	68.9	55.0	54.2	54.6	73.7	74.1	**73.9**	57.1	75.7	**60.6**
Corry-C	79.8	76.4	78.1	70.9	67.9	**69.4**	54.7	55.5	55.1	73.8	73.1	73.5	57.4	63.8	59.4
Corry-M	79.8	76.4	78.1	66.3	63.5	64.8	61.5	53.4	**57.2**	76.8	66.5	71.3	58.5	56.2	57.1
German															
closed×gold															
SUCRE	100	100	100	72.9	72.9	72.9	74.4	48.1	**58.4**	90.4	73.6	81.1	78.2	61.8	**66.4**
TANL-1	100	100	100	77.7	77.7	**77.7**	16.4	60.6	25.9	77.2	96.7	**85.9**	54.4	75.1	57.4
UBIU	92.6	95.5	94.0	67.4	68.9	68.2	22.1	21.7	21.9	73.7	77.9	75.7	60.0	77.2	64.5
closed×regular															
SUCRE	79.3	77.5	78.4	60.6	59.2	**59.9**	49.3	35.0	**40.9**	69.1	60.1	**64.3**	52.7	59.3	**53.6**
TANL-1	60.9	57.7	59.2	50.9	48.2	49.5	10.2	31.5	15.4	47.2	54.9	50.7	50.2	63.0	44.7
UBIU	50.6	66.8	57.6	39.4	51.9	44.8	9.5	11.4	10.4	41.2	53.7	46.6	50.2	54.4	48.0
open×gold															
BART	94.3	93.7	94.0	67.1	66.7	**66.9**	70.5	40.1	**51.1**	85.3	64.4	**73.4**	65.5	61.0	**62.8**
open×regular															
BART	82.5	82.3	82.4	61.4	61.2	**61.3**	61.4	36.1	**45.5**	75.3	58.3	**65.7**	55.9	60.3	**57.3**
Italian															
closed×gold															
SUCRE	98.4	98.4	98.4	66.0	66.0	**66.0**	48.1	42.3	**45.0**	76.7	76.9	**76.8**	54.8	63.5	**56.9**
closed×regular															
SUCRE	84.6	98.1	90.8	57.1	66.2	**61.3**	50.1	50.7	**50.4**	63.6	79.2	**70.6**	55.2	68.3	**57.7**
UBIU	46.8	35.9	40.6	37.9	29.0	32.9	2.9	4.6	3.6	38.4	31.9	34.8	50.0	46.6	37.2
open×gold															
open×regular															
BART	42.8	80.7	55.9	35.0	66.1	45.8	35.3	54.0	**42.7**	34.6	70.6	46.4	57.1	68.1	**59.6**
TANL-1	90.5	73.8	81.3	62.2	50.7	**55.9**	37.2	28.3	32.1	66.8	56.5	**61.2**	50.7	69.3	48.5
Spanish															
closed×gold															
RelaxCor	100	100	100	66.6	66.6	66.6	14.8	73.8	24.7	65.3	97.5	**78.2**	53.4	81.8	55.6
SUCRE	100	100	100	69.8	69.8	**69.8**	52.7	58.3	**55.3**	75.8	79.0	77.4	67.3	62.5	**64.5**
TANL-1	100	96.8	98.4	66.9	64.7	65.8	16.6	56.5	25.7	65.2	93.4	76.8	52.5	79.0	54.1
UBIU	73.8	96.4	83.6	45.7	59.6	51.7	9.6	18.8	12.7	46.8	77.1	58.3	52.9	63.9	54.3
closed×regular															
SUCRE	74.9	66.3	70.3	56.3	49.9	52.9	35.8	36.8	**36.3**	56.6	54.6	55.6	52.1	61.2	**51.4**
TANL-1	82.2	84.1	83.1	58.6	60.0	**59.3**	14.0	48.4	21.7	56.6	79.0	**66.0**	51.4	74.7	**51.4**
UBIU	51.1	72.7	60.0	33.6	47.6	39.4	7.6	14.4	10.0	32.8	57.1	41.6	50.4	54.6	48.4
open×gold															
open×regular															

Table 5: Official results of the participating systems for all languages, settings, and metrics.

References

Giuseppe Attardi, Stefano Dei Rossi, and Maria Simi. 2010. TANL-1: coreference resolution by parse analysis and similarity clustering. In *Proceedings of SemEval-2*.

Amit Bagga and Breck Baldwin. 1998. Algorithms for scoring coreference chains. In *Proceedings of the LREC Workshop on Linguistic Coreference*, pages 563–566.

Samuel Broscheit, Massimo Poesio, Simone Paolo Ponzetto, Kepa Joseba Rodríguez, Lorenza Romano, Olga Uryupina, Yannick Versley, and Roberto Zanoli. 2010. BART: A multilingual anaphora resolution system. In *Proceedings of SemEval-2*.

Walter Daelemans, Sabine Buchholz, and Jorn Veenstra. 1999. Memory-based shallow parsing. In *Proceedings of CoNLL 1999*.

George Doddington, Alexis Mitchell, Mark Przybocki, Lance Ramshaw, Stephanie Strassel, and Ralph Weischedel. 2004. The Automatic Content Extraction (ACE) program – Tasks, data, and evaluation. In *Proceedings of LREC 2004*, pages 837–840.

Katrin Erk and Carlo Strapparava, editors. 2010. *Proceedings of SemEval-2*.

Johan Hall and Joakim Nivre. 2008. A dependency-driven parser for German dependency and constituency representations. In *Proceedings of the ACL Workshop on Parsing German (PaGe 2008)*, pages 47–54.

Erhard W. Hinrichs, Sandra Kübler, and Karin Naumann. 2005. A unified representation for morphological, syntactic, semantic, and referential annotations. In *Proceedings of the ACL Workshop on Frontiers in Corpus Annotation II: Pie in the Sky*, pages 13–20.

Lynette Hirschman and Nancy Chinchor. 1997. MUC-7 Coreference Task Definition – Version 3.0. In *Proceedings of MUC-7*.

Véronique Hoste and Guy De Pauw. 2006. KNACK-2002: A richly annotated corpus of Dutch written text. In *Proceedings of LREC 2006*, pages 1432–1437.

Hamidreza Kobdani and Hinrich Schütze. 2010. SUCRE: A modular system for coreference resolution. In *Proceedings of SemEval-2*.

Xiaoqiang Luo. 2005. On coreference resolution performance metrics. In *Proceedings of HLT-EMNLP 2005*, pages 25–32.

Joseph F. McCarthy and Wendy G. Lehnert. 1995. Using decision trees for coreference resolution. In *Proceedings of IJCAI 1995*, pages 1050–1055.

Thomas S. Morton. 1999. Using coreference in question answering. In *Proceedings of TREC-8*, pages 85–89.

Constantin Orasan, Dan Cristea, Ruslan Mitkov, and António Branco. 2008. Anaphora Resolution Exercise: An overview. In *Proceedings of LREC 2008*.

Sameer S. Pradhan, Eduard Hovy, Mitch Marcus, Martha Palmer, Lance Ramshaw, and Ralph Weischedel. 2007. Ontonotes: A unified relational semantic representation. In *Proceedings of the International Conference on Semantic Computing (ICSC 2007)*, pages 517–526.

Marta Recasens and Eduard Hovy. in prep. BLANC: Implementing the Rand Index for Coreference Evaluation.

Marta Recasens and M. Antònia Martí. 2009. AnCora-CO: Coreferentially annotated corpora for Spanish and Catalan. *Language Resources and Evaluation*, DOI:10.1007/s10579-009-9108-x.

Kepa Joseba Rodríguez, Francesca Delogu, Yannick Versley, Egon Stemle, and Massimo Poesio. 2010. Anaphoric annotation of Wikipedia and blogs in the Live Memories Corpus. In *Proceedings of LREC 2010*, pages 157–163.

Emili Sapena, Lluís Padró, and Jordi Turmo. 2010. RelaxCor: A global relaxation labeling approach to coreference resolution for the SemEval-2 Coreference Task. In *Proceedings of SemEval-2*.

Helmut Schmid and Florian Laws. 2008. Estimation of conditional probabilities with decision trees and an application to fine-grained POS tagging. In *Proceedings of COLING 2008*, pages 777–784.

Helmut Schmid. 1995. Improvements in part-of-speech tagging with an application to German. In *Proceedings of the ACL SIGDAT Workshop*, pages 47–50.

Josef Steinberger, Massimo Poesio, Mijail A. Kabadjov, and Karel Jeek. 2007. Two uses of anaphora resolution in summarization. *Information Processing and Management: an International Journal*, 43(6):1663–1680.

Olga Uryupina. 2010. Corry: A system for coreference resolution. In *Proceedings of SemEval-2*.

Gertjan van Noord, Ineke Schuurman, and Vincent Vandeghinste. 2006. Syntactic annotation of large corpora in STEVIN. In *Proceedings of LREC 2006*.

Marc Vilain, John Burger, John Aberdeen, Dennis Connolly, and Lynette Hirschman. 1995. A model-theoretic coreference scoring scheme. In *Proceedings of MUC-6*, pages 45–52.

Desislava Zhekova and Sandra Kübler. 2010. UBIU: A language-independent system for coreference resolution. In *Proceedings of SemEval-2*.

SemEval-2010 Task 2: Cross-Lingual Lexical Substitution

Rada Mihalcea
University of North Texas
rada@cs.unt.edu

Ravi Sinha
University of North Texas
ravisinha@unt.edu

Diana McCarthy
Lexical Computing Ltd.
diana@dianamccarthy.co.uk

Abstract

In this paper we describe the SemEval-2010 Cross-Lingual Lexical Substitution task, where given an English target word in context, participating systems had to find an alternative substitute word or phrase in Spanish. The task is based on the English Lexical Substitution task run at SemEval-2007. In this paper we provide background and motivation for the task, we describe the data annotation process and the scoring system, and present the results of the participating systems.

1 Introduction

In the Cross-Lingual Lexical Substitution task, annotators and systems had to find an alternative substitute word or phrase in Spanish for an English target word in context. The task is based on the English Lexical Substitution task run at SemEval-2007, where both target words and substitutes were in English.

An automatic system for cross-lingual lexical substitution would be useful for a number of applications. For instance, such a system could be used to assist human translators in their work, by providing a number of correct translations that the human translator can choose from. Similarly, the system could be used to assist language learners, by providing them with the interpretation of the unknown words in a text written in the language they are learning. Last but not least, the output of a cross-lingual lexical substitution system could be used as input to existing systems for cross-language information retrieval or automatic machine translation.

2 Motivation and Related Work

While there has been a lot of discussion on the relevant sense distinctions for monolingual WSD systems, for machine translation applications there is a consensus that the relevant sense distinctions are those that reflect different translations. One early and notable work was the SENSEVAL-2 Japanese Translation task (Kurohashi, 2001) that obtained alternative translation records of typical usages of a test word, also referred to as a *translation memory*. Systems could either select the most appropriate translation memory record for each instance and were scored against a gold-standard set of annotations, or they could provide a translation that was scored by translation experts after the results were submitted. In contrast to this work, in our task we provided actual translations for target instances in advance, rather than predetermine translations using lexicographers or rely on post-hoc evaluation, which does not permit evaluation of new systems after the competition.

Previous standalone WSD tasks based on parallel data have obtained distinct translations for senses as listed in a dictionary (Ng and Chan, 2007). In this way fine-grained senses with the same translations can be lumped together, however this does not fully allow for the fact that some senses for the same words may have some translations in common but also others that are not (Sinha et al., 2009).

In our task, we collected a dataset which allows instances of the same word to have some translations in common, while not necessitating a clustering of translations from a specific resource into senses (in comparison to Lefever and Hoste (2010)). [1] Resnik and Yarowsky (2000) also

[1]Though in that task note that it is possible for a translation to occur in more than one cluster. It will be interesting to

Proceedings of the 5th International Workshop on Semantic Evaluation, ACL 2010, pages 9–14,
Uppsala, Sweden, 15-16 July 2010.

conducted experiments using words in context, rather than a predefined sense-inventory however in these experiments the annotators were asked for a single preferred translation. In our case, we allowed annotators to supply as many translations as they felt were equally valid. This allows us to examine more subtle relationships between usages and to allow partial credit to systems that get a close approximation to the annotators' translations. Unlike a full blown machine translation task (Carpuat and Wu, 2007), annotators and systems are not required to translate the whole context but just the target word.

3 Background: The English Lexical Substitution Task

The English Lexical substitution task (hereafter referred to as LEXSUB) was run at SemEval-2007 (McCarthy and Navigli, 2007; McCarthy and Navigli, 2009). LEXSUB was proposed as a task which, while requiring contextual disambiguation, did not presuppose a specific sense inventory. In fact, it is quite possible to use alternative representations of meaning, such as those proposed by Schütze (1998) and Pantel and Lin (2002).

The motivation for a substitution task was that it would reflect capabilities that might be useful for natural language processing tasks such as paraphrasing and textual entailment, while not requiring a complete system that might mask system capabilities at a lexical level and make participation in the task difficult for small research teams.

The task required systems to produce a substitute word for a word in context. The data was collected for 201 words from open class parts-of-speech (PoS) (i.e. nouns, verbs, adjectives and adverbs). Words were selected that have more than one meaning with at least one near synonym. Ten sentences for each word were extracted from the English Internet Corpus (Sharoff, 2006). There were five annotators who annotated each target word as it occurred in the context of a sentence. The annotators were each allowed to provide up to three substitutes, though they could also provide a NIL response if they could not come up with a substitute. They had to indicate if the target word was an integral part of a multiword.

see the extent that this actually occurred in their data and the extent that the translations that our annotators provided might be clustered.

4 The Cross-Lingual Lexical Substitution Task

The Cross-Lingual Lexical Substitution task follows LEXSUB except that the annotations are translations rather than paraphrases. Given a target word in context, the task is to provide several correct translations for that word in a given language. We used English as the source language and Spanish as the target language.

We provided both development and test sets, but no training data. As for LEXSUB, any systems requiring training data had to obtain it from other sources. We included nouns, verbs, adjectives and adverbs in both development and test data. We used the same set of 30 development words as in LEXSUB, and a subset of 100 words from the LEXSUB test set, selected so that they exhibit a wide variety of substitutes. For each word, the same example sentences were used as in LEXSUB.

4.1 Annotation

We used four annotators for the task, all native Spanish speakers from Mexico, with a high level of proficiency in English. As in LEXSUB, the annotators were allowed to use any resources they wanted to, and were required to provide as many substitutes as they could think of.

The inter-tagger agreement (ITA) was calculated as pairwise agreement between sets of substitutes from annotators, as done in LEXSUB. The ITA without mode was determined as 0.2777, which is comparable with the ITA of 0.2775 determined for LEXSUB.

4.2 An Example

One significant outcome of this task is that there are not necessarily clear divisions between usages and senses because we do not use a predefined sense inventory, or restrict the annotations to distinctive translations. This means that there can be usages that overlap to different extents with each other but do not have identical translations. An example is the target adverb *severely*. Four sentences are shown in Figure 1 with the translations provided by one annotator marked in italics and {} braces. Here, all the token occurrences seem related to each other in that they share some translations, but not all. There are sentences like 1 and 2 that appear not to have anything in common. However 1, 3, and 4 seem to be partly related (they share *severamente*), and 2, 3, and 4 are also partly related (they share *seriamente*). When we look again, sentences 1 and 2, though not directly related, both have translations in common with sentences 3 and 4.

4.3 Scoring

We adopted the **best** and **out-of-ten** precision and recall scores from LEXSUB (oot in the equations below). The systems were allowed to supply as many translations as they feel fit the context. The system translations are then given credit depending on the number of annotators that picked each translation. The credit is divided by the number of annotator responses for the item and since for the **best** score the credit for the system answers for an item is also divided by the number of answers the system provides, this allows more credit to be given to instances where there is less variation. For that reason, a system is better guessing the translation that is most frequent unless it really wants to hedge its bets. Thus if i is an item in the set of instances I, and T_i is the multiset of gold standard translations from the human annotators for i, and a system provides a set of answers S_i for i, then the **best** score for item i is[2]:

$$best\ score(i) = \frac{\sum_{s \in S_i} frequency(s \in T_i)}{|S_i| \cdot |T_i|} \quad (1)$$

Precision is calculated by summing the scores for each item and dividing by the number of items that the system attempted whereas recall divides the sum of scores for each item by $|I|$. Thus:

$$best\ precision = \frac{\sum_i best\ score(i)}{|i \in I : defined(S_i)|} \quad (2)$$

$$best\ recall = \frac{\sum_i best\ score(i)}{|I|} \quad (3)$$

The **out-of-ten** scorer allows up to ten system responses and does not divide the credit attributed to each answer by the number of system responses. This allows a system to be less cautious and for the fact that there is considerable variation on the task and there may be cases where systems select a perfectly good translation that the annotators had not thought of. By allowing up to ten translations in the **out-of-ten** task the systems can hedge their bets to find the translations that the annotators supplied.

[2]NB scores are multiplied by 100, though for **out-of-ten** this is not strictly a percentage.

$$oot\ score(i) = \frac{\sum_{s \in S_i} frequency(s \in T_i)}{|T_i|} \quad (4)$$

$$oot\ precision = \frac{\sum_i oot\ score(i)}{|i \in I : defined(S_i)|} \quad (5)$$

$$oot\ recall = \frac{\sum_i oot\ score(i)}{|I|} \quad (6)$$

We note that there was an issue that the original LEXSUB **out-of-ten** scorer allowed duplicates (McCarthy and Navigli, 2009). The effect of duplicates is that systems can get inflated scores because the credit for each item is not divided by the number of substitutes and because the frequency of each annotator response is used. McCarthy and Navigli (2009) describe this oversight, identify the systems that had included duplicates and explain the implications. For our task, we decided to continue to allow for duplicates, so that systems can boost their scores with duplicates on translations with higher probability.

For both the **best** and **out-of-ten** measures, we also report a *mode* score, which is calculated against the mode from the annotators responses as was done in LEXSUB. Unlike the LEXSUB task, we did not run a separate multi-word subtask and evaluation.

5 Baselines and Upper bound

To place results in perspective, several baselines as well as the upper bound were calculated.

5.1 Baselines

We calculated two baselines, one dictionary-based and one dictionary and corpus-based. The baselines were produced with the help of an online Spanish-English dictionary[3] and the Spanish Wikipedia. For the first baseline, denoted by DICT, for all target words, we collected all the Spanish translations provided by the dictionary, in the order returned on the online query page. The **best** baseline was produced by taking the first translation provided by the online dictionary, while the **out-of-ten** baseline was produced by taking the first 10 translations provided.

The second baseline, DICTCORP, also accounted for the frequency of the translations within a Spanish dictionary. All the translations

[3]www.spanishdict.com

1. Perhaps the effect of West Nile Virus is sufficient to extinguish endemic birds already **severely** stressed by habitat losses. {*fuertemente, severamente, duramente, exageradamente*}
2. She looked as **severely** as she could muster at Draco. {*rigurosamente, seriamente*}
3. A day before he was due to return to the United States Patton was **severely** injured in a road accident. {*seriamente, duramente, severamente*}
4. Use market tools to address environmental issues , such as eliminating subsidies for industries that **severely** harm the environment, like coal. {*peligrosamente, seriamente, severamente*}
5. This picture was **severely** damaged in the flood of 1913 and has rarely been seen until now. {*altamente, seriamente, exageradamente*}

Figure 1: Translations from one annotator for the adverb *severely*

provided by the online dictionary for a given target word were ranked according to their frequencies in the Spanish Wikipedia, producing the DICTCORP baseline.

5.2 Upper bound

The results for the **best** task reflect the inherent variability as less credit is given where annotators express differences. The theoretical upper bound for the **best** recall (and precision if all items are attempted) score is calculated as:

$$\begin{aligned} best_{ub} &= \frac{\sum_{i \in I} \frac{freq_{most\ freq\ substitute_i}}{|T_i|}}{|I|} \times 100 \\ &= 40.57 \end{aligned} \quad (7)$$

Note of course that this upper bound is theoretical and assumes a human could find the most frequent substitute selected by all annotators. Performance of annotators will undoubtedly be lower than the theoretical upper bound because of human variability on this task. Since we allow for duplicates, the **out-of-ten** upper bound assumes the most frequent word type in T_i is selected for all ten answers. Thus we would obtain ten times the **best** upper bound (equation 7).

$$\begin{aligned} oot_{ub} &= \frac{\sum_{i \in I} \frac{freq_{most\ freq\ substitute_i} \times 10}{|T_i|}}{|I|} \times 100 \\ &= 405.78 \end{aligned} \quad (8)$$

If we had not allowed duplicates then the **out-of-ten** upper bound would have been just less than 100% (99.97). This is calculated by assuming the top 10 most frequent responses from the annotators are picked in every case. There are only a couple of cases where there are more than 10 translations from the annotators.

6 Systems

Nine teams participated in the task, and several of them entered two systems. The systems used various resources, including bilingual dictionaries, parallel corpora such as Europarl or corpora built from Wikipedia, monolingual corpora such as Web1T or newswire collections, and translation software such as Moses, GIZA or Google. Some systems attempted to select the substitutes on the English side, using a lexical substitution framework or word sense disambiguation, whereas some systems made the selection on the Spanish side using lexical substitution in Spanish.

In the following, we briefly describe each participating system.

CU-SMT relies on a phrase-based statistical machine translation system, trained on the Europarl English-Spanish parallel corpora.

The UvT-v and UvT-g systems make use of k-nearest neighbour classifiers to build one word expert for each target word, and select translations on the basis of a GIZA alignment of the Europarl parallel corpus.

The UBA-T and UBA-W systems both use candidates from Google dictionary, SpanishDict.com and Babylon, which are then confirmed using parallel texts. UBA-T relies on the automatic translation of the source sentence using the Google Translation API, combined with several heuristics. The UBA-W system uses a parallel corpus automatically constructed from DBpedia.

SWAT-E and SWAT-S use a lexical substitution framework applied to either English or Spanish. The SWAT-E system first performs lexical substitution in English, and then each substitute is translated into Spanish. SWAT-S translates the source sentences into Spanish, identifies the Spanish word corresponding to the target word, and then it performs lexical substitution in Spanish.

TYO uses an English monolingual substitution module, and then it translates the substitution candidates into Spanish using the Freedict and the Google English-Spanish dictionary.

FCC-LS uses the probability of a word to be translated into a candidate based on estimates obtained from the GIZA alignment of the Europarl corpus. These translations are subsequently filtered to include only those that appear in a translation of the target word using Google translate.

WLVUSP determines candidates using the best N translations of the test sentences obtained with the Moses system, which are further filtered using an English-Spanish dictionary. USPWLV uses candidates from an alignment of Europarl, which are then selected using various features and a classifier tuned on the development data.

IRST-1 generates the **best** substitute using a PoS constrained alignment of Moses translations of the source sentences, with a back-off to a bilingual dictionary. For **out-of-ten**, dictionary translations are filtered using the LSA similarity between candidates and the sentence translation into Spanish. IRSTbs is intended as a baseline, and it uses only the PoS constrained Moses translation for **best**, and the dictionary translations for **out-of-ten**.

ColEur and ColSlm use a supervised word sense disambiguation algorithm to distinguish between senses in the English source sentences. Translations are then assigned by using GIZA alignments from a parallel corpus, collected for the word senses of interest.

7 Results

Tables 1 and 2 show the precision P and recall R for the **best** and **out-of-ten** tasks respectively, for normal and mode. The rows are ordered by R. The **out-of-ten** systems were allowed to provide up to 10 substitutes and did not have any advantage by providing less. Since duplicates were allowed so that a system can put more emphasis on items it is more confident of, this means that **out-of-ten** R and P scores might exceed 100% because the credit for each of the human answers is used for each of the duplicates (McCarthy and Navigli, 2009). Duplicates will not help the mode scores, and can be detrimental as valuable guesses which would not be penalised are taken up with

Systems	R	P	$Mode\ R$	$Mode\ P$
UBA-T	27.15	27.15	57.20	57.20
USPWLV	26.81	26.81	58.85	58.85
ColSlm	25.99	27.59	56.24	59.16
WLVUSP	25.27	25.27	52.81	52.81
SWAT-E	21.46	21.46	43.21	43.21
UvT-v	21.09	21.09	43.76	43.76
CU-SMT	20.56	21.62	44.58	45.01
UBA-W	19.68	19.68	39.09	39.09
UvT-g	19.59	19.59	41.02	41.02
SWAT-S	18.87	18.87	36.63	36.63
ColEur	18.15	19.47	37.72	40.03
IRST-1	15.38	22.16	33.47	45.95
IRSTbs	13.21	22.51	28.26	45.27
TYO	8.39	8.62	14.95	15.31
DICT	24.34	24.34	50.34	50.34
DICTCORP	15.09	15.09	29.22	29.22

Table 1: **best** results

duplicates. In table 2, in the column marked dups, we display the number of test items for which at least one duplicate answer was provided. [4] Although systems were perfectly free to use duplicates, some may not have realised this. [5] Duplicates help when a system is fairly confident of a subset of its 10 answers.

We had anticipated a practical issue to come up with all participants, which is the issue of different character encodings, especially when using bilingual dictionaries from the Web. While we were counting on the participants to clean their files and provide us with clean characters only, we ended up with result files following different encodings (e.g, UTF-8, ANSI), some of them including diacritics, and some of them containing malformed characters. We were able to perform a basic cleaning of the files, and transform the diacritics into their diacriticless counterparts, however it was not possible to clean all the malformed characters without a significant manual effort that was not possible due to time constraints. As a result, a few of the participants ended up losing a few points because their translations, while being correct, contained an invalid, malformed character that was not recognized as correct by the scorer.

There is some variation in rank order of the systems depending on which measures are used. [6]

[4] Please note that any residual character encoding issues were not considered by the scorer and so the number of duplicates may be slightly higher than if diacritics/different encodings had been considered.

[5] Also, note that some systems did not supply 10 translations. Their scores would possibly have improved if they had done so.

[6] There is not a big difference between P and R because

Systems	R	P	$Mode\ R$	$Mode\ P$	dups
SWAT-E	174.59	174.59	66.94	66.94	968
SWAT-S	97.98	97.98	79.01	79.01	872
UvT-v	58.91	58.91	62.96	62.96	345
UvT-g	55.29	55.29	73.94	73.94	146
UBA-W	52.75	52.75	83.54	83.54	-
WLVUSP	48.48	48.48	77.91	77.91	64
UBA-T	47.99	47.99	81.07	81.07	-
USPWLV	47.60	47.60	79.84	79.84	30
Colslm	43.91	46.61	65.98	69.41	509
ColEur	41.72	44.77	67.35	71.47	125
TYO	34.54	35.46	58.02	59.16	-
IRST-1	31.48	33.14	55.42	58.30	-
FCC-LS	23.90	23.90	31.96	31.96	308
IRSTbs	8.33	29.74	19.89	64.44	-
DICT	44.04	44.04	73.53	73.53	30
DICTCORP	42.65	42.65	71.60	71.60	-

Table 2: **out-of-ten** results

UBA-T has the highest ranking on R for **best**. USPWLV is best at finding the mode, for **best** however the UBA-W and UBA-T systems (particularly the former) both have exceptional performance for finding the mode in the **out-of-ten** task, though note that SWAT-S performs competitively given that its duplicate responses will reduce its chances on this metric. SWAT-E is the best system for **out-of-ten**, as several of the items that were emphasized through duplication were also correct.

The results are much higher than for LEXSUB (McCarthy and Navigli, 2007). There are several possible causes for this. It is perhaps easier for humans, and machines to come up with translations compared to paraphrases. Though the ITA figures are comparable on both tasks, our task contained only a subset of the data in LEXSUB and we specifically avoided data where the LEXSUB annotators had not been able to come up with a substitute or had labelled the instance as a name e.g. measurements such as *pound, yard* or terms such as *mad* in *mad cow disease*. Another reason for this difference may be that there are many parallel corpora available for training a system for this task whereas that was not the case for LEXSUB.

8 Conclusions

In this paper we described the SemEval-2010 cross-lingual lexical substitution task, including the motivation behind the task, the annotation process and the scoring system, as well as the participating systems. Nine different teams with a total of 15 different systems participated in the task, using a variety of resources and approaches. Comparative evaluations using different metrics helped determine what works well for the selection of cross-lingual lexical substitutes.

systems typically supplied answers for most items. However, IRST-1 and IRSTbs did considerably better on precision compared to recall since they did not cover all test items.

9 Acknowledgements

The work of the first and second authors has been partially supported by a National Science Foundation CAREER award #0747340. The work of the third author has been supported by a Royal Society UK Dorothy Hodgkin Fellowship. The authors are grateful to Samer Hassan for his help with the annotation interface.

References

Marine Carpuat and Dekai Wu. 2007. Improving statistical machine translation using word sense disambiguation. In *Proceedings of the Joint Conference on Empirical Methods in Natural Language Processing and Computational Natural Language Learning (EMNLP-CoNLL 2007)*, pages 61–72, Prague, Czech Republic, June. Association for Computational Linguistics.

Sadao Kurohashi. 2001. SENSEVAL-2 japanese translation task. In *Proceedings of the* SENSEVAL-2 *workshop*, pages 37–44.

Els Lefever and Veronique Hoste. 2010. SemEval-2007 task 3: Cross-lingual word sense disambiguation. In *Proceedings of the 5th International Workshop on Semantic Evaluations (SemEval-2010)*, Uppsala, Sweden.

Diana McCarthy and Roberto Navigli. 2007. SemEval-2007 task 10: English lexical substitution task. In *Proceedings of the 4th International Workshop on Semantic Evaluations (SemEval-2007)*, pages 48–53, Prague, Czech Republic.

Diana McCarthy and Roberto Navigli. 2009. The English lexical substitution task. *Language Resources and Evaluation Special Issue on Computational Semantic Analysis of Language: SemEval-2007 and Beyond*, 43(2):139–159.

Hwee Tou Ng and Yee Seng Chan. 2007. SemEval-2007 task 11: English lexical sample task via English-Chinese parallel text. In *Proceedings of the 4th International Workshop on Semantic Evaluations (SemEval-2007)*, pages 54–58, Prague, Czech Republic.

Patrick Pantel and Dekang Lin. 2002. Discovering word senses from text. In *Proceedings of ACM SIGKDD Conference on Knowledge Discovery and Data Mining*, pages 613–619, Edmonton, Canada.

Philip Resnik and David Yarowsky. 2000. Distinguishing systems and distinguishing senses: New evaluation methods for word sense disambiguation. *Natural Language Engineering*, 5(3):113–133.

Hinrich Schütze. 1998. Automatic word sense discrimination. *Computational Linguistics*, 24(1):97–123.

Serge Sharoff. 2006. Open-source corpora: Using the net to fish for linguistic data. *International Journal of Corpus Linguistics*, 11(4):435–462.

Ravi Sinha, Diana McCarthy, and Rada Mihalcea. 2009. Semeval-2010 task 2: Cross-lingual lexical substitution. In *Proceedings of the NAACL-HLT Workshop SEW-2009 - Semantic Evaluations: Recent Achievements and Future Directions*, Boulder, Colorado, USA.

SemEval-2010 Task 3: Cross-Lingual Word Sense Disambiguation

Els Lefever[1,2] and Veronique Hoste[1,2]

[1]LT3, Language and Translation Technology Team, University College Ghent, Belgium
[2]Department of Applied Mathematics and Computer Science, Ghent University, Belgium

{Els.Lefever,Veronique.Hoste}@hogent.be

Abstract

The goal of this task is to evaluate the feasibility of multilingual WSD on a newly developed multilingual lexical sample data set. Participants were asked to automatically determine the contextually appropriate translation of a given English noun in five languages, viz. Dutch, German, Italian, Spanish and French. This paper reports on the sixteen submissions from the five different participating teams.

1 Introduction

Word Sense Disambiguation, the task of selecting the correct sense of an ambiguous word in a given context, is a well-researched NLP problem (see for example Agirre and Edmonds (2006) and Navigli (2009)), largely boosted by the various Senseval and SemEval editions. The SemEval-2010 Cross-lingual Word Sense Disambiguation task focuses on two bottlenecks in current WSD research, namely the scarcity of sense inventories and sense-tagged corpora (especially for languages other than English) and the growing tendency to evaluate the performance of WSD systems in a real application such as machine translation and cross-language information retrieval (see for example Agirre et al. (2007)).

The Cross-lingual WSD task aims at the development of a multilingual data set to test the feasibility of multilingual WSD. Many studies have already shown the validity of this cross-lingual evidence idea (Gale et al., 1993; Ide et al., 2002; Ng et al., 2003; Apidianaki, 2009), but until now no benchmark data sets have been available. For the SemEval-2010 competition we developed (i) a sense inventory in which the sense distinctions were extracted from the multilingual corpus Europarl[1] and (ii) a data set in which the ambiguous words were annotated with the senses from the multilingual sense inventory. The Cross-Lingual WSD task is a lexical sample task for English nouns, in which the word senses are made up of the translations in five languages, viz. Dutch, French, Italian, Spanish and German. Both the sense inventory and the annotated data set were constructed for a sample of 25 nouns. The data set was divided into a trial set of 5 ambiguous nouns and a test set of 20 nouns. The participants had to automatically determine the contextually appropriate translation for a given English noun in each or a subset of the five target languages. Only translations present in Europarl were considered as valid translations.

The remainder of this article is organized as follows. Section 2 focuses on the task description and gives a short overview of the construction of the sense inventory and the annotation of the benchmark data set with the senses from the multilingual sense inventory. Section 3 clarifies the scoring metrics and presents two frequency-based baselines. The participating systems are presented in Section 4, while the results of the task are discussed in Section 5. Section 6 concludes this paper.

2 Task setup

2.1 Data sets

Two types of data sets were used in the Cross-lingual WSD task: (a) a parallel corpus on the basis of which the gold standard sense inventory was created and (b) a collection of English sentences containing the lexical sample words annotated with their contextually appropriate translations in five languages.

[1]http://www.statmt.org/europarl/

Proceedings of the 5th International Workshop on Semantic Evaluation, ACL 2010, pages 15–20,
Uppsala, Sweden, 15-16 July 2010.

Below, we provide a short summary of the complete data construction process. For a more detailed description, we refer to Lefever and Hoste (2009; 2010).

The gold standard sense inventory was derived from the Europarl parallel corpus[2], which is extracted from the proceedings of the European Parliament (Koehn, 2005). We selected 6 languages from the 11 European languages represented in the corpus, viz. English (our target language), Dutch, French, German, Italian and Spanish. All data were already sentence-aligned using a tool based on the Gale and Church (1991) algorithm, which was part of the Europarl corpus. We only considered the 1-1 sentence alignments between English and the five other languages. These sentence alignments were made available to the task participants for the five trial words. The sense inventory extracted from the parallel data set (Section 2.2) was used to annotate the sentences in the trial set and the test set, which were extracted from the JRC-ACQUIS Multilingual Parallel Corpus[3] and BNC[4].

2.2 Creation of the sense inventory

Two steps were taken to obtain a multilingual sense inventory: (1) word alignment on the sentences to find the set of possible translations for the set of ambiguous nouns and (2) clustering by meaning (per target word) of the resulting translations.

GIZA++ (Och and Ney, 2003) was used to generate the initial word alignments, which were manually verified by certified translators in all six involved languages. The human annotators were asked to assign a "NULL" link to words for which no valid translation could be identified. Furthermore, they were also asked to provide extra information on compound translations (e.g. the Dutch word *Investeringsbank* as a translation of the English multiword *Investment Bank*), fuzzy links, or target words with a different PoS (e.g. the verb *to bank*).

The manually verified translations were clustered by meaning by one annotator. In order to do so, the translations were linked across languages on the basis of unique sentence IDs. After the selection of all unique translation combinations, the translations were grouped into clusters. The clusters were organized in two levels, in which the top level reflects the main sense categories (e.g. for the word *coach* we have (1) (sports) manager, (2) bus, (3) carriage and (4) part of a train), and the subclusters represent the finer sense distinctions. Translations that correspond to English multiword units were identified and in case of non-apparent compounds, i.e. compounds which are not marked with a "-", the different compound parts were separated by §§ in the clustering file (e.g. the German *Post§§kutsche*). All clustered translations were also manually lemmatized.

2.3 Sense annotation of the test data

The resulting sense inventory was used to annotate the sentences in the trial set (20 sentences per ambiguous word) and the test set (50 sentences per ambiguous word). In total, 1100 sentences were annotated. The annotators were asked to (a) pick the contextually appropriate sense cluster and to (b) choose their three preferred translations from this cluster. In case they were not able to find three appropriate translations, they were also allowed to provide fewer. These potentially different translations were used to assign frequency weights (shown in example (2)) to the gold standard translations per sentence. The example (1) below shows the annotation result in both German and Dutch for an English source sentence containing *coach*.

(1) SENTENCE 12. STRANGELY , the national coach of the Irish teams down the years has had little direct contact with the four provincial coaches .

German 1: Nationaltrainer
German 2: Trainer
German 3: Coach

Dutch 1: trainer
Dutch 2: coach
Dutch 3: voetbaltrainer

For each instance, the gold standard that results from the manual annotation contains a set of translations that are enriched with

[2] http://www.statmt.org/europarl/
[3] http://wt.jrc.it/lt/Acquis/
[4] http://www.natcorp.ox.ac.uk/

frequency information. The format of both the input file and gold standard is similar to the format that will be used for the SemEval Cross-Lingual Lexical Substitution task (Sinha and Mihalcea, 2009). The following example illustrates the six-language gold standard format for the trial sentence in (1). The first field contains the target word, PoS-tag and language code, the second field contains the sentence ID and the third field contains the gold standard translations in the target language, enriched with their frequency weight:

(2) coach.n.nl 12 :: coach 3; speler-trainer 1; trainer 3; voetbaltrainer 1;
coach.n.fr 12 :: capitaine 1; entraîneur 3;
coach.n.de 12 :: Coach 1; Fußbaltrainer 1; Nationaltrainer 2; Trainer 3;
coach.n.it 12 :: allenatore 3;
coach.n.es 12 :: entrenador 3;

3 Evaluation

3.1 Scoring

To score the participating systems, we use an evaluation scheme which is inspired by the English lexical substitution task in SemEval 2007 (McCarthy and Navigli, 2007). We perform both a *best result* evaluation and a more relaxed evaluation for the *top five results*. The evaluation is performed using precision and recall ($Prec$ and Rec in the equations below), and Mode precision (M_P) and Mode recall (M_R), where we calculate precision and recall against the translation that is preferred by the majority of annotators, provided that one translation is more frequent than the others.

For the precision and recall formula we use the following variables. Let H be the set of annotators, T the set of test items and h_i the set of responses for an item $i \in T$ for annotator $h \in H$. For each $i \in T$ we calculate the mode (m_i) which corresponds to the translation with the highest frequency weight. For a detailed overview of the M_P and M_R calculations, we refer to McCarthy and Navigli (2007). Let A be the set of items from T (and TM) where the system provides at least one answer and $a_i : i \in A$ the set of guesses from the system for item i. For each i, we calculate the multiset union (H_i) for all h_i for all $h \in H$ and for each unique type (res) in H_i that has an associated frequency ($freq_{res}$). In order to assign frequency weights to our gold standard translations, we asked our human annotators to indicate their top 3 translations, which enables us to also obtain meaningful associated frequencies ($freq_{res}$) viz. "1" in case a translation is picked by 1 annotator, "2" if picked by two annotators and "3" if chosen by all three annotators.

Best result evaluation For the *best result* evaluation, systems can propose as many guesses as the system believes are correct, but the resulting score is divided by the number of guesses. In this way, systems that output a lot of guesses are not favoured.

$$Prec = \frac{\sum_{a_i : i \in A} \frac{\frac{\sum_{res \in a_i} freq_{res}}{|a_i|}}{|H_i|}}{|A|} \quad (1)$$

$$Rec = \frac{\sum_{a_i : i \in T} \frac{\frac{\sum_{res \in a_i} freq_{res}}{|a_i|}}{|H_i|}}{|T|} \quad (2)$$

Out-of-five (Oof) evaluation For the more relaxed evaluation, systems can propose up to five guesses. For this evaluation, the resulting score is not divided by the number of guesses.

$$Prec = \frac{\sum_{a_i : i \in A} \frac{\sum_{res \in a_i} freq_{res}}{|H_i|}}{|A|} \quad (3)$$

$$Rec = \frac{\sum_{a_i : i \in T} \frac{\sum_{res \in a_i} freq_{res}}{|H_i|}}{|T|} \quad (4)$$

3.2 Baselines

We produced two frequency-based baselines:

1. For the *Best result* evaluation, we select the most frequent lemmatized translation that results from the automated word alignment process (GIZA++).

2. For the *Out-of-five* or *more relaxed* evaluation, we select the five most frequent (lemmatized) translations that result from the GIZA++ alignment.

Table 1 shows the baselines for the *Best* evaluation, while Table 2 gives an overview per language of the baselines for the *Out-of-five* evaluation.

	Prec	Rec	M_P	M_R
Spanish	18.36	18.36	23.38	23.38
French	20.71	20.71	15.21	15.21
Italian	14.03	14.03	11.23	11.23
Dutch	15.69	15.69	8.71	8.71
German	13.16	13.16	6.95	6.95

Table 1: *Best* Baselines

	Prec	Rec	M_P	M_R
Spanish	48.41	48.41	42.62	42.62
French	45.99	45.99	36.45	36.45
Italian	34.51	34.51	29.70	29.70
Dutch	37.43	37.43	24.58	24.58
German	32.89	32.89	29.80	29.80

Table 2: *Out-of-five* Baselines

4 Systems

We received sixteen submissions from five different participating teams. One group tackled all five target languages, whereas the other groups focused on four (one team), two (one team) or one (two teams) target language(s). For both the *best* and the *Out-of-five* evaluation tasks, there were between three and seven participating systems per language.

The OWNS system identifies the nearest neighbors of the test instances from the training data using a pairwise similarity measure (weighted sum of the word overlap and semantic overlap between two sentences). They use WordNet similarity measures as an additional information source, while the other teams merely rely on parallel corpora to extract all lexical information. The UvT-WSD systems use a k-nearest neighbour classifier in the form of one word expert per lemma–Part-of-Speech pair to be disambiguated. The classifier takes as input a variety of local and global context features. Both the FCC-WSD and T3-COLEUR systems use bilingual translation probability tables that are derived from the Europarl corpus. The FCC-WSD system uses a Naive Bayes classifier, while the T3-COLEUR system uses an unsupervised graph-based method. Finally, the UHD systems build for each target word a multilingual co-occurrence graph based on the target word's aligned contexts found in parallel corpora. The cross-lingual nodes are first linked by translation edges, that are labeled with the translations of the target word in the corresponding contexts. The graph is transformed into a minimum spanning tree which is used to select the most relevant words in context to disambiguate a given test instance.

5 Results

For the system evaluation results, we show precision (*Prec*), recall (*Rec*), Mode precision (M_P) and Mode recall (M_R). We ranked all system results according to recall, as was done for the Lexical Substitution task. Table 3 shows the system ranking on the *best* task, while Table 4 shows the results for the *Oof* task.

	Prec	Rec	M_P	M_R
Spanish				
UvT-v	23.42	24.98	24.98	24.98
UvT-g	19.92	19.92	24.17	24.17
T3-COLEUR	19.78	19.59	24.59	24.59
UHD-1	20.48	16.33	28.48	22.19
UHD-2	20.2	16.09	28.18	22.65
FCC-WSD1	15.09	15.09	14.31	14.31
FCC-WSD3	14.43	14.43	13.41	13.41
French				
T3-COLEUR	21.96	21.73	16.15	15.93
UHD-2	20.93	16.65	17.78	14.15
UHD-1	20.22	16.21	17.59	14.56
OWNS2	16.05	16.05	14.21	14.21
OWNS1	16.05	16.05	14.21	14.21
OWNS3	12.53	12.53	14.21	14.21
OWNS4	10.49	10.49	14.21	14.21
Italian				
T3-COLEUR	15.55	15.4	10.2	10.12
UHD-2	16.28	13.03	14.89	9.46
UHD-1	15.94	12.78	12.34	8.48
Dutch				
UvT-v	17.7	17.7	12.05	12.05
UvT-g	15.93	15.93	10.54	10.54
T3-COLEUR	10.71	10.56	6.18	6.16
German				
T3-COLEUR	13.79	13.63	8.1	8.1
UHD-1	12.2	9.32	11.05	7.78
UHD-2	12.03	9.23	12.91	9.22

Table 3: *Best* System Results

Beating the baseline seems to be quite challenging for this WSD task. While the best systems outperform the baseline for the *best* task,

	Prec	Rec	M_P	M_R
Spanish				
UvT-g	43.12	43.12	43.94	43.94
UvT-v	42.17	42.17	40.62	40.62
FCC-WSD2	40.76	40.76	44.84	44.84
FCC-WSD4	38.46	38.46	39.49	39.49
T3-COLEUR	35.84	35.46	39.01	38.78
UHD-1	38.78	31.81	40.68	32.38
UHD-2	37.74	31.3	39.09	32.05
French				
T3-COLEUR	49.44	48.96	42.13	41.77
OWNS1	43.11	43.11	38.29	38.29
OWNS2	38.74	38.74	37.73	37.73
UHD-1	39.06	32	37.00	26.79
UHD-2	37.92	31.38	37.66	27.08
Italian				
T3-COLEUR	40.7	40.34	38.99	38.70
UHD-1	33.72	27.49	27.54	21.81
UHD-2	32.68	27.42	29.82	23.20
Dutch				
UvT-v	34.95	34.95	24.62	24.62
UvT-g	34.92	34.92	19.72	19.72
T3-COLEUR	21.47	21.27	12.05	12.03
German				
T3-COLEUR	33.21	32.82	33.60	33.56
UHD-1	27.62	22.82	25.68	21.16
UHD-2	27.24	22.55	27.19	22.30

Table 4: *Out-of-five* System Results

this is not always the case for the *Out-of-five* task. This is not surprising though, as the *Oof* baseline contains the five most frequent Europarl translations. As a consequence, these translations usually contain the most frequent translations from different sense clusters, and in addition they also contain the most generic translation that often covers multiple senses of the target word.

The best results are achieved by the UvT-WSD (Spanish, Dutch) and ColEur (French, Italian and German) systems. An interesting feature that these systems have in common, is that they extract all lexical information from the parallel corpus at hand, and do not need any additional data sources. As a consequence, the systems can easily be applied to other languages as well. This is clearly illustrated by the ColEur system, that participated for all supported languages, and outperformed the other systems for three of the five languages.

In general, we notice that Spanish and French have the highest scores, followed by Italian, whereas Dutch and German seem to be more challenging. The same observation can be made for both the *Oof* and *Best* results, except for Italian that performs worse than Dutch for the latter. However, given the low participation rate for Italian, we do not have sufficient information to explain this different behaviour on the two tasks. The discrepancy between the performance figures for Spanish and French on the one hand, and German and Dutch on the other hand, seems more readily explicable. A likely explanation could be the number of classes (or translations) the systems have to choose from. As both Dutch and German are characterized by a rich compounding system, these compound translations also result in a higher number of different translations. Figure 1 illustrates this by listing the number of different translations (or classes in the context of WSD) for all trial and test words. As a result, the broader set of translations makes the WSD task, that consists in choosing the most appropriate translation from all possible translations for a given instance, more complicated for Dutch and German.

6 Concluding remarks

We believe that the Cross-lingual Word Sense Disambiguation task is an interesting contribution to the domain, as it attempts to address two WSD problems which have received a lot of attention lately, namely (1) the scarcity of hand-crafted sense inventories and sense-tagged corpora and (2) the need to make WSD more suited for practical applications.

The system results lead to the following observations. Firstly, languages which make extensive use of single word compounds seem harder to tackle, which is also reflected in the baseline scores. A possible explanation for this phenomenon could lie in the number of translations the systems have to choose from. Secondly, it is striking that the systems with the highest performance solely rely on parallel corpora as a source of information. This would seem very promising for future multilingual WSD research; by eliminating the need

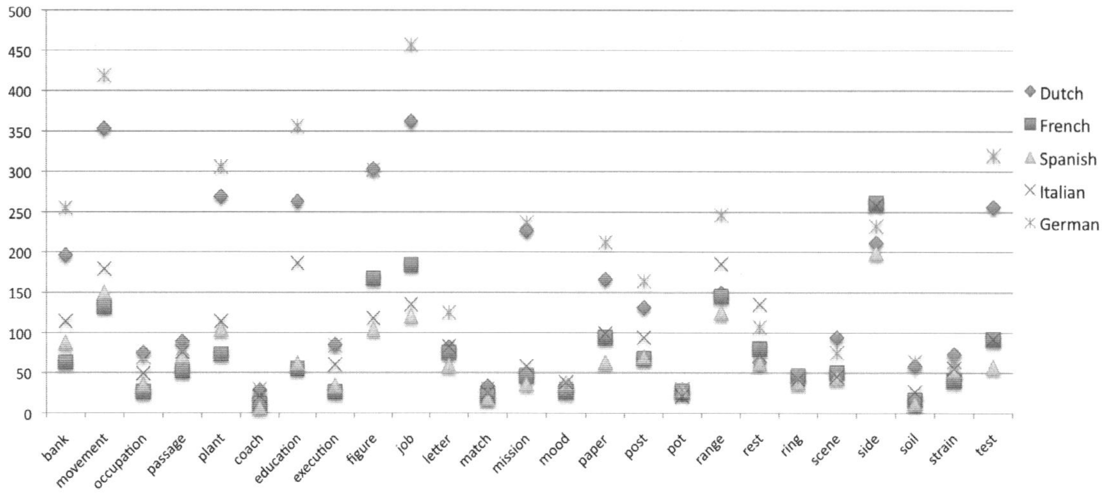

Figure 1: Number of different translations per word for Dutch, French, Spanish, Italian and German.

for external information sources, these systems present a more flexible and language-independent approach to WSD.

References

E. Agirre and P. Edmonds, editors. 2006. *Word Sense Disambiguation.* Text, Speech and Language Technology. Springer, Dordrecht.

E. Agirre, B. Magnini, O. Lopez de Lacalle, A. Otegi, G. Rigau, and P. Vossen. 2007. Semeval-2007 task01: Evaluating wsd on cross-language information retrieval. In *Proceedings of CLEF 2007 Workshop, pp. 908 - 917. ISSN: 1818-8044. ISBN: 2-912335-31-0.*

M. Apidianaki. 2009. Data-driven semantic analysis for multilingual wsd and lexical selection in translation. In *Proceedings of the 12th Conference of the European Chapter of the Association for Computational Linguistics (EACL)*, Athens, Greece.

W.A. Gale and K.W. Church. 1991. A program for aligning sentences in bilingual corpora. In *Computational Linguistics*, pages 177–184.

W.A. Gale, K.W. Church, and D. Yarowsky. 1993. A method for disambiguating word senses in a large corpus. In *Computers and the Humanities*, volume 26, pages 415–439.

N. Ide, T. Erjavec, and D. Tufis. 2002. Sense discrimination with parallel corpora. In *Proceedings of ACL Workshop on Word Sense Disambiguation: Recent Successes and Future Directions*, pages 54–60.

P. Koehn. 2005. Europarl: A parallel corpus for statistical machine translation. In *Proceedings of the MT Summit.*

E. Lefever and V. Hoste. 2009. Semeval-2010 task 3: Cross-lingual word sense disambiguation. In *Proceedings of the NAACL-HLT 2009 Workshop: SEW-2009 - Semantic Evaluations*, pages 82–87, Boulder, Colorado.

E. Lefever and V. Hoste. 2010. Construction of a benchmark data set for cross-lingual word sense disambiguation. In *Proceedings of the seventh international conference on Language Resources and Evaluation.*, Malta.

D. McCarthy and R. Navigli. 2007. Semeval-2007 task 10: English lexical substitution task. In *Proceedings of the 4th International Workshop on Semantic Evaluations (SemEval-2007)*, pages 48–53, Prague, Czech Republic.

R. Navigli. 2009. Word sense disambiguation: a survey. In *ACM Computing Surveys*, volume 41, pages 1–69.

H.T. Ng, B. Wang, and Y.S. Chan. 2003. Exploiting parallel texts for word sense disambiguation: An empirical study. In *Proceedings of the 41st Annual Meeting of the Association for Computational Linguistics*, pages 455–462, Santa Cruz.

F.J. Och and H. Ney. 2003. A systematic comparison of various statistical alignment models. *Computational Linguistics*, 29(1):19–51.

McCarthy D. Sinha, R. D. and R. Mihalcea. 2009. Semeval-2010 task 2: Cross-lingual lexical substitution. In *Proceedings of the NAACL-HLT 2009 Workshop: SEW-2009 - Semantic Evaluations*, Boulder, Colorado.

SemEval-2010 Task 5: Automatic Keyphrase Extraction from Scientific Articles

Su Nam Kim,♠ Olena Medelyan,♡ Min-Yen Kan◇ and **Timothy Baldwin♠**
♠ Dept of Computer Science and Software Engineering, University of Melbourne, Australia
♡ Pingar LP, Auckland, New Zealand
◇ School of Computing, National University of Singapore, Singapore
sunamkim@gmail.com, medelyan@gmail.com,
kanmy@comp.nus.edu.sg, tb@ldwin.net

Abstract

This paper describes Task 5 of the Workshop on Semantic Evaluation 2010 (SemEval-2010). Systems are to automatically assign keyphrases or keywords to given scientific articles. The participating systems were evaluated by matching their extracted keyphrases against manually assigned ones. We present the overall ranking of the submitted systems and discuss our findings to suggest future directions for this task.

1 Task Description

Keyphrases[1] are words that capture the main topics of a document. As they represent these key ideas, extracting high-quality keyphrases can benefit various natural language processing (NLP) applications such as summarization, information retrieval and question-answering. In summarization, keyphrases can be used as a form of semantic metadata (Barzilay and Elhadad, 1997; Lawrie et al., 2001; D'Avanzo and Magnini, 2005). In search engines, keyphrases can supplement full-text indexing and assist users in formulating queries.

Recently, a resurgence of interest in keyphrase extraction has led to the development of several new systems and techniques for the task (Frank et al., 1999; Witten et al., 1999; Turney, 1999; Hulth, 2003; Turney, 2003; Park et al., 2004; Barker and Corrnacchia, 2000; Hulth, 2004; Matsuo and Ishizuka, 2004; Mihalcea and Tarau, 2004; Medelyan and Witten, 2006; Nguyen and Kan, 2007; Wan and Xiao, 2008; Liu et al., 2009; Medelyan, 2009; Nguyen and Phan, 2009). These have showcased the potential benefits of keyphrase extraction to downstream NLP applications.

In light of these developments, we felt that this was an appropriate time to conduct a shared task for keyphrase extraction, to provide a standard assessment to benchmark current approaches. A second goal of the task was to contribute an additional public dataset to spur future research in the area.

Currently, there are several publicly available data sets.[2] For example, Hulth (2003) contributed 2,000 abstracts of journal articles present in Inspec between the years 1998 and 2002. The data set contains keyphrases (i.e. controlled and uncontrolled terms) assigned by professional indexers — 1,000 for training, 500 for validation and 500 for testing. Nguyen and Kan (2007) collected a dataset containing 120 computer science articles, ranging in length from 4 to 12 pages. The articles contain author-assigned keyphrases as well as reader-assigned keyphrases contributed by undergraduate CS students. In the general newswire domain, Wan and Xiao (2008) developed a dataset of 308 documents taken from DUC 2001 which contain up to 10 manually-assigned keyphrases per document. Several databases, including the ACM Digital Library, IEEE Xplore, Inspec and PubMed provide articles with author-assigned keyphrases and, occasionally, reader-assigned ones. Medelyan (2009) automatically generated a dataset using tags assigned by the users of the collaborative citation platform CiteULike. This dataset additionally records how many people have assigned the same keyword to the same publication. In total, 180 full-text publications were annotated by over 300 users.[3] Despite the availability of these datasets, a standardized benchmark dataset with a well-defined train-

[1]We use "keyphrase" and "keywords" interchangeably to refer to both single words and phrases.

◇ Min-Yen Kan's work was funded by National Research Foundation grant "Interactive Media Search" (grant # R-252-000-325-279).

[2]All data sets listed below are available for download from http://github.com/snkim/AutomaticKeyphraseExtraction

[3]http://bit.ly/maui-datasets

Proceedings of the 5th International Workshop on Semantic Evaluation, ACL 2010, pages 21–26,
Uppsala, Sweden, 15-16 July 2010.

ing and test split is needed to maximize comparability of results.

For the SemEval-2010 Task 5, we have compiled a set of 284 scientific articles with keyphrases carefully chosen by both their authors and readers. The participants' task was to develop systems which automatically produce keyphrases for each paper. Each team was allowed to submit up to three system runs, to benchmark the contributions of different parameter settings and approaches. Each run consisted of extracting a ranked list of 15 keyphrases from each document, ranked by their probability of being reader-assigned keyphrases.

In the remainder of the paper, we describe the competition setup, including how data collection was managed and the evaluation methodology (Section 2). We present the results of the shared task, and discuss the immediate findings of the competition in Section 3. In Section 4 we assess the human performance by comparing reader-assigned keyphrases to those assigned by the authors. This gives an approximation of an upper-bound performance for this task.

2 Competition Setup

2.1 Data

We collected trial, training and test data from the ACM Digital Library (conference and workshop papers). The input papers ranged from 6 to 8 pages, including tables and pictures. To ensure a variety of different topics was represented in the corpus, we purposefully selected papers from four different research areas for the dataset. In particular, the selected articles belong to the following four 1998 ACM classifications: C2.4 (Distributed Systems), H3.3 (Information Search and Retrieval), I2.11 (Distributed Artificial Intelligence – Multiagent Systems) and J4 (Social and Behavioral Sciences – Economics). All three datasets (trial, training and test) had an equal distribution of documents from among the categories (see Table 1). This domain specific information was provided with the papers (e.g. I2.4-1 or H3.3-2), in case participant systems wanted to utilize this information. We specifically decided to straddle different areas to see whether participant approaches would work better within specific areas.

Participants were provided with 40, 144, and 100 articles, respectively, in the trial, training and test data, distributed evenly across the four research areas in each case. Note that the trial data is a subset of the training data. Since the original format for the articles was PDF, we converted them into (UTF-8) plain text using pdftotext, and systematically restored full words that were originally hyphenated and broken across two lines. This policy potentially resulted in valid hyphenated forms having their hyphen (-) removed.

All collected papers contain author-assigned keyphrases, part of the original PDF file. We additionally collected reader-assigned keyphrases for each paper. We first performed a pilot annotation task with a group of students to check the stability of the annotations, finalize the guidelines, and discover and resolve potential issues that may occur during the actual annotation. To collect the actual reader-assigned keyphrases, we then hired 50 student annotators from the Computer Science department of the National University of Singapore.

We assigned 5 papers to each annotator, estimating that assigning keyphrases to each paper should take about 10-15 minutes. Annotators were explicitly told to extract keyphrases that actually appear in the text of each paper, rather than to create semantically-equivalent phrases, but could extract phrases from any part of the document (including headers and captions). In reality, on average 15% of the reader-assigned keyphrases did not appear in the text of the paper, but this is still less than the 19% of author-assigned keyphrases that did not appear in the papers. These values were computed using the test documents only. In other words, the maximum recall that the participating systems can achieve on these documents is 85% and 81% for the reader- and author-assigned keyphrases, respectively.

As some keyphrases may occur in multiple forms, in our evaluation we accepted two different versions of genitive keyphrases: *A of B* $\rightarrow$ *B A* (e.g. *policy of school* = *school policy*) and *A's B* $\rightarrow$ *A B* (e.g. *school's policy* = *school policy*). In certain cases, such alternations change the semantics of the candidate phrase (e.g., *matter of fact* vs. *?fact matter*). We judged borderline cases by committee and do not include alternations that were judged to be semantically distinct.

Table 1 shows the distribution of the trial, training and test documents over the four different research areas, while Table 2 shows the distribution of author- and reader-assigned keyphrases.

Interestingly, among the 387 author-assigned

Dataset	Total	Document Topic			
		C	H	I	J
Trial	40	10	10	10	10
Training	144	34	39	35	36
Test	100	25	25	25	25

Table 1: Number of documents per topic in the trial, training and test datasets, across the four ACM document classifications

Dataset	Author	Reader	Combined
Trial	149	526	621
Training	559	1824	2223
Test	387	1217	1482

Table 2: Number of author- and reader-assigned keyphrases in the different datasets

keywords, 125 keywords match exactly with reader-assigned keywords, while many more near-misses (i.e. partial matches) occur.

2.2 Evaluation Method and Baseline

Traditionally, automatic keyphrase extraction systems have been assessed using the proportion of top-N candidates that exactly match the gold-standard keyphrases (Frank et al., 1999; Witten et al., 1999; Turney, 1999). In some cases, inexact matches, or near-misses, have also been considered. Some have suggested treating semantically-similar keyphrases as correct based on similarities computed over a large corpus (Jarmasz and Barriere, 2004; Mihalcea and Tarau, 2004), or using semantic relations defined in a thesaurus (Medelyan and Witten, 2006). Zesch and Gurevych (2009) compute near-misses using an n-gram based approach relative to the gold standard. For our shared task, we follow the traditional exact match evaluation metric. That is, we match the keyphrases in the answer set with those the systems provide, and calculate micro-averaged precision, recall and F-score ($\beta = 1$). In the evaluation, we check the performance over the top 5, 10 and 15 candidates returned by each system. We rank the participating systems by F-score over the top 15 candidates.

Participants were required to extract existing phrases from the documents. Since it is theoretically possible to retrieve author-assigned keyphrases from the original PDF articles, we evaluate the participating systems over the independently-generated and held-out reader-assigned keyphrases, as well as the combined set of keyphrases (author- and reader-assigned).

All keyphrases in the answer set are stemmed using the English Porter stemmer for both the training and test dataset.[4]

We computed a TF$\times$IDF n-gram based baseline using both supervised and unsupervised learning systems. We use 1, 2, 3-grams as keyphrase candidates, used Naïve Bayes (NB) and Maximum Entropy (ME) classifiers to learn two supervised baseline systems based on the keyphrase candidates and gold-standard annotations for the training documents. In total, there are three baselines: two supervised and one unsupervised. The performance of the baselines is presented in Table 3, where *R* indicates reader-assigned keyphrases and *C* indicates combined (both author- and reader-assigned) keyphrases.

3 Competition Results

The trial data was downloaded by 73 different teams, of which 36 teams subsequently downloaded the training and test data. 21 teams participated in the final competition, of which two teams withdrew their systems.

Table 4 shows the performance of the final 19 submitted systems. 5 teams submitted one run, 6 teams submitted two runs and 8 teams submitted the maximum number of three runs. We rank the best-performing system from each team by micro-averaged F-score over the top 15 candidates. We also show system performance over reader-assigned keywords in Table 5, and over author-assigned keywords in Table 6. In all these tables, P, R and F denote precision, recall and F-score, respectively.

The best results over the reader-assigned and combined keyphrase sets are **23.5%** and **27.5%**, respectively, achieved by the *HUMB* team. Most systems outperformed the baselines. Systems also generally did better over the combined set, as the presence of a larger gold-standard answer set improved recall.

In Tables 7 and 8, we ranked the teams by F-score, computed over the top 15 candidates for each of the four ACM document classifications. The numbers in brackets are the actual F-scores

[4]Using the Perl implementation available at `http://tartarus.org/~martin/PorterStemmer/`; we informed participants that this was the stemmer we would be using for the task, to avoid possible stemming variations between implementations.

Method	by	Top 5 candidates			Top 10 candidates			Top 15 candidates		
		P	R	F	P	R	F	P	R	F
TF×IDF	R	17.8%	7.4%	10.4%	13.9%	11.5%	12.6%	11.6%	14.5%	12.9%
	C	22.0%	7.5%	11.2%	17.7%	12.1%	14.4%	14.9%	15.3%	15.1%
NB	R	16.8%	7.0%	9.9%	13.3%	11.1%	12.1%	11.4%	14.2%	12.7%
	C	21.4%	7.3%	10.9%	17.3%	11.8%	14.0%	14.5%	14.9%	14.7%
ME	R	16.8%	7.0%	9.9%	13.3%	11.1%	12.1%	11.4%	14.2%	12.7%
	C	21.4%	7.3%	10.9%	17.3%	11.8%	14.0%	14.5%	14.9%	14.7%

Table 3: Baseline keyphrase extraction performance for one unsupervised (TF×IDF) and two supervised (NB and ME) systems

System	Rank	Top 5 candidates			Top 10 candidates			Top 15 candidates		
		P	R	F	P	R	F	P	R	F
HUMB	1	39.0%	13.3%	19.8%	32.0%	21.8%	26.0%	27.2%	27.8%	27.5%
WINGNUS	2	40.2%	13.7%	20.5%	30.5%	20.8%	24.7%	24.9%	25.5%	25.2%
KP-Miner	3	36.0%	12.3%	18.3%	28.6%	19.5%	23.2%	24.9%	25.5%	25.2%
SZTERGAK	4	34.2%	11.7%	17.4%	28.5%	19.4%	23.1%	24.8%	25.4%	25.1%
ICL	5	34.4%	11.7%	17.5%	29.2%	19.9%	23.7%	24.6%	25.2%	24.9%
SEERLAB	6	39.0%	13.3%	19.8%	29.7%	20.3%	24.1%	24.1%	24.6%	24.3%
KX_FBK	7	34.2%	11.7%	17.4%	27.0%	18.4%	21.9%	23.6%	24.2%	23.9%
DERIUNLP	8	27.4%	9.4%	13.9%	23.0%	15.7%	18.7%	22.0%	22.5%	22.3%
Maui	9	35.0%	11.9%	17.8%	25.2%	17.2%	20.4%	20.3%	20.8%	20.6%
DFKI	10	29.2%	10.0%	14.9%	23.3%	15.9%	18.9%	20.3%	20.7%	20.5%
BUAP	11	13.6%	4.6%	6.9%	17.6%	12.0%	14.3%	19.0%	19.4%	19.2%
SJTULTLAB	12	30.2%	10.3%	15.4%	22.7%	15.5%	18.4%	18.4%	18.8%	18.6%
UNICE	13	27.4%	9.4%	13.9%	22.4%	15.3%	18.2%	18.3%	18.8%	18.5%
UNPMC	14	18.0%	6.1%	9.2%	19.0%	13.0%	15.4%	18.1%	18.6%	18.3%
JU_CSE	15	28.4%	9.7%	14.5%	21.5%	14.7%	17.4%	17.8%	18.2%	18.0%
LIKEY	16	29.2%	10.0%	14.9%	21.1%	14.4%	17.1%	16.3%	16.7%	16.5%
UvT	17	24.8%	8.5%	12.6%	18.6%	12.7%	15.1%	14.6%	14.9%	14.8%
POLYU	18	15.6%	5.3%	7.9%	14.6%	10.0%	11.8%	13.9%	14.2%	14.0%
UKP	19	9.4%	3.2%	4.8%	5.9%	4.0%	4.8%	5.3%	5.4%	5.3%

Table 4: Performance of the submitted systems over the combined author- and reader-assigned keywords, ranked by F-score

for each team. Note that in the case of a tie in F-score, we ordered teams by descending F-score over all the data.

4 Discussion of the Upper-Bound Performance

The current evaluation is a testament to the gains made by keyphrase extraction systems. The system performance over the different keyword categories (reader-assigned and author-assigned) and numbers of keyword candidates (top 5, 10 and 15 candidates) attest to this fact.

The top-performing systems return F-scores in the upper twenties. Superficially, this number is low, and it is instructive to examine how much room there is for improvement. Keyphrase extraction is a subjective task, and an F-score of 100% is infeasible. On the author-assigned keyphrases in our test collection, the highest a system could theoretically achieve was 81% recall[5] and 100% precision, which gives a maximum F-score of 89%. However, such a high value would only be possible if the number of keyphrases extracted per document could vary; in our task, we fixed the thresholds at 5, 10 and 15 keyphrases.

[5]The remaining 19% of keyphrases do not actually appear in the documents and thus cannot be extracted.

Another way of computing the upper-bound performance would be to look into how well people perform the same task. We analyzed the performance of our readers, taking the author-assigned keyphrases as the gold standard. The authors assigned an average of 4 keyphrases to each paper, whereas the readers assigned 12 on average. These 12 keyphrases cover 77.8% of the authors' keyphrases, which corresponds to a precision of 21.5%. The F-score achieved by the readers on the author-assigned keyphrases is 33.6%, whereas the F-score of the best-performing system on the same data is 19.3% (for top 15, not top 12 keyphrases, see Table 6).

We conclude that there is definitely still room for improvement, and for any future shared tasks, we recommend against fixing any threshold on the number of keyphrases to be extracted per document. Finally, as we use a strict exact matching metric for evaluation, the presented evaluation figures are a lower bound for performance, as semantically equivalent keyphrases are not counted as correct. For future runs of this challenge, we believe a more semantically-motivated evaluation should be employed to give a more accurate impression of keyphrase acceptability.

System	Rank	Top 5 candidates			Top 10 candidates			Top 15 candidates		
		P	R	F	P	R	F	P	R	F
HUMB	1	30.4%	12.6%	17.8%	24.8%	20.6%	22.5%	21.2%	26.4%	23.5%
KX_FBK	2	29.2%	12.1%	17.1%	23.2%	19.3%	21.1%	20.3%	25.3%	22.6%
SZTERGAK	3	28.2%	11.7%	16.6%	23.2%	19.3%	21.1%	19.9%	24.8%	22.1%
WINGNUS	4	30.6%	12.7%	18.0%	23.6%	19.6%	21.4%	19.8%	24.7	22.0%
ICL	5	27.2%	11.3%	16.0%	22.4%	18.6%	20.3%	19.5%	24.3%	21.6%
SEERLAB	6	31.0%	12.9%	18.2%	24.1%	20.0%	21.9%	19.3%	24.1%	21.5%
KP-Miner	7	28.2%	11.7%	16.5%	22.0%	18.3%	20.0%	19.3%	24.1%	21.5%
DERIUNLP	8	22.2%	9.2%	13.0%	18.9%	15.7%	17.2%	17.5%	21.8%	19.5%
DFKI	9	24.4%	10.1%	14.3%	19.8%	16.5%	18.0%	17.4%	21.7%	19.3%
UNICE	10	25.0%	10.4%	14.7%	20.1%	16.7%	18.2%	16.0%	19.9%	17.8%
SJTULTLAB	11	26.6%	11.1%	15.6%	19.4%	16.1%	17.6%	15.6%	19.4%	17.3%
BUAP	12	10.4%	4.3%	6.1%	13.9%	11.5%	12.6%	14.9%	18.6%	16.6%
Maui	13	25.0%	10.4%	14.7%	18.1%	15.0%	16.4%	14.9%	18.5%	16.1%
UNPMC	14	13.8%	5.7%	8.1%	15.1%	12.5%	13.7%	14.5%	18.0%	16.1%
JU_CSE	15	23.4%	9.7%	13.7%	18.1%	15.0%	16.4%	14.4%	17.9%	16.0%
LIKEY	16	24.6%	10.2%	14.4%	17.9%	14.9%	16.2%	13.8%	17.2%	15.3%
POLYU	17	13.6%	5.7%	8.0%	12.6%	10.5%	11.4%	12.0%	14.9%	13.3%
UvT	18	20.4%	8.5%	12.0%	15.6%	13.0%	14.2%	11.9%	14.9%	13.2%
UKP	19	8.2%	3.4%	4.8%	5.3%	4.4%	4.8%	4.7%	5.8%	5.2%

Table 5: Performance of the submitted systems over the reader-assigned keywords, ranked by F-score

System	Rank	Top 5 candidates			Top 10 candidates			Top 15 candidates		
		P	R	F	P	R	F	P	R	F
HUMB	1	21.2%	27.4%	23.9%	15.4%	39.8%	22.2%	12.1%	47.0%	19.3%
KP-Miner	2	19.0%	24.6%	21.4%	13.4%	34.6%	19.3%	10.7%	41.6%	17.1%
ICL	3	17.0%	22.0%	19.2%	13.5%	34.9%	19.5%	10.5%	40.6%	16.6%
Maui	4	20.4%	26.4%	23.0%	13.7%	35.4%	19.8%	10.2%	39.5%	16.2%
SEERLAB	5	18.8%	24.3%	21.2%	13.1%	33.9%	18.9%	10.1%	39.0%	16.0%
SZTERGAK	6	14.6%	18.9%	16.5%	12.2%	31.5%	17.6%	9.9%	38.5%	15.8%
WINGNUS	7	18.6%	24.0%	21.0%	12.6%	32.6%	18.2%	9.3%	36.2%	14.8%
DERIUNLP	8	12.6%	16.3%	14.2%	9.7%	25.1%	14.0%	9.3%	35.9%	14.7%
KX_FBK	9	13.6%	17.6%	15.3%	10.0%	25.8%	14.4%	8.5%	32.8%	13.5%
BUAP	10	5.6%	7.2%	6.3%	8.1%	20.9%	11.7%	8.3%	32.0%	13.2%
JU_CSE	11	12.0%	15.5%	13.5%	8.5%	22.0%	12.3%	7.5%	29.0%	11.9%
UNPMC	12	7.0%	9.0%	7.9%	7.7%	19.9%	11.1%	7.1%	27.4%	11.2%
DFKI	13	12.8%	16.5%	14.4%	8.5%	22.0%	12.3%	6.6%	25.6%	10.5%
SJTULTLAB	14	9.6%	12.4%	10.8%	7.8%	20.2%	11.3%	6.2%	24.0%	9.9%
Likey	15	11.6%	15.0%	13.1%	7.9%	20.4%	11.4%	5.9%	22.7%	9.3%
UvT	16	11.4%	14.7%	12.9%	7.6%	19.6%	11.0%	5.8%	22.5%	9.2%
UNICE	17	8.8%	11.4%	9.9%	6.4%	16.5%	9.2%	5.5%	21.5%	8.8%
POLYU	18	3.8%	4.9%	4.3%	4.1%	10.6%	5.9%	4.1%	16.0%	6.6%
UKP	19	1.6%	2.1%	1.8%	0.9%	2.3%	1.3%	0.8%	3.1%	1.3%

Table 6: Performance of the submitted systems over the author-assigned keywords, ranked by F-score

5 Conclusion

This paper has described Task 5 of the Workshop on Semantic Evaluation 2010 (SemEval-2010), focusing on keyphrase extraction. We outlined the design of the datasets used in the shared task and the evaluation metrics, before presenting the official results for the task and summarising the immediate findings. We also analyzed the upper-bound performance for this task, and demonstrated that there is still room for improvement over the task. We look forward to future advances in automatic keyphrase extraction based on this and other datasets.

References

Ken Barker and Nadia Corrnacchia. Using noun phrase heads to extract document keyphrases. In *Proceedings of BCCSCSI : Advances in Artificial Intelligence*. 2000, pp.96–103.

Regina Barzilay and Michael Elhadad. Using lexical chains for text summarization. In *Proceedings of ACL/EACL Workshop on Intelligent Scalable Text Summarization*. 1997, pp. 10–17.

Ernesto D'Avanzo and Bernado Magnini. A Keyphrase-Based Approach to Summarization: the LAKE System at DUC-2005. In *Proceedings of DUC*. 2005.

Eibe Frank and Gordon W. Paynter and Ian H. Witten and Carl Gutwin and Craig G. Nevill-Manning. Domain Specific Keyphrase Extraction. In *Proceedings of IJCAI*. 1999, pp.668–673.

Annette Hulth. Improved automatic keyword extraction given more linguistic knowledge. In *Proceedings of EMNLP*. 2003, 216–223.

Annette Hulth. Enhancing Linguistically Oriented Automatic Keyword Extraction. In *Proceedings of HLT/NAACL*. 2004, pp. 17–20.

Mario Jarmasz and Caroline Barriere. Using semantic similarity over tera-byte corpus, compute the performance of keyphrase extraction. In *Proceedings of CLINE*. 2004.

Dawn Lawrie and W. Bruce Croft and Arnold Rosenberg. Finding Topic Words for Hierarchical Summarization. In *Proceedings of SIGIR*. 2001, pp. 349–357.

Rank	Group C	Group H	Group I	Group J
1	HUMB(28.3%)	HUMB(30.2%)	HUMB(24.2%)	HUMB(27.4%)
2	ICL(27.2%)	WINGNUS(28.9%)	SEERLAB(24.2%)	WINGNUS(25.4%)
3	KP-Miner(25.5%)	SEERLAB(27.8%)	KP-Miner(22.8%)	ICL(25.4%)
4	SZTERGAK(25.3%)	KP-Miner(27.6%)	KX_FBK(22.8%)	SZTERGAK(25.17%)
5	WINGNUS(24.2%)	SZTERGAK(27.6%)	WINGNUS(22.3%)	KP-Miner(24.9%)
6	KX_FBK(24.2%)	ICL(25.5%)	SZTERGAK(22.25%)	KX_FBK(24.6%)
7	DERIUNLP(23.6%)	KX_FBK(23.9%)	ICL(21.4%)	UNICE(23.5%)
8	SEERLAB(22.0%)	Maui(23.9%)	DERIUNLP(20.1%)	SEERLAB(23.3%)
9	DFKI(21.7%)	DERIUNLP(23.6%)	DFKI(19.3%)	DFKI(22.2%)
10	Maui(19.3%)	UNPMC(22.6%)	BUAP(18.5%)	Maui(21.3%)
11	BUAP(18.5%)	SJTULTLAB(22.1%)	SJTULTLAB(17.9%)	DERIUNLP(20.3%)
12	JU_CSE(18.2%)	UNICE(21.8%)	JU_CSE(17.9%)	BUAP(19.7%)
13	Likey(18.2%)	DFKI(20.5%)	Maui(17.6%)	JU_CSE(18.6%)
14	SJTULTLAB(17.7%)	BUAP(20.2%)	UNPMC(17.6%)	UNPMC(17.8%)
15	UvT(15.8%)	UvT(20.2%)	UNICE(14.7%)	Likey(17.2%)
16	UNPMC(15.2%)	Likey(19.4%)	Likey(11.3%)	SJTULTLAB(16.7%)
17	UNIC(14.3%)	JU_CSE(17.3%)	POLYU(13.6%)	POLYU(14.3%)
18	POLYU(12.5%)	POLYU(15.8%)	UvT(10.3%)	UvT(12.6%)
19	UKP(4.4%)	UKP(5.0%)	UKP(5.4%)	UKP(6.8%)

Table 7: System ranking (and F-score) for each ACM classification: combined keywords

Rank	Group C	Group H	Group I	Group J
1	ICL(23.3%)	HUMB(25.0%)	HUMB(21.7%)	HUMB(24.7%)
2	KX_FBK(23.3%)	WINGNUS(23.5%)	KX_FBK(21.4%)	WINGNUS(24.4%)
3	HUMB(22.7%)	SEERLAB(23.2%)	SEERLAB(21.1%)	SZTERGAK(24.4%)
4	SZTERGAK(22.7%)	KP-Miner(22.4%)	WINGNUS(19.9%)	KX_FBK(24.4%)
5	DERIUNLP(21.5%)	SZTERGAK(21.8%)	KP-Miner(19.6%)	UNICE(23.8%)
6	KP-Miner(21.2%)	KX_FBK(21.2%)	SZTERGAK(19.6%)	ICL(23.5%)
7	WINGNUS(20.0%)	ICL(20.1%)	ICL(19.6%)	KP-Miner(22.6%)
8	SEERLAB(19.4%)	DERIUNLP(20.1%)	DFKI(18.5%)	SEERLAB(22.0%)
9	DFKI(19.4%)	DFKI(19.5%)	SJTULTLAB(17.6%)	DFKI(21.7%)
10	JU_CSE(17.0%)	SJTULTLAB(19.5%)	DERIUNLP(17.3%)	BUAP(19.6%)
11	Likey(16.4%)	UNICE(19.2%)	JU_CSE(16.7%)	DERIUNLP(19.0%)
12	SJTULTLAB(15.8%)	Maui(18.1%)	BUAP(16.4%)	Maui(17.8%)
13	BUAP(15.5%)	UNPMC(18.1%)	UNPMC(16.1%)	JU_CSE(17.9%)
14	Maui(15.2%)	Likey(16.9%)	Maui(14.9%)	Likey(17.5%)
15	UNICE(14.0%)	UvT(16.4%)	UNICE(14.0%)	UNPMC(16.6%)
16	UvT(14.0%)	POLYU(15.5%)	POLYU(11.9%)	SJTULTLAB(16.3%)
17	UNPMC(13.4%)	BUAP(14.9%)	Likey(10.4%)	POLYU(13.3%)
18	POLYU(12.5%)	JU_CSE(12.6%)	UvT(9.5%)	UvT(13.0%)
19	UKP(4.5%)	UKP(4.3%)	UKP(5.4%)	UKP(6.9%)

Table 8: System ranking (and F-score) for each ACM classification: reader-assigned keywords

Zhiyuan Liu and Peng Li and Yabin Zheng and Sun Maosong. Clustering to Find Exemplar Terms for Keyphrase Extraction. In *Proceedings of EMNLP*. 2009, pp. 257–266.

Yutaka Matsuo and Mitsuru Ishizuka. Keyword Extraction from a Single Document using Word Co-occurrence Statistical Information. *International Journal on Artificial Intelligence Tools*. 2004, 13(1), pp. 157–169.

Olena Medelyan and Ian H. Witten. Thesaurus based automatic keyphrase indexing. In *Proceedings of ACM/IEED-CS JCDL*. 2006, pp. 296–297.

Olena Medelyan. Human-competitive automatic topic indexing. PhD Thesis. University of Waikato. 2009.

Rada Mihalcea and Paul Tarau. TextRank: Bringing Order into Texts. In *Proceedings of EMNLP*. 2004, pp. 404–411.

Thuy Dung Nguyen and Min-Yen Kan. Key phrase Extraction in Scientific Publications. In *Proceedings of ICADL*. 2007, pp. 317–326.

Chau Q. Nguyen and Tuoi T. Phan. An ontology-based approach for key phrase extraction. In *Proceedings of the ACL-IJCNLP*. 2009, pp. 181–184.

Youngja Park and Roy J. Byrd and Branimir Boguraev. Automatic Glossary Extraction Beyond Terminology Identification. In *Proceedings of COLING*. 2004, pp. 48–55.

Peter Turney. Learning to Extract Keyphrases from Text. In *National Research Council, Institute for Information Technology, Technical Report ERB-1057*. 1999.

Peter Turney. Coherent keyphrase extraction via Web mining. In *Proceedings of IJCAI*. 2003, pp. 434–439.

Xiaojun Wan and Jianguo Xiao. CollabRank: towards a collaborative approach to single-document keyphrase extraction. In *Proceedings of COLING*. 2008, pp. 969–976.

Ian H. Witten and Gordon Paynter and Eibe Frank and Car Gutwin and Graig Nevill-Manning. KEA:Practical Automatic Key phrase Extraction. In *Proceedings of ACM conference on Digital libraries*. 1999, pp. 254–256.

Torsten Zesch and Iryna Gurevych. Approximate Matching for Evaluating Keyphrase Extraction. In *Proceedings of RANLP*. 2009.

SemEval-2010 Task 7: Argument Selection and Coercion

James Pustejovsky and **Anna Rumshisky** and **Alex Plotnick**
Dept. of Computer Science
Brandeis University
Waltham, MA, USA

Elisabetta Jezek
Dept. of Linguistics
University of Pavia
Pavia, Italy

Olga Batiukova
Dept. of Humanities
Carlos III University of Madrid
Madrid, Spain

Valeria Quochi
ILC-CNR
Pisa, Italy

Abstract

We describe the *Argument Selection and Coercion* task for the SemEval-2010 evaluation exercise. This task involves characterizing the type of compositional operation that exists between a predicate and the arguments it selects. Specifically, the goal is to identify whether the type that a verb selects is satisfied directly by the argument, or whether the argument must change type to satisfy the verb typing. We discuss the problem in detail, describe the data preparation for the task, and analyze the results of the submissions.

1 Introduction

In recent years, a number of annotation schemes that encode semantic information have been developed and used to produce data sets for training machine learning algorithms. Semantic markup schemes that have focused on annotating entity types and, more generally, word senses, have been extended to include semantic relationships between sentence elements, such as the semantic role (or label) assigned to the argument by the predicate (Palmer et al., 2005; Ruppenhofer et al., 2006; Kipper, 2005; Burchardt et al., 2006; Subirats, 2004).

In this task, we take this one step further and attempt to capture the "compositional history" of the argument selection relative to the predicate. In particular, this task attempts to identify the operations of type adjustment induced by a predicate over its arguments when they do not match its selectional properties. The task is defined as follows: for each argument of a predicate, identify whether the entity in that argument position satisfies the type expected by the predicate. If not, then identify how the entity in that position satisfies the typing expected by the predicate; that is, identify the source and target types in a type-shifting or *coercion* operation.

Consider the example below, where the verb *report* normally selects for a human in subject position, as in (1a). Notice, however, that through a metonymic interpretation, this constraint can be violated, as demonstrated in (1b).

(1) a. John reported in late from Washington.
b. Washington reported in late.

Neither the surface annotation of entity extents and types nor assigning semantic roles associated with the predicate would reflect in this case a crucial point: namely, that in order for the typing requirements of the predicate to be satisfied, a *type coercion* or a *metonymy* (Hobbs et al., 1993; Pustejovsky, 1991; Nunberg, 1979; Egg, 2005) has taken place.

The SemEval Metonymy task (Markert and Nissim, 2007) was a good attempt to annotate such metonymic relations over a larger data set. This task involved two types with their metonymic variants: *categories-for-locations* (e.g., place-for-people) and *categories-for-organizations* (e.g., organization-for-members). One of the limitations of this approach, however, is that while appropriate for these specialized metonymy relations, the annotation specification and resulting corpus are not an informative guide for extending the annotation of argument selection more broadly.

In fact, the metonymy example in (1) is an instance of a much more pervasive phenomenon of type shifting and coercion in argument selection. For example, in (2) below, the sense annotation for the verb *enjoy* should arguably assign similar values to both (2a) and (2b).

Proceedings of the 5th International Workshop on Semantic Evaluation, ACL 2010, pages 27–32,
Uppsala, Sweden, 15-16 July 2010.

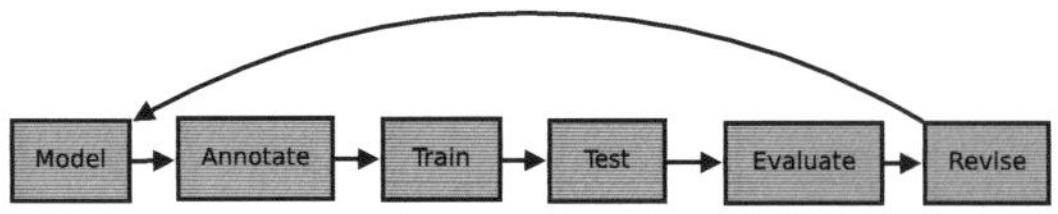

Figure 1: The MATTER Methodology

(2) a. Mary enjoyed drinking her beer.
b. Mary enjoyed her beer.

The consequence of this is that under current sense and role annotation strategies, the mapping to a syntactic realization for a given sense is made more complex, and is in fact perplexing for a clustering or learning algorithm operating over subcategorization types for the verb.

2 Methodology of Annotation

Before introducing the specifics of the argument selection and coercion task, we will briefly review our assumptions regarding the role of annotation in computational linguistic systems.

We assume that the features we use for encoding a specific linguistic phenomenon are rich enough to capture the desired behavior. These linguistic descriptions are typically distilled from extensive theoretical modeling of the phenomenon. The descriptions in turn form the basis for the annotation values of the specification language, which are themselves the features used in a development cycle for training and testing a labeling algorithm over a text. Finally, based on an analysis and evaluation of the performance of a system, the model of the phenomenon may be revised.

We call this cycle of development the MATTER methodology (Fig. 1):

Model: Structural descriptions provide theoretically informed attributes derived from empirical observations over the data;

Annotate: Annotation scheme assumes a feature set that encodes specific structural descriptions and properties of the input data;

Train: Algorithm is trained over a corpus annotated with the target feature set;

Test: Algorithm is tested against held-out data;

Evaluate: Standardized evaluation of results;

Revise: Revisit the model, annotation specification, or algorithm, in order to make the annotation more robust and reliable.

Some of the current and completed annotation efforts that have undergone such a development cycle include PropBank (Palmer et al., 2005), NomBank (Meyers et al., 2004), and TimeBank (Pustejovsky et al., 2005).

3 Task Description

The argument selection and coercion (ASC) task involves identifying the selectional mechanism used by the predicate over a particular argument.[1] For the purposes of this task, the possible relations between the predicate and a given argument are restricted to *selection* and *coercion*. In *selection*, the argument NP satisfies the typing requirements of the predicate, as in (3):

(3) a. The spokesman denied the statement (PROPOSITION).
b. The child threw the stone (PHYSICAL OBJECT).
c. The audience didn't believe the rumor (PROPOSITION).

Coercion occurs when a type-shifting operation must be performed on the complement NP in order to satisfy selectional requirements of the predicate, as in (4). Note that coercion operations may apply to any argument position in a sentence, including the subject, as seen in (4b). Coercion can also be seen as an object of a proposition, as in (4c).

(4) a. The president denied the attack (EVENT → PROPOSITION).
b. The White House (LOCATION → HUMAN) denied this statement.
c. The Boston office called with an update (EVENT → INFO).

In order to determine whether type-shifting has taken place, the classification task must then involve (1) identifying the verb sense and the associated syntactic frame, (2) identifying selectional requirements imposed by that verb sense on the target argument, and (3) identifying the semantic type of the target argument.

4 Resources and Corpus Development

We prepared the data for this task in two phases: the *data set construction phase* and the *annotation phase* (see Fig. 2). The first phase consisted of (1) selecting the target verbs to be annotated and compiling a sense inventory for each target, and (2) data extraction and preprocessing. The prepared data was then loaded into the annotation interface. During the annotation phase, the annotation judgments were entered into the database, and an adjudicator resolved disagreements. The resulting database was then exported in an XML format.

[1]This task is part of a larger effort to annotate text with compositional operations (Pustejovsky et al., 2009).

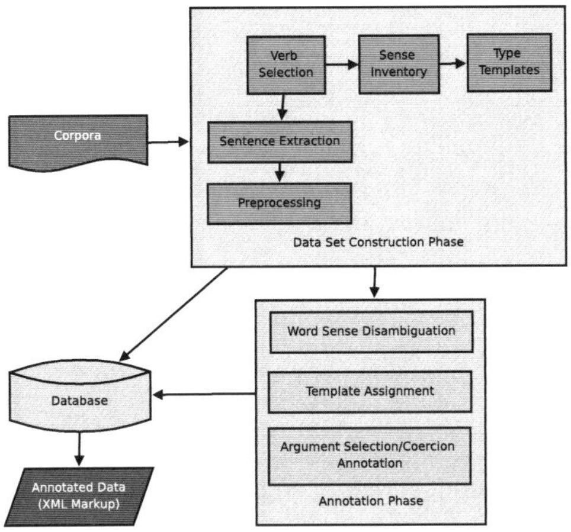

Figure 2: Corpus Development Architecture

4.1 Data Set Construction Phase: English

For the English data set, the data construction phase was combined with the annotation phase. The data for the task was created using the following steps:

1. The verbs were selected by examining the data from the BNC, using the Sketch Engine (Kilgarriff et al., 2004) as described in (Rumshisky and Batiukova, 2008). Verbs that consistently impose semantic typing on one of their arguments in at least one of their senses (strongly coercive verbs) were included into the final data set: *arrive (at)*, *cancel*, *deny*, *finish*, and *hear*.

2. Sense inventories were compiled for each verb, with the senses mapped to OntoNotes (Pradhan et al., 2007) whenever possible. For each sense, a set of type templates was compiled using a modification of the CPA technique (Hanks and Pustejovsky, 2005; Pustejovsky et al., 2004): every argument in the syntactic pattern associated with a given sense was assigned a type specification. Although a particular sense is often compatible with more than one semantic type for a given argument, this was never the case in our data set, where no disjoint types were tested. The coercive senses of the chosen verbs were associated with the following type templates:

   a. *Arrive (at)*, sense *reach a destination or goal*: HUMAN arrive at LOCATION
   b. *Cancel*, sense *call off*: HUMAN cancel EVENT
   c. *Deny*, sense *state or maintain that something is untrue*: HUMAN deny PROPOSITION
   d. *Finish*, sense *complete an activity*: HUMAN finish EVENT
   e. *Hear*, sense *perceive physical sound*: HUMAN hear SOUND

   We used a subset of semantic types from the Brandeis Shallow Ontology (BSO), which is a shallow hierarchy of types developed as a part of the CPA effort (Hanks, 2009; Pustejovsky et al., 2004; Rumshisky et al., 2006). Types were selected for their prevalence in manually identified selection context patterns developed for several hundred English verbs. That is, they capture common semantic distinctions associated with the selectional properties of many verbs. The types used for annotation were:

   ABSTRACT ENTITY, ANIMATE, ARTIFACT, ATTITUDE, DOCUMENT, DRINK, EMOTION, ENTITY, EVENT, FOOD, HUMAN, HUMAN GROUP, IDEA, INFORMATION, LOCATION, OBLIGATION, ORGANIZATION, PATH, PHYSICAL OBJECT, PROPERTY, PROPOSITION, RULE, SENSATION, SOUND, SUBSTANCE, TIME PERIOD, VEHICLE

   This set of types is purposefully shallow and non-hierarchical. For example, HUMAN is a subtype of both ANIMATE and PHYSICAL OBJECT, but annotators and system developers were instructed to choose the most relevant type (e.g., HUMAN) and to ignore inheritance.

3. A set of sentences was randomly extracted for each target verb from the BNC (Burnard, 1995). The extracted sentences were parsed automatically, and the sentences organized according to the grammatical relation the target verb was involved in. Sentences were excluded from the set if the target argument was expressed as anaphor, or was not present in the sentence. The semantic head for the target grammatical relation was identified in each case.

4. Word sense disambiguation of the target predicate was performed manually on each extracted sentence, matching the target against the sense inventory and the corresponding type templates as described above. The appropriate senses were then saved into the database along with the associated type template.

5. The sentences containing coercive senses of the target verbs were loaded into the Brandeis Annotation Tool (Verhagen, 2010). Annotators were presented with a list of sentences and asked to determine whether the argument in the specified grammatical relation to the target belongs to the type associated with that sense in the corresponding template. Disagreements were resolved by adjudication.

Coerion Type	Verb	Train	Test
EVENT→LOCATION	*arrive at*	38	37
ARTIFACT→EVENT	*cancel*	35	35
	finish	91	92
EVENT→PROPOSITION	*deny*	56	54
ARTIFACT→SOUND	*hear*	28	30
EVENT→SOUND	*hear*	24	26
DOCUMENT→EVENT	*finish*	39	40

Table 1: Coercions in the English data set

6. To guarantee robustness of the data, two additional steps were taken. First, only the six most recurrent coercion types were selected; these are given in table 1. Preference was given to cross-domain coercions, where the source and the target types are not related ontologically. Second, the distribution of selection and coercion instances were skewed to increase the number of coercions. The final English data set contains about 30% coercions.

7. Finally, the data set was randomly split in half into a training set and a test set. The training data has 1032 instances, 311 of which are coercions, and the test data has 1039 instances, 314 of which are coercions.

4.2 Data Set Construction Phase: Italian

In constructing the Italian data set, we adopted the same methodology used for the English data set, with the following differences:

1. The list of coercive verbs was selected by examining data from the ItWaC (Baroni and Kilgarriff, 2006) using the Sketch Engine (Kilgarriff et al., 2004):

   accusare 'accuse', *annunciare* 'announce', *arrivare* 'arrive', *ascoltare* 'listen', *avvisare* 'inform', *chiamare* 'call', *cominciare* 'begin', *completare* 'complete', *concludere* 'conclude', *contattare* 'contact', *divorare* 'devour', *echeggiare* 'echo', *finire* 'finish', *informare* 'inform', *interrompere* 'interrupt', *leggere* 'read', *raggiungere* 'reach', *recar(si)* 'go to', *rimbombare* 'resound', *sentire* 'hear', *udire* 'hear', *visitare* 'visit'.

2. The coercive senses of the chosen verbs were associated with type templates, some of which are listed listed below. Whenever possible, senses and type templates were adapted from the Italian Pattern Dictionary (Hanks and Jezek, 2007) and mapped to their SIMPLE equivalents (Lenci et al., 2000).

   a. *arrivare*, sense *reach a location*: HUMAN arriva [prep] LOCATION
   b. *cominciare*, sense *initiate an undertaking*: HUMAN comincia EVENT
   c. *completare*, sense *finish an activity*: HUMAN completa EVENT
   d. *udire*, sense *perceive a sound*: HUMAN ode SOUND
   e. *visitare*, sense *visit a place*: HUMAN visita LOCATION

   The following types were used to annotate the Italian dataset:

   ABSTRACT ENTITY, ANIMATE, ARTIFACT, ATTITUDE, CONTAINER, DOCUMENT, DRINK, EMOTION, ENTITY, EVENT, FOOD, HUMAN, HUMAN GROUP, IDEA, INFORMATION, LIQUID, LOCATION, ORGANIZATION, PHYSICAL OBJECT, PROPERTY, SENSATION, SOUND, TIME PERIOD, VEHICLE

   The annotators were provided with a set of definitions and examples of each type.

3. A set of sentences for each target verb was extracted and parsed from the *PAROLE sottoinsieme corpus* (Bindi et al., 2000). They were skimmed to ensure that the final data set contained a sufficient number of coercions, with proportionally more selections than coercions. Sentences were preselected to include instances representing one of the chosen senses.

4. In order to exclude instances that may have been wrongly selected, a judge performed word sense disambiguation of the target predicate in the extracted sentences.

5. Annotators were presented with a list of sentences and asked to determine the usual semantic type associated with the argument in the specified grammatical relation. Every sentence was annotated by two annotators and one judge, who resolved disagreements.

6. Some of the coercion types selected for Italian were:

   a. LOCATION → HUMAN (*accusare, annunciare*)
   b. ARTIFACT → HUMAN (*annunciare, avvisare*)
   c. EVENT → LOCATION (*arrivare, raggiungere*)
   d. ARTIFACT → EVENT (*cominciare, completare*)
   e. EVENT → DOCUMENT (*leggere, divorare*)
   f. HUMAN → DOCUMENT (*leggere, divorare*)
   g. EVENT → SOUND (*ascoltare, echeggiare*)
   h. ARTIFACT → SOUND (*ascoltare, echeggiare*)

7. The Italian training data contained 1466 instances, 381 of which are coercions; the test data had 1463 instances, with 384 coercions.

5 Data Format

The test and training data were provided in XML. The relation between the predicate (viewed as a function) and its argument were represented by composition link elements (`CompLink`), as shown below. The test data differed from the training data in the omission of `CompLink` elements.

In case of *coercion*, there is a mismatch between the source and the target types, and both types need to be identified; e.g., *The State Department repeatedly denied the attack*:

```
The State Department repeatedly
<SELECTOR sid="s1">denied</SELECTOR>
the <TARGET id="t1">attack</TARGET>.
<CompLink cid="cid1"
          compType="COERCION"
          selector_id="s1"
          relatedToTarget="t1"
          sourceType="EVENT"
          targetType="PROPOSITION"/>
```

When the compositional operation is *selection*, the source and target types must match; e.g., *The State Department repeatedly denied the statement*:

```
The State Department repeatedly
<SELECTOR sid="s2">denied</SELECTOR>
the <TARGET id="t2">statement</TARGET>.
<CompLink cid="cid2"
          compType="SELECTION"
          selector_id="s2"
          relatedToTarget="t2"
          sourceType="PROPOSITION"
          targetType="PROPOSITION"/>
```

6 Results & Analysis

We received only a single submission for the ASC task. The **UTDMet** system was an SVM-based system with features derived from two main sources: a PageRank-style algorithm over WordNet hypernyms used to define semantic classes, and statistics from a PropBank-style parse of some 8 million documents from the English Gigaword corpus. The results, shown in Table 2, were computed from confusion matrices constructed for each of four classification tasks for the 1039 link instances in the English test data: determination of argument selection or coercion, identification of the argument source type, identification of the argument target type, and the joint identification of the source/target type pair.

Clearly, the UTDMet system did quite well at this task. The one immediately noticeable outlier is the macro-averaged precision for the joint type, which reflects a small number of miscategorizations of rare types. For example, eliminating the single miscategorized ARTIFACT-LOCATION link in the submitted test data bumps this score up to a respectable 94%. This large discrepancy can explained by the lack of *any* coercions with those types in the gold-standard data.

	Prec.	Recall	Averaging
Selection *vs.* Coercion:	95	96	(macro)
	96	96	(micro)
Source Type:	96	96	(macro)
	96	96	(micro)
Target Type:	100	100	(both)
Joint Type:	86	95	(macro)
	96	96	(micro)

Table 2: Results for the UTDMet submission.

In the absence of any other submissions, it is difficult to provide a point of comparison for this performance. However, we can provide a baseline by taking each link to be a selection whose source and target types are the most common type (EVENT for the gold-standard English data). This yields micro-averaged precision scores of 69% for selection *vs.* coercion, 33% for source type identification, 37% for the target type identification, and 22% for the joint type.

The performance of the UTDMet system suggests that most of the type coercions were identifiable based largely on examination of lexical clues associated with selection contexts. This is in fact to be expected for the type coercions that were the focus of the English data set. It will be interesting to see how systems perform on the Italian data set and an expanded corpus for English and Italian, where more subtle and complex type exploitations and manipulations are at play. These will hopefully be explored in future competitions.

7 Conclusion

In this paper, we have described the Argument Selection and Coercion task for SemEval-2010. This task involves identifying the relation between a predicate and its argument as one that encodes the compositional history of the selection process. This allows us to distinguish surface forms that directly satisfy the selectional (type) requirements of a predicate from those that are coerced in context. We described some details of a specification language for selection, the annotation task using this specification to identify argument selection behavior, and the preparation of the data for the task. Finally, we analyzed the results of the task submissions.

References

M. Baroni and A. Kilgarriff. 2006. Large linguistically-processed web corpora for multiple languages. In *Proceedings of European ACL.*

R. Bindi, P. Baroni, M. Monachini, and E. Gola. 2000. PAROLE-Sottoinsieme. *ILC-CNR Internal Report.*

Aljoscha Burchardt, Katrin Erk, Anette Frank, Andrea Kowalski, Sebastian Pado, and Manfred Pinkal. 2006. The salsa corpus: a german corpus resource for lexical semantics. In *Proceedings of LREC*, Genoa, Italy.

L. Burnard, 1995. *Users' Reference Guide, British National Corpus.* British National Corpus Consortium, Oxford, England.

Marcus Egg. 2005. *Flexible semantics for reinterpretation phenomena.* CSLI, Stanford.

P. Hanks and E. Jezek. 2007. Building Pattern Dictionaries with Corpus Analysis. In *International Colloquium on Possible Dictionaries*, Rome, June, 6-7. Oral Presentation.

P. Hanks and J. Pustejovsky. 2005. A pattern dictionary for natural language processing. *Revue Française de Linguistique Appliquée.*

P. Hanks. 2009. Corpus pattern analysis. CPA Project Page. Retrieved April 11, 2009, from http://nlp.fi.muni.cz/projekty/cpa/.

J. R. Hobbs, M. Stickel, and P. Martin. 1993. Interpretation as abduction. *Artificial Intelligence*, 63:69–142.

A. Kilgarriff, P. Rychly, P. Smrz, and D. Tugwell. 2004. The Sketch Engine. *Proceedings of Euralex, Lorient, France*, pages 105–116.

Karin Kipper. 2005. *VerbNet: A broad-coverage, comprehensive verb lexicon.* Phd dissertation, University of Pennsylvania, PA.

A. Lenci, N. Bel, F. Busa, N. Calzolari, E. Gola, M. Monachini, A. Ogonowski, I. Peters, W. Peters, N. Ruimy, et al. 2000. SIMPLE: A general framework for the development of multilingual lexicons. *International Journal of Lexicography*, 13(4):249.

K. Markert and M. Nissim. 2007. SemEval-2007 task 8: Metonymy resolution. In Eneko Agirre, Lluís Màrquez, and Richard Wicentowski, editors, *Proceedings of the Fourth International Workshop on Semantic Evaluations (SemEval-2007)*, Prague, Czech Republic, June. Association for Computational Linguistics.

A. Meyers, R. Reeves, C. Macleod, R. Szekely, V. Zielinska, B. Young, and R. Grishman. 2004. The NomBank project: An interim report. In *HLT-NAACL 2004 Workshop: Frontiers in Corpus Annotation*, pages 24–31.

Geoffrey Nunberg. 1979. The non-uniqueness of semantic solutions: Polysemy. *Linguistics and Philosophy*, 3:143–184.

M. Palmer, D. Gildea, and P. Kingsbury. 2005. The proposition bank: An annotated corpus of semantic roles. *Computational Linguistics*, 31(1):71–106.

S. Pradhan, E. Hovy, MS Marcus, M. Palmer, L. Ramshaw, and R. Weischedel. 2007. Ontonotes: A unified relational semantic representation. In *International Conference on Semantic Computing, 2007*, pages 517–526.

J. Pustejovsky, P. Hanks, and A. Rumshisky. 2004. Automated Induction of Sense in Context. In *COLING 2004, Geneva, Switzerland*, pages 924–931.

J. Pustejovsky, R. Knippen, J. Littman, and R. Sauri. 2005. Temporal and event information in natural language text. *Language Resources and Evaluation*, 39(2):123–164.

J. Pustejovsky, A. Rumshisky, J. Moszkowicz, and O. Batiukova. 2009. GLML: Annotating argument selection and coercion. *IWCS-8: Eighth International Conference on Computational Semantics.*

J. Pustejovsky. 1991. The generative lexicon. *Computational Linguistics*, 17(4).

A. Rumshisky and O. Batiukova. 2008. Polysemy in verbs: systematic relations between senses and their effect on annotation. In *COLING Workshop on Human Judgement in Computational Linguistics (HJCL-2008)*, Manchester, England.

A. Rumshisky, P. Hanks, C. Havasi, and J. Pustejovsky. 2006. Constructing a corpus-based ontology using model bias. In *The 19th International FLAIRS Conference, FLAIRS 2006*, Melbourne Beach, Florida, USA.

J. Ruppenhofer, M. Ellsworth, M. Petruck, C. Johnson, and J. Scheffczyk. 2006. *FrameNet II: Extended Theory and Practice.*

Carlos Subirats. 2004. FrameNet Español. Una red semántica de marcos conceptuales. In *VI International Congress of Hispanic Linguistics*, Leipzig.

Marc Verhagen. 2010. The Brandeis Annotation Tool. In *Language Resources and Evaluation Conference, LREC 2010*, Malta.

SemEval-2010 Task 8: Multi-Way Classification of Semantic Relations Between Pairs of Nominals

Iris Hendrickx[*], **Su Nam Kim**[†], **Zornitsa Kozareva**[‡], **Preslav Nakov**[§], **Diarmuid Ó Séaghdha**[¶], **Sebastian Padó**[||], **Marco Pennacchiotti**[**], **Lorenza Romano**[††], **Stan Szpakowicz**[‡‡]

Abstract

SemEval-2 Task 8 focuses on *Multi-way classification of semantic relations between pairs of nominals*. The task was designed to compare different approaches to semantic relation classification and to provide a standard testbed for future research. This paper defines the task, describes the training and test data and the process of their creation, lists the participating systems (10 teams, 28 runs), and discusses their results.

1 Introduction

SemEval-2010 Task 8 focused on *semantic relations between pairs of nominals*. For example, *tea* and *ginseng* are in an ENTITY-ORIGIN relation in "*The cup contained tea from dried ginseng.*". The automatic recognition of semantic relations has many applications, such as information extraction, document summarization, machine translation, or construction of thesauri and semantic networks. It can also facilitate auxiliary tasks such as word sense disambiguation, language modeling, paraphrasing, and recognizing textual entailment.

Our goal was to create a testbed for automatic classification of semantic relations. In developing the task we met several challenges: selecting a suitable set of relations, specifying the annotation procedure, and deciding on the details of the task itself. They are discussed briefly in Section 2; see also Hendrickx et al. (2009), which includes a survey of related work. The direct predecessor of Task 8 was *Classification of semantic relations between nominals*, Task 4 at SemEval-1 (Girju et al., 2009), which had a separate binary-labeled dataset for each of seven relations. We have defined SemEval-2010 Task 8 as a multi-way classification task in which the label for each example must be chosen from the complete set of ten relations and the mapping from nouns to argument slots is not provided in advance. We also provide more data: 10,717 annotated examples, compared to 1,529 in SemEval-1 Task 4.

2 Dataset Creation

2.1 The Inventory of Semantic Relations

We first decided on an inventory of semantic relations. Ideally, it should be exhaustive (enable the description of relations between any pair of nominals) and mutually exclusive (each pair of nominals *in context* should map onto only one relation). The literature, however, suggests that no relation inventory satisfies both needs, and, in practice, some trade-off between them must be accepted.

As a pragmatic compromise, we selected nine relations with coverage sufficiently broad to be of general and practical interest. We aimed at avoiding semantic overlap as much as possible. We included, however, two groups of strongly related relations (ENTITY-ORIGIN / ENTITY-DESTINATION and CONTENT-CONTAINER / COMPONENT-WHOLE / MEMBER-COLLECTION) to assess models' ability to make such fine-grained distinctions. Our inventory is given below. The first four were also used in SemEval-1 Task 4, but the annotation guidelines have been revised, and thus no complete continuity should be assumed.

Cause-Effect (CE). An event or object leads to an effect. Example: *those cancers were caused by radiation exposures*

Instrument-Agency (IA). An agent uses an instrument. Example: *phone operator*

Product-Producer (PP). A producer causes a product to exist. Example: *a factory manufactures suits*

[*] University of Lisbon, iris@clul.ul.pt
[†] University of Melbourne, snkim@csse.unimelb.edu.au
[‡] Information Sciences Institute/University of Southern California, kozareva@isi.edu
[§] National University of Singapore, nakov@comp.nus.edu.sg
[¶] University of Cambridge, do242@cl.cam.ac.uk
[||] University of Stuttgart, pado@ims.uni-stuttgart.de
[**] Yahoo! Inc., pennacc@yahoo-inc.com
[††] Fondazione Bruno Kessler, romano@fbk.eu
[‡‡] University of Ottawa *and* Polish Academy of Sciences, szpak@site.uottawa.ca

Proceedings of the 5th International Workshop on Semantic Evaluation, ACL 2010, pages 33–38,
Uppsala, Sweden, 15-16 July 2010. ©2010 Association for Computational Linguistics

Content-Container (CC). An object is physically stored in a delineated area of space. Example: *a bottle full of honey was weighed*

Entity-Origin (EO). An entity is coming or is derived from an origin (e.g., position or material). Example: *letters from foreign countries*

Entity-Destination (ED). An entity is moving towards a destination. Example: *the boy went to bed*

Component-Whole (CW). An object is a component of a larger whole. Example: *my apartment has a large kitchen*

Member-Collection (MC). A member forms a nonfunctional part of a collection. Example: *there are many trees in the forest*

Message-Topic (MT). A message, written or spoken, is about a topic. Example: *the lecture was about semantics*

2.2 Annotation Guidelines

We defined a set of general annotation guidelines as well as detailed guidelines for each semantic relation. Here, we describe the general guidelines, which delineate the scope of the data to be collected and state general principles relevant to the annotation of all relations.[1]

Our objective is to annotate instances of semantic relations which are true in the sense of holding in the most plausible truth-conditional interpretation of the sentence. This is in the tradition of the Textual Entailment or Information Validation paradigm (Dagan et al., 2009), and in contrast to "aboutness" annotation such as semantic roles (Carreras and Màrquez, 2004) or the BioNLP 2009 task (Kim et al., 2009) where negated relations are also labelled as positive. Similarly, we exclude instances of semantic relations which hold only in speculative or counterfactural scenarios. In practice, this means disallowing annotations within the scope of modals or negations, e.g., "*Smoking may/may not have caused cancer in this case.*"

We accept as relation arguments only noun phrases with common-noun heads. This distinguishes our task from much work in Information Extraction, which tends to focus on specific classes of named entities and on considerably more fine-grained relations than we do. Named entities are a specific category of nominal expressions best dealt with using techniques which do not apply to common nouns. We only mark up the semantic heads of nominals, which usually span a single word, except for lexicalized terms such as *science fiction*.

We also impose a syntactic locality requirement on example candidates, thus excluding instances where the relation arguments occur in separate sentential clauses. Permissible syntactic patterns include simple and relative clauses, compounds, and pre- and post-nominal modification. In addition, we did not annotate examples whose interpretation relied on discourse knowledge, which led to the exclusion of pronouns as arguments. Please see the guidelines for details on other issues, including noun compounds, aspectual phenomena and temporal relations.

2.3 The Annotation Process

The annotation took place in three rounds. First, we manually collected around 1,200 sentences for each relation through pattern-based Web search. In order to ensure a wide variety of example sentences, we used a substantial number of patterns for each relation, typically between one hundred and several hundred. Importantly, in the first round, the relation itself was not annotated: the goal was merely to collect positive and near-miss candidate instances. A rough aim was to have 90% of candidates which instantiate the target relation ("positive instances").

In the second round, the collected candidates for each relation went to two independent annotators for labeling. Since we have a multi-way classification task, the annotators used the full inventory of nine relations plus OTHER. The annotation was made easier by the fact that the cases of overlap were largely systematic, arising from general phenomena like metaphorical use and situations where more than one relation holds. For example, there is a systematic potential overlap between CONTENT-CONTAINER and ENTITY-DESTINATION depending on whether the situation described in the sentence is static or dynamic, e.g., "*When I came, the <e1>apples</e1> were already put in the <e2>basket</e2>.*" is CC(e1, e2), while "*Then, the <e1>apples</e1> were quickly put in the <e2>basket</e2>.*" is ED(e1, e2).

In the third round, the remaining disagreements were resolved, and, if no consensus could be achieved, the examples were removed. Finally, we merged all nine datasets to create a set of 10,717 instances. We released 8,000 for training and kept

[1]The full task guidelines are available at `http://docs.google.com/View?id=dfhkmm46_0f63mfvf7`

the rest for testing.[2]

Table 1 shows some statistics about the dataset. The first column (Freq) shows the absolute and relative frequencies of each relation. The second column (Pos) shows that the average share of positive instances was closer to 75% than to 90%, indicating that the patterns catch a substantial amount of "near-miss" cases. However, this effect varies a lot across relations, causing the non-uniform relation distribution in the dataset (first column).[3] After the second round, we also computed inter-annotator agreement (third column, IAA). Inter-annotator agreement was computed on the sentence level, as the percentage of sentences for which the two annotations were identical. That is, these figures can be interpreted as exact-match accuracies. We do not report Kappa, since chance agreement on preselected candidates is difficult to estimate.[4] IAA is between 60% and 95%, again with large relation-dependent variation. Some of the relations were particularly easy to annotate, notably CONTENT-CONTAINER, which can be resolved through relatively clear criteria, despite the systematic ambiguity mentioned above. ENTITY-ORIGIN was the hardest relation to annotate. We encountered ontological difficulties in defining both Entity (e.g., in contrast to Effect) and Origin (as opposed to Cause). Our numbers are on average around 10% higher than those reported by Girju et al. (2009). This may be a side effect of our data collection method. To gather 1,200 examples in realistic time, we had to seek productive search query patterns, which invited certain homogeneity. For example, many queries for CONTENT-CONTAINER centered on "usual suspect" such as *box* or *suitcase*. Many instances of MEMBER-COLLECTION were collected on the basis of from available lists of collective names.

3 The Task

The participating systems had to solve the following task: given a sentence and two tagged nominals, predict the relation between those nominals *and* the direction of the relation.

We released a detailed scorer which outputs (1) a confusion matrix, (2) accuracy and coverage, (3) precision (P), recall (R), and F_1-Score for each relation, (4) micro-averaged P, R, F_1, (5) macro-averaged P, R, F_1. For (4) and (5), the calculations ignored the OTHER relation. Our official scoring metric is macro-averaged F_1-Score for (9+1)-way classification, taking directionality into account.

The teams were asked to submit test data predictions for varying fractions of the training data. Specifically, we requested results for the first 1000, 2000, 4000, and 8000 training instances, called TD1 through TD4. TD4 was the full training set.

Relation	Freq	Pos	IAA
Cause-Effect	1331 (12.4%)	91.2%	79.0%
Component-Whole	1253 (11.7%)	84.3%	70.0%
Entity-Destination	1137 (10.6%)	80.1%	75.2%
Entity-Origin	974 (9.1%)	69.2%	58.2%
Product-Producer	948 (8.8%)	66.3%	84.8%
Member-Collection	923 (8.6%)	74.7%	68.2%
Message-Topic	895 (8.4%)	74.4%	72.4%
Content-Container	732 (6.8%)	59.3%	95.8%
Instrument-Agency	660 (6.2%)	60.8%	65.0%
Other	1864 (17.4%)	N/A[4]	N/A[4]
Total	10717 (100%)		

Table 1: Annotation Statistics. Freq: Absolute and relative frequency in the dataset; Pos: percentage of "positive" relation instances in the candidate set; IAA: inter-annotator agreement

4 Participants and Results

Table 2 lists the participants and provides a rough overview of the system features. Table 3 shows the results. Unless noted otherwise, all quoted numbers are F_1-Scores.

Overall Ranking and Training Data. We rank the teams by the performance of their best system on TD4, since a per-system ranking would favor teams with many submitted runs. UTD submitted the best system, with a performance of over 82%, more than 4% better than the second-best system. FBK_IRST places second, with 77.62%, a tiny margin ahead of ISI (77.57%). Notably, the ISI system outperforms the FBK_IRST system for TD1 to TD3, where it was second-best. The accuracy numbers for TD4 (Acc TD4) lead to the same overall ranking: micro- versus macro-averaging does not appear to make much difference either. A random baseline gives an uninteresting score of 6%. Our competitive baseline system is a simple Naive Bayes classifier which relies on words in the sentential context only; two systems scored below this baseline.

[2]This set includes 891 examples from SemEval-1 Task 4. We re-annotated them and assigned them as the last examples of our *training* dataset to ensure that the test set was unseen.

[3]To what extent our candidate selection produces a biased sample is a question that we cannot address within this paper.

[4]We do not report Pos or IAA for OTHER, since OTHER is a pseudo-relation that was not annotated in its own right. The numbers would therefore not be comparable to other relations.

System	Institution	Team	Description	Res.	Class.
Baseline	Task organizers		local context of 2 words only		BN
ECNU-SR-1	East China Normal University	Man Lan, Yuan Chen, Zhimin Zhou, Yu Xu	stem, POS, syntactic patterns	S	SVM (multi)
ECNU-SR-2,3			features like ECNU-SR-1, different prob. thresholds		SVM (binary)
ECNU-SR-4			stem, POS, syntactic patterns, hyponymy and meronymy relations	WN, S	SVM (multi)
ECNU-SR-5,6			features like ECNU-SR-4, different prob. thresholds		SVM (binary)
ECNU-SR-7			majority vote of ECNU-1,2,4,5		
FBK_IRST-6C32	Fondazione Bruno Kessler	Claudio Giuliano, Kateryna Tymoshenko	3-word window context features (word form, part of speech, orthography) + Cyc; parameter estimation by optimization on training set	Cyc	SVM
FBK_IRST-12C32			FBK_IRST-6C32 + distance features		
FBK_IRST-12VBC32			FBK_IRST-12C32 + verbs		
FBK_IRST-6CA, -12CA, -12VBCA			features as above, parameter estimation by cross-validation		
FBK_NK-RES1	Fondazione Bruno Kessler	Matteo Negri, Milen Kouylekov	collocations, glosses, semantic relations of nominals + context features	WN	BN
FBK_NK-RES 2,3,4			like FBK_NK-RES1 with different context windows and collocation cutoffs		
ISI	Information Sciences Institute, University of Southern California	Stephen Tratz	features from different resources, a noun compound relation system, and various feature related to capitalization, affixes, closed-class words	WN, RT, G	ME
ISTI-1,2	Istituto di scienca e tecnologie dell'informazione "A. Faedo"	Andrea Esuli, Diego Marcheggiani, Fabrizio Sebastiani	Boosting-based classification. Runs differ in their initialization.	WN	2S
JU	Jadavpur University	Santanu Pal, Partha Pakray, Dipankar Das, Sivaji Bandyopadhyay	Verbs, nouns, and prepositions; seed lists for semantic relations; parse features and NEs	WN, S	CRF
SEKA	Hungarian Academy of Sciences	Eszter Simon, Andras Kornai	Levin and Roget classes, n-grams; other grammatical and formal features	RT, LC	ME
TUD-base	Technische Universität Darmstadt	György Szarvas, Iryna Gurevych	word, POS n-grams, dependency path, distance	S	ME
TUD-wp			TUD-base + ESA semantic relatedness scores	+WP	
TUD-comb			TUD-base + own semantic relatedness scores	+WP,WN	
TUD-comb-threshold			TUD-comb with higher threshold for OTHER		
UNITN	University of Trento	Fabio Celli	punctuation, context words, prepositional patterns, estimation of semantic relation	–	DR
UTD	University of Texas at Dallas	Bryan Rink, Sanda Harabagiu	context wods, hypernyms, POS, dependencies, distance, semantic roles, Levin classes, paraphrases	WN, S, G, PB/NB, LC	SVM, 2S

Table 2: Participants of SemEval-2010 Task 8. Res: Resources used (WN: WordNet data; WP: Wikipedia data; S: syntax; LC: Levin classes; G: Google n-grams, RT: Roget's Thesaurus, PB/NB: PropBank/NomBank). Class: Classification style (ME: Maximum Entropy; BN: Bayes Net; DR: Decision Rules/Trees; CRF: Conditional Random Fields; 2S: two-step classification)

System	TD1	TD2	TD3	TD4	Acc TD4	Rank	Best Cat	Worst Cat-9
Baseline	33.04	42.41	50.89	57.52	50.0	-	MC (75.1)	IA (28.0)
ECNU-SR-1	52.13	56.58	58.16	60.08	57.1		CE (79.7)	IA (32.2)
ECNU-SR-2	46.24	47.99	69.83	72.59	67.1		CE (84.4)	IA (52.2)
ECNU-SR-3	39.89	42.29	65.47	68.50	62.0		CE (83.4)	IA (46.5)
ECNU-SR-4	67.95	70.58	72.99	74.82	70.5	4	CE (84.6)	IA (61.4)
ECNU-SR-5	49.32	50.70	72.63	75.43	70.2		CE (85.1)	IA (60.7)
ECNU-SR-6	42.88	45.54	68.87	72.19	65.8		CE (85.2)	IA (56.7)
ECNU-SR-7	58.67	58.87	72.79	75.21	70.2		CE (86.1)	IA (61.8)
FBK_IRST-6C32	60.19	67.31	71.78	76.81	72.4		ED (82.6)	IA (69.4)
FBK_IRST-12C32	60.66	67.91	72.04	76.91	72.4		MC (84.2)	IA (68.8)
FBK_IRST-12VBC32	62.64	69.86	73.19	77.11	72.3	2	ED (85.9)	PP (68.1)
FBK_IRST-6CA	60.58	67.14	71.63	76.28	71.4		CE (82.3)	IA (67.7)
FBK_IRST-12CA	61.33	67.80	71.65	76.39	71.4		ED (81.8)	IA (67.5)
FBK_IRST-12VBCA	63.61	70.20	73.40	77.62	72.8		ED (86.5)	IA (67.3)
FBK_NK-RES1	55.71*	64.06*	67.80*	68.02	62.1		ED (77.6)	IA (52.9)
FBK_NK-RES2	54.27*	63.68*	67.08*	67.48	61.4	7	ED (77.4)	PP (55.2)
FBK_NK-RES3	54.25*	62.73*	66.11*	66.90	60.5		MC (76.7)	IA (56.3)
FBK_NK-RES4	44.11*	58.85*	63.06*	65.84	59.4		MC (76.1)	IA/PP (58.0)
ISI	66.68	71.01	75.51	77.57	72.7	3	CE (87.6)	IA (61.5)
ISTI-1	50.49*	55.80*	61.14*	68.42	63.2	6	ED (80.7)	PP (53.8)
ISTI-2	50.69*	54.29*	59.77*	66.65	61.5		ED (80.2)	IA (48.9)
JU	41.62*	44.98*	47.81*	52.16	50.2	9	CE (75.6)	IA (27.8)
SEKA	51.81	56.34	61.10	66.33	61.9	8	CE (84.0)	PP (43.7)
TUD-base	50.81	54.61	56.98	60.50	56.1		CE (80.7)	IA (31.1)
TUD-wp	55.34	60.90	63.78	68.00	63.5	5	ED (82.9)	IA (44.1)
TUD-comb	57.84	62.52	66.41	68.88	64.6		CE (83.8)	IA (46.8)
TUD-comb-θ	58.35	62.45	66.86	69.23	65.4		CE (83.4)	IA (46.9)
UNITN	16.57*	18.56*	22.45*	26.67	27.4	10	ED (46.4)	PP (0)
UTD	**73.08**	**77.02**	**79.93**	**82.19**	77.9	1	CE (89.6)	IA (68.5)

Table 3: F_1-Score of all submitted systems on the test dataset as a function of training data: TD1=1000, TD2=2000, TD3=4000, TD4=8000 training examples. Official results are calculated on TD4. The results marked with * were submitted after the deadline. The best-performing run for each participant is *italicized*.

As for the amount of training data, we see a substantial improvement for all systems between TD1 and TD4, with diminishing returns for the transition between TD3 and TD4 for many, but not all, systems. Overall, the differences between systems are smaller for TD4 than they are for TD1. The spread between the top three systems is around 10% at TD1, but below 5% at TD4. Still, there are clear differences in the influence of training data size even among systems with the same overall architecture. Notably, ECNU-SR-4 is the second-best system at TD1 (67.95%), but gains only 7% from the eightfold increase of the size of the training data. At the same time, ECNU-SR-3 improves from less than 40% to almost 69%. The difference between the systems is that ECNU-SR-4 uses a multi-way classifier including the class OTHER, while ECNU-SR-3 uses binary classifiers and assigns OTHER if no other relation was assigned with $p>0.5$. It appears that these probability estimates for classes are only reliable enough for TD3 and TD4.

The Influence of System Architecture. Almost all systems used either MaxEnt or SVM classifiers, with no clear advantage for either. Similarly, two systems, UTD and ISTI (rank 1 and 6) split the task into two classification steps (relation and direction), but the 2nd- and 3rd-ranked systems do not. The use of a sequence model such as a CRF did not show a benefit either.

The systems use a variety of resources. Generally, richer feature sets lead to better performance (although the differences are often small – compare the different FBK_IRST systems). This improvement can be explained by the need for semantic generalization from training to test data. This need can be addressed using WordNet (contrast ECNU-1 to -3 with ECNU-4 to -6), the Google n-gram collection (see ISI and UTD), or a "deep" semantic resource (FBK_IRST uses Cyc). Yet, most of these resources are also included in the less successful systems, so beneficial integration of knowledge sources into semantic relation classification seems to be difficult.

System Combination. The differences between the systems suggest that it might be possible to achieve improvements by building an ensemble system. When we combine the top three systems (UTD, FBK_IRST-12VBCA, and ISI) by predicting their majority vote, or OTHER if there was none, we obtain a small improvement over the UTD system with an F_1-Score of 82.79%. A combination of the top five systems using the same method shows a worse performance, however (80.42%). This suggests that the best system outperforms the rest by a margin that cannot be compensated with system combination, at least not with a crude majority vote. We see a similar pattern among the ECNU systems, where the ECNU-SR-7 combination system is outperformed by ECNU-SR-5, presumably since it incorporates the inferior ECNU-SR-1 system.

Relation-specific Analysis. We also analyze the performance on individual relations, especially the extremes. There are very stable patterns across all systems. The best relation (presumably the easiest to classify) is CE, far ahead of ED and MC. Notably, the performance for the best relation is 75% or above for almost all systems, with comparatively small differences between the systems. The hardest relation is generally IA, followed by PP.[5] Here, the spread among the systems is much larger: the highest-ranking systems outperform others on the difficult relations. Recall was the main problem for both IA and PP: many examples of these two relations are misclassified, most frequently as OTHER. Even at TD4, these datasets seem to be less homogeneous than the others. Intriguingly, PP shows a very high inter-annotator agreement (Table 1). Its difficulty may therefore be due not to questionable annotation, but to genuine variability, or at least the selection of difficult patterns by the dataset creator. Conversely, MC, among the easiest relations to model, shows only a modest IAA.

Difficult Instances. There were 152 examples that are classified incorrectly by all systems. We analyze them, looking for sources of errors. In addition to a handful of annotation errors and some borderline cases, they are made up of instances which illustrate the limits of current shallow modeling approaches in that they require more lexical knowledge and complex reasoning. A case in point: *The bottle carrier converts your <e1>bottle</e1> into a <e2>canteen</e2>*. This instance of OTHER is misclassified either as CC (due to the nominals) or as ED (because of the preposition *into*). Another example: *[...] <e1>Rudders</e1> are used by <e2>towboats</e2> and other vessels that require a high degree of manoeuvrability.* This is an instance of CW misclassified as IA, probably on account of the verb *use* which is a frequent indicator of an agentive relation.

[5]The relation OTHER, which we ignore in the overall F_1-score, does even worse, often below 40%. This is to be expected, since the OTHER examples in our datasets are near misses for other relations, thus making a very incoherent class.

5 Discussion and Conclusion

There is little doubt that 19-way classification is a non-trivial challenge. It is even harder when the domain is lexical semantics, with its idiosyncrasies, and when the classes are not necessarily disjoint, despite our best intentions. It speaks to the success of the exercise that the participating systems' performance was generally high, well over an order of magnitude above random guessing. This may be due to the impressive array of tools and lexical-semantic resources deployed by the participants.

Section 4 suggests a few ways of interpreting and analyzing the results. Long-term lessons will undoubtedly emerge from the workshop discussion. One optimistic-pessimistic conclusion concerns the size of the training data. The notable gain TD3 $\rightarrow$ TD4 suggests that even more data would be helpful, but that is so much easier said than done: it took the organizers well in excess of 1000 person-hours to pin down the problem, hone the guidelines and relation definitions, construct sufficient amounts of trustworthy training data, and run the task.

References

X. Carreras and L. Màrquez. 2004. Introduction to the CoNLL-2004 shared task: Semantic role labeling. In *Proc. CoNLL-04*, Boston, MA.

I. Dagan, B. Dolan, B. Magnini, and D. Roth. 2009. Recognizing textual entailment: Rational, evaluation and approaches. *Natural Language Engineering*, 15(4):i–xvii.

R. Girju, P. Nakov, V. Nastase, S. Szpakowicz, P. Turney, and D. Yuret. 2009. Classification of semantic relations between nominals. *Language Resources and Evaluation*, 43(2):105–121.

I. Hendrickx, S. Kim, Z. Kozareva, P. Nakov, D. Ó Séaghdha, S. Padó, M. Pennacchiotti, L. Romano, and S. Szpakowicz. 2009. SemEval-2010 Task 8: Multi-way classification of semantic relations between pairs of nominals. In *Proc. NAACL Workshop on Semantic Evaluations*, Boulder, CO.

J. Kim, T. Ohta, S. Pyysalo, Y. Kano, and J. Tsujii. 2009. Overview of BioNLP'09 shared task on event extraction. In *Proc. BioNLP-09*, Boulder, CO.

SemEval-2010 Task 9: The Interpretation of Noun Compounds Using Paraphrasing Verbs and Prepositions

Cristina Butnariu
University College Dublin
ioana.butnariu@ucd.ie

Su Nam Kim
University of Melbourne
nkim@csse.unimelb.edu.au

Preslav Nakov
National University of Singapore
nakov@comp.nus.edu.sg

Diarmuid Ó Séaghdha
University of Cambridge
do242@cam.ac.uk

Stan Szpakowicz
University of Ottawa
Polish Academy of Sciences
szpak@site.uottawa.ca

Tony Veale
University College Dublin
tony.veale@ucd.ie

Abstract

Previous research has shown that the meaning of many noun-noun compounds N_1 N_2 can be approximated reasonably well by paraphrasing clauses of the form 'N_2 that ... N_1', where '...' stands for a verb with or without a preposition. For example, *malaria mosquito* is a '*mosquito that carries malaria*'. Evaluating the quality of such paraphrases is the theme of Task 9 at SemEval-2010. This paper describes some background, the task definition, the process of data collection and the task results. We also venture a few general conclusions before the participating teams present their systems at the SemEval-2010 workshop. There were 5 teams who submitted 7 systems.

1 Introduction

Noun compounds (NCs) are sequences of two or more nouns that act as a single noun,[1] e.g., *stem cell, stem cell research, stem cell research organization*, etc. Lapata and Lascarides (2003) observe that NCs pose syntactic and semantic challenges for three basic reasons: (1) the compounding process is extremely productive in English; (2) the semantic relation between the head and the modifier is implicit; (3) the interpretation can be influenced by contextual and pragmatic factors. Corpus studies have shown that while NCs are very common in English, their frequency distribution follows a Zipfian or power-law distribution and the majority of NCs encountered will be rare types (Tanaka and Baldwin, 2003; Lapata and Lascarides, 2003; Baldwin and Tanaka, 2004; Ó Séaghdha, 2008). As a consequence, Natural Language Processing (NLP) applications cannot afford either to ignore NCs or to assume that they can be handled by relying on a dictionary or other static resource.

Trouble with lexical resources for NCs notwithstanding, NC semantics plays a central role in complex knowledge discovery and applications, including but not limited to Question Answering (QA), Machine Translation (MT), and Information Retrieval (IR). For example, knowing the (implicit) semantic relation between the NC components can help rank and refine queries in QA and IR, or select promising translation pairs in MT (Nakov, 2008a). Thus, robust semantic interpretation of NCs should be of much help in broad-coverage semantic processing.

Proposed approaches to modelling NC semantics have used semantic similarity (Nastase and Szpakowicz, 2003; Moldovan et al., 2004; Kim and Baldwin, 2005; Nastase and Szpakowicz, 2006; Girju, 2007; Ó Séaghdha and Copestake, 2007) and paraphrasing (Vanderwende, 1994; Kim and Baldwin, 2006; Butnariu and Veale, 2008; Nakov and Hearst, 2008). The former body of work seeks to measure the similarity between known and unseen NCs by considering various features, usually context-related. In contrast, the latter group uses verb semantics to interpret NCs directly, e.g., *olive oil* as '*oil that is extracted from olive(s)*', *drug death* as '*death that is caused by drug(s)*', *flu shot* as a '*shot that prevents flu*'.

The growing popularity – and expected direct utility – of paraphrase-based NC semantics has encouraged us to propose an evaluation exercise for the 2010 edition of SemEval. This paper gives a bird's-eye view of the task. Section 2 presents its objective, data, data collection, and evaluation method. Section 3 lists the participating teams. Section 4 shows the results and our analysis. In Section 5, we sum up our experience so far.

[1] We follow the definition in (Downing, 1977).

Proceedings of the 5th International Workshop on Semantic Evaluation, ACL 2010, pages 39–44,
Uppsala, Sweden, 15-16 July 2010.

2 Task Description

2.1 The Objective

For the purpose of the task, we focused on two-word NCs which are modifier-head pairs of nouns, such as *apple pie* or *malaria mosquito*. There are several ways to "attack" the paraphrase-based semantics of such NCs.

We have proposed a rather simple problem: assume that many paraphrases can be found – perhaps via clever Web search – but their relevance is up in the air. Given sufficient training data, we seek to estimate the quality of candidate paraphrases in a test set. Each NC in the training set comes with a long list of verbs in the infinitive (often with a preposition) which may paraphrase the NC adequately. Examples of apt paraphrasing verbs: olive oil – *be extracted from*, drug death – *be caused by*, flu shot – *prevent*. These lists have been constructed from human-proposed paraphrases. For the training data, we also provide the participants with a quality score for each paraphrase, which is a simple count of the number of human subjects who proposed that paraphrase. At test time, given a noun compound and a list of paraphrasing verbs, a participating system needs to produce aptness scores that correlate well (in terms of relative ranking) with the held out human judgments. There may be a diverse range of paraphrases for a given compound, some of them in fact might be inappropriate, but it can be expected that the distribution over paraphrases estimated from a large number of subjects will indeed be representative of the compound's meaning.

2.2 The Datasets

Following Nakov (2008b), we took advantage of the *Amazon Mechanical Turk*[2] (MTurk) to acquire paraphrasing verbs from human annotators. The service offers inexpensive access to subjects for tasks which require human intelligence. Its API allows a computer program to run tasks easily and collate the subjects' responses. MTurk is becoming a popular means of eliciting and collecting linguistic intuitions for NLP research; see Snow et al. (2008) for an overview and a further discussion.

Even though we recruited human subjects, whom we required to take a qualification test,[3] data collection was time-consuming since many annotators did not follow the instructions. We had to monitor their progress and to send them timely messages, pointing out mistakes. Although the MTurk service allows task owners to accept or reject individual submissions, rejection was the last resort since it has the triply unpleasant effect of (1) denying the worker her fee, (2) negatively affecting her rating, and (3) lowering our rating as a requester. We thus chose to try and educate our workers "on the fly". Even so, we ended up with many examples which we had to correct manually by labor-intensive post-processing. The flaws were not different from those already described by Nakov (2008b). Post-editing was also necessary to lemmatize the paraphrasing verbs systematically.

Trial Data. At the end of August 2009, we released as trial data the previously collected paraphrase sets (Nakov, 2008b) for the *Levi-250* dataset (after further review and cleaning). This dataset consisted of 250 noun-noun compounds form (Levi, 1978), each paraphrased by 25-30 MTurk workers (without a qualification test).

Training Data. The training dataset was an extension of the trial dataset. It consisted of the same 250 noun-noun compounds, but the number of annotators per compound increased significantly. We aimed to recruit at least 30 additional MTurk workers per compound; for some compounds we managed to get many more. For example, when we added the paraphrasing verbs from the trial dataset to the newly collected verbs, we had 131 different workers for *neighborhood bars*, compared to just 50 for *tear gas*. On the average, we had 72.7 workers per compound. Each worker was instructed to try to produce at least three paraphrasing verbs, so we ended up with 191.8 paraphrasing verbs per compound, 84.6 of them being unique. See Table 1 for more details.

Test Data. The test dataset consisted of 388 noun compounds collected from two data sources: (1) the Nastase and Szpakowicz (2003) dataset; and (2) the Lauer (1995) dataset. The former contains 328 noun-noun compounds (there are also a number of adjective-noun and adverb-noun pairs), while the latter contains 266 noun-noun compounds. Since these datasets overlap between themselves and with the training dataset, we had to exclude some examples. In the end, we had 388

[2] `www.mturk.com`

[3] We soon realized that we also had to offer a version of our assignments without a qualification test (at a lower pay rate) since very few people were willing to take a test. Overall, we found little difference in the quality of work of subjects recruited with and without the test.

	Training: 250 NCs		Testing: 388 NCs		All: 638 NCs	
	Total	Min/Max/Avg	Total	Min/Max/Avg	Total	Min/Max/Avg
MTurk workers	28,199	50/131/72.7	17,067	57/96/68.3	45,266	50/131/71.0
Verb types	32,832	25/173/84.6	17,730	41/133/70.9	50,562	25/173/79.3
Verb tokens	74,407	92/462/191.8	46,247	129/291/185.0	120,654	92/462/189.1

Table 1: Statistics about the the training/test datasets. Shown are the total number of verbs proposed as well as the minimum, maximum and average number of paraphrasing verb types/tokens per compound.

unique noun-noun compounds for testing, distinct from those used for training. We aimed for 100 human workers per testing NC, but we could only get 68.3, with a minimum of 57 and a maximum of 96; there were 185.0 paraphrasing verbs per compound, 70.9 of them being unique, which is close to what we had for the training data.

Data format. We distribute the training data as a raw text file. Each line has the following tab-separated format:

```
NC paraphrase frequency
```

where `NC` is a noun-noun compound (e.g., *apple cake*, *flu virus*), `paraphrase` is a human-proposed paraphrasing verb optionally followed by a preposition, and `frequency` is the number of annotators who proposed that paraphrase. Here is an illustrative extract from the training dataset:

```
flu virus  cause             38
flu virus  spread            13
flu virus  create            6
flu virus  give              5
flu virus  produce           5
...
flu virus  be made up of     1
flu virus  be observed in    1
flu virus  exacerbate        1
```

The test file has a similar format, except that the frequency is not included and the paraphrases for each noun compound appear in random order:

```
...
chest pain  originate
chest pain  start in
chest pain  descend in
chest pain  be in
...
```

License. All datasets are released under the *Creative Commons Attribution 3.0 Unported license.*[4]

[4] `creativecommons.org/licenses/by/3.0`

2.3 Evaluation

All evaluation was performed by computing an appropriate measure of similarity/correlation between system predictions and the compiled judgements of the human annotators. We did it on a compound-by-compound basis and averaged over all compounds in the test dataset. Section 4 shows results for three measures: Spearman rank correlation, Pearson correlation, and cosine similarity.

Spearman Rank Correlation (ρ) was adopted as the official evaluation measure for the competition. As a rank correlation statistic, it does not use the numerical values of the predictions or human judgements, only their relative ordering encoded as integer ranks. For a sample of n items ranked by two methods x and y, the rank correlation ρ is calculated as follows:

$$\rho = \frac{n\sum x_i y_i - (\sum x_i)(\sum y_i)}{\sqrt{n\sum x_i^2 - (\sum x_i)^2}\sqrt{n\sum y_i^2 - (\sum y_i)^2} \quad (1)$$

where x_i, y_i are the ranks given by x and y to the ith item, respectively. The value of ρ ranges between -1.0 (total negative correlation) and 1.0 (total positive correlation).

Pearson Correlation (r) is a standard measure of correlation strength between real-valued variables. The formula is the same as (1), but with x_i, y_i taking real values rather than rank values; just like ρ, r's values fall between -1.0 and 1.0.

Cosine similarity is frequently used in NLP to compare numerical vectors:

$$\cos = \frac{\sum_i^n x_i y_i}{\sqrt{\sum_i^n x_i^2 \sum_i^n y_i^2}} \quad (2)$$

For non-negative data, the cosine similarity takes values between 0.0 and 1.0. Pearson's r can be viewed as a version of the cosine similarity which performs centering on x and y.

Baseline: To help interpret these evaluation measures, we implemented a simple baseline. A distribution over the paraphrases was estimated by

System	Institution	Team	Description
NC-INTERP	International Institute of Information Technology, Hyderabad	Prashant Mathur	Unsupervised model using verb-argument frequencies from parsed Web snippets and WordNet smoothing
UCAM	University of Cambridge	Clemens Heppner	Unsupervised model using verb-argument frequencies from the British National Corpus
UCD-GOGGLE-I	University College Dublin	Guofu Li	Unsupervised probabilistic model using pattern frequencies estimated from the Google N-Gram corpus
UCD-GOGGLE-II			Paraphrase ranking model learned from training data
UCD-GOGGLE-III			Combination of UCD-GOGGLE-I and UCD-GOGGLE-II
UCD-PN	University College Dublin	Paul Nulty	Scoring according to the probability of a paraphrase appearing in the same set as other paraphrases provided
UVT-MEPHISTO	Tilburg University	Sander Wubben	Supervised memory-based ranker using features from Google N-Gram Corpus and WordNet

Table 2: Teams participating in SemEval-2010 Task 9

summing the frequencies for all compounds in the training dataset, and the paraphrases for the test examples were scored according to this distribution. Note that this baseline entirely ignores the identity of the nouns in the compound.

3 Participants

The task attracted five teams, one of which (UCD-GOGGLE) submitted three runs. The participants are listed in Table 2 along with brief system descriptions; for more details please see the teams' own description papers.

4 Results and Discussion

The task results appear in Table 3. In an evaluation by Spearman's ρ (the official ranking measure), the winning system was UVT-MEPHISTO, which scored 0.450. UVT also achieved the top Pearson's r score. UCD-PN is the top-scoring system according to the cosine measure. One participant submitted part of his results after the official deadline, which is marked by an asterisk.

The participants used a variety of information sources and estimation methods. UVT-MEPHISTO is a supervised system that uses frequency information from the Google N-Gram Corpus and features from WordNet (Fellbaum, 1998) to rank candidate paraphrases. On the other hand, UCD-PN uses no external resources and no supervised training, yet came within 0.009 of UVT-MEPHISTO in the official evaluation. The basic idea of UCD-PN – that one can predict the plausibility of a paraphrase simply by knowing which other paraphrases have been given for that compound *regardless of their frequency* – is clearly a powerful one. Unlike the other systems, UCD-PN used information about the test examples (not their ranks, of course) for model estimation; this has similarities to "transductive" methods for semi-supervised learning. However, post-hoc analysis shows that UCD-PN would have preserved its rank if it had estimated its model on the training data only. On the other hand, if the task had been designed differently – by asking systems to propose paraphrases from the set of all possible verb/preposition combinations – then we would not expect UCD-PN's approach to work as well as models that use corpus information.

The other systems are comparable to UVT-MEPHISTO in that they use corpus frequencies to evaluate paraphrases and apply some kind of semantic smoothing to handle sparsity. However, UCD-GOGGLE-I, UCAM and NC-INTERP are unsupervised systems. UCAM uses the 100-million word BNC corpus, while the other systems use Web-scale resources; this has presumably exacerbated sparsity issues and contributed to a relatively poor performance.

The *hybrid* approach exemplified by UCD-GOGGLE-III combines the predictions of a system that models paraphrase correlations and one that learns from corpus frequencies and thus attains better performance. Given that the two top-scoring systems can also be characterized as using these two distinct information sources, it is natural to consider combining these systems. Simply normalizing (to unit sum) and averaging the two sets of prediction values for each compound does

Rank	System	Supervised?	Hybrid?	Spearman ρ	Pearson r	Cosine
1	UVT-MEPHISTO	yes	no	**0.450**	**0.411**	0.635
2	UCD-PN	no	no	0.441	0.361	**0.669**
3	UCD-GOGGLE-III	yes	yes	0.432	0.395	0.652
4	UCD-GOGGLE-II	yes	no	0.418	0.375	0.660
5	UCD-GOGGLE-I	no	no	0.380	0.252	0.629
6	UCAM	no	no	0.267	0.219	0.374
7	NC-INTERP*	no	no	0.186	0.070	0.466
	Baseline	yes	no	0.425	0.344	0.524
	Combining UVT and UCD-PN	yes	yes	0.472	0.431	0.685

Table 3: Evaluation results for SemEval-2010 Task 9 (* denotes a late submission).

indeed give better scores: Spearman $\rho = 0.472$, $r = 0.431$, Cosine = 0.685.

The baseline from Section 2.3 turns out to be very strong. Evaluating with Spearman's ρ, only three systems outperform it. It is less competitive on the other evaluation measures though. This suggests that global paraphrase frequencies may be useful for telling sensible paraphrases from bad ones, but will not do for quantifying the plausibility of a paraphrase for a given noun compound.

5 Conclusion

Given that it is a newly-proposed task, this initial experiment in paraphrasing noun compounds has been a moderate success. The participation rate has been sufficient for the purposes of comparing and contrasting different approaches to the role of paraphrases in the interpretation of noun-noun compounds. We have seen a variety of approaches applied to the same dataset, and we have been able to compare the performance of *pure* approaches to *hybrid* approaches, and of supervised approaches to unsupervised approaches. The results reported here are also encouraging, though clearly there is considerable room for improvement.

This task has established a high baseline for systems to beat. We can take heart from the fact that the best performance is apparently obtained from a combination of corpus-derived usage features and dictionary-derived linguistic knowledge. Although clever but simple approaches can do quite well on such a task, it is encouraging to note that the best results await those who employ the most robust and the most informed treatments of NCs and their paraphrases. Despite a good start, this is a challenge that remains resolutely open. We expect that the dataset created for the task will be a valuable resource for future research.

Acknowledgements

This work is partially supported by grants from Amazon and from the Bulgarian National Science Foundation (D002-111/15.12.2008 – *SmartBook*).

References

Timothy Baldwin and Takaaki Tanaka. 2004. Translation by Machine of Compound Nominals: Getting it Right. In *Proceedings of the ACL-04 Workshop on Multiword Expressions: Integrating Processing*, pages 24–31, Barcelona, Spain.

Cristina Butnariu and Tony Veale. 2008. A Concept-Centered Approach to Noun-Compound Interpretation. In *Proceedings of the 22nd International Conference on Computational Linguistics (COLING-08)*, pages 81–88, Manchester, UK.

Pamela Downing. 1977. On the creation and use of English compound nouns. *Language*, 53(4):810–842.

Christiane Fellbaum, editor. 1998. *WordNet: an electronic lexical database*. MIT Press.

Roxana Girju. 2007. Improving the Interpretation of Noun Phrases with Cross-linguistic Information. In *Proceedings of the 45th Annual Meeting of the Association of Computational Linguistics (ACL-07)*, pages 568–575, Prague, Czech Republic.

Su Nam Kim and Timothy Baldwin. 2005. Automatic interpretation of noun compounds using WordNet similarity. In *Proceedings of the 2nd International Joint Conference on Natural Language Processing (IJCNLP-05)*, pages 945–956, Jeju Island, South Korea.

Su Nam Kim and Timothy Baldwin. 2006. Interpreting Semantic Relations in Noun Compounds via Verb Semantics. In *Proceedings of the COLING-ACL-06 Main Conference Poster Sessions*, pages 491–498, Sydney, Australia.

Mirella Lapata and Alex Lascarides. 2003. Detecting novel compounds: The role of distributional evidence. In *Proceedings of the 10th Conference of the*

European Chapter of the Association for Computational Linguistics (EACL-03), pages 235–242, Budapest, Hungary.

Mark Lauer. 1995. *Designing Statistical Language Learners: Experiments on Noun Compounds*. Ph.D. thesis, Macquarie University.

Judith Levi. 1978. *The Syntax and Semantics of Complex Nominals*. Academic Press, New York, NY.

Dan Moldovan, Adriana Badulescu, Marta Tatu, Daniel Antohe, and Roxana Girju. 2004. Models for the Semantic Classification of Noun Phrases. In *Proceedings of the HLT-NAACL-04 Workshop on Computational Lexical Semantics*, pages 60–67, Boston, MA.

Preslav Nakov and Marti A. Hearst. 2008. Solving Relational Similarity Problems Using the Web as a Corpus. In *Proceedings of the 46th Annual Meeting of the Association of Computational Linguistics (ACL-08)*, pages 452–460, Columbus, OH.

Preslav Nakov. 2008a. Improved Statistical Machine Translation Using Monolingual Paraphrases. In *Proceedings of the 18th European Conference on Artificial Intelligence (ECAI-08)*, pages 338–342, Patras, Greece.

Preslav Nakov. 2008b. Noun Compound Interpretation Using Paraphrasing Verbs: Feasibility Study. In *Proceedings of the 13th International Conference on Artificial Intelligence: Methodology, Systems and Applications (AIMSA-08)*, pages 103–117, Varna, Bulgaria.

Vivi Nastase and Stan Szpakowicz. 2003. Exploring noun-modifier semantic relations. In *Proceedings of the 5th International Workshop on Computational Semantics (IWCS-03)*, pages 285–301, Tilburg, The Netherlands.

Vivi Nastase and Stan Szpakowicz. 2006. Matching syntactic-semantic graphs for semantic relation assignment. In *Proceedings of the 1st Workshop on Graph Based Methods for Natural Language Processing (TextGraphs-06)*, pages 81–88, New York, NY.

Diarmuid Ó Séaghdha and Ann Copestake. 2007. Cooccurrence Contexts for Noun Compound Interpretation. In *Proceedings of the ACL-07 Workshop on A Broader Perspective on Multiword Expressions (MWE-07)*, pages 57–64, Prague, Czech Republic.

Diarmuid Ó Séaghdha. 2008. *Learning Compound Noun Semantics*. Ph.D. thesis, University of Cambridge.

Rion Snow, Brendan O'Connor, Daniel Jurafsky, and Andrew Ng. 2008. Cheap and Fast – But is it Good? Evaluating Non-Expert Annotations for Natural Language Tasks. In *Proceedings of the 2008 Conference on Empirical Methods in Natural Language Processing (EMNLP-08)*, pages 254–263, Honolulu, HI.

Takaaki Tanaka and Timothy Baldwin. 2003. Noun-noun compound machine translation: A feasibility study on shallow processing. In *Proceedings of the ACL-03 Workshop on Multiword Expressions (MWE-03)*, pages 17–24, Sapporo, Japan.

Lucy Vanderwende. 1994. Algorithm for Automatic Interpretation of Noun Sequences. In *Proceedings of the 15th International Conference on Computational Linguistics (COLING-94)*, pages 782–788, Kyoto, Japan.

SemEval-2010 Task 10:
Linking Events and Their Participants in Discourse

Josef Ruppenhofer and **Caroline Sporleder**
Computational Linguistics
Saarland University
{josefr,csporled}@coli.uni-sb.de

Roser Morante
CNTS
University of Antwerp
Roser.Morante@ua.ac.be

Collin Baker
ICSI
Berkeley, CA 94704
collin@icsi.berkeley.edu

Martha Palmer
Department of Linguistics
University of Colorado at Boulder
martha.palmer@colorado.edu

Abstract

We describe the SemEval-2010 shared task on "Linking Events and Their Participants in Discourse". This task is an extension to the classical semantic role labeling task. While semantic role labeling is traditionally viewed as a sentence-internal task, local semantic argument structures clearly interact with each other in a larger context, e.g., by sharing references to specific discourse entities or events. In the shared task we looked at one particular aspect of cross-sentence links between argument structures, namely linking locally uninstantiated roles to their co-referents in the wider discourse context (if such co-referents exist). This task is potentially beneficial for a number of NLP applications, such as information extraction, question answering or text summarization.

1 Introduction

Semantic role labeling (SRL) has been defined as a sentence-level natural-language processing task in which semantic roles are assigned to the syntactic arguments of a predicate (Gildea and Jurafsky, 2002). Semantic roles describe the function of the participants in an event. Identifying the semantic roles of the predicates in a text allows knowing who did what to whom when where how, etc.

However, semantic role labeling as it is currently defined misses a lot of information due to the fact that it is viewed as a sentence-internal task. Hence, relations between different local semantic argument structures are disregarded. This view of SRL as a sentence-internal task is partly due to the fact that large-scale manual annotation projects such as FrameNet[1] and PropBank[2] typically present their annotations lexicographically by lemma rather than by source text.

It is clear that there is an interplay between local argument structure and the surrounding discourse (Fillmore, 1977). In early work, Palmer et al. (1986) discussed filling null complements from context by using knowledge about individual predicates and tendencies of referential chaining across sentences. But so far there have been few attempts to find links between argument structures across clause and sentence boundaries explicitly on the basis of semantic relations between the predicates involved. Two notable exceptions are Fillmore and Baker (2001) and Burchardt et al. (2005). Fillmore and Baker (2001) analyse a short newspaper article and discuss how frame semantics could benefit discourse processing but without making concrete suggestions of how to model this. Burchardt et al. (2005) provide a detailed analysis of the links between the local semantic argument structures in a short text; however their system is not fully implemented either.

With the shared task, we aimed to make a first step towards taking SRL beyond the domain of individual sentences by linking local semantic argument structures to the wider discourse context. The task addresses the problem of finding fillers for roles which are neither instantiated as direct dependents of our target predicates nor displaced through long-distance dependency or coinstantiation constructions. Often a referent for an uninstantiated role can be found in the wider context, i.e. in preceding or following sentences. An example is given in (1), where the CHARGES role

[1] http://framenet.icsi.berkeley.edu/
[2] http://verbs.colorado.edu/~mpalmer/projects/ace.html

Proceedings of the 5th International Workshop on Semantic Evaluation, ACL 2010, pages 45–50,
Uppsala, Sweden, 15-16 July 2010.

(ARG2 in PropBank) of *cleared* is left empty but can be linked to *murder* in the previous sentence.

(1) In a lengthy court case the defendant was tried for murder. In the end, he was cleared.

Another very rich example is provided by (2), where, for instance, the experiencer and the object of jealousy are not overtly expressed as dependents of the noun *jealousy* but can be inferred to be Watson and the speaker, Holmes, respectively.

(2) Watson won't allow that I know anything of art but that is mere jealousy because our views upon the subject differ.

This paper is organized as follows. In Section 2 we define how the concept of Null Instantiation is understood in the task. Section 3 describes the tasks to be performed, and Section 4, how they are evaluated. Section 5 presents the participant systems, and Section 6, their results. Finally, in Section 7, we put forward some conclusions.

2 Null Instantiations

The theory of null complementation used here is the one adopted by FrameNet, which derives from the work of Fillmore (1986).[3] Briefly, omissions of core arguments of predicates are categorized along two dimensions, the licensor and the interpretation they receive. The idea of a licensor refers to the fact that either a particular lexical item or a particular grammatical construction must be present for the omission of a frame element (FE) to occur. For instance, the omission of the agent in (3) is licensed by the passive construction.

(3) No doubt, mistakes were made $0^{Protagonist}$.

The omission is a constructional omission because it can apply to any predicate with an appropriate semantics that allows it to combine with the passive construction. On the other hand, the omission in (4) is lexically specific: the verb *arrive* allows the Goal to be unspecified but the verb *reach*, also a member of the Arriving frame, does not.

(4) We arrived 0^{Goal} at 8pm.

[3] Palmer et al.'s (1986) treatment of uninstantiated 'essential roles' is very similar (see also Palmer (1990)).

The above two examples also illustrate the second major dimension of variation. Whereas, in (3) the protagonist making the mistake is only existentially bound within the discourse (instance of indefinite null instantiation, INI), the Goal location in (4) is an entity that must be accessible to speaker and hearer from the discourse or its context (definite null instantiation, DNI). Finally, note that the licensing construction or lexical item fully and reliably determines the interpretation. Whereas missing by-phrases have always an indefinite interpretation, whenever *arrive* omits the Goal lexically, the Goal has to be interpreted as definite, as it is in (4).

The import of this classification to the task here is that we will concentrate on cases of DNI, be they licensed lexically or constructionally.

3 Description of the Task

3.1 Tasks

We originally intended to offer the participants a choice of two different tasks: a **full task**, in which the test set was only annotated with gold standard word senses (i.e., frames) for the target words and the participants had to perform role recognition/labeling and null instantiation linking, and a **NI only** task, in which the test set was already annotated with gold standard semantic argument structures and the participants only had to recognize definite null instantiations and find links to antecedents in the wider context (NI linking).

However, it turned out that the basic semantic role labeling task was already quite challenging for our data set. Previous shared tasks have shown that frame-semantic SRL of running text is a hard problem (Baker et al., 2007), partly due to the fact that running text is bound to contain many frames for which no or little annotated training data are available. In our case the difficulty was increased because our data came from a new genre and domain (i.e., crime fiction, see Section 3.2). Hence, we decided to add standard SRL, i.e., role recognition and labeling, as a third task (**SRL only**). This task did not involve NI linking.

3.2 Data

The participants were allowed to make use of a variety of data sources. We provided a training set annotated with semantic argument structure and null instantiation information. The annotations were originally made using FrameNet-style and later mapped semi-automatically to PropBank annotations, so that participants could choose which framework they wanted to work in. The data formats we used were TIGER/SALSA XML (Erk and Padó, 2004) (FrameNet-style) and a modified CoNLL-format (PropBank-style). As it turned out, all participants chose to work on FrameNet-style annotations, so we will not describe the PropBank annotation in this paper (see Ruppenhofer et al. (2009) for more details).

FrameNet-style annotation of full text is extremely time-consuming. Since we also had to annotate null instantiations and co-reference chains (for evaluation purposes, see Section 4), we could only make available a limited amount of data. Hence, we allowed participants to make use of additional data, in particular the FrameNet and PropBank releases.[4] We envisaged that the participants would want to use these additional data sets to train SRL systems for the full task and to learn something about typical fillers for different roles in order to solve the NI linking task. The annotated data sets we made available were meant to provide additional information, e.g., about the typical distance between an NI and its filler and about how to distinguish DNIs and INIs.

We annotated texts from two of Arthur Conan Doyle's fiction works. The text that served as training data was taken from "The Adventure of Wisteria Lodge". Of this lengthy, two-part story we annotated the second part, titled "The Tiger of San Pedro". The test set was made up of the last two chapters of "The Hound of the Baskervilles". We chose fiction rather than news because we believe that fiction texts with a linear narrative generally contain more context-resolvable NIs. They also tend to be longer and have a simpler structure than news texts, which typically revisit the same facts repeatedly at different levels of detail (in the so-called 'inverted pyramid' structure) and which mix event reports with commentary and evaluation, thus sequencing material that is understood as running in parallel. Fiction texts should lend themselves more readily to a first attempt at integrating discourse structure into semantic role labeling. We chose Conan Doyle's work because most of his books are not subject to copyright anymore, which allows us to freely release the annotated data. Note, however, that this choice of data means that our texts come from a different domain and genre than many of the examples in FrameNet and PropBank as well as making use of a somewhat older variety of English.[5]

Table 1 provides basic statistics of the data sets. The training data had 3.1 frames per sentence and the test data 3.2, which is lower than the 8.8 frames per sentence in the test data of the 2007 SemEval task on Frame Semantic Structure Extraction.[6] We think this is mainly the result of switching to a domain different from the bulk of what FrameNet has made available in the way of full-text annotation. In doing so, we encountered many new frames and lexical units for which we could not ourselves create the necessary frames and provide lexicographic annotations. The statistics also show that null-instantiation is relatively common: in the training data, about 18.7% of all FEs are omitted, and in the test set, about 18.4%. Of the DNIs, 80.9% had an antecedent in the training data, and 74.2% in the test data.

To ensure a high quality of the annotations, both data sets were annotated by more than one person and then adjudicated. The training set was annotated independently by two experienced annotators and then adjudicated by the same two people. The test set was annotated by three annotators and then adjudicated by the two experienced annotators. Throughout the annotation and adjudication process, we discussed difficult cases and also maintained a wiki. Additionally, we created a software tool that checked the consistency of our annotations against the frame, frame element and FE-relation specifications of FrameNet and alerted annotators to problems with their annotations. The average agreement (F-score) for frame assignment for pairs of annotators on the two chapters in the test set ranges from 0.7385 to 0.7870. The agreement of individual annotators with the adjudicated gold standard ranges from 0.666 to 0.798. Given that the gold standard for the two chapters features 228 and 229 different frame types, respectively, this level of agreement seems quite good.

[4]For FrameNet we provided an intermediate release, FrameNet 1.4 alpha, which contained more frames and lexical units than release 1.3.

[5]While PropBank provides annotations for the Penn Treebank and is thus news-based, the lexicographic annotations in FrameNet are extracted from the BNC, a balanced corpus. The FrameNet full-text annotations, however, only cover three domains: news, travel guides, and nuclear proliferation reports.

[6]The statistics in Table 1 and all our discussion of the data includes only instances of semantic frames and ignores the instances of the Coreference, Support, and Relativization frames, which we labeled on the data as auxiliary information.

data set	sentences	tokens	frame inst.	frame types	overt FEs	DNIs (resolved)	INIs
train	438	7,941	1,370	317	2,526	303 (245)	277
test	525	9,131	1,703	452	3,141	349 (259)	361

Table 1: Statistics for the provided data sets

For the annotation of NIs and their links to the surrounding discourse we created new guidelines as this was a novel annotation task. We adopted ideas from the annotation of co-reference information, linking locally unrealized roles to all mentions of the referents in the surrounding discourse, where available. We marked only identity relations but not part-whole or bridging relations between referents. The set of unrealized roles under consideration includes only the core arguments but not adjuncts (peripheral or extra-thematic roles in FrameNet's terminology). Possible antecedents are not restricted to noun phrases but include all constituents that can be (local) role fillers for some predicate plus complete sentences (which can sometimes fill roles such as MESSAGE).

4 Evaluation

As noted above, we allowed participants to address three different tasks: SRL only, NI only, full task. For role recognition and labeling we used a standard evaluation set-up, i.e., accuracy for role labeling and precision, recall, F-Score for role recognition.

The NI linkings were evaluated slightly differently. In the gold standard, we identified referents for null instantiations in the discourse context. In some cases, more than one referent might be appropriate, e.g., because the omitted argument refers to an entity that is mentioned multiple times in the context. In this case, a system is given credit if the NI is linked to any of these expressions. To achieve this we create equivalence sets for the referents of NIs (by annotating coreference chains). If the NI is linked to any item in the equivalence set, the link is counted as a true positive. We can then define **NI linking precision** as the number of all true positive links divided by the number of links made by a system, and **NI linking recall** as the number of true positive links divided by the number of links between an NI and its equivalence set in the gold standard. **NI linking F-Score** is then the harmonic mean between NI linking precision and recall.

Since it may sometimes be difficult to determine the correct extent of the filler of an NI, we score an automatic annotation as correct if it includes the head of the gold standard filler in the predicted filler. However, in order to not favor systems which link NIs to very large spans of text to maximize the likelihood of linking to a correct referent, we introduce a second evaluation measure, which computes the overlap (Dice coefficient) between the words in the predicted filler (P) of an NI and the words in the gold standard one (G):

$$\textbf{NI linking overlap} = \frac{2|P \cap G|}{|P| + |G|} \qquad (5)$$

Example (6) illustrates this point. The verb *won* in the second sentence evokes the Finish_competition frame whose COMPETITION role is omitted. From the context it is clear that the competition role is semantically filled by *their first TV debate* (head: *debate*) and *last night's debate* (head: *debate*) in the previous sentences. These two expressions form the equivalence set for the COMPETITION role in the last sentence. Any system that would predict a linkage to a filler that covers the head of either of these two expressions would score a true positive for this NI. However, a system that linked to *last night's debate* would have an NI linking overlap of 1 (i.e., 2*3/(3+3)) while a system linking the whole second sentence *Last night's debate was eagerly anticipated* to the NI would have an overlap of 0.67 (i.e., 2*3/(6+3))

(6) US presidential rivals Republican John McCain and Democrat Barack Obama have yesterday evening attacked each other over foreign policy and the economy, in [their first TV debate]$_{Competition}$. [Last night's debate]$_{Competition}$ was eagerly anticipated. Two national flash polls suggest that [Obama]$_{Competitor}$ won$_{Finish_competition}$ $0^{Competition}$.

5 Participating Systems

While a fair number of people expressed an interest in the task and 26 groups or individuals downloaded the data sets, only three groups submitted results for evaluation. Feedback from the teams that downloaded the data suggests that this was due to coinciding deadlines and to the difficulty and novelty of the task. Only the SEMAFOR group addressed the full task, using a pipeline of argument recognition followed by NI identification and resolution. Two groups (GETARUNS++ and SEMAFOR) tackled the NI only task, and also two groups, the SRL only task (CLR and SEMAFOR[7]).

All participating systems were built upon existing systems for semantic processing which were modified for the task. Two of the groups, GETARUNS++ and CLR, employed relatively deep semantic processing, while the third, SEMAFOR, employed a shallower probabilistic system. Different approaches were taken for NI linking. The SEMAFOR group modeled NI linking as a variant of role recognition and labeling by extending the set of potential arguments beyond the locally available arguments to also include noun phrases from the previous sentence. The system then uses, among other information, distributional semantic similarity between the heads of potential arguments and role fillers in the training data. The GETARUNS++ group applied an existing system for deep semantic processing, anaphora resolution and recognition of textual entailment, to the task. The system analyzes the sentences and assigns its own set of labels, which are subsequently mapped to frame semantic categories. For more details of the participating systems please consult the separate system papers.

6 Results and Analysis

6.1 SRL Task

	Argument Recognition			Label
	Prec.	Rec.	F1	Acc.
SHA	0.6332	0.3884	0.4812	0.3471
SEM	0.6528	0.4674	0.5448	0.4184
CLR	0.6702	0.1121	0.1921	0.1093

Table 2: Shalmaneser (SHA), SEMAFOR (SEM) and CLR performance on the SRL task (across both chapters)

The results on the SRL task are shown in Table 2. To get a better sense of how good the performance of the submitted systems was on this task, we applied the Shalmaneser statistical semantic parser (Erk and Padó, 2006) to our test data and report the results. Note, however, that we used a Shalmaneser trained only on FrameNet version 1.3 which is different from the version 1.4 alpha that was used in the task, so its results are lower than what can be expected with release 1.4 alpha.

We observe that although the SEMAFOR and the CLR systems score a higher precision than Shalmaneser for argument recognition, the SEMAFOR system scores considerably higher recall than Shalmaneser, whereas the CLR system scores a much lower recall.

6.2 NI Task

Tackling the resolution of NIs proved to be a difficult problem due to a variety of factors. First, the NI sub-task was completely new and involves several steps of linguistic processing. It also is inherently difficult in that a given FE is not always omitted with the same interpretation. For instance, the Content FE of the Awareness frame evoked by *know* is interpreted as indefinite in the blog headline *More babbling about what it means to know* but as definite in a discourse like *Don't tell me you didn't know!*. Second, prior to this SemEval task there was no full-text training data available that contained annotations with all the kinds of information that is relevant to the task, namely overt FEs, null-instantiated FEs, resolutions of null-instantiations, and coreference. Third, the data we used also represented a switch to a new domain compared to existing FrameNet full-text annotation, which comes from newspapers, travel guides, and the nuclear proliferation domain. Our most frequent frame was Observable_bodyparts, whereas it is Weapons in FrameNet full-text. Fourth, it was not well understood at the beginning of the task that, in certain cases, FrameNet's null-instantiation annotations for a given FE cannot be treated in isolation of the annotations of other FEs. Specifically, null-instantiation annotations interact with the set of relations between core FEs that FrameNet uses in its analyses. As an example, consider the CoreSet relation, which specifies that from a set of core FEs at least one must be instantiated overtly, though more of them can be. As long as one of the FEs in the set is expressed overtly, null-instantiation is not annotated for the other FEs in the set. For instance, in the Statement frame, the two FEs

[7]For SEMAFOR, this was the first step of their pipeline.

Topic and Message are in one CoreSet and the two FEs Speaker and Medium are in another. If a frame instance occurs with an overt Speaker and an overt Topic, the Medium and Message FEs are not marked as null-instantiated. Automatic systems that treat each core FE separately, may propose DNI annotations for Medium and Message, resulting in false positives.

Therefore, we think that the evaluation that we initially defined was too demanding for a novel task. It would have been better to give separate scores for 1) ability to recognize when a core FE has to be treated as null-instantiated; 2) ability to distinguish INI and DNI; and 3) ability to find antecedents. The systems did have to tackle these steps anyway and an analysis of the system output shows that they did so with different success. The two chapters of our test data contained a total of 710 null instantiations, of which 349 were DNI and 361 INI. The SEMAFOR system recognized 63.4% (450/710) of the cases of NI, while the GETARUNS++ system found only 8.0% (57/710). The distinction between DNI and INI proved very difficult, too. Of the NIs that the SEMAFOR system correctly identified, 54.7% (246/450) received the correct interpretation type (DNI or INI). For GETARUNS++, the percentage is higher at 64.2% (35/57), but also based on fewer proposed classifications. A simple majority-class baseline gives a 50.8% accuracy. Interestingly, the SEMAFOR system labeled many more INIs than DNIs, thus often misclassifying DNIs as INI. The GETARUNS++ system applied both labels about equally often.

7 Conclusion

In this paper we described the SemEval-2010 shared task on "Linking Events and Their Participants in Discourse". The task is novel, in that it tackles a semantic cross-clausal phenomenon that has not been treated before in a task, namely, linking locally uninstantiated roles to their coreferents at the text level. In that sense the task represents a first step towards taking SRL beyond the sentence level. A new corpus of fiction texts has been annotated for the task with several types of semantic information: semantic argument structure, coreference chains and NIs. The results scored by the systems in the NI task and the feedback from participant teams shows that the task was more difficult than initially estimated and that the evaluation should have focused on more specific aspects of the NI phenomenon, rather than on the completeness of the task. Future work will focus on modeling the task taking this into account.

Acknowledgements

Josef Ruppenhofer and Caroline Sporleder are supported by the German Research Foundation DFG (under grant PI 154/9-3 and the Cluster of Excellence Multimodal Computing and Interaction (MMCI), respectively). Roser Morante's research is funded by the GOA project BIOGRAPH of the University of Antwerp. We would like to thank Jinho Choi, Markus Dräger, Lisa Fuchs, Philip John Gorinski, Russell Lee-Goldman, Ines Rehbein, and Corinna Schorr for their help with preparing the data and/or implementing software for the task. Thanks also to the SemEval-2010 Chairs Katrin Erk and Carlo Strapparava for their support during the task organization period.

References

C. Baker, M. Ellsworth, K. Erk. 2007. SemEval-2007 Task 19: Frame semantic structure extraction. In *Proceedings of SemEval-07*.

A. Burchardt, A. Frank, M. Pinkal. 2005. Building text meaning representations from contextually related frames – A case study. In *Proceedings of IWCS-6*.

K. Erk, S. Padó. 2004. A powerful and versatile XML format for representing role-semantic annotation. In *Proceedings of LREC-2004*.

K. Erk, S. Padó. 2006. Shalmaneser - a flexible toolbox for semantic role assignment. In *Proceedings of LREC-06*.

C. Fillmore, C. Baker. 2001. Frame semantics for text understanding. In *Proc. of the NAACL-01 Workshop on WordNet and Other Lexical Resources*.

C. Fillmore. 1977. Scenes-and-frames semantics, linguistic structures processing. In A. Zampolli, ed., *Fundamental Studies in Computer Science, No. 59*, 55–88. North Holland Publishing.

C. Fillmore. 1986. Pragmatically controlled zero anaphora. In *Proceedings of the Twelfth Annual Meeting of the Berkeley Liguistics Society*.

D. Gildea, D. Jurafsky. 2002. Automatic labeling of semantic roles. *Computational Linguistics*, 28(3):245–288.

M. Palmer, D. Dahl, R. Passonneau, L. Hirschman, M. Linebarger, J. Dowding. 1986. Recovering implicit information. In *Proceedings of ACL-1986*.

M. Palmer. 1990. *Semantic Processing for Finite Domains*. CUP, Cambridge, England.

J. Ruppenhofer, C. Sporleder, R. Morante, C. Baker, M. Palmer. 2009. Semeval-2010 task 10: Linking events and their participants in discourse. In *The NAACL-HLT 2009 Workshop on Semantic Evaluations: Recent Achievements and Future Directions (SEW-09)*.

SemEval-2010 Task 12: Parser Evaluation using Textual Entailments

Deniz Yuret
Koç University
İstanbul, Turkey
dyuret@ku.edu.tr

Aydın Han
Koç University
İstanbul, Turkey
ahan@ku.edu.tr

Zehra Turgut
Koç University
İstanbul, Turkey
zturgut@ku.edu.tr

Abstract

Parser Evaluation using Textual Entailments (PETE) is a shared task in the SemEval-2010 Evaluation Exercises on Semantic Evaluation. The task involves recognizing textual entailments based on syntactic information alone. PETE introduces a new parser evaluation scheme that is formalism independent, less prone to annotation error, and focused on semantically relevant distinctions.

1 Introduction

Parser Evaluation using Textual Entailments (PETE) is a shared task that involves recognizing textual entailments based on syntactic information alone. Given two text fragments called "text" and "hypothesis", textual entailment recognition is the task of determining whether the meaning of the hypothesis is entailed (can be inferred) from the text. In contrast with general RTE tasks (Dagan et al., 2009) the PETE task focuses on syntactic entailments:

Text: The man with the hat was tired.
Hypothesis-1: The man was tired. *(yes)*
Hypothesis-2: The hat was tired. *(no)*

PETE is an evaluation scheme based on a natural human linguistic competence (i.e. the ability to comprehend sentences and answer simple yes/no questions about them). We believe systems should try to model natural human linguistic competence rather than their dubious competence in artificial tagging tasks.

The PARSEVAL measures introduced nearly two decades ago (Black et al., 1991) still dominate the field of parser evaluation. These methods compare phrase-structure bracketings produced by the parser with bracketings in the annotated corpus, or "treebank". Parser evaluation using short textual entailments has the following advantages compared to treebank based evaluation.

Consistency: Recognizing syntactic entailments is a more natural task for people than treebank annotation. Focusing on a natural human competence makes it practical to collect high quality evaluation data from untrained annotators. The PETE dataset was annotated by untrained Amazon Mechanical Turk workers at an insignificant cost and each annotation is based on the unanimous agreement of at least three workers. In contrast, of the 36306 constituent strings that appear multiple times in the Penn Treebank (Marcus et al., 1994), 5646 (15%) have multiple conflicting annotations. If indicative of the general level of inconsistency, 15% is a very high number given that the state of the art parsers claim f-scores above 90% (Charniak and Johnson, 2005).

Relevance: PETE automatically focuses attention on semantically relevant phenomena rather than differences in annotation style or linguistic convention. Whether a phrase is tagged ADJP vs ADVP rarely affects semantic interpretation. Attaching the wrong subject to a verb or the wrong prepositional phrase to a noun changes the meaning of the sentence. Standard treebank based evaluation metrics do not distinguish between semantically relevant and irrelevant errors (Bonnema et al., 1997). In PETE semantically relevant differences lead to different entailments, semantically irrelevant differences do not.

Framework independence: Entailment recognition is a formalism independent task. A common evaluation method for parsers that do not use the Penn Treebank formalism is to automatically convert the Penn Treebank to the appropriate formalism and to perform treebank based evaluation (Nivre et al., 2007a; Hockenmaier and Steedman,

Proceedings of the 5th International Workshop on Semantic Evaluation, ACL 2010, pages 51–56,
Uppsala, Sweden, 15-16 July 2010.

2007). The inevitable conversion errors compound the already mentioned problems of treebank based evaluation. In addition, manually designed treebanks do not naturally lend themselves to unsupervised parser evaluation. Unlike treebank based evaluation, PETE can compare phrase structure parsers, dependency parsers, unsupervised parsers and other approaches on an equal footing.

PETE was inspired by earlier work on representations of grammatical dependency, proposed for ease of use by end users and suitable for parser evaluation. These include the grammatical relations (GR) by (Carroll et al., 1999), the PARC representation (King et al., 2003), and Stanford typed dependencies (SD) (De Marneffe et al., 2006) (See (Bos and others, 2008) for other proposals). Each use a set of binary relations between words in a sentence as the primary unit of representation. They share some common motivations: usability by people who are not (computational) linguists and suitability for relation extraction applications. Here is an example sentence and its SD representation (De Marneffe and Manning, 2008):

Bell, based in Los Angeles, makes and distributes electronic, computer and building products.

nsubj(makes-8, Bell-1)
nsubj(distributes-10, Bell-1)
partmod(Bell-1, based-3)
nn(Angeles-6, Los-5)
prep-in(based-3, Angeles-6)
conj-and(makes-8, distributes-10)
amod(products-16, electronic-11)
conj-and(electronic-11, computer-13)
amod(products-16, computer-13)
conj-and(electronic-11, building-15)
amod(products-16, building-15)
dobj(makes-8, products-16)

PETE goes one step further by translating most of these dependencies into natural language entailments.

Bell makes something.
Bell distributes something.
Someone is based in Los Angeles.
Someone makes products.

PETE has some advantages over representations based on grammatical relations. For example SD defines 55 relations organized in a hierarchy, and it may be non-trivial for a non-linguist to understand the difference between *ccomp* (clausal complement with internal subject) and *xcomp* (clausal complement with external subject) or between *nsubj* (nominal subject) and *xsubj* (controlling subject). In fact it could be argued that proposals like SD replace one artificial annotation formalism with another and no two such proposals agree on the ideal set of binary relations to use. In contrast, untrained annotators have no difficulty unanimously agreeing on the validity of most PETE type entailments.

However there are also significant challenges associated with an evaluation scheme like PETE. It is not always clear how to convert certain relations into grammatical hypothesis sentences without including most of the original sentence in the hypothesis. Including too much of the sentence in the hypothesis would increase the chances of getting the right answer with the wrong parse. Grammatical hypothesis sentences are especially difficult to construct when a (negative) entailment is based on a bad parse of the sentence. Introducing dummy words like "someone" or "something" alleviates part of the problem but does not help in the case of clausal complements. In summary, PETE makes the annotation phase more practical and consistent but shifts the difficulty to the entailment creation phase.

PETE gets closer to an extrinsic evaluation by focusing on semantically relevant, application oriented differences that can be expressed in natural language sentences. This makes the evaluation procedure indirect: a parser developer has to write an extension that can handle entailment questions. However, given the simplicity of the entailments, the complexity of such an extension is comparable to one that extracts grammatical relations.

The balance of what is being evaluated is also important. A treebank based evaluation scheme may mix semantically relevant and irrelevant mistakes, but at least it covers every sentence at a uniform level of detail. In this evaluation, we focused on sentences and relations where state of the art parsers disagree. We hope this methodology will uncover weaknesses that the next generation systems can focus on.

The remaining sections will go into more detail about these challenges and the solutions we have chosen to implement. Section 2 explains the method followed to create the PETE dataset. Section 3 evaluates the baseline systems the task organizers created by implementing simple entailment extensions for several state of the art parsers. Section 4 presents the participating systems, their methods and results. Section 5 summarizes our contribution.

2 Dataset

To generate the entailments for the PETE task we followed the following three steps:

1. Identify syntactic dependencies that are challenging to state of the art parsers.

2. Construct short entailment sentences that paraphrase those dependencies.

3. Identify the subset of the entailments with high inter-annotator agreement.

2.1 Identifying Challenging Dependencies

To identify syntactic dependencies that are challenging for current state of the art parsers, we used example sentences from the following sources:

- The "Unbounded Dependency Corpus" (Rimell et al., 2009). An unbounded dependency construction contains a word or phrase which appears to have been moved, while being interpreted in the position of the resulting "gap". An unlimited number of clause boundaries may intervene between the moved element and the gap (hence "unbounded").

- A list of sentences from the Penn Treebank on which the Charniak parser (Charniak and Johnson, 2005) performs poorly[1].

- The Brown section of the Penn Treebank.

We tested a number of parsers (both phrase structure and dependency) on these sentences and identified the differences in their output. We took sentences where at least one of the parsers gave a different answer than the others or the gold parse. Some of these differences reflected linguistic convention rather than semantic disagreement (e.g. representation of coordination) and some did not represent meaningful differences that can be expressed with entailments (e.g. labeling a phrase ADJP vs ADVP). The remaining differences typically reflected genuine semantic disagreements that would effect downstream applications. These were chosen to turn into entailments in the next step.

2.2 Constructing Entailments

We tried to make the entailments as targeted as possible by building them around two content words that are syntactically related. When the two content words were not sufficient to construct a grammatical sentence we used one of the following techniques:

- Complete the mandatory elements using the words "somebody" or "something". (e.g. To test the subject-verb dependency in "John kissed Mary." we construct the entailment "John kissed somebody.")

- Make a passive sentence to avoid using a spurious subject. (e.g. To test the verb-object dependency in "John kissed Mary." we construct the entailment "Mary was kissed.")

- Make a copular sentence or use existential "there" to express noun modification. (e.g. To test the noun-modifier dependency in "The big red boat sank." we construct the entailment "The boat was big." or "There was a big boat.")

2.3 Filtering Entailments

To identify the entailments that are clear to human judgement we used the following procedure:

1. Each entailment was tagged by 5 untrained annotators from the Amazon Mechanical Turk crowdsourcing service.

2. The results from the annotators whose agreement with the gold parse fell below 70% were eliminated.

3. The entailments for which there was unanimous agreement of at least 3 annotators were kept.

The instructions for the annotators were brief and targeted people with no linguistic background:

> Computers try to understand long sentences by dividing them into a set of short facts. You will help judge whether the computer extracted the right facts from a given set of 25 English sentences. Each of the following examples consists of a sentence (T), and a short statement (H) derived from this sentence by a computer. Please

[1] http://www.cs.brown.edu/~ec/papers/badPars.txt.gz

read both of them carefully and choose "Yes" if the meaning of (H) can be inferred from the meaning of (T). Here is an example:

(T) *Any lingering suspicion that this was a trick Al Budd had thought up was dispelled.*
(H) *The suspicion was dispelled.* Answer: YES
(H) *The suspicion was a trick.* Answer: NO

You can choose the third option "Not sure" when the (H) statement is unrelated, unclear, ungrammatical or confusing in any other manner.

The "Not sure" answers were grouped with the "No" answers during evaluation. Approximately 50% of the original entailments were retained after the inter-annotator agreement filtering.

2.4 Dataset statistics

The final dataset contained 367 entailments which were randomly divided into a 66 sentence development test and a 301 sentence test set. 52% of the entailments in the test set were positive.

Approximately half of the final entailments were from the Unbounded Dependency Corpus, a third were from the Brown section of the Penn Treebank, and the remaining were from the Charniak sentences. Table 1 lists the most frequent grammatical relations encountered in the entailments.

GR	Entailments
Direct object	42%
Nominal subject	33%
Reduced relative clause	21%
Relative clause	13%
Passive nominal subject	6%
Object of preposition	5%
Prepositional modifier	4%
Conjunct	2%
Adverbial modifier	2%
Free relative	2%

Table 1: Most frequent grammatical relations encountered in the entailments.

3 Baselines

In order to establish baseline results for this task, we built an entailment decision system for CoNLL format dependency files and tested several publicly available parsers. The parsers used were the Berkeley Parser (Petrov and Klein, 2007), Charniak Parser (Charniak and Johnson, 2005), Collins Parser (Collins, 2003), Malt Parser (Nivre et al., 2007b), MSTParser (McDonald et al., 2005) and Stanford Parser (Klein and Manning, 2003). Each parser was trained on sections 02-21 of the WSJ section of Penn Treebank. Outputs of phrase structure parsers were automatically annotated with function tags using Blaheta's function tagger (Blaheta and Charniak, 2000) and converted to the dependency structure with LTH Constituent-to-Dependency Conversion Tool (Johansson and Nugues, 2007).

To decide the entailments both the test and hypothesis sentences were parsed. All the content words in the hypothesis sentence were determined by using part-of-speech tags and dependency relations. After applying some heuristics such as active-passive conversion, the extracted dependency path between the content words was searched in the dependency graph of the test sentence. In this search process, same relation types for the direct relations between the content word pairs and isomorphic subgraphs in the test and hypothesis sentences were required for the "YES" answer.

Table 2 lists the baseline results achieved. There are significant differences in the entailment accuracies of systems that have comparable unlabeled attachment scores. One potential reason for this difference is the composition of the PETE dataset which emphasizes challenging syntactic constructions that some parsers may be better at. Another reason is the complete indifference of treebank based measures like UAS to the semantic significance of various dependencies and their impact on potential applications.

System	PETE	UAS
Berkeley Parser	68.1%	91.2
Stanford Parser	66.1%	90.2
Malt Parser	65.5%	89.8
Charniak Parser	64.5%	93.2
Collins Parser	63.5%	91.6
MST Parser	59.8%	92.0

Table 2: Baseline systems: The second column gives the performance on the PETE test set, the third column gives the unlabeled attachment score on section 23 of the Penn Treebank.

4 Systems

There were 20 systems from 7 teams participating in the PETE task. Table 3 gives the percentage of correct answers for each system. 12 sys-

System	Accuracy	Precision	Recall	F1
360-418-Cambridge	0.7243	0.7967	0.6282	0.7025
459-505-SCHWA	0.7043	0.6831	0.8013	0.7375
473-568-MARS-3	0.6678	0.6591	0.7436	0.6988
372-404-MDParser	0.6545	0.7407	0.5128	0.6061
372-509-MaltParser	0.6512	0.7429	0.5000	0.5977
473-582-MARS-5	0.6346	0.6278	0.7244	0.6726
166-415-JU-CSE-TASK12-2	0.5781	0.5714	0.7436	0.6462
166-370-JU-CSE-TASK12	0.5482	0.5820	0.4551	0.5108
390-433-Berkeley Parser Based	0.5415	0.5425	0.7372	0.6250
473-566-MARS-1	0.5282	0.5547	0.4551	0.5108
473-569-MARS-4	0.5249	0.5419	0.5385	0.5402
390-431-Brown Parser Based	0.5216	0.5349	0.5897	0.5610
473-567-MARS-2	0.5116	0.5328	0.4679	0.4983
363-450-VENSES	0.5083	0.5220	0.6090	0.5621
473-583-MARS-6	0.5050	0.5207	0.5641	0.5415
390-432-Brown Reranker Parser Based	0.5017	0.5217	0.4615	0.4898
390-435-Berkeley Parser with substates	0.5017	0.5395	0.2628	0.3534
390-434-Berkeley Parser with Self Training	0.4983	0.5248	0.3397	0.4125
390-437-Combined	0.4850	0.5050	0.3269	0.3969
390-436-Berkeley Parser with Viterbi Decoding	0.4784	0.4964	0.4359	0.4642

Table 3: Participating systems and their scores. The system identifier consists of the participant ID, system ID, and the system name given by the participant. Accuracy gives the percentage of correct entailments. Precision, Recall and F1 are calculated for positive entailments.

tems performed above the "always yes" baseline of 51.83%.

Most systems started the entailment decision process by extracting syntactic dependencies, grammatical relations, or predicates by parsing the text and hypothesis sentences. Several submissions, including the top two scoring systems used the C&C Parser (Clark and Curran, 2007) which is based on Combinatory Categorical Grammar (CCG) formalism. Others used dependency structures produced by Malt Parser (Nivre et al., 2007b), MSTParser (McDonald et al., 2005) and Stanford Parser (Klein and Manning, 2003).

After the parsing step, the decision for the entailment was based on the comparison of relations, predicates, or dependency paths between the text and the hypothesis. Most systems relied on heuristic methods of comparison. A notable exception is the MARS-3 system which used an SVM-based classifier to decide on the entailment using dependency path features.

Table 4 lists the frequency of various grammatical relations in the instances where the top system made mistakes. A comparison with Table 1 shows the direct objects and reduced relative clauses to be the frequent causes of error.

GR	Entailments
Direct object	51%
Reduced relative clause	36%
Nominal subject	20%
Object of preposition	7%
Passive nominal subject	7%

Table 4: Frequency of grammatical relations in entailment instances that got wrong answers from the Cambridge system.

5 Contributions

We introduced PETE, a new method for parser evaluation using textual entailments. By basing the entailments on dependencies that current state of the art parsers disagree on, we hoped to create a dataset that would focus attention on the long tail of parsing problems that do not get sufficient attention using common evaluation metrics. By further restricting ourselves to differences that can be expressed by natural language entailments, we hoped to focus on semantically relevant decisions rather than accidents of convention which get mixed up in common evaluation metrics. We chose to rely on untrained annotators on a natural inference task rather than trained annotators on an artificial tagging task because we believe (i) many subfields of computational linguistics are struggling to make progress because of the noise in artificially tagged data, and (ii) systems should try to model natural human linguistic competence rather than their dubious competence in artificial tagging tasks. Our hope is datasets like PETE will be used not only for evaluation but also for training and fine-tuning of systems in the future. Further work is needed to automate the entailment generation process and to balance the composition of syntactic phenomena covered in a PETE dataset.

Acknowledgments

We would like to thank Laura Rimell, Stephan Oepen and Anna Mac for their careful analysis and valuable suggestions. Önder Eker contributed to the early development of the PETE task.

References

E. Black, S. Abney, D. Flickenger, C. Gdaniec, R. Grishman, P. Harrison, D. Hindle, R. Ingria, F. Jelinek, J. Klavans, et al. 1991. A Procedure for Quantitatively Comparing the Syntactic Coverage of English Grammars. In *Speech and natural language: proceedings of a workshop, held at Pacific Grove, California, February 19-22, 1991*, page 306. Morgan Kaufmann Pub.

D. Blaheta and E. Charniak. 2000. Assigning function tags to parsed text. In *Proceedings of the 1st North American chapter of the Association for Computational Linguistics conference*, page 240. Morgan Kaufmann Publishers Inc.

R. Bonnema, R. Bod, and R. Scha. 1997. A DOP model for semantic interpretation. In *Proceedings of the eighth conference on European chapter of the Association for Computational Linguistics*, pages 159–167. Association for Computational Linguistics.

Johan Bos et al., editors. 2008. *Proceedings of the Workshop on Cross-Framework and Cross-Domain Parser Evaluation*. In connection with the 22nd International Conference on Computational Linguistics.

J. Carroll, G. Minnen, and T. Briscoe. 1999. Corpus annotation for parser evaluation. In *Proceedings of the EACL workshop on Linguistically Interpreted Corpora (LINC)*.

E. Charniak and M. Johnson. 2005. Coarse-to-fine n-best parsing and MaxEnt discriminative reranking. In *Proceedings of the 43rd Annual Meeting on Association for Computational Linguistics*, page 180. Association for Computational Linguistics.

S. Clark and J.R. Curran. 2007. Wide-coverage efficient statistical parsing with CCG and log-linear models. *Computational Linguistics*, 33(4):493–552.

M. Collins. 2003. Head-driven statistical models for natural language parsing. *Computational linguistics*, 29(4):589–637.

I. Dagan, B. Dolan, B. Magnini, and D. Roth. 2009. Recognizing textual entailment: Rational, evaluation and approaches. *Natural Language Engineering*, 15(04).

M.C. De Marneffe and C.D. Manning, 2008. *Stanford typed dependencies manual*.

M.C. De Marneffe, B. MacCartney, and C.D. Manning. 2006. Generating typed dependency parses from phrase structure parses. In *LREC 2006*.

J. Hockenmaier and M. Steedman. 2007. CCGbank: a corpus of CCG derivations and dependency structures extracted from the Penn Treebank. *Computational Linguistics*, 33(3):355–396.

R. Johansson and P. Nugues. 2007. Extended constituent-to-dependency conversion for English. In *Proc. of the 16th Nordic Conference on Computational Linguistics (NODALIDA)*.

T.H. King, R. Crouch, S. Riezler, M. Dalrymple, and R. Kaplan. 2003. The PARC 700 dependency bank. In *Proceedings of the EACL03: 4th International Workshop on Linguistically Interpreted Corpora (LINC-03)*, pages 1–8.

D. Klein and C.D. Manning. 2003. Accurate unlexicalized parsing. In *Proceedings of the 41st Annual Meeting on Association for Computational Linguistics-Volume 1*, pages 423–430. Association for Computational Linguistics.

M.P. Marcus, B. Santorini, and M.A. Marcinkiewicz. 1994. Building a large annotated corpus of English: The Penn Treebank. *Computational linguistics*, 19(2):313–330.

R. McDonald, F. Pereira, K. Ribarov, and J. Hajic. 2005. Non-projective dependency parsing using spanning tree algorithms. In *Proceedings of HLT/EMNLP*, pages 523–530.

J. Nivre, J. Hall, S. Kübler, R. McDonald, J. Nilsson, S. Riedel, and D. Yuret. 2007a. The CoNLL 2007 shared task on dependency parsing. In *Proceedings of the CoNLL Shared Task Session of EMNLP-CoNLL*, volume 7, pages 915–932.

J. Nivre, J. Hall, J. Nilsson, A. Chanev, G. Eryigit, S. Kübler, S. Marinov, and E. Marsi. 2007b. Malt-Parser: A language-independent system for data-driven dependency parsing. *Natural Language Engineering*, 13(02):95–135.

S. Petrov and D. Klein. 2007. Improved inference for unlexicalized parsing. In *Proceedings of NAACL HLT 2007*, pages 404–411.

L. Rimell, S. Clark, and M. Steedman. 2009. Unbounded dependency recovery for parser evaluation. In *Proceedings of the 2009 Conference on Empirical Methods in Natural Language Processing*, pages 813–821. Association for Computational Linguistics.

SemEval-2010 Task 13: TempEval-2

Marc Verhagen[†], **Roser Saurí** [‡], **Tommaso Caselli**[*] **and James Pustejovsky**[†]

† Computer Science Department, Brandeis University, Massachusetts, USA
‡Barcelona Media, Barcelona, Spain ∗ ILC-CNR, Pisa, Italy

marc@cs.brandeis.edu roser.sauri@barcelonamedia.org
tommaso.caselli@ilc.cnr.it jamesp@cs.brandeis.edu

Abstract

Tempeval-2 comprises evaluation tasks for time expressions, events and temporal relations, the latter of which was split up in four sub tasks, motivated by the notion that smaller subtasks would make both data preparation and temporal relation extraction easier. Manually annotated data were provided for six languages: Chinese, English, French, Italian, Korean and Spanish.

1 Introduction

The ultimate aim of temporal processing is the automatic identification of all temporal referring expressions, events and temporal relations within a text. However, addressing this aim is beyond the scope of an evaluation challenge and a more modest approach is appropriate.

The 2007 SemEval task, TempEval-1 (Verhagen et al., 2007; Verhagen et al., 2009), was an initial evaluation exercise based on three limited temporal ordering and anchoring tasks that were considered realistic both from the perspective of assembling resources for development and testing and from the perspective of developing systems capable of addressing the tasks.[1]

TempEval-2 is based on TempEval-1, but is more elaborate in two respects: (i) it is a multilingual task, and (ii) it consists of six subtasks rather than three.

In the rest of this paper, we first introduce the data that we are dealing with. Which gets us in a position to present the list of task introduced by TempEval-2, including some motivation as to why we feel that it is a good idea to split up temporal relation classification into sub tasks. We proceed by shortly describing the data resources and their creation, followed by the performance of the systems that participated in the tasks.

[1]The Semeval-2007 task was actually known simply as TempEval, but here we use Tempeval-1 to avoid confusion.

2 TempEval Annotation

The TempEval annotation language is a simplified version of TimeML.[2] using three TimeML tags: TIMEX3, EVENT and TLINK.

TIMEX3 tags the time expressions in the text and is identical to the TIMEX3 tag in TimeML. Times can be expressed syntactically by adverbial or prepositional phrases, as shown in the following example.

(1) a. on Thursday
b. November 15, 2004
c. Thursday evening
d. in the late 80's
e. later this afternoon

The two main attributes of the TIMEX3 tag are TYPE and VAL, both shown in the example (2).

(2) *November 22, 2004*
`type="DATE" val="2004-11-22"`

For TempEval-2, we distinguish four temporal types: TIME (*at 2:45 p.m.*), DATE (*January 27, 1920, yesterday*), DURATION (*two weeks*) and SET (*every Monday morning*). The VAL attribute assumes values according to an extension of the ISO 8601 standard, as enhanced by TIMEX2.

Each document has one special TIMEX3 tag, the Document Creation Time (DCT), which is interpreted as an interval that spans a whole day.

The EVENT tag is used to annotate those elements in a text that describe what is conventionally referred to as an *eventuality*. Syntactically, events are typically expressed as inflected verbs, although event nominals, such as "crash" in *killed by the crash*, should also be annotated as EVENTs. The most salient event attributes encode tense, aspect, modality and polarity information. Examples of some of these features are shown below:

[2]See http://www.timeml.org for language specifications and annotation guidelines

Proceedings of the 5th International Workshop on Semantic Evaluation, ACL 2010, pages 57–62,
Uppsala, Sweden, 15-16 July 2010.

(3) should have *bought*
`tense="PAST" aspect="PERFECTIVE"`
`modality="SHOULD" polarity="POS"`

(4) did not *teach*
`tense="PAST" aspect="NONE"`
`modality="NONE" polarity="NEG"`

The relation types for the TimeML TLINK tag form a fine-grained set based on James Allen's interval logic (Allen, 1983). For TempEval, the set of labels was simplified to aid data preparation and to reduce the complexity of the task. We use only six relation types including the three core relations BEFORE, AFTER, and OVERLAP, the two less specific relations BEFORE-OR-OVERLAP and OVERLAP-OR-AFTER for ambiguous cases, and finally the relation VAGUE for those cases where no particular relation can be established.

Temporal relations come in two broad flavours: anchorings of events to time expressions and orderings of events. Events can be anchored to an adjacent time expression as in examples 5 and 6 or to the document creation time as in 7.

(5) Mary $taught_{e1}$ on *Tuesday* $morning_{t1}$
OVERLAP(e1,t1)

(6) They cancelled the $evening_{t2}$ $class_{e2}$
OVERLAP(e2,t2)

(7) Most troops will $leave_{e1}$ Iraq by August of 2010. AFTER(e1,dct)
The country $defaulted_{e2}$ on debts for that entire year. BEFORE(e2,dct)

In addition, events can be ordered relative to other events, as in the examples below.

(8) The President $spoke_{e1}$ to the nation on Tuesday on the financial crisis. He had $conferred_{e2}$ with his cabinet regarding policy the day before. AFTER(e1,e2)

(9) The students $heard_{e1}$ a *fire* $alarm_{e2}$.
OVERLAP(e1,e2)

(10) He $said_{e1}$ they had $postponed_{e2}$ the meeting.
AFTER(e1,e2)

3 TempEval-2 Tasks

We can now define the six TempEval tasks:

A. Determine the extent of the time expressions in a text as defined by the TimeML TIMEX3 tag. In addition, determine value of the features TYPE and VAL.

B. Determine the extent of the events in a text as defined by the TimeML EVENT tag. In addition, determine the value of the features CLASS, TENSE, ASPECT, POLARITY, and MODALITY.

C. Determine the temporal relation between an event and a time expression in the same sentence. This task is further restricted by requiring that either the event syntactically dominates the time expression or the event and time expression occur in the same noun phrase.

D. Determine the temporal relation between an event and the document creation time.

E. Determine the temporal relation between two main events in consecutive sentences.

F. Determine the temporal relation between two events where one event syntactically dominates the other event.

Of these tasks, C, D and E were also defined for TempEval-1. However, the syntactic locality restriction in task C was not present in TempEval-1.

Task participants could choose to either do all tasks, focus on the time expression task, focus on the event task, or focus on the four temporal relation tasks. In addition, participants could choose one or more of the six languages for which we provided data: Chinese, English, French, Italian, Korean, and Spanish.

We feel that well-defined tasks allow us to structure the workflow, allowing us to create task-specific guidelines and using task-specific annotation tools to speed up annotation. More importantly, each task can be evaluated in a fairly straightforward way, contrary to for example the problems that pop up when evaluating two complex temporal graphs for the same document. In addition, tasks can be ranked, allowing systems to feed the results of one (more precise) task as a feature into another task.

Splitting the task into substask reduces the error rate in the manual annotation, and that merging the different sub-task into a unique layer as a post-processing operation (see figure 1) provides better

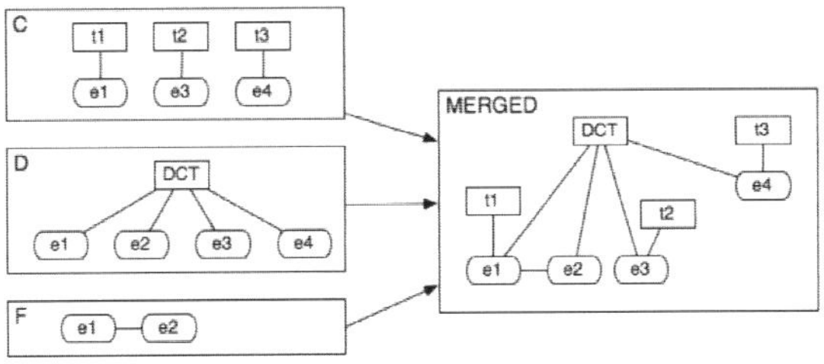

Figure 1: Merging Relations

and more reliable results (annotated data) than doing a complex task all at once.

4 Data Preparation

The data for the five languages were prepared independently of each other and do not comprise a parallel corpus. However, annotation specifications and guidelines for the five languages were developed in conjunction with one other, in many cases based on version 1.2.1 of the TimeML annotation guidelines for English[3]. Not all corpora contained data for all six tasks. Table 1 gives the size of the training set and the relation tasks that were included.

language	tokens	C	D	E	F	X
Chinese	23,000	✓	✓	✓	✓	
English	63,000	✓	✓	✓	✓	
Italian	27,000	✓	✓	✓		
French	19,000					✓
Korean	14,000					
Spanish	68,000	✓	✓			

Table 1: Corpus size and relation tasks

All corpora include event and timex annotation. The French corpus contained a subcorpus with temporal relations but these relations were not split into the four tasks C through F.

Annotation proceeded in two phases: a dual annotation phase where two annotators annotate each document and an adjudication phase where a judge resolves disagreements between the annotators. Most languages used BAT, the Brandeis Annotation Tool (Verhagen, 2010), a generic web-based annotation tool that is centered around the notion of annotation tasks. With the task decomposition allowed by BAT, it is possible to structure the complex task of temporal annotation by splitting it up in as many sub tasks as seems useful. As such, BAT was well-suited for TempEval-2 annotation.

We now give a few more details on the English and Spanish data, skipping the other languages for reasons that will become obvious at the beginning of section 6.

The English data sets were based on TimeBank (Pustejovsky et al., 2003; Boguraev et al., 2007), a hand-built gold standard of annotated texts using the TimeML markup scheme.[4] However, all event annotation was reviewed to make sure that the annotation complied with the latest guidelines and all temporal relations were added according to the Tempeval-2 relation tasks, using the specified relation types.

The data released for the TempEval-2 Spanish edition is a fragment of the Spanish TimeBank, currently under development. Its documents are originally from the Spanish part of the AnCora corpus (Taulé et al., 2008). Data preparation followed the annotation guidelines created to deal with the specificities of event and timex expressions in Spanish (Saurí et al., 2009a; Saurí et al., 2009b).

5 Evaluation Metrics

For the extents of events and time expressions (tasks A and B), precision, recall and the f1-measure are used as evaluation metrics, using the following formulas:

$$\begin{aligned} precision &= tp/(tp+fp) \\ recall &= tp/(tp+fn) \\ f\text{-}measure &= 2*(P*R)/(P+R) \end{aligned}$$

Where *tp* is the number of tokens that are part of an extent in both key and response, *fp* is the number of tokens that are part of an extent in the response but not in the key, and *fn* is the number of tokens that are part of an extent in the key but not in the response.

For attributes of events and time expressions (the second part of tasks A and B) and for relation types (tasks C through F) we use an even simpler metric: the number of correct answers divided by the number of answers.

[3]See http://www.timeml.org.

[4]See www.timeml.org for details on TimeML, TimeBank is distributed free of charge by the Linguistic Data Consortium (www.ldc.upenn.edu), catalog number LDC2006T08.

6 System Results

Eight teams participated in TempEval-2, submitting a grand total of eighteen systems. Some of these systems only participated in one or two tasks while others participated in all tasks. The distribution over the six languages was very uneven: sixteen systems for English, two for Spanish and one for English and Spanish.

The results for task A, recognition and normalization of time expressions, are given in tables 2 and 3.

team	p	r	f	type	val
UC3M	0.90	0.87	0.88	0.91	0.83
TIPSem	0.95	0.87	0.91	0.91	0.78
TIPSem-B	0.97	0.81	0.88	0.99	0.75

Table 2: Task A results for Spanish

team	p	r	f	type	val
Edinburgh	0.85	0.82	0.84	0.84	0.63
HeidelTime1	0.90	0.82	0.86	0.96	0.85
HeidelTime2	0.82	0.91	0.86	0.92	0.77
JU_CSE	0.55	0.17	0.26	0.00	0.00
KUL	0.78	0.82	0.80	0.91	0.55
KUL Run 2	0.73	0.88	0.80	0.91	0.55
KUL Run 3	0.85	0.84	0.84	0.91	0.55
KUL Run 4	0.76	0.83	0.80	0.91	0.51
KUL Run 5	0.75	0.85	0.80	0.91	0.51
TERSEO	0.76	0.66	0.71	0.98	0.65
TIPSem	0.92	0.80	0.85	0.92	0.65
TIPSem-B	0.88	0.60	0.71	0.88	0.59
TRIOS	0.85	0.85	0.85	0.94	0.76
TRIPS	0.85	0.85	0.85	0.94	0.76
USFD2	0.84	0.79	0.82	0.90	0.17

Table 3: Task A results for English

The results for Spanish are more uniform and generally higher than the results for English. For Spanish, the f-measure for TIMEX3 extents ranges from 0.88 through 0.91 with an average of 0.89; for English the f-measure ranges from 0.26 through 0.86, for an average of 0.78. However, due to the small sample size it is hard to make any generalizations. In both languages, type detection clearly was a simpler task than determining the value.

The results for task B, event recognition, are given in tables 4 and 5. Both tables contain results for both Spanish and English, the first part of each table contains the results for Spanish and the next part the results for English.

team	p	r	f
TIPSem	0.90	0.86	0.88
TIPSem-B	0.92	0.85	0.88
team	p	r	f
Edinburgh	0.75	0.85	0.80
JU_CSE	0.48	0.56	0.52
TIPSem	0.81	0.86	0.83
TIPSem-B	0.83	0.81	0.82
TRIOS	0.80	0.74	0.77
TRIPS	0.55	0.88	0.68

Table 4: Event extent results

The column headers in table 5 are abbreviations for polarity (pol), mood (moo), modality (mod), tense (tns), aspect (asp) and class (cl). Note that the English team chose to include modality whereas the Spanish team used mood.

team	pol	moo	tns	asp	cl
TIPSem	0.92	0.80	0.96	0.89	0.66
TIPSem-B	0.92	0.79	0.96	0.89	0.66
team	pol	mod	tns	asp	cl
Edinburgh	0.99	0.99	0.92	0.98	0.76
JU_CSE	0.98	0.98	0.30	0.95	0.53
TIPSem	0.98	0.97	0.86	0.97	0.79
TIPSem-B	0.98	0.98	0.85	0.97	0.79
TRIOS	0.99	0.95	0.91	0.98	0.77
TRIPS	0.99	0.96	0.67	0.97	0.67

Table 5: Event attribute results

As with the time expressions results, the sample size for Spanish is small, but note again the higher f-measure for event extents in Spanish.

Table 6 shows the results for all relation tasks, with the Spanish systems in the first two rows and the English systems in the last six rows. Recall that for Spanish the training and test sets only contained data for tasks C and D.

Interestingly, the version of the TIPSem systems that were applied to the Spanish data did much better on task C compared to its English cousins, but much worse on task D, which is rather puzzling.

Such a difference in performance of the systems could be due to differences in annotation accurateness, or it could be due to some particularities of how the two languages express certain temporal

team	C	D	E	F
TIPSem	0.81	0.59	-	-
TIPSem-B	0.81	0.59	-	-
JU_CSE	0.63	0.80	0.56	0.56
NCSU-indi	0.63	0.68	0.48	0.66
NCSU-joint	0.62	0.21	0.51	0.25
TIPSem	0.55	0.82	0.55	0.59
TIPSem-B	0.54	0.81	0.55	0.60
TRIOS	0.65	0.79	0.56	0.60
TRIPS	0.63	0.76	0.58	0.59
USFD2	0.63	-	0.45	-

Table 6: Results for relation tasks

aspects, or perhaps the one corpus is more homogeneous than the other. Again, there are not enough data points, but the issue deserves further attention.

For each task, the test data provided the event pairs or event-timex pairs with the relation type set to NONE and participating systems would replace that value with one of the six allowed relation types. However, participating systems were allowed to not replace NONE and not be penalized for it. Those cases would not be counted when compiling the scores in table 6. Table 7 lists those systems that did not classify all relation and the percentage of relations for each task that those systems did not classify.

team	C	D	E	F
TRIOS	25%	19%	36%	31%
TRIPS	20%	10%	17%	10%

Table 7: Percentage not classified

A comparison with the Tempeval-1 results from Semeval-2007 may be of interest. Six systems participated in the TempEval-1 tasks, compared to seven or eight systems for TempEval-2. Table 8 lists the average scores and the standard deviations for all the tasks (on the English data) that Tempeval-1 and Tempeval-2 have in common.

		C	D	E
tempeval-1	average	0.59	0.76	0.51
	stddev	0.03	0.03	0.05
tempeval-2	average	0.61	0.70	0.53
	stddev	0.04	0.22	0.05

Table 8: Comparing Tempevals

The results are very similar except for task D, but if we take a away the one outlier (the NCSU-joint score of 0.21) then the average becomes 0.78 with a standard deviation of 0.05. However, we had expected that for TempEval-2 the systems would score better on task C since we added the restriction that the event and time expression had to be syntactically adjacent. It is not clear why the results on task C have not improved.

7 Conclusion

In this paper, we described the TempEval-2 task within the SemEval 2010 competition. This task involves identifying the temporal relations between events and temporal expressions in text. Using a subset of TimeML temporal relations, we show how temporal relations and anchorings can be annotated and identified in six different languages. The markup language adopted presents a descriptive framework with which to examine the temporal aspects of natural language information, demonstrating in particular, how tense and temporal information is encoded in specific sentences, and how temporal relations are encoded between events and temporal expressions. This work paves the way towards establishing a broad and open standard metadata markup language for natural language texts, examining events, temporal expressions, and their orderings.

One thing that would need to be addressed in a follow-up task is what the optimal number of tasks is. Tempeval-2 had six tasks, spread out over six languages. This brought about some logistical challenges that delayed data delivery and may have given rise to a situation where there was simply not enough time for many systems to properly prepare. And clearly, the shared task was not successful in attracting systems to four of the six languages.

8 Acknowledgements

Many people were involved in TempEval-2. We want to express our gratitude to the following key contributors: Nianwen Xue, Estela Saquete, Lotus Goldberg, Seohyun Im, André Bittar, Nicoletta Calzolari, Jessica Moszkowicz and Hyopil Shin.

Additional thanks to Joan Banach, Judith Domingo, Pau Giménez, Jimena del Solar, Teresa Suñol, Allyson Ettinger, Sharon Spivak, Nahed Abul-Hassan, Ari Abelman, John Polson, Alexandra Nunez, Virginia Partridge, , Amber Stubbs, Alex Plotnick, Yuping Zhou, Philippe Muller and

Irina Prodanof.

The work on the Spanish corpus was supported by a EU Marie Curie International Reintegration Grant (PIRG04-GA-2008-239414). Work on the English corpus was supported under the NSF-CRI grant 0551615, "Towards a Comprehensive Linguistic Annotation of Language" and the NSF-INT-0753069 project "Sustainable Interoperability for Language Technology (SILT)", funded by the National Science Foundation.

Finally, thanks to all the participants, for sticking with a task that was not always as flawless and timely as it could have been in a perfect world.

References

James Allen. 1983. Maintaining knowledge about temporal intervals. *Communications of the ACM*, 26(11):832–843.

Bran Boguraev, James Pustejovsky, Rie Ando, and Marc Verhagen. 2007. Timebank evolution as a community resource for timeml parsing. *Language Resource and Evaluation*, 41(1):91–115.

James Pustejovsky, David Day, Lisa Ferro, Robert Gaizauskas, Patrick Hanks, Marcia Lazo, Roser Saurí, Andrew See, Andrea Setzer, and Beth Sundheim. 2003. The TimeBank Corpus. *Corpus Linguistics*, March.

Roser Saurí, Olga Batiukova, and James Pustejovsky. 2009a. Annotating events in spanish. timeml annotation guidelines. Technical Report Version TempEval-2010., Barcelona Media - Innovation Center.

Roser Saurí, Estela Saquete, and James Pustejovsky. 2009b. Annotating time expressions in spanish. timeml annotation guidelines. Technical Report Version TempEval-2010, Barcelona Media - Innovation Center.

Mariona Taulé, Toni Martí, and Marta Recasens. 2008. Ancora: Multilevel annotated corpora for catalan and spanish. In *Proceedings of the LREC 2008*, Marrakesh, Morocco.

Marc Verhagen, Robert Gaizauskas, Frank Schilder, Mark Hepple, Graham Katz, and James Pustejovsky. 2007. Semeval-2007 task 15: Tempeval temporal relation identification. In *Proc. of the Fourth Int. Workshop on Semantic Evaluations (SemEval-2007)*, pages 75–80, Prague, Czech Republic, June. Association for Computational Linguistics.

Marc Verhagen, Robert Gaizauskas, Frank Schilder, Mark Hepple, Jessica Moszkowicz, and James Pustejovsky. 2009. The tempeval challenge: identifying temporal relations in text. *Language Resources and Evaluation*.

Marc Verhagen. 2010. The Brandeis Annotation Tool. In *Language Resources and Evaluation Conference, LREC 2010*, Malta.

SemEval-2010 Task 14: Word Sense Induction & Disambiguation

Suresh Manandhar
Department of Computer Science
University of York, UK

Ioannis P. Klapaftis
Department of Computer Science
University of York, UK

Dmitriy Dligach
Department of Computer Science
University of Colorado, USA

Sameer S. Pradhan
BBN Technologies
Cambridge, USA

Abstract

This paper presents the description and evaluation framework of SemEval-2010 Word Sense Induction & Disambiguation task, as well as the evaluation results of 26 participating systems. In this task, participants were required to induce the senses of 100 target words using a training set, and then disambiguate unseen instances of the same words using the induced senses. Systems' answers were evaluated in: (1) an unsupervised manner by using two clustering evaluation measures, and (2) a supervised manner in a WSD task.

1 Introduction

Word senses are more beneficial than simple word forms for a variety of tasks including Information Retrieval, Machine Translation and others (Pantel and Lin, 2002). However, word senses are usually represented as a fixed-list of definitions of a manually constructed lexical database. Several deficiencies are caused by this representation, e.g. lexical databases miss main domain-specific senses (Pantel and Lin, 2002), they often contain general definitions and suffer from the lack of explicit semantic or contextual links between concepts (Agirre et al., 2001). More importantly, the definitions of hand-crafted lexical databases often do not reflect the exact meaning of a target word in a given context (Véronis, 2004).

Unsupervised Word Sense Induction (WSI) aims to overcome these limitations of hand-constructed lexicons by learning the senses of a target word directly from text without relying on any hand-crafted resources. The primary aim of SemEval-2010 WSI task is to allow comparison of unsupervised word sense induction and disambiguation systems.

The target word dataset consists of 100 words, 50 nouns and 50 verbs. For each target word, participants were provided with a training set in order to learn the senses of that word. In the next step, participating systems were asked to disambiguate unseen instances of the same words using their learned senses. The answers of the systems were then sent to organisers for evaluation.

2 Task description

Figure 1 provides an overview of the task. As can be observed, the task consisted of three separate phases. In the first phase, *training phase*, participating systems were provided with a training dataset that consisted of a set of target word (noun/verb) instances (sentences/paragraphs). Participants were then asked to use this training dataset to induce the senses of the target word. No other resources were allowed with the exception of NLP components for morphology and syntax. In the second phase, *testing phase*, participating systems were provided with a testing dataset that consisted of a set of target word (noun/verb) instances (sentences/paragraphs). Participants were then asked to tag (disambiguate) each testing instance with the senses induced during the *training phase*. In the third and final phase, the tagged test instances were received by the organisers in order to evaluate the answers of the systems in a supervised and an unsupervised framework. Table 1 shows the total number of target word instances in the training and testing set, as well as the average number of senses in the gold standard.

The main difference of the SemEval-2010 as compared to the SemEval-2007 sense induction task is that the training and testing data are treated separately, i.e the testing data are only used for sense tagging, while the training data are only used

Proceedings of the 5th International Workshop on Semantic Evaluation, ACL 2010, pages 63–68,
Uppsala, Sweden, 15-16 July 2010.

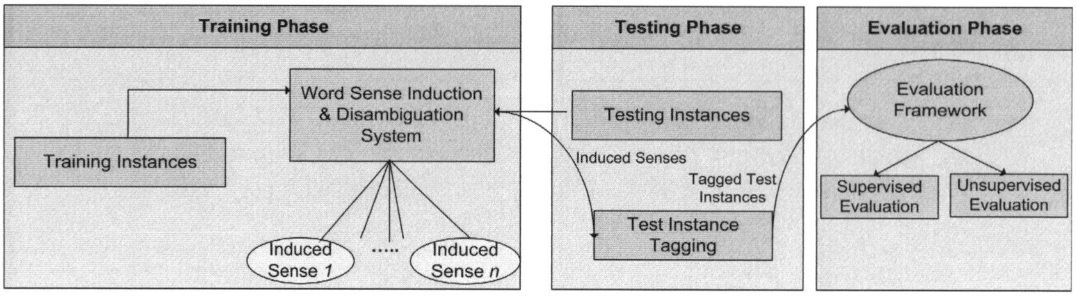

Figure 1: Training, testing and evaluation phases of SemEval-2010 Task 14

	Training set	Testing set	Senses (#)
All	879807	8915	3.79
Nouns	716945	5285	4.46
Verbs	162862	3630	3.12

Table 1: Training & testing set details

for sense induction. Treating the testing data as new unseen instances ensures a realistic evaluation that allows to evaluate the clustering models of each participating system.

The evaluation framework of SemEval-2010 WSI task considered two types of evaluation. In the first one, *unsupervised evaluation*, systems' answers were evaluated according to: (1) *V-Measure* (Rosenberg and Hirschberg, 2007), and (2) *paired F-Score* (Artiles et al., 2009). Neither of these measures were used in the SemEval-2007 WSI task. Manandhar & Klapaftis (2009) provide more details on the choice of this evaluation setting and its differences with the previous evaluation. The second type of evaluation, *supervised evaluation*, follows the supervised evaluation of the SemEval-2007 WSI task (Agirre and Soroa, 2007). In this evaluation, induced senses are mapped to gold standard senses using a mapping corpus, and systems are then evaluated in a standard WSD task.

2.1 Training dataset

The target word dataset consisted of 100 words, i.e. 50 nouns and 50 verbs. The training dataset for each target noun or verb was created by following a web-based semi-automatic method, similar to the method for the construction of *Topic Signatures* (Agirre et al., 2001). Specifically, for each WordNet (Fellbaum, 1998) sense of a target word, we created a query of the following form:

<Target Word> ***AND*** *<Relative Set>*

The *<Target Word>* consisted of the target word stem. The *<Relative Set>* consisted of a disjunctive set of word lemmas that were related

Word Sense	Query
Sense 1	failure AND (loss OR nonconformity OR test OR surrender OR "force play" OR ...)
Sense 2	failure AND (ruination OR flop OR bust OR stall OR ruin OR walloping OR ...)

Table 2: Training set creation: example queries for target word *failure*

to the target word sense for which the query was created. The relations considered were WordNet's hypernyms, hyponyms, synonyms, meronyms and holonyms. Each query was manually checked by one of the organisers to remove ambiguous words. The following example shows the query created for the first[1] and second[2] WordNet sense of the target noun *failure*.

The created queries were issued to Yahoo! search API[3] and for each query a maximum of 1000 pages were downloaded. For each page we extracted fragments of text that occurred in <p> </p> html tags and contained the target word stem. In the final stage, each extracted fragment of text was POS-tagged using the Genia tagger (Tsuruoka and Tsujii, 2005) and was only retained, if the POS of the target word in the extracted text matched the POS of the target word in our dataset.

2.2 Testing dataset

The testing dataset consisted of instances of the same target words from the training dataset. This dataset is part of OntoNotes (Hovy et al., 2006). We used the sense-tagged dataset in which sentences containing target word instances are tagged with OntoNotes (Hovy et al., 2006) senses. The texts come from various news sources including CNN, ABC and others.

[1] An act that fails

[2] An event that does not accomplish its intended purpose

[3] http://developer.yahoo.com/search/ [Access:10/04/2010]

	G_1	G_2	G_3
C_1	10	10	15
C_2	20	50	0
C_3	1	10	60
C_4	5	0	0

Table 3: Clusters & GS senses matrix.

3 Evaluation framework

For the purposes of this section we provide an example (Table 3) in which a target word has 181 instances and 3 GS senses. A system has generated a clustering solution with 4 clusters covering all instances. Table 3 shows the number of common instances between clusters and GS senses.

3.1 Unsupervised evaluation

This section presents the measures of unsupervised evaluation, i.e *V-Measure* (Rosenberg and Hirschberg, 2007) and (2) *paired F-Score* (Artiles et al., 2009).

3.1.1 V-Measure evaluation

Let w be a target word with N instances (data points) in the testing dataset. Let $K = \{C_j | j = 1 \dots n\}$ be a set of automatically generated clusters grouping these instances, and $S = \{G_i | i = 1 \dots m\}$ the set of gold standard classes containing the desirable groupings of w instances.

V-Measure (Rosenberg and Hirschberg, 2007) assesses the quality of a clustering solution by explicitly measuring its *homogeneity* and its *completeness*. Homogeneity refers to the degree that each cluster consists of data points primarily belonging to a single GS class, while completeness refers to the degree that each GS class consists of data points primarily assigned to a single cluster (Rosenberg and Hirschberg, 2007). Let h be homogeneity and c completeness. V-Measure is the harmonic mean of h and c, i.e. $VM = \frac{2 \cdot h \cdot c}{h+c}$.

Homogeneity. The homogeneity, h, of a clustering solution is defined in Formula 1, where $H(S|K)$ is the conditional entropy of the class distribution given the proposed clustering and $H(S)$ is the class entropy.

$$h = \begin{cases} 1, & \text{if } H(S) = 0 \\ 1 - \frac{H(S|K)}{H(S)}, & \text{otherwise} \end{cases} \quad (1)$$

$$H(S) = -\sum_{i=1}^{|S|} \frac{\sum_{j=1}^{|K|} a_{ij}}{N} \log \frac{\sum_{j=1}^{|K|} a_{ij}}{N} \quad (2)$$

$$H(S|K) = -\sum_{j=1}^{|K|} \sum_{i=1}^{|S|} \frac{a_{ij}}{N} \log \frac{a_{ij}}{\sum_{k=1}^{|S|} a_{kj}} \quad (3)$$

When $H(S|K)$ is 0, the solution is perfectly homogeneous, because each cluster only contains data points that belong to a single class. However in an imperfect situation, $H(S|K)$ depends on the size of the dataset and the distribution of class sizes. Hence, instead of taking the raw conditional entropy, V-Measure normalises it by the maximum reduction in entropy the clustering information could provide, i.e. $H(S)$. When there is only a single class ($H(S) = 0$), any clustering would produce a perfectly homogeneous solution.

Completeness. Symmetrically to homogeneity, the completeness, c, of a clustering solution is defined in Formula 4, where $H(K|S)$ is the conditional entropy of the cluster distribution given the class distribution and $H(K)$ is the clustering entropy. When $H(K|S)$ is 0, the solution is perfectly complete, because all data points of a class belong to the same cluster.

For the clustering example in Table 3, homogeneity is equal to 0.404, completeness is equal to 0.37 and V-Measure is equal to 0.386.

$$c = \begin{cases} 1, & \text{if } H(K) = 0 \\ 1 - \frac{H(K|S)}{H(K)}, & \text{otherwise} \end{cases} \quad (4)$$

$$H(K) = -\sum_{j=1}^{|K|} \frac{\sum_{i=1}^{|S|} a_{ij}}{N} \log \frac{\sum_{i=1}^{|S|} a_{ij}}{N} \quad (5)$$

$$H(K|S) = -\sum_{i=1}^{|S|} \sum_{j=1}^{|K|} \frac{a_{ij}}{N} \log \frac{a_{ij}}{\sum_{k=1}^{|K|} a_{ik}} \quad (6)$$

3.1.2 Paired F-Score evaluation

In this evaluation, the clustering problem is transformed into a classification problem. For each cluster C_i we generate $\binom{|C_i|}{2}$ instance pairs, where $|C_i|$ is the total number of instances that belong to cluster C_i. Similarly, for each GS class G_i we generate $\binom{|G_i|}{2}$ instance pairs, where $|G_i|$ is the total number of instances that belong to GS class G_i.

Let $F(K)$ be the set of instance pairs that exist in the automatically induced clusters and $F(S)$ be the set of instance pairs that exist in the gold standard. Precision can be defined as the number of common instance pairs between the two sets to the total number of pairs in the clustering solution (Equation 7), while recall can be defined as the number of common instance pairs between the two sets to the total number of pairs in the gold standard (Equation 8). Finally, precision and recall are combined to produce the harmonic mean ($FS = \frac{2 \cdot P \cdot R}{P+R}$).

$$P = \frac{|F(K) \cap F(S)|}{|F(K)|} \quad (7)$$

$$R = \frac{|F(K) \cap F(S)|}{|F(S)|} \quad (8)$$

For example in Table 3, we can generate $\binom{35}{2}$ instance pairs for C_1 , $\binom{70}{2}$ for C_2, $\binom{71}{2}$ for C_3 and $\binom{5}{2}$ for C_4, resulting in a total of 5505 instance pairs. In the same vein, we can generate $\binom{36}{2}$ instance pairs for G_1, $\binom{70}{2}$ for G_2 and $\binom{75}{2}$ for G_3. In total, the GS classes contain 5820 instance pairs. There are 3435 common instance pairs, hence precision is equal to 62.39%, recall is equal to 59.09% and paired F-Score is equal to 60.69%.

3.2 Supervised evaluation

In this evaluation, the testing dataset is split into a mapping and an evaluation corpus. The first one is used to map the automatically induced clusters to GS senses, while the second is used to evaluate methods in a WSD setting. This evaluation follows the supervised evaluation of SemEval-2007 WSI task (Agirre and Soroa, 2007), with the difference that the reported results are an average of 5 random splits. This repeated random sampling was performed to avoid the problems of the SemEval-2007 WSI challenge, in which different splits were providing different system rankings.

Let us consider the example in Table 3 and assume that this matrix has been created by using the mapping corpus. Table 3 shows that C_1 is more likely to be associated with G_3, C_2 is more likely to be associated with G_2, C_3 is more likely to be associated with G_3 and C_4 is more likely to be associated with G_1. This information can be utilised to map the clusters to GS senses.

Particularly, the matrix shown in Table 3 is normalised to produce a matrix M, in which each entry depicts the estimated conditional probability $P(G_i|C_j)$. Given an instance I of tw from the evaluation corpus, a row cluster vector IC is created, in which each entry k corresponds to the score assigned to C_k to be the winning cluster for instance I. The product of IC and M provides a row sense vector, IG, in which the highest scoring entry a denotes that G_a is the winning sense. For example, if we produce the row cluster vector $[C_1 = 0.8, C_2 = 0.1, C_3 = 0.1, C_4 = 0.0]$, and multiply it with the normalised matrix of Table 3, then we would get a row sense vector in which G_3 would be the winning sense with a score equal to 0.43.

System	VM (%) (All)	VM (%) (Nouns)	VM (%) (Verbs)	#Cl
Hermit	16.2	16.7	15.6	10.78
UoY	15.7	20.6	8.5	11.54
KSU KDD	15.7	18	12.4	17.5
Duluth-WSI	9	11.4	5.7	4.15
Duluth-WSI-SVD	9	11.4	5.7	4.15
Duluth-R-110	8.6	8.6	8.5	9.71
Duluth-WSI-Co	7.9	9.2	6	2.49
KCDC-PCGD	7.8	7.3	8.4	2.9
KCDC-PC	7.5	7.7	7.3	2.92
KCDC-PC-2	7.1	7.7	6.1	2.93
Duluth-Mix-Narrow-Gap	6.9	8	5.1	2.42
KCDC-GD-2	6.9	6.1	8	2.82
KCDC-GD	6.9	5.9	8.5	2.78
Duluth-Mix-Narrow-PK2	6.8	7.8	5.5	2.68
Duluth-MIX-PK2	5.6	5.8	5.2	2.66
Duluth-R-15	5.3	5.4	5.1	4.97
Duluth-WSI-Co-Gap	4.8	5.6	3.6	1.6
Random	4.4	4.2	4.6	4
Duluth-R-13	3.6	3.5	3.7	3
Duluth-WSI-Gap	3.1	4.2	1.5	1.4
Duluth-Mix-Gap	3	2.9	3	1.61
Duluth-Mix-Uni-PK2	2.4	0.8	4.7	2.04
Duluth-R-12	2.3	2.2	2.5	2
KCDC-PT	1.9	1	3.1	1.5
Duluth-Mix-Uni-Gap	1.4	0.2	3	1.39
KCDC-GDC	7	6.2	7.8	2.83
MFS	0	0	0	1
Duluth-WSI-SVD-Gap	0	0	0.1	1.02

Table 4: V-Measure unsupervised evaluation

4 Evaluation results

In this section, we present the results of the 26 systems along with two baselines. The first baseline, Most Frequent Sense (*MFS*), groups all testing instances of a target word into one cluster. The second baseline, *Random*, randomly assigns an instance to one out of four clusters. The number of clusters of *Random* was chosen to be roughly equal to the average number of senses in the GS. This baseline is executed five times and the results are averaged.

4.1 Unsupervised evaluation

Table 4 shows the V-Measure (VM) performance of the 26 systems participating in the task. The last column shows the number of induced clusters of each system in the test set.The *MFS* baseline has a V-Measure equal to 0, since by definition its completeness is 1 and homogeneity is 0. All systems outperform this baseline, apart from one, whose V-Measure is equal to 0. Regarding the *Random* baseline, we observe that 17 perform better, which indicates that they have learned useful information better than chance.

Table 4 also shows that V-Measure tends to favour systems producing a higher number of clus-

System	FS (%) (All)	FS (%) (Nouns)	FS (%) (Verbs)	#Cl
MFS	63.5	57.0	72.7	1
Duluth-WSI-SVD-Gap	63.3	57.0	72.4	1.02
KCDC-PT	61.8	56.4	69.7	1.5
KCDC-GD	59.2	51.6	70.0	2.78
Duluth-Mix-Gap	59.1	54.5	65.8	1.61
Duluth-Mix-Uni-Gap	58.7	57.0	61.2	1.39
KCDC-GD-2	58.2	50.4	69.3	2.82
KCDC-GDC	57.3	48.5	70.0	2.83
Duluth-Mix-Uni-PK2	56.6	57.1	55.9	2.04
KCDC-PC	55.5	50.4	62.9	2.92
KCDC-PC-2	54.7	49.7	61.7	2.93
Duluth-WSI-Gap	53.7	53.4	53.9	1.4
KCDC-PCGD	53.3	44.8	65.6	2.9
Duluth-WSI-Co-Gap	52.6	53.3	51.5	1.6
Duluth-MIX-PK2	50.4	51.7	48.3	2.66
UoY	49.8	38.2	66.6	11.54
Duluth-Mix-Narrow-Gap	49.7	47.4	51.3	2.42
Duluth-WSI-Co	49.5	50.2	48.2	2.49
Duluth-Mix-Narrow-PK2	47.8	37.1	48.2	2.68
Duluth-R-12	47.8	44.3	52.6	2
Duluth-WSI-SVD	41.1	37.1	46.7	4.15
Duluth-WSI	41.1	37.1	46.7	4.15
Duluth-R-13	38.4	36.2	41.5	3
KSU KDD	36.9	24.6	54.7	17.5
Random	31.9	30.4	34.1	4
Duluth-R-15	27.6	26.7	28.9	4.97
Hermit	26.7	24.4	30.1	10.78
Duluth-R-110	16.1	15.8	16.4	9.71

Table 5: Paired F-Score unsupervised evaluation

ters than the number of GS senses, although V-Measure does not increase monotonically with the number of clusters increasing. For that reason, we introduced the second unsupervised evaluation measure (paired F-Score) that penalises systems when they produce: (1) a higher number of clusters (low recall) or (2) a lower number of clusters (low precision), than the GS number of senses.

Table 5 shows the performance of systems using the second unsupervised evaluation measure. In this evaluation, we observe that most of the systems perform better than *Random*. Despite that, none of the systems outperform the *MFS* baseline. It seems that systems generating a smaller number of clusters than the GS number of senses are biased towards the *MFS*, hence they are not able to perform better. On the other hand, systems generating a higher number of clusters are penalised by this measure. Systems generating a number of clusters roughly the same as the GS tend to conflate the GS senses lot more than the *MFS*.

4.2 Supervised evaluation results

Table 6 shows the results of this evaluation for a 80-20 test set split, i.e. 80% for mapping and 20% for evaluation. The last columns shows the average number of GS senses identified by each system in the five splits of the evaluation datasets. Overall, 14 systems outperform the *MFS*, while 17 of them perform better than *Random*. The ranking of systems in nouns and verbs is different. For instance, the highest ranked system in nouns is *UoY*, while in verbs *Duluth-Mix-Narrow-Gap*. It seems that depending on the part-of-speech of the target word, different algorithms, features and parameters' tuning have different impact.

System	SR (%) (All)	SR (%) (Nouns)	SR (%) (Verbs)	#S
UoY	62.4	59.4	66.8	1.51
Duluth-WSI	60.5	54.7	68.9	1.66
Duluth-WSI-SVD	60.5	54.7	68.9	1.66
Duluth-WSI-Co-Gap	60.3	54.1	68.6	1.19
Duluth-WSI-Co	60.8	54.7	67.6	1.51
Duluth-WSI-Gap	59.8	54.4	67.8	1.11
KCDC-PC-2	59.8	54.1	68.0	1.21
KCDC-PC	59.7	54.6	67.3	1.39
KCDC-PCGD	59.5	53.3	68.6	1.47
KCDC-GDC	59.1	53.4	67.4	1.34
KCDC-GD	59.0	53.0	67.9	1.33
KCDC-PT	58.9	53.1	67.4	1.08
KCDC-GD-2	58.7	52.8	67.4	1.33
Duluth-WSI-SVD-Gap	58.7	53.2	66.7	1.01
MFS	58.7	53.2	66.6	1
Duluth-R-12	58.5	53.1	66.4	1.25
Hermit	58.3	53.6	65.3	2.06
Duluth-R-13	58.0	52.3	66.4	1.46
Random	57.3	51.5	65.7	1.53
Duluth-R-15	56.8	50.9	65.3	1.61
Duluth-Mix-Narrow-Gap	56.6	48.1	69.1	1.43
Duluth-Mix-Narrow-PK2	56.1	47.5	68.7	1.41
Duluth-R-110	54.8	48.3	64.2	1.94
KSU KDD	52.2	46.6	60.3	1.69
Duluth-MIX-PK2	51.6	41.1	67.0	1.23
Duluth-Mix-Gap	50.6	40.0	66.0	1.01
Duluth-Mix-Uni-PK2	19.3	1.8	44.8	0.62
Duluth-Mix-Uni-Gap	18.7	1.6	43.8	0.56

Table 6: Supervised recall (SR) (test set split:80% mapping, 20% evaluation)

The supervised evaluation changes the distribution of clusters by mapping each cluster to a weighted vector of senses. Hence, it can potentially favour systems generating a high number of homogeneous clusters. For that reason, we applied a second testing set split, where 60% of the testing corpus was used for mapping and 40% for evaluation. Reducing the size of the mapping corpus allows us to observe, whether the above statement is correct, since systems with a high number of clusters would suffer from unreliable mapping.

Table 7 shows the results of the second supervised evaluation. The ranking of participants did not change significantly, i.e. we observe only different rankings among systems belonging to the same participant. Despite that, Table 7 also shows that the reduction of the mapping corpus has a different impact on systems generating a larger number of clusters than the GS number of senses.

For instance, *UoY* that generates 11.54 clusters outperformed the *MFS* by 3.77% in the 80-20 split and by 3.71% in the 60-40 split. The reduction of the mapping corpus had a minimal impact on its performance. In contrast, *KSU KDD* that generates 17.5 clusters was below the *MFS* by 6.49%

System	SR (%) (All)	SR (%) (Nouns)	SR (%) (Verbs)	#S
UoY	62.0	58.6	66.8	1.66
Duluth-WSI-Co	60.1	54.6	68.1	1.56
Duluth-WSI-Co-Gap	59.5	53.5	68.3	1.2
Duluth-WSI-SVD	59.5	53.5	68.3	1.73
Duluth-WSI	59.5	53.5	68.3	1.73
Duluth-WSI-Gap	59.3	53.2	68.2	1.11
KCDC-PCGD	59.1	52.6	68.6	1.54
KCDC-PC-2	58.9	53.4	67.0	1.25
KCDC-PC	58.9	53.6	66.6	1.44
KCDC-GDC	58.3	52.1	67.3	1.41
KCDC-GD	58.3	51.9	67.6	1.42
MFS	58.3	52.5	66.7	1
KCDC-PT	58.3	52.2	67.1	1.11
Duluth-WSI-SVD-Gap	58.2	52.5	66.7	1.01
KCDC-GD-2	57.9	51.7	67.0	1.44
Duluth-R-12	57.7	51.7	66.4	1.27
Duluth-R-13	57.6	51.1	67.0	1.48
Hermit	57.3	52.5	64.2	2.27
Duluth-R-15	56.5	50.0	66.1	1.76
Random	56.5	50.2	65.7	1.65
Duluth-Mix-Narrow-Gap	56.2	47.7	68.6	1.51
Duluth-Mix-Narrow-PK2	55.7	46.9	68.5	1.51
Duluth-R-110	53.6	46.7	63.6	2.18
Duluth-MIX-PK2	50.5	39.7	66.1	1.31
KSU KDD	50.4	44.3	59.4	1.92
Duluth-Mix-Gap	49.8	38.9	65.6	1.04
Duluth-Mix-Uni-PK2	19.1	1.8	44.4	0.63
Duluth-Mix-Uni-Gap	18.9	1.5	44.2	0.56

Table 7: Supervised recall (SR) (test set split:60% mapping, 40% evaluation)

in the 80-20 split and by 7.83% in the 60-40 split. The reduction of the mapping corpus had a larger impact in this case. This result indicates that the performance in this evaluation also depends on the distribution of instances within the clusters. Systems generating a skewed distribution, in which a small number of homogeneous clusters tag the majority of instances and a larger number of clusters tag only a few instances, are likely to have a better performance than systems that produce a more uniform distribution.

5 Conclusion

We presented the description, evaluation framework and assessment of systems participating in the SemEval-2010 sense induction task. The evaluation has shown that the current state-of-the-art lacks unbiased measures that objectively evaluate clustering.

The results of systems have shown that their performance in the unsupervised and supervised evaluation settings depends on cluster granularity along with the distribution of instances within the clusters. Our future work will focus on the assessment of sense induction on a task-oriented basis as well as on clustering evaluation.

Acknowledgements

We gratefully acknowledge the support of the EU FP7 INDECT project, Grant No. 218086, the National Science Foundation Grant NSF-0715078, Consistent Criteria for Word Sense Disambiguation, and the GALE program of the Defense Advanced Research Projects Agency, Contract No. HR0011-06-C-0022, a subcontract from the BBN-AGILE Team.

References

Eneko Agirre and Aitor Soroa. 2007. SemEval-2007 Task 02: Evaluating Word Sense Induction and Discrimination Systems. In *Proceedings of SemEval-2007*, pages 7–12, Prague, Czech Republic. ACL.

Eneko Agirre, Olatz Ansa, David Martinez, and Eduard Hovy. 2001. Enriching Wordnet Concepts With Topic Signatures. *ArXiv Computer Science e-prints*.

Javier Artiles, Enrique Amigó, and Julio Gonzalo. 2009. The role of named entities in web people search. In *Proceedings of EMNLP*, pages 534–542. ACL.

Christiane Fellbaum. 1998. *Wordnet: An Electronic Lexical Database*. MIT Press, Cambridge, Massachusetts, USA.

Eduard Hovy, Mitchell Marcus, Martha Palmer, Lance Ramshaw, and Ralph Weischedel. 2006. Ontonotes: the 90% solution. In *Proceedings of NAACL, Companion Volume: Short Papers on XX*, pages 57–60. ACL.

Suresh Manandhar and Ioannis P. Klapaftis. 2009. Semeval-2010 Task 14: Evaluation Setting for Word Sense Induction & Disambiguation Systems. In *DEW '09: Proceedings of the Workshop on Semantic Evaluations: Recent Achievements and Future Directions*, pages 117–122, Boulder, Colorado, USA. ACL.

Patrick Pantel and Dekang Lin. 2002. Discovering Word Senses from Text. In *KDD '02: Proceedings of the 8th ACM SIGKDD Conference*, pages 613–619, New York, NY, USA. ACM.

Andrew Rosenberg and Julia Hirschberg. 2007. V-measure: A Conditional Entropy-based External Cluster Evaluation Measure. In *Proceedings of the 2007 EMNLP-CoNLL Joint Conference*, pages 410–420, Prague, Czech Republic.

Yoshimasa Tsuruoka and Junichi Tsujii. 2005. Bidirectional Inference With the Easiest-first Strategy for Tagging Sequence Data. In *Proceedings of the HLT-EMNLP Joint Conference*, pages 467–474, Morristown, NJ, USA.

Jean Véronis. 2004. Hyperlex: Lexical Cartography for Information Retrieval. *Computer Speech & Language*, 18(3):223–252.

SemEval-2010 Task: Japanese WSD

Manabu Okumura
Tokyo Institute of Technology
oku@pi.titech.ac.jp

Kiyoaki Shirai
Japan Advanced Institute of Science and Technology
kshirai@jaist.ac.jp

Kanako Komiya
Tokyo University of Agriculture and Technology
kkomiya@cc.tuat.ac.jp

Hikaru Yokono
Tokyo Institute of Technology
yokono@lr.pi.titech.ac.jp

Abstract

An overview of the SemEval-2 Japanese WSD task is presented. It is a lexical sample task, and word senses are defined according to a Japanese dictionary, the Iwanami Kokugo Jiten. This dictionary and a training corpus were distributed to participants. The number of target words was 50, with 22 nouns, 23 verbs, and 5 adjectives. Fifty instances of each target word were provided, consisting of a total of 2,500 instances for the evaluation. Nine systems from four organizations participated in the task.

1 Introduction

This paper reports an overview of the SemEval-2 Japanese Word Sense Disambiguation (WSD) task. It can be considered an extension of the SENSEVAL-2 Japanese monolingual dictionary-based task (Shirai, 2001), so it is a lexical sample task. Word senses are defined according to the Iwanami Kokugo Jiten (Nishio et al., 1994), a Japanese dictionary published by Iwanami Shoten. It was distributed to participants as a sense inventory. Our task has the following two new characteristics:

1. All previous Japanese sense-tagged corpora were from newspaper articles, while sense-tagged corpora were constructed in English on balanced corpora, such as Brown corpus and BNC corpus. The first balanced corpus of contemporary written Japanese (BCCWJ corpus) is now being constructed as part of a national project in Japan (Maekawa, 2008), and we are now constructing a sense-tagged corpus based on it. Therefore, the task will use the first balanced Japanese sense-tagged corpus.

   Because a balanced corpus consists of documents from multiple genres, the corpus can be divided into multiple sub-corpora of a genre. In supervised learning approaches on word sense disambiguation, because word sense distribution might vary across different sub-corpora, we need to take into account the genres of training and test corpora. Therefore, word sense disambiguation on a balanced corpus requires tackling a kind of domain (genre) adaptation problem (Chang and Ng, 2006; Agirre and de Lacalle, 2008).

2. In previous WSD tasks, systems have been required to select a sense from a given set of senses in a dictionary for a word in one context (an instance). However, the set of senses in the dictionary is not always complete. New word senses sometimes appear after the dictionary has been compiled. Therefore, some instances might have a sense that cannot be found in the dictionary's set. The task will take into account not only the instances that have a sense in the given set but also the instances that have a sense that cannot be found in the set. In the latter case, systems should output that the instances have a sense that is not in the set.

Training data, a corpus that consists of three genres (books, newspaper articles, and white papers) and is manually annotated with sense IDs, was also distributed to participants. For the evaluation, we distributed a corpus that consists of four genres (books, newspaper articles, white papers, and documents from a Q&A site on the WWW) with marked target words as test data. Participants were requested to assign one or more sense IDs to each target word, optionally with associated probabilities. The number of target words was 50, with 22 nouns, 23 verbs, and 5 adjectives. Fifty instances of each target word were provided, con-

Proceedings of the 5th International Workshop on Semantic Evaluation, ACL 2010, pages 69–74,
Uppsala, Sweden, 15-16 July 2010.

sisting of a total of 2,500 instances for the evaluation.

In what follows, section two describes the details of the data used in the Japanese WSD task. Section three describes the process to construct the sense tagged data, including the analysis of an inter-annotator agreement. Section four briefly introduces participating systems and section five describes their results. Finally, section six concludes the paper.

2 Data

In the Japanese WSD task, three types of data were distributed to all participants: a sense inventory, training data, and test data[1].

2.1 Sense Inventory

As described in section one, word senses are defined according to a Japanese dictionary, the Iwanami Kokugo Jiten. The number of headwords and word senses in the Iwanami Kokugo Jiten is 60,321 and 85,870.

As described in the task description of SENSEVAL-2 Japanese dictionary task (Shirai, 2001), the Iwanami Kokugo Jiten has hierarchical structures in word sense descriptions. The Iwanami Kokugo Jiten has at most three hierarchical layers.

2.2 Training Data

An annotated corpus was distributed as the training data. It consists of 240 documents of three genres (books, newspaper articles, and white papers) from the BCCWJ corpus. The annotated information in the training data is as follows:

- Morphological information
  The document was annotated with morphological information (word boundaries, a part-of-speech (POS) tag, a base form, and a reading) for all words. All the morphological information was automatically annotated using chasen[2] with unidic and was manually post-edited.

- Genre code
  Each document was assigned a code indicating its genre from the aforementioned list.

- Word sense IDs
  3,437 word types in the data were annotated for sense IDs, and the data contain 31,611 sense-tagged instances that include 2,500 instances for the 50 target words. Words assigned with sense IDs satisfied the following conditions:

  1. The Iwanami Kokugo Jiten gave their sense description.
  2. Their POSs were either a noun, a verb, or an adjective.
  3. They were ambiguous, that is, there were more than two word senses for them in the dictionary.

  Word sense IDs were manually annotated.

2.3 Test Data

The test data consists of 695 documents of four genres (books, newspaper articles, white papers, and documents from a Q&A site on the WWW) from the BCCWJ corpus, with marked target words. The documents used for the training and test data are not mutually exclusive. The number of overlapping documents between the training and test data is 185. The instances used for the evaluation were not provided as the training data[3]. The annotated information in the test data is as follows:

- Morphological information
  Similar to the training data, the document was annotated with morphological information (word boundaries, a POS tag, a base form, and a reading) for all words. All morphological information was automatically annotated using chasen with unidic and was manually post-edited.

- Genre code
  As in the training data, each document was assigned a code indicating its genre from the aforementioned list.

- Word sense IDs
  Word sense IDs were manually annotated for

[1] Due to space limits, we unfortunately cannot present the statistics of the training and test data, such as the number of instances in different genres, the number of instances for a new word sense, and the Jensen Shannon (JS) divergence (Lin, 1991; Dagan et al., 1997) between the word sense distributions of two different genres. We hope we will present them in another paper in the near future.

[2] `http://chasen-legacy.sourceforge.jp/`

[3] The word sense IDs for them were hidden from the participants.

the target words[4].

The number of target words was 50, with 22 nouns, 23 verbs, and 5 adjectives. Fifty instances of each target word were provided, consisting of a total of 2,500 instances for the evaluation.

3 Word Sense Tagging

Except for the word sense IDs, the data described in section two was developed by the National Institute of Japanese Language. However, the word sense IDs were newly annotated on the data. This section presents the process of annotating the word sense IDs, and the analysis of the inter-annotator agreement.

3.1 Sampling Target Words

When we chose target words, we considered the following conditions:

- The POSs of target words were either a noun, a verb, or an adjective.
- We chose words that occurred more than 50 times in the training data.
- The relative "difficulty" in disambiguating the sense of words was taken into account. The difficulty of the word w was defined by the entropy of the word sense distribution $E(w)$ in the test data (Kilgarriff and Rosenzweig, 2000). Obviously, the higher $E(w)$ is, the more difficult the WSD for w is.
- The number of instances for a new sense was also taken into account.

3.2 Manual Annotation

Nine annotators assigned the correct word sense IDs for the training and test data. All of them had a certain level of linguistic knowledge. The process of manual annotation was as follows:

1. An annotator chose a sense ID for each word separately in accordance with the following guidelines:
   - One sense ID was to be chosen for each word.
   - Sense IDs at any layers in the hierarchical structures were assignable.
   - The "new word sense" tag was to be chosen only when all sense IDs were not absolutely applicable.
2. For the instances that had a 'new word sense' tag, another annotator reexamined carefully whether those instances really had a new sense.

Because a fragment of the corpus was tagged by multiple annotators in a preliminary annotation, the inter-annotator agreement between the two annotators in step 1 was calculated with Kappa statistics. It was 0.678.

4 Evaluation Methodology

The evaluation was returned in the following two ways:

1. The outputted sense IDs were evaluated, assuming the 'new sense' as another sense ID. The outputted sense IDs were compared to the given gold standard word senses, and the usual precision measure for supervised word sense disambiguation systems was computed using the scorer. The Iwanami Kokugo Jiten has three levels for sense IDs, and we used the middle-level sense in the task. Therefore, the scoring in the task was 'middle-grained scoring.'
2. The ability of finding the instances of new senses was evaluated, assuming the task as classifying each instance into a 'known sense' or 'new sense' class. The outputted sense IDs (same as in 1.) were compared to the given gold standard word senses, and the usual accuracy for binary classification was computed, assuming all sense IDs in the dictionary were in the 'known sense' class.

5 Participating Systems

In the Japanese WSD task, 10 organizations registered for participation. However, only the nine systems from four organizations submitted the results. In what follows, we outline them with the following description:

1. learning algorithm used,
2. features used,
3. language resources used,

[4] They were hidden from the participants during the formal run.

4. level of analysis performed in the system,
5. whether and how the difference in the text genre was taken into account,
6. method to detect new senses of words, if any.

Note that most of the systems used supervised learning techniques.

- HIT-1
  1. Naive Bayes, 2. Word form/POS of the target word, word form/POS before or after the target word, content words in the context, classes in a thesaurus for those words in the context, the text genre, 3. 'Bunrui-Goi-Hyou', a Japanese thesaurus (National Institute of Japanese Language, 1964), 4. Morphological analysis, 5. A genre is included in the features. 6. Assuming that the posterior probability has a normal distribution, the system judges those instances deviating from the distribution at the 0.05 significance level as a new word sense

- JAIST-1
  1. Agglomerative clustering, 2. Bag-of-words in context, etc. 3. None, 4. Morphological analysis, 5. The system does not merge example sentences in different genre sub-corpus into a cluster. 6. First, the system makes clusters of example sentences, then measures the similarity between a cluster and a sense in the dictionary, finally regarding the cluster as a collection of new senses when the similarity is small. For WSD, the system chooses the most similar sense for each cluster, then it considers all the instances in the cluster to have that sense.

- JAIST-2
  1. SVM, 2. Word form/POS before or after the target word, content words in the context, etc. 3. None, 4. Morphological analysis, 5. The system was trained with the feature set where features are distinguished whether or not they are derived from only one genre sub-corpus. 6. 'New sense' is treated as one of the sense classes.

- JAIST-3
  The system is an ensemble of JAIST-1 and JAIST-2. The judgment of a new sense is performed by JAIST-1. The output of JAIST-1 is chosen when the similarity between a cluster and a sense in the dictionary is sufficiently high. Otherwise, the output of JAIST-2 is used.

- MSS-1,2,3
  1. Maximum entropy, 2. Three word forms/lemmas/POSs before or after the target word, bigrams, and skip bigrams in the context, bag-of-words in the document, a class of the document categorized by a topic classifier, etc. 3. None, 4. None, 5. For each target word, the system selected the genre and dictionary examples combinations for training data, which got the best results in cross-validation. 6. The system calculated the entropy for each target word given by the Maximum Entropy Model (MEM). It assumed that high entropy (when probabilities of classes are uniformly dispersed) was indicative of a new sense. The threshold was tuned by using the words with a new sense tag in the training data. Three official submissions correspond to different thresholds.

- RALI-1, RALI-2
  1. Naive Bayes, 2. Only the 'writing' of the words (inside of <mor> tag), 3. The Mainichi 2005 corpus of NTCIR, parsed with chasen+unidic, 4. None, 5. Not taken into account, 6. 'New sense' is only used when it is evident in the training data

For more details, please refer to their description papers.

6 Their Results

The evaluation results of all the systems are shown in tables 1 and 2. "Baseline" for WSD indicates the results of the baseline system that used SVM with the following features:

- Morphological features
  Bag-of-words (BOW), Part-of-speech (POS), and detailed POS classification. We extract these features from the target word itself and the two words to the right and left of it.

- Syntactic features
  - If the POS of a target word is a noun, extract the verb in a grammatical dependency relation with the noun.

Table 1: Results: Word sense disambiguation

	Precision
Baseline	0.7528
HIT-1	0.6612
JAIST-1	0.6864
JAIST-2	0.7476
JAIST-3	0.7208
MSS-1	0.6404
MSS-2	0.6384
MSS-3	0.6604
RALI-1	0.7592
RALI-2	0.7636

Table 2: Results: New sense detection

	Accuracy	Precision	Recall
Baseline	0.9844	-	0
HIT-1	0.9132	0.0297	0.0769
JAIST-1	0.9512	0.0337	0.0769
JAIST-2	0.9872	1	0.1795
JAIST-3	0.9532	0.0851	0.2051
MSS-1	0.9416	0.1409	0.5385
MSS-2	0.9384	0.1338	0.5385
MSS-3	0.9652	0.2333	0.5385
RALI-1	0.9864	0.7778	0.1795
RALI-2	0.9872	0.8182	0.2308

  - If the POS of a target word is a verb, extract the noun in a grammatical dependency relation with the verb.

- Figures in Bunrui-Goi-Hyou
  4 and 5 digits regarding the content word to the right and left of the target word.

The baseline system did not take into account any information on the text genre. "Baseline" for new sense detection (NSD) indicates the results of the baseline system, which outputs a sense in the dictionary and never outputs the new sense tag. Precision and recall for NSD are shown just for reference. Because relatively few instances for a new word sense were found (39 out of 2500), the task of the new sense detection was found to be rather difficult.

Tables 3 and 4 show the results for nouns, verbs, and adjectives. In our comparison of the baseline system scores for WSD, the score for nouns was the biggest, and the score for verbs was the smallest (table 3). However, the average entropy of nouns was the second biggest (0.7257), and that of verbs was the biggest (1.194)[5].

Table 3: Results for each POS (Precision): Word sense disambiguation

	Noun	Verb	Adjective
Baseline	0.8255	0.6878	0.732
HIT-1	0.7436	0.5739	0.7
JAIST-1	0.7645	0.5957	0.76
JAIST-2	0.84	0.6626	0.732
JAIST-3	0.8236	0.6217	0.724
MSS-1	0.7	0.5504	0.792
MSS-2	0.6991	0.5470	0.792
MSS-3	0.7218	0.5713	0.8
RALI-1	0.8236	0.6965	0.764
RALI-2	0.8127	0.7191	0.752

Table 4: Results for each POS (Accuracy): New sense detection

	Noun	Verb	Adjective
Baseline	0.97	0.9948	1
HIT-1	0.8881	0.9304	0.944
JAIST-1	0.9518	0.9470	0.968
JAIST-2	0.9764	0.9948	1
JAIST-3	0.9564	0.9470	0.968
MSS-1	0.9355	0.9409	0.972
MSS-2	0.9336	0.9357	0.972
MSS-3	0.96	0.9670	0.98
RALI-1	0.9745	0.9948	1
RALI-2	0.9764	0.9948	1

We set up three word classes, $D_{diff}(E(w) \geq 1)$, $D_{mid}(0.5 \leq E(w) < 1)$, and $D_{easy}(E(w) < 0.5)$. D_{diff}, D_{mid}, and D_{easy} consist of 20, 19 and 11 words, respectively. Tables 5 and 6 show the results for each word class. The results of WSD are quite natural in that the higher $E(w)$ is, the more difficult WSD is, and the more the performance degrades.

7 Conclusion

This paper reported an overview of the SemEval-2 Japanese WSD task. The data used in this task will be available when you contact the task organizer and sign a copyright agreement form. We hope this valuable data helps many researchers improve their WSD systems.

[5]The average entropy of adjectives was 0.6326.

Table 5: Results for entropy classes (Precision): Word sense disambiguation

	D_{easy}	D_{mid}	D_{diff}
Baseline	0.9418	0.7411	0.66
HIT-1	0.8436	0.6832	0.54
JAIST-1	0.8782	0.7158	0.553
JAIST-2	0.9509	0.7484	0.635
JAIST-3	0.92	0.7368	0.596
MSS-1	0.8291	0.6558	0.522
MSS-2	0.8273	0.6558	0.518
MSS-3	0.8345	0.6905	0.536
RALI-1	0.9455	0.7653	0.651
RALI-2	0.94	0.7558	0.674

Table 6: Results for Entropy classes (Accuracy): New sense detection

	D_{easy}	D_{mid}	D_{diff}
Baseline	1	0.9737	0.986
HIT-1	0.8909	0.9095	0.929
JAIST-1	0.9672	0.9505	0.943
JAIST-2	1	0.9811	0.986
JAIST-3	0.9673	0.9558	0.943
MSS-1	0.9818	0.9221	0.938
MSS-2	0.98	0.9221	0.931
MSS-3	0.9873	0.9611	0.957
RALI-1	1	0.9789	0.986
RALI-2	1	0.9811	0.986

Acknowledgments

We would like to thank all the participants and the annotators for constructing this sense tagged corpus.

References

Eneko Agirre and Oier Lopez de Lacalle. 2008. On robustness and domain adaptation using svd for word sense disambiguation. In *Proc. of COLING'08.*

Yee Seng Chang and Hwee Tou Ng. 2006. Estimating class priors in domain adaptation for wsd. In *Proc. of ACL'06.*

Ido Dagan, Lillian Lee, and Fernando Pereira. 1997. Similarity-based methods for word sense disambiguation. In *Proceedings of the Thirty-Fifth Annual Meeting of the Association for Computational Linguistics and Eighth Conference of the European Chapter of the Association for Computational Linguistics*, pages 56–63.

A. Kilgarriff and J. Rosenzweig. 2000. English senseval: Report and results. In *Proc. LREC'00.*

J. Lin. 1991. Divergence measures based on the shannon entropy. *IEEE Transactions on Information Theory*, 37(1):145–151.

Kikuo Maekawa. 2008. Balanced corpus of contemporary written japanese. In *Proceedings of the 6th Workshop on Asian Language Resources (ALR)*, pages 101–102.

National Institute of Japanese Language. 1964. *Bunruigoihyou.* Shuuei Shuppan. In Japanese.

Minoru Nishio, Etsutaro Iwabuchi, and Shizuo Mizutani. 1994. *Iwanami Kokugo Jiten Dai Go Han.* Iwanami Publisher. In Japanese.

Kiyoaki Shirai. 2001. Senseval-2 japanese dictionary task. In *Proceedings of SENSEVAL-2: Second International Workshop on Evaluating Word Sense Disambiguation Systems*, pages 33–36.

SemEval-2010 Task 17: All-words Word Sense Disambiguation on a Specific Domain

Eneko Agirre, Oier Lopez de Lacalle
IXA NLP group
UBC
Donostia, Basque Country
{e.agirre,oier.lopezdelacalle}@ehu.es

Christiane Fellbaum
Department of Computer Science
Princeton University
Princeton, USA
fellbaum@princeton.edu

Shu-Kai Hsieh
Department of English
National Taiwan Normal University
Taipei, Taiwan
shukai@ntnu.edu.tw

Maurizio Tesconi
IIT
CNR
Pisa, Italy
maurizio.tesconi@iit.cnr.it

Monica Monachini
ILC
CNR
Pisa, Italy
monica.monachini@ilc.cnr.it

Piek Vossen, Roxanne Segers
Faculteit der Letteren
Vrije Universiteit Amsterdam
Amsterdam, Netherlands
p.vossen@let.vu.nl,roxane.segers@gmail.com

Abstract

Domain portability and adaptation of NLP components and Word Sense Disambiguation systems present new challenges. The difficulties found by supervised systems to adapt might change the way we assess the strengths and weaknesses of supervised and knowledge-based WSD systems. Unfortunately, all existing evaluation datasets for specific domains are lexical-sample corpora. This task presented all-words datasets on the environment domain for WSD in four languages (Chinese, Dutch, English, Italian). 11 teams participated, with supervised and knowledge-based systems, mainly in the English dataset. The results show that in all languages the participants where able to beat the most frequent sense heuristic as estimated from general corpora. The most successful approaches used some sort of supervision in the form of hand-tagged examples from the domain.

1 Introduction

Word Sense Disambiguation (WSD) competitions have focused on general domain texts, as attested in previous Senseval and SemEval competitions (Kilgarriff, 2001; Mihalcea et al., 2004; Snyder and Palmer, 2004; Pradhan et al., 2007). Specific domains pose fresh challenges to WSD systems: the context in which the senses occur might change, different domains involve different sense distributions and predominant senses, some words tend to occur in fewer senses in specific domains, the context of the senses might change, and new senses and terms might be involved. Both supervised and knowledge-based systems are affected by these issues: while the first suffer from different context and sense priors, the later suffer from lack of coverage of domain-related words and information.

The main goal of this task is to provide a multilingual testbed to evaluate WSD systems when faced with full-texts from a specific domain. All datasets and related information are publicly available from the task websites[1].

This task was designed in the context of Kyoto (Vossen et al., 2008)[2], an Asian-European project that develops a community platform for modeling knowledge and finding facts across languages and cultures. The platform operates as a Wiki system with an ontological support that social communities can use to agree on the meaning of terms in specific domains of their interest. Kyoto focuses on the environmental domain because it poses interesting challenges for information sharing, but the techniques and platforms are

[1] http://xmlgroup.iit.cnr.it/SemEval2010/ and http://semeval2.fbk.eu/
[2] http://www.kyoto-project.eu/

Proceedings of the 5th International Workshop on Semantic Evaluation, ACL 2010, pages 75–80,
Uppsala, Sweden, 15-16 July 2010.

independent of the application domain.

The paper is structured as follows. We first present the preparation of the data. Section 3 reviews participant systems and Section 4 the results. Finally, Section 5 presents the conclusions.

2 Data preparation

The data made available to the participants included the test set proper, and background texts. Participants had one week to work on the test set, but the background texts where provided months earlier.

2.1 Test datasets

The WSD-domain comprises comparable all-words test corpora on the environment domain. Three texts were compiled for each language by the European Center for Nature Conservation[3] and Worldwide Wildlife Forum[4]. They are documents written for a general but interested public and involve specific terms from the domain. The document content is comparable across languages. Table 1 shows the numbers for the datasets.

Although the original plan was to annotate multiword terms, and domain terminology, due to time constraints we focused on single-word nouns and verbs. The test set clearly marked which were the words to be annotated. In the case of Dutch, we also marked components of single-word compounds. The format of the test set followed that of previous all-word exercises, which we extended to accommodate Dutch compounds. For further details check the datasets in the task website.

The sense inventory was based on publicly available wordnets of the respective languages (see task website for details). The annotation procedure involved double-blind annotation by experts plus adjudication, which allowed us to also provide Inter Annotator Agreement (IAA) figures for the dataset. The procedure was carried out using KAFnotator tool (Tesconi et al., 2010). Due to limitations in resources and time, the English dataset was annotated by a single expert annotator. For the rest of languages, the agreement was very good, as reported in Table 1.

Table 1 includes the results of the random baseline, as an indication of the polysemy in each dataset. Average polysemy is highest for English, and lowest for Dutch.

[3]http://www.ecnc.org

[4]http://www.wwf.org

	Total	Noun	Verb	IAA	Random
Chinese	3989	754	450	0.96	0.321
Dutch	8157	997	635	0.90	0.328
English	5342	1032	366	n/a	0.232
Italian	8560	1340	513	0.72	0.294

Table 1: Dataset numbers, including number of tokens, nouns and verbs to be tagged, Inter-Annotator Agreement (IAA) and precision of random baseline.

	Documents	Words
Chinese	58	455359
Dutch	98	21089
English	113	2737202
Italian	27	240158

Table 2: Size of the background data.

2.2 Background data

In addition to the test datasets proper, we also provided additional documents on related subjects, kindly provided by ECNC and WWF. Table 2 shows the number of documents and words made available for each language. The full list with the urls of the documents are available from the task website, together with the background documents.

3 Participants

Eleven participants submitted more than thirty runs (cf. Table 3). The authors classified their runs into supervised (S in the tables, three runs), weakly supervised (WS, four runs), unsupervised (no runs) and knowledge-based (KB, the rest of runs)[5]. Only one group used hand-tagged data from the domain, which they produced on their own. We will briefly review each of the participant groups, ordered following the rank obtained for English. They all participated on the English task, with one exception as noted below, so we report their rank in the English task. Please refer to their respective paper in these proceedings for more details.

CFILT: They participated with a domain-specific knowledge-based method based on Hopfield networks (Khapra et al., 2010). They first identify domain-dependant words using the background texts, use a graph based on hyponyms in WordNet, and a breadth-first search to select the most representative synsets within domain. In addition they added manually disambiguated around one hundred examples from the domain as seeds.

[5]Note that boundaries are slippery. We show the classifications as reported by the authors.

English

Rank	Participant	System ID	Type	P	R	R nouns	R verbs
1	Anup Kulkarni	CFILT-2	WS	0.570	0.555 ±0.024	0.594 ±0.028	0.445 ±0.047
2	Anup Kulkarni	CFILT-1	WS	0.554	0.540 ±0.021	0.580 ±0.025	0.426 ±0.043
3	Siva Reddy	IIITH1-d.l.ppr.05	WS	0.534	0.528 ±0.027	0.553 ±0.023	0.456 ±0.041
4	Abhilash Inumella	IIITH2-d.r.l.ppr.05	WS	0.522	0.516 ±0.023	0.529 ±0.027	0.478 ±0.041
5	Ruben Izquierdo	BLC20SemcorBackground	S	0.513	0.513 ±0.022	0.534 ±0.026	0.454 ±0.044
-	-	*Most Frequent Sense*	-	0.505	0.505 ±0.023	0.519 ±0.026	0.464 ±0.043
6	Ruben Izquierdo	BLC20Semcor	S	0.505	0.505 ±0.025	0.527 ±0.031	0.443 ±0.045
7	Anup Kulkarni	CFILT-3	KB	0.512	0.495 ±0.023	0.516 ±0.027	0.434 ±0.048
8	Andrew Tran	Treematch	KB	0.506	0.493 ±0.021	0.516 ±0.028	0.426 ±0.046
9	Andrew Tran	Treematch-2	KB	0.504	0.491 ±0.021	0.515 ±0.030	0.425 ±0.044
10	Aitor Soroa	kyoto-2	KB	0.481	0.481 ±0.022	0.487 ±0.025	0.462 ±0.039
11	Andrew Tran	Treematch-3	KB	0.492	0.479 ±0.022	0.494 ±0.028	0.434 ±0.039
12	Radu Ion	RACAI-MFS	KB	0.461	0.460 ±0.022	0.458 ±0.025	0.464 ±0.046
13	Hansen A. Schwartz	UCF-WS	KB	0.447	0.441 ±0.022	0.440 ±0.025	0.445 ±0.043
14	Yuhang Guo	HIT-CIR-DMFS-1.ans	KB	0.436	0.435 ±0.023	0.428 ±0.027	0.454 ±0.043
15	Hansen A. Schwartz	UCF-WS-domain	KB	0.440	0.434 ±0.024	0.434 ±0.029	0.434 ±0.044
16	Abhilash Inumella	IIITH2-d.r.l.baseline.05	KB	0.496	0.433 ±0.024	0.452 ±0.023	0.390 ±0.044
17	Siva Reddy	IIITH1-d.l.baseline.05	KB	0.498	0.432 ±0.021	0.463 ±0.026	0.344 ±0.038
18	Radu Ion	RACAI-2MFS	KB	0.433	0.431 ±0.022	0.434 ±0.027	0.399 ±0.049
19	Siva Reddy	IIITH1-d.l.ppv.05	KB	0.426	0.425 ±0.026	0.434 ±0.028	0.399 ±0.043
20	Abhilash Inumella	IIITH2-d.r.l.ppv.05	KB	0.424	0.422 ±0.023	0.456 ±0.025	0.325 ±0.044
21	Hansen A. Schwartz	UCF-WS-domain.noPropers	KB	0.437	0.392 ±0.025	0.377 ±0.025	0.434 ±0.043
22	Aitor Soroa	kyoto-1	KB	0.384	0.384 ±0.022	0.382 ±0.024	0.391 ±0.047
23	Ruben Izquierdo	BLC20Background	S	0.380	0.380 ±0.022	0.385 ±0.026	0.366 ±0.037
24	Davide Buscaldi	NLEL-WSD-PDB	WS	0.381	0.356 ±0.022	0.357 ±0.027	0.352 ±0.049
25	Radu Ion	RACAI-Lexical-Chains	KB	0.351	0.350 ±0.015	0.344 ±0.017	0.368 ±0.030
26	Davide Buscaldi	NLEL-WSD	WS	0.370	0.345 ±0.022	0.352 ±0.027	0.328 ±0.037
27	Yoan Gutierrez	Relevant Semantic Trees	KB	0.328	0.322 ±0.022	0.335 ±0.026	0.284 ±0.044
28	Yoan Gutierrez	Relevant Semantic Trees-2	KB	0.321	0.315 ±0.022	0.327 ±0.024	0.281 ±0.040
29	Yoan Gutierrez	Relevant Cliques	KB	0.312	0.303 ±0.021	0.304 ±0.024	0.301 ±0.041
-	-	*Random baseline*	-	0.232	0.232	0.253	0.172

Chinese

Rank	Participant	System ID	Type	P	R	R nouns	R verbs
-	-	*Most Frequent Sense*	-	0.562	0.562 ±0.026	0.589 ±0.027	0.518 ±0.039
1	Meng-Hsien Shih	HR	KB	0.559	0.559 ±0.024	0.615 ±0.026	0.464 ±0.039
2	Meng-Hsien Shih	GHR	KB	0.517	0.517 ±0.024	0.533 ±0.035	0.491 ±0.038
-	-	*Random baseline*	-	0.321	0.321	0.326	0.312
4	Aitor Soroa	kyoto-3	KB	0.322	0.296 ±0.022	0.257 ±0.027	0.360 ±0.038
3	Aitor Soroa	kyoto-2	KB	0.342	0.285 ±0.021	0.251 ±0.026	0.342 ±0.040
5	Aitor Soroa	kyoto-1	KB	0.310	0.258 ±0.023	0.256 ±0.029	0.261 ±0.031

Dutch

Rank	Participant	System ID	Type	P	R	R nouns	R verbs
1	Aitor Soroa	kyoto-3	KB	0.526	0.526 ±0.022	0.575 ±0.029	0.450 ±0.034
2	Aitor Soroa	kyoto-2	KB	0.519	0.519 ±0.022	0.561 ±0.027	0.454 ±0.034
-	-	*Most Frequent Sense*	-	0.480	0.480 ±0.022	0.600 ±0.027	0.291 ±0.025
3	Aitor Soroa	kyoto-1	KB	0.465	0.465 ±0.021	0.505 ±0.026	0.403 ±0.033
-	-	*Random baseline*	-	0.328	0.328	0.350	0.293

Italian

Rank	Participant	System ID	Type	P	R	R nouns	R verbs
1	Aitor Soroa	kyoto-3	KB	0.529	0.529 ±0.021	0.530 ±0.024	0.528 ±0.038
2	Aitor Soroa	kyoto-2	KB	0.521	0.521 ±0.018	0.522 ±0.023	0.519 ±0.035
3	Aitor Soroa	kyoto-1	KB	0.496	0.496 ±0.019	0.507 ±0.020	0.468 ±0.037
-	-	*Most Frequent Sense*	-	0.462	0.462 ±0.020	0.472 ±0.024	0.437 ±0.035
-	-	*Random baseline*	-	0.294	0.294	0.308	0.257

Table 3: Overall results for the domain WSD datasets, ordered by recall.

This is the only group using hand-tagged data from the target domain. Their best run ranked 1st.

IIITTH: They presented a personalized PageRank algorithm over a graph constructed from WordNet similar to (Agirre and Soroa, 2009), with two variants. In the first (IIITH1), the vertices of the graph are initialized following the ranking scores obtained from predominant senses as in (McCarthy et al., 2007). In the second (IIITH2), the graph is initialized with keyness values as in

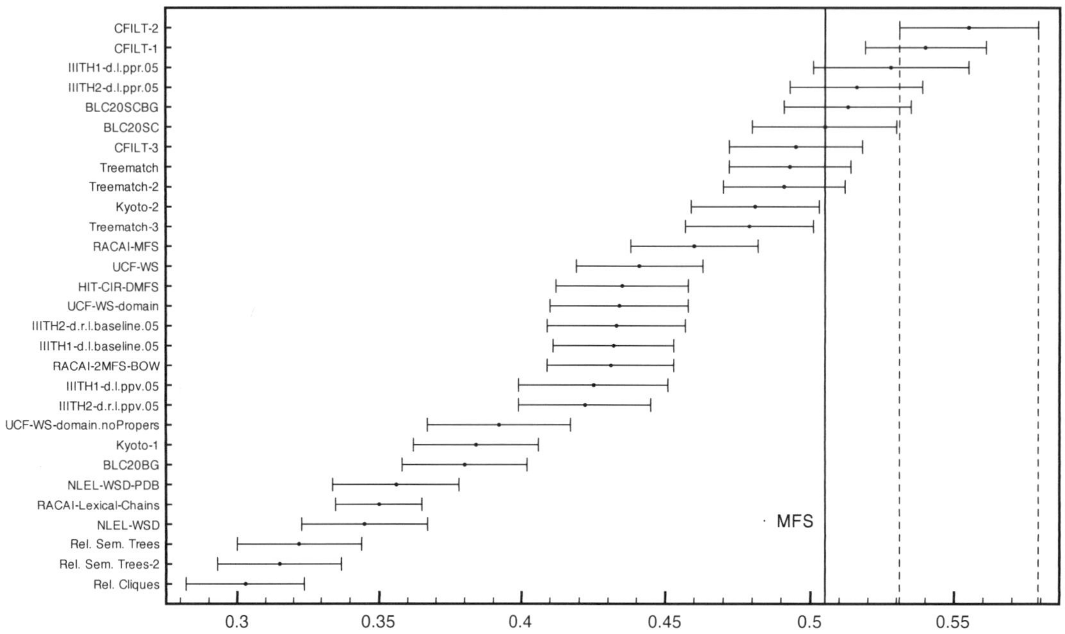

Figure 1: Plot for all the systems which participated in English domain WSD. Each point correspond to one system (denoted in axis $\mathcal{Y}$) according each recall and confidence interval (axis $\mathcal{X}$). Systems are ordered depending on their rank.

(Rayson and Garside, 2000). Some of the runs use sense statistics from SemCor, and have been classified as weakly supervised. They submitted a total of six runs, with the best run ranking 3rd.

BLC20(SC/BG/SCBG): This system is supervised. A Support Vector Machine was trained using the usual set of features extracted from context and the most frequent class of the target word. Semantic class-based classifiers were built from SemCor (Izquierdo et al., 2009), where the classes were automatically obtained exploiting the structural properties of WordNet. Their best run ranked 5th.

Treematch: This system uses a knowledge-based disambiguation method that requires a dictionary and untagged text as input. A previously developed system (Chen et al., 2009) was adapted to handle domain specific WSD. They built a domain-specific corpus using words mined from relevant web sites (e.g. WWF and ECNC) as seeds. Once parsed the corpus, the used the dependency knowledge to build a nodeset that was used for WSD. The background documents provided by the organizers were only used to test how exhaustive the initial seeds were. Their best run ranked 8th.

Kyoto: This system participated in all four languages, with a free reimplementation of the domain-specific knowledge-based method for WSD presented in (Agirre et al., 2009). It uses a module to construct a distributional thesaurus, which was run on the background text, and a disambiguation module based on Personalized PageRank over wordnet graphs. Different WordNet were used as the LKB depending on the language. Their best run ranked 10th. Note that this team includes some of the organizers of the task. A strict separation was kept, in order to keep the test dataset hidden from the actual developers of the system.

RACAI: This participant submitted three different knowledge-based systems. In the first, they use the mapping to domains of WordNet (version 2.0) in order to constraint the domains of the content words of the test text. In the second, they choose among senses using lexical chains (Ion and Stefanescu, 2009). The third system combines the previous two. Their best system ranked 12th.

HIT-CIR: They presented a knowledge-based system which estimates predominant sense from raw test. The predominant senses were calculated with the frequency information in the provided background text, and automatically constructed thesauri from bilingual parallel corpora. The system ranked 14.

UCFWS: This knowledge-based WSD system was based on an algorithm originally described in (Schwartz and Gomez, 2008), in which selectors are acquired from the Web via searching with local context of a given word. The sense is chosen based on the similarity or relatedness between the senses of the target word and various types of selectors. In some runs they include predominant senses(McCarthy et al., 2007). The best run ranked 13th.

NLEL-WSD(-PDB): The system used for the participation is based on an ensemble of different methods using fuzzy-Borda voting. A similar system was proposed in SemEval-2007 task-7 (Buscaldi and Rosso, 2007). In this case, the component method used where the following ones: 1) Most Frequent Sense from SemCor; 2) Conceptual Density ; 3) Supervised Domain Relative Entropy classifier based on WordNet Domains; 4) Supervised Bayesian classifier based on WordNet Domains probabilities; and 5) Unsupervised Knownet-20 classifiers. The best run ranked 24th.

UMCC-DLSI (Relevant): The team submitted three different runs using a knowledge-based system. The first two runs use domain vectors and the third is based on cliques, which measure how much a concept is correlated to the sentence by obtaining Relevant Semantic Trees. Their best run ranked 27th.

(G)HR: They presented a Knowledge-based WSD system, which make use of two heuristic rules (Li et al., 1995). The system enriched the Chinese WordNet by adding semantic relations for English domain specific words (e.g. ecology, environment). When in-domain senses are not available, the system relies on the first sense in the Chinese WordNet. In addition, they also use sense definitions. They only participated in the Chinese task, with their best system ranking 1st.

4 Results

The evaluation has been carried out using the standard Senseval/SemEval scorer `scorer2` as included in the trial dataset, which computes precision and recall. Table 3 shows the results in each dataset. Note that the main evaluation measure is recall (R). In addition we also report precision (P) and the recall for nouns and verbs. Recall measures are accompanied by a 95% confidence interval calculated using bootstrap resampling procedure (Noreen, 1989). The difference between two systems is deemed to be statistically significant if there is no overlap between the confidence intervals. We show graphically the results in Figure 1. For instance, the differences between the highest scoring system and the following four systems are not statistically significant. Note that this method of estimating statistical significance might be more strict than other pairwise methods.

We also include the results of two baselines. The random baseline was calculated analytically. The first sense baseline for each language was taken from each wordnet. The first sense baseline in English and Chinese corresponds to the most frequent sense, as estimated from out-of-domain corpora. In Dutch and Italian, it followed the intuitions of the lexicographer. Note that we don't have the most frequent sense baseline from the domain texts, which would surely show higher results (Koeling et al., 2005).

5 Conclusions

Domain portability and adaptation of NLP components and Word Sense Disambiguation systems present new challenges. The difficulties found by supervised systems to adapt might change the way we assess the strengths and weaknesses of supervised and knowledge-based WSD systems. With this paper we have motivated the creation of an all-words test dataset for WSD on the environment domain in several languages, and presented the overall design of this SemEval task.

One of the goals of the exercise was to show that WSD systems could make use of unannotated background corpora to adapt to the domain and improve their results. Although it's early to reach hard conclusions, the results show that in each of the datasets, knowledge-based systems are able to improve their results using background text, and in two datasets the adaptation of knowledge-based systems leads to results over the MFS baseline. The evidence of domain adaptation of supervised systems is weaker, as only one team tried, and the differences with respect to MFS are very small. The best results for English are obtained by a system that combines a knowledge-based system with some targeted hand-tagging. Regarding the techniques used, graph-based methods over WordNet and distributional thesaurus acquisition methods have been used by several teams.

All datasets and related information are publicly available from the task websites[6].

Acknowledgments

We thank the collaboration of Lawrence Jones-Walters, Amor Torre-Marin (ECNC) and Karin de Boom (WWF), compiling the test and background documents. This work task is partially funded by the European Commission (KYOTO ICT-2007-211423), the Spanish Research Department (KNOW-2 TIN2009-14715-C04-01) and the Basque Government (BERBATEK IE09-262).

References

Eneko Agirre and Aitor Soroa. 2009. Personalizing pagerank for word sense disambiguation. In *Proceedings of the 12th Conference of the European Chapter of the Association for Computational Linguistics (EACL09)*, pages 33–41. Association for Computational Linguistics.

Eneko Agirre, Oier Lopez de Lacalle, and Aitor Soroa. 2009. Knowledge-based wsd on specific domains: Performing better than generic supervised wsd. In *Proceedigns of IJCAI. pp. 1501-1506."*.

Davide Buscaldi and Paolo Rosso. 2007. Upv-wsd : Combining different wsd methods by means of fuzzy borda voting. In *Proceedings of the Fourth International Workshop on Semantic Evaluations (SemEval-2007)*, pages 434–437.

P. Chen, W. Ding, and D. Brown. 2009. A fully unsupervised word sense disambiguation method and its evaluation on coarse-grained all-words task. In *Proceeding of the North American Chapter of the Association for Computational Linguistics (NAACL09)*.

Radu Ion and Dan Stefanescu. 2009. Unsupervised word sense disambiguation with lexical chains and graph-based context formalization. In *Proceedings of the 4th Language and Technology Conference: Human Language Technologies as a Challenge for Computer Science and Linguistics*, pages 190–194.

Rubén Izquierdo, Armando Suárez, and German Rigau. 2009. An empirical study on class-based word sense disambiguation. In *EACL '09: Proceedings of the 12th Conference of the European Chapter of the Association for Computational Linguistics*, pages 389–397, Morristown, NJ, USA. Association for Computational Linguistics.

Mitesh Khapra, Sapan Shah, Piyush Kedia, and Pushpak Bhattacharyya. 2010. Domain-specific word sense disambiguation combining corpus based and wordnet based parameters. In *Proceedings of the 5th International Conference on Global Wordnet (GWC2010)*.

A. Kilgarriff. 2001. English Lexical Sample Task Description. In *Proceedings of the Second International Workshop on evaluating Word Sense Disambiguation Systems*, Toulouse, France.

R. Koeling, D. McCarthy, and J. Carroll. 2005. Domain-specific sense distributions and predominant sense acquisition. In *Proceedings of the Human Language Technology Conference and Conference on Empirical Methods in Natural Language Processing. HLT/EMNLP*, pages 419–426, Ann Arbor, Michigan.

Xiaobin Li, Stan Szpakowicz, and Stan Matwin. 1995. A wordnet-based algorithm for word sense disambiguation. In *Proceedings of The 14th International Joint Conference on Artificial Intelligence (IJCAI95)*.

Diana McCarthy, Rob Koeling, Julie Weeds, and John Carroll. 2007. Unsupervised acquisition of predominant word senses. *Computational Linguistics*, 33(4).

R. Mihalcea, T. Chklovski, and Adam Killgariff. 2004. The Senseval-3 English lexical sample task. In *Proceedings of the 3rd ACL workshop on the Evaluation of Systems for the Semantic Analysis of Text (SENSEVAL)*, Barcelona, Spain.

Eric W. Noreen. 1989. *Computer-Intensive Methods for Testing Hypotheses*. John Wiley & Sons.

Sameer Pradhan, Edward Loper, Dmitriy Dligach, and Martha Palmer. 2007. Semeval-2007 task-17: English lexical sample, srl and all words. In *Proceedings of the Fourth International Workshop on Semantic Evaluations (SemEval-2007)*, pages 87–92, Prague, Czech Republic.

Paul Rayson and Roger Garside. 2000. Comparing corpora using frequency profiling. In *Proceedings of the workshop on Comparing corpora*, pages 1–6.

Hansen A. Schwartz and Fernando Gomez. 2008. Acquiring knowledge from the web to be used as selectors for noun sense disambiguation. In *Proceedings of the Twelfth Conference on Computational Natural Language Learning (CONLL08)*.

B. Snyder and M. Palmer. 2004. The English all-words task. In *Proceedings of the 3rd ACL workshop on the Evaluation of Systems for the Semantic Analysis of Text (SENSEVAL)*, Barcelona, Spain.

M. Tesconi, F. Ronzano, S. Minutoli, C. Aliprandi, and A. Marchetti. 2010. Kafnotator: a multilingual semantic text annotation tool. In *In Proceedings of the Second International Conference on Global Interoperability for Language Resources*.

Piek Vossen, Eneko Agirre, Nicoletta Calzolari, Christiane Fellbaum, Shu kai Hsieh, Chu-Ren Huang, Hitoshi Isahara, Kyoko Kanzaki, Andrea Marchetti, Monica Monachini, Federico Neri, Remo Raffaelli, German Rigau, Maurizio Tescon, and Joop VanGent. 2008. Kyoto: a system for mining, structuring and distributing knowledge across languages and cultures. In *Proceedings of the Sixth International Language Resources and Evaluation (LREC'08)*, Marrakech, Morocco, may. European Language Resources Association (ELRA). http://www.lrec-conf.org/proceedings/lrec2008/.

[6] `http://xmlgroup.iit.cnr.it/SemEval2010/` and `http://semeval2.fbk.eu/`

SemEval-2010 Task 18: Disambiguating Sentiment Ambiguous Adjectives

Yunfang Wu
Key Laboratory of Computational Linguistics (Peking University), Ministry of Education, China
wuyf@pku.edu.cn

Peng Jin
Laboratory of Intelligent Information Processing and Application, Leshan Normal University, China
jinp@lstc.edu.cn

Abstract

Sentiment ambiguous adjectives cause major difficulties for existing algorithms of sentiment analysis. We present an evaluation task designed to provide a framework for comparing different approaches in this problem. We define the task, describe the data creation, list the participating systems and discuss their results. There are 8 teams and 16 systems.

1 Introduction

In recent years, sentiment analysis has attracted considerable attention (Pang and Lee, 2008). It is the task of mining positive and negative opinions from natural language, which can be applied to many natural language processing tasks, such as document summarization and question answering. Previous work on this problem falls into three groups: opinion mining of documents, sentiment classification of sentences and polarity prediction of words. Sentiment analysis both at document and sentence level rely heavily on word level.

The most frequently explored task at word level is to determine the semantic orientation (SO) of words, in which most work centers on assigning a prior polarity to words or word senses in the lexicon out of context. However, for some words, the polarity varies strongly with context, making it hard to attach each to a specific sentiment category in the lexicon. For example, consider "low cost" versus "low salary". The word "low" has a positive orientation in the first case but a negative orientation in the second case.

Turney and Littman (2003) claimed that sentiment ambiguous words could not be avoided easily in a real-world application in the future research. But unfortunately, sentiment ambiguous words are discarded by most research concerning sentiment analysis (Hatzivassiloglou and McKeown, 1997; Turney and Littman, 2003; Kim and Hovy, 2004). The exception work is Ding et al. (2008). They call these words as *context dependant opinions* and propose a holistic lexicon-based approach to solve this problem. The language they deal with is English.

The disambiguation of sentiment ambiguous words can also be considered as a problem of phrase-level sentiment analysis. Wilson et al. (2005) present a two-step process to recognize contextual polarity that employs machine learning and a variety of features. Takamura et al. (2006, 2007) propose latent variable model and lexical network to determine SO of phrases, focusing on "noun+adjective" pairs. Their experimental results suggest that the classification of pairs containing ambiguous adjectives is much harder than those with unambiguous adjectives.

The task 18 at SemEval 2010 provides a benchmark data set to encourage studies on this problem. This paper is organized as follows. Section 2 defines the task. Section 3 describes the data annotation. Section 4 gives a brief summary of 16 participating systems. Finally Section 5 draws conclusions.

2 Task Set up

2.1 Task description

In this task, we focus on 14 frequently used sentiment ambiguous adjectives in Chinese, which all have the meaning of measurement, as shown below.

Proceedings of the 5th International Workshop on Semantic Evaluation, ACL 2010, pages 81–85,
Uppsala, Sweden, 15-16 July 2010.

(1) Sentiment ambiguous adjectives(SAAs) ={大 da "large", 多 duo "many", 高 gao "high", 厚 hou "thick", 深 shen "deep", 重 zhong "heavy", 巨大 ju-da "huge", 重大 zhong-da "great", 小 xiao "small", 少 shao "few", 低 di "low", 薄 bao "thin", 浅 qian "shallow", 轻 qing "light"}

These adjectives are neutral out of context, but when they co-occur with some target nouns, positive or negative emotion will be evoked. Although the number of such ambiguous adjectives is not large, they are frequently used in real text, especially in the texts expressing opinions and emotions.

The task is designed to automatically determine the SO of these sentiment ambiguous adjectives within context: positive or negative. For example, 高 gao "high" should be assigned as positive in 工资高 gong-zi-gao "salary is high" but negative in 价格高 jia-ge-gao "price is high".

This task was carried out in an unsupervised setting. No training data was provided, but external resources are encouraged to use.

2.2 Data Creation

We collected data from two sources. The main part was extracted from Xinhua News Agency of Chinese Gigaword (Second Edition) released by LDC. The texts were automatically word-segmented and POS-tagged using the open software *ICTCLAS*[1]. In order to concentrate on the disambiguation of sentiment ambiguous adjectives, and reduce the noise introduced by the parser, we extracted sentences containing strings in pattern of (2), where the target nouns are modified by the adjectives in most cases.

(2) noun+adverb+adjective (adjective∈SAAs)
e.g. 成本/n 较/d 低/a cheng-ben-jiao-di
"the cost is low."

Another small part of data was extracted from the Web. Using the search engine Google[2], we searched the queries as in (3):

(3) 很 hen "very"+ adjective (adjective∈SAAs)

From the returned snippets, we manually picked out some sentences that contain the strings of (2). Also, the sentences were automatically segmented and POS-tagged using *ICTCLAS*.

Sentiment ambiguous adjectives in the data were assigned as positive, negative or neutral, independently by two annotators. Since we focus on the distinction between positive and negative categories, the neutral instances were removed. The inter-annotator agreement is in a high level with a kappa of 0.91. After cases with disagreement were negotiated between the two annotators, a gold standard annotation was agreed upon. In total 2917 instances were provided as the test data in the task, and the number of sentences of per target adjective is listed in Table 2.

Evaluation was performed in micro accuracy and macro accuracy:

$$P_{mir} = \sum_{i=1}^{N} m_i / \sum_{i=1}^{N} n_i \qquad (1)$$

$$P_{mar} = \sum_{i=1}^{N} P_i / N \qquad P_i = m_i / n_i \qquad (2)$$

where N is the number of all target words, n_i is the number of all test instances for a specific word, and m_i is the number of correctly labeled instances.

2.3 Baseline

We group 14 sentiment ambiguous adjectives into two categories: positive-like adjectives and negative-like adjectives. The former has the connotation towards large measurement, whereas the latter towards small measurement.

(4) Positive-like adjectives (Pa) ={大 da "large", 多 duo "many", 高 gao "high", 厚 hou "thick", 深 shen "deep", 重 zhong "heavy", 巨大 ju-da "huge", 重大 zhong-da "great"}

(5) Negative-like adjectives (Na) ={小 xiao "small", 少 shao "few", 低 di "low", 薄 bao "thin", 浅 qian "shallow", 轻 qing "light"}

We conduct a baseline in the dataset. Not considering the context, assign all positive-like adjectives as positive and all negative-like adjectives as negative. The micro accuracy of the baseline is 61.20%.

The inter-annotator agreement of 0.91 can be considered as the upper bound of the dataset.

3 Systems and Results

We published firstly trial data and then test data. In total 11 different teams downloaded both the trial and test data. Finally 8 teams submitted their experimental results, including 16 systems.

[1] http://www.ictclas.org/.
[2] http://www.google.com/.

3.1 Results

Table 1 lists all systems' scores, ranked from best to worst performance measured by micro accuracy. To our surprise, the performance of different systems differs greatly. The micro accuracy of the best system is 94.20% that is 43.12% higher than the worst system. The accuracy of the best three systems is even higher than inter-annotator agreement. The performance of the worst system is only a little higher than random baseline, which is 50% when we randomly assign the SO of sentiment ambiguous adjectives.

Table 1: The scores of 16 systems

System	Micro Acc.(%)	Macro Acc.(%)
YSC-DSAA	94.20	92.93
HITSZ_CITYU_1	93.62	95.32
HITSZ_CITYU_2	93.32	95.79
Dsaa	88.07	86.20
OpAL	76.04	70.38
CityUHK4	72.47	69.80
CityUHK3	71.55	75.54
HITSZ_CITYU_3	66.58	62.94
QLK_DSAA_R	64.18	69.54
CityUHK2	62.63	60.85
CityUHK1	61.98	67.89
QLK_DSAA_NR	59.72	65.68
Twitter Sentiment	59.00	62.27
Twitter Sentiment_ext	56.77	61.09
Twitter Sentiment_zh	56.46	59.63
Biparty	51.08	51.26

Table 2 shows that the performance of different systems differs greatly on each of 14 target adjectives. For example, the accuracy of 大 da "large" is 95.53% by one system but only 46.51% by another system.

Table 2: The scores of 14 ambiguous adjectives

Words	Ins#	Max%	Min%	Stdev
大 |large	559	95.53	46.51	0.155
多|many	222	95.50	49.10	0.152
高 ||high	546	95.60	54.95	0.139
厚 |thick	20	95.00	35.00	0.160
深 |deep	45	100.00	51.11	0.176
重|heavy	259	96.91	34.75	0.184
巨大 |huge	49	100.00	10.20	0.273
重大 |great	28	100.00	7.14	0.243
小 |small	290	93.10	49.66	0.167
少 few	310	95.81	41.29	0.184
低 |low	521	93.67	48.37	0.147
薄 |thin	33	100.00	18.18	0.248
浅 |shallow	8	100.00	37.50	0.155
轻 |light	26	100.00	34.62	0.197

3.2 Systems

In this section, we give a brief description of the systems.

YSC-DSAA This system creates a new word library named SAAOL (SAA-Oriented Library), which is built manually with the help of software. SAAOL consists of positive words, negative words, NSSA, PSSA, and inverse words. The system divides the sentences into clauses using heuristic rules, and disambiguates SAA by analyzing the relationship between SAA and the keywords.

HITSZ_CITYU This group submitted three systems, including one baseline system and two improved systems.

HITSZ_CITYU_3: The baseline system is based on collocation of opinion words and their targets. For the given adjectives, their collocations are extracted from People's Daily Corpus. With human annotation, the system obtained 412 positive and 191 negative collocations, which are regarded as seed collocations. Using the context words of seed collocations as features, the system trains a one-class SVM classifier.

HITSZ_CITYU_2 and HITSZ_CITYU_1: Using HowNet-based word similarity as clue, the authors expand the seed collocations on both ambiguous adjectives side and collocated targets side. The authors then exploit sentence-level opinion analysis to further improve performance. The strategy is that if the neighboring sentences on both sides have the same polarity, the ambiguous adjective is assigned as the same polarity; if the neighboring sentences have conflicted polarity, the SO of ambiguous adjective is determined by its context words and the transitive probability of sentence polarity. The two systems use different parameters and combination strategy.

OpAL This system combines supervised methods with unsupervised ones. The authors employ Google translator to translate the task dataset from Chinese to English, since their system is working in English. The system explores three types of judgments. The first one trains a SVM classifier based on NTCIR data and EmotiBlog annotations. The second one uses search engine, issuing queries of "noun + SAA + AND + non-ambiguous adjective". The non-ambiguous adjectives include positive set ("positive, beautiful, good") and negative set ("negative, ugly, bad"). An example is "price high and good". The third one uses "too, very-rules". The final result is determined by the majority vote of the three components.

CityUHK This group submitted four systems. Both machine learning method and lexicon-based method are employed in their systems. In the machine learning method, maximum entropy model is used to train a classifier based on the Chinese data from NTCIR opinion task. Clause-level and sentence-level classifiers are compared. In the lexicon-based method, the authors classify SAAs into two clusters: intensifiers (our positive-like adjectives in (4)) and suppressors (our negative-like adjectives in (5)), and then use the polarity of context to determine the SO of SAAs.

CityUHK4: clause-level machine learning + lexicon.

CityUHK3: sentence-level machine learning + lexicon.

CityUHK2: clause-level machine learning.

CityUHK2: sentence-level machine learning.

QLK_DSAA This group submitted two systems. The authors adopt their SELC model (Qiu, et al., 2009), which is proposed to exploit the complementarities between lexicon-based and corpus-based methods to improve the whole performance. They determine the sentence polarity by SELC model, and simply regard the sentence polarity as the polarity of SAA in the sentence.

QLK_DSAA_NR: Based on the result of SELC model, they inverse the SO of SAA when it is modified by negative terms. Our task includes only positive and negative categories, so they replace the neutral value obtained by SELC model by the predominant polarity of the adjective.

QLK_DSAA_R: Based on the result of QLK_DSAA_NR, they add a rule to cope with two modifiers 偏 pian "specially" and 太 tai "too", which always have the negative meaning.

Twitter sentiment This group submitted three systems. The authors use a training data collected from microblogging platform. By exploiting Twitter, they collected automatically a dataset consisting of negative and positive expressions. The sentiment classifier is trained using Naive Bayes with n-grams of words as features.

Twitter Sentiment: Translating the task dataset from Chinese to English using Google translator, and then based on training data in English texts from Twitter.

Twitter Sentiment_ext: With Twitter Sentiment as basis, using extended data.

Twitter Sentiment_zh: Based on training data in Chinese texts from Twitter.

Biparty This system transforms the problem of disambiguating SAAs to predict the polarity of target nouns. The system presents a bootstrapping method to automatically build the sentiment lexicon, by building a nouns-verbs biparty graph from a large corpus. Firstly they select a few nouns as seed words, and then they use a cross inducing method to expand more nouns and verbs into the lexicon. The strategy is based on a random walk model.

4 Discussion

The experimental results of some systems are promising. The micro accuracy of the best three systems is over 93%. Therefore, the inter-annotator agreement (91%) is not an upper bound on the accuracy that can be achieved. On the contrary, the experimental results of some systems are disappointing, which are below our predefined simple baseline (61.20%), and are only a little higher than random baseline (50%). The accuracy variance of different systems makes this task more interesting.

The participating 8 teams exploit totally different methods.

Human annotation. In YSC-DSAA system, the word library of SAAOL is verified by human. In HITSZ_CITYU systems, the seed collocations are annotated by human. The three systems rank top 3. Undoubtedly, human labor can help improve the performance in this task.

Training data. The OpAL system employs SVM machine learning based on NTCIR data and EmotiBlog annotations. The CityUHK systems trains a maximum entropy classifier based on the annotated Chinese data from NTCIR. The Twitter Sentiment systems use a training data automatically collected from Twitter. The results show that some of these supervised methods based on training data cannot rival unsupervised ones, partly due to the poor quality of the training data.

English resources. Our task is in Chinese. Some systems use English resources by translating Chinese into English, as OpAL and Twitter Sentiment. The OpAL system achieves a quite good result, making this method a promising direction. This also shows that disambiguating SAAs is a common problem in natural language.

5 Conclusion

This paper describes task 18 at SemEval-2010, disambiguating sentiment ambiguous adjectives. The experimental results of the 16 participating systems are promising, and the used approaches are quite novel.

We encourage further research into this issue, and integration of the disambiguation of sentiment ambiguous adjectives into applications of sentiment analysis.

Acknowledgments

This work was supported by National Natural Science Foundation of China (No. 60703063), National Social Science Foundation of China (No. 08CYY016), and the Open Projects Program of Key Laboratory of Computational Linguistics(Peking University), Ministry of Education. We thank Miaomiao Wen and Tao Guo for careful annotation of the data.

References

Ding X., Liu B. and Yu, P. 2008. A holistic lexicon-based approach to opinion mining. *Proceedings of WSDM'08.*

Hatzivassiloglou, V. and McKeown, K. 1997 Predicting the semantic orientation of adjectives. *Proceedings of ACL'97.*

Kim, S and Hovy, E. 2004. Determining the sentiment of opinions. *Proceedings of COLING'04.*

Pang, B. and Lee, L. 2008. Opinion mining and sentiment analysis. *Foundations and Trends in Information Retrieval.*

Qiu L., Zhang W., Hu, C. and Zhao, K. 2009. SELC: A self-supervised model for sentiment analysis. In *Proceedings of CIKM'09.*

Takamura, H., Inui,T. and Okumura, M. 2006. Latent Variable Models for Semantic Orientations of phrases. *Proceedings of EACL'06.*

Takamura, H., Inui,T. and Okumura, M. 2007. Extracting Semantic Orientations of Phrases from Dictionary. *Proceedings of NAACL HLT '07.*

Turney, P. and Littman, M. 2003. Measuring praise and criticism: inference of semantic orientation from association. *ACM transaction on information systems.*

Wilson, T., Wiebe, J. and Hoffmann, P. 2005. Recognizing contextual polarity in phrase-level sentiment analysis. *Proceedings of HLT/EMNLP'05.*

SemEval-2010 Task 11: Event detection in Chinese news sentences

Qiang Zhou
Tsinghua University, Beijing 100084, P. R. China
zq-lxd@mail.tsinghua.edu.cn

The goal of the task is to detect and analyze the event contents in real world Chinese news texts. It consists of finding key verbs or verb phrases to describe these events in the Chinese sentences after word segmentation and part-of-speech tagging, selecting suitable situation descriptions for them, and anchoring different situation arguments with suitable syntactic chunks in the sentence. Three main sub-tasks are as follows: (1) Target verb WSD; (2) Sentence SRL; (3) Event detection.

We will select 100 high-frequency Chinese target verbs for this task. Among them, 30 verbs have multiple senses and 70 verbs have single sense. Each target verb will be assigned more than 50 annotated sentences to consist of training and test sets. Each annotated sentence will have following event information: (1) word segmentation and POS tags; (2) the target verb (or verb phrase) and its position in the sentence; (3) the event description (situation description formula or natural explanation text) of the target verb (or verb phrase) in the context of the sentences; (4) the chunks annotated with suitable syntactic constituent tags, functional tags and event argument role tags. The training and test set will be extracted from the data set with ratio 8:2.

For the WSD subtask, we give two evaluation measures: WSD-Micro-Accuracy and WSD-Macro-Accuracy. The correct conditions are: the selected situation description formula and natural explanation text of the target verbs will be same with the gold-standard codes. We evaluated 27 multiple-sense target verbs in the test set.

For the SRL subtask, we give three evaluation measures: Chunk-Precision, Chunk-Recall, and Chunk-F-measure. The correct conditions are: the recognized chunks should have the same boundaries, syntactic constituent and functional tags, and situation argument tags with the gold-standard argument chunks of the key verbs or verb phrases. We only select the key argument chunks (with semantic role tags: x, y, z, L or O) for evaluation.

For the event detection subtask, we give two evaluation measures: Event-Micro-Accuracy and Event-Macro-Accuracy. The correct conditions are: (1) The event situation description formula and natural explanation text of the target verb should be same with the gold-standard ones; (2) All the argument chunks of the event descriptions should be same with the gold-standard ones; (3) The number of the recognized argument chunks should be same with the gold-standard one.

8 participants downloaded the training and test data. Only 3 participants uploaded the final results. Among them, 1 participant (User ID = 156) submitted 4 results and 1 participant (User ID = 485) submitted 2 results. So we received 7 uploaded results for evaluation. The mean elaboration time of the test data is about 30 hours. The following is the evaluation result table. All the results are ranked with Event-Macro-Accuracy.

User ID	System ID	WSD-Micro-A	WSD-Macro-A	Chunk-P	Chunk-R	Chunk-F	Event-Micro-A	Event-Macro-A	Rank
485	480-a	87.54	89.59	80.91	77.91	79.38	52.12	53.76	1
485	480-b	87.24	89.18	80.91	76.95	78.88	50.59	52.05	2
303	109	73.00	70.64	63.50	57.39	60.29	22.85	23.05	3
156	348	79.23	82.18	58.33	53.32	55.71	20.05	20.23	4
156	350	77.74	81.42	58.33	53.32	55.71	20.05	20.22	5
156	347	81.30	83.81	58.33	53.32	55.71	20.33	20.19	6
156	349	79.82	82.58	58.33	53.32	55.71	20.05	20.14	7

The results show the event detection task is still an open problem for exploring in the Chinese language.

Proceedings of the 5th International Workshop on Semantic Evaluation, ACL 2010, page 86,
Uppsala, Sweden, 15-16 July 2010.

SemEval-2 Task 15: Infrequent Sense Identification for Mandarin Text to Speech Systems

Peng Jin[1] and Yunfang Wu[2]
[1]Laboratory of Intelligent Information Processing and Application, Leshan Normal University, Leshan China
[2]Institute of Computational Linguistics Peking University, Beijing China
{jandp, wuyf}@pku.edu.cn

1 Introduction

There are seven cases of grapheme to phoneme in a text to speech system (Yarowsky, 1997). Among them, the most difficult task is disambiguating the homograph word, which has the same POS but different pronunciation. In this case, different pronunciations of the same word always correspond to different word senses. Once the word senses are disambiguated, the problem of GTP is resolved.

There is a little different from traditional WSD, in this task two or more senses may correspond to one pronunciation. That is, the sense granularity is coarser than WSD. For example, the preposition "为" has three senses: sense1 and sense2 have the same pronunciation {wei 4}, while sense3 corresponds to {wei 2}. In this task, to the target word, not only the pronunciations but also the sense labels are provided for training; but for test, only the pronunciations are evaluated. The challenge of this task is the much skewed distribution in real text: the most frequent pronunciation occupies usually over 80%.

In this task, we will provide a large volume of training data (each homograph word has at least 300 instances) accordance with the truly distribution in real text. In the test data, we will provide at least 100 instances for each target word. The senses distribution in test data is the same as in training data.All instances come from People Daily newspaper (the most popular newspaper in Mandarin). Double blind annotations are executed manually, and a third annotator checks the annotation.

2 Participating Systems

Two kinds of precisions are evaluated. One is micro-average:

$$P_{mir} = \sum_{i=1}^{N} m_i / \sum_{i=1}^{N} n_i$$

N is the number of all target word-types. m_i is the number of labeled correctly to one specific target word-type and n_i is the number of all test instances for this word-type. The other is macro-average:

$$P_{mar} = \sum_{i=1}^{N} p_i / N \text{, } p_i = m_i / n_i$$

There are two teams participated in and submitted nine systems. Table 1 shows the results, all systems are better than baseline (Baseline is using the most frequent sense to tag all the tokens).

System	Micro-average	Macro-average
156-419	0.974432	0.951696
205-332	0.97028	0.938844
205-417	0.97028	0.938844
205-423	0.97028	0.938844
205-425	0.97028	0.938844
205-424	0.968531	0.938871
156-420	0.965472	0.942086
156-421	0.965472	0.94146
156-422	0.965472	0.942086
baseline	0.923514	0.895368

Table 1: The scores of all participating systems

References

Yarowsky, David. 1997. "Homograph disambiguation in text-to-speech synthesis." In van Santen, Jan T. H.; Sproat, Richard; Olive, Joseph P.; and Hirschberg, Julia. Progress in Speech Synthesis. Springer-Verlag, New York, 157-172.

Proceedings of the 5th International Workshop on Semantic Evaluation, ACL 2010, page 87,
Uppsala, Sweden, 15-16 July 2010. ©2010 Association for Computational Linguistics

RelaxCor: A Global Relaxation Labeling Approach to Coreference Resolution

Emili Sapena, Lluís Padró and Jordi Turmo
TALP Research Center
Universitat Politècnica de Catalunya
Barcelona, Spain
{esapena, padro, turmo}@lsi.upc.edu

Abstract

This paper describes the participation of RelaxCor in the Semeval-2010 task number 1: "Coreference Resolution in Multiple Languages". RelaxCor is a constraint-based graph partitioning approach to coreference resolution solved by relaxation labeling. The approach combines the strengths of groupwise classifiers and chain formation methods in one global method.

1 Introduction

The Semeval-2010 task is concerned with intra-document coreference resolution for six different languages: Catalan, Dutch, English, German, Italian and Spanish. The core of the task is to identify which noun phrases (NPs) in a text refer to the same discourse entity (Recasens et al., 2010).

RelaxCor (Sapena et al., 2010) is a graph representation of the problem solved by a relaxation labeling process, reducing coreference resolution to a graph partitioning problem given a set of constraints. In this manner, decisions are taken considering the whole set of mentions, ensuring consistency and avoiding that classification decisions are independently taken.

The paper is organized as follows. Section 2 describes RelaxCor, the system used in the Semeval task. Next, Section 3 describes the tuning needed by the system to adapt it to different languages and other task issues. The same section also analyzes the obtained results. Finally, Section 4 concludes the paper.

2 System Description

This section briefly describes RelaxCor. First, the graph representation is presented. Next, there is an explanation of the methodology used to learn constraints and train the system. Finally, the algorithm used for resolution is described.

2.1 Problem Representation

Let $G = G(V, E)$ be an undirected graph where V is a set of vertices and E a set of edges. Let $\mathbf{m} = (m_1, ..., m_n)$ be the set of mentions of a document with n mentions to resolve. Each mention m_i in the document is represented as a vertex $v_i \in V$ in the graph. An edge $e_{ij} \in E$ is added to the graph for pairs of vertices (v_i, v_j) representing the possibility that both mentions corefer.

Let C be our set of constraints. Given a pair of mentions (m_i, m_j), a subset of constraints $C_{ij} \subseteq C$ restrict the compatibility of both mentions. C_{ij} is used to compute the weight value of the edge connecting v_i and v_j. Let $w_{ij} \in W$ be the weight of the edge e_{ij}:

$$w_{ij} = \sum_{k \in C_{ij}} \lambda_k f_k(m_i, m_j) \qquad (1)$$

where $f_k(\cdot)$ is a function that evaluates the constraint k and λ_k is the weight associated to the constraint. Note that λ_k and w_{ij} can be negative.

In our approach, each vertex (v_i) in the graph is a variable (v_i) for the algorithm. Let L_i be the number of different values (labels) that are possible for v_i. The possible labels of each variable are the partitions that the vertex can be assigned. A vertex with index i can be in the first i partitions (i.e. $L_i = i$).

Proceedings of the 5th International Workshop on Semantic Evaluation, ACL 2010, pages 88–91,
Uppsala, Sweden, 15-16 July 2010.

Distance and position:
- DIST: Distance between m_i and m_j in sentences: number
- DIST_MEN: Distance between m_i and m_j in mentions: number
- APPOSITIVE: One mention is in apposition with the other: y,n
- I/J_IN_QUOTES: $m_{i/j}$ is in quotes or inside a NP or a sentence in quotes: y,n
- I/J_FIRST: $m_{i/j}$ is the first mention in the sentence: y,n

Lexical:
- I/J_DEF_NP: $m_{i/j}$ is a definitive NP: y,n
- I/J_DEM_NP: $m_{i/j}$ is a demonstrative NP: y,n
- I/J_INDEF_NP: $m_{i/j}$ is an indefinite NP: y,n
- STR_MATCH: String matching of m_i and m_j: y,n
- PRO_STR: Both are pronouns and their strings match: y,n
- PN_STR: Both are proper names and their strings match: y,n
- NONPRO_STR: String matching like in Soon et al. (2001) and mentions are not pronouns: y,n
- HEAD_MATCH: String matching of NP heads: y,n

Morphological:
- NUMBER: The number of both mentions match: y,n,u
- GENDER: The gender of both mentions match: y,n,u
- AGREEMENT: Gender and number of both mentions match: y,n,u
- I/J_THIRD_PERSON: $m_{i/j}$ is 3rd person: y,n
- PROPER_NAME: Both mentions are proper names: y,n,u
- I/J_PERSON: $m_{i/j}$ is a person (pronoun or proper name in a list): y,n
- ANIMACY: Animacy of both mentions match (persons, objects): y,n
- I/J_REFLEXIVE: $m_{i/j}$ is a reflexive pronoun: y,n
- I/J_TYPE: $m_{i/j}$ is a pronoun (p), entity (e) or nominal (n)

Syntactic:
- NESTED: One mention is included in the other: y,n
- MAXIMALNP: Both mentions have the same NP parent or they are nested: y,n
- I/J_MAXIMALNP: $m_{i/j}$ is not included in any other mention: y,n
- I/J_EMBEDDED: $m_{i/j}$ is a noun and is not a maximal NP: y,n
- BINDING: Conditions B and C of binding theory: y,n

Semantic:
- SEMCLASS: Semantic class of both mentions match: y,n,u (the same as (Soon et al., 2001))
- ALIAS: One mention is an alias of the other: y,n,u (only entities, else unknown)
- I/J_SRL_ARG: Semantic role of $m_{i/j}$: N,0,1,2,3,4,M,L
- SRL_SAMEVERB: Both mentions have a semantic role for the same verb: y,n

Figure 1: Feature functions used.

2.2 Training Process

Each pair of mentions (m_i, m_j) in a training document is evaluated by the set of feature functions shown in Figure 1. The values returned by these functions form a positive example when the pair of mentions corefer, and a negative one otherwise. Three specialized models are constructed depending on the type of anaphor mention (m_j) of the pair: pronoun, named entity or nominal.

A decision tree is generated for each specialized model and a set of rules is extracted with C4.5 rule-learning algorithm (Quinlan, 1993). These rules are our set of constraints. The C4.5rules algorithm generates a set of rules for each path from the learned tree. It then checks if the rules can be generalized by dropping conditions.

Given the training corpus, the weight of a constraint C_k is related with the number of examples where the constraint applies A_{C_k} and how many of them corefer C_{C_k}. We define λ_k as the weight of constraint C_k calculated as follows: $\lambda_k = \frac{C_{C_k}}{A_{C_k}} - 0.5$

2.3 Resolution Algorithm

Relaxation labeling (Relax) is a generic name for a family of iterative algorithms which perform function optimization, based on local information (Hummel and Zucker, 1987). The algorithm solves our weighted constraint satisfaction problem dealing with the edge weights. In this manner, each vertex is assigned to a partition satisfying as many constraints as possible. To do that, the algorithm assigns a probability for each possible label of each variable. Let $\mathbf{H} = (\mathbf{h}^1, \mathbf{h}^2, \ldots, \mathbf{h}^n)$ be the weighted labeling to optimize, where each $\mathbf{h}^i$ is a vector containing the probability distribution of v_i, that is: $\mathbf{h}^i = (h^i_1, h^i_2, \ldots, h^i_{L_i})$. Given that the resolution process is iterative, the probability for label l of variable v_i at time step t is $h^i_l(t)$, or simply h^i_l when the time step is not relevant.

Initialize:
  $H := H_0$,

Main loop:
  repeat
  For each variable v_i
    For each possible label l for v_i
      $S_{il} = \sum_{j \in A(v_i)} w_{ij} \times h^j_l$
    End for
    For each possible label l for v_i
      $h^i_l(t+1) = \frac{h^i_l(t) \times (1+S_{il})}{\sum_{k=1}^{L_i} h^i_k(t) \times (1+S_{ik})}$
    End for
  End for
  Until no more significant changes

Figure 2: Relaxation labeling algorithm

The support for a pair variable-label (S_{il}) expresses how compatible is the assignment of label l to variable v_i taking into account the labels of adjacent variables and the edge weights. The support is defined as the sum of the edge weights that relate variable v_i with each adjacent variable v_j multiplied by the weight for the same label l of variable v_j: $S_{il} = \sum_{j \in A(v_i)} w_{ij} \times h^j_l$ where w_{ij} is the edge weight obtained in Equation 1 and vertex v_i has $|A(v_i)|$ adjacent vertices. In our version of the algorithm for coreference resolution $A(v_i)$ is the list of adjacent vertices of v_i but only considering the ones with an index $k < i$.

The aim of the algorithm is to find a weighted labeling such that global consistency is maximized. Maximizing global consistency is defined

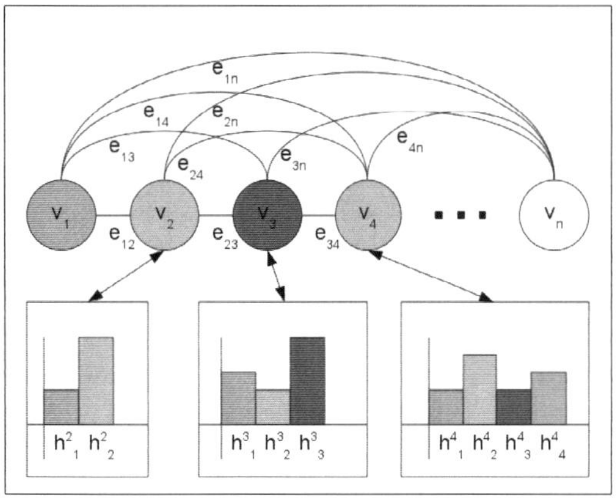

Figure 3: Representation of Relax. The vertices representing mentions are connected by weighted edges e_{ij}. Each vertex has a vector $\mathbf{h}^i$ of probabilities to belong to different partitions. The figure shows $\mathbf{h}^2$, $\mathbf{h}^3$ and $\mathbf{h}^4$.

as maximizing the average support for each variable. The final partitioning is directly obtained from the weighted labeling **H** assigning to each variable the label with maximum probability.

The pseudo-code of the relaxation algorithm can be found in Figure 2. The process updates the weights of the labels in each step until convergence, i.e. when no more significant changes are done in an iteration. Finally, the assigned label for a variable is the one with the highest weight. Figure 3 shows an example of the process.

3 Semeval task participation

RelaxCor have participated in the Semeval task for English, Catalan and Spanish. The system does not detect the mentions of the text by itself. Thus, the participation has been restricted to the gold-standard evaluation, which includes the manual annotated information and also provides the mention boundaries.

All the knowledge required by the feature functions (Figure 1) is obtained from the annotations of the corpora and no external resources have been used, with the exception of WordNet (Miller, 1995) for English. In this case, the system has been run two times for English: English-open, using WordNet, and English-closed, without WordNet.

3.1 Language and format adaptation

The whole methodology of RelaxCor including the resolution algorithm and the training process is totally independent of the language of the document. The only parts that need few adjustments are the preprocess and the set of feature functions. In most cases, the modifications in the feature functions are just for the different format of the data for different languages rather than for specific language issues. Moreover, given that the task includes many information about the mentions of the documents such as part of speech, syntactic dependency, head and semantic role, no preprocess has been needed.

One of the problems we have found adapting the system to the task corpora was the large amount of available data. As described in Section 2.2, the training process generates a feature vector for each pair of mentions into a document for all the documents of the training data set. However, the great number of training documents and their length overwhelmed the software that learns the constraints. In order to reduce the amount of pair examples, we run a clustering process to reduce the number of negative examples using the positive examples as the centroids. Note that negative examples are near 94% of the training examples, and many of them are repeated. For each positive example (a corefering pair of mentions), only the negative examples with distance less than a threshold d are included in the final training data. The distance is computed as the number of different values inside the feature vector. After some experiments over development data, the value of d was assigned to 3. Thus, the negative examples were discarded when they have more than three features different than any positive example.

Our results for the development data set are shown in Table 1.

3.2 Results analysis

Results of RelaxCor for the test data set are shown in Table 2. One of the characteristics of the system is that the resolution process always takes into account the whole set of mentions and avoids any possible pair-linkage contradiction as well as forces transitivity. Therefore, the system favors the precision, which results on high scores with metrics CEAF and B^3. However, the system is penalized with the metrics based on pair-linkage, specially with MUC. Although RelaxCor has the highest precision scores even for MUC, the recall is low enough to finally obtain low scores for F_1.

Regarding the test scores of the task comparing with the other participants (Recasens et al., 2010), RelaxCor obtains the best performances for Cata-

-	CEAF			MUC			B^3		
language	R	P	F_1	R	P	F_1	R	P	F_1
ca	69.7	69.7	69.7	27.4	77.9	40.6	67.9	96.1	79.6
es	70.8	70.8	70.8	30.3	76.2	43.4	68.9	95.0	79.8
en-closed	74.8	74.8	74.8	21.4	67.8	32.6	74.1	96.0	83.7
en-open	75.0	75.0	75.0	22.0	66.6	33.0	74.2	95.9	83.7

Table 1: Results on the development data set

-	CEAF			MUC			B^3			BLANC		
language	R	P	F_1	R	P	F_1	R	P	F_1	R	P	Blanc
Information: closed Annotation: gold												
ca	70.5	70.5	70.5	29.3	77.3	42.5	68.6	95.8	79.9	56.0	81.8	59.7
es	66.6	66.6	66.6	14.8	73.8	24.7	65.3	97.5	78.2	53.4	81.8	55.6
en	75.6	75.6	75.6	21.9	72.4	33.7	74.8	97.0	84.5	57.0	83.4	61.3
Information: open Annotation: gold												
en	75.8	75.8	75.8	22.6	70.5	34.2	75.2	96.7	84.6	58.0	83.8	62.7

Table 2: Results of the task

lan (CEAF and B^3), English (closed: CEAF and B^3; open: B^3) and Spanish (B^3). Moreover, RelaxCor is the most precise system for all the metrics in all the languages except for CEAF in English-open and Spanish. This confirms the robustness of the results of RelaxCor but also remarks that more knowledge or more information is needed to increase the recall of the system without loosing this precision

The incorporation of WordNet to the English run is the only difference between English-open and English-closed. The scores are slightly higher when using WordNet but not significant. Analyzing the MUC scores, note that the recall is improved, while precision decreases a little which corresponds with the information and the noise that WordNet typically provides.

The results for the test and development are very similar as expected, except the Spanish (es) ones. The recall considerably falls from development to test. It is clearly shown in the MUC recall and also is indirectly affecting on the other scores.

4 Conclusion

The participation of RelaxCor to the Semeval coreference resolution task has been useful to evaluate the system in multiple languages using data never seen before. Many published systems typically use the same data sets (ACE and MUC) and it is easy to unintentionally adapt the system to the corpora and not just to the problem. This kind of tasks favor comparisons between systems with the same framework and initial conditions.

The results obtained confirm the robustness of the RelaxCor, and the performance is considerably good in the state of the art. The system avoids contradictions in the results which causes a high precision. However, more knowledge is needed about the mentions in order to increase the recall without loosing that precision. A further error analysis is needed, but one of the main problem is the lack of semantic information and world knowledge specially for the nominal mentions – the mentions that are NPs but not including named entities neither pronouns–.

Acknowledgments

The research leading to these results has received funding from the European Community's Seventh Framework Programme (FP7/2007-2013) under Grant Agreement number 247762 (FAUST), and from the Spanish Science and Innovation Ministry, via the KNOW2 project (TIN2009-14715-C04-04).

References

R. A. Hummel and S. W. Zucker. 1987. On the foundations of relaxation labeling processes. pages 585–605.

G.A. Miller. 1995. WordNet: a lexical database for English.

J.R. Quinlan. 1993. *C4.5: Programs for Machine Learning*. Morgan Kaufmann.

M. Recasens, L. Màrquez, E. Sapena, M.A. Martí, M. Taulé, V. Hoste, M. Poesio, and Y. Versley. 2010. SemEval-2010 Task 1: Coreference resolution in multiple languages. In *Proceedings of the 5th International Workshop on Semantic Evaluations (SemEval-2010)*, Uppsala, Sweden.

E. Sapena, L. Padró, and J. Turmo. 2010. A Global Relaxation Labeling Approach to Coreference Resolution. *Submitted*.

W.M. Soon, H.T. Ng, and D.C.Y. Lim. 2001. A Machine Learning Approach to Coreference Resolution of Noun Phrases. *Computational Linguistics*, 27(4):521–544.

SUCRE: A Modular System for Coreference Resolution

Hamidreza Kobdani and Hinrich Schütze
Institute for Natural Language Processing
University of Stuttgart, Germany
kobdani@ims.uni-stuttgart.de

Abstract

This paper presents SUCRE, a new software tool for coreference resolution and its feature engineering. It is able to separately do noun, pronoun and full coreference resolution. SUCRE introduces a new approach to the feature engineering of coreference resolution based on a relational database model and a regular feature definition language. SUCRE successfully participated in SemEval-2010 Task 1 on Coreference Resolution in Multiple Languages (Recasens et al., 2010) for gold and regular closed annotation tracks of six languages. It obtained the best results in several categories, including the regular closed annotation tracks of English and German.

1 Introduction

In this paper, we introduce a new software tool for coreference resolution. Coreference resolution is the process of finding discourse entities (markables) referring to the same real-world entity or concept. In other words, this process groups the markables of a document into equivalence classes (coreference entities) so that all markables in an entity are coreferent.

There are various publicly available systems that perform coreference resolution, such as BART (Versley et al., 2008) and GUITAR (Steinberger et al., 2007). A considerable engineering effort is needed for the full coreference resolution task, and a significant part of this effort concerns feature engineering. Thus, a system which is able to extract the features based on a feature definition language can help the researcher reduce the implementation effort needed for feature extraction. Most methods of coreference resolution, if providing a baseline, usually use a feature set similar to (Soon et al., 2001) or (Ng and Cardie, 2002) and do the feature extraction in the preprocessing stage. SUCRE has been developed to provide a more flexible method for feature engineering of coreference resolution. It has a novel approach to model an unstructured text corpus in a structured framework by using a relational database model and a regular feature definition language to define and extract the features. Relational databases are a well-known technology for structured data modeling and are supported by a wide array of software and tools. Converting a text corpus to/from its equivalent relational database model is straightforward in our framework.

A regular language for feature definition is a very flexible method to extract different features from text. In addition to features defined directly in SUCRE, it accepts also externally extracted/generated features. Its modular architecture makes it possible to use any externally available classification method too. In addition to link features (features related to a markable pair), it is also possible to define other kinds of features: atomic word and markable features. This approach to feature engineering is suitable not only for knowledge-rich but also for knowledge-poor datasets. It is also language independent. The results of SUCRE in SemEval-2010 Task 1 show the promise of our framework.

2 Architecture

The architecture of SUCRE has two main parts: preprocessing and coreference resolution.

In preprocessing the text corpus is converted to a relational database model. These are the main functionalities in this stage:

1. Preliminary text conversion
2. Extracting atomic word features
3. Markable detection

Proceedings of the 5th International Workshop on Semantic Evaluation, ACL 2010, pages 92–95,
Uppsala, Sweden, 15-16 July 2010.

Column	Characteristic
Word Table	
Word-ID	Primary Key
Document-ID	Foreign Key
Paragraph-ID	Foreign Key
Sentence-ID	Foreign Key
Word-String	Attribute
Word-Feature-0	Attribute
Word-Feature-1	Attribute
...	Attribute
Word-Feature-N	Attribute
Markable Table	
Markable-ID	Primary Key
Begin-Word-ID	Foreign Key
End-Word-ID	Foreign Key
Head-Word-ID	Foreign Key
Markable-Feature-0	Attribute
Markable-Feature-1	Attribute
...	Attribute
Markable-Feature-N	Attribute
Links Table	
Link-ID	Primary Key
First-Markable-ID	Foreign Key
Second-Markable-ID	Foreign Key
Coreference-Status	Attribute
Status-Confidence-Level	Attribute

Table 1: Relational Database Model of Text Corpus

4. Extracting atomic markable features

After converting (modeling) the text corpus to the database, coreference resolution can be performed. Its functional components are:

1. Relational Database Model of Text Corpus
2. Link Generator
3. Link Feature Extractor
4. Learning (Applicable on Train Data)
5. Decoding (Applicable on Test Data)

2.1 Relational Database Model of Text Corpus

The Relational Database model of text thev corpus is an easy to generate format. Three tables are needed to have a minimum running system: Word, Markable and Link.

Table 1 presents the database model of the text corpus. In the word table, Word-ID is the index of the word, starting from the beginning of the corpus. It is used as the primary key to uniquely identify each token. Document-ID, Paragraph-ID and Sentence-ID are each counted from the beginning of the corpus, and also act as the foreign keys pointing to the primary keys of the document, paragraph and sentence tables, which are optional (the system can also work without them). It is obvious that the raw text as well as any other format of the corpus can be generated from the word table. Any word features (Word-Feature-#X columns) can be defined and will then be added to the word table in preprocessing. In the markable table, Markable-ID is the primary key. Begin-Word-ID, End-Word-ID and Head-Word-ID refer to the word table. Like the word features, the markable features are not mandatory and in the preprocessing we can decide which features are added to the table. In the link table, Link-ID is the primary key; First-Markable-ID and Second-Markable-ID refer to the markable table.

2.2 Link Generator

For training, the system generates a positive training instance for each adjacent coreferent markable pair and negative training instances for a markable m and all markables disreferent with m that occur before m (Soon et al., 2001). For decoding it generates all the possible links inside a window of 100 markables.

2.3 Link Feature Extractor

There are two main categories of features in SUCRE: Atomic Features and Link Features

We first explain atomic features in detail and then turn to link features and the extraction method we use.

Atomic Features: The current version of SUCRE supports the atomic features of words and markables but in the next versions we are going to extend it to sentences, paragraphs and documents. An atomic feature is an attribute. For example the position of the word in the corpus is an atomic word feature. Atomic word features are stored in the columns of the word table called Word-Feature-X.

In addition to word position in the corpus, document number, paragraph number and sentence number, the following are examples of atomic word features which can be extracted in preprocessing: Part of speech tag, Grammatical Gender (male, female or neutral), Natural Gender (male or female), Number (e.g. singular, plural or both), Semantic Class, Type (e.g. pronoun types: personal, reflexive, demonstrative ...), Case (e.g. nominative, accusative, dative or genitive in German) and Pronoun Person (first, second or third). Other possible atomic markable features include:

number of words in markable, named entity, alias, syntactic role and semantic class.

For sentences, the following could be extracted: number of words in the sentence and sentence type (e.g. simple, compound or complex). For paragraphs these features are possible: number of words and number of sentences in the paragraph. Finally, examples of document features include document type (e.g. news, article or book), number of words, sentences and paragraphs in the document.

Link Features: Link features are defined over a pair of markables. For link feature extraction, the head words of the markables are usually used, but in some cases the head word may not be a suitable choice. For example, consider the two markables *the books* and *a book*. In both cases *book* is the head word, but to distinguish which markable is definite and which indefinite, the article must be taken into account. Now consider the two markables *the university student from Germany* and *the university student from France*. In this case, the head words and the first four words of each markable are the same but they can not be coreferent; this can be detected only by looking at the last words. Sometimes we need to consider all words in the two markables, or even define a feature for a markable as a unit. To cover all such cases we need a regular feature definition language with some keywords to select different word combinations of two markables. For this purpose, we define the following variables. **m1** is the first markable in the pair. **m1b**, **m1e** and **m1h** are the first, last and head words of the first markable in the pair. **m1a** refers to all words of the first markable in the pair. **m2, m2b, m2e, m2h** and **m2a** have the same definitions as above but for the second markable in the pair.

In addition to the above keywords there are some other keywords that this paper does not have enough space to mention (e.g. for accessing the constant values, syntax relations or roles). The currently available functions are: exact- and substring matching (in two forms: case-sensitive and case-insensitive), edit distance, alias, word relation, markable parse tree path, absolute value.

Two examples of link features are as follows:

- $(seqmatch(m1a, m2a) > 0)$
  $\&\&\ (m1h.f0 == f0.N)$
  $\&\&\ (m2h.f0 == f0.N)$
  means that there is at least one exact match between the words of the markables and that the head words of both are nouns (f0 means Word-Feature-0, which is part of speech in our system).

- $(abs(m2b.stcnum - m1b.stcnum) == 0)$
  $\&\&\ (m2h.f3 == f3.reflexive)$
  means that two markables are in the same sentence and that the type of the second markable head word is reflexive (f3 means Word-Feature-3, which is morphological type in our system).

2.4 Learning

There are four classifiers integrated in SUCRE: Decision-Tree, Naive-Bayes, Support Vector Machine (Joachims, 2002) and Maximum-Entropy (Tsuruoka, 2006).

When we compared these classifiers, the best results, which are reported in Section 3, were achieved with the Decision-Tree.

2.5 Decoding

In decoding, the coreference chains are created. SUCRE uses best-first clustering for this purpose. It searches for the best predicted antecedent from right-to-left starting from the end of the document.

3 Results

Table 2 shows the results of SUCRE and the best competitor system on the test portions of the six languages from SemEval-2010 Task 1. Four different evaluation metrics were used to rank the participating systems: MUC (Vilain et al., 1995), B^3 (Bagga and Baldwin, 1998), CEAF (Luo, 2005) and BLANC (Recasens and Hovy, in prep).

SUCRE has the best results in regular closed annotation track of English and German (for all metrics). Its results for gold closed annotation track of both English and German are the best in MUC and BLANC scoring metrics (MUC: English +27.1 German +32.5, BLANC: English +9.5 German +9.0) and for CEAF and B^3 (CEAF: English -1.3 German -4.8, B^3: English -2.1 German -4.8); in comparison to the second ranked system, the performance is clearly better in the first case and slightly better in the second. This result shows that SUCRE has been optimized in a way that achieves good results on the four different scoring metrics. We view this good performance as a demonstration of the strength of SUCRE: our method of feature extraction, definition and tuning is uniform and can be optimized and applied to all languages and tracks.

Results of SUCRE show a correlation between the MUC and BLANC scores (the best MUC scores of all tracks and the best BLANC scores in 11 tracks of a total 12), in our opinion this correlation is not because of the high similarity between MUC and BLANC, but it is because of the balanced scores.

Language	ca	de	en	es	it	nl
System	SUCRE (Gold Annotation)					
MD-F1	100	100	100	100	98.4	100
CEAF-F1	68.7	72.9	74.3	69.8	66.0	58.8
MUC-F1	**56.2**	**58.4**	**60.8**	**55.3**	**45.0**	**69.8**
B^3-F1	77.0	81.1	82.4	77.4	**76.8**	**67.0**
BLANC	**63.6**	**66.4**	**70.8**	**64.5**	**56.9**	**65.3**
System	SUCRE (Regular Annotation)					
MD-F1	69.7	**78.4**	**80.7**	70.3	**90.8**	**42.3**
CEAF-F1	47.2	**59.9**	**62.7**	52.9	**61.3**	15.9
MUC-F1	**37.3**	**40.9**	**52.5**	**36.3**	**50.4**	**29.7**
B^3-F1	51.1	**64.3**	**67.1**	55.6	**70.6**	11.7
BLANC	**54.2**	**53.6**	**61.2**	**51.4**	57.7	**46.9**
System	Best Competitor (Gold Annotation)					
MD-F1	100	100	100	100	N/A	N/A
CEAF-F1	**70.5**	**77.7**	**75.6**	66.6	N/A	N/A
MUC-F1	42.5	25.9	33.7	24.7	N/A	N/A
B^3-F1	**79.9**	**85.9**	**84.5**	**78.2**	N/A	N/A
BLANC	59.7	57.4	61.3	55.6	N/A	N/A
System	Best Competitor (Regular Annotation)					
MD-F1	**82.7**	59.2	73.9	**83.1**	55.9	34.7
CEAF-F1	**57.1**	49.5	57.3	**59.3**	45.8	**17.0**
MUC-F1	22.9	15.4	24.6	21.7	42.7	8.3
B^3-F1	**64.6**	50.7	61.3	**66.0**	46.4	**17.0**
BLANC	51.0	44.7	49.3	51.4	**59.6**	32.3

Table 2: Results of SUCRE and the best competitor system. Bold F1 scores indicate that the result is the best SemEval result. MD: Markable Detection, ca: Catalan, de: German, en:English, es: Spanish, it: Italian, nl: Dutch

4 Conclusion

In this paper, we have presented a new modular system for coreference resolution. In comparison with the existing systems the most important advantage of our system is its flexible method of feature engineering based on relational database and a regular feature definition language. There are four classifiers integrated in SUCRE: Decision-Tree, Naive-Bayes, SVM and Maximum-Entropy. The system is able to separately do noun, pronoun and full coreference resolution. The system uses best-first clustering. It searches for the best predicted antecedent from right-to-left starting from the end of the document.

References

Amit Bagga and Breck Baldwin. 1998. Algorithms for scoring coreference chains. In *In The First International Conference on Language Resources and Evaluation Workshop on Linguistics Coreference*, pages 563–566.

Thorsten Joachims. 2002. *Learning to Classify Text Using Support Vector Machines, Methods, Theory, and Algorithms*. Kluwer/Springer.

Xiaoqiang Luo. 2005. On coreference resolution performance metrics. In *HLT '05: Proceedings of the conference on Human Language Technology and Empirical Methods in Natural Language Processing*, pages 25–32, Morristown, NJ, USA. Association for Computational Linguistics.

Vincent Ng and Claire Cardie. 2002. Improving machine learning approaches to coreference resolution. In *Proceedings of the ACL*, pages 104–111.

Marta Recasens and Eduard Hovy. in prep. BLANC: Implementing the Rand Index for Coreference Evaluation.

Marta Recasens, Lluís Màrquez, Emili Sapena, M.Antònia Martí, Mariona Taulé, Véronique Hoste, Massimo Poesio, and Yannick Versley. 2010. SemEval-2010 Task 1: Coreference resolution in multiple languages. In *Proceedings of the 5th International Workshop on Semantic Evaluations (SemEval-2010)*, Uppsala, Sweden.

Wee Meng Soon, Hwee Tou Ng, and Daniel Chung Yong Lim. 2001. A machine learning approach to coreference resolution of noun phrases. In *Computational Linguistics*, pages 521–544.

Josef Steinberger, Massimo Poesio, Mijail A. Kabadjovb, and Karel Jezek. 2007. Two uses of anaphora resolution in summarization. In *Information Processing and Management, Special issue on Summarization*, pages 1663–1680.

Yoshimasa Tsuruoka. 2006. A simple c++ library for maximum entropy classification. *Tsujii laboratory, Department of Computer Science, University of Tokyo*.

Yannick Versley, Simone Paolo Ponzetto, Massimo Poesio, Vladimir Eidelman, Alan Jern, Jason Smith, and Xiaofeng Yang. 2008. Bart: A modular toolkit for coreference resolution. In *Proceedings of the 46nd Annual Meeting of the Association for Computational Linguistics*, pages 9–12.

Marc Vilain, John Burger, John Aberdeen, Dennis Connolly, and Lynette Hirschman. 1995. A model-theoretic coreference scoring scheme. In *MUC6 '95: Proceedings of the 6th conference on Message understanding*, pages 45–52, Morristown, NJ, USA. Association for Computational Linguistics.

UBIU: A Language-Independent System for Coreference Resolution

Desislava Zhekova
University of Bremen
zhekova@uni-bremen.de

Sandra Kübler
Indiana University
skuebler@indiana.edu

Abstract

We present UBIU, a language independent system for detecting full coreference chains, composed of named entities, pronouns, and full noun phrases which makes use of memory based learning and a feature model following Rahman and Ng (2009). UBIU is evaluated on the task "Coreference Resolution in Multiple Languages" (SemEval Task 1 (Recasens et al., 2010)) in the context of the 5th International Workshop on Semantic Evaluation.

1 Introduction

Coreference resolution is a field in which major progress has been made in the last decade. After a concentration on rule-based systems (cf. e.g. (Mitkov, 1998; Poesio et al., 2002; Markert and Nissim, 2005)), machine learning methods were embraced (cf. e.g. (Soon et al., 2001; Ng and Cardie, 2002)). However, machine learning based coreference resolution is only possible for a very small number of languages. In order to make such resources available for a wider range of languages, language independent systems are often regarded as a partial solution. To this day, there have been only a few systems reported that work on multiple languages (Mitkov, 1999; Harabagiu and Maiorano, 2000; Luo and Zitouni, 2005). However, all of those systems were geared towards predefined language sets.

In this paper, we present a language independent system that does require syntactic resources for each language but does not require any effort for adapting the system to a new language, except for minimal effort required to adapt the feature extractor to the new language. The system was completely developed within 4 months, and will be extended to new languages in the future.

2 UBIU: System Structure

The UBIU system aims at being a language-independent system in that it uses a combination of machine learning, in the form of memory-based learning (MBL) in the implementation of TiMBL (Daelemans et al., 2007), and language independent features. MBL uses a similarity metric to find the k nearest neighbors in the training data in order to classify a new example, and it has been shown to work well for NLP problems (Daelemans and van den Bosch, 2005). Similar to the approach by Rahman and Ng (2009), classification in UBUI is based on mention pairs (having been shown to work well for German (Wunsch, 2009)) and uses as features standard types of linguistic annotation that are available for a wide range of languages and are provided by the task.

Figure 1 shows an overview of the system. In preprocessing, we slightly change the formatting of the data in order to make it suitable for the next step in which language dependent feature extraction modules are used, from which the training and test sets for the classification are extracted. Our approach is untypical in that it first extracts the heads of possible antecedents during feature extraction. The full yield of an antecedent in the test set is determined after classification in a separate module. During postprocessing, final decisions are made concerning which of the mention pairs are considered for the final coreference chains.

In the following sections, we will describe feature extraction, classification, markable extraction, and postprocessing in more detail.

2.1 Feature Extraction

The language dependent modules contain finite state expressions that detect the heads based on the linguistic annotations. Such a language module requires a development time of approximately 1 person hour in order to adapt the regular expressions

Proceedings of the 5th International Workshop on Semantic Evaluation, ACL 2010, pages 96–99,
Uppsala, Sweden, 15-16 July 2010.

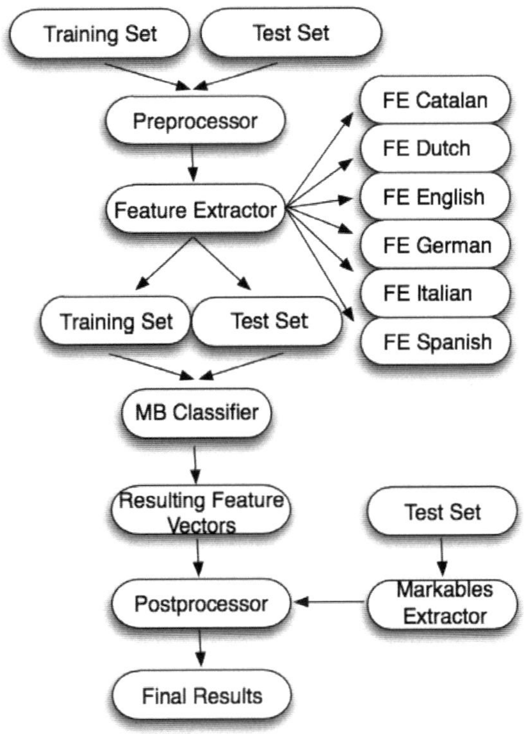

Figure 1: Overview of the system.

#	Feature Description
1	m_j - the antecedent
2	m_k - the mention to be resolved
3	Y if m_j is pron.; else N
4	Y if m_j is subject; else N
5	Y if m_j is a nested NP; else N
6	number - Sg. or Pl.
7	gender - F(emale), M(ale), N(euter), U(nknown)
8	Y if m_k is a pronoun; else N
9	Y if m_k is a nested NP; else N
10	semantic class – extracted from the NEs in the data
11	the nominative case of m_k if pron.; else NA
12	C if the mentions are the same string; else I
13	C if one mention is a substring of the other; else I
14	C if both mentions are pron. and same string; else I
15	C if both mentions are both non-pron. and same string; else I
16	C if both m. are pron. and either same pron. or diff. w.r.t. case; NA if at least one is not pron.; else I
17	C if the mentions agree in number; I if not; NA if the number for one or both is unknown
18	C if both m. are pron. I if neither
19	C if both m. are proper nouns; I if neither; else NA
20	C if the m. have same sem. class; I if not; NA if the sem. class for one or both m. is unknown
21	sentence distance between the mentions
22	concat. values for f. 6 for m_j and m_k
23	concat. values for f. 7 for m_j and m_k
24	concat. values for f. 3 for m_j and m_k
25	concat. values for f. 5 for m_j and m_k
26	concat. values for f. 10 for m_j and m_k
27	concat. values for f. 11 for m_j and m_k

Table 1: The pool of features for all languages.

to the given language data (different POS tagsets, differences in the provided annotations). This is the only language dependent part of the system.

We decided to separate the task of finding heads of markables, which then serve as the basis for the generation of the feature vectors, from the identification of the scope of a markable. For the English sentence "Any details or speculation on who specifically, we don't know that at this point.", we first detect the heads of possible antecedents, for example "details". However, the decision on the scope of the markable, i.e. the decision between "details" or "Any details or speculation on who specifically" is made in the postprocessing phase.

One major task of the language modules is the check for cyclic dependencies. Our system relies on the assumption that cyclic dependencies do not occur, which is a standard assumption in dependency parsing (Kübler et al., 2009). However, since some of the data sets in the multilingual task contained cycles, we integrated a module in the preprocessing step that takes care of such cycles.

After the identification of the heads of markables, the actual feature extraction is performed. The features that were used for training a classifier (see Table 1) were selected from the feature pool presented by Rahman and Ng (2009). Note that not all features could be used for all languages. We extracted all the features in Table 1 if the corresponding type of annotation was available; otherwise, a null value was assigned.

A good example for the latter concerns the gender information represented by feature 7 (for possible feature values cf. Table 1). Let us consider the following two entries - the first from the German data set and the second from English:

1. Regierung Regierung Regierung NN NN cas=d|num=sg|gend=fem cas=d|num=sg|gend=fem 31 31 PN PN . . .
2. law _ law NN NN NN NN 2 2 PMOD PMOD . . .

Extracting the value from entry 1, where *gend=fem*, is straightforward; the value being *F*. However, there is no gender information provided in the English data (entry 2). As a result, the value for feature 7 is *U* for the closed task.

2.2 Classifier Training

Based on the features extracted with the feature extractors described above, we trained TiMBL. Then we performed a non-exhaustive parameter optimization across all languages. Since a full optimization strategy would lead to an unmanageable number of system runs, we concentrated on varying k, the number of nearest neighbors considered in classification, and on the distance metric.

Furthermore, the optimization is focused on language independence. Hence, we did not optimize each classifier separately but selected parameters that lead to best average results across all languages of the shared task. In our opinion, this ensures an acceptable performance for new languages without further adaptation. The optimal settings for all the given languages were k=3 with the Overlap distance and gain ratio weighting.

2.3 Markable Extraction

The markable extractor makes use of the dependency relation labels. Each syntactic head together with all its dependents is identified as a separate markable. This approach is very sensitive to incorrect annotations and to dependency cycles in the data set. It is also sensitive to differences between the syntactic annotation and markables. In the Dutch data, for example, markables for named entities (NE) often exclude the determiner, a nominal dependent in the dependency annotation. Thus, the markable extractor suggests the whole phrase as a markable, rather than just the NE.

During the development phase, we determined experimentally that the recognition of markables is one of the most important steps in order to achieve high accuracy in coreference resolution: We conducted an ablation study on the training data set. We used the *train* data as training set and the *devel* data as testing set and investigated three different settings:

1. Gold standard setting: Uses gold markable annotations as well as gold linguistic annotations (upper bound).
2. Gold linguistic setting: Uses automatically determined markables and gold linguistic annotations.
3. Regular setting: Uses automatically determined markables and automatic linguistic information.

Note that we did not include all six languages: we excluded Italian and Dutch because there is no gold-standard linguistic annotation provided. The results of the experiment are shown in Table 2. From those results, we can conclude that the

S	Lang.	IM	CEAF	MUC	B^3	BLANC
1	Spanish	85.8	52.3	12.8	60.0	56.9
	Catalan	85.5	56.0	11.6	59.4	51.9
	English	96.1	68.7	17.9	74.9	52.7
	German	93.6	70.0	19.7	73.4	64.5
2	Spanish	61.0	41.5	11.3	42.4	48.7
	Catalan	60.8	40.5	9.6	41.4	48.3
	English	72.1	54.1	11.6	57.3	50.3
	German	57.7	45.5	12.2	45.7	44.3
3	Spanish	61.2	41.8	10.3	42.3	48.5
	Catalan	61.3	40.9	11.3	41.9	48.5
	English	71.9	54.7	13.3	57.4	50.3
	German	57.5	45.4	12.0	45.6	44.2

Table 2: Experiment results (as F1 scores) where IM is identification of mentions and S - Setting.

figures in Setting 2 and 3 are very similar. This means that the deterioration from gold to automatically annotated linguistic information is barely visible in the coreference results. This is a great advantage, since gold-standard data has always proved to be very expensive and difficult or impossible to obtain. The information that proved to be extremely important for the performance of the system is the one providing the boundaries of the markables. As shown in Table 2, the latter leads to an improvement of about 20%, which is observable in the difference in the figures of Setting 1 and 2. The results for the different languages show that it is more important to improve markable detection than the linguistic information.

2.4 Postprocessing

In Section 2.1, we described that we decided to separate the task of finding heads of markables from the identification of the scope of a markable. Thus, in the postprocessing step, we perform the latter (by the Markables Extractor module) as well as reformat the data for evaluation.

Another very important step during postprocessing is the selection of possible antecedents. In cases where more than one mention pair is classified as coreferent, only the pair with highest confidence by TiMBL is selected. Since nouns can be discourse-new, they do not necessarily have a coreferent antecedent; pronouns however, require an antecedent. Thus, in cases where all possible antecedents for a given pronoun are classified as not coreferent, we select the closest subject as antecedent; or if this heuristic is not successful, the antecedent that has been classified as not coreferent with the lowest confidence score (i.e. the highest distance) by TiMBL.

Lang.	S	IM	CEAF	MUC	B^3	BLANC
Catalan	G	84.4	52.3	11.7	58.8	52.2
	R	59.6	38.4	8.6	40.9	47.8
English	G	95.9	65.7	20.5	74.8	54.0
	R	74.2	53.6	14.2	58.7	51.0
German	G	94.0	68.2	21.9	75.7	64.5
	R	57.6	44.8	10.4	46.6	48.0
Spanish	G	83.6	51.7	12.7	58.3	54.3
	R	60.0	39.4	10.0	41.6	48.4
Italian	R	40.6	32.9	3.6	34.8	37.2
Dutch	R	34.7	17.0	8.3	17.0	32.3

Table 3: Final system results (as F1 scores) where IM is identification of mentions and S - Setting. For more details cf. (Recasens et al., 2010).

3 Results

UBIU participated in the closed task (i.e. only information provided in the data sets could be used), in the gold and regular setting. It was one of two systems that submitted results for all languages, which we count as preliminary confirmation that our system is language independent. The final results of UBIU are shown in Table 3. The figures for the identification of mentions show that this is an area in which the system needs to be improved. The errors in the gold setting result from an incompatibility of our two-stage markable annotation with the gold setting. We are planning to use a classifier for mention identification in the future.

The results for coreference detection show that English has a higher accuracy than all the other languages. We assume that this is a consequence of using a feature set that was developed for English (Rahman and Ng, 2009). This also means that an optimization of the feature set for individual languages should result in improved system performance.

4 Conclusion and Future Work

We have presented UBIU, a coreference resolution system that is language independent (given different linguistic annotations for languages). UBIU is easy to maintain, and it allows the inclusion of new languages with minimal effort.

For the future, we are planning to improve the system while strictly adhering to the language independence. We are planning to separate pronoun and definite noun classification, with the possibility of using different feature sets. We will also investigate language independent features and implement a markable classifier and a negative instance sampling module.

References

Walter Daelemans and Antal van den Bosch. 2005. *Memory Based Language Processing*. Cambridge University Press.

Walter Daelemans, Jakub Zavrel, Ko van der Sloot, and Antal van den Bosch. 2007. TiMBL: Tilburg memory based learner – version 6.1 – reference guide. Technical Report ILK 07-07, Induction of Linguistic Knowledge, Computational Linguistics, Tilburg University.

Sanda M. Harabagiu and Steven J. Maiorano. 2000. Multilingual coreference resolution. In *Proceedings of ANLP 2000*, Seattle, WA.

Sandra Kübler, Ryan McDonald, and Joakim Nivre. 2009. *Dependency Parsing*. Morgan Claypool.

Xiaoqiang Luo and Imed Zitouni. 2005. Multilingual coreference resolution with syntactic features. In *Proceedings of HLT/EMNLP 2005*, Vancouver, Canada.

Katja Markert and Malvina Nissim. 2005. Comparing knowledge sources for nominal anaphora resolution. *Computational Linguistics*, 31(3).

Ruslan Mitkov. 1998. Robust pronoun resolution with limited knowledge. In *Proceedings of ACL/COLING 1998*, Montreal, Canada.

Ruslan Mitkov. 1999. Multilingual anaphora resolution. *Machine Translation*, 14(3-4):281–299.

Vincent Ng and Claire Cardie. 2002. Improving machine learning approaches to coreference resolution. In *Proceedings of ACL 2002*, pages 104–111, Philadelphia, PA.

Massimo Poesio, Tomonori Ishikawa, Sabine Schulte im Walde, and Renata Vieira. 2002. Acquiring lexical knowledge for anaphora resolution. In *Proceedings of LREC 2002*, Las Palmas, Gran Canaria.

Altaf Rahman and Vincent Ng. 2009. Supervised models for coreference resolution. In *Proceedings of EMNLP 2009*, Singapore.

Marta Recasens, Lluís Màrquez, Emili Sapena, M.Antònia Martí, Mariona Taulé, Véronique Hoste, Massimo Poesio, and Yannick Versley. 2010. Semeval-2010 task 1: Coreference resolution in multiple languages. In *Proceedings of the 5th International Workshop on Semantic Evaluations (SemEval-2010)*, Uppsala, Sweden.

Wee Meng Soon, Hwee Tou Ng, and Daniel Chung Yong Lim. 2001. A machine learning approach to coreference resolution of noun phrases. *Computational Linguistics*, 27(4):521–544.

Holger Wunsch. 2009. *Rule-Based and Memory-Based Pronoun Resolution for German: A Comparison and Assessment of Data Sources*. Ph.D. thesis, Universität Tübingen.

Corry: A System for Coreference Resolution

Olga Uryupina
CiMeC, University of Trento
uryupina@gmail.com

Abstract

Corry is a system for coreference resolution in English. It supports both local (Soon et al. (2001)-style) and global (Integer Linear Programming, Denis and Baldridge (2007)-style) models of coreference. Corry relies on a rich linguistically motivated feature set, which has, however, been manually reduced to 64 features for efficiency reasons. Three runs have been submitted for the SemEval task 1 on Coreference Resolution (Recasens et al., 2010), optimizing Corry's performance for BLANC (Recasens and Hovy, in prep), MUC (Vilain et al., 1995) and CEAF (Luo, 2005). Corry runs have shown the best performance level among all the systems in their track for the corresponding metric.

1 Introduction

Corry is a system for coreference resolution in English. It supports both local (Soon et al. (2001)-style) and global (ILP, Denis and Baldridge (2007)-style) models of coreference. The backbone of the system is a family of SVM classifiers for pairs of mentions: each mention type receives its own classifier. A separate anaphoricity classifier is learned for the ILP setting. Corry relies on a rich linguistically motivated feature set, which has, however, been manually reduced to 64 features for efficiency reasons.

Corry has only participated in the "open" setting, as it has already a number of preprocessing modules integrated into the system: the Stanford NLP toolkit for parsing (Klein and Manning, 2003) and NE-tagging (Finkel et al., 2005), Wordnet for semantic classes and the U.S. census data for assigning gender values to person names.

Three runs have been submitted for the SemEval task 1 on Coreference Resolution, optimizing Corry's performance for BLANC, MUC and CEAF. The runs differ with respect to the model (local for BLANC, global for MUC and CEAF) and the definition of mention types.

2 Preprocessing and Mention Extraction

In our previous study (Uryupina, 2008) we have shown that up to 35% recall and 20% precision errors in coreference resolution for MUC corpora are due to inaccurate mention detection. We have therefore invested substantial efforts into our mention detection module.

Most state-of-the-art coreference resolution systems operate either on *gold* markables or on the output of an ACE-style mention detection module. We are not aware of extensive studies on mention extraction algorithms for such datasets as SemEval (OntoNotes) where mentions are complex NPs not constrained with respect to their semantic types.

We rely on the Stanford NLP toolkit for extracting named entities (Finkel et al., 2005) and parse trees for each sentence (Klein and Manning, 2003). We then merge the output of the NE-tagger and the parser to create a list of mentions in the following way:

1. Named entities are considered mentions if they correspond to a sequence of parsing constraints.

2. Pronouns are considered mentions if they are not a part of an NE-mention.

3. NPs are considered "candidate mentions" if they are not a part of an NE-mention. The set of

Proceedings of the 5th International Workshop on Semantic Evaluation, ACL 2010, pages 100–103,
Uppsala, Sweden, 15-16 July 2010.

candidate mentions is then filtered to eliminate pairs of NPs with the same head noun (coordinate NPs receive unique artificial heads). For possessive NPs we adjust the boundaries and the head to exclude the "'s" token. The remaining candidates are aligned with NE-mentions – if an NE and an NP have the same last word, they are considered the same mention of a special type. Finally, the list of candidates is optionally filtered using a small stop-list (for example, all the "there" NPs in "There is .." are discarded).

We rely on the Stanford NLP toolkit, WordNet and the U.S. census data to assign numerous properties to our mentions: semantic type, number, gender and others.

3 Features

Corry relies on two SVM[1] classifiers for *coreference* and *anaphoricity*. The former determines whether two given mentions M_i and M_j are coreferent or not. The latter determines whether a given mention M_i is anaphoric or discourse new. In Section 4 we show how these classifiers help us build coreference chains. We use the SVM-Light package (Joachims, 1999) for learning our classifiers.

The strength of our system lies in its rich feature set for the coreference classifier. In our previous studies (Uryupina, 2006; 2007) we have tested up to 351 nominal/continuous (1096 boolean/continuous) features showing significant improvements over basic feature sets advocated in the literature. For the SemEval task 1, we have reduced our rich feature set to 64 nominal/continuous features for efficiency reasons: on the one hand, our new set is large enough to cover complex linguistic patterns of coreference, on the other hand, it allows us to test different settings and investigate possibilities for global modeling.

Our *anaphoricity* classifier is used by the ILP model. It relies on 26 boolean/continuous features. More details on the classifier itself can be found in (Uryupina, 2003).

[1]Corry supports a number of machine learning algorithms: C4.5, TiMBL, Ripper, MaxEnt and SVM. See Uryupina (2006) for a comparison of Corry's performance with different learners.

4 Modeling

Corry supports both global and local views of coreference. Our evaluation experiments (cf. Section 5) show that the choice of a particular model should be motivated by the desired scoring metric.

Our local model of coreference is a reimplementation of the algorithm, proposed by Soon et al. (2001) with an extended feature set. The core of Soon et al.'s (2001) approach is a *link*-based classifier: it determines whether a given pair of markables are coreferent or not. During testing, a greedy clustering algorithm (link-first) is next used to build coreference chains on the output of the classifier.

We have slightly extended this model to allow separate classifiers for different *mention types*: each candidate anaphor receives a type (e.g. "pronoun") and is processed with a corresponding classifier. We, thus, rely on a family of classifiers, with the same feature set and the same machine learner. The exact definition of mention types is a parameter to be determined empirically on the development set.

Our global model is largely motivated by Denis and Baldridge (2007; 2008) and Finkel and Manning (2008). Following these studies, we use Integer Linear Programming to find the most globally optimal solution, given the decisions made by our *coreference* and *anaphoricity* classifiers.

In general, an ILP problem is determined by an objective function to be maximized (or minimized) and a set of task-specific constraints. The function is defined by costs $link_{<i,j>}$, and $dnew_j$ reflecting potential gains and losses for committing to specific variable assignments. We assume that costs can be positive (for pairs of markables that are likely to be coreferent) or negative (for pairs of markables that are unlikely to be coreferent). The costs are computed by an external module (such as a family of local classifiers described above). The objective function then takes the form:

$$max\Big(\sum_{<i,j>} link_{<i,j>} * L_{<i,j>} - \sum_{j} dnew_j * D_j\Big) \quad (1)$$

Binary variables $L_{<i,j>}$ indicate that two markables M_i and M_j are coreferent in the output assignment. Binary variables D_j indicate that the markable M_j is considered anaphoric in the output assignment. The ILP solver thus assigns values to

$L_{<i,j>}, \forall i,j : i < j$ and $D_j, \forall j$ whilst maximizing the objective in (1). We take the transitive closure of all the proposed $L_{<i,j>}$ to build the output partition.

Note that the objective in (1) is not constrained in any way and will thus allow illegal variable assignments. For example it does not constrain the assignment of L and D variables to be consistent with one another and does not enforce transitivity. The following constraints suggested in the literature (Denis and Baldridge, 2007; Denis and Baldridge, 2008; Finkel and Manning, 2008) ensure that these and other coreference properties are respected:

1. Best-link constraint

$$B : \sum_i L_{<i,j>} \leq 1, \forall j \tag{2}$$

2. Transitivity constraints

$$\forall i,j,k : i < j < k$$
$$T: \quad L_{<i,j>} + L_{<j,k>} - 1 \leq L_{<i,k>} \tag{3}$$
$$L: \quad L_{<j,k>} + L_{<i,k>} - 1 \leq L_{<i,j>} \tag{4}$$
$$R: \quad L_{<i,j>} + L_{<i,k>} - 1 \leq L_{<j,k>} \tag{5}$$

3. Anaphoricity constraints

$$A: \quad \textstyle\sum_i L_{<i,j>} >= D_j \, \forall j \tag{6}$$
$$D: \quad L_{<i,j>} \leq D_j \, \forall i,j \tag{7}$$

We refer the reader to the above-mentioned papers for detailed discussions of these constraints and their impact on coreference resolution. As we show in Section 5 below, the usability of a particular constraint should be determined experimentally based on the desired system behaviour.

5 Evaluation

5.1 Development

Corry has participated in the *gold* and *regular* open settings for English. We have collected a number of runs on the development data to optimize the performance level for a particular score: BLANC (Recasens and Hovy, in prep), MUC (Vilain et al., 1995) or CEAF (Luo, 2005). The runs differ with respect to the model (local vs. global with varying sets of constraints) and the definition of mention types. We deliberately left the B-CUBE score (Bagga and Baldwin, 1998) completely out of our preliminary experiments. The official SemEval scorer was used for these experiments.

Our experiments on the development set show that no configuration is able to produce equally reliable scores according to all the metrics (note, for example, that on the test set the BLANC difference between Corry-M and Corry-B in the *gold* setting is almost 10%). We believe that it is a challenging point for future research.

We have selected the best configurations for each score and submitted them as separate runs. The Corry-C system, optimized for CEAF-$\phi 4$, is a global model with the L, D and A constraints. For the *gold* setting, mention types are defined as pronouns and non-pronouns. For the *regular* setting, the system distinguishes between "speech" pronouns, 3rd person pronouns, names and nominals.

Corry-M, optimized for MUC, is a global model with the D constraint and separate classifiers for pronouns, names and nominals. Note that, compared to Corry-C, this setting allows for more coreference links – it is well known from the literature (cf., for example, Bagga and Baldwin (1998)) that the MUC metric is biased towards recall.

Finally, Corry-B, optimized for BLANC, is a local model that distinguishes between pronouns, nominals and names. The fact that such a simple model is able to outperform much more complex versions of Corry strengthens the importance of feature engineering.

5.2 Testing

Table 1 shows the SemEval task 1 scores for the gold/regular open setting. Corry has shown reliable performance for both mention detection and coreference resolution. For mention detection, Corry's F-score is 4% higher than the one of the competing approach. For coreference, all the Corry runs yielded the best performance level for a score under optimization.

Finally, for the B-CUBE metric that had not been optimized at all, Corry lost only marginally to the RelaxCor system in the gold setting and came first in the regular setting.

6 Conclusion

We have presented Corry – a system for coreference resolution in English. Our plans include extending it to cover multiple languages. However, as the main strength of Corry lies in its rich linguistically motivated feature set, this remains an issue.

	Mention detection			CEAF			MUC			B^3			BLANC		
	R	P	F1	R	P	F1	R	P	F1	R	P	F1	R	P	F1
Language: en, Information: open, Annotation: gold															
Corry-B	100	100	100	77.5	77.5	77.5	56.1	57.5	56.8	82.6	85.7	84.1	69.3	75.3	**71.8**
Corry-C	100	100	100	77.7	77.7	**77.7**	57.4	58.3	57.9	83.1	84.7	83.9	71.3	71.6	71.5
Corry-M	100	100	100	73.8	73.8	73.8	62.5	56.2	**59.2**	85.5	78.6	81.9	76.2	58.8	62.7
RelaxCor	100	100	100	75.8	75.8	75.8	22.6	70.5	34.2	75.2	96.7	**84.6**	58.0	83.8	62.7
Language: en, Information: open, Annotation: regular															
BART	76.1	69.8	72.8	70.1	64.3	67.1	62.8	52.4	57.1	74.9	67.7	71.1	55.3	73.2	57.7
Corry-B	79.8	76.4	**78.1**	70.4	67.4	68.9	55.0	54.2	54.6	73.7	74.1	**73.9**	57.1	75.7	**60.6**
Corry-C	79.8	76.4	**78.1**	70.9	67.9	**69.4**	54.7	55.5	55.1	73.8	73.1	73.5	57.4	63.8	59.4
Corry-M	79.8	76.4	**78.1**	66.3	63.5	64.8	61.5	53.4	**57.2**	76.8	66.5	71.3	58.5	56.2	57.1

Table 1: System scores for the gold/regular open setting. The best F-score for each metric shown in bold.

An important advantage of Corry is its flexibility: the system allows for a number of modeling solutions that can be tested on the development set to optimize the performance level for a particular objective. Our SemEval task 1 results confirm that a system might benefit a lot from a direct optimization for a given performance metric.

References

Amit Bagga and Breck Baldwin. 1998. Algorithms for scoring coreference chains. In *Proceedings of the Linguistic Coreference Workshop at the International Conference on Language Resources and Evaluation (LREC-1998)*, pages 563–566.

Pascal Denis and Jason Baldridge. 2007. Joint determination of anaphoricity and coreference resolution using integer programming. In *Proceedings of the Annual Meeting of the North American Chapter of the Association for Computational Linguistics - Human Language Technology Conference (NAACL/HLT-2007)*.

Pascal Denis and Jason Baldridge. 2008. Coreference with named entity classification and transitivity constraints and evaluation with MUC, B-CUBED, and CEAF. In *Proceedings of Corpus-Based Approaches to Coreference Resolution in Romance Languages (CBA 2008)*.

Jenny Rose Finkel and Christopher D. Manning. 2008. Enforcing transitivity in coreference resolution. In *Proceedings of the 46th Annual Meeting of the Association for Computational Linguistics (ACL 2008), Short Papers*, pages 45–48.

Jenny Rose Finkel, Trond Grenager, and Christopher Manning. 2005. Incorporating non-local information into information extraction systems by Gibbs sampling. In *Proceedings of the 43rd Annual Meeting of the Association for Computational Linguistics*, pages 363–370.

Thorsten Joachims. 1999. Making large-scale SVM learning practical. In B. Schölkopf, C. Burges, and A. Smola, editors, *Advances in Kernel Methods - Support Vector Learning*. MIT-Press.

Dan Klein and Christopher Manning. 2003. Accurate unlexicalized parsing. In *Proceedings of the 41st Annual Meeting of the Association for Computational Linguistics*, pages 423–430.

Xiaoqiang Luo. 2005. On coreference resolution performance metrics. In *Proceedings of the Annual Meeting of the North American Chapter of the Association for Computational Linguistics - Human Language Technology Conference (NAACL/HLT-2005)*, pages 25–32.

Marta Recasens and Eduard Hovy. in prep. BLANC: Implementing the rand index for coreference evaluation.

Marta Recasens, Lluís Màrquez, Emili Sapena, M.Antònia Martí, Mariona Taulé, Véronique Hoste, Massimo Poesio, and Yannick Versley. 2010. SemEval-2010 Task 1: Coreference resolution in multiple languages. In *Proceedings of the 5th International Workshop on Semantic Evaluations (SemEval-2010)*, Uppsala, Sweden.

Wee Meng Soon, Hwee Tou Ng, and Daniel Chung Yong Lim. 2001. A machine learning approach to coreference resolution of noun phrases. *Computational Linguistics (Special Issue on Computational Anaphora Resolution)*, 27(4):521–544.

Olga Uryupina. 2003. High-precision identification of discourse-new and unique noun phrases. In *Proceedings of the ACL'03 Student Workshop*, pages 80–86.

Olga Uryupina. 2006. Coreference resolution with and without linguistic knowledge. In *Proceedings of the Language Resources and Evaluation Conference*.

Olga Uryupina. 2007. *Knowledge Acquisition for Coreference Resolution*. Ph.D. thesis, Saarland University.

Olga Uryupina. 2008. Error analysis for learning-based coreference resolution. In *Proceedings of the Language Resources and Evaluation Conference*.

Marc Vilain, John Burger, John Aberdeen, Dennis Connolly, and Lynette Hirschman. 1995. A model-theoretic coreference scoring scheme. In *Proceedings of the 6th Message Understanding Conference*, pages 45–52.

BART: A Multilingual Anaphora Resolution System

Samuel Broscheit*, **Massimo Poesio**[‡], **Simone Paolo Ponzetto***, **Kepa Joseba Rodriguez**[‡], **Lorenza Romano**[†], **Olga Uryupina**[‡], **Yannick Versley**[◇], **Roberto Zanoli**[†]
*Seminar für Computerlinguistik, University of Heidelberg
[‡]CiMeC, University of Trento
[†]Fondazione Bruno Kessler
[◇]SFB 833, University of Tübingen
broscheit@cl.uni-heidelberg.de, massimo.poesio@unitn.it,
ponzetto@cl.uni-heidelberg.de, kepa.rodriguez@unitn.it,
romano@fbk.eu, uryupina@gmail.com,
versley@sfs.uni-tuebingen.de, zanoli@fbk.eu

Abstract

BART (Versley et al., 2008) is a highly modular toolkit for coreference resolution that supports state-of-the-art statistical approaches and enables efficient feature engineering. For the SemEval task 1 on Coreference Resolution, BART runs have been submitted for German, English, and Italian.

BART relies on a maximum entropy-based classifier for pairs of mentions. A novel entity-mention approach based on Semantic Trees is at the moment only supported for English.

1 Introduction

This paper presents a multilingual coreference resolution system based on BART (Versley et al., 2008). BART is a modular toolkit for coreference resolution that supports state-of-the-art statistical approaches to the task and enables efficient feature engineering. BART has originally been created and tested for English, but its flexible modular architecture ensures its portability to other languages and domains. In SemEval-2010 task 1 on Coreference Resolution, BART has shown reliable performance for English, German and Italian.

In our SemEval experiments, we mainly focus on extending BART to cover multiple languages. Given a corpus in a new language, one can re-train BART to obtain baseline results. Such a language-agnostic system, however, is only used as a starting point: substantial improvements can be achieved by incorporating language-specific information with the help of the *Language Plugin*. This design provides effective separation between linguistic and machine learning aspects of the problem.

2 BART Architecture

The BART toolkit has five main components: preprocessing pipeline, mention factory, feature extraction module, decoder and encoder. In addition, an independent *LanguagePlugin* module handles all the language specific information and is accessible from any component. The architecture is shown on Figure 1. Each module can be accessed independently and thus adjusted to leverage the system's performance on a particular language or domain.

The preprocessing pipeline converts an input document into a set of lingustic layers, represented as separate XML files. The mention factory uses these layers to extract mentions and assign their basic properties (number, gender etc). The feature extraction module describes pairs of mentions $\{M_i, M_j\}$, $i < j$ as a set of features.

The decoder generates training examples through a process of sample selection and learns a pairwise classifier. Finally, the encoder generates testing examples through a (possibly distinct) process of sample selection, runs the classifier and partitions the mentions into coreference chains.

3 Language-specific issues

Below we briefly describe our language-specific extensions to BART. These issues are addressed in more details in our recent papers (Broscheit et al., 2010; Poesio et al., 2010).

3.1 Mention Detection

Robust mention detection is an essential component of any coreference resolution system. BART supports different pipelines for mention detection. The

Proceedings of the 5th International Workshop on Semantic Evaluation, ACL 2010, pages 104–107,
Uppsala, Sweden, 15-16 July 2010.

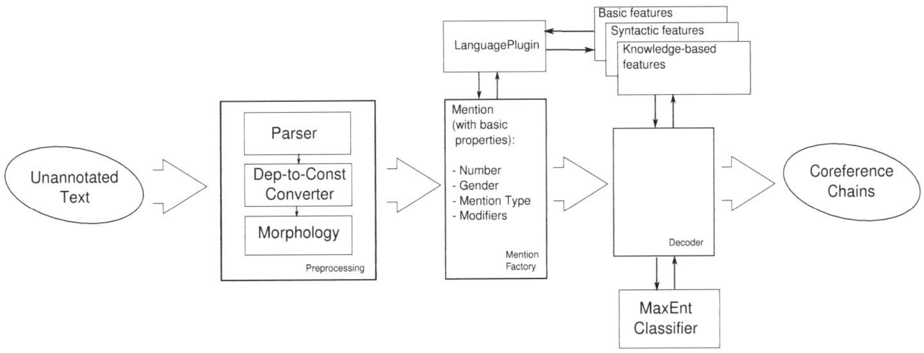

Figure 1: BART architecture

choice of a pipeline depends crucially on the availability of linguistic resources for a given language.

For English and German, we use the *Parsing Pipeline and Mention Factory* to extract mentions. The parse trees are used to identify minimal and maximal noun projections, as well as additional features such as number, gender, and semantic class.

For **English**, we use parses from a state-of-the-art constituent parser (Petrov et al., 2006) and extract all base noun phrases as mentions. For **German**, the SemEval dependency tree is transformed to a constituent representation and minimal and maximal phrases are extracted for all nominal elements (pronouns, common nouns, names), except when the noun phrase is in a non-referring syntactic position (for example, expletive "es", predicates in copula constructions).

For **Italian**, we use the *EMD Pipeline and Mention Factory*. The Typhoon (Zanoli et al., 2009) and DEMention (Biggio et al., 2009) systems were used to recognize mentions in the test set. For each mention, its head and extension were considered. The extension was learned by using the mention annotation provided in the training set (13th column) whereas the head annotation was learned by exploiting the information produced by MaltParser (Nivre et al., 2007). In addition to the features extracted from the training set, such as prefixes and suffixes (1-4 characters) and orthographic information (capitalization and hyphenation), a number of features extracted by using external resources were used: mentions recognized by TextPro (http://textpro.fbk.eu), gazetteers of generic proper nouns extracted from the Italian phone-book and Wikipedia, and other features derived from WordNet. Each of these features was extracted in a local context of ± 2 words.

3.2 Features

We view coreference resolution as a binary classification problem. Each classification instance consists of two markables, i.e. an anaphor and potential antecedent. Instances are modeled as feature vectors (cf. Table 1) and are handed over to a binary classifier that decides, given the features, whether the anaphor and the candidate are coreferent or not. All the feature values are computed automatically, without any manual intervention.

Basic feature set. We use the same set of relatively language-independent features as a backbone of our system, extending it with a few language-specific features for each subtask. Most of them are used by virtually all the state-of-the-art coreference resolution systems. A detailed description can be found, for example, in (Soon et al., 2001).

English. Our English system is based on a novel model of coreference. The key concept of our model is a *Semantic Tree* – a filecard associated with each discourse entity containing the following fields:

- **Types:** the list of types for mentions of a given entity. For example, if an entity contains the mention "software from India", the shallow predicate "software" is added to the types.
- **Attributes:** this field collects the premodifiers. For instance, if one of the mentions is "the expensive software" the shallow attribute "expensive" is added to the list of attributes.
- **Relations:** this field collects the prepositional postmodifiers. If an entity contains the mention "software from India", the shallow relation "from(India)" is added to the list of relations.

For each mention BART creates such a filecard using syntactic information. If the classifier decides that both mentions are corefering, the filecard of the anaphora is merged into the filecard of the antecedent (cf. Section 3.3 below).

The `SemanticTreeCompatibility` feature extractor checks whether individual slots of the anaphor's filecard are compatible with those of the antecedent's.

The `StrudelRelatedness` feature relies on Strudel – a distributional semantic model (Baroni et al., 2010). We compute Strudel vectors for the sets of types of the anaphor and the antecedent. The relatedness value is determined as the cosine between the two.

German. We have tested extra features for German in our previous study (Broscheit et al., 2010).

The `NodeDistance` feature measures the number of clause nodes (SIMPX, R-SIMPX) and prepositional phrase nodes (PX) along the path between M_j and M_i in the parse tree.

The `PartialMorphMatch` feature is a substring match with a morphological extension for common nouns. In German the frequent use of noun composition makes a simple string match for common nouns unfeasible. The feature checks for a match between the noun stems of M_i and M_j. We extract the morphology with SMOR/Morphisto (Schmid et al., 2004).

The `GermanetRelatedness` feature uses the Pathfinder library for GermaNet (Finthammer and Cramer, 2008) that computes and discretizes raw scores into three categories of semantic relatedness. In our experiments we use the measure from Wu and Palmer (1994), which has been found to be the best performing on our development data.

Italian. We have designed a feature to cover Italian aliasing patterns. A list of company/person designators (e.g., "S.p.a" or "D.ssa") has been manually crafted. We have collected patterns of name variants for locations. Finally, we have relaxed abbreviation constraints, allowing for lower-case characters in the abbreviations. Our pilot experiments suggest that, although a universal aliasing algorithm is able to resolve some coreference links between NEs, creating a language-specific module boosts the system's performance for Italian substantially.

Basic feature set
MentionType(M_i),MentionType(M_j) SemanticClass(M_i), SemanticClass(M_j) GenderAgreement(M_i,M_j) NumberAgreement(M_i,M_j) AnimacyAgreement(M_i,M_j) StringMatch(M_i,M_j) Distance(M_i,M_j)
Basic features used for English and Italian
Alias(M_i,M_j) Apposition(M_i,M_j) FirstMention(M_i)
English
IsSubject(M_i) SemanticTreeCompatibility(M_i,M_j) StrudelRelatedness(M_i,M_j)
German
InQuotedSpeech(M_i), InQuotedSpeech(M_j) NodeDistance(M_i,M_j) PartialMorphMatch(M_i,M_j) GermanetRelatedness(M_i,M_j)
Italian
AliasItalian(M_i,M_j)

Table 1: Features used by BART: each feature describes a pair of mentions $\{M_i, M_j\}$, $i < j$, where M_i is a candidate antecedent and M_j is a candidate anaphor

3.3 Resolution Algorithm

The BART toolkit supports several models of coreference (pairwise modeling, rankers, semantic trees), as well as different machine learning algorithms. Our final setting relies on a pairwise maximum entropy classifier for Italian and German.

Our English system is based on an entity-mention model of coreference. The key concept of our model is a Semantic Tree - a filecard associated to each discourse entity (cf. Section 3.2). Semantic trees are used for both computing feature values and guiding the resolution process.

We start by creating a Semantic Tree for each mention. We process the document from left to right, trying to find an antecedent for each mention (candidate anaphor). When the antecedent is found, we extend its Semantic Tree with the types, attributes and relations of the anaphor, provided they are mutually compatible. Consider, for example, a list of mentions, containing, among others, "software from India", "the software" and "software from China". Initially, BART creates the following semantic trees: "(type: software) (relation: from(India))", "(type: software)" and "(type: software) (relation: from(China))". When the second mention gets resolved to the first one, their semantic trees are merged to "(type: software) (relation: from(India)". Therefore, when we attempt to resolve the third mention, both candidate antecedents are rejected, as their relation attributes are incompatible with "from(China)". This approach helps us avoid erroneous links (such as the link between the second and the third mentions in our example) by leveraging entity-level information.

4 Evaluation

The system was evaluated on the SemEval task 1 corpus by using the SemEval scorer.

First, we have evaluated our mention detection modules: the system's ability to recognize both the mention extensions and the heads in the *regular* setting. BART has achieved the best score for mention detection in German and has shown reliable figures for English. For Italian, the moderate performance level is due to the different algorithms for identifying the heads: the MaltParser (trained on TUT: http://www.di.unito.it/tutreeb) produces a more semantic representation, while the SemEval scorer seems to adopt a more syntactic approach.

Second, we have evaluated the quality of our coreference resolution modules. For German, BART has shown better performance than all the other systems on the *regular* track.

For English, the only language targeted by all systems, BART shows good performance over all metrics in the *regular* setting, usually only outperformed by systems that were tuned to a particular metric.

Finally, the Italian version of BART shows reliable figures for coreference resolution, given the mention alignment problem discussed above.

5 Conclusion

We have presented BART – a multilingual toolkit for coreference resolution. Due to its highly modular architecture, BART allows for efficient language-specific feature engineering. Our effort represents the first steps towards building a freely available coreference resolution system for many languages.

References

Marco Baroni, Brian Murphy, Eduard Barbu, and Massimo Poesio. 2010. Strudel: A corpus-based semantic model based on properties and types. *Cognitive Science*, 34(2):222–254.

Silvana Marianela Bernaola Biggio, Claudio Giuliano, Massimo Poesio, Yannick Versley, Olga Uryupina, and Roberto Zanoli. 2009. Local entity detection and recognition task. In *Proc. of Evalita-09*.

Samuel Broscheit, Simone Paolo Ponzetto, Yannick Versley, and Massimo Poesio. 2010. Extending BART to provide a coreference resolution system for German. In *Proc. of LREC '10*.

Marc Finthammer and Irene Cramer. 2008. Exploring and navigating: Tools for GermaNet. In *Proc. of LREC '08*.

Joakim Nivre, Johan Hall, Jens Nilsson, Atanas Chanev, Gulsen Eryigit, Sandra Kübler, Svetoslav Marinov, and Erwin Marsi. 2007. Maltparser: A language-independent system for data-driven dependency parsing. *Natural Language Engineering*, 13(2):95–135.

Slav Petrov, Leon Barett, Romain Thibaux, and Dan Klein. 2006. Learning accurate, compact, and interpretable tree annotation. In *Proc. of COLING-ACL-06*.

Massimo Poesio, Olga Uryupina, and Yannick Versley. 2010. Creating a coreference resolution system for Italian. In *Proc. of LREC '10*.

Helmut Schmid, Arne Fitschen, and Ulrich Heid. 2004. SMOR: A German computational morphology covering derivation, composition and inflection. In *Proc. of LREC '04*.

Wee Meng Soon, Hwee Tou Ng, and Daniel Chung Yong Lim. 2001. A machine learning approach to coreference resolution of noun phrases. *Computational Linguistics (Special Issue on Computational Anaphora Resolution)*, 27(4):521–544.

Yannick Versley, Simone Paolo Ponzetto, Massimo Poesio, Vladimir Eidelman, Alan Jern, Jason Smith, Xiaofeng Yang, and Alessandro Moschitti. 2008. BART: A modular toolkit for coreference resolution. In *Proceedings of the Linguistic Coreference Workshop at the International Conference on Language Resources and Evaluation (LREC-2008)*.

Zhibiao Wu and Martha Palmer. 1994. Verb semantics and lexical selection. In *Proc. of ACL-94*, pages 133–138.

Roberto Zanoli, Emiliano Pianta, and Claudio Giuliano. 2009. Named entity recognition through redundancy driven classifier. In *Proc. of Evalita-09*.

TANL-1: Coreference Resolution by Parse Analysis and Similarity Clustering

Giuseppe Attardi
Dipartimento di Informatica
Università di Pisa
Largo B. Pontecorvo, 3
attardi@di.unipi.it

Stefano Dei Rossi
Dipartimento di Informatica
Università di Pisa
Largo B. Pontecorvo, 3
deirossi@di.unipi.it

Maria Simi
Dipartimento di Informatica
Università di Pisa
Largo B. Pontecorvo, 3
simi@di.unipi.it

Abstract

Our submission to the Semeval 2010 task on coreference resolution in multiple languages is based on parse analysis and similarity clustering. The system uses a binary classifier, based on Maximum Entropy, to decide whether or not there is a relationship between each pair of mentions extracted from a textual document. Mention detection is based on the analysis of the dependency parse tree.

1 Overview

Coreference resolution can be described as the problem of clustering noun phrases (NP), also called *mentions*, into sets referring to the same discourse entity.

The "Coreference Resolution in Multiple Languages task" at SemEval-2010 is meant to assess different machine learning techniques in a multilingual context, and by means of different evaluation metrics. Two different scenarios are considered: a *gold standard* scenario (only available for Catalan and Spanish), where correct mention boundaries are provided to the participants, and a *regular* scenario, where mention boundaries are to be inferred from other linguistic annotations provided in the input data. In particular the linguistic annotations provided for each token in a sentence are: position in sentence (ID), word (TOKEN), lemma and predicted lemma (LEMMA and PLEMMA), morphosyntactic information, both gold and/or predicted (POS and PPOS, FEAT and PFEAT), dependency parsing annotations (HEAD and PHEAD, DEPREL and PDEPREL), named entities (NE and PNE), and semantic roles (PRED, PPRED, and corresponding roles in the following columns). In the gold scenario, mention boundaries annotations (in column COREF) can also be used as input.

Our approach to the task was to split coreference resolution into two sub-problems: mention identification and creation of entities. Mention recognition was based on the analysis of parse trees produced from input data, which were produced by manual annotation or state-of-the-art dependency parsers. Once the mentions are identified, coreference resolution involves partitioning them into subsets corresponding to the same entity. This problem is cast into the binary classification problem of deciding whether two given mentions are coreferent. A Maximum Entropy classifier is trained to predict how likely two mentions refer to the same entity. This is followed by a greedy procedure whose purpose is to cluster mentions into entities.

According to Ng (2005), most learning based coreference systems can be defined by four elements: the *learning algorithm* used to train the coreference classifier, the *method of creating training instances* for the learner, the *feature set* used to represent a training or test instance, and the *clustering algorithm* used to coordinate the coreference classification decisions. In the following we will detail our approach by making explicit the strategies used in each of above mentioned components.

The data model used by our system is based on the concepts of *entity* and *mention*. The collection of mentions referring to the same object in a document forms an *entity*. A mention is an instance referring to an object: it is represented by the *start* and *end* positions in a sentence, a type and a sequence number. For convenience it also contains a frequency count and a reference to the containing sentence.

Proceedings of the 5th International Workshop on Semantic Evaluation, ACL 2010, pages 108–111,
Uppsala, Sweden, 15-16 July 2010.

2 Mention detection

The first stage of the coreference resolution process tries to identify the occurrence of mentions in documents.

In the training phase mentions are obtained from the NE (or PNE) column of the corpus and are partitioned into entities using the information provided in the COREF column.

In the regular setting, we used an algorithm for predicting boundaries that relies on the parse tree of the sentence produced from the gold annotations in columns HEAD and DEP, if available, or else from columns PHEAD and PDEP, the output of a dependency parser provided as input data.

This analysis relied on minimal language knowledge, in order to determine possible heads of sub-trees counting as mentions, i.e. noun phrases or adverbial phrases referring to quantities, times and locations. POS tags and morphological features, when available, were mostly taken into account in determining mention heads. The leaves of the sub-trees of each detected head were collected as possible mentions.

The mentions identified by the NE column were then added to this set, discarding duplicates or partial overlaps. Partial overlaps in principle should not occur, but were present occasionally in the data. When this occurred, we applied a strategy to split them into a pair of mentions.

The same mention detection strategy was used also in the gold task, where we could have just returned the boundaries present in the data, scoring 100% in accuracy. This explains the small loss in accuracy we achieved in mention identification in the gold setting.

Relying on parse trees turned out to be quite effective, especially for languages where gold parses where available. For some other languages, the strategy was less effective. This was due to different annotation policies across different languages, and, in part, to inconsistencies in the data. For example in the Italian data set, named entities may include prepositions, which are typically the head of the noun phrase, while our strategy of looking for noun heads leaves the preposition out of the mention boundaries. Moreover this strategy obviously fails when mentions span across sentences as was the case, again, for Italian.

3 Determining coreference

For determining which mentions belong to the same entity, we applied a machine learning technique. We trained a Maximum Entropy classifier written in Python (Le, 2004) to determine whether two mentions refer to the same entity.

We did do not make any effort to optimize the number of training instances for the pair-wise learner: a positive instance is created for each anaphoric NP, paired with each of its antecedents with the same number, and a negative instance is created by pairing each NP with each of its preceding non-coreferent noun phrases.

The classifier is trained using the following features, extracted for each pair of mentions.

Lexical features

- *Same:* whether two mentions are equal;
- *Prefix:* whether one mention is a prefix of the other;
- *Suffix:* whether one mention is a suffix of the other;
- *Acronym:* whether one mention is the acronym of the other.
- *Edit distance:* quantized editing distance between two mentions.

Distance features

- *Sentence distance:* quantized distance between the sentences containing the two mentions;
- *Token distance:* quantized distance between the start tokens of the two mentions;
- *Mention distance:* quantized number of other mentions between two mentions.

Syntax features

- *Head:* whether the heads of two mentions have the same POS;
- *Head POS:* pairs of POS of the two mentions heads;

Count features

- *Count*: pairs of quantized numbers, each counting how many times a mention occurs.

Type features

- *Type*: whether two mentions have the same associated NE (Named Entity) type.

Pronoun features

When the most recent mention is a pronominal anaphora, the following features are extracted:

- *Gender*: pair of attributes {female, male or undetermined};
- *Number*: pair of attributes {singular, plural, undetermined};
- *Pronoun type*: this feature is language dependent and represents the type of pronominal mention, i.e. whether the pronoun is *reflexive*, *possessive*, *relative*, …

In the submitted run we used the GIS (Generalized Iterative Scaling) algorithm for parameter estimation, with 600 iterations, which appeared to provide better results than using L-BFGS (a limited-memory algorithm for unconstrained optimization). Training times ranged from one minute for German to 8 minutes for Italian, hence the slower speed of GIS was not an issue.

3.1 Entity creation

The mentions detected in the first phase were clustered, according to the output of the classifier, using a greedy clustering algorithm.

Each mention is compared to all previous mentions, which are collected in a global mentions table. If the pair-wise classifier assigns a probability greater than a given threshold to the fact that a new mention belongs to a previously identified entity, it is assigned to that entity. In case more than one entity has a probability greater than the threshold, the mention is assigned to the one with highest probability. This strategy has been described as *best-first clustering* by Ng (2005).

In principle the process is not optimal since, once a mention is assigned to an entity, it cannot be later assigned to another entity to which it more likely refers. Luo et al. (2004) propose an approach based on the Bell tree to address this problem. Despite this potential limitation, our system performed quite well.

4 Data preparation

We used the data as supplied by the task organizers for all languages except Italian. A modified version of the Hunpos tagger (Halácsy, Kornai & Oravecz, 2007; Attardi et al., 2009) was used to add to the Italian training and development corpora more accurate POS tags than those supplied, as well as missing information about morphology. The POS tagger we used, in fact is capable of tagging sentences with detailed POS tags, which include morphological information; this was added to column PFEATS in the data. Just for this reason our submission for Italian is to be considered an open task submission.

The Italian training corpus appears to contain several errors related to mention boundaries. In particular there are cases of entities starting in a sentence and ending in the following one. This appears to be due to sentence splitting (for instance at semicolons) performed after named entities had been tagged. As explained in section 2, our system was not prepared to deal with these situations.

Other errors in the annotations of entities occurred in the Italian test data, in particular incorrect balancing of openings and closings named entities, which caused problems to our submission. We could only complete the run after the deadline, so we could only report unofficial results for Italian.

5 Results

We submitted results to the gold and regular challenges for the following languages: Catalan, English, German and Spanish.

Table 1 summarizes the performance of our system, according to the different accuracy scores for the gold task, Table 2 for the regular task. We have outlined in bold the cases where we achieved the best scores among the participating systems.

	Mention	CEAF	MUC	B^3	BLANC
Catalan	98.4	64.9	26.5	76.2	54.4
German	**100**	**77.7**	25.9	**85.9**	57.4
English	89.8	67.6	24.0	73.4	52.1
Spanish	98.4	65.8	25.7	76.8	54.1

Table 1. Gold task, Accuracy scores.

	Mention	CEAF	MUC	B^3	BLANC
Catalan	**82.7**	**57.1**	22.9	**64.6**	51.0
German	59.2	49.5	15.4	50.7	44.7
English	73.9	57.3	24.6	61.3	49.3
Spanish	**83.1**	**59.3**	21.7	**66.0**	**51.4**

Table 2. Regular task. Accuracy scores.

6 Error analysis

We performed some preliminary error analysis. The goal was to identify systematic errors and possible corrections for improving the performance of our system.

We limited our analysis to the mention boundaries detection for the regular tasks. A similar analysis for coreference detection, would require the availability of gold test data.

7 Mention detection errors

As described above, the strategy used for the extraction of mentions boundaries is based on dependency parse trees and named entities. This proved to be a good strategy in some languages such as Catalan (F1 score: 82.7) and Spanish (F1 score: 83.1) in which the dependency data available in the corpora were very accurate and consistent with the annotation of named entities. Instead, there have been unexpected problems in other languages like English or German, where the dependencies information were annotated using a different approach.

For German, while we achieved the best B^3 accuracy on coreference analysis in the gold settings, we had a quite low accuracy in mention detection (F1: 59.2), which was responsible of a significant drop in coreference accuracy for the regular task. This degradation in performance was mainly due to punctuations, which in German are linked to the sub-tree containing the noun phrase rather than to the root of the sentence or tokens outside the noun phrase, as it happens in Catalan and Spanish. This misled our mention detection algorithm to create many mentions with wrong boundaries, just because punctuation marks were included.

In the English corpus different conventions were apparently used for dependency parsing and named entity annotations (Table 3), which produced discrepancies between the boundaries of the named entities present in the data and those predicted by our algorithm. This in turn affected negatively the coreference detection algorithm that uses both types of information.

ID	TOKEN	HEAD	DEPREL	NE	COREF
1	Defense	2	NAME	(org)	(25
2	Secretary	4	NMOD	_	_
3	William	4	NAME	(person	_
4	Cohen	5	SBJ	person)	25)

Table 3. Example of different conventions for NE and COREF in the English corpus.

Error analysis also has shown that further improvements could be obtained, for all languages, by using more accurate language specific extraction rules. For example, we missed to consider a number of specific POS tags as possible identifiers for the head of noun phrases. By some simple tuning of the algorithm we obtained some improvements.

8 Conclusions

We reported our experiments on coreference resolution in multiple languages. We applied an approach based on analyzing the parse trees in order to detect mention boundaries and a Maximum Entropy classifier to cluster mentions into entities.

Despite a very simplistic approach, the results were satisfactory and further improvements are possible by tuning the parameters of the algorithms.

References

G. Attardi et al., 2009. Tanl (Text Analytics and Natural Language Processing). SemaWiki project: http://medialab.di.unipi.it/wiki/SemaWiki.

P. Halácsy, A. Kornai, and C. Oravecz, 2007. HunPos: an open source trigram tagger. *Proceedings of the ACL 2007*, Prague.

Z. Le, Maximum Entropy Modeling Toolkit for Pytho and C++, Reference Manual.

X. Luo, A. Ittycheriah, H. Jing, N. Kambhatla & S. Roukos. 2004. A Mention-Synchronous Coreference Resolution Algorithm Based on the Bell Tree. *Proceedings of the ACL 2004*, Barcelona.

V. Ng, Machine Learning for Coreference Resolution: From Local Classification to Global Ranking, *Proceedings of the 43rd Annual Meeting of the Association for Computational Linguistics* (ACL), Ann Arbor, MI, June 2005, pp. 157-164.

M. Recasens, L. Màrquez, E. Sapena, M. A. Martí, M. Taulé, V. Hoste, M. Poesio and Y. Versley, SemEval-2010 Task 1: Coreference resolution in multiple languages, in Proceedings of the 5th International Workshop on Semantic Evaluations (SemEval-2010), Uppsala, Sweden, 2010.

FCC: Modeling Probabilities with GIZA++ for Task #2 and #3 of SemEval-2

Darnes Vilariño, Carlos Balderas, David Pinto, Miguel Rodríguez, Saul León
Faculty of Computer Science, BUAP
Puebla, Mexico
{darnes,mrodriguez,dpinto}@cs.buap.mx

Abstract

In this paper we present a naïve approach to tackle the problem of cross-lingual WSD and cross-lingual lexical substitution which correspond to the Task #2 and #3 of the SemEval-2 competition. We used a bilingual statistical dictionary, which is calculated with Giza++ by using the EUROPARL parallel corpus, in order to calculate the probability of a source word to be translated to a target word (which is assumed to be the correct sense of the source word but in a different language). Two versions of the probabilistic model are tested: unweighted and weighted. The obtained values show that the unweighted version performs better thant the weighted one.

1 Introduction

Word Sense Disambiguation (WSD) is considered one of the most important problems in Natural Language Processing (Agirre and Edmonds, 2006). It is claimed that WSD is essential for those applications that require of language comprehension modules such as search engines, machine translation systems, automatic answer machines, second life agents, etc. Moreover, with the huge amounts of information in Internet and the fact that this information is continuosly growing in different languages, we are encourage to deal with cross-lingual scenarios where WSD systems are also needed. Despite the WSD task has been studied for a long time, the expected feeling is that WSD should be integrated into real applications such as mono and multi-lingual search engines, machine translation systems, automatic answer machines, etc (Agirre and Edmonds, 2006). Different studies on this issue have demonstrated that those applications benefit from WSD, such as in the case of machine translation (Chan et al., 2007; Carpuat and Wu., 2007). On the other hand, Lexical Substitution (LS) refers to the process of finding a substitute word for a source word in a given sentence. The LS task needs to be approached by firstly disambiguating the source word, therefore, these two tasks (WSD and LS) are somehow related.

Since we are describing the modules of our system, we did not provide information of the datasets used. For details about the corpora, see the task description paper for both tasks (#2 and #3) in this volume (Mihalcea et al., 2010; Lefever and Hoste, 2010). Description about the other teams are also described in the same papers.

2 A Naïve Approach to WSD and LS

In this section it is presented an overview of the presented system, but also we further discuss the particularities of the general approach for each task evaluated. We will start this section by explaining the manner we deal with the Cross-Lingual Word Sense Disambiguation (C-WSD) problem.

2.1 Cross-Lingual Word Sense Disambiguation

We have approached the cross-lingual word sense disambiguation task by means of a probabilistic system which considers the probability of a word sense (in a target language), given a sentence (in a source language) containing the ambiguous word. In particular, we used the Naive Bayes classifier in two different ways. First, we calculated the probability of each word in the source language of being associated/translated to the corresponding word (in the target language). The probabilities were estimated by means of a bilingual statistical dictionary which is calculated using the Giza++ system over the EUROPARL parallel corpus. We filtered this corpus by selecting only those sen-

Proceedings of the 5th International Workshop on Semantic Evaluation, ACL 2010, pages 112–116,
Uppsala, Sweden, 15-16 July 2010. ©2010 Association for Computational Linguistics

tences which included some senses of the ambiguous word which were obtained by translating this ambiguous word on the Google search engine.

In Figure 1 we may see the complete process for approaching the problem of cross-lingual WSD.

The second approach considered a weighted probability for each word in the source sentence. The closer a word of the sentence to the ambiguous word, the higher the weight given to it.

In other words, given an English sentence $S = \{w_1, w_2, \cdots, w_k, \cdots, w_{k+1}, \cdots\}$ with the ambiguous word w_k in position k. Let us consider N candidate translations of w_k, $\{t_1^k, t_2^k, \cdots, t_N^k\}$ obtained somehow (we will further discuss about this issue in this section). We are insterested on finding the most probable candidate translations for the polysemous word w_k. Therefore, we may use a Naïve Bayes classifier which considers the probability of t_i^k given w_k. A formal description of the classifier is given as follows.

$$p(t_i^k|S) = p(t_i^k|w_1, w_2, \cdots, w_k, \cdots) \quad (1)$$

$$p(t_i^k|S) = \frac{p(t_i^k)p(w_1, w_2, \cdots, w_k, \cdots|t_i^k)}{p(w_1, w_2, \cdots, w_k, \cdots)} \quad (2)$$

We are interested on finding the argument that maximizes $p(t_i^k|S)$, therefore, we may to calculate the denominator. Moreover, if we assume that all the different translations are equally distributed, then Eq. (2) may be approximated by Eq. (3).

$$p(t_i^k|w_1, w_2, \cdots, w_k, \cdots) \approx p(w_1, w_2, \cdots, w_k, \cdots|t_i^k) \quad (3)$$

The complete calculation of Eq. (3) requires to apply the chain rule. However, if we assumed that the words of the sentence are independent, then we may rewrite Eq. (3) as Eq. (4).

$$p(t_i^k|w_1, w_2, \cdots, w_k, \cdots) \approx \prod_{j=1}^{|S|} p(w_j|t_i^k) \quad (4)$$

The best translation is obtained as shown in Eq. (5). Nevertheless the position of the ambiguous word, we are only considering a product of the probabilites of translation. Thus, we named this approach, the *unweighted version*. Algorithm 1 provides details about the implementation.

$$BestSense_u(w_k) = \arg\max_{t_i^k} \prod_{j=1}^{|S|} p(w_j|t_i^k) \quad (5)$$

with $i = 1, \cdots, N$.

Algorithm 1: An unweighted naïve Bayes approach to cross-lingual WSD

Input: A set Q of sentences:
$Q = \{S_1, S_2, \cdots\}$;
$Dictionary = p(w|t)$: A bilingual statistical dictionary;
Output: The best word/sense for each ambiguous word $w_j \in S_l$

for $l = 1$ *to* $|Q|$ **do**
  for $i = 1$ *to* N **do**
    $P_{l,i} = 1$;
    for $j = 1$ *to* $|S_l|$ **do**
      foreach $w_j \in S_l$ **do**
        if $w_j \in Dictionary$ **then**
          $P_{l,i} = P_{l,i} * p(w_j|t_i^k)$;
        else
          $P_{l,i} = P_{l,i} * \epsilon$;
        end
      end
    end
  end
end
return $\arg\max_{t_i^k} \prod_{j=1}^{|S|} p(w_j|t_i^k)$

A second approach (*weighted version*) is also proposed as shown in Eq. (6). Algorithm 2 provides details about its implementation.

$$BestSense_w(w_k) =$$

$$\arg\max_{t_i^k} \prod_{j=1}^{|S|} p(w_j|t_i^k) * \frac{1}{k-j+1} \quad (6)$$

With respect to the N candidate translations of the polysemous word w_k, $\{t_1^k, t_2^k, \cdots, t_N^k\}$, we have used of the Google translator[1]. Google provides all the possible translations for w_k with the corresponding grammatical category. Therefore, we are able to use those translations that match with the same grammatical category of the

[1] http://translate.google.com.mx/

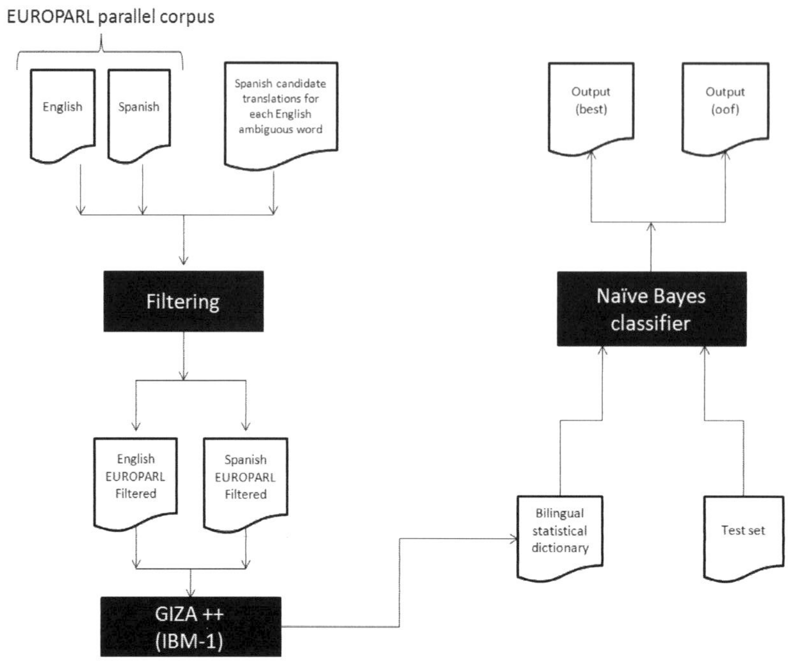

Figure 1: An overview of the presented approach for cross-lingual word sense disambiguation

---

Algorithm 2: A weighted naïve Bayes approach to cross-lingual WSD

Input: A set Q of sentences: $Q = \{S_1, S_2, \cdots\}$;
$Dictionary = p(w|t)$: A bilingual statistical dictionary;
Output: The best word/sense for each ambiguous word $w_j \in S_l$

for $l = 1$ *to* $|Q|$ **do**
  for $i = 1$ *to* N **do**
    $P_{l,i} = 1$;
    for $j = 1$ *to* $|S_l|$ **do**
      foreach $w_j \in S_l$ **do**
        if $w_j \in Dictionary$ **then**
          $P_{l,i} = P_{l,i} * p(w_j|t_i^k) * \frac{1}{k-j+1}$;
        else
          $P_{l,i} = P_{l,i} * \epsilon$;
        end
      end
    end
  end
end
return $\arg\max_{t_i^k} \prod_{j=1}^{|S|} p(w_j|t_i^k) * \frac{1}{k-j+1}$

---

ambiguous word. Even if we attempted other approaches such as selecting the most probable translations from the statistical dictionary, we confirmed that by using the Google online translator we obtain the best results. We consider that this result is derived from the fact that Google has a better language model than we have, because our bilingual statistical dictionary was trained only with the EUROPARL parallel corpus.

The experimental results of both, the *unweighted* and the *weighted* versions of the presented approach for cross-lingual word sense disambiguation are given in Section 3.

2.2 Cross-Lingual Lexical Substitution

This module is based on the cross-lingual word sense disambiguation system. Once we knew the best word/sense (Spanish) for the ambiguous word(English), we lemmatized the Spanish word. Thereafter, we searched, at WordNet, the synonyms of this word (sense) that agree with the grammatical category (noun, verb, etc) of the query (source polysemous word), and we return those synonyms as possible lexical substitutes. Notice again that this task is complemented by the WSD solver.

In Figure 2 we may see the complete process of approaching the problem of cross-lingual lexical substitution.

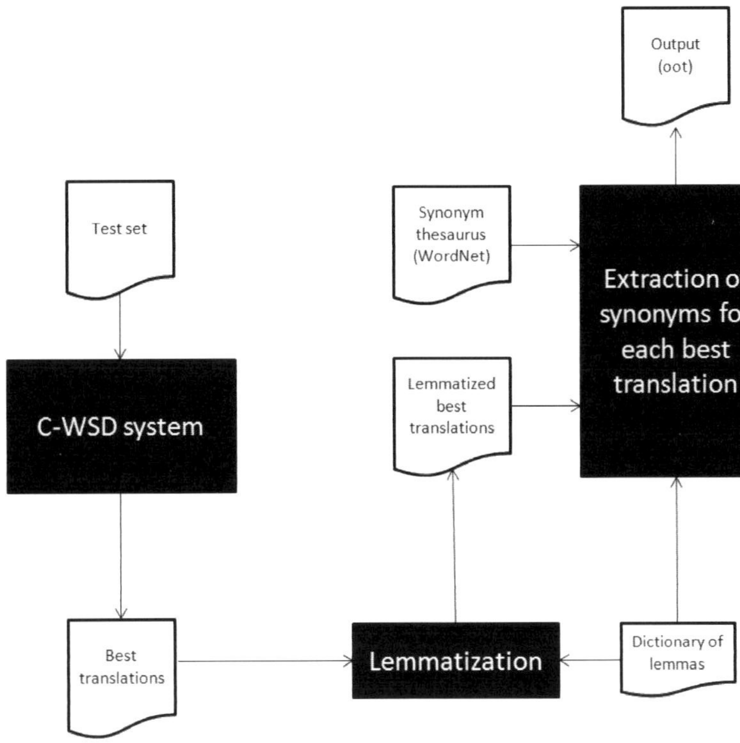

Figure 2: An overview of the presented approach for cross-lingual lexical substitution

3 Experimental Results

In this section we present the obtained results for both, the cross-lingual word sense disambiguation task and the cross-lingual lexical substitution task.

3.1 Cross-Lingual Word Sense Disambiguation

In Table 2 we may see the results we have obtained with the different versions of the presented approach. In the same Table we can find a comparison of our runs with others presented at the SemEval-2 competition. In particular, we have tested four different runs which correspond to two evaluations for each different version of the probabilistic classifier. The description of each run is given in Table 1.

We obtained a better performance with those runs that were evaluated with the five best translations (oof) than with those that were evaluated with only the best ones. This fact lead us to consider in further work to improve the ranking of the translations found by our system. On other hand, the unweighted version of the proposed classifier improved the weighted one. This behavior was unexpected, because in the development dataset, the results were opposite. We consider that the problem comes from taking into account the entire sentence instead of a neighborhood (windows) around the ambiguous word. We will further investigate about this issue. We got a better performance than other systems, and those runs that outperformed our system runs did it by around 3% of precision and recall in the case of the oof evaluation.

3.2 Cross-Lingual Lexical Substitution

In Table 3 we may see the obtained results for the cross-lingual lexical substitution task. The obtained results are low in comparison with the best one. Since this task relies on the C-WSD task, then a lower performance on the C-WSD task will conduct to a even lower performance in C-LS. Firstly, we need to improve the C-WSD solver. In particular, we need to improve the ranking procedure in order to obtain a better translation of the source ambiguous word. Moreover, we consider that the use of language modeling would be of high benefit, since we could test whether or not a given translation together with the terms in its context would have high probability in the target language.

Run name		Description
FCC-WSD1	:	Best translation (one target word) / unweighted version
FCC-WSD2	:	Five best translations (five target words - *oof*) / unweighted version
FCC-WSD3	:	Best translation (one target word) / weighted version
FCC-WSD4	:	Five best translations (five target words - *oof*) / weighted version

Table 1: Description of runs

System name	Precision (%)	Recall (%)
UvT-v	23.42	23.42
UvT-g	19.92	19.92
FCC-WSD1	15.09	15.09
FCC-WSD3	14.43	14.43
UHD-1	20.48	16.33
UHD-2	20.2	16.09
T3-COLEUR	19.78	19.59

a) Best translation

System name	Precision (%)	Recall (%)
UvT-v	42.17	42.17
UvT-g	43.12	43.12
FCC-WSD2	40.76	40.76
FCC-WSD4	38.46	38.46
UHD-1	38.78	31.81
UHD-2	37.74	31.3
T3-COLEUR	35.84	35.46

b) Five best translations (oof)

Table 2: Evaluation of the cross-lingual word sense disambiguation task

System name	Precision (%)	Recall (%)
SWAT-E	174.59	174.59
SWAT-S	97.98	97.98
UvT-v	58.91	58.91
UvT-g	55.29	55.29
UBA-W	52.75	52.75
WLVUSP	48.48	48.48
UBA-T	47.99	47.99
USPWLV	47.6	47.6
ColSlm	43.91	46.61
ColEur	41.72	44.77
TYO	34.54	35.46
IRST-1	31.48	33.14
FCC-LS	23.9	23.9
IRSTbs	8.33	29.74
DICT	44.04	44.04
DICTCORP	42.65	42.65

Table 3: Evaluation of the cross-lingual lexical substitution task (the ten best results - *oot*)

4 Conclusions and Further Work

In this paper we have presented a system for cross-lingual word sense disambiguation and cross-lingual lexical substitution. The approach uses a Naïve Bayes classifier which is fed with the probabilities obtained from a bilingual statistical dictionary. Two different versions of the classifier, unweighted and weighted were tested. The results were compared with those of an international competition, obtaining a good performance. As further work, we need to improve the ranking module of the cross-lingual WSD classifier. Moreover, we consider that the use of a language model for Spanish would highly improve the results on the cross-lingual lexical substitution task.

Acknowledgments

This work has been partially supported by CONACYT (Project #106625) and PROMEP (Grant #103.5/09/4213).

References

[Agirre and Edmonds2006] E. Agirre and P. Edmonds. 2006. *Word Sense Disambiguation, Text, Speech and Language Technology*. Springer.

[Carpuat and Wu.2007] M. Carpuat and D. Wu. 2007. Improving statistical machine translation using word sense disambiguation. In *Proceedings of the 2007 Joint Conference on Empirical Methods in Natural Language Processing and Computational Natural Language Learning (EMNLPCoNLL)*, pages 61–72.

[Chan et al.2007] Y.S. Chan, H.T. Ng, and D. Chiang. 2007. Word sense disambiguation improves statistical machine translation. In *Proceedings of the 45th Annual Meeting of the Association of Computational Linguistics*, pages 33–40.

[Lefever and Hoste2010] E. Lefever and V. Hoste. 2010. Semeval-2010 task3:cross-lingual word sense disambiguation. In *Proceedings of the Fifth International Workshop on Semantic Evaluations (SemEval-2010)*. Association for Computational Linguistics.

[Mihalcea et al.2010] R. Mihalcea, R. Sinha, and D. McCarthy. 2010. Semeval-2010 task2:cross-lingual lexical substitution. In *Proceedings of the Fifth International Workshop on Semantic Evaluations (SemEval-2010)*. Association for Computational Linguistics.

USP*wlv* and WLV*usp*: Combining Dictionaries and Contextual Information for Cross-Lingual Lexical Substitution

Wilker Aziz
University of São Paulo
São Carlos, SP, Brazil
wilker.aziz@usp.br

Lucia Specia
University of Wolverhampton
Wolverhampton, UK
l.specia@wlv.ac.uk

Abstract

We describe two systems participating in Semeval-2010's *Cross-Lingual Lexical Substitution* task: USP*wlv* and WLV*usp*. Both systems are based on two main components: (i) a dictionary to provide a number of possible translations for each source word, and (ii) a contextual model to select the best translation according to the context where the source word occurs. These components and the way they are integrated are different in the two systems: they exploit corpus-based and linguistic resources, and supervised and unsupervised learning methods. Among the 14 participants in the subtask to identify the *best* translation, our systems were ranked 2nd and 4th in terms of recall, 3rd and 4th in terms of precision. Both systems outperformed the baselines in all subtasks according to all metrics used.

1 Introduction

The goal of the *Cross-Lingual Lexical Substitution* task in Semeval-2010 (Mihalcea et al., 2010) is to find the best (***best*** subtask) Spanish translation or the 10-best (***oot*** subtask) translations for 100 different English source words depending on their context of occurrence. Source words include nouns, adjectives, adverbs and verbs. $1,000$ occurrences of such words are given along with a short context (a sentence).

This task resembles that of Word Sense Disambiguation (WSD) within Machine Translation (MT). A few approaches have recently been proposed using standard WSD features to learn models using *translations* instead of *senses* (Specia et al., 2007; Carpuat and Wu, 2007; Chan and Ng, 2007). In such approaches, the global WSD score is added as a feature to statistical MT systems, along with additional features, to help the system on its choice for the best translation of a source word or phrase.

We exploit contextual information in alternative ways to standard WSD features and supervised approaches. Our two systems - USP*wlv* and WLV *usp* - use two main components: (i) a list of possible translations for the source word regardless of its context; and (ii) a contextual model that ranks such translations for each occurrence of the source word given its context.

While these components constitute the core of most WSD systems, the way they are created and integrated in our systems differs from standard approaches. Our systems do not require a model to disambiguate / translate each particular source word, but instead use general models. We experimented with both corpus-based and standard dictionaries, and different learning methodologies to rank the candidate translations. Our main goal was to maximize the accuracy of the system in choosing the ***best*** translation.

WLV*usp* is a very simple system based essentially on (i) a Statistical Machine Translation (SMT) system trained using a large parallel corpus to generate the n-best translations for each occurrence of the source words and (ii) a standard English-Spanish dictionary to filter out noisy translations and provide additional translations in case the SMT system was not able to produce a large enough number of legitimate translations, particularly for the ***oot*** subtask.

USP*wlv* uses a dictionary built from a large parallel corpus using inter-language information theory metrics and an online-learning supervised algorithm to rank the options from the dictionary. The ranking is based on global and local contextual features, such as the mutual information between the translation and the words in the source context, which are trained using human annotation on the trial dataset.

Proceedings of the 5th International Workshop on Semantic Evaluation, ACL 2010, pages 117–122,
Uppsala, Sweden, 15-16 July 2010. ©2010 Association for Computational Linguistics

2 Resources

2.1 Parallel corpus

The English-Spanish part of Europarl (Koehn, 2005), a parallel corpus from the European Parliament proceedings, was used as a source of sentence level aligned data. The nearly 1.7M sentence pairs of English-Spanish translations, as provided by the Fourth Workshop on Machine Translation (WMT09[1]), sum up to approximately 48M tokens in each language. Europarl was used both to train the SMT system and to generate dictionaries based on inter-language mutual information.

2.2 Dictionaries

The dictionary used by WLV*usp* was extracted using the free online service *Word Reference*[2], which provides two dictionaries: Espasa Concise and Pocket Oxford Spanish Dictionary. Regular expressions were used to extract the content of the webpages, keeping only the translations of the words or phrasal expressions, and the outcome was manually revised. The manual revision was necessary to remove translations of long idiomatic expressions which were only defined through examples, for example, for the verb *check*: "we *checked* up and found out he was lying – hicimos averiguaciones y comprobamos que mentía". The resulting dictionary contains a number of open domain (single or multi-word) translations for each of the 100 source words. This number varies from 3 to 91, with an average of 12.87 translations per word. For example:

- **yet.r** = todavía, aún, ya, hasta ahora, sin embargo
- **paper.n** = artículo, papel, envoltorio, diario, periódico, trabajo, ponencia, examen, parte, documento, libro

Any other dictionary can in principle be used to produce the list of translations, possibly without manual intervention. More comprehensive dictionaries could result in better results, particularly those with explicit information about the frequencies of different translations. Automatic metrics based on parallel corpus to learn the dictionary can also be used, but we would expect the accuracy of the system to drop in that case.

The process to generate the corpus-based dictionary for USP*wlv* is described in Section 4.

2.3 Pre-processing techniques

The Europarl parallel corpus was tokenized and lowercased using standard tools provided by the WMT09 competition. Additionally, the sentences that were longer than 100 tokens after tokenization were discarded.

Since the task specifies that translations should be given in their basic forms, and also in order to decrease the sparsity due to the rich morphology of Spanish, the parallel corpus was lemmatized using TreeTagger (Schmid, 2006), a freely available part-of-speech (POS) tagger and lemmatizer. Two different versions of the parallel corpus were built using both lemmatized words and their POS tags:

Lemma Words are represented by their lemmatized form. In case of ambiguity, the original form was kept, in order to avoid incorrect choices. Words that could not be lemmatized were also kept as in their original form.

Lemma.pos Words are represented by their lemmatized form followed by their POS tags. POS tags representing content words are generalized into four groups: verbs, nouns, adjectives and adverbs. When the system could not identify a POS tag, a dummy tag was used.

The same techniques were used to pre-process the trial and test data.

2.4 Training samples

The trial data available for this task was used as a training set for the USP*wlv* system, which uses a supervised learning algorithm to learn the weights of a number of global features. For the 300 occurrences of 30 words in the trial data, the expected lexical substitutions were given by the task organizers, and therefore the feature weights could be optimized in a way to make the system result in good translations. These sentences were preprocessed in the same way the parallel corpus.

3 WLV*usp* system

This system is based on a combination of the Statistical Machine Translation (SMT) framework using the English-Spanish Europarl data and an English-Spanish dictionary built semi-automatically (Section 2.2). The parallel corpus

[1] http://www.statmt.org/wmt09/translation-task.html

[2] http://www.wordreference.com/

was lowercased, tokenized and lemmatized (Section 2.3) and then used to train the standard SMT system Moses (Koehn et al., 2007) and translate the trial/test sentences, producing the 1000-best translations for each input sentence.

Moses produces its own dictionary from the parallel corpus by using a word alignment tool and heuristics to build parallel phrases of up to seven source words and their corresponding target words, to which are assigned translation probabilities using frequency counts in the corpus. This methodology provides some very localized contextual information, which can help guiding the system towards choosing a correct translation. Additional contextual information is used by the language model component in Moses, which considers how likely the sentence translation is in the Spanish language (with a 5-gram language model).

Using the phrase alignment information, the translation of each occurrence of a source word is identified in the output of Moses. Since the phrase translations are learned using the Europarl corpus, some translations are very specific to that domain. Moreover, translations can be very noisy, given that the process is unsupervised. We therefore filter the translations given by Moses to keep only those also given as possible Spanish translations according to the semi-automatically built English-Spanish dictionary (Section 2.2). This is a general-domain dictionary, but it is less likely to contain noise.

For *best* results, only the top translation produced by Moses is considered. If the actual translation does not belong to the dictionary, the first translation in that dictionary is used. Although there is no information about the order of the translations in the dictionaries used, by looking at the translations provided, we believe that the first translation is in general one of the most frequent.

For *oot* results, the alternative translations provided by the 1000-best translations are considered. In cases where fewer than 10 translations are found, we extract the remaining ones from the handcrafted dictionary following their given order until 10 translations (when available) are found, without repetition.

WLV*usp* system therefore combines contextual information as provided by Moses (via its phrases and language model) and general translation information as provided by a dictionary.

4 USP*wlv* System

For each source word occurring in the context of a specific sentence, this system uses a linear combination of features to rank the options from an automatically built English-Spanish dictionary.

For the ***best*** subtask, the translation ranked first is chosen, while for the ***oot*** subtask, the 10 best ranked translations are used without repetition.

The building of the dictionary, the features used and the learning scheme are described in what follows.

Dictionary Building The dictionary building is based on the concept of inter-language Mutual Information (MI) (Raybaud et al., 2009). It consists in detecting which words in a source-language sentence trigger the appearance of other words in its target-language translation. The inter-language MI in Equation 3 can be defined for pairs of source (s) and target (t) words by observing their occurrences at the sentence level in a parallel, sentence aligned corpus. Both simple (Equation 1) and joint distributions (Equation 2) were built based on the English-Spanish Europarl corpus using its *Lemma.pos* version (Section 2.3).

$$p_l(x) = \frac{count_l(x)}{Total} \quad (1)$$

$$p_{en,es}(s,t) = \frac{f_{en,es}(s,t)}{Total} \quad (2)$$

$$MI(s,t) = p_{en,es}(s,t) log\left(\frac{p_{en,es}(s,t)}{p_{en}(s)p_{es}(t)}\right) \quad (3)$$

$$Avg_{MI}(t_j) = \frac{\sum_{i=1}^{l} w(|i-j|) MI(s_i, t_j)}{\sum_{i=1}^{l} w(|i-j|)} \quad (4)$$

In the equations, $count_l(x)$ is the number of sentences in which the word x appear in a corpus of l-language texts; $count_{en,es}(s,t)$ is the number of sentences in which source and target words co-occur in the parallel corpus; and $Total$ is the total number of sentences in the corpus of the language(s) under consideration. The distributions p_{en} and p_{es} are monolingual and can been extracted from any monolingual corpus.

To prevent discontinuities in Equation 3, we used a smoothing technique to avoid null probabilities. We assume that any monolingual event occurs at least once and the joint distribution is smoothed by a Guo's factor $\alpha = 0.1$ (Guo et al., 2004):

$$p_{en,es}(s,t) \leftarrow \frac{p_{en,es}(s,t) + \alpha p_{en}(s)p_{es}(t)}{1+\alpha}$$

For each English source word, a list of Spanish translations was produced and ranked according to inter-language MI. From the resulting list, the 50-best translations constrained by the POS of the original English word were selected.

Features The inter-language MI is a feature which indicates the global suitability of translating a source token s into a target one t. However, inter-language MI is not able to provide local contextual information, since it does not take into account the source context sentence c. The following features were defined to achieve such capability:

Weighted Average MI (aMI) consists in averaging the inter-language MI between the target word t_j and every source word s in the context sentence c (Raybaud et al., 2009). The MI component is scaled in a way that long range dependencies are considered less important, as shown in Equation 4. The scaling factor $w(\cdot)$ is assigned 1 for verbs, nouns, adjectives and adverbs up to five positions from the source word, and 0 otherwise. This feature gives an idea of how well the elements in a window centered in the source word *head* (s_j) align to the target word t_j, representing the suitability of t_j translating s_j in the given context.

Modified Weighted Average MI (mMI) takes the average MI as previously defined, except that the source word *head* is not taken into account. In other words, the scaling function in Equation 4 equals 0 also when $|i - j| = 0$. It gives an idea of how well the source words align to the target word t_j without the strong influence of its source translation s_j. This should provide less biased information to the learning.

Best from WLV*usp* (B) consists in a flag that indicates whether a candidate t is taken as the best ranked option according to the WLV*usp* system. The goal is to exploit the information from the SMT system and handcrafted dictionary used by that system.

10-*best* from WLV*usp* (T) this feature is a flag which indicates whether a candidate t was among the 10 best ranked translations provided by the WLV*usp* system.

Online Learning In order to train a binary ranking system based on the trial dataset as our *training set*, we used the online passive-aggressive algorithm MIRA (Crammer et al., 2006). MIRA is said to be passive-aggressive because it updates the parameters only when a misprediction is detected. At training time, for each sentence a set of pairs of candidate translations is retrieved. For each of these pairs, the rank given by the system with the current parameters is compared to the correct $rank_h(\cdot)$. A loss function $loss(\cdot)$ controls the updates attributing non 0 values only for mispredictions. In our implementation, it equals 1 for any mistake made by the model.

Each element of the kind (c, s, t) = (*source context sentence, source head, translation candidate*) is assigned a feature vector $f(c, s, t) = \langle MI, aMI, mMI, B, T\rangle$, which is modeled by a vector of parameters $w \in R^5$.

The binary ranking is defined as the task of finding the best parameters w which maximize the number of successful predictions. A successful prediction happens when the system is able to rank two translation candidates as expected. For doing so, we define an oriented pair $x = (a, b)$ of candidate translations of s in the context of c and a feature vector $F(x) = f(c, s, a) - f(c, s, b)$. $signal(w \cdot F(x))$ is the orientation the model gives to x, that is, whether the system believes a is better than b or vice versa. Based on whether or not that orientation is the same as that of the reference [3], the algorithm takes the decision between updating or not the parameters. When an update occurs, it is the one that results in the minimal changes in the parameters leading to correct labeling x, that is, guaranteeing that after the update the system will rank (a, b) correctly. Algorithm 1 presents the general method, as proposed in (Crammer et al., 2006).

In the case of this binary ranking, the minimization problem has an analytic solution well defined as long as $f(c, s, a) \neq f(c, s, b)$ and $rank_h(a) \neq rank_h(b)$, otherwise $signal(w \cdot F(x))$ or the human label would not be defined, respectively. These conditions have an impact on the content of $Pairs(c)$, the set of training points built upon the system outputs for c, which can only contain pairs of differently ranked translations.

The learning scheme was initialized with a uni-

[3]Given s in the context of c and (a, b) a pair of candidate translations of s, the reference produces 1 if $rank_h(a) > rank_h(b)$ and -1 if $rank_h(b) > rank_h(a)$.

Algorithm 1 MIRA

for $c \in$ *Training Set* **do**
  for $x = (a, b) \in Pairs(c)$ **do**
    $\hat{y} \leftarrow signal(w \cdot F(x))$
    $z \leftarrow$ *correct label*(x)
    $w = argmax_u \frac{1}{2}||w - u||^2$
    s.t. $u \cdot F(x) \geq loss(\hat{y}, z)$
    $v \leftarrow v + w$
    $T \leftarrow T + 1$
  end for
end for
return $\frac{1}{T}v$

form vector. The average parameters after $N = 5$ iterations over the training set was taken.

5 Results

5.1 Official results

Tables 1 and 2 show the main results obtained by our two systems in the official competition. We contrast our systems' results against the best baseline provided by the organizers, *DIC*, which considers translations from a dictionary and frequency information from WordNet, and show the relative position of the system among the 14 participants. The metrics are defined in (Mihalcea et al., 2010).

Subtask	Metric	Baseline	WLV*usp*	Position
Best	R	24.34	25.27	4th
	P	24.34	25.27	3rd
	Mode R	50.34	52.81	3rd
	Mode P	50.34	52.81	4th
OOT	R	44.04	48.48	6th
	P	44.04	48.48	6th
	Mode R	73.53	77.91	5th
	Mode P	73.53	77.91	5th

Table 1: Official results for WLV*usp* on the test set, compared to the highest baseline, *DICT*. P = precision, R = recall. The last column shows the relative position of the system.

Subtask	Metric	Baseline	USP*wlv*	Position
Best	R	24.34	26.81	2nd
	P	24.34	26.81	3rd
	Mode R	50.34	58.85	1st
	Mode P	50.34	58.85	2nd
OOT	R	44.04	47.60	8th
	P	44.04	47.60	8th
	Mode R	73.53	79.84	3rd
	Mode P	73.53	79.84	3rd

Table 2: Official results for USP*wlv* on the test set, compared to the highest baseline, *DICT*. The last column shows the relative position of the system.

In the ***oot*** subtask, the original systems were able to output the mode translation approximately 80% of the times. From those translations, nearly 50% were actually considered as best options according to human annotators. It is worth noticing that we focused on the ***best*** subtask. Therefore, for the ***oot*** subtask we did not exploit the fact that translations could be repeated to form the set of 10 best translations. For certain source words, our resulting set of translations is smaller than 10. For example, in the WLV*usp* system, whenever the set of alternative translations identified in Moses' top 1000-best list did not contain 10 *legitimate* translations, that is, 10 translations also found in the handcrafted dictionary, we simply copied other translations from that dictionary to amount 10 different translations. If they did not sum to 10 because the list of translations in the dictionary was too short, we left the set as it was. As a result, 58% of the 1000 test cases had fewer than 10 translations, many of them with as few as two or three translations. In fact, the list of ***oot*** results for the complete test set resulted in only 1,950 translations, when there could be 10,000 (1,000 test case occurrences $*$ 10 translations). In the next section we describe some additional experiments to take this issue into account.

5.2 Additional results

After receiving the gold-standard data, we computed the scores for a number of variations of our two systems. For example, we checked whether the performance of USP*wlv* is too dependent on the handcrafted dictionary, via the features **B** and **T**. Table 3 presents the performance of two variations of USP*wlv*: MI-aMI-mMI was trained without the two contextual flag features which depend on WLV*usp*. MI-B-T was trained without the mutual information contextual features. The variation MI-aMI-mMI of USP*wlv* performs well even in the absence of the features coming from WLV*usp*, although the scores are lower. These results show the effectiveness of the learning scheme, since USP*wlv* achieves better performance by combining these feature variations, as compared to their individual performance.

To provide an intuition on the contribution of the two different components in the system WLV*usp*, we checked the proportion of times a translation was provided by each of the components. In the ***best*** subtask, 48% of the translations came from Moses, while the remaining 52% pro-

Subtask	Metric	Baseline	MI-aMI-mMI	MI-B-T
Best	R	24.34	22.59	20.50
	P	24.34	22.59	20.50
	Mode R	50.34	50.21	44.01
	Mode P	50.34	50.21	44.01
OOT	R	39.65	47.60	32.75
	P	44.04	39.65	32.75
	Mode R	73.53	74.19	56.70
	Mode P	73.53	74.19	56.70

Table 3: Comparing between variations of the system USP*wlv* on the test set and the highest baseline, *DICT*. The variations are different sources of contextual knowledge: MI (MI–aMI–mMI) and the WLV*usp* (MI–B–T) system.

vided by Moses were not found in the dictionary. In those cases, the first translation in the dictionary was used. In the ***oot*** subtask, only 12% (246) of the translations came from Moses, while the remaining (1,704) came from the dictionary. This can be explained by the little variation in the n-best lists produced by Moses: most of the variations account for word-order, punctuation, etc.

Finally, we performed additional experiments in order to exploit the possibility of replicating well ranked translations for the ***oot*** subtask. Table 4 presents the results of some strategies arbitrarily chosen for such replications. For example, in the colums labelled "5" we show the scores for repeating (once) the 5 top translations. Notice that precision and recall increase as we take fewer top translation and repeat them more times. In terms of mode metrics, by reducing the number of distinct translations from 10 to 5, USP*wlv* still outperforms (marginally) the baseline. In general, the new *systems* outperform the baseline and our previous results (see Table 1 and 2) in terms of precision and recall. However, according to the other *mode* metrics, they are below our official systems.

System	Metric	*5*	*4*	*3*	*2*
WLV*usp*	R	69.09	88.36	105.32	122.29
	P	69.09	88.36	105.32	122.29
	Mode R	68.27	63.05	63.05	52.47
	Mode P	68.27	63.05	63.05	52.47
USP*wlv*	R	73.50	94.78	102.96	129.09
	P	73.50	94.78	102.96	129.09
	Mode R	73.77	68.27	62.62	57.40
	Mode P	73.77	68.27	62.62	57.40

Table 4: Comparison between different strategies for duplicating answers in the task ***oot***. The systems output a number of distinct guesses and through arbitrarily schemes replicate them in order to complete a list of 10 translations.

6 Discussion and future work

We have presented two systems combining contextual information and a pre-defined set of translations for cross-lingual lexical substitution. Both systems performed particularly well in the ***best*** subtask. A handcrafted dictionary has shown to be essential for the WLV*usp* system and also helpful for the USP*wlv* system, which uses an additional dictionary automatically build from a parallel corpus. We plan to investigate how such systems can be improved by enhancing the corpus-based resources to further minimize the dependency on the handcrafted dictionary.

References

Marine Carpuat and Dekai Wu. 2007. Improving statistical machine translation using word sense disambiguation. In *Joint Conference on Empirical Methods in Natural Language Processing and Computational Natural Language Learning*, pages 61–72.

Yee Seng Chan and Hwee Tou Ng. 2007. Word sense disambiguation improves statistical machine translation. In *45th Annual Meeting of the Association for Computational Linguistics*, pages 33–40.

Koby Crammer, Ofer Dekel, Joseph Keshet, Shai Shalev-Shwartz, and Yoram Singer. 2006. Online passive-agressive algorithms. *Jornal of Machine Learning Research*, 7:551–585.

Gang Guo, Chao Huang, Hui Jiang, and Ren-Hua Wang. 2004. A comparative study on various confidence measures in large vocabulary speech recognition. In *International Symposium on Chinese Spoken Language Processing*, pages 9–12.

Philipp Koehn. 2005. Europarl: A parallel corpus for statistical machine translation. In *MT Summit*.

Rada Mihalcea, Ravi Sinha, and Diana McCarthy. 2010. Semeval-2010 task 2: Cross-lingual lexical substitution. In *SemEval-2010: 5th International Workshop on Semantic Evaluations*.

Sylvain Raybaud, Caroline Lavecchia, David Langlois, and Kamel Smaili. 2009. Word- and sentence-level confidence measures for machine translation. In *13th Annual Conference of the European Association for Machine Translation*, pages 104–111.

Helmut Schmid. 2006. Probabilistic part-of-speech tagging using decision trees. In *International Conference on New Methods in Natural Language Processing*, pages 44–49.

Lucia Specia, Mark Stevenson, and Maria das Graças Volpe Nunes. 2007. Learning expressive models for word sense disambiguation. In *45th Annual Meeting of the Association for Computational Linguistics*, pages 41–148.

SWAT: Cross-Lingual Lexical Substitution using Local Context Matching, Bilingual Dictionaries and Machine Translation

Richard Wicentowski, Maria Kelly, Rachel Lee
Department of Computer Science
Swarthmore College
Swarthmore, PA 19081 USA
richardw@cs.swarthmore.edu, {mkelly1,rlee1}@sccs.swarthmore.edu

Abstract

We present two systems that select the most appropriate Spanish substitutes for a marked word in an English test sentence. These systems were official entries to the SemEval-2010 Cross-Lingual Lexical Substitution task. The first system, SWAT-E, finds Spanish substitutions by first finding English substitutions in the English sentence and then translating these substitutions into Spanish using an English-Spanish dictionary. The second system, SWAT-S, translates each English sentence into Spanish and then finds the Spanish substitutions in the Spanish sentence. Both systems exceeded the baseline and all other participating systems by a wide margin using one of the two official scoring metrics.

1 Introduction

We present two systems submitted as official entries to the SemEval-2010 Cross-Lingual Lexical Substitution task (Mihalcea et al., 2010). In this task, participants were asked to substitute a single marked word in an English sentence with the most appropriate Spanish translation(s) given the context. On the surface, our two systems are very similar, performing monolingual lexical substitution and using translation tools and bilingual dictionaries to make the transition from English to Spanish.

2 Scoring

The task organizers used two scoring metrics adapted from the SemEval-2007 English Lexical Substitution task (McCarthy and Navigli, 2007). For each test item i, human annotators provided a multiset of substitutions, T_i, that formed the gold standard. Given a system-provided multiset answer S_i for test item i, the *best* score for a single test item is computed using (1). Systems were allowed to provide an unlimited number of responses in S_i, but each item's *best* score was divided by the number of answers provided in S_i.

$$\textit{best}\text{ score} = \frac{\sum_{s \in S_i} \text{frequency}(s \in T_i)}{|S_i| \cdot |T_i|} \tag{1}$$

The out-of-ten score, henceforth *oot*, limited systems to a maximum of 10 responses for each test item. Unlike the *best* scoring method, the final score for each test item in the *oot* method is not divided by the actual number of responses provided by the system; therefore, systems could maximize their score by always providing exactly 10 responses. In addition, since S_i is a multiset, the 10 responses in S_i need not be unique.

$$\textit{oot}\text{ score} = \frac{\sum_{s \in S_i} \text{frequency}(s \in T_i)}{|T_i|} \tag{2}$$

Further details on the *oot* scoring method and its impact on our systems can be found in Section 3.4.

The final *best* and *oot* score for the system is computed by summing the individual scores for each item and, for recall, dividing by the number of tests items, and for precision, dividing by the number of test items answered. Our systems provided a response to every test item, so precision and recall are the same by this definition.

For both *best* and *oot*, the Mode recall (similarly, Mode precision) measures the system's ability to identify the substitute that was the annotators' most frequently chosen substitute, when such a most frequent substitute existed (McCarthy and Navigli, 2007).

3 Systems

Our two entries were SWAT-E and SWAT-S. Both systems used a two-step process to obtain a ranked list of substitutes. The SWAT-E system first used a monolingual lexical substitution algorithm to provide a ranked list of English substitutes and then

Proceedings of the 5th International Workshop on Semantic Evaluation, ACL 2010, pages 123–128,
Uppsala, Sweden, 15-16 July 2010.

these substitutes were translated into Spanish to obtain the cross-lingual result. The SWAT-S system performed these two steps in the reverse order: first, the English sentences were translated into Spanish and then the monolingual lexical substitution algorithm was run on the translated output to provide a ranked list of Spanish substitutes.

3.1 Syntagmatic coherence

The monolingual lexical substitution algorithm used by both systems is an implementation of the syntagmatic coherence criterion used by the IRST2 system (Giuliano et al., 2007) in the SemEval-2007 Lexical Substitution task.

For a sentence H_w containing the target word w, the IRST2 algorithm first compiles a set, E, of candidate substitutes for w from a dictionary, thesaurus, or other lexical resource. For each $e \in E$, H_e is formed by substituting e for w in H_w. Each n-gram ($2 \leq n \leq 5$) of H_e containing the substitute e is assigned a score, f, equal to how frequently the n-gram appeared in a large corpus.

For all triples (e, n, f) where $f > 0$, we add (e, n, f) to E'. E' is then sorted by n, with ties broken by f. The highest ranked item in E', therefore, is the triple containing the synonym e that appeared in the longest, most frequently occurring n-gram. Note that each candidate substitute e can appear multiple times in E': once for each value of n.

The list E' becomes the final output of the syntagmatic coherence criterion, providing a ranking for all candidate substitutes in E.

3.2 The SWAT-E system

3.2.1 Resources

The SWAT-E system used the English Web1T 5-gram corpus (Brants and Franz, 2006), the Spanish section of the Web1T European 5-gram corpus (Brants and Franz, 2009), Roget's online thesaurus[1], NLTK's implementation of the Lancaster Stemmer (Loper and Bird, 2002), Google's online English-Spanish dictionary[2], and SpanishDict's online dictionary[3]. We formed a single Spanish-English dictionary by combining the translations found in both dictionaries.

[1] http://thesaurus.com
[2] http://www.google.com/dictionary
[3] http://www.spanishdict.com

3.2.2 Ranking substitutes

The first step in the SWAT-E algorithm is to create a ranked list of English substitutes. For each English test sentence H_w containing the target word w, we use the syntagmatic coherence criterion described above to create E', a ranking of the synonyms of w taken from Roget's thesaurus. We use the Lancaster stemmer to ensure that we count all morphologically similar lexical substitutes.

Next, we use a bilingual dictionary to convert our candidate English substitutes into candidate Spanish substitutes, forming a new ranked list S'. For each item (e, n, f) in E', and for each Spanish translation s of e, we add the triple (s, n, f) to S'. Since different English words can have the same Spanish translation s, we can end up with multiple triples in S' that have the same values for s and n. For example, if s_1 is a translation of both e_1 and e_2, and the triples $(e_1, 4, 87)$ and $(e_2, 4, 61)$ appear in E', then S' will contain the triples $(s_1, 4, 87)$ and $(s_1, 4, 61)$. We merge all such "duplicates" by summing their frequencies. In this example, we would replace the two triples containing s_1 with a new triple, $(s_1, 4, 148)$. After merging all duplicates, we re-sort S' by n, breaking ties by f. Notice that since triples are merged only when both s and n are the same, Spanish substitutes can appear multiple times in S': once for each value of n.

At this point, we have a ranked list of candidate Spanish substitutes, S'. From this list S', we keep only those Spanish substitutes that are direct translations of our original word w. The reason for doing this is that some of the translations of the synonyms of w have no overlapping meaning with w. For example, the polysemous English noun "bug" can mean a flaw in a computer program (cf. test item 572). Our thesaurus lists "hitch" as a synonym for this sense of "bug". Of course, "hitch" is also polysemous, and not every translation of "hitch" into Spanish will have a meaning that overlaps with the original "bug" sense. Translations such as "enganche", having the "trailer hitch" sense, are certainly not appropriate substitutes for this, or any, sense of the word "bug". By keeping only those substitutes that are also translations of the original word w, we maintain a cleaner list of candidate substitutes. We call this filtered list of candidates S.

3.2.3 Selecting substitutes

For each English sentence in the test set, we now have a ranked list of cross-lingual lexical substi-

$best = \{(s_1, n_1, f_1)\}$
$j \leftarrow 2$
while $(n_j == n_1)$ and $(f_j \geq 0.75 * f_1)$ **do**
  $best \leftarrow best \cup \{(s_j, n_j, f_j)\}$
  $j \leftarrow j + 1$
end while

Figure 1: The method for selecting multiple answers in the *best* method used by SWAT-E

tutes, S. In the *oot* scoring method, we selected the top 10 substitutes in the ranked list S. If there were less than 10 items (but at least one item) in S, we duplicated answers from our ranked list until we had made 10 guesses. (See Section 3.4 for further details on this process.) If there were no items in our ranked list, we returned the most frequent translations of w as determined by the unigram counts of these translations in the Spanish Web1T corpus.

For our *best* answer, we returned multiple responses when the highest ranked substitutes had similar frequencies. Since S was formed by transferring the frequency of each English substitute e onto all of its Spanish translations, a single English substitute that had appeared with high frequency would lead to many Spanish substitutes, each with high frequencies. (The frequencies need not be exactly the same due to the merging step described above.) In these cases, we hedged our bet by returning each of these translations.

Representing the i-th item in S as (s_i, n_i, f_i), our procedure for creating the *best* answer can be found in Figure 1. We allow all items from S that have the same value of n as the top ranked item and have a frequency at least 75% that of the most frequent item to be included in the best answer.

Of the 1000 test instances, we provided a single "best" candidate 630 times, two candidates 253 times, three candidates 70 times, four candidates 30 times, and six candidates 17 times. (We never returned five candidates).

3.3 SWAT-S

3.3.1 Resources

The SWAT-S system used both Google's[4] and Yahoo's[5] online translation tools, the Spanish section of the Web1T European 5-gram corpus, Roget's online thesaurus, TreeTagger (Schmid, 1994) for morphological analysis and both Google's and Yahoo's[6] English-Spanish dictionaries. We formed a single Spanish-English dictionary by combining the translations found in both dictionaries.

3.3.2 Ranking substitutes

To find the cross-lingual lexical substitutes for a target word in an English sentence, we first translate the sentence into Spanish and then use the syntagmatic coherence criterion on the translated Spanish sentence.

In order to perform this monolingual Spanish lexical substitution, we need to be able to identify the target word we are attempting to substitute in the translated sentence. We experimented with using Moses (Koehn et al., 2007) to perform the machine translation and produce a word alignment but we found that Google's online translation tool produced better translations than Moses did when trained on the Europarl data we had available.

In the original English sentence, the target word is marked with an XML tag. We had hoped that Google's translation tool would preserve the XML tag around the translated target word, but that was not the case. We also experimented with using quotation marks around the target word instead of the XML tag. The translation tool often preserved quotation marks around the target word, but also yielded a different, and anecdotally worse, translation than the same sentence without the quotation marks. (We will, however, return to this strategy as a backoff method.) Although we did not experiment with using a stand-alone word alignment algorithm to find the target word in the Spanish sentence, Section 4.3 provides insights into the possible performance gains possible by doing so.

Without a word alignment, we were left with the following problem: Given a translated Spanish sentence H, how could we identify the word w that is the translation of the original English target word, v? Our search strategy proceeded as follows.

1. We looked up v in our English-Spanish dictionary and searched H for one of these translations (or a morphological variant), choosing the matching translation as the Spanish target word. If the search yielded multiple matches, we chose the match that was in the most similar position in the sentence to the position of v in

[4] http://translate.google.com/
[5] http://babelfish.yahoo.com/
[6] http://education.yahoo.com/reference/dict_en_es/

the English sentence. This method identified a match in 801 of the 1000 test sentences.

2. If we had not found a match, we translated each word in H back into English, one word at a time. If one of the re-translated words was a synonym of v, we chose that word as the target word. If there were multiple matches, we again used position to choose the target.

3. If we still had no match, we used Yahoo's translation tool instead of Google's, and repeated steps 1. and 2. above.

4. If we still had no match, we reverted to using Google's translation tool, this time explicitly offsetting the English target word with quotation marks.

In 992 of the 1000 test sentences, this four-step procedure produced a Spanish sentence H_w with a target w. For each of these sentences, we produced E', the list of ranked Spanish substitutes using the syntagmatic selection coherence criterion described in Section 3.1. We used the Spanish Web1T corpus as a source of n-gram counts, and we used the Spanish translations of v as the candidate substitution set E. For the remaining 8 test sentences where we could not identify the target word, we set E' equal to the top 10 most frequently occurring Spanish translations of v as determined by the unigram counts of these translations in the Spanish Web1T corpus.

3.3.3 Selecting substitutes

For each English sentence in the test set, we selected the single best item in E' as our answer for the *best* scoring method.

For the *oot* scoring method, we wanted to ensure that the translated target word w, identified in Section 3.3.2, was represented in our output, even if this substitute was poorly ranked in E'. If w appeared in E', then our *oot* answer was simply the first 10 entries in E'. If w was not in E', then our answer was the top 9 entries in E' followed by w.

As we had done with our SWAT-E system, if the *oot* answer contained less than 10 items, we repeated answers until we had made 10 guesses. See the following section for more information.

3.4 *oot* selection details

The metric used to calculate *oot* precision in this task (Mihalcea et al., 2010) favors systems that always propose 10 candidate substitutes over those that propose fewer than 10 substitutes. For each test item the *oot* score is calculated as follows:

$$\textit{oot}\text{ score} = \frac{\sum_{s \in S_i} \text{frequency}(s \in T_i)}{|T_i|}$$

The final *oot* recall is just the average of these scores over all test items. For test item i, S_i is the multiset of candidates provided by the system, T_i is the multiset of responses provided by the annotators, and frequency$(s \in T_i)$ is the number of times each item s appeared in T_i.

Assume that T_i = {*feliz, feliz, contento, alegre*}. A system that produces S_i = {*feliz, contento*} would receive a score of $\frac{2+1}{4} = 0.75$. However a system that produces S_i with *feliz* and *contento* each appearing 5 times would receive a score of $\frac{5*2+5*1}{4} = 3.75$. Importantly, a system that produced S_i = {*feliz, contento*} plus 8 other responses that were not in the gold standard would receive the same score as the system that produced only S_i = {*feliz, contento*}, so there is never a penalty for providing all 10 answers.

For this reason, in both of our systems, we ensure that our *oot* response always contains exactly 10 answers. To do this, we repeatedly append our list of candidates to itself until the length of the list is equal to or exceeds 10, then we truncate the list to exactly 10 answers. For example, if our original candidate list was [a, b, c, d], our final *oot* response would be [a, b, c, d, a, b, c, d, a, b].

Notice that this is not the only way to produce a response with 10 answers. An alternative would be to produce a response containing [a, b, c, d] followed by 6 other unique translations from the English-Spanish dictionary. However, we found that padding the response with unique answers was far less effective than repeating the answers returned by the syntagmatic coherence algorithm.

4 Analysis of Results

Table 1 shows the results of our two systems compared to two baselines, DICT and DICTCORP, and the upper bound for the task.[7] Since all of these systems provide an answer for every test instance, precision and recall are always the same. The upper bound for the *best* metric results from returning a single answer equal to the annotators' most frequent substitute. The upper bound for the *oot* metric is obtained by returning the annotator's most frequent substitute repeated 10 times.

[7]Details on the baselines and the upper bound can be found in (Mihalcea et al., 2010).

System	*best* R	*best* Mode R	*oot* R	*oot* Mode R
SWAT-E	21.5	43.2	174.6	66.9
SWAT-S	18.9	36.6	98.0	79.0
DICT	24.3	50.3	44.0	73.5
DICTCORP	15.1	29.2	29.2	29.2
upper bound	40.6	100.0	405.9	100.0

Table 1: System performance using the two scoring metrics, *best* and *oot*. All test instances were answered, so precision equals recall. DICT and DICTCORP are the two baselines.

System	*filled oot* R	*filled oot* P	*oot* R	*oot* P
SWAT-E	174.6	174.6	174.6	174.6
IRST-1	126.0	132.6	31.5	33.1
SWAT-S	98.0	98.0	98.0	98.0
WLVUSP	86.1	86.1	48.5	48.5
DICT	71.1	71.1	44.0	44.0
DICTCORP	66.7	66.7	15.1	15.1

Table 2: System performance using *oot* for the top 4 systems when providing exactly 10 substitutes for all answered test items ("filled oot"), as well as the score as submitted ("oot").

Like the IRST2 system (Giuliano et al., 2007) submitted in the 2007 Lexical Substitution task, our system performed extremely well on the *oot* scoring method while performing no better than average on the *best* method. Further analysis should be done to determine if this is due to a flaw in the approach, or if there are other factors at work.

4.1 Analysis of the *oot* method

Our *oot* performance was certainly helped by the fact that we chose to provide 10 answers for each test item. One way to measure this is to score both of our systems with all duplicate candidates removed. We can see that the recall of both systems drops off sharply: SWAT-E drops from 174.6 to 36.3, and SWAT-S drops from 98.0 to 46.7. As was shown in Section 3.4, the *oot* system should always provide 10 answers; however, 12.8% of the SWAT-S test responses, and only 3.2% of the SWAT-E test responses contained no duplicates. In fact, 38.4% of the SWAT-E responses contained only a single unique answer. Providing duplicate answers allowed us to express confidence in the substitutes found. If duplicates were forbidden, simply filling any remaining answers with other translations taken from the English-Spanish dictionary could only serve to increase performance.

Another way to measure the effect of always providing 10 answers is to modify the responses provided by the other systems so that they, too, always provide 10 answers. Of the 14 submitted systems, only 5 (including our systems) provided 10 answers for each test item. Neither of the two baseline systems, DICT and DICTCORP, provided 10 answers for each test item. Using the algorithm described in Section 3.4, we re-scored each of the systems with answers duplicated so that each response contained exactly 10 substitutes. As shown in Table 2, both systems still far exceed the baseline, SWAT-E remains the top scoring system, and SWAT-S drops to 3rd place behind IRST-1, which had finished 12th with its original submission.

4.2 Analysis of *oot* Mode R

Although the SWAT-E system outperformed the SWAT-S system in *best* recall, *best* Mode recall ("Mode R"), and *oot* recall, the SWAT-S system outperformed the SWAT-E system by a large margin in *oot* Mode R (see Table 1). This result is easily explained by first referring to the method used to compute Mode recall: a score of 1 was given to each test instance where the *oot* response contained the annotators' most frequently chosen substitute; otherwise 0 was given. The average of these scores yields Mode R. A system can maximize its Mode R score by always providing 10 unique answers. SWAT-E provided an average of 3.3 unique answers per test item and SWAT-S provided 6.9 unique answers per test item. By providing more than twice the number of unique answers per test item, it is not at all surprising that SWAT-S outperformed SWAT-E in the Mode R measure.

4.3 Analysis of SWAT-S

In the SWAT-S system, 801 (of 1000) test sentences had a direct translation of the target word present in Google's Spanish translation (identified by step 1 in Section 3.3.2). In these cases, the resulting output was better than those cases where a more indirect approach (steps 2-4) was necessary. The *oot* precision on the test sentences where the target was found directly was 101.3, whereas the precision of the test sentences where a target was found more indirectly was only 84.6. The 8 sentences where the unigram backoff was

	best		*oot*	
SWAT-E	P	Mode P	P	Mode P
adjective	25.94	50.67	192.78	85.78
noun	22.34	40.44	197.87	59.11
verb	18.62	41.46	155.16	55.12
adverb	15.68	33.78	119.51	66.22
SWAT-S	P	Mode P	P	Mode P
adjective	21.70	40.00	126.41	86.67
noun	24.77	45.78	107.85	82.22
verb	13.58	27.80	69.04	71.71
adverb	10.46	22.97	80.26	66.22

Table 3: Precision of *best* and *oot* for both systems, analyzed by part of speech.

used had a precision of 77.4. This analysis indicates that using a word alignment tool on the translated sentence pairs would improve the performance of the method. However, since the precision in those cases where the target word could be identified was only 101.3, using a word alignment tool would almost certainly leave SWAT-S as a distant second to the 174.6 precision achieved by SWAT-E.

4.4 Analysis by part-of-speech

Table 3 shows the performance of both systems broken down by part-of-speech. In the IRST2 system submitted to the 2007 Lexical Substitution task, adverbs were the best performing word class, followed distantly by adjectives, then nouns, and finally verbs. However, in this task, we found that adverbs were the hardest word class to correctly substitute. Further analysis should be done to determine if this is due to the difficulty of the particular words and sentences chosen in this task, the added complexity of performing the lexical substitution across two languages, or some independent factor such as the choice of thesaurus used to form the candidate set of substitutes.

5 Conclusions

We presented two systems that participated in the SemEval-2010 Cross-Lingual Lexical Substitution task. Both systems use a two-step process to obtain the lexical substitutes. SWAT-E first finds English lexical substitutes in the English sentence and then translates these substitutes into Spanish. SWAT-S first translates the English sentences into Spanish and then finds Spanish lexical substitutes using these translations.

The official competition results showed that our two systems performed much better than the other systems on the *oot* scoring method, but that we performed only about average on the *best* scoring method.

The analysis provided here indicates that the *oot* score for SWAT-E would hold even if every system had its answers duplicated in order to ensure 10 answers were provided for each test item. We also we showed that a word alignment tool would likely improve the performance of SWAT-S, but that this improvement would not be enough to surpass SWAT-E.

References

T. Brants and A. Franz. 2006. Web 1T 5-gram, ver. 1. LDC2006T13, Linguistic Data Consortium, Philadelphia.

T. Brants and A. Franz. 2009. Web 1T 5-gram, 10 European Languages, ver. 1. LDC2009T25, Linguistic Data Consortium, Philadelphia.

Claudio Giuliano, Alfio Gliozzo, and Carlo Strapparava. 2007. FBK-irst: Lexical Substitution Task Exploiting Domain and Syntagmatic Coherence. In *Proceedings of the Fourth International Workshop on Semantic Evaluations (SemEval-2007)*.

Philipp Koehn, Hieu Hoang, Alexandra Birch, Chris Callison-Burch, Marcello Federico, Nicola Bertoldi, Brooke Cowan, Wade Shen, Christine Moran, Richard Zens, Chris Dyer, Ondrej Bojar, Alexandra Constantin, and Evan Herbst. 2007. Moses: Open source toolkit for statistical machine translation. In *Proceedings of the 45th Annual Meeting of the Association for Computational Linguistics Companion Volume Proceedings of the Demo and Poster Sessions*.

E. Loper and S. Bird. 2002. NLTK: The Natural Language Toolkit. In *Proceedings of the ACL-02 Workshop on Effective Tools and Methodologies for Teaching Natural Language Processing and Computational Linguistics*.

D. McCarthy and R. Navigli. 2007. SemEval-2007 Task 10: English lexical substitution task. In *Proceedings of SemEval-2007*.

Rada Mihalcea, Ravi Sinha, and Diana McCarthy. 2010. Semeval-2010 Task 2: Cross-lingual lexical substitution. In *Proceedings of the 5th International Workshop on Semantic Evaluations (SemEval-2010)*.

Helmut Schmid. 1994. Probabilistic part-of-speech tagging using decision trees. In *International Conference on New Methods in Language Processing*.

COLEUR and COLSLM: A WSD approach to Multilingual Lexical Substitution, Tasks 2 and 3 SemEval 2010

Weiwei Guo and Mona Diab
Center for Computational Learning Systems
Columbia University
{weiwei,mdiab}@ccls.columbia.edu

Abstract

In this paper, we present a word sense disambiguation (WSD) based system for multilingual lexical substitution. Our method depends on having a WSD system for English and an automatic word alignment method. Crucially the approach relies on having parallel corpora. For Task 2 (Sinha *et al.*, 2009) we apply a supervised WSD system to derive the English word senses. For Task 3 (Lefever & Hoste, 2009), we apply an unsupervised approach to the training and test data. Both of our systems that participated in Task 2 achieve a decent ranking among the participating systems. For Task 3 we achieve the highest ranking on several of the language pairs: French, German and Italian.

1 Introduction

In this paper, we present our system that was applied to the cross lingual substitution for two tasks in SEMEVAL 2010, Tasks 2 and 3. We adopt the same approach for both tasks with some differences in the basic set-up. Our basic approach relies on applying a word sense disambiguation (WSD) system to the English data that comes from a parallel corpus for English and a language of relevance to the task, language 2 (l2). Then we automatically induce the English word sense correspondences to l2. Accordingly, for a given test target word, we return its equivalent l2 words assuming that we are able to disambiguate the target word in context.

2 Our Detailed Approach

We approach the problem of multilingual lexical substitution from a WSD perspective. We adopt the hypothesis that the different word senses of ambiguous words in one language probably translate to different lexical items in another language. Hence, our approach relies on two crucial components: a WSD module for the source language (our target test words, in our case these are the English target test words) and an automatic word alignment module to discover the target word sense correspondences with the foreign words in a second language. Our approach to both tasks is unsupervised since we don't have real training data annotated with the target words and their corresponding translations into l2 at the onset of the problem.

Accordingly, at training time, we rely on automatically tagging large amounts of English data (target word instances) with their relevant senses and finding their l2 correspondences based on automatically induced word alignments. Each of these English sense and l2 correspondence pairs has an associated translation probability value depending on frequency of co-occurrence. This information is aggregated in a look-up table over the entire training set. An entry in the table would have a target word sense type paired with all the observed translation correspondences l2 word types. Each of the l2 word types has a probability of translation that is calculated as a normalized weighted average of all the instances of this l2 word type with the English sense aggregated across the whole parallel corpus. This process results in an English word sense translation table (WSTT). The word senses are derived from WordNet (Fellbaum, 1998). We expand the English word sense entry correspondences by adding the translations of the members of target word sense synonym set as listed in WordNet.

For alignment, we specifically use the GIZA++ software for inducing word alignments across the parallel corpora (Och & Ney, 2003). We apply GIZA++ to the parallel corpus in both directions English to l2 and l2 to English then take only the intersection of the two alignment sets, hence fo-

Proceedings of the 5th International Workshop on Semantic Evaluation, ACL 2010, pages 129–133,
Uppsala, Sweden, 15-16 July 2010.

cusing more on precision of alignment rather than recall.

For each language in Task 3 and Task 2, we use TreeTagger[1] to do the preprocessing for all languages. The preprocessing includes segmentation, POS tagging and lemmatization. Since TreeTagger is independent of languages, our system does not rely on anything that is language specific; our system can be easily applied to other languages. We run GIZA++ on the parallel corpus, and obtain the intersection of the alignments in both directions. Meanwhile, every time a target English word appears in a sentence, we apply our WSD system on it, using the sentence as context. From this information, we build a WSST from the English sense(s) to their corresponding foreign words. Moreover, we use WordNet as a means of augmenting the translation correspondences. We expand the word sense to its synset from WordNet adding the l2 words that corresponded to all the member senses in the synset yielding more translation variability.

At test time, given a test data target word, we apply the same WSD system that is applied to the training corpus to create the WSTT. Once the target word instance is disambiguated in context, we look up the corresponding entry in the WSTT and return the ranked list of l2 correspondences. We present results for best and for oot which vary only in the cut off threshold. In the BEST condition we return the highest ranked candidate, in the oot condition we return the top 10 (where available).[2]

Given the above mentioned pipeline, Tasks 2 and 3 are very similar. Their main difference lies in the underlying WSD system applied.

3 Task 2

3.1 System Details

We use a relatively simple monolingual supervised WSD system to create the sense tags on the English data. We use the SemCor word sense annotated corpus. SemCor is a subset of the Brown Corpus. For each of our target English words found disambiguated in the SemCor corpus, we create a sense profile for each of its senses. A sense profile is a vector of all the content words that occur in the context of this sense in the SemCor corpus. The dimensions of the vector are word types, as in a bag of words model, and the vector entries are the co-occurrence frequency of the word sense and the word type. At test time, given a a target English word, we create a bag of word types contextual vector for each instance of the word using the surrounding context. We compare the created test vector to the SemCor vectors and choose the highest most similar sense and use that for sense disambiguation. In case of ties, we return more than one sense tag.

Corpus	best		oot	
	P	R	P	R
T2-COLSLM	27.59	25.99	46.61	43.91
T2-COLEUR	19.47	18.15	44.77	41.72

Table 1: Precision and Recall results per corpus on Task 2 test set

3.2 Data

We use both naturally occurring parallel data and machine translation data. The data for our first Task 2 submission, T2-COLEUR, comprises naturally occurring parallel data, namely, the Spanish English portion of the EuroParl data provided by Task 3 organizers. For the machine translation data, we use translations of the source English data pertaining to the following corpora: the Brown corpus, WSJ, SensEval1, SensEval2 datasets as translated by two machine translation systems: Global Link (GL), Systran (SYS) (Guo & Diab, 2010). We refer to the translated corpus as the SALAAM corpus. The intuition for creating SALAAM (an artificial parallel corpus) is to create a balanced translation corpus that is less domain and genre skewed than the EuroParl data. This latter corpus results in our 2nd system for this task T2-COLSLM.

3.3 Results

Table 1 presents our overall results as evaluated by the organizers.

It is clear that the T2-COLSLM outperforms T2-COLEUR.

4 Task 3

4.1 System Details

Contrary to Task 2, we apply a context based unsupervised WSD module to the English side of the parallel data. Our unsupervised WSD method, as described in (Guo & Diab, 2009), is a graph based

[1] http://www.ims.uni-stuttgart.de/projekte/corplex/TreeTagger/

[2] Some of the target word senses had less than 10 l2 word correspondences.

unsupervised WSD method. Given a sequence of words $W = \{w_1, w_2 ... w_n\}$, each word w_i with several senses $\{s_{i1}, s_{i2} ... s_{im}\}$. A graph G = (V,E) is defined such that there exists a vertex v for each sense. Two senses of two different words may be connected by an edge e, depending on their distance. That two senses are connected suggests they should have influence on each other, accordingly a maximum allowable distance is set. They explore 4 different graph based algorithms.We focus on the `In-Degree` graph based algorithm. The `In-Degree` algorithm presents the problem as a weighted graph with senses as nodes and similarity between senses as weights on edges. The `In-Degree` of a vertex refers to the number of edges incident on that vertex. In the weighted graph, the `In-Degree` for each vertex is calculated by summing the weights on the edges that are incident on it. After all the `In-Degree` values for each sense are computed, the sense with maximum value is chosen as the final sense for that word. In our implementation of the `In-Degree` algorithm, we use the JCN similarity measure for both Noun-Noun and Verb-Verb similarity calculation.

4.2 Data

We use the training data from EuroParl provided by the task organizers for the 5 different language pairs. We participate in all the language competitions. We refer to our system as T3-COLEUR.

4.3 Results

Table 2 shows our system results on Task 3, specified by languages.

4.4 Error Analysis and Discussion

As shown in Table 2, our system T3-COLEUR ranks the highest for the French, German and Italian language tasks on both best and oot. However the overall F-measures are very low. Our system ranks last for Dutch among 3 systems and it is middle of the pack for the Spanish language task. In general we note that the results for oot are naturally higher than for BEST since by design it is a more relaxed measure.

5 Related works

Our work mainly investigates the influence of WSD on providing machine translation candidates. Carpuat & Wu (2007) and Chan et al.(2007) show WSD improves MT. However, in (Carpuat & Wu, 2007) classical WSD is missing by ignoring predefined senses. They treat translation candidates as sense labels, then find linguistic features in the English side, and cast the disambiguation process as a classification problem. Of relevance also to our work is that related to the task of English monolingual lexical substitution. For example some of the approaches that participated in the SemEval 2007 excercise include the following. Yuret (2007) used a statistical language model based on a large corpus to assign likelihoods to each candidate substitutes for a target word in a sentence. Martinez et al. (2007) uses WordNet to find candidate substitutes, produce word sequence including substitutes. They rank the substitutes by ranking the word sequence including that substitutes using web queries. In (Giuliano C. *et al.*, 2007), they extract synonyms from dictionaries. They have 2 ways of ranking of the synonyms: by similarity metric based on LSA and by occurrence in a large 5-gram web corpus. Dahl et al. (2007) also extract synonyms from dictionaries. They present two systems. The first one scores substitutes based on how frequently the local context match the target word. The second one incorporates cosine similarity. Finally, Hassan et al. (2007) extract candidates from several linguistic resources, and combine many techniques and evidences to compute the scores such as machine translation, most common sense, language model and so on to pick the most suitable lexical substitution candidates.

6 Conclusions and Future Directions

In this paper we presented a word sense disambiguation based system for multilingual lexical substitution. The approach relies on having a WSD system for English and an automatic word alignment method. Crucially the approach relies on having parallel corpora. For Task 2 we apply a supervised WSD system to derive the English word senses. For Task 3, we apply an unsupervised approach to the training and test data. Both of our systems that participated in Task 2 achieve a decent ranking among the participating systems. For Task 3 we achieve the highest ranking on several of the language pairs: French, German and Italian.

In the future, we would like to investigate the usage of the Spanish and Italian WordNets for the

Language	best			oot		
	P	R	rank	P	R	rank
Dutch	10.71	10.56	3/3	21.47	21.27	3/3
Spanish	19.78	19.59	3/7	35.84	35.46	5/7
French	21.96	21.73	1/7	49.44	48.96	1/5
German	13.79	13.63	1/3	33.21	32.82	1/3
Italian	15.55	15.4	1/3	40.7	40.34	1/3

Table 2: Results of T3-COLEUR per language on Task 3 Test set

task. We would like to also expand our examination to other sources of bilingual data such as comparable corpora. Finally, we would like to investigate using unsupervised clustering of senses (Word Sense Induction) methods in lieu of the WSD approaches that rely on WordNet.

References

CARPUAT M. & WU D. (2007). Improving statistical machine translation using word sense disambiguation. In *Proceedings of the 2007 Joint Conference on Empirical Methods in Natural Language Processing and Computational Natural Language Learning (EMNLP-CoNLL)*, p. 61–72, Prague, Czech Republic: Association for Computational Linguistics.

CHAN Y. S., NG H. T. & CHIANG D. (2007). Word sense disambiguation improves statistical machine translation. In *Proceedings of the 45th Annual Meeting of the Association of Computational Linguistics*, p. 33–40, Prague, Czech Republic: Association for Computational Linguistics.

DAHL G., FRASSICA A. & WICENTOWSKI R. (2007). SW-AG: Local Context Matching for English Lexical Substitution. In *Proceedings of the 4th workshop on Semantic Evaluations (SemEval-2007)*, Prague, Czech Republic.

FELLBAUM C. (1998). "wordnet: An electronic lexical database". MIT Press.

GIULIANO C., GLIOZZO A. & STRAPPARAVA C (2007). FBK-irst: Lexical Substitution Task Exploiting Domain and Syntagmatic Coherence. In *Proceedings of the 4th workshop on Semantic Evaluations (SemEval-2007)*, Prague, Czech Republic.

GUO W. & DIAB M. (2009). "Improvements to monolingual English word sense disambiguation". In *ACL Workshop on Semantics Evaluations*.

GUO W. & DIAB M. (2010). "Combining orthogonal monolingual and multilingual sources of evidence for All Words WSD". In *ACL 2010*.

HASSAN S., CSOMAI A., BANEA C., SINHA R. & MIHALCEA R. (2007). UNT: SubFinder: Combining Knowledge Sources for Automatic Lexical Substitution. In *Proceedings of the 4th workshop on Semantic Evaluations (SemEval-2007)*, Prague, Czech Republic.

IDE N. & V RONIS J. (1998). Word sense disambiguation: The state of the art. In *Computational Linguistics*, p. 1–40.

JIANG J. & CONRATH. D. (1997). Semantic similarity based on corpus statistics and lexical taxonomy. In *Proceedings of the International Conference on Research in Computational Linguistics*, Taiwan.

LEACOCK C. & CHODOROW M. (1998). Combining local context and wordnet sense similarity for word sense identification. In *WordNet, An Electronic Lexical Database*: The MIT Press.

LEFEVER C. & HOSTE V. (2009). SemEval-2010 Task 3: Cross-lingual Word Sense Disambiguation. In *Proceedings of the NAACL HLT Workshop on Semantic Evaluations: Recent Achievements and Future Directions*, Boulder, Colorado.

LESK M. (1986). Automatic sense disambiguation using machine readable dictionaries: How to tell a pine cone from an ice cream cone. In *In Proceedings of the SIGDOC Conference*, Toronto.

MARTINEZ D., KIM S. & BALDWIN T. (2007). MELB-MKB: Lexical Substitution system based on Relatives in Context In *Proceedings of the 4th workshop on Semantic Evaluations (SemEval-2007)*, Prague, Czech Republic.

M. PALMER, C. FELLBAUM S. C. L. D. & DANG H. (2001). English tasks: all-words and verb lexical sample. In *In Proceedings of ACL/SIGLEX Senseval-2*, Toulouse, France.

MIHALCEA R. (2005). Unsupervised large-vocabulary word sense disambiguation with graph-based algorithms for sequence data labeling. In *Proceedings of Human Language Technology Conference and Conference on Empirical Methods in Natural Language Processing*, p. 411–418, Vancouver, British Columbia, Canada: Association for Computational Linguistics.

MILLER G. A. (1990). Wordnet: a lexical database for english. In *Communications of the ACM*, p. 39–41.

NAVIGLI R. (2009). Word sense disambiguation: a survey. In *ACM Computing Surveys*, p. 1–69: ACM Press.

OCH F. J. & NEY H. (2003). A systematic comparison of various statistical alignment models. *Computational Linguistics*, **29(1)**, 19–51.

PEDERSEN B. & PATWARDHAN (2005). Maximizing semantic relatedness to perform word sense disambiguation. In *University of Minnesota Supercomputing Institute Research Report UMSI 2005/25*, Minnesotta.

PRADHAN S., LOPER E., DLIGACH D. & PALMER M. (2007). Semeval-2007 task-17: English lexical sample, srl and all words. In *Proceedings of the Fourth International Workshop on Semantic Evaluations (SemEval-2007)*, p. 87–92, Prague, Czech Republic: Association for Computational Linguistics.

SINHA R. & MIHALCEA R. (2007). Unsupervised graph-based word sense disambiguation using measures of word semantic similarity. In *Proceedings of the IEEE International Conference on Semantic Computing (ICSC 2007)*, Irvine, CA.

SINHA R., MCCARTHY D. & MIHALCEA R. (2009). SemEval-2010 Task 2: Cross-Lingual Lexical Substitution. In *Proceedings of the NAACL HLT Workshop on Semantic Evaluations: Recent Achievements and Future Directions*, Irvine, CA.

SNYDER B. & PALMER M. (2004). The english all-words task. In R. MIHALCEA & P. EDMONDS, Eds., *Senseval-3: Third International Workshop on the Evaluation of Systems for the Semantic Analysis of Text*, p. 41–43, Barcelona, Spain: Association for Computational Linguistics.

YURET D. (2007). KU: Word sense disambiguation by substitution. In *Proceedings of the 4th workshop on Semantic Evaluations (SemEval-2007)*, Prague, Czech Republic.

UHD: Cross-Lingual Word Sense Disambiguation Using Multilingual Co-occurrence Graphs

Carina Silberer and **Simone Paolo Ponzetto**
Department of Computational Linguistics
Heidelberg University
{silberer,ponzetto}@cl.uni-heidelberg.de

Abstract

We describe the University of Heidelberg (UHD) system for the Cross-Lingual Word Sense Disambiguation SemEval-2010 task (CL-WSD). The system performs CL-WSD by applying graph algorithms previously developed for monolingual Word Sense Disambiguation to multilingual co-occurrence graphs. UHD has participated in the BEST and out-of-five (OOF) evaluations and ranked among the most competitive systems for this task, thus indicating that graph-based approaches represent a powerful alternative for this task.

1 Introduction

This paper describes a graph-based system for Cross-Lingual Word Sense Disambiguation, i.e. the task of disambiguating a word in context by providing its most appropriate translations in different languages (Lefever and Hoste, 2010, CL-WSD henceforth). Our goal at SemEval-2010 was to assess whether graph-based approaches, which have been successfully developed for monolingual Word Sense Disambiguation, represent a valid framework for CL-WSD. These typically transform a knowledge resource such as WordNet (Fellbaum, 1998) into a graph and apply graph algorithms to perform WSD. In our work, we follow this line of research and apply graph-based methods to *multilingual co-occurrence graphs* which are automatically created from parallel corpora.

2 Related Work

Our method is heavily inspired by previous proposals from Véronis (2004, Hyperlex) and Agirre et al. (2006). Hyperlex performs graph-based WSD based on *co-occurrence graphs*: given a monolingual corpus, for each target word a graph is built where nodes represent content words co-occurring with the target word in context, and edges connect the words which co-occur in these contexts. The second step iteratively selects the node with highest degree in the graph (root hub) and removes it along with its adjacent nodes. Each such selection corresponds to isolating a high-density component of the graph, in order to select a sense of the target word. In the last step the root hubs are linked to the target word and the Minimum Spanning Tree (MST) of the graph is computed to disambiguate the target word in context. Agirre et al. (2006) compare Hyperlex with an alternative method to detect the root hubs based on PageRank (Brin and Page, 1998). PageRank has the advantage of requiring less parameters than Hyperlex, whereas the authors ascertain equal performance of the two methods.

3 Graph-based Cross-Lingual WSD

We start by building for each target word a multilingual co-occurrence graph based on the target word's aligned contexts found in parallel corpora (Sections 3.1 and 3.2). Multilingual nodes are linked by translation edges, labeled with the target word's translations observed in the corresponding contexts. We then use an adapted PageRank algorithm to select the nodes which represent the target word's different senses (Section 3.3) and, given these nodes, we compute the MST, which is used to select the most relevant words in context to disambiguate a given test instance (Section 3.4). Translations are finally given by the incoming translation edges of the selected context words.

Proceedings of the 5th International Workshop on Semantic Evaluation, ACL 2010, pages 134–137,
Uppsala, Sweden, 15-16 July 2010.

3.1 Monolingual Graph

Let C_s be all contexts of a target word w in a source language s, i.e. English in our case, within a (PoS-tagged and lemmatized) monolingual corpus. We first construct a monolingual co-occurrence graph $G_s = \langle V_s, E_s \rangle$. We collect all pairs (cw_i, cw_j) of co-occurring nouns or adjectives in C_s (excluding the target word itself) and add each word as a node into the initially empty graph. Each co-occurring word pair is connected with an edge $(v_i, v_j) \in E_s$, which is assigned a weight $w(v_i, v_j)$ based on the strength of association between the respective words cw_i and cw_j:

$$w(v_i, v_j) = 1 - \max\,[p(cw_i|cw_j), p(cw_j|cw_i)].$$

The conditional probability of word cw_i given word cw_j is estimated by the number of contexts in which cw_i and cw_j co-occur divided by the number of contexts containing cw_j.

3.2 Multilingual Graph

Given a set of target languages L, we then extend G_s to a labeled multilingual graph $G_{ML} = \langle V_{ML}, E_{ML} \rangle$ where:

1. $V_{ML} = V_s \cup \bigcup_{l \in L} V_l$ is a set of nodes representing content words from either the source (V_s) or the target (V_l) languages;
2. $E_{ML} = E_s \cup \bigcup_{l \in L} \{E_l \cup E_{s,l}\}$ is a set of edges. These include (a) *co-occurrence edges* $E_l \subseteq V_l \times V_l$ between nodes representing words in a target language (V_l), weighted in the same way as the edges in the monolingual graph; (b) labeled *translation edges* $E_{s,l}$ which represent translations of words from the source language into a target language. These edges are assigned a complex label $t \in \mathcal{T}_{w,l}$ comprising a translation of the word w in the target language l and its frequency of translation, i.e. $E_{s,l} \subseteq V_s \times \mathcal{T}_{w,l} \times V_l$.

The multilingual graph is built based on a word-aligned multilingual parallel corpus and a multilingual dictionary. The pseudocode is presented in Algorithm 1. We start with the monolingual graph from the source language (line 1) and then for each target language $l \in L$ in turn, we add the translation edges $(v_s, t, v_l) \in E_{s,l}$ of each word in the source language (lines 5-15). In order to include the information about the translations of w in the different target languages, each translation edge

Algorithm 1 Multilingual co-occurrence graph.

Input: target word w and its contexts C_s
monolingual graph $G_s = \langle V_s, E_s \rangle$
set of target languages L
Output: a multilingual graph G_{ML}

1: $G_{ML} = \langle V_{ML}, E_{ML} \rangle \leftarrow G_s = \langle V_s, E_s \rangle$
2: **for each** $l \in L$
3: $V_l \leftarrow \emptyset$
4: C_l := aligned sentences of C_s in lang. l
5: **for each** $v_s \in V_s$
6: $T_{v_s,l}$:= translations of v_s found in C_l
7: $C_{v_s} \subseteq C_s$:= contexts containing w and v_s
8: **for each** translation $v_l \in T_{v_s,l}$
9: C_{v_l} := aligned sentences of C_{v_s} in lang. l
10: $\mathcal{T}_{w,C_{v_l}} \leftarrow$ translation labels of w from C_{v_l}
11: **if** $v_l \notin V_{ML}$ **then**
12: $V_{ML} \leftarrow V_{ML} \cup v_l$
13: $V_l \leftarrow V_l \cup v_l$
14: **for each** $t \in \mathcal{T}_{w,C_{v_l}}$
15: $E_{ML} \leftarrow E_{ML} \cup (v_s, t, v_l)$
16: **for each** $v_i \in V_l$
17: **for each** $v_j \in V_l,\ i \neq j$
18: **if** v_i and v_j co-occur in C_l **then**
19: $E_{ML} \leftarrow E_{ML} \cup (v_i, v_j)$
20: **return** G_{ML}

(v_s, t, v_l) receives a translation label t. Formally, let $C_{v_s} \subseteq C_s$ be the contexts where v_s and w co-occur, and C_{v_l} the word-aligned contexts in language l of C_{v_s}, where v_s is translated as v_l. Then each edge between nodes v_s and v_l is labeled with a translation label t (lines 14-15): this includes a translation of w in C_{v_l}, its frequency of translation and the information of whether the translation is monosemous, as found in a multilingual dictionary, i.e. EuroWordNet (Vossen, 1998) and PanDictionary (Mausam et al., 2009). Finally, the multilingual graph is further extended by inserting all possible co-occurrence edges $(v_i, v_j) \in E_l$ between the nodes for the target language l (lines 16-19, i.e. we apply the step from Section 3.1 to l and C_l). As a result of the algorithm, the multilingual graph is returned (line 20).

3.3 Computing Root Hubs

We compute the root hubs in the multilingual graph to discriminate the senses of the target word in the source language. Hubs are found using the adapted PageRank from Agirre et al. (2006):

$$PR(v_i) = (1-d) + d \sum_{j \in deg(v_i)} \frac{w_{ij}}{\sum_{k \in deg(v_j)} w_{jk}} PR(v_j)$$

where d is the so-called damping factor (typically set to 0.85), $deg(v_i)$ is the number of adjacent nodes of node v_i and w_{ij} is the weight of the co-occurrence edge between nodes v_i and v_j.

Since this step aims to induce the senses for the target word, only nodes referring to words in English can become root hubs. However, in order to use additional evidence from other languages, we furthermore include in the computation of PageRank co-occurrence edges from the target languages, as long as these occur in contexts with 'safe', i.e. *monosemous*, translations of the target word. Given an English co-occurrence edge $(v_{s,i}, v_{s,j})$ and translation edges $(v_{s,i}, v_{l,i})$ and $(v_{s,j}, v_{l,j})$ to nodes in the target language l, labeled with monosemous translations, we include the co-occurrence edge $(v_{l,i}, v_{l,j})$ in the PageRank computation. For instance, animal and biotechnology are translated in German as Tier and Biotechnologie, both with edges labeled with the monosemous Pflanze: accordingly, we include the edge (Tier, Biotechnologie) in the computation of $PR(v_i)$, where v_i is either animal or biotechnology.

Finally, following Véronis (2004), a MST is built with the target word as its root and the root hubs of G_{ML} forming its first level. By using a multilingual graph, we are able to obtain MSTs which contain translation nodes and edges.

3.4 Multilingual Disambiguation

Given a context W for the target word w in the source language, we use the MST to find the most relevant words in W for disambiguating w. We first map each content word $cw \in W$ to nodes in the MST. Since each word is dominated by exactly one hub, we can find the relevant nodes by computing the correct hub $disHub$ (i.e. sense) and then only retain those nodes linked to $disHub$. Let W_h be the set of mapped content words dominated by hub h. Then, $disHub$ can be found as:

$$disHub = \underset{h}{\operatorname{argmax}} \sum_{cw \in W_h} \frac{d(cw)}{dist(cw, h) + 1}$$

where $d(cw)$ is a function which assigns a weight to cw according to its distance to w, i.e. the more words occur between w and cw within W, the smaller the weight, and $dist(cw, h)$ is given by the number of edges between cw and h in the MST. Finally, we collect the translation edges of the retained context nodes W_{disHub} and we sum the translation counts to rank each translation.

4 Results and Analysis

Experimental Setting. We submitted two runs for the task (UHD-1 and UHD-2 henceforth). Since we were interested in assessing the impact of using different resources with our methodology, we automatically built multilingual graphs from different sentence-aligned corpora, i.e. Europarl (Koehn, 2005) for UHD-1, augmented with the JRC-Acquis corpus (Steinberger et al., 2006) for UHD-2[1]. Both corpora were tagged and lemmatized with TreeTagger (Schmid, 1994) and word aligned using GIZA++ (Och and Ney, 2003). For German, in order to avoid the sparseness deriving from the high productivity of compounds, we performed a morphological analysis using Morphisto (Zielinski et al., 2009).

To build the multilingual graph (Section 3.2), we used a minimum frequency threshold of 2 occurrences for a word to be inserted as a node, and retained only those edges with a weight less or equal to 0.7. After constructing the multilingual graph, we additionally removed those translations with a frequency count lower than 10 (7 in the case of German, due to the large amount of compounds). Finally, the translations generated for the BEST evaluation setting were obtained by applying the following rule onto the ranked answer translations: add translation tr_i while $count(tr_i) \geq count(tr_{i-1})/3$, where i is the i-th ranked translation.

Results and discussion. The results for the BEST and out-of-five (OOF) evaluations are presented in Tables 1 and 2 respectively. Results are computed using the official scorer (Lefever and Hoste, 2010) and no post-processing is applied to the system's output, i.e. we do not back-off to the baseline most frequent translation in case the system fails to provide an answer for a test instance. For the sake of brevity, we present the results for UHD-1, since we found no statistically significant difference in the performance of the two systems (e.g. UHD-2 outperforms UHD-1 only by $+0.7\%$ on the BEST evaluation for French).

[1]As in the case of Europarl, only 1-to-1-aligned sentences were extracted.

Language	P	R	Mode P	Mode R
FRENCH	20.22	16.21	17.59	14.56
GERMAN	12.20	9.32	11.05	7.78
ITALIAN	15.94	12.78	12.34	8.48
SPANISH	20.48	16.33	28.48	22.19

Table 1: BEST results (UHD-1).

Language	P	R	Mode P	Mode R
FRENCH	39.06	32.00	37.00	26.79
GERMAN	27.62	22.82	25.68	21.16
ITALIAN	33.72	27.49	27.54	21.81
SPANISH	38.78	31.81	40.68	32.38

Table 2: OOF results (UHD-1).

Overall, in the BEST evaluation our system ranked in the middle for those languages where the majority of systems participated – i.e. second and fourth out of 7 submissions for FRENCH and SPANISH. When compared against the baseline, i.e. the most frequent translation found in Europarl, our method was able to achieve in the BEST evaluation a higher precision for ITALIAN and SPANISH (+1.9% and +2.1%, respectively), whereas FRENCH and GERMAN lie near below the baseline scores (−0.5% and −1.0%, respectively). The trade-off is a recall always below the baseline. In contrast, we beat the Mode precision baseline for all languages, i.e. up to +5.1% for SPANISH. The fact that our system is strongly precision-oriented is additionally proved by a low performance in the OOF evaluation, where we always perform below the baseline (i.e. the five most frequent translations in Europarl).

5 Conclusions

We presented in this paper a graph-based system to perform CL-WSD. Key to our approach is the use of a co-occurrence graph built from multilingual parallel corpora, and the application of well-studied graph algorithms for monolingual WSD (Véronis, 2004; Agirre et al., 2006). Future work will concentrate on extensions of the algorithms, e.g. computing hubs in each language independently and combining them as a joint problem, as well as developing robust techniques for unsupervised tuning of the graph weights, given the observation that the most frequent translations tend to receive too much weight and accordingly crowd out more appropriate translations. Finally, we plan to investigate the application of our approach directly to multilingual lexical resources such as PanDictionary (Mausam et al., 2009) and BabelNet (Navigli and Ponzetto, 2010).

References

Eneko Agirre, David Martínez, Oier López de Lacalle, and Aitor Soroa. 2006. Two graph-based algorithms for state-of-the-art WSD. In *Proc. of EMNLP-06*, pages 585–593.

Sergey Brin and Lawrence Page. 1998. The anatomy of a large-scale hypertextual web search engine. *Computer Networks and ISDN Systems*, 30(1–7):107–117.

Christiane Fellbaum, editor. 1998. *WordNet: An Electronic Database*. MIT Press, Cambridge, MA.

Philipp Koehn. 2005. Europarl: A parallel corpus for statistical machine translation. In *Proceedings of Machine Translation Summit X*.

Els Lefever and Veronique Hoste. 2010. SemEval-2010 Task 3: Cross-lingual Word Sense Disambiguation. In *Proc. of SemEval-2010*.

Mausam, Stephen Soderland, Oren Etzioni, Daniel Weld, Michael Skinner, and Jeff Bilmes. 2009. Compiling a massive, multilingual dictionary via probabilistic inference. In *Proc. of ACL-IJCNLP-09*, pages 262–270.

Roberto Navigli and Simone Paolo Ponzetto. 2010. BabelNet: Building a very large multilingual semantic network. In *Proc. of ACL-10*.

Franz Josef Och and Hermann Ney. 2003. A systematic comparison of various statistical alignment models. *Computational Linguistics*, 29(1):19–51.

Helmut Schmid. 1994. Probabilistic part-of-speech tagging using decision trees. In *Proceedings of the International Conference on New Methods in Language Processing (NeMLaP '94)*, pages 44–49.

Ralf Steinberger, Bruno Pouliquen, Anna Widiger, Camelia Ignat, Tomaž Erjavec, Dan Tufiş, and Dániel Varga. 2006. The JRC-Acquis: A multilingual aligned parallel corpus with 20+ languages. In *Proc. of LREC '06*.

Jean Véronis. 2004. Hyperlex: lexical cartography for information retrieval. *Computer Speech & Language*, 18(3):223–252.

Piek Vossen, editor. 1998. *EuroWordNet: A Multilingual Database with Lexical Semantic Networks*. Kluwer, Dordrecht, The Netherlands.

Andrea Zielinski, Christian Simon, and Tilman Wittl. 2009. Morphisto: Service-oriented open source morphology for German. In *State of the Art in Computational Morphology*, volume 41 of *Communications in Computer and Information Science*, pages 64–75. Springer.

OWNS: Cross-lingual Word Sense Disambiguation Using Weighted Overlap Counts and Wordnet Based Similarity Measures

Lipta Mahapatra **Meera Mohan**
Dharmsinh Desai University
Nadiad, India
lipta.mahapatra89@gmail.com
mu.mohan@gmail.com

Mitesh M. Khapra **Pushpak Bhattacharyya**
Indian Institute of Technology Bombay
Powai, Mumbai 400076,India
miteshk@cse.iitb.ac.in
pb@cse.iitb.ac.in

Abstract

We report here our work on English French Cross-lingual Word Sense Disambiguation where the task is to find the best French translation for a target English word depending on the context in which it is used. Our approach relies on identifying the nearest neighbors of the test sentence from the training data using a pairwise similarity measure. The proposed measure finds the affinity between two sentences by calculating a weighted sum of the word overlap and the semantic overlap between them. The semantic overlap is calculated using standard Wordnet Similarity measures. Once the nearest neighbors have been identified, the best translation is found by taking a majority vote over the French translations of the nearest neighbors.

1 Introduction

Cross Language Word Sense Disambiguation (CL-WSD) is the problem of finding the correct target language translation of a word given the context in which it appears in the source language. In many cases a full disambiguation may not be necessary as it is common for different meanings of a word to have the same translation. This is especially true in cases where the sense distinction is very fine and two or more senses of a word are closely related. For example, the two senses of the word *letter*, namely, *"formal document'* and *"written/printed message"* have the same French translation *"lettre"*. The problem is thus reduced to distinguishing between the coarser senses of a word and ignoring the finer sense distinctions which is known to be a common cause of errors in conventional WSD. CL-WSD can thus be seen as a slightly relaxed version of the conventional WSD problem. However, CL-WSD has its own set of challenges as described below.

The translations learnt from a parallel corpus may contain a lot of errors. Such errors are hard to avoid due to the inherent noise associated with statistical alignment models. This problem can be overcome if good bilingual dictionaries are available between the source and target language. EuroWordNet[1] can be used to construct such a bilingual dictionary between English and French but it is not freely available. Instead, in this work, we use a noisy statistical dictionary learnt from the Europarl parallel corpus (Koehn, 2005) which is freely downloadable.

Another challenge arises in the form of matching the lexical choice of a native speaker. For example, the word *coach* (as in, *vehicle*) may get translated differently as *autocar*, *autobus* or *bus* even when it appears in very similar contexts. Such decisions depend on the native speaker's intuition and are very difficult for a machine to replicate due to their inconsistent usage in a parallel training corpus.

The above challenges are indeed hard to overcome, especially in an unsupervised setting, as evidenced by the lower accuracies reported by all systems participating in the SEMEVAL Shared Task on Cross-lingual Word Sense Disambiguation (Lefever and Hoste, 2010). Our system ranked second in the English French task (in the *out-of-five* evaluation). Even though its average performance was lower than the baseline by 3% it performed better than the baseline for 12 out of the 20 target nouns.

Our approach identifies the *top-five* translations of a word by taking a majority vote over the translations appearing in the nearest neighbors of the test sentence as found in the training data. We use a pairwise similarity measure which finds the affinity between two sentences by calculating a

[1] http://www.illc.uva.nl/EuroWordNet

Proceedings of the 5th International Workshop on Semantic Evaluation, ACL 2010, pages 138–141,
Uppsala, Sweden, 15-16 July 2010.

weighted sum of the word overlap and the semantic overlap between them. The semantic overlap is calculated using standard Wordnet Similarity measures.

The remainder of this paper is organized as follows. In section 2 we describe related work on WSD. In section 3 we describe our approach. In Section 4 we present the results followed by conclusion in section 5.

2 Related Work

Knowledge based approaches to WSD such as Lesk's algorithm (Lesk, 1986), Walker's algorithm (Walker and Amsler, 1986), Conceptual Density (Agirre and Rigau, 1996) and Random Walk Algorithm (Mihalcea, 2005) are fundamentally overlap based algorithms which suffer from data sparsity. While these approaches do well in cases where there is a surface match (*i.e., exact word match*) between two occurrences of the target word (say, training and test sentence) they fail in cases where their is a semantic match between two occurrences of the target word even though there is no surface match between them. The main reason for this failure is that these approaches do not take into account semantic generalizations (*e.g.*, `train` *is-a* `vehicle`).

On the other hand, WSD approaches which use Wordnet based semantic similarity measures (Patwardhan et al., 2003) account for such semantic generalizations and can be used in conjunction with overlap based approaches. We therefore propose a scoring function which combines the strength of overlap based approaches – frequently co-occurring words indeed provide strong clues – with semantic generalizations using Wordnet based similarity measures. The disambiguation is then done using k-NN (Ng and Lee, 1996) where the k nearest neighbors of the test sentence are identified using this scoring function. Once the nearest neighbors have been identified, the best translation is found by taking a majority vote over the translations of these nearest neighbors.

3 Our approach

In this section we explain our approach for Cross Language Word Sense Disambiguation. The main emphasis is on disambiguation *i.e.* finding English sentences from the training data which are closely related to the test sentence.

3.1 Motivating Examples

To explain our approach we start with two motivating examples. First, consider the following occurrences of the word *coach*:

- S_1*:...carriage of passengers by* ***coach*** *and* ***bus***...
- S_2*:...occasional services by* ***coach*** *and* ***bus*** *and the transit operations...*
- S_3*:...the Gloucester* ***coach*** *saw the game...*

In the first two cases, the word ***coach*** appears in the sense of a ***vehicle*** and in both the cases the word ***bus*** appears in the context. Hence, the surface similarity (*i.e.,* word-overlap count) of S_1 and S_2 would be higher than that of S_1 and S_3 and S_2 and S_3. This highlights the strength of overlap based approaches – frequently co-occurring words can provide strong clues for identifying similar usage patterns of a word.

Next, consider the following two occurrences of the word *coach*:

- S_1*:...I* ***boarded*** *the* ***last coach*** *of the* ***train***...
- S_2*:...I* ***alighted*** *from the* ***first coach*** *of the* ***bus***...

Here, the surface similarity (*i.e.,* word-overlap count) of S_1 and S_2 is zero even though in both the cases the word ***coach*** appears in the sense of ***vehicle***. This problem can be overcome by using a suitable Wordnet based similarity measure which can uncover the hidden semantic similarity between these two sentences by identifying that {bus, train} and {boarded, alighted} are closely related words.

3.2 Scoring function

Based on the above motivating examples, we propose a scoring function for calculating the similarity between two sentences containing the target word. Let S_1 be the test sentence containing m words and let S_2 be a training sentence containing n words. Further, let w_{1i} be the i-th word of S_1 and let w_{2j} be the j-th word of S_2. The similarity between S_1 and S_2 is then given by,

$$Sim(S_1, S_2) = \lambda * Overlap(S_1, S_2) + (1 - \lambda) * Semantic\_Sim(S_1, S_2) \quad (1)$$

where,

$$Overlap(S_1, S_2) = \frac{1}{m+n} \sum_{i=1}^{m} \sum_{j=1}^{n} freq(w_{1i}) * \mathbf{1}_{\{w_{1i}=w_{2j}\}}$$

and,

$$Semantic\_Sim(S_1, S_2) = \frac{1}{m} \sum_{i=1}^{m} Best\_Sim(w_{1i}, S_2)$$

where,

$$Best\_Sim(w_{1i}, S_2) = \max_{w_{2j} \in S_2} lch(w_{1i}, w_{2j})$$

We used the *lch* measure (Leacock and Chodorow, 1998) for calculating semantic similarity of two words. The semantic similarity between S_1 and S_2 is then calculated by simply summing over the maximum semantic similarity of each constituent word of S_1 over all words of S_2. Also note that the overlap count is weighted according to the frequency of the overlapping words. This frequency is calculated from all the sentences in the training data containing the target word. The rational behind using a frequency-weighted sum is that more frequently appearing co-occurring words are better indicators of the sense of the target word (of course, stop words and function words are not considered). For example, the word ***bus*** appeared very frequently with ***coach*** in the training data and was a strong indicator of the ***vehicle*** sense of ***coach***. The values of $Overlap(S_1, S_2)$ and $Semantic\_Sim(S_1, S_2)$ are appropriately normalized before summing them in Equation (1). To prevent the semantic similarity measure from introducing noise by over-generalizing we chose a very high value of λ. This effectively ensured that the $Semantic\_Sim(S_1, S_2)$ term in Equation (1) became active only when the $Overlap(S_1, S_2)$ measure suffered data sparsity. In other words, we placed a higher bet on $Overlap(S_1, S_2)$ than on $Semantic\_Sim(S_1, S_2)$ as we found the former to be more reliable.

3.3 Finding translations of the target word

We used GIZA++[2] (Och and Ney, 2003), a freely available implementation of the IBM alignment models (Brown et al., 1993) to get word level alignments for the sentences in the English-French portion of the Europarl corpus. Under this alignment, each word in the source sentence is aligned to zero or more words in the corresponding target sentence. Once the nearest neighbors for a test sentence are identified using the similarity score described earlier, we use the word alignment models to find the French translation of the target word in the top-k nearest training sentences. These translations are then ranked according to the number of times they appear in these top-k nearest neighbors. The top-5 most frequent translations are then returned as the output.

4 Results

We report results on the English-French Cross-Lingual Word Sense Disambiguation task. The test data contained 50 instances for 20 polysemous nouns, namely, *coach, education, execution, figure, job, letter, match, mission, mood, paper, post, pot, range, rest, ring, scene, side, soil, strain and test*. We first extracted the sentences containing these words from the English-French portion of the Europarl corpus. These sentences served as the training data to be compared with each test sentence for identifying the nearest neighbors. The appropriate translations for the target word in the test sentence were then identified using the approach outlined in section 3.2 and 3.3. For the *best evaluation* we submitted two runs: one containing only the top-1 translation and another containing top-2 translations. For the *oof evaluation* we submitted one run containing the top-5 translations. The system was evaluated using Precision and Recall measures as described in the task paper (Lefever and Hoste, 2010). In the *oof evaluation* our system gave the second best performance among all the participants. However, the average precision was 3% lower than the baseline calculated by simply identifying the five most frequent translations of a word according to GIZA++ word alignments. A detailed analysis showed that in the *oof evaluation* we did better than the baseline for 12 out of the 20 nouns and in the *best evaluation* we did better than the baseline for 5 out of the 20 nouns. Table 1 summarizes the performance of our system in the *best evaluation* and Table 2 gives the detailed performance of our system in the *oof evaluation*. In both the evaluations our system provided a translation for every word in the test data and hence the precision was same as recall in all cases. We refer to our system as OWNS (**O**verlap

[2]`http://sourceforge.net/projects/giza/`

and WordNet Similarity).

System	Precision	Recall
OWNS	16.05	16.05
Baseline	20.71	20.71

Table 1: Performance of our system in *best evaluation*

Word	OWNS (Precision)	Baseline (Precision)
coach	**45.11**	39.04
education	**82.15**	80.4
execution	**59.22**	39.63
figure	30.56	35.67
job	**43.93**	40.98
letter	**46.01**	42.34
match	**31.01**	15.73
mission	55.33	97.19
mood	35.22	64.81
paper	**48.93**	40.95
post	36.65	41.76
pot	26.8	65.23
range	16.28	17.02
rest	**39.89**	38.72
ring	**39.74**	33.74
scene	33.89	38.7
side	**37.85**	36.58
soil	**67.79**	59.9
strain	21.13	30.02
test	**64.65**	61.31
Average	43.11	45.99

Table 2: Performance of our system in *oof evaluation*

5 Conclusion

We described our system for English French Cross-Lingual Word Sense Disambiguation which calculates the affinity between two sentences by combining the weighted word overlap counts with semantic similarity measures. This similarity score is used to find the nearest neighbors of the test sentence from the training data. Once the nearest neighbors have been identified, the best translation is found by taking a majority vote over the translations of these nearest neighbors. Our system gave the second best performance in the *oof evaluation* among all the systems that participated in the English French Cross-Lingual Word Sense Disambiguation task. Even though the average performance of our system was less than the baseline by around 3%, it outperformed the baseline system for 12 out of the 20 nouns.

References

Eneko Agirre and German Rigau. 1996. Word sense disambiguation using conceptual density. In *In Proceedings of the 16th International Conference on Computational Linguistics (COLING)*.

Peter E Brown, Vincent J. Della Pietra, Stephen A. Della Pietra, and Robert L. Mercer. 1993. The mathematics of statistical machine translation: parameter estimation. *Computational Linguistics*, 19:263–311.

P. Koehn. 2005. Europarl: A parallel corpus for statistical machine translation. In *In Proceedings of the MT Summit*.

C. Leacock and M. Chodorow, 1998. *Combining local context and WordNet similarity for word sense identification*, pages 305–332. In C. Fellbaum (Ed.), MIT Press.

Els Lefever and Veronique Hoste. 2010. Semeval-2010 task 3: Cross-lingual word sense disambiguation. In *Proceedings of the 5th International Workshop on Semantic Evaluations (SemEval-2010), Association for Computational Linguistics*.

Michael Lesk. 1986. Automatic sense disambiguation using machine readable dictionaries: how to tell a pine cone from an ice cream cone. In *In Proceedings of the 5th annual international conference on Systems documentation*.

Rada Mihalcea. 2005. Large vocabulary unsupervised word sense disambiguation with graph-based algorithms for sequence data labeling. In *In Proceedings of the Joint Human Language Technology and Empirical Methods in Natural Language Processing Conference (HLT/EMNLP)*, pages 411–418.

Hwee Tou Ng and Hian Beng Lee. 1996. Integrating multiple knowledge sources to disambiguate word senses: An exemplar-based approach. In *In Proceedings of the 34th Annual Meeting of the Association for Computational Linguistics (ACL)*, pages 40–47.

Franz Josef Och and Hermann Ney. 2003. A systematic comparison of various statistical alignment models. *Computational Linguistics*, 29(1):19–51.

Siddharth Patwardhan, Satanjeev Banerjee, and Ted Pedersen. 2003. Using measures of semantic relatedness for word sense disambiguation. In *In proceedings of the Fourth International Conference on Intelligent Text Processing and Computation Linguistics (CICLing*.

D. Walker and R. Amsler. 1986. The use of machine readable dictionaries in sublanguage analysis. In *In Analyzing Language in Restricted Domains, Grishman and Kittredge (eds), LEA Press*, pages 69–83.

273. Task 5. Keyphrase Extraction Based on Core Word Identification and Word Expansion

You Ouyang Wenjie Li Renxian Zhang
The Hong Kong Polytechnic University
{csyouyang,cswjli,csrzhang}@comp.polyu.edu.hk

Abstract

This paper provides a description of the Hong Kong Polytechnic University (PolyU) System that participated in the task #5 of SemEval-2, i.e., the *Automatic Keyphrase Extraction from Scientific Articles* task. We followed a novel framework to develop our keyphrase extraction system, motivated by differentiating the roles of the words in a keyphrase. We first identified the core words which are defined as the most essential words in the article, and then expanded the identified core words to the target keyphrases by a word expansion approach.

1 Introduction

The task #5 in SemEval-2 requires extracting the keyphrases for scientific articles. According to the task definition, keyphrases are the words that capture the main topic of the given document. Currently, keyphrase extraction is usually carried out by a two-stage process, including candidate phrase identification and key phrase selection. The first stage is to identify the candidate phrases that are potential keyphrases. Usually, it is implemented as a process that filters out the obviously unimportant phrases. After the candidate identification stage, the target keyphrases can then be selected from the candidates according to their importance scores, which are usually estimated by some features, such as word frequencies, phrase frequencies, POS-tags, etc.. The features can be combined either by heuristics or by learning models to obtain the final selection strategy.

In most existing keyphrase extraction methods, the importance of a phrase is estimated by a composite score of the features. Different features indicate preferences to phrases with specific characteristics. As to the common features, the phrases that consist of important and correlated words are usually preferred. Moreover, it is indeed implied in these features that the words are uniform in the phrase, that is, their degrees of importance are evaluated by the same criteria. However, we think that this may not always be true. For example, in the phrase "video encoding/decoding", the word "video" appears frequently in the article and thus can be easily identified by simple features, while the word "encoding/decoding" is very rare and thus is very hard to discover. Therefore, a uniform view on the words is not able to discover this kind of keyphrases. On the other hand, we observe that there is usually at least one word in a keyphrase which is very important to the article, such as the word "video" in the above example. In this paper, we call this kind of words *core words*. For each phrase, there may be one or more core words in it, which serve as the core component of the phrase. Moreover, the phrase may contain some words that support the core words, such as "encoding/decoding" in the above example. These words may be less important to the article, but they are highly correlated with the core word and are able to form an integrated concept with the core words. Motivated by this, we consider a new keyphrase extraction framework, which includes two stages: identifying the core words and expanding the core words to keyphrases. The methodology of the proposed approaches and the performance of the resulting system are introduced below. We also provide further discussions and modifications.

2 Methodology

According to our motivation, our extraction framework consists of three processes, including

(1) The pre-processing to obtain the necessary information for the following processes;
(2) The core word identification process to discover the core words to be expanded;
(3) The word expansion process to generate the final keyphrases.

In the pre-processing, we first identify the text fields for each scientific article, including its title, abstract and main text (defined as all the section titles and section contents). The texts are then processed by the language toolkit GATE [1] to carry out sentence segmentation, word stemming and POS (part-of-speech) tagging. Stop-words

[1] Publicly available at http://gate.ac.uk/gate

Proceedings of the 5th International Workshop on Semantic Evaluation, ACL 2010, pages 142–145,
Uppsala, Sweden, 15-16 July 2010.

are not considered to be parts of the target keyphrases.

2.1 Core Word Identification

Core words are the words that represent the dominant concepts in the article. To identify the core words, we consider the features below.

Frequencies: In a science article, the words with higher frequencies are usually more important. To differentiate the text fields, in our system we consider three frequency-based features, i.e., **Title-Frequency (TF)**, **Abstract-Frequency (AF)** and **MainText-Frequency (MF)**, to represent the frequencies of one word in different text fields. For a word *w* in an article *t*, the frequencies are denoted by

$TF(w)$ = Frequency of *w* in the title of *t*;

$AF(w)$ = Frequency of *w* in the abstract of *t*;

$MF(w)$ = Frequency of *w* in the main text of *t*.

POS tag: The part-of-speech tag of a word is a good indicator of core words. Here we adopt a simple constraint, i.e., only nouns or adjectives can be potential core words.

In our system, we use a progressive algorithm to identify all the core words. The effects of different text fields are considered to improve the accuracy of the identification result. First of all, for each word *w* in the title, it is identified to be a core word when satisfying

$\{ TF(w) > 0 \wedge AF(w) > 0 \}$

Since the abstract is usually less indicative than the title, we use stricter conditions for the words in the abstract by considering their co-occurrence with the already-identified core words in the title. For a word *w* in the abstract, a co-occurrence-based feature $CO_T(w)$ is defined as $|S(w)|$, where $S(w)$ is the set of sentences which contain both *w* and at least one title core word. For a word *w* in the abstract, it is identified as an abstract core word when satisfying

$\{ AF(w) > 0 \wedge MF(w) > \alpha_1 \wedge CO_T(w) > \alpha_2 \}$

Similarly, for a word *w* in the main text, it is identified as a general core word when satisfying

$\{ MF(w) > \beta_1 \wedge CO_{TA}(w) > \beta_2 \}$

where $CO_{TA}(w) = |S'(w)|$ and $S'(w)$ is the set of sentences which contain both *w* and at least one identified title core word or abstract core word.

With this progressive algorithm, new core words can be more accurately identified with the previously identified core words. In the above heuristics, the parameters α and β are pre-defined thresholds, which are manually assigned[2].

[2] $(\alpha_1, \alpha_2, \beta_1, \beta_2) = (10, 5, 20, 10)$ in the system

As a matter of fact, this heuristic-based identification approach is simple and preliminary. More sophisticated approaches, such as training machine learning models to classify the words, can be applied for better performance. Moreover, more useful features can also be considered. Nevertheless, we adopted the heuristic-based implementation to test the applicability of the framework as an initial study.

An example of the identified core words is illustrated in Table 1 below:

Type	Core Word
Title	grid, service, discovery, UDDI
Abstract	distributed, multiple, web, computing, registry, deployment, scalability, DHT, DUDE, architecture
Main	proxy, search, node, key, etc.

Table 1: Different types of core words

2.2 Core Word Expansion

Given the identified core words, the keyphrases can then be generated by expanding the core words. An example of the expansion process is illustrated below as

grid ➔ grid service ➔ grid service discovery ➔ scalable grid service discovery

For a core word, each appearance of it can be viewed as a potential expanding point. For each expanding point of the word, we need to judge if the context words can form a keyphrase along with it. Formally, for a candidate word *w* and the current phrase *e* (here we assume that *w* is the previous word, the case for the next word is similar), we consider the following features to judge if *e* should be expanded to *w+e*.

Frequencies: the frequency of *w* (denoted by $Freq(w)$) and the frequency of the combination of *w* and *e* (denoted by $phraseFreq(w, e)$) which reflects the degree of *w* and *e* forming an integrated phrase.

POS pattern: The part-of-speech tag of the word *w* is also considered here, i.e., we only try to expand *w* to *w+e* when *w* is a noun, an adjective or the specific conjunction "of".

A heuristic-based approach is adopted here again. We intend to define some loose heuristics, which prefer long keyphrases. The heuristics include (1) If *w* and *e* are in the title or abstract, expand *e* to *e+w* when *w* satisfies the POS constraint and $Freq(w) > 1$; (2) If *w* and *e* are in the main text, expand *e* to *e+w* when *w* satisfies the POS constraint and $phraseFreq(w, e) > 1$.

More examples are provided in Table 2 below.

Core Word	Expanded Key Phrase
grid	scalable grid service discovery, grid computing
UDDI	UDDI registry, UDDI key
web	web service,
scalability	Scalability issue
DHT	DHT node

Table 2: Core words and corresponding key phrases

3 Results

3.1 The Initial PolyU System in SemEval-2

In the Semeval-2 test set, a total of 100 articles are provided. Systems are required to generate 15 keyphrases for each article. Also, 15 keyphrases are generated by human readers as standard answers. Precision, recall and F-value are used to evaluate the performance.

To generate exactly 15 keyphrases with the framework, we expand the core words in the title, abstract and main text in turn. Moreover, the core words in one fixed field are expanded following the descending order of frequency. When 15 keyphrases are obtained, the process is stopped.

For each new phrase, a redundancy check is also conducted to make sure that the final 15 keyphrases can best cover the core concepts of the article, i.e.,
(1) the new keyphrase should contain at least one word that is not included in any of the selected keyphrases;
(2) if a selected keyphrase is totally covered by the new keyphrase, the covered keyphrase will be substituted by the new keyphrase.

The resulting system based on the above method is the one we submitted to SemEval-2.

3.2 Phrase Filtering and Ranking

Initially, we intend to use just the proposed framework to develop our system, i.e., using the expanded phrases as the keyphrases. However, we find out later that it must be adjusted to suit the requirement of the SemEval-2 task. In our subsequent study, we consider two adjustments, i.e., phrase filtering and phrase ranking.

In SemEval-2, the evaluation criteria require exact match between the phrases. A phrase that covers a reference keyphrase but is not equal to it will not be counted as a successful match. For example, the candidate phrase "scalable grid service discovery" is not counted as a match when compared to the reference keyphrase "grid service discovery". We call this the "partial matching problem". In our original framework, we followed the idea of "expanding the phrase as much as possible" and adopted loose conditions. Consequently, the partial matching problem is indeed very serious. This unavoidably affects its performance under the criteria in SemEval-2 that requires exact matches. Therefore, we consider a simple filtering strategy here, i.e., filtering any keyphrase which only appears once in the article.

Another issue is that the given task requires a total of exactly 15 keyphrases. Naturally we need a selection process to handle this. As to our framework, a keyphrase ranking process is necessary for discovering the best 15 keyphrases, not the best 15 core words. For this reason, we also try a simple method that re-ranks the expanded phrases by their frequencies. The top 15 phrases are then selected finally.

3.3 Results

Table 3 below shows the precision, recall and F-value of our submitted system (**PolyU**), the best and worst systems submitted to SemEval-2 and the baseline system that uses simple TF-IDF statistics to select keyphrases.

On the SemEval-2 test data, the performance of the **PolyU** system was not good, just a little better than the baseline. A reason is that we just developed the PolyU system with our past experiences but did not adjust it much for better performance (since we were focusing on designing the new framework). After the competition, we examined two refined systems with the methods introduced in section 3.2.

First, the PolyU system is adapted with the phrase filtering method. The performance of the resulting system (denoted by **PolyU+**) is given in Table 4. As shown in Table 4, the performance is much better just with this simple refinement to meet the requirement on extract matches for the evaluation criteria. Then, the phrase ranking method is also incorporated into the system. The performance of the resulting system (denoted by **PolyU++**) is also provided in Table 4. The performance is again much improved with the phrase ranking process.

3.4 Discussion

In our participation in SemEval-2, we submitted the PolyU system with the proposed extraction framework, which is based on expanding the core words to keyphrases. However, the PolyU system did not perform well in SemEval-2. However, we also showed later that the framework can be much improved after some

Simple but necessary refinements are made according to the given task. The final PolyU++ system with two simple refinements is much better. These refinements, including phrase filtering and ranking, are similar to traditional techniques. So it seems that our expansion-based framework is more applicable along with some traditional techniques. Though this conflicts our initial objective to develop a totally novel framework, the framework shows its ability of finding those keyphrases which contain different types of words. As to the PolyU++ system, when adapted with just two very simple post-processing methods, the extracted candidate phrases can already perform quite well in SemEval-2. This may suggest that the framework can be considered as a new way for candidate keyphrase identification for the traditional extraction process.

4 Conclusion and future work

In this paper, we introduced our system in our participation in SemEval-2. We proposed a new framework for the keyphrase extraction task, which is based on expanding core words to keyphrases. Heuristic approaches are developed to implement the framework. We also analyzed the errors of the system in SemEval-2 and conducted some refinements. Finally, we concluded that the framework is indeed appropriate as a candidate phrase identification method. Another issue is that we just consider some simple information such as frequency or POS tag in this initial study. This indeed limits the power of the resulting systems. In future work, we'd like to develop more sophisticated implementations to testify the effectiveness of the framework. More syntactic and semantic features should be considered. Also, learning models can be applied to improve both the core word identification approach and the word expansion approach.

Acknowledgments

The work described in this paper is supported by Hong Kong RGC Projects (PolyU5217/07E and PolyU5230/08E).

References

Frank, E., Paynter, G.W., Witten, I., Gutwin, C. and Nevill-Manning, C.G.. 1999. Domain Specific Keyphrase Extraction. Proceedings of the IJCAI 1999, pp.668--673.

Medelyan, O. and Witten, I. H.. 2006. Thesaurus based automatic keyphrase indexing. Proceedings of the JCDL 2006, Chapel Hill, NC, USA.

Medelyan, O. and Witten, I. H.. 2008. Domain independent automatic keyphrase indexing with small training sets. Journal of American Society for Information Science and Technology. Vol. 59 (7), pp. 1026-1040

SemEval-2. Evaluation Exercises on Semantic Evaluation. http://semeval2.fbk.eu/

Turney, P.. 1999. Learning to Extract Keyphrases from Text. National Research Council, Institute for Information Technology, Technical Report ERB-1057. (NRC \#41622), 1999.

Wan, X. Xiao, J.. 2008. Single document keyphrase extraction using neighborhood knowledge. In Proceedings of AAAI 2008, pp 885-860.

System	5 Keyphrases			10 Keyphrases			15 Keyphrases		
	P	R	F	P	R	F	P	R	F
Best	34.6%	14.4%	20.3%	26.1%	21.7%	23.7%	21.5%	26.7%	23.8%
Worst	8.2%	3.4%	4.8%	5.3%	4.4%	4.8%	4.7%	5.8%	5.2%
PolyU	13.6%	5.65%	7.98%	12.6%	10.5%	11.4%	12.0%	15.0%	13.3%
Baseline	17.8%	7.4%	10.4%	13.9%	11.5%	12.6%	11.6%	14.5%	12.9%

Table 3: Results from SemEval-2

System	5 Keyphrases			10 Keyphrases			15 Keyphrases		
	P	R	F	P	R	F	P	R	F
PolyU	13.6%	5.65%	7.98%	12.6%	10.5%	11.4%	12.0%	15.0%	13.3%
PolyU+	21.2%	8.8%	12.4%	16.9%	14.0%	15.3%	13.9%	17.3%	15.4%
PolyU++	31.2%	13.0%	18.3%	22.1%	18.4%	20.1%	20.3%	20.6%	20.5%

Table 4: The performance of the refined systems

DERIUNLP: A Context Based Approach to Automatic Keyphrase Extraction

Georgeta Bordea
Unit for Natural Language Processing
Digital Enterprise Research Institute
National University of Ireland, Galway
georgeta.bordea@deri.org

Paul Buitelaar
Unit for Natural Language Processing
Digital Enterprise Research Institute
National University of Ireland, Galway
paul.buitelaar@deri.org

Abstract

The DERI UNLP team participated in the SemEval 2010 Task #5 with an unsupervised system that automatically extracts keyphrases from scientific articles. Our approach does not only consider a general description of a term to select keyphrase candidates but also context information in the form of "skill types". Even though our system analyses only a limited set of candidates, it is still able to outperform baseline unsupervised and supervised approaches.

1 Introduction

Keyphrases provide users overwhelmed by the richness of information currently available with useful insight into document content but at the same time they are a valuable input for a variety of NLP applications such as summarization, clustering and searching. The SemEval 2010 competition included a task targeting the Automatic Keyphrase Extraction from Scientific Articles (Kim et al., 2010). Given a set of scientific articles participants are required to assign to each document keyphrases extracted from text.

We participated in this task with an unsupervised approach for keyphrase extraction that does not only consider a general description of a term to select candidates but also takes into consideration context information. The larger context of our work is the extraction of expertise topics for Expertise Mining (Bordea, 2010).

Expertise Mining is the task of automatically extracting expertise topics and expertise profiles from a collection of documents. Even though the Expertise Mining task and the Keyphrase Extraction task are essentially different, it is important to assess the keyphraseness of extracted expertise topics, i.e., their ability to represent the content of a document. Here we will report only relevant findings for the Keyphrase Extraction task, focusing on the overlapping aspects of the two aforementioned tasks.

After giving an overview of related work in section 2 we introduce skill types and present our candidate selection method in section 3. Section 4 describes the features used for ranking and filtering the candidate keyphrases and Section 5 presents our results before we conclude in Section 6.

2 Related Work

The current methods for keyphrase extraction can be categorized in supervised and unsupervised approaches. Typically any keyphrase extraction system works in two stages. In the first stage a general set of candidates is selected by extracting the tokens of a text. In the second stage unsupervised approaches combine a set of features in a rank to select the most important keyphrases and supervised approaches use a training corpus to learn a keyphrase extraction model.

Mihalcea and Tarau (2004) propose an unsupervised approach that considers single tokens as vertices of a graph and co-occurrence relations between tokens as edges. Candidates are ranked using PageRank and adjacent keywords are merged into keyphrases in a post-processing step. The frequency of noun phrase heads is exploited by Barker and Cornacchia (2000), using noun phrases as candidates and ranking them based on term frequency and term length.

Kea is a supervised system that uses all n-grams of a certain length, a Naive Bayes classifier and tf-idf and position features (Frank et al., 1999). Turney (2000) introduces Extractor, a supervised system that selects stems and stemmed n-grams as candidates and tunes its parameters (mainly related to frequency, position, length) with a genetic algorithm. Hulth (2004) experiments with three types of candidate terms (i.e., n-grams, noun phrase chunks and part-of-speech tagged words

Proceedings of the 5th International Workshop on Semantic Evaluation, ACL 2010, pages 146–149,
Uppsala, Sweden, 15-16 July 2010.

that match a set of patterns) and constructs classifiers by rule induction using features such as term frequency, collection frequency, relative position and PoS tags.

The candidate selection method is the main difference between our approach and previous work. We did not use only a general description of a term to select candidates, but we also took into consideration context information.

3 The Skill Types Candidate Selection Method

Skill types are important domain words that are general enough to be used in different subfields and that reflect theoretical or practical expertise. Consider for instance the following extracts from scientific articles:

*...**analysis** of historical trends...*
*...duplicate photo detection **algorithm** ...*
*...**approach** for data assimilation...*
*...**methodology** for reservoir characterization...*

In all four examples the expertise topic (e.g., "historical trends", "duplicate photo detection algorithm", "data assimilation", "reservoir characterization") is introduced by a skill type (e.g., "analysis", "algorithm", "approach", "methodology"). Some of these skill types are valid for any scientific area (e.g. "approach", "method", "analysis", "solution") but we can also identify domain specific skill types, e.g., for computer science "implementation", "algorithm", "development", "framework", for physics "proof", "principles", "explanation" and for chemistry "law", "composition", "mechanism", "reaction", "structure".

Our system is based on the GATE natural language processing framework (Cunningham et al., 2002) and it uses the ANNIE IE system included in the standard GATE distribution for text tokenization, sentence splitting and part-of-speech tagging. The GATE processing pipeline is depicted in Figure 1, where the light grey boxes embody components available as part of the GATE framework whereas the dark grey boxes represent components implemented as part of our system.

We manually extract a set of 81 single word skill types for the Computer Science field by analysing word frequencies for topics from the ACM classification system[1]. The skill types that appear most

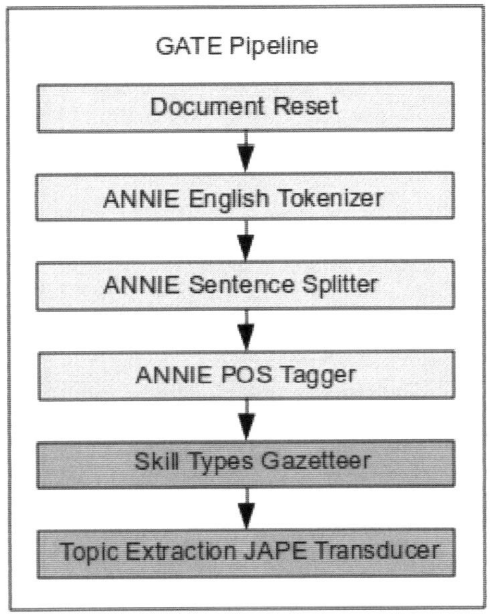

Figure 1: GATE Processing Pipeline

frequently in keyphrases given in the training set are "system", "model" and "information". The Skill Types Gazetteer adds annotations for skill types and then the JAPE Transducer uses regular expressions to annotate candidates.

We rely on a syntactic description of a term to discover candidate keyphrases that appear in the right context of a skill type or that include a skill type. The syntactic pattern for a term is defined by a sequence of part-of-speech tags, mainly a noun phrase. We consider that a noun phrase is a head noun accompanied by a set of modifiers (i.e nouns, adjectives) that includes proper nouns, cardinal numbers (e.g., "P2P systems") and gerunds (e.g., "ontology mapping", "data mining"). Terms that contain the preposition "of" (e.g., "quality of service") or the conjunction "and" (e.g., "search and rescue") were also allowed.

4 Ranking and Filtering

For the ranking stage we use several features already proposed in the literature such as length of a keyphrase, tf-idf and position. We also take into consideration the collection frequency in the context of a skill type.

Ranking. Longer candidates in terms of number of words are ranked higher, because they are more descriptive. Keyphrases that appear more frequently with a skill type in the collection of documents are also ranked higher. Therefore we define the rank for a topic as:

[1]ACM classification system: `http://www.acm.org/about/class/`

Method	5P	5R	5F	10P	10R	10F	15P	15R	15F
TF-IDF	22	7.5	11.19	17.7	12.07	14.35	14.93	15.28	15.1
NB	21.4	7.3	10.89	17.3	11.8	14.03	14.53	14.87	14.7
ME	21.4	7.3	10.89	17.3	11.8	14.03	14.53	14.87	14.7
DERIUNLP	**27.4**	**9.35**	**13.94**	**23**	**15.69**	**18.65**	**22**	**22.51**	**22.25**
DUB	15.83	5.13	7.75	13.40	8.68	10.54	13.33	12.96	13.14

Table 1: Baseline and DERIUNLP Performance aver Combined Keywords

System	5P	5R	5F	10P	10R	10F	15P	15R	15F
Best	39.0	13.3	19.8	32.0	21.8	26.0	27.2	27.8	27.5
Average	29.6	10.1	15	26.1	17.8	21.2	21.9	22.4	22.2
Worst	9.4	3.2	4.8	5.9	4.0	4.8	5.3	5.4	5.3
DERIUNLP	27.4	9.4	13.9	23.0	15.7	18.7	22.0	22.5	22.3

Table 2: Performance over Combined Keywords

$$R_{i,j} = Tn_i * Fn_i * tfidf_{i,j}$$

Where R_i is the rank for the candidate i and the document j, Tn_i is the normalized number of tokens (number of tokens divided by the maximum number of tokens for a keyphrase), Fn_i is the normalized collection frequency of the candidate in the context of a skill type (collection frequency divided by the maximum collection frequency), and $tfidf_i$ is the TF-IDF for candidate i and topic j (computed based on extracted topics not based on all words).

Filtering. Several approaches (Paukkeri et al., 2008; Tomokiyo and Hurst, 2003) use a reference corpus for keyphrase extraction. We decided to use the documents available on the Web as a reference corpus, therefore we use an external web search engine to filter out the candidates that are too general from the final result set. If a candidate has more than 10^9 hits on the web it is too general to be included in the final result set. A lot of noise is introduced by general combination of words that could appear in any document. We remove candidates longer than eight words and we ignore keyphrases that have one letter words or that include non-alphanumerical characters.

Acronyms. Acronyms usually replace long or frequently referenced terms. Results are improved by analysing acronyms (Krulwich and Burkey, 1996) because most of the times the expanded acronym is reported as a keyphrase, not the acronym and because our rank is sensitive to the number of words in a keyphrase. We consider the length of an acronym to be the same as the length of its expansion and we report only the expansion as a keyphrase.

Position. The candidates that appear in the title or the introduction of a document are more likely to be relevant for the document. We divide each document in 10 sections relative to document size and we increase the ranks for keyphrases first mentioned in one of these sections (200% increase for the first section, 100% increase for the second section and 25% for the third section). Candidates with a first appearance in the last section of a document are penalised by 25%.

5 Evaluation

The SemEval task organizers provided two sets of scientific articles, a set of 144 documents for training and a set of 100 documents for testing. No information was provided about the scientific domain of the articles but at least some of them are from Computer Science. The average length of the articles is between 6 and 8 pages including tables and pictures. Three sets of answers were provided: author-assigned keyphrases, reader-assigned keyphrases and combined keyphrases (combination of the first two sets). The participants were asked to assign a number of exactly 15 keyphrases per document.

All reader-assigned keyphrases are extracted from the papers, whereas some of the author-assigned keyphrases do not occur explicitly in the text. Two alternations of keyphrase are accepted: A of B / B A and A's B. In case that the semantics changes due to the alternation, the alternation is not included in the answer set. The traditional evaluation metric was followed, matching the extracted keyphrases with the keyphrases in the answer sets and calculating precision, recall and F-score. In both tables the column labels start with a number which stands for the top 5, 10 or 15 candidates. The characters P, R, F mean micro-averaged precision, recall and F-scores. For baselines, 1, 2, 3 grams were used as candidates and TF-IDF as features.

In Table 1 the keyphrases extracted by our system are compared with keyphrases extracted by an unsupervised method that ranks the candidates based on TF-IDF scores and two supervised methods using Naive Bayes (NB) and maximum entropy(ME) in WEKA[2]. Our performance is well above the baseline in all cases.

To show the contribution of skill types we included the results for a baseline version of our system (DUB) that does not rank the candidates using the normalized collection frequency in the context of a skill type Fn_i but the overall collection frequency (i.e., the number of occurrences of a keyphrase in the corpus). The significantly increased results compared to our baseline version show the effectiveness of skill types for keyphrase candidate ranking.

Table 2 presents our results in comparison with results of other participants. Even though our system considers in the first stage a significantly limited set of candidates the results are very close to the average results of other participants. Our system performed 8th best out of 19 participants for top 15 keyphrases, 10th best for top 10 keyphrases and 13th best for top 5 keyphrases, which indicates that our approach could be improved by using a more sophisticated ranking method.

6 Conclusions

In this paper we have reported the performance of an unsupervised approach for keyphrase extraction that does not only consider a general description of a term to select keyphrase candidates but also takes into consideration context information. The method proposed here uses term extraction techniques (the syntactic description of a term), classical keyword extraction techniques(TF-IDF, length, position) and contextual evidence (skill types).

We argued that so called "skill types" (e.g., "methods", "approach", "analysis") are a useful instrument for selecting keyphrases from a document. Another novel aspect of this approach is using the collection of documents available on the Web (i.e., number of hits for a keyphrase) instead of a reference corpus. It would be interesting to evaluate the individual contributions of skill types for Keyphrase Extraction by adding them as a feature in a classical system like KEA.

Future work will include an algorithm for automatic extraction of skill types for a domain and an analysis of the performance of each skill type.

[2]WEKA:`http://www.cs.waikato.ac.nz/ml/weka/`

7 Aknowledgements

This work is supported by Science Foundation Ireland under Grant No. SFI/08/CE/I1380 (Lion-2).

References

Ken Barker and Nadia Cornacchia. 2000. Using Noun Phrase Heads to Extract Document Keyphrases. In *Canadian Conference on AI*, pages 40–52. Springer.

Georgeta Bordea. 2010. Concept Extraction Applied to the Task of Expert Finding. In *Extended Semantic Web Conference 2010, PhD Symposium*. Springer.

H. Cunningham, D. Maynard, K. Bontcheva, and V. Tablan. 2002. GATE: A Framework and Graphical Development Environment for Robust NLP Tools and Applications. In *Proceedings of the 40th Anniversary Meeting of the Association for Computational Linguistics.*

Eibe Frank, Gordon W Paynter, Ian H Witten, Carl Gutwin, and Craig G Nevill-Manning. 1999. Domain-Specific Keyphrase Extraction. In *Proceedings of the 16th International Joint Conference on Aritficial Intelligence*, pages 668–673.

Anette Hulth. 2004. Enhancing Linguistically Oriented Automatic Keyword Extraction. In *Proceedings of HLT/NAACL: Short Papers*, pages 17–20.

Su Nam Kim, Alyona Medelyan, Min-Yen Kan, and Timothy Baldwin. 2010. SemEval-2010 Task 5: Automatic Keyphrase Extraction from Scientific Articles. In *Proceedings of the ACL 2010 Workshop on Evaluation Exercises on Semantic Evaluation (SemEval 2010).*

Bruce Krulwich and Chad Burkey. 1996. Learning user information interests through extraction of semantically significant phrases. In *Proc. AAAI Spring Symp. Machine Learning in Information Access*, Menlo Park, Calif. Amer. Assoc. for Artificial Intelligence.

Rada Mihalcea and Paul Tarau. 2004. Textrank: Bringing order into texts. In *Proceedings of the Conference on Empirical Methods in Natural Language Processing*, pages 404–411.

Mari-Sanna Paukkeri, Ilari T. Nieminen, Polla Matti, and Timo Honkela. 2008. A Language-Independent Approach to Keyphrase Extraction and Evaluation. In *Coling 2008 Posters*, number August, pages 83–86.

Takashi Tomokiyo and Matthew Hurst. 2003. A Language Model Approach to Keyphrase Extraction. In *Proceedings of the ACL 2003 work- shop on Multiword expressions*, pages 33–40.

Peter D Turney. 2000. Learning algorithms for keyphrase extraction. *Information Retrieval*, 2:303–336.

DFKI KeyWE: Ranking keyphrases extracted from scientific articles

Kathrin Eichler
DFKI - Language Technology
Berlin, Germany
kathrin.eichler@dfki.de

Günter Neumann
DFKI - Language Technology
Saarbrücken, Germany
neumann@dfki.de

Abstract

A central issue for making the content of a scientific document quickly accessible to a potential reader is the extraction of keyphrases, which capture the main topic of the document. Keyphrases can be extracted automatically by generating a list of keyphrase candidates, ranking these candidates, and selecting the top-ranked candidates as keyphrases. We present the KeyWE system, which uses an adapted nominal group chunker for candidate extraction and a supervised ranking algorithm based on support vector machines for ranking the extracted candidates. The system was evaluated on data provided for the SemEval 2010 Shared Task on Keyphrase Extraction.

1 Introduction

Keyphrases capture the main topic of the document in which they appear and can be useful for making the content of a document quickly accessible to a potential reader. They can be presented to the reader directly, in order to provide a short overview of the document, but can also be processed further, e.g. for text summarization, document clustering, question-answering or relation extraction. The task of extracting keyphrases automatically can be performed by generating a list of keyphrase candidates, ranking these candidates, and selecting the top-ranked candidates as keyphrases. In the KeyWE system, candidates are generated based on an adapted nominal group chunker described in section 3 and ranked using the SVM^{rank} algorithm (Joachims, 2006), as described in section 4. The used features are specified in section 5. In section 6, we present the results achieved on the test data provided for the SemEval 2010 Shared Task on Keyphrase Extraction[1] by selecting as keyphrases the top 5, 10, and 15 top-ranked candidates, respectively.

2 Related work

The task of keyphrase extraction came up in the 1990s and was first treated as a supervised learning problem in the GenEx system (Turney, 1999). Since then, the task has evolved and various new approaches have been proposed. The task is usually performed in two steps: 1. candidate extraction (or generation) and 2. keyphrase selection. The most common approach towards candidate extraction is to generate all n-grams up to a particular length and filter them using stopword lists. Lately, more sophisticated candidate extraction methods, usually based on additional linguistic information (e.g. POS tags), have been proposed and shown to produce better results (e.g. Hulth (2004)). Liu et al. (2009) restrict their candidate list to verb, noun and adjective words. Kim and Kan (2009) generate regular expression rules to extract simplex nouns and nominal phrases. As the majority of technical terms is in nominal group positions[2], we assume that the same holds true for keyphrases and apply an adapted nominal group chunker to extract keyphrase candidates.

The selection process is usually based on some supervised learning algorithm, e.g. Naive Bayes (Frank et al., 1999), genetic algorithms (Turney, 1999), neural networks (Wang et al., 2005) or decision trees (Medelyan et al., 2009). Unsupervised approaches have also been proposed, e.g. by Mihalcea and Tarau (2004) and Liu et al. (2009). However, as for the shared task, annotated training data was available, we opted for an approach based on supervised learning.

[1] http://semeval2.fbk.eu/semeval2.php?location=tasks#T6

[2] Experiments on 100 manually annotated scientific abstracts from the biology domain showed that 94% of technical terms are in nominal group position (Eichler et al., 2009).

Proceedings of the 5th International Workshop on Semantic Evaluation, ACL 2010, pages 150–153,
Uppsala, Sweden, 15-16 July 2010.

3 Candidate extraction

Rather than extracting candidates from the full text of the article, we restrict our search for candidates to the first 2000 characters starting with the abstract[3]. We also extract title and general terms for use in the feature construction process. From the reduced input text, we extract keyphrase candidates based on the output of a nominal group chunker.

This approach is inspired by findings from cognitive linguistics. Talmy (2000) divides the concepts expressed in language into two subsystems: the grammatical subsystem and the lexical subsystem. Concepts associated with the grammatical subsystem provide a structuring function and are expressed using so-called closed-class forms (function words, such as conjunctions, determiners, pronouns, and prepositions, but also suffixes such as plural markers and tense markers). Closed-class elements (CCEs) provide a scaffolding, across which concepts associated with the lexical subsystem (i.e. nouns, verbs, adjectives and adverbs) can be draped (Evans and Pourcel, 2009). Spurk (2006) developed a nominal group (NG) chunker that makes use of this grammatical subsystem. Using a finite list of CCEs and learned word class models for identifying verbs and adverbs, a small set of linguistically motivated extraction patterns is stated to extract NGs. The rules are based on the following four types of occurrences of NGs in English: 1. at the sentence beginning, 2. within a determiner phrase, 3. following a preposition and 4. following a verb. Not being trained on a particular corpus, the chunker works in a domain-independent way. In addition, it scales well to large amounts of textual data.

In order to use the chunker for keyphrase extraction, we manually analysed annotated keyphrases in scientific texts, and, based on the outcome of the evaluation, made some adaptations to the chunker, which take care of the fact that the boundaries of a keyphrase do not always coincide with the boundaries of a NG. In particular, we remove determiners, split NGs on conjunctions, and process text within parentheses separately from the main text. An evaluation on the provided training data showed that the adapted chunker extracts 80% of the reader-annotated keyphrases found in the text.

[3]This usually covers the introductory part of the article and is assumed to contain most of the keyphrases. Partial sentences at the end of this input are cut off.

4 Candidate ranking

The problem of ranking keyphrase candidates can be formalized as follows: For a document d and a collection of n keyword candidates C = $c_1 ... c_n$, the goal is to compute a ranking r that orders the candidates in C according to their degree of keyphraseness in d.

The problem can be transformed into an ordinal regression problem. In ordinal regression, the label assigned to an example indicates a rank (rather than a nominal class, as in classification problems). The ranking algorithm we use is SVM^{rank}, developed by Joachims (2006). This algorithm learns a linear ranking function and has shown to outperform classification algorithms in keyphrase extraction (Jiang et al., 2009).

The target (i.e. rank) value defines the order of the examples (i.e. keyphrase candidates). During training, the target values are used to generate pairwise preference constraints. A preference constraint is included for all pairs of examples in the training file, for which the target value differs. Two examples are considered for a pairwise preference constraint only if they appear within the same document.

The model that is learned from the training data is then used to make predictions on the test examples. For each line in the test data, the model predicts a ranking score, from which the ranking of the test examples can be recovered via sorting.

For ranking the candidates, they are transformed into vectors based on the features described in section 5.

During training, the set of candidates is made up of the annotated reader and author keywords as well as all NG chunks extracted from the text. These candidates are mapped to three different ranking values: All annotated keywords are given a ranking value of 2; all extracted NG chunks that were annotated somewhere else in the training data are given a ranking value of 1; all other NG chunks are assigned a ranking value of 0. Giving a special ranking value to chunks annotated somewhere else in the corpus is a way of exploiting domain-specific information about keyphrases. Even though not annotated in this particular document, a candidate that has been annotated in some other document of the domain, is more likely to be a keyphrase than a candidate that has never been annotated before (cf. Frank et al. (1999)).

5 Features

We used two types of features: term-specific features and document-specific features. Term-specific features cover properties of the candidate term itself (e.g. term length). Document-specific features relate properties of the candidate to the text, in which it appears (e.g. frequency of the term in the document). Our term-specific features concern the following properties:

- **Term length** refers to the length of a candidate in number of tokens. We express this property in terms of five boolean features: *has1token*, *has2tokens*, *has3tokens*, *has4tokens*, *has5orMoreTokens*. The advantage over expressing term length as a numeric value is that using binary features, we allow the algorithm to learn that candidates of medium lengths are more likely to be keyphrases than very short or very long candidates.

- The **MSN score** of a candidate refers to the number of results retrieved when querying the candidate string using the MSN search engine[4]. The usefulness of MSN scores for technical term extraction has been shown by Eichler et al. (2009). We normalize the MSN scores based on the number of digits of the score and store the normalized value in the feature *normalizedMsn*. We also use a binary feature *isZeroMsn* expressing whether querying the candidate returns no results at all.

- **Special characters** can indicate whether a candidate is (un)likely to be a keyphrase. We use two features concerning special characters: *containsDigit* and *containsHyphen*.

- **Wikipedia** has shown to be a valuable source for extracting keywords (Medelyan et al., 2009). We use a feature *isWikipediaTerm*, expressing whether the term candidate corresponds to an entry in Wikipedia.

In addition, we use the following document-specific features:

- **TFIDF**, a commonly used feature introduced by Salton and McGill (1983), relates the frequency of a candidate in a document to its frequency in other documents of the corpus.

- **Term position** relates the position of the first appearance of the candidate in the document to the length of the document. In addition, our feature *appearsInTitle* covers the fact that candidates appearing in the document title are very likely to be keyphrases.

- **Average token count** measures the average occurrence of the individual (lemmatized) tokens of the term in the document. Our assumption is that candidates with a high average token count are more likely to be keyphrases.

- **Point-wise mutual information** (PMI, Church and Hanks (1989)) is used to capture the semantic relatedness of the candidate to the topic of the document. A similar feature is introduced by Turney (2003), who, in a first pass, ranks the candidates based on a base feature set, and then reranks them by calculating the statistical association between the given candidate and the top K candidates from the first pass. To avoid the two-pass method, rather than calculating inter-candidate association, we calculate the association of each candidate to the terms specified in the General Terms section of the paper. Like Turney, we calculate PMI based on web search results (in our case, using MSN). The feature *maxPmi* captures the maximum PMI score achieved with the lemmatized candidate and any of the general terms.

6 Results and critical evaluation

Table 1 presents the results achieved by applying the KeyWE system on the data set of scientific articles provided by the organizers of the shared task along with two sets of manually assigned keyphrases for each article (reader-assigned and author-assigned keyphrases). Our model was trained on the trial and training data (144 articles) and evaluated on the test data set (100 articles). The evaluation is based on stemmed keyphrases, where stemming is performed using the Porter stemmer (Porter, 1980).
Since SVM^{rank} learns a linear function, one can analyze the individual features by studying the learned weights. Roughly speaking, a high positive (negative) weight indicates that candidates with this feature should be higher (lower) in the

[4] http://de.msn.com/

Top	Set	P	R	F
5	reader	24.40%	10.13%	14.32%
	combined	29.20%	9.96%	14.85%
10	reader	19.80%	16.45%	17.97%
	combined	23.30%	15.89%	18.89%
15	reader	17.40%	21.68%	19.31%
	combined	20.27%	20.74%	20.50%

Table 1: Results on the two keyword sets: reader (reader-assigned keyphrases) and combined (reader- and author-assigned keyphrases)

ranking. In our learned model, the four most important features (i.e. those with the highest absolute weight) were *containsDigit* (-1.17), *isZeroMsn* (-1.12), *normalizedMsn* (-1.00), and *avgTokenCount* (+0.97). This result confirms that web frequencies can be used as a valuable source for ranking keyphrases. It also validates our assumption that a high average token count indicates a good keyphrase candidate. The *maxPMI* feature turned out to be of minor importance (-0.16). This may be due to the fact that we used the terms from the General Terms section of the paper to calculate the association scores, which may be too general for this purpose.

Acknowledgments

We thank Angela Schneider for her adaptations to the chunker and helpful evaluations. The research project DiLiA is co-funded by the European Regional Development Fund (ERDF) in the context of Investitionsbank Berlins ProFIT program under grant number 10140159. We gratefully acknowledge this support.

References

K. W. Church and P. Hanks. 1989. Word association norms, mutual information and lexicography. In *Proceedings of the 27th Annual Conference of the Association of Computational Linguistics*.

K. Eichler, H. Hemsen, and G. Neumann. 2009. Unsupervised and domain-independent extraction of technical terms from scientifc articles in digital libraries. In *Proceedings of the LWA Information Retrieval Workshop*, TU Darmstadt, Germany.

V. Evans and S. Pourcel. 2009. *New Directions in Cognitive Linguistics*. John Benjamins Publishing Company.

E. Frank, G. W. Paynter, I. H. Witten, C. Gutwin, and C. G. Nevill-Manning. 1999. Domain-specific keyphrase extraction. In *Proceedings of the 16th International Joint Conference on Artificial Intelligence*.

A. Hulth. 2004. *Combining Machine Learning and Natural Language Processing for Automatic Keyword Extraction*. Ph.D. thesis, Department of Computer and Systems Sciences, Stockholm University.

X. Jiang, Y. Hu, and H. Li. 2009. A ranking approach to keyphrase extraction. In *Proceedings of the 32nd Annual International ACM SIGIR Conference on Research and Development in Information Retrieval*.

T. Joachims. 2006. Training linear svms in linear time. In *Proceedings of the ACM Conference on Knowledge Discovery and Data Mining*.

S. N. Kim and M. Y. Kan. 2009. Re-examining automatic keyphrase extraction approaches in scientific articles. In *Proceedings of the ACL/IJCNLP Multiword Expressions Workshop*.

F. Liu, D. Pennell, F. Liu, and Y. Liu. 2009. Unsupervised approaches for automatic keyword extraction using meeting transcripts. In *Proceedings of the Conference of the NAACL, HLT*.

O. Medelyan, E. Frank, and I.H. Witten. 2009. Human-competitive tagging using automatic keyphrase extraction. In *Proceedings of the International Conference of Empirical Methods in Natural Language Processing (EMNLP)*.

R. Mihalcea and P. Tarau. 2004. TextRank: Bringing order into texts. In *Proceedings of the EMNLP*.

M. F. Porter. 1980. An algorithm for suffix stripping. *Program*, 14(3):130–137.

G. Salton and M. J. McGill. 1983. *Introduction to modern information retrieval*. McGraw-Hill.

C. Spurk. 2006. Ein minimal überwachtes Verfahren zur Erkennung generischer Eigennamen in freien Texten. Diplomarbeit, Saarland University, Germany.

L. Talmy. 2000. *Towards a cognitive semantics*. MIT Press, Cambridge, MA.

P. D. Turney. 1999. Learning to extract keyphrases from text. Technical report, National Research Council, Institute for Information Technology.

P. D. Turney. 2003. Coherent keyphrase extraction via web mining. In *Proceedings of the Eighteenth International Joint Conference on Artificial Intelligence*.

J.-B. Wang, H. Peng, and J.-S. Hu. 2005. Automatic keyphrases extraction from document using backpropagation. In *Proceedings of 2005 international conference on Machine Learning and Cybernetics*.

Task 5: Single document keyphrase extraction using sentence clustering and Latent Dirichlet Allocation

Claude Pasquier
Institute of Developmental Biology & Cancer
University of Nice Sophia-Antipolis
UNSA/CNRS UMR-6543
Parc Valrose
06108 NICE Cedex 2, France
claude.pasquier@unice.fr

Abstract

This paper describes the design of a system for extracting keyphrases from a single document The principle of the algorithm is to cluster sentences of the documents in order to highlight parts of text that are semantically related. The clusters of sentences, that reflect the themes of the document, are then analyzed to find the main topics of the text. Finally, the most important words, or groups of words, from these topics are proposed as keyphrases.

1 Introduction

Keyphrases are words, or groups of words, that capture the key ideas of a document. They represent important information concerning a document and constitute an alternative, or a complement, to full-text indexing. Pertinent keyphrases are also useful to potential readers who can have a quick overview of the content of a document and can select easily which document to read.

Currently, the most powerful keyphrases extraction algorithms are based on supervised learning. These methods address the problem of associating keyphrases to documents as a classification task. However, the fact that this approach requires a corpus of similar documents, which is not always readily available, constitutes a major drawback. For example, if one encounters a new Web page, one might like to know quickly the main topics addressed. In this case, a domain-independent keyword extraction system that applies to a single document is needed.

Several methods have been proposed for extracting keywords from a single document (Matsuo and Ishizuka, 2004; Palshikar, 2007). The reported performances were slightly higher than that obtained using a corpus and selecting the words with the highest TF-IDF [1] measure (Salton et al., 1975).

The paper describes a new keyphrase extraction algorithm from a single document. We show that our system performs well without the need for a corpus.

The paper is organized as follows. The next section describes the principles of our keyphrase extraction system. We present the main parts of the algorithm in section 3, we detail the methods in section 4 and we conclude the paper.

2 Principles

When authors write documents, they have to think first at the way they will present their ideas. Most of the time, they establish content summaries that highlight the main topics of their texts. Then, they write the content of the documents by carefully selecting the most appropriate words to describe each topic. In this paper, we make the assumption that the words, or the set of words, that are representative of each topic constitute the keyphrases of the document. In the following of this paper, we call *terms*, the components of a document that constitute the vocabulary (see the detail of the identification of terms in subsection 4.3).

In statistical natural language processing, one common way of modeling the contributions of different topics to a document is to treat each topic as a probability distribution over words. Therefore, a document is considered as a probabilistic mixture of these topics (Griffiths and Steyvers, 2004).

Generative models can be used to relate a set of observations (in our case, the terms used in a document) to a set of latent variables (the topics). A particular generative model, which is well suited for the modeling of text, is called Latent Dirichlet

[1] The TF-IDF weight gives the degree of importance of a word in a collection of documents. The importance increases if the word is frequently used in the set of documents but decreases if it is used by too many documents.

Proceedings of the 5th International Workshop on Semantic Evaluation, ACL 2010, pages 154–157,
Uppsala, Sweden, 15-16 July 2010.

Allocation (LDA) (Blei et al., 2003). Given a set of documents, the algorithms describes each document as a mixture over topics, where each topic is characterized by a distribution over words.

The idea is to perform first a clustering of the sentences of the document based on their semantic similarity. Intuitively, one can see each cluster as a part of the text dealing with semantically related content. Therefore, the initial document is divided into a set of clusters and LDA can then be applied on this new representation.

3 Algorithm

The algorithm is composed of 8 steps:

1. Identification and expansion of abbreviations.
2. Splitting the content of the document into m sentences.
3. Identification of the n unique terms in the document that are potential keyphrases.
4. Creation of a $m \times n$ sentence-term matrix X to identify the occurrences of the n terms within a collection of m sentences.
5. Dimensionality reduction to transform data in the high-dimensional matrix X to a space of fewer dimensions.
6. Data clustering performed in the reduced space. The result of the clustering is used to build a new representation of the source document, which is now considered as a set of clusters, with each cluster consisting of a bag of terms.
7. Execution of LDA on the new document representation.
8. Selection of best keyphrases by analyzing LDA's results.

4 Methods

Our implementation is build on UIMA (Unstructured Information Management Architecture) (*http://incubator.apache.org/uima/*), a robust and flexible framework that facilitates interoperability between tools dedicated to unstructured information processsing. The method processes one document at a time by performing the steps described below.

4.1 Abbreviation Expansion

The program *ExtractAbbrev* (Schwartz and Hearst, 2003) is used to identify abbreviations (short forms) and their corresponding definitions (long forms). Once abbreviations have been identified, each short form is replaced by its corresponding long form in the processed document.

4.2 Sentence Detection

Splitting the content of a document into sentences is an important step of the method. To perform this task, we used the OpenNLP's sentence detector module (*http://opennlp.sourceforge.net/*) trained on a corpus of general English texts.

4.3 Term Identification

Word categories are identified by using the LingPipe's general English part-of-speech (POS) tagger trained on the Brown Corpus (*http://alias-i.com/lingpipe/*). We leverage POS information to collect, for each sentence, nominal groups that are potential keyphrases.

4.4 Matrix Creation

Let $D = \{d_1, d_2, \ldots, d_n\}$ be the complete vocabulary set of the document identified in subsection 4.3 above. We build a $m \times n$ matrix $X = [x_{ij}]$ where m is the number of sentences in the document, n is the number of terms and x_{ij} is the weight of the j_{th} term in the i_{th} sentence. The weight of a term in a sentence is the product of a local and global weight given by $x_{ij} = l_{ij} \times g_j$, where l_{ij} is the local weight of term j within sentence i, and g_j is the global weight of term j in the document. The local weighting function measures the importance of a term within a sentence and the global weighting function measures the importance of a term across the entire document. Three local weighting functions were investigated: term frequency, log of term frequency and binary. Five global weighting functions were also investigated: Normal, GFIDF (Global frequency $\times$ Inverse document frequency, IDF (Inverse document frequency), Entropy and none (details of calculation can be found in Dumais (1991) paper).

4.5 Dimensionality Reduction

The matrix X is a representation of a document in a high-dimensional space. Singular Value Decomposition (SVD) (Forsythe et al., 1977) and Non-Negative Matrix Factorization (NMF) (Lee and

Seung, 1999) are two matrix decomposition techniques that can be used to transform data in the high-dimensional space to a space of fewer dimensions.

With SVD, the original matrix X is decomposed as a factor of three other matrices U, Σ and V such as:

$$X = U \Sigma V^T$$

where U is an $m \times m$ matrix, Σ is a $m \times n$ diagonal matrix with nonnegative real numbers on the diagonal, and V^T denotes the transpose of V, an $n \times n$ matrix. It is often useful to approximate X using only r singular values (with $r < min(m, n)$), so that we have $X = U_r \Sigma_k V_r^T + E$, where E is an error or residual matrix, U_r is an $m \times r$ matrix, Σ_r is a $k \times r$ diagonal matrix, and V_r is an $n \times r$ matrix.

NMF is a matrix factorization algorithm that decomposes a matrix with only positive elements into two positive elements matrices, with $X = WH + E$. Usually, only r components are fit, so E is an error or residual matrix, W is a non-negative $m \times r$ matrix and H is a non-negative $r \times n$ matrix. There are several ways in which W and H may be found. In our system, we use Lee and Seung's multiplicative update method (Lee and Seung, 1999).

4.6 Sentence Clustering

The clustering of sentences is performed in the reduced space by using the cosine similarity between sentence vectors. Several clustering techniques have been investigated: k-means clustering, Markov Cluster Process (MCL) (Dongen, 2008) and ClassDens (Guénoche, 2004).

The latent semantic space derived by SVD does not provide a direct indication of the data partitions. However, with NMF, the cluster membership of each document can be easily identified directly using the W matrix (Xu et al., 2003). Each value w_{ij} of matrix W, indicates, indeed, to which degree sentence i is associated with cluster j. If NMF was calculated with the rank r, then r clusters are represented on the matrix. We use a simple rule to determine the content of each cluster: sentence i belongs to cluster j if $w_{ij} > a \max_{k \in \{1 \ldots m\}} w_{ik}$. In our system, we fixed $a = 0.1$.

4.7 Applying Latent Dirichlet Allocation

By using the result of the clustering, the source document is now represented by c clusters of terms. The terms associated with a cluster c_i is the sum of the terms belonging to all the sentences in the cluster. JGibbLDA (*http://jgibblda.sourceforge.net/*) is used to execute LDA on the new dataset. We tried to extract different numbers of topics t (with $t \in \{2, 5, 10, 20, 50, 100\}$) and we choose the Dirichlet hyperparameters such as $\alpha = 0.1$ and $\beta = 50/t$. LDA inferences a topic model by estimating the cluster-topic distribution Θ and the topic-word distribution Φ (Blei et al., 2003).

4.8 Term Ranking and Keyphrase Selection

We assume that topics covering a significant portion of the document content are more important than those covering little content. To reflect this assumption, we calculate the importance of a term in the document (its score) with a function that takes into account the distribution of topics over clusters given by θ, the distribution of terms over topics given by Φ and the clusters' size.

$$score(i) = \max_{j \in \{1 \ldots n\}} (\Phi_{ji} \sum_{k=1}^{c} (\Theta_{kj} p(s(k)))$$

where $score(i)$ represents the score of term i and $s(k)$ is the size of the cluster k. We tested three different functions for p: the constant function $p(i) = 1$, the linear function $p(i) = i$ and the exponential function $p(i) = i^2$.

When a score is attributed to each term of the vocabulary, our system simply selects the top terms with the highest score and proposes them as keyphrases.

4.9 Setting Tuning Parameters

Numerous parameters have influence on the method: the weighting of the terms in the document matrix, the dimension reduction method used, the number of dimension retained, the clustering algorithm, the number of topics used to execute LDA and the way best keyphrases are selected.

The parameter that most affects the performance is the method used to perform the dimension reduction. In all cases, whatever the other parameters, NMF performs better than SVD. We found that using only 10 components for the factorization is sufficient. There was no significant performance increase by using more factors.

The second most important parameter is the clustering method used. When NMF is used, the best results were achieved by retrieving clusters from the W matrix. With SVD, ClassDens gets the best results. We tested the performance of k-means clustering by specifying a number of clusters varying from 5 to 100. The best performances were achieved with a number of clusters ≥ 20. However, k-means scores a little bit below ClassDens and MCL is found to be the worst method.

The choice of the global weighting function is also important. In our experiments, the use of IDF and no global weighting gave the worst results. Entropy and normal weighting gave the best results but, on average, entropy performs a little better than normal weight. In the final version, the global weighting function used is entropy.

The last parameter that has a visible influence on the quality of extracted keyphrases is the selection of keyphrases from LDA's results. In our experiments, the exponential function performs best.

The remaining parameters do not have notable influence on the results. As already stated by Lee et al. (2005), the choice of local weighting function makes relatively little difference. Similarly, the number of topics used for LDA has little influence. In our implementation we used term frequency as local weighting and executed LDA with a number of expected topics of 10.

5 Results and Conclusion

In Task 5, participants are invited to provide the keyphrases for 100 scientific papers provided by the organizers. Performances (precision, recall and F-score) are calculated by comparing the proposed keyphrases to keywords given by the authors of documents, keywords selected by independant readers and a combination of both. Compared to other systems, our method gives the best results on the keywords assigned by readers. By performing the calculation on the first 5 keyphrases, our system ranks 9th out of 20 submitted systems, with an F-score of 14.7%. This is below the best method that obtains 18.2%, but above the TD-IDF baseline of 10.44%. The same calculation performed on the first 15 kephrases gives a F-score of 17.80% for our method (10th best F-score). This is still below the best method, which obtains an F-score of 23.50%, but a lot better than the TD-IDF baseline (F-score=12.87%).

The evaluation shows that the performance of our system is near the average of other submitted systems. However, one has to note that our system uses only the information available from a single document. Compared to a selection of keywords based on TF-IDF, which is often used as a reference, our system provides a notable improvement. Therefore, the algorithm described here is an interesting alternative to supervised learning methods when no corpus of similar documents is available.

References

David M. Blei, Andrew Y. Ng, and Michael I. Jordan. 2003. Latent dirichlet allocation. *J. Mach. Learn. Res.*, 3:993–1022.

Stijn Van Dongen. 2008. Graph clustering via a discrete uncoupling process. *SIAM J. Matrix Anal. Appl.*, 30(1):121–141.

Susan T. Dumais. 1991. Improving the retrieval of information from external sources. *Behavior Research Methods, Instruments, & Comp.*, 23(2):229–236.

George Forsythe, Michael Malcolm, and Cleve Moler. 1977. *Computer Methods for Mathematical Computations*. Englewood Cliffs, NJ: Prentice Hall.

Thomas L. Griffiths and Mark Steyvers. 2004. Finding scientific topics. *Proceedings of the National Academy of Sciences*, 101:5228–5235.

Alain Guénoche. 2004. Clustering by vertex density in a graph. In *Classification, Clustering and Data Mining, D. Banks et al. (Eds.), Springer, 15-23.*

Daniel D. Lee and H. Sebastian Seung. 1999. Learning the parts of objects by non-negative matrix factorization. *Nature*, 401:788.

Michael D. Lee, Brandon Pincombe, and Matthew Welsh. 2005. A comparison of machine measures of text document similarity with human judgments. In *proceedings of CogSci2005*, pages 1254–1259.

Yutaka Matsuo and Mitsuru Ishizuka. 2004. Keyword extraction from a single document using word co-occurrence statistical information. *Int. Journal on Artificial Intelligence Tools*, 13(1):157–169.

Girish Keshav Palshikar. 2007. Keyword extraction from a single document using centrality measures. *LNCS*, 4815/2007:503–510.

G Salton, C. S. Yang, and C. T. Yu. 1975. A theory of term importance in automatic text analysis. *Journal of the American Society for Information Science*, 26(1):33–44.

Ariel S. Schwartz and Marti A. Hearst. 2003. A simple algorithm for identifying abbreviation definitions in biomedical text. In *proceedings of PSB 2003*, pages 451–462.

Wei Xu, Xin Liu, and Yihong Gong. 2003. Document clustering based on non-negative matrix factorization. In *proceedings of SIGIR 03*, pages 267–273.

SJTULTLAB: Chunk Based Method for Keyphrase Extraction

Letian Wang
Department of
Computer Science & Engineering
Shanghai Jiao Tong University
Shanghai, China
koh@sjtu.edu.cn

Fang Li
Department of
Computer Science & Engineering
Shanghai Jiao Tong University
Shanghai, China
fli@sjtu.edu.cn

Abstract

In this paper we present a chunk based keyphrase extraction method for scientific articles. Different from most previous systems, supervised machine learning algorithms are not used in our system. Instead, document structure information is used to remove unimportant contents; Chunk extraction and filtering is used to reduce the quantity of candidates; Keywords are used to filter the candidates before generating final keyphrases. Our experimental results on test data show that the method works better than the baseline systems and is comparable with other known algorithms.

1 Introduction

Keyphrases are sequences of words which capture the main topics discussed in a document. Keyphrases are very useful in many natural language processing (NLP) applications such as document summarization, classification and clustering. But it is an expensive and time-consuming job for users to tag keyphrases of a document. These needs motivate methods for automatic keyphrase extraction.

Most existing algorithms for keyphrase extraction treat this task as a supervised classification task. The KEA algorithm (Gordon et al., 1999) identifies candidate keyphrases using lexical methods, calculates feature values for each candidate, and uses a machine-learning algorithm to predict which candidates are good keyphrases. A domain-specific method (Frank et al., 1999) was proposed based on the Naive Bayes learning scheme. Turney (Turney, 2000) treated a document as a set of phrases, which the learning algorithm must learn to classify as positive or negative examples of keyphrases. Turney (Turney, 2003) also presented enhancements to the KEA keyphrase extraction algorithm that are designed to increase the coherence of the extracted keyphrases. Nguyen and yen Kan (Nguyen and yen Kan, 2007) presented a keyphrase extraction algorithm for scientific publications. They also introduced two features that capture the positions of phrases and salient morphological phenomena. Wu and Agogino (Wu and Agogino, 2004) proposed an automated keyphrase extraction algorithm using a nondominated sorting multi-objective genetic algorithm. Kumar and Srinathan (Kumar and Srinathan, 2008) used n-gram filtration technique and weight of words for keyphrase extraction from scientific articles.

For this evaluation task, Kim and Kan (Kim and Kan, 2009) tackled two major issues in automatic keyphrase extraction using scientific articles: candidate selection and feature engineering. They also re-examined the existing features broadly used for the supervised approach.

Different from previous systems, our system uses a chunk based method to extract keyphrases from scientific articles. Domain-specific information is used to find out useful parts in a document. The chunk based method is used to extract candidates of keyphrases in a document. Keywords of a document are used to select keyphrases from candidates.

In the following, Section 2 will describe the architecture of the system. Section 3 will introduce functions and implementation of each part in the system. Experiment results will be showed in Section 4. The conclusion will be given in Section 5.

2 System Architecture

Figure 1 shows the architecture of our system. The system accepts a document as input (go through arrows with solid lines), then does the preprocessing job and identifies the structure of the document. After these two steps, the formatted document is sent to the candidate selection module

Proceedings of the 5th International Workshop on Semantic Evaluation, ACL 2010, pages 158–161,
Uppsala, Sweden, 15-16 July 2010.

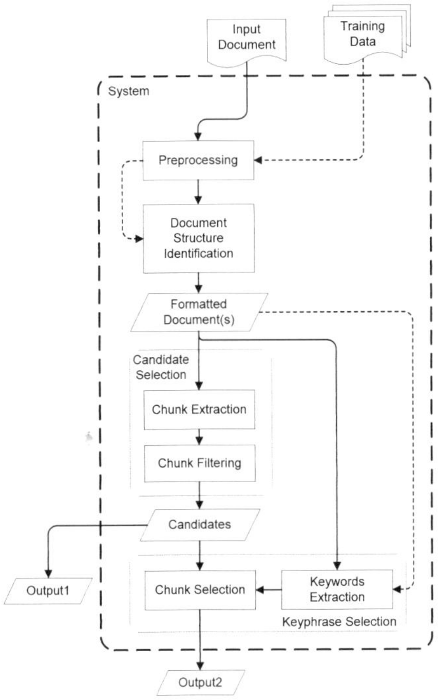

Figure 1: System architecture

which first extracts chunks from the document, then uses some rules to filter the extracted chunks. After candidate selection, the system will choose top fifteen (ordered by the position of the first occurrence in the original document) chunks from the candidates as the keyphrases and output the result ("Output1" in Figure 1) which is our submitted result. The candidates will also be sent to keyphrase selection module which first extracts keywords from the formatted document, then uses keywords to choose keyphrases from the candidates. Keywords extraction needs some training data (go through arrows with dotted lines) which also needs first two steps of our system. The result of keywords selection module will be sent to "Output2" as the final result after choosing top fifteen chunks.

`OpenNLP`[1] and `KEA`[2] are used in chunk extraction and keywords extraction respectively.

3 System Description

3.1 Preprocessing

In preprocessing, our system first deletes line breaks between each broken lines to reconnect the broken sentences while line breaks after title and section titles will be reserved. Title and section titles are recognized through some heuristic rules that title occupies first few lines of a document and section titles are started with numbers except abstract and reference. The system then deletes brackets blocks in the documents to make sure no keyphrases will be splitted by brackets blocks (e.g., the brackets in "natural language processing (NLP) applications" could be an obstacle to extracting phrase "natural language processing applications").

3.2 Document Structure Identification

Scientific articles often have similar structures which start with title, abstract and end with conclusion, reference. The structure information is used in our system to remove unimportant contents in the input document. Based on the analysis of training documents, we assume that each article can be divided into several parts: *Title*, *Abstract*, *Introduction*, *Related Work*, *Content*, *Experiment*, *Conclusion*, *Acknowledgement* and *Reference*, where *Content* often contains the description of theories, methods or algorithms.

To implement the identification of document structure, our system first maps each section title (including document title) to one of the parts in the document structure with some rules derived from the analysis of training documents. For each part except *Content*, we have a pattern to map the section titles. For example, the section title of *Abstract* should be equal to "abstract", the section title of *Introduction* should contain "introduction", the section title of *Related Work* should contain "related work" or "background", the section title of *Experiment* should contain "experiment", "result" or "evaluation", the section title of *Conclusion* should contain "conclusion" or "discussion". Section titles which do not match any of the patterns will be mapped to the *Content* part. After mapping section titles, the content between two section titles will be mapped to the same part as the first section title (e.g., the content between the section title "1. Introduction" and "2. Related Work" will be mapped to the *Introduction* part).

In our keyphrase analysis, we observed that most keyphrases appear in the first few parts of a document, such as *Title*, *Abstract*, and *Introduction*. We also found that parts like *Experiment*, *Acknowledgement* and *Reference* almost have no

[1] http://opennlp.sourceforge.net/
[2] http://nzdl.org/Kea/

keyphrases. Thus, *Experiment*, *Acknowledgement* and *Reference* are removed by our system and other parts are sorted in their original order and outputted as formatted document(s) (see in Figure 1) for further process.

3.3 Candidate Selection

The purpose of candidate selection is to find out potential keyphrases in a document. Traditional approaches just choose all the possible words sequences and filters them with part-of-speech tags. This approach may result in huge amount of candidates and lots of meaningless candidates for each document.

Our system uses chunk based method to solve these problems.

> "A chunk is a textual unit of adjacent word tokens which can be mutually linked through unambiguously identified dependency chains with no recourse to idiosyncratic lexical information."[3]

Our approach significantly reduces the quantity of candidates and keep the meanings of original documents. For example, for an article title, "Evaluating adaptive resource management for distributed real-time embedded systems", the traditional method will extract lots of meaningless candidates like "adaptive resource" and "distributed real-time", while our method just extract "adaptive resource management" and "distributed real-time embedded systems" as candidates.

3.3.1 Chunk Extraction

The first step of candidate selection is chunk extraction which extract chunks from a document. Four tools in `OpenNLP`, *SentenceDetector*, *Tokenizer*, *PosTagger* and *TreebankChunker*, are utilized in our system. The system first evokes *SentenceDetector* to split the formatted document into sentences. Then uses *Tokenizer* and *PosTagger* to label all the words with part-of-speech tag. At last, *TreebankChunker* is used to extract chunks from the document.

3.3.2 Chunk filtering

Not all the extracted chunks can be the candidates of keyphrases. Our system uses some heuristic rules to select candidates from extracted chunks. The types of rules range from statistic information to syntactic structures. The rules that our system uses are based on some traditional methods for candidate filtering. They are:

1. Any chunks in candidates should have less than 5 words.
2. Any single word chunks in candidates should be found at least twice in a document.
3. Any chunks in candidates should be noun phrases.
4. Any chunks in candidates must start with the word with the part-of-speech tag (defined in `OpenNLP`) NN, NNS, NNP, NNPS, JJ, JJR or JJS and end with the word with the part-of-speech tag NN, NNS, NNP or NNPS. Chunks that do not match these rules will be removed. Chunks that haven't been removed will be the candidate keyphrases of the document.

3.4 Keyphrase Selection

Our analysis shows that keywords are helpful to extract keyphrases from a document. Thus, keywords are used to select keyphrases from candidate chunks.

3.4.1 Keywords Extraction

`KEA` is a keyphrase extraction tool, it can also be used to extract keywords with some appropriate parameters. We observed that most keyphrases extracted by `KEA` only contain one word or two words which describe the key meaning of the document, even when the max length is set to 5 or more. There are four parameters to be set, in order to get best results, we set maximum length of a keyphrase to 2, minimum length of a keyphrase to 1, minimum occurrence of a phrase to 1 and number of keyphrases to extract to 30. Then, the output of the `KEA` system contains thirty keywords per document.

As showed in Figure 1, `KEA` needs training data (provided by the task owner). Our system uses formatted documents (generated by the first two steps of our system) of training data as the input training data to `KEA`.

3.4.2 Chunk Selection

After extracting thirty keywords from each document, our system uses these keywords to filter out non-keyphrase chunks from the candidates. The

[3]http://www.ilc.cnr.it/sparkle/wp1-prefinal/node24.html

system completes the task in two steps: 1) Remove candidates of a document that do not have any keywords of the document extracted by KEA; 2) Choose the top fifteen (ordered by the position of the first occurrence in the orginal document) keyphrases as the answer of a document ("Output2" in Figure 1).

4 Experiment Result

Table 1 shows the F-score of two outputs of our system and some baseline systems. The first three methods are the baselines provided by the task owner. TFIDF is an unsupervised method to rank the candidates based on TFIDF scores. NB and ME are supervised methods using Navie Bayes and maximum entropy in WEKA[4]. KEA refers to the KEA system with the parameters that can output the best results. OP1 is our system with the "Output1" as result and OP2 is our system with the "Output2" as result (see Figure 1). In second column, "R" means to use the reader-assigned keyphrases set as gold-standard data and "C" means to use both author-assigned and reader-assigned keyphrases sets as answers.

Method	by	Top05	Top10	Top15
TFIDF	R	10.44%	12.61%	12.87%
	C	11.19%	14.35%	15.10%
NB	R	9.86%	12.07%	12.65%
	C	10.89%	14.03%	14.70%
ME	R	9.86%	12.07%	12.65%
	C	10.89%	14.03%	14.70%
KEA	R	14.55%	17.24%	16.42%
	C	14.45%	17.68%	17.74%
OP1	R	**15.61%**	**17.60%**	**17.31%**
	C	**15.36%**	**18.41%**	**18.61%**
OP2	R	16.08%	18.42%	18.05%
	C	17.91%	20.52%	20.36%

Table 1: The comparison of F-score of our system with other systems.

From the table, we can see that, both two outputs of our system made an improvement over the baseline systems and got better results than the well known KEA system.

We submitted both results of OP1 and OP2 to the evaluation task. Because of some misunderstanding over the result upload system, only the result of OP1 (with bold style) was successfully submitted.

[4] http://www.cs.waikato.ac.nz/ml/weka/

5 Conclusion

We proposed a chunk based method for keyphrase extraction in this paper. In our system, document structure information of scientific articles is used to pick up significant contents, chunk based candidate selection is used to reduce the quantity of candidates and reserve their original meanings, keywords are used to select keyphrases from a document. All these factors contribute to the result of our system.

References

Eibe Frank, Gordon W. Paynter, Ian H. Witten, Carl Gutwin, and Craig G. Nevill-manning. 1999. Domain-specific keyphrase extraction. pages 668–673. Morgan Kaufmann Publishers.

Ian Witten Gordon, Gordon W. Paynter, Eibe Frank, Carl Gutwin, and Craig G. Nevill-manning. 1999. Kea: Practical automatic keyphrase extraction. In *Proceedings of Digital Libraries 99 (DL'99*, pages 254–255. ACM Press.

Su Nam Kim and Min-Yen Kan. 2009. Re-examining automatic keyphrase extraction approaches in scientific articles. In *Proceedings of the Workshop on Multiword Expressions: Identification, Interpretation, Disambiguation and Applications*, pages 9–16, Singapore, August. Association for Computational Linguistics.

Niraj Kumar and Kannan Srinathan. 2008. Automatic keyphrase extraction from scientific documents using n-gram filtration technique. In *DocEng '08: Proceeding of the eighth ACM symposium on Document engineering*, pages 199–208, New York, NY, USA. ACM.

Thuy Dung Nguyen and Min yen Kan. 2007. Keyphrase extraction in scientific publications. In *In Proc. of International Conference on Asian Digital Libraries (ICADL 07*, pages 317–326. Springer.

Peter Turney. 2000. Learning algorithms for keyphrase extraction. *Information Retrieval*, 2:303–336.

Peter Turney. 2003. Coherent keyphrase extraction via web mining. In *In Proceedings of IJCAI*, pages 434–439.

Jia-Long Wu and Alice M. Agogino. 2004. Automating keyphrase extraction with multi-objective genetic algorithms. In *HICSS '04: Proceedings of the Proceedings of the 37th Annual Hawaii International Conference on System Sciences (HICSS'04) - Track 4*, page 40104.3, Washington, DC, USA. IEEE Computer Society.

Likey: Unsupervised Language-independent Keyphrase Extraction

Mari-Sanna Paukkeri and Timo Honkela
Adaptive Informatics Research Centre
Aalto University School of Science and Technology
P.O. Box 15400, FI-00076 AALTO, Finland
mari-sanna.paukkeri@tkk.fi

Abstract

Likey is an unsupervised statistical approach for keyphrase extraction. The method is language-independent and the only language-dependent component is the reference corpus with which the documents to be analyzed are compared. In this study, we have also used another language-dependent component: an English-specific Porter stemmer as a preprocessing step. In our experiments of keyphrase extraction from scientific articles, the *Likey* method outperforms both supervised and unsupervised baseline methods.

1 Introduction

Keyphrase extraction is a natural language processing task for collecting the main topics of a document into a list of phrases. Keyphrases are supposed to be available in the processed documents themselves, and the aim is to extract these most meaningful words and phrases from the documents. Keyphrase extraction summarises the content of a document as few phrases and thus provides a quick way to find out what the document is about. Keyphrase extraction is a basic text mining procedure that can be used as a ground for other, more sophisticated text analysis methods. Automatically extracted keyphrases may be used to improve the performance of information retrieval, automatic user model generation, document collection clustering and visualisation, summarisation and question-answering, among others.

This article describes the participation of the *Likey* method in the Task 5 of the SemEval 2010 challenge, automatic keyphrase extraction from scientific articles (Kim et al., 2010).

1.1 Related work

In statistical keyphrase extraction, many variations for term frequency counts have been proposed in the literature including relative frequencies (Damerau, 1993), collection frequency (Hulth, 2003), term frequency–inverse document frequency (*tf-idf*) (Salton and Buckley, 1988), among others. Additional features to frequency that have been experimented are e.g., relative position of the first occurrence of the term (Frank et al., 1999), importance of the sentence in which the term occurs (HaCohen-Kerner, 2003), and widely studied part-of-speech tag patterns, e.g. Hulth (2003). Matsuo and Ishizuka (2004) present keyword extraction method using word co-occurrence statistics. An unsupervised keyphrase extraction method by Liu et al. (2009) uses clustering to find exemplar terms that are then used for keyphrase extraction. Most of the presented methods require a reference corpus or a training corpus to produce keyphrases. Statistical keyphrase extraction methods without reference corpora have also been proposed, e.g. (Matsuo and Ishizuka, 2004; Bracewell et al., 2005). The later study is carried out for bilingual corpus.

2 Data

The data used in this work are from the SemEval 2010 challenge Task 5, automatic keyphrase extraction from scientific articles. The data consist of train, trial, and test data sets. The number of scientific articles and the total number of word tokens in each of the original data sets (before preprocessing) are given in Table 1.

Three sets of "correct" keyphrases are provided for each article in each data set: reader-assigned keyphrases, author-provided keyphrases, and a combination of them. All reader-assigned keyphrases have been extracted manually from the papers whereas some of author-provided

Proceedings of the 5th International Workshop on Semantic Evaluation, ACL 2010, pages 162–165,
Uppsala, Sweden, 15-16 July 2010. ©2010 Association for Computational Linguistics

Data set	Articles	Word tokens
train	144	1 159 015
trial	40	334 379
test	100	798 049

Table 1: Number of scientific articles and total number of word tokens in the data sets.

keyphrases may not occur in the content. The numbers of correct keyphrases in each data set are shown in Table 2.

Data set	Reader	Author	Combined
train	1 824	559	2 223
trial	526	149	621
test	1 204	387	1 466

Table 2: Number of correct answers in reader, author, and combined answer sets for each data set.

More detailed information on the data set can be found in (Kim et al., 2010).

3 Methods

Likey keyphrase extraction approach comes from the tradition of statistical machine learning (Paukkeri et al., 2008). The method has been developed to be as language-independent as possible. The only language-specific component needed is a corpus in each language. This kind of data is readily available online or from other sources.

Likey selects the words and phrases that best crystallize the meaning of the documents by comparing ranks of frequencies in the documents to those in the reference corpus. The *Likey ratio* (Paukkeri et al., 2008) for each phrase is defined as

$$L(p, d) = \frac{rank_d(p)}{rank_r(p)}, \quad (1)$$

where $rank_d(p)$ is the rank value of phrase p in document d and $rank_r(p)$ is the rank value of phrase p in the reference corpus. The rank values are calculated according to the frequencies of phrases of the same length n. If the phrase p does not exist in the reference corpus, the value of the maximum rank for phrases of length n is used: $rank_r(p) = max\_rank_r(n) + 1$. The *Likey ratio* orders the phrases in a document in such a way that the phrases that have the smallest ratio are the best candidates for being a keyphrase.

As a post-processing step, the phrases of length $n > 1$ face an extra removal process: if one of the words composing the phrase has a rank of less than a threshold ξ in the reference corpus, the phrase is removed from the keyphrase list. This procedure excludes phrases that contain function words such as "of" or "the". As another post-processing step, phrases that are subphrases of those that have occurred earlier on the keyphrase list are removed, excluding e.g. "language model" if "unigram language model" has been already accepted as a keyphrase.

3.1 Reference corpus

Likey needs a reference corpus that is seen as a sample of the general language. In the present study, we use a combination of the English part of Europarl, European Parliament plenary speeches (Koehn, 2005) and the preprocessed training set as the reference corpus. All XML tags of meta information are excluded from the Europarl data. The size of the Europarl corpus is 35 800 000 words after removal of XML tags.

3.2 Preprocessing

The scientific articles are preprocessed by removing all headers including the names and addresses of the authors. Also the reference section is removed from the articles, as well as all tables, figures, equations and citations. Both scientific articles and the Europarl data is lowercased, punctuation is removed (the hyphens surrounded by word characters and apostrophes are kept) and the numbers are changed to `<NUM>` tag.

The data is stemmed with English Porter stemmer implementation provided by the challenge organizers, which differs from our earlier experiments.

3.3 Baselines

We use three baseline methods for keyphrase extraction. The baselines use uni-, bi-, and trigrams as candidates of keyphrases with *tf-idf* weighting scheme. One of the baselines is unsupervised and the other two are supervised approaches. The unsupervised method is to rank the candidates according to their *tf-idf* scores. The supervised methods are *Naïve Bayes (NB)* and *Maximum Entropy (ME)* implementations from WEKA package[1].

[1] http://www.cs.waikato.ac.nz/~ml/weka/

4 Experiments

We participated the challenge with *Likey* results of three different parameter settings. The settings are given in Table 3. *Likey-1* has phrases up to 3 words and *Likey-2* and *Likey-3* up to 4 words. The threshold value for postprocessing was selected against the trial set, with $\xi = 100$ performing best. It is used for *Likey-1* and *Likey-2*. Also a bit larger threshold $\xi = 130$ was tried for *Likey-3* to exclude more function words.

Repr.	n	ξ
Likey-1	1–3	100
Likey-2	1–4	100
Likey-3	1–4	130

Table 3: Different parametrizations for *Likey*: n-gram length and threshold value ξ.

An example of the resulting keyphrases extracted by *Likey-1* from the first scientific article in the test set (article C-1) is given in Table 4. Also the corresponding "correct" answers in reader-assigned and author-provided answer sets are shown. The keyphrases are given in stemmed versions. *Likey* keyphrases that can be found in the reader or author answer sets are emphasized.

Likey-1	*uddi registri*, proxi registri, servic discoveri, *grid servic discoveri*, uddi kei, uniqu uddi kei, servic discoveri mechan, distribut hash tabl, *web servic*, *dht*, servic name, web servic discoveri, local proxi registri, local uddi registri, queri multipl registri
Reader	*grid servic discoveri*, uddi, distribut web-servic discoveri architectur, dht base uddi registri hierarchi, deploy issu, bamboo dht code, case-insensit search, queri, longest avail prefix, qo-base servic discoveri, autonom control, *uddi registri*, scalabl issu, soft state
Author	uddi, *dht*, *web servic*, grid comput, md, discoveri

Table 4: Extracted keyphrases by *Likey-1* from article C-1 and the corresponding correct answers in reader and author answer sets.

The example shows clearly that many of the extracted keyphrases contain the same words that can be found in the correct answer sets but the length of the phrases vary and thus they cannot be counted as successfully extracted keyphrases.

The results for the three different *Likey* parametrizations and the three baselines are given in Table 5 for reader-assigned keyphrases and Table 6 for the combined set of reader and author-assigned keyphrases. The evaluation is conducted by calculating precision (P), recall (R) and F-measure (F) for top 5, 10, and 15 keyphrase candidates for each method, using the reader-assigned and author-provided lists as correct answers. The baseline methods are unsupervised *tf-idf* and supervised *Naïve Bayes (NB)* and *Maximum Entropy (ME)*.

Likey-1 performed best in the competition and is thus selected as the official result of *Likey* in the task. Anyway, all *Likey* parametrizations outperform the baselines, *Likey-1* having the best precision 24.60% for top-5 candidates in the reader data set and 29.20% for top-5 candidates in the combined data set. The best F-measure is obtained with *Likey-1* for top-10 candidates for both reader and combined data set: 16.24% and 17.11%, respectively. *Likey* seems to produce the best keyphrases in the beginning of the keyphrase list: for reader-assigned keyphrases the top 5 keyphrase precision for *Likey-1* is 6.8 points better than the best-performing baseline *tf-idf* and the corresponding F-measure is 4.0 points better. For the combined set, the numbers are 7.2 and 3.7 points, respectively. The difference decreases for the larger keyphrase sets.

5 Conclusions and discussion

This article describes our submission to SemEval 2010 Task 5, keyphrase extraction from scientific articles. Our unsupervised and language-independent method *Likey* uses reference corpus and is able to outperform both the unsupervised and supervised baseline methods. The best results are obtained with the top-5 keyphrases: precision of 24.60% with reader-assigned keyphrases and 29.20% with the combination of reader-assigned and author-provided keyphrases.

There are some keyphrases in the answer sets that our method does not find: due to the comparatively large threshold value ξ many phrases that contain function words, e.g. "of", cannot be found. We also extract keyphrases of maximum length of three or four words and thus cannot find keyphrases longer than that. The next step of this research would be to take these problems into account.

Method	Top 5 candidates			Top 10 candidates			Top 15 candidates		
	P %	R %	F %	P %	R %	F %	P %	R %	F %
Likey-1	**24.60**	10.22	14.44	17.90	14.87	**16.24**	13.80	**17.19**	15.31
Likey-2	23.80	9.88	13.96	16.90	14.04	15.34	13.40	16.69	14.87
Likey-3	23.40	9.72	13.73	16.80	13.95	15.24	13.73	17.11	15.23
tf-idf	17.80	7.39	10.44	13.90	11.54	12.61	11.60	14.45	12.87
NB	16.80	6.98	9.86	13.30	11.05	12.07	11.40	14.20	12.65
ME	16.80	6.98	9.86	13.30	11.05	12.07	11.40	14.20	12.65

Table 5: Results for *Likey* and the baselines for the reader data set. The best precision (P), recall (R) and F-measure (F) are highlighted.

Method	Top 5 candidates			Top 10 candidates			Top 15 candidates		
	P %	R %	F %	P %	R %	F %	P %	R %	F %
Likey-1	**29.20**	9.96	14.85	21.10	14.39	**17.11**	16.33	**16.71**	16.52
Likey-2	28.40	9.69	14.45	19.90	13.57	16.14	15.73	16.10	15.91
Likey-3	28.00	9.55	14.24	19.60	13.37	15.90	16.07	16.44	16.25
tf-idf	22.00	7.50	11.19	17.70	12.07	14.35	14.93	15.28	15.10
NB	21.40	7.30	10.89	17.30	11.80	14.03	14.53	14.87	14.70
ME	21.40	7.30	10.89	17.30	11.80	14.03	14.53	14.87	14.70

Table 6: Results for *Likey* and the baselines for the combined (reader+author) data set. The best precision (P), recall (R) and F-measure (F) are highlighted.

Acknowledgements

This work was supported by the Finnish Graduate School in Language Studies (Langnet) funded by Ministry of Education of Finland.

References

David B. Bracewell, Fuji Ren, and Shingo Kuriowa. 2005. Multilingual single document keyword extraction for information retrieval. In *Proceedings of NLP-KE'05*.

Fred Damerau. 1993. Generating and evaluating domain-oriented multi-word terms from text. *Information Processing and Management*, 29(4):433–447.

Eibe Frank, Gordon W. Paynter, Ian H. Witten, Carl Gutwin, and Craig G. Nevill-Manning. 1999. Domain-specific keyphrase extraction. In *Proceedings of IJCAI'99*, pages 668–673.

Yaakov HaCohen-Kerner. 2003. Automatic extraction of keywords from abstracts. In V. Palade, R.J. Howlett, and L.C. Jain, editors, *KES 2003, LNAI 2773*, pages 843–849. Springer-Verlag.

Anette Hulth. 2003. Improved automatic keyword extraction given more linguistic knowledge. In *Proceedings of the Conference on Empirical Methods in Natural Language Processing*, pages 216–223.

Su Nam Kim, Alyona Medelyan, Min-Yen Kan, and Timothy Baldwin. 2010. SemEval-2010 Task 5: Automatic Keyphrase Extraction from Scientific Articles. In *Proceedings of the ACL 2010 Workshop on Evaluation Exercises on Semantic Evaluation (SemEval 2010)*. to appear.

Philipp Koehn. 2005. Europarl: A parallel corpus for statistical machine translation. In *MT Summit 2005*.

Zhiyuan Liu, Peng Li, Yabin Zheng, and Maosong Sun. 2009. Clustering to find exemplar terms for keyphrase extraction. In *Proceedings of the 2009 Conference on Empirical Methods in Natural Language Processing*, pages 257–266, Singapore, August. Association for Computational Linguistics.

Yutaka Matsuo and Mitsuru Ishizuka. 2004. Keyword extraction from a single document using word co-occurrence statistical information. *International Journal on Artificial Intelligence Tools*, 13(1):157–169.

Mari-Sanna Paukkeri, Ilari T. Nieminen, Matti Pöllä, and Timo Honkela. 2008. A language-independent approach to keyphrase extraction and evaluation. In *Coling 2008: Companion volume: Posters*, pages 83–86, Manchester, UK, August. Coling 2008 Organizing Committee.

Gerard Salton and Chris Buckley. 1988. Term weighting approaches in automatic text retrieval. *Information Processing and Management*, 24(5):513–523.

WINGNUS: Keyphrase Extraction Utilizing Document Logical Structure

Thuy Dung Nguyen
Department of Computer Science
School of Computing
National University of Singapore
nguyen14@comp.nus.edu.sg

Minh-Thang Luong
Department of Computer Science
School of Computing
National University of Singapore
luongmin@comp.nus.edu.sg

Abstract

We present a system description of the WINGNUS team work[1] for the SemEval-2010 task #5 Automatic Keyphrase Extraction from Scientific Articles. A key feature of our system is that it utilizes an inferred document logical structure in our candidate identification process, to limit the number of phrases in the candidate list, while maintaining its coverage of important phrases. Our top performing system achieves an F_1 of 25.22% for the combined keyphrases (author and reader assigned) in the final test data. We note that the method we report here is novel and orthogonal from other systems, so it can be combined with other techniques to potentially achieve higher performance.

1 Introduction

Keyphrases are noun phrases (NPs) that capture the primary topics of a document. While beneficial for applications such as summarization, clustering and indexing, only a minority of documents have manually-assigned keyphrases, as it is a time-consuming process. Automatic keyphrase generation is thus a focus for many researchers.

Most existing keyphrase extraction systems view this task as a supervised classification task in two stages: generating a list of candidates – *candidate identification*; and using answer keyphrases to distinguish true keyphrases – *candidate selection*. The selection model uses a set of features that capture the saliency of a phrase as a keyphrase. A major challenge of the keyphrase extraction task lies in the candidate identification process. A narrow candidate list will overlook some true keyphrases (favoring precision), whereas a broad list will produce more errors and require more processing in latter selection stage (favoring recall).

In our previous system (Nguyen and Kan, 2007), we made use of the document logical structure in the proposed features. The premise of this earlier work was that keyphrases are distributed non-uniformly in different logical sections of a paper, favoring sections such as *introduction*, and *related work*. We introduced features indicating which sections a candidate occurrs in. For our fielded system in this task (Kim et al., 2010), we further leverage the document logical structure for both candidate identification and selection stages.

Our contributions are as follows: 1) We suggest the use of Google Scholar-based crawler to automatically find PDF files to enhance logical structure extraction; 2) We provide a keyphrase distribution study with respect to different logical structures; and 3) From the study result, we propose a candidate identification approach that uses logical structures to effectively limit the number of candidates considered while ensuring good coverage.

2 Preprocessing

Although we have plain text for all test input, we posit that logical structure recovery is much more robust given the original richly-formatted document (*e.g.*, PDF), as font and formatting information can be used for detection. As a bridge between plain text data provided by the organizer and PDF input required to extract formatting features, we first describe our *Google Scholar-based crawler* to find PDFs given plain texts. We then detail on the *logical structure extraction* process.

Google Scholar-based Paper Crawler

Our crawler[2] takes inputs as titles to query Google Scholar (GS) by means of web scraping. It pro-

[1]This work was supported by a National Research Foundation grant "Interactive Media Search" (grant # R-252-000-325-279).

[2]http://wing.comp.nus.edu.sg/~lmthang/GS/

Proceedings of the 5th International Workshop on Semantic Evaluation, ACL 2010, pages 166–169,
Uppsala, Sweden, 15-16 July 2010. ©2010 Association for Computational Linguistics

cesses GS results and performs approximate title matching using character-based *Longest Common Subsequence* similarity. Once a matching title with high similarity score (> 0.7 experimentally) is found, the crawler retrieves the list of available PDFs, and starts downloading until one is correctly stored. We enforce that PDFs accepted should have the OCR texts closely match the provided plain texts in terms of lines and tokens.

In the keyphrase task, we approximate the title inputs to our crawler by considering the first two lines of each plain text provided. For 140 train and 100 test input documents, the crawler downloaded 117 and 80 PDFs, of which 116 and 76 files are correct, respectively. This yields an acceptable level of performance in terms of (Precision, Recall) of (99.15%, 82.86%) for train and (95%, 76%) for test data.

Logical Structure Extraction

Logical structure is defined as "a hierarchy of logical components, for example, titles, authors, affiliations, abstracts, sections, etc." in (Mao et al., 2003). Operationalizing this definition, we employ an in-house software, called SectLabel (Luong et al., to appear), to obtain comprehensive logical structure information for each document. SectLabel classifies each text line in a scholarly document with a semantic class (*e.g., title, header, bodyText*). Header lines are furthered classified into generic roles (*e.g., abstract, intro, method*).

A prominent feature of SectLabel is that it is capable of utilizing rich information, such as font format and spatial layout, from an optical character recognition (OCR) output if PDF files are present[3]. In case PDFs are unavailable, SectLabel still handles plain text based logical structure discovery, but with degraded performance.

3 Candidate Phrase Identification

Phrase Distribution Study

We perform a study of keyphrase distribution on the training data over different logical structures (LSs) to understand the importance of each section within documents. These LSs include: *title, headers, abstract, introduction* (intro), *related work* (rw), *conclusion*, and *body text*[4] (body).

[3]We note that the PDFs have author assigned keyphrases of the document, but we filtered this information before passing to our keyphrases system to ensure a fair test.

[4]We utilize the comprehensive output of our logical structure system to filter out *copyright, email, equation, figure, caption, footnote*, and *reference* lines.

We make a key observation that within a paragraph, important phrases occur mostly in the first n sentences. To validate our hypothesis, we consider keyphrase distribution over *body*$_n$, which is the subset of all of the *body* LS, limited to the first n sentences of each paragraph ($n = 1, 2, 3$ experimentally).

	Ath	**Rder**	**Com**	**Sent**	**Den**
title	142	175	251	122	**2.06**
headers	158	342	425	1,893	0.22
abstract	276	745	897	1,124	**0.80**
intro	335	984	**1,166**	4,338	0.27
rw	160	345	443	1,945	0.23
concl	227	488	616	1,869	0.33
body	398	1,175	**1,411**	39,179	0.04
full	465	1,720	**1,994**	50,512	0.04
body$_1$	333	839	**1,035**	11,280	0.09
body$_2$	366	980	1,197	20,024	0.06
body$_3$	382	1,042	1,269	26,163	0.05
fulltext	480	1,773	**2,059**	166,471	0.01

Table 1: Keyphrase distribution over different logical structures computed from the 144 training documents. The type counts of author-assigned (ath), reader-assigned (rder) and combined (comb) keyphrases are shown. *Sent* indicates the number of sentences in each LS. The *Den* column gives the density of keyphrases for each LS.

Results in Table 1 show that individual LSs (title, headers, abstract, intro, rw, concl) contain a high concentration (i.e., density > 0.2) of keyphrases, with *title* and *abstract* having the highest density, and *intro* being the most dominant LS in terms of keyphrase count. With all these LSs and *body*, we obtain the *full* setting, covering 1994/2059=96.84% of all keyphrases appearing in the original text, *fulltext*, while effectively reducing the number of processed sentences by more than two-thirds.

Considering only the first sentence of each paragraph in the body text, *body*$_1$, yields fair keyphrase coverage of 1035/1411=73.35% relative to that of *fulltext*. The number of lines to be processed is much smaller, about a third, which validates our aforementioned hypothesis.

Keyphrase Extraction

Results from the keyphrase distribution study motivates us to further explore the use of logical structures (LS). The idea is to limit the search scope of our candidate identification system while maintaining coverage. We propose a new approach, which extracts candidates according to the regular expression rules discussed in (Kim and Kan, 2009). However, instead of using the whole document text as input, we abridge the input text at different levels from *full* to *minimal*.

Input	Description	Cand	Com	Recall
minimal	title + headers + abs + intro	30,702	1,312	63.72%
medium	*min* + rw + conclusion	44,975	1,414	68.67%
full_1	*med* + body_1	**73,958**	**1,580**	**76.74%**
full_2	*med* + body_2	90,624	1,635	79.41%
full_3	*med* + body_3	101,006	1,672	81.20%
full	*med* + body	121,378	1,737	84.36%
fulltext	original text	**148,411**	**1,766**	**85.77%**

Table 2: Different levels of abridged inputs computed on the training data. *Cand* shows the number of candidate keyphrases extracted for each input type; *Com* gives the number of correct keyphrases appear as candidates; *Recall* is computed with respect to the total number of keyphrases in the original texts (2059).

Results in Table 2 show that we could gather a recall of 63.72% when considering a significantly abridged form of the input culled from title, headers, abstract (abs) and introduction (intro) – *minimal*. Further adding related work (rw) and conclusion – *medium* – enhances the recall by 4.95%. When adding only the first line of each paragraph in the body text, we achieve a good recall of 76.74% while effectively reducing the number of candidate phrases to be process by a half with respect to the *fulltext* input. Even though $full_2$, $full_3$, and *full* show further improvements in terms of recall, we opt to use $full_1$ in our experimental runs, which trades off recall for less computational complexity, which may influence downstream classification.

4 Candidate Phrase Selection

Following (Nguyen and Kan, 2007), we use the Naïve Bayes model implemented in Weka (Hall et al., 2009) for candidate phrase selection. As different learning models have been discussed much previous work, we just list the different features with which we experimented with. Our features[5] are as follows (where *n* indicates a numeric feature; *b*, a boolean one):

[5]Detailed feature definitions are described in (Nguyen and Kan, 2007; Kim and Kan, 2009).

F1-F3 (*n*): TF×IDF, term frequency, term frequency of substrings.

F4-F5 (*n*): First and last occurrences (word offset).

F6 (*n*): Length of phrases in words.

F7 (*b*): Typeface attribute (available when PDF is present) – Indicates if any part of the candidate phrase has appeared in the document with bold or italic format, a good hint for its relevance as a keyphrase.

F8 (*b*): InTitle – shows whether a phrase is also part of the document title.

F9 (*n*): TitleOverlap – the number of times a phrase appears in the title of other scholarly documents (obtained from a dump of the DBLP database).

F10-F14 (*b*): Header, Abstract, Intro, RW, Concl – indicate whether a phrase appears in headers, abstract, introduction, related work or conclusion sections, respectively.

F15-F19 (*n*): HeaderF, AbstractF, IntroF, RWF, ConclF - indicate the frequency of a phrase in the headers, abstract, introduction, related work or conclusion sections, respectively.

5 Experiments

5.1 Datasets

For this task (Kim et al., 2010), we are given two datasets: *train* (144 docs) and *test* (100 docs) with detailed answers for *train*. To tune our system, we split the train dataset into train and validation subsets: $train_t$ (104 docs) and $train_v$ (40 docs). Once the best setting is derived from $train_t$-$train_v$, we obtain the final model trained on the full data, and apply it to the test set for the final results.

5.2 Evaluation

Our evaluation process is accomplished in two stages: we first experiment different feature combinations by using the input types *fulltext* and $full_1$. We then fix the best feature set, and vary our different abridged inputs to find the optimal one.

Feature Combination

To evaluate the performance of individual features, we define a *base* feature set, as $F_{1,4}$, and measure the performance of each feature added separately to the base. Results in Table 3 have highlighted the set of positive features, which is $F_{3,5,6,13,16}$.

From the positive set $F_{3,5,6,13,16}$, we tried different combinations for the two input types shown

System	F Score	System	F Score
base	*23.42%*	+ F_{11}	23.42%
+ F_2	21.13%	+ F_{12}	23.42%
+ F_3	**24.57%**	+ F_{13}	**23.75%**
+ F_5	**24.08%**	+ F_{14}	22.28%
+ F_6	**25.06%**	+ F_{15}	22.11%
+ F_7	23.42%	+ F_{16}	**23.59%**
+ F_8	22.77%	+ F_{17}	22.60%
+ F_9	22.28%	+ F_{18}	23.26%
+ F_{10}	23.42%	+ F_{19}	21.95%

Table 3: Performance of individual features (on *fulltext*) added separately to the base set $F_{1,4}$.

in Table 4. The results indicate that while *fulltext* obtains the best performance with $F_{3,6,5}$ added, using *full*$_1$ shows superior performance at 28.18% F Score with $F_{3,6}$ added. Hence, we have identified our best feature set as $F_{1,3,4,6}$.

	fulltext	full$_1$
base ($F_{1,4}$)	23.42%	22.60%
+ $F_{3,6}$	25.88%	**28.18%**
+ $F_{3,6,5}$	**26.21%**	26.21%
+ $F_{3,6,5,13}$	24.90%	26.21%
+ $F_{3,6,5,16}$	24.24%	26.70%
+ $F_{3,6,5,13,16}$	23.42%	26.70%

Table 4: Performance (F_1) over difference feature combinations for *fulltext* and *full*$_1$ inputs.

Abridged Inputs

Table 5 gives the performance for the abridged inputs we tried with the best feature set $F_{1,3,4,6}$. All *full*$_1$, *full*$_2$, *full*$_3$ and *full* show improved performance compared to those on the *fulltext*. We achieve our best performance with *full*$_1$ at 28.18% F Score. These results validate the effectiveness of our approach in utilizing logical structure for the candidate identification. We report our results submitted in Table 6. These figures are achieved using the best feature combination $F_{1,3,4,6}$.

6 Conclusion

We have described and evaluated our keyphrase extraction system for the SemEval-2 Task #5. With the use of logical structure in the candidate identification, our system has demonstrated its superior performance over systems that do not use such information. Moreover, we have effectively reduced the numbers of text lines and candidate phrases to be processed in the candidate identification and selection respectively by about half.

Input	@5	@10	@15	Fscore
min	62	110	145	23.75%
med	79	130	158	25.88%
full$_1$	84	135	172	**28.18%**
full$_2$	90	132	164	26.86%
full$_3$	89	134	162	26.54%
full	84	130	164	26.86%
fulltext	82	127	158	**25.88%**

Table 5: Performance over different abridged inputs using the best feature set $F_{1,3,4,6}$. "@N" indicates the number of top N keyphrase matches.

System	Description	F@5	F@10	F@15
WINGNUS$_1$	full, $F_{1,3,4,6}$	20.65%	24.66%	24.95%
WINGNUS$_2$	full$_1$, $F_{1,3,4,6}$	20.45%	24.73%	**25.22%**

Table 6: Final results on the test data.

Our system takes advantage of the logical structure analysis but not to the extent we had hoped. We had hypothesized that formatting features (F_7) such as bold and italics, would help discriminate key phrases, but in our limited experiments for this task did not validate this. Similarly, external knowledge should help in the keyphrase task, but the prior knowledge about keyphrase likelihood (F_9) in DBLP hurt performance in our tests. We plan to further explore these issues for the future.

References

Mark Hall, Eibe Frank, Geoffrey Holmes, Bernhard Pfahringer, Peter Reutemann, and Ian H. Witten. 2009. The WEKA data mining software: an update. *SIGKDD Explor. Newsl.*, 11(1):10–18.

Su Nam Kim and Min-Yen Kan. 2009. Re-examining automatic keyphrase extraction approaches in scientific articles. In *MWE '09*.

Su Nam Kim, Alyona Medelyan, Min-Yen Kan, and Timothy Baldwin. 2010. Task 5: Automatic keyphrase extraction from scientific articles. In *SemEval*.

Minh-Thang Luong, Thuy Dung Nguyen, and Min-Yen Kan. to appear. Logical structure recovery in scholarly articles with rich document features. IJDLS. Forthcoming, accepted for publication.

Song Mao, Azriel Rosenfeld, and Tapas Kanungo. 2003. Document structure analysis algorithms: a literature survey. In *Proc. SPIE Electronic Imaging*.

Thuy Dung Nguyen and Min-Yen Kan. 2007. Keyphrase extraction in scientific publications. In *ICADL*.

KX: A flexible system for Keyphrase eXtraction

Emanuele Pianta
Fondazione Bruno Kessler
Trento, Italy.
pianta@fbk.eu

Sara Tonelli
Fondazione Bruno Kessler
Trento, Italy.
satonelli@fbk.eu

Abstract

In this paper we present KX, a system for keyphrase extraction developed at FBK-IRST, which exploits basic linguistic annotation combined with simple statistical measures to select a list of weighted keywords from a document. The system is flexible in that it offers to the user the possibility of setting parameters such as frequency thresholds for collocation extraction and indicators for keyphrase relevance, as well as it allows for domain adaptation exploiting a corpus of documents in an unsupervised way. KX is also easily adaptable to new languages in that it requires only a PoS-Tagger to derive lexical patterns. In the SemEval task 5 "Automatic Keyphrase Extraction from Scientific Articles", KX performance achieved satisfactory results both in finding *reader-assigned keywords* and in the *combined keywords* subtask.

1 Introduction

Keyphrases are expressions, either single words or phrases, describing the most important concepts of a document. As such, a list of keyphrases provides an approximate but useful characterization of the content of a text and can be used in a number of interesting ways both for human and automatic processing. For example, keyphrases provide a sort of quick summary of a document. This can be exploited not only in automatic *summarization* tasks, but also to enable quick *topic search* over a number of documents indexed according to their keywords, which is more precise and efficient than full-text search. Once the keywords of a document collection are known, they can also be used to calculate *semantic similarity* between documents and to *cluster* the texts according to such similarity (Ricca et al, 2004). Also, keyword extraction can be used as an intermediate step for *automatic sense extraction* (Jones et al, 2002).

For these reasons, the keyphrase extraction task proposed at SemEval 2010 raised much attention among NLP researchers, with 20 groups participating to the competition. In this framework, we presented the KX system, specifically tuned to identify keyphrases in scientific articles. In particular, the challenge comprised two subtasks: the extraction of *reader-assigned* and of *author-assigned* keyphrases in scientific articles from the ACM digital library. The former are assigned to the articles by annotators, who can choose only keyphrases that occur in the document, while author-assigned keyphrases are not necessarily included in the text.

2 KX architecture

A previous version of the KX system, named KXPat (Pianta, 2009), was developed to extract keyphrases from patent documents in the PatExpert project (www.patexpert.org). The system employed in the SemEval task has additional parameters and has been tailored to identify keyphrases in scientific articles.

With KX, the identification of keyphrases can be accomplished with or without the help of a reference corpus, from which some statistical measures are computed in an unsupervised way. We present here the general KX architecture, including the corpus-based pre-processing, even if in the SemEval task the information extracted from the corpus did not contribute as expected (see Section 3).

KX keyphrase extraction combines linguistic and statistical information, similar to (Frantzi et al., 2000) and is based on 4 steps. The first three steps are carried out at corpus level, whereas the fourth one extracts information specific to each single document to be processed. This means that the first three steps require a corpus *C*, preferably sharing the same domain of the document *d* from which the keyphrases should be extracted. The fourth step, instead, is focused only on the

Proceedings of the 5th International Workshop on Semantic Evaluation, ACL 2010, pages 170–173,
Uppsala, Sweden, 15-16 July 2010.

document *d*. The steps can be summarized as follows:

Step 1: Extract from *C* the list *NG-c* of *corpus* n-grams, where an n-gram is any sequence of tokens in the text, for instance "the system", "of the", "specifically built".

Step 2: Select from the list *NG-c* a sub-list of multiword terms *MW-c*, that is combinations of words expressing a unitary concept, for instance "light beam" or "access control"

Step 3: For each document in *C*, recognize and mark the multiword terms. Calculate the inverse document frequency (IDF) for all words and multiword terms in the corpus.

Step 4: Given a document *d* from which a set of relevant keyphrases should be extracted, count all words and multiword terms and rank them.

Step 1 is aimed at building a list of all possible n-grams in *C*. The maximum length of the selected n-grams can be set by the user. For SemEval, beside one-token n-grams, we select 2-, 3- and 4-grams. Since n-grams occurring only a few times are very unlikely to be useful for keyphrase recognition, they are cut off from the extracted list and excluded for further processing. The frequency threshold can be set according to the reference corpus dimensions. For SemEval, we fixed the frequency threshold to 4. In this step, a black-list was also used in order to exclude n-grams containing any of the stopwords in the list. Such stopwords include for example "everything", "exemplary", "preceding", etc.

In Step 2, we select as multiword terms those n-grams that match certain lexical patterns. To this purpose, we first analyze all n-grams with the MorphoPro morphological analyzer of the TextPro toolsuite (Pianta et al., 2006). Then, we filter out the n-grams whose analysis does not correspond to a predefined set of lexical patterns. For example, one of the patterns admitted for 4-grams is the following: [N]~[O]~[ASPGLU]~[NU]. This means that a 4-gram is a candidate multiword term if it is composed by a Noun, followed by "of" or "for" (defined as O), followed by either an Adjective, Singular noun, Past participle, Gerund, punctuation (L) or Unknown word, followed by either a Noun or Unknown word. This is matched for example by the 4-gram "subset [S] of [O] parent [S] peers [N]". Both the lexical categories (e.g. S for singular noun) and the admissible lexical patterns can be defined by the user.

In Step 3, multiword terms are recognized by combining local (document) and global (corpus) evidence. To this purpose, we do not exploit association measures such as Log-Likelihood, or Mutual Information, but a simple frequency based criterion. Two thresholds are defined: *MinCorpus*, which corresponds to the minimum number of occurrences of an n-gram in a *reference corpus*, and *MinDoc*, i.e. the minimum number of occurrences in the *current document*. KX marks an n-gram in a document as a multiword term if it occurs at least *MinCorpus* times in the corpus or at least *MinDoc* times in the document. The two parameters depend on the size of the corpus and the document respectively. In SemEval, we found that the best thresholds are *MinDoc*=4 and *MinCorpus*=8. A similar, frequency-based, strategy is used to solve ambiguities in how sequences of contiguous multiwords should be segmented. For instance, given the sequence "combined storage capability of sensors" we need to decide whether we recognize "combined storage capability" or "storage capability of sensors". To this purpose, we calculate the strength of each alternative collocation as *docFrequency * corpusFrequency*, and then choose the stronger one. To calculate IDF for each word and multiword term, we use the usual formula: *log(TotDocs / DocsContaningTerm)*.

In step 4, we take into account a new document *d*, possibly not included in *C*, from which the keyphrases should be extracted. First we recognize and mark multiword terms, through the same algorithm used in Step 3. Note that KX can recognize multiwords also in isolated documents, independently of any reference corpus, by activating only the *MinDoc* parameter (see above). Then, we count the frequency of words and multiword terms in *d*, obtaining a first list of keyphrases, ranked according to frequency. Thus, *frequency* is the *baseline* ranking parameter, based on the assumption that important concepts are mentioned more frequently than less important ones.

After the creation of a frequency-based list of keyphrases, various techniques are used to re-rank it according to relevance. In order to find the best ranking mechanism for the type of keyphrases we want to extract, different parameters can be set:

- *Inverse document frequency* (*IDF*): this parameter takes into account the fact that a concept that is mentioned in all documents is less relevant to our task than a concept occurring in few documents

- *Keyphrase length*: number of tokens in a keyphrase. Concepts expressed by longer phrases are expected to be more specific, and thus more relevant. When this parameter is activated, frequency is multiplied by the keyphrase length.
- *Position of first occurrence*: important concepts are expected to be mentioned before less relevant ones. If the parameter is activated, the frequency score will be multiplied by the *PosFact* factor computed as $(DistFromEnd\ /\ MaxIndex)^{pwr2}$, where *MaxIndex* is the length of the current document and *DistFromEnd* is *MaxIndex* minus the position of the first keyphrase occurrence in the text.
- *Shorter concept subsumption*: In the keyphrase list, two concepts can occur, such that one is a specification of the other. Concept subsumption and boosting are used to merge or re-rank such couples of concepts. If a keyphrase is (stringwise) included in a longer keyphrase with a *higher frequency*, the frequency of the shorter keyphrase is transferred to the count of the longer one. E.g. "grid service discovery"=6 and "grid service"=4 are re-ranked as "grid service discovery"=10 and "grid service"=0
- *Longer concept boosting:* If a keyphrase is included in a longer one with a *lower frequency*, the average score between the two keyphrase frequency is computed. Such score is assigned to the less frequent keyphrase and subtracted from the frequency score of the higher ranked one. For example, if "grid service discovery"=4 and "grid service"=6, the average frequency is 5, so that "grid service discovery"=5 and "grid service" = 6–5=1. This parameter can be activated alone or together with another one that modifies the criterion for computing the boosting. With this second option, the longer keyphrase is assigned the frequency of the shorter one. For example, if "grid service discovery"=4 and "grid service"=6, the boosting gives "grid service discovery"=6 and "grid service"=6.

After the list of ranked keyphrases is extracted for each document, it is finally *post-processed* in two steps. The post-processing phase has been added specifically for SemEval, because keyphrases do not usually need to be stemmed and acronym expansion is relevant only for the specific genre of scientific articles. For this reason, the two processes are not part of the official system architecture.

First, acronyms are replaced by the extended form, which is automatically extracted from the current document. The algorithm for acronym detection scans for parenthetical expressions in the text and checks if a preceding text span can be considered a suitable correspondence (Nguyen and Kan, 2007). The algorithm should detect cases in which the acronym appears after or before the extended form, like in "Immediate Predecessors Tracking (IPT)" and "IPT (Immediate Predecessors Tracking)". If the acronym and the extended form appear both in the keyphrase list, only the extended form is kept and the acronym frequency is added.

The second step is stemming with the (Porter Stemmer). Then, we check if the list of stemmed keyphrases contains duplicate entries. If yes, we sum the frequencies of the double keyphrases and remove one of the two from the list.

3 Experimental Setup

In the SemEval task, 144 training files were made available before the test data release. We split them into a training/development set of 100 documents and a test set of 44 documents, in order to find the best parameter combination. Keyphrase assignment is a subjective task and criteria for keyphrase identification depend on the domain and on the goal for which the keyphrases are needed. For example in scientific articles longer keyphrases are often more informative than shorter ones, so the parameters for boosting longer concepts are particularly relevant.

We first tested all parameters in isolation to compute the improvement over the frequency-based baseline. Results are reported in Table 1. F1 is computed as the harmonic mean of precision and recall over the 15 top-ranked keyphrases after stemming. We report the *combined F1*, as computed by the task scorer in order to combine *reader-assigned* and *author-assigned* keyword sets.

Parameter	F1 (combined)
Baseline(MinDoc = 2)	13.63
Baseline(MinDoc = 4)	14.84
+CorpusColloc(small)	13.48
+CorpusColloc(big)	13.33
+IDF	17.98

+KeyphraseLength	16.78
+FirstPosition	16.18
+ShortConcSubsumption	16.03
+LongConcBoost(version1)	14.38
+LongConcBoost(version2)	13.93
MinDoc = 4, +FirstPosition, +IDF, +KeyphraseLength, +ShortConcSubsumption, +LongConcBoost(version1)	**25.62**

Table 1: Parameter performance over development set

The parameter scoring the highest improvement over the baseline is IDF. Also the parameters boosting longer keyphrases and those that occur at the beginning of the text are effective. Note that the *LongConcBoost* parameter achieves better results in the first version, which has a higher impact on the re-ranking. Surprisingly, using a domain corpus to extract information about multiword terms, as described in Section 2, steps 1 - 3, does not achieve any improvement. This means that KX can better recognize keyphrases in single documents without any corpus reference. Besides, the best setting for *MinDoc*, the minimum number of multiword occurrences in the current document (see Section 2) is 4. We tested the *CorpusColloc* parameter using two different reference corpora: one contained the 100 articles of the training set (*CorpusColloc small*), while the other (*CorpusColloc big*) included both the 100 training articles and the 200 scientific publications of the NUS Keyphrase Corpus (Nguyen and Kan, 2007). The performance is worse using the larger corpus than the smaller one, and in both cases it is below the baseline obtained without any reference corpus.

In the bottom row of Table 1, the best parameter combination is reported with the score obtained over the development set. The improvement over the baseline reaches 11.99 F1.

4 Evaluation

In the SemEval task, the system was run on the test set (100 articles) with the best performing parameter combination described in the previous section. The results obtained over the 15 top-ranked keyphrases are reported in Table 2.

Keyphrase type	**P**	**R**	**F1**
Reader-assigned	20.33	25.33	**22.56**
Combined	23.60	24.15	**23.87**

Table 2: System performance over test set

In the competition, the F1 score over reader-assigned keyphrases was ranked 3rd out of 20 participants, while the combined measure achieved the 7th best result out of 20.

5 Conclusions

In this work we have described KX, a flexible system for keyphrase extraction, which achieved promising results in the SemEval task 5. The good KX performance is due to its adaptable architecture, based on a set of parameters that can be tailored to the document type, the preferred keyphrase length, etc. The system can also exploit multiword lists (with frequency) extracted from a reference corpus, even if this feature did not improve KX performance in this specific task. However, this proved to be relevant when applied to keyphrase extraction in the patent domain, using a large domain-specific corpus of 10.000 very long documents (Pianta, 2009).

A limitation of KX in the task was that it extracts only keyphrases already present in a given document, while the *author-assigned* subtask in the SemEval competition included also keyphrases that do not occur in the text. Another improvement, which is now being implemented, is the extraction of the best parameter combination using machine-learning techniques.

References

Jones, S., Lundy, S. and Paynter, G. W. 2002. Interactive Document Summarization Using Automatically Extracted Keyphrases. In *Proc. of the 35th Hawaii International Conference on System Sciences*.

Frantzi, K., Ananiadou, S. and Mima, H. 2000. Automatic recognition of multi-word terms: the C-value/NC-value method. *Journal on Digital Libraries*. 3 (2), pp.115-130.

Thuy Dung Nguyen and Min-Yen Kan. 2007. Keyphrase Extraction in Scientific Documents. In D.H.-L. Goh et al. (eds.): *ICADL 2007*, LNCS 4822, pp. 317-326.

Pianta, E., Girardi, C and Zanoli, R. 2006. The TextPro tool suite. In *Proc. of LREC*.

Pianta, E. 2009. *Content Distillation from Patent Material*, FBK Technical Report.

Ricca, F., Tonella, P., Girardi, C and Pianta, E. 2004. An empirical study on Keyword-based Web Site Clustering. In *Proceedings of the 12th IWPC*.

PorterStemmer: http://tartarus.org/~martin/PorterStemmer/perl.txt.

BUAP: An Unsupervised Approach to Automatic Keyphrase Extraction from Scientific Articles

Roberto Ortiz, David Pinto, Mireya Tovar
Faculty of Computer Science, BUAP
Puebla, Mexico
korn_resorte2003@hotmail.com,
{dpinto, mtovar}@cs.buap.mx

Héctor Jiménez-Salazar
Information Technologies Dept., UAM
DF, Mexico
hgimenezs@gmail.com

Abstract

In this paper, it is presented an unsupervised approach to automatically discover the latent keyphrases contained in scientific articles. The proposed technique is constructed on the basis of the combination of two techniques: maximal frequent sequences and pageranking. We evaluated the obtained results by using micro-averaged precision, recall and F-scores with respect to two different gold standards: 1) reader's keyphrases, and 2) a combined set of author's and reader's keyphrases. The obtained results were also compared against three different baselines: one unsupervised (TF-IDF based) and two supervised (Naïve Bayes and Maximum Entropy).

1 Introduction

The task of automatic keyphrase extraction has been studied for several years. Firstly, as semantic metadata useful for tasks such as summarization (Barzilay and Elhadad, 1997; Lawrie et al., 2001; DAvanzo and Magnini, 2005), but later recognizing the impact that good keyphrases would have on the quality of various Natural Language Processing (NLP) applications (Frank et al., 1999; Witten et al., 1999; Turney, 1999; Barker and Corrnacchia, 2000; Medelyan and Witten, 2008). Thus, the selection of important, topical phrases from within the body of a document may be used in order to improve the performance of systems dealing with different NLP problems such as, clustering, question-answering, named entity recognition, information retrieval, etc.

In general, a keyphrase may be considered as a sequence of one or more words that capture the main topic of the document, as that keyphrase is expected to represent one of the key ideas expressed by the document author. Following the previously mentioned hypothesis, we may take advantage of two different techniques of text analysis: maximal frequent sequences to extract a sequence of one or more words from a given text, and pageranking, expecting to extract those word sequences that represent the key ideas of the author.

The interest on extracting high quality keyphrases from raw text has motivated forums, such as SemEval, where different systems may evaluate their performances. The purpose of SemEval is to evaluate semantic analysis systems. In particular, in this paper we are reporting the results obtained in Task #5 of SemEval-2 2010, which has been named: "Automatic Keyphrase Extraction from Scientific Articles". We focused this paper on the description of our approach and, therefore, we do not describe into detail the task nor the dataset used. For more information about this information read the "Task #5 Description paper", also published in this proceedings volume (Nam Kim et al., 2010).

The rest of this paper is structured as follows. Section 2 describes into detail the components of the proposed approach. In Section 3 it is shown the performance of the presented system. Finally, in Section 4 a discussion of findings and further work is given.

2 Description of the approach

The approach presented in this paper relies on the combination of two different techniques for selecting the most prominent terms of a given text: maximal frequent sequences and pageranking. In Figure 1 we may see this two step approach, where we are considering a sequence to be equivalent to an n-gram. The complete description of the procedure is given as follows.

We select maximal frequent sequences which

Proceedings of the 5th International Workshop on Semantic Evaluation, ACL 2010, pages 174–177,
Uppsala, Sweden, 15-16 July 2010.

we consider to be candidate keyphrases and, thereafter, we ranking them in order to determine which ones are the most importants (according to the pageranking algorithm). In the following subsections we give a brief description of these two techniques. Afterwards, we provide an algorithm of the presented approach.

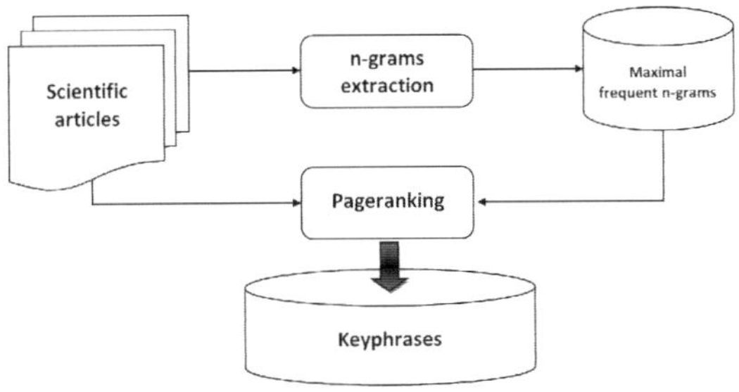

Figure 1: Two step approach of BUAP Team at the Task #5 of SemEval-2

2.1 Maximal Frequent Sequences

Definition: If a sequence p is a subsequence of q and the number of elements in p is equal to n, then the p is called an n-gram in q.

Definition: A sequence $p = a_1 \cdots a_k$ is a subsequence of a sequence q if all the items a_i occur in q and they occur in the same order as in p. If a sequence p is a subsequence of a sequence q we say that p occurs in q.

Definition: A sequence p is frequent in S if p is a subsequence of at least β documents in S where β is a given frequency threshold. Only one occurrence of sequence in the document is counted. Several occurrences within one document do not make the sequence more frequent.

Definition: A sequence p is a maximal frequent sequence in S if there does not exists any sequence q in S such that p is a subsequence of q and p is frequent in S.

2.2 PageRanking

The algorithm of PageRanking was defined by Brin and Page in (Brin and Page, 1998). It is a graph-based algorithm used for ranking webpages. The algorithm considers input and output links of each page in order to construct a graph, where each vertex is a webpage and each edge may be the input or output links for this webpage. They denote as $In(V_i)$ the set of input links of webpage V_i, and $Out(V_i)$ their output links. The algorithm proposed to rank each webpage based on the voting or recommendation of other webpages. The higher the number of votes that are cast for a vertex, the higher the importance of the vertex. Moreover, the importance of the vertex casting the vote determines how important the vote itself is, and this information is also taken into account by the ranking model.

Although this algoritm has been initially proposed for webpages ranking, it has been also used for other NLP applications which may model their corresponding problem in a graph structure. Eq. (1) is the formula proposed by Brin and Page.

$$S(V_i) = (1-d) + d * \sum_{j \in In(V_i)} \frac{1}{|Out(V_j)|} S(V_j) \qquad (1)$$

where d is a damping factor that can be set between 0 and 1, which has the role of integrating into the model the probability of jumping from a given vertex to another random vertex in the graph. This factor is usually set to 0.85 (Brin and Page, 1998).

There are some other propossals, like the one presented in (Mihalcea and Tarau, 2004), where a textranking algorithm is presented. The authors consider a weighted version of PageRank and present some applications to NLP using unigrams. They also construct multi-word terms by exploring the conections among ranked words in the graph. Our algorithm differs from textranking in that we use MFS for feeding the PageRanking algorithm.

2.3 Algorithm

The complete algoritmic description of the presented approach is given in Algorithm 1. Readers and writers keyphrases may be quite different. In particular, writers usually introduce acronyms in their text, but they use the complete or expanded representation of these acronyms for their keyphrases. Therefore, we have included a module ($Extract\_Acronyms$) for extracting both, acronyms with their corresponding expanded version, which are used afterwards as output of our system. We have preprocessed the dataset removing stopwords and punctuation symbols. Lemmatization (TreeTagger[1]) and stemming (Porter Stemmer (Porter, 1980)) were also applied in some stages of preprocessing.

The $Maximal\_Freq\_Sequences$ module extracts maximal frequent sequences of words and we feed the PageRaking module ($PageRanking$)

[1] http://www.ims.uni-stuttgart.de/projekte/corplex/TreeTagger/

with all these sequences for determining the most important ones. We use the structure of the scientific articles in order to determine *in* and *out* links of the sequences found. In fact, we use a neighborhood criterion (a pair of MFS in the same sentence) for determining the links between those MFS's. Once the ranking is calculated, we may select those sequences of a given length (unigrams, bigrams and trigrams) as output of our system. We also return a maximum of three acronyms, and their associated multiterm phrases ($MultiTerm$), as candidate keyphrases. Determining the length and quantity of the sequences (n-grams) was experimentally deduced from the training corpus.

Algorithm 1: Algorithm of the Two Step approach for the Task #5 at SemEval-2

```
Input: A document set: D = {d_1, d_2, ···}
Output: A set K = {K_1, K_2, ···} of
        keyphrases for each document d_i:
        K_i = {k_{i,1}, k_{i,2}, ···}
foreach d_i ∈ D do
    AcronymSet = Extract_Acronyms(d_i);
    d_i^1 = Pre_Processing(d_i);
    MFS = Maximal_Freq_Sequences(d_i^1);
    CK = PageRanking(d_i^1, MFS);
    CU = Top_Nine_Unigrams(CK);
    CT = Top_Three_Trigrams(CK);
    K_i = CT;
    NU = 0;
    Acronyms = 0;
    foreach unigram ∈ CU do
        if unigram ∈ AcronymSet then
            if Acronyms < 3 then
                K_i = K_i ⋃ {unigram};
                EA = MultiTerm(unigram);
                K_i = K_i ⋃ {EA};
                Acronyms++;
            end
        else
            K_i = K_i ⋃ {unigram};
            NU++;
        end
    end
    N = (15−(2∗Acronyms+|CT|+NU));
    CB = Top_N_Bigrams(CK, N);
    K_i = K_i ⋃ CB;
end
return K = {K_1, K_2, ···}
```

In this edition of the Task #5 of SemEval-2 2010, we tested three different runs, which were named: $BUAP-1$, $BUAP-2$ and $BUAP-3$. Definition and differences among the three runs are given in Table 3.

The results obtained with each run, together with three different baselines are given in the following section.

3 Experimental results

In all tables, P, R, F mean micro-averaged precision, recall and F-scores. For baselines, there were provided 1,2,-3 grams as candidates and $TFIDF$ as features. In Table 2, $TFIDF$ is an unsupervised method to rank the candidates based on $TFIDF$ scores. NB and ME are supervised methods using Naïve Bayes and maximum entropy in WEKA. In second column, R means to use the reader-assigned keyword set as gold-standard data and C means to use both author-assigned and reader-assigned keyword sets as answers.

Notice from Tables 2 and 3 that we outperformed all the baselines for the Top 15 candidates. However, the Top 10 candidates were only outperformed by the *Reader*-Assigned keyphrases found. This implies that the *Writer* keyphrases we obtained were not of as good as the *Reader* ones. As we mentioned, readers and writers assign different keywords. The former write keyphrases based on the lecture done, by the latter has a wider context and their keyphrases used to be more complex. We plan to investigate this issue in the future.

4 Conclusions

We have presented an approach based on the extraction of maximal frequent sequences which are then ranked by using the pageranking algorithm. Three different runs were tested, modifying the preprocessing stage and the number of bigrams given as output. We did not see an improvement when we used lemmatization of the documents. The run which obtained the best results was ranking by the organizer according to the top 15 best keyphrases, however, we may see that our runs need to be analysed more into detail in order to provide a re-ranking procedure for the best 15 keyphrases found. This procedure may improve the top 5 candidates precision.

Run name		*Description*
$BUAP-1$	:	This run is exactly the one described in Algorithm 1.
$BUAP-2$	:	Same as $BUAP-1$ but lemmatization was applied a priori and stemming at the end.
$BUAP-3$	:	Same as $BUAP-2$ but output twice the number of bigrams.

Table 1: Description of the three runs submitted to the Task #5 of SemEval-2 2010

Method	by	top 5 candidates			top 10 candidates			top 15 candidates		
		P	R	F	P	R	F	P	R	F
$TF-IDF$	R	17.80%	7.39%	10.44%	13.90%	11.54%	12.61%	11.60%	14.45%	12.87%
	C	22.00%	7.50%	11.19%	17.70%	12.07%	14.35%	14.93%	15.28%	15.10%
NB	R	16.80%	6.98%	9.86%	13.30%	11.05%	12.07%	11.40%	14.20%	12.65%
	C	21.40%	7.30%	10.89%	17.30%	11.80%	14.03%	14.53%	14.87%	14.70%
ME	R	16.80%	6.98%	9.86%	13.30%	11.05%	12.07%	11.40%	14.20%	12.65%
	C	21.40%	7.30%	10.89%	17.30%	11.80%	14.03%	14.53%	14.87%	14.70%

Table 2: Baselines

Method	by	top 5 candidates			top 10 candidates			top 15 candidates		
		P	R	F	P	R	F	P	R	F
$BUAP-1$	R	10.40%	4.32%	6.10%	13.90%	11.54%	12.61%	14.93%	18.60%	16.56%
	C	13.60%	4.64%	6.92%	17.60%	12.01%	14.28%	19.00%	19.44%	19.22%
$BUAP-2$	R	10.40%	4.32%	6.10%	13.80%	11.46%	12.52%	14.67%	18.27%	16.27%
	C	14.40%	4.91%	7.32%	17.80%	12.14%	14.44%	18.73%	19.17%	18.95%
$BUAP-3$	R	10.40%	4.32%	6.10%	12.10%	10.05%	10.98%	12.33%	15.37%	13.68%
	C	14.40%	4.91%	7.32%	15.60%	10.64%	12.65%	15.67%	16.03%	15.85%

Table 3: The three different runs submitted to the competition

Acknowledgments

This work has been partially supported by CONACYT (Project #106625) and PROMEP (Grant #103.5/09/4213).

References

[Barker and Corrnacchia2000] K. Barker and N. Cornacchia. 2000. Using noun phrase heads to extract document keyphrases. In *13th Biennial Conference of the Canadian Society on Computational Studies of Intelligence: Advances in Artificial Intelligence.*

[Barzilay and Elhadad1997] R. Barzilay and M. Elhadad. 1997. Using lexical chains for text summarization. In *ACL/EACL 1997 Workshop on Intelligent Scalable Text Summarization*, pages 10–17.

[Brin and Page1998] S. Brin and L. Page. 1998. The anatomy of a large-scale hypertextual web search engine. In *COMPUTER NETWORKS AND ISDN SYSTEMS*, pages 107–117. Elsevier Science Publishers B. V.

[DAvanzo and Magnini2005] E. DAvanzo and B. Magnini. 2005. A keyphrase-based approach to summarization:the lake system. In *Document Understanding Conferences (DUC-2005).*

[Frank et al.1999] E. Frank, G.W. Paynter, I. Witten, C. Gutwin, and C.G. Nevill-Manning. 1999. Domain specific keyphrase extraction. In *16th International Joint Conference on AI*, pages 668–673.

[Lawrie et al.2001] D. Lawrie, W. B. Croft, and A. Rosenberg. 2001. Finding topic words for hierarchical summarization. In *SIGIR 2001*.

[Medelyan and Witten2008] O. Medelyan and I. H. Witten. 2008. Domain independent automatic keyphrase indexing with small training sets. *Journal of American Society for Information Science and Technology*, 59(7):1026–1040.

[Mihalcea and Tarau2004] R. Mihalcea and P. Tarau. 2004. Textrank: Bringing order into texts. In *EMNLP 2004, ACL*, pages 404–411.

[Nam Kim et al.2010] S. Nam Kim, O. Medelyan, and M.Y. Kan. 2010. Semeval-2010 task5: Automatic keyphrase extraction from scientific articles. In *Proceedings of the Fifth International Workshop on Semantic Evaluations (SemEval-2010)*. Association for Computational Linguistics.

[Porter1980] M. F. Porter. 1980. An algorithm for suffix stripping. *Program*, 14(3).

[Turney1999] P. Turney. 1999. Learning to extract keyphrases from text. Technical Report ERB-1057. (NRC #41622), National Research Council, Institute for Information Technology.

[Witten et al.1999] I. Witten, G. Paynter, E. Frank, C. Gutwin, and G. Nevill-Manning. 1999. Kea:practical automatic key phrase extraction. In *fourth ACM conference on Digital libraries*, pages 254–256.

UNPMC: Naïve Approach to Extract Keyphrases from Scientific Articles

Jungyeul Park
LINA,
Université de Nantes
Nantes, France
jungyeul.park
@univ-nantes.fr

Jong Gun Lee
LIP6-CNRS,
UPMC (Paris 6)
Paris, France
jonggun.lee
@lip6.fr

Béatrice Daille
LINA,
Université de Nantes
Nantes, France
beatrice.daille
@univ-nantes.fr

Abstract

We describe our method for extracting keyphrases from scientific articles which we participate in the shared task of SemEval-2 Evaluation Exercise. Even though general-purpose term extractors along with linguistically-motivated analysis allow us to extract elaborated morpho-syntactic variation forms of terms, a naïve statistic approach proposed in this paper is very simple and quite efficient for extracting keyphrases especially from well-structured scientific articles. Based on the characteristics of keyphrases with section information, we obtain 18.34% for f-measure using top 15 candidates. We also show further improvement without any complications and we discuss this at the end of the paper.

1 Introduction[1]

Key phrases are a set of words to capture the main topic of the document. Since key phrases contain the substance of the document, they are used in the large spectrum of areas; from applications which explicitly use key phrases such as automatic indexing, documents classification and search engine optimization in information retrieval, to applications which implicitly use key phrases such as summarization and question-answering systems. During the last decade, many previous works have dealt with the various methods for automatically extracting key phrases (e.g., Frank et al., 1999; Barker and Corrnacchia, 2000; Turney, 2003; Medelyan and Witten, 2006; Nguyen and Kan, 2007; Wan and Xiao, 2008).

The task of extracting key phrases would be considered as a subtask of extracting terminology if key phrases are a kind of terms. Typical approaches for automatically extracting terms use linguistic preprocessing which involves morpho-syntactic analysis such as part-of-speech tagging and phrase chunking, and statistical postprocessing such as log likelihood which compares the term frequencies in a document against their expected frequencies derived in a bigger text. Besides, extracting terms prefers syntactically plausible noun phrases (NPs) which are mainly multi-words terms. Kim and Kan (2009) report that most of key phrases are often simple words than less often compound words[2].

The task for extracting key phrases tend to include analyzing the document structure. Especially, extracting key phrases from well-structured scientific articles should consider cross-section information (Nguyen and Kan, 2007). This information has been explored to assess the suitability of features during learning in Kim and Kan (2009).

Extracting key phrases, however, is more than to extracting terminology or analyzing the document structure. While terms are words which appear in specific contexts and analyse concept structures in *domains* of human activity, key phrases are words that capture the key idea of *documents*. In addition, while terms usually occur in the given document more often than we would expect to occur, key phrases do not necessarily occur frequently or key phrases do not occur at all in the document. Consequently, the task for extracting key phrases should not be considered as the subtask of extracting terminology and we are not able to directly apply general-purpose term extractors to extract key phrases.

In this paper, we describe our method for "Automatic Keyphrase Extraction from Scientific Ar-

[1] UNPMC means the collaborative team from Laboratoire d'Informatique de Nantes Atlantique of the Université de Nantes and Laboratoire d'Informatique de Paris 6 of the Université Pierre et Marie Curie.

[2] In training data, only 23.4% of keyphrases, however, are single words.

Proceedings of the 5th International Workshop on Semantic Evaluation, ACL 2010, pages 178–181,
Uppsala, Sweden, 15-16 July 2010. ©2010 Association for Computational Linguistics

ticles", the shared task of SemEval-2 Evaluation Exercise which we participated in. Although term extractors along with linguistically-motivated analysis allow us to extract even elaborated morpho-syntactic variation forms of terms, the naïve statistic approach proposed in this paper is very simple and quite efficient for extracting keyphrases especially from well-structured scientific articles. In a nutshell, our method is based on empirical rules without any linguistically-motivated preprocessing. Empirical rules are obtained from the analysis of the characteristics of keyphrases by observing training data.

The remaining of this paper is organized as follows: Section 2 explains the characteristics of keyphrases in scientific articles. Section 3 and 4 detail our naïve statistic approach and experiment, respectively. We conclude this paper and discuss a further improvement in Section 6.

2 Characteristics of Keyphrases in Scientific Articles

In this section, we investigate the characteristics of keyphrases in training data. Table 1 shows statistics of training data. In Table 1, `D-author` means the keyphrases assigned by authors, `D-reader` the keyphrases assigned by readers, and `D-combined` the combined keyphrases assigned by both of authors and readers.

	# of papers (p)	# of key phrases (k)	k / p
D-author	144	563	3.91
D-reader	144	1,865	12.95
D-combined	144	2,265	15.73

Table 1: Statistics of training data

2.1 Word length of keyphrases

We measure the distribution of word length of key phrases in training data and present it in Figure 1. Over half of key phrases are two-word key phrases in both author- and reader-assigned key phrases. Differently with Kim and Kan (2009) which they reported that most of key phrases are often simple words than less often compound words, only 29.7% and 17.7% of key phrases are one-word key phrases. There are also more than four-word key phrases which hold 4.3% and 7.2% of author and reader assigned key phrases, respectively.

2.2 Occurrences of keyphrases

In which section do keyphrases occur frequently? To answer this question, we count the number of

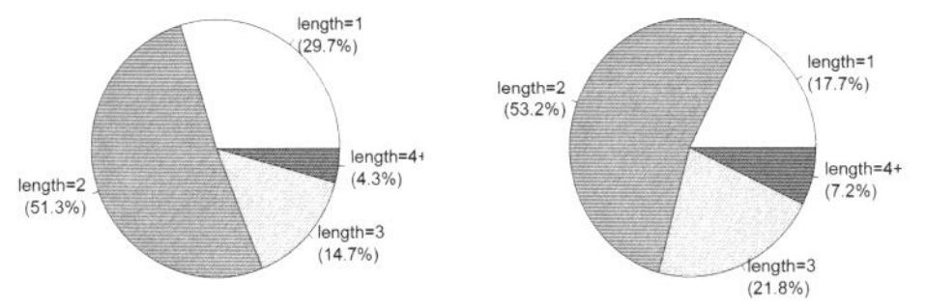

(a) D-author (b) D-reader

Figure 1: Word length of keyphrases in training data

occurrences of keyphrases of each section. Due to the variation of the naming of the section, we divide sections into title and abstract, introduction, conclusion, and the rest including references. Table 2 and 3 show the number of occurrences and the accumulative number of unique occurrences of keyphrases in each section, respectively. We also show the accumulative number of words in each section in Table 4. Including the rest sections exponentially diminishes the ratio of the number of gold keyphrases to the number of candidate keyphrases. Note that m words produce $\sum_{i=0}^{n-1}(m-i)$ candidate keyphrases for up to n-word keyphrases by supposing that candidate keyphrases are simple n-word terms.

Note also that both author- and reader-assigned keyphrases hold only 75.49% and 89.44%, respectively. Even some keyphrases are different with surface forms in the document and our naïve method with no linguistic intervention is not able to recognize them. For example, one of reader-assigned keyphrases *distributed real-time embedded system* for C-41 actually appears as *distributed real-time and embedded (DRE) systems.*

	D-author	D-reader
Title and Abstract	277	802
Introduction	215	491
Conclusion	313	982
Other	387	1,210

Table 2: Number of occurrences of keyphrases in each section

	D-author	D-reader
Total	563 (100.0%)	1,865 (100.0%)
Title and Abstract	277 (49.20%)	802 (43.00%)
'+' Introduction	317 (56.30%)	937 (50.24%)
'+' Conclusion	367 (65.19%)	1,311 (70.29%)
'+' Other	425 (75.49%)	1,668 (89.44%)

Table 3: Accumulative number of unique occurrences of keyphrases in each section

	# words (W)	# gold (G)	G/W
Title and Abstract	28435	802	0.0282
'+' Introduction	72729	937	0.0128
'+' Conclusion	178473	1311	0.0073
'+' Other	948007	1668	0.0018

Table 4: Number of words in training data and gold data (`D-reader`)

2.3 Coincidence of keyphrases

Figure 2 shows the coincidence of keyphrases[3]. Almost half of keyphrases (58.44% and 45.74% for author- and reader-assigned keyphrases, respectively) occur coincidentally in keysections and the rest sections. Keysections hold 65.19% and 70.29% of keyphrases and the rest sections besides keysections hold 68.74% and 64.88% of whole keyphrases. Note that the rest sections occupy over 70% of the document on the average.

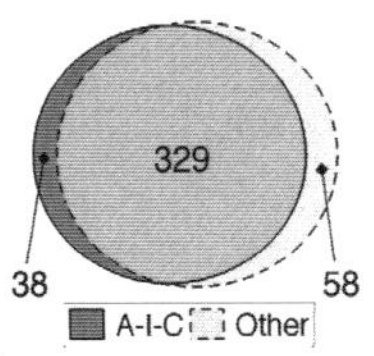

(a) `D-author`

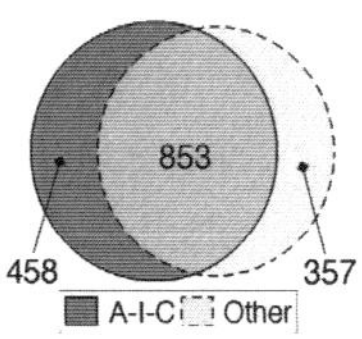

(b) `D-reader`

Figure 2: Coincidence of keyphrases

3 Methodology

From training data, we observe and decide the followings:

- More than four-word keyphrases hold only 4.3% and 7.2% of whole keyphrases. We decide that our approach limits the word length as three for extracting keyphrases. Thus we extract only up to three-word keyphrases. This choice might lead the performance degradation of our method because we explicitly exclude more than four-word keyphrases.

- Keysections hold 65.19% and 70.29% of keyphrases. We decide that our approach limits keysections from which we extract keyphrases. Including the rest sections may improve recall, but probably diminish precision since the rest sections occupy over 70% of the document.

- Almost half of keyphrases occur coincidentally in keysections and the rest sections. We decide that our approach limits coincident keyphrases in both of them. This decision is made empirically and improve precision.

The following procedure explains and details our approach for extracting keyphrases.

- Extract up to three-word terms from keysections as candidate keyphrases.
- Filter them out if they contain one or more of stop words or non-content-containing words (see Table 5 for non-content-containing words).
- Count the number of occurrences of extracted terms from each keysection.
- Check the coincidence whether candidate keyphrases occurs in more than two keysections. If so, we assign weight.
- Calculate a score for candidate keyphrases and list them by order of the score.

4 Experiment results

This section shows the experiment results with training and test data.

4.1 Training data

To optimize our results, we use various thresholds for the number of n-word keyphrases and weight.

We try to find the $(i : j : k)$ pattern which means i one-word, j two-word, and K three-word keyphrases to produce the best results. We also try to find the threshold for weight d to calculate the score as follows: if keyphrases appear in more than two keysections, $score = d * \#\ of\ total\ occurences$, otherwise $score = \#\ of\ total\ occurences$. Table 6 shows our best results for training data where $(i : j : k) = (3 : 9 : 3)$ and $d = 2$. Empirically, we found these thresholds from training data by iterating several possibilities[4].

4.2 Test data

Table 7 shows our test data results published by organizers of the shared task of SemEval-2 Evaluation Exercise.

[3]We denote title and abstract as `A`, introduction as `I`, conclusion as `C`, and the rest sections including references as `Other`.

[4]These thresholds will be more examined in future work.

Type	Examples
Noun	section, abstract, introduction, conclusion, reference, future work, figure, paper, result, laboratory, university
Verb	present, how, introduce, become, improve, find, help, improve, consider, call, yield, allow, give, assume
Adverb	always, formally, necessarily, successfully, previously, usually,mainly, final, essentially, ultinately, commonly, severely, significantly, dramatically, clearly, still, well, who, whose, whom, which, whether, therefore,
Other POSs	that, this, those, these, many, several, more, over, less, behind, above, below, each, few, different, under, both, within, through, prior, various, better, following, between, possible, via, before,even, such, if, new, show, important, simple, good, tranditional, current, varying, necessary, previous, clear

Table 5: Example of (heuristically obtained) non-content-containing terms

AUTHOR.STEM.FINAL

# Gold: 559	Match	Precision	Recall	F-score
Top 05	43	5.97%	7.69%	6.72%
Top 10	101	7.01%	18.07%	10.10%
Top 15	139	6.44%	24.87%	10.23%

READER.STEM.FINAL

# Gold: 1824	Match	Precision	Recall	F-score
Top 05	118	16.39%	6.47%	9.28%
Top 10	249	17.29%	13.65%	15.26%
Top 15	361	16.71%	19.79%	18.12%

COMBINED.STEM.FINAL

# Gold: 2223	Match	Precision	Recall	F-score
Top 05	143	19.86%	6.43%	9.71%
Top 10	309	21.46%	13.90%	16.87%
Top 15	441	20.42%	19.84%	20.13%

Table 6: Training data results

READER.STEM.FINAL

# Gold: 1204	Precision	Recall	Fscore
Top 05	13.80%	5.73%	8.10%
Top 10	15.10%	12.54%	13.70%
Top 15	14.47%	18.02%	16.05%

COMBINED.STEM.FINAL

# Gold: 1466	Precision	Recall	Fscore
Top 05	18.00%	6.14%	9.16%
Top 10	19.00%	12.96%	15.41%
Top 15	18.13%	18.55%	18.34%

Table 7: Test data results

5 Conclusion and Discussion

In this paper, we described our simple method for extracting keyphrases from scientific articles which we participate in the shared task of SemEval-2 Evaluation Exercise. The naïve approach was proposed. This approach turned out very simple and quite efficient for extracting keyphrases from well-structured scientific articles. Based on learning the distribution of keyphrases with section information, we obtain 18.34% for f-measure using top 15 candidates.

Our naïve approach still has much room for improvement. For example, we are able to improve the result for same test data up to 20.71% and 25.55% for f-measure using top 15 candidates simply by adding the rest sections and normalizing the number of occurrences of terms from each section[5].

Moreover, our n-word terms based extraction can be benefited by linguistic preprocessing such as normalizing surface forms. Handcrafted regular expression rules along with part-of-speech tagging and phrase chunking would be also introduced to improve candidate selection. We have not explored thoroughly feature engineering, neither. For example, more fine-grained section information and weight re-assignment might help filter out irrelevant candidates. We leave these possibilities for future work.

[5]The result is not improved only by adding the rest sections.

References

Ken Barker and Nadia Cornacchia. 2000. Using noun phrase heads to extract document keyphrases. In *Proceedings of the 13th Biennial Conference of the Canadian Society on Computational Studies of Intelligence: Advances in Artificial Intelligence*, pages 40-52. May 14-17, 2000. Montréal, Quebec, Canada.

Eibe Frank , Gordon W. Paynter , Ian H. Witten , Carl Gutwin, and Craig G. Nevill-Manning. 1999. Domain-Specific Keyphrase Extraction. In *Proceedings of the 16th International Joint Conference on Artificial Intelligence*, pages 668-673. July 31-August 6, 1999. Stockholm, Sweden.

Su Nam Kim and Min-Yen Kan. 2009. Re-examining Automatic Keyphrase Extraction Approaches in Scientific Articles. In *Proceedings of the Workshop on Multiword Expressions: Identification, Interpretation, Disambiguation and Applications (MWE 2009), ACL-IJCNLP 2009*, pages 9-12. August 6, 2009. Singapore.

Olena Medelyan and Ian H. Witten. 2006. Thesaurus based automatic keyphrase indexing. In *Proceedings of the 6th ACM/IEEE-CS joint conference on Digital libraries*, pages 296-297. June 11-15, 2006. Chapel Hill, NC, USA.

Thuy Dung Nguyen and Min-Yen Kan. 2007. Key phrase Extraction in Scientific Publications. *Asian Digital Libraries. Looking Back 10 Years and Forging New Frontiers*, pages 317-326. Springer Berlin, Heidelberg.

Peter D. Turney. 2003. Coherent keyphrase extraction via Web mining. In *Proceedings of the 18th International Joint Conference on Artificial Intelligence*, pages 434-439. August 9-15, 2003. Acapulco, Mexico.

Xiaojun Wan and Jianguo Xiao. 2008. CollabRank: towards a collaborative approach to single-document keyphrase extraction. In *Proceedings of the 22nd International Conference on Computational Linguistics (Coling 2008)*, pages 969-976. 18-22 August, 2008. Manchester, UK.

SEERLAB: A System for Extracting Keyphrases from Scholarly Documents

Pucktada Treeratpituk[1] **Pradeep Teregowda**[2] **Jian Huang**[1] **C. Lee Giles**[1,2]
[1] Information Sciences and Technology
[2] Computer Science and Engineering
Pennsylvania State University, University Park, PA, USA

Abstract

We describe the SEERLAB system that participated in the SemEval 2010's Keyphrase Extraction Task. SEERLAB utilizes the DBLP corpus for generating a set of candidate keyphrases from a document. Random Forest, a supervised ensemble classifier, is then used to select the top keyphrases from the candidate set. SEERLAB achieved a 0.24 F-score in generating the top 15 keyphrases, which places it sixth among 19 participating systems. Additionally, SEERLAB performed particularly well in generating the top 5 keyphrases with an F-score that ranked third.

1 Introduction

Keyphrases are phrases that represent the important topics of a document. There are two types of keyphrases associated with scholarly publications: author-assigned ones and reader-assigned ones. In the Keyphrase Extraction Task (Kim et al., 2010), each system receives two set of scientific papers from the ACM digital library; a training set and a testing set. The author-assigned keyphrases and reader-assigned keyphrases are given for each paper in the training set. The objective is to produce the keyphrases for each article in the testing set.

This paper is organized as followed. First, We describe our keyphrase extraction system, SEERLAB. We then discuss its performance in SemEval 2010. Lastly, we analyze the effectiveness of each feature used by SEERLAB, and provide a summary of our findings.

2 System Description

SEERLAB consists of three main components: a section parser, a candidate keyphrase extractor, and a keyphrase ranker. To generate keyphrases for a paper, the section parser first segments the document into pre-defined generic section types. Secondly, the candidate keyphrase extractor generates a list of candidate phrases based on the document content. Then, the keyphrase ranker ranks each candidate according to the likelihood that it is a keyphrase. The top candidates are selected as keyphrases of the paper.

2.1 Section Parser

The goal of the section parser is to parse each document into the same set of pre-defined sections. However, segmenting a scientific article into pre-defined section types is not trivial. While scholarly publications generally contains similar sections (such as *Abstract* and *Conclusion*), a section's exact header description and the order in which it appears can vary from document to document. For example, the "*Related Work*" section is sometimes referred to as "*Previous Research*" or "*Previous Work*." Also, while the "*Related Work*" section often appears right after the introduction, it could also appear near the end of a paper.

(Nguyen and Kan, 2007) had success in using a maximum entropy (ME) classifier to classify sections into 14 generic section types including those such as *Motivation, Acknowledgement, References*. However, their approach requires annotated training data, which is not always available. Instead, SEERLAB uses regular expressions to parse each document into 6 generic section types: *Title, Abstract, Introduction, Related Work, Methodology + Experiments, and Conclusion + Future Work*. We decided to go with the smaller number of section types (only 6), unlike previous work in (Nguyen and Kan, 2007), because we believed that many sections, such as *Acknowledgement*, are irrelevant to the task.

Proceedings of the 5th International Workshop on Semantic Evaluation, ACL 2010, pages 182–185,
Uppsala, Sweden, 15-16 July 2010.

2.2 Extracting Candidate Keyphrases

In this section, we describe how SEERLAB derives a set of candidate keyphrases for a given document. The goal of the candidate extractor is to include as many actual keyphrases in the candidate set as possible, while keeping the number of candidates small. The performance of the candidate extractor determines the maximum achievable Recall of the whole system. The more correct candidates extracted at this step, the higher the possible Recall. But a bigger candidate set potentially could lower Precision. In our implementation, we decided to ignore the *Methodology + Experiments* sections to limit the size of candidate sets.

First, SEERLAB extracts a list of bigrams, trigrams and quadgrams that appear at least 3 times in titles of papers in DBLP[1], ignoring those that contain stopwords. Prepositions such as "of", "for", "to" are allowed to be present in the ngrams. From 2,144,390 titles in DBLP, there are 376,577 of such ngrams. It then constructs a trie (a prefix-tree) of all ngrams so that it can later perform the longest-prefix matching lookup efficiently.

To generate candidates from a body of text, we start the cursor at the beginning of the text. The DBLP trie is then used to find the longest-prefix match. If no match is found, the cursor is moved to the next word in the text. If a match is found, the matched phrase is extracted and added to the candidate set, while the cursor is moved to the end of the matched phrase. The process is repeated until the cursor reaches the end of the text.

However, the trie constructed as described above can only produce non-unigram candidates that appear in the DBLP corpus. For example, it is incapable of generating candidates such as *"preference elicitation problem,"* which does not appear in DBLP, and *"bet,"* which is an unigram. To remedy such limitations, for each document we also include its top 30 most frequent unigrams, its top 30 non-unigram ngrams and the acronyms found in the document as candidates.

Our method of extracting candidate keyphrases differs from most previous work. Previous work (Kim and Kan, 2009; Nguyen and Kan, 2007) uses hand-crafted regular expressions for candidate extractions. Many of these rules also require POS (part of speech) inputs. In contrast, our method is corpus-driven and requires no additional input from the POS tagger. Additionally, our approach allows us to effectively include phrases that appear only once in the document as candidates, as long as they appear more than twice in the DBLP data.

[1]http://www.informatik.uni-trier.de/ ley/db/index.html

2.3 Ranking Keyphrases

We train a supervised Random Forest (RF) classifier to identify keyphrases from a candidate set. A Random Forest is a collection of decision trees, where its prediction is simply the aggregated votes of each tree. Thus, for each candidate phrase, the number of votes that it receives is used as its fitness score. Candidates with the top fitness scores are then chosen as keyphrases. The detail of the Random Forest algorithm and the features used in the model are given below.

2.3.1 Features

We represent each candidate as a vector of features. There are the total of 11 features.

N: The length of the keyphrase.

ACRO: A binary feature indicating whether the keyphrase appears as an acronym in the document.

$\mathbf{TF}_{doc}$: The number of times that the keyphrase appears in the document.

DF: The document frequency. This is computed based on the DBLP data. For document-specific candidates (unigrams and those not found in DBLP), their DFs are set to 1.

TFIDF: The TFIDF weight of the keyphrase, computed using TF_{doc} and DF.

$\mathbf{TF}_{headers}$: The number of occurrences that the keyphrase appears in any section headers and subsection headers.

$\mathbf{TF}_{section_i}$: The number of occurrences that the keyphrase appears in the $section_i$, where $section_i \in$ {*Title, Abstract, Introduction, Related Work, Conclusion*}. These accounted for the total of 5 features.

2.3.2 Random Forest

Since a random forest (RF) is an ensemble classifier combining multiple decision trees (Breiman, 2001), it makes predictions by aggregating votes of each of the trees. To built a random forest, multiple bootstrap samples are drawn from the original training data, and an unpruned decision tree is built from each bootstrap sample. At each node in a tree, when selecting a feature to split, the selection is done not on the full feature set but on a randomly selected subset of features instead. The

Gini index[2], which measures the class dispersion within a node, is used to determine the best splits.

RFs have been successfully applied to various classification problems with comparable results to other state-of-the-art classifiers such as SVM (Breiman, 2001; Treeratpituk and Giles, 2009). It achieves high accuracy by keeping a low bias of decision trees while reducing the variance through the introduction of randomness.

One concern in training Random Forests for identifying keyphrases is the data imbalanced problem. On average, 130 candidates are extracted per document but only 8 out of 130 are correct keyphrases (positive examples). Since the training data is highly imbalanced, the resulting RF classifier tends to be biased towards the negative class examples. There are two methods for dealing with imbalanced data in Random Forests (Chen et al., 2004). The first approach is to incorporate class weights into the algorithm, giving higher weights to the minority classes, so that misclassifying a minority class is penalized more. The other approach is to adjust the sampling strategy by down-sampling the majority class so that each tree is grown on a more balanced data. In SEERLAB, we employ the down-sampling strategy to correct the imbalanced data problem (See Section 3).

3 Results

In this section, we discuss the performance and the implementation detail of our system in the Keyphrase Extraction Task. Each model in the experiment is trained on the training data, containing 144 documents, and is evaluated on a separate data set of 100 documents. The performance of each model is measured using Precision (P), Recall (R) and F-measure (F) for the top 5, 10 and 15 candidates. A keyphrase is considered correct if and only if it exactly matches one of the answer keys. No partial credit is given.

Three baseline systems were provided by the organizer: *TF.IDF*, *NB* and *ME*. All baselines use the simple unigrams, bigrams and trigrams as candidates and *TFIDF* as features. *TF.IDF* is an unsupervised method that ranks each candidate based on *TFIDF* scores. NB and ME are supervised Naive Bayes and Maximum Entropy respectively.

We use the randomForest package in R for our keyphrase ranker (Liaw and Wiener, 2002). All RF models are built with the following parameters: the number of trees = 200 and the number of features considered at each split = 3. The average training and testing time are around 15s and 5s.

[2]For a set S of data with K classes, its Gini index is defined as: $Gini(S) = \sum_{j=1}^{K} p_j^2$, where p_i denotes the probability of observing class i in S.

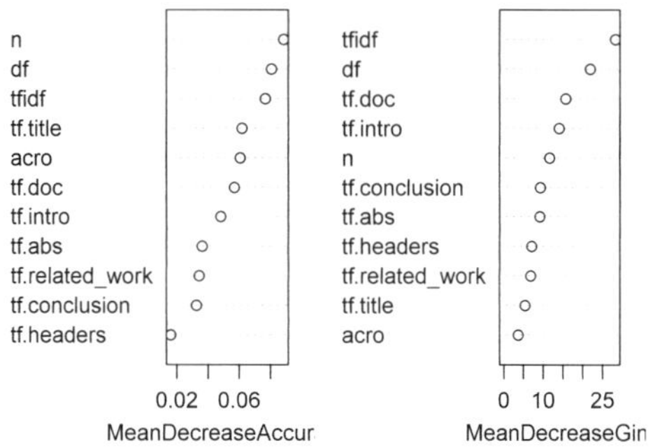

Figure 1: Variable importance for each feature

Table 1. compares the performance of three different SEERLAB models against the baselines. RF_0 is the basic model, where the training data is imbalanced. For $RF_{1:1}$, the negative examples are down-sampled to make the data balanced. For $RF_{1:7}$, the negative examples are down-sampled to where its ratio with the positive examples is 7 to 1. All three models significantly outperform the baselines. The $RF_{1:7}$ model has the highest performance, while the $RF_{1:1}$ model performs slightly worse than the basic model RF_0. This shows that while the sampling strategy helps, overdoing it can hurt the performance. The optimal sampling ratio ($RF_{1:7}$) is chosen according to a 10-fold cross-validation on the training data. For the top 15 candidates, $RF_{1:7}$'s F-score (C) ranks sixth among the 19 participants with a 24.34% F-score approximately 1% lower than the third place team. We also observed that SEERLAB performs quite well for the top 5 candidates with 39% Precision (C). Its F-scores at the top 5, 19.84% (C) and 18.19% (R), place SEERLAB third and second respectively among other participants.

Figure 1. shows two variable importance indicators for each feature: *mean decrease accuracy (MDA)* and *mean decrease Gini (MDG)*. Both indicators measure each feature's contribution in identifying whether a candidate phrase is a keyphrase. The *MDA* of a feature is computed by randomly permuting the value of that feature in the training data and then measuring the decrease in prediction accuracy. If the permuted feature is

System	by	top 5 candidates			top 10 candidates			top 15 candidates		
		P	R	F	P	R	F	P	R	F
TF.IDF	R	17.80	7.39	10.44	13.90	11.54	12.61	11.60	14.45	12.87
	C	22.00	7.50	11.19	17.70	12.07	14.35	14.93	15.28	15.10
NB	R	16.80	6.98	9.86	13.30	11.05	12.07	11.40	14.20	12.65
	C	21.40	7.30	10.89	17.30	11.80	14.03	14.53	14.87	14.70
ME	R	16.80	6.98	9.86	13.30	11.05	12.07	11.40	14.20	12.65
	C	21.40	7.30	10.89	17.30	11.80	14.03	14.53	14.87	14.70
SEERLAB (RF_0)	R	29.00	12.04	17.02	22.50	18.69	20.42	18.20	22.67	20.19
	C	36.00	12.28	18.31	28.20	19.24	22.87	22.53	23.06	22.79
SEERLAB ($RF_{1:1}$)	R	26.00	10.80	15.26	20.80	17.28	18.88	17.40	21.68	19.31
	C	32.00	10.91	16.27	26.00	17.74	21.09	21.93	22.44	22.18
SEERLAB ($RF_{1:7}$)	R	31.00	12.87	18.19	24.10	20.02	21.87	19.33	24.09	21.45
	C	**39.00**	**13.30**	**19.84**	**29.70**	**20.26**	**24.09**	**24.07**	**24.62**	**24.34**

Table 1: Performance (%) comparison for the Keyphrase Extraction Task. R (Reader) indicates that the reader-assigned keyword is used as the gold-standard and C (Combined) means that both author-assigned and reader-assigned keyword sets are used.

a very good predictor, then the prediction accuracy should decrease substantially from the original model. The *MDG* of a feature implies that average Gini decreases for the nodes in the forest that use that feature as the splitting criteria.

TFIDF and *DF* are good indicators of performance according to both *MDA* and *MDG*. Both are very effective when used as splitting criteria, and the prediction accuracy is very sensitive to them. Surprisingly, the length of the phrase (*N*) also has high importance. Also, TF_{title} and *ACRO* have high *MDA* but low *MDG*. They have high *MDA* because if a candidate phrase is an acronym or appears in the title, it is highly likely that it is a keyphrase. However, most keyphrases are not acronyms and do not appear in titles. Thus, on average as splitting criteria, they do not decrease Gini index by much, resulting in a low *MDG*. Also, $\text{TF}_{related\_work}$ and $\text{TF}_{headers}$ have lower *MDA* and *MDG* than TF of other sections (TF_{intro}, TF_{abs}, and $\text{TF}_{conclusion}$). This might suggest that the occurrences in the "*Related Work*" section or section headers are not strong indicators of being a keyphrase as the occurrences in the sections "*Introduction*," "*Abstract*" and "*Conclusion*."

4 Conclusion

We have described our SEERLAB system that participated in the Keyphrase Extraction Task. SEERLAB combines unsupervised corpus-based approach with Random Forests to identify keyphrases. The experimental results show that our system performs well in the Keyphrase Extraction Task, especially on the top 5 key phrase candidates. We also show that the down-sampling strategy can be used to enhance our performance.

References

Leo Breiman. 2001. Random forests. *Machine Learning*, Jan.

Chao Chen, Andy Liaw, and Leo Breiman. 2004. Using random forest to learn imbalanced data. *Technical Report, University of California, Berkeley*.

Su Nam Kim and Min-Yen Kan. 2009. Re-examining automatic keyphrase extraction approaches in scientific articles. *Proceedings of the Workshop on Multiword Expressions, ACL-IJCNLP*, Jan.

Su Nam Kim, Olena Medelyan, Min-Yen Kan, and Timothy Baldwin. 2010. Semeval-2010 task 5: Automatic keyphrase extraction from scienctific article. *ACL workshop on Semantic Evaluations (SemEval 2010)*.

Andy Liaw and Matthew Wiener. 2002. Classification and regression by randomforest. *R News*.

Thuy Dung Nguyen and Min-Yen Kan. 2007. Keyphrase extraction in scientific publications. *Proceedings of International Conference on Asian Digital Libraries (ICADL'07)*, Jan.

Pucktada Treeratpituk and C Lee Giles. 2009. Disambiguating authors in academic publications using random forests. *In Proceedings of the Joint Conference on Digital Libraries (JCDL'09)*, Jan.

SZTERGAK : Feature Engineering for Keyphrase Extraction

Gábor Berend
Department of Informatics
University of Szeged
2. Árpád tér Szeged, H-6720, Hungary
berendg@inf.u-szeged.hu

Richárd Farkas
Hungarian Academy of Sciences
103. Tisza Lajos körút
Szeged, H-6720, Hungary
rfarkas@inf.u-szeged.hu

Abstract

Automatically assigning keyphrases to documents has a great variety of applications. Here we focus on the keyphrase extraction of scientific publications and present a novel set of features for the supervised learning of keyphraseness. Although these features are intended for extracting keyphrases from scientific papers, because of their generality and robustness, they should have uses in other domains as well. With the help of these features SZTERGAK achieved top results on the *SemEval-2 shared task on Automatic Keyphrase Extraction from Scientific Articles* and exceeded its baseline by 10%.

1 Introduction

Keyphrases summarize the content of documents with the most important phrases. They can be valuable in many application areas, ranging from information retrieval to topic detection. However, since manually assigned keyphrases are rarely provided and creating them by hand would be costly and time-consuming, their automatic generation is of great interest nowadays. Recent state-of-the-art systems treat this kind of task as a supervised learning task, in which phrases of a document should be classified with respect to their key phrase characteristics based on manually labeled corpora and various feature values.

This paper focuses on the task of keyphrase extraction from scientific papers and we shall introduce new features that can significantly improve the overall performance. Although the experimental results presented here are solely based on scientific articles, due to the robustness and universality of the features, our approach is expected to achieve good results when applied on other domains as well.

2 Related work

In **keyphrase extraction** tasks, phrases are extracted from one document that are the most characteristic of its content (Liu et al., 2009; Witten et al., 1999). In these approaches keyphrase extraction is treated as a classification task, in which certain n-grams of a specific document act as keyphrase candidates, and the task is to classify them as proper keyphrases or not.

While Frank et al. (1999) exploited domain specific knowledge to improve the quality of automatic tagging, others like Liu et al. (2009) analyze term co-occurence graphs. It was Nguyen and Kan (2007) who dealt with the special characteristics of scientific papers and introduced the state-of-the-art feature set to keyphrase extraction tasks. Here we will follow a similar approach and make significant improvements by the introduction of novel features.

3 The SZTERGAK system

The SZTERGAK framework treats the reproduction of reader-assigned keyphrases as a supervised learning task. In our setting a restricted set of token sequences extracted from the documents was used as classification instances. These instances were ranked regarding to their posteriori probabilities of the `keyphrase` class, estimated by a Naïve Bayes classifier. Finally, we chose the top-15 candidates as keyphrases.

Our features can be grouped into four main categories: those that were calculated solely from the surface characteristics of phrases, those that took into account the document that contained a keyphrase, those that were obtained from the given document set and those that were based on external sources of information.

Proceedings of the 5th International Workshop on Semantic Evaluation, ACL 2010, pages 186–189,
Uppsala, Sweden, 15-16 July 2010.

3.1 Preprocessing

Since there are parts of a document (e.g. tables or author affiliations) that can not really contribute to the keyphrase extractor, several preprocessing steps were carried out. Preprocessing included the elimination of author affiliations and messy lines.

The determination of the full title of an article would be useful, however, it is not straightforward because of multi-line titles. To solve this problem, a web query was sent with the first line of a document and its most likely title was chosen by simply selecting the most frequently occurring one among the top 10 responses provided by the Google API. This title was added to the document, and all the lines before the first occurrence of the line `Abstract` were omitted.

Lines unlikely to contain valuable information were also excluded from the documents. These lines were identified according to statistical data of their surface forms (e.g. the average and the deviation of line lengths) and regular expressions. Lastly, section and sentence boundaries were found in a rule-based way, and the POS and syntactic tagging (using the Stanford parser (Klein and Manning, 2003)) of each sentence were carried out.

When syntactically parsed sentences were obtained, keyphrase aspirants were extracted. The 1 to 4-long token sequences that did not start or end with a stopword and consisted only of POS-codes of an `adjective`, a `noun` or a `verb` were defined to be possible keyphrases (resulting in classification instances). Tokens of key phrase aspirants were stemmed to store them in a uniform way, but they were also appended by the POS-code of the derived form, so that the same root forms were distinguished if they came from tokens having different POS-codes, like there shown in Table 1.

Textual Appearance	Canonical form
regulations	regul_nns
Regulation	regul_nn
regulates	regul_vbz
regulated	regul_vbn

Table 1: Standardization of document terms.

3.2 The extended feature set

The features characterizing the extracted keyphrase aspirants can be grouped into four main types, namely phrase-, document-, corpus-level and external knowledge-based features. Below we will describe the different types of features as well as those of KEA (Witten et al., 1999) which are cited as default features by most of the literature dealing with keyphrase extraction.

3.2.1 Standard features

Features belonging to this set contain those of KEA, namely Tf-idf and the first occurrence.

The **Tf-idf feature** assigns the tf-idf metric to each keyphrase aspirant.

The **first occurrence feature** contains the relative first position for each keyphrase aspirant. The feature value was obtained by dividing the absolute first token position of a phrase by the number of tokens of the document in question.

3.2.2 Phrase-level features

Features belonging to this group were calculated solely based on the keyphrase aspirants themselves. Such features are able to get the general characteristics of phrases functioning as keyphrases.

Phrase length feature contains the number of tokens a keyphrase aspirant consists of.

POS feature is a nominal one that stores the POS-code sequence of each keyphrase aspirant. (For example, for the phrase `full_JJ space_NN` its value was `JJ NN`.)

Suffix feature is a binary feature that stores information about whether the original form of a keyphrase aspirant finished with some specific ending according to a subset of the Michigan Sufficiency Exams' Suffix List. [1]

3.2.3 Document-level features

Since keyphrases should summarize the particular document they represent, and phrase-level features introduced above were independent of their context, document-level features were also invented.

Acronymity feature functions as a binary feature that is assigned a true value iff a phrase is likely to be an extended form of an acronym in the same document. A phrase is treated as an extended form of an acronym if it starts with the same letter as the acronym present in its document and it also contains all the letters of the acronym in the very same order as they occur in the acronym.

PMI feature provides a measure of the multiword expression nature of multi-token phrases,

[1] http://www.michigan-proficiency-exams.com/suffix-list.html

and it is defined in Eq. (1), where $p(t_i)$ is the document-level probability of the occurrence of ith token in the phrase. This feature value is a generalized form of pointwise mutual information for phrases with an arbitrary number of tokens.

$$pmi(t_1, t_2, ..., t_n) = \frac{log(\frac{p(t_1,t_2,...,t_n)}{p(t_1)\cdot p(t_2)\cdot ... \cdot p(t_n)})}{log(p(t_1, t_2, ..., t_n))^{n-1}} \quad (1)$$

Syntactic feature values refer to the average minimal normalized depth of the NP-rooted parse subtrees that contain a given keyphrase aspirant at the leaf nodes in a given document.

3.2.4 Corpus-level features

Corpus-level features are used to determine the relative importance of keyphrase aspirants based on a comparison of corpus-level and document-level frequencies.

The **sf-isf feature** was created to deal with logical positions of keyphrases and the formula shown in Eq. (2) resembles that of tf-idf scores (hence its name, i.e. Section Frequency-Inverted Section Frequency). This feature value favors keyphrase aspirants k that are included in several sections of document d (sf), but are present in a relatively small number of sections in the overall corpus (isf). Phrases with higher sf-isf scores for a given document are those that are more relevant with respect to that document.

$$sfisf(k, d) = sf(k, d) * isf(k) \quad (2)$$

Keyphraseness feature is a binary one which has a true value iff a phrase is one of the 785 different author-assigned keyphrases provided in the training and test corpora.

3.2.5 External knowledge-based features

Apart from relying on the given corpus, further enhancements in performance can be obtained by relying on external knowledge sources.

Wikipedia-feature is assigned a true value for keyphrase aspirants for which there exists a Wikipedia article with the same title. Preliminary experiments showed that this feature is noisy, thus we also investigated a relaxed version of it, where occurrences of Wikipedia article titles were looked for only in the title and abstract of a paper.

Besides using Wikipedia for feature calculation, it was also utilized to retrieve semantic orientations of phrases. Making use of **redirect links of Wikipedia**, the semantic relation of synonymity can be exploited. For example, as there exists a redirection between Wikipedia articles `XML` and `Extensible Markup Language`, it may be assumed that these phrases mean the same. For this reason during the training phase we treated a phrase equivalent to its redirected version, i.e. if there is a keyphrase aspirant that is not assigned in the gold-standard reader annotation but the Wikipedia article with the same title has a redirection to such a phrase that is present among positive keyphrase instances of a particular document, the original phrase can be treated as a positive instance as well. In this way the ratio of positive examples could be increased from 0.99% to 1.14%.

Feature combinations	**F-score**
Standard features (SF)	14.57
SF + phrase length feature	20.93
SF + POS feature	19.60
SF + suffix feature	16.35
SF + acronymity feature	16.87
SF + PMI feature	15.68
SF + syntactic feature	14.20
SF + sf-isf feature	14.79
SF + keyphraseness feature	15.17
SF + Wikipedia feature - full paper	14.37
SF + Wikipedia feature - abstract	16.50
SF + Wikipedia redirect	14.50
Shared Task best baseline	12.87
All features	23.82
All features - keyphraseness excluded	22.11

Table 2: Results obtained with different features.

4 Results and discussion

The training and test sets of the shared task (Kim et al., 2010) consisted of 144 and 100 scientific publications from the ACL repository, respectively. Since the primary evaluation of the shared task was based on the top-15 ranked automatic keyphrases compared to the keyphrases assigned by the readers of the articles, these results are reported here. The evaluation results can be seen in Table 2 where the individual effect of each feature is given in combination with the standard features.

It is interesting to note the improvement obtained by extending standard features with the simple feature of phrase length. This indicates that though the basic features were quite good, they did not take into account the point that reader keyphrases are likely to consist of several words.

Morphological features, such as POS or suffix features were also among the top-performing ones, which seems to show that most of the keyphrases tend to have some common structure. In contrast, the syntactic feature made some decrease in the performance when it was combined just with the standard ones. This can be due to the fact that the input data were quite noisy, i.e. some inconsistencies arose in the data during the pdf to text conversion of articles, which made it difficult to parse some sentences correctly.

It was also interesting to see that Wikipedia feature did not improve the result when it was applied to the whole document. However, our previous experiences on keyphrase extraction from scientific abstracts showed that this feature can be very useful. Hence, we relaxed the feature to handle occurrences just from the abstract. This modification of the feature yielded a 14.8% improvement in the F-measure. A possible explanation for this is that Wikipedia has articles of very common phrases (such as `Calculation` or `Result`) and the distribution of such non-keyphrase terms is higher in the body of the articles than in abstracts.

The last row of Table 2 contains the result achieved by the complete feature set excluding *keyphraseness*. As keyphraseness exploits author-assigned keyphrases and – to the best of our knowledge – other participants of the shared task did not utilize author-assigned keyphrases, this result is present in the final ranking of the shared task systems. However, we believe that if the task is to extract keyphrases from an article to gain semantic meta-data for an NLP application (e.g. for information retrieval or summarization), author-assigned keyphrases are often present and can be very useful. This latter statement was proved by one of our experiments where we used the author keyphrases assigned to the document itself as a binary feature (instead of using the pool of all keyphrases). This feature set could achieve an F-score of 27.44 on the evaluation set and we believe that this should be the complete feature set in a real-world semantic indexing application.

5 Conclusions

In this paper we introduced a wide set of new features that are able to enhance the overall performance of supervised keyphrase extraction applications. Our features include those calculated simply on surface forms of keyphrase aspirants, those that make use of the document- and corpus-level environment of phrases and those that rely on external knowledge. Although features were designed to the specific task of extracting keyphrases from scientific papers, due to their generality it is highly assumable that they can be successfully utilized on different domains as well.

The features we selected in SZTERGAK performed well enough to actually achieve the third place on the shared task by excluding the keyphraseness feature and would be the first by using any author-assigned keyphrase-based feature. It is also worth emphasizing that we think that there are many possibilities to further extend the feature set (e.g. with features that take the semantic relatedness among keyphrase aspirants into account) and significant improvement could be achievable.

Acknowledgement

The authors would like to thank the annotators of the shared task for the datasets used in the shared task. This work was supported in part by the NKTH grant (project codename TEXTREND).

References

Eibe Frank, Gordon W. Paynter, Ian H. Witten, Carl Gutwin, and Craig G. Nevill-Manning. 1999. Domain-specific keyphrase extraction. In *Proceeding of 16th IJCAI*, pages 668–673.

Su Nam Kim, Olena Medelyan, Min-Yen Kan, and Timothy Baldwin. 2010. Semeval-2010 task 5 : Automatic keyphrase extraction from scientific articles. In *Proc. of the 5th SIGLEX Workshop on Semantic Evaluation*.

Dan Klein and Christopher D. Manning. 2003. Accurate unlexicalized parsing. In *Proceedings of the 41st Meeting of the Association for Computational Linguistics*, pages 423–430.

Zhiyuan Liu, Peng Li, Yabin Zheng, and Maosong Sun. 2009. Clustering to find exemplar terms for keyphrase extraction. In *Proceedings of the 2009 Conference on EMNLP*.

Thuy Dung Nguyen and Minyen Kan. 2007. Keyphrase extraction in scientific publications. In *Proc. of International Conference on Asian Digital Libraries (ICADL 07)*, pages 317–326.

Ian H. Witten, Gordon W. Paynter, Eibe Frank, Carl Gutwin, and Craig G. Nevill-Manning. 1999. Kea: Practical automatic keyphrase extraction. In *ACM DL*, pages 254–255.

KP-Miner: Participation in SemEval-2

Samhaa R. El-Beltagy
Cairo University
Giza, Egypt.
samhaa@computer.org

Ahmed Rafea
The American University in Cairo
New Cairo, Egypt.
rafea@aucegypt.edu

Abstract

This paper briefly describes the KP-Miner system which is a system developed for the extraction of keyphrases from English and Arabic documents, irrespective of their nature. The paper also outlines the performance of the system in the "Automatic Keyphrase Extraction from Scientific Articles" task which is part of SemEval-2.

1 Introduction

KP-Miner (El-Beltagy, 2006) (El-Beltagy, 2009) is a system for the extraction of keyphrases from English and Arabic documents. When developing the system, the goal was to build a general purpose keyphrase extraction system that can be easily configured by users based on their understanding of the documents from which keyphrases are to be extracted and without the need for any training documents or the use of any sophisticated natural language processing or linguistic tools. As such, the keyphrase extraction process in KP-Miner is an un-supervised one. When building a general purpose keyphrase extraction system, this was an important objective, as training data is not always readily available for any type of data. The goal of entering the KP-Miner system into the SemEval-2 competition, was to see how well it will perform on a specific task, without making any changes in its default parameters.

2 System Overview

Keyphrase extraction in the KP-Miner system is a three step process: candidate keyphrase selection, candidate keyphrase weight calculation and finally keyphrase refinement. Each of these steps, is explained in the following sub-sections. More details about the employed algorithm, and justification for using certain values for selected parameters, can be found in (El-Beltagy, 2009).

2.1 Candidate keyphrase selection

In KP-Miner, a set of rules is employed in order to elicit candidate keyphrases. As a phrase will never be separated by punctuation marks within some given text and will rarely have stop words within it, the first condition a sequence of words has to display in order to be considered a candidate keyphrase, is that it is not be separated by punctuation marks or stop words. A total of 187 common stopwords (the, then, in, above, etc) are used in the candidate keyphrase extraction step. After applying this first condition on any given document, too many candidates will be generated; some of which will make no sense to a human reader. To filter these out, two further conditions are applied. The first condition states that a phrase has to have appeared at least ***n*** times in the document from which keyphrases are to be extracted, in order to be considered a candidate keyphrase. This is called the least allowable seen frequency(lasf) factor and in the English version of the system, this is set to 3. However, if a document is short, ***n*** is decremented depending on the length of the document.

The second condition is related to the position where a candidate keyphrase first appears within an input document. Through observation as well as experimentation, it was found that in long documents, phrases occurring for the first time after a given threshold, are very rarely keyphrases. So a cutoff constant CutOff is defined in terms of a number of words after which if a phrase appears for the first time, it is filtered out and ignored. The initial prototype of the KP-Miner system (El-Beltagy, 2006), set this cutoff value to a constant (850). Further experimentation carried out in (El-Beltagy, 2009) revealed that an optimum value for this constant is 400. In

Proceedings of the 5th International Workshop on Semantic Evaluation, ACL 2010, pages 190–193,
Uppsala, Sweden, 15-16 July 2010.

the implementation of the KP-Miner system, the phrase extraction step described above is carried out in two phases. In the first phase, words are scanned until either a punctuation mark or a stop word is encountered. The scanned sequence of words and all possible n-grams within the encountered sequence where ***n*** can vary from 1 to sequence length-1, are stemmed and stored in both their original and stemmed forms. If the phrase (in its stemmed or original form) or any of its sub-phrases, has been seen before, then the count of the previously seen term is incremented by one, otherwise the previously unseen term is assigned a count of one. Very weak stemming is performed in this step using only the first step of the Porter stemmer (Porter, 1980). In the second phase, the document is scanned again for the longest possible sequence that fulfills the conditions mentioned above. This is then considered as a candidate keyphrase. Unlike most of the other keyphrase extraction systems, the devised algorithm places no limit on the length of keyphrases, but it was found that extracted keyphrases rarely exceed three terms.

2.2 Candidate keyphrases weight calculation

Single key features obtained from documents by models such as TF-IDF (Salton and Buckley, 1988) have already been shown to be representative of documents from which they've been extracted as demonstrated by their wide and successful use in clustering and classification tasks. However, when applied to the task of keyphrase extraction, these same models performed very poorly (Turney, 1999). By looking at almost any document, it can be observed that the occurrences of phrases is much less frequent than the occurrence of single terms within the same document. So it can be concluded that one of the reasons that TF-IDF performs poorly on its own when applied to the task of keyphrase extraction, is that it does not take this fact into consideration which results in a bias towards single words as they occur in larger numbers. So, a boosting factor is needed for compound terms in order to balance this bias towards single terms. In this work for each input document ***d*** from which keyphrases are to be extracted, a boosting factor B_d is calculated as follows:

$$B_d = |N_d| / (|P_d| * \propto)$$

and if $B_d > \sigma$ then $B_d = \sigma$

Here $|N_d|$ is the number of all candidate terms in document **d**, $|P_d|$ is the number of candidate terms whose length exceeds one in document ***d*** and $\propto$ and σ are weight adjustment constants. The values used by the implemented system are 3 for σ and 2.3 for $\propto$.

To calculate the weights of document terms, the TF-IDF model in conjunction with the introduced boosting factor, is used. However, another thing to consider when applying TF-IDF for a general application rather than a corpus specific one, is that keyphrase combinations do not occur as frequently within a document set as do single terms. In other words, while it is possible to collect frequency information for use by a general single keyword extractor from a moderately large set of random documents, the same is not true for keyphrase information. There are two possible approaches to address this observation. In the first, a very large corpus of a varied nature can be used to collect keyphrase related frequency information. In the second, which is adopted in this work, any encountered phrase is considered to have appeared only once in the corpus. This means that for compound phrases, frequency within a document as well as the boosting factor are really what determine its weight as the idf value for all compound phrases will be a constant ***c*** determined by the size of the corpus used to build frequency information for single terms. If the position rules described in (El-Beltagy, 2009) are also employed, then the position factor is also used in the calculation for the term weights. In summary, the following equation is used to calculate the weight of candidate keyphrases whether single or compound:

$$w_{ij} = tf_{ij} * idf * B_i * P_f$$

Where:

w_{ij} = weight of term t_j in Document D_i

tf_{ij} = frequency of term t_j in Document D_i

idf = log_2 N/n where N is the number of documents in the collection and n is number of documents where term t_j occurs at least once. If the term is compound, n is set to 1.

B_i = *the boosting factor associated with document* D_i

P_f = *the term position associated factor. If position rules are not used this is set to 1.*

2.3 Final Candidate Phrase List Refinement

The KP-Miner system, allows the user to specify a number ***n*** of keyphrases s/he wants back and uses the sorted list to return the top ***n*** keyphrases requested by the user. The default number of ***n*** is five. As stated in step one, when generating candidate keyphrases, the longest possible sequence of words that are uninterrupted by possible phrase terminators, are sought and stored and so are sub-phrases contained within that sequence provided that they appear somewhere in the text on their own. For example, if the phrase 'excess body weight' is encountered five times in a document, the phrase itself will be stored along with a count of five. If the sub-phrase , 'body weight', is also encountered on its own, than it will also be stored along with the number of times it appeared in the text including the number of times it appeared as part of the phrase 'excess body weight'. This means that an overlap between the count of two or more phrases can exist. Aiming to eliminate this overlap in counting early on can contribute to the dominance of possibly noisy phrases or to overlooking potential keyphrases that are encountered as sub-phrases. However, once the weight calculation step has been performed and a clear picture of which phrases are most likely to be key ones is obtained, this overlap can be addressed through refinement. To refine results in the KP-Miner system, the top ***n*** keys are scanned to see if any of them is a sub-phrase of another. If any of them are, then its count is decremented by the frequency of the term of which it is a part. After this step is completed, weights are recalculated and a final list of phrases sorted by weight, is produced. The reason the top ***n*** keys rather than all candidates, are used in this step is so that lower weighted keywords do not affect the outcome of the final keyphrase list. It is important to note that the refinement step is an optional one, but experiments have shown that in the English version of the system, omitting this step leads to the production of keyphrase lists that match better with author assigned keyword. In (El-Beltagy, 2009) the authors suggested that employing this step leads to the extraction of higher quality keyphrases. Experimentation carried out on the Gold standard dataset provided by the organizers of the SemEval-2 competition on "Keyphrase Extraction from Scientific Documents" and described in the next section, seems to suggest that this idea is a valid one.

3 Participation in the SemEval-2 Competition

One of the new tracks introduced to SemEval this year is a track dedicated entirely to keyphrase extraction from scientific articles. The task was proposed with the aim of providing participants with "the chance to compete and benchmark" this technology (SemEval2, 2010).

In this competition, participants were provided with 40 trial documents, 144 training documents, and 100 test documents. For the trial and training data, three sets of answers were provided: author-assigned keyphrases, reader-assigned keyphrases, and finally a set that is simply a combination between the 2 previous sets. Unlike author-assigned keyphrases, which may or may not occur in the content, all reader-assigned keyphrases were said to have been extracted from the papers. The participants were then asked to produce the top 15 keyphrases for each article in the test document set and to submit the stemmed version of these to the organizers.

Evaluation was carried out in the traditional way in which keyphrase sets extracted by each of the participants were matched against answer sets (i.e. author-assigned keyphrases and reader-assigned keyphrases) to calculate precision, recall and F-score. Participants were then ranked by F-score when extracting all 15 keyphrases.

Since the KP-miner system is an unsupervised keyphrase extraction system, no use was made of the trial and training data. The system was simply run of the set of test documents, and the output was sent to the organizers. 2 different runs were submitted: one produced used the initial prototype of the system, (El-Beltagy, 2006), while the second was produced using the more mature version of the system (El-Beltagy, 2009). Both systems were run without making any changes to their default parameters. The idea was to see how well the KP-Miner would fair among other keyphrase extraction systems without any additional configuration. The more mature version of the system performed better when its results were compared to the author-reader combined keyphrase set and consequently was the one whose final results were taken into consideration in the competition. The system ranked at 2 , with a tie between it and another system when extracting 15 keyphrases from the combined keypharse set. The results are shown in table 1.

	Precision	Recall	F-Score
HUMB	27.2%	27.8%	27.5%
WINGNUS	24.9%	25.5%	25.2%
KP-Miner	**24.9%**	**25.5%**	**25.2%**
SZTERGAK	24.8%	25.4%	25.1%
ICL	24.6%	25.2%	24.9%
SEERLAB	24.1%	24.6%	24.3%

KX_FBK	23.6%	24.2%	23.9%
DERIUNLP	22.0%	22.5%	22.3%
Maui	20.3%	20.8%	20.6%
DFKI	20.3%	20.7%	20.5%
BUAP	19.0%	19.4%	19.2%
SJTULTLAB	18.4%	18.8%	18.6%
UNICE	18.3%	18.8%	18.5%
UNPMC	18.1%	18.6%	18.3%
JU_CSE	17.8%	18.2%	18.0%
LIKEY	16.3%	16.7%	16.5%
UvT	14.6%	14.9%	14.8%
NIRAJIIITH	14.1%	14.5%	14.3%
POLYU	13.9%	14.2%	14.0%
UKP	5.3%	5.4%	5.3%

Table 1: Performance of all participating systems over combined keywords when extracting 15 keyphrases

When evaluating the system on reader assigned keyphrases only (again when extracting 15 keyphrases), the KP-Miner system ranked at 6 with a tie between it and another system. The system's precision, recall, and f-score were: 19.3%, 24.1% , 21.5% respectively.

To test whether the phrase refinement step described in section 2.3 would improve the results or not, this option was turned on, and the results were evaluated using the script and the golden dataset provided by the competition organizers. The results are shown in tables 2 and 3.

	Precision	Recall	F-Score
Top 5	29.6%	12.3%	17.4%
Top 10	23.3%	20.5%	24.3%
Top 15	25.3%	26.1%	25.8%

Table 2: Performance over combined keywords when extracting, 5, 10, and 15 keyphrases

	Precision	Recall	F-Score
Top 5	37.8%	12.9%	19.2%
Top 10	30.3%	19.4%	21.1%
Top 15	20.1%	25.1%	22.3%

Table 3: Performance over reader assigned keywords when extracting, 5, 10, and 15 keyphrases

Had these results been submitted, the system would have still ranked at number 2 (but more comfortably so) when comparing its results to the combined author-reader set of keywords, but it would jumped to third place for the reader assigned keyphrases. This improvement confirms what the authors hypothesized in (El-Beltagy, 2009) which is that the usage of the final refinement step does lead to better quality keyphrases.

4 Conclusion and future work

Despite the fact that the KP-Miner was designed as a general purpose keyphrase extraction system, and despite the simplicity of the system and the fact that it requires no training to function, it seems to have performed relatively well when carrying out the task of keyphrase extraction from scientific documents. The fact that it was outperformed, seems to indicate that for optimal performance for this specific task, further tweaking of the system's parameters should be carried out. In future work, the authors will investigate the usage of machine learning techniques for configuring the system for specific tasks. A further improvement to the system can entail allowing certain stopwords to appear within the produced keyphrases. It is worth noting that the organizers stated that 55 of the reader assigned keyphrases and 6 of the author assigned keyphrases (making a total of 61 keyphrases in the combined dataset), contained the "of" stopword. However, none of these would have been detected by the KP-Miner system as currently "of" is considered as a phrase terminator.

References

M Porter. 1980. An Algorithm for Suffix Stripping, *Program*, 14, 130-137.

G. Salton and C. Buckley. 1988. Term-weighting Approaches in Automatic Text Retrieval, *Information Processing and Management*, 24:513-523.

Peter D. Turney. 1999. Learning to Extract Keyphrases from Text, *National Research Council*, Institute for Information Technology, ERB-1057.

Samhaa. R. El-Beltagy and Ahmed Rafea. 2009. KP-Miner: A Keyphrase Extraction System for English and Arabic Documents *Information Systems*, 34(1):132-144.

Samhaa R. El-Beltagy. 2006. KP-Miner: A Simple System for Effective Keyphrase Extraction. *Proceeding of the 3rd IEEE International Conference on Innovations in Information Technology (IIT '06)*, Dubai, UAE.

SemEval. 2010. http://semeval2.fbk.eu/semeval2.php

UvT: The UvT Term Extraction System in the Keyphrase Extraction task

Kalliopi Zervanou
ILK / TiCC - Tilburg centre for Cognition and Communication
University of Tilburg, P.O. Box 90153, 5000 LE Tilburg, The Netherlands
K.Zervanou@uvt.nl

Abstract

The UvT system is based on a hybrid, linguistic and statistical approach, originally proposed for the recognition of multi-word terminological phrases, the C-value method (Frantzi et al., 2000). In the UvT implementation, we use an extended noun phrase rule set and take into consideration orthographic and morphological variation, term abbreviations and acronyms, and basic document structure information.

1 Introduction

The increasing amount of documents in electronic form makes imperative the need for document content classification and semantic labelling. Keyphrase extraction contributes to this goal by the identification of important and discriminative concepts expressed as keyphrases. Keyphrases as reduced document content representations may find applications in document retrieval, classification and summarisation (D'Avanzo and Magnini, 2005). The literature distinguishes between two principal processes: keyphrase extraction and keyphrase assignment. In the case of keyphrase assignment, suitable keyphrases from an existing knowledge resource, such as a controlled vocabulary, or a thesaurus are assigned to documents based on classification of their content. In keyphrase extraction, the phrases are mined from the document itself. Supervised approaches to the problem of keyphrase extraction include the Naive Bayes-based KEA algorithms (Gordon et al., 1999) (Medelyan and Witten, 2006), decision tree-based and the genetic algorithm-based GenEx (Turney, 1999), and the probabilistic KL divergence-based language model (Tomokiyo and Hurst, 2003). Research in keyphrase extraction proposes the detection of keyphrases based on various statistics-based, or pattern-based features. Statistical measures investigated focus primarily on keyphrase frequency measures, whereas pattern-features include noun phrase pattern filtering, identification of keyphrase head and respective frequencies (Barker and Cornacchia, 2000), document section position of the keyphrase (e.g., (Medelyan and Witten, 2006)) and keyphrase coherence (Turney, 2003). In this paper, we present an unsupervised approach which combines pattern-based morphosyntactic rules with a statistical measure, the C-value measure (Frantzi et al., 2000) which originates from research in the field of automatic term recognition and was initially designed for specialised domain terminology acquisition.

2 System description

The input documents in the Keyphrase Extraction task were scientific articles converted from their originally published form to plain text. Due to this process, some compound hyphenated words are erroneously converted into a single word (e.g., "resourcemanagement" vs. "resource-management"). Moreover, document sections such as tables, figures, footnotes, headers and footers, often intercept sentence and paragraph text. Finally, due to the particularity of the scientific articles domain, input documents often contain irregular text, such as URLs, inline bibliographic references, mathematical formulas and symbols. In our approach, we attempted to address some of these issues by document structuring, treatment of orthographic variation and filtering of irregular text.

The approach adopted first applies part-of-speech tagging and basic document structuring (sec. 2.1 and 2.2). Subsequently, keyphrase candidates conforming to pre-defined morphosyntactic rule patterns are identified (sec. 2.3). In the next stage, orthographic, morphological and abbreviation variation phenomena are addressed

Proceedings of the 5th International Workshop on Semantic Evaluation, ACL 2010, pages 194–197,
Uppsala, Sweden, 15-16 July 2010. ©2010 Association for Computational Linguistics

(sec. 2.4) and, finally, candidate keyphrases are selected based on C-value statistical measure (sec. 2.5).

2.1 Linguistic pre-processing

For morphosyntactic analysis, we used the Maxent (Ratnaparkhi, 1996) POS tagger implementation of the openNLP toolsuite[1]. In order to improve tagging accuracy, irregular text, such as URLs, inline references, and recurrent patterns indicating footers and mathematical formulas are filtered prior to tagging.

2.2 Basic document structuring

Document structuring is based on identified recurrent patterns, such as common section titles and legend indicators (e.g., "Abstract", "Table..."), section headers numbering and preserved formatting, such as newline characters. Thus, the document sections that the system may recognise are: Title, Abstract, Introduction, Conclusion, Acknowledgements, References, Header (for any other section headers and legends) and Main (for any other document section text).

2.3 Rule pattern filtering

The UvT system considers as candidate keyphrases, those multi-word noun phrases conforming to pre-defined morphosyntactic rule patterns. In particular, the patterns considered are:

$M^+ N$

$M\ C\ M\ N$

$M^+ N\ C\ N$

$N\ P\ M^* N$

$N\ P\ M^* N\ C\ N$

$N\ C\ N\ P\ M^* N$

$M\ C\ M\ N$

$M^+ N\ C\ N$

where M is a modifier, such as an adjective, a noun, a present or past participle, or a proper noun including a possessive ending, N is a noun, P a preposition and C a conjunction. For every sentence input, the matching process is exhaustive: after the longest valid match is identified, the rules are re-applied, so as to identify all possible shorter valid matches for nested noun phrases. At this stage, the rules also allow for inclusion of potential abbreviations and acronyms in the identified noun phrase of the form:

$M^+ (A)\ N$

$M^+ N\ (A)$

where (A) is a potential acronym appearing as a single token in uppercase, enclosed by parentheses and tagged as a proper noun.

2.4 Text normalisation

In this processing stage, the objective is the recognition and reduction of variation phenomena which, if left untreated, will affect the C-value statistical measures at the keyphrase selection stage. Variation is a pervasive phenomenon in terminology and is generally defined as the alteration of the surface form of a terminological concept (Jacquemin, 2001). In our approach, we attempt to address morphological variation, i.e., variation due to morphological affixes and orthographic variation, such as hyphenated vs. non-hyphenated compound phrases and abbreviated phrase forms vs. full noun phrase forms.

In order to reduce morphological variation, UvT system uses the J.Renie interface[2] to WordNet lexicon[3] to acquire lemmas for the respective candidate phrases. Orthographic variation phenomena are treated by rule matching techniques. In this process, for every candidate keyphrase matching a rule, the respective string alternations are generated and added as variant phrases. For example, for patterns including acronyms and the respective full form, alternative variant phrases generated may contain either the full form only, or the acronym replacing its respective full form. Similarly, for hyphenated words, non-hyphenated forms are generated.

2.5 C-value measure

The statistical measure used for keyphrase ranking and selection is the C-value measure (Frantzi et al., 2000). C-value was originally proposed for defining potential terminological phrases and is based on normalising frequency of occurrence measures

[1] http://opennlp.sourceforge.net/

[2] http://www.ai.mit.edu/ jrennie/WordNet/

[3] http://wordnet.princeton.edu/

Performance over Reader-Assigned Keywords									
System	top 5 candidates			top 10 candidates			top 15 candidates		
	P	R	F	P	R	F	P	R	F
TF·IDF	17.80%	7.39%	10.44%	13.90%	11.54%	12.61%	11.60%	14.45%	12.87%
NB & ME	16.80%	6.98%	9.86%	13.30%	11.05%	12.07%	11.40%	14.20%	12.65%
UvT	**20.40%**	**8.47%**	**11.97%**	**15.60%**	**12.96%**	**14.16%**	**11.93%**	**14.87%**	**13.24%**
UvT - A	23.60%	9.80%	13.85%	16.10%	13.37%	14.61%	12.00%	14.95%	13.31%
UvT - I	21.20%	8.80%	12.44%	14.50%	12.04%	13.16%	12.00%	14.95%	13.31%
UvT - M	20.40%	8.47%	11.97%	15.10%	12.54%	13.70%	11.40%	14.20%	12.65%
UvT - IC	23.20%	9.63%	13.61%	16.00%	13.29%	14.52%	13.07%	16.28%	14.50%

Performance over Combined Keywords									
System	top 5 candidates			top 10 candidates			top 15 candidates		
	P	R	F	P	R	F	P	R	F
TF·IDF	22.00%	7.50%	11.19%	17.70%	12.07%	14.35%	14.93%	15.28%	15.10%
NB & ME	21.40%	7.30%	10.89%	17.30%	11.80%	14.03%	14.53%	14.87%	14.70%
UvT	**24.80%**	**8.46%**	**12.62%**	**18.60%**	**12.69%**	**15.09%**	**14.60%**	**14.94%**	**14.77%**
UvT - A	28.80%	9.82%	14.65%	19.60%	13.37%	15.90%	14.67%	15.01%	14.84%
UvT - I	26.40%	9.00%	13.42%	17.80%	12.14%	14.44%	14.73%	15.08%	14.90%
UvT - M	24.80%	8.46%	12.62%	17.90%	12.21%	14.52%	14.07%	14.39%	14.23%
UvT - IC	28.60%	9.75%	14.54%	19.70%	13.44%	15.98%	16.13%	16.51%	16.32%

Table 1: UvT, UvT variants and baseline systems performance on the Keyphrase Extraction Task

by taking into consideration the candidate multi-word phrase constituent length and terms appearing as nested within longer terms. In particular, depending on whether a candidate multi-word phrase is nested or not, C-value is defined as:

$$\text{C-value} = \begin{cases} \log_2 |a| f(a) \\ \log_2 |a|(f(a) - \frac{1}{P(T_a)} \sum_{b \in T_a} f(b)) \end{cases}$$

In the above, the first C-value measurement is for non-nested terms and the second for nested terms, where a denotes the word sequence that is proposed as a term, $|a|$ is the length of this term in words, $f(a)$ is the frequency of occurrence of this term in the corpus, both as an independent term and as a nested term within larger terms, and $P(T_a)$ denotes the probability of a term string occurring as nested term.

In this processing stage of keyphrase selection, we start by measuring frequency of occurrence for all our candidate phrases, taking into consideration phrase variants, as identified in the *Text normalisation* stage. Then, we proceed by calculating nested phrases frequences and, finally, we estimate C-value.

The result of this process is a list of proposed keyphrases, ranked by decreasing C-value measure, wherefrom the top 15 were selected for the evaluation of the system results.

3 Results

The overall official results of the UvT system are shown in Table 1, where P, R and F correspond to micro-averaged precision, recall and F-score for the respective sets of candidate keyphrases, based on reader-assigned and combined author- and reader-assigned gold standards. Table 1 also illustrates the reported performance of the task baseline systems (i.e., TF·IDF, Naive Bayes (NB) and maximum entropy (ME)[4]) and the UvT system performance variance based on document section candidates (-A: Abstract, -I: Introduction, -M: Main, -IC: Introduction and Conclusion combination). In these system variants, rather than selecting the top 15 C-value candidates from the system output, we also apply restrictions based on the candidate keyphrase document section information, thus skipping candidates which do not appear in the respective document section.

Overall, the UvT system performance is close to the baseline systems results. We observe that the system exhibits higher performance for its top

[4]The reported performance of both NB and ME for the respective gold-standard sets in the Keyphrase Extraction Task is identical.

5 candidate set and this performance drops rapidly as we include more terms in the answer set. One possible reason for its average performance could be attributed to increased "noise" in the results set. In particular, our text filtering method failed to accurately remove a large amount of irregular text in form of mathematical formulas and symbols which were erroneously tagged as proper nouns. As indicated in Table 1, the improved results of system variants based on document sections, such as Abstract, Introduction and Conclusion, where these symbols and formulas are rather uncommon, could be partly attributed to "noise" reduction.

Interestingly, the best system performance in these document section results is demonstrated by the Introduction-Conclusion combination (UvT-IC). Other tested combinations (not illustrated in Table 1), such as abstract-intro, abstract-intro-conclusions, abstract-intro-conclusions-references, display similar results on the reader-assigned set and a performance ranging between 15,6-16% for the 15 candidates on the combined set, while the inclusion of the Main section candidates reduces the performance to the overall system output (i.e., UvT results). Further experiments are required for refining the criteria for document section information, when the text filtering process for "noise" is improved.

Finally, another reason that contributes to the system's average performance lies in its inherent limitation for the detection of multi-word phrases, rather than both single and multi-word. In particular, single word keyphrases account for approx. 20% of the correct keyphrases in the gold standard sets.

4 Conclusion

We have presented an approach to keyphrase extraction mainly based on adaptation and implementation of the C-value method. This method was originally proposed for the detection of terminological phrases and although domain terms may express the principal informational content of a scientific article document, a method designed for their exhaustive identification (including both nested and longer multi-word terms) has not been proven more effective than baseline methods in the keyphrase detection task. Potential improvements in performance could be investigated by (1) improving document structure detection, so as to reduce irregular text, (2) refinement of document section information in keyphrase selection, (3) adaptation of the C-value measure, so as to possibly combine keyphrase frequency with a discriminative measure, such as *idf*.

References

Ken Barker and Nadia Cornacchia. 2000. Using noun phrase heads to extract document keyphrases. In *Proceedings of the 13th Biennial Conference of the Canadian Society on Computational Studies of Intelligence: Advances in Artificial Intelligence*, pages 40–52, Montreal, Canada, May.

Ernesto D'Avanzo and Bernado Magnini. 2005. A keyphrase-based approach to summarization: the LAKE system. In *Proceedings of Document Understanding Conferences*, pages 6–8, Vancouver, BC, Canada, October 9-10.

Katerina Frantzi, Sophia Ananiadou, and Hideki Mima. 2000. Automatic recognition of multi-word terms: The C-Value/NC-value Method. *Intern. Journal of Digital Libraries*, 3(2):117–132.

Ian Witten Gordon, Gordon W. Paynter, Eibe Frank, Carl Gutwin, and Craig G. Nevill-manning. 1999. Kea: Practical automatic keyphrase extraction. In *Proceedings of the Fourth ACM conference on Digital Libraries*, pages 254–256, Berkeley, CA, USA, August 11-14. ACM Press.

Christian Jacquemin. 2001. *Spotting and Discovering Terms through Natural Language Processing*. MIT Press, Cambridge, MA, USA.

Olena Medelyan and Ian H. Witten. 2006. Thesaurus based automatic keyphrase indexing. In *JCDL '06: Proceedings of the 6th ACM/IEEE-CS joint conference on Digital libraries*, pages 296–297, New York, NY, USA. ACM.

Adwait Ratnaparkhi. 1996. A maximum entropy model for part-of-speech tagging. In Eric Brill and Kenneth Church, editors, *Proceedings of the Empirical Methods in Natural Language Processing*, pages 133–142.

Takashi Tomokiyo and Matthew Hurst. 2003. A language model approach to keyphrase extraction. In *Proceedings of the ACL 2003 workshop on Multiword expressions*, pages 33–40, Morristown, NJ, USA. Association for Computational Linguistics.

Peter Turney. 1999. Learning to extract keyphrases from text. Technical Report ERB-1057, National Research Council, Institute for Information Technology, February 17.

Peter Turney. 2003. Coherent keyphrase extraction via web mining. In *IJCAI'03: Proceedings of the 18th international joint conference on Artificial intelligence*, pages 434–439, San Francisco, CA, USA. Morgan Kaufmann Publishers Inc.

UNITN: Part-Of-Speech Counting in Relation Extraction

Fabio Celli
University of Trento
Italy
fabio.celli@unitn.it

Abstract

This report describes the UNITN system, a Part-Of-Speech Context Counter, that participated at Semeval 2010 Task 8: Multi-Way Classification of Semantic Relations Between Pairs of Nominals. Given a text annotated with Part-of-Speech, the system outputs a vector representation of a sentence containing 20 features in total. There are three steps in the system's pipeline: first the system produces an estimation of the entities' position in the relation, then an estimation of the semantic relation type by means of decision trees and finally it gives a predicition of semantic relation plus entities' position. The system obtained good results in the estimation of entities' position (F1=98.3%) but a critically poor performance in relation classification (F1=26.6%), indicating that lexical and semantic information is essential in relation extraction. The system can be used as an integration for other systems or for purposes different from relation extraction.

1 Introduction and Background

This technical report describes the UNITN system (a Part-Of-Speech Context Counter) that participated to Semeval 2010 Task 8: Multi-Way Classification of Semantic Relations Between Pairs of Nominals (see Hendrickx *et al.*, 2009). A different version of this system based on Part-Of-Speech counting has been previously used for the automatic annotation of three general and separable semantic relation classes (taxonomy, location, association) obtaining an average F1-measure of 0.789 for english and 0.781 for italian, see Celli 2010 for details. The organizers of Semeval 2010 Task 8 provided ten different semantic relation types in context, namely:

- **Cause-Effect** (CE). An event or object leads to an effect. Example: *Smoking causes cancer.*
- **Instrument-Agency** (IA). An agent uses an instrument. Example: *Laser printer.*
- **Product-Producer** (PP). A producer causes a product to exist. Example: *The growth hormone produced by the pituitary gland.*
- **Content-Container** (CC). An object is physically stored in a delineated area of space, the container. Example: *The boxes contained books.*
- **Entity-Origin** (EO). An entity is coming or is derived from an origin (e.g., position or material). Example: *Letters from foreign countries.*
- **Entity-Destination** (ED). An entity is moving towards a destination. Example: *The boy went to bed.*
- **Component-Whole** (CW). An object is a component of a larger whole. Example: *My apartment has a large kitchen.*
- **Member-Collection** (MC). A member forms a nonfunctional part of a collection. Example: *There are many trees in the forest.*
- **Message-Topic** (CT). An act of communication, whether written or spoken, is about a topic. Example: *The lecture was about semantics.*
- **Other**. The entities are related in a way that do not fall under any of the previous mentioned classes. Example: *Batteries stored in a discharged state are susceptible to freezing.*

Proceedings of the 5th International Workshop on Semantic Evaluation, ACL 2010, pages 198–201,
Uppsala, Sweden, 15-16 July 2010.

The task was to predict, given a sentence and two marked-up entities, which one of the relation labels to apply and the position of the entities in the relation (except from "Other"). An example is reported below:

```
''The <e1>bag</e1>
contained <e2>books</e2>,
a cell phone and notepads,
but no explosives.''
Content-Container(e2,e1)
```

The task organizers also provided 8000 sentences for training and 2717 sentences for testing. Part of the task was to discover whether it is better to predict entities' position before semantic relation or viceversa.
In the next section there is a description of the UNITN system, in section 3 are reported the results of the system on the dataset provided for Semeval Task 8, in section 4 there is the discussion, then some conclusions follow in section 5.

2 System Description

UNITN is a Part-Of-Speech Context Counter. Given as input a plain text with Part-Of-Speech and end-of-sentence markers annotated it outputs a numerical feature vector that gives a representation of a sentence. For Part-Of-Speech and end-of-sentence annotation I used Textpro, a tool for NLP that showed state-of-the-art performance for POS tagging (see Pianta *et al.*, 2008). The POS tagset is the one used in the BNC, described at `http://pie.usna.edu/POScodes.html`.
Features in the vector can be tailored for specific tasks, in this case 20 features were used in total. They are:

1. Number of prepositions in sentence.
2. Number of nouns and proper names in sentence.
3. Number of lexical verbs in sentence.
4. Number of "be" verbs in sentence.
5. Number of "have" verbs in sentence.
6. Number of "do" verbs in sentence.
7. Number of modal verbs in sentence.
8. Number of conjunctions in sentence.
9. Number of adjectives in sentence.
10. Number of determiners in sentence.
11. Number of pronouns in sentence.
12. Number of punctuations in sentence.
13. Number of negative particles in sentence.
14. Number of words in the context between the first and the second entity.
15. Number of verbs in the context between the first and the second entity.
16. patterns (from, in, on, by, of, to).
17. POS of entity 1 (noun, adjective, other).
18. POS of entity 2 (noun, adjective, other).
19. Estimate of entities' position in the relation (e1-e2, e2-e1, 00).
20. Estimate of semantic relation (relations described in section 1 above).

Prepositional patterns in feature 16 were chosen for their high cooccurrence frequency with a semantic relation type and their low cooccurrence with the other ones.
The system works in three steps: in the first one features 1-18 are used for predicting feature 19, in the second one features 1-19 are used for predicting feature 20. In the third step, after the application of Hall 1998's attribute selection filter (that evaluates the worth of a subset of attributes by considering the individual predictive ability of each feature along with the degree of redundancy between them) features 12, 14, 16, 19 and 20 are used for the prediction of semantic relation plus entities' position (19 relations in total).
For all the steps I used C4.5 decision trees (see Quinlan 1993) and Cohen 1995's RIPPER algorithm (Repeated Incremental Pruning to Produce Error Reduction). Evaluation for steps 1, 2 and 3 have been run on the training set, with a 10-fold cross-validation, since the test set was relased in a second time. Results of evaluation of step 1, 2 and 3 are reported in table 1 below, chance values (100/number of classes) are taken as baselines, all experiments have been run in Weka (see Witten and Frank, 2005).
I also inverted step 1 and 2 for predicting seman-

Prediction	Baseline	average F1
step 1	33.33%	98.3%
step 2	10%	29.8%
step 3	5.26%	28.1%

Table 1: Evaluation for steps 1, 2 and 3.

tic relation estimate before entities' position estimate and the average F1-measure is even worse (0.271), demonstrating that entities' position estimate has a positive weight on semantic relation estimate. There are instead some problems with step 2, and I will return on this later in the discussion (section 4).

3 Results

As it was requested by the task, the system has been run 4 times in the testing phase: the first time (r1) using 1000 examples from the training set for building the model, the second time (r2) 2000 examples, the third (r3) 4000 example and the last one (r4) using the entire training set.
The results obtained by UNITN in the competition are not good, overall performance is poor, especially for some relations, in particular Product-Producer and Message-Topic. The best performance is achieved by the Member-Collection relation (47.30%), that changed from 0% in the first run to 42.71% in the second one. Scores are reported, relation by relation, in table 2 below, the discussion follows in section 4.

Rel	**F1** (r1)	**F1** (r2)	**F1** (r3)	**F1** (r4)
CE	23.08%	17.24%	22.37%	26.86%
CW	13.64%	0.00%	13.85%	25.23%
CC	26.43%	25.36%	26.72%	28.39%
ED	37.26%	37.25%	46.27%	46.35%
EO	36.60%	36.49%	37.61%	41.79%
IA	10.68%	7.95%	5.59%	17.32%
MC	0.00%	42.71%	43.08%	47.30%
CT	1.48%	0.00%	4.93%	6.81%
PP	0.00%	0.00%	1.67%	0.00%
Other	27.14%	26.15%	25.80%	20.64%
avg*	16.57%	18.56%	22.45%	26.67%

Table 2: Results. *Macro average excuding "Other".

4 Discussion

On the one hand the POSCo system showed an high performance in step 1 (entities' position detection), indicating that the numerical sentence representation obtained by means of Part-Of-Speech can be a good way for extracting syntactic information.
On the other hand the POSCo system proved not to be good for the classification of semantic relations. This clearly indicates that lexical and semantic information is essential in relation extraction. This fact is highlighted also by the attribute selection filter algorithm that choosed, among others, feature 16 (prepositional patterns), which was the only attribute providing lexical information in the system.
It is interesting to note that it chose feature 12 (punctuation) and 14 (number of words in the context between the first and the second entity). Punctuation can be used to provide, to a certain level, information about how much the sentence is complex (the higher the number of the punctuation, the higher the subordinated phrases), while feature 14 provides information about the distance between the related entities and this could be useful for the classification between presence or absence of a semantic relation (the longer the distance, the lower the probability to have a relation between entities) but it is useless for a multi-way classification with many semantic relations, like in this case.

5 Conclusions

In this report we have seen that Part-Of-Speech Counting does not yield good performances in relation extraction. Despite this it provides some information about the complexity of the sentence and this can be useful for predicting the position of the entities in the relation. The results confirm the fact that lexical and semantic information is essential in relation extraction, but also that there are some useful non-lexical features, like the complexity of the sentence and the distance between the first and the second related entities, that can be used as a complement for systems based on lexical and semantic resources.

References

Fabio Celli. 2010. Automatic Semantic Relation Annotation for Italian and English. (technical report available at `http://clic.cimec.unitn.it/fabio`).

William W. Cohen. 1995. Fast effective rule induction. In *Proceedings of the 12th International Conference on Machine Learning*. Lake Tahoe, CA.

Mark A. Hall. 1998. Correlation-based Feature Selection for Discrete and Numeric Class Machine Learning. Technical report available at `http://citeseerx.ist.psu.edu/viewdoc/download?doi=10.1.1.148.6025&rep=rep1&type=pdf`.

Iris Hendrickx and Su Nam Kim and Zornitsa Kozareva and Preslav Nakov and Diarmuid Ó Séaghdha and Sebastian Padó and Marco Pennacchiotti and Lorenza Romano and Stan Szpakowicz. 2010. SemEval-2010 Task 8: Multi-Way Classification of Semantic Relations Between Pairs of Nominals. In *Proceedings of the 5th SIGLEX Workshop on Semantic Evaluation*, Uppsala, Sweden.

Emanuele Pianta and Christian Girardi and Roberto Zanoli. 2008. The TextPro tool suite. *In Proceedings of LREC*, Marrakech, Morocco.

John Ross Quinlan. 1993. C4.5: Programs for Machine Learning. *Morgan Kaufmann Publishers*, San Mateo, CA.

Ian H. Witten and Eibe Frank. 2005. *Data Mining. Practical Machine Learning Tools and Techniques with Java implementations*. Morgan and Kaufman, San Francisco, CA.

FBK_NK: a WordNet-based System for Multi-Way Classification of Semantic Relations

Matteo Negri and Milen Kouylekov
FBK-Irst
Trento, Italy
{negri,kouylekov}@fbk.eu

Abstract

We describe a WordNet-based system for the extraction of semantic relations between pairs of nominals appearing in English texts. The system adopts a lightweight approach, based on training a Bayesian Network classifier using large sets of binary features. Our features consider: *i)* the context surrounding the annotated nominals, and *ii)* different types of knowledge extracted from WordNet, including direct and explicit relations between the annotated nominals, and more general and implicit evidence (*e.g.* semantic boundary collocations). The system achieved a Macro-averaged F1 of 68.02% on the "Multi-Way Classification of Semantic Relations Between Pairs of Nominals" task (Task #8) at SemEval-2010.

1 Introduction

The "Multi-Way Classification of Semantic Relations Between Pairs of Nominals" task at SemEval-2010 (Hendrickx et al., 2010) consists in: *i)* selecting from an inventory of nine possible relations the one that most likely holds between two annotated nominals appearing in the input sentence, and *ii)* specifying the order of the nominals as the arguments of the relation. In contrast with the semantic relations classification task (Task #4) at SemEval-2007 (Girju et al., 2007), which treated each semantic relation separately as a single two-class (positive vs. negative) classification task, this year's edition of the challenge presented participating systems with a more difficult and realistic *multi-way* setup, where the relation *Other* can also be assigned if none of the nine relations is suitable for a given sentence. Examples of the possible markable relations are reported in Table 1[1].

The objective of our experiments with the proposed task is to develop a Relation Extraction system based on shallow linguistic processing, taking the most from available thesauri and ontologies. As a first step in this direction, our submitted runs have been obtained by processing the input sentences only to lemmatize their terms, and by using WordNet as the sole source of knowledge.

Similar to other approaches (Moldovan and Badulescu, 2009; Beamer et al., 2009), our system makes use of *semantic boundaries* extracted from the WordNet IS-A backbone. Such boundaries (*i.e.* divisions in the WordNet hierarchy that best generalize over the training examples) are used to define pairs of high-level synsets with high correlation with specific relations. For instance, <*microorganism#1, happening#1*> and <*writing#1, consequence#1*> are extracted from the training data as valid high-level collocations respectively for the relations *Cause-Effect* and *Message-Topic*. Besides exploiting the WordNet IS-A hierarchy, the system also uses the holo-/meronymy relations, and information derived from the WordNet glosses to capture specific relations such as *Member-Collection* and *Product-Producer*. In addition, the context surrounding the annotated nominals is represented as a *bag-of-words/synonyms* to enhance the relation extraction process. Several experiments have been carried out encoding all the information as large sets of binary features (up to ~6200) to train a Bayesian Network classifier available in the Weka[2] toolkit. To capture both the *relations* and the *order* of

[1] In the first example the order of the nominals is (<e2>,<e1>), while in the others is (<e1>,<e2>)

[2] http://www.cs.waikato.ac.nz/ml/weka/

Proceedings of the 5th International Workshop on Semantic Evaluation, ACL 2010, pages 202–205,
Uppsala, Sweden, 15-16 July 2010. ©2010 Association for Computational Linguistics

1	Cause-Effect(e2,e1)	A person infected with a particular <e1>flu</e1> <e2>virus</e2> strain develops an antibody against that virus.
2	Instrument-Agency(e1,e2)	The <e1>river</e1> once powered a <e2>grist mill</e2>.
3	Product-Producer(e1,e2)	The <e1>honey</e1> <e2>bee</e2> is the third insect genome published by scientists, after a lab workhorse, the fruit fly, and a health menace, the mosquito.
4	Content-Container(e1,e2)	I emptied the <e1>wine</e1> <e2>bottle</e2> into my glass and toasted my friends.
5	Entity-Origin(e1,e2)	<e1>This book</e1>is from the 17th <e2>century</e2>.
6	Entity-Destination(e1,e2)	<e1>Suspects</e1> were handed over to the <e2>police station</e2>.
7	Component-Whole(e1,e2)	<e1>Headlights</e1> are considered as the eyes of the <e2>vehicle</e2>.
8	Member-Collection(e1,e2)	Mary looked back and whispered: 'I know every <e1>tree</e1> in this <e2>forest</e2>, every scent'.
9	Message-Topic(e1,e2)	Here we offer a selection of our favourite <e1>books</e1> on military <e2>history</e2>.

Table 1: SemEval-2010 Task #8 semantic relations.

their arguments, training sentences having opposite argument directions for the same relation have been handled separately, and assigned to different classes (thus obtaining 18 classes for the nine target relations, plus one for the *Other* relation).

The following sections overview our experiments, describing the features used by the system (Section 2), and the submitted runs with the achieved results (Section 3). A concluding discussion on the results is provided in Section 4.

2 Features used

The system uses two types of boolean features: WordNet features, and context features.

2.1 WordNet features

WordNet features consider different types of knowledge extracted from WordNet 3.0.

Semantic boundary collocations. Collocations of high-level synsets featuring a high correlation with specific relations are acquired from the training set using a bottom-up approach. Starting from the nominals annotated in the training sentences (<e1> and <e2>), the WordNet IS-A backbone is climbed to collect all their ancestors. Then, all the ancestors' collocations occurring at least n times for at most m relations are retained, and treated as boolean features (set to 1 for a given sentence if its annotated nominals appear among their hyponyms). The n and m parameters are optimized on the training set.

Holo-/meronymy relations. These boolean features are set to 1 every time a pair of annotated nominals in a sentence is *directly* connected by holo-/meronyny relations. They are particularly appropriate to capture the *Component-Whole* and *Member-Collection* relations, as in the 8th example in Table 1 (where *tree#1* is an *holonym* of *forest#1*). Due to time constraints, we did not explore the possibility to generalize these features considering transitive closures of the nominals' hypo-/hypernyms. This possibility could allow to handle sentences like *"A <e1>herd</e1> is a large group of <e2>animals</e2>."* Here, though *herd#1* and *animal#1* are not directly connected by the meronymy relation, all the *herd#1* meronyms have *animal#1* as a common ancestor.

Glosses. Given a pair of annotated nominals <e1>,<e2>, these features are set to 1 every time either <e1> appears in the gloss of <e2>, or vice-versa. They are intended to support the discovery of relations in the case of consecutive nominals (*e.g. honey#1* and *bee#1* in the 3rd example in Table 1), where contextual information does not provide sufficient clues to make a choice. In our experiments we extracted features from both tokenized and lemmatized words (both nominals, and gloss words). Also in this case, due to time constraints we did not explore the possibility to generalize the feature considering the nominals' hypo-/hypernyms. This possibility could allow to handle sentences like examples 1 and 4 in Table 1. For instance in example 4, the gloss of *"bottle"* contains two hypernyms of *wine#1*, namely *drink#3* and *liquid#1*, that could successfully trigger the *Content-Container* relation.

Synonyms. While the previous features operate with the annotated nominals, WordNet synonyms are used to generalize the other terms in the sentence, allowing to extract different types of contextual features (see the next Section).

2.2 Context features

Besides the annotated nominals, also specific words (and word combinations) appearing in the surrounding context often contribute to trigger the target relations. Distributional evidence is captured by considering word contexts *before*, *between*, and *after* the annotated nominals. To this aim, we experimented with windows of different size, containing words that occur in the training set a variable number of times. Both the parameters (*i.e.* the size of the windows, and the number of occurrences) are optimized on training data. In our experiments we extracted contextual features from lemmatized sentences.

3 Submitted runs and results

Our participation to the SemEval-2010 Task #8 consisted in four runs, with the best one (FBK_NK-RES1) achieving a Macro-averaged F1 of 68.02% on the test data. For this submission, the overall training and test running times are about 12'30" and 1'30" respectively, on an Intel Core2 Quad 2.66GHz with 4GB RAM.

FBK_NK-RES1. This run has been obtained adopting a conservative approach, trying to minimize the risk of overfitting the training data. The features used can be summarized as follows:

- Semantic boundary collocations: all the collocations of <e1> and <e2> ancestors occurring at least 10 times in the training set (*m* param.), for at most 3 relations (*n* param.);
- Holo-/meronymy relations between the annotated nominals;
- Glosses: handled at the level of *tokens*;
- Context features: *left*, *between*, and *right* context windows of size 3-ALL-3 words respectively. Number of occurrences: 25 (*left*), 10 (*between*), 25 (*right*).

On the **training set**, the Bayesian Network classifier (trained with 2239 features, and evaluated with 10-fold cross-validation) achieves an Accuracy of 65.62% (5249 correctly classified instances out of 8000), and a Macro F1 of 78.15%.

FBK_NK-RES2. Similar to the first run, but:

- Semantic boundary collocations: *m*=9, *n*=3;
- Glosses: handled at the level of *lemmas*;
- Context features: *left*, *between*, and *right* context windows of size 4-ALL-1 words respectively (occurrences: 25-10-25).

Run	1000	2000	4000	8000
FBK_NK-RES1	55.71	64.06	67.80	**68.02**
FBK_NK-RES2	54.27	63.68	67.08	67.48
FBK_NK-RES3	54.25	62.73	66.11	66.90
FBK_NK-RES4	44.11	58.85	63.06	65.84

Table 2: Test results (Macro-averaged F1) using different amounts of training sentences.

Based on the observation of system's behaviour on the training data, the objectives of this run were to: *i)* add more collocations as features, *ii)* increase the importance of terms appearing in the *left* context, *iii)* reduce the importance of terms appearing in the *right* context, and *iv)* increase the possibility of matching the nominals with gloss terms by considering their respective lemmas. On the **training set**, the classifier (trained with 2998 features) achieves 66.92% Accuracy (5353 correctly classified instances), and a Macro F1 of 79.56%.

FBK_NK-RES3. Similar to the second run, but considering the synonyms of the most frequent sense of the words *between* <e1> and <e2>.

The goal of this run was to generalize the context *between* nominals, by considering word lemmas. On the **training set**, the classifier (trained with 2998 features) achieves an Accuracy of 64.94% (5195 correctly classified instances), and a Macro F1 of 77.38%.

FBK_NK-RES4. Similar to the second run, but considering semantic boundary collocations occurring at least 7 times in the training set (*m* param.), for at most 3 relations (*n* param.).

The goal of this run was to further increase the number of collocations used as features. On the **training set**, the classifier (trained with 6233 features) achieves achieves 68.12% Accuracy (5449 correct classifications), and 82.24% Macro F1.

As regards the results on the test set, Table 2 reports the scores achieved by each run using different portions of the training set (1000, 2000, 4000, 8000 examples), while Figure 1 shows the learning curves for each relation of our best run.

4 Discussion and conclusion

As can be seen from Table 2, the results contradict our expectations about the effectiveness of our less conservative configurations and, in particular, about the utility of using larger amounts of semantic boundary collocations. The performance

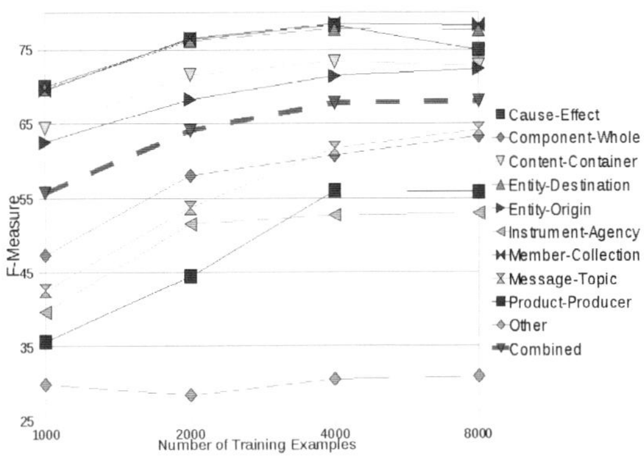

Figure 1: Learning curves on the test set (FBK_NK-RES1).

decrease from Run2 to Run4[3] clearly indicates an overfitting problem. Though suitable to model the training data, the additional collocations were not encountered in the test set. This caused a bias towards the *Other* relation, which reduced the overall performance of the system.

Regarding our best run, Figure 1 shows different system's behaviours with the different target relations. For some of them (*e.g. Entity-Destination, Cause-Effect*) better results are motivated by the fact that they are often triggered by frequent unambiguous word patterns (*e.g.* "*<e1>has been moved to a <e2>*", "*<e1> causes <e2>*"). Such relations are effectively handled by the context features which, in contrast, are inadequate for those expressed with high lexical variability. This is particularly evident with the *Other* relation, for which the acquired context features poorly discriminate positive from negative examples even on the training set.

For some relations additional evidence is successfully brought by the WordNet features. For instance, the good results for *Member-Collection* demonstrate the usefulness of the holo-/meronymy features.

As regards semantic boundary collocations, to check their effectiveness we performed a *post-hoc* analysis of those used in our best run. Such analysis was done in two ways: *i)* by counting the number of collocations acquired on the training set for each relation R_i, and *ii)* by calculating the ambiguity of each R_i's collocation on the training set (*i.e.* the average number of other relations activated by the collocation). The analysis revealed that the top performing relations (*Member-Collection, Entity-Destination, Cause-Effect*, and *Content-Container*) are those for which we acquired lots of unambiguous collocations. These findings also explain the poor performance on the *Instrument-Agency* and the *Other* relation. For *Instrument-Agency* we extracted the lowest number of collocations, which were also the most ambiguous ones. For the *Other* relation the high ambiguity of the collocations extracted is not compensated by their huge number (around 50% of the total collocations acquired).

In conclusion, considering *i)* the level of processing required (only lemmatization), *ii)* the fact that WordNet is used as the sole source of knowledge, and *iii)* the many possible solutions left unexplored due to time constraints, our results demonstrate the validity of our approach, despite its simplicity. Future research will focus on a better use of semantic boundary collocations, on more refined ways to extract knowledge from WordNet, and on integrating other knowledge sources (*e.g.* SUMO, YAGO, Cyc).

[3]The only difference between Run2 and Run4 is the addition of around 4000 semantic boundary collocations, which lead to an overall 2.4% F1 performance decrease. The decrease mainly comes in terms of Recall (from 65.91% in Run2 to 63.35% in Run4).

Acknowledgments

The research leading to these results has received funding from the European Community's Seventh Framework Programme (FP7/2007-2013) under Grant Agreement n. 248531 (CoSyne project).

References

B. Beamer, A. Rozovskaya, and R. Girju 2008. *Automatic Semantic Relation Extraction with Multiple Boundary Generation.* Proceedings of The National Conference on Artificial Intelligence (AAAI).

R. Girju, P. Nakov, V. Nastase, S. Szpakowicz, P. Turney, and D. Yuret 2007. *SemEval-2007 task 04: Classification of semantic relations between nominals.* Proceedings of the 4th Semantic Evaluation Workshop (SemEval-2007).

I. Hendrickx et al. 2010. *SemEval-2010 Task 8: Multi-Way Classification of Semantic Relations Between Pairs of Nominals* Proceedings of the 5th SIGLEX Workshop on Semantic Evaluation.

D. Moldovan, A. Badulescu 2005. *A Semantic Scattering Model for the Automatic Interpretation of Genitives.* Proceedings of The Human Language Technology Conference (HLT).

JU: A Supervised Approach to Identify Semantic Relations from Paired Nominals

Santanu Pal **Partha Pakray** **Dipankar Das** **Sivaji Bandyopadhyay**
Department of Computer Science & Engineering, Jadavpur University, Kolkata, India
santanupersonal1@gmail.com, parthapakray@gmail.com,
dipankar.dipnil2005@gmail.com, sivaji_cse_ju@yahoo.com

Abstract

This article presents the experiments carried out at Jadavpur University as part of the participation in Multi-Way Classification of Semantic Relations between Pairs of Nominals in the SemEval 2010 exercise. Separate rules for each type of the relations are identified in the baseline model based on the verbs and prepositions present in the segment between each pair of nominals. Inclusion of WordNet features associated with the paired nominals play an important role in distinguishing the relations from each other. The Conditional Random Field (CRF) based machine-learning framework is adopted for classifying the pair of nominals. Application of dependency relations, Named Entities (NE) and various types of WordNet features along with several combinations of these features help to improve the performance of the system. Error analysis suggests that the performance can be improved by applying suitable strategies to differentiate each paired nominal in an already identified relation. Evaluation result gives an overall macro-averaged F1 score of 52.16%.

1 Introduction

Semantic Relations describe the relations between concepts or meanings that are crucial but hard to identify. The present shared task aims to develop the systems for automatically recognizing semantic relations between pairs of nominals. Nine relations such as Cause-Effect, Instrument-Agency, Product-Producer, Content-Container, Entity-Origin, Entity-Destination, Component-Whole, Member-Collection and Message-Topic are given for SemEval-2010 Task #8 (Hendrix *et al.*, 2010). The relation that does not belong to any of the nine relations is tagged as *Other*. The first five relations also featured in the previous SemEval-2007 Task #4.

The present paper describes the approach of identifying semantic relations between pair of nominals. The baseline system is developed based on the verbs and prepositions present in the sentential segment between the two nominals. Some WordNet (Miller, 1990) features are also used in the baseline for extracting the relation specific attributes (e.g. *Content* type *hypernym* feature used for extracting the relation of *Content-Container*). The performance of the baseline system is limited due to the consideration of only the verb and preposition words in between the two nominals along with a small set of WordNet features. Hence, the Conditional Random Field (CRF) (McCallum *et al.*, 2001) based framework is considered to accomplish the present task. The incorporation of different lexical features (e.g. WordNet *hyponyms*, *Common-parents, distance*), Named Entities (NE) and syntactic features (direct or transitive dependency relations of parsing) has noticeably improved the performance of the system. It is observed that *nominalization* feature plays an effective role for identifying as well as distinguishing the relations. The test set containing 2717 sentences is evaluated against four different training sets. Some of the relations, e.g. *Cause-Effect*, *Member-Collection* perform well in comparison to other relations in all the four test results. Reviewing of the confusion matrices suggests that the system performance can be improved by reducing the errors that occur in distinguishing the two individual nominals in each relation.

The rest of the paper is organized as follows. The pre-processing of resources and the baseline system are described in Section 2 and Section 3 respectively. Development of CRF-based model is discussed in Section 4. Experimental results along

Proceedings of the 5th International Workshop on Semantic Evaluation, ACL 2010, pages 206–209,
Uppsala, Sweden, 15-16 July 2010.

with error analysis are specified in Section 5. Finally Section 6 concludes the paper.

2 Resource Pre-Processing

The annotated training corpus containing 8000 sentences was made available by the respective task organizers. The objective is to evaluate the effectiveness of the system in terms of identifying semantic relations between pair of nominals. The rule-based baseline system is evaluated against the whole training corpus. But, for in-house experiments regarding CRF based framework, the development data is prepared by randomly selecting 500 sentences from the 8000 training sentences. Rest 7500 sentences are used for training of the CRF-model. The format of one example entry in training file is as follows.

"The system as described above has its greatest application in an arrayed <e1>configuration</e1> of antenna <e2>elements</e2>."

Component-Whole (e2, e1)

Comment: Not a collection: there is structure here, organisation.

Each of the training sentences is annotated by the paired nominals tagged as *<e1>* and *<e2>*. The relation of the paired nominals and a comment portion describing the detail of the input type follows the input sentence.

The sentences are filtered and passed through Stanford Dependency Parser (Marneffe *et al.*, 2006) to identify direct as well as transitive dependencies between the nominals. The direct dependency is identified based on the simultaneous presence of both nominals, *<e1>* as well as *<e2>* in the same dependency relation whereas the transitive dependencies are verified if *<e1>* and *<e2>* are connected via one or more intermediate dependency relations.

Each of the sentences is passed through a Stanford Named Entity Recognizer (NER)[1] for identifying the named entities. The named entities are the useful hints to separately identify the relations like *Entity-Origin* and *Entity-Destination* from other relations as the *Origin* and *Destination* entities are tagged by the NER frequently than other entities.

Different seed lists are prepared for different types of verbs. For example, the lists for *causal* and *motion* verbs are developed by processing the XML files of English VerbNet (Kipper-Schuler, 2005). The list of the *causal* and *motion* verbs are prepared by collecting the member verbs if their corresponding class contain the semantic type "*CAUSE*" or "*MOTION*". The other verb lists are prepared manually by reviewing the frequency of verbs in the training corpus. The WordNet stemmer is used to identify the root forms of the verbs.

3 Baseline Model

The baseline model is developed based on the similarity clues present in the phrasal pattern containing verbs and prepositions. Different rules are identified separately for the nine different relations. A few WordNet features such as *hypernym*, *meronym*, *distance* and *Common-Parents* are added into the rule-based baseline model. Some of the relation specific rules are mentioned below.

For example, if any of the nominals contain their *meronym* property as "*whole*" and if the *hypernym* tree for one of the nominals contains the word "*whole*", the relation is identified as a *Component-Whole* relation. But, the ordering of the nominals *<e1>* and *<e2>* is done based on the combination of "*has*", "*with*" and "*of*" with other word level components.

The relations *Cause-Effect*, *Entity-Destination* are identified based on the *causal verbs* (cause, lead etc.) and *motion verbs* (go, run etc.) respectively. One of the main criteria for extracting these relations is to verify the presence of *causal* and *motion* verbs in between the text segment of *<e1>* and *<e2>*. Different types of specific *relaters* (as, because etc.) are identified from the text segment as well. It is observed that such specific causal *relaters* help in distinguishing other relations from *Cause-Effect*.

If one of the nominals is described as *instrument* type in its *hypernym* tree, the corresponding relation is identified as *Instrument-Agency* but the base level filtering criterion is applied if both the nominals belong to *instrument* type. On the other hand, if any of the nominals belong to the *hypernym* tree as *content* or *container* or *hold* type, it returns the relation *Content-Container* as a probable answer. Similarly, if both of them belong to the same type, the condition is fixed as false criterion for that particular category. The nominals identified as the part of *collective nouns* and associated with

[1] http://nlp.stanford.edu/software/CRF-NER.shtml

phrases like "*of*", "*in*", "*from*" between *<e1>* and *<e2>* contain the relation of *Member-Collection*. The relations e.g. *Message-Topic* uses seed list of verbs that satisfy the *communication* type in the *hypernym* tree and *Product-Producer* relation concerns the *hypernym* feature as *Product* type.

But, the identification of the proper ordering of the entities in the relation, i.e., whether the relation is valid between *<e1, e2>* or *<e2, e1>* is done by considering the passive sense of the sentence with the help of the keyword "*by*" as well as by some passive dependency relations.

The evaluation of the rule-based baseline system on the 8000 training data gives an average F1-score of 22.45%. The error analysis has shown that use of lexical features only is not sufficient to analyze the semantic relation between two nominals and the performance can be improved by adopting strategies for differentiating the nominals of a particular pair.

4 CRF-based Model

To improve the baseline system performance, CRF-based machine learning framework (McCallum *et al.*, 2001) is considered for classifying the semantic relations that exist among the ordered pair of nominals. Identification of appropriate features plays a crucial role in any machine-learning framework. The following features are identified heuristically by manually reviewing the corpus and based on the frequency of different verbs in different relations.

- 11 WordNet features (*Synset, Synonym, Gloss, Hyponym, Nominalization, Holonym, Common-parents, WordNet distance, Sense ID, Sense count, Meronym*)
- Named Entities (NE)
- Direct Dependency
- Transitive Dependency
- 9 separate verb list containing relation specific verbs, each for 9 different semantic relations

Different singleton features and their combinations are generated from the training corpus. Instead of considering the whole sentence as an input to the CRF-based system, only the pairs of nominals are passed for classification. The previous and next token of the current token with respect to each of the relations are added in the template to identify their co-occurrence nature that in turn help in the classification process. Synsets containing synonymous verbs of the same and different senses are considered as individual features.

4.1 Feature Analysis

The importance of different features varies according to the genre of the relations. For example, the *Common-parents* WordNet feature plays an effective role in identifying the *Content-Container* and *Product-Producer* relations. If the nominals in a pair share a common *Sense ID* and *Sense Count* then this is considered as a feature. The combination of multiple features in comparison with a single feature generally shows a reasonable performance enhancement of the present classification system. Evaluation on the development data for the various feature combinations has shown that the *nominalization* feature effectively performs for all the relations. WordNet *distance* feature is used for capturing the relations like *Content-Container* and *Component-Whole*. The direct and transitive dependency syntactic features contribute in identifying the relation as well as identify the ordering of the entities *<e1>* and *<e2>* in the relation.

The *Named-Entity* (NE) relation plays an important role in distinguishing the relations, e.g., *Entity-Origin* and *Entity-Destination* from other relations. The *person* tagged NEs have been excluded from the present task as such NEs are not present in the *Entity-Origin* and *Entity-Destination* relations. It has been observed that the relation specific verbs supply useful clues to the training phrase for differentiating relations among nominals.

The system is trained on 7500 sentences and the evaluation is carried out on 500 development sentences achieving an F1-Score of 57.56% F1-Score. The tuning on the development set has been carried out based on the performance produced by the individual features that effectively contains *WordNet* relations. In addition to that, the combination of dependency features with verb feature plays an contributory role on the system evaluation results.

Relations	TD1			TD2			TD3			TD4		
	Prec.	Recall	F1	Prec.	Recall	F1	Prec.	Recall	F1	Prec.	Recall	F1
Cause-Effect	76.33	65.85	70.70	78.55	65.85	71.64	79.86	68.90	73.98	79.26	72.26	75.60
Component-Whole	49.25	31.41	38.36	48.76	37.82	42.60	50.77	42.31	46.15	58.40	49.04	53.31
Content-Container	31.35	30.21	30.77	37.93	34.38	36.07	40.65	32.81	36.31	51.15	34.90	41.49
Entity-Destination	37.58	62.67	46.98	43.43	63.36	51.53	43.09	63.01	51.18	47.07	60.62	52.99
Entity-Origin	62.50	46.51	53.33	61.95	49.22	54.86	60.18	52.71	56.20	64.02	53.10	58.05
Instrument-Agency	19.46	23.08	21.11	21.18	27.56	23.96	26.43	23.72	25.00	32.48	24.36	27.84
Member-Collection	50.97	67.81	58.20	54.82	70.82	61.80	59.93	72.53	65.63	66.80	71.67	69.15
Message-Topic	41.70	41.38	41.54	50.23	42.15	45.83	52.81	46.74	49.59	57.78	49.81	53.50
Product-Producer	52.94	7.79	13.58	48.94	9.96	16.55	59.09	16.88	26.26	53.17	29.00	37.54
Other	21.10	27.09	23.72	24.48	33.70	28.36	26.28	37.44	30.88	26.64	42.07	32.62
Average F1 score	**42.62**			**44.98**			**47.81**			**52.16**		

Table 1: Precision, Recall and F1-scores (in %) of semantic relations in (9+1) way directionality-based evaluation

5 Experimental Results

The active feature list is prepared after achieving the best possible F1-score of 61.82% on the development set of 500 sentences. The final training of the CRF-based model is carried out on four different sets containing 1000, 2000, 4000 and 8000 sentences. These four training sets are prepared by extracting sentences from the beginning of the training corpus and the final evaluation is carried out on 2717 test sentences as provided by the organizers. The results on the four test sets termed as TD1, TD2, TD3 and TD4 are shown in Table 1. The error analysis is done based on the information present in the confusion matrices. The fewer occurrence of *Entity-Destination (e2, e1)* instance in the training corpus plays the negative role in identifying the relation. Mainly, the strategy used for assigning the order among the entities, i.e., either *<e1, e2>* or *<e2, e1>* in the already identified relations is the main cause of errors of the system. The *Entity-Origin, Product-Producer* and *Message-Topic* relations suffer from overlapping problem with other relations. Each of the tested nominal pairs is tagged with more than one relation. But, selecting the first output tag produced by CRF is considered as the final relational tag for each of the nominal pairs. Hence, a distinguishing strategy needs to be adopted for fine-grained selection.

6 Conclusion and Future Task

In our approach to automatic classification of semantic relations between nominals, the system achieves its best performance using the lexical feature such as *nominalization* of WordNet and syntactic information such as dependency relations. These facts lead us to conclude that semantic features from WordNet, in general, play a key role in the classification task. The present system aims for assigning class labels to discrete word level entities but the context feature is not taken into consideration. The future task is to evaluate the performance of the system by capturing the context present between the pair of nominals.

References

Andrew McCallum, Fernando Pereira and John Lafferty. 2001. Conditional Random Fields: Probabilistic Models for Segmenting and labeling Sequence Data. ICML-01, 282 – 289.

George A. Miller. 1990. WordNet: An on-line lexical database. *International Journal of Lexicography*, 3(4): 235–312.

Karin Kipper-Schuler. 2005. VerbNet. A broad-coverage, comprehensive verb lexicon. Ph.D. thesis, University of Pennsylvania, Philadelphia, PA.

Marie-Catherine de Marneffe, Bill MacCartney, and Christopher D. Manning. 2006. Generating Typed Dependency Parses from Phrase Structure Parses. *(LREC 2006).*

Iris Hendrickx, Su Nam Kim, Zornitsa Kozareva, Preslav Nakov, Diarmuid ´O S´eaghdha, Sebastian Padok , Marco Pennacchiotti, Lorenza Romano, Stan Szpakowicz. 2010. SemEval-2010 Task 8: Multi-Way Classification of Semantic Relations Between Pairs of Nominals. *5th SIGLEX Workshop.*

TUD: semantic relatedness for relation classification

György Szarvas* and **Iryna Gurevych**
Ubiquitous Knowledge Processing (UKP) Lab
Computer Science Department
Technische Universität Darmstadt
Hochschulstraße 10., D-64289 Darmstadt, Germany
http://www.ukp.tu-darmstadt.de/

Abstract

In this paper, we describe the system submitted by the team TUD to Task 8 at SemEval 2010. The challenge focused on the identification of semantic relations between pairs of nominals in sentences collected from the web. We applied maximum entropy classification using both lexical and syntactic features to describe the nominals and their context. In addition, we experimented with features describing the semantic relatedness (SR) between the target nominals and a set of clue words characteristic to the relations. Our best submission with SR features achieved 69.23% macro-averaged F-measure, providing 8.73% improvement over our baseline system. Thus, we think SR can serve as a natural way to incorporate external knowledge to relation classification.

1 Introduction

Automatic extraction of typed semantic relations between sentence constituents is an important step towards deep semantic analysis and understanding the semantic content of natural language texts. Identification of relations between a nominal and the main verb, and between pairs of nominals are important steps for the extraction of structured semantic information from text, and can benefit various applications ranging from Information Extraction and Information Retrieval to Machine Translation or Question Answering.

The Multi-Way Classification of Semantic Relations Between Pairs of Nominals challenge (Hendrickx et al., 2010) focused on the identification of specific relation types between nominals (nouns or base noun phrases) in natural language sentences collected from the web. The main task of the challenge was to identify and classify instances of 9 abstract semantic relations between noun phrases, i.e. *Cause-Effect, Instrument-Agency, Product-Producer, Content-Container, Entity-Origin, Entity-Destination, Component-Whole, Member-Collection, Message-Topic*. That is, given two nominals (*e1* and *e2*) in a sentence, systems had to decide whether *relation(e1,e2)*, *relation(e2,e1)* holds for one of the relation types or the nominals' relation is *other* (falls to a category not listed above or they are unrelated). In this sense, the challenge was an important pilot task towards large scale semantic processing of text.

In this paper, we describe the system we submitted to Semeval 2010, Task 8. We applied maximum entropy classification to the problem using both lexical and contextual features to describe the nominals themselves and their context (i.e. the sentence). In addition, we experimented with features exploiting the strength of association between the target nominals and a predefined set of clue words characteristic to the nine relation types. In order to measure the semantic relatedness (SR) of targets and clues, we used the Explicit Semantic Analysis (Gabrilovich and Markovitch, 2007) SR measure (based on Wikipedia, Wiktionary and WordNet). Our best submission, benefiting from SR features, achieved 69.23% macro-averaged F-measure for the 9 relation types used. Providing 8.73% improvement over our baseline system, we found the SR-based features to be beneficial for the classification of semantic relations.

2 Experimental setup

2.1 Feature set and selection

Feature set In our system, we used both lexical (1-3) and contextual features (4-8) to describe the nominals and their context (i.e. the sentence). Additionally, we experimented with a set of features (9) that exploit the co-occurrence statistics of the

* On leave from the Research Group on Artificial Intelligence of the Hungarian Academy of Sciences

Proceedings of the 5th International Workshop on Semantic Evaluation, ACL 2010, pages 210–213,
Uppsala, Sweden, 15-16 July 2010.

nominals and a set of clue words chosen manually, examining the relation definitions and examples provided by the organizers. The clues characterize the relations addressed in the task (e.g. *cargo, goods, content, box, bottle* characterize the *Content-Container* relation)[1]. Each feature type was distinguished from the others using a prefix. All but the semantic relatedness features we used were binary, denoting whether a specific word, lemma, POS tag, etc. is found in the example sentence, or not. SR features were real valued, scaled to $[0, 1]$ for each clue word separately (on train, and the same scaling factores were applied on the test data). The feature types used:

1. *Token:* word unigrams in the sentence in their inflected form. ***2.*** *Lemma:* word uni- and bigrams in the sentence in their lemmatized form. ***3.*** *Target Nouns:* the syntactic head words of the target nouns. ***4.*** *POS:* the part of speech uni- and bi- and trigrams in the sentence. ***5.*** *Between POS:* the part of speech sequence between the target nouns. ***6.*** *Dependency Path:* the dependency path (syntactic relations and directions) between the target nouns. The whole path constituted a single feature. ***7.*** *Target Distance:* the distance between the target nouns (in tokens). ***8.*** *Sentence Length:* the length of the sentence (in tokens). ***9.*** *Semantic Relatedness:* the semantic relatedness scores measuring the strength of association between the target nominals and the set of clue words we collected. In order to measure the semantic relatedness (SR) of targets and clues, we used the Explicit Semantic Analysis (ESA) SR measure.

Feature selection In order to discard uninformative features automatically, we performed feature selection on the binary features. We kept features that satisfied the following three conditions:

$$freq(x) > 3 \quad (1)$$

$$p = argmax_y P(y|x) > t_1 \quad (2)$$

$$p^5 \times freq(x) > t_2 \quad (3)$$

where $freq(x)$ denotes the frequency of feature x observed in the training dataset, y denotes a class label, p denotes the highest posterior probability (for feature x) over the nine relations (undirected) and the *other* class. Finally, t_1, t_2 are filtering thresholds chosen arbitrarily. We used $t_1 = 0.25$ for all features but the dependency path, where we used $t_1 = 0.2$. We set the thresold t_2 to 1.9 for lexical features (i.e. token and lemma features), to 0.3 for dependency path features and to 0.9 for all other features. All parameters for the feature selection process were chosen manually (cross-validating the parameters was omitted due to lack of time during the challenge development period). The higher t_2 value for lexical features was motivated by the aim to avoid overfitting, and the lower thresholds for dependency-based features by the hypothesis that these can be most efficient to determine the direction of relationships (c.f. we disregarded direction during feature selection). As the numeric SR features were all bound to clue words selected specifically for the task, we did not perform any feature selection for that feature type.

relation type	size	c4.5	SMO	maxent
cause-effect	1003	75.2%	**78.9%**	78.2%
component-whole	941	46.7%	53.0%	**54.7%**
content-container	540	72.9%	**78.1%**	75.1%
entity-destination	845	77.6%	**82.3%**	82.0%
entity-origin	716	61.8%	65.0%	**68.7%**
instrument-agency	534	40.7%	42.7%	**47.6%**
member-collection	690	68.2%	72.1%	**75.3%**
message-topic	634	41.3%	47.3%	**56.4%**
product-producer	717	43.8%	50.3%	**53.4%**
macro AVG F1	6590	58.7%	63.3%	**65.7%**

Table 1: Performance of different learning methods on train (10-fold).

2.2 Learning models

We compared three learning algorithms, using the baseline feature types (1-8), namely a C4.5 decision tree learner, a support vector classifier (SMO), and a maximum entropy (logistic regression) classifier, all implemented in the Weka package (Hall et al., 2009). We trained the SMO model with polynomial kernel of degree 2, fitting logistic models to the output to get valid probability estimates and the C4.5 model with pruning confidence factor set to 0.33. All other parameters were set to their default values as defined in Weka. We found the maxent model to perform best in 10-fold cross validation on the training set (see Table 1). Thus, we used maxent in our submissions.

3 Results

We submitted 4 runs to the challenge. Table 2 shows the per-class and the macro average F-measures of the 9 relation classes and the accuracy over all classes including *other*, on the train (10-fold) and the test sets (official evaluation):

[1]The clue list is available at: `http://www.ukp.tu-darmstadt.de/research/data/relation-classification/`

	Train				Test			
relation type	**Base**	**WP**	**cSR**	**cSR-t**	**Base**	**WP**	**cSR**	**cSR-t**
cause-effect	78.17%	78.25%	**79.42%**	79.10%	80.69%	81.90%	**83.76%**	83.38%
component-whole	54.68%	58.71%	60.18%	**60.79%**	50.52%	57.90%	61.67%	**62.15%**
content-container	75.09%	77.55%	**78.26%**	78.11%	75.27%	**78.96%**	78.33%	78.87%
entity-destination	81.99%	82.97%	**83.12%**	82.90%	77.59%	**82.86%**	81.54%	81.12%
entity-origin	68.74%	70.39%	71.14%	**71.18%**	67.08%	**72.05%**	71.03%	70.36%
instrument-agency	47.59%	56.71%	59.60%	**59.80%**	31.09%	44.06%	46.78%	**46.91%**
member-collection	75.27%	79.43%	80.71%	**80.89%**	66.37%	71.24%	**72.65%**	**72.65%**
message-topic	56.40%	62.68%	64.77%	**65.15%**	49.88%	65.06%	68.15%	**69.83%**
product-producer	53.36%	57.98%	59.97%	**60.70%**	46.04%	**57.94%**	56.00%	**57.85%**
macro AVG F1	65.70%	69.40%	70.80%	**70.96%**	60.50%	68.00%	68.88%	**69.23%**
accuracy (incl. *other*)	62.10%	65.42%	66.83%	**67.12%**	56.13%	63.49%	64.63%	**65.37%**

Table 2: Performance of 4 submissions on train (10-fold) and test.

Baseline (Base) As our baseline system, we used the information extracted from the sentence itself (i.e. lexical and contextual features, types 1-8).

Wikipedia (WP) As a first extension, we added SR features (9) exploiting term co-occurrence information, using the ESA model with Wikipedia.

Combined Semantic Relatedness (cSR) Second, we replaced the ESA measure with a combined measure developed by us, exploiting term co-occurrence not only in Wikipedia, but also in WordNet and Wiktionary glosses. We found this measure to perform better than the Wikipedia-based ESA in earlier experiments.

cSR threshold (cSR-t) We submitted the predictions of the cSR system, with less emphasis on the *other* class: we predicted *other* label only when the following held for the posteriors predicted by cSR: $\frac{argmax_y P(y|x)}{p(other)} < 0.7$. The threshold 0.7 was chosen based on the training dataset.

First, the SR features improved the performance of our system by a wide marging (see Table 2). The difference in performance is even more prominent on the Test dataset, which suggests that these features efficiently incorporated useful external evidence on the relation between the nominals and this not just improved the accuracy of the system, but also helped to avoid overfitting. Thus we conclude that the SR features with the encoded external knowledge helped the maxent model to learn a hypothesis that clearly generalized better.

Second, we notice that the combined SR measure proved to be more useful than the standard ESA measure (Gabrilovich and Markovitch, 2007) improving the performance by approximately 1 percent over ESA, both in terms of macro averaged F-measure and overall accuracy. This confirms our hypothesis that the combined measure is more robust than ESA with just Wikipedia.

prediction category	**cSR**	**cSR-t**
true positive relation (TP)	1555	1612
true positive *other* (TN)	201	164
wrong relation type (FP & FN)	291	341
wrong relation direction (FP & FN)	50	58
relation classified as *other* (FN)	367	252
other classified as relation (FP)	253	290
total	2717	2717

Table 3: Prediction error statistics.

3.1 Error Analysis

Table 3 shows the breakdown of system predictions to different categories, and their contribution to the official ranking as true/false positives and negatives. The submission that manipulated the decision threshold for the *other* class improved the overall performance by a small margin. This fact, and Table 3 confirm that our approach had major difficulties in correctly discriminating the 9 relation categories from *other*. Since this class is an umbrella class for unrelated nominals and the numerous semantic relations not considered in the challenge, it proved to be extremely difficult to accurately characterize this class. On the other hand, the confusion of the 9 specified relations (between each other) and directionality were less prominent error types. The most frequent cross-relation confusion types were the misclassification of *Component-Whole* as *Instrument-Agency* and *Member-Collection*; *Content-Container* as *Component-Whole*; *Instrument-Agency* as *Product-Producer* and vice versa. Interestingly, *Component-Whole* and *Cause-Effect* relations were the most typical sources for wrong direction errors. Lowering the decision threshold for *other* in our system naturally resulted in more true positive relation classifications, but unfortunately not only raised the number of *other* instances falsely classified as being one of the valuable relations, but also introduced several wrong relation classification errors (see Table 3). That is why this step resulted only in marginal improvement.

4 Conclusions & Future Work

In this paper, we presented our system submitted to the Multi-Way Classification of Semantic Relations Between Pairs of Nominals challenge at SemEval 2010. We submitted 4 different system runs. Our first submission was a baseline system (Base) exploiting lexical and contextual information collected solely from the sentence to be classified. A second run (WP) complemented this baseline configuration with a set of features that used Explicit Semantic Analysis (Wikipedia) to model the SR of the nominals to be classified and a set of clue words characteristic of the relations used in the challenge. Our third run (cSR) used a combined semantic relatedness measure that exploits multiple lexical semantic resources (Wikipedia, Wiktionary and WordNet) to provide more reliable relatedness estimates. Our final run (cSR-t) exploited that our system in general was inaccurate in predicting instances of the *other* class. Thus, it used the same predictions as cSR, but favored the prediction of one of the 9 specified classes instead of *other*, when a comparably high posterior for such a class was predicted by the system.

Our approach is fairly simple, in the sense that it used mostly just local information collected from the sentence. It is clear though that encoding as much general world knowledge to the representation as possible is crucial for efficient classification of semantic relations. In the light of the above fact, the results we obtained are reasonable.

As the main goal of our study, we attempted to use semantic relatedness features that exploit texts in an external knowledge source (Wikipedia, Wiktionary or WordNet in our case) to incorporate some world knowledge in the form of term co-occurrence scores. We found that our SR features significantly contribute to system performance. Thus, we think this kind of information is useful in general for relation classification. The experimental results showed that our combined SR measure performed better than the standard ESA using Wikipedia. This confirms our hypothesis that exploiting multiple resources for modeling term relatedness is beneficial in general.

Obviously, our system leaves much space for improvement – the feature selection parameters and the clue word set for the SR features were chosen manually, without any cross-validation (on the training set), due to lack of time. One of the participating teams used an SVM-based system and gained a lot from manipulating the decision thresholds. Thus, despite our preliminary results, it is also an interesting option to use SVMs.

In general, we think that more features are needed to achieve significantly better performance than we reported here. Top performing systems in the challenge typically exploited web frequency information (n-gram data) and manually encoded relations from an ontology (mainly WordNet). Thus, future work is to incorporate such features.

We demonstrated that SR features are helpful to move away from lexicalized systems using token- or lemma-based features. Probably the same holds for web-based and ontology-based features extensively used by top performing systems. This suggests that experimenting with all these to see if their value is complementary is an especially interesting piece of future work.

Acknowledgments

This work was supported by the German Ministry of Education and Research (BMBF) under grant 'Semantics- and Emotion-Based Conversation Management in Customer Support (SIGMUND)', No. 01ISO8042D, and by the Volkswagen Foundation as part of the Lichtenberg-Professorship Program under the grant No. I/82806.

References

Evgeniy Gabrilovich and Shaul Markovitch. 2007. Computing Semantic Relatedness using Wikipedia-based Explicit Semantic Analysis. In *Proceedings of The 20th International Joint Conference on Artificial Intelligence*, pages 1606–1611.

Mark Hall, Eibe Frank, Geoffrey Holmes, Bernhard Pfahringer, Peter Reutemann, and Ian H. Witten. 2009. The WEKA Data Mining Software: An Update. *SIGKDD Explorations*, 11(1):10–18.

Iris Hendrickx, Su Nam Kim, Zornitsa Kozareva, Preslav Nakov, Diarmuid Ó Séaghdha, Sebastian Padó, Marco Pennacchiotti, Lorenza Romano, and Stan Szpakowicz. 2010. Semeval-2010 task 8: Multi-way classification of semantic relations between pairs of nominals. In *Proceedings of the 5th SIGLEX Workshop on Semantic Evaluation*.

FBK-IRST: Semantic Relation Extraction using Cyc

Kateryna Tymoshenko and **Claudio Giuliano**
FBK-IRST
I-38050, Povo (TN), Italy
tymoshenko@fbk.eu, giuliano@fbk.eu

Abstract

We present an approach for semantic relation extraction between nominals that combines semantic information with shallow syntactic processing. We propose to use the ResearchCyc knowledge base as a source of semantic information about nominals. Each source of information is represented by a specific kernel function. The experiments were carried out using support vector machines as a classifier. The system achieves an overall F_1 of 77.62% on the "Multi-Way Classification of Semantic Relations Between Pairs of Nominals" task at SemEval-2010.

1 Introduction

The SemEval-2010 Task 8 "Multi-Way Classification of Semantic Relations Between Pairs of Nominals" consists in identifying which semantic relation holds between two nominals in a sentence (Hendrickx et al., 2010). The set of relations is composed of nine mutually exclusive semantic relations and the *Other* relation. Specifically, the task requires to return the most informative relation between the specified pair of nominals e_1 and e_2 taking into account their order. Annotation guidelines show that semantic knowledge about e_1 and e_2 plays a very important role in distinguishing among different relations. For example, relations *Cause-Effect* and *Product-Producer* are closely related. One of the restrictions which might help to distinguish between them is that products must be concrete physical entities, while effects must not.

Recently, there has emerged a large number of freely available large-scale knowledge bases. The ground idea of our research is to use them as source of semantic information. Among such resources there are DBpedia,[1] YAGO,[2] and OpenCyc.[3] On the one hand, DBpedia and YAGO have been automatically extracted from Wikipedia. They have a good coverage of named entities, but their coverage of common nouns is poorer. They seem to be more suitable for relation extraction between named entities. On the other hand, Cyc is a manually designed knowledge base, which describes actions and entities both in common life and in specific domains (Lenat, 1995). Cyc has a good coverage of common nouns, making it interesting for our task. The full version of Cyc is freely available to the research community as ResearchCyc.[4]

We approached the task using the system introduced by Giuliano et al. (2007) as a basis. They exploited two information sources: the whole sentence where the relation appears, and WordNet synonymy and hyperonymy information. In this paper, we (i) investigate usage of Cyc as a source of semantic knowledge and (ii) linguistic information, which give useful clues to semantic relation extraction. From Cyc, we obtain information about super-classes (in the Cyc terminology *generalizations*) of the classes which correspond to nominals in a sentence. The sentence itself provides linguistic information, such as local contexts of entities, bag of verbs and distance between nominals in the context.

The different sources of information are represented by kernel functions. The final system is based on four kernels (i.e., local context kernel, distance kernel, verbs kernel and generalization kernel). The experiments were carried out using support vector machines (Vapnik, 1998) as a classifier. The system achieves an overall F_1 of

[1] http://dbpedia.org/
[2] http://www.mpi-inf.mpg.de/yago-naga/yago/
[3] http://www.cyc.com/opencyc
[4] http://research.cyc.com/

Proceedings of the 5th International Workshop on Semantic Evaluation, ACL 2010, pages 214–217,
Uppsala, Sweden, 15-16 July 2010.

77.62%.

2 Kernel Methods for Relation Extraction

In order to implement the approach based on shallow syntactic and semantic information, we employed a linear combination of kernels, using the support vector machines as a classifier. We developed two types of basic kernels: syntactic and semantic kernels. They were combined by exploiting the closure properties of kernels. We define the composite kernel $K_C(x_1, x_2)$ as follows.

$$\sum_{i=1}^{n} \frac{K_i(x_1, x_2)}{\sqrt{K_i(x_1, x_1)K_i(x_2, x_2)}}. \quad (1)$$

Each basic kernel K_i is normalized.

All the basic kernels are explicitly calculated as follows

$$K_i(x_1, x_2) = \langle \varphi(x_1), \varphi(x_2) \rangle, \quad (2)$$

where $\varphi(\cdot)$ is the embedding vector. The resulting feature space has high dimensionality. However, Equation 2 can be efficiently computed explicitly because the representations of input are extremely sparse.

2.1 Local context kernel

Local context is represented by terms, lemmata, PoS tags, and orthographic features extracted from a window around the nominals considering the token order. Formally, given a relation example R, we represent a local context $LC = t_{-w}, ..., t_{-1}, t_0, t_{+1}, ..., t_{+w}$ as a row vector

$$\psi_{LC}(R) = (tf_1(LC), tf_2(LC), ..., tf_m(LC)) \in \{0, 1\}^m, \quad (3)$$

where tf_i is a feature function which returns 1 if the feature is active in the specified position of LC; 0 otherwise. The local context kernel $K_{LC}(R_1, R_2)$ is defined as

$$K_{LC\_e1}(R_1, R_2) + K_{LC\_e2}(R_1, R_2), \quad (4)$$

where K_{LC_e1} and K_{LC_e2} are defined by substituting the embedding of the local contexts of e_1 and e_2 into Equation 2, respectively.

2.2 Verb kernel

The verb kernel operates on the verbs present in the sentence,[5] representing it as a *bag-of-verbs*. More formally, given a relation example R, we represent the verbs from it as a row vector

$$\psi_V(R) = (vf(v_1, R), ..., vf(v_l, R)) \in \{0, 1\}^l, \quad (5)$$

where the binary function $vf(v_i, R)$ shows if a particular verb is used in R. By substituting $\psi_V(R)$ into Equation 2 we obtain the bag-of-verbs kernel K_V.

2.3 Distance kernel

Given a relation example $R(e_1, e_2)$, we represent the distance between the nominals as a one-dimensional vector

$$\psi_D(R) = \frac{1}{dist(e_1, e_2)} \in \Re^1, \quad (6)$$

where $dist(e_1, e_2)$ is number of tokens between the nominals e_1 and e_2 in a sentence. By substituting $\psi_D(R)$ into Equation 2 we obtain the distance kernel K_D.

2.4 Cyc-based kernel

Cyc is a comprehensive, manually-build knowledge base developed since 1984 by CycCorp. According to Lenat (1995) it can be considered as an expert system with domain spanning all everyday actions and entities, like *Fish live in water*. The open-source version of Cyc named OpenCyc, which contains the full Cyc ontology and restricted number of assertions, is freely available on the web. Also the full power of Cyc has been made available to the research community via ResearchCyc. Cyc knowledge base contains more than 500,000 concepts and more than 5 million assertions about them. They may refer both to common human knowledge like food or drinks and to specialized knowledge in domains like physics or chemistry. The knowledge base has been formulated using CycL language. A Cyc constant represents a thing or a concept in the world. It may be an individual, e.g. *BarackObama*, or a collection, e.g. *Gun*, *Screaming*.

2.4.1 Generalization kernel

Given a nominal e, we map it to a set of Cyc constants $EC = \{c_i\}$, using the Cyc function *denotation-mapper*. Nominals in Cyc usually denote constants-collections. Notice that we do not perform word sense disambiguation. For each $c_i \in EC$, we query Cyc for collections which generalize it. In Cyc collection X generalizes collection

[5] On average there are 2.65 verbs per sentence

Y if each element of Y is also an element of collection X. For instance, collection *Gun* is generalized by *Weapon, ConventionalWeapon, MechanicalDevice* and others.

The semantic kernel incorporates the data from Cyc described above. More formally, given a relation example R each nominal e is represented as

$$\psi_{EC}(R) = (fc(c_1, e), ..., fc(c_k, e)) \in \{0, 1\}^k, \quad (7)$$

where the binary function $fc(c_i, e)$ shows if a particular Cyc collection c_i is a generalization of e.

The *bag-of-generalizations* kernel $K_{genls}(R_1, R_2)$ is defined as

$$K_{genls\_e1}(R_1, R_2) + K_{genls\_e2}(R_1, R_2), \quad (8)$$

where K_{genls_e1} and K_{genls_e2} are defined by substituting the embedding of generalizations e_1 and e_2 into Equation 2 respectively.

3 Experimental setup and Results

Sentences have been tokenized, lemmatized and PoS tagged with TextPro.[6] Information for generalization kernel has been obtained from ResearchCyc. All the experiments were performed using jSRE customized to embed our kernels.[7] jSRE uses the SVM package LIBSVM (Chang and Lin, 2001). The task is casted as multi-class classification problem with 19 classes (2 classes for each relation to encode the directionality and 1 class to encode *Other*). The multiple classification task is handled with One-Against-One technique. The SVM parameters have been set as follows. The cost-factor W_i for a given class i is set to be the ratio between the number of negative and positive examples. We used two values of regularization parameter C: (i) $C_{def} = \frac{1}{\sum K(x,x)}$ where x are all examples from the training set, (ii) optimized C_{grid} value obtained by brute-force grid search method. The default value is used for the other parameters.

Table 1 shows the performance of different kernel combinations, trained on 8000 training examples, on the test set. The system achieves the best overall macro-average F_1 of 77.62% using $K_{LC} + K_V + K_D + K_{genls}$. Figure 1 shows the learning curves on the test set. Our experimental study has shown that the size of the training set influences the performance of the system. We observe that when the system is trained on 8000 examples the overall F_1 increases for 14.01% as compared to the case of 1000 examples.

[6]http://textpro.fbk.eu/

[7]jSRE is a Java tool for relation extraction available at http://tcc.itc.it/research/textec/tools-resources/jsre.html.

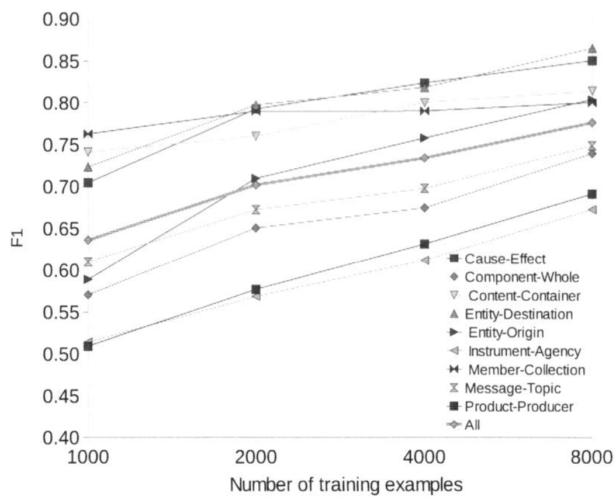

Figure 1: Learning curves on the test set per relation

Kernels	P	R	F_1
$K_{LC} + K_V + K_D + K_{genls}$	74.98	80.69	77.62
$K_{LC} + K_V + K_D + K_{genls}*$	78.51	76.03	77.11
$K_{LC} + K_D + K_{genls}*$	78.14	75.93	76.91
$K_{LC} + K_{genls}*$	78.19	75.70	76.81
$K_{LC} + K_D + K_{genls}$	72.98	80.28	76.39
$K_{LC} + K_{genls}$	73.05	79.98	76.28

Table 1: Performance on the test set. Combinations marked with * were run with C_{grid}, others with C_{def}.

4 Discussion and error analysis

The experiments have shown that K_{LC} is the core kernel of our approach. It has good performance on its own. For instance, it achieves precision of 66.16%, recall 72.67% and F_1 of 69.13% evaluated using 10-fold cross-validation on the training set.

Relation	K_{LC}	$K_{LC} + K_{genls}$	ΔF_1
Cause-Effect	74.29	76.41	2.12
Component-Whole	61.24	66.13	4.89
Content-Container	76.36	79.12	2.76
Entity-Destination	82.85	83.95	1.10
Entity-Origin	72.09	74.13	2.04
Instrument-Agency	57.71	65.51	7.80
Member-Collection	81.30	83.40	2.10
Message-Topic	60.41	69.09	8.68
Product-Producer	55.95	63.52	7.57

Table 2: The contribution of Cyc evaluated on the training set.

Generalization kernel combined with local context kernel gives precision of 70.38%, recall of 76.96%, and F_1 73.47% with the same experimental setting. The increase of F_1 per relation is shown in the Table 2 in the column ΔF_1. The largest F_1 increase is observed for *Instrument-Agency* (+7.80%), *Message-Topic* (+8.68%) and *Product-Producer* (+7.57%). K_{genls} reduces the number of misclassifications between the two directions of the same relation, like *Product-Producer(artist,design)*. It also captures the differences among relations, specified in the annotation guidelines. For instance, the system based only on K_{LC} misclassfied "The <e1>species</e1> makes a squelching <e2>noise</e2>" as *Product-Producer(e2,e1)*. Generalizations for *<e2>noise</e2>* provided by Cyc include *Event, MovementEvent, Sound*. According to the annotation guidelines a product must not be an event. A system based on the combination of K_{LC} and K_{genls} correctly labels this example as *Cause-Effect(e1,e2)*.

K_{genls} improves the performance in general. However, in some cases using Cyc as a source of semantic information is a source of errors. Firstly, sometimes the set of constants for a given nominal is empty (e.g., *disassembler*, *babel*) or does not include the correct one (noun *surge* is mapped to the constant *IncreaseEvent*). In other cases, an ambiguous nominal is mapped to many constants at once. For instance, *notes* is mapped to a set of constants, which includes *MusicalNote*, *Note-Document* and *InformationRecordingProcess*. Word sense disambiguation should help to solve this problem. Other knowledge bases like DBpedia and FreeBase[8] can be used to overcome the problem of lack of coverage.

Bag-of-word kernel with all words from the sentence did not impact the final result.[9] However, the information about verbs present in the sentence represented by K_V helped to improve the performance. A preliminary error analysis shows that a deeper syntactic analysis could help to further improve the performance.

For comparison purposes, we also exploited WordNet information by means of the supersense kernel K_{SS} (Giuliano et al., 2007). In all experiments, K_{SS} was outperformed by K_{genls}. For instance, $K_{LC} + K_{SS}$ gives overall F_1 measure of 70.29% with the same experimental setting as described in the beginning of this section.

5 Conclusion

The paper describes a system for semantic relations extraction, based on the usage of semantic information provided by ResearchCyc and shallow syntactic features. The experiments have shown that the external knowledge, encoded as super-class information from ResearchCyc without any word sense disambiguation, significantly contributes to improve overall performance of the system. The problem of the lack of coverage may be overcome by the usage of other large-scale knowledge bases, such as DBpedia. For future work, we will try to use the Cyc inference engine to obtain implicit information about nominals in addition to the information about their superclasses and perform word sense disambiguation.

Acknowledgments

The research leading to these results has received funding from the ITCH project (`http://itch.fbk.eu`), sponsored by the Italian Ministry of University and Research and by the Autonomous Province of Trento and the Copilosk project (`http://copilosk.fbk.eu`), a Joint Research Project under Future Internet - Internet of Content program of the Information Technology Center, Fondazione Bruno Kessler.

References

Chih-Chung Chang and Chih-Jen Lin. 2001. *LIBSVM: a library for support vector machines*. Software available at `http://www.csie.ntu.edu.tw/~cjlin/libsvm`.

Claudio Giuliano, Alberto Lavelli, Daniele Pighin, and Lorenza Romano. 2007. Fbk-irst: Kernel methods for semantic relation extraction. In *Proceedings of the Fourth International Workshop on Semantic Evaluations (SemEval-2007)*, Prague, Czech Republic, June. Association for Computational Linguistics.

Iris Hendrickx, Su Nam Kim, Zornitsa Kozareva, Preslav Nakov, Diarmuid Ó Séaghdha, Sebastian Padó, Marco Pennacchiotti, Lorenza Romano, and Stan Szpakowicz. 2010. Semeval-2010 task 8: Multi-way classification of semantic relations between pairs of nominals. In *Proceedings of the 5th SIGLEX Workshop on Semantic Evaluation*, Uppsala, Sweden.

Douglas B. Lenat. 1995. CYC: A large-scale investment in knowledge infrastructure. *Communications of the ACM*, 38(11):33–38.

Vladimir N. Vapnik. 1998. *Statistical Learning Theory*. Wiley-Interscience, September.

---
[8] `http://www.freebase.com/`

[9] This kernel has been evaluated only on the training data.

ISTI@SemEval-2 Task #8: Boosting-Based Multiway Relation Classification

Andrea Esuli, Diego Marcheggiani, Fabrizio Sebastiani
Istituto di Scienza e Tecnologie dell'Informazione
Consiglio Nazionale delle Ricerche
56124 Pisa, Italy
firstname.lastname@isti.cnr.it

Abstract

We describe a boosting-based supervised learning approach to the "Multi-Way Classification of Semantic Relations between Pairs of Nominals" task #8 of SemEval-2. Participants were asked to determine which relation, from a set of nine relations plus "Other", exists between two nominals, and also to determine the roles of the two nominals in the relation.

Our participation has focused, rather than on the choice of a rich set of features, on the classification model adopted to determine the correct assignment of relation and roles.

1 Introduction

The "Multi-Way Classification of Semantic Relations between Pairs of Nominals" (Hendrickx et al., 2010) we faced can be seen as the composition of two sub-tasks:

1. Determining which relation r, from a set of relations R (see Table 1), exists between two entities e_1 and e_2.

2. Determining the direction of the relation, i.e., determining which of $r(e_1, e_2)$ or $r(e_2, e_1)$ holds.

The set R is composed by nine "semantically determined" relations, plus a special Other relation which includes all the pairs which do not belong to any of the nine previously mentioned relations.
The two novel aspects of this task with respect to the similar task # 4 of SemEval-2007 (Girju et al., 2007) ("Classification of Semantic Relations between Nominals") are (i) the definition of the task as a "single-label" classification task and (ii) the need of determining the direction of the relation (i.e., Item 2 above).

1	Cause-Effect
2	Instrument-Agency
3	Product-Producer
4	Content-Container
5	Entity-Origin
6	Entity-Destination
7	Component-Whole
8	Member-Collection
9	Message-Topic

Table 1: The nine relations defined for the task.

The classification task described can be formalized as a *single-label* (aka "multiclass") text classification (SLTC) task, i.e., as one in which exactly one class must be picked for a given object out of a set of m available classes.

Given a set of objects D (ordered pairs of nominals, in our case) and a predefined set of *classes* (aka *labels*, or *categories*) $C = \{c_1, \ldots, c_m\}$, SLTC can be defined as the task of estimating an unknown *target function* $\Phi : D \rightarrow C$, that describes how objects ought to be classified, by means of a function $\hat{\Phi} : D \rightarrow C$ called the *classifier*[1].

In the relation classification task which is the object of this evaluation, the set C of classes is composed of 19 elements, i.e., the nine relations of Table 1, each one considered twice because it may take two possible directions, plus Other.

2 The learner

As the learner for our experiments we have used a boosting-based learner called MP-BOOST (Esuli et al., 2006). Boosting is among the classes of supervised learning devices that have obtained the best performance in several learning tasks and, at the same time, have strong justifications from computational learning theory. MP-BOOST is a

[1]Consistently with most mathematical literature we use the caret symbol (^) to indicate estimation.

Proceedings of the 5th International Workshop on Semantic Evaluation, ACL 2010, pages 218–221,
Uppsala, Sweden, 15-16 July 2010.

variant of AdaBoost.MH (Schapire and Singer, 2000), which has been shown in (Esuli et al., 2006) to obtain considerable effectiveness improvements with respect to AdaBoost.MH.

MP-Boost works by iteratively generating, for each class c_j, a sequence $\hat{\Phi}^j_1, \ldots, \hat{\Phi}^j_S$ of classifiers (called *weak hypotheses*). A weak hypothesis is a function $\hat{\Phi}^j_s : D \rightarrow \mathbf{R}$, where D is the set of documents and $\mathbf{R}$ is the set of real numbers. The sign of $\hat{\Phi}^j_s(d_i)$ (denoted by $sgn(\hat{\Phi}^j_s(d_i))$) represents the binary decision of $\hat{\Phi}^j_s$ on whether d_i belongs to c_j, i.e. $sgn(\hat{\Phi}^j_s(d_i)) = +1$ (resp., -1) means that d_i is believed to belong (resp., not to belong) to c_j. The absolute value of $\hat{\Phi}^j_s(d_i)$ (denoted by $|\hat{\Phi}^j_s(d_i)|$) represents instead the confidence that $\hat{\Phi}^j_s$ has in this decision, with higher values indicating higher confidence.

At each iteration s MP-Boost tests the effectiveness of the most recently generated weak hypothesis $\hat{\Phi}^j_s$ on the training set, and uses the results to update a distribution D^j_s of weights on the training examples. The initial distribution D^j_1 is uniform by default. At each iteration s all the weights $D^j_s(d_i)$ are updated, yielding $D^j_{s+1}(d_i)$, so that the weight assigned to an example correctly (resp., incorrectly) classified by $\hat{\Phi}^j_s$ is decreased (resp., increased). The weight $D^j_{s+1}(d_i)$ is thus meant to capture how ineffective $\hat{\Phi}^j_1, \ldots, \hat{\Phi}^j_s$ have been in guessing the correct c_j*-assignment* of d_i (denoted by $\Phi^j(d_i)$), i.e., in guessing whether training document d_i belongs to class c_j or not. By using this distribution, MP-Boost generates a new weak hypothesis $\hat{\Phi}^j_{s+1}$ that concentrates on the examples with the highest weights, i.e. those that had proven harder to classify for the previous weak hypotheses.

The overall prediction on whether d_i belongs to c_j is obtained as a sum $\hat{\Phi}^j(d_i) = \sum_{s=1}^{S} \hat{\Phi}^j_s(d_i)$ of the predictions made by the weak hypotheses. The final classifier $\hat{\Phi}^j$ is thus a *committee* of S classifiers, a committee whose S members each cast a weighted vote (the vote being the binary decision $sgn(\hat{\Phi}^j_s(d_i))$, the weight being the confidence $|\hat{\Phi}^j_s(d_i)|$) on whether d_i belongs to c_j. For the final classifier $\hat{\Phi}^j$ too, $sgn(\hat{\Phi}^j(d_i))$ represents the binary decision as to whether d_i belongs to c_j, while $|\hat{\Phi}^j(d_i)|$ represents the confidence in this decision.

MP-Boost produces a *multi-label* classifier, i.e., a classifier which independently classifies a document against each class, possibly assigning a document to multiple classes or no class at all. In order to obtain a single-label classifier, we compare the outcome of the $|C|$ binary classifiers, and the class which has obtained the highest $\hat{\Phi}^j(d_i)$ value is assigned to d_i, i.e., $\hat{\Phi}(d_i) = \arg\max_j \hat{\Phi}^j(d_i)$.

"<e1>People</e1> have been moving back into <e2>downtown</e2>."

Entity-Destination(e1,e2)

F_People FS_Peopl FH_group FP_NNP
FS1_have FS1S_have FS1H_have FS1P_VBP
FS2_been FS2S_been FS2H_be FS2P_VBN
FP3_moving FP3S_move FP3H_travel FP3P_VBG
SP3_moving SP3S_move SP3H_travel SP3P_VBG
SP2_back SP2S_back SP2H_O SP2P_RB
SP1_into SP1S_into SP1H_O SP1P_IN
S_downtown SS_downtown SH_city_district SP_NN
SS1_. SS1S_. SS1H_O SS1P_.

Table 2: A training sentence and the features extracted from it.

3 Vectorial representation

We have generated the vectorial representations of the training and test objects by extracting a number of contextual features from the text surrounding the two nominals whose relation is to be identified.

An important choice we have made is to "normalize" the representation of the two nominals with respect to the order in which they appear *in the relation*, and not in the sentence. Thus, if e_2 appears in a relation $r(e_2, e_1)$, then e_2 is considered to be the *first* (F) entity in the feature generation process and e_1 is the second (S) entity.

We have generated a number of features for each term denoting an entity and also for the three terms preceding each nominal (P1, P2, P3) and for the three terms following it (S1, S2, S3):

T : the term itself;

S : the stemmed version of the term, obtained using a Porter stemmer;

P : the POS of the term, obtained using the Brill Tagger;

H : the hypernym of the term, taken from WordNet ("O" if not available).

Features are prefixed with a proper composition of the above labels in order to identify their role in the sentence. Table 2 illustrates a sentence from the training set and its extracted features.

If an entity is composed by $k > 1$ terms, entity-specific features are generated for all the term n-grams contained in the entity, for all $n \in [1, ..., k]$. E.g., for "phone call" features are generated for the n-grams: "phone", "call", "phone_call".

In all the experiments described in this paper, MP-BOOST has been run for $S = 1000$ iterations. No feature weighting has been performed, since MP-BOOST requires binary input only.

4 Classification model

The classification model we adopted in our experiments splits the two tasks of recognizing the relation type and the one of determining the direction of the relation in two well distinct phases.

4.1 Relation type determination

Given the training set Tr of all the sentences for which the classifier outcome is known, vectorial representations (see Section 3) are built in a way that "normalizes" the direction of the relation, i.e.:

- if the training object belongs to one of the nine relevant relations, the features extracted from the documents are given proper identifiers in order to mark their role in the relation, not the order of appearance in the sentence;
- if the training object belongs to Other the *two* distinct vectorial representations are generated, one for relation Other(e_1, e_2) and one for Other(e_2, e_1).

The produced training set has thus a larger number of examples than the one actually provided. The training set provided for the task yielded 9410 training examples from the original 8000 sentences. A 10-way classifier is then trained on the vectorial representation.

4.2 Relation direction determination

The 10-way classifier is thus able to assign a relation, or the Other relation, to a sentence, but not to return the direction of the relation. The direction of the relation is determined at test time, by classifying *two* instances of each test sentence, and then combining the outcome of the two classifications in order to produce the final classification result.

More formally, given a test sentence d belonging to an unknown relation r, two vectorial representations are built: one, $d_{1,2}$, under the hypothesis that $r(e_1, e_2)$ holds, and one, $d_{2,1}$, under the hypothesis that $r(e_2, e_1)$ holds.

Both $d_{1,2}$ and $d_{2,1}$ are classified by $\hat{\Phi}$:

- if both classifications return Other, then d is assigned to Other;
- if one classification returns Other and the other returns a relation r, then r, with the proper direction determined by which vectorial representation determined the assignment, is assigned to d;
- if the two classifications return two relations $r_{1,2}$ and $r_{2,1}$ different from Other (of the same or of different relation type), then the one that obtains the highest $\hat{\Phi}$ value determines the relation and the direction to be assigned to d.

5 Experiments

We have produced two official runs.

The ISTI-2 run uses the learner, vectorial representation, and classification model described in the previous sections.

The ISTI-1 run uses the same configuration of ISTI-2, with the only difference being how the initial distribution D_1^j of the boosting method is defined. Concerning this, we followed the observations of (Schapire et al., 1998, Section 3.2) on boosting with general utility functions; the initial distribution in the ISTI-1 run is thus set to be equidistributed between the portion Tr_j^+ of positive examples of the training set and the portion Tr_j^- of negative examples, for each class j, i.e.,

$$D_1^j(d_i) = \frac{1}{2|Tr_j^+|} \quad \text{iff } d_i \in Tr_j^+ \qquad (1)$$

$$D_1^j(d_i) = \frac{1}{2|Tr_j^-|} \quad \text{iff } d_i \in Tr_j^- \qquad (2)$$

This choice of initial distribution, which gives more relevance to the less frequent type of elements of the training set (namely, the positive examples), is meant to improve the performance on highly imbalanced classes, thus improving effectiveness at the the macro-averaged level.

We have also defined a third method for an additional run, ISTI-3; unfortunately we were not able to produce it in time, and there is thus no official evaluation for this run on the test data. The method upon which the ISTI-3 run is based relies on a more "traditional" approach to the classification task, i.e., a single-label classifier trained

	Run	π^{μ}	ρ^{μ}	F_1^{μ}	π^{M}	ρ^{M}	F_1^{M}
Official results	ISTI-1	72.01%	**67.08%**	**69.46%**	71.12%	**66.24%**	**68.42%**
	ISTI-2	**73.55%**	63.54%	68.18%	**72.38%**	62.34%	66.65%
10-fold cross-validation	ISTI-1	73.60%	**69.34%**	**71.41%**	72.44%	**68.17%**	**69.95%**
	ISTI-2	**75.34%**	65.92%	70.32%	**73.96%**	64.65%	68.52%
	ISTI-3	68.52%	61.58%	64.86%	66.19%	59.75%	62.31%

Table 3: Official results (upper part), and results of the three relation classification methods when used in a 10-fold cross-validation experiment on training data (lower part). Precision, recall, and F_1 are reported as percentages for more convenience.

on the nine relations plus Other, not considering the direction, coupled with nine binary classifiers trained to determined the direction of each relation. We consider this configuration as a reasonable baseline to evaluate the impact of the original classification model adopted in the other two runs.

Table 3 summarizes the experimental results. The upper part of the table reports the official results for the two official runs. The lower part reports the results obtained by the three relation classification methods when used in a 10-fold cross-validation experiment on the training data. The evaluation measures are *precison* (π), *recall* (ρ), and the F_1 score, computed both in a *microaveraged* ($*^{\mu}$) and a *macroaveraged* ($*^{M}$) way (Yang, 1999).

The results for ISTI-1 and ISTI-2 in the 10-fold validation experiment are similar both in trend and in absolute value to the official results, allowing us to consider the ISTI-3 results in the 10-fold validation experiment as a good prediction of the efficacy of the ISTI-3 method on the test data. The classification model of ISTI-2, which uses an initial uniform distribution for the MP-BOOST learner as ISTI-3, improves F_1^M over ISTI-3 by 9.97%, and F_1^{μ} by 8.42%.

The use of a F_1-customized distribution in ISTI-1 results in a F_1 improvement with respect to ISTI-2 (F_1^M improves by 2.66% in official results, 2.09% in 10-fold validation results), which is mainly due to a relevant improvement in recall.

Comparing ISTI-1 with ISTI-3 the total improvement is 12.26% for F_1^M and 10.10% for F_1^{μ}.

6 Conclusion and future work

The original relation classification model we have adopted has produced a relevant improvement in efficacy with respect to a "traditional" approach.

We have not focused on the development of a rich set of features. In the future we would like to apply our classification model to the vectorial representations generated by the other participants, in order to evaluate the distinct contributions of the feature set and the classification model.

The use of a F_1-customized initial distribution for the MP-BOOST learner has also produced a relevant improvement, and it will be further investigated on more traditional text classification tasks.

References

Andrea Esuli, Tiziano Fagni, and Fabrizio Sebastiani. 2006. MP-Boost: A multiple-pivot boosting algorithm and its application to text categorization. In *Proceedings of the 13th International Symposium on String Processing and Information Retrieval (SPIRE'06)*, pages 1–12, Glasgow, UK.

Roxana Girju, Preslav Nakov, Vivi Nastase, Stan Szpakowicz, Peter Turney, and Deniz Yuret. 2007. Semeval-2007 task 04: Classification of semantic relations between nominals. In *Proceedings of the Fourth International Workshop on Semantic Evaluations (SemEval-2007)*, pages 13–18, Prague, CZ. Association for Computational Linguistics.

Iris Hendrickx, Su Nam Kim, Zornitsa Kozareva, Preslav Nakov, Diarmuid Ó Séaghdha, Sebastian Padó, Marco Pennacchiotti, Lorenza Romano, and Stan Szpakowicz. 2010. Semeval-2010 task 8: Multi-way classification of semantic relations between pairs of nominals. In *Proceedings of the 5th SIGLEX Workshop on Semantic Evaluation*, Uppsala, Sweden.

Robert E. Schapire and Yoram Singer. 2000. Boostexter: A boosting-based system for text categorization. *Machine Learning*, 39(2/3):135–168.

Robert E. Schapire, Yoram Singer, and Amit Singhal. 1998. Boosting and rocchio applied to text filtering. In *SIGIR '98: Proceedings of the 21st annual international ACM SIGIR conference on Research and development in information retrieval*, pages 215–223, New York, NY, USA. ACM.

Yiming Yang. 1999. An evaluation of statistical approaches to text categorization. *Information Retrieval*, 1(1/2):69–90.

ISI: Automatic Classification of Relations Between Nominals Using a Maximum Entropy Classifier

Stephen Tratz and **Eduard Hovy**
Information Sciences Institute
University of Southern California
Marina del Rey, CA 90292
{stratz,hovy}@isi.edu

Abstract

The automatic interpretation of semantic relations between nominals is an important subproblem within natural language understanding applications and is an area of increasing interest. In this paper, we present the system we used to participate in the SEMEVAL 2010 Task 8 Multi-Way Classification of Semantic Relations between Pairs of Nominals. Our system, based upon a Maximum Entropy classifier trained using a large number of boolean features, received the third highest score.

1 Introduction

Semantic interpretation of the relations between nominals in text is an area of growing interest within natural language processing (NLP). It has potential uses for a variety of tasks including machine translation (Baldwin and Tanaka, 2004) and question answering (Ahn et al., 2005). The related and more narrowly-focused problem of automatic interpretation of noun compounds is the focus of another SEMEVAL task (Butnariu et al., 2009).

In this paper, we discuss the overall setup of SEMEVAL 2010 Task 8 (Hendrickx et al., 2010), present the system we used to participate, and discuss our system's performance. Our system, which consists of a Maximum Entropy classifier trained using a large variety of boolean features, received the third highest official score of all the entries.

2 Related Work

The groundwork for SEMEVAL 2010 Task 8 was laid by an earlier SEMEVAL task (Girju et al., 2007). For SEMEVAL 2007 Task 4, participants provided *yes* or *no* answers as to whether a particular relation held for each test example. For SEMEVAL 2010, instead of providing a binary output for a single class, participants were required to perform multi-way classification, that is, select the most appropriate relation from a set of 10 relations including the OTHER relation.

The selection of a semantic relation for a pair of nominals within a sentence is somewhat similar to the task of noun compound interpretation, which is a more restricted problem focused only upon the nouns within noun compounds. Some of the recent work on this problem includes that of Butnariu et al. (2009), Girju (2007), Girju et al. (2005), Kim and Baldwin (2005), Nakov (2008), Nastase et al. (2006), Turney (2006), and Ó Séaghdha and Copestake (2009).

3 Task Overview

The task is, given a pair of nominals within their sentence context, select the most appropriate semantic relation from the set of available relations and indicate the direction of the relation. Though the final score was based upon the output of the system trained using the whole training dataset, participants were also required to submit three additional label sets using the first 12.5%, 25%, and 50% of the training data.

3.1 Relation Scheme

The relations were taken from earlier work on noun compounds by Nastase and Szpakowicz (2003).

A total of 10 relations were used including CAUSE-EFFECT, COMPONENT-WHOLE, CONTENT-CONTAINER, ENTITY-ORIGIN, ENTITY-DESTINATION, INSTRUMENT-AGENCY, MEMBER-COLLECTION, MESSAGE-TOPIC, OTHER, and PRODUCT-PRODUCER. Since each relation except the OTHER relation must have its direction specified, there are a total of 19 possible labels.

Proceedings of the 5th International Workshop on Semantic Evaluation, ACL 2010, pages 222–225,
Uppsala, Sweden, 15-16 July 2010.

3.2 Data

The training and testing datasets consist of 8000 and 2717 examples respectively. Each example consists of a single sentence with two of its nominals marked as being the nominals of interest. The training data also provides the correct relation for each example.

4 Method

4.1 Classifier

We use a Maximum Entropy (Berger et al., 1996) classifier trained using a large number of boolean features. Maximum Entropy classifiers have proven effective for a variety of NLP problems including word sense disambiguation (Tratz et al., 2007; Ye and Baldwin, 2007). We use the implementation provided in the MALLET machine learning toolkit (McCallum, 2002). We used the default Gaussian prior parameter value of 1.0.

4.2 Features Used

We generate features from individual words, including both the nominals and their context, and from combinations of the nominals.

To generate the features for individual words, we first use a set of word selection rules to select the words of interest and then run these words of interest through a variety of feature-generating functions. Some words may be selected by multiple word selection rules. For example, the word to the right of the first nominal will be identified by the *word 1 to the right of the 1st nominal* rule, the *words that are 3 or less to the right of the 1st nominal* rule, and the *all words between the nominals* rule. In these cases, the actual feature is the combination of an identifier for the word selection rule and the output from the feature-generating function. The 19 word-selection rules are listed below:

Word-Selection Rules

- The {1st, 2nd} nominal (2 rules)
- Word {1, 2, 3} to the {left, right} of the {1st, 2nd} nominal (12 rules)
- Words that are 3 or less to the {left, right} of the {1st, 2nd} nominal (4 rules)
- All words between the two nominals (1 rule)

The features generated from the individual words come from a variety of sources including word orthography, simple gazetteers, pattern matching, WordNet (Fellbaum, 1998), and Roget's Thesaurus.

Orthographic Features

- Capitalization indicator
- The {first, last} {two, three} letters of each word
- Indicator if the first letter of the word is a/A.
- Indicator for the overall form of the word (e.g. jump -> a, Mr. -> Aa., SemEval2 -> AaAa0)
- Indicators for the suffix types (e.g., de-adjectival, de-nominal [non]agentive, de-verbal [non]agentive)
- Indicators for a wide variety of affixes including those related to degree, number, order, etc. (e.g., ultra-, poly-, post-)
- Indicators for whether or not a preposition occurs within either term (e.g., 'down' in 'breakdown')

Gazetteer and Pattern Features

- Indicators if the word is one of a number of closed classes (e.g. articles, prepositions)
- Indicator if the word is listed in the U.S. Census 2000's most common surnames list
- Indicator if the word is listed in the U.S. Census 2000's most common first names list
- Indicator if the word is a name or location based upon some simple regular expressions

WordNet-based Features

- Lemmatized version of the word
- Synonyms for all NN and VB entries for the word
- Hypernyms for all NN and VB entries for the word
- All terms in the definitions ('gloss') for the word
- Lexicographer file names for the word
- Lists of all link types (e.g., meronym links) associated with the word
- Part-of-speech indicators for the existence of NN/VB/JJ/RB entries for the word
- All sentence frames for the word
- All part, member, substance-of holonyms for the word

Roget's Thesaurus-based Features

- Roget's divisions for all noun (and verb) entries for the word

Some additional features were extracted using combinations of the nominals. These include features generated using The Web 1T corpus (Brants and Franz, 2006), and the output of a noun compound interpretation system.

Web 1T N-gram Features

To provide information related to term usage to the classifier, we extracted trigram and 4-gram features from the Web 1T Corpus (Brants and Franz, 2006). Only n-grams containing lowercase words were used. The nominals were converted to lowercase if needed. Only n-grams containing both terms (including plural forms) were extracted. We included the n-gram, with the nominals replaced with N1 and N2 respectively, as individual boolean features. We also included versions of the n-gram features with the words replaced with wild cards. For example, if the nominals were 'food' and 'basket' and the extracted n-gram was 'put_N1_in_the_N2', we also included '*_N1_in_the_N2', '*_N1_*_the_N2', etc. as features.

Noun Compound System Features

We also ran the nominals through an in-house noun compound interpretation system and took its output as features. We will not be discussing the noun compound interpretation system in detail in this paper. It uses a similar approach to that described in this paper including a Maximum Entropy classifier trained with similar features that outputs a ranked list of a fixed set of semantic relations. The relations ranked within the top 5 and bottom 5 were included as features. For example, if "Topic of Communication" was the third highest relation, both "top:3:Topic of Communication" and "top:*:Topic of Communication" would be included as features.

4.3 Feature Filtering

The aforementioned feature generation process creates a very large number of features. To determine the final feature set, we first ranked the features according to the Chi-Squared metric. Then, by holding out one tenth of the training data and trying different thresholds, we concluded that 100,000 features was roughly optimal. For the cases where we used 12.5%, 25%, and 50%, we tested on the remaining training data and came up different cutoffs: 25,000, 40,000, and 60,000, respectively.

5 Results

Each participating site was allowed to submit multiple runs based upon different systems or configurations thereof. The results for the best performing submissions from each team are presented in Table 1. The official metric for the task was F1 macroaveraged across the different relations. We are pleased to see that our system received the third highest score.

Our results by the different relation types are shown in Table 2. We note that the performance on the OTHER relation is relatively low.

Top Results				
System	Macroaveraged F1			
	12.5%	25%	50%	100%
UTD	73.08	77.02	79.93	82.19
FBK_IRST	63.61	70.20	73.40	77.62
ISI	**66.68**	**71.01**	**75.51**	**77.57**
ECNU	49.32	50.70	72.63	75.43
TUD	58.35	62.45	66.86	69.23
ISTI	50.49	55.80	61.14	68.42
FBK_NK	55.71	64.06	67.80	68.02
SEKA	51.81	56.34	61.10	66.33
JU	41.62	44.98	47.81	52.16
UNITN	16.57	18.56	22.45	26.67

Table 1: Final results (macroaveraged F1) for the highest ranking (based upon result for training with the complete training set) submissions for each site. 12.5%, 25%, 50%, and 100% indicate the amount of training data used.

Results by Relation			
Relation	P	R	F1
Cause-Effect	87.77	87.50	87.63
Component-Whole	73.21	75.32	74.25
Content-Container	82.74	84.90	83.80
Entity-Destination	81.51	81.51	81.51
Entity-Origin	81.86	75.19	78.38
Instrument-Agency	64.34	58.97	61.54
Member-Collection	84.62	84.98	84.80
Message-Topic	75.91	79.69	77.76
Product-Producer	70.83	66.23	68.46
Other	43.28	45.37	44.30

Table 2: Precision, recall, and F1 results for our system by semantic relation.

6 Conclusion

We explain the system we used to participate in the SEMEVAL 2010 Task 8: Multi-Way Classification of Semantic Relations Between Pairs of Nominals and present its results. The overall approach is straight forward, consisting of a single Maximum Entropy classifier using a large number of boolean features, and proves effective, with our system receiving the third highest score of all the submissions.

7 Future Work

In the future, we are interested in utilizing parsing and part-of-speech tagging to enrich the feature set. We also want to investigate the relatively low performance for the OTHER category and see if we could develop a method to improve this.

Acknowledgements

Stephen Tratz is supported by a National Defense Science and Engineering Graduate Fellowship. We would like to thank the organizers of this task for their hard work in putting this task together.

References

Ahn, K., J. Bos, J. R. Curran, D. Kor, M. Nissim, and B. Webber. 2005. Question Answering with QED at TREC-2005. In *Proc. of TREC-2005*.

Baldwin, T. & T. Tanaka 2004. Translation by machine of compound nominals: Getting it right. In *Proc. of the ACL 2004 Workshop on Multiword Expressions: Integrating Processing*.

Berger, A., S. A. Della Pietra, and V. J. Della Pietra. 1996. A Maximum Entropy Approach to Natural Language Processing. *Computational Linguistics*, 22.

Brants, T. and A. Franz. 2006. Web 1T 5-gram Corpus Version 1.1. Linguistic Data Consortium.

Butnariu, C. and T. Veale. 2008. A concept-centered approach to noun-compound interpretation. In *Proc. of 22nd International Conference on Computational Linguistics (COLING 2008)*.

Butnariu, C., S.N. Kim, P. Nakov, D. Ó Séaghdha, S. Szpakowicz, and T. Veale. 2009. SemEval Task 9: The Interpretation of Noun Compounds Using Paraphrasing Verbs and Prepositions. In *Proc. of the NAACL HLT Workshop on Semantic Evaluations: Recent Achievements and Future Directions*.

Fellbaum, C., editor. 1998. WordNet: An Electronic Lexical Database. MIT Press, Cambridge, MA.

Girju, R., D. Moldovan, M. Tatu and D. Antohe. 2005. On the semantics of noun compounds. *Computer Speech and Language*, 19.

Girju, R., P. Nakov, V. Nastase, S. Szpakowicz, P. Turney, and D. Yuret. 2007. SemEval-2007 Task 04: Classification of Semantic Relations between Nominals In *Proc. of the 4th Semantic Evaluation Workshop (SemEval-2007)*.

Hendrickx, I., S. N. Kim, Z. Kozareva, P. Nakov, D. Ó Séaghdha, Sebastian Padó, M. Pennacchiotti, L. Romano, and S. Szpakowicz. 2010. Improving the interpretation of noun phrases with cross-linguistic information. In *Proc. of the 5th SIGLEX Workshop on Semantic Evaluation*.

Girju, R. 2007. Improving the interpretation of noun phrases with cross-linguistic information. In *Proc. of the 45th Annual Meeting of the Association of Computational Linguistics (ACL 2007)*.

Kim, S.N. and T. Baldwin. 2005. Automatic Interpretation of Compound Nouns using WordNet::Similarity. In *Proc. of 2nd International Joint Conf. on Natural Language Processing*.

McCallum, A. K. MALLET: A Machine Learning for Language Toolkit. http://mallet.cs.umass.edu. 2002.

Nakov, P. 2008. Noun Compound Interpretation Using Paraphrasing Verbs: Feasibility Study. In *Proc. the 13th International Conference on Artificial Intelligence: Methodology, Systems, Applications (AIMSA'08)*.

Nastase V. and S. Szpakowicz. 2003. Exploring noun-modifier semantic relations. In *Proc. the 5th International Workshop on Computational Semantics*.

Nastase, V., J. S. Shirabad, M. Sokolova, and S. Szpakowicz 2006. Learning noun-modifier semantic relations with corpus-based and Wordnet-based features. In *Proc. of the 21st National Conference on Artificial Intelligence (AAAI-06)*.

Ó Séaghdha, D. and A. Copestake. 2009. Using lexical and relational similarity to classify semantic relations. In *Proc. of the 12th Conference of the European Chapter of the Association for Computational Linguistics (EACL 2009)*.

Tratz, S., A. Sanfilippo, M. Gregory, A. Chappell, C. Posse, and P. Whitney. 2007. PNNL: A Supervised Maximum Entropy Approach to Word Sense Disambiguation In *Proc. of the 4th International Workshop on Semantic Evaluations (SemEval-2007)*.

Turney, P. D. 2006. Similarity of semantic relations. *Computation Linguistics*, 32(3):379-416

Ye, P. and T. Baldwin. 2007. MELB-YB: Preposition Sense Disambiguation Using Rich Semantic Features. In *Proc. of the 4th International Workshop on Semantic Evaluations (SemEval-2007)*.

ECNU: Effective Semantic Relations Classification without Complicated Features or Multiple External Corpora

Yuan Chen[†], **Man Lan**[†,§], **Jian Su**[§], **Zhi Min Zhou**[†], **Yu Xu**[†]
[†]East China Normal University, Shanghai, PRC.
[§]Institute for Infocomm Research, Singapore.
lanman.sg@gmail.com

Abstract

This paper describes our approach to the automatic identification of semantic relations between nominals in English sentences. The basic idea of our strategy is to develop machine-learning classifiers which: (1) make use of class-independent features and classifier; (2) make use of a simple and effective feature set without high computational cost; (3) make no use of external annotated or unannotated corpus at all. At SemEval 2010 Task 8 our system achieved an F-measure of 75.43% and a accuracy of 70.22%.

1 Introduction

Knowledge extraction of semantic relations between pairs of nominals from English text is one important application both as an end in itself and as an intermediate step in various downstream NLP applications, such as information extraction, summarization, machine translation, QA etc. It is also useful for many auxiliary tasks such as word sense disambiguation, language modeling, paraphrasing and discourse relation processing.

In the past decade, semantic relation classification has attracted a lot of interest from researchers and a wide variety of relation classification schemes exist in the literature. However, most research work is quite different in definition of relations and granularities of various applications. That is, there is little agreement on relation inventories. SemEval 2010 Task 8 (Hendrickx et al., 2008) provides a new standard benchmark for semantic relation classification to a wider community, where it defines 9 relations including CAUSE-EFFECT, COMPONENT-WHOLE, CONTENT-CONTAINER, ENTITY-DESTINATION, ENTITY-ORIGIN, INSTRUMENT-AGENCY, MEMBER-COLLECTION, MESSAGE-TOPIC, PRODUCT-PRODUCER, and a tenth pseudo-relation OTHER (where relation is not one of the 9 annotated relations).

Unlike the previous semantic relation task in SemEval 2007 Task 4, the current evaluation provides neither query pattern for each sentence nor manually annotated word sense (in WordNet semantic) for each nominals. Since its initiative is to provide a more realistic real-world application design that is practical, any classification system must be usable without too much effort. It needs to be easily computable. So we need to take into account the following special considerations.

1. The extracted features for relation are expected to be easily computable. That is, the steps in the feature extraction process are to be simple and direct for the purpose of reducing errors possibly introduced by many NLP tools. Furthermore, a unified (global) feature set is set up for all relations rather than for each relation.

2. Most previous work at SemEval 2007 Task 4 leveraged on external theauri or corpora (whether unannotated or annotated) (Davidov and Rappoport, 2008), (Costello, 2007), (Beamer et al., 2007) and (Nakov and Hearst, 2008) that make the task adaption to different domains and languages more difficult, since they would not have such manually classified or annotated corpus available. From a practical point of view, our system would make use of less resources.

3. Most previous work at Semeval 2007 Task 4 constructed several local classifiers on different algorithms or different feature subsets, one for each relation (Hendrickx et al., 2007) and (Davidov and Rappoport, 2008). Our approach is to build a global classifier for all relations in practical NLP settings.

Proceedings of the 5th International Workshop on Semantic Evaluation, ACL 2010, pages 226–229,
Uppsala, Sweden, 15-16 July 2010.

Based on the above considerations, the idea of our system is to make use of external resources as less as possible. The purpose of this work is two-fold. First, it provides an overview of our simple and effective process for this task. Second, it compares different features and classification strategies for semantic relation.

Section 2 presents the system description. Section 3 describes the results and discussions. Section 4 concludes this work.

2 System Description

2.1 Features Extraction

For each training and test sentence, we reduce the annotated target entities *e1* and *e2* to single nouns *noun1* and *noun2*, by keeping their last nouns only, which we assume to be heads.

We create a global feature set for all relations. The features extracted are of three types, i.e., lexical, morpho-syntactic and semantic. The feature set consists of the following 6 types of features.

Feature set 1: Lemma of target entities *e1* and *e2*. The lemma of the entities annotated in the given sentence.

Feature set 2: Stem and POS of words between *e1* and *e2*. The stem and POS tag of the words between two nominals. First all the words between two nominals were extracted and then the Porter's stemming was performed to reduce words to their base forms (Porter, 1980). Meanwhile, OpenNLP postag tool was used to return part-of-speech tagging for each word.

Feature set 3: syntactic pattern derived from syntactic parser between *e1* and *e2*. Typically, the verb phrase or preposition phrase which contain the nominals are important for relation classification. Therefore, OpenNLP Parser was performed to do full syntactic parsing for each sentence. Then for each nominal, we look for its parent node in the syntactic tree until the parent node is a verb phrase or preposition phrase. Then the label of this phrase and the verb or preposition of this phrase were extracted as the syntactic features.

Besides, we also extracted other 3 feature types with the aid of WordNet.

Feature set 4: WordNet semantic class of *e1* and *e2*. The WordNet semantic class of each annotated entity in the relation. If the nominal has two and more words, then we examine the semantic class of "*w1_w2*" in WordNet. If no result returned from WordNet, we examine the semantic class of head in the nominal. Since the cost of manually WSD is expensive, the system simply used the first (most frequent) noun senses for those words.

Feature set 5: meronym-holonym relation between *e1* and *e2*. The meronym-holonym relation between nominals. These information are quite important for COMPONENT-WHOLE and MEMBER-COLLECTION relations. WordNet3.0 provides meronym and holonym information for some nouns. The features are extracted in the following steps. First, for nominal *e1*, we extract its holonym from WN and for nominal *e2*, we extract its Synonyms/Hypernyms. Then, the system will check if there is same word between *e1*'s holonym and *e2*'s synonym & hypernym. The yes or no result will be a binary feature. If yes, we also examine the type of this match is "*part_of*" or "*member_of*" in holonym result. Then this type is also a binary feature. After that, we exchange the position of *e1* and *e2* and perform the same processing. By creating these features, the system can also take the direction of relations into account.

Feature set 6: hyponym-hypernym relation between nominal and the word of "container". This feature is designed for CONTENT-CONTAINER relation. For each nominal, WordNet returns its hypernym set. Then the system examine if the hypernym set contains the word "container". The result leads to a binary feature.

2.2 Classifier Construction

Our system is to build up a global classifier based on global feature set for all 9 non-Other relations. Generally, for this multi-class task, there are two strategies for building classifier, which both construct classifier on a global feature set. The first scheme is to treat this multi-class task as an multi-way classification. Since each pair of nominals corresponds to one relation, i.e., single label classification, we build up a 10-way SVM classifier for all 10 relations. Here, we call it multi-way classification. That is, the system will construct one single global classifier which can classify 10 relations simultaneously in a run. The second scheme is to split this multi-class task into multiple binary classification tasks. Thus, we build 9 binary SVM classifiers, one for each non-Other relation. Noted that in both strategies the classifiers are built on global feature set for all relations. For the second multiple binary classification, we also experimented on different prob. thresholds, i.e., 0.25 and 0.5. Furthermore, in order to reduce errors and boost performance, we also adopt the majority voting strategy to combine different classifiers.

3 Results and Discussion

3.1 System Configurations and Results

The classifiers for all relations were optimized independently in a number of 10-fold cross-validation (CV) experiments on the provided training sets. The feature sets and learning algorithms which were found to obtain the highest accuracies for each relation were then used when applying the classifiers to the unseen test data.

Table 1 summaries the 7 system configurations we submitted and their performance on the test data.

Among the above 7 system, SR5 system shows the best macro-averaged F1 measure. Table 2 describes the statistics and performance obtained per relation on the SR5 system.

Table 3 shows the performance of these 7 systems on the test data as a function of training set size.

3.2 Discussion

The first three systems are based on three feature sets, i.e.,F1-F3, with different classification strategy. The next three systems are based on all six feature sets with different classification strategy. The last system adopts majority voting scheme on the results of four systems, i.e., SR1, SR2, SR4 and SR5. Based on the above series of experiments and results shown in the above 3 tables, some interesting observations can be found as follows.

Obviously, although we did not perform WSD on each nominal and only took the first noun sense as semantic class, WordNet significantly improved the performance. This result is consistent with many previous work on Semeval 2007 Task 4 and once again it shows that WordNet is important for semantic relation classification. Specifically, whether for multi-way classification or multiple binary classification, the systems involved features extracted from WordNet performed better than the others not involved WN, for example, SR4 better than SR1 (74.82% vs 60.08%), SR5 better than SR2 (75.43% vs 72.59%), SR6 better than SR3 (72.19% vs 68.50%).

Generally, the performance of multiple binary classifier is better than multi-way classifier. That means, given a global feature set for 9 relations, the performance of 9 binary classifiers is better than a 10-way classifier. Specifically, when F1-F3 are involved, SR2 (72.59%) and SR3 (68.50%) are both better than SR1 (60.08%). However, when F1-F6 feature sets are involved, the performance of SR4 is between that of SR5 and SR6 in terms of macro-averaged F_1 measure. With respect to accuracy measure (Acc), SR4 system performs the best.

Moreover, for multiple binary classification, the threshold of probability has impact on the performance. Generally, the system with prob. threshold 0.25 is better than that with 0.5, for example, SR2 better than SR3 (72.59% vs 68.50%), SR5 better than SR6 (75.43% vs 72.19%).

As an ensemble system, SR7 combines the results of SR1, SR2, SR4 and SR5. However, this majority voting strategy has not shown significant improvements. The possible reason may be that these classifiers come from a family of SVM classifiers and thus the random errors are not significantly different.

Besides, one interesting observation is that SR4 system achieved the top 2 performance on TD1 data amongst all participating systems. This shows that, even with less training data, SR4 system achieves good performance.

Acknowledgments

This work is supported by grants from National Natural Science Foundation of China (No.60903093), Shanghai Pujiang Talent Program (No.09PJ1404500) and Doctoral Fund of Ministry of Education of China (No.20090076120029).

References

I. Hendrickx, S. N. Kim, Z. Kozareva, P. Nakov, D. Ó Séaghdha, S. Padó, M. Pennacchiotti, L. Romano and S. Szpakowicz. SemEval-2010 Task 8: Multi-Way Classification of Semantic Relations Between Pairs of Nominals. In *Proceedings of the 5th SIGLEX Workshop on Semantic Evaluation*, pp.94-99, 2010, Uppsala, Sweden.

D. Davidov and A. Rappoport. Classification of Semantic Relationships between Nominals Using Pattern Clusters. *Proceedings of ACL-08: HLT*, pp.227-235, 2008.

F. J. Costello. UCD-FC: Deducing semantic relations using WordNet senses that occur frequently

Run	Feature Set	Classifier	P (%)	R (%)	F_1 (%)	Acc (%)
SR1	F1-F3	multi-way classification	70.69	58.05	60.08	57.05
SR2	F1-F3	multiple binary (prob. threshold =0.25)	74.02	71.61	72.59	67.10
SR3	F1-F3	multiple binary (prob. threshold =0.5)	80.25	60.92	68.50	62.02
SR4	F1-F6	multi-way classification	75.72	74.16	74.82	70.52
SR5	F1-F6	multiple binary (prob. threshold =0.25)	75.88	75.29	**75.43**	70.22
SR6	F1-F6	multiple binary (prob. threshold =0.5)	83.08	64.72	72.19	65.81
SR7	F1-F6	majority voting based on SR1, SR2, SR4 and SR5	74.83	75.97	75.21	70.15

Table 1: Summary of 7 system configurations and performance on the test data. Precision, Recall, F1 are macro-averaged for system's performance on 9 non-Other relations and evaluated with directionality taken into account.

Run	Total #	P(%)	R (%)	F_1 (%)	Acc (%)
Cause-Effect	328	83.33	86.89	85.07	86.89
Component-Whole	312	74.82	65.71	69.97	65.71
Content-Container	192	79.19	81.25	80.21	81.25
Entity-Destination	292	79.38	86.99	83.01	86.99
Entity-Origin	258	81.01	81.01	81.01	81.01
Instrument-Agency	156	63.19	58.33	60.67	58.33
Member-Collection	233	73.76	83.26	78.23	83.26
Message-Topic	261	75.2	73.18	74.17	73.18
Product-Producer	231	73.06	61.04	66.51	61.04
Other	454	38.56	40.09	39.31	40.09
Micro-Average		76.88	76.27	76.57	70.22
Macro-Average		75.88	75.29	75.43	70.22

Table 2: Performance obtained per relation on SR5 system. Precision, Recall, F1 are macro-averaged for system's performance on 9 non-Other relations and evaluated with directionality taken into account.

Run	TD1		TD2		TD3		TD4	
	F_1 (%)	Acc (%)	F_1 (%)	Acc (%)	F_1 (%)	Acc (%)	F_1 (%)	Acc (%)
SR1	52.13	49.50	56.58	54.84	58.16	56.16	60.08	57.05
SR2	46.24	38.90	47.99	40.45	69.83	64.67	72.59	67.10
SR3	39.89	34.56	42.29	36.66	65.47	59.59	68.50	62.02
SR4	**67.95**	**63.45**	**70.58**	**66.14**	**72.99**	**68.94**	74.82	**70.52**
SR5	49.32	41.59	50.70	42.77	72.63	67.72	**75.43**	70.22
SR6	42.88	36.99	45.54	39.57	69.87	64.00	72.19	65.81
SR7	58.67	52.71	58.87	53.18	72.79	68.09	75.21	70.15

Table 3: Performance of these 7 systems on the test data as a function of training set size. The four training subsets, TD1, TD2, TD3 and TD4, have 1000, 2000, 4000 and 8000 (complete) training samples respectively. F1 is macro-averaged for system's performance on 9 non-Other relations and evaluated with directionality taken into account.

in a database of noun-noun compounds. *ACL SemEval'07 Workshop*, pp.370C373, 2007.

B. Beamer, S. Bhat, B. Chee, A. Fister, A. Rozovskaya and R.Girju. UIUC: A knowledge-rich approach to identifying semantic relations between nominals. *ACL SemEval'07 Workshop*, pp.386-389, 2007.

I. Hendrickx, R. Morante, C. Sporleder and A. Bosch. ILK: machine learning of semantic relations with shallow features and almost no data. *ACL SemEval'07 Workshop*, pp.187C190, 2007.

P. Nakov and M. A. Hearst. Solving Relational Similarity Problems Using the Web as a Corpus. In *Proceedings of ACL*, pp.452-460, 2008.

M. Porter. An algorithm for suffix stripping. In *Program*, vol. 14, no. 3, pp.130-137, 1980.

UCD-Goggle: A Hybrid System for Noun Compound Paraphrasing

Guofu Li
School of Computer Science and Informatics
University College Dublin
guofu.li@ucd.ie

Alejandra Lopez-Fernandez
School of Computer Science and Informatics
University College Dublin
alejandra.lopez-fernandez@ucd.ie

Tony Veale
School of Computer Science and Informatics
University College Dublin
tony.veale@ucd.ie

Abstract

This paper addresses the problem of ranking a list of paraphrases associated with a noun-noun compound as closely as possible to human raters (Butnariu et al., 2010). UCD-Goggle tackles this task using semantic knowledge learnt from the Google n-grams together with human-preferences for paraphrases mined from training data. Empirical evaluation shows that UCD-Goggle achieves 0.432 Spearman correlation with human judgments.

1 Introduction

Noun compounds (NC) are sequences of nouns acting as a single noun (Downing, 1977). Research on noun compounds involves two main tasks: NC detection and NC interpretation. The latter has been studied in the context of many natural language applications, including question-answering, machine translation, information retrieval, and information extraction.

The use of multiple *paraphrases* as a semantic intepretation of noun compounds has recently become popular (Kim and Baldwin, 2006; Nakov and Hearst, 2006; Butnariu and Veale, 2008; Nakov, 2008). The best paraphrases are those which most aptly characterize the relationship between the *modifier* noun and the *head* noun.

The aim of this current work is to provide a ranking for a list of paraphrases that best approximates human rankings for the same paraphrases. We have created a system called UCD-Goggle, which uses semantic knowledge acquired from Google n-grams together with human-preferences mined from training data. Three major components are involved in our system: B-score, produced by a Bayesian algorithm using semantic knowledge from the n-grams corpus with a smoothing layer of additional inference; R_t-score captures human preferences observed in the tail distribution of training data; and R_p-score captures pairwise paraphrase preferences calculated from the training data. Our best system for SemEval-2 task 9 combines all three components and achieves a Spearman correlation of 0.432 with human rankings.

This paper is organized as follows: the Bayesian B-score is introduced in section 2. In section 3 we describe two supervised approaches to mining the preferences of human raters from training data. Finally, section 4 presents the results of our empirical evaluation of the UCD-Goggle system.

2 Semantic Approach

2.1 Collecting Data

Google have made their web n-grams, also known as Web-1T corpus, public via the Linguistic Data Consortium (Brants and Franz, 2006). This corpus contains sequences of n terms that occur more than 40 times on the web.

We view the paraphrase task as that of suggesting the right verb phrase for two nouns (Butnariu and Veale, 2008). Previous work has shown the n-grams corpus to be a promising resource for retrieving semantic evidence for this approach. However, the corpus itself needs to be tailored to serve our purpose. Since the n-grams corpus is a collection of raw snippets from the web, together with their web frequency, certain pre-processing steps are essential before it can be used as a semi-structured knowledge base. Following a syntactic pattern approach, snippets in the n-grams that agree with the following patterns are harvested:

1. *Head VP Mod*
2. *Head VP DET Mod*
3. *Head* $[that|which]$ *VP Mod*
4. *Head* $[that|which]$ *VP DET Mod*

Here, *DET* denotes any of the determiners (*i.e.*,

Proceedings of the 5th International Workshop on Semantic Evaluation, ACL 2010, pages 230–233, Uppsala, Sweden, 15-16 July 2010.

the set of $\{an, a, the\}$ for English), *Head* and *Mod* are nouns for heads and modifiers, and *VP* stands for verb-based paraphrases observed in the test data. It must be highlighted that, when we collect snippets for the KB, any *Head* or *Mod* that falls out of the range of the dataset are also accepted via a process of semantic slippage (to be discussed in Sect. 2.4). The patterns listed above enable us to collect examples such as:

1. *"bread containing nut"*
2. *"pill alleviates the headache"*
3. *"novel which is about crimes"*
4. *"problem that involves the students"*

After a shallow parse, these snippets are formalized into the triple format $\langle Head, Para, Mod\rangle$. The sample snippets above are represented as:

1. ⟨`bread, contain, nut`⟩
2. ⟨`pill, alleviate, headache`⟩
3. ⟨`novel, be about, crime`⟩
4. ⟨`problem, involve, student`⟩

We use $\|Head, Para, Mod\|$ to denote the frequency of $\langle Head, Para, Mod\rangle$ in the n-grams.

2.2 Loosely Coupled Compound Analysis

Tens of millions of snippets are harvested and cleaned up in this way, yet expecting even this large set to provide decent coverage over the test data is still unrealistic. We calculated the probability of an example in the test data to appear in KB at less than 1%. To overcome the coverage issue, a loosely coupled analysis and representation of compounds is employed. Despite the fact that both modifier and head can influence the ranking of a paraphrase, we believe that either the modifier or the head is the dominating factor in most cases. This assumption has been shown to be plausible by earlier work (Butnariu and Veale, 2008). Thus, instead of storing complete triples in our KB, we divide each complete triple into two partial triples as shown below:

$$\langle Head, Para, Mod\rangle \rightarrow \begin{cases} \langle Head, Para, ?\rangle \\ \langle ?, Para, Mod\rangle \end{cases}$$

We can also retrieve these partial triples directly from the n-grams corpus using partial patterns like *"Head Para"* and *"Para Mod"*. However, just as shorter incomplete patterns can produce a larger KB, they also accept much more noise. For instance, single-verb paraphrases are very common among the test data. In these cases, the partial pattern approach would need to harvest snippets with the form *"NN VV"* or *"VV NN"* from 2-grams, which are too common to be reliable.

2.3 Probabilistic Framework

In the probabilistic framework, we define the B-score as the conditional probability of a paraphrase, $Para$, being suggested for a given compound $Comp$:

$$B(Para; Comp) \equiv P(Para|Comp) \quad (1)$$

Using the KB, we can estimate this conditional probability by applying the Bayes theorem:

$$P(Para|Comp) = \frac{P(Comp|Para)P(Para)}{P(Comp)} \quad (2)$$

The loose-coupling assumption (Sect. 2.2) allows us to estimate $P(Comp)$ as:

$$P(Comp) \equiv P(Mod \vee Head). \quad (3)$$

Meanwhile, *a priori* probabilities such as $P(Para)$ can be easily inferred from the KB.

2.4 Inferential Smoothing Layer

After applying the loose-coupling technique described in Section 2.2, the coverage of the KB rises to 31.78% (see Figure 1). To further increase this coverage, an inference layer is added to the system. This layer aims to stretch the contents of the KB via semantic slippage to the KB, as guided by the maximization of a fitness function. A WordNet-based similarity matrix is employed (Seco et al., 2004) to provide a similarity measure between nouns (so $sim(x, x)$ is 1). Then, a superset of *Head* or *Mod* (denoted as $\mathcal{H}$ and $\mathcal{M}$ respectively) can be extracted by including all nouns with similarity greater than 0 to any of them in the test data. Formally, for *Head* we have:

$$\mathcal{H} = \{h|sim(h, Head) \geq 0, Head \text{ in dataset}\}. \quad (4)$$

The definition of $\mathcal{M}$ is analogous to that of $\mathcal{H}$.

A system of equations is defined to produce alternatives for *Head* and *Mod* and their smoothed corpus frequencies (we show only the functions for head here):

$$h_0 = Head \quad (5)$$

$$fit(h) = sim^2(h, h_n) \times \|h, p, ?\| \quad (6)$$

$$h_{n+1} = \arg\max_{h \in \mathcal{H}} fit(h) \quad (7)$$

Here, $fit(h)$ is a fitness function of the candidate head h, in the context of a paraphrase p. Empirically, we use h_1 for $Head$ and $fit(h_1)$ for $\|Head, Para, ?\|$ when calculating the B-score back in the probabilistic framework (Sect. 2.3). In theory, we can apply this smoothing step repeatedly until convergence is obtained.

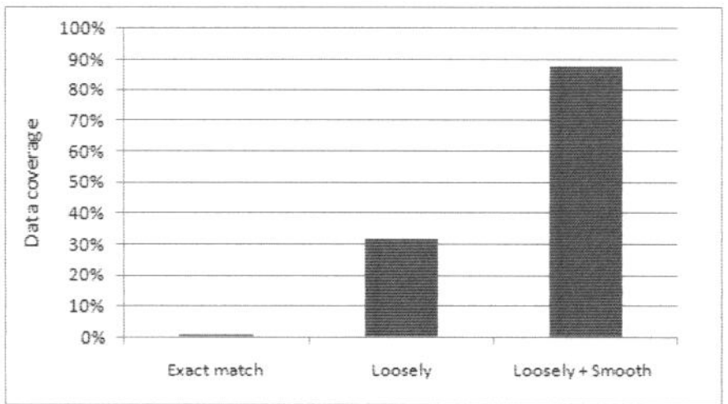

Figure 1: Comparison on coverage.

This semantic slippage mechanism allows a computer to infer the missing parts of the KB, by building a bridge between the limitations of a finite KB and the knowledge demands of an application. Figure 1 above shows how the coverage of the system increases when using partial matching and the smoothing technique, over the use of exact matching with the KB.

3 Preferences for Paraphrases

3.1 Tail-based Preference

Similar to various types of data studied by social scientists, the distribution of strings in our corpus tends to obey Zipf's law (Zipf, 1936). The same Zipfian trend was also observed in the compound-paraphrase dataset: more than 190 out of 250 compounds in the training data have 60% of their paraphrases in an undiscriminating tail, while 245 of 250 have 50% of their paraphrases in the tail. We thus assume the existence of a long *tail* in the paraphrase list for each compound.

The tail of each paraphrase list can be a valuable heuristic for modeling human paraphrase preferences. We refer to this model as the *tail-based preference* model. We assume that an occurrence of a paraphrase is deemed to occur in the tail *iff* it is mentioned by the human raters only once. Thus, the tail preference is defined as the probability that a paraphrase appears in the non-tail part of the list for all compounds in the training data. Formally, it can be expressed as:

$$R_t(p) = \frac{\sum_{c \in \mathcal{C}} \delta(c,p) f(c,p)}{\sum_{c \in \mathcal{C}} f(c,p)} \quad (8)$$

where $\mathcal{C}$ is the set of all compounds in the training data and $f(c,p)$ is the frequency of paraphrase p on compound c as given by the human raters. The $\delta(c,p)$ is a filter coefficient as shown below:

$$\delta(c,p) = \begin{cases} 1, & f(c,p) > 1, \\ 0, & f(c,p) = 1. \end{cases} \quad (9)$$

The *tail-based preference* model is simple but effective when used in conjunction with semantic ranking via the KB acquired from n-grams. However, an important drawback is that the tail model assigns a static preference to paraphrase (i.e., tail preferences are assumed to be context-independent). More than that, this preference does not take information from non-tail paraphrases into consideration. Due to these downsides, we use pairwise preferences described below.

3.2 Pairwise Preference

To fully utilize the training data, we employ another preference mining approach called *pairwise preference* modeling. This approach applies the principle of *pairwise comparison* (David, 1988) to determine the rank of a paraphrase inside a list.

We build a pairwise comparison matrix Π for paraphrases using the values of Equation 10 (here we have assumed that each of the paraphrases has been mapped into numeric values):

$$\Pi_{i,j} = \begin{cases} \frac{n(p_i,p_j)}{n(p_i,p_j)+n(p_j,p_i)}, & n(p_i,p_j) > n(p_j,p_i), \\ 0, & otherwise. \end{cases} \quad (10)$$

where $n(p_i, p_j)$ is the relative preferability of p_i to p_j. To illustrate the logic behind $n(x, y)$, we imagine a scenario with three compounds shown in Table 1:

	abor. prob.	*abor. vote*	*arti. desc.*
involve	12	8	3
concern	10	9	5
be about	3	9	15

Table 1: An example[1] to illustrate $n(x, y)$

[1] In this example, *abor. prob.* stands for *abortion problem*, *abor. vote* stands for *abortion vote*, and *arti. desc.* stands for *artifact description*

The relative preferability is given by the number of times that the frequency of p_i from human raters is greater than that of p_j. Observing that 1 out of 3 times *involve* is ranked higher than *concern*, we can calculate their relative preferability as:

$$n(involve, concern) = 1$$
$$n(concern, involve) = 2$$

Once the matrix is built, the preference score for a paraphrase i is calculated as:

$$R_p(i;c) = \frac{\sum_{j \in \mathcal{P}_c} \Pi_{i,j}}{|\mathcal{P}_c|} \quad (11)$$

where $\mathcal{P}_c$ is the list of paraphrases for a given compound c in the test data. The pairwise preference puts a paraphrase in the context of its company, so that the opinions of human raters can be approximated more precisely.

4 Empirical Results

We evaluated our system by tackling theSemEval-2 task 9 test data. We created three systems with different combinations of the three components (B, R_t, R_p). Table 2 below shows the performance of UCD-Goggle for each setting:

	System Config	Spearman ρ	Pearson r
I	$B + R_t$	0.380	0.252
II	R_p	0.418	0.375
III	$B + R_t + R_p$	**0.432**	**0.395**
*	Baseline	0.425	0.344

Table 2: Evaluation results on different settings of the UCD-Goggle system.

The first setting is a hybrid system which first calculates a ranking according to the $n$grams corpus and then applies a very simple preference heuristic (Sect. 2.3 and 3.1). The second setting simply applies the pairwise preference algorithm to the training data to learn ranking preferences (Sect. 3.2). Finally, the third setting integrates both of these settings in a single approach.

The individual contribution of B-score and R_t was tested by two-fold cross validation applied to the training data. The training data was split into two subsets and preferences were learnt from one part and then applied to the other. As an unsupervised algorithm, B-score produced Spearman correlation of 0.31 while the R_t-score gave 0.33. We noticed that more than 78% of the paraphrases had 0 score by R_t. This number not only reconfirmed the existence of the long-tail phenomenon, but also suggested that R_t-score alone could hardly capture the preference on the non-tail part. On the other hand, with more than 80% chance we could expect B to produce a non-zero score for a paraphrase, even if the paraphrase fell out of the topic. When combined together, B and R_t complemented each other and improved the performance considerably. However, this combined effort still could not beat the pairwise preference R_p or the baseline system, which had no semantic knowledge involved. The major limitation of our system is that the semantic approach is totally ignorant of the training data. In future work, we will intend to use it as a valuable resource in both KB construction and ranking stage.

References

T. Brants and A. Franz. 2006. *Web 1T 5-gram Version 1.* Linguistic Data Consortium.

C. Butnariu and T. Veale. 2008. A concept-centered approach to noun-compound interpretation. In *Proc. of the 22nd COLING*, pages 81–88, Manchester, UK.

C. Butnariu, S. N. Kim, P. Nakov, D. Ó Séaghdha, S. Szpakowicz, and T. Veale. 2010. Semeval-2 task 9: The interpretation of noun compounds using paraphrasing verbs and prepositions. In *Workshop on Semantic Evaluation*, Uppsala, Sweden.

H. A. David. 1988. *The Method of Paired Comparisons.* Oxford University Press, New York.

P. Downing. 1977. On the creation and use of English compound nouns. In *Language 53*, pages 810–842.

S. N. Kim and T. Baldwin. 2006. Interpreting semantic relations in noun compounds via verb semantics. In *Proc. of the COLING/ACL*, pages 491–498, Morristown, NJ, USA.

P. Nakov and M. A. Hearst. 2006. Using verbs to characterize noun-noun relations. In *Proc. of AIMSA*, pages 233–244.

P. Nakov. 2008. Noun compound interpretation using paraphrasing verbs: Feasibility study. In *Proc. of the 13th AIMSA*, pages 103–117, Berlin, Heidelberg. Springer-Verlag.

N. Seco, T. Veale, and J. Hayes. 2004. An intrinsic information content metric for semantic similarity in WordNet. In *Proc. of the 16th ECAI*, Valencia, Spain. John Wiley.

G. K. Zipf. 1936. *The Psycho-Biology of Language: An Introdution to Dynamic Philology.* Routledge, London.

UCD-PN: Selecting General Paraphrases Using Conditional Probability

Paul Nulty
University College Dublin
Dublin, Ireland
paul.nulty@ucd.ie

Fintan Costello
University College Dublin
Dublin, Ireland
fintan.costello@ucd.ie

Abstract

We describe a system which ranks human-provided paraphrases of noun compounds, where the frequency with which a given paraphrase was provided by human volunteers is the gold standard for ranking. Our system assigns a score to a paraphrase of a given compound according to the number of times it has co-occurred with other paraphrases in the rest of the dataset. We use these co-occurrence statistics to compute conditional probabilities to estimate a sub-typing or Is-A relation between paraphrases. This method clusters together paraphrases which have similar meanings and also favours frequent, general paraphrases rather than infrequent paraphrases with more specific meanings.

1 Introduction

SemEval 2010 Task 9, "Noun Compound Interpretation Using Paraphrasing Verbs", requires systems to rank paraphrases of noun compounds according to which paraphrases were most frequently produced for each compound by human annotators (Butnariu et al., 2010). This paper describes a system which ranks a paraphrase for a given compound by computing the probability of the paraphrase occurring given that we have previously observed that paraphrase co-occurring with other paraphrases in the candidate paraphrase list. These co-occurrence statistics can be built using either the compounds from the test set or the training set, with no significant difference in results.

The model is informed by two observations: people tend to use general, semantically light paraphrases more often than detailed, semantically heavy ones, and most paraphrases provided for a specific compound indicate the same interpretation of that compound, varying mainly according to level of semantic detail.

Given these two properties of the data, the objective of our system was to test the theory that conditional probabilities can be used to estimate a sub-typing or Is-A relation between paraphrases. No information about the compounds was used, nor were the frequencies provided in the training set used.

2 Motivation

Most research on the disambiguation of noun compounds involves automatically categorizing the compound into one of a pre-defined list of semantic relations. Paraphrasing compounds is an alternative approach to the disambiguation task which has been explored by (Lauer, 1995) and (Nakov, 2008). Paraphrases of semantic relations may be verbs, prepositions, or "prepositional verbs" like *found in* and *caused by*. (Lauer, 1995) categorized compounds using only prepositions. (Nakov, 2008) and the current task use only verbs and prepositional verbs, however, many of the paraphrases in the task data are effectively just prepositions with a copula, e.g. *be in*, *be for*, *be of*.

The paraphrasing approach may be easier to integrate into applications such as translation, query-expansion and question-answering — its output is a set of natural language phrases rather than an abstract relation category. Also, most sets of pre-defined semantic relations have only one or maybe two levels of granularity. This can often lead to semantically converse relations falling under the same abstract category, for example a *headache tablet* is a tablet for preventing headaches, while *headache weather* is weather that induces headaches — but both compounds would be assigned the same relation (perhaps *instrumental* or *causal*) in many taxonomies of semantic relations. Paraphrases of compounds using verbs or verb-preposition combinations can provide as much or as little detail as is required to adequately disambiguate the compound.

Proceedings of the 5th International Workshop on Semantic Evaluation, ACL 2010, pages 234–237,
Uppsala, Sweden, 15-16 July 2010.

2.1 General paraphrases are frequent

The object of SemEval 2010 Task 9 is to rank paraphrases for noun compounds given by 50-100 human annotators. When deciding on a model we took into account several observations about the data.

Firstly, the model does not need to produce plausible paraphrases for noun compounds, it simply needs to rank paraphrases that have been provided. Given that all of the paraphrases in the training and test sets have been produced by people, we presume that all of them will have at least some plausible interpretation, and most paraphrases for a given compound will indicate generally the same interpretation of that compound. This will not always be the case; some compounds are genuinely ambiguous rather than vague. For example a *stone bowl* could *be a bowl for holding stones* or a *bowl made of stone*. However, the mere fact that a compound has occurred in text is evidence that the speaker who produced the text believed that the compound was unambiguous, at least in the given context.

Given that most of the compounds in the dataset have one clear plausible meaning to readers, when asked to paraphrase a compound people tend to observe the Grician maxim of brevity (Grice, 1975) by using simple, frequent terms rather than detailed, semantically weighty paraphrases. For the compound *alligator leather* in the training data, the two most popular paraphrases were *be made from* and *come from*. Also provided as paraphrases for this compound were *hide of* and *be skinned from*. These are more detailed, specific, and more useful than the most popular paraphrases, but they were only produced once each, while *be made from* and *come from* were provided by 28 and 20 annotators respectively. This trend is noticeable in most of the compounds in the training data - the most specific and detailed paraphrases are not the most frequently produced.

According to the lesser-known of Zipf's laws — the law of meaning (Zipf, 1945) — words that are more frequent overall in a language tend to have more sub-senses. Frequent terms have a shorter lexical access time (Broadbent, 1967), so to minimize the effort required to communicate meaning of a compound, speakers should tend to use the most common words - which tend to be semantically general and have many possible sub-senses. This seems to hold for paraphrasing verbs and prepositions; terms that have a high overall frequency in English such as *be in*, *have* and *be of* are vague — there are many more specific paraphrases which could be considered sub-senses of these common terms.

2.2 Using conditional probability to detect subtypes

Our model uses conditional probabilities to detect this sub-typing structure based on the theory that observing a specific, detailed paraphrase is good evidence that a more general parent sense of that paraphrase would be acceptable in the same context. The reverse is not true - observing a frequently occurring, semantically light paraphrase is not strong evidence that any sub-sense of that paraphrase would be acceptable in the same context. For example, consider the spatial and temporal sub-senses of the paraphrase *be in*. A possible spatial sub-sense of this paraphrase is *be located in*, while a possible temporal sub-sense would be *occur during*. The fact that *occur during* is provided as a paraphrase for a compound almost always means that *be in* is also a plausible paraphrase. However, observing *be in* as a paraphrase does not provide such strong evidence for *occur during* also being plausible, as we do not know which sub-sense of *in* is intended.

If this is correct, then we would expect that the conditional probability of a paraphrase B occurring given that we have observed another paraphrase A in the same context is a measure of the extent to which B is a more general type (parent sense) of A.

3 System Description

The first step in our model is to generate a conditional probability table by going over all the compounds in the data and calculating the probability of each paraphrase occurring given that we observed another given paraphrase co-occurring for the same compound. We compute the conditional probability of every paraphrase with all other paraphrases individually. We could use either the training or the test set to collect these co-occurrence statistics, as the frequencies with which the paraphrases are ranked are not used — we simply note how many times each paraphrase co-occurred as a possible paraphrase for the same compound with each other paraphrase. For the submitted system we used the test data, but subsequently we confirmed that using only the training data for this step is not detrimental to the system's performance.

For each paraphrase in the data, the conditional probability of that paraphrase is computed with respect to all other paraphrases in the data. For any two paraphrases B and A:

$$P(B|A) = \frac{P(A \wedge B)}{P(A)}$$

As described in the previous section, we anticipate that more general, less specific paraphrases will be produced more often than their more detailed sub-senses. Therefore, we score each paraphrase by summing its conditional probability with each other paraphrase provided for the same compound.

For a list of paraphrases A provided for a given compound, we score a paraphrase b in that list by summing its conditional probability individually with every other paraphrase in the list.

$$score(b) = \sum_{a \in A} P(b|a)$$

This gives the more general, broad coverage, paraphrases a higher score, and also has a clustering effect whereby paraphrases that have not co-occurred with the other paraphrases in the list very often for other compounds are given a lower score — they are unusual in the context of this paraphrase list.

4 Results and Analysis

4.1 Task results

Table 1 shows the results of the top 3 systems in the task. Our system achieved the second highest correlation according to the official evaluation measure, Spearman's rank correlation coefficient. Results were also provided using Pearson's correlation coefficient and the cosine of the vector of scores for the gold standard and submitted predictions. Our system performed best using the cosine measure, which measures how closely the predicted scores match the gold standard frequencies, rather than the rank correlation. This could be helpful as the scores provide a scale of acceptability.

As mentioned in the system description, we collected the co-occurrence statistics for our submitted prediction from the test set of paraphrases alone. Since our model does not use the frequencies provided in the training set, we chose to use the test set as it was larger and had more annotators. This could be perceived as an unfair use of the test data, as we are using all of the test compounds and their paraphrases to calculate the position of a given paraphrase relative to other paraphrases.

System	Spearman	Pearson	Cosine
UVT	**.450**	**.411**	.635
UCD-PN	.441	.361	**.669**
UCD-GOG	.432	.395	.652
baseline	.425	.344	.524

Table 1: Results for the top three systems.

This is a kind of clustering which would not be possible if only a few test cases were provided. To check that our system did not need to collect co-occurrence probabilities on exactly the same data as it made predictions on, we submitted a second set of predictions for the test based on the probabilities from the training compounds alone. [1]

These predictions actually achieved a slightly better score for the official evaluation measure, with a Spearman rho of 0.444, and a cosine of 0.631. This suggests that the model does not need to collect co-occurrence statistics from the same compounds as it makes predictions on, as long as sufficient data is available.

4.2 Error Analysis

The most significant drawback of this system is that it cannot generate paraphrases for noun compounds - it is designed to rank paraphrases that have already been provided.

Using the conditional probability to rank paraphrases has two effects. Firstly there is a clustering effect which favours paraphrases that are more similar to the other paraphrases in a list for a given compound. Secondly, paraphrases which are more frequent overall receive a higher score, as frequent verbs and prepositions may co-occur with a wide variety of more specific terms.

These effects lead to two possible drawbacks. Firstly, the system would not perform well if detailed, specific paraphrases of compounds were needed. Although less frequent, more specific paraphrases may be more useful for some applications, these are not the kind of paraphrases that people seem to produce spontaneously.

[1]Thanks to Diarmuid Ó Séaghdha for pointing this out and scoring the second set of predictions

Also, because of the clustering effect, this system would not work well for compounds that are genuinely ambiguous e.g. *stone bowl* (*bowl made of stone* vs *bowl contains stones*). Most examples are not this ambiguous, and therefore almost all of the provided paraphrases for a given compound are plausible, and indicate the same relation. They vary mainly in how specific/detailed their explanation of the relation is.

The three compounds which our system produced the worst rank correlation for were *diesel engine*, *midnight train*, and *bathing suit*. Without access to the gold-standard scores for these compounds it is difficult to explain the poor performance, but examining the list of possible paraphrases for the first two of these suggests that the annotators identified two distinct senses for each: *diesel engine* is paraphrased by verbs of containment (e.g. *be in*) and verbs of function (e.g. *runs on*), while midnight train is paraphrased by verbs of location (e.g. *be found in*, *be located in*) and verbs of movement (e.g. *run in*, *arrive at*). Our model works by separating paraphrases according to granularity, and cannot disambiguate these distinct senses. The list of possible paraphrases for *bathing suit* suggests that our model is not robust if implausible paraphrases are in the candidate list - the model ranked *be in*, *be found in* and *emerge from* among the top 8 paraphrases for this compound, even though they are barely comprehensible as plausible paraphrases. The difficulty here is that even if only one annotator suggests a paraphrase, it is deemed to have co-occurred with other paraphrases in that list, since we do not use the frequencies from the training set.

The compounds for which the highest correlations were achieved were *wilderness areas*, *consonant systems* and *fiber optics*. The candidate paraphrases for the first two of these seem to be fairly homogeneous in semantic intent. *Fiber optics* is probably a lexicalised compound which hardly needs paraphrasing. This would lead people to use short and semantically general paraphrases.

5 Conclusion

We have described a system which uses a simple statistical method, conditional probability, to estimate a sub-typing relationship between possible paraphrases of noun compounds. From a list of candidate paraphrases for each noun compound, those which were judged by this method to be good "parent senses" of other paraphrases in the list were scored highly in the rankings.

The system does require a large dataset of compounds with associated plausible paraphrases, but it does not require a training set of human provided rankings and does not use any information about the noun compound itself, aside from the list of plausible paraphrases that were provided by the human annotators.

Given the simplicity of our model and its performance compared to other systems which used more intensive approaches, we believe that our initial observations on the data are valid: people tend to produce general, semantically light paraphrases more often than specific or detailed paraphrases, and most of the paraphrases provided for a given compound indicate a similar interpretation, varying instead mainly in level of semantic weight or detail.

We have also shown that conditional probability is an effective way to compute the sub-typing relation between paraphrases.

Acknowledgement

This research was supported by a grant under the FP6 NEST Programme of the European Commission (ANALOGY: Humans the Analogy-Making Species: STREP Contr. No 029088).

References

Donald E. Broadbent 1967. Word-frequency effect and response bias.. *Psychological Review*, 74,

Cristina Butnariu and Su Nam Kim and Preslav Nakov and Diarmuid Ó Séaghdha and Stan Szpakowicz and Tony Veale. 2010. SemEval-2 Task 9: The Interpretation of Noun Compounds Using Paraphrasing Verbs and Prepositions, *Proceedings of the 5th SIGLEX Workshop on Semantic Evaluation*, Uppsala, Sweden

Paul Grice. 1975. *Studies in the Way of Words*. Harvard University Press, Cambridge, Mass.

Mark Lauer 1995. *Designing statistical language learners: experiments on noun compound*, PhD Thesis Macquarie University, Australia

Preslav Nakov and Marti Hearst 2008. Solving Relational Similarity Problems using the Web as a Corpus. *In Proceedings of the 46th Annual Meeting of the Association for Computational Linguistics* (ACL-08), Columbus, OH.

George Kingsley Zipf. 1945. The Meaning-Frequency Relationship of Words. *Journal of General Psychology*, 33,

UvT-WSD1: a Cross-Lingual Word Sense Disambiguation system

Maarten van Gompel
Tilburg centre for Cognition and Communication
Tilburg University
proycon@anaproy.nl

Abstract

This paper describes the Cross-Lingual Word Sense Disambiguation system UvT-WSD1, developed at Tilburg University, for participation in two SemEval-2 tasks: the Cross-Lingual Word Sense Disambiguation task and the Cross-Lingual Lexical Substitution task. The UvT-WSD1 system makes use of k-nearest neighbour classifiers, in the form of single-word experts for each target word to be disambiguated. These classifiers can be constructed using a variety of local and global context features, and these are mapped onto the translations, i.e. the senses, of the words. The system works for a given language-pair, either English-Dutch or English-Spanish in the current implementation, and takes a word-aligned parallel corpus as its input.

1 Introduction

The UvT-WSD1 system described in this paper took part in two similar SemEval-2 tasks: Cross-Lingual Word Sense Disambiguation (Lefever and Hoste, 2010) and Cross-Lingual Lexical Substitution (Mihalcea et al., 2010). In each task, a number of words is selected for which the senses are to be determined for a number of instances of these words. For each word, a number of samples in context is provided, where each sample consists of one sentence, with the word to be disambiguated marked.

Because of the cross-lingual nature of the tasks, a word sense corresponds to a translation in another language, rather than a sense description in the same language. In the Cross-lingual Lexical Substitution task, the target language is Spanish. The task is to find Spanish substitutes for the English words marked in the test samples. In the Cross-Lingual Word Sense Disambiguation task, we participate for English-Dutch and English-Spanish. The Word Sense Disambiguation task provides training data for all five languages, in the form of the sentence-aligned EuroParl parallel corpus (Koehn, 2005). This is the source of training data the UvT-WSD1 system uses for both tasks.

The system may output several senses per instance, rather than producing just one sense prediction. These are evaluated in two different ways. The scoring type "**best**" expects that the system outputs the best senses, in the order of its confidence. The scoring type "**out of five/ten**" expects five or ten guesses, and each answer weighs the same. These metrics are more extensively described in (Mihalcea et al., 2010). The UvT-WSD1 system participates in both scoring types, for both tasks. The system put forth in this paper follows a similar approach as described in earlier research by (Hoste et al., 2002).

2 System Description

The UvT-WSD1 system uses machine learning techniques to learn what senses/translations are associated with any of the target words. It does so on the basis of a variety of local and global context features, discussed in Section 2.2. At the core of the system are the classifiers, or so called "word experts", one per target word. These are built using the Tilburg Memory Based Learner (TiMBL) (Daelemans et al., 2009), making use of the IB1 algorithm, an implementation of the k-nearest neighbour classifier.

The core of the system can be subdivided into roughly three stages. In the first stage, the word-aligned parallel corpus is read and for each found instance of one of the target words, features are extracted to be used in the classifier. The class consists of the word aligned to the found instance of the target word, i.e. the translation/sense. In this way a word expert is built for each of the target

Proceedings of the 5th International Workshop on Semantic Evaluation, ACL 2010, pages 238–241,
Uppsala, Sweden, 15-16 July 2010.

words in the task, yielding a total amount of classifiers equal to the total amount of target words. The test data is processed in a similar way, for each marked occurrence of any of the target words, features are extracted and test instances are created. Subsequently, the word experts are trained and tested, and on the basis of the training data, a parameter search algorithm (Van den Bosch, 2004) determines the optimal set of classifier parameters for each word expert, including for example the value of k and the distance weighting metric used.

In the last phase, the classifier output of each word expert is parsed. The classifiers yield a distribution of classes per test instance, and these are converted to the appropriate formats for "best" and "out of five/ten" evaluation. For the latter scoring type, the five/ten highest scoring senses are selected, for the former scoring type, all classes scoring above a certain threshold are considered "best". The threshold is set at 90% of the score of the highest scoring class.

2.1 Word-Alignment, Tokenisation, Lemmatisation and Part-of-Speech-tagging

The Europarl parallel corpus, English-Spanish and English-Dutch, is delivered as a sentence-aligned parallel corpus. We subsequently run GIZA++ (Och and Ney, 2000) to compute a word-aligned parallel corpus.

This, however, is not the sole input. The target words in both tasks are actually specified as a lemma and part-of-speech tag pair, rather than words. In the Word Sense Disambiguation task, all target lemmas are simply nouns, but in the Cross-Lingual Lexical Substitution task, they can also be verbs, adjectives or adverbs. Likewise, both tasks expect the sense/translation output to also be in the form of lemmas. Therefore the system internally has to be aware of the lemma and part-of-speech tag of each word in the parallel corpus and test data, only then can it successfully find all occurrences of the target words. In order to get this information, both sides of the word-aligned parallel corpus are run through tokenisers, lemmatisers and Part-of-Speech taggers, and the tokenised output is realigned with the untokenised input so the word alignments are retained. The test data is also processed this way. For English and Spanish, the software suite Freeling (Atserias et al., 2006) performed all these tasks, and for Dutch it was done by Tadpole (Van den Bosch et al., 2007).

2.2 Feature Extraction

The system can extract a variety of features to be used in training and testing. A distinction can be made between *local context features* and *global context features*. Local context features are extracted from the immediate neighbours of the occurrence of the target word. One or more of the following local context features are extractable by the UvT-WSD1 system: word features, lemma features, and part-of-speech tag features. In each case, n features both to the right and left of the focus word are selected. Moreover, the system also supports the extraction of bigram features, but these did not perform well in the experiments.

The global context features are made up of a bag-of-words representation of keywords that *may* be indicative for a given word to sense/translation mapping. The idea is that words are collected which have a certain power of discrimination for the specific target word with a specific sense, and all such words are then put in a bag-of-word representation, yielding as many features as the amount of keywords found. A global count over the full corpus is needed to find these keywords. Each keyword acts as a binary feature, indicating whether or not that particular keyword is found in the context of the occurrence of the target word. The context in which these keywords are searched for is exactly one sentence, i.e. the sentence in which the target word occurs. This is due to the test data simply not supplying a wider context.

The method used to extract these keywords (k) is proposed by (Ng and Lee, 1996) and used also in the research of (Hoste et al., 2002). Assume we have a focus word f, more precisely, a lemma and part-of-speech tag pair of one of the target words. We also have one of its aligned translations/senses s, which in this implementation is also a lemma. We can now estimate $P(s|k)$, the probability of sense s, given a keyword k, by dividing $N_{s,k_{local}}$. (the number of occurrences of a possible local context word k with particular focus word lemma-PoS combination and with a particular sense s) by $N_{k_{local}}$ (the number of occurrences of a possible local context keyword k_{loc} with a particular focus word-PoS combination regardless of its sense). If we also take into account the frequency of a possible keyword k in the complete training corpus ($N_{k_{corpus}}$), we get:

$$P(s|k) = \frac{N_{s,k_{local}}}{N_{k_{local}}}(\frac{1}{N_{k_{corpus}}}) \quad (1)$$

(Hoste et al., 2002) select a keyword k for inclusion in the bag-of-words representation if that keyword occurs more than T_1 times in that sense s, and if $P(s|k) \geq T_2$. Both T_1 and T_2 are predefined thresholds, which by default were set to 3 and 0.001 respectively. In addition, UvT-WSD1 contains an extra parameter which can be enabled to automatically adjust the T_1 threshold when it yields too many or too few keywords. The selection of bag-of-word features is computed prior to the extraction of the training instances, as this information is a prerequisite for the successful generation of both training and test instances.

2.3 Voting system

The local and global context features, and the various parameters that can be configured for extraction, yield a lot of possible classifier combinations. Rather than merging all local context and global context features together in a single classifier, they can also be split over several classifiers and have an arbiter voting system do the final classification step. UvT-WSD1 also supports this approach. A voter is constructed by taking as features the class output of up to three different classifiers, trained and tested on the training data, and mapping these features onto the actual correct sense in the training data. For testing, the same approach is taken: up to three classifiers run on the test data; their output is taken as feature vector, and the voting system predicts a sense. This approach may be useful in boosting results and smoothing out errors. In our experiments we see that a voter combination often performs better than taking all features together in one single classifier. Finally, also in the voter system there is a stage of automatic parameter optimisation for TiMBL.

3 Experiments and Results

Both SemEval-2 tasks have provided trial data upon which the system could be tested during the development stage. Considering the high configurability of the various parameters for feature extraction, the search space in possible configurations and classifier parameters is vast, also due to fact that the TiMBL classifier used may take a wealth of possible parameters. As already mentioned, for the latter an automatic algorithm of parameter optimisation was used (Van den Bosch, 2004), but optimisation of the feature extraction parameters has not been automated. Rather, a selection of configurations has been manually chosen and tested during the development stage.

BEST	UvT-WSD1-v	UvT-WSD1-g
Precision & Recall	21.09	19.59
Mode Prec. & Rec.	43.76	41.02
Ranking (out of 14)	6	9
OUT OF TEN	UvT-WSD1-v	UvT-WSD1-g
Precision & Recall	58.91	55.29
Mode Prec. & Rec.	62.96	73.94
Ranking	3	4

Table 1: UvT-WSD1 results in the Cross-Lingual Lexical Substitution task

The following two configurations of features were found to perform amongst the best on the trial data. Therefore they have been selected and submitted for the contest:

1. **UvT-WSD1-v** (aka *UvT-v*) – An arbiter-voting system over three classifiers: 1) Word experts with two word features and lemma features on both sides of the focus word. 2)Word experts with global features[1]. 3) Word experts with two word features, two lemma features *and* two part-of-speech tag features.

2. **UvT-WSD1-g** (aka *UvT-g*) – Word experts with global features only.

Table 1 shows a condensed view of the results for the Cross-Lingual Lexical Substitution task. Table 2 shows the final results for the Word-Sense Disambiguation task. Note that UvT-WSD1-v and UvT-WSD1-g are two different configurations of the UvT-WSD1 system, and to conserve space these are abbreviated as UvT-v and UvT-g respectively. These are also the names used in both tasks (Lefever and Hoste, 2010; Mihalcea et al., 2010) to refer to our system.

4 Discussion and Conclusion

Cross-Lingual Word Sense Disambiguation and Cross-Lingual Lexical Substitution have proven to be hard tasks, with scores that are relatively close to baseline. This can be attributed to a noticeable trait in the system output to be inclined to assign the same majority sense to all instances.

[1]For the Cross-Lingual Lexical Substitution task only, the parameter to recompute the T_1 threshold automatically was enabled.

Dutch BEST	UvT-v	UvT-g	T3-COLEUR		
Precision & Recall	17.7	15.93	10.72 & 10.56		
Mode Prec. & Rec.	12.06	10.54	6.18 & 6.16		
Dutch OUT OF FIVE	UvT-v	UvT-g	T3-COLEUR		
Precision & Recall	34.95	34.92	21.54 & 21.22		
Mode Prec. & Rec.	24.62	19.72	12.05 & 12.03		
Spanish BEST	UvT-v	UHD-1	UvT-g	T3-COLEUR	FCC-WSD1
Precision & Recall	23.42	20.48 & 16.33	19.92	19.78 & 19.59	15.09
Mode Prec. & Rec.	24.98	28.48 & 22.19	24.17	24.59	14.31
Spanish OUT OF FIVE	UvT-g	UvT-v	FCC-WSD2	UHD-1	T3-COLEUR
Precision & Recall	43.12	42.17	40.76	38.78 & 31.81	35.84 & 35.46
Mode Prec. & Rec.	43.94	40.62	44.84	40.68 & 32.38	39.01 & 38.78

Table 2: UvT-WSD1 results in comparison to other participants in the Word-Sense Disambiguation task

In our system, we used the same configuration of feature extraction, or a voter over a set of configurations, for all word experts. The actual classifier parameters however, do differ per word expert, as they are the result of the automatic parameter optimisation algorithm. Selecting different feature extraction configurations per word expert would be a logical next step to attempt to boost results even further, as been done in (Decadt et al., 2004).

Keeping in mind the fact that different word experts may perform differently, some *general* conclusions can be drawn from the experiments on the trial data. It appears to be beneficial to include lemma features, rather than just word features. However, adding Part-of-speech features tends to have a negative impact. For these local context features, the optimum context size is often two features to the left and two features to the right of the focus word, cf. (Hendrickx et al., 2002). The global keyword features perform well, but best results are achieved if they are not mixed with the local context features in one classifier.

An arbiter voting approach over multiple classifiers helps to smooth out errors and yields the highest scores (see Tables 1 and 2). When compared to the other participants, the UvT-WSD1 system, in the voting configuration, ranks first in the Word Sense Disambiguation task, for the two language pairs in which we participated.

References

Jordi Atserias, Bernardino Casas, Elisabet Comelles, Meritxell Gonzlez, Lluís Padró, and Muntsa Padró. 2006. FreeLing 1.3: Syntactic and semantic services in an open-source NLP library . In *Proceedings of the Fifth International Conference on Language Resources and Evaluation (LREC 2006)*, Genoa, Italy. ELRA.

W. Daelemans, J. Zavrel, K. Van der Sloot, and A. Van den Bosch. 2009. TiMBL: Tilburg memory based learner, version 6.2, reference guide. Technical Report ILK 09-01, ILK Research Group, Tilburg University.

B. Decadt, V. Hoste, W. Daelemans, and A. Van den Bosch. 2004. GAMBL, genetic algorithm optimization of memory-based WSD. In R. Mihalcea and P. Edmonds, editors, *Proceedings of the Third International Workshop on the Evaluation of Systems for the Semantic Analysis of Text (Senseval-3)*, pages 108–112, New Brunswick, NJ. ACL.

I. Hendrickx, A. Van den Bosch, V. Hoste, and W. Daelemans. 2002. Dutch word sense disambiguation: Optimizing the localness of context. In *Proceedings of the Workshop on word sense disambiguation: Recent successes and future directions*, pages 61–65, Philadelphia, PA.

V. Hoste, I. Hendrickx, W. Daelemans, and A. Van den Bosch. 2002. Parameter optimization for machine learning of word sense disambiguation. *Natural Language Engineering*, 8(4):311–325.

Philipp Koehn. 2005. Europarl: A parallel corpus for statistical machine translation. In *In Proceedings of the Machine Translation Summit X ([MT]'05).*, pages 79–86.

Els Lefever and Veronique Hoste. 2010. Semeval 2010 task 3: Cross-lingual word sense disambiguation. In *Proceedings of the 5th International Workshop on Semantic Evaluations (SemEval-2010)*, Uppsala, Sweden.

Rada Mihalcea, Ravi Sinha, and Diana McCarthy. 2010. Semeval 2010 task 2: Cross-lingual lexical substitution. In *Proceedings of the 5th International Workshop on Semantic Evaluations (SemEval-2010)*, Uppsala, Sweden.

Hwee Tou Ng and Hian Beng Lee. 1996. Integrating multiple knowledge sources to disambiguate word sense: An exemplar-based approach. In *ACL*, pages 40–47.

F.J. Och and H. Ney. 2000. Giza++: Training of statistical translation models. Technical report, RWTH Aachen, University of Technology.

A. Van den Bosch, G.J. Busser, S. Canisius, and W. Daelemans. 2007. An efficient memory-based morphosyntactic tagger and parser for Dutch. In P. Dirix, I. Schuurman, V. Vandeghinste, , and F. Van Eynde, editors, *Computational Linguistics in the Netherlands: Selected Papers from the Seventeenth CLIN Meeting*, pages 99–114, Leuven, Belgium.

A. Van den Bosch. 2004. Wrapped progressive sampling search for optimizing learning algorithm parameters. In R. Verbrugge, N. Taatgen, and L. Schomaker, editors, *Proceedings of the Sixteenth Belgian-Dutch Conference on Artificial Intelligence*, pages 219–226, Groningen, The Netherlands.

UBA: Using Automatic Translation and Wikipedia for Cross-Lingual Lexical Substitution

Pierpaolo Basile
Dept. of Computer Science
University of Bari "Aldo Moro"
Via E. Orabona, 4
70125 Bari (ITALY)
basilepp@di.uniba.it

Giovanni Semeraro
Dept. of Computer Science
University of Bari "Aldo Moro"
Via E. Orabona, 4
70125 Bari (ITALY)
semeraro@di.uniba.it

Abstract

This paper presents the participation of the University of Bari (UBA) at the SemEval-2010 Cross-Lingual Lexical Substitution Task. The goal of the task is to substitute a word in a language L_s, which occurs in a particular context, by providing the best synonyms in a different language L_t which fit in that context. This task has a strict relation with the task of automatic machine translation, but there are some differences: Cross-lingual lexical substitution targets one word at a time and the main goal is to find as many good translations as possible for the given target word. Moreover, there are some connections with Word Sense Disambiguation (WSD) algorithms. Indeed, understanding the meaning of the target word is necessary to find the best substitutions. An important aspect of this kind of task is the possibility of finding synonyms without using a particular sense inventory or a specific parallel corpus, thus allowing the participation of unsupervised approaches. UBA proposes two systems: the former is based on an automatic translation system which exploits Google Translator, the latter is based on a parallel corpus approach which relies on Wikipedia in order to find the best substitutions.

1 Introduction

The goal of the Cross-Lingual Lexical Substitution (CLLS) task is to substitute a word in a language L_s, which occurs in a particular context, by providing the best substitutions in a different language L_t. In SemEval-2010 the source language L_s is English, while the target language L_t is Spanish. Clearly, this task is related to Lexical Substitution (LS) (McCarthy and Navigli, 2007) which consists in selecting an alternative word for a given one in a particular context by preserving its meaning. The main difference between the LS task and the CLLS one is that in LS source and target languages are the same. CLLS is not a easy task since neither a list of candidate words nor a specific parallel corpus are supplied by the organizers. However, this opens the possibility of using several knowledge sources, instead of a single one fixed by the task organizers. Therefore, the system must identify a set of candidate words in L_t and then select only those words which fit the context. From another point of view, the cross-lingual nature of the task allows to exploit automatic machine translation methods, hence the goal is to find as many good translations as possible for the given target word. A thorough description of the task can be found in (Mihalcea et al., 2010; Sinha et al., 2009).

To easily understand the task, an example follows. Consider the sentence:

> *During the siege, George Robertson had appointed Shuja-ul-Mulk , who was a* ***bright*** *boy only 12 years old and the youngest surviving son of Aman-ul-Mulk, as the ruler of Chitral.*

In the previous sentence the target word is "**bright**". Taking into account the meaning of the word "**bright**" in this particular context, the best substitutions in Spanish are: "**inteligente**", "**brillante**" and "**listo**".

We propose two systems to tackle the problem of CLLS: the first is based on an automatic translation system which exploits the API of Google Translator[1], the second is based on a parallel corpus approach which relies on Wikipedia. In particular, in the second approach we use a structured version of Wikipedia called DBpedia (Bizer

[1] http://code.google.com/p/google-api-translate-java/

Proceedings of the 5th International Workshop on Semantic Evaluation, ACL 2010, pages 242–247,
Uppsala, Sweden, 15-16 July 2010. ©2010 Association for Computational Linguistics

et al., 2009). Both systems adopt several lexical resources to select the list of possible substitutions for a given word. Specifically, we use three different dictionaries: Google Dictionary, Babylon Dictionary and Spanishdict. Then, we combine the dictionaries into a single one, as described in Section 2.1.

The paper is organized as follows: Section 2 describes the strategy we adopted to tackle the CLLS task, while results of an experimental session we carried out in order to evaluate the proposed approaches are presented in Section 3. Conclusions are discussed in Section 4.

2 Methodology

Generally speaking, the problem of CLLS can be coped with a strategy which consists of two steps, as suggested in (Sinha et al., 2009):

- *candidate collection*: in this step several resources are queried to retrieve a list of potential translation candidates for each target word and part of speech;
- *candidate selection*: this step concerns the ranking of potential candidates, which are the most suitable ones for each instance, by using information about the context.

Regarding the candidate collection, we exploit three dictionaries: Google Dictionary, Babylon Dictionary and Spanishdict. Each dictionary is modeled using a strategy described in Section 2.1. We use the same approach to model each dictionary in order to make easy both the inclusion of future dictionaries and the integration with the candidate selection step.

Candidate selection is performed in two different ways. The first one relies on the automatic translation of the sentence in which the target word occurs, in order to find the best substitutions. The second method uses a parallel corpus built on DBpedia to discover the number of documents in which the target word is translated by one of the potential translation candidates. Details about both methods are reported in Section 2.2

2.1 Candidate collection

This section describes the method adopted to retrieve the list of potential translation candidates for each target word and part of speech.

Our strategy combines several bi-lingual dictionaries and builds a single list of candidates for each target word. The involved dictionaries meet the following requirements:

1. the source language L_s must be English and the target one L_t must be Spanish;
2. each dictionary must provide information about the part of speech;
3. the dictionary must be freely available.

Moreover, each candidate has a score s_{ij} computed by taking into account its rank in the list of possible translations supplied by the $i-th$ dictionary. Formally, let us denote by $D = \{d_1, d_2, \ldots, d_n\}$ the set of n dictionaries and by $L_i = \{c_1, c_2, \ldots, c_{m_i}\}$ the list of potential candidates provided by d_i. The score s_{ij} is computed by the following equation:

$$s_{ij} = 1 - \frac{j}{m_i} \quad j \in \{1, 2, \ldots, m_i\} \tag{1}$$

Since each list L_i has a different size, we adopt a score normalization strategy based on Z-score to merge the lists in a unique one. Z-score normalizes the scores according to the average μ and standard deviation σ. Given the list of scores $L = \{s_1, s_2, \ldots, s_n\}$, μ and σ are computed on L and the normalized score is defined as:

$$\overline{s_i} = \frac{s_i - \mu}{\sigma} \tag{2}$$

Then, all the lists L_i are merged in a single list M. The list M contains all the potential candidates belonging to all the dictionaries with the related score. If a candidate occurs in more than one dictionary, only the occurrence with the maximum score is chosen.

At the end of the candidate collection step the list M of potential translation candidates for each target word is computed. It is important to point out that the list M is sorted and supplies an initial rank, which can be then modified by the candidate selection step.

2.2 Candidate selection

While the candidate collection step is common to the two proposed systems, the problem of candidate selection is faced by using different strategies in the two systems.

The first system, called `unibaTranslate`, uses a method based on google-api-translate-java[2]. The main idea behind `unibaTranslate` is to look for a potential candidate in the translation of the target sentence. Sometimes, no potential candidates occur into the translation. When this happens the system uses some heuristics to discover a possible translation.

For example, given the target word **"raw"** and the potential candidates $M = \{$*puro, crudo, sin refinar, de baja calidad, agrietado, al natural, bozal, asado, frito and bruto*$\}$, the two possible scenarios are:

1. a potential candidate occurs into the translation:
   - S_{en}: *The **raw** honesty of that basic crudeness makes you feel stronger in a way.*
   - S_{es}: *La **cruda** honestidad de esa crudeza de base que te hace sentir mas fuerte en un camino.*
2. no potential candidates occur into the translation, but a correct translation of the target word is provided:
   - S_{en}: *Many institutional investors are now deciding that they are getting a **raw** deal from the company boards of Australia.*
   - S_{es}: *Muchos inversores institucionales estan ahora decidiendo que estan recibiendo un trato **injusto** de los directorios de las empresas de Australia.*

In detail, the strategy can be split in several steps:

1. Retrieve the list M of potential translation candidates using the method described in Section 2.1.
2. Translate the target sentence S_{en} from English to Spanish, using the google-api-translate-java, which results into the sentence S_{es}.
3. Enrich M by adding multiword expressions. To implement this step, the two bigrams which contain the target word and the only trigram in which the target word is the 2nd term are taken into to account.

   Coming back to the first sentence in the previous example, the following n-grams are built: *"the raw"*, *"raw honesty"* and *"the raw honesty"*. For each n-gram, candidate translations are looked for using Google Dictionary. If translations are found, they are added to M with an initial score equal to 0.
4. Fix a window W^3 of n words to the right and to the left of the target word, and perform the following steps:
   (a) for each candidate c_k in M, try to find c_k in W. If c_k occurs in W, then add 2 to the score of c_k in M;
   (b) if no exact match is found in the previous step, perform a new search by comparing c_k with the words in W using the Levenshtein distance[4](Levenshtein, 1966). If the Levenshtein distance is greater than 0.8, then add 2 to the score of c_k in M.
5. If no exact/partial match is found in the previous steps, probably the target word is translated with a word which does not belong to M. To overcome this problem, we implement a strategy able to discover a possible translation in S_{es} which is not in M. This approach involves three steps:
   (a) for each word w_i in S_{en}, a list of potential translations P_i is retrieved;
   (b) if a word in P_i is found in S_{es}, the word is removed from S_{es}[5];
   (c) at this point, S_{es} contains a list R of words with no candidate translations. A score is assigned to those words by taking into account their position in S_{es} with respect to the position of the target word in S_{en}, using the following equation:

$$1 - \frac{|pos_c - pos_t|}{L_{max}} \quad (3)$$

   where pos_c is the translation candidate position in S_{es}, pos_t is the target word position in S_{en} and L_{max} is the maximum length between the length of S_{en} and S_{es}.

[2]http://code.google.com/p/google-api-translate-java/

[3]The window W is the same for both S_{en} and S_{es}.

[4]A normalized Levenshtein distance is adopted to obtain a value in [0, 1].

[5]A partial match based on normalized Levenshtein distance is implemented.

Moreover, the words not semantically related to the potential candidates (found using Spanish WordNet[6]) are removed from R. In detail, for each candidate in M a list of semantically related words in Spanish WordNet[7] is retrieved which results in a set WN of related words. Words in R but not in WN are removed from R. In the final step, the list R is sorted and the first word in R is added to M assigning a score equal to 2.

6. In the last step, the list M is sorted. The output of this process is the ranked list of potential candidates.

It is important to underline that both S_{en} and S_{es} are tokenized, part-of-speech tagged and lemmatized. Lemmatization plays a key role in the matching step, while part-of-speech tagging is needed to query both the dictionaries and the Spanish WordNet. We adopt META (Basile et al., 2008) and FreeLing (Atserias et al., 2006) to perform text processing for English and Spanish respectively.

The second proposed system, called `unibaWiki`, is based on the idea of automatically building a parallel corpus from Wikipedia. We use a structured version of Wikipedia called DBpedia (Bizer et al., 2009). The main idea behind DBpedia is to extract structured information from Wikipedia and then to make this information available. The main goal is to have access easily to the large amount of information in Wikipedia. DBpedia opens new and interesting ways to use Wikipedia in NLP applications.

In CLLS task, we use the extended abstracts of English and Spanish provided by DBpedia. For each extended abstract in Spanish which has the corresponding extended abstract in English, we build a document composed by two fields: the former contains the English text ($text_{en}$) and the latter contains the Spanish text ($text_{es}$). We adopt Lucene[8] as storage and retrieval engine to make the documents access fast and easy.

The idea behind `unibaWiki` is to count, for each potential candidate, the number of documents in which the target word occurs in $text_{en}$ and the potential candidate occurs in $text_{es}$. A score equal to the number of retrieved documents is assigned, then the candidates are sorted according to that score.

Given the list M of potential candidates and the target word t, for each $c_k \in M$ we perform the following query:

$$text_{en} : t \text{ AND } text_{es} : c_k$$

where the field name is followed by a colon and by the term you are looking for.

It is important to underline here that multiword expressions require a specific kind of query. For each multiword expression we adopt the PhraseQuery which is able to retrieve documents that contain a specific sequence of words instead of a single keyword.

2.3 Implementation

To implement the candidate collection step we developed a Java application able to retrieve information from dictionaries. For each dictionary, a different strategy has been adopted. In particular:

1. *Google Dictionary*: Google Dictionary website is queried by using the HTTP protocol and the answer page is parsed;

2. *Spanishdict*: the same strategy adopted for Google Dictionary is used for the Spanishdict website[9];

3. *Babylon Dictionary*: the original file available from the Babylon website[10] is converted to obtain a plain text file by using the Unix utility *dictconv*. After that, an application queries the text file in an efficient way by means of a hash map.

Both candidate selection systems are developed in Java. Regarding the `unibaWiki` system, we adopt Lucene to index DBpedia abstracts. The output of Lucene is an index of about 680 Mbytes, 277,685 documents and about 1,500,000 terms.

3 Evaluation

The goal of the evaluation is to measure the systems' ability to find correct Spanish substitutions for a given word. The dataset supplied by the organizers contains 1,000 instances in XML format.

[6] http://www.lsi.upc.edu/~nlp/projectes/ewn.html

[7] The semantic relations of hyperonymy, hyponymy and "similar to" are exploited.

[8] http://lucene.apache.org/

[9] http://www.spanishdict.com/

[10] www.babylon.com

Moreover, the organizers provide trial data composed by 300 instances to help the participants during the development of their systems.

The systems are evaluated using two scoring types: **best** scores the best guessed substitution, while out-of-ten (**oot**) scores the best 10 guessed substitutions. For each scoring type, precision (*P*) and recall (*R*) are computed. Mode precision (*P-mode*) and mode recall (*R-mode*) calculate precision and recall against the substitution chosen by the majority of the annotators (if there is a majority), respectively. Details about evaluation and scoring types are provided in the task guidelines (McCarthy et al., 2009).

Results of the evaluation using trial data are reported in Table 1 and Table 2. Our systems are tagged as **UBA-T** and **UBA-W**, which denote `unibaTranslate` and `unibaWiki`, respectively. Systems marked as *BL-1* and *BL-2* are the two baselines provided by the organizers. The baselines use Spanishdict dictionary to retrieve candidates. The system *BL-1* ranks the candidates according to the order returned on the online query page, while the *BL-2* rank is based on candidate frequencies in the Spanish Wikipedia.

Table 1: **best** results (trial data)

System	P	R	P-mode	R-Mode
BL-1	24.50	24.50	51.80	51.80
BL-2	14.10	14.10	28.38	28.38
UBA-T	**26.39**	**26.39**	**59.01**	**59.01**
UBA-W	22.18	22.18	48.65	48.65

Table 2: **oot** results (trial data)

System	P	R	P-mode	R-Mode
BL-1	38.58	38.58	71.62	71.62
BL-2	37.83	37.83	68.02	68.02
UBA-T	44.16	44.16	**78.38**	**78.38**
UBA-W	**45.15**	**45.15**	72.52	72.52

Results obtained using trial data show that our systems are able to overcome the baselines. Only the best score achieved by *UBA-W* is below *BL-1*. Moreover, our strategy based on Wikipedia (*UBA-W*) works better than the one proposed by the organizers (*BL-2*).

Results of the evaluation using test data are reported in Table 3 and Table 4, which include all the participants. Results show that *UBA-T* obtains the highest recall using **best** scoring strategy. Moreover, both systems *UBA-T* and *UBA-W* achieve the highest *R*-mode and *P*-mode using **oot** scoring strategy. It is worthwhile to point out that the presence of duplicates affect recall (*R*) and precision (*P*), but not *R*-mode and *P*-mode. For this reason some systems, such as *SWAT-E*, obtain very high recall (*R*) and low *R*-mode using **oot** scoring. Duplicates are not produced by our systems, but we performed an a posteriori experiment in which duplicates are allowed. In that experiment, the first candidate provided by *UBA-T* has been duplicated ten times in the results. Using that strategy, *UBA-T* achieves a recall (and precision) equal to 271.51. This experiment proves that also our system is able to obtain the highest recall when duplicates are allowed into the results. Moreover, it is important to underline here that we do not know how other participants generate duplicates in their results. We adopted a trivial strategy to introduce duplicates.

Table 3: **best** results (test data)

System	P	R	P-mode	R-Mode
BL-1	24.34	24.34	50.34	50.34
BL-2	15.09	15.09	29.22	29.22
UBA-T	**27.15**	**27.15**	57.20	57.20
UBA-W	19.68	19.68	39.09	39.09
USPWLV	26.81	26.81	**58.85**	**58.85**
Colslm	27.59	25.99	59.16	56.24
WLVUSP	25.27	25.27	52.81	52.81
SWAT-E	21.46	21.46	43.21	43.21
UvT-v	21.09	21.09	43.76	43.76
CU-SMT	21.62	20.56	45.01	44.58
UvT-g	19.59	19.59	41.02	41.02
SWAT-S	18.87	18.87	36.63	36.63
ColEur	19.47	18.15	40.03	37.72
IRST-1	22.16	15.38	45.95	33.47
IRSTbs	22.51	13.21	45.27	28.26
TYO	8.62	8.39	15.31	14.95

Table 4: **oot** results (test data)

System	P	R	P-mode	R-Mode
BL-1	44.04	44.04	73.53	73.53
BL-2	42.65	42.65	71.60	71.60
UBA-T	47.99	47.99	81.07	81.07
UBA-W	52.75	52.75	**83.54**	**83.54**
USPWLV	47.60	47.60	79.84	79.84
Colslm	46.61	43.91	69.41	65.98
WLVUSP	48.48	48.48	77.91	77.91
SWAT-E	**174.59**	**174.59**	66.94	66.94
UvT-v	58.91	58.91	62.96	62.96
UvT-g	55.29	55.29	73.94	73.94
SWAT-S	97.98	97.98	79.01	79.01
ColEur	44.77	41.72	71.47	67.35
IRST-1	33.14	31.48	58.30	55.42
IRSTbs	29.74	8.33	64.44	19.89
TYO	35.46	34.54	59.16	58.02
FCC-LS	23.90	23.90	31.96	31.96

Finally, Table 5 reports some statistics about *UBA-T* and the number of times (*N*) the candidate translation is taken from Spanish WordNet (*Spanish WN*) or multiword expressions (*Multiword exp.*). The number of instances in which the candidate is a correct substitution is reported in column *C*. Analyzing the results we note that most errors are due to part-of-speech tagging. For example, given the following sentence:

S_{en}: You will still be responsible for the shipping and handling fees, and for the cost of **returning** the merchandise.

S_{es}: Usted seguira siendo responsable de los gastos de envio y manipulacion y, para los gastos de **devolucion** de la mercancia.

where the target word is the verb *return*. In this case the verb is used as noun and the algorithm suggests correctly *devolucion* (noun) as substitution instead of *devolver* (verb). The gold standard provided by the organizers contains *devolver* as substitution and there is no match between *devolucion* and *devolver* during the scoring.

Table 5: *UBA-T* statistics.

Strategy	N	C
Spanish WN	34	11
Multiword exp.	21	11

4 Conclusions

We described our participation at SemEval-2 Cross-Lingual Lexical Substitution Task, proposing two systems called *UBA-T* and *UBA-W*. The first relies on Google Translator, the second is based on DBpedia, a structured version of Wikipedia. Moreover, we exploited several dictionaries to retrieve the list of candidate substitutions.

UBA-T achieves the highest recall among all the participants to the task. Moreover, the results proved that the method based on Google Translator is more effective than the one based on DBpedia.

Acknowledgments

This research was partially funded by Regione Puglia under the contract POR PUGLIA 2007-2013 - Asse I Linea 1.1 Azione 1.1.2 - Bando "Aiuti agli Investimenti in Ricerca per le PMI" - Fondo per le Agevolazioni alla Ricerca, project title: "Natural Browsing".

References

Jordi Atserias, Bernardino Casas, Elisabet Comelles, Meritxell González, Lluís Padró, and Muntsa Padró. 2006. FreeLing 1.3: Syntactic and semantic services in an open-source NLP library. In *Proceedings of the 5th International Conference on Language Resources and Evaluation (LREC06)*, pages 48–55.

Pierpaolo Basile, Marco de Gemmis, Anna Lisa Gentile, Leo Iaquinta, Pasquale Lops, and Giovanni Semeraro. 2008. META - MultilanguagE Text Analyzer. In *Proceedings of the Language and Speech Technnology Conference - LangTech 2008, Rome, Italy, February 28-29*, pages 137–140.

Christian Bizer, Jens Lehmann, Georgi Kobilarov, Sören Auer, Christian Becker, Richard Cyganiak, and Sebastian Hellmann. 2009. DBpedia-A crystallization point for the Web of Data. *Web Semantics: Science, Services and Agents on the World Wide Web*, Issue 7:154–165.

Vladimir Iosifovich Levenshtein. 1966. Binary codes capable of correcting deletions, insertions, and reversals. In *Soviet Physics-Doklady*, volume 10.

Diana McCarthy and Roberto Navigli. 2007. SemEval-2007 Task 10: English Lexical Substitution Task. In *Proceedings of the Fourth International Workshop on Semantic Evaluations (SemEval-2007)*, pages 48–53, Prague, Czech Republic, June. Association for Computational Linguistics.

Diana McCarthy, Rada Sinha, and Ravi Mihalcea. 2009. Cross Lingual Lexical Substitution. http://lit.csci.unt.edu/DOCS/task2clls-documentation.pdf.

Rada Mihalcea, Ravi Sinha, and Diana McCarthy. 2010. SemEval-2010 Task 2: Cross-Lingual Lexical Substitution. In *Proceedings of the 5th International Workshop on Semantic Evaluations (SemEval-2010)*. Association for Computational Linguistics.

Ravi Sinha, Diana McCarthy, and Rada Mihalcea. 2009. SemEval-2010 Task 2: cross-lingual lexical substitution. In *SEW '09: Proceedings of the Workshop on Semantic Evaluations: Recent Achievements and Future Directions*, pages 76–81, Morristown, NJ, USA. Association for Computational Linguistics.

HUMB: Automatic Key Term Extraction from Scientific Articles in GROBID

Patrice Lopez
INRIA
Berlin, Germany
patrice_lopez@hotmail.com

Laurent Romary
INRIA & HUB-IDSL
Berlin, Germany
laurent.romary@inria.fr

Abstract

The Semeval task 5 was an opportunity for experimenting with the key term extraction module of GROBID, a system for extracting and generating bibliographical information from technical and scientific documents. The tool first uses GROBID's facilities for analyzing the structure of scientific articles, resulting in a first set of structural features. A second set of features captures content properties based on phraseness, informativeness and keywordness measures. Two knowledge bases, GRISP and Wikipedia, are then exploited for producing a last set of lexical/semantic features. Bagged decision trees appeared to be the most efficient machine learning algorithm for generating a list of ranked key term candidates. Finally a post ranking was realized based on statistics of co-usage of keywords in HAL, a large Open Access publication repository.

1 Introduction

Key terms (or keyphrases or keywords) are metadata providing general information about the content of a document. Their selection by authors or readers is, to a large extent, subjective which makes automatic extraction difficult. This is, however, a valuable exercise, because such key terms constitute good topic descriptions of documents which can be used in particular for information retrieval, automatic document clustering and classification. Used as subject headings, better keywords can lead to higher retrieval rates of an article in a digital library.

We view automatic key term extraction as a subtask of the general problem of extraction of technical terms which is crucial in technical and scientific documents (Ahmad and Collingham, 1996). Among the extracted terms for a given scientific document in a given collection, which key terms best characterize this document?

This article describes the system realized for the Semeval 2010 task 5, based on GROBID's (**G**ene**R**ation **O**f **BI**bilographic **D**ata) module dedicated to key term extraction. GROBID is a tool for analyzing technical and scientific documents, focusing on automatic bibliographical data extraction (header, citations, etc.) (Lopez, 2009) and structure recognition (section titles, figures, etc).

As the space for the system description is very limited, this presentation focuses on key aspects. We present first an overview of our approach, then our selection of features (section 3), the different tested machine learning models (section 4) and the final post-ranking (section 5). We briefly describe our unsuccessful experiments (section 6) and we conclude by discussing future works.

2 Bases

Principle As most of the successful works for keyphrase extraction, our approach relies on Machine Learning (ML). The following steps are applied to each document to be processed:

1. Analysis of the structure of the article.
2. Selection of candidate terms.
3. Calculation of features.
4. Application of a ML model for evaluating each candidate term independently.
5. Final re-ranking for capturing relationships between the term candidates.

For creating the ML model, steps 1-3 are applied to the articles of the training set. We view steps 1 and 5 as our main novel contributions. The structure analysis permits the usage of reliable features in relation to the logical composition of the article to be processed. The final re-ranking exploits

Proceedings of the 5th International Workshop on Semantic Evaluation, ACL 2010, pages 248–251,
Uppsala, Sweden, 15-16 July 2010.

general relationships between the set of candidates which cannot be captured by the ML models.

Candidate term selection In the following, *word* should be understood as similar to *token* in the sense of MAF[1]. Step 2 has been implemented in a standard manner, as follows:

1. Extract all n-grams up to 5 words,
2. Remove all candidate n-grams starting or ending with a stop word,
3. Filter from these candidates terms having mathematical symbols,
4. Normalize each candidate by lowercasing and by stemming using the Porter stemmer.

Training data The task's collection consists of articles from the ACM (Association for Computational Machinery) in four narrow domains (*C.2.4* Distributed Systems, *H.3.3* Information Search and Retrieval, *I.2.6* Learning and *J.4* Social and Behavioral Sciences). As training data, we used this task's training resources (144 articles from ACM) and the National University of Singapore (NUS) corpus[2] (156 ACM articles from all computing domains). Adding the additional NUS training data improved our final results (+7.4% for the F-score at top 15, i.e. from 25.6 to 27.5).

3 Features

3.1 Structural features

One of the goals of GROBID is to realize reliable conversions of technical and scientific documents in PDF to fully compliant TEI[3] documents. This conversion implies first the recognition of the different sections of the document, then the extraction of all header metadata and references. The analysis is realized in GROBID with Conditional Random Fields (CRF) (Peng and McCallum, 2004) exploiting a large amount of training data. We added to this training set a few ACM documents manually annotated and obtained a very high performance for field recognitions, between 97% (section titles, reference titles) and 99% (title, abstract) accuracy for the task's collection.

Authors commonly introduce the main concepts of a written communication in the header (title, abstract, table of contents), the introduction, the section titles, the conclusion and the reference list. Similarly human readers/annotators typically focus their attention on the same document parts. We introduced thus the following 6 binary features characterizing the position of a term with respect to the document structure for each candidate: present in the *title*, in the *abstract*, in the *introduction*, in at least one *section titles*, in the *conclusion*, in at least one *reference or book title*.

In addition, we used the following standard feature: the *position of the first occurrence*, calculated as the number of words which precede the first occurrence of the term divided by the number of words in the document, similarly as, for instance, (Witten et al., 1999).

3.2 Content features

The second set of features used in this work tries to captures distributional properties of a term relatively to the overall textual content of the document where the term appears or the collection.

Phraseness The phraseness measures the lexical cohesion of a sequence of words in a given document, i.e. the degree to which it can be considered as a phrase. This measure is classically used for term extraction and can rely on different techniques, usually evaluating the ability of a sequence of words to appear as a stable phrase more often than just by chance. We applied here the Generalized Dice Coeficient (GDC) as introduced by (Park et al., 2002), applicable to any arbitrary n-gram of words ($n \geq 2$). For a given term T, $\mid T \mid$ being the number of words in T, $freq(T)$ the frequency of occurrence of T and $freq(w_i)$ the frequency of occurrence of the word w_i, we have:

$$GDC(T) = \frac{\mid T \mid log_{10}(freq(T))freq(T)}{\sum_{w_i \in T} freq(w_i)}$$

We used a default value for a single word, because, in this case, the association measure is not meaningful as it depends only on the frequency.

Informativeness The *informativeness* of a term is the degree to which the term is representative of a document given a collection of documents. Once again many measures can be relevant, and we opt for the standard TF-IDF value which is used in most of the keyphrase extraction systems, see for instance (Witten et al., 1999) or (Medelyan and

[1] Morpho-syntactic Annotation Framework, see http://pauillac.inria.fr/ clerger/MAF/
[2] http://wing.comp.nus.edu.sg/downloads/keyphraseCorpus
[3] Text Encoding Initiative (TEI), http://www.tei-c.org.

Witten, 2008). The TF-IDF score for a Term T in document D is given by:

$$\text{TF-IDF}(T, D) = \frac{freq(T, D)}{\mid D \mid} \times -log_2 \frac{count(T)}{N}$$

where $\mid D \mid$ is the number of words in D, $count(T)$ is the number of occurrence of the term T in the global corpus, and N is the number of documents in the corpus.

Keywordness Introduced by (Witten et al., 1999), the keywordness reflects the degree to which a term is selected as a keyword. In practice, it is simply the frequency of the keyword in the global corpus. The efficiency of this feature depends, however, on the amount of training data available and the variety of technical domains considered. As the training set of documents for this task is relatively large and narrow in term of technical domains, this feature was relevant.

3.3 Lexical/Semantic features

GRISP is a large scale terminological database for technical and scientific domains resulting from the fusion of terminological resources (MeSH, the Gene Ontology, etc.), linguistic resources (part of WordNet) and part of Wikipedia. It has been created for improving patent retrieval and classification (Lopez and Romary, 2010). The assumption is that a phrase which has been identified as controlled term in these resources tend to be a more important keyphrase. A binary feature is used to indicate if the term is part of GRISP or not.

We use Wikipedia similarly as the *Wikipedia keyphraseness* in Maui (Medelyan, 2009). The *Wikipedia keyphraseness* of a term T is the probability of an appearance of T in a document being an anchor (Medelyan, 2009). We use Wikipedia Miner[4] for obtaining this value.

Finally we introduced an additional feature commonly used in keyword extraction, the *length* of the term candidate, i.e. its number of words.

4 Machine learning model

We experimented different ML models: Decision tree (C4.5), Multi-Layer perceptron (MLP) and Support Vector Machine (SVM). In addition, we combined these models with boosting and bagging techniques. We used WEKA (Witten and Frank, 2005) for all our experiments, except for SVM where LIBSVM (Chang and Lin, 2001) was used. We failed to obtain reasonable results with SVM. Our hypothesis is that SVM is sensitive to the very large number of negative examples compared to the positive ones and additional techniques should be used for balancing the training data. Results for decision tree and MLP were similar but the latter is approx. 57 times more time-consuming for training. Bagged decision tree appeared to perform constantly better than boosting (+8,4% for F-score). The selected model for the final run was, therefore, bagged decision tree, similarly as, for instance, in (Medelyan, 2009).

5 Post-ranking

Post-ranking uses the selected candidates as a whole for improving the results, while in the previous step, each candidate was selected independently from the other. If we have a ranked list of term T_{1-N}, each having a score $s(T_i)$, the new score s' for the term T_i is obtained as follow:

$$s'(T_i) = s(T_i) + \alpha^{-1} \sum_{j \neq i} P(T_j | T_i) s(T_j)$$

where α is a constant in $[0 - 1]$ for controlling the re-ranking factor. α has been set experimentally to 0.8. $P(T_j|T_i)$ is the probability that the keyword T_j is chosen by the author when the keyword T_i has been selected. For obtaining these probabilities, we use statistics for the HAL[5] research archive. HAL contains approx. 139,000 full texts articles described by a rich set of metadata, often including author's keywords. We use the keywords appearing in English and in the Computer Science domain (a subset of 29,000 articles), corresponding to a total of 16,412 different keywords. No smoothing was used. The usage of open publication repository as a research resource is in its infancy and very promising.

6 Results

Our system was ranked first of the competition among 19 participants. Table 1 presents our official results (**P**recision, **R**ecall, **F**-score) for *combined* keywords and *reader* keywords, together with the scores of the systems ranked second (WINGNUS and KX FBK).

[4] http://wikipedia-miner.sourceforge.net

[5] HAL (Hyper Article en Ligne) is the French Institutional repository for research publications: http://hal.archives-ouvertes.fr/index.php?langue=en

Set	System	top 5	top 10	top 15
Comb.	HUMB	**P**:39.0 **R**:13.3 **F**:19.8	**F**:32.0 **R**:21.8 **F**:25.9	**P**:27.2 **R**:27.8 **F**:27.5
	WINGNUS	**P**:40.2 **R**:13.7 **F**:20.5	**P**:30.5 **R**:20.8 **F**:24.7	**P**:24.9 **R**:25.5 **F**:25.2
Reader	HUMB	**P**:30.4 **R**:12.6 **F**:17.8	**P**:24.8 **R**:20.6 **F**:22.5	**P**:21.2 **R**:26.4 **F**:23.5
	KX FBK	**P**:29.2 **R**:12.1 **F**:17.1	**P**:23.2 **R**:19.3 **F**:21.1	**P**:20.3 **R**:25.3 **F**:22.6

Table 1: Performance of our system (HUMB) and of the systems ranked second.

7 What did not work

The previously described features were selected because they all had a positive impact on the extraction accuracy based on our experiments on the task's collection. The following intuitively pertinent ideas appeared, however, to deteriorate or to be neutral for the results.

Noun phrase filtering We applied a filtering of noun phrases based on a POS tagging and extraction of all possible NP based on typical patterns. This filtering lowered both the recall and the precision (-7.6% for F-score at top 15).

Term variants We tried to apply a post-ranking by conflating term variants using FASTR[6], resulting in a disappointing -11.5% for the F-score.

Global keywordness We evaluated the keywordness using also the overall HAL keyword frequencies rather than only the training corpus. It had no impact on the results.

Language Model deviation We experimented the usage of HMM deviation using LingPipe[7] as alternative informativeness measure, resulting in -3.7% for the F-score at top 15.

Wikipedia term Relatedness Using Wikipedia Miner, we tried to apply as post-ranking a boosting of related terms, but saw no impact on the results.

8 Future work

We think that automatic key term extraction can be highly valuable for assisting self-archiving of research papers by authors in scholarly repositories such as arXiv or HAL. We plan to experiment keyword suggestions in HAL based on the present system. Many archived research papers are currently not associated with any keyword.

We also plan to adapt our module to a large collection of approx. 2.6 million patent documents in the context of CLEF IP 2010. This will be the opportunity to evaluate the relevance of the extracted key terms for large scale topic-based IR.

[6] http://perso.limsi.fr/jacquemi/FASTR

[7] http://alias-i.com/lingpipe

References

K. Ahmad and S. Collingham. 1996. Pointer project final report. Technical report, University of Surrey. http://www.computing.surrey.ac.uk/ai/pointer/report.

C.-C. Chang and C.-J. Lin. 2001. Libsvm: a library for support vector machines. Technical report.

P. Lopez and L. Romary. 2010. GRISP: A Massive Multilingual Terminological Database for Scientific and Technical Domains. In *Seventh international conference on Language Resources and Evaluation (LREC)*, Valletta, Malta.

P. Lopez. 2009. GROBID: Combining Automatic Bibliographic Data Recognition and Term Extraction for Scholarship Publications. In *Proceedings of ECDL 2009, 13th European Conference on Digital Library*, Corfu, Greece.

O. Medelyan and I.H. Witten. 2008. Domain-independent automatic keyphrase indexing with small training sets. *Journal of the American Society for Information Science and Technology*, 59(7):1026–1040.

O. Medelyan. 2009. *Human-competitive automatic topic indexing*. Ph.D. thesis.

Y. Park, R.J. Byrd, and B.K. Boguraev. 2002. Automatic glossary extraction: beyond terminology identification. In *Proceedings of the 19th international conference on Computational linguistics-Volume 1*, pages 1–7. Association for Computational Linguistics.

F. Peng and A. McCallum. 2004. Accurate information extraction from research papers using conditional random fields. In *Proceedings of HLT-NAACL*, Boston, USA.

I.H. Witten and E. Frank. 2005. *Data Mining: Practical machine learning tools and techniques*. Morgan Kaufmann, San Francisco, 2nd edition edition.

I.H. Witten, G.W. Paynter, E. Frank, C. Gutwin, and C.G. Nevill-Manning. 1999. KEA: Practical automatic keyphrase extraction. In *Proceedings of the fourth ACM conference on Digital libraries*, page 255. ACM.

UTDMet: Combining WordNet and Corpus Data for Argument Coercion Detection

Kirk Roberts and Sanda Harabagiu
Human Language Technology Research Institute
University of Texas at Dallas
Richardson, Texas, USA
{kirk,sanda}@hlt.utdallas.edu

Abstract

This paper describes our system for the classification of argument coercion for SemEval-2010 Task 7. We present two approaches to classifying an argument's semantic class, which is then compared to the predicate's expected semantic class to detect coercions. The first approach is based on learning the members of an arbitrary semantic class using WordNet's hypernymy structure. The second approach leverages automatically extracted semantic parse information from a large corpus to identify similar arguments by the predicates that select them. We show the results these approaches obtain on the task as well as how they can improve a traditional feature-based approach.

1 Introduction

Argument coercion (a type of *metonymy*) occurs when the expected semantic class (relative to the a predicate) is substituted for an object of a different semantic class. Metonymy is a pervasive phenomenon in language and the interpretation of metonymic expressions can impact tasks from semantic parsing (Scheffczyk et al., 2006) to question answering (Harabagiu et al., 2005). A seminal example in metonymy from (Lakoff and Johnson, 1980) is:

(1) The ham sandwich is waiting for his check.

The ARG1 for the predicate *wait* is typically an animate, but the "*ham sandwich*" is clearly not an animate. Rather, the argument is coerced to fulfill the predicate's typing requirement. This coercion is allowed because an object that would normally fulfill the typing requirement (the customer) can be uniquely identified by an attribute (the ham sandwich he ordered).

SemEval-2010 Task 7 ("Argument Selection and Coercion") (Pustejovsky and Rumshisky, 2009) was designed to evaluate systems that detect such coercions and provide a "compositional history" of argument selection relative to the predicate. In order to accomplish this, an argument is annotated with both the semantic class to which it belongs (the "source" type) as well as the class expected by the predicate (the "target" type). However, in the data provided, the target type was unambiguous given the lemmatized predicate, so the remainder of this paper discusses source type classification. The detection of coercion is then simply performed by checking if the classified source type and target type are different.

In our system, we explore two approaches with separate underlying assumptions about how arbitrary semantic classes can be learned. In our first approach, we assume a semantic class can be defined a priori from a set of seed terms and that WordNet is capable of defining the membership of that semantic class. We apply the PageRank algorithm in order to weight WordNet synsets given a set of seed concepts. In our second approach, we assume that arguments in the same semantic class will be selected by similar verbs. We apply a statistical test to determine the most representative predicates for an argument. This approach benefits from a large corpus from which we automatically extracted 200 million predicate-argument pairs.

The remainder of this paper is organized as follows. Section 2 discusses our WordNet-based approach. Section 3 describes our corpus approach. Section 4 discusses our experiments and results. Section 5 provides a conclusion and direction for future work. Due to space limitations, previous work is discussed when relevant.

2 PageRanking WordNet Hypernyms

Our first approach assumes that semantic class members can be defined and acquired a priori.

Proceedings of the 5th International Workshop on Semantic Evaluation, ACL 2010, pages 252–255,
Uppsala, Sweden, 15-16 July 2010.

Given a set of seed concepts, we mine WordNet for other concepts that may be in the same semantic class. Clearly, this approach has both practical limitations (WordNet does not contain every possible concept) and linguistic limitations (concepts may belong to different semantic classes based on their context). However, given the often vague nature of semantic classes (is a *building* an ARTIFACT or a LOCATION?), access to a weighted list of semantic class members can prove useful for arguments not seen in the train set.

Using (Esuli and Sebastiani, 2007) as inspiration, we have implemented our own naive version of WordNet PageRank. They use sense-disambiguated glosses provided by eXtended WordNet (Harabagiu et al., 1999) to link synsets by starting with positive (or negative) sentiment concepts in order to find other concepts with positive (or negative) sentiment values. For our task, however, hypernymy relations are more appropriate for determining a given synset's membership in a semantic class. Hypernymy defines an IS-A relationship between the parent class (the *hypernym*) and one of its child classes (the *hyponym*). Furthermore, while PageRank assumes directed edges (e.g., hyperlinks in a web page), we use undirected edges. In this way, if HYPERNYMOF(A, B), then A's membership in a semantic class strengthens B's and vice versa.

Briefly, the formula for PageRank is:

$$\mathbf{a}^{(k)} = \alpha \mathbf{a}^{(k-1)} \mathbf{W} + (1-\alpha)\mathbf{e} \qquad (1)$$

where $\mathbf{a}^{(k)}$ is the weight vector containing weights for every synset in WordNet at time k; $\mathbf{W}_{i,j}$ is the inverse of the total number of hypernyms and hyponyms for synset i if synset j is a hypernym or hyponym of synset i; $\mathbf{e}$ is the initial score vector; and α is a tuning parameter. In our implementation, $\mathbf{a}^{(0)}$ is initialized to all zeros; α is fixed at 0.5; and $\mathbf{e}_i = 1$ if synset i is in the seed set S, and zero otherwise. The process is then run until convergence, defined by $|\mathbf{a}_i^{(k)} - \mathbf{a}_i^{(k-1)}| < 0.0001$ for all i.

The result of this PageRank is a weighted list containing every synset reachable by a hypernym/hyponym relation from a seed concept. We ran the PageRank algorithm six times, once for each semantic class, using the arguments in the train set as seeds. For arguments that are polysemous, we make a first WordNet sense assumption. Representative examples of the concepts generated from this approach are shown in Table 1.

ARTIFACT		DOCUMENT	
funny_wagon	.377	white_paper	.342
liquor	.353	progress_report	.342
iced_tea	.338	screenplay	.324
tartan	.325	papyrus	.313
alpaca	.325	pie_chart	.308
EVENT		LOCATION	
rock_concert	.382	heliport	.381
rodeo	.369	mukataa	.380
radium_therapy	.357	subway_station	.342
seminar	.347	dairy_farm	.326
pub_crawl	.346	gateway	.320
PROPOSITION		SOUND	
dibs	.363	whoosh	.353
white_paper	.322	squish	.353
tall_tale	.319	yodel	.339
commendation	.310	theme_song	.320
field_theory	.309	oldie	.312

Table 1: Some of the concepts (and scores) learned from applying PageRank to WordNet hypernyms.

3 Leveraging a Large Corpus of Semantic Parse Annotations

Our second approach assumes that semantic class members are arguments of similar predicates. As (Pustejovsky and Rumshisky, 2009) elaborate, predicates select an argument from a specific semantic class, therefore terms that belong in the same semantic class should be selected by similar predicates. However, this assumption is often violated: type coercion allows predicates to have arguments outside their intended semantic class. Our solution to this problem, partially inspired by (Lapata and Lascarides, 2003), is to collect statistics from an enormous amount of data in order to statistically filter out these coercions.

The English Gigaword Forth Edition corpus[1] contains over 8.5 million documents of newswire text collected over a 15 year period. We processed these documents with the SENNA[2] (Collobert and Weston, 2009) suite of natural language tools, which includes a part-of-speech tagger, phrase chunker, named entity recognizer, and PropBank semantic role labeler. We chose SENNA due to its speed, yet it still performs comparably with many state-of-the-art systems. Of the 8.5 million documents in English Gigaword, 8 million were successfully processed. For each predicate-argument pair in these documents, we gathered counts by argument type and argument head. The head was determined with simple heuristics from the chunk parse and parts-of-speech for each argument (arguments consisting of more than three phrase chunks were discarded). When available, named entity types (e.g., PERSON, ORGANIZATION, LO-

[1] LDC2009T13

[2] http://ml.nec-labs.com/senna/

coffee	*book*	*meeting*	*station*	*report*	*voice*
drink	write	hold	own	release	hear
sip	read	attend	build	publish	raise
brew	publish	schedule	open	confirm	give
serve	title	chair	attack	issue	add
spill	sell	convene	close	comment	have
smell	buy	arrange	operate	submit	silence
sell	balance	call	fill	deny	sound
pour	illustrate	host	shut	file	lend
buy	research	plan	storm	prepare	crack
rise	review	make	set	voice	find

Table 2: Top ten predicates for the most common word in the train set for the six semantic classes.

CATION) were substituted for heads. This resulted in over 511 million predicate-argument pairs for argument types ARG0, ARG1, and ARG2. For this task, however, we chose only to use ARG1 arguments (direct objects), which resulted in 210 million pairs, 7.65 million of which were unique. The ARG1 argument was chosen because most of the arguments in the data are direct objects [3].

The "best" predicates for a given argument are defined by a ranking based on Fisher's exact test (Fisher, 1922):

$$p = \frac{(a+b)!(c+d)!(a+c)!(b+d)!}{n!a!b!c!d!} \quad (2)$$

where a is the number of times the given argument was used with the given predicate, b is the number of times the argument was used with a different predicate, c is the number of times the predicate was used with a different argument, d is the number of times neither the given argument or predicate was used, and $n = a+b+c+d$. The top ranked (lowest p) predicates for the most common arguments in the training data are shown in Table 2.

4 Experiments

We have conducted several experiments to test the performance of the approaches outlined in Sections 2 and 3 along with additional features commonly found in information extraction literature. All experiments were conducted using the SVM^{multiclass} support vector machine library[4].

4.1 WordNet PageRank

We experimented with the output of our WordNet PageRank implementation along three separate dimensions: (1) which sense to use (since we did not incorporate a word sense disambiguation system), (2) whether to use the highest scoring semantic class or every class an argument belonged to, and (3) how to use the weight output by the algorithm. The results of these experiments yielded a single feature for each class that returns true if the argument is in that class, regardless of weight. This resulted in a micro-precision score of 75.6%.

4.2 Gigaword Predicates

We experimented with both (i) the number of predicates to use for an argument and (ii) the score threshold to use. Ultimately, the Fisher score did not prove nearly as useful as a classifier as it did as a ranker. Since the distribution of predicates for each argument varied significantly, choosing a high number of predicates would yield good results for some arguments but not others. However, because of size of the training data, we were able to choose the top 5 predicates for each argument as features and still achieve a reasonable micro-precision score of 89.6%.

4.3 Other Features

Many other features common in information extraction are well-suited for this task. Given that SVMs can support millions of features, we chose to add many features simpler than those previously described in order to improve the final performance of the classifier. These include the lemma of the argument (both the last word's lemma and every word's lemma), the lemma of the predicate, the number of words in the argument, the casing of the argument, the part-of-speech of the argument's last word, the WordNet synset and all (recursive) hypernyms of the argument. Additionally, since the EVENT class is both the most common and the most often confused, we introduced two features based on annotated resources. The first feature indicates the most common part-of-speech for the un-lemmatized argument in the Treebank corpus. This helped classify examples such as *thinking* which was confused with a PROPOSITION for the predicate *deny*. Second, we introduced a feature that indicated if the un-lemmatized argument was considered an event in the TimeBank corpus (Pustejovsky et al., 2003) at least five times. This helped to distinguish events such as *meeting*, which was confused with a LOCATION for the predicate *arrive*.

4.4 Ablation Test

We conducted an ablation test using combinations of five feature sets: (1) our WordNet PageR-

[3]The notable exception to this, however, is *arrive*, where the data uses the destination argument. In the PropBank scheme (Palmer et al., 2005), this would correspond to the ARG4, which usually signifies an end state.

[4]http://svmlight.joachims.org/svm_multiclass.html

		+WNSH	+WNPR	+GWPA	+EVNT
WORD	89.2	94.2	95.0	95.6	96.1
EVNT	31.1	89.7	89.9	90.8	
GWPA	89.6	90.8	91.0		
WNPR	75.6	89.4			
WNSH	89.0				

Table 3: Ablation test of feature sets showing micro-precision scores.

		Precision	Recall
Selection vs. Coercion	Macro	95.4	95.7
	Micro	96.3	96.3
Source Type	Macro	96.5	95.7
	Micro	96.1	96.1
Target Type	Macro	100.0	100.0
	Micro	100.0	100.0
Joint Type	Macro	85.5	95.2
	Micro	96.1	96.1

Table 4: Results for UTDMET on SemEval-2010 Task 7.

ank feature (WNPR), (2) our Gigaword Predicates feature (GWPA), (3) word, lemma, and part-of-speech features (WORD), (4) WordNet synset and hypernym features (WNSH), and (5) Treebank and TimeBank features (EVNT). Of these $2^5 - 1 = 31$ tests, 15 are shown in Table 3. The Gigaword Predicates (GWPA) was the best overall feature, but each feature set ended up helping the final score. WordNet PageRank (WNPR) even improved the score when combined WordNet hypernym features (WNSH) despite the fact that they are heavily related. Ultimately, WordNet PageRank had a greater precision, while the other WordNet features had greater recall.

4.5 Task 7 Results

Table 4 shows the official results for UTDMET on the Task 7 data. The target type was unambiguous given the lemmatized predicate. For classifying selection vs. coercion, we simply checked to see if the classified source type was the same as the target type. If this was the case, we returned selection, otherwise a coercion existed.

5 Conclusion

We have presented two approaches for determining the semantic class of a predicate's argument. The two approaches capture different information and combine well to classify the "source" type in SemEval-2010 Task 7. We showed how this can be incorporated into a system to detect coercions as well as the argument's compositional history relative to its predicate. In future work we plan to extend this system to more complex tasks such as when the predicate may be polysemous or unseen predicates may be encountered.

Acknowledgments

The authors would like to thank Bryan Rink for several insights during the course of this work.

References

Ronan Collobert and Jason Weston. 2009. Deep Learning in Natural Language Processing. Tutorial at NIPS.

Andrea Esuli and Fabrizio Sebastiani. 2007. PageRanking WordNet Synsets: An Application to Opinion Mining. In *Proceedings of the 45th Annual Meeting of the Association for Computational Linguistics*, pages 424–431.

Ronald A. Fisher. 1922. On the interpretation of χ^2 from contingency tables, and the calculation of p. 85(1):87–94.

Sanda Harabagiu, George Miller, and Dan Moldovan. 1999. WordNet 2 - A Morphologically and Semantically Enhanced Resource. In *Proceedings of the SIGLEX Workshop on Standardizing Lexical Resources*, pages 1–7.

Sanda Harabagiu, Andrew Hickl, John Lehmann, and Dan Moldovan. 2005. Experiments with Interactive Question-Answering. In *Proceedings of the 43rd Annual Meeting of the Association for Computational Linguistics*, pages 205–214.

George Lakoff and Mark Johnson. 1980. *Metaphors We Live By*. University of Chicago Press.

Maria Lapata and Alex Lascarides. 2003. A Probabilistic Account of Logical Metonymy. *Computational Linguistics*, 21(2):261–315.

Martha Palmer, Paul Kingsbury, and Daniel Gildea. 2005. The Proposition Bank: An Annotated Corpus of Semantic Roles. *Computational Linguistics*, 31(1):71–106.

James Pustejovsky and Anna Rumshisky. 2009. SemEval-2010 Task 7: Argument Selection and Coercion. In *Proceedings of the NAACL HLT Workshop on Semantic Evaluations: Recent Achievements and Future Directions*, pages 88–93.

James Pustejovsky, Patrick Hanks, Roser Saurí, Andrew See, Robert Gaizauskas, Andrea Setzer, Dragomir Radev, Beth Sundheim, David Day, Lisa Ferro, and Marcia Lazo. 2003. The TIMEBANK Corpus. In *Proceedings of Corpus Linguistics*, pages 647–656.

Jan Scheffczyk, Adam Pease, and Michael Ellsworth. 2006. Linking FrameNet to the Suggested Upper Merged Ontology. In *Proceedings of Formal Ontology in Information Systems*, pages 289–300.

UTD: Classifying Semantic Relations by Combining Lexical and Semantic Resources

Bryan Rink and Sanda Harabagiu
Human Language Technology Research Institute
University of Texas at Dallas
Richardson, Texas
{bryan,sanda}@hlt.utdallas.edu

Abstract

This paper describes our system for SemEval-2010 Task 8 on multi-way classification of semantic relations between nominals. First, the type of semantic relation is classified. Then a relation type-specific classifier determines the relation direction. Classification is performed using SVM classifiers and a number of features that capture the context, semantic role affiliation, and possible pre-existing relations of the nominals. This approach achieved an F1 score of 82.19% and an accuracy of 77.92%.

1 Introduction

SemEval-2010 Task 8 evaluated the multi-way classification of semantic relations between nominals in a sentence (Hendrickx et al., 2010). Given two nominals embedded in a sentence, the task requires identifying which of the following nine semantic relations holds between the nominals: *Cause-Effect*, *Instrument-Agency*, *Product-Producer*, *Content-Container*, *Entity-Origin*, *Entity-Destination*, *Component-Whole*, *Member-Collection*, *Message-Topic*, or *Other* if no other relation is appropriate. For instance, the following sentence provides an example of the *Entity-Destination* relation:

"A small [piece]$_{E1}$ of rock landed into the [trunk]$_{E2}$."

The two nominals given for this sentence are E_1 (*piece*) and E_2 (*trunk*). This is an *Entity-Destination* relation because the piece of rock originated from outside of the trunk, but ended up there. Finally, the direction of the relation is (E_1,E_2) because E_1, the *piece*, is the *Entity* and E_2, the *trunk*, is the *Destination*.

Analysis of the training data revealed three major classes of knowledge required for recognizing semantic relations: (i) examples that require background knowledge of an existing relation between the nominals (e.g., example 5884 below), (ii) examples using background knowledge regarding the typical role of one of the nominals (e.g., example 3402), and (iii) examples that require contextual cues to disambiguate the role between the nominals (e.g., example 5710).

Example 5884 *"The Ca content in the [corn]$_{E1}$ [flour]$_{E2}$ has also a strong dependence on the pericarp thickness."*

Example 3402 *"The [rootball]$_{E1}$ was in a [crate]$_{E2}$ the size of a refrigerator, and some of the arms were over 12 feet tall."*

Example 5710 *"The seniors poured [flour]$_{E1}$ into wax [paper]$_{E2}$ and threw the items as projectiles on freshmen during a morning pep rally."*

In example 5884, the background knowledge that flour is often made or derived from corn can directly lead to the classification of the example as containing an *Entity-Origin* relation. Likewise, knowing that crates often act as containers is a strong reason for believing that example 3402 is a *Content-Container* relation. However, in example 5710, neither the combination of the nominals nor their individual affiliations lead to an obvious semantic relation. After taking the context into account, it becomes clear that this is an *Entity-Destination* relation because E_1 is going *into* E_2.

2 Approach

We cast the task of determining a semantic relation and its direction as a classification task. Rather than classifying both pieces of information (relation and direction) simultaneously, one classifier is used to determine the relation type, and then, for each relation type, a separate classifier determines the direction. We used a total of 45 feature types (henceforth: features), which

Proceedings of the 5th International Workshop on Semantic Evaluation, ACL 2010, pages 256–259,
Uppsala, Sweden, 15-16 July 2010.

were shared among all of the direction classifiers and the one relation classifier. These feature types can be partitioned into 8 groups: lexical features, hypernyms from WordNet[1], dependency parse, PropBank parse, FrameNet parse, nominalization, predicates from TextRunner, and nominal similarity derived from the Google N-Gram data set. All features were treated as FEATURE-TYPE:VALUE pairs which were then presented to the SVM[2] classifier as a boolean feature (0 or 1).

We further group our features into the three classes described above: Contextual, Nominal affiliation, and Pre-existing relations. Table 1 illustrates sample feature values from example 117 of the training set.

3 Contextual and Lexical Features

The contextual features consist of lexical features and features based on dependency, PropBank, and FrameNet parses. For lexical features, we extract the words and parts of speech for E_1 and E_2, the words, parts of speech, and prefixes of length 5 for tokens between the nominals, and the words before and single word after E_1 and E_2 respectively. The words between the nominals can be strong indicators for the type of relation. For example the words *into*, *produced*, and *caused* are likely to occur in *Entity-Destination*, *Product-Producer*, and *Cause-Effect* relations, respectively. Using the prefixes of length 5 for the words between the nominals provides a kind of stemming (*produced* → *produ*, *caused* → *cause*).

Inspired by a feature from (Beamer et al., 2007), we extract a coarse-grained part of speech sequence for the words between the nominals. This is accomplished by building a string using the first letter of each token's Treebank POS tag. This feature is motivated by the fact that relations such as *Member-Collection* usually invoke prepositional phrases such as: *of*, *in the*, and *of various*. The corresponding POS sequences we extract are: "I", "I_D", and "I_J". Finally, we also use the number of words between the nominals as a feature because relations such as *Product-Producer* and *Entity-Origin* often have no intervening tokens (e.g., *organ builder* or *Coconut oil*).

Syntactic and semantic parses capture long distance relationships between phrases in a sentence. Instead of a traditional syntactic parser, we chose the Stanford dependency parser[3] for the simpler syntactic structure it produces. Our dependency features are based on paths in the dependency tree of length 1 and length 2. The paths encode the dependencies and words those dependencies attach to. To generalize the paths, some of the features replace verbs in the path with their top-level Levin class, as determined by running a word sense disambiguation system (Mihalcea and Csomai, 2005) followed by a lookup in VerbNet[4]. One of the features for length 2 paths generalizes further by replacing all words with their location relative to the nominals, either BEFORE, BETWEEN, or AFTER.

Consider example 117 from Table 1. The length 2 dependency path (feature *depPathLen2VerbNet*) neatly captures the fact that E_1 is the subject of a verb falling into Levin class 27, and E_2 is the direct object. Levin class 27 is the class of engender verbs, such as *cause*, *spawn*, and *generate*. This path is indicative of a *Cause-Effect* relation.

Semantic parses such as ASSERT's PropBank parse[5] and LTH's FrameNet parse[6] identify predicates in text and their semantic roles. These parses go beyond the dependency parse and identify the specific role each nominal assumes for the predicates in the sentence, so the parses should be a more reliable indicator for the relation type between nominals. We have features for the identified predicates and for the roles assigned to each nominal. Several of the features are only triggered if both nominals are arguments for the same predicate. The values from Table 1 show that the features correctly determined that E_1 and E_2 are governed by a verb of Levin class 27, and that the lexical unit is *cause.v*.

4 Nominal Role Affiliation Features

Although context can be critical to identifying the semantic relation present in some examples, in others we must bring some background knowledge to bear regarding the types of nominals involved. Knowing that a *writer* is a person provides supporting evidence for that nominal taking part in a PRODUCER role. Additionally, *writer* nominalizes the verb *write* which is classified by Levin (Levin, 1993) as an "Image creation" or "Creation and Transformation" verb. This provides further support for assigning *writer* to a PRODUCER role.

[1]http://wordnet.princeton.edu/
[2]We used Weka's SMO classifier http://www.cs.waikato.ac.nz/ml/weka/
[3]http://nlp.stanford.edu/software/lex-parser.shtml
[4]http://verbs.colorado.edu/ mpalmer/projects/verbnet.html
[5]http://cemantix.org/assert.html
[6]http://nlp.cs.lth.se/software/semantic_parsing:_framenet_frames/

Example 117: Forward [motion]$_{E1}$ of the vehicle through the air caused a [suction]$_{E2}$ on the road draft tube.	
Feature Set	**Feature Values**
Lexical	e1Word=motion, e2Word=suction, e1OrE2Word={motion,suction}, wordsBetween={of, the, vehicle, through, the, air, caused, a}, posE1=NN, posE2=NN, posE1orE2=NN posBetween=I_D_N_I_D_N_V_D, distance=8, wordsOutside={Forward, on}, prefix5Between={air, cause, a, of, the, vehic, throu, the}
Dependency	depPathLen1={caused→nsubj→<E1>, caused→dobj→<E2>,...} depPathLen1VerbNet={vn:27→nsubj→<E1>, vn:27→dobj→<E2>,...} depPathLen2VerbNet={<E1>←nsubj←vn:27→dobj→<E2>}, depPathLen2Location={<E1>←nsubj←BETWEEN→dobj→<E2>}
PropBank	pbPredStem=caus, pbVerbNet=27, pbE1CoarseRole=ARG0, pbE2CoarseRole=ARG1, pbE1orE2CoarseRole={ARG1,ARG2}, pbNumPredToks=1, pbE1orE2PredHyper = {cause#v#1, create#v#1}
FrameNet	fnAnyLU={cause.v, vehicle.n, road.n}, fnAnyTarget={cause,vehicle,road}, fnE2LU=cause.v, fnE1OrE2LU=cause.v
Hypernym	hyperE1={gesture#n#2, communication#n#2, entity#n#1, ...}, hyperE2={suction#n#1, phenomenon#n#1, entity#n#1,...}, hyperE1orE2={gesture#n#2, communication#n#2, entity#n#1, suction#n#1, phenomenon#n#1, ...}, hyperBetween={quality#n#1, cause#v#1, create#v#1, ...}
NomLex-Plus	*Features did not fire*
NGrams	knnE1={motion, amendment, action, appeal, decision}, knnE2={suction, hose, pump, vacuum, nozzle}, knnE1Role=Message, knnE2Role=Component
TextRunner	trE1_E2={may result from, to contact, created, moves, applies, causes, falls below, corresponds to which}, trE2_E1={including, are moved under, will cause, according to, are effected by, repeats, can match}, trE1_E2Hyper={be#v#6, agree#v#3, cause#v#1, ensue#v#1, contact#v#1, apply#v#1, ...}

Table 1: All of the feature types and values for example 117 from the training data. Despite the errors in disambiguation the system still correctly classifies this as Cause-Effect(E_1,E_2)

We capture this background knowledge by leveraging four sources of lexical and semantic knowledge: WordNet, NomLex-Plus[7], VerbNet, and the Google N-Gram data[8].

We utilize a word sense disambiguation system (Mihalcea and Csomai, 2005) to determine the best sense for each nominal and use all of the hypernyms as a feature. Hypernyms are also determined for the words between the nominals, however only the top three levels are used as a feature. Following (Beamer et al., 2007), we also incorporate a nominalization feature for each nominal based on NomLex-Plus. Rather than use the agential information as they did, we determine the verb being nominalized and retrieve the verb's top-level Levin class from VerbNet. This reduces the sparsity problem for nominalizations while still capturing their semantics.

Our final role-affiliation features make use of the Google N-Gram data. Using the 5-grams we determined the top 1,000 words that occur most often in the context of each nominal. Nominals were then compared to each other using Jaccard similarity of their contexts and the 4 closest neighbors were retained. For each nominal, we have a feature containing the nominal itself and its 4 nearest neighbors from the training set. Additional features determine the most frequent role assigned to the neighbors. Examples of all these features can be seen in Table 1 in the row for NGrams. The neighbors for *motion* in the table show the difficulty this feature has with ambiguity, incorrectly picking up words similar to the sense meaning a proposal for action.

[7]http://nlp.cs.nyu.edu/meyers/NomBank.html

[8]Available from LDC as LDC2006T13

5 Pre-existing Relation Features

For some examples the context and the individual nominal affiliations provide little help in determining the semantic relation, such as example 5884 from before (i.e., *corn flour*). These examples require knowledge of the interaction between the nominals and we cannot rely solely on determining the role of one nominal or the other. We turned to TextRunner (Yates et al., 2007) as a large source of background knowledge about pre-existing relations between nominals. TextRunner is a queryable database of NOUN-VERB-NOUN triples extracted from a large corpus of webpages. For example, the phrases retrieved from TextRunner for "corn _____ flour" include: "is ground into", "to make", "to obtain", and "makes". Querying in the reverse direction, for "flour _____ corn" returns phrases such as: "contain", "filled with", "comprises", and "is made from". We use the top ten phrases for the "<E_1> _____ <E_2>" query results, and also for the "<E_2> _____ <E_1>" results, forming two features. In addition, we include a feature that has all of the hypernyms for the content words in the verb phrases from the queries for the E_1-E_2 direction.

Relation	P	R	F1
Cause-Effect	89.63	89.63	89.63
Component-Whole	74.34	81.73	77.86
Content-Container	84.62	85.94	85.27
Entity-Destination	88.22	89.73	88.96
Entity-Origin	83.87	80.62	82.21
Instrument-Agency	71.83	65.38	68.46
Member-Collection	84.30	87.55	85.89
Message-Topic	81.02	85.06	82.99
Product-Producer	82.38	74.89	78.46
Other	52.97	51.10	52.02
Overall	82.25	82.28	82.19

Table 2: Overall and individual relation scores on the test set, along with precision and recall

6 Results

Our system achieved the best overall score as measured by macro-averaged F1 (for scoring details see (Hendrickx et al., 2010)) among the ten teams that participated in the semantic relation task at SemEval-2010. The results in Table 2 show the performance of the system on the test set for each relation type and the overall score.

The training data consisted of 8,000 annotated instances, including the numbered examples introduced earlier, and the test set contained 2,717 examples. To assess the learning curve for this task we trained on sets of size 1000, 2000, 4000, and 8000, obtaining test scores of 73.08, 77.02, 79.93, and 82.19, respectively. These results indicate that more training data does help, but going from 1,000 training instances to 8,000 only boosts the score by about 9 points of F-measure.

Because our approach makes use of many different features, we ran ablation tests on the 8 sets of features from Table 1 to determine which types of features contributed the most to classifying semantic relations. We evaluated all 256 (2^8) combinations of the feature sets on the training data using 10-fold cross validation. The results are shown in Table 3. The last lines of Tables 2 and 3 correspond to the system submitted for SemEval-2010 Task 8. The score on the training data is lower because the data includes examples from SemEval-2007, which has more of the harder to classify *Other* relations[9].

These tests have shown that the NomLex-Plus feature likely did not help. Further, the dependency parse feature added little beyond PropBank and FrameNet. Given the high score for the lexical feature set we split it into smaller sets to see their contributions in the top portion of Table 3. This reveals the best individual feature is for the words between the two nominals.

[9]To confirm this we performed a 10 fold cross validation of examples 1-7109, adding examples 7110-8000 (the 2007 data) to each training set. This resulted in an F1 of 82.18

	Feature Sets	F1
	E_1 and E_2 only	48.7
	Words between only	64.0
	E_1, E_2, and words between	72.5
	All word features (incl. before and after)	73.1
1	Lexical	73.8
2	+Hypernym	77.8
3	+FrameNet	78.9
4	+NGrams	79.7
5	-FrameNet +PropBank +TextRunner	80.5
6	+FrameNet	81.1
7	+Dependency	81.3
8	+NomLex-Plus	81.3

Table 3: Scores obtained for various sets of features on the training set. The bottom portion of the table shows the best combination containing 1 to 8 feature sets

7 Conclusion

By combining various linguistic resources we were able to build a state of the art system for recognizing semantic relations in text. While the large training size available in SemEval-2010 Task 8 enables achieving high scores using only word-based features, richer linguistic and background-knowledge resources still provide additional aid in identifying semantic relations.

Acknowledgments

The authors would like to thank Kirk Roberts for providing code and insightful comments.

References

B. Beamer, S. Bhat, B. Chee, A. Fister, A. Rozovskaya, and R. Girju. 2007. UIUC: a knowledge-rich approach to identifying semantic relations between nominals. In *ACL SemEval07 Workshop*.

I. Hendrickx, S.N. Kim, Z. Kozareva, P. Nakov, D. Ó Séaghdha, S. Padó, M. Pennacchiotti, L. Romano, and S. Szpakowicz. 2010. Semeval-2010 task 8: Multi-way classification of semantic relations between pairs of nominals. In *Proceedings of the 5th SIGLEX Workshop on Semantic Evaluation*, Uppsala, Sweden.

B. Levin. 1993. English verb classes and alternations: A preliminary investigation. *Chicago, Il.*

R. Mihalcea and A. Csomai. 2005. SenseLearner: word sense disambiguation for all words in unrestricted text. In *Proceedings of the ACL 2005 on Interactive poster and demonstration sessions*. ACL.

A. Yates, M. Cafarella, M. Banko, O. Etzioni, M. Broadhead, and S. Soderland. 2007. TextRunner: open information extraction on the web. In *Proceedings of HLT: NAACL: Demonstrations*.

UvT: Memory-based pairwise ranking of paraphrasing verbs

Sander Wubben
Tilburg centre for Cognition and Communication
Tilburg University
The Netherlands
s.wubben@uvt.nl

Abstract

In this paper we describe Mephisto, our system for Task 9 of the SemEval-2 workshop. Our approach to this task is to develop a machine learning classifier which determines for each verb pair describing a noun compound which verb should be ranked higher. These classifications are then combined into one ranking. Our classifier uses features from the Google N-gram Corpus, WordNet and the provided training data.

1 Introduction

We interpret the task of ranking a set of given paraphrasing verbs as described by Butnariu et al (2010) as a competition between these verbs. Each verb competes with every other verb in the set and receives a positive score if it is more likely to describe the given noun compound (NC) than the other verb and a negative score if it is less likely to describe the NC. In line with this approach we regard the task as a classification problem where for each comparison our classification algorithm picks the paraphrasing verb that is more likely to describe the NC. This brings the classification problem down to three classes: higher, equal or lower. Sometimes the paraphrasing verbs are accompanied by a preposition. In this paper we will simply refer to all verbs and verb-prepositions as verbs.

The distribution of the verbs in the training data provides us already with valuable information. We incorporate basic features describing this distribution to train our classifier. We also need additional semantic features that provide us with insight into the relation between the NC and the verb, therefore we use features constructed from WordNet and the Google N-gram Corpus to train our Memory-based paraphrase interpretation scoring tool (Mephisto).

2 System Description

The system consists of three components: the feature extraction component, the classification component and the ranking component. We will describe all three components.

2.1 Feature Extraction

For each verb describing an NC we try to extract those features that describe the probability that this verb is a good interpretation of the NC. We assume that given a NC N_1N_2 and a verb V, the NC interpretation should be N_2VN_1. The phrase "Butter made from peanuts" adequately describes peanut butter.

The training data provides us with a total of 17,727 instances of NC verb pairs scored by human judges. This can be broken down into 4,360 unique verb phrases describing 250 NCs. This distribution already gives us a good clue when we are generating new rankings. The following are the features we used:

Weighted mean in training data For each NC that has to be ranked we find the most similar NC in the training data by measuring the overlap in verb phrases between the two NCs. We do this by calculating the Jaccard coefficient over the sets of verbs associated with the NCs. We adapt the highest ranking NC as most similar to our candidate NC (the NC with most matching verbs). For each verb V we then calculate the score as follows:

$$Score = J * S_{sim} + (1 - J) * M$$

where J is the Jaccard score, S_{sim} is the assigned score of the verb in the most similar set and M is the mean score for the verb in the training data.

Rank in training data For this feature we directly compare the two verbs V_1 and V_2. We just

Proceedings of the 5th International Workshop on Semantic Evaluation, ACL 2010, pages 260–263,
Uppsala, Sweden, 15-16 July 2010.

feature	values	info gain	gain ratio
verb1	4,093	0.24	0.02
verb2	4,093	0.24	0.02
verb1-verb2	768,543	1.06	0.06
verb1-verb2-LCS	986,031	1.29	0.07
n-gram score1	7	0.07	0.02
n-gram score2	7	0.01	0.08
weighted mean	7	0.29	0.12
rank	3	0.68	0.43

Table 1: Features used in our system

count the number of times that V_1 is ranked higher than V_2 and vice versa for every NC where both verbs occur. We end up with a positive, equal or negative class.

WordNet Least Common Subsumer In order to distinguish between different kinds of NCs we use WordNet (Fellbaum, 1998) to determine the kind of relation between the nouns. This idea is supported by work by Levi (1978), Warren (1978) and Nastase & Szpakowicz (2003). Our intuition is that the ranking of verb phrases is very dependent on this relation between the nouns. To determine this we use the WordNet::QueryData (Rennie, 2000) module. In the WordNet graph we look for the Least Common Subsumer (LCS) of the two nouns. The LCS is the lowest parent node of both nouns. We combine the LCS with both verb phrases into one feature.

Google N-gram features We use the Google N-gram corpus to count co-occurence frequencies of certain n-grams. An NC occurring often together with a certain verb should indicate that that verb is a good paraphrase for the NC. Using web text for various NLP-tasks has been proven to be useful (Lapata and Keller, 2005), also for NC interpretation (Nakov and Hearst, 2005). Because of data sparseness and the unlikelihood of finding a perfect match for a certain n-gram, we adopt different strategies for constructing features. First of all, we try to relax the matching conditions by applying certain regular expression. Given the NC "abortion problem" and the paraphrasing verb "be related to" , it seems unlikely you will ever encounter the n-gram "problem be related to abortion", yet in the training data "be related to" is the number three verb for "abortion problem". Therefore, we first apply some simple inflection. Instead of "be" we match on "is/are/being". and we do a comparable inflection for other verbs transforming a verb such as "involve" into "involves/involving". Additionally we also match on singular and plural nouns. We then use two different techniques to find the n-gram frequencies:

	+up+	-dwn-	=eq=
+up+	23,494	7,099	8,912
-dwn-	7,168	23,425	8,912
=eq=	22,118	22,084	22,408

Table 2: Confusion matrix of the classes, with horizontally the output classes and vertically the target classes

$$N - gram_1 = \frac{f(N_2V) + f(VN_1)}{f(V)}$$

$$N - gram_2 = \frac{f(N_2VN_1)}{f(V)}$$

where f stands for the occurrences of the given sequences of nouns and verb. We do not divide by noun occurrences because they are constant for every pair of verbs we compare.

Pairwise comparison of features For each verb pair in an NC set we compare all numeric features and assign one of the following symbols to characterize the relation of the two verbs:

+++: V_1 score is more than 10 times V_2 score
++: V_1 score is between 2 and 10 times V_2 score
+: V_1 score is between 1 and 2 times verb2 score
=: scores are equal
-: V_2 score is between 1 and 2 times V_1 score
- -: V_2 score is between 2 and 10 times V_1 score
- - -: V_2 score is more than 10 times V_1 score

An overview of the features is displayed in Table 1.

2.2 Classification

Our system makes use of Memory-Based Learning (MBL) for classification. MBL stores feature representations of training instances in memory without abstraction and classifies unseen instances by matching their feature representation to all instances in memory, finding the most similar instances. The class of these most similar instances is then copied to the new instance The learning algorithm our system uses is the IB1 classier as implemented in TiMBL (version 6.1.5). IB1 is a supervised decision-tree-based implementation of

Settings	TiMBL F-score	Spearman ρ	Pearson r	KullbackLeibler div.
k=3 all features	0.48	**0.50**	0.44	1.91
k=3 no external features	0.53	0.48	0.41	2.05
k=11 all features	0.51	0.50	0.42	1.97
k=11 no external features	0.20	-	-	-

Table 3: Results for different settings on the development set

the k-nearest neighbor algorithm for learning classification tasks (Aha et al., 1991). The TiMBL parameters we used in the Mephisto system for the IB1 classifier are the overlap metric, weighting using GainRatio, and k=3, taking into account the instances on the 3 most similar positions to extrapolate the class of the instance. More information about these settings can be found in the TiMBL reference guide (Daelemans et al., 2009). We train our classifier on the provided training data to classify instances into one of three classes; **+up+** if V_1 ranks higher than V_2 , **=eq=** if both verbs rank equally and **-dwn-** if V_1 ranks lower than V_2.

2.3 Ranking

The final step is to combine all the classification into one score per verb. This is done in a very straight forward way: a verb receives one point every time it is classified as +up+. This results in scores for each verb paraphrasing an NC. We then perform a simple post processing step: we reassign classes to each verb based on the final scores they have received and recalculate their scores. We repeat this process until the scores converge.

3 Results

For development the original training set was divided in a development training set of 15,966 lines and a development test set of 1,761 lines, which contains 23 NCs. The distribution and ranking features were calculated using only the development training set. Because we compare for each NC every verb to every other verb the TiMBL training instance-base contains 1,253,872 lines, and the development test set 145,620. The results for different settings are in Table 3. Although the TiMBL F-score (macro-averaged) of using all features is actually lower than using only semantic features at k=3, the final correlations are in favor of using all features. There does not seem to be an improvement when extrapolating from 11 neighbouring instances in the instance-base over 3. In fact, when using no external features and k=11, the classifier overgeneralizes and classifies every instance as =eq= and consequently does not provide a ranking at all. Additionally, classifying with k=11 takes considerably longer than with k=3. The settings we use for our final system are k=3 and we use all features. Table 2 displays a confusion matrix of the classification on the development test set. Not surprisingly the classifier is very bad at recognizing the =eq= class. These mistakes are not as bad as miss-classifying a +up+ instance as -dwn- and vice versa, and fortunately these mistakes happen less often.

System	Spearman ρ	Pearson r	Cosine
UvT-MEPHISTO	0.450	0.411	0.635
UCD-PN	0.441	0.361	0.669
UCD-GOGGLE-III	0.432	0.395	0.652
UCD-GOGGLE-II	0.418	0.375	0.660
UCD-GOGGLE-I	0.380	0.252	0.629
UCAM	0.267	0.219	0.374
NC-INTERP	0.186	0.070	0.466
Baseline	0.425	0.344	0.524

Table 4: Final results for SemEval-2 Task 9

The official test set contains 32,830 instances, almost twice as many as the training set. This breaks down into 2,837,226 cases to classify. In Table 4 are the final results of the task with all participating systems and their macro-averaged Spearman, Pearson and Cosine correlation. Also shown is the baseline, which involves scoring a given verb paraphrase by its frequency in the training set. The final results are quite a bit lower than the results on the development set. This could be coincidence (the final test set is about twenty times larger than our development test set), but it could also be due to overfitting on the development set. The ten best and worst scoring compounds are shown in Table 5 with their Least Common Subsumer as taken from WordNet. The best-scoring NC "jute products" achieves a Spearman ρ of 0.75 while the worst-scoring compound, "electron microscope" only achieves 0.12.

4 Conclusion

We have shown that a Memory-based pairwise approach to ranking with features taken from WordNet and the Google N-gram corpus achieves

Best scoring NCs	LCS	Spearman ρ
jute products	physical entity	0.75
ceramics products	artifact	0.75
steel frame	physical entity	0.74
cattle population	entity	0.74
metal body	physical entity	0.74
winter blooming	entity	0.73
warbler family	entity	0.72
wool scarf	artifact	0.71
fiber optics	physical entity	0.70
petroleum products	physical entity	0.70
Worst scoring NCs	**LCS**	**Spearman ρ**
electron microscope	whole	0.12
light bulb	physical entity	0.15
yesterday evening	measure	0.16
student loan	entity	0.16
theater orchestra	entity	0.17
sunday restrictions	abstraction	0.20
yesterday afternoon	measure	0.20
relations agency	abstraction	0.21
crime novelist	entity	0.21
office buildings	structure	0.21

Table 5: Best and worst scoring noun compounds with their Least Common Subsumer and Spearman ρ correlation

good results on the task of ranking verbs paraphrasing noun compounds. We outperform the strong baseline and also systems using an unsupervised approach. If we analyse our results we see that our system scores particularly well on noun compounds describing materials: in Table 5 we see that all top ten compounds are either "artifacts", "physical entities" or "entities" according to WordNet and the relation is quite direct: generally a *made of* relation seems appropriate. If we look at the bottom ten on the other hand, we see relations such as "abstraction" and "measure": these are harder to qualify. Also, an "electron microscope" will generally not be perceived as a microscope made of electrons. We can conclude that for NCs where the relation between the nouns is more obscure the verbs are harder to rank.

If we look at the Information Gain Ratio, of all features the rank difference of the verbs in the training data seems to be the strongest feature, and of the external features the frequency difference of the entire phrase containing the NC and the verb. A lot more investigations could be made into the viability of using large n-gram collections such as the Google N-gram corpus for paraphrase tasks.

It might also be interesting to explore a somewhat more challenging variant of this task by not providing the verbs to be ranked a priori. This would probably be more interesting for real world applications because often the task is not only ranking but finding the verbs in the first place. Our system should be able to handle this task with minor modifications: we simply regards all verbs in the training-data candidates to be ranked. Then, a pre-filtering step should take place to weed out irrelevant verbs based on an indicator such as the LCS of the nouns. In addition a threshold could be implemented to only accept a (further) limited set of verbs in the final ranking.

References

David W. Aha, Dennis Kibler, and Marc K. Albert. 1991. Instance-based learning algorithms. *Mach. Learn.*

Cristina Butnariu, Su Nam Kim, Preslav Nakov, Diarmuid Ó Séaghdha, Stan Szpakowicz, and Tony Veale. 2010. Semeval-2 task 9: The interpretation of noun compounds using paraphrasing verbs and prepositions. In *Proceedings of the 5th SIGLEX Workshop on Semantic Evaluation.*

Walter Daelemans, Jakub Zavrel, Ko van der Sloot, and Antal van den Bosch. 2009. Timbl: Tilburg memory-based learner - version 6.2 - reference guide.

Christiane Fellbaum. 1998. *WordNet: An Electronic Lexical Database.*

Mirella Lapata and Frank Keller. 2005. Web-based models for natural language processing. *ACM Trans. Speech Lang. Process.*

Judith N. Levi. 1978. *The Syntax and Semantics of Complex Nominals.*

Preslav Nakov and Marti Hearst. 2005. Search engine statistics beyond the n-gram: Application to noun compound bracketing. In *Proceedings of the 9th Conference on Computational Natural Language Learning.*

Vivi Nastase and Stan Szpakowicz. 2003. Exploring noun-modifier semantic relations. In *Proceedings of the 5th International Workshop on Computational Semantics.*

Jason Rennie. 2000. Wordnet::querydata: a perl module for accessing the wordnet database.

Beatrice Warren. 1978. *Semantic Patterns of Noun-Noun Compounds.*

SEMAFOR: Frame Argument Resolution with Log-Linear Models

Desai Chen Nathan Schneider Dipanjan Das Noah A. Smith
School of Computer Science, Carnegie Mellon University, Pittsburgh, PA 15213, USA
{desaic@andrew,dipanjan@cs,nschneid@cs,nasmith@cs}.cmu.edu

Abstract

This paper describes the SEMAFOR system's performance in the SemEval 2010 task on linking events and their participants in discourse. Our entry is based upon SEMAFOR 1.0 (Das et al., 2010a), a frame-semantic probabilistic parser built from log-linear models. The extended system models *null instantiations*, including non-local argument reference. Performance is evaluated on the task data with and without gold-standard overt arguments. In both settings, it fares the best of the submitted systems with respect to recall and F_1.

1 Introduction

The theory of frame semantics (Fillmore, 1982) holds that meaning is largely structured by holistic units of knowledge, called *frames*. Each frame encodes a conventionalized gestalt event or scenario, often with conceptual dependents (participants, props, or attributes) filling roles to elaborate the specific instance of the frame. In the FrameNet lexicon (Fillmore et al., 2003), each frame defines **core roles** tightly coupled with the particular meaning of the frame, as well as more generic **non-core** roles (Ruppenhofer et al., 2006). Frames can be evoked with linguistic predicates, known as **lexical units (LUs)**; role fillers can be expressed overtly and linked to the frame via (morpho)syntactic constructions. However, a great deal of conceptually-relevant content is left unexpressed or is not explicitly linked to the frame via linguistic conventions; rather, it is expected that the listener will be able to infer the appropriate relationships pragmatically. Certain types of implicit content and implicit reference are formalized in the theory of **null instantiations (NIs)** (Fillmore, 1986; Ruppenhofer, 2005). A complete frame-semantic analysis of text thus incorporates covert *and* overt predicate-argument information.

In this paper, we describe a system for frame-semantic analysis, evaluated on a semantic role labeling task for explicit and implicit arguments (§2). Extending the SEMAFOR 1.0 frame-semantic parser (Das et al., 2010a; outlined in §3), we detect null instantiations via a simple two-stage pipeline: the first stage predicts *whether* a given role is null-instantiated, and the second stage (§4) predicts *how* it is null-instantiated, if it is not overt. We report performance on the SemEval 2010 test set under the full-SRL and NI-only conditions.

2 Data

The SemEval 2007 task on frame-semantic parsing (Baker et al., 2007) provided a small (about 50,000 words and 2,000 sentences) dataset of news text, travel guides, and bureaucratic accounts of weapons stockpiles. Sentences in this dataset were fully annotated with frames and their arguments. The SemEval 2010 task (Ruppenhofer et al., 2010) adds annotated data in the fiction domain: parts of two Sherlock Holmes stories by Arthur Conan Doyle. The SemEval 2010 **training set** consists of the SemEval 2007 data plus one document from the new domain. This document has about 7800 words in 438 sentences; it has 1492 annotated frame instances, including 3169 (overt and null-instantiated) argument annotations. The **test set** consists of two chapters from another story: Chapter 13 contains about 4000 words, 249 sentences, and 791 frames; Chapter 14 contains about 5000 words, 276 sentences, and 941 frames (see also Table 3). Figure 1 shows two annotated test sentences. All data released for the 2010 task include part-of-speech tags, lemmas, and phrase-structure trees from a parser, with head annotations for constituents.

3 Argument identification

Our starting point is SEMAFOR 1.0 (Das et al., 2010a), a discriminative probabilistic frame-semantic parsing model that operates in three stages: (a) rule-based target selection, (b) probabilistic disambiguation that resolves each target to a FrameNet frame, and (c) joint selection of text spans to fill the roles of each target through a second probabilistic model.[1]

[1]Das et al. (2010a) report the performance of this system on the complete SemEval 2007 task at 46.49% F_1.

Proceedings of the 5th International Workshop on Semantic Evaluation, ACL 2010, pages 264–267,
Uppsala, Sweden, 15-16 July 2010.

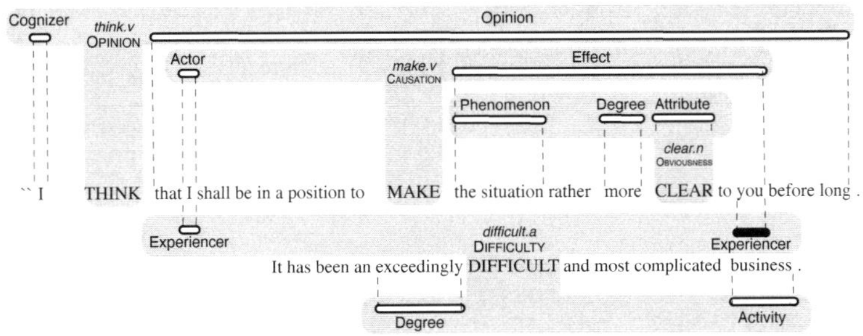

Figure 1. Two consecutive sentences in the test set, with frame-semantic annotations. Shaded regions represent frames: they include the target word in the sentence, the corresponding frame name and lexical unit, and arguments. Horizontal bars mark gold argument spans—white bars are gold annotations and black bars show mistakes of our NI-only system.

Training Data	Chapter 13 Prec.	Chapter 13 Rec.	Chapter 13 F_1	Chapter 14 Prec.	Chapter 14 Rec.	Chapter 14 F_1
SemEval 2010 data (includes SemEval 2007 data)	0.69	0.50	0.58	0.66	0.48	0.56
SemEval 2007 data + 50% new, in-domain data	0.68	0.47	0.55	0.66	0.45	0.54
SemEval 2007 data only	0.67	0.41	0.50	0.64	0.40	0.50

Table 1. Overt argument labeling performance.

Stage (c), known as **argument identification** or SRL, is most relevant here. In this step, the system takes the target (frame-evoking) phrase t and corresponding frame type f predicted by the previous stages, and independently fills each role of f with a word or phrase from the sentence, or the symbol OTHER to indicate that the role has no (local) overt argument. Features used to inform this decision include aspects of the syntactic dependency parse (e.g. the path in the parse from the target to the argument); voice; word overlap of the argument with respect to the target; and part-of-speech tags within and around the argument. SEMAFOR as described in (Das et al., 2010a) does not distinguish between different types of null instantiations or find non-local referents. Given perfect input to stage (c), the system achieved 68.5% F_1 on the SemEval 2007 data (exact match, evaluating overt arguments only). The only difference in our use of SEMAFOR's argument identification module is in preprocessing the training data: we use dependency parses transformed from the head-augmented phrase-structure parses in the task data.

Table 1 shows the performance of our argument identification model on this task's test data. The SRL systems compared in (Ruppenhofer et al., 2010) all achieved precision in the mid 60% range, but SEMAFOR achieved substantially higher recall, F_1, and label accuracy on this subtask. (The table also shows how performance of our model degrades when half or all of the new data are not used for training; the 9% difference in recall suggests the importance of in-domain training data.)

4 Null instantiation detection

In this subtask, which follows the argument identification subtask (§3), our system seeks to characterize non-overt core roles given gold standard local frame-argument annotations. Consider the following passage from the test data:

> "That's lucky for him—in fact, it's lucky for all of you, since you are all on the wrong side of the law in this matter. I am not sure that as a conscientious detective [$_{\text{Authorities}}$ my] first duty is not to arrest [$_{\text{Suspect}}$ the whole household]. [$_{\text{Charges}}^{\text{DNI}}$ $\emptyset$]

The frame we are interested in, ARREST, has four core roles, two of which (Authorities and Suspect) have overt (local) arguments. The third core role, Charges, is annotated as having anaphoric or **definite null instantiation (DNI)**. "Definite" means that the discourse implies a specific referent that should be recoverable from context, without marking that referent linguistically. Some DNIs in the data are linked to phrases in syntactically non-local positions, such as in another sentence (see Figure 1). This one is not (though our model incorrectly labels *this matter* from the previous sentence as a DNI referent for this role). The fourth core role, Offense, is not annotated as a null instantiation because it belongs to the same **CoreSet** as Charges—which is to say they are relevant in a similar way to the frame as a whole (both pertain to the rationale for the arrest) and only one is typically expressed.[2] We will use the term **masked** to refer to any non-overt core role which does not need to be specified as null-instantiated due to a structural connection to another role in its frame.

The typology of NIs given in Ruppenhofer (2005) and employed in the annotation distinguishes anaphoric/definite NIs from existential or **indefinite null instantiations (INIs)**. Rather than having a specific referent accessible in the discourse, INIs are left vague or deemphasized, as in

[2] If the FrameNet lexicon marks a pair of roles within a frame as being in a CoreSet or Excludes relationship, then filling one of them satisfies the requirement that the other be (expressly or implicitly) present in the use of the frame.

	Training Data	Chapter 13 Prec.	Rec.	F_1	Chapter 14 Prec.	Rec.	F_1
NI-only	SemEval 2010 new: 100%	0.40	0.64	0.50	0.53	0.60	0.56
	SemEval 2010 new: 75%	0.66	0.37	0.50	0.70	0.37	0.48
	SemEval 2010 new: 50%	0.73	0.38	0.51	0.75	0.35	0.48
Full	All	0.35	0.55	0.43	0.56	0.49	0.52

Table 2. Performance on the full task and the NI-only task. The NI model was trained on the new SemEval 2010 document, "The Tiger of San Pedro" (data from the 2007 task was excluded because none of the null instantiations in that data had annotated referents).

Gold \ *Predicted*	overt	DNI	INI	masked	inc.	total
overt	**2068 (1630)**	5	362	327	0	2762
DNI	64	**12 (3)**	182	90	0	348
INI	41	2	**214**	96	0	353
masked	73	0	240	**1394**	0	1707
inc.	12	2	55	2	**0**	71
total	2258	21	1053	1909	0	**3688 correct**

Table 3. Instantiation type confusion matrix for the full model (argument identification plus NI detection). Parenthesized numbers count the predictions of the correct type which also predicted the same (argument or referent) span. On the NI-only task, our system has a similar distribution of NI detection errors.

the thing(s) eaten in the sentence *We ate.*

The problem can be decomposed into two steps: (a) *classifying* each null instantiation as definite, indefinite, or masked; and (b) *resolving* the DNIs, which entails finding referents in the non-local context. Instead, our model makes a single NI prediction for any role that received no local argument (OTHER) in the argument identification phase (§3), thereby combining classification and resolution.[3]

4.1 Model

Our model for this subtask is analogous to the argument identification model: it chooses one from among many possible fillers for each role. However, whereas the argument identification model considers parse constituents as potential local fillers (which might constitute an overt argument within the sentence) along with a special category, OTHER, here the set of candidate fillers consists of phrases from outside the sentence, along with special categories INI or MASKED. When selected, a non-local phrase will be interpreted as a non-local argument and labeled as a DNI referent.

These non-local candidate fillers are handled differently from candidates within the sentence considered in the argument identification model: they are selected using more restrictive criteria, and are associated with a different set of features.

Restricted search space for DNI referents. We consider nouns, pronouns, and noun phrases from the previous three sentences as candidate DNI referents. This narrows the search space considerably to make learning tractable, but at a cost: many gold DNI referents will not even be considered. In the training data, there are about 250 DNI instances with explicit referents; their distribution is chaotic.[4] Judging by the training data, our heuristics thus limit oracle recall to about 20% of DNIs.[5]

Modified feature set. Since it is not obvious how to calculate a syntactic path between two words in different sentences, we replaced dependency path features with simpler features derived from FrameNet's lexicographic exemplar annotations. For each candidate span, we use two types of features to model the affinity between the head word and the role. The first indicates whether the head word is used as a filler for this role in at least one of the lexicographic exemplars. The second encodes the maximum distributional similarity to any word heading a filler of that role in the exemplars.[6] In practice, we found that these features received negligible weight and had virtually no effect on performance, possibly due to data sparseness. An additional change in the feature set is that ordering/distance features (Das et al., 2010b, p. 13) were replaced with a feature indicating the number of *sentences* away the candidate is from the target.[7] Otherwise, the null identifica-

[3]Investigation of separate modeling is left to future work.

[4]91 DNI referents are found no more than three sentences prior; another 90 are in the same sentence as the target. 20 DNIs have referents which are not noun phrases. Six appear *after* the sentence containing its frame target; 28 appear at least 25 sentences prior. 60 have no referent.

[5]Our system ignores DNIs with no referent or with a referent in the same sentence as the target. Experiments with variants on these assumptions show that the larger the search space (i.e. the more candidate DNI referents are under consideration), the worse the trained model performs at distinguishing NIs from non-NIs (though DNI vs. INI precision improves). This suggests that data sparseness is hindering our system's ability to learn useful generalizations about NIs.

[6]Distributional similarity scores are obtained from D. Lin's Proximity-based Thesaurus (`http://webdocs.cs.ualberta.ca/~lindek/Downloads/sims.lsp.gz`) and quantized into binary features for intervals: $[0, .03)$, $[.03, .06)$, $[.06, .08)$, $[.08, \infty)$.

[7]All of the new features are instantiated in three forms:

tion model uses the same features as the argument identification model.

The theory of null instantiations holds that the grammaticality of lexically-licensed NI for a role in a given frame depends on the LU: for example, the verbs *buy* and *sell* share the same frame but differ as to whether the Buyer or Seller role may be lexically null-instantiated. Our model's feature set is rich enough to capture this in a soft way, with lexicalized features that fire, e.g., when the Seller role is null-instantiated and the target is *buy*. Moreover, (Ruppenhofer, 2005) hypothesizes that each role has a strong preference for one interpretation (INI or DNI) when it is lexically null-instantiated, regardless of LU. This, too, is modeled in our feature set. In theory these trends should be learnable given sufficient data, though it is doubtful that there are enough examples of null instantiations in the currently available dataset for this learning to take place.

4.2 Evaluation

We trained the model on the non-overt arguments in the new SemEval 2010 training document, which has 580 null instantiations—303 DNIs and 277 INIs.[8,9] Then we used the task scoring procedure to evaluate the NI detection subtask in isolation (given gold-standard overt arguments) as well as the full task (when this module is combined in a pipeline with argument identification). Results are shown in Table 2.[10]

Table 3 provides a breakdown of our system's predictions on the test data by instantiation type: overt local arguments, DNIs, INIs, and the MASKED category (marking the role as redundant or irrelevant for the particular use of the frame, given the other arguments). It also shows counts for **incorporated** ("inc.") roles, which are filled by the frame-evoking target, e.g. *clear* in Figure 1.[11] This table shows that the system is reasonably effective at discriminating NIs from masked roles, but DNI identification suffers from low recall and INI identification from low precision. Data sparseness is likely the biggest obstacle here. To put this in perspective, there are over 20,000 training examples of overt arguments, but fewer than 600 examples of null instantiations, two thirds of which do not have referents. Without an order of magnitude more NI data (at least), it is unlikely that a supervised learner could generalize well enough to recognize on new data null instantiations of the over 7000 roles in the lexicon.

5 Conclusion

We have described a system that implements a clean probabilistic model of frame-semantic structure, considering overt arguments as well as various forms of null instantion of roles. The system was evaluated on SemEval 2010 data, with mixed success at detecting null instantiations. We believe in-domain data sparseness is the predominant factor limiting the robustness of our supervised model.

Acknowledgments

This work was supported by DARPA grant NBCH-1080004 and computational resources provided by Yahoo. We thank the task organizers for providing data and conducting the evaluation, and two reviewers for their comments.

References

C. Baker, M. Ellsworth, and K. Erk. 2007. SemEval-2007 Task 19: Frame Semantic Structure Extraction. In *Proc. of SemEval*.

D. Das, N. Schneider, D. Chen, and N. A. Smith. 2010a. Probabilistic frame-semantic parsing. In *Proc. of NAACL-HLT*.

D. Das, N. Schneider, D. Chen, and N. A. Smith. 2010b. SEMAFOR 1.0: A probabilistic frame-semantic parser. Technical Report CMU-LTI-10-001, Carnegie Mellon University.

C. J. Fillmore, C. R. Johnson, and M. R.L. Petruck. 2003. Background to FrameNet. *International Journal of Lexicography*, 16(3).

C. J. Fillmore. 1982. Frame semantics. In *Linguistics in the Morning Calm*, pages 111–137. Hanshin Publishing Co., Seoul, South Korea.

C. J. Fillmore. 1986. Pragmatically controlled zero anaphora. In *Proc. of Berkeley Linguistics Society*, pages 95–107, Berkeley, CA.

J. Ruppenhofer, M. Ellsworth, M. R.L. Petruck, C. R. Johnson, and J. Scheffczyk. 2006. FrameNet II: extended theory and practice.

J. Ruppenhofer, C. Sporleder, R. Morante, C. Baker, and M. Palmer. 2010. SemEval-2010 Task 10: Linking Events and Their Participants in Discourse. In *Proc. of SemEval*.

J. Ruppenhofer. 2005. Regularities in null instantiation.

one specific to the frame and the role, one specific to the role name only, and one to learn the overall bias of the data.

[8]For feature engineering we held out the last 25% of sentences from the new training document as development data, retraining on the full training set for final evaluation.

[9]We used Nils Reiter's FrameNet API, version 0.4 (`http://www.cl.uni-heidelberg.de/trac/FrameNetAPI`) in processing the data.

[10]The other system participating in the NI-only subtask had much lower NI recall of 8% (Ruppenhofer et al., 2010).

[11]We do not predict any DNIs without referents or incorporated roles, though the evaluation script gives us credit when we predict INI for these cases.

Cambridge: Parser Evaluation using Textual Entailment by Grammatical Relation Comparison

Laura Rimell and **Stephen Clark**
University of Cambridge
Computer Laboratory
{laura.rimell,stephen.clark}@cl.cam.ac.uk

Abstract

This paper describes the Cambridge submission to the SemEval-2010 Parser Evaluation using Textual Entailment (PETE) task. We used a simple definition of entailment, parsing both T and H with the C&C parser and checking whether the core grammatical relations (subject and object) produced for H were a subset of those for T. This simple system achieved the top score for the task out of those systems submitted. We analyze the errors made by the system and the potential role of the task in parser evaluation.

1 Introduction

SemEval-2010 Task 12, Parser Evaluation using Textual Entailment (PETE) (Yuret et al., 2010), was designed as a new, formalism-independent type of parser evaluation scheme. The task is broadly Recognizing Textual Entailment (RTE), but unlike typical RTE tasks, its intention is to focus on purely syntactic entailments, assuming no background knowledge or reasoning ability. For example, given a text (T) *The man with the hat was tired.*, the hypothesis (H) *The man was tired.* is entailed, but *The hat was tired.* is not. A correct decision on whether H is entailed can be used as a diagnostic for the parser's analysis of (some aspect of) T. By requiring only a binary decision on the entailment, instead of a full syntactic analysis, a parser can be evaluated while its underlying formalism remains a "black box".

Our system had two components: a parser, and an entailment system which decided whether T entails H based on the parser's output. We distinguish two types of evaluation. *Task evaluation*, i.e. the official task scoring, indicates whether the entailment decisions – made by the parser and entailment system together – tally with the gold standard dataset. *Entailment system evaluation*, on the other hand, indicates whether the entailment system is an appropriate parser evaluation tool. In the PETE task the parser is not evaluated directly on the dataset, since the entailment system acts as intermediary. Therefore, for PETE to be a viable parser evaluation scheme, each parser must be coupled with an entailment system which accurately reflects the parser's analysis of the data.

2 System

We used the C&C parser (Clark and Curran, 2007), which can produce output in the form of grammatical relations (GRs), i.e. labelled head-dependencies. For example, `(nsubj tired man)` for the example in Section 1 represents the fact that the NP headed by *man* is the subject of the predicate headed by *tired*. We chose to use the Stanford Dependency GR scheme (de Marneffe et al., 2006), but the same approach should work for other schemes (and other parsers producing GRs).

Our entailment system was very simple, and based on the assumption that H is a simplified version of T (true for this task though not for RTE in general). We parsed both T and H with the C&C parser. Let grs(S) be the GRs the parser produces for a sentence S. In principle, if grs(H) $\subseteq$ grs(T), then we would consider H an entailment. In practice, a few refinements to this rule are necessary.

We identified three exceptional cases. First, syntactic transformations between T and H may change GR labels. The most common transformation in this dataset was passivization, meaning that a direct object in T could be a passive subject in H.

Second, H could contain tokens not present in T. Auxiliary verbs were introduced by passivization. Pronouns such as *somebody* and *something* were introduced into some H sentences to indicate an NP or other phrase not targeted for evaluation. Determiners were sometimes introduced or changed, e.g. *prices* to *the prices*. Expletive subjects were also sometimes introduced.

Proceedings of the 5th International Workshop on Semantic Evaluation, ACL 2010, pages 268–271,
Uppsala, Sweden, 15-16 July 2010.

Third, the parses of T and H might be inconsistent in an incidental way. Consider the pair *I reached into that funny little pocket that is high up on my dress.* $\Rightarrow$ *The pocket is high up on something.* The intended focus of the evaluation (as indicated by the content word pair supplied as a supplement to the gold standard development data) is *(pocket, high)*. As long as the parser analyzes *pocket* as the subject of *high*, we want to avoid penalizing it for, say, treating the PP *up on X* differently in T and H.

To address these issues we used a small set of heuristics. First, we ignored any GR in grs(H) containing a token not in T. This addressed the passive auxiliaries, pronouns, determiners, and expletive subjects. Second, we equated passive subjects with direct objects. Similar rules could be defined for other transformations, but we implemented only this one based on the prevalence of passivization in the development data. Third, when checking whether grs(H) $\subseteq$ grs(T), we considered only the core relations subject and object. The intention was that incidental differences between the parses of T and H would not be counted as errors. We chose these GR types based on the nature of the entailments in the development data, but the system could easily be reconfigured to focus on other relation types. Finally, we required grs(H) $\cap$ grs(T) to be non-empty (no vacuous positives), but did not restrict this criterion to subjects and objects.

We used a PTB tokenizer[1] for consistency with the parser's training data. We used the morpha lemmatizer (Minnen et al., 2000), which is built into the C&C tools, to match tokens across T and H; and we converted all tokens to lowercase. If the parser failed to find a spanning analysis for either T or H, the entailment decision was NO. The full pipeline is shown in Figure 1.

Tokenize T and H with PTB tokenizer

$\Downarrow$

Parse T and H with C&C parser

$\Downarrow$

Lowercase and lemmatize all tokens

$\Downarrow$

Discard any GR in grs(H) containing a token not in T

$\Downarrow$

YES if core(H) $\subseteq$ core(T) and grs(H) $\cap$ grs(T) $\neq \emptyset$, NO otherwise

Figure 1: Full pipeline for parser and entailment system. core(S): the set of core (subject and object) GRs in grs(S).

3 Results

A total of 19 systems were submitted. The baseline score for "always YES" was 51.8% accuracy. Our system achieved 72.4% accuracy, which was the highest score among the submitted systems. Table 1 shows the results for our system, as well as SCHWA (University of Sydney), also based on the C&C parser and the next-highest scorer (see Section 6 for a comparison), and the median and lowest scores. The parser found an analysis for 99.0% of T sentences and 99.7% of H sentences in the test data.

4 Error Analysis

Table 2 shows the results for our system on the development data (66 sentences). The parser found an analysis for 100% of sentences and the overall accuracy was 66.7%. In the majority of cases the parser and entailment system worked together to find the correct answer as expected. For example, for *Trading in AMR shares was suspended shortly after 3 p.m. EDT Friday and didn't resume.* $\Rightarrow$ *Trading didn't resume.*, the parser produced three GRs for H (tokens are shown lemmatized and lowercase): `(nsubj resume trading)`, `(neg do n't)`, and `(aux resume do)`. All of these were also in grs(T), and the correct YES decision was made. For *Moreland sat brooding for a full minute, during which I made each of us a new drink.* $\Rightarrow$ *Minute is made.*, the parser produced two GRs for H. One, `(auxpass make be)`, was ignored because the passive auxiliary *be* is not in T. The second, passive subject GR `(nsubjpass make minute)` was equated with a direct object `(dobj make minute)`. This GR was not in grs(T), so the correct NO decision was made.

In some cases a correct YES answer was reached via arguably insufficient positive evidence. For *He would wake up in the middle of the night and fret about it.* $\Rightarrow$ *He would wake up.*, the parser produces incorrect analyses for the VP *would wake up* for both T and H. However, these GRs are ignored since they are non-core (not subject or object), and a YES decision is based on the single GR match `(nsubj would he)`. This

[1]http://www.cis.upenn.edu/~treebank/tokenizer.sed.

System	Score on YES entailments correct	incorrect	accuracy (%)	Score on NO entailments correct	incorrect	accuracy (%)	Overall accuracy (%)
Cambridge	98	58	62.8	120	25	82.8	72.4
SCHWA	125	31	80.1	87	58	60.0	70.4
Median	71	85	45.5	88	57	60.7	52.8
Low	68	88	43.6	76	69	52.4	47.8

Table 1: Results on the test data.

System	Score on YES entailments correct	incorrect	accuracy (%)	Score on NO entailments correct	incorrect	accuracy (%)	Overall accuracy (%)
Cambridge	22	16	57.9	22	6	78.6	66.7

Table 2: Results on the development data.

Type	FN	FP	Total
Unbounded dependency	8	1	9
Other parser error	6	2	8
Entailment system	1	3	4
Difficult entailment	1	0	1
Total	16	6	22

Table 3: Error breakdown on the development data. FN: false negative, FP: false positive.

is not entirely a lucky guess, since the entailment system has correctly ignored the odd analyses of *would wake up* and focused on the role of *he* as the subject of the sentence. However, especially since the target content word pair was *(he, wake)*, more positive evidence would be desirable. Of the 22 correct YES decisions, only two were truly lucky guesses in that the single match was a determiner; others had at least one core match.

Table 3 shows the breakdown of errors. The largest category was false negatives due to unbounded dependencies not recovered by the parser, for example *It required an energy he no longer possessed to be satirical about his father. ⇒ Somebody no longer possessed the energy.*. Here the parser fails to recover the direct object relation between *possess* and *energy* in T. It is known that parsers have difficulty with unbounded dependencies (Rimell et al., 2009, from which the unbounded examples in this dataset were obtained), so this result is not surprising.

The next category was other parser errors. This is a miscellaneous category including e.g. errors on coordination, parenthetical elements, identifying the head of a clausal subject, and one due to the POS tagger. For example, for *Then at least he would have a place to hang his tools and something to work on. ⇒ He would have something to work on.*, the parser incorrectly coordinated *tools* and *something* for T. As a result `(dobj have something)` was in grs(H) but not grs(T), yielding an incorrect NO.

Four errors were due to the entailment system rather than the parser; these will be dicsussed in Section 5. We also identified one sentence where the gold standard entailment appears to rely on extra-syntactic information, or at least information that is difficult for a parser to recover. This is *Index-arbitrage trading is "something we want to watch closely," an official at London's Stock Exchange said. ⇒ We want to watch index-arbitrage trading.* Recovering the entailment would require resolving the reference of *something*, arguably the role of a semantic rather than syntactic module.

5 Entailment System Evaluation

We now consider whether our entailment system was an appropriate tool for evaluating the C&C parser on the PETE dataset. It is easy to imagine a poor entailment system that makes incorrect guesses in spite of good parser output, or conversely one that uses additional reasoning to supplement the parser's analysis. To be an appropriate *parser evaluation tool*, the entailment system must decide whether the information in H is also contained in the parse of T, without "introducing" or "correcting" any errors.

Assuming our GR-based approach is valid, then given gold-standard GRs for T and H, we expect an appropriate entailment system to result in 100% accuracy on the task evaluation. To perform this oracle experiment we annotated the development data with gold-standard GRs. Using our entailment system with the gold GRs we achieved 90.9% task accuracy. Six incorrect entailment decisions were made, of which one was on the arguably extra-syntactic entailment discussed in Section 4.

Three errors were due to transformations between T and H which changed the GR label or head. For example, consider *Occasionally, the children find steamed, whole-wheat grains for cereal which they call "buckshot".* ⇒ *Grains are steamed.*. In T, *steamed* is a prenominal adjective, with *grains* as its head; while in H, it is a passive, with *grains* as its subject. The entailment system did not account for this transformation, although in principle it could have. The other two errors occurred because GRs involving a non-core relation or a pronoun introduced in H, both of which our system ignored, were crucial for the correct entailment decision.

Table 3 shows that with automatically-generated GRs, four errors on the task evaluation were attributable to the entailment system. Three of these were also found in the oracle experiment. The fourth resulted from a POS change between T and H for *There was the revolution in Tibet which we pretended did not exist.* ⇒ *The pretended did not exist.*. The crucial GR was `(nsubj exist pretended)` in grs(H), but the entailment system ignored it because the lemmatizer did not give *pretend* as the lemma for *pretended* as a noun. This type of error might be prevented by answering NO if the POS of any word changes between T and H, but the implementation is non-trivial since word indices may also change. There were eight POS changes in the development data, most of which did not result in errors. We also observed two cases where the entailment system "corrected" parser errors, yielding a correct entailment decision despite the parser's incorrect analysis of T. When compared with a manual analysis of whether T entailed H based on automatically-generated GRs, the entailment system achieved 89.4% overall accuracy.

6 Conclusion

We achieved a successful result on the PETE task using a state-of-the-art parser and a simple entailment system, which tested syntactic entailments by comparing the GRs produced by the parser for T and H. We also showed that our entailment system had accuracy of approximately 90% as a tool for evaluating the C&C parser (or potentially any parser producing GR-style output) on the PETE development data. This latter result is perhaps even more important than the task score since it suggests that PETE is worth pursuing as a viable approach to parser evaluation.

The second-highest scoring system, SCHWA (University of Sydney), was also based on the C&C parser and used a similar approach (though using CCG dependency output rather than GRs). It achieved almost identical task accuracy to the Cambridge system, but interestingly with higher accuracy on YES entailments, while our system was more accurate on NO entailments (Table 1). We attribute this difference to the decision criteria: both systems required at least one matching relation between T and H for a YES answer; but we additionally answered NO if any core GR in grs(H) was not in grs(T). This difference shows that a GR-based entailment system can be tuned to favour precision or recall.

Finally, we note that although this was a simple entailment system with some dataset-specific characteristics – such as a focus on subject and object relations rather than, say, PP-attachment – these aspects should be amenable to customization or generalization for other related tasks.

Acknowledgments

The authors were supported by EPSRC grant EP/E035698/1. We thank Matthew Honnibal for his help in producing the gold-standard GRs.

References

Stephen Clark and James R. Curran. 2007. Wide-coverage efficient statistical parsing with CCG and log-linear models. *Computational Linguistics*, 33(4):493–552.

Marie-Catherine de Marneffe, Bill MacCartney, and Christopher D. Manning. 2006. Generating typed dependency parses from phrase structure parses. In *Proceedings of LREC*, Genoa, Italy.

Guido Minnen, John Carroll, and Darren Pearce. 2000. Robust, applied morphological generation. In *Proceedings of INLG*, Mitzpe Ramon, Israel.

Laura Rimell, Stephen Clark, and Mark Steedman. 2009. Unbounded dependency recovery for parser evaluation. In *Proceedings of EMNLP*, Singapore.

Deniz Yuret, Aydın Han, and Zehra Turgut. 2010. Semeval-2010 task 12: Parser evaluation using textual entailments. In *Proceedings of SemEval-2010*, Uppsala, Sweden.

MARS: A Specialized RTE System for Parser Evaluation

Rui Wang[†] **Yi Zhang**[†‡]
† Department of Computational Linguistics, Saarland University
‡ LT-Lab, German Research Center for Artificial Intelligence
Im Stadtwald, 66123 Saarbrücken, Germany
{rwang,yzhang}@coli.uni-sb.de

Abstract

This paper describes our participation in the the SemEval-2010 Task #12, *Parser Evaluation using Textual Entailment*. Our system incorporated two dependency parsers, one semantic role labeler, and a deep parser based on hand-crafted grammars. The shortest path algorithm is applied on the graph representation of the parser outputs. Then, different types of features are extracted and the entailment recognition is casted into a machine-learning-based classification task. The best setting of the system achieves 66.78% of accuracy, which ranks the 3rd place.

1 Introduction

The SemEval-2010 Task #12, *Parser Evaluation using Textual Entailment* (PETE) (Yuret et al., 2010), is an interesting task connecting two areas of research, parsing and recognizing textual entailment (RTE) (Dagan et al., 2005). The former is usually concerned with syntactic analysis in specific linguistic frameworks, while the latter is believed to involve more semantic aspects of the human languages. However, no clear-cut boundary can be drawn between syntax and semantics for both tasks. In recent years, the parsing community has been reaching beyond what was usually accepted as syntactic structures. Many deep linguistic frameworks allow the construction of semantic representations in parallel to the syntactic structure. Meanwhile, data-driven shallow semantic parsers (or semantic role labelers) are another popular type of extension to enrich the information in the parser outputs.

Although *entailment* is described as a semantic relation, RTE, in practice, covers linguistic phenomena at various levels, from surface text to the meaning, even to the context and discourse. One proposal of solving the problem is to deal with different cases of entailment using different specialized RTE modules (Wang and Neumann, 2009). Then, the PETE data can be naturally classified into the syntactic and shallow semantic categories.

By participating in this shared task, we aim to investigate whether different parsing outputs leads to different RTE accuracy, and on the contrary, whether the "application"-based evaluation provides insights to the parser comparison. Further, we investigate if strict grammaticality checking with a linguistic grammar is helpful in this task.

2 System Description

The workflow of the system is shown in Figure 1 and the details of the three components will be elaborated on in the following sections.

2.1 Preprocessing

In this paper, we generally refer all the linguistic analyses on the text as *preprocessing*. The output of this procedure is a graph representation, which approximates the meaning of the input text. In particular, after tokenization and POS tagging, we did dependency parsing and semantic role labeling. In addition, HPSG parsing is a filter for ungrammatical hypotheses.

Tokenization and POS Tagging We use the Penn Treebank style tokenization throughout the various processing stages. **TnT**, an HMM-based POS tagger trained with Wall Street Journal sections of the PTB, was used to automatically predict the part-of-speech of each token in the texts and hypotheses.

Dependency Parsing For obtaining the syntactic dependencies, we use two dependency parsers, MSTParser (McDonald et al., 2005) and MaltParser (Nivre et al., 2007). MSTParser is a graph-based dependency parser where the best parse tree is acquired by searching for a spanning tree

Proceedings of the 5th International Workshop on Semantic Evaluation, ACL 2010, pages 272–275,
Uppsala, Sweden, 15-16 July 2010.

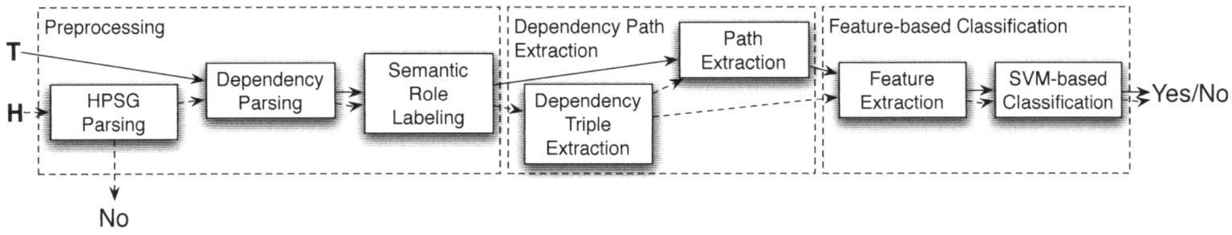

Figure 1: Workflow of the System

which maximize the score on an either partially or fully connected dependency graph. MaltParser is a transition-based incremental dependency parser, which is language-independent and data-driven. It contains a deterministic algorithm, which can be viewed as a variant of the basic shift-reduce algorithm. Both parsers can achieve state-of-the-art performance and Figure 2 shows the resulting syntactic dependency trees of the following T-H pair,

> ID: *2036*; Entailment: *YES*
> **T**: *Devotees of the market question the value of the work national service would perform.*
> **H**: *Value is questioned.*

Semantic Role Labeling The statistical dependency parsers provide shallow syntactic analyses of the entailment pairs through the limited vocabulary of the dependency relations. In our case, the CoNLL shared task dataset from 2008 were used to train the statistical dependency parsing models. While such dependencies capture interesting syntactic relations, when compared to the parsing systems with deeper representations, the contained information is not as detailed. To compensate for this, we used a shallow semantic parser to predict the semantic role relations in the **T** and **H** of entailment pairs. The shallow semantic parser was also trained with CoNLL 2008 shared task dataset, with semantic roles extracted from the Propbank and Nombank annotations (Zhang et al., 2008). Figure 3 shows the resulting semantic dependency graphs of the T-H pair.

HPSG Parsing We employ the English Resource Grammar (Flickinger, 2000), a hand-written linguistic grammar in the framework of HPSG, and the PET HPSG parser (Callmeier, 2001) to check the grammaticality of each hypothesis sentence. As the hypotheses in this PETE shared task were automatically generated, some ungrammatical hypotheses occur in non-entailment pairs. the grammaticality checking allows us to quickly identify these instances.

2.2 Dependency Path Extraction

According to the task definition, we need to verify whether those dependency relations in H also appear in T. We firstly find out all the important dependency triples in H, like <word, dependency relation, word>, excluding those having stop words. The extracted syntactic dependency triples of the example T-H pair would be none, since the only content words "value" and "questioned" have no direct syntactic dependency in-between (Figure 2). The extracted semantic dependency triples would be <"questioned", "A1", "value"> (Figure 3).

After that, we use the word pairs contained in the extracted dependency triples as anchors to find out the corresponding dependency relations in T. Notice that it is not necessarily that we can always find a direct dependency relation in T between the same word pair, so we need to traverse the dependency tree or graph to find the *dependency paths*. In general, we treat all the dependency trees and graphs as undirected graphs with loops, but keep records for the directions of the edges we traverse. For the following three representations, we apply slightly different algorithms to find the dependency path between two words,

Syntactic Dependency Tree We simply traverse the tree and find the corresponding dependency path connecting the two words;

Semantic Dependency Graph We apply Dijkstra's algorithm (Dijkstra, 1959) to find the shortest path between the two words;

Joint Dependency Graph We assign different weights to syntactic and semantic dependencies and apply Dijkstra's algorithm to find the shortest path (with the lowest cost)[1].

2.3 Feature-based Classification

Based on the meaning representation we have discussed above (Section 2.1 and Section 2.2), we ex-

[1] In practice, we simply give semantic dependencies 0.5 cost and syntactic dependencies 1.0 cost, to show the preferences on the former when both exist.

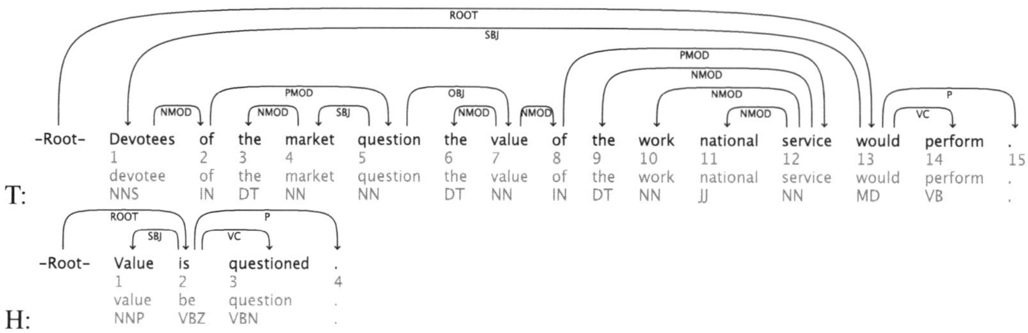

Figure 2: Syntactic dependency of the example T-H pair by MaltParser.

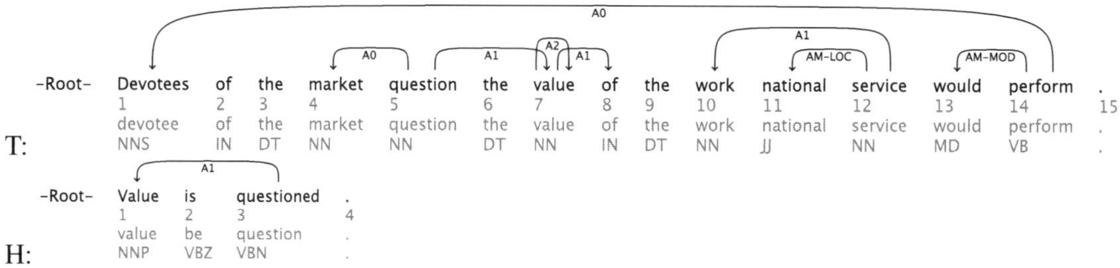

Figure 3: Semantic dependency of the example T-H pair by MaltParser and our SRL system.

tract features for the machine-learning-based classifier. First of all, we should check whether there are dependency triples extracted from H, otherwise for our system, there is no meaning representation for that sentence. Then we also need to check whether the same words can be found in T as well. Only if the corresponding dependency paths are successfully located in T, we could extract the following features.

The direction of each dependency relation or path could be interesting. The direction of the H-path is clear, so we only need to check the direction of the T-path. In practice, we simply use a boolean value to represent whether T-path contains dependency relations with different directions. For instance, in Figure 3, if we extract the path from "market" to "value", the directions of the dependency relations contained in the path would be $\leftarrow$ and $\rightarrow$, one of which would be inconsistent with the dependency relation in H.

Notice that all the dependency paths from H have length 1[2], but the lengths of the dependency paths from T are varied. If the latter length is also 1, we can simply compare the two dependency relations; otherwise, we compare each of the dependency relation contained the T-path with H-path one by one[3]. By comparison, we mainly focus on two values, the category of the dependency relation (e.g. syntactic dependency vs. semantic dependency) and the content of the dependency relation (e.g. A1 vs. AM-LOC).

We also incorporate the string value of the dependency relation pair and make it boolean according to whether it occurs or not. Table 1 shows the feature types we extract from each T-H pair.

3 Experiments

As we mentioned in the preprocessing section (Section 2.1), we utilize the open source dependency parsers, MSTParser[4] and MaltParser[5], our own semantic role labeler (Zhang et al., 2008), and the PET HPSG parser[6]. For the shortest path algorithm, we use the jGraphT package[7]; and for the machine learning toolkit, we use the UniverSVM

[2]The length of one dependency path is defined as the number of dependency relations contained in the path.

[3]Enlightened by Wang and Neumann (2007), we exclude some dependency relations like "CONJ", "COORD", "APPO", etc., heuristically, since in most of the cases, they will not change the relationship between the two words at both ends of the path.

[4]`http://sourceforge.net/projects/mstparser/`

[5]`http://maltparser.org/`

[6]`http://heartofgold.dfki.de/PET.html`

[7]`http://jgrapht.sourceforge.net/`

	H_Null?	T_Null?	Dir	Multi?	Dep_Same?	Rel_Sim?	Rel_Same?	Rel_Pair
Joint	+	+	+	+	+	+	+	+
No Sem		+	+	+			+	+
No Syn	+	+	+	+		+	+	+

Table 1: Feature types of different settings of the system. *H_Null?* means whether H has dependencies; *T_Null?* means whether T has the corresponding paths (using the same word pairs found in H); *Dir* is whether the direction of the path T the same as H; *Multi?* adds a prefix, *m_*, to the *Rel_Pair* features, if the T-path is longer than one dependency relation; *Dep_Same?* checks whether the two dependency types are the same, i.e. syntactic and semantic dependencies; *Rel_Sim?* only occurs when two semantic dependencies are compared, meaning whether they have the same prefixes, e.g. *C-*, *AM-*, etc.; *Rel_Same?* checks whether the two dependency relations are the same; and *Rel_Pair* simple concatenates the two relation labels together. Notice that, the first seven feature types all contain boolean values, and for the last one, we make it boolean as well, by observing whether that pair of dependency labels appear or not.

package[8]. We test different dependency graphs and feature sets as mentioned before (Table 1), and the results are shown in Table 2.

	MSTParser+SRL			MaltParser+SRL		
	Joint	No Sem	No Syn	Joint	No Sem	No Syn
+GC	0.5249	0.5116 (-1.3%)	0.5050 (-2.0%)	0.6678	0.5282 (-14.0%)	0.6346 (-3.3%)
-GC	0.5216	0.5050	0.4950	0.6545	0.5282	0.6179

Table 2: Experiment results of our system with different settings.

First of all, in almost all the cases, the grammaticality checking based on HPSG parsing is helpful, if we compare each pair of results at the two rows, +GC and -GC. In all cases, the joint graph representation achieves better results. This indicates that features extracted from both syntactic dependency and shallow semantic dependency are useful for the entailment recognition. For the MaltParser case, the semantic features show great importance. Notice that the performance of the whole system does not necessarily reflect the performance of the parser itself, since it also depends on our entailment modules. In all, the best setting of our system ranks the 3rd place in the evaluation.

4 Conclusion

In this paper, we present our system used in the PETE task, which consists of preprocessing, dependency path extraction, and feature-based classification. We use MSTParser and MaltParser as dependency parsers, our SRL system as a shallow semantic parser, and a deep parser based on hand-crafted grammars for grammaticality checking. The entailment recognition is done by an SVM-based classifier using features extracted from the graph representation of the parser outputs. Based on the results, we tentatively conclude that both the syntactic and the shallow semantic features are useful. A detailed error analysis would be our ongoing work in the near future.

[8] `http://www.kyb.mpg.de/bs/people/fabee/universvm.html`

Acknowledgment

The authors thank the PIRE PhD scholarship and the German Excellence Cluster of MMCI for the support of the work.

References

Ulrich Callmeier. 2001. Efficient parsing with large-scale unification grammars. Master's thesis, Universität des Saarlandes, Saarbrücken, Germany.

Ido Dagan, Oren Glickman, and Bernardo Magnini. 2005. The pascal recognising textual entailment challenge. In Quiñonero-Candela et al., editor, *MLCW 2005*, volume LNAI Volume 3944, pages 177–190. Springer-Verlag.

E. W. Dijkstra. 1959. A note on two problems in connexion with graphs. *Numerische Mathematik*, 1:269–271.

Dan Flickinger. 2000. On building a more efficient grammar by exploiting types. *Natural Language Engineering*, 6(1):15–28.

Ryan McDonald, Fernando Pereira, Kiril Ribarov, and Jan Hajic. 2005. Non-Projective Dependency Parsing using Spanning Tree Algorithms. In *Proceedings of HLT-EMNLP 2005*, pages 523–530, Vancouver, Canada.

Joakim Nivre, Jens Nilsson, Johan Hall, Atanas Chanev, Gülsen Eryigit, Sandra Kübler, Svetoslav Marinov, and Erwin Marsi. 2007. Maltparser: A language-independent system for data-driven dependency parsing. *Natural Language Engineering*, 13(1):1–41.

Rui Wang and Günter Neumann. 2007. Recognizing textual entailment using a subsequence kernel method. In *Proceedings of AAAI-07*, Vancouver, Canada, July.

Rui Wang and Günter Neumann. 2009. An accuracy-oriented divide-and-conquer strategy for recognizing textual entailment. In *Proceedings of TAC 2008*, Gaithersburg, Maryland, USA.

Deniz Yuret, Aydın Han, and Zehra Turgut. 2010. Semeval-2010 task 12: Parser evaluation using textual entailments. In *Proceedings of the SemEval-2010 Evaluation Exercises on Semantic Evaluation*.

Yi Zhang, Rui Wang, and Hans Uszkoreit. 2008. Hybrid learning of dependency structures from heterogeneous linguistic resources. In *Proceedings of the Twelfth Conference on Computational Natural Language Learning (CoNLL 2008)*, pages 198–202, Manchester, UK.

TRIPS and TRIOS System for TempEval-2: Extracting Temporal Information from Text

Naushad UzZaman
University of Rochester
Rochester, NY, USA
naushad@cs.rochester.edu

James F. Allen
University of Rochester
Rochester, NY, USA
james@cs.rochester.edu

Abstract

Extracting temporal information from raw text is fundamental for deep language understanding, and key to many applications like question answering, information extraction, and document summarization. In this paper, we describe two systems we submitted to the TempEval 2 challenge, for extracting temporal information from raw text. The systems use a combination of deep semantic parsing, Markov Logic Networks and Conditional Random Field classifiers. Our two submitted systems, TRIPS and TRIOS, approached all tasks and outperformed all teams in two tasks. Furthermore, TRIOS mostly had second-best performances in other tasks. TRIOS also outperformed the other teams that attempted all the tasks. Our system is notable in that for tasks C – F, they operated on raw text while all other systems used tagged events and temporal expressions in the corpus as input.

1 Introduction

The recent emergence of language processing applications like question answering, information extraction, and document summarization has drawn attention to the need for systems that are temporally aware. For example, for a QA system in newswire domain, if we want to know who was the President of Bangladesh in the January of 1983, and we only had documents that tell us about the President from 1980 to 1985 then a temporally aware system will help the QA system to infer who was president in the January of 1983 as well. In medical domain for patient's history record, doctors write all the information about patients' medical record, usually not in chronological order. Extracting a temporal structure of the medical record will help practitioner understand the patient's medical history easily. For people who have trouble reading and understanding, be it dyslexic people, or people who are not native English speakers, a temporal structure of document could help them to follow the story better. Extracting temporal information will benefit in almost any application processing natural language text.

In this paper, we present the first step towards our goal of building such temporal structures. We participated in all tasks in TempEval 2, which includes work on extracting events, event features, temporal expressions, and various temporal relations.

We first describe our systems. Next, we show the performance of our system and compare with best performing systems on TempEval-2. Finally, we describe our future directions.

2 Our System Modules

Our approach for all the tasks is best described as hybrid between linguistically motivated solutions and machine learning classifiers. We do deep semantic parsing and use hand-coded rules to extract events, features and temporal expressions from the logical forms produced by the parser. In parallel, we filter events, extract event features, temporal expressions, classify temporal relations using machine-learning classifiers. We describe these modules briefly here and in the next sections will describe how these modules are used in solving different subtasks.

2.1 TRIPS Parser

We use the existing TRIPS parser (Allen et al, 2008) to produce deep logical forms from text. The system is generic and no grammatical rules or lexical entries were added specifically for this task. The TRIPS grammar is lexicalized context-free grammar, augmented with feature structures and feature unification. The grammar is motivated from X-bar theory, and draws on principles from GPSG (e.g., head and foot features) and HPSG. The parser uses a packed-forest chart representation and builds constituents bottom-up using a best-first search strategy similar to A*,

Proceedings of the 5th International Workshop on Semantic Evaluation, ACL 2010, pages 276–283,
Uppsala, Sweden, 15-16 July 2010. ©2010 Association for Computational Linguistics

based on rule and lexical weights and the influences of statistical preprocessing. The search terminates when a pre-specified number of spanning constituents have been found or a pre-specified maximum chart size is reached. The chart is then searched using a dynamic programming algorithm to find the least cost sequence of logical forms according to a cost table that can be varied by genre.

The TRIPS system here uses a wide range of statistically driven preprocessing, including part of speech tagging, constituent bracketing, interpretation of unknown words using WordNet, and named-entity recognition (Allen et al, 2008). All these are generic off-the-shelf resources that extend and help guide the deep parsing process.

The TRIPS LF (logical form) ontology[1] is designed to be linguistically motivated and domain independent. The semantic types and selectional restrictions are driven by linguistic considerations rather than requirements from reasoning components in the system (Dzikovska et al. 2003). As much as possible the semantic types in the LF ontology are compatible with types found in FrameNet (Johnson & Fillmore 2000). FrameNet generally provides a good level of abstraction for applications since the frames are derived from corpus examples and can be reliably distinguished by human annotators. However TRIPS parser uses a smaller, more general set of semantic roles for linking the syntactic and semantic arguments rather than FrameNet's extensive set of specialized frame elements. The LF ontology defines approximately 2500 semantic types and 30 semantic roles. The TRIPS parser will produce LF representations in terms of this linguistically motivated ontology[1].

As an example, the result of parsing the sentence, *He fought in the war*, is expressed as set of expressions in an unscoped logical formalism with reified events and semantic roles.

```
(SPEECHACT V1 SA-TELL :CONTENT V2)
(F V2 (:* FIGHTING FIGHT) :AGENT V3 :MODS
(V4) :TMA ((TENSE PAST)))
(PRO V3 (:* PERSON HE) :CONTEXT-REL HE)
(F V4 (:* SITUATED-IN IN) :OF V2 :VAL V5)
(THE V5 (:* ACTION WAR))
```

The main event (V2) is of ontology type *fighting*, which is a subclass of *intentional-action*, and which corresponds to the first WordNet sense of fight, and includes verbs such as *fight*, *defend*, *contend* and *struggle*. The *agent* role of this event is the referent of the pronoun *he*, and the event is situated in an event described by the word *war*. For words not in the TRIPS core lexicon, the system looks up the WordNet senses and maps them to the TRIPS ontology. The word *war* is not in the core lexicon, and via WordNet is classified into the TRIPS ontology as the abstract type *action*.

2.2 Markov Logic Network (MLN)

One of the statistical relational learning (SRL) frameworks that has recently gained momentum as a platform for global learning and inference in AI is Markov Logic (Richardson and Domingos, 2006). Markov logic is a combination of first order logic and Markov networks. It can be seen as a formalism that extends first-order logic to allow formulae to be violated with some penalty.

For our different classification tasks, we used different classifiers based on MLNs. We used an off-the-shelf MLN classifier *Markov thebeast*[2], using Cutting Plane Inference (Riedel, 2008) with an Integer Linear Programming (ILP) solver for inference.

To use *thebeast* or any other MLN framework, at first we have to write the formulas, which corresponds to defining features for other machine learning approaches. The Markov network then learns the weights for these formulas from the training corpus and uses these weights for inference in testing phase.

One easy example will give a brief idea about these weights. To classify the event feature *class*, we have a formula that captures influence of both *tense* and *aspect* together. Here are two examples that show the learned weights for the formula from training data.

```
tense(e1, INFINITIVE) & aspect(e1, NONE) =>
class(e1, OCCURRENCE)        weight = 0.3199
tense(e1, PRESPART) & aspect(e1, NONE) =>
class(e1, REPORTING) weight = -0.2681
```

The MLN then uses these weights for reasoning about the *class*. Generally, larger the weights are, the more likely the formula holds. These weights could be negative as well, i.e. the formulas are most likely not to hold.

Finding useful features for MLNs is the same as any other ML algorithm. However, the MLN framework gives the opportunity to capture the relations between different features in first order logic, which can lead to better inference. For example, when filtering events, we have formula combining *word and pos*, or *word and previous*

[1] TRIPS ontology browser: http://www.cs.rochester.edu/research/trips/lexicon/browse-ont-lex.html

[2] http://code.google.com/p/thebeast/

word, or *pos and next pos*, where we can capture relationship of two predicates together. Many of these predicates (features) could be encoded in other classifiers concatenating the features. But when the size of relations between features increases it complicates matters and we have to regenerate the whole classifier data, every time we introduce a new relationship.

3 Event and Event Feature Extraction (Task B)

Because event extraction from the raw text is a prerequisite to everything else we do, we discuss this capability first.

3.1 Event Extraction

For event extraction, we parse the raw text with the TRIPS parser. Then we take the resulting Logical Form (LF) and apply around hundred of hand-coded extraction patterns to extract events and features, by matching semantic patterns of phrases. These hand-coded rules are devised by checking the parse output in our development set. It was 2-3 weeks of work to come up with most of the extraction rules that extract the events. There were minor incremental improvements in rules afterwards. It is worth mentioning, these rules are very generic and can be used in a new domain without any extra work, because, the TRIPS parser and ontology are domain independent, and use mappings from WordNet to interpret unknown words. Hence, the extraction rules will apply (and can be tested) for any natural language text without any extra work.

Because of the ontology, we can usually express general rules that capture a wide range of phenomena. For instance, all noun-phrases describing objects that fall under the TRIPS Ontology's top-level type *situation-root* are extracted as described events. This situation is captured by the extraction rule:

```
((THE ?x (? type SITUATION-ROOT))
    -extract-noms>
    (EVENT ?x (? type SITUATION-ROOT)
        :pos NOUN :class OCCURRENCE ))
```

Since *war* has the type *action*, which falls under *situation-root* in TRIPS ontology, this extraction rule will match the LF `(THE V5 (:* ACTION WAR))` and will extract *war* as event. Beside matching *war* under *situation-root* in ontology, it also matches the specifier *the*, which indicates that it is a definite noun phrase.

The result of matching around hundred of such rules to the sentence above is:

```
<EVENT eid=V2 word=FIGHT
      pos=VERBAL ont-type=FIGHTING
      class=OCCURRENCE tense=PAST
      voice=ACTIVE aspect=NONE
      polarity=POSITIVE
      nf-morph=NONE>
<RLINK eventInstanceID=V2
      ref-word=HE
      ref-ont-type=PERSON
      relType=AGENT>
<SLINK signal=IN
      eventInstanceID=V2
      subordinatedEventInstance=V5
      relType=SITUATED-IN>
<EVENT eid=V5 word=WAR pos=NOUN
      ont-type=ACTION
      class=OCCURRENCE
      voice=ACTIVE
      polarity=POSITIVE
      aspect=NONE tense=NONE>
```

In this way, we extract events and TimeML-suggested event features (*class, tense, aspect, pos, polarity, modality*). We also extract a few additional features such as ontology type (ont-type). TimeML tries to capture event information by very coarse-grained event features *class* or *pos*. The ontology type feature captures more fine-grained information about the event, but still coarse-grained than the words. The extraction rules also map our fine-grained types to the coarse-grained TimeML event class. We also extract relations between events (SLINK), whenever one event syntactically dominates the other, so it extracts more than TimeML's SLINKs and another new relation, relation between event and its arguments (RLINK). Details about these new additions can be found in UzZaman and Allen (2010).

This system extracts events from the TempEval-2 corpus with high recall. However, this high performance comes with the expense of precision. The reasons for lower precision include, (i) the fact that generic events are not coded as events in TempEval, (ii) errors in parsing and, (iii) legitimate events found by the parser but missed by TempEval annotators. To remedy this problem, we introduced a MLN based filtering classifier, using the event features extracted from the TRIPS parser. The formulas in MLN for filtering were derived by linguistic intuition and by checking the errors in our development set. We devised around 30 formulas.

There were two goals for this filtering step: (1) Eliminating events that result from errors in the parse, and (2) Removing event-classes, such as generics, that were not coded in TempEval.

The second goal is needed to perform a meaningful evaluation on the TempEval challenge. For our long-term goal of using the

For our long-term goal of using the temporal summary in natural language understanding task, however, we would retain these other events. The resulting system, including parsing, extraction, and post-filtering, is named as **TRIOS system**.

2.3 Event Feature Extraction

The TRIPS parser and extraction rules already give us event features along with events, which is reported in the results as the **TRIPS system**. To improve performance, we implemented MLN classifiers **(TRIOS system)** for the *class, tense, aspect* and *pos* features, using the features generated from the TRIPS parser plus lexical and syntactical features generated from the text using the Stanford POS tagger[3]. The TRIOS system reports the *polarity* and *modality* performance of TRIPS system, i.e. we don't have any extra classifiers to classify those features in TRIOS system. The Table 1 gives a summary of features used to classify these event features.

<table>
<tr><th>Event feature</th><th>Common features</th><th>Extra features</th></tr>
<tr><td>Pos</td><td rowspan="4">Event word, event penn tag, verb pos sequence [4], verb word sequence, previous word of verb sequence, previous pos of verb sequence, next word, next pos</td><td>none</td></tr>
<tr><td>Tense</td><td>pos, polarity, modality, voice (active or passive)</td></tr>
<tr><td>Aspect</td><td>pos, polarity, modality, voice (active or passive), pos+previous-pos, pos+next-pos</td></tr>
<tr><td>Class</td><td>TRIPS class suggestion, ont-type, slink_core_rel [5], tense+aspect, pos, stem, contains dollar</td></tr>
</table>

Table 1: Attributes/features used for classifying event features *pos, tense, aspect* and *class*

3 Temporal Expression Extraction (Task A)

3.1 Recognizing Temporal Expression

The TRIPS parser extracts temporal expressions the same way as we extract events. The performance of TRIPS parser's temporal extraction doesn't outperform state-of-the-art techniques on the evaluation measures. To improve on this, we also use a traditional machine learning classifier straight from the text. We used a token-by-token classification for temporal expressions represented by B-I-O encoding with a set of lexical and syntactic features, using Conditional Random Field (CRF) classifier[6]. CRF is widely used for labeling and segmenting sequence data. Unlike Hidden Markov Models, CRFs are based on exponential models in which probabilities are computed based on the values of a set of features induced from both the observation and label sequences. They have been used in POS tagging, shallow parsing, named entity recognition and also for temporal expression extraction in TERN dataset [Ahn et al. (2005), Hacioglu et al. (2005) and Poveda et al. (2007)].

We used lexical features like *word, shape, is year, is date of week, is month, is number, is time, is day, is quarter, is punctuation, if belong to word-list like init-list*[7], *follow-list*[8], etc. We then use CRF++ templates to capture relation between different features to extract the sequence. For example, we will write a template to capture the current word is in *init-list* and the next word is in *follow-list*, this rule will train the model to capture sequences like *this weekend, earlier morning, several years*, etc.

On the other hand, the TRIPS parser does extract temporal relations between events and temporal expressions, which helps us in the temporal relation identification tasks. So we take the temporal expressions from the CRF based extractor and for the cases where TRIPS parser extracts the temporal expression, we use TRIPS parser id, so that we can relate to relations generated by the parser.

The temporal expressions that are suggested by CRF based system, are passed to a filtering step that tries to extract a normalized *value* and *type* of the temporal expression. If we can find a normalized *value* and *type*, we accept the tempo-

[3] http://nlp.stanford.edu/software/tagger.shtml

[4] One Penn tag derived features is *verb word sequence*, which captures all previous verbs, or TO (infinitive), or modal verbs, of the event word. That is, it will capture all consecutive verbs before the event until we get non-verbal word. Similarly *verb pos sequence* is the penn tag sequence of these verbs.

[5] SLINK captures relation between two events, when one syntactically dominates other. This feature captures the relation-type as feature for core events.

[6] We used off the shelf CRF++ implementation. http://crfpp.sourceforge.net/

[7] *init-list* contains words like: *this, mid, first, almost, last, next, early, recent, earlier, beginning, nearly, few, following, several, around, the, less, than, more, no, of, each, late.*

[8] *follow-list* contains words like: *century, centuries, day, days, era, hour, hours, millisecond, minute, minutes, moment, month, months, night, nights, sec, second, time, week, weeks, year, years, am, pm, weekend, summer, fall, winter, fiscal, morning, evening, afternoon, noon, EST, GMT, PST, CST, ago, half.*

ral expressions. We reported this CRF based system with filtering as both **TRIPS and TRIOS systems**.

3.2 Determining The Normalized Value and Type of temporal expression

Temporal expressions are most useful for later processing when a normalized *value* and *type* is determined. We implemented a rule-based technique to determine the *types* and *values*. We match regular expressions to identify the *type* of temporal expressions. *Type* could be either of *time, date, duration and set.*

Then in next step we extract the normalized value of temporal expression, as suggested by TimeML scheme. We take the Document Creation Time (DCT) and then calculate the values for different dates in terms of document creation date, e.g. *last month, Sunday, today*. We will make our type and value extractor and temporal expression extractor modules available[9] for public use.

4 Temporal Relation Identification (Task C – F)

We identify temporal relations using a Markov Logic Network classifier, namely *thebeast*, by using linguistically motivated features that we extracted in previous steps. Our work matches closely with the work of Yoshikawa et al. (2009). We only consider the local classifiers, but we use more linguistically motivated features and features generated from text, whereas they used TempEval-1's (Verhagen et al., 2007) annotations as input, along with their derived features. Other participants in TempEval 2 also used features from annotated corpus, making us the only group in TempEval-2 to use own-generated entities (events and temporal expression) and features.

TempEval-2 has four subtasks for identifying temporal relations. The tasks are:

(C) Determine the temporal relation between an event and temporal expression in the same sentence;

(D) Determine the temporal relation between an event and the document creation time (DCT);

(E) Determine the temporal relation between the main events in two adjacent sentences; and

(F) Determine the temporal relation between two events, where one event syntactically dominates the other event.

Both TRIPS and TRIOS use the same MLN classifier with same feature-set for each task. However the difference is, they take events and temporal expressions from respective systems, e.g. in Task C (temporal relation between events and temporal expressions), TRIPS system will classify relations for instances where TRIPS event extractor extracted events (in task B) and TRIPS temporal expression extractor extracted temporal expression (in task A). The recall measure of task C will represent the accuracy of extracting events, temporal expression and identifying temporal relations together. This applies for all C – F tasks and for both TRIOS and TRIPS systems.

Tables 2 and 3 show the features we used for each of these tasks. We used some features that we extracted from TRIPS parser. Related information about these concepts can be found in UzZaman and Allen (2010).

Features	**Task C**	**Task D**
Event Class	YES	YES
Event Tense	YES	YES
Event Aspect	YES	YES
Event Polarity	YES	YES
Event Stem	YES	YES
Event Word	YES	YES
Event Constituent[10]		YES
Event Ont-type [11]		YES
Event LexAspect [12] *x Tense*		YES
Event Pos	YES	YES
Timex Word		YES
Timex Type	YES	YES
Timex Value	YES	YES
Timex DCT relation	YES	YES
Event to Argument connective ont-type[13]	YES	YES
Event's argument's ont-type	YES	YES
TLINK event-time signal[14]	YES	

[9] Available online at: http://www.cs.rochester.edu/u/naushad/temporal

[10] TRIPS parser identifies the event constituent along with event word.

[11] Ontology-type is described in Event Extraction subsection.

[12] LexicalAspect feature is a subset of feature *class* and it classifies the events into *Event, State and Reporting* class.

[13] Ontology type of connective that connects the event and its argument

Table 2: Features used for TempEval-2 Task C and D

Features	**Task E**	**Task F**
Event Class	e1 x e2	e1 x e2[15]
Event Tense	e1 x e2	e1 x e2
Event Aspect	e1 x e2	e1 x e2
Event Polarity	e1 x e2	e1 x e2
Event Stem	e1 x e2	e1 x e2
Event Word	YES	YES
Event Constituent	e1 x e2	e1 x e2
Event Ont-type	e1 x e2	e1 x e2
Event LexAspect x Tense	e1 x e2	e1 x e2
Event Pos	e1 x e2	e1 x e2
SLINK event-event relation type[16]		e1 x e2

Table 3: Features used for TempEval-2 Task E and F

5 Results

5.1 Event and Event Feature Extraction (Task B)

On event extraction, the TRIPS system has the highest recall, while the TRIOS system is second best in precision with the highest scoring system, TIPSem. But overall they do very well compared to our system on event extraction. Performance of our both systems and the best performing TIPSem system is reported in Table 4.

	Precision	Recall	Fscore
TRIPS	0.55	**0.88**	0.67
TRIOS	0.80	0.74	0.77
Best (TIPSem)	**0.81**	0.86	**0.84**

Table 4: Performance of Event Extraction (Task B)

On event feature extraction, our TRIOS system, which is based on MLN based classifiers, has the best performance on *aspect* and *polarity*; we also do very well (second-best performances mostly) on *tense, class, pos* and *modality*.

Feature	TRIPS	TRIOS	Best
Class	0.67	0.77	0.79 (TIPSem)
Tense	0.67	0.91	0.92 (Ed.-LTG)
Aspect	0.97	**0.98**	0.98
Pos	0.88	0.96	0.97 (TIPSem, Edinburg-LTG)
Polarity	**0.99**	**0.99**	0.98
Modality	0.95	0.95	0.99 (Ed.-LTG)

Table 5: Performance of Event Features (Task B)

5.2 Temporal Expression Extraction (Task A)

Both the TRIPS and TRIOS systems use the same CRF-based approach for temporal expression extraction. Our system has the second best performance on combined temporal expression extraction and normalization task (identifying type and value). It is worth mentioning that the average of identifying value performance is 0.61 and if we remove our systems and the best system, HeidelTime-1, the average is only 0.56. Hence, our freely distributed normalization tool could be beneficiary to many people. Performance of our system and the best system on task A is reported in Table 5.

		TRIPS TRIOS	Best (HeidelTime-1)
Timex extraction	Precision	0.85	0.90
	Recall	0.85	0.82
Normalization	*type*	0.94	0.96
	value	0.76	0.85

Table 5: Performance on Temporal Expression extraction (Task A)

5.3 Temporal Relation Identification (Task C – F)

For temporal relation identification (Task C – F), other teams used events, temporal expressions and their features from human-annotated corpus, whereas, we used our extracted entities and their features that we extracted in Task A and B. So our performances represent the capability of identifying these relationships from raw text and it is also harder classification task, since we are starting with imperfect features.

Even though we are using our own generated features, we outperformed other groups in task C (temporal relation between event and temporal expression) and task E (temporal relation between main events of consecutive sentences). We also have second-best/equivalent performance for other two tasks (temporal relation between event and DCT; and temporal relation between events, where one syntactically dominates other).

Table 6 reports our systems' performances with precision (P) and recall (R). For others,

[14] TRIPS parser generated event-time TLINK connective or signal (similar to TimeML)

[15] Task E and F is temporal relations between events. In MLN framework, we can write formula in first-order logic. e1 x e2 instances are cases, where we capture both events together. For example, in case of Tense, it will learn the weights for temporal relations given first event's tense is PRESENT and second event's tense is PAST. Instead of just considering first event is PRESENT and second event is PAST, we are considering first event is PRESENT and second event is PAST together.

[16] The SLINK relation type that connects two events, more at UzZaman and Allen (2010).

since they take annotated events and features, they don't actually have a recall, so their recall is not reported.

Since TRIPS system for these tasks uses events (task B) from TRIPS system, which has higher recall, it will have higher recall in relations as well.

	TRIPS		TRIOS		Best
Task	P	R	P	R	P
Task C	0.63	**0.52**	**0.65**	**0.52**	0.65
Task D	0.76	**0.69**	0.79	0.67	0.82 (TIPSem)
Task E	**0.58**	**0.50**	0.56	0.42	0.58
Task F	0.59	**0.54**	0.6	0.46	0.66 (NCSU-indi)

Table 6: Performance on identifying temporal relations (Task C – F)

5.4 Overall Performance

Many teams chose just to attempt one task between task A and B, or both, or only attempt some of tasks C to F. Only three teams attempted all tasks, our team, TIPSem and JU_CSE_TEMP. For tasks C – F, we used our generated features, whereas all other teams used the features provided in the corpus.

In this section, we will show head-to-head comparison of the performance of these three systems to see which team handles the overall challenge of TempEval-2 better. Table 6 summarizes our analysis.

Task	Description	Best
Task A	Temporal expression extraction	TRIOS
Task B	Event extraction	TIPSem
Task C	Event-Timex relationship	TRIOS
Task D	Event-DCT relationship	TIPSem
Task E	Main event-event relationship	TRIOS
Task F	Subordinate event-event relationship	TRIOS

Table 6: Head-to-head comparison of TRIOS, TIPSem and JU_CSE_TEMP (teams that approached all tasks) in TempEval-2 challenge

Note that JU_CSE_TEMP didn't perform best in any particular task. However, they do a little better than us in Task D (TRIOS 0.79, JU_CSE_TEMP .80). They also didn't extract temporal expression *type* and *value*.

Both TRIOS and TIPSem teams submitted two systems. For this comparison, we pick the best system of each team then compare between them. On temporal expression extraction, we have very close extraction scores (TRIOS fscore 0.85 and TIPSem fscore 0.855). However on temporal expression attributes, we are far superior to TIP-Sem. So overall in Task A, we claim we did better. TIPSem clearly did better on the event extraction task.

On the other hand, given that task A and task B has many subtasks, if we split them into entity extraction and attribute extraction, then we have four tasks of extraction and four tasks on relation identification. In that case, TIPSem does better than us on event extraction, but on event feature extraction we have a tie; for temporal expression extraction, we have another tie, but we outperform in temporal expression attribute extraction.

6 Future Work

Our interest is in constructing a domain-independent system for temporal information extraction. We expect that our system will perform closely to TRIPS system (not the better TRIOS) in new domains, since it uses a domain independent semantic parser and domain independent extraction rules. On the other hand, the TRIOS system is dependent on machine learning classifiers, which depends on having a training corpus. So in those cases, we plan to explore bootstrapping a corpus in the new domain using TRIPS, to obtain performance similar to the TRIOS system.

In parallel to that, we plan to build a system that generates reliable temporal structure of documents that can be used in information extraction and language understanding in general. We are particularly interested in generating the temporal structure of documents in medical applications, and in applications that would help people who have trouble reading and understanding documents. To do that, we plan to represent our events, temporal expressions, and temporal relations in a representation like Timegraph (Miller and Schubert, 1990), which is very easy-to-understand representation for humans and also very scalable and efficient solution for temporal reasoning. This would also open the door for applications that require sophisticated temporal reasoning.

Finally, we plan to use the system to semi-automatically create a larger temporally annotated corpus based on TimeML scheme. The system would produce an initial version that could be reviewed by human judges before making it public.

7 Conclusion

We have shown that a hybrid system combining domain-independent deep understanding techniques with machine learning can extract significant amounts of temporal information from documents. Our submitted systems, TRIPS and TRIOS for TempEval-2 challenge, approached all tasks and outperformed all teams in two tasks (out of six) and TRIOS mostly had second-best performances in other tasks. TRIOS also outperforms the other teams that approached all tasks, even though for task C - F we operated on features automatically computed from raw text rather than using the tagged events and temporal expressions in the corpus.

Acknowledgments

This work was supported in part by the National Science Foundation, grant #0748942, and the Office of Naval Research (N000140510314). We thank Mary Swift and William DeBeaumont for help with the TRIPS parser, Benjamin van Durme for many useful suggestions and Sebestian Reidel for help on using the very useful MLN tool *TheBeast*. We are also very thankful to Marc Verhagen and other organizers and annotators of TempEval-2 challenge for organizing a very successful event and also for being very cooperative. Finally, we are thankful to the SemEval-2 chairs, Katrin Erk and Carlo Strapparava for granting us extra pages to describe our approach to all tasks with two systems.

References

D. Ahn, S.F. Adafre, M. de Rijke, 2005. Extracting Temporal Information from Open Domain Text: A Comparative Exploration, *Digital Information Management,* 2005.

J. Allen, M. Swift, and W. de Beaumont, 2008. Deep semantic analysis of text. In *Symposium on Semantics in Systems for Text Processing (STEP)*, 2008.

M. Dzikovska, J. Allen and M. Swift. 2003. Integrating linguistic and domain knowledge for spoken dialogue systems in multiple domains. *Workshop on Knowledge and Reasoning in Practical Dialogue Systems, IJCAI*, Acapulco.

K. Hachioglu, Y. Chen and B. Douglas, 2005. Automatic Time Expression Labeling for English and Chinese Text. In *Proceedings of CICLing-2005.*

C. Johnson and C. Fillmore. 2000. The FrameNet tagset for frame-semantic and syntactic coding of predicate-argument structure. *ANLP-NAACL*, Seattle, WA.

J. Poveda, M. Surdeanu and J. Turmo, 2007. A Comparison of Statistical and Rule-Induction Learners for Automatic Tagging of Time Expressions in English. In *Proceedings of the International Symposium on Temporal Representation and Reasoning, 2007.*

S.A. Miller and L.K. Schubert, Time Revisited, *Computational Intelligence* 6(2), 108-118, 1990.

James Pustejovsky, Jos M. Castao, Robert Ingria, Roser Sauri, Robert J. Gaizauskas, Andrea Setzer, Graham Katz, and Dragomir R. Radev, 2003. TimeML: Robust Specification of Event and Temporal Expressions in Text. In Mark T. Maybury, editor, *New Directions in Question Answering*, pages 28–34. AAAI Press, 2003.

Matthew Richardson and Pedro Domingos, 2006. Markov logic networks. *Machine Learning*, 2006.

Sebastian Riedel. 2008. Improving the accuracy and efficiency of map inference for markov logic. *In Proceedings of UAI 2008.*

Naushad UzZaman and James Allen, 2010, TRIOS-TimeBank Corpus: Extended TimeBank corpus with help of Deep Understanding of Text, To Appear in the Proceedings of *The seventh international conference on Language Resources and Evaluation (LREC), Malta, 2010.*

Marc Verhagen, Robert Gaizauskas, Frank Schilder, Mark Hepple, Graham Katz and James Pustejovsky, 2007. SemEval-2007 Task 15: TempEval Temporal Relation Identification, Proceedings of *4th International Workshop on Semantic Evaluations (SemEval 2007).*

Katsumasa Yoshikawa, Sebastian Riedel, Masayuki Asahara and Yuji Matsumoto. 2009. Jointly Identifying Temporal Relations with Markov Logic. Proceedings of the *Joint Conference of the 47th Annual Meeting of the ACL and the 4th International Joint Conference on Natural Language Processing of the AFNLP, 2009.*

TIPSem (English and Spanish): Evaluating CRFs and Semantic Roles in TempEval-2

Hector Llorens, Estela Saquete, Borja Navarro
University of Alicante
Alicante, Spain
{hllorens,stela,borja}@dlsi.ua.es

Abstract

This paper presents TIPSem, a system to extract temporal information from natural language texts for English and Spanish. TIPSem, learns CRF models from training data. Although the used features include different language analysis levels, the approach is focused on semantic information. For Spanish, TIPSem achieved the best F1 score in all the tasks. For English, it obtained the best F1 in tasks B (events) and D (event-dct links); and was among the best systems in the rest.

1 Introduction

The automatic treatment of time expressions, events and their relations over natural language text consists of making temporal elements explicit through a system that identifies and annotates them following a standard scheme. This information is crucial for other natural language processing (NLP) areas, such as summarization or question answering. The relevance of temporal information has been reflected in specialized conferences (Schilder et al., 2007) and evaluation forums (Verhagen et al., 2007).

We present a system to tackle the six different tasks related to multilingual temporal information treatment proposed in TempEval-2. Particularly, in this evaluation exercise, TimeML (Pustejovsky et al., 2003) is adopted as temporal annotation scheme. In this manner, the tasks require participating systems to automatically annotate different TimeML elements. Firstly, task A consists of determining the extent of time expressions as defined by the TimeML TIMEX3 tag, as well as the attributes "type" and "value". Secondly, task B addresses the recognition and classification of events as defined by TimeML EVENT tag. Finally, tasks C to F comprise the categorization of different temporal links (TimeML LINKs). Figure 1 illustrates the TimeML elements in a sentence.

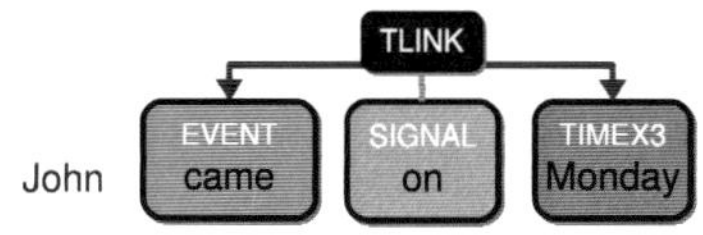

Figure 1: TimeML example

In the context of TempEval-2, we tackle all tasks for English and Spanish with a data-driven system. This consists of CRF models inferred from lexical, syntactic and semantic information of given training data.

Our main approach, TIPSem (Temporal Information Processing based on Semantic information), is focused on semantic roles and semantic networks. Furthermore, we present a secondary approach, TIPSem-B (TIPSem-Baseline), which contrary to the former does not consider semantic information.

The main objectives of this paper are (1) evaluating the performance of TIPSem comparing it to other participating systems and (2) measuring the contribution of semantic information to different TempEval-2 tasks though the comparison between our systems: TIPSem and TIPSem-B.

This paper is structured as follows. Our approach to address the TempEval-2 tasks is motivated in Section 2 and described in Section 3. The results obtained in the evaluation are shown and analyzed in Section 4. Finally, conclusions are drawn in Section 5.

2 Approach motivation

The next two subsections describe the two main characteristics of our approach, CRFs and semantic roles, and the reasons why we think they could be useful to tackle TimeML annotation.

Proceedings of the 5th International Workshop on Semantic Evaluation, ACL 2010, pages 284–291,
Uppsala, Sweden, 15-16 July 2010. ©2010 Association for Computational Linguistics

2.1 CRF probabilistic model

Conditional Random Fields is a popular and efficient ML technique for supervised sequence labeling (Lafferty et al., 2001). In the recognition problem raised by TempEval-2 tasks A and B, assume X is a random variable over data sequences to be labeled, and Y is a random variable over the corresponding label sequences, being all Y components (Y_i) members of a finite label alphabet γ. X might range over the sentences and Y range over possible annotations of those sentences, with γ the set of possible event IOB2[1] labels. The following example illustrates the problem.

(1)	X	Y		
	That	?		B-TIMEX3
	was	?		B-EVENT
	another	?	? =	I-TIMEX3
	bad	?		I-EVENT
	week	?		O

Then, CRFs construct a conditional model from paired observations and label sequences: $p(Y|X)$.

To extend the problem to classification, X is replaced with elements to be classified and γ is replaced with the possible classes, for instance, in task A $X = \{\text{TIMEX3 instances in text}\}$ and $\gamma = \{\text{DATE, DURATION, SET, TIME}\}$.

From our point of view, CRFs are well suited to address TempEval-2 tasks. Firstly, TimeML elements depend on structural properties of sentences. Not only the word sequence, but morphological, syntactic and semantic structure is related with them. Secondly, some TIMEX3 and EVENT elements are denoted by sequences of words, therefore the CRFs are very appropriate.

2.2 Semantic roles

Semantic role labeling (SRL) has achieved important results in the last years (Gildea and Jurafsky, 2002; Moreda et al., 2007). For each predicate in a sentence, semantic roles identify all constituents, determining their arguments (agent, patient, etc.) and their adjuncts (locative, temporal, etc.). Figure 2 illustrates a semantic role labeled sentence.

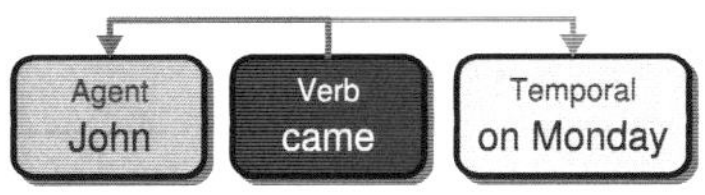

Figure 2: Semantic roles example

Semantic roles provide structural relations of the predicates in which TimeML elements may participate. Beyond syntactic relations expressed by means of the different types of phrases, semantic roles give further information about semantic relations between the arguments of a predicate. Due to the fact that roles represent high level information, they are more independent from word tokens. Hence, roles may aid in learning more general models that could improve the results of approaches focused on lower level information.

3 Our approach: TIPSem

As defined in previous section, this paper proposes CRF as learning method to infer models to face the TempEval-2 tasks. Specifically, CRF++ toolkit[2] was used for training and testing our approach. The learning process was done using the parameters: *CRF-L2* algorithm and hyperparameter C=1.

In order to set out the approach architecture and select the features for learning, we divided the tasks proposed in the evaluation exercise into four groups: recognition, classification, normalization and link-categorization. Each group represents a kind of problem to be resolved. Recognition problem is present in TIMEX3 and EVENT bounding (tasks A and B). Classification problem appears in TIMEX3 type and EVENT class attributes (tasks A and B). Normalization arises in TIMEX3 value attribute (task A). And link-categorization is applied to different kind of link relations (tasks C to F). Each group uses a particular feature set to learn an annotation model. The features of these sets are grouped in two subsets. On the one hand, general features, which are widely used in different NLP fields and represent lower language analysis levels. On the other hand, semantic features, which are a novelty in the task and our main focus.

TIPSem system uses all the features defined above. However, to measure the influence of semantic information in temporal information treatment, TIPSem-B system was implemented excluding the semantic features.

3.1 Recognition

In recognition, the features are obtained at token level, that is to say, each token has its own set of features.

Regarding each language analysis level, the general features used to train our CRF model are:

[1]IOB2 format: (B)egin, (I)nside, and (O)utside

[2]http://crfpp.sourceforge.net/

- **Morphological**: The lemma and part-of-speech (PoS) context, in a 5-window (-2,+2), was employed due to the good results it achieved in other NLP tasks. Tokenization, PoS and lemmatization were obtained using TreeTagger (Schmid, 1994) for English, and were got from AnCora (Taulé et al., 2008) for Spanish.

- **Syntactic**: Different TimeML elements are contained in particular types of phrases. This feature tries to capture this fact by considering phrase level syntactic information. The syntactic tree was obtained using Charniak parser (Charniak and Johnson, 2005) for English, and AnCora for Spanish.

- **Polarity, tense and aspect**: These were obtained using PoS and a set of handcrafted rules (e.g., will+verb → future).

The semantic level features used to enhance the training framework of the CRF model are:

- **Role**: For each token, we considered the role regarding the verb the token depends on. To get semantic roles, CCG SRL tool (Punyakanok et al., 2004) was used for English, and AnCora for Spanish.

- **Governing verb**: The verb to which the current token holds a particular role. This may distinguish tokens appearing under the influence of different verbs.

- **Role+verb combination**: The previous two features were combined to capture the relation between them. This introduces additional information by distinguishing roles depending on different verbs. The importance of this falls especially on the numbered roles (A0, A1, etc.) meaning different things when depending on different verbs.

- **Role configuration**: This feature is only present in verb tokens heading a sentence or sub-sentence. This consists of the set of roles depending on the verb. This may be particularly useful for distinguish different sentence settings.

- **Lexical semantics**: WordNet (Fellbaum, 1998) top ontology classes have been widely used to represent word meaning at ontological level, and demonstrated its worth in many tasks. TIPSem uses the top four classes for each word. For Spanish, EuroWordNet (Vossen, 1998) was used.

In this manner, given a list of tokens and its features, the trained recognition model will assign to each token one of the valid labels. For instance, in the case of TIMEX3 recognition: B-TIMEX3, I-TIMEX3 or O.

3.2 Classification

Classification features, used to get TIMEX3 types and EVENT classes, are basically the same as the ones used for recognition. However, the main difference is that the features are not obtained at token level but at TIMEX3 or EVENT level. This implies that the word context is set to the extent of each element (TIMEX3 and EVENT), as well as all the features have as many values as tokens comprises the element (e.g., element-tokens="next Monday", PoS-feature="JJ+NNP"). Hence, following this description, the classification models will assign to each element one of the valid classes. For example, in the case of TIMEX3 typing: DATE, DURATION, SET or TIME.

3.3 Normalization

As in classification the features are obtained at TIMEX3 level. Furthermore, word-spelled numbers contained in the TIMEX3 extent are translated to their numerical value (e.g., "three days" → "3 days").

Normalization process consists of two main steps: (1) obtain the normalization type and (2) apply the corresponding normalization rules.

The first step applies a CRF model that uses the same features as the previous two plus TIMEX3 pattern. This new feature consists of the tokens comprised by the TIMEX3 but replacing numbers by NUM, temporal units, such as years or days, by TUNIT, months by MONTH, and weekdays by WEEKDAY. In other words, "next Monday" would result in "next WEEKDAY" and "June 1999" in "MONTH NUM". Once the model is trained, for each new TIMEX3 it assigns a normalization type. We define seven normalization types: Period, ISO, ISO_set, ISO_function, present_ref, past_ref and future_ref.

The second step uses as input the output of the first one. Each normalization type has its own normalization rules.

- **Period**: Apply rules to convert period-like TIMEX3 ("3 days") into P_NUM_TUNIT normalized period ("P3D").

- **ISO**: Apply rules to convert any-format explicit date or time into a valid ISO 8601 standard date.

- **ISO_set**: Apply rules to get a valid ISO-like set from a TIMEX3 set ("monthly" → XXXX-XX).

- **ISO_function**: This is the most complex type. The system applies different functions to get a valid ISO date or time in a valid granularity from DCT[3] dates. Here, time direction indicators like "next" or "previous", as well as verbal tenses are used.

- **Present_ref, past_ref and future_ref**: these are already normalized.

3.4 Link-categorization

Each one of link-related tasks (C to F) has its own link-categorization features. Nevertheless, all link types share some of them.

- **Task C**: For categorizing the relation between an EVENT and a TIMEX3, the system takes into account the following features:
  - *Heading preposition* if the event or the TIMEX3 are contained by a prepositional phrase as in "before the meeting", where "meeting" is the event and "before" the heading preposition.
  - *Syntactic relation* of the event and the TIMEX3 in the sentence. This feature may be evaluated as: same sentence, same subsentence or same phrase.
  - *Time position*. If the event is not directly linked with the relation TIMEX3 but related to another TIMEX3, the time position represents whether the event is before, overlap or after the relation TIMEX3.
  - *Interval*. This feature is 0 unless there appears some interval indicator token near the TIMEX3. This is useful to identify overlap-and-after and overlap-and-before categories.
  - *TIMEX3 type*.
  - *Semantic roles* if the event or the TIMEX3 are contained by a temporal subordination (labeled with temporal role), for example, in "after he left home", "left" is the event and "after" the subordinating element (role feature).

- **Task D**: To determine the relationship between an event and the DCT, TIPSem uses the same features as in task C except *interval*. In addition, all the features related to TIMEX3 are now related to the closer TIMEX3 (if exists) in the event sentence. In this manner, the *time position* is calculated by comparing DCT and that TIMEX3.

- **Task E**: Relations between two main events are categorized using only four features: the *tense and aspect* of the two events, the *syntactic relation* between them, and the *time position*, calculated using the closer TIMEX3 to each event.

- **Task F**: For categorizing subordinated events, TIPSem uses the subordinating element of temporal *roles* containing each event (if present), the *heading preposition* of a prepositional phrases containing each event (if present), as well as the *tense and aspect*.

To illustrate the system architecture, Figure 3 summarizes the strategies that TIPSem follows to tackle the tasks proposed in the TempEval-2 framework.

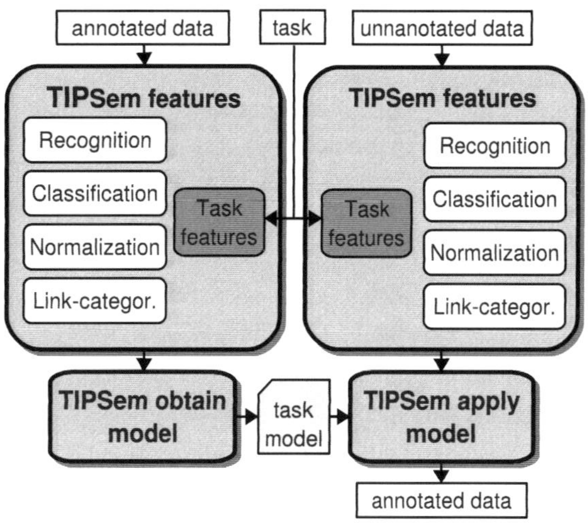

Figure 3: TIPSem architecture

[3] Date Creation Time

4 Evaluation

The test corpus consists of 17K words for English and 10K words for Spanish, in which approximately a half part correspond to tasks A and B, and the other half to tasks C, D, E and F. The performance is measured using precision, recall and $F_{\beta=1}$ metrics. A scoring script is provided. This counts correct instances at token level for tasks A and B, and at temporal link level for the rest.

Next subsections show the results obtained by TIPSem system in each one of the TempEval-2 tasks for English (EN) and Spanish (ES). Moreover, a final subsection illustrates the $F_{\beta=1}$ results in three comparative graphs. In tasks A and B, precision, recall and $F_{\beta=1}$ are given. In tasks C to E, links tasks precision, recall and $F_{\beta=1}$ are the same because our system does not consider the NONE value. Hence, only $F_{\beta=1}$ is given. Tasks E and F were not considered for Spanish in TempEval-2 evaluation and thus Spanish is excluded from those subsections.

For each task, scores in which our system obtained the first place in the evaluation exercise are in bold. Furthermore, in all cases the best score obtained by participating systems is reported. Finally, the influence of semantic information in terms of improvement is indicated and analyzed through the comparison with TIPSem-B system, which exclude the features related with semantics.

4.1 Task A: TIMEX3

Table 1 shows the results obtained by our approaches in TIMEX3 recognition, typing and ISO 8601 normalization (value).

System *lang*	Prec.	Rec.	$F_{\beta=1}$	type	value
TIPSem *EN*	**0.92**	0.80	0.85	0.92	0.65
TIPSem *ES*	0.95	**0.87**	**0.91**	**0.91**	0.78
TIPSem-B *EN*	0.88	0.60	0.71	0.88	0.59
TIPSem-B *ES*	**0.97**	0.81	0.88	0.99	0.75

Table 1: Task A - English and Spanish

As shown in results, TIPSem obtains the best results for Spanish in all measures except for "value" attribute, in which the best system obtained a 0.83. Another system obtained the same recall (0.87) but a lower precision (0.90), and thus a $F_{\beta=1}$ of (0.88) below TIPSem score (0.91). For English, our main approach obtained the best precision. However, another system obtained the best recall (0.91). The best $F_{\beta=1}$ was 0.86. Regarding type attribute, TIPSem obtained values closer to best system (0.98). Finally, in normalization, which is the only attribute that is not annotated by a purely data-driven process, best system surpassed TIPSem in 0.20.

These results indicate that CRFs represent an appropriate ML technique to learn models for annotating TIMEX3. Furthermore, they show that normalization process used by TIPSem could be improved using other techniques.

Specifically, the usage of semantic information improved the capability of learned models to generalize rules. For instance in time expressions, if an unseen instance is contained by a temporal role is a clear candidate to be a time expression. Hence, they improve system recall (33% EN, 7% ES).

4.2 Task B: EVENT

Table 2 shows the results obtained by our approaches in recognizing and classifying events.

System *lang*	Prec.	Recall	$F_{\beta=1}$	class
TIPSem *EN*	0.81	0.86	**0.83**	**0.79**
TIPSem *ES*	0.90	**0.86**	**0.88**	**0.66**
TIPSem-B *EN*	**0.83**	0.81	0.82	0.79
TIPSem-B *ES*	**0.92**	0.85	0.88	0.66

Table 2: Task B - English and Spanish

In this tasks, TIPSem obtained the best results in TempEval-2 for Spanish and English in both recognition and classification. Although for English another system achieved the best recall (0.88), it obtained a lower precision (0.55); and thus a 0.68 $F_{\beta=1}$. This indicates that our approach obtains the best $F_{\beta=1}$ (0.83) with a well-balanced precision and recall.

Again, the usage of semantic information improves the capability of learned models to generalize, which improves the recall (6% EN, 1% ES). For events, the improvement is lower than for TIMEX3 because, contrary to TIMEX3, they are not clearly defined by specific roles. In this case, features like role configuration, semantic classes, or role-governing verb are more useful.

Other attributes present in events such as polarity, mood and tense obtained values of about 90%. However, to get the values for these attributes the system applies a set of handcrafted rules and then the results are not relevant for our approach.

4.3 Task C: LINKS - Events and TIMEXs

Table 3 shows the results obtained by our approaches in categorizing EVENT-TIMEX3 links.

System *lang*	$F_{\beta=1}$
TIPSem *EN*	0.55
TIPSem *ES*	**0.81**
TIPSem-B *EN*	0.54
TIPSem-B *ES*	0.81

Table 3: Task C - English and Spanish

TIPSem was the only system participating in this task for Spanish. Nevertheless, 0.81 is a high score comparing it to English best score (0.63). Our system, for English, is 8 points below top scored system.

In this task, the application of semantic roles introduced an improvement of 2% in $F_{\beta=1}$.

4.4 Task D: LINKS - Events and DCTs

Table 4 shows the results obtained by our approaches in categorizing events with respect to the creation time of a document.

System *lang*	$F_{\beta=1}$
TIPSem *EN*	**0.82**
TIPSem *ES*	**0.59**
TIPSem-B *EN*	0.81
TIPSem-B *ES*	0.59

Table 4: Task D - English and Spanish

Task D is successfully covered by TIPSem obtaining the best results in the evaluation.

It seems that the relation of events with document creation time strongly depends on tense and aspect, as well as the event position in time with respect to DCT when defined by neighboring TIMEX3.

Furthermore, the learned CRF models take advantage of using temporal semantic roles information. Specifically, the usefulness of semantic roles in this task was quantified to 2%.

4.5 Task E: LINKS - Main events

Table 5 shows the results obtained by our approaches in categorizing main events relations in text.

System *lang*	$F_{\beta=1}$
TIPSem *EN*	0.55
TIPSem-B *EN*	0.55

Table 5: Task E - English

In this task, our system obtains the second place. However, the top scored achieved a 0.56. Again, the tense and aspect features, as well as the events position in time resulted useful to tackle this task. In this case, semantic roles information is not used so TIPSem and TIPSem-B are equivalent.

4.6 Task F: LINKS - Subordinated events

Table 6 shows the results obtained by our approaches in categorizing events relations with the events they syntactically govern.

System *lang*	$F_{\beta=1}$
TIPSem *EN*	0.59
TIPSem-B *EN*	0.60

Table 6: Task F - English

Categorizing subordinated events TIPSem obtained the second place. Best score was 0.66. In this task, the application of roles did not help and decreased the score in one point. The cause may be that for this task roles are not relevant but noisy. In this case, some extra information extending semantic roles is needed to turn them into a useful feature.

4.7 Comparative graphs

This subsection presents the TIPSem $F_{\beta=1}$ results in three graphs. Figure 4 illustrates the results for English indicating the higher and lower scores achieved by TempEval-2 participating systems. Figure 5 shows the same for Spanish but, due to the fact that TIPSem was the only participant in tasks B, C and D, the graph includes English min. and max. scores as indirect assessment. Finally, Figure 6, compares the TIPSem results for English and Spanish.

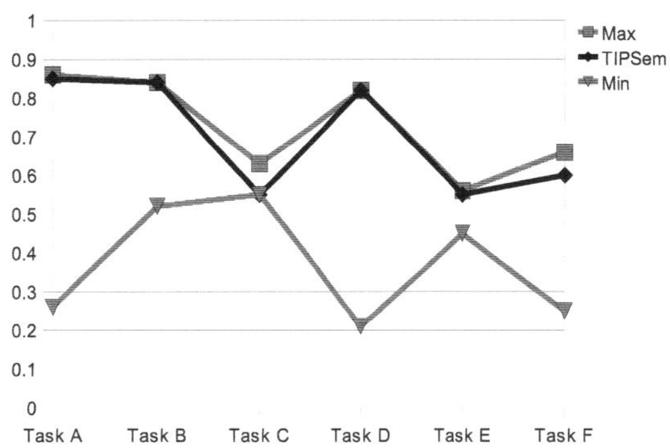

Figure 4: English $F_{\beta=1}$ comparative

Figure 4 shows how TIPSem achieved, in general, a high performance for English.

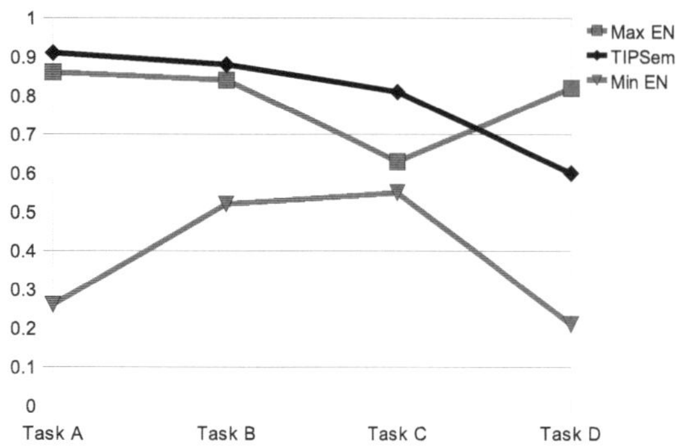

Figure 5: Spanish $F_{\beta=1}$ indirect assessment

For Spanish we can only report indirect assessment comparing the results to English scores. It can be seen that the quality of the results is similar for tasks A and B, but seems to be inverted in tasks C and D.

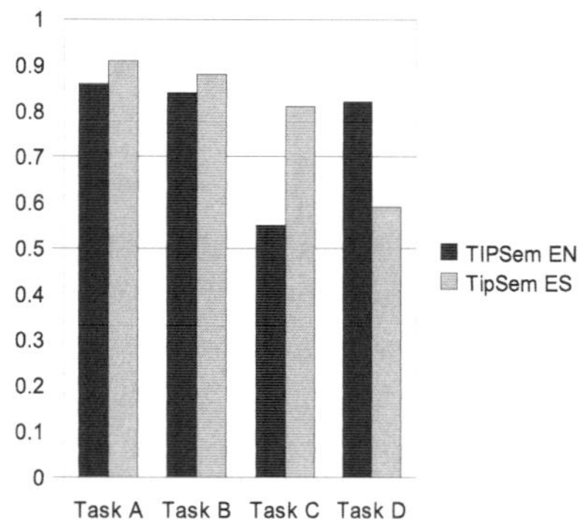

Figure 6: TIPSem EN - ES $F_{\beta=1}$ comparative

Finally, in this graph comparing TIPSem results, we observe that our approach achieved similar performance for both languages in tasks A and B. This indicates that for this tasks, the approach is valid for both languages. However, as in the previous graph, it seems that for English TIPSem performs worse in task C and better in task D while for Spanish it does right the opposite.

The train and test corpora were reviewed to analyze this fact. On the one hand, the reason for the high performance in task C for Spanish was the high amount of "overlap" instances in both corpora. This trained the CRF model for categorizing event-timex links as "overlap" in most of cases. On the other hand, the cause of the Spanish low performance in task D is "vague" links. The features defined in TIPSem cannot distinguish between "overlap" and "vague". Due to the fact that "vague" links are quite popular in Spanish test set, the results decreased. This did not affect to English results because of the spareness of "vague" links.

5 Conclusions and Further Work

This paper presented a system for automatically treating temporal information of natural language texts as required in the TempEval-2 evaluation exercise, in particular, following TimeML specifications.

Our system, TIPSem, is a data-driven approach and consists of different CRF models learned using semantic information as main feature. CRFs were used taking into account that data-driven approaches have obtained good results in many NLP tasks, and due to their appropriateness in sequence labeling problems and problems in which structural properties are relevant, as those proposed in TempEval-2. Furthermore, the models were enhanced using semantic information. Roles have been applied in other NLP fields with successful results, but never employed before for this purpose. With these two main characteristics, we designed a complete learning environment selecting, in addition to roles, different language analysis level properties as features to train the models.

The results obtained for English and Spanish in the evaluation exercise were satisfactory and well-balanced between precision and recall. For Spanish, TIPSem achieved the best $F_{\beta=1}$ in all tasks. For English, it obtained the best $F_{\beta=1}$ in event recognition and classification (task B), and event and document creation time links categorization (task D). Furthermore, in general, all the results of TIPSem were very competitive and were among the top scored systems. This verifies that our approach is appropriate to address TempEval-2 tasks.

Regarding multilinguality, the approach was proven to be valid for different languages (English and Spanish). This was also verified for Catalan language by earlier versions of TIPSem (Llorens et al., 2009). In fact, the data-driven part of the system could be considered language independent because it has been applied to different languages and could be applied to other languages without adaptation, provided that there are tools available to get the morphosyntactic and semantic information required by the approach. It has to be highlighted that to apply TIPSem-B only morphosyntactic information is required. Only the normalization of time expressions is a language dependent process in our system and requires the construction of a set of rules for each target language.

The contribution of semantic information to temporal information treatment was more significant in recall and the improvement was concentrated in tasks A and B (approx. 12% recall improvement). Although, TIPSem-B achieved lower results they are high enough to confirm that that most of temporal elements strongly depends on lexical and morphosyntactic information.

The main errors and difficulties of our approach in this evaluation exercise are related to TIMEX3 normalization (value attribute). A pure ML approach for solving this problem is not trivial, at least, using our approach philosophy. The treatment of normalization functions is an inherently complex task and requires many training data to be automatically learned. This required us to include in the system some handcrafted rules to enable the system for this task.

As further work we propose improving the TIMEX3 normalization by replacing handcrafted normalization rules with machine learned ones by combining statistic techniques and multilingual temporal knowledge resources (ontologies). Furthermore, link-categorization will be analyzed in more detail in order to include more features to improve the models. Finally, the suggested language independence of the approach will be tested using TempEval-2 available data for other languages.

Acknowledgments

This paper has been supported by the Spanish Government, projects TIN-2006-15265-C06-01, TIN-2009-13391-C04-01 and PROMETEO/2009/119, where Hector Llorens is funded under a FPI grant (BES-2007-16256).

References

Eugene Charniak and Mark Johnson. 2005. Coarse-to-fine n-best parsing and maxent discriminative reranking. In *43rd Annual Meeting of the ACL*.

Christiane Fellbaum. 1998. *WordNet: An Electronic Lexical Database (Language, Speech, and Communication)*. MIT Press.

Daniel Gildea and Daniel Jurafsky. 2002. Automatic labeling of semantic roles. *Computational Linguistics*, 28(3):245–288.

John D. Lafferty, Andrew McCallum, and Fernando C. N. Pereira. 2001. Conditional random fields: Probabilistic models for segmenting and labeling sequence data. In *Proceedings of the 18th ICML*, pages 282–289. Morgan Kaufmann.

Hector Llorens, Borja Navarro, and Estela Saquete. 2009. Detección de Expresiones Temporales TimeML en Catalán mediante Roles Semánticos y Redes Semánticas. In *Procesamiento del Lenguaje Natural (SEPLN)*, number 43, pages 13–21.

Paloma Moreda, Borja Navarro, and Manuel Palomar. 2007. Corpus-based semantic role approach in information retrieval. *Data Knowledge Engineering*, 61(3):467–483.

Vasin Punyakanok, Dan Roth, W. Yih, D. Zimak, and Y. Tu. 2004. Semantic role labeling via generalized inference over classifiers. In *HLT-NAACL (CoNLL)*, pages 130–133. ACL.

James Pustejovsky, José M. Castaño, Robert Ingria, Roser Saurí, Robert Gaizauskas, Andrea Setzer, and Graham Katz. 2003. TimeML: Robust Specification of Event and Temporal Expressions in Text. In *IWCS-5*.

Frank Schilder, Graham Katz, and James Pustejovsky. 2007. *Annotating, Extracting and Reasoning About Time and Events (Dagstuhl 2005)*, volume 4795 of *LNCS*. Springer.

Helmut Schmid. 1994. Probabilistic part-of-speech tagging using decision trees. In *Proceedings of the International Conference on New Methods in Language Processing*, pages 44–49.

Mariona Taulé, M. Antonia Martí, and Marta Recasens. 2008. AnCora: Multilevel Annotated Corpora for Catalan and Spanish. In ELRA, editor, *LREC*, Marrakech, Morocco.

Marc Verhagen, Robert Gaizauskas, Mark Hepple, Frank Schilder, Graham Katz, and James Pustejovsky. 2007. Semeval-2007 task 15: Tempeval temporal relation identification. In *Proceedings of the 4th International Workshop on Semantic Evaluations*, pages 75–80, Prague. ACL.

Piek Vossen. 1998. *EuroWordNet: a multilingual database with lexical semantic networks*. Kluwer Academic Publishers, MA, USA.

CityU-DAC: Disambiguating Sentiment-Ambiguous Adjectives within Context

Bin LU and Benjamin K. TSOU
Department of Chinese, Translation and Linguistics &
Language Information Sciences Research Centre
City University of Hong Kong
{lubin2010, rlbtsou}@gmail.com

Abstract

This paper describes our system participating in task 18 of SemEval-2010, i.e. disambiguating Sentiment-Ambiguous Adjectives (SAAs). To disambiguating SAAs, we compare the machine learning-based and lexicon-based methods in our submissions: 1) Maximum entropy is used to train classifiers based on the annotated Chinese data from the NTCIR opinion analysis tasks, and the clause-level and sentence-level classifiers are compared; 2) For the lexicon-based method, we first classify the adjectives into two classes: intensifiers (i.e. adjectives intensifying the intensity of context) and suppressors (i.e. adjectives decreasing the intensity of context), and then use the polarity of context to get the SAAs' contextual polarity based on a sentiment lexicon. The results show that the performance of maximum entropy is not quite high due to little training data; on the other hand, the lexicon-based method could improve the precision by considering the polarity of context.

1 Introduction

In recent years, *sentiment analysis*, which mines opinions from information sources such as news, blogs, and product reviews, has drawn much attention in the NLP field (Hatzivassiloglou and McKeown, 1997; Pang et al., 2002; Turney, 2002; Hu and Liu, 2004; Pang and Lee, 2008). It has many applications such as social media monitoring, market research, and public relations.

Some adjectives are neutral in sentiment polarity out of context, but they could show positive, neutral or negative meaning within specific context. Such words can be called dynamic sentiment-ambiguous adjectives (SAAs). However, SAAs have not been intentionally tackled in the researches of sentiment analysis, and usually have been discarded or ignored by most previous work. Wu et al., (2008) presents an approach of combining collocation information and SVM to disambiguate SAAs, in which the collocation-based method was first used to disambiguate adjectives within the context of collocation (i.e. a sub-sentence marked by comma), and then the SVM algorithm was explored for those instances not covered by the collocation-based method. According to their experiments, their supervised algorithm achieves encouraging performance.

The task 18 at SemEval-2010 is intended to create a benchmark dataset for disambiguating SAAs. Given only 100 trial sentences, but not provided with any official training data, participants are required to tackle this problem data by unsupervised approaches or use their own training data. The task consists of 14 SAAs, which are all high-frequency words in Mandarin Chinese. They are 大|big, 小|small, 多|many, 少|few, 高|high, 低|low, 厚|thick, 薄|thin, 深|deep, 浅|shallow, 重|heavy, 轻|light, 巨大|huge, 重大|grave. This task deals with Chinese SAAs, but the disambiguating techniques should be language-independent. Please refer to (Wu and Jin, 2010) for more descriptions of the task.

In our participating system, the annotated Chinese data from the NTCIR opinion analysis tasks is used as training data with the help of a combined sentiment lexicon. A machine learning-based method (namely maximum entropy) and the lexicon-based method are compared in our submissions. The results show that the performance of maximum entropy is not quite high due to little training data; on the other hand, the lexicon-based method could improve

Proceedings of the 5th International Workshop on Semantic Evaluation, ACL 2010, pages 292–295,
Uppsala, Sweden, 15-16 July 2010. ©2010 Association for Computational Linguistics

the precision by considering the context of SAAs. In Section 2, we briefly describe data preparation of sentiment lexicon and training data. Our approaches for disambiguating SAAs are given in Section 3. The experiment and results are presented in Section 4, followed by a conclusion in Section 5.

2 Data Preparation

2.1 Sentiment Lexicon

Several traditional Chinese resources of polar words/phrases are collected, including NTU Sentiment Dictionary[1], *The Lexicon of Chinese Positive Words* (Shi and Zhu, 2006), *The Lexicon of Chinese Negative Words* (Yang and Zhu, 2006) 0, and CityU's sentiment-bearing word/phrase list (Lu et al, 2008), which were manually marked in the political news data by trained annotators (Benjamin and Lu, 2008). Sentiment-bearing items marked with the *SENTIMENT_KW* tag (SKPI), including only positive and negative items but not neutral ones, were also automatically extracted from the Chinese sample data of NTCIR-6 OAPT (Seki et al., 2007). All these polar item lexicons were combined, and the combined polar item lexicon consists of 13,437 positive items and 18,365 negative items, a total of 31,802 items.

2.2 Training Data

The training data is extracted from the Chinese sample and test data from the NTCIR opinion analysis task, including NTCIR-6 (Seki et al., 2007), NTCIR-7 (Seki et al., 2008) and NTCIR-8 (Seki et al., 2010). The NTCIR opinion analysis tasks provide an opportunity to evaluate the techniques used by different participants based on a common evaluation framework in Chinese (simplified and traditional), Japanese and English.

For data from NTCIR-6 and NTCIR-7, three annotators manually marked the polarity of each opinionated sentence, and the lenient polarity is used here as the gold standard (please refer to Seki et al., 2008 for explanation of lenient and strict standard). For each opinionated sentence from NTCIR-8, only two annotators marked and the strict polarity is used as the gold standard. The traditional Chinese sentences are transferred into simplified Chinese. In total, there are about 12K opinionated sentences annotated with polarity, out of which about 9K are marked as positive or negative, and others neutral. All the 9K sentences plus the 100 sentences from the trial data are used as the sentence-level training data.

Meanwhile, we also try to get the clause-level training data since the context of collocation within sub-sentences are quite crucial for disambiguating SAAs according to Wu et al. (2008). From the 9K positive/ negative sentences above, we automatically extract the clause for each occurrence of SAAs.

Note the polarity for a whole sentence is not necessarily the same with that of the clause containing SAAs. Consider the sentence *在 当前 的 世界* **大** *格局 中 ， 中俄 两国 相互 支持 (In the current large circumstance of the world, China and Russia support each other)*. The polarity of the whole sentence is positive, while the clause *在当前的世界大格局中(In the current large circumstance of the world)* containing a SAA *大 (large)* is neutral, and the polarity lies in the second part of the whole sentence, i.e. *相互 支持* (support each other).

Thus, we manually checked the polarity of clauses containing SAAs. Due to time limitation, we only checked 465 clauses. Plus the clauses extracted from 100 trial sentences, the final clause-level training data consist of 565 positive/negative clauses containing SAAs.

3 Our Approach for Disambiguating SAAs

To disambiguating SAAs, we use the maximum entropy algorithm and the sentiment lexicon-based method, and also combine them together.

3.1 The Maximum Entropy-based Method

Maximum entropy classification (MaxEnt) is a technique which has proven effective in a number of natural language processing applications (Berger et al., 1996). Le Zhang's maximum entropy tool[2] is used for classification.

The Chinese sentences are segmented into words using a production segmentation system. Unigrams of words are used as basic features for classification. Bigrams are also tried, but does not show improvement, and thus are not described in details here.

3.2 The Lexicon-based Method

For the lexicon-based method, we first classify the 14 adjectives into two classes: intensifiers

[1] http://nlg18.csie.ntu.edu.tw:8080/opinion/index.html

[2] http:// homepages.inf.ed.ac.uk/lzhang10/maxent_toolkit.html

and suppressors. Intensifiers refer to adjectives intensifying the intensity of context, including 大|big, 多|many, 高|high, 厚|thick, 深|deep, 重|heavy, 巨大|huge, 重大|grave, while suppressors refer to adjectives decreasing the intensity of context, including 小|small, 少|few, 低|low, 薄|thin, 浅|shallow, 轻|light.

Meanwhile, the collocation nouns are also classified into two classes: positive and negative. Positive nouns include 素质|quality, 标准|standard, 水平|level, 效益|benefit, 成就|achievement, etc. Negative nouns include 压力|pressure, 差距|disparity, 问题|problem, 风险|risk, 污染|pollution etc.

The hypothesis here is that intensifiers will receive the polarity of their collocations while suppressors will get the opposite polarity of their collocations. For example, 成就|achievement could be collocated with one of the following intensifiers: 大|big, 多|many or 高|high, and the adjectives just receive the polarity of 成就|achievement, which is positive. Meanwhile, 污染|pollution could be collocated with one of the following suppressors: 小|small, 少|few, 低|low, and the adjectives just receive the opposite polarity of 污染|pollution, which is also positive.

Based on this hypothesis, we could get the polarity of SAAs through theirs collocation nouns within the clauses containing SAAs. The context of SAAs is a sub-sentence marked by comma. The sentiment lexicon mentioned in Section 2.1 is used to find polarity of collocation nouns.

3.3 Combining Maximum Entropy and Lexicon

To combine the two methods above, the lexicon-based method is first used to disambiguate the sentiment of SAAs, and the context of collocation is a sub-sentence marked by comma. Then for those instances that are not covered by the lexicon-based method, the maximum entropy algorithm is explored.

4 Experiment and Results

The dataset contains two parts: some sentences were extracted from Chinese Gigaword (LDC corpus: LDC2005T14), and other sentences were gathered through the search engine like Google. Firstly, these sentences were automatically segmented and POS-tagged, and then the ambiguous adjectives were manually annotated with the correct sentiment polarity within the sentence context. Two annotators annotated the sentences double blindly, and the third annotator checks the annotation. All the data of 2,917 sentences is provided as the test set, and evaluation is performed in terms of micro accuracy and macro accuracy.

We submitted 4 runs: run 1 is based on the sentence-level MaxEnt classifier; run 2 on the clause-level MaxEnt classifier; run 3 is got by combining the lexicon-based method and the sentence-level MaxEnt classifier; and run 4 by combining the lexicon-based method and the clause-level MaxEnt classifier. The official scores for the 4 runs are shown in Table 2.

Table 2. Results of 4 Runs

Run	Micro Acc. (%)	Macro Acc. (%)
1	61.98	67.89
2	62.63	60.85
3	71.55	75.54
4	72.47	69.80

From Table 2, we can observe that:

1) Compared the highest scores achieved by other teams, the performance of maximum entropy (run 1 and 2) is not quite high due to little training data;

2) By integrating the lexicon-based method and maximum entropy (run 3 and 4), we improve the accuracy by considering the context of SAAs;

3) The sentence-level maximum entropy classifier shows better macro accuracy, and clause-level one better micro accuracy.

In addition to the official scores, we also evaluate the performance of the lexicon-based method alone. The micro and macro accuracy are respectively 0.847 and 0.835665, showing that the lexicon-based method is more accurate than the maximum entropy algorithm (run 1 and 2). But it only covers 1,436 (49%) of 2,917 test instances.

Because the data from the NTCIR opinion analysis task is not specifically annotated for this task, and the manually checked clauses are less than 600, the performance of our system is not quite high compared to the highest performance achieved by other teams.

5 Conclusion

To disambiguating SAAs, we compare machine learning-based and lexicon-based methods in our submissions: 1) Maximum entropy is used to train classifiers based on the annotated Chinese data from the NTCIR opinion analysis tasks, and the clause-level and sentence-level classifiers are compared; 2) For the lexicon-based method, we first classify the adjectives into two classes: intensifiers (i.e. adjectives intensifying the intensity of context) and suppressors (i.e. adjectives decreasing the intensity of context), and then use the polarity of context to get the SAAs' contextual polarity. The results show that the performance of maximum entropy is not quite high due to little training data; on the other hand, the lexicon-based method could improve the precision by considering the context of SAAs.

References

Adam L. Berger, Stephen A. Della Pietra, and Vincent J. Della Pietra. 1996. A maximum entropy approach to natural language processing. *Computational Linguistics*, 22(1):39-71.

Vasileios Hatzivassiloglou and Kathleen McKeown. 1997. Predicting the Semantic Orientation of Adjectives. *Proceedings of ACL-97*. 174-181.

Minqing Hu and Bing Liu. 2004. Mining Opinion Features in Customer Reviews. In *Proceedings of the 19th National Conference on Artificial Intelligence*, pp. 755-760.

Bin Lu, Benjamin K. Tsou and Oi Yee Kwong. 2008. Supervised Approaches and Ensemble Techniques for Chinese Opinion Analysis at NTCIR-7. In *Proceedings of the Seventh NTCIR Workshop (NTCIR-7)*. pp. 218-225. Tokyo, Japan.

Bo Pang and Lillian Lee. 2008. *Opinion mining and sentiment analysis, Foundations and Trends in Information Retrieval*, Now Publishers.

Bo Pang, Lillian Lee, and Shivakumar Vaithyanathan. 2002. Thumbs up? Sentiment classification using machine learning techniques. In *Proceedings of EMNLP 2002*, pp.79–86.

Yohei Seki, David Kirk Evans, Lun-Wei Ku, Le Sun, Hsin-His Chen, Noriko Kando. 2007. Overview of Opinion Analysis Pilot Task at NTCIR-6. *Proc. of the Seventh NTCIR Workshop*. Japan. 2007.6.

Yohei Seki, David Kirk Evans, Lun-Wei Ku, Le Sun, Hsin-His Chen, Noriko Kando and Chin-Yew Lin. 2008. Overview of Multilingual Opinion Analysis Task at NTCIR-7. *Proc. of the Seventh NTCIR Workshop*. Japan. Dec. 2008.

Yohei Seki, Lun-Wei Ku, Le Sun, Hsin-His Chen, Noriko Kando. 2010. Overview of Multilingual Opinion Analysis Task at NTCIR-8. *Proc. of the Seventh NTCIR Workshop*. Japan. June, 2010.

Jilin Shi and Yinggui Zhu. 2006. The Lexicon of Chinese Positive Words (褒義詞詞典). Sichuan Lexicon Press.

Benjamin K. Tsou and Bin Lu. 2008. A Political News Corpus in Chinese for Opinion Analysis. In *Proceedings of the Second International Workshop on Evaluating Information Access (EVIA2008)*. pp. 6-7. Tokyo, Japan.

Peter D. Turney. 2002. Thumbs up or thumbs down? Semantic orientation applied to unsupervised classification of reviews, In *Proceedings of ACL-02*, Philadelphia, Pennsylvania, 417-424.

Yunfang Wu, Miao Wang, Peng Jin and Shiwen Yu. 2008. Disambiguate sentiment ambiguous adjectives. In *Proceedings of IEEE International Conference on Natural Language Processing and Knowledge Engineering (NLP-KE'08)*.

Yunfang Wu, and Peng Jin. 2010. SemEval-2010 Task 18: Disambiguate sentiment ambiguous adjectives. In *Proceedings of SemEval-2010*.

Ruifeng Xu, Kam-Fai Wong and Yunqing Xia. 2008. Coarse-Fine Opinion Mining - WIA in NTCIR-7 MOAT Task. In *Proceedings of the Seventh NTCIR Workshop (NTCIR-7)*. Tokyo, Japan, Dec. 16-19.

Ling Yang and Yinggui Zhu. 2006. The Lexicon of Chinese Negative Words (貶義詞詞典). Sichuan Lexicon Press.

VENSES++: Adapting a deep semantic processing system to the identification of null instantiations

Sara Tonelli
Fondazione Bruno Kessler
Trento, Italy.
satonelli@fbk.eu

Rodolfo Delmonte
Università Ca' Foscari
Venezia, Italy.
delmont@unive.it

Abstract

The system to spot INIs, DNIs and their antecedents is an adaptation of VENSES, a system for semantic evaluation that has been used for RTE challenges in the last 6 years. In the following we will briefly describe the system and then the additions we made to cope with the new task. In particular, we will discuss how we mapped the VENSES analysis to the representation of frame information in order to identify null instantiations in the text.

1 Introduction

The SemEval-2010 task for linking events and their participants in discourse (Ruppenhofer et al., 2009) introduced a new issue w.r.t. the SemEval-2007 task "Frame Semantic Structure Extraction" (Baker et al., 2007), in that it focused on linking local semantic argument structures across sentence boundaries. Specifically, the task included first the identification of frames and frame elements in a text following the FrameNet paradigm (Baker et al., 1998), then the identification of locally uninstantiated roles (NIs). If these roles are indefinite (INI), they have to be marked as such and no antecedent has to be found. On the contrary, if they are definite (DNI), their coreferents have to be found in the wider discourse context. The challenge comprised two tasks, namely the *full task* (semantic role recognition and labelling + NI linking) and the *NIs only task*, i.e. the identification of null instantiations and their referents given a test set with gold standard local semantic argument structure.

We took part to the NIs only task by modifying the VENSES system for deep semantic processing and entailment recognition (Delmonte et al., 2005). In our approach, we assume that the identification of null instantiations is a complex task requiring different levels of semantic knowledge and several processing steps. For this reason, we believe that the rich analysis performed by the pipeline architecture of VENSES is particularly suitable for the task, also due to the small amount of training data available and the heterogeneity of NI phenomena.

2 The VENSES system

VENSES is a reduced version of GETARUNS (Delmonte, 2008), a complete system for text understanding, whose backbone is LFG theory in its original version (Bresnan, 1982 and 2000). The system produces different levels of analysis, from syntax to discourse. However, three of them contribute most to the NI identification task: the lexico-semantic, the anaphora resolution and the deep semantic module.

2.1 The syntactic and lexico-semantic module

The system produces a c(onstituent)-structure representation by means of a cascade of augmented FSA, then it uses this output to map lexical information from a number of different lexica which however contain similar information related to verb/adjective and noun subcategorization. The mapping is done by splitting sentences into main and subordinate clauses. Other clauses are computed in their embedded position and can be either complement or relative clauses.

The system output is an Augmented Head Dependent Structure (AHDS), which is a fully indexed logical form, with Grammatical Relations and Semantic Roles. The inventory of semantic roles we use is however very small – 35, even though it is partly overlapping the one proposed in the first FrameNet project. We prefer to use generic roles rather than specific Frame Elements (FEs) because sense disambiguation at this stage of computation may not be effective.

Proceedings of the 5th International Workshop on Semantic Evaluation, ACL 2010, pages 296–299,
Uppsala, Sweden, 15-16 July 2010.

2.2 The anaphora resolution module

The AHDS structure is passed to and used by a full-fledged module for pronominal and anaphora resolution, which is in turn split into *two submodules*. The resolution procedure takes care only of third person pronouns of all kinds – reciprocals, reflexives, possessive and personal. Its mechanisms are quite complex, as described in (Delmonte et al., 2006). The *first submodule* basically treats all pronouns at sentence level – that is, taking into account their position – and if they are left free, they receive the annotation "external". If they are bound, they are associated to an antecedent's index; else they might also be interpreted as expletives, i.e. they receive a label that prevents the following submodule to consider them for further computation.
The *second submodule* receives as input the external pronouns, and tries to find an antecedent in the previous stretch of text or discourse. To do that, the systems computes a *topic hierarchy* that is built following suggestions by (Sidner and Grosz, 1986) and is used in a centering-like manner.

2.3 The semantic module

The output of the anaphora resolution module is used by the semantic module to substitute the pronoun's head with the antecedent's head. After this operation, the module produces Predicate-Argument Structures or PAS on the basis of a previously produced Logical Form. PAS are produced for each clause and they separate obligatory from non-obligatory arguments, and these from adjuncts and modifiers. Some adjuncts, like spatiotemporal locations, are only bound at propositional level.

3 From VENSES output to NIs identification and binding

After computing PAS information for each sentence, we first map the test set gold standard annotation of frame information to VENSES output. Starting from the PAS with frames and FE labels attached to the predicates and the arguments, we run a module for DNI/INI spotting and DNI binding. It is composed by two different submodules, one for *verbal* predicates and one for *nominal* ones.

3.1 NIs identification and binding with verbal predicates

As pointed out in (Ruppenhofer et al., 2009), the identification of DNI/INIs includes three main steps: i) recognizing that a core role is missing ii) ascertaining if it has a definite interpretation and iii) if yes, finding a role filler for it.
For verbal predicates, the two first steps are accomplished starting from the PAS structure produced by VENSES and trying to map them with the valence patterns in FrameNet. To this purpose, we take into account the list of all valence patterns extracted for every LU and every frame from FrameNet 1.4 and from the training data, in which all possible sequences of FEs (both overtly expressed and null instantiated) are listed with their grammatical functions, coreness status and frequencies. For example, the predicate "barbecue.v" in the APPLY_HEAT frame is characterized by two patterns, both occurring once. In the first, *Food* is the subject (ext) and *Cook* is constructionally not instantiated (cni). In the second, the peripheral FE *Time* is also present:

```
ssr(barbecue-v,apply_heat,[[[[food-
c,np,ext],[cook-c,cni,null]],1],[[[time-
p,pp,dep],[food-c,np,ext],[cook-
c,cni,null]],1]]).
```

The first step in our computation is selecting for the current predicate those patterns or templates that contain the same number of core arguments of the clause under analysis plus one. This is due to the fact that NIs are always core FEs. For example, if a test sentence contains the "barbecue.v" lexical unit labelled with the APPLY_HEAT frame and only the *Food* FE is overtly annotated, we look in the template list for all patterns in which "barbecue.v" appears with the *Food* FE and another implicit core FE (either INI or DNI). If "barbecue.v" is not present in the template list, we consider the templates of the other verbal lexical units in the same frame.

The second step is assessing the licensor of the omission, whether lexical or constructional. Here we only distinguish complement governing predicates and passive constructions. For example, if "barbecue.v" is attested in the template list both with an indefinite and with a definite instantiation of the *Cook* FE, we check if it occurs in the passive form in the test sentence. If yes, we infer that *Cook* has to be labelled as an indefinite null instantiation (INI). Another licensor of the omission could be the imperative form of the verb, which however has not been considered yet by our system.

If we assess that the null instantiation is not indefinite, we look for an antecedent of the NI and, if we find it, we label it as a DNI. Otherwise, we don't encode any information about omitted roles. The strategy devised for searching for possible referential expressions is as follows:

1. Given the current PAS (with frame labels), look in the previous sentence(s) for comparable PAS. *Comparable* means that the predicate is the same or semantically related based on WordNet synsets.
2. If a comparable PAS is found, check if they share at least one argument slot – typically they should share the subject role.
3. If yes, look for the best head available in that PAS by semantic matching with the FE label as a referent for the DNI label in the current sentence. In case that does not produce any matching, we look into the list of all heads in FrameNet associated to the FE label and select the one present in the PAS that matches.

3.2 NIs identification and binding with nominal predicates

In order to identify DNI/INIs of *nominal* predicates, we take into account the History List produced by VENSES in the AHDS analysis, where all nominal heads describing Events, Spatial and Temporal Locations and Body Parts in the document are collected together with their current sentence ID. Such list is derived from WordNet general nouns.

Based on a computational lexicon of Common Sense Reasoning relations made available with ConceptNet 2.0 by MIT AI Lab (Liu and Singh, 2004), we first process the history list in order to identify the relations between nominal heads in different sentences. Such relations include inheritance and inferences. For instance, if the current sentence contains the nominal heads "door" or "window", they are connected to the "house" head, if it is present in the History List as a spatial location occurring in a previous sentence. For instance, sentence 42 of the test document n. 13 contains the noun "wall" as lexical unit of the ARCHITECTURAL_PART frame. In the History List, it is classified as a place. Also the noun "house" in sentence n. 7 (token 7) is classified as a place in the History List. Since ConceptNet allows us to infer a meronymy relation between "wall" and "house", we can derive the following information, saying that "place" in sent. 45, token 25, is related to "house", in sent. 7, token 7:

```
loc(42-25, place, wall, house-[7-7]).
```

Starting from this information, we then check which core FEs are overtly expressed in the test sentence for the "wall" lexical unit. As encoded in the FrameNet database, the ARCHITECTURAL_PART frame has two core FEs, namely *Part* and *Whole*. Since *Part* is already present in sentence n. 45, we assume that *Whole* could be a candidate DNI. After looking up the relations between nominal heads identified in the previous step, we make the hypothesis that "house" be the antecedent of the *Whole* DNI. We then check if "house" appears as a head of the *Whole* FE either in the FrameNet database or in the training data of the SemEval task in order to perform some semantic verification. If this hypothesis is confirmed, we finally take the syntactic node headed by the antecedent as the best DNI referent. In our example, "house" is the head of the node 501, so we generate the following output, in which the Whole FE is identified with the node 501 (headed by "house") in sentence 7:

```
<fe id="s42_f5_e2" name="Whole">
<fenode idref="s7_501"/>
<flag name="Definite_Interpretation">
```

Note that, in case the antecedent does not appear as the head of the candidate FE, it is discarded and no information about NIs is generated. This is clearly a limit of our approach, because nominal predicates are never assigned an INI label.

4 System output and evaluation

The SemEval test data comprise two annotated documents extracted from Conan Doyle's novels. We report some statistics about the test data with gold standard annotation and a comparison with our system output in Table 1.

	Text 1	Text 2
N. of sentences	249	276
Gold standard data		
N. of DNIs	158	191
N. of INIs	115	245
System output		
N. of DNIs	35	30
N. of INIs	16	20
F-score	0.0121	

Table 1: Comparison between gold standard and system output

The amount of NIs detected by our system is much lower than the gold standard one, particularly for INIs. This depends partly on the fact that no specific strategy for INI detection with nominal predicates has been devised so far, as described in Section 3.2. Another problem is that a lot of DNIs in the gold standard don't get resolved, while our system always looks for a referent in case of DNIs and if it is not found, the procedure fails.

The issue of detecting which DNIs are liable not to have an explicit antecedent remains an open problem. In general, Ruppenhofer et al. (2009) suggest to treat the DNI identification and binding as a coreference resolution task. However, the only information available is in fact the label of the missing FE. The authors propose to obtain information about the likely fillers of a missing FE from annotated data sets, but the task showed that this procedure could be successful only in case all FE labels are semantically well identifiable: in fact many FE labels are devoid of any specific associated meaning. Furthermore, lexical fillers of a given semantic role in the FrameNet data sets can be as diverse as possible. For example, a complete search in the FrameNet database for the FE *Charges* will reveal heads like "possession, innocent, actions", where the significant portion of text addressed by the FE would be in the specification - i.e. "possession of a gun" etc. Only in case of highly specialized FEs there will be some help in the semantic characterization of a possible antecedent. Another open issue is the notion of context where the antecedent should be searched for, which is lacking an appropriate definition.

If we take into account our system results on Text 1, we notice that only 3 DNIs have been identified and linked to the correct antecedent, while the overall amount of exact matches including INIs is 7. However, in 21 other cases the system correctly identifies a null instantiated role and assigns the right FE label, but it either detects an INI instead of a DNI (and vice-versa), or it finds the wrong antecedent for the DNI. A similar performance is achieved on Text 2: no DNI has been linked to the correct antecedent, and in only 8 cases there is an exact match between the INIs identified by the system and those in the gold standard. However, in 18 cases a null instantiation is detected and assigned the correct FE label, even if either the referent or the definiteness label is wrong. Some evaluation metrics taking into account the different information layers conveyed by the system would help highlighting such differences and pointing out the NI identification steps that need to be consolidated.

5 Conclusions

In this paper, we have introduced VENSES++, a modified version of the VENSES system for deep semantic processing and entailment detection. We described two strategies for the identification of null instantiations in a text, depending on the predicate class (either nominal or verbal).

The system took part to the SemEval task for NIs identification and binding. Even if the preliminary results are far from satisfactory, we were able to devise a general strategy for dealing with the task. Only 2 teams took part to the competition, and the first ranked system achieved F1 = 0.0140. This confirms that NI identification is a very challenging issue which can be hardly modeled. Anyway, it deserves further efforts, as various NLP applications could benefit from the effective identification of null instantiated roles, from SRL to coreference resolution and information extraction.

References

Baker, C., Ellsworth, M. and Erk, K. 2007. *Frame Semantic Structure Extraction*. In Proceedings of the 4th International Workshop on Semantic Evaluations. Prague, Czech Republic.

Baker, C. F., Fillmore, C. J., & Lowe, J. B. 1998. *The Berkeley FrameNet project*. In Proceedings of COLING-ACL-98, Montreal, Canada.

Bresnan, J. 2000. *Lexical-functional syntax*. Oxford: Blackwell.

Bresnan, J. (ed.). 1982. *The mental representation of grammatical relations*, The MIT Press, Cambridge.

Delmonte R., 2008. *Computational Linguistic Text Processing – Lexicon, Grammar, Parsing and Anaphora Resolution*, Nova Science, New York.

Delmonte, R., Tonelli, S., Piccolino Boniforti, M. A., Bristot, A., and Pianta, E. 2005. VENSES – A Linguistically-based System for Semantic Evaluation. In Proc. of the 1st PASCAL RTE Workshop.

Delmonte, R., Bristot, A., Piccolino Boniforti, M.A., and Tonelli, S. 2006. *Another Evaluation of Anaphora Resolution Algorithms and a Comparison with GETARUNS' Knowledge Rich Approach*, In Proc. of ROMAND 2006, Trento, pp. 3-10.

Grosz, B., and Sidner, C. 1986. *Attention, intentions and the structure of discourse*. Computational Linguistics, 12, 175–204.

Liu, H., and Singh, P. 2004. ConceptNet: a practical commonsense reasoning toolkit. At http://web.media.mit.edu/~push/ConceptNet.pdf.

Ruppenhofer, J., Sporleder, C., Morante, R., Baker, C. and Palmer, M. 2009. *SemEval-2010 Task 10: Linking Events and Their Participants in Discourse*. In Proc. of the HLT-NAACL Workshop on Semantic Evaluations: Recent Achievements and Future Directions. Boulder, Colorado.

CLR: Linking Events and Their Participants in Discourse Using a Comprehensive FrameNet Dictionary

Ken Litkowski
CL Research
Damascus, MD USA.
ken@clres.com

Abstract

The CL Research system for SemEval-2 Task 10 for linking events and their participants in discourse is an exploration of the use of a specially created FrameNet dictionary that captures all FrameNet information about frames, lexical units, and frame-to-frame relations. This system is embedded in a specially designed interface, the Linguistic Task Analyzer. The implementation of this system was quite minimal at the time of submission, allowing only an initial completion of the role recognition and labeling task, with recall of 0.112, precision of 0.670, and F-score of 0.192. We describe the design of the system and the continuing efforts to determine how much of this task can be performed with the available lexical resources. Changes since the official submission have improved the F-score to 0.266.

1 Introduction

The semantic role labeling (SRL) task has received considerable attention in recent years, with previous tasks in Senseval-2 (Litkowski, 2004), Semeval-1 (Baker et al., 2007), and CoNLL (Carreras & Marquez, 2004; Carreras & Marquez, 2005). The current task, Linking Events and their Participants in Discourse, continues the evolution of SRL tasks with the intent of identifying Null Instantiations, i.e., frame elements that are absent from the local context, but potentially recoverable from the wider discourse context.

CL Research participated in one subtask, role recognition and labeling, unable to implement techniques for the null instantiation subtask. This paper describes our efforts thus far (clearly a work in progress), specifically the implementation of a development interface (section 2), the use of a specially constructed FrameNet dictionary (section 3), techniques for performing the role recognition and labeling task (section 4), our results (section 5), and future developments (section 6).

2 The Linguistic Task Analyzer

CL Research participated in the linking task by extending its Linguistic Task Analyzer (LTA), an interface also used for such tasks as word-sense disambiguation and recognizing textual entailment. LTA includes a wide array of modules, including a full-scale parser, post-parsing semantic analysis routines, the use of XML functionality for creating and analyzing input and output, and access to several integrated dictionaries (used for semantic analysis). Modification of LTA for the linking task involves using existing functionality and implementing new functionality specific to the task. We describe LTA in some detail to illustrate steps that might be relevant to a symbolic approach to the linking task.

Each task in LTA consists of a set of items to be analyzed, in this case, an identifier for each sentence in the document being analyzed. LTA loads the appropriate XML files (usually the annotation file and the gold file) and provides various data for each sentence, including the number of terminals, non-terminals, frames, frame elements that have been recognized, true positives, false positives, false negatives, and a characterization of problems that have been encountered. Summary statistics are given, showing such things as the total number of frames and the scoring for the current annotation (when a gold file is available).

Whenever a sentence is selected in the LTA, the text is shown (accomplished by querying the XML for the selected sentence and retrieving all its terminals). LTA provides a capability for se-

Proceedings of the 5th International Workshop on Semantic Evaluation, ACL 2010, pages 300–303,
Uppsala, Sweden, 15-16 July 2010. ©2010 Association for Computational Linguistics

lecting all sentences matching particular criteria, e.g., all sentences containing a **Color** frame or all sentences having targets that have problematic entries in the FrameNet dictionary.

LTA contains a basic command to run and evaluate the system against the selected sentences. This can be used during development to test the effect of changes to the underlying code for performing any of the tasks. During the test phase, all sentences are selected, the **Run and Evaluate** command is executed, the XML test file is modified with the insertion of frame elements constituting the system's answers, and the XML file is saved for the official submission. For the official submission, this took less than a minute for each of the two chapters.

A single sentence can be selected in the LTA for detailed examination. This **Sentence Detail** shows (1) the sentence itself (as in the main form), (2) a tree of the frames in the sentence, along with each of the frame elements that have been identified, minimally showing the target, and the text that has been identified for the frame element, and (3) from the training data, the frame element differences from the gold file, along with their terminal or non-terminal id references.

The **Sentence Detail** also has buttons to (1) score the annotation against the gold file for the sentence, (2) identify the missing core frame elements, (3) examine the FrameNet entries for the targets, and (4) perform the task. The functionality underlying the scoring and the task performance are called from the main form when all or selected sentences are to be processed (e.g., in the **Run and Evaluate** command).

Implementation of the scoring functionality for the **Sentence Detail** form attempts to follow the implementation in the official scorer. We have not yet captured every nuance of the scorer; however, we seem to have 99.9 percent agreement.

The **Sentence Detail** functionality is at the heart of the investigation and implementation of techniques for performing the tasks. At this time, we must view the implementation as only in its initial stages, minimally capable of performing the role recognition and labeling task. Further details about the implementation, including its shortcomings, will be described below.

3 The FrameNet Dictionary

Central to the performance of the linking task is the use of a dictionary constructed from the FrameNet data. This dictionary is in a format used by the CL Research DIMAP dictionary maintenance program.[1] The FrameNet dictionary attempts to capture all the information in FrameNet, in a form that can be easily accessed and used for tasks such as the linking task. This dictionary is also used in general word-sense disambiguation tasks, when all words in a text are simultaneously disambiguated with several dictionaries. The FrameNet dictionary has almost 11,000 entries[2] of four main types: frames, frame-to-frame relations, normal entries, and frame elements[3]. This dictionary was initially described in Litkowski (2007), but is described in more detail in the following subsections in order to show how the information in these entries is used in the linking task.

3.1 Frame Entries

A FrameNet frame is entered in the dictionary by preceding its name with a "#" sign to distinguish it from other types of entries. A frame entry, such as **#Abandonment**, consists of one sense with no part of speech. This sense contains a list of its frame elements and the coreness of each frame element. The sense also lists all the lexical units associated with the frame, along with the identifying number for each so that a link can be made if necessary to the appropriate lexical unit and lexical entry XML files. The sense identifies any frame-to-frame relations in which the frame participates, such as "IS_INHERITED_BY" with a link to the inheriting frame. Thus, whenever a specific frame is signaled in the linking task, its properties can be accessed and we can investigate which of the frame elements might be present in the context.

3.2 Frame-to-Frame Relations

While the entries for the individual frames identify the frame-to-frame relations in which a frame participates, separate entries are created to

---

[1] These dictionaries are stored in a Btree file format for rapid access. A free demonstration version of DIMAP is available at CL Research (http://www.clres.com). This version can be used to manipulate any of several dictionaries that are also available. These include WordNet and the basic FrameNet. CL Research also makes available a publicly available FrameNet Explorer and a DIMAP Frame Element Hierarchy dictionary.

[2] By contrast, the DIMAP dictionary for WordNet contains 147,000 entries.

[3] When a new version of FrameNet is made available, a new version of the DIMAP dictionary is created. This was the case with the preliminary FrameNet version 1.4a made available by the task organizers. This creation takes about two hours.

hold the mappings between the frame elements of the two frames. These entries are prefixed with an "@" sign, followed by the name of a frame, the frame relation, and the name of the second frame, as in the name "@Abounding_with INHERITS Locative_relation". The single sense for such an entry shows the mapping, e.g., of the Location frame element of **Abounding_with** to the Figure frame element of **Locative_relation**. The information in these entries has not yet been used in the linking task.

3.3 Frame Elements

Frame element entries are preceded with a "%", as in **%Toxic_substance**. We have a taxonomy of the 1131 uniquely-named frame elements in all the FrameNet frames.[4] Each frame element entry identifies its superordinate frame element (or none for the 12 roots) and the frame elements in which it is used. The information in these entries has not yet been used in the linking task.

3.4 Main Entries

The bulk of the entries in the FrameNet dictionary are for the lexical units. An entry was created for each unique form, with senses for each lexical unit of the base form. Thus, **beat** has four senses, two verb, one noun, and one adjective. Minimally, each sense contains its part of speech, its frame, and its id number. A sense may also contain a definition and its source, if present n the FrameNet lexical unit files.

If available, the information available in the lexical entry (LE) files is encapsulated in the sense, from the FERealization elements. This captures the phrase type, the grammatical function, the frame element, and the frequency in the FrameNet annotation files. An example of what information is available for one verb sense of **beat** is shown in Table 1.

Table 1. Lexical Entry Syntactic Patterns for "beat"

Feature Name	Feature Value
NP(Ext)	Loser (12)
NP(Obj)	Loser (28)
PP[by](Dep)	Winner (5)
CNI()	Winner (5)
PP[against](Dep)	Winner (2)
NP(Ext)	Winner (31)

[4] This taxonomy can be viewed at http://www.clres.com/db/feindex.html, which provides links describing how it was constructed and which can be downloaded in DIMAP or MySQL format.

At the present time, this type of information is the primary information used in the linking task.

4 Role Recognition and Labeling

To perform the role recognition and labeling task, the system first retrieves all the frames for the sentence and then iterates over each. The frame name and the target are retrieved. From the target XML, the id reference is used to retrieve the part of speech and lemma from the targets terminal node. With this information, an attempt is made to add child nodes to the frame node in the XML, thus supplying the system's performance of the task. After any nodes have thus been added, it is only necessary to save the modified XML as the output file.

The first step in adding child nodes is to obtain the lexical entries from the FrameNet dictionary for the frame and the lemma. Since the lemma may have multiple senses, we obtain the specific sense that corresponds to the frame. We iterate through the features for the sense, focusing on those providing syntactic patterns, such as those in Table 1. We deconstruct the feature value into its frame element name and its frequency. We then call a function with the feature name and the target's id reference to see if we can find a matching constituent; if successful, we create a child node of the frame with the frame element name and the id reference (for the child <fenode> of frame element <fe> node).

The matching constituent function operates on the syntactic pattern, calling specific functions to search the XML terminals and non-terminals for constituent that fit the syntactic criterion. At present, this only operates on four patterns: **DEN()**, **Poss(Gen)**, **NP(Ext)**, and **N(Head)**.[5] As an example, for **Poss(Gen)**, we select the non-terminals with the target as the "head" and search these for a terminal node marked as **PRP$**. A special constituent matching function was also written to look for the **Supported** frame element in the **Support** frame.

5 System Results

CL Research's results for the role recognition and labeling task are shown in Table 2. These results are generally consistent across the two chapters in the test and with results obtained with the training data during development. Combining

[5] The DEN pattern identifies incorporated frame elements. Since the official submission, two patterns (**NP(OBJ)** and **PP(Dep)** have been added.

the two chapters, the recall was 0.112, the precision was 0.670, and the F-score was 0.192.[6]

Table 2. Scores for Chapters 13 and 14

Measure	Ch. 13	Ch. 14
True Positives	191	246
False Positives	82	133
False Negatives	1587	1874
Correct Labels	189	237
Precision	0.700	0.649
Recall	0.107	0.116
F-Score	0.186	0.197
Label Accuracy	0.106	0.112

As can be seen, for entries with patterns (albeit a low recall), a substantial number of frame elements could be recognized with high precision from a very small number of constituent matching functions. A detailed analysis of the results, identifying the contribution of each pattern recognition and the problem of false positives, has not yet been completed. One such observation is that when the same syntactic pattern is present for more than one frame element, such as **NP(Ext)** for both **Loser** and **Winner** in the case of **beat** as shown in Table 1, the same constituent will be identified for both.

A significant shortcoming in the system occurs when there are no syntactic patterns available for a particular sense (27 percent of the targets). For example, the lemma **hour** frequently appears in the training set as the target of either the **Measure_duration** or **Calendric_unit** frames, but it has no syntactic patterns (i.e., the FrameNet data contain no annotations for this lexical unit), while **decade**, also used in the same frames, does have syntactic patterns. This is a frequent occurrence with the FrameNet dictionary.

6 Future Developments

As should be clear from the preceding description, there are many opportunities for improvement. First, several improvements can be made in the LTA to improve the ability to facilitate development. The LTA has only barely begun exploitation of the many integrated modules that are available. Additional functionality needs to be developed so that it will be possible to determine the effect of any changes in constituent matching, i.e., what is the effect on recall and precision. The sentence detail form can be improved to provide better insights into the relation between syntactic patterns and their matching constituents.

Secondly, major improvements appear likely from greater exploitation of the FrameNet dictionary. At present, no use is made of the frequency information or the weighting of choices for matching constituents. When a given lemma has no syntactic patterns, it is likely that some use of the patterns for other lexical units in the frame can be made. It is also possible that some general patterns can be discerned using the frame element taxonomy.

It is important to see how far the FrameNet data can be further exploited and where other lexical data, such as available in WordNet or in more traditional lexical databases, can be used. The data developed for this linking task provide many opportunities for further exploration.

[6]The additional patterns described in the previous footnote have improved recall to 0.166 and F-score to 0.266, while maintaining a high precision (0.676).

References

Collin Baker, Michael Ellsworth, and Katrin Erk. 2007. Semeval-2007 Task 19: Frame Semantic Structure Extraction. *Proceedings of the Fourth International Workshop on Semantic Evaluations (SemEval-2007)*. Prague, Czech Republic, Association for Computational Linguistics, pp. 99-104.

Xavier Carreras and Luis Marquez. 2004. Introduction to the CoNLL-2004 Shared Task Semantic Role Labeling. *Proceedings of the Eighth Conference on Computational Natural Language Learning (CoNLL-2004) International Workshop on Semantic Evaluations (SemEval-2007)*. Boston, MA Association for Computational Linguistics, pp. 89-97.

Xavier Carreras and Luis Marquez. 2005. Introduction to the CoNLL-2005 Shared Task Semantic Role Labeling. *Proceedings of the Eighth Conference on Computational Natural Language Learning (CoNLL-2004) International Workshop on Semantic Evaluations (SemEval-2007)*. Ann Arbor, MI Association for Computational Linguistics, pp. 152-164.

Kenneth C. Litkowski. 2004. Senseval-3 Task: Automatic Labeling of Semantic Roles. *Proceedings of Senseval-3: The Third International Workshop on the Evaluation of Systems for the Semantic Analysis of Text*. Barcelona, Spain, Association for Computational Linguistics, pp. 9-12.

Kenneth C. Litkowski. 2007. CLR: Integration of FrameNet in a Text Representation System. *Proceedings of the Fourth International Workshop on Semantic Evaluations (SemEval-2007)*. Prague, Czech Republic, Association for Computational Linguistics, pp. 113-6.

PKU_HIT: An Event Detection System Based on Instances Expansion and Rich Syntactic Features

Shiqi Li[1], Pengyuan Liu[2], Tiejun Zhao[1], Qin Lu[3] and Hanjing Li[1]
[1]School of Computer Science and Technology,
Harbin Institute of Technology, Harbin 150001, China
{sqli,tjzhao,hjlee}@mtlab.hit.edu.cn
[2]Institute of Computational Linguistics,
Peking University, Beijing 100871, China
liupengyuan@pku.edu.cn
[3]Department of Computing,
The Hong Kong Polytechnic University, Hong Kong, China
csluqin@comp.polyu.edu.hk

Abstract

This paper describes the PKU_HIT system on event detection in the SemEval-2010 Task. We construct three modules for the three sub-tasks of this evaluation. For target verb WSD, we build a Naïve Bayesian classifier which uses additional training instances expanded from an untagged Chinese corpus automatically. For sentence SRL and event detection, we use a feature-based machine learning method which makes combined use of both constituent-based and dependency-based features. Experimental results show that the Macro Accuracy of the WSD module reaches 83.81% and F-Score of the SRL module is 55.71%.

1 Introduction

In this paper, we describe the system submitted to the SemEval-2010 Task 11 on event detection in Chinese news sentences (Zhou, 2010). The objective of the task is to detect and analyze basic event contents in Chinese news sentences, similar to the frame semantic structure extraction task in SemEval-2007. However, this task is a more complex as it involves three interrelated subtasks: (1) target verb word sense disambiguation (WSD), (2) sentence semantic role labeling (SRL) and (3) event detection (ED).

Therefore, the architecture of the system that we develop for the task consists of three modules: WSD, SRL and ED. First, the WSD module is to recognize key verbs or verb phrases which describe the basic event in a sentence, and then select an appropriate situation description formula for the recognized key verbs (or verb phrases); Then, the SRL module anchors the arguments to suitable constituents in the sentence, and then label each argument with three functional tags, namely constituent type tag, semantic role tags and event role tag. Finally, in the ED module, complete situation description of the sentence can be achieved by combining the results of the WSD module and the SRL module.

For the WSD module, we consider the subtask as a general WSD problem. First of all, we automatically extract many instances from an untagged Chinese corpus using a heuristic rule inspired by Yarowsky (1993). Then we train a Naïve Bayesian (NB) classifier based on both the extracted instances and the official training data. We then use the NB classifier to predict situation the description formula and natural explanation of each target verb in testing data.

For the SRL module, we use a rich syntactic feature-based learning method. As the state-of-the-art method in the field of SRL, feature-based method represents a predicate-argument structure (PAS) by a flat vector using a set of linguistic features. Then PAS can be directly classified by machine learning algorithms based on the corresponding vectors. In feature-based SRL, the

Proceedings of the 5th International Workshop on Semantic Evaluation, ACL 2010, pages 304–307,
Uppsala, Sweden, 15-16 July 2010. ©2010 Association for Computational Linguistics

significance of syntactic information in SRL was proven by (Punyakanok et al., 2005). In our method, we exploit a rich set of syntactic features from two syntactic views: constituent and dependency. As the two syntactic views focus on different syntactic elements, constituent-based features and dependency-based features can complement each other in SRL to some extent. Finally, the ED module can be readily implemented by combining the SRL and the WSD result using some simply rules.

2 System Description

2.1 Target Verb WSD

The WSD module is based on a simple heuristic rule by which we can extract sense-labeled instances automatically. The heuristic rule assumes that one sense per 3-gram which is proposed by us initially through investigating a Chinese sense-tagged corpus STC (Wu et al., 2006). The assumption is similar to the celebrated one sense per collocation supposition (Yarowsky, 1993), whereas ours has more expansibility. STC is an ongoing project which is to build a sense-tagged corpus containing sense-tagged 1, 2 and 3 months of People's Daily 2000 now. According to our investigation, given a specific 3-gram ($w_{-1}w_{\text{verb}}w_1$) to any target verb, on average, we expect to see the same label 95.4% of the time. Based on this observation, we consider one sense per 3-gram ($w_{-1}w_{\text{verb}}w_1$) or at least we can extract instances with this pattern.

For all the 27 multiple-sense target verbs in the official training data, we found their 3-gram ($w_{-1}w_{\text{verb}}w_1$) and extracted the instances with the same 3-gram from a Chinese monolingual corpus – the 2001 People's Daily (about 116M bytes). We consider the same 3-gram instances should have the same label. Then an additional sense-labeled training corpus is built automatically in expectation of having 95.4% precision at most. And this corpus has 2145 instances in total (official training data have 4608 instances).

We build four systems to investigate the effect of our instances expansion using the Naïve Bayesian classifier. System configuration is shown in Table 1. In column 1, BL means baseline, X means instance expansion, 3 and 15 means the window size. In column 2, w_i is the *i-th* word relative to the target word, $w_{i-1}w_i$ is the 2-gram of words, w_j/j is the word with position information ($j\in[-3,+3]$). In the last column, 'O' means using only the original training data and 'O+A' means using both the original and additional training data. Syntactic feature and parameter optimizing are not used in this module.

System	Features	Window Size	Training Data
BL_3	w_i, $w_{i-1}w_i$, w_j/j	±3	O
X_3		±3	O+A
BL_15		±15	O
X_15		±15	O+A

Table 1: The system configuration

2.2 Sentence SRL and Event Detection

We use a feature-based machine learning method to implement the SRL module in which three tags are labeled, namely the semantic role tag, the event role tag and the phrase type tag. We consider the SRL task as a four-step pipeline: (1) **parsing** which generates a constituent parse tree for the input sentence; (2) **pruning** which filters out many apparently impossible constituents (Xue and Palmer, 2004); (3) **semantic role identification (SRI)** which identifies the constituent that will be the semantic role of a predicate in a sentence, and (4) **semantic role classification (SRC)** which determines the type of identified semantic role. The machine learning method takes PAS as the classification unit which consists of a target predicate and an argument candidate. The SRI step utilizes a binary classifier to determine whether the argument candidate in the PAS is a real argument. Finally, in the SRC step, the semantic role tag and the event role tag of each identified argument can be obtained by two multi-value classifications on the SRI results. The remaining phrase type tag can be directly extracted from the constituent parsing tree.

The selection of the feature set is the most important factor for the feature-based SRL method. In addition to constituent-based features and dependency-based features, we also consider WSD-based features. To our knowledge, the combined use of constituents-based syntactic features and dependency-based syntactic features is the first attempts to use them both on the feature level of SRL. As a prevalent kind of syntactic features for SRL, constituent-based features have been extensively studied by many researchers. In this module, we use 34 constituent-based features, 35 dependency-based features, and 2 WSD-based features. Among the constituent-based features, 26 features are manually selected from effective features proven by existing SRL studies and 8 new features are defined by us. Firstly, the 26 constituent-based features used by others are:

- *predicate* (c1), *path* (c2), *phrase type* (c3), *position* (c4), *voice* (c5), *head word* (c6), *predicate subcategorization* (c7), *syntactic frame* (c8), *head word POS* (c9), *partial path* (c10), *first/last word* (c11/c12), *first/last POS* (c13/c14), *left/right sibling type* (c15/c16), *left/right sibling head* (c17/c18), *left/right sibling POS* (c19/c20), *constituent tree distance* (c21), *temporal cue words* (c22), *Predicate POS* (c23), *argument's parent type*(c24), *argument's parent head* (c25) and *argument's parent POS* (c26).

And the 8 new features we define are:

- *Locational cue words* (c27): a binary feature indicating whether the constituent contains location cue word.
- *POS pattern of argument* (c28): the left-to-right chain of POS tags of argument's children.
- *Phrase type pattern of argument* (c29): the left-to-right chain of phrase type labels of argument's children.
- *Type of LCA and left child* (c30): The phrase type of the Lowest Common Ancestor (LCA) combined with its left child.
- *Type of LCA and right child* (c31): The phrase type of the LCA combined with its right child.
- Three features: *word bag of path* (c32), *word bag of POS pattern* (c33) and *word bag of type pattern* (c34), for generalizing three sparse features: *path* (c7), *POS pattern argument* (c28) and *phrase type pattern of argument* (c29) by the bag-of-words representation.

Secondly, the selection of dependency-based features is similar to that of constituent-based features. But dependency parsing lacks constituent information. If we want to use dependency-based features to label constituents, we should map a constituent to one or more appropriate words in dependency trees. Here we use head word of a constituent to represent it in dependency parses. The 35 dependency-based features we adopt are:

- *Predicate/Argument relation* (d1/d2), *relation path* (d3), *POS pattern of predicate's children* (d4), *relation pattern of predicate's children* (d5) , *child relation set* (d6), *child POS set* (d7), *predicate/argument parent word* (d8/d9), *predicate/argument parent POS* (d10/d11), *left/right word* (d12/d13), *left/right POS* (d14/d15), *left/right relation* (d16/d17), *left/right sibling word* (d18/d19), *left/right sibling POS* (d20/d21), *left/right sibling relation* (d22/d23), *dep-exists* (d24) and *dep-type* (d25), *POS path* (d26), *POS path length* (d27), *relation path length* (d28), *high/low support verb* (d29/d30), *high/low support noun* (d31/d32) and *LCA's word/POS/relation* (d33/d34/d35).

In this work, the dependency parse trees are generated from the constituent parse trees using a constituent-to-dependency converter (Marneffe et al., 2006). The converter is suitable for semantic analysis as it can retrieve the semantic head rather than the general syntactic head.

Lastly, the 2 WSD-based features are:

- *Situation description formula* (s1): predicate's situation description formula generated by the WSD module.
- *Natural explanation* (s2): predicate's natural explanation generated by the WSD module.

3 Experimental Results and Discussion

3.1 Target Verb WSD

System	Micro-A (%)	Macro-A (%)	Rank
BL_3	81.30	83.81	3/7
X_3	79.82	82.58	4/7
BL_15	79.23	82.18	5/7
X_15	77.74	81.42	6/7

Table 2: Official results of the WSD systems

Table 2 shows the official result of the WSD system. BL_3 with window size three using the original training corpus achieves the best result in our submission. It indicates the local features are more effective in our systems. There are two possible reasons why the performances of the X system with instance expansion are lower than the BL system. First, the additional instances extracted based on 3-gram provide a few local features but many topical features. But, local features are more effective for our systems as mentioned above. The local feature related information that the classifier gets from the additional instances is not sufficient. Second, the granularity of the WSD module is too small to be distinguished by 3-grams. As a result, the additional corpus built upon 3-gram has more exceptional instances (noises), and therefore it impairs the performance of X_3 and X_15. Taking the verb '属于' (belong to) as an example, it has two senses in the task, but both senses have the same natural explanation: '归一某方面或为某方所有' (part of or belong to), which is always considered as the sense in general SRL. The difference between the two senses is in their situation description formulas: 'partof (x,y)+NULL' vs. 'belongto (x,y)+NULL'.

3.2 Sentence SRL and Event Detection

In the SRL module, we use the training data provided by SemEval-2010 to train the SVM classifiers without any external resources. The training data contain 4,608 sentences, 100 target predicates and 13,926 arguments. We use the SVM-Light Toolkit (Joachims, 1999) for the implementation of SVM, and use the Stanford Parser (Levy and Manning, 2003) as the parser and the constituent-to-dependency converter. We employ the linear kernel for SVM and set the regularization parameter to the default value which is the reciprocal of the average Euclidean norm of the training data. The evaluation results of our SRL module on the official test data are shown in Table 3, where 'AB', 'SR', 'PT' and 'ER' represent argument boundary, semantic role tag, phrase type tag, and event role tag.

Tag	Precision(%)	Recall(%)	F-Score(%)
AB	73.10	66.83	69.82
AB+SR	67.44	61.65	64.42
AB+PT	61.78	56.48	59.01
AB+ER	69.05	63.12	65.95
Overall	58.33	53.32	55.71

Table 3: Official results of the SRL system

It is clear that 'AB' plays an important role as the labeling of the other three tags is directly based on it. Through analyzing the results, we find that errors in the recognition of 'AB' are mainly caused by two factors: the automatic constituent parsing and the pruning algorithm. It is inevitable that some constituents and hierarchical relations are misidentified in automatic parsing of Chinese. These errors are further enlarged by the heuristic-based pruning algorithm because the algorithm is built upon the gold-standard paring trees, and therefore a lot of real arguments are pruned out when using the noisy automatic parses. So the pruning algorithm is the current bottleneck of SRL in the evaluation.

System	Micro-A (%)	Macro-A (%)	Rank
BL_3	20.33	20.19	4/7
X_3	20.05	20.23	5/7
BL_15	20.05	20.22	6/7
X_15	20.05	20.14	7/7

Table 4: Official results of the ED systems

From the fact that the results of 'AB+SR' and 'AB+ER' are close to that of 'AB', it can be inferred that the SR and ER results should be satisfactory if the errors in 'AB' are not propagated. Furthermore, the result of 'AB+PT' is low as the phrase types here is inconsistent with those in Stanford Parser. The problem should be improved by a set of mapping rules.

Finally, in the ED module, we combine the results of WSD and SRL by filling variables of the situation description formula obtained by the WSD module with the arguments obtained by the SRL module according to their event role tags. Table 4 shows the final results which are generated by combining the results of WSD and SRL. Obviously the reduced overall ranking comparing to WSD is due to the SRL module.

4 Conclusions

In this paper, we propose a modular approach for the SemEval-2010 Task on Chinese event detection. Our system consists of three modules: WSD, SRL and ED. The WSD module is based on instances expansion, and the SRL module is based on rich syntactic features. Evaluation results show that our system is good at WSD, semantic role tagging and event role tagging, but poor at pruning and boundary detection. In future studies, we will modify the pruning algorithm to reduce the bottleneck of the current system.

Acknowledgments

This work is partially supported by the Hong Kong Polytechnic University under Grant No. G-U297 and G-U596, and by the National Natural Science Foundation of China under Grant No. 60736014 and 60803094.

References

Thorsten Joachims. 1999. Making large-Scale SVM Learning Practical. Advances in Kernel Methods. *Support Vector Learning*, B. Schölkopf and C. Burges and A. Smola (ed), MIT Press.

Roger Levy and Christopher D. Manning. 2003. Is it harder to parse Chinese, or the Chinese Treebank. *Proceedings of ACL-2003.*

Vasin Punyakanok, Dan Roth, and Wentau Yih. 2005. The necessity of syntactic parsing for semantic role labeling. *Proceedings of IJCAI-2005.*

Yunfang Wu, Peng Jin, Yangsen Zhang, and Shiwen Yu. 2006. A Chinese corpus with word sense annotation. *Proceedings of ICCPOL-2006.*

David Yarowsky. 1993. One sense per collocation. *Proceedings of the ARPA Workshop on Human Language Technology.*

Qiang Zhou. 2010. SemEval-2010 task 11: Event detection in Chinese News Sentences. *Proceedings of SemEval-2010.*

372:Comparing the Benefit of Different Dependency Parsers for Textual Entailment Using Syntactic Constraints Only

Alexander Volokh
alexander.volokh@dfki.de
DFKI
Stuhlsatzenhausweg 3
66123 Saarbrücken, Germany

Günter Neumann
neumann@dfki.de
DFKI
Stuhlsatzenhausweg 3
66123 Saarbrücken, Germany

Abstract

We compare several state of the art dependency parsers with our own parser based on a linear classification technique. Our primary goal is therefore to use syntactic information only, in order to keep the comparison of the parsers as fair as possible. We demonstrate, that despite the inferior result using the standard evaluation metrics for parsers like UAS or LAS on standard test data, our system achieves comparable results when used in an application, such as the SemEval-2 #12 evaluation exercise PETE. Our submission achieved the 4th position out of 19 participating systems. However, since it only uses a linear classifier it works 17-20 times faster than other state of the parsers, as for instance MaltParser or Stanford Parser.

1 Introduction

Parsing is the process of mapping sentences to their syntactic representations. These representations can be used by computers for performing many interesting natural language processing tasks, such as question answering or information extraction. In recent years a lot of parsers have been developed for this purpose.

A very interesting and important issue is the comparison between a large number of such parsing systems. The most widespread method is to evaluate the number of correctly recognized units according to a certain gold standard. For dependency-based units unlabeled or labeled attachment scores (percentage of correctly classified dependency relations, either with or without the dependency relation type) are usually used (cf. Buchholz and Marsi, 2006).

However, parsing is very rarely a goal in itself. In most cases it is a necessary preprocessing step for a certain application. Therefore it is usually not the best option to decide which parser suits one's goals best by purely looking on its performance on some standard test data set. It is rather more sensible to analyse whether the parser is able to recognise those syntactic units or relations, which are most relevant for one's application.

The shared task #12 PETE in the SemEval-2010 Evaluation Exercises on Semantic Evaluation (Yuret, Han and Turgut, 2010) involved recognizing textual entailments (RTE). RTE is a binary classification task, whose goal is to determine, whether for a pair of texts T and H the meaning of H is contained in T (Dagan et al., 2006). This task can be very complex depending on the properties of these texts. However, for the data, released by the organisers of PETE, only the syntactic information should be sufficient to reliably perform this task. Thus it offers an ideal setting for evaluating the performance of different parsers.

To our mind evaluation of parsers via RTE is a very good additional possibility, besides the usual evaluation metrics, since in most cases the main thing in real-word applications is to recognize the primary units, such as the subject, the predicate,

Proceedings of the 5th International Workshop on Semantic Evaluation, ACL 2010, pages 308–312,
Uppsala, Sweden, 15-16 July 2010. ©2010 Association for Computational Linguistics

the objects, as well as their modifiers, rather than the other subordinate relations.

We have been developing our own a multilingual dependency parser (called MDParser), which is based on linear classification[1]. Whereas the system is quite fast because the classification is linear, it usually achieves inferior results (using UAS/LAS evaluation metrics) in comparison to other parsers, which for example use kernel-based classification or other more sophisticated methods.

Therefore the PETE shared task was a perfect opportunity for us to investigate whether the inferior result of our parser is also relevant for its applicability in a concrete task. We have compared our system with three state of the art parsers made available on the PETE web page: MaltParser, MiniPar and StandfordParser. We have achieved the total score of 0.6545 (200/301 correct answers on the test data), which is the 4th rank out of 19 submissions.

2 MDParser

MDParser stands for multilingual dependency parser and is a data-driven system, which can be used to parse text of an arbitrary language for which training data is available. It is a transition-based parser and uses a deterministic version of the Covington's algorithm (Covington, 2000).

The models of the system are based on various features, which are extracted from the words of the sentence, including word forms and part of speech tags. No additional morphological features or lemmas are currently used in our models, even if they are available in the training data, since the system is especially designed for processing plain text in different languages, and such components are not available for every language.

The preprocessing components of MDParser include a.) a sentence splitter[2], since the parser constructs a dependency structure for individual sentences, b.) a tokenizer, in order to recognise the elements between which the dependency relations will be built[3], and c.) a part of speech tagger, in order to determine the part of speech tags, which are intensively used in the feature models[4].

MDParser is an especially fast system because it uses a linear classification algorithm L1R-LR(L1 regularised logistic regression) from the machine learning package LibLinear (Lin et al., 2008) for constructing its dependency structures and therefore it is particularly suitable for processing very large amounts of data. Thus it can be used as a part of larger applications in which dependency structures are desired.

Additionally, significant efforts were made in order to make the gap between our linear classification and more advanced methods as small as possible, e.g. by introducing features conjunctions, which are complex features built out of ordinary features, as well as methods for automatically measuring feature usefulness in order to automate and optimise feature engineering.

3 Triple Representation

Every parser usually produces its own somehow special representation of the sentence. We have created such a representation, which we will call *triple representation* and have implemented an automatic transformation of the results of Minipar, MaltParser, Stanford Parser and of course MDParser into it (cf. Wang and Neumann, 2007).

The triple representation of a sentence is a set of triple elements of the form <*parent*, *label*, *child*>, where *child* and *parent* elements stand for the head and the modifier words and their parts of speech, and *label* stands for the relation between them. E.g. <have:VBZ, SBJ, Somebody:NN>. This information is extractable from the results of any dependency parser.

4 Predicting Entailment

Whereas the first part of the PETE shared task was to construct syntactic representations for all T-H-pairs, the second important subtask was to determine whether the structure of H is entailed by the structure of T. The PETE guide[5] states that the following three phenomena were particularly important to recognise the entailment relation:

[1]http://www.dfki.de/~avolokh/mdparser.pdf

[2]http://morphadorner.northwestern.edu/morphadorner/sentencesplitter/

[3]http://morphadorner.northwestern.edu/morphadorner/wordtokenizer/

[4]The part of speech tagger was trained with the SVMTool http://www.lsi.upc.edu/~nlp/SVMTool/

[5]http://pete.yuret.com/guide

1. subject-verb dependency (*John kissed Mary. → John kissed somebody.*)
2. verb-object dependency (*John kissed Mary → Mary was kissed.*)
3. noun-modifier dependency (*The big red boat sank. → The boat was big.*)

Thus we have manually formulated the following **generic decision rule** for determining the entailment relation between T and H:

1. identify the root triple of H <null:null, ROOT, x>
2. check whether the subject and the complements(objects, verb complements) of the root word in H are present in T. Formally: all triples of H of the form <x, z, y> should be contained in T(x in 1 and 2 is thus the same word).
3. if 2 returns false we have to check whether H is a structure in passive and T contains the same content in active voice(a) or the other way around(b). Formally:

3a. For triples of the form <be:VBZ, SBJ, s> and <be:VBZ, VC, t> in H check whether there is a triple of the form <s, NMOD, t> in T.

3b. For triples of the form <u, OBJ,v> in H check whether there is a triple of the form <v, NMOD, u> in T.

It turned out that few **additional modifications** to the base rule were necessary for some sentences: 1.) For sentences containing conjunctions: If we were looking for a subject of a certain verb and could not find it, we investigated whether this verb is connected via a conjunction with another one. If true, we compared the subject in H with the subject of the conjunct verb. 2.) For sentences containing special verbs, e.g. modal verbs *may* or *can* or auxiliary verbs like *to have* it turned out to be important to go one level deeper into the dependency structure and to check whether all of their arguments in H are also present in T, the same way as in 3.

A triple <x,z,y> is contained in a set of triples S, when there exists at least one of the triples in S <u,w,v>, such that x=u, w=z and y=v. This is also true if the words *somebody, someone* or *something* are used on one of the equation sides. Moreover, we use an English lemmatizer for all word forms, so when checking the equality of two words we actually check their lemmas, e.g., *is* and *are* are also treated equally.

5 Results

We have parsed the 66 pairs of the development data with 4 parsers:[6] MiniPar, Stanford Parser, MaltParser and MDParser. After applying our rule we have achieved the following result:

	Accuracy	Parsing Speed
MiniPar	45/66	1233 ms
Stanford Parser	50/66	32889 ms
MaltParser	51/66	37149 ms
MDParser	50/66	1785 ms

We used the latest versions of MiniPar[7] and Stanford Parser[8]. We did not re-test the performance of these parsers on standard data, since we were sure that these versions provide the best possible results of these systems.

As far as the MaltParser is concerned we had to train our own model. We have trained the model with the following LibSVM options: “-s_0_-t_1_-d_2_-g_0.18_-c_0.4_-r_0.4_-e_1.0”. We were able to achieve a result of 83.86% LAS and 87.25% UAS on the standard CoNLL English test data, a result which is only slightly worse than those reported in the literature, where the options are probably better tuned for the data. The training data used for training was the same as for MDParser.

The application of our rule for MDParser and MaltParser was fully automated, since both use the same training data and thus work over the same tag sets. For MiniPar and Stanford Parser, which construct different dependency structures with different relation types, we had to go through all pairs manually in order to investigate how the rule should be adopted to their tag sets and structures. However, since we have already counted the number of structures, for which an adoptation of the rule would work during this investigation, we did not implement it in the end. Therefore these results might be taken with a pinch of salt, despite the fact that we have tried to stay as fair as possible and treated some pairs as correct, even if a quite large modification of the

[6]For all results reported in this section a desktop PC with an Intel Core 2 Duo E8400 3.00 GHz processor and 4.00 GB RAM was used.

[7]http://webdocs.cs.ualberta.ca/~lindek/minipar

[8]http://nlp.stanford.edu/downloads/lex-parser.shtml

rule was necessary in order to adopt it to the different tag set and/or dependency structure.

For test data we were only able to apply our rule for the results of MDParser and MaltParser, since for such a large number of pairs (301) only the fully automated version of our mechanism for predicting entailment could be applied. For MiniPar and Stanford Parser it was too tedious to apply it to them manually or to develop a mapping between their dependency annotations and the ones used in MDParser or MaltParser. Here are the official results of our submissions for MaltParser and MDParser:

	Accuracy	Parsing Speed
MDParser	197/301	8704 ms
MaltParser	196/301	147938 ms

6 Discussion

We were able to show that our parser based on a linear classification technique is especially fast compared to other state of the art parsers. Furthermore, despite the fact, that it achieves an inferior result, when using usual evaluation metrics like UAS or LAS, it is absolutely suitable for being used in applications, since the most important dependency relations are recognized correctly even with a less sophisticated linear classifier as the one being used in MDParser.

As far as the overall score is concerned we think a much better result could be achieved, if we would put more effort into our mechanism for recognizing entailment using triple representations. However, many of the pairs required more than only syntactical information. In many cases one would need to extend one's mechanism with logic, semantics and the possibility to resolve anaphoric expressions, which to our mind goes beyond the idea behind the PETE task. Since we were primarly interested in the comparison between MaltParser and MDParser, we have not tried to include solutions for such cases. Here are some of the pairs we think require more than only syntax:

(4069 entailment="YES") <t>Mr. Sherwood speculated that the leeway that Sea Containers has means that Temple would have to "substantially increase their bid if they're going to top us."</t>

<h>Someone would have to increase the bid.</h>

(7003 entailment="YES") <t>After all, if you were going to set up a workshop you had to have the proper equipment and that was that.</t>

<h>Somebody had to have the equipment.</h>

(3132.N entailment="YES") <t>The first was that America had become -- or was in danger of becoming -- a second-rate military power.</t>

<h>America was in danger.</h>

→ 4069, 7003 and 3132.N are examples for sentences were beyond syntactical information logic is required. Moreover we are surprised that sentences of the form "if **A**, then **B**" entail **B** and a sentence of the form "**A** or **B**" entails **B**, since "*or*" in this case means uncertainty.

(4071.N entailment="NO") <t>Interpublic Group said its television programming operations -- which it expanded earlier this year -- agreed to supply more than 4,000 hours of original programming across Europe in 1990.</t>

<h>Interpublic Group expanded.</h>

(6034 entailment="YES") <t>"Oh," said the woman, "I've seen that picture already."</t>

<h>The woman has seen something.</h>

→ In 4071.N one has to resolve "*it*" in "*it expanded*" to *Interpublic Group*. In 6034 one has to resolve "*I*" in "*I've seen*" to "*the woman*". Both cases are examples for the necessity of anaphora resolution, which goes beyond syntax as well.

(2055) <t>The Big Board also added computer capacity to handle huge surges in trading volume.</t>

<h>Surges were handled.</h>

→ If something is added in order to do something it does not entail that this something is thus automatically done. Anyways pure syntax is not sufficient, since the entailment depends on the verb used in such a construction.

(3151.N) <t>Most of them are Democrats and nearly all consider themselves, and are viewed as, liberals.</t>

<h>Some consider themselves liberal.</h>

→ One has to know that the semantics of "consider themselves as liberals" and "consider themselves liberal" is the same.

Acknowledgements

The work presented here was partially supported by a research grant from the German Federal Ministry of Economics and Technology (BMWi) to the DFKI project Theseus Ordo TechWatch (FKZ: 01MQ07016). We thank Joakim Nivre and Johan Hall for their support and tips when training models with MaltParser. Additionally, we are very grateful to Sven Schmeier for providing us with a trained part of speech tagger for English and for his support when using this tool.

References

Michael A. Covington, 2000. *A Fundamental Algorithm for Dependency Parsing*. In Proceedings of the 39th Annual ACM Southeast Conference.

Dan Klein and Christopher D. Manning, 2003. *Accurate Unlexicalized Parsing*. Proceedings of the 41st Meeting of the Association for Computational Linguistics, pp. 423-430.

Lin D, 2003. *Dependency-Based Evaluation Of Minipar.* In Building and using Parsed Corpora Edited by: Abeillé A. Dordrecht: Kluwer; 2003.

Sabine Buchholz and Erwin Marsi. 2006. *CoNLL-X shared task on multilingual dependency parsing*. In Proceedings of CONLL-X, pages 149–164, New York.

Ido Dagan, Oren Glickman and Bernardo Magnini. *The PASCAL Recognising Textual Entailment Challenge*. In Quinonero-Candela, J.; Dagan, I.; Magnini, B.; d'Alche-Buc, F. (Eds.), Machine Learning Challenges. Lecture Notes in Computer Science, Vol. 3944, pp. 177-190, Springer, 2006.

Nivre, J., J. Hall and J. Nilsson, 2006. *MaltParser: A Data-Driven Parser-Generator for Dependency Parsing*. In Proceedings of the fifth international conference on Language Resources and Evaluation (LREC2006), May 24-26, 2006, Genoa, Italy, pp. 2216-2219.

Rui Wang and Günter Neumann, 2007. *Recognizing Textual Entailment Using a Subsequence Kernel Method.* In Proceedings of AAAI 2007.

R. Fan, K. Chang, C. Hsieh, X. Wang, and C. Lin, 2008. *LIBLINEAR: A Library for Large Linear Classification*. Journal of Machine Learning Research, 9(4): 1871–1874.

Deniz Yuret, Aydın Han and Zehra Turgut, 2010. *SemEval-2010 Task 12: Parser Evaluation using Textual Entailments.* In Proceedings of the SemEval-2010 Evaluation Exercises on Semantic Evaluation.

The Stanford Parser: A Statistical Parser. http://nlp.stanford.edu/downloads/lex-parser.shtml

Maltparser. http://maltparser.org/

Minipar. http://webdocs.cs.ualberta.ca/~lindek/minipar.htm

MDParser: Multilingual Dependency Parser. http://mdparser.sb.dfki.de/

SCHWA: PETE using CCG Dependencies with the C&C Parser

Dominick Ng, James W. D. Constable, Matthew Honnibal and **James R. Curran**
ə-lab, School of Information Technologies
University of Sydney
NSW 2006, Australia
{dong7223,jcon6353,mhonn,james}@it.usyd.edu.au

Abstract

This paper describes the SCHWA system entered by the University of Sydney in SemEval 2010 Task 12 – Parser Evaluation using Textual Entailments (Yuret et al., 2010). Our system achieved an overall accuracy of 70% in the task evaluation.

We used the C&C parser to build CCG dependency parses of the truth and hypothesis sentences. We then used partial match heuristics to determine whether the system should predict entailment. Heuristics were used because the dependencies generated by the parser are construction specific, making full compatibility unlikely. We also manually annotated the development set with CCG analyses, establishing an upper bound for our entailment system of 87%.

1 Introduction

The SemEval 2010 Parser Evaluation using Textual Entailments (PETE) task attempts to address the long-standing problems in parser evaluation caused by the diversity of syntactic formalisms and analyses in use. The task investigates the feasibility of a minimalist extrinsic evaluation – that of detecting textual entailment between a truth sentence and a hypothesis sentence. It is extrinsic in the sense that it evaluates parsers on a task, rather than a direct comparison of their output against some gold standard. However, it requires only minimal task-specific logic, and the proposed entailments are designed to be inferrable based on syntactic information alone.

Our system used the C&C parser (Clark and Curran, 2007a), which uses the Combinatory Categorial Grammar formalism (CCG, Steedman, 2000). We used the CCGbank-style dependency output of the parser (Hockenmaier and Steedman, 2007), which is a directed graph of head-child relations labelled with the head's lexical category and the argument slot filled by the child.

We divided the dependency graphs of the truth and hypothesis sentences into *predicates* that consisted of a head word and its immediate children. For instance, the parser's analysis of the sentence *Totals include only vehicle sales reported in period* might produce predicates like *include(Totals, sales)*, *only(include)*, and *reported(sales)*. If at least one such predicate matches in the two parses, we predict entailment. We consider a single predicate match sufficient for entailment because the lexical categories and slots that constitute our dependency labels are often different in the hypothesis sentence due to the generation process used in the task.

The single predicate heuristic gives us an overall accuracy of 70% on the test set. Our precision and recall over the test set was 68% and 80% respectively giving an F-score of 74%.

To investigate how many of the errors were due to parse failures, and how many were failures of our entailment recognition process, we manually annotated the 66 development truth sentences with gold standard CCG derivations. This established an upper bound of 87% F-score for our approach.

This upper bound suggests that there is still work to be done before the system allows transparent evaluation of the parser. However, cross-framework parser evaluation is a difficult problem: previous attempts to evaluate the C&C parser on grammatical relations (Clark and Curran, 2007b) and Penn Treebank-trees (Clark and Curran, 2009) have also produced upper bounds between 80 and 90% F-score. Our PETE system was much easier to produce than either of these previous attempts at cross-framework parser evaluation, suggesting that this may be a promising approach to a difficult problem.

Proceedings of the 5th International Workshop on Semantic Evaluation, ACL 2010, pages 313–316,
Uppsala, Sweden, 15-16 July 2010.

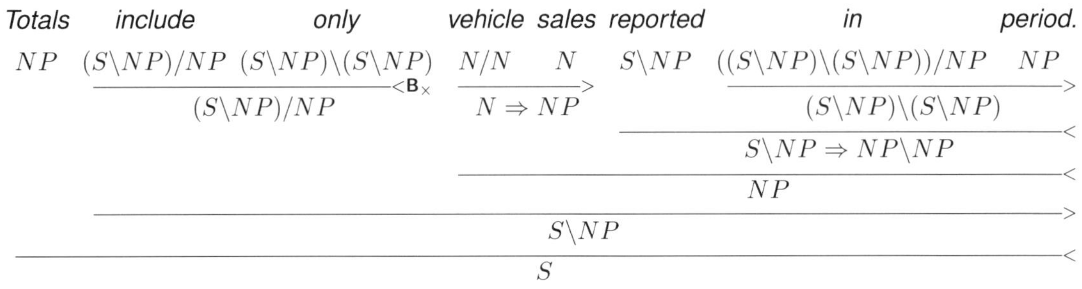

Figure 1: An example CCG derivation, showing how the categories assigned to words are combined to form a sentence. The arrows indicate the direction of application.

2 Background

Combinatory Categorial Grammar (CCG, Steedman, 2000) is a lexicalised grammar formalism based on combinatory logic. The grammar is directly encoded in the lexicon in the form of combinatory categories that govern how each word combines with its neighbours. The parsing process determines the most likely assignment of categories to words, and finds a sequence of combinators that allows them to form a sentence.

A sample CCG derivation for a sentence from the test set is shown in Figure 1. The category for each word is indicated beneath it. It can be seen that some categories take other categories as arguments; each argument slot in a category is numbered based on the order of application, from latest to earliest. For example:

$$((S/NP_1)/(S/NP)_2)\backslash NP_3$$

Figure 2 shows how the argument slots are mapped to dependencies. The first two columns list the predicate words and their categories, while the second two show how each argument slot is filled. For example, in the first row, *only* has the category $(S\backslash NP)\backslash(S\backslash NP)$, with argument slot 1 filled by *include*). It is these dependencies that form the basis for our predicates in this task.

only	$(S\backslash NP)\backslash(S\backslash NP)$	1	*include*
vehicle	N/N	1	*sales*
in	$((S\backslash NP)\backslash(S\backslash NP))/NP$	2	*period*
in	$((S\backslash NP)\backslash(S\backslash NP))/NP$	1	*reported*
reported	$S\backslash NP$	1	*sales*
include	$(S\backslash NP)/NP$	2	*sales*
include	$(S\backslash NP)/NP$	1	*Totals*

Figure 2: The dependencies represented by the derivation in Figure 1.

Recent work has seen the development of high-performance parsers built on the CCG formalism. Clark and Curran (2007a) demonstrate the use of techniques like adaptive supertagging, parallelisation and a dynamic-programming chart parsing algorithm to implement the C&C parser, a highly efficient CCG parser that performs well against parsers built on different formalisms (Rimell et al., 2009). We use this parser for the PETE task.

The performance of statistical parsers is largely a function of the quality of the corpora they are trained on. For this task, we used models derived from the CCGbank corpus – a transformation of the Penn Treebank (Marcus et al., 1993) including CCG derivations and dependencies (Hockenmaier, 2003a). It was created to further CCG research by providing a large corpus of appropriately annotated data, and has been shown to be suitable for the training of high-performance parsers (Hockenmaier, 2003b; Clark and Curran, 2004).

3 Method

Our system used the C&C parser to parse the truth and hypothesis sentences. We took the dependencies generated by the parser and processed these to generate predicates encoding the canonical form of the head word, its required arguments, and their order. We then attempted to unify the predicates from the hypothesis sentence with the predicates in the truth sentence. A successful unification of predicates a and b occurs when the head words of a and b are identical and their argument slots are also identical. If any predicate from the hypothesis sentence unified with a predicate from the truth sentence, our system returned YES, otherwise the system returned NO.

We used the 66 sentence development set to tune our approach. While analysing the hypothesis sentences, we noticed that many examples re-

System	YES entailment correct	YES entailment incorrect	YES entailment A (%)	NO entailment correct	NO entailment incorrect	NO entailment A (%)	Overall accuracy (%)	F-score
SCHWA	125	31	80	87	58	60	70	74
median	71	85	46	88	57	61	53	50
baseline	156	0	100	0	145	0	52	68
low	68	88	44	76	69	52	48	46

Table 1: Final results over the test set

System	YES entailment correct	YES entailment incorrect	YES entailment A (%)	NO entailment correct	NO entailment incorrect	NO entailment A (%)	Overall accuracy (%)	F-score
Gold deps	34	6	85	22	4	90	87	87
Parsed deps	32	8	80	20	6	77	79	82

Table 2: Results over the development set

placed nouns from the truth sentence with indefinite pronouns such as *someone* or *something* (e.g. *Someone bought something*). In most of these cases the indefinite would not be present in the truth sentence at all, so to deal with this we converted indefinite pronouns into wildcard markers that could be matched to any argument. We also incorporated sensitivity to passive sentences by adjusting the argument numbers of dependents.

In its most naive form our system is heavily biased towards excellent recall but poor precision. We evaluated a number of heuristics to prune the predicate space and selected those which improved the performance over the development set. Our final system used the part-of-speech tags generated by the parser to remove predicates headed by determiners, prepositions and adjectives. We note that even after predicate pruning our system is still likely to return better recall performance than precision, but this discrepancy was masked in part by the nature of the development set: most hypotheses are short and so the potential number of predicates after pruning is likely to be small. The final predicates generated by the system for the example derivation given in Figure 1 after heuristic pruning are:

```
only(include)
reported(sales)
include(totals, sales)
```

4 Results

We report results over the 301 sentence test set in Table 1. Our overall accuracy was 70%, and performance over YES entailments was roughly 20% higher than accuracy over NO entailments. This bias towards YES entailments is a reflection of our single match heuristic that only required one predicate match before answering YES. Our system performed nearly 20% better than the baseline system (all YES responses) and placed second overall in the task evaluation.

Table 2 shows our results over the development corpus. The 17% drop in accuracy and 8% drop in F-score between the development data and the test data suggests that our heuristics may have overfitted to the limited development data. More sophisticated heuristics over a larger corpus would be useful for further fine-tuning our system.

4.1 Results with Gold Standard Parses

Our entailment system's errors could be broadly divided into two classes: those due to incorrect parses, and those due to incorrect comparison of the parses. To investigate the relative contributions of these two classes of errors, we manually annotated the 66 development sentences with CCG derivations. This allowed us to evaluate our system using gold standard parses. Only one annotator was available, so we were unable to calculate inter-annotator agreement scores to examine the quality of our annotations.

The annotation was prepared with the annotation tool used by Honnibal et al. (2009). The tool presents the user with a CCG derivation produced by the C&C parser. The user can then correct the lexical categories, or add bracket constraints to the parser using the algorithm described by Djordjevic and Curran (2006), and reparse the sentence until the derivation desired is produced.

Our results with gold standard dependencies are

shown in Table 2. The accuracy is 87%, establishing a fairly low upper bound for our approach to the task. Manual inspection of the remaining errors showed that some were due to incorrect parses for the hypothesis sentence, and some were due to entailments which the parser's dependency analyses could not resolve, such as *They ate whole steamed grains* ⇒ *The grains were steamed*. The largest source of errors was our matching heuristics, suggesting that our approach to the task must be improved before it can be considered a transparent evaluation of the parser.

5 Conclusion

We constructed a system to evaluate the C&C parser using textual entailments. We converted the parser output into a set of predicate structures and used these to establish the presence of entailment. Our system achieved an overall accuracy of 79% on the development set and 70% over the test set. The gap between our development and test accuracies suggests our heuristics may have been overfitted to the development data.

Our investigation using gold-standard dependencies established an upper bound of 87% on the development set for our approach to the task. While this is not ideal, we note that previous efforts at cross-parser evaluation have shown that it is a difficult problem (Clark and Curran (2007b) and Clark and Curran (2009)). We conclue that the concept of a minimal extrinsic evaluation put forward in this task is a promising avenue for formalism-independent parser comparison.

References

Stephen Clark and James R. Curran. Parsing the WSJ using CCG and log-linear models. In *Proceedings of the 42nd Annual Meeting of the Association for Computational Linguistics*, pages 104–111, 2004.

Stephen Clark and James R. Curran. Wide-Coverage Efficient Statistical Parsing with CCG and Log-Linear Models. *Computational Linguistics*, 33(4):493–552, 2007a.

Stephen Clark and James R. Curran. Formalism-independent parser evaluation with CCG and DepBank. In *Proceedings of the 45th Annual Meeting of the Association for Computational Linguistics*, pages 248–255, Prague, Czech Republic, 25–27 June 2007b.

Stephen Clark and James R. Curran. Comparing the accuracy of CCG and Penn Treebank Parsers. In *Proceedings of the ACL-IJCNLP 2009 Conference Short Papers*, pages 53–56, Suntec, Singapore, August 2009.

Bojan Djordjevic and James R. Curran. Faster wide-coverage CCG parsing. In *Proceedings of the Australasian Language Technology Workshop 2006*, pages 3–10, Sydney, Australia, December 2006.

Julia Hockenmaier. *Data and models for statistical parsing with Combinatory Categorial Grammar*. PhD thesis, 2003a.

Julia Hockenmaier. Parsing with generative models of predicate-argument structure. In *Proceedings of the 41st Annual Meeting of the Association for Computational Linguistics*, pages 359–366. Association for Computational Linguistics Morristown, NJ, USA, 2003b.

Julia Hockenmaier and Mark Steedman. CCGbank: a corpus of CCG derivations and dependency structures extracted from the Penn Treebank. *Computational Linguistics*, 33(3):355–396, 2007.

Matthew Honnibal, Joel Nothman, and James R. Curran. Evaluating a Statistical CCG Parser on Wikipedia. In *Proceedings of the 2009 Workshop on The People's Web Meets NLP: Collaboratively Constructed Semantic Resources*, pages 38–41, Singapore, August 2009.

Mitchell P. Marcus, Mary Ann Marcinkiewicz, and Beatrice Santorini. Building a large annotated corpus of English: The Penn Treebank. *Computational Linguistics*, 19(2):313–330, 1993.

Laura Rimell, Stephen Clark, and Mark Steedman. Unbounded Dependency Recovery for Parser Evaluation. In *Proceedings of the 2009 Conference on Empirical Methods in Natural Language Processing*, volume 2, pages 813–821, 2009.

Mark Steedman. *The Syntactic Process*. MIT Press, Massachusetts Institute of Technology, USA, 2000.

Deniz Yuret, Aydın Han, and Zehra Turgut. SemEval-2010 Task 12: Parser Evaluation using Textual Entailments. In *Proceedings of the SemEval-2010 Evaluation Exercises on Semantic Evaluation*, 2010.

ID 392:TERSEO + T2T3 Transducer. A systems for recognizing and normalizing TIMEX3

Estela Saquete
Natural Language Processing and Information System Group
University of Alicante
stela@dlsi.ua.es

Abstract

The system described in this paper has participated in the Tempeval 2 competition, specifically in the Task A, which aim is to determine the extent of the time expressions in a text as defined by the TimeML TIMEX3 tag, and the value of the features type and val. For this purpose, a combination of TERSEO system and the T2T3 Transducer was used. TERSEO system is able to annotate text with TIDES TIMEX2 tags, and T2T3 transducer performs the translation from this TIMEX2 tags to TIMEX3 tags.

1 Introduction

Identification and extraction of explicit and implicit temporal information has become a very important field of research within the computational linguistics area since some years ago (Allen, 1983) (Allen, 1984). Moreover, a large number of NLP applications are exploiting this extracted information, such as question answering and summarization systems, allowing these applications to perform in a more complex level.

When dealing with temporal information identification and normalization, different approaches can be taken, depending on the available resources of the target language and the requirements of the system being developed. The most extended approaches to the problem are: a) rule-based approaches, such as Chronos (ITC-irst): recognizes and normalizes temporal expressions in English and Italian (Negri, 2007); TERSEO (University of Alicante, the system used for this work): a knowledge based system for Spanish that has been automatically extended to other languages, such as English, Italian and Catalan (Saquete et al., 2006), b) machine learning approaches, such as TimexTag (University of Amsterdam): applies data-driven methods for recognition and normalization tasks (Ahn et al., 2005) (Ahn, 2006); CU-TMP (University of Colorado): uses machine learning for automatic annotation (Bethard and Martin, 2007), and c) mixed combination of rules and ML approaches, such as, TempEx (MITRE Corporation): combines hand-coded patterns with machine learning rules to tag documents (TempEx, 2008) (Mani and Wilson, 2000); TARSQI (Brandeis University): currently uses GUTime (2008) for temporal expression annotation, which extends the capabilities of the TempEx tagger while generating `TIMEX3` annotations (Verhagen et al., 2005). However, whatever the approach, the output of these systems is a standardized annotation scheme.

The most popular annotation schemes are TIDES (Mani et al., 2001) and TimeML (Pustejovsky et al., 2003b). TIDES program followed the efforts started in the context of the Message Understanding Conference, MUC (1998), and defined the TIMEX2 tag, with the goal of interpreting temporal expressions within a normalized representation of the times they denote, adopting the ISO 8601 standard (Technical Committee ISO/TC 154, 2004). In 2004, within the ACE program, the Time Expression Recognition and Normalization (TERN, 2004) evaluation workshop was held, requiring by the participation systems to detect and normalize the temporal expressions mentioned in the source data, according to the TIDES annotation standard [1]. In spite of the widespread use of this annotation scheme within NLP researchers, it is necessary to identify other types of temporal information such as events or the relations between events and temporal expressions. Motivated by such considerations, the TimeML annotation scheme (Pustejovsky et al., 2003a) (Pustejovsky et al., 2005) (Lee et al., 2007) was developed, specifying four major data structures (elements) for an-

[1] http://fofoca.mitre.org/annotation_guidelines/2005_timex2_standard_v1.1.pdf

Proceedings of the 5th International Workshop on Semantic Evaluation, ACL 2010, pages 317–320,
Uppsala, Sweden, 15-16 July 2010.

notation: EVENT, TIMEX3, SIGNAL and LINK (Pustejovsky et al., 2005).

2 System Description

The system presented in this paper is a combination of two separated systems. First of all, TERSEO system, which is a knowledge-based system for Spanish automatically extended to English, performs an identification and normalization of all the temporal expressions in the text, annotating them with TIMEX2 tags. Once the text has been annotated with TIMEX2, the T2T3 transducer applies a set of translation rules to convert this TIMEX2 output to a TIMEX3 output.

2.1 Description of TERSEO system

TERSEO system first implementation used a hand-made knowledge database in Spanish. However, our main goal was the possibility of working with TERSEO on a multilingual level, but building the different knowledge databases for the new languages through the automatic acquisition of rules (Negri et al., 2006). Therefore, it is possible to create a multilingual system with no need of a previous knowledge of the other languages to which TERSEO system is going to be extended. For this purpose, an architecture similar to the one used by EuroWordNet (Vossen, 2000) was implemented, in order to obtain knowledge databases for the different languages, but all of them connected though a unit denominated TER-ILI or Temporal Expression Rules Interlingua Index. In doing that, TERSEO system have a new knowledge database for each new language and is able to solve any expression in this language. Besides, the system is easily extensible to other new languages. The output of TERSEO system is following the guidelines of TIDES annotation scheme.

This system participated in TERN2004 for English, obtaining the results shown in Table 1.

It is important to consider the results of the system annotating TIMEX2 tags, due to the fact that the final results after the translation depends on how correct the annotation was made by TERSEO.

2.2 Description of T2T3 Transducer

The T2T3 Transducer, developed by University of Alicante and Brandeis University, implements an automatic mapping between TIDES annotation scheme and TimeML, only in English in a first step. This mapping is performed applying a set of rules in two steps:

- **Step 1: Rules for the adaptation of the extent**: the temporal expression extent is adapted from TIMEX2 to TIMEX3. The extension of the expression is related to recognition of the expression. Most expressions which are considered as markable in TIDES are also considered as markable in TimeML. However, TimeML differs from TIDES with respect to the tag span in some cases. Therefore, following the outline of both TIDES 2005 guidelines[2] and TimeML 1.2.1 guidelines[3], a mapping is performed in order to properly adapt the TIMEX2 extent to the TIMEX3 extent. Besides, all the possible adaptations from one scheme to the other are clustered in a set of transformation rules.
- **Step 2: Rules for the transformation of the attributes**: TIMEX2 attributes are transformed to TIMEX3 attributes. The attributes are related to normalization of the expression. The transducer has one rule for each TimeML TIMEX3 attribute, extracting and combining the information provided by the TIMEX2 attributes of each temporal expression. In Tempeval 2 competition only type and val attributes are considered. Therefore, only these two transformation rules are presented here:
  - Attribute type: The **Type Assignment** rule defines the following steps:
    1. If the <TIMEX2> tag has a SET attribute which value is "YES", then type="SET" must be added to the TIMEX3 tag.
    2. If the VAL attribute of the <TIMEX2> tag starts with "P", then type="DURATION" must be added to the TIMEX3 tag.
    3. If the VAL attribute of the <TIMEX2> tag contains a "T", then type="TIME" must be added to the TIMEX3 tag.
    4. In any other case, type="DATE" must be added to the TIMEX3 tag.
  - Attribute value: The attribute value is equivalent to the VAL attribute in

[2]Section 5 in TIDES guidelines http://fofoca.mitre.org

[3]Section 2.2.1.2 in TimeML guidelines http://www.timeml.org

Tag	Precision	Recall	F-Measure
TIMEX2	0.954	0.786	0.862
TIMEX2:ANCHOR_DIR	0.818	0.566	0.669
TIMEX2:ANCHOR_VAL	0.703	0.487	0.575
TIMEX2:MOD	0.444	0.111	0.178
TIMEX2:SET	0.882	0.455	0.600
TIMEX2:TEXT	0.687	0.567	0.621
TIMEX2:VAL	0.686	0.709	0.698

Table 1: Results obtained by TERSEO in TERN2004 competition for TIMEX2

TIMEX2 in most cases. Therefore, in general, the translation is direct. However, there is an exception to this rule in the case of time-anchored expressions. Whereas in TimeML, the value of the head expression is always a period, according to TIDES, there are two different types of time-anchored expressions: a) Anchored point expressions and b) Anchored duration expressions. Therefore, when the T2T3 transducer detects one of these anchored point expressions, a special treatment with the TIMEX2 attributes is performed in order to obtain the proper period value. Moreover, the "DURATION" type is established for the expression.

3 Evaluation results

In this section all the evaluation results for Task A in English are presented. Table 2 shows the results of the system using the trial corpus provided by the organization, the results of the system using the first delivered training corpus and the whole training data, and finally, the score of the system with the test corpus. Accuracy value is not given in the test results and it can not be calculated from the results data provided.

As shown in the results of the different evaluations, test results are very similar to training results, what means that the system is performing steadily. Besides, in the test evaluation, the type attribute result is the best one obtained, being close to 100%. It would be interesting to have the corpus annotated also with TIMEX2 in order to determine which errors derive from TERSEO and which errors derive from the Transducer.

4 Conclusions

Our participation in Tempeval 2 competition was only in Task A, due to the fact that the system presented is a extension of TERSEO system, which only performs identification and normalization of temporal expressions generating TIMEX2 annotation output. Events and links are out of the scope of this system currently.

However, our motivation for participating in Tempeval 2 competition was the possibility to determine the performance of the extension applied to TERSEO, by means of a transducer that is able to convert TIMEX2 annotation to TIMEX3, only using the information of the TIMEX2 tags as input. The transducer applies a set of rules, in order to transform the extent of the temporal expression according to TimeML annotation guidelines, and a set of rules to translate the TIMEX2 attributes to the attributes established by TimeML also. It is important to consider that TERSEO system is a knowledge-based system, with hand-made rules for Spanish. These rules were automatically extended to other languages (English is one of them) using only automatic resources and without manual revision. This automatic extension is very interesting since it is possible to create a new knowledge for the system very fast and with satisfactory results.

The results of the evaluation of this combination (TERSEO + T2T3 Transducer) are 76% precision, 66% recall and 71% F1-Measure. For the case of the attributes, it obtained 98% for type and 65% for value.

Acknowledgments

This research has been partially supported by the Spanish government, projects TIN-2009-13391-C04-01 and PROMETEO/2009/119. Furthermore, I want thank James Pustejovsky for being the co-author of T2T3 Transducer.

References

David Ahn, Sisay Fissaha Adafre, and Maarten de Rijke. 2005. Towards task-based temporal extraction and recognition. In Graham Katz, James Pustejovsky, and Frank Schilder, editors, *Annotating, Extracting and Reasoning about Time and Events*, volume 05151 of *Dagstuhl Seminar Proceedings*. Inter-

Measure	Trial	Training 1	Training 2	Test
PRECISION	0.83	0.78	0.83	0.76
RECALL	0.72	0.66	0.55	0.66
F1-MEASURE	0.77	0.72	0.66	0.71
ACCURACY	0.99	0.98	0.98	-
ATT. TYPE	0.86	0.87	0.87	0.98
ATT. VAL	0.64	0.58	0.63	0.65

Table 2: Results obtained by TERSEO+T2T3 Transducer with trial corpus for English

nationales Begegnungs- und Forschungszentrum für Informatik (IBFI), Schloss Dagstuhl, Germany Internationales Begegnungs- und Forschungszentrum für Informatik (IBFI), Schloss Dagstuhl, Germany.

D. Ahn. 2006. The stages of event extraction. In Association for Computational Linguistics, editor, *ARTE: Workshop of 44th Annual Meeting of the Association for Computational Linguistics*, pages 1–8, Sydney, Australia.

J. Allen. 1983. Maintaining knowledge about temporal intervals. *Communications of the ACM 26*, (11):832–843.

J. Allen. 1984. Towards a general theory of action and time. *Artificial Intelligence*, (23):123–154.

S. Bethard and J.H. Martin. 2007. CU-TMP: Temporal Classification Using Syntactic and Semantic Features. In *Proceedings of the 4th International Workshop of SemEval-2007*, pages 129–132.

GUTime. 2008. Georgetown University. `http://www.timeml.org/site/tarsqi/modules/gutime/index.html`.

K. Lee, B. Boguaraev, H. Bunt, and J. Pustejovsky. 2007. ISO-TimeML and its Applications. In *Proceedings of the 2007 Conference for ISO Technical Committee 37*.

I. Mani and G. Wilson. 2000. Processing of news. In *Proceedings of the 38th Annual Meeting of the Association for Computational Linguistics (ACL2000)*, pages 69–76.

I. Mani, G. Wilson, B. Sundheim, and L. Ferro. 2001. Guidelines for annotating temporal information. In *Proceedings of HLT 2001, First International Conference on Human Language Technology Research, J. Allan ed., Morgan Kaufmann, San Francisco*, pages 142–144.

1998. *MUC-7: Proc. of the Seventh Message Understanding Conf.* Defense Advanced Research Projects Agency.

M. Negri, E. Saquete, P. Martnez-Barco, and R. Muoz. 2006. Evaluating Knowledge-based Approaches to the Multilingual Extension of a Temporal Expression Normalizer. In Association for Computational Linguistics, editor, *ARTE: Workshop of 44th Annual Meeting of the Association for Computational Linguistics*, pages 30–37, Sydney, Australia.

M. Negri. 2007. Dealing with italian temporal expressions: The ita-chronos system. In *Proceedings of EVALITA 2007, Workshop held in conjunction with AI*IA*.

J. Pustejovsky, J. Castao, R. Ingria, R. Saur, R. Gaizauskas, A. Setzer, and G. Katz. 2003a. TimeML: Robust Specification of Event and Temporal Expressions in Text. In *Proc. of the Fifth Int. Workshop on Computational Semantics(IWCS-5)*.

James Pustejovsky, José M. Castaño, Robert Ingria, Roser Sauri, Robert J. Gaizauskas, Andrea Setzer, Graham Katz, and Dragomir R. Radev. 2003b. TimeML: Robust Specification of Event and Temporal Expressions in Text. In *New Directions in Question Answering*, pages 28–34.

J. Pustejovsky, R. Knippen, J. Littman, and R. Saur. 2005. Temporal and event information in natural language text. *Language Resources and Evaluation*, 39:123–164.

E. Saquete, R. Muoz, and P. Martnez-Barco. 2006. Event ordering using terseo system. *Data and Knowledge Engineering Journal*, (58):70–89.

Technical Committee ISO/TC 154. 2004. Processes, data elements and documents in commerce, industry and administration "ISO 8601:2004(E)".

TempEx. 2008. MITRE Corporation. `http://timex2.mitre.org/taggers/timex2_taggers.html`.

TERN. 2004. Time Expression Recognition and Normalization. `http://timex2.mitre.org/tern.html`.

Marc Verhagen, Inderjeet Mani, Roser Sauri, Jessica Littman, Robert Knippen, Seok Bae Jang, Anna Rumshisky, John Phillips, and James Pustejovsky. 2005. Automating Temporal Annotation with TARSQI. In *ACL*. The Association for Computer Linguistics.

P. Vossen. 2000. EuroWordNet: Building a Multilingual Database with WordNets in 8 European Languages. *The ELRA Newsletter*, 5(1):9–10.

HeidelTime: High Quality Rule-based Extraction and Normalization of Temporal Expressions

Jannik Strötgen
Institute of Computer Science
University of Heidelberg
Heidelberg, Germany
stroetgen@uni-hd.de

Michael Gertz
Institute of Computer Science
University of Heidelberg
Heidelberg, Germany
gertz@uni-hd.de

Abstract

In this paper, we describe HeidelTime, a system for the extraction and normalization of temporal expressions. HeidelTime is a rule-based system mainly using regular expression patterns for the extraction of temporal expressions and knowledge resources as well as linguistic clues for their normalization. In the TempEval-2 challenge, HeidelTime achieved the highest F-Score (86%) for the extraction and the best results in assigning the correct value attribute, i.e., in understanding the semantics of the temporal expressions.

1 Introduction

Temporal annotation of documents, i.e., the extraction and chronological ordering of events, is crucial to many NLP applications, e.g., text summarization or machine translation. In this paper, we describe our system HeidelTime for the extraction and normalization of temporal expressions in English documents. It was the best-performing system in Task A for English of the TempEval-2 challenge[1]. The purpose of this challenge was to evaluate different systems for temporal tagging as well as event and temporal relation extraction since a competitive evaluation helps to drive forward research, and temporal annotation is important for many NLP tasks (Pustejovsky and Verhagen, 2009). The annotation scheme for temporal expressions, events, and relations is based on TimeML, the ISO standard for temporal annotation[2].

Before using temporal information in other applications is possible, the first task to solve is to extract and normalize temporal expressions (Task A of the challenge, annotated as Timex3). There are two types of approaches to address this problem: rule-based and machine learning ones. We decided to develop a rule-based system since normalization can then be supervised in a much easier way. Furthermore, respective systems allow for modular extensions.

Although we only participated in Task A, we do not consider the extraction and normalization of temporal expressions in isolation, but use temporal information in combination with other extracted facts, e.g., for the exploration of spatio-temporal information in documents (Strötgen et al., 2010). One of our primary objectives is therefore to develop a system that can be used in other scenarios without any adaptations. Thus, we implement HeidelTime as a UIMA[3] (Unstructured Information Management Architecture) component to integrate the system into our existing document processing pipeline. Another advantage of our temporal tagger is that the user can choose between a precision- and a recall-optimized rule set. In the TempEval-2 challenge, both rule sets achieved top scores in the extraction (F-scores of 86%) and the precision-optimized set achieved the best results for assigning the correct value attributes to the temporal expressions (85% accuracy).

The remainder of the paper is structured as follows: The system architecture is outlined in the next section. In Section 3, we present the evaluation results of HeidelTime in comparison to other systems that participated in the challenge. We conclude our paper in Section 4.

2 System Architecture

In this section, the system architecture of HeidelTime is explained. First, UIMA and our UIMA-based document processing pipeline are detailed, followed by a description of the extraction and normalization tasks, the functionality of the rules

[1] http://semeval2.fbk.eu/
[2] http://www.timeml.org/
[3] http://uima.apache.org/

Proceedings of the 5th International Workshop on Semantic Evaluation, ACL 2010, pages 321–324,
Uppsala, Sweden, 15-16 July 2010.

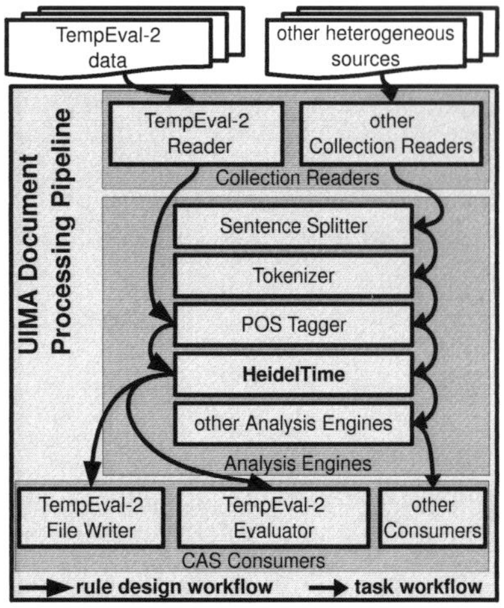

Figure 1: UIMA pipeline with two workflows, one for rule design and one for using HeidelTime.

and the post-processing steps.

2.1 Document Processing Pipeline

HeidelTime is developed as a UIMA component so that we are able to integrate our temporal tagger into our existing document processing pipeline. It is an extension of the temporal tagger we already use for the extraction and exploration of spatio-temporal information in documents (Strötgen et al., 2010). UIMA is widely used for processing unstructured content such as audio, images, or text. Different components can be combined to create a pipeline of modular tools, and all components use the same data structure, the Common Analysis Structure (CAS). This allows to combine tools that were not originally built to be used together, an advantage we are using for preprocessing tasks as well.

In general, a UIMA pipeline consists of three types of components, a Collection Reader for accessing the documents from a source and initializing a CAS object for each document. The analysis of the documents is performed by Analysis Engines that add annotations to the CAS objects. Finally, CAS Consumers are used for final processing, e.g., for storing the annotated information in a database or performing an evaluation.

In Figure 1, the document processing pipeline for designing and using our temporal tagger HeidelTime is depicted. The design workflow (left arrows) contains the TempEval-2 Reader, which reads the TempEval-2 data, initializes a CAS object for each textual document and adds the annotated data to the CAS. For the test set of the temporal expression task, these include the sentence and token information, and for the training set also the gold standard Timex3 entities. Next, the OpenNLP part-of-speech tagger[4] is used, which assigns the corresponding part-of-speech (POS) tag to each token. The information about sentences, tokens, and POS tags is then used by our temporal tagger HeidelTime for extracting and normalizing temporal expressions mentioned in the documents. The CAS Consumer TempEval-2 File Writer is used for creating the files needed for applying the scorer and which had to be submitted for evaluation. During the rule development phase of HeidelTime, the CAS Consumer TempEval-2 Evaluator was used, which compares the gold standard Timex3 annotations with the Timex3 annotations extracted by HeidelTime, resulting in lists of true positives, false positives, and false negatives. These lists were then used for adapting existing or creating new rules.

On the right-hand side of Figure 1, a workflow for using HeidelTime in other scenarios is shown. This workflow reflects the fact that temporal tagging is just one intermediate component of our document processing pipeline. Here, the documents have to be split into sentences and tokens using the two analysis engines Sentence Splitter and Tokenizer. The POS tagger and HeidelTime are used in the same way as described for the other workflow. In addition, other Analysis Engines can be used, e.g., for combining the extracted temporal information with spatial information. Finally, CAS Consumers are used, e.g., for storing the spatio-temporal information in a database.

2.2 Extraction and Normalization Tasks

Every temporal expression te can be viewed as a three-tuple $te_i = \langle e_i, t_i, v_i \rangle$, where e_i is the expression itself as it occurs in the textual document, t_i represents the type of the expression, and v_i is the normalized value. There are four possible types, namely *Date*, *Time*, *Duration*, and *Set*. The normalized value represents the temporal semantics of an expression as it is specified by the markup language TimeML, regardless of the expression used in the document. The goal of HeidelTime is to extract for every temporal expression the expression e_i and to correctly assign the type and value attributes t_i and v_i, respectively.

For this, HeidelTime uses hand-crafted rules,

[4] http://opennlp.sourceforge.net

Expression resources	$reMonth$ = "(... |June|July|...)"	
	$reSeason$ = "(... |summer|...)"	
Normalization functions	$normMonth$("June") = "06"	
	$normSeason$("summer") = "SU"	

Table 1: Examples for extraction and normalization resources for months and seasons.

which are grouped into four types, namely the four possible types of temporal expressions. More precisely, every rule is a triple of an expression rule, a normalization function and the type information. The extraction rules mainly consist of regular expression patterns. However, other features can be used as well, e.g., a constraint what part-of-speech the previous or next token has to have. HeidelTime contains resources for both the extraction and the normalization tasks of the rules. For instance, there are resources for weekdays, months, or seasons, which are realized as regular expressions and can be accessed by multiple extraction rules. In addition, there are knowledge resources for the normalization of such expressions. Examples are given in Table 1.

Algorithm 1 illustrates how rules are used in HeidelTime. First, the rules are applied to every sentence of a document, and extracted timexes are added to the CAS object. Then, two post-processing steps are executed to disambiguate underspecified values and to remove invalid temporal expressions from the CAS. This functionality is detailed in the next sections with a focus on the linguistic clues for the normalization task.

Algorithm 1 ApplyRules.

```
foreach sentence in document
    addDatesToCAS(date_rules, CAS);
    addTimesToCAS(time_rules, CAS);
    addDurationsToCAS(dur_rules, CAS);
    addSetsToCAS(set_rules, CAS);
end foreach
foreach timex3 in CAS
    disambiguateValues(CAS);
end foreach
removeInvalidsFromCAS(CAS);
```

2.3 Functionality of HeidelTime

There are many ways to textually describe temporal expressions, either explicitly, implicitly or relatively (Schilder and Habel, 2001). The extraction for all temporal expressions works in the same way, but assigning the value attributes has to be done differently. Explicit temporal expressions are fully specified, i.e., the value attribute can directly

explicit temporal expressions
$date\_r1 = (reMonth)_{g1}\ (reDay)_{g2},\ (reFullYear)_{g3}$
norm_r1(g1,g2,g3) = g3-normMonth(g1)-normDay(g2)
implicit temporal expressions
$date\_r2 = (reHoliday)_{g1}\ (reFullYear)_{g2}$
norm_r2(g1,g2) = g2-normHoliday(g1)

Table 2: Extraction parts and normalization parts of two sample rules.

be assigned using the corresponding normalization function of the rule. For example, the explicit expression *March 11, 1982* can be extracted with the rule date_r1 of Table 2 containing the resources $reMonth$, $reDay$, and $reFullYear$ (regular expressions for possible month, day and year tokens of a date phrase, respectively). The matched tokens can be accessed using the group ids so that the normalization function can be called with the extracted tokens resulting in the value 1982-03-11.

The value attribute of implicit expressions can be assigned once the implicit temporal semantics of such expressions is known. Holidays, for example, can be extracted using date_r2 with the resource $reHoliday$ and normalized using the knowledge resource for normalization as shown in Table 2. An example is *Independence Day 2010* to which the value 2010-07-04 is assigned.

The normalization of relative expressions for which a reference time is needed is the most challenging task. Examples are *last June*, just *June* in phrases such as *in June*, or *year-earlier* in *the year-earlier results*. To such expressions, HeidelTime assigns the values in an underspecified format depending on the assumed reference time and disambiguates them in a post-processing step. The underspecified values for the examples are UNDEF-last-June, UNDEF-June, and UNDEF-REF-last-year, respectively. For the first two examples, the document creation time (dct) is assumed to be the reference time while for the last example the previously mentioned date is used for reference. In news texts (as used in TempEval-2) the dct is meaningful while other documents may not contain such a reference time. Then, the previously mentioned date is used for all underspecified values. The disambiguation of such expressions is detailed in the next section.

2.4 Post-Processing

The first post-processing step is to disambiguate underspecified value attributes (see Algorithm 1). If the value starts with UNDEF-REF, the previously mentioned date is used for disambiguation, otherwise the document creation time (dct) if meaningful. The value UNDEF-last-June of the previous section is disambiguated by calculating the June before the dct. More complex are even less underspecified values like UNDEF-June. Here, linguistic knowledge is used to disambiguate which June is meant: The tense of the sentence is determined by using the part-of-speech information of the tokens and checking the semantics of the verbs in the sentence. This method identifies whether a sentence is past, present, or future tense. E.g., the tense of the sentence *In June, new results will be published* will be determined to be future tense and the new value UNDEF-next-June can be assigned instead of UNDEF-last-June if past tense was identified. Such values are then disambiguated using the methods described above.

If the reference time is assumed to be the previously mentioned date all previous extracted Timex3 are checked to be of the type *Date*. The value v_{ref} of the closest previously mentioned date is then used for further disambiguation. For example, UNDEF-REF-last-year is calculated by subtracting one year from v_{ref}. This can result in a specific day but also in a specific quarter if the last mentioned timex was a quarter.

The last post-processing step is to remove all extracted timex annotations that are invalid. Invalid are all expressions that are included in other expressions. For instance, having the phrase *June 11* the whole phrase is found by a rule as well as just *June*. Since *June* is in *June 11*, it is removed.

3 Evaluation

In this section, we outline the evaluation of HeidelTime and compare our results with other systems that participated in the TempEval-2 challenge Task A for English. For this challenge, we developed two rule sets, one precision- and one recall-optimized set, reflecting the user's choice between precision and recall. The first set consists of 43 rules, 25 for dates, and 6 for times, durations, and sets, respectively. The recall-optimized rule set contains two more rules, one for dates and one for durations. These rules are very general and thus negatively influence precision.

Our results for the extraction in the two runs are shown in Figure 2 together with the results of the other participating systems. As one can see, both our runs achieved the best F-score results (86%)

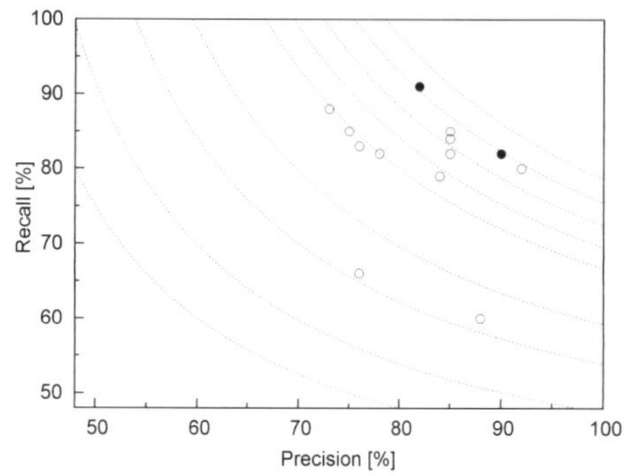

Figure 2: Performance of participating systems with an F-score contour for reference. Our runs are shown as full circles.

with a precision of 90% (82%) and a recall of 82% (91%) for the two sets.

HeidelTime, with the precision-optimized rule set, was the best system in assigning the value attributes (85% values are assigned correctly). In addition, the type attribute was correctly assigned to 96% of the extracted expressions.

4 Conclusions

HeidelTime achieves high quality results for the extraction and normalization of temporal expressions. The precision-optimized rule set achieved the best results for interpreting the semantics of the temporal expressions. In our opinion, this aspect, i.e., assigning the correct value attribute, is crucial since the value is used for further analysis of the documents, e.g., when ordering events or doing a temporal analysis of documents.

The rule-based approach makes it possible to include further knowledge easily, e.g., to assign temporal information directly to historic events.

References

James Pustejovsky and Marc Verhagen. 2009. SemEval-2010 Task 13: Evaluating Events, Time Expressions, and Temporal Relations (TempEval-2). In *Proceedings of the Workshop on Semantic Evaluations (SEW-2009)*, pages 112–116. ACL.

Frank Schilder and Christopher Habel. 2001. From Temporal Expressions to Temporal Information: Semantic Tagging of News Messages. In *Proceedings of the ACL-2001 Workshop on Temporal and Spatial Information Processing*, pages 65–72. ACL.

Jannik Strötgen, Michael Gertz, and Pavel Popov. 2010. Extraction and Exploration of Spatio-Temporal Information in Documents. In *GIR '10*, pages 1–8. ACM.

KUL: Recognition and Normalization of Temporal Expressions

Oleksandr Kolomiyets, Marie-Francine Moens
Department of Computer Science
Katholieke Universiteit Leuven
{oleksandr.kolomiyets, sien.moens}@cs.kuleuven.be

Abstract

In this paper we describe a system for the recognition and normalization of temporal expressions (Task 13: TempEval-2, Task A). The recognition task is approached as a classification problem of sentence constituents and the normalization is implemented in a rule-based manner. One of the system features is extending positive annotations in the corpus by semantically similar words automatically obtained from a large unannotated textual corpus. The best results obtained by the system are 0.85 and 0.84 for precision and recall respectively for recognition of temporal expressions; the accuracy values of 0.91 and 0.55 were obtained for the feature values `TYPE` and `VAL` respectively.

1 Introduction

Recognition of temporal expressions[1] is a task of proper identification of phrases with temporal semantics in running text. After several evaluation campaigns targeted at temporal processing of text, such as MUC, ACE TERN and TempEval-1 (Verhagen et al., 2007), the recognition and normalization task has been again newly reintroduced in TempEval-2 (Pustejovsky & Verhagen, 2009). The task is defined as follows: determine the extent of the time expressions; in addition, determine the value of the features `TYPE` for the type of the temporal expression and its temporal value `VAL`. In this paper we describe the KUL system that has participated in this task.

Architecturally, the system employs a pipelined information processing chain and implements a number of machine learning classifiers for extracting the necessary information for the temporal value estimation. The normalization step employs a number of hand-crafted vocabularies for tagging single elements of a temporal expression and a rule-based system for estimating the temporal value. The performance of the system obtained the values of 0.85 and 0.84 for precision and recall respectively for the recognition of temporal expressions. The accuracy for the type and value is 0.91 and 0.55 respectively.

The remainder of the paper is organized as follows: Section 2 reports on the architecture of the system with single modules and describes theirs functions. Section 3 presents the results and error analysis; the conclusions are provided in Section 4.

2 System Architecture

The system is implemented in Java and follows a pipelined method for information processing. Regarding the problems it solves, it can be split in two sub-systems: recognition and normalization.

2.1 Recognition of Temporal Expressions

This sub-system is employed for finding temporal expressions in the text. It takes a sentence as input and looks for temporal expressions in it.

Pre-processing: At this step the input text undergoes syntactic analysis. Sentence detection, tokenization, part-of-speech tagging and parsing are applied[2].

Candidate selection: Since only certain lexical categories can be temporal expressions and they are defined in the TIDES standard (Ferro et

---

[1] Temporal expressions are sometimes referenced as time expressions and timexes.

[2] For preprocessing we use the OpenNLP package (http://opennlp.sourceforge.net).

Proceedings of the 5th International Workshop on Semantic Evaluation, ACL 2010, pages 325–328,
Uppsala, Sweden, 15-16 July 2010.

al., 2003), in our implementation we consider the following chunk-phrases as candidates for temporal expressions: nouns (*week*, *day*), proper names (*Tuesday*, *May*), noun phrases (*last Tuesday*), adjectives (*current*), adjective phrases (*then current*), adverbs (*currently*), adverbial phrases (*a year ago*), and numbers (*2000*). As input it takes the sentences with provided syntactic information and marks phrases in the parse tree belonging to the above types for temporal expressions.

Annotation alignment: If the system is used for training classifiers, all the candidates in a sentence are examined against the available annotations. The candidates, whose parse and annotation extents aligned, are taken as positive examples and the rest is considered as negative.

Feature Design: To produce a feature-vector we use most valuable features extracted for phrase-candidate. After a number of experiments the following features were selected:

- Last token in the phrase, most probable token to be a temporal trigger;
- Lemma of the last phrasal token;
- Part-of-speech of the last phrasal token;
- Character pattern of the last phrasal token as introduced in (Ahn et al., 2007);
- Neighbor POS's. The concatenated part-of-speech tags of the last phrasal token and its preceding token;
- Character pattern of the entire phrase;
- Phrase surface. A concatenated string of sub-parse types for the phrase;
- A Boolean feature indicating nested complex phrasal parses, such as noun verb, adverbial, adjective or prepositional phrase;
- Depth of the phrase. The number of the nested sub-parses to the deepest pre-terminal sub-parse.

All the features are considered as Boolean.

Classification: Once the classifiers are trained they can be used for recognition of temporal expressions on test sentences. A preprocessed sentence is taken as input and starting from its parse-tree root the candidate-phrases are classified. The most probable class will be assigned to the candidate under consideration. Once the phrase is classified as temporal expression no further classification of nested phrases is performed, since no embedded timexes are allowed in the corpus. After a series of experiments with different machine learning techniques on the training data the maximum entropy classifier was chosen.

Extending positive instances: Sparseness of annotated corpora is the biggest challenge for any supervised machine learning technique. To overcome this problem we hypothesize that knowledge of semantic similar words could be found by associating words that do not occur in the training set to similar words that did occur in the training set. Furthermore, we would like to learn these similarities automatically in order to be as much as possible independent of knowledge sources that might not be available for all languages or domains. For example, there is in TimeBank a temporal expression "*last summer*" with the temporal trigger *summer*, but there is no annotation of temporal expressions built around the temporal trigger *winter*, and this means that no temporal expression with the trigger *winter* can be recognized. Something similar usually happens to any annotated corpus and we want to find a way how to find other temporal expressions outside the available data, which can be used for training. On the other hand, we want to avoid a naïve selection of words as, for example, from a gazetteer with temporal triggers, which may contradict with grammatical rules and the lexical context of a timex in text, e.g.:

on *Tuesday* said....

But grammatically wrong by naïve replacement from a gazetteer:

... on ***week*** said*...
... on ***day*** said*...
... on ***month*** said* ...

In order to find these words, which are legitimate at a certain position in a certain context we use the latent word language model (LWLM) (Deschacht & Moens, 2009) with a Hidden Markov Model approach for estimating the latent word parameters.

Complementary, we use WordNet (Miller, 1995) as a source that can provide a most complete set of words similar to the given one. One should note that the use of WordNet is not straight-forward. Due to the polysemy, the word sense disambiguation (WSD) problem has to be solved. Our system uses latent words obtained by the LWLM and chooses the synset with the highest overlap between WordNet synonyms and coordinate terms, and the latent words. The overlap value is calculated as the sum of LWLM probabilities for matching words.

Having these two sets of synonyms and after a series of preliminary tests we found the setting, at which the system produces the highest results and submitted several runs with different strategies:

- Baseline (no expansion) (KUL Run 1)
- 3 LWLM words with highest probabilities (KUL Run 2)
- 3 WordNet coordinate terms; WSD is solved by means of LWLM[3] (KUL Run 3)

For each available annotation in the corpus a positive instance is generated. After that, the token at the most probable position for a temporal trigger is replaced by a synonym from the synonym set found to the available token.

2.2 Normalization of Temporal Expressions

Normalization of temporal expressions is a process of estimating standardized temporal values and types. For example, the temporal expression "*summer 1990*" has to be resolved to its value of `1990-SU` and the type of `DATE`. In contrast, for the expression "*last year*" the value cannot be estimated directly, rather it gets a modified value of another time expression.

Due to a large variance of expressions denoting the same date and vagueness in language, rule-based systems have been proven to perform better than machine-learning ones for the normalization task. The current implementation follows a rule-based approach and takes a pre-processed document with recognized temporal expressions (as it is described in Section 2.1) and estimates a standardized ISO-based date/time value. In the following sections we provide implementation details of the system.

Before the temporal value is estimated, we employ a classifier, which uses the same feature sets and classify the temporal expression among type classes `DATE`, `TIME`, `DURATION` and `SET`.

Labeling: Labeling text is a process of providing tags to tokens of chunk-phrases from a defined set of tags. We carefully examined available annotated temporal expressions and annotation standards to determine categories of words participating in temporal expressions. The following set of categories with labels based on semantics of temporally relevant information and simple syntax was defined: ordinal numbers (*first*, *30th* etc.), cardinal numbers (*one*, *two*, *10* etc.), month names (*Jan.*, *January* etc.), week day names (*Mo.*, *Monday* etc.), season names (*summer*, *winter* etc.), parts of day (*morning*, *afternoon* etc.), temporal directions (*ago*, *later*, *earlier* etc.), quantifiers (*several*, *few* etc.), modifiers (*recent*, *last* etc.), approximators (*almost*, *nearly* etc.), temporal co-references (*time*, *period* etc.), fixed single token timexes (*tomorrow*, *today* etc.), holidays (*Christmas*, *Easter* etc.) and temporal units (*days*, *months*, *years* etc.). Also fine-grained categories are introduced: day number, month number and year number. For each category we manually construct a vocabulary, in which each entry specifies a value of a temporal field or a final date/time value, or a method with parameters to apply.

As input, the normalization takes a recognized temporal expression and its properties, such as the temporal type and the discourse type[4]. During labeling each token in a temporal expression is tagged with one or multiple labels corresponding to the categories defined above. For each of the categories a custom detector is implemented. The detector declares the method to run and the expected type of the result. The rules that implement the logics for the detector are inherited from an abstract class for this specific detector, so that if a new rule needs to be implemented its realization is limited to the development of one class, all the rest the detector does automatically. Besides, the order, in which detectors have to be run, can be specified (as for example, in case of fine-grained detectors). As output, the module provides labels of the categories to the tokens in the temporal expression. If there is no entry in the vocabulary for a token, its part-of-speech tag is used as the label.

Value estimation: Value estimation is implemented in the way of aggregating the values defined for entries in the vocabulary and/or executing instructions or methods specified. Also a set of predefined resolution

[3] Preliminary experiments, when the most common sense in WordNet is chosen for increasing the number of positive examples, showed a low performance level and thus has not been proposed for evaluations.

[4] Since in TempEval-2 the reference to the timex with respect to which the value estimated is given, the normalization module considers all timexes as deictic.

rules is provided and can be extended with new implementations of resolution strategies.

For resolution of complex relative temporal expressions, the value for which cannot be estimated directly, we need to rely on additional information found at the recognition step. This includes the semantic type of the timex, discourse type and contextual temporal information (speech or document creation time, or previously mentioned timexes). Let's consider the following temporal expression as an example: *10 days ago*. In this example the temporal expression receives a modified value of another timex, namely the value of the document creation time. The temporal expression is recognized and classified as a date (`SEM TYPE: DATE`), which refers to another timex (`DISCOURSE TYPE: DEICTIC`). It takes the value of the referenced timex and modifies it with respect to the number (*10*), magnitude (*days*) and temporal direction (*ago*). Thus, the final value is calculated by subtracting a number of days for the value of the referenced timex.

3 Results and Error Analysis

In the Table 1 the results of the best-performing runs are presented.

Run	Recognition			Normalization	
	P	*R*	*F1*	TYPE Acc.	VAL Acc.
1	0.78	0.82	0.8	0.91	0.55
2	0.75	0.85	0.797	0.91	0.51
3	0.85	0.84	0.845	0.91	0.55

Table 1. Results of different runs of the system.

As we can see the best results were obtained by extending available annotations with maximum 3 additional instances, which are extracted as coordinate terms in WordNet, whereas the WSD problem was solved as the greatest overlap between coordinate terms and latent words obtained by the LWLM.

Most of the errors at the recognition step were caused by misaligned parses and annotations.

For normalization we acknowledge the significance of estimating a proper temporal value with a correct link to the temporal expression with its value. In the TempEval-2 training data the links to the temporal expressions indicating how the value is calculated were not provided, and thus, the use of machine learning tools for training and automatic disambiguation was not possible. We choose a fixed strategy and all relative temporal expressions were resolved with respect to the document creation time, which caused errors with wrong temporal values and a low performance level.

4 Conclusions

For TempEval-2 we proposed a system for the recognition and normalization of temporal expressions. Multiple runs were submitted, among which the best results were obtained with automatically expanded positive instances by words derived as coordinate terms from WordNet for which the proper sense was found as the greatest overlap between coordinate terms and latent words found by the LWLM.

Acknowledgements

This work has been funded by the Flemish government as a part of the project AMASS++ (Grant: IWT-60051) and by Space Applications Services NV as part of the ITEA2 project LINDO (ITEA2-06011, IWT-70043).

References

Ahn, D., van Rantwijk, J., and de Rijke, M. 2007. A Cascaded Machine Learning Approach to Interpreting Temporal Expressions. In *Proceedings of NAACL-HLT 2007*.

Deschacht, K., and Moens M.-F. 2009. Using the Latent Words Language Model for Semi-Supervised Semantic Role Labeling. In *Proceedings of the Conference on Empirical Methods in Natural Language Processing*.

Ferro, L., Gerber, L., Mani, I., Sundheim, B., and Wilson, G. 2003. TIDES 2003 Standard for the Annotation of Temporal Expressions.

Miller, G. A. 1995. WordNet: A Lexical Database for English. *Communications of the ACM*, 38(11): 39-41.

Pustejovsky, J. and Verhagen, M. 2009. SemEval-2010 Task 13: Evaluating Events, Time Expressions, and Temporal Relations (TempEval-2). In *Proceedings of the Workshop on Semantic Evaluations: Recent Achievements and Future Directions*.

Verhagen, M., Gaizauskas, R., Schilder, F., Hepple, M., and Pustejovsky, J. 2007. Semeval-2007 Task 15: Tempeval Temporal Relation Identification. In *SemEval-2007: 4th International Workshop on Semantic Evaluations*.

UC3M system: Determining the Extent, Type and Value of Time Expressions in TempEval-2

María Teresa Vicente-Díez, Julián Moreno Schneider, Paloma Martínez
Department of Computer Science
Universidad Carlos III de Madrid
Avda. Universidad, 30
Leganés, 28911, Madrid, Spain.
{tvicente, jmschnei, pmf}@inf.uc3m.es

Abstract

This paper describes the participation of Universidad Carlos III de Madrid in Task A of the TempEval-2 evaluation. The UC3M system was originally developed for the temporal expressions recognition and normalization (TERN task) in Spanish texts, according to the TIDES standard. Current version supposes an almost-total refactoring of the earliest system. Additionally, it has been adapted to the TimeML annotation schema and a considerable effort has been done with the aim of increasing its coverage. It takes a rule-based design both in the identification and the resolution phases. It adopts an inductive approach based on the empirical study of frequency of temporal expressions in Spanish corpora. Detecting the extent of the temporal expressions the system achieved a Precision/Recall of 0.90/0.87 whereas, in determining the TYPE and VALUE of those expressions, system results were 0.91 and 0.83, respectively.

1 Introduction

The study of temporality in NLP is not a new task. However, in the last years it has witnessed a huge interest. Initiatives like TempEval task or the Automatic Context Extraction[1] (ACE) TERN competitions have boosted research on the field and have promoted the development of new resources to the scientific community.

There are two main advantages in participating in these evaluations. On the one hand it is possible to measure the systems' performance under standardized metrics, sharing datasets and other resources. On the other hand, it is possible to make comparative evaluations among distinct participants looking forward the same objectives but using different approaches.

Until recently, most of temporally annotated corpora, as well as temporal taggers, were available in English. Since languages as Spanish start to become prominent in the field it seems interesting the development of specific resources. Tempeval-2 has contributed to this target in a significant way thanks to the release of annotated corpora and the publication of specific guidelines (Sauri et al., 2009), (Saurí et al., 2010).

This paper resumes the participation of the UC3M system in the task of determining the extent and resolving the value of time expressions in texts (Task A). This system was originally developed for the Spanish TERN task proposed in ACE 2007 evaluation (Vicente-Díez et al., 2007), achieving encouraging results although it was in a early stage of development.

The system follows a ruled-based approach whose knowledge base has been inducted from the study of annotated temporal corpora (Vicente-Díez et al., 2008). A machine learning approach was initially discarded due to the limitation of annotated Spanish corpora.

The aims of this work were to improve the coverage of the original system and test its performance against new available datasets with a view to its integration in future domains of application. Main challenges were to move to a new temporal model where interval is considered as the basic time unit as well as the isolation of the internal representation of temporal information from the annotation schema.

[1] Automatic Content Extraction Evaluation. National Institute of Standards and Technology (NIST) http://www.itl.nist.gov/iad/mig//tests/ace/

Proceedings of the 5th International Workshop on Semantic Evaluation, ACL 2010, pages 329–332,
Uppsala, Sweden, 15-16 July 2010.

This paper is organized as follows: Section 2 describes the system operation; Section 3 presents experimentation and results; conclusions and future work are discussed in Section 4.

2 System Description

The UC3M system recognizes and annotates temporal expressions in texts based on a linguistic rules engine for Spanish language.

Our system is divided into three different parts: recognition of temporal expressions, normalization of the detections, and annotation of the temporal expressions according to the TimeML schema.

Following the definition of the Task A, the system is able to determine not only the extent of the temporal expressions but also the value of the features TYPE and VAL. It differentiates among the four TYPE values (dates, durations, sets and times) thanks to the classification of the recognition rules. The system straightforwardly provides a VAL attribute that accomplishes the format defined by TIMEX2 and TIMEX3 standards through its internal model for representing time.

2.1 Recognition

The recognizer detects temporal expressions by means of a set of linguistic rules, focusing on those which are most frequent in Spanish.

We adopted an empirical inductive approach through the analysis of the different types of temporal expressions in news corpora, and we could outline a typology of most common time expressions in the language. The typology together with the patterns that define these expressions form up the knowledge base for a successful automatic identification and resolution of temporal expressions.

The rule engine allows managing different sets of rules independently of the target. In this case, the rules have been created attending to each pattern that is likely to match a temporal expression. Each rule determines the set of tokens that form an expression, the normalization type to be applied and the expression type.

In Table 1 an example of a rule to identify dates is shown. The first line represents the name of the rule. The second line specifies the normalization method that will be used once the expression is recognized. The third line specifies the type of the temporal expression and the annotation pattern. Finally, the fourth line shows the tokens that trigger the rule.

1.	*TEMPORAL_RULE(r1.3)*
2.	*TEMPORAL_ANALYSIS_NORMALIZATION_ TYPE=(abs_dia_mes_anio_3)*
3.	*TEMPORAL_ANALYSIS_TYPE= (date:init:YYYY-MM-DD)*
4.	*RULE= [[el/_] [DIC(DIASEMANA)/_] [dia/_] DIC(DIA) de DIC(MES) DIC(PREP) METHOD(year)]*

Table 1 Rule definition example

The operation of the system is described as follows: first, the text is parsed token by token. Then, for each token, every rule is checked to find out if it triggers through a given token and the following ones.

This operation implies that the higher the number of rules, the slower the text processing. The disadvantage of the processing speed has been accepted as a design criterion for the sake of the simplicity of creating new rules.

2.2 Normalization

The temporal expression normalization is done as an intermediate step between recognition and annotation, isolating the extraction of semantics from the annotation schema while trying to facilitate the second step.

Normalization is important since recognized time expressions are managed and returned in a standard format that avoids semantic ambiguities.

UC3M system applies an interval-based temporal normalization. It means that every temporal expression is represented as an interval with two boundaries: an initial and a final date (including time). This approach is motivated by the belief that the use of intervals as a basic time unit leads to a lower loss of semantics. For instance, when an expression like “en enero” (“in January”) is detected, current task proposes the annotation “2010-01”. However, we think that for many applications that are likely to use this system it would be more useful to have the complete interval that the expression refers (“2010-01-01 - 2010-01-31”). Through a set of procedures (as getting the length of a given month), our system tries to define the interval boundaries as much as possible. Every normalized expression is made up of two dates although it refers to a concrete date or time.

In the internal representation model normalized dates and times adopts the ISO-8601 form, durations are captured as a length related to the unit of measure, and sets are managed in a similar way to durations, adding quantity and frequency modifiers.

The normalization process is dependent on the rule used to recognize each expression. For each new rule added to the engine a new normalization clause is needed.

In Table 2 some temporal expression normalization examples are presented:

Expression	Init Date	Final Date
18 de abril de 2005 *18th of April of 2005*	20050418	20050418
mayo de 1999 *May of 1999*	19990501	19990531
en 1975 *in 1975*	19750101	19751231
el próximo mes *next month*	20100501	20100531

Table 2 Interval-based normalization sample

2.3 Annotation

The annotation process starts from the normalized form of the temporal expression. The system implements a transformation procedure based on patterns. This transformation is dependent on the temporal expression type.

Dates: when dealing with dates, the VAL value is extracted from the initial boundary of the interval in accordance with the annotation pattern defined in the corresponding rule (see Table 1). Some examples are shown in Table 3.

Expression	Norm. Init Date	Pattern	VAL
mayo de 1999 *May of 1999*	19990501	YYYY-MM	1999-05
la semana pasada *last week*	20100405	YYYY-WXX	2010-W14
los años 80 *the 80's*	19800101	YYY	198

Table 3 Annotation patterns for dates

Durations: the model represents durations by capturing the length of action as a quantity. This quantity is stored in the position of the initial boundary whose granularity corresponds with the unit of measure. The annotation patterns indicate the granularity to be considered (Table 4).

Expression	*Norm. Init Date*	*Pattern*	*VAL*
4 años *4 años*	00040000	PXY	P4Y
4 meses, 3 días y 2 horas *4 moths,3 days and 2 hours*	00040003-02:00:00	COMBINED	P4M3DT2H

Table 4 Annotation patterns for durations

Sets are managed similarly to durations. In this case also frequency and quantity modifiers are captured internally together with the interval representation, so that the transformation is immediate.

Expression	Norm. Init Date	Pattern	VAL	FREQ	QUANT
cada 2 años *each 2 years*	00020000 F1QEv	PXY	P2Y	1x	EVERY
2 veces al día *twice a day*	00000001 F2QEv	PXD	P1D	2x	EVERY

Table 5 Annotation patterns for sets

Times: the representation model allows capturing hours, minutes, seconds and milliseconds if they are specified. Similarly to the annotation of dates, VAL value is obtained of the information in the initial boundary in the way the pattern determines (Table 6).

Expression	Norm. Init Date	Pattern	VAL
a las 12:30 PM *at 12:30 PM*	20100405 12:30:00	THXMX	2010-04-05T12H30M
por la tarde *in the evening*	20100405 12:00:00	TDP	2010-04-05TAF

Table 6 Annotation patterns for times

3 Experiments and Results

Precision and recall and f-measure are used as evaluation metrics according to the evaluation methodology (Pustejovsky et al., 2009). To determine the quality of annotation, results are completed with figures concerning to the resolution of TYPE and VAL attributes.

Before evaluation, the system was tested on the training corpus and, once the test datasets were released, it was tested on the corpus for relations detection (tasks C-F) since it contained both files "*timex-extents.tab*" and "*timex-attributes.tab*". The results are shown in Table 7.

Corpus	Timex Extent			Timex Attbs.	
	P	*R*	*F*	*TYPE*	*VAL*
Training	0.93	0.67	**0.78**	0.87	0.82
Relation-Test	0.89	0.63	**0.74**	0.86	0.83

Table 7 Results on training corpus

In Table 8 results of final evaluation are presented and compared with the other participants' figures for the same task and language. Since the test corpora were not aligned, further comparisons for different languages have not been proposed.

Our system achieved a precision rate of 90% and a recall of 87%, being the f-measure of 88%. Thus, it supposes a significant improvement over our earlier work. In more, determining the value of TIMEX3 attributes the system raises good figures, obtaining the best VAL score, what means that normalization is working well.

Team	Timex Extent			Timex Attrbs.	
	P	*R*	*F*	*TYPE*	*VAL*
UC3M	0.90	0.87	**0.88**	0.91	0.83
TIPSem	0.95	0.87	**0.91**	0.91	0.78
TIPSem-B	0.97	0.81	**0.88**	0.99	0.75

Table 8 Results on test corpus

Analyzing the experimental errors several facts can be highlighted:

The percentage of expressions completely and correctly recognized and normalized is good but there are some missing expressions, mainly due to their complexity (or fuzziness) and to the absence of a rule to manage them, i.e.: "durante un largo periodo" (*during a long period*).

Errors in determining the extent of the temporal expressions were mainly due to the inclusion of prepositions or articles that precede to the kernel of the expression, i.e.: "a corto plazo" vs. "corto plazo" (*in short term*).

A number of false positives were due to some inconsistencies in the annotation of the corpus. An example has been observed in fuzzy time expressions that denotes a future reference: "el próximo técnico" (*the next trainer*) (not annotated) vs. "el próximo preparador" (*the next coach*) (FUTURE_REF)

Although normalization figures are good, some annotations are incorrect if their resolution implies context-aware mechanisms.

4 Conclusions and Future Work

In this paper a rule based approach for automatically detecting and annotating temporal expressions according to TimeML TIMEX3 tag has been presented. It is based on an empirical study of temporal expressions frequencies in Spanish that provides the main recognition rules of the knowledge base. At the normalization stage, a representation model based on intervals has been adopted with the aim of capturing most semantics. The annotation process relies on patterns that distinguish among different types and granularities of the expressions to be tagged.

Obtained results suppose a significant improvement over our previous work. Part of this success is due to the specific annotation guidelines for Spanish that have been released with occasion of the TempEval-2. It is a helpful tool to optimize the system performance, since each language has its own peculiarities that should be taken into account. The promotion of a common framework and the development of resources like specific corpora are also very interesting topics to boost research in the field, since both comparative and standardized evaluation of the systems are needed.

Several aspects should be taken into account in future versions of the system. In order to improve the recall new knowledge must be incorporated to the rule engine. That supposes the addition of new rules and annotation patterns. This objective includes the implementation of dictionaries with a broader coverage of translatable temporal expressions, such as holidays, festivities, etc.

We will also explore context extraction techniques that facilitate the resolution of context-aware temporal expressions.

Another pending issue is the enlargement of the system to span the detection of events and the relations among events and time expressions.

Finally, the system will be integrated into a NLP application that benefits from the temporal information management. We want to check the improvement that the extraction of temporal entities supposes on a traditional approach.

Acknowledgments

This work has been partially supported by the Research Network MAVIR (S-0505/TIC-0267), and project BRAVO (TIN2007-67407-C03-01).

References

James Pustejovsky, Marc Verhagen, Xue Nianwen, Robert Gaizauskas, Mark Hepple, Frank Schilder, Graham Katz, Roser Saurí, Estela Saquete, Tommaso Caselli, Nicoletta Calzolari, Kiyong Lee, and Seohyun Im. 2009. TempEval2: Evaluating Events, Time Expressions and Temporal Relations. SemEval Task Proposal.

María Teresa Vicente-Díez, Doaa Samy and Paloma Martínez. 2008. An empirical approach to a preliminary successful identification and resolution of temporal expressions in Spanish news corpora. In Proceedings of the LREC'08.

María Teresa Vicente-Díez, César de Pablo-Sánchez and Paloma Martínez. Evaluación de un Sistema de Reconocimiento y Normalización de Expresiones Temporales en Español. Procesamiento del lenguaje natural. N. 39 pp. 113-120, Sept. 2007.

Roser Saurí, Estela Saquete and James Pustejovsky. 2010. Annotating Time Expressions in Spanish. TimeML Annotation Guidelines. Version TempEval-2010.

Roser Saurí, Olga Batiukova, James Pustejovsky. 2009. Annotating Events in Spanish. TimeML Annotation Guidelines. Version TempEval-2010.

Edinburgh-LTG: TempEval-2 System Description

Claire Grover, Richard Tobin, Beatrice Alex and Kate Byrne
University of Edinburgh
Edinburgh, United Kingdom
{grover, richard, balex, kbyrne3}@inf.ed.ac.uk

Abstract

We describe the Edinburgh information extraction system which we are currently adapting for analysis of newspaper text as part of the SYNC3 project. Our most recent focus is geospatial and temporal grounding of entities and it has been useful to participate in TempEval-2 to measure the performance of our system and to guide further development. We took part in Tasks A and B for English.

1 Background

The Language Technology Group (LTG) at Edinburgh has been active in the field of information extraction (IE) for a number of years. Up until recently our main focus has been in biomedical IE (Alex et al., 2008) but we have also been pursuing projects in other domains, e.g. digitised historical documents (Grover et al., 2010) and we are currently participants in the EU-funded SYNC3 project where our role is to analyse news articles and establish spatio-temporal and other relations between news events. As a step towards this goal, we have been extending and adapting our IE pipeline to ground spatial and temporal entities. We have developed the Edinburgh Geoparser for georeferencing documents and have evaluated our system against the SpatialML corpus, as reported in Tobin et al. (2010). We are currently in the process of developing a rule-based date and time grounding component and it is this component that we used for Task A, which requires systems to identify the extents of temporal named entities and provide their interpretation. The TempEval-2 data also contains event entities and we have adapted the output of our inhouse chunker (Grover and Tobin, 2006) to identify events for Task B, which requires systems to identify event denoting words and to compute a range of attributes for them. In future work we will adapt our machine-learning-based relation extraction component (Haddow, 2008) to recognise relations between spatial and temporal entities and event entities along the lines of the linking tasks.

2 The Edinburgh IE System

Our IE system is a modular pipeline system built around the LT-XML2[1] and LT-TTT2[2] toolsets. Documents are converted into our internal document format and are then passed through a sequence of linguistic components which each add XML mark-up. Early stages identify paragraphs, sentences and tokens. Part-of-speech (POS) tagging is done using the C&C tagger (Curran and Clark, 2003a) and lemmatisation is done using morpha (Minnen et al., 2000).

We use both rule-based and machine-learning named entity recognition (NER) components, the former implemented using LT-TTT2 and the latter using the C&C maximum entropy NER tagger (Curran and Clark, 2003b). We are experimenting to find the best combination of the two different NER views but this is not an issue in the case of date and time entities since we have taken the decision to use the rule-based output for these. The main motivation for this decision arises from the need to ground (provide temporal values for) these entities and the rules for the grounding are most naturally implemented as an elaboration of the rules for recognition.

Our IE pipeline also uses the LT-TTT2 chunker to provide a very shallow syntactic analysis. Figure 1 shows an example of the results of processing at the point where the rule-based NER and chunker have both applied. As can be seen from Figure 1, a positive feature for TempEval-2 is that the verb group analysis provides information about tense, aspect, voice, modality and polarity which translate relatively straightforwardly into the Task B attributes. The noun group analysis provides verbal stem information (e.g.

[1]www.ltg.ed.ac.uk/software/ltxml2
[2]www.ltg.ed.ac.uk/software/lt-ttt2

Proceedings of the 5th International Workshop on Semantic Evaluation, ACL 2010, pages 333–336,
Uppsala, Sweden, 15-16 July 2010.

```
<s id="s1">
 <ng>
  <w p="DT" id="w13">The</w>
  <w p="NN" id="w17" l="announcement" vstem="announce" headn="yes">announcement</w>
 </ng>
 <vg tense="pres" voice="pass" asp="simple" modal="yes" neg="yes">
  <w p="MD" id="w30" pws="yes" l="must" neg="yes">must</w>
  <w p="RB" id="w35" pws="yes" neg="yes">not</w>
  <w p="VB" id="w39" pws="yes" l="be">be</w>
  <w p="VBN" id="w42" pws="yes" l="make" headv="yes">made</w>
 </vg>
 <ng>
  <timex unit="day" trel="same" type="date" id="rb1">
   <w unit="day" trel="same" p="NN" id="w47" l="today">today</w>
  </timex>
 </ng>
 <w p="." id="w52" sb="true">.</w>
</s>
```

Figure 1: Example of NER tagger and chunker output for the sentence "The announcement must not be made today."

vstem="announce") about nominalisations.

Various attributes are computed for <timex> elements and these are used by a temporal resolution component to provide a grounding for them. The final output of the IE pipeline contains entity mark-up in "standoff" format where the entities point at the word elements using ids. The date and event entities for "made" and "today" are as follows:

```
<ent tense="pres" voice="pass" neg="yes"
     modal="yes" asp="simple" id="ev1"
     subtype="make" type="event">
  <parts>
    <part ew="w39" sw="w39">made</part>
  </parts>
</ent>

<ent wdaynum="5" day="Friday" date="16"
     month="4" year="2010" unit="day"
     day-number="733877" trel="same"
     type="date" id="rb1">
  <parts>
    <part ew="w47" sw="w47">today</part>
  </parts>
</ent>
```

The date entity has been grounded with respect to the date of writing (16th April 2010). To do the grounding we calculate a day-number value for each date where the day number count starts from 1st January 1 AD. Using this unique day number we are able to calculate the date for any given day number as well as the day of the week. We use the day number to perform simple arithmetic to ground date expressions such as "last Monday", "the day after tomorrow" etc. Grounding information is spread across the attributes for day, date, month and year. A fully grounded date has a value for all of these while an underspecified date, e.g. "2009", "March 13th", "next year", etc., only has values for some of these attributes.

3 Adaptations for TempEval-2

Our system has been developed independently of TimeML or TempEval-2 and there is therefore a gap between what our system outputs and what is contained in the TempEval-2 data. In order to run our system over the data we needed to convert it into our XML input format while preserving the tokenisation decisions from the original. Certain tokenisation mismatches required that we extend various rules to allow for alternative token boundaries, for example, we tokenise "wasn't" as was + n't whereas the TempEval-2 data contains was + n + 't or occasionally wasn + 't.

Other adaptations fall broadly into two classes: extension of our system to cover entities in TempEval-2 that we didn't previously recognise, and mapping of our output to fit TempEval-2 requirements.

3.1 Extensions

The date and time entities that our system recognises are more like the MUC7 TIMEX entities (Chinchor, 1998) than TIMEX3 ones. In particular, we have focused on dates which can either be fully grounded or which, though underspecified, can be grounded to a precise range, e.g. "last month" can be grounded to a particular month and year given a document creation date and it can be precisely specified if we take it to express a range from the first to last days of the month. TIMEX3 entities can be vaguer than this, for example, entities of type DURATION such as "twenty years", "some time", etc. can be recognised as denoting a temporal period but cannot easily be grounded. To align our output more closely to TempEval-2, we added NER rules to recognise examples such as "a long time", "recent years", "the past", "years", "some weeks", "10 minutes". In addition we needed to compute appropriate information to allow us to create TempEval-2 values such as `P1W` (period of 1 week).

For event recognition, our initial system created an event entity for every head verb and for every head noun which was a nominalisation. This simple approach goes a long way towards capturing the TempEval-2 events but results in too many false positives and false negatives for nouns. In addition our system did not calculate the information needed to compute the TempEval-2 class attribute. To help improve performance we added attributes to potential event entities based on look-up in lexicons compiled from the training data and from WordNet (Fellbaum, 1998). These attributes contribute to the decision as to whether a noun or verb chunk head should be an event entity or not[3]. The lexicons derived from the training data contain the stems of all the nouns which acted more than once as events as well as information about those predicates which occurred more than once as class ASPECTUAL, I_STATE, REPORTING or STATE in the training data. Where look-up succeeds for event, if class look-up also succeeds then the class attribute is set accordingly. If class look-up fails, the default, OCCURRENCE, is used. The WordNet derived lexicon contains information about whether the first sense of a noun has event or state as a hypernym. As a result of the lexical look-up stage, the noun "work", for example, is marked as having occurred in the training data as an event and as having event as a hypernym for its first sense. The conjunction of these cause it to be considered to be an event entity. For verbs, the only substantive change in our system was to not consider as events all main verb uses of "be" (be happy), "have" (have a meal) and "do" (do the dishes).

3.2 Mapping

For both timex and event entities the creation of the extents files was a straightforward mapping. For the creation of the attributes files, on the other hand, we used stylesheets to construct appropriate values for the TempEval-2 attributes based on the attributes in our output XML. The construction of event attributes is not overly complex: for example, where an event entity is specified as `tense="nonfin"` and `voice="pass"` the TempEval-2 tense attribute is given the value PASTPART. For modality our attribute only records whether a modal verb is present or not, so it was necessary to set the TempEval-2 modality attribute to the actual modal verb inside the verb group.

For timex entities, a single value for the value attribute had to be constructed from the values of a set of attributes on our entity. For example, the information in `date="16", month="4" year="2010"` has to be converted to 2010-04-16. For durations other attributes provide the relevant information, for example for "two days" the attributes `unit="day", quty="2"` are used to create the value P2D (period of 2 days).

4 Evaluation and Error Analysis

The recognition results for both timex and event extents are shown in Table 1. For Task A (timex) we achieved a close balance between precision and recall, while for Task B (events) we erred towards recall at some cost to precision.

Task	Precision	Recall	F1
Task A	0.85	0.82	0.84
Task B	0.75	0.85	0.80

Table 1: Extent Results

For timex entities our false negatives were all entities of the vaguest kind, for example, "10-hour", "currently", "third-quarter", "overnight", "the week": these are ones which the original system did not recognise and for which we added extra rules, though evidently we were not thorough enough. The false positives were mostly of the kind that would usually be a date entity but which were not considered to be so in the key, for example, "1969", "Oct 25", "now", "the past", "a few days". In two cases the system mistakenly identified numbers as times ("1.02", "2.41").

For event entities we had 73 false negatives. Some of these were caused by verbs being mistagged as nouns ("complies", "stretch", "suit") while others were nouns which didn't occur in the WordNet derived lexicon as events. There were 143 event false positives. Some of these are clearly wrong, for example, "destruction" in "weapons of mass destruction" while others are a consequence of the subtle distinctions that the TempEval-2 guidelines make and which our shallow approach cannot easily mimic.

Table 2 shows the results for attribute detection for both tasks. In the case of timex attributes

[3] Our system does not recognise adjective events. However, passive participles, which are sometimes treated as adjectives in TempEval-2, are frequently treated as verbs in our system and are therefore recognised.

Task	Attribute	Score
Task A	type	0.84
	value	0.63
Task B	polarity	0.99
	pos	0.97
	modality	0.99
	tense	0.92
	aspect	0.98
	class	0.76

Table 2: Attribute Results

there was a set of entities which had systematically wrong values for both type and value: these were dates such as "this week" and "last week". These should have had DATE as their type and a value such as 1998-W19 to indicate exactly which week in which year they denote. Our date grounding does not currently cover the numbering of weeks in a year and so it would not have been possible to create appropriate values. Instead we incorrectly treated these entities as being of type DURATION with value P1W. Many of the remaining errors were value errors where the system resolved relative dates as past references when they should have been future or vice versa. For example, the value for "Monday" in "He and Palestinian leader Yasser Arafat meet separately Monday with ..." should have been 1998-05-04 but our system interpreted it as the past Monday, 1998-04-27. There were a few cases where the value was correct but insufficient, for example for "a year ago" the system returned 1988 when it should have produced 1988-Q3.

Our scores for event attributes were high for all attributes except for class. The high scoring attributes were derived from the output of our chunker and demonstrate the quality of this component. There does not appear to be a particular pattern behind the small number of errors for these attributes except that errors for the pos attribute reflect POS tagger errors and there were some combined tense and modality errors where "will" and "would" should have been interpreted as future tense but were instead treated as modals. The class attribute represents information that our system had not previously been designed to determine. We computed the class attribute in a relatively minimal way. Since the class value is OCCURRENCE in nearly 60% of events in the training data, we use this as the default but, as described in Section 3, we override this for events which are in our training data-derived lexicon as REPORTING, ASPECTUAL, I_STATE or STATE. We do not attempt to assign the I_ACTION class value and nearly half of our class errors result from this. Another set of errors comes from missing REPORTING events such as "alleging", "telegraphed" and "acknowledged".

Acknowledgements

The current phase of development of the Edinburgh IE system is supported by the SYNC3 project (FP7-231854)[4].

References

Beatrice Alex, Claire Grover, Barry Haddow, Mijail Kabadjov, Ewan Klein, Michael Matthews, Richard Tobin, and Xinglong Wang. 2008. Automating curation using a natural language processing pipeline. *Genome Biology*, 9(Suppl 2).

Nancy A. Chinchor. 1998. *Proceedings of the Seventh Message Understanding Conference (MUC-7).* Fairfax, Virginia.

James R. Curran and Stephen Clark. 2003a. Investigating GIS and smoothing for maximum entropy taggers. In *Proceedings of the 11th Meeting of the European Chapter of the Association for Computational Linguistics (EACL-03)*, pages 91–98. Budapest, Hungary.

James R. Curran and Stephen Clark. 2003b. Language independent NER using a maximum entropy tagger. In *Proceedings of the 7th Conference on Natural Language Learning*, Edmonton, Alberta, Canada.

Christiane Fellbaum, editor. 1998. *WordNet: An Electronic Lexical Database.* MIT Press, Cambridge, MA.

Claire Grover and Richard Tobin. 2006. Rule-based chunking and reusability. In *Proceedings of the Fifth International Conference on Language Resources and Evaluation (LREC 2006).*

Claire Grover, Richard Tobin, Kate Byrne, Matthew Woollard, James Reid, Stuart Dunn, and Julian Ball. 2010. Use of the Edinburgh geoparser for georeferencing digitised historical collections. *Phil. Trans. R. Soc. A.*

Barry Haddow. 2008. Using automated feature optimisation to create an adaptable relation extraction system. In *Proc. of BioNLP 2008*, Columbus, Ohio.

Guido Minnen, John Carroll, and Darren Pearce. 2000. Robust, applied morphological generation. In *Proceedings of the 1st International Natural Language Generation Conference*, Mitzpe Ramon, Israel.

Richard Tobin, Claire Grover, Kate Byrne, James Reid, and Jo Walsh. 2010. Evaluation of georeferencing. In *Proceedings of Workshop on Geographic Information Retrieval (GIR'10).*

[4] http://www.sync3.eu/

USFD2: Annotating Temporal Expresions and TLINKs for TempEval-2

Leon Derczynski
Dept of Computer Science
University of Sheffield
Regent Court
211 Portobello
Sheffield S1 4DP, UK
leon@dcs.shef.ac.uk

Robert Gaizauskas
Dept of Computer Science
University of Sheffield
Regent Court
211 Portobello
Sheffield S1 4DP, UK
robertg@dcs.shef.ac.uk

Abstract

We describe the University of Sheffield system used in the TempEval-2 challenge, USFD2. The challenge requires the automatic identification of temporal entities and relations in text.

USFD2 identifies and anchors temporal expressions, and also attempts two of the four temporal relation assignment tasks. A rule-based system picks out and anchors temporal expressions, and a maximum entropy classifier assigns temporal link labels, based on features that include descriptions of associated temporal signal words. USFD2 identified temporal expressions successfully, and correctly classified their type in 90% of cases. Determining the relation between an event and time expression in the same sentence was performed at 63% accuracy, the second highest score in this part of the challenge.

1 Introduction

The TempEval-2 (Pustejovsky and Verhagen, 2009) challenge proposes six tasks. Our system tackles three of these: task A – identifying time expressions, assigning TIMEX3 attribute values, and anchoring them; task C – determining the temporal relation between an event and time in the same sentence; and task E – determining the temporal relation between two main events in consecutive sentences. For our participation in the task, we decided to employ both rule- and ML-classifier-based approaches. Temporal expressions are dealt with by sets of rules and regular expressions, and relation labelling performed by NLTK's[1] maximum entropy classifier with rule-based processing applied during feature generation. The features (described in full in Section 2) included attributes from the TempEval-2 training data annotation, augmented by features that can be directly derived from the annotated texts. There are two main aims of this work: (1) to create a rule-based temporal expression annotator that includes knowledge from work published since GUTime (Mani and Wilson, 2000) and measure its performance, and (2) to measure the performance of a classifier that includes features based on temporal signals.

Our entry to the challenge, USFD2, is a successor to USFD (Hepple et al., 2007). In the rest of this paper, we will describe how USFD2 is constructed (Section 2), and then go on to discuss its overall performance and the impact of some internal parameters on specific TempEval tasks. Regarding classifiers, we found that despite using identical feature sets across relation classification tasks, performance varied significantly. We also found that USFD2 performance trends with TempEval-2 did not match those seen when classifiers were trained on other data while performing similar tasks. The paper closes with comments about future work.

2 System Description

The TempEval-2 training and test sets are partitioned into data for entity recognition and description, and data for temporal relation classification. We will first discuss our approach for temporal expression recognition, description and anchoring, and then discuss our approach to two of the relation labelling tasks.

2.1 Identifying, describing and anchoring temporal expressions

Task A of TempEval-2 requires the identification of temporal expressions (or **timex**es) by defining a start and end boundary for each expression, and assigning an ID to it. After this, systems should attempt to describe the temporal expression, determining its type and value (described below).

[1] See http://www.nltk.org/ .

Proceedings of the 5th International Workshop on Semantic Evaluation, ACL 2010, pages 337–340,
Uppsala, Sweden, 15-16 July 2010.

Our timex recogniser works by building a set of n-grams from the data to be annotated ($1 \leq n \leq 5$), and comparing each n-gram against a hand-crafted set of regular expressions. This approach has been shown to achieve high precision, with recall increasing in proportion to ruleset size (Han et al., 2006; Mani and Wilson, 2000; Ahn et al., 2005). The recogniser chooses the largest possible sequence of words that could be a single temporal expression, discarding any sub-parts that independently match any of our set of regular expressions. The result is a set of boundary-pairs that describe temporal expression locations within documents. This part of the system achieved 0.84 precision and 0.79 recall, for a balanced f1-measure of 0.82.

The next part of the task is to assign a type to each temporal expression. These can be one of `TIME`, `DATE`, `DURATION`, or `SET`. USFD2 only distinguishes between `DATE` and `DURATION` timexes. If the words *for* or *during* occur in the three words before the timex, the timex ends with an *s* (such as in *seven years*), or the timex is a bi-gram whose first token is *a* (e.g. in *a month*), then the timex is deemed to be of type `DURATION`; otherwise it is a `DATE`. These three rules for determining type were created based on observation of output over the test data, and are correct 90% of the time with the evaluation data.

The final part of task A is to provide a value for the timex. As we only annotate `DATE`s and `DURATION`s, these will be either a fixed calendrical reference in the format YYYY-MM-DD, or a duration in according to the TIMEX2 standard (Ferro et al., 2005). Timex strings of *today* or *now* were assigned the special value `PRESENT_REF`, which assumes that *today* is being used in a literal and not figurative manner, an assumption which holds around 90% of the time in newswire text (Ahn et al., 2005) such as that provided for TempEval-2. In an effort to calculate a temporal distance from the document creation time (DCT), USFD2 then checks to see if numeric words (e.g. *one*, *seven hundred*) are in the timex, as well as words like *last* or *next* which determine temporal offset direction. This distance figure supplies either the second parameter to a `DURATION` value, or helps calculate DCT offset. Strings that describe an imprecise amount, such as *few*, are represented in duration values with an `X`, as per the TIMEX2 standard. We next search the timex for temporal unit strings (e.g. *quarter*, *day*).

Table 1: Features used by USFD2 to train a temporal relation classifier.

Feature	Type
For events	
Tense	String
Aspect	String
Polarity	pos or neg
Modality	String
For timexes	
Type	Timex type
Value	String
Describing signals	
Signal text	String
Signal hint	Relation type
Arg 1 before signal?	Boolean
Signal before Arg 2?	Boolean
For every relation	
Arguments are same tense	Boolean
Arguments are same aspect	Boolean
Arg 1 before Arg 2?	Boolean
For every interval	
Token number in sentence / 5	Integer
Text annotated	String
Interval type	event or timex

This helps build either a duration length or an offset. If we are anchoring a date, the offset is applied to DCT, and date granularity adjusted according to the coarsest temporal primitive present – for example, if DCT is 1997-06-12 and our timex is *six months ago*, a value of 1997-01 is assigned, as it is unlikely that the temporal expression refers to the day precisely six months ago, unless followed by the word *today*.

Where weekday names are found, we used Baldwin's 7-day window (Baldwin, 2002) to anchor these to a calendrical timeline. This technique has been found to be accurate over 94% of the time with newswire text (Mazur and Dale, 2008). Where dates are found that do not specify a year or a clear temporal direction marker (e.g., *April 17* vs. *last July*), our algorithm counts the number of days between DCT and the next occurrence of that date. If this is over a limit f, then the date is assumed to be last year. This is a very general rule and does not take into account the tendency of very-precisely-described dates to be closer to DCT, and far off dates to be loosely specified. An f of 14 days gives the highest performance based on the TempEval-2 training data.

Anchoring dates / specifying duration lengths was the most complex part of task A and our naïve rule set was correct only 17% of the time.

Table 2: A sample of signals and the TempEval-2 temporal relation they suggest.

Signal phrase	Suggested relation
previous	AFTER
ahead of	BEFORE
so far	OVERLAP
thereafter	BEFORE
in anticipation of	BEFORE
follows	AFTER
since then	BEFORE
soon after	AFTER
as of	OVERLAP-OR-AFTER
throughout	OVERLAP

2.2 Labelling temporal relations

Our approach for labelling temporal relations (or **TLINK**s) is based on NLTK's maximum entropy classifier, using the feature sets initially proposed in Mani et al. (2006). Features that describe temporal signals have been shown to give a 30% performance boost in TLINKs that employ a signal (Derczynski and Gaizauskas, 2010). Thus, the features in Mani et al. (2006) are augmented with those used to describe signals detailed in Derczynski and Gaizauskas (2010), with some slight changes. Firstly, as there are no specific TLINK/signal associations in the TempEval-2 data (unlike TimeBank (Pustejovsky et al., 2003)), USFD2 needs to perform signal identification and then associate signals with a temporal relation between two events or timexes. Secondly, a look-up list is used to provide TLINK label hints based on a signal word. A list of features employed by USFD2 is in Table 1.

We used a simplified version of the approach in Cheng et al. (2007) to identify signal words. This involved the creation of a list of signal phrases that occur in TimeBank with a frequency of 2 or more, and associating a signal from this list with a temporal entity if it is in the same sentence and clause. The textually nearest signal is chosen in the case of conflict.

As this list of signal phrases only contained 42 entries, we also decided to define a "most-likely" temporal relation for each signal. This was done by imagining a short sentence of the form *event1 – signal – event2*, and describing the type of relation between event 1 and event 2. An excerpt from these entries is shown in Table 2. The hint from this table was included as a feature. Determining whether or not to invert the suggested relation type based on word order was left to the classifier, which is already provided with word order features. It would be possible to build these suggestions from data such as TimeBank, but a number of problems stand in the way; the TimeML and TempEval-2 relation types are not identical, word order often affects the actual relationship type suggested by a signal (e.g. compare *He ran home before he showered* and *Before he ran home, he showered*), and noise in mined data is a problem with the low corpus occurrence frequency of most signals.

This approach was used for both the intra-sentence timex/event TLINK labelling task and also the task of labelling relations between main events in adjacent sentences.

3 Discussion

USFD2's rule-based element for timex identification and description performs well, even achieving above-average recall despite a much smaller rule set than comparable and more complex systems. However, the temporal anchoring component performs less strongly. The "all-or-nothing" metric employed for evaluating the annotation of timex values gives non-strict matches a zero score (e.g. if the expected answer is 1990-05-14, no reward is given for 1990-05) even if values are close, which many were.

In previous approaches that used a maximum entropy classifier and comparable feature set (Mani et al., 2006; Derczynski and Gaizauskas, 2010), the accuracy of event-event relation classification was higher than that of event-timex classification. Contrary to this, USFD2's event-event classification of relations between main events of successive sentences (Task E) was less accurate than the classification of event-timex relations between events and timexes in the same sentence (Task C). Accuracy in Task C was good (63%), despite the lack of explicit signal/TLINK associations and the absence of a sophisticated signal recognition and association mechanism. This is higher than USFD2's accuracy in Task E (45%) though the latter is a harder task, as most TempEval-2 systems performed significantly worse at this task than event/timex relation classification.

Signal information was not relied on by many TempEval 2007 systems (Min et al. (2007) discusses signals to some extent but the system described only includes a single feature – the signal text), and certainly no processing of this data was performed for that challenge. USFD2 begins to leverage this information, and gives very competitive performance at event/timex classification. In this case, the signals provided an increase from 61.5% to 63.1% predictive accuracy in task C. The small size of the improvement might be due to the crude and unevaluated signal identification and association system that we implemented.

The performance of classifier based approaches to temporal link labelling seems to be levelling off – the 60%-70% relation labelling accuracy of work such as Mani et al. (2006) has not been greatly exceeded. This performance level is still the peak of the current generation of systems. Recent improvements, while employing novel approaches to the task that rely on constraints between temporal link types or on complex linguistic information beyond that describable by TimeML attributes, still yield marginal improvements (e.g. Yoshikawa et al. (2009)). It seems that to break through this performance "wall", we need to continue to innovate with and discuss temporal relation labelling, using information and knowledge from many sources to build practical high-performance systems.

4 Conclusion

In this paper, we have presented USFD2, a novel system that annotates temporal expressions and temporal links in text. The system relies on new hand-crafted rules, existing rule sets, machine learning and temporal signal information to make its decisions. Although some of the TempEval-2 tasks are difficult, USFD2 manages to create good and useful annotations of temporal information. USFD2 is available via Google Code[2].

Acknowledgments

Both authors are grateful for the efforts of the TempEval-2 team and appreciate their hard work. The first author would like to acknowledge the UK Engineering and Physical Science Research Council for support in the form of a doctoral studentship.

[2]See http://code.google.com/p/usfd2/ .

References

D. Ahn, S.F. Adafre, and MD Rijke. 2005. Towards task-based temporal extraction and recognition. In *Dagstuhl Seminar Proceedings*, volume 5151.

J.A. Baldwin. 2002. *Learning temporal annotation of French news*. Ph.D. thesis, Georgetown University.

Y. Cheng, M. Asahara, and Y. Matsumoto. 2007. Temporal relation identification using dependency parsed tree. In *Proceedings of the 4th International Workshop on Semantic Evaluations*, pages 245–248.

L. Derczynski and R. Gaizauskas. 2010. Using signals to improve automatic classification of temporal relations. In *Proceedings of the ESSLLI StuS*. Submitted.

L. Ferro, L. Gerber, I. Mani, B. Sundheim, and G. Wilson. 2005. TIDES 2005 standard for the annotation of temporal expressions. Technical report, MITRE.

B. Han, D. Gates, and L. Levin. 2006. From language to time: A temporal expression anchorer. In *Temporal Representation and Reasoning (TIME)*, pages 196–203.

M. Hepple, A. Setzer, and R. Gaizauskas. 2007. USFD: preliminary exploration of features and classifiers for the TempEval-2007 tasks. In *Proceedings of SemEval-2007*, pages 438–441.

I. Mani and G. Wilson. 2000. Robust temporal processing of news. In *Proceedings of the 38th Annual Meeting on ACL*, pages 69–76. ACL.

I. Mani, M. Verhagen, B. Wellner, C.M. Lee, and J. Pustejovsky. 2006. Machine learning of temporal relations. In *Proceedings of the 21st International Conference on Computational Linguistics*, page 760. ACL.

P. Mazur and R. Dale. 2008. Whats the date? High accuracy interpretation of weekday. In *22nd International Conference on Computational Linguistics (Coling 2008), Manchester, UK*, pages 553–560.

C. Min, M. Srikanth, and A. Fowler. 2007. LCC-TE: a hybrid approach to temporal relation identification in news text. In *Proceedings of the 4th International Workshop on Semantic Evaluations*, pages 219–222.

J. Pustejovsky and M. Verhagen. 2009. SemEval-2010 task 13: evaluating events, time expressions, and temporal relations (TempEval-2). In *Proceedings of the Workshop on Semantic Evaluations*, pages 112–116. ACL.

J. Pustejovsky, P. Hanks, R. Sauri, A. See, R. Gaizauskas, A. Setzer, D. Radev, D. Day, L. Ferro, et al. 2003. The Timebank Corpus. In *Corpus Linguistics*, volume 2003, page 40.

K. Yoshikawa, S. Riedel, M. Asahara, and Y. Matsumoto. 2009. Jointly identifying temporal relations with markov logic. In *IJCNLP: Proceedings of 47th Annual Meeting of the ACL*, pages 405–413.

NCSU: Modeling Temporal Relations with Markov Logic and Lexical Ontology

Eun Young Ha **Alok Baikadi** **Carlyle Licata** **James C. Lester**
Department of Computer Science
North Carolina State University
Raleigh, NC, USA
{eha,abaikad,cjlicata,lester}@ncsu.edu

Abstract

As a participant in TempEval-2, we address the temporal relations task consisting of four related subtasks. We take a supervised machine-learning technique using Markov Logic in combination with rich lexical relations beyond basic and syntactic features. One of our two submitted systems achieved the highest score for the Task F (66% precision), untied, and the second highest score (63% precision) for the Task C, which tied with three other systems.

1 Introduction

Time plays a key role in narrative. However, correctly recognizing temporal order among events is a challenging task. As a follow-up to the first TempEval competition, TempEval-2 addresses this challenge. Among the three proposed tasks of TempEval-2, we address the temporal relations task consisting of four subtasks: predicting temporal relations that hold between events and time expressions in the same sentence (Task C), events and the document creation time (Task D), main events in adjacent sentences (Task E), and main events and syntactically dominated events, such as those in subordinated clauses (Task F). We are primarily concerned with Task C, E, and F, because D is not relevant to our application domain.[1] However, rather than eliminating Task D altogether, we build a very simple model for this task by using only those features that are shared with other task models (i.e., the document creation time data are not used because none of the other task models need them as features). It was expected that this approach would support more interesting comparisons with other systems that take a more sophisticated approach to the task. Further, we experiment with a joint modeling technique to examine if the communication with other task models brings a boost to a performance of the simple model.

Taking a supervised machine-learning approach with *Markov Logic (ML)* (Richardson and Domingos, 2006), we constructed two systems, NCSU-INDI and NCSU-JOINT. NCSU-INDI consists of four independently trained classifiers, one for each task, whereas NCSU-JOINT models all four tasks jointly. The choice of ML as learning technique for temporal relations is motivated both theoretically and practically. Theoretically, it is a statistical relational learning framework that does not make the *i.i.d.* assumption for the data. This is a desirable characteristic for complex problems such as temporal relation classification, as well as many other natural language problems, in which the features representing a given problem are often correlated with one another. Practically, ML allows us to build both individual and joint models in a uniform framework; individual models can be easily combined together into a joint model with a set of global formulae governing over them.

In previous work (Yoshikawa et al., 2009), ML was successfully applied to temporal relation classification task. Our approach is different from this work in two primary respects. First, we introduce new lexical relation features derived from English lexical ontologies. Second, our model addresses a new task introduced in TempEval-2, which is to identify temporal relations between main and syntactically dominated events in the same sentence. We also employ phrase-based syntactic features (Bethard and

[1] Our application domain concerns analysis of narrative stories written by middle school students, with the analysis being conducted a single story at a time.

Proceedings of the 5th International Workshop on Semantic Evaluation, ACL 2010, pages 341–344,
Uppsala, Sweden, 15-16 July 2010.

Martin 2007) rather than dependency-based syntactic features.

2 Features

We consider three types of features: basic, syntactic, and lexical relation features. Basic features represent the information directly available from the original data provided by the task organizer; syntactic features are extracted from syntactic parses generated by Charniak parser (Charniak, 2000); and lexical semantic relations that are derived from two external lexical databases, VERBOCEAN (Chklovski and Pantel, 2004) and WordNet (Fellbaum, 1998).

2.1 Basic Features

Basic features include the word tokens, stems of the words, and the manually annotated attributes of events and time expressions. In the TempEval-2 data, an event always consists of a single word token, but time expressions often consist of multiple tokens. We treat each word in time expressions as a different feature. For example, two word features, *'this'* and *'afternoon'*, are extracted from a given time expression *'this afternoon'*. Stemming is done with the Porter Stemmer in NLTK (Loper and Bird, 2002). The value attributes of time expressions are treated as symbolic features, rather than being decomposed into actual integer values representing dates and times.

2.2 Syntactic Features

Our syntactic features draw upon the features previously shown to be effective for temporal relation classification (Bethard and Martin, 2007), including the following:

- `pos`: the part-of-speech (pos) tags of the event and the time expression word tokens, assigned by Charniak parser.
- `gov-prep`: any prepositions governing the event or time expression (e.g., *'for'* in *'for ten years'*).
- `gov-verb`: the verb governing the event or time expression, similar to *gov-prep*.
- `gov-verb-pos`: the *pos* tag of the governing verb.

We also investigate both full and partial syntactic paths between a pair of event and time expressions, but including these features does not improve the classification results on our development data set.

2.3 Lexical Relation Features

VERBOCEAN is a graph of semantic relations between verbs. There are 22,306 relations between 3,477 verbs that have been mined using Google searches for lexico-syntactic patterns. VERBOCEAN contains five different types of relations (Table 1). Verbs are stored in the lemmatized forms and senses are not disambiguated. A connection between two verbs indicates that the relation holds between some senses of the verbs.

VERBOCEAN'S database is presented as a list of verb pair relations, along with a confidence score. Both the transitive and symmetric closure over the relations were taken before storage in a SQLite database for queries. The transitive closure was calculated using the Warshall algorithm (Agrawal and Jagadish, 1990). The confidence score for the new arc was calculated as the average of the two constituents. The symmetric closure was calculated using a simple pass. The confidence score is the same as the reflected edge for symmetric relations. A set of VERBOCEAN features were calculated for each target event pair within each of the temporal relations tasks. Each verb was lemmatized using the WordNet lemmatizer in NLTK before being compared against the database. Rather than focusing only on HAPPENS-BEFORE relation as in Mani et al. (2006), we consider all five verb relations in two different versions, unweighted and weighted. The unweighted version is a binary feature indicating the existence of an arc between the two target verbs in VERBOCEAN. In the weighted version, the existence of an arc is weighted by the associated confidence score.

In addition to VerbOcean, WordNet was used for its conceptual relations. WordNet is a large lexical database, which contains information on verbs, nouns, adjectives and adverbs, grouped into hierarchically organized cognitive synonym

Relation	Example
SIMILARITY ‡†	*produce* :: *create*
STRENGTH †	*wound* :: *kill*
ANTONYMY ‡	*open* :: *close*
ENABLEMENT	*fight* :: *win*
HAPPENS-BEFORE †	*buy* :: *own*

Table 1: Semantic relations between verbs in VERBOCEAN (‡ and † denotes symmetric and transitive closure, respectively, holds for the given relation)[2]

[2] Examples are taken from http://demo.patrickpantel.com/Content/Verbocean/.

sets (*synsets*). WordNet was accessed through the WordNetCorpusReader module of NLTK. For each target event pair within each of the temporal relations tasks, a semantic distance between the associated tokens was computed using the path-similarity metric present within the API. The *synset* chosen was simply the first synset returned by the reader. Similar to the VERBOCEAN features, we consider both unweighted and weighted versions of the feature.

3 The Systems

ML is a probabilistic extension of first-order logic that allows formulae to be violated. It assigns a weight to each formula, reflecting the strength of the constraint represented by the formula. A *Markov logic network (MLN)* is a set of weighted first-order clauses, which, together with constants, defines a Markov network. We constructed two systems, NCSU-INDI and NCSU-JOINT using an off-the-shelf tool for ML (Riedel, 2008).

3.1 NCSU-INDI

NCSU-INDI consists of four independently trained MLNs, one for each task. Each MLN is defined by a set of local formulae that are conjunctions of predicates representing the features. An example local formula used for Task C is

$$eventTimex(e, t) \wedge eventWord(e, w) \rightarrow relEventTimex(e, t, r) \quad (1)$$

If a pair of event *e* and time expression *t* exists and the event consists of a word token *w*, formula (1) assigns a temporal relation *t* to the given pair of *e* and *t* with some weights.

For each task, the features described in Section 2 were examined on a held-out development data set (about 10% of the training data) for their effectiveness in predicting temporal relations and removed if they do not improve the results. Table 2 lists the features actually used for the tasks. Interestingly, none of the time expression features were effective on the development data.

3.2 NCSU-JOINT

As well as the local formulae from the four local MLNs, a set of global formulae are added to NCSU-JOINT as hard constraints to ensure the consistency between the classification decisions of local MLNs. For example, formula (2) ensures that if an event *e1* happens before the document creation time (*dct*) and another event *e2* happens after *dct*, then *e1* happens before *e2* and vice versa.

$$relDctEvent(e1,t,\text{BEFORE}) \wedge relDctEvent(e2,t,\text{ AFTER}) \rightarrow relEvents(e1, e2, \text{BEFORE}) \quad (2)$$

A set of global constraints is defined between Tasks C and F, D and F, as well as D and E, respectively.

Feature		Task C	Task D	Task E	Task F
Event	*event-word*	√	√	$\surd_{e2}$	$\surd_{e1,e2}$
	event-stem	√	√	$\surd_{e1.e2}$	$\surd_{e1,e2}$
Event Attribute	*event-polarity*	√	√	$\surd_{e1.e2}$	$\surd_{e1,e2}$
	event-modal	√	√	$\surd_{e1.e2}$	$\surd_{e1,e2}$
	event-pos	√	√	$\surd_{e1.e2}$	$\surd_{e2}$
	event-tense	√		$\surd_{e1.e2}$	$\surd_{e1,e2}$
	event-aspect	√	√	$\surd_{e1.e2}$	$\surd_{e1,e2}$
	event-class	√	√	$\surd_{e1.e2}$	$\surd_{e1,e2}$
Timex	*timex-word*				
	timex-stem				
Timex Attribute	*timex-type*				
	timex-value				
Syntactic Parse	*pos*		$\surd_{e}$	$\surd_{e1.e2}$	
	gov-prep	$\surd_{e,t}$	$\surd_{e}$	$\surd_{e1.e2}$	$\surd_{e1,e2}$
	gov-verb	$\surd_{e,t}$	$\surd_{e}$	$\surd_{e1.e2}$	$\surd_{e1,e2}$
	gov-verb-pos	$\surd_{e,t}$		$\surd_{e1.e2}$	$\surd_{e1,e2}$
Verb-Ocean	*verb-rel*				√
	verb-rel-w			√	
WordNet	*word-dist*			√	
	word-dist-w				

Table 2: Features used for each task (subscripts *e* and *t* mean event and time expression, respectively. Subscripts *e1* and *e2* mean the first and the second main events for the Task E and the main and the syntactically dominated events for the Task F, respectively)

4 Results and Discussion

The predicted outputs from our systems exhibit mixed results. NCSU-INDI achieves the highest precision score on the test data for Task F by a relatively large margin (6%) from the second-place system, as well as the second highest precision score on Task C, tied with three other systems. Given the encouraging result for Task F, we would preliminarily conclude that the VEBOCEAN relations are effective predictors of temporal relations between main and syntactically dominated events. However, the same system does not achieve the same level of accuracy

System	Precision / Recall (%)			
	Task C	Task D	Task E	Task F
NCSU-INDI	63/63	68/68	48/48	66/66
NCSU-JOINT	62/62	21/21	51/51	25/25

Table 3: Accuracy of the systems on each task

for Task E, even though it is closely related to Task F. The major difference between the models of Task E and F is that the Task E model uses weighted VERBOCEAN relations along with a WordNet feature, while the Task F model uses unweighted VERBOCEAN relations without the WordNet feature. We suspect these two features might negatively impact the classification decisions on the test data, even though they preliminarily appeared to be effective predictors on the development data.

NCSU-JOINT also yields mixed results. The performance on both Task D and F dramatically drops with the joint modeling approach, while there is a modest improvement on Task E. Manual examination of the results on the test data revealed that the majority of the relations in Task D and F were classified as *OVERLAP*, which may be due to overly strict global constraints; rather than violating global constraints, the system resorted to rather neutral predictions.

5 Conclusions

Temporal event order recognition is a challenging task. Using basic, syntactic, and lexical relation features, we built two systems with ML: NCSU-INDI models each subtask independently, and NCSU-JOINT models all four tasks jointly. NCSU-INDI was most effective in predicting temporal relations between main events and syntactically dominated events (66% precision), as well as temporal relations between time expressions and events (63% precision). Future directions include conducting a more rigorous examination of the predictive power of the features, as well as the impact of global formulae for the joint model.

Acknowledgments
This research was supported by the National Science Foundation under Grant IIS-0757535. Any opinions, findings, and conclusions or recommendations expressed in this material are those of the authors and do not necessarily reflect the views of the National Science Foundation.

References

R. Agrawal, S. Dar, and H. V. Jagadish. 1990. Direct transitive closure algorithms: design and performance evaluation. *ACM Transactions on Database Systems*, 15(3): 427-458.

S. Bethard and J. H. Martin. 2007. CU-TMP: temporal relation classification using syntactic and semantic features. In *Proceedings of the 4th International Workshop on Semantic Evaluations*, pages 129-132, Prague, Czech Republic.

E. Charniak. 2000. A maximum-entropy-inspired parser. In *Proceedings of the 1st North American chapter of the Association for Computational Linguistics conference*, pages 132-139, Seattle, WA.

Y. Cheng, M. Asahara, and Y. Matsumoto. 2007. NAIST.Japan: Temporal relation identification using dependency parsed tree. In *Proceedings of the 4th International Workshop on Semantic Evaluations*, pages 245-248, Prague, Czech Republic.

T. Chklovski and P. Pantel. 2004.VerbOcean: Mining the Web for Fine-Grained Semantic Verb Relations. In *Proceedings of Conference on Empirical Methods in Natural Language Processing*, pages 33-40, Barcelona, Spain.

C. Fellbaum. 1998. *WordNet: An Electronic Lexical Database*. Cambridge, MA: MIT Press.

E. Loper and S. Bird. 2002. NLTK: The Natural Language Toolkit. In *Proceedings of ACL Workshop on Effective Tools and Methodologies for Teaching Natural Language Processing and Computational Linguistics*, pages 62–69, Philadelphia, PA.

I. Mani, M. Verhagen, B. Wellner, C. M. Lee, and J. Pustejovsky. 2006. Machine learning of temporal relations. In *Proceedings of the 21st International Conference on Computational Linguistics and the 44th annual meeting of the Association for Computational Linguistics*, pages 753-760, Sydney, Australia.

M. Richardson and P. Domingos. 2006. Markov Logic Networks. *Machine Learning*, 62(1): 107-136.

S. Riedel. 2008. Improving the accuracy and efficiency of MAP inference for Markov Logic. In *Proceedings of the 24th Conference in Uncertainty in Artificial Intelligence*, pages 468-475, Helsinki, Finland.

K. Yoshikawa, S. Riedel, M. Asahara, and Y. Matsumoto. 2009. Jointly Identifying Temporal Relations with Markov Logic. In *Proceedings of the Joint Conference of the 47th Annual Meeting of the ACL and the 4th International Joint Conference on Natural Language Processing of the AFNLP*, pages 405-413, Suntec, Singapore.

JU_CSE_TEMP: A First Step towards Evaluating Events, Time Expressions and Temporal Relations

Anup Kumar Kolya[1], Asif Ekbal[2] and Sivaji Bandyopadhyay[3]

[1,3]Department of Computer Science and Engineering, Jadavpur University, Kolkata-700032, India
[2]Department of Computational Linguistics, Heidelberg University, Heidelberg-69120, Germany
Email: anup.kolya@gmail.com[1], asif.ekbal@gmail.com[2] and sivaji_cse_ju@yahoo.com[3]

Abstract

Temporal information extraction is a popular and interesting research field in the area of Natural Language Processing (NLP). In this paper, we report our works on TempEval-2 shared task. This is our first participation and we participated in all the tasks, i.e., A, B, C, D, E and F. We develop rule-based systems for Tasks A and B, whereas the remaining tasks are based on a machine learning approach, namely Conditional Random Field (CRF). All our systems are still in their development stages, and we report the very initial results. Evaluation results on the shared task English datasets yield the precision, recall and F-measure values of 55%, 17% and 26%, respectively for Task A and 48%, 56% and 52%, respectively for Task B (event recognition). The rest of tasks, namely C, D, E and F were evaluated with a relatively simpler metric: the number of correct answers divided by the number of answers. Experiments on the English datasets yield the accuracies of 63%, 80%, 56% and 56% for tasks C, D, E and F, respectively.

1 Introduction

Temporal information extraction is, nowadays, a popular and interesting research area of Natural Language Processing (NLP). Generally, events are described in different newspaper texts, stories and other important documents where events happen in time and the temporal location and ordering of these events are specified. One of the important tasks of text analysis clearly requires identifying events described in a text and locating these in time. This is also important in a wide range of NLP applications that include temporal question answering, machine translation and document summarization.

In the literature, temporal relation identification based on machine learning approaches can be found in Boguraev et el. (2005), Mani et al. (2006), Chambers et al. (2007) and some of the TempEval 2007 participants (Verhagen et al., 2007). Most of these works tried to improve classification accuracies through feature engineering. The performance of any machine learning based system is often limited by the amount of available training data. Mani et al. (2006) introduced a temporal reasoning component that greatly expands the available training data. The training set was increased by a factor of 10 by computing the closure of the various temporal relations that exist in the training data. They reported significant improvement of the classification accuracies on event-event and event-time relations. Their experimental result showed the accuracies of 62.5%-94.95% and 73.68%-90.16% for event-event and event-time relations, respectively. However, this has two shortcomings, namely feature vector duplication caused by the data normalization process and the unrealistic evaluation scheme. The solutions to these issues are briefly described in Mani et al. (2007). In TempEval 2007 task, a common standard dataset was introduced that involves three temporal relations. The participants reported F-measure scores for event-event relations ranging from 42% to 55% and for event-time relations from 73% to 80%. Unlike (Mani et al., 2007; 2006), event-event temporal relations were not discourse-wide (i.e., *any* pair of events can be temporally linked) in TempEval 2007. Here, the event-event relations were restricted to events within two consecutive sentences. Thus, these two frameworks produced highly dissimilar re-

Proceedings of the 5th International Workshop on Semantic Evaluation, ACL 2010, pages 345–350,
Uppsala, Sweden, 15-16 July 2010.

sults for solving the problem of temporal relation classification.

In order to apply various machine learning algorithms, most of the authors formulated temporal relation as an event paired with a time or another event and translated these into a set of feature values. Some of the popularly used machine learning techniques were Naive-Bayes, Decision Tree (C5.0), Maximum Entropy (ME) and Support Vector Machine (SVM). Machine learning techniques alone cannot always yield good accuracies. To achieve reasonable accuracy, some researchers (Mao et al., 2006) used hybrid approach. The basic principle of hybrid approach is to combine the rule-based component with machine learning. It has been shown in (Mao et al., 2006) that classifiers make most mistakes near the decision plane in feature space. The authors carried out a series of experiments for each of the three tasks on four models, namely naive-Bayes, decision tree (C5.0), maximum entropy and support vector machine. The system was designed in such a way that they can take the advantage of rule-based as well as machine learning during final decision making. But, they did not explain exactly in what situations machine learning or rule based system should be used given a particular instance. They had the option to call either component on the fly in different situations so that they can take advantage of the two empirical approaches in an integrated way.

The rest of the paper is structured as follows. We present very brief descriptions of the different tasks in Section 2. Section 3 describes our approach in details with rule-based techniques for tasks A and B in Subsection 3.1, CRF based techniques in Subsection 3.2 for tasks C, D, E and F, and features in Subsection 3.3. Detailed evaluation results are reported in Section 4. Finally, Section 5 concludes the paper with a direction to future works.

2 Task Description

The main research in this area involves identification of all temporal referring expressions, events and temporal relations within a text. The main challenges involved in this task were first addressed during TempEval-1 in 2007 (Verhagen et al., 2007). This was an initial evaluation exercise based on three limited tasks that were considered realistic both from the perspective of assembling resources for development and testing and from the perspective of developing systems capable of addressing the tasks. In TempEval 2007, following types of event-time temporal relations were considered: **Task A** (relation between the events and times within the same sentence), **Task B** (relation between events and document creation time) and **Task C** (relation between verb events in adjacent sentences). The data sets were based on TimeBank, a hand-built gold standard of annotated texts using the TimeML markup scheme[1]. The data sets included sentence boundaries, timex3 tags (including the special document creation time tag), and event tags. For tasks A and B, a restricted set of events was used, namely those events that occur more than 5 times in TimeBank. For all three tasks, the relation labels used were before, after, overlap, before-or-overlap, overlap-or-after and vague. Six teams participated in the TempEval tasks. Three of the teams used statistics exclusively, one used a rule-based system and the other two employed a hybrid approach. For task A, the range of F-measure scores were from 0.34 to 0.62 for the *strict scheme* and from 0.41 to 0.63 for the *relaxed scheme*. For task B, the scores were from 0.66 to 0.80 (*strict*) and 0.71 to 0.81 (*relaxed*). Finally, task C scores range from 0.42 to 0.55 (*strict*) and from 0.56 to 0.66 (*relaxed*).

In TempEval-2, the following six tasks were proposed:

A: The main task was to determine the *extent of the time expressions* in a text as defined by the TimeML timex3 tag. In addition, values of the features *type* and *val* had to be determined. The possible values of *type* are time, date, duration, and set; the value of *val* is a normalized value as defined by the timex2 and timex3 standards.

B. Task was to determine the *extent of the events* in a text as defined by the TimeML event tag. In addition, the values of the features tense, aspect, polarity, and modality had to be determined.

C. Task was to determine the *temporal relation* between an *event* and a *time expression* in the same sentence.

D. *Temporal* relation between an *event* and the *document creation* time had to be determined.

E. *Temporal* relation between two *main events* in consecutive sentences had to be determined.

F. *Temporal relation* between two *events*, where one event syntactically dominates the other event.

In our present work, use handcrafted rules for Task A and Task B. All the other tasks, i.e., C, D, E and F are developed based on the well known statistical algorithm, Conditional Random

[1]www.timeml.org for details on TimeML

Field (CRF). For CRF, we use only those features that are available in the training data. All the systems are evaluated on the TempEval-2 shared task English datasets. Evaluation results yield the precision, recall and F-measure values of 55%, 17% and 26%, respectively for Task A and 48%, 56% and 52%, respectively for Task B. Experiments on the other tasks demonstrate the accuracies of 63%, 80%, 56% and 56% for C, D, E and F, respectively.

3 Our Approach

In this section, we present our systematic approach for *evaluating events*, *time expressions* and *temporal relations* as part of our first participation in the TempEval shared task. We participated in all the six tasks of TempEval-2. Rule-based systems are developed using a preliminary handcrafted set of rules for tasks A and B. We use machine learning approach, namely CRF for solving the remaining tasks, i.e., C, D, E and F.

3.1 Rules for Task A and Task B

We manually identify a set of rules studying the various features available in the training data. There were some exceptions to these rules. However, a rule is used if it is found to be correct most of the time throughout the training data. It is to be noted that these are the very preliminary rules, and we are still working on finding out more robust rules. Below, we present the rules for tasks A and B.

Task A. The time expression is identified by defining appropriate regular expression. The regular expressions are based on several entities that denote month names, year, weekdays and the various digit expressions. We also use a list of keywords (e.g., day, time, AM, PM etc.) that denote the various time expressions. The values of various attributes (e.g., *type* and *value*) of time expressions are computed by some simple template matching algorithms.

Task B. In case of Task B, the training data is initially passed through the Stanford PoS tagger[2]. We consider the tokens as the events that are tagged with POS tags such as *VB*, *VBG*, *VBN*, *VBP*, *VBZ* and *VBD*, denoting the various verb expressions. Values of different attributes are computed as follows.

[2] http://nlp.stanford.edu/software/tagger.shtml

a. Tense: A manually augmented suffix list such as: "*ed*","*d*","*t*" etc. is used to capture the proper tense of any event verb from surface level orthographic variations.
b. Aspect: The Tense-Aspect-Modality (TAM) for English verbs is generally associated with auxiliaries. A list is manually prepared. Any occurrence of main verb with continuous aspect leads to search for the adjacent previous auxiliary and rules are formulated to extract TAM relation using the manually generated checklist. A separate list of auxiliaries is prepared and successfully used for detection of progressive verbs.
c. Polarity: Verb-wise polarity is assigned by the occurrence of previous negation words. If any negation word appears before any event verb then the resultant polarity is negative; otherwise, the verb considered as positive by default.
d. Modality: We prepare a manual list that contains the words such as: *may*, *could*, *would* etc. The presence of these modal auxiliaries gives modal tag to the targeted verb in a sentence otherwise it is considered a non-modal.
e. Class: We select '*occurrence*' to be class value by default.

3.2 Machine Learning Approach for Tasks C, D, E and F

For tasks C-F, we use a supervised machine learning approach that is based on CRF. We consider the temporal relation identification task as a pair-wise classification problem in which the target pairs–a TIMEX3 tag and an EVENT–are modelled using CRF, which can include arbitrary set of features, and still can avoid overfitting in a principled manner.

Introduction to CRF. CRF (Lafferty et al., 2001), is used to calculate the conditional probability of values on designated output nodes given values on other designated input nodes. The conditional probability of a state sequence $S = < s_1, s_2, ..., s_T >$ given an observation sequence $O = < o_1, o_2, ..., o_T)$ is calculated as:

$$P_\wedge(s \mid o) = \frac{1}{Z_o} \exp(\sum_{t=1}^{T} \sum_{k=1}^{K} \lambda_k f_k(s_{t-1}, s_t, o, t))$$

where, $f_k(s_{t-1}, s_t, o, t)$ is a feature function whose weight λ_k is to be learned via training. The values of the feature functions may range between $-\infty .....+\infty$, but typically they are binary. To make all conditional probabilities sum up to 1, we must calculate the normalization factor,

$$Z_0 = \sum_s \exp(\sum_{t=1}^{T} \sum_{k=1}^{K} \lambda_k f_k(s_{t-1}, s_t, o, t)),$$

which, as in HMMs, can be obtained efficiently by dynamic programming.

To train a CRF, the objective function to be maximized is the penalized log-likelihood of the state sequences given the observation sequence:

$$L_\wedge = \sum_{i=1}^{N} \log(P_\wedge(s^{(i)} \mid o^{(i)})) - \sum_{k=1}^{K} \frac{\lambda_k^2}{2\sigma^2},$$

where, $\{<o^{(i)}, s^{(i)}>\}$ is the labeled training data. The second sum corresponds to a zero-mean, σ^2 -variance Gaussian prior over parameters, which facilitates optimization by making the likelihood surface strictly convex.

CRFs generally can use real-valued functions but it is often required to incorporate the binary valued features. A feature function $f_k(s_{t-1}, s_t, o, t)$ has a value of 0 for most cases and is only set to 1, when s_{t-1}, s_t are certain states and the observation has certain properties. Here, we set parameters λ to maximize the penalized log-likelihood using Limited-memory BFGS (Sha and Pereira, 2003) a quasi-Newton method that is significantly more efficient, and which results in only minor changes in accuracy due to changes in σ.

We use the OpenNLP C^{++} based CRF++ package[3], a simple, customizable, and open source implementation of CRF for segmenting /labeling sequential data.

3.3 Features of Tasks C, D, E and F

We extract the gold-standard TimeBank features for events and times in order to train/test the CRF. In the present work, we mainly use the various combinations of the following features:

(i). **Part of Speech (POS)** of event terms: It denotes the POS information of the event. The features values may be either of ADJECTIVE, NOUN, VERB, and PREP.

(ii). **Event Tense**: This feature is useful to capture the standard distinctions among the grammatical categories of verbal phrases. The tense attribute can have values, PRESENT, PAST, FUTURE, INFINITIVE, PRESPART, PASTPART, or NONE.

(iii). **Event Aspect**: It denotes the aspect of the events. The aspect attribute may take values**,** PROGRESSIVE, PERFECTIVE and PERFECTIVE PROGRESSIVE or NONE.

(iv). **Event Polarity**: The polarity of an event instance is a required attribute represented by the boolean attribute, polarity. If it is set to 'NEG', the event instance is negated. If it is set to 'POS' or not present in the annotation, the event instance is not negated.

(v). **Event Modality**: The modality attribute is only present if there is a modal word that modifies the instance.

(vi). **Event Class**: This is denoted by the 'EVENT' tag and used to annotate those elements in a text that mark the semantic events described by it. Typically, events are verbs but can be nominal also. It may belong to one of the following classes:

REPORTING: Describes the action of a person or an organization declaring something, narrating an event, informing about an event, etc. For example, *say*, *report*, *tell*, *explain*, *state* etc.

PERCEPTION: Includes events involving the physical perception of another event. Such events are typically expressed by verbs like: *see*, *watch*, *glimpse*, *behold*, *view*, *hear*, *listen*, *overhear* etc.

ASPECTUAL: Focuses on different facets of event history. For example, *initiation*, *reinitiation*, *termination*, *culmination*, *continuation* etc.

I_ACTION: An intentional action. It introduces an event argument which must be in the text explicitly describing an action or situation from which we can infer something given its relation with the I_ ACTION.

I_STATE: Similar to the I_ACTION class. This class includes states that refer to alternative or possible words, which can be introduced by subordinated clauses, nominalizations, or untensed verb phrases (VPs).

STATE: Describes circumstances in which something obtains or holds true.

Occurrence: Includes all of the many other kinds of events that describe something that happens or occurs in the world.

(vii). **Type of temporal expression:** It represents the temporal relationship holding between events, times, or between an event and a time of the event.

(viii). **Event Stem**: It denotes the stem of the head event.

[3]http://crfpp.sourceforge.net

(ix). **Document Creation Time**: The document creation time of the event.

4 Evaluation Results

Each of the tasks is evaluated with the TempEval-2 shared task datasets.

4.1 Evaluation Scheme

For the extents of events and time expressions (tasks A and B), precision, recall and the F-measure are used as evaluation metrics, using the following formulas:

Precision (P) = tp/ (tp + fp)

Recall (R) = tp/ (tp + fn)

F-measure = 2 *(P * R)/ (P + R)

Where, tp is the number of tokens that are part of an extent in both keys and response,

fp is the number of tokens that are part of an extent in the response but not in the key, and

fn is the number of tokens that are part of an extent in the key but not in the response.

An even simpler evaluation metric similar to the definition of 'accuracy' is used to evaluate the attributes of events and time expressions (the second part of tasks, A and B) and for relation types (tasks C through F). The metric, henceforth referred to as 'accuracy', is defined as below:

Number of correct answers/ Number of answers present in the test data

4.2 Results

For tasks A and B, we identify a set of rules from the training set and apply them on the respective test sets.

The tasks C, D, E and F are based on CRF. We develop a number of models based on CRF using the different features included into it. A feature vector consisting of the subset of the available features as described in Section 2.3 is extracted for each of <event, timex>, <event, DCT>, <event, event> and <event, event> pairs in tasks C, D, E and F, respectively. Now, we have a training data in the form (W_i, T_i), where, W_i is the ith pair along with its feature vector and T_i is it's corresponding TempEval relation class. Models are built based on the training data and the feature template. The procedure of training is summarized below:

1. Define the training corpus, C.
2. Extract the corresponding relation from the training corpus.
3. Create a file of candidate features, including lexical features derived from the training corpus.
4. Define a feature template.
5. Compute the CRF weights λ_k for every f_K using the CRF toolkit with the training file and feature template as input.

During evaluation, we consider the following feature templates for the respective tasks:

(i) **Task C**: Feature vector consisting of current token, polarity, POS, tense, class and value; combination of token and type, combination of tense and value of the current token, combination of aspect and type of current token, combination of aspect, value and type of the current token.

(ii) **Task D**: Feature vector consisting of current token and POS; combination of POS and tense of the current token, combination of polarity and POS of the current token, combination of POS and aspect of current token, combination of polarity and POS of current token, combination of POS, tense and aspect of the current token.

(iii). **Task E**: Current token, combination of event-class and event-id of the current token, combination of POS tags of the pair of events, combination of (tense, aspect) values of the event pairs.

(iv). **Task F**: Current token, combination of POS tags of the pair of events, combination of tense values of the event pairs, combination of the aspect values of the event pairs, combination of the event classes of the event pairs.

Experimental results of tasks A and B are reported in Table 1 for English datasets. The results for task A, i.e., recognition and normalization of time expressions, yield the precision, recall and F-measure values of 55%, 17% and 26%, respectively. For task B, i.e., event recognition, the system yields precision, recall and F-measure values of 48%, 56% and 52%, respectively. Event attribute identification shows the accuracies of 98%, 98%, 30%, 95% and 53% for *polarity*, *mood*, *modality*, *tense*, *aspect* and *class*, respectively. These systems are the *baseline* models, and the performance can further be improved with a more carefully handcrafted set of robust rules. In further experiments, we would also like to apply machine learning methods to these problems.

Task	precision (in %)	recall (in %)	F-measure (in %)
A	55%	17%	26%
B	48%	56%	52%

Table 1. Experimental results on tasks A and B

Evaluation results on the English datasets for tasks C, D, E and F are presented in Table 2. Experiments show the accuracies of 63%, 80%, 56% and 56% for tasks C, D, E and F, respectively. Results show that our system performs best for task D, i.e., relationships between *event* and *document creation time*. The system achieves an accuracy of 63% for task C that finds the temporal relation between an *event* and a *time expression* in the same sentence. The system performs quite similarly for tasks E and F. It is to be noted that there is still the room for performance improvement. In the present work, we did not carry out sufficient experiments to identify the most suitable feature templates for each of the tasks. In future, we would experiment after selecting a development set for each task; and find out appropriate feature template depending upon the performance on the development set.

Task	Accuracy (in %)
C	63%
D	80%
E	56%
F	56%

Table 2. Experimental results on tasks C, D, E and F

5 Conclusion and Future Works

In this paper, we report very preliminary results of our first participation in the TempEval shared task. We participated in all the tasks of TempEval-2, i.e., A, B, C, D, E and F for English. We develop the rule-based systems for tasks A and B, whereas the remaining tasks are based on a machine learning approach, namely CRF. All our systems are still in their development stages. Evaluation results on the shared task English datasets yield the precision, recall and F-measure values of 55%, 17% and 26%, respectively for Task A and 48%, 56% and 52%, respectively for Task B (event recognition). Experiments on the English datasets yield the accuracies of 63%, 80%, 56% and 56% for tasks C, D, E and F, respectively.

Future works include identification of more precise rules for tasks A and B. We would also like to experiment with CRF for these two tasks. We would experiment with the various feature templates for tasks C, D, E and F. Future works also include experimentations with other machine learning techniques like maximum entropy and support vector machine.

References

Boguraev, B. and R. K. Ando. 2005. TimeML Compliant Text Analysis for Temporal Reasoning. In *Proceedings of Nineteenth International Joint Conference on Artificial Intelligence (IJCAI-05)*, Edinburgh, Scotland, August, pages 997–1003.

Chambers, N., S., Wang, and D., Jurafsky. , 2007. Classifying Temporal Relations between Events. In *Proceedings of the ACL 2007 Demo and Poster Sessions*, Prague, Czech Republic, June, pages 173–176.

Lafferty, J., McCallum, A., and Pereira, F. Conditional Random Fields: Probabilistic Models for Segmenting and Labeling Sequence Data. In *Proceedings of 18th International Conference on Machine Learning*, 2001.

Mani, I., B., Wellner, M., Verhagen, and J. Pustejovsky. 2007. Three Approaches to Learning TLINKs in TimeML. *Technical Report CS-07-268*, Computer Science Department, Brandeis University, Waltham, USA.

Mani, I., Wellner, B., Verhagen, M., Lee C.M., Pustejovsky, J. 2006. Machine Learning of Temporal Relation. In *Proceedings of the COLING/ACL*, Sydney, Australia, ACL.

Mao, T., Li., T., Huang, D., Yang, Y. 2006. Hybrid Models for Chinese Named Entity Recognition. In *Proceedings of the Fifth SIGHAN Workshop on Chinese Language Processing.*

Sha, F., Pereira, F. 2003. Shallow Parsing with Conditional Random Fields. In *Proceedings of HLT-NAACL*, 2003.

Verhagen, M., Gaizauskas, R., Schilder, F., Hepple, M., Katz, G., Pustejovsky, and J.: SemEval-2007 Task 15: TempEval Temporal Relation Identification. 2007. In *Proceedings of the SemEval-2007*, Prague, June 2007, pages 75-80.

KCDC: Word Sense Induction by Using Grammatical Dependencies and Sentence Phrase Structure

Roman Kern
Know-Center
Graz, Austria
rkern@know-center.at

Markus Muhr
Know-Center
Graz, Austria
mmuhr@know-center.at

Michael Granitzer
Graz University of Technology,
Know-Center
Graz, Austria
mgrani@know-center.at

Abstract

Word sense induction and discrimination (WSID) identifies the senses of an ambiguous word and assigns instances of this word to one of these senses. We have build a WSID system that exploits syntactic and semantic features based on the results of a natural language parser component. To achieve high robustness and good generalization capabilities, we designed our system to work on a restricted, but grammatically rich set of features. Based on the results of the evaluations our system provides a promising performance and robustness.

1 Introduction

The goal of the SemEval-2 word sense induction and discrimination task, see Manandhar et al. (2010), is to identify the senses of ambiguous nouns and verbs in an unsupervised manner and to label unseen instances of these words with one of the induced senses. The most common approach towards this task is to apply clustering or graph partitioning algorithms on a representation of the words that surround an ambiguous target word, see for example Niu et al. (2007) and Pedersen (2007). We followed this approach by employing a clustering algorithm to detect the individual senses, but focused on generating feature sets different to the mainstream approach. Our feature sets utilize the output of a linguistic processing pipeline that captures the syntax and semantics of sentence parts closely related with the target word.

2 System Overview

The base of our system is to apply a parser on the sentence in which the target word occurs. Contextual information, for example the sentences surrounding the target sentence, are currently not exploited by our system. To analyze the sentences we applied the Stanford Parser (Version 1.6.2), which is based on lexicalized probabilistic context free grammars, see Klein and Manning (2003). This open-source parser not only extracts the phrase structure of a given sentence, but also provides a list of so called grammatical relations (typed dependencies), see de Marneffe et al. (2006). These relations reflect the dependencies between the words within the sentence, for example the relationship between the verb and the subject. See Chen et al. (2009) for an application of grammatical dependencies for word sense disambiguation.

2.1 Feature Extraction

The phrase structure and the grammatical dependencies are sources for the feature extraction stage. To illustrate the result of the parser and feature extraction stages we use an example sentence, where the target word is the verb "file":

> Afterward , I watched as a butt-ton of good , but misguided people **filed** out of the theater , and immediately lit up a smoke .

2.1.1 Grammatical Dependency Features

The Stanford Parser provides 55 different grammatical dependency types. Figure 2 depicts the list of the grammatical dependencies identified by the Stanford Parser for the example sentence. Only a limited subset of these dependencies are selected to build the grammatical feature set. This subset has been defined based on preliminary tests on the trial dataset. For verbs only dependencies that represent the association of a verb with prepositional modifiers and phrasal verb particles are selected (`prep`, `prepc`, `prt`). If the verb is not associated with a preposition or particle, a synthetic "missing" feature is added instead (`!prep`, `!prt`). For nouns the selected dependencies are the prepositions (for head nouns that are the object of a preposition) and noun compound modifiers (`pobj`, `nn`).

Proceedings of the 5th International Workshop on Semantic Evaluation, ACL 2010, pages 351–354,
Uppsala, Sweden, 15-16 July 2010.

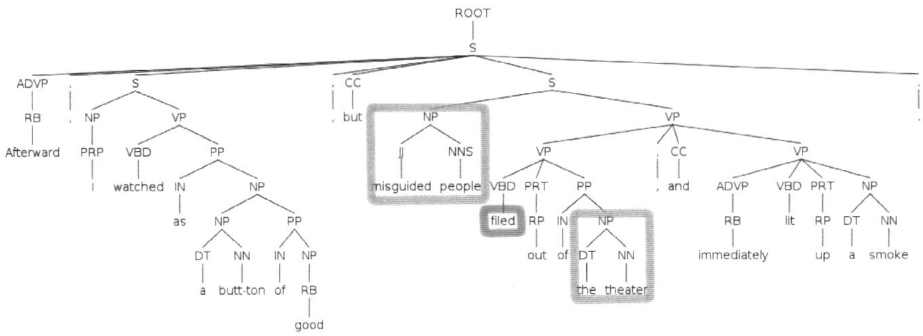

Figure 1: Phrase tree of the example sentence. The noun phrase "misguided people" is connected to the target word via the `nsubj` dependency and the phrase "the theater" is associated with the target verb via the `prep` and `pobj` dependencies.

relation	gov	dep
pobj	as-5	butt-ton-7
det	butt-ton-7	a-6
prep	butt-ton-7	of-8
nsubj	filed-14	people-13
prt	filed-14	out-15
prep	filed-14	of-16
cc	filed-14	and-20
conj	filed-14	lit-22
advmod	lit-22	immediat...
prt	lit-22	up-23
dobj	lit-22	smoke-25
pobj	of-16	theater-18
pobj	of-8	good-9
amod	people-13	misguide...
det	smoke-25	a-24
det	theater-18	the-17
advmod	watched-4	Afterwar...
nsubj	watched-4	I-3
prep	watched-4	as-5
cc	watched-4	but-11
conj	watched-4	filed-14

Figure 2: List of grammatical dependencies as detected by the Stanford Parser.

If the noun is associated with a verb the grammatical dependencies of this verb are also added to the feature set.

The name of the dependency and the word (i.e. preposition or particle) are used to construct the grammatical feature. The different features are weighted. The weights have been derived from their frequencies within the trial dataset and listed in table 1. For the example sentence the extracted grammatical features are:

```
'out', 'of', prep, prt
```

2.1.2 Phrase Term Features

The second set of features are generated from the sentence phrase structure. In figure 1 the parse tree for the example sentence is depicted.

Again we tried to keep the feature set as small as possible. Starting with the target word only phrases that are directly associated with the ambiguous word are selected. To identify these phrases the grammatical dependencies are exploited. For nouns as target words the associated verb is searched at first. Given a verb the phrases containing the head noun of a subject or object relationship are identified. If the verb is accompanied by a preposition, the phrase carrying the object of the preposition is also added. All nouns and adjectives from these these phrases are then collected. The phrase words together with the verb, prepositions and particles are lemmatized using tools also provided by the Stanford Parser project.

Feature	Weight
prepc, prt, nn, pobj	0.9
prep	0.45
!prep, !prt	0.5
'prepositions', 'particles'	0.97

Table 1: Weights of the grammatical features, which were derived from their distribution within the trial dataset.

The weights of the phrase term features are based on the frequency of the words within the training dataset, where N is the total number of sentences and N_f is the number of sentences in which the lemmatized phrase term occurs in:

$$weight_f = log(\frac{N}{N_f + 1}) + 1 \quad (1)$$

In our example sentence the extracted phrase term features are:

```
of, misguided, file, theater, people, out
```

2.2 Phrase Term Expansion

The feature space of the phrase terms is expected to be very sparse. Additionally different phrase terms may have similar semantics. Therefore the phrase terms are optionally expanded with associated terms, where semantically similar terms should be associated with the same terms.

To calculate the statistics for term expansion we used the training dataset (although other datasets would be more suitable for this purpose). The dataset is split into sentences. Stopwords and rarely used words, which occur in less than 3 sentences, were removed. The remaining words were finally lemmatized. For a given phrase term the top 100 associated terms are used to build the feature set. The association weight between two terms is based on the Pointwise Mutual Information:

$$weight_{pmi}(t_i, t_j) = \frac{log_2(\frac{P(t_i|t_j)}{P(t_j)})}{log_2(\frac{1}{P(t_j)})} \quad (2)$$

For example the top 10 associated terms for `theater` are:

```
theater.n, movie.n, opera.n,
vaudeville.n, wnxt-abc.n, imax.n,
orpheum.n, pullulate.v, projector.n,
psychomania.n
```

2.3 Sense Induction

To detect the individual senses within the training dataset we applied unsupervised machine learning techniques. For each ambiguous word a matrix - $M_{|Instances| \times |Features|}$ - is created and a clustering algorithm is applied, namely the Growing k-Means, see Daszykowski et al. (2002). This algorithm needs the number of clusters and centroids as initialization parameters, where the initial centroids are calculated using a directed random seed finder as described in Arthur and Vassilvitskii (2007). We used the Jensen-Shannon Divergence function for the grammatical dependency features and the Cosine Similarity for the phrase term feature sets as relatedness function.

For each cluster number we re-run the clustering with different random initial centroids (30 times) and for each run we calculate a cluster quality criterion. The overall cluster quality criterion is the mean of all feature quality criteria, which are calculated based on the set of clusters the feature occurs in - C_f - the number of instances of each cluster - N_c - and the number of instances within a cluster where the feature occurs in - $N_{c,f}$:

$$FQC_f = \frac{weight_f}{|C_f|} * \sum_{c \in C_f} \frac{N_{c,f}}{N_c} \quad (3)$$

$$QC_{run} = \overline{FQC_f} \quad (4)$$

The cluster quality criterion is calculated for each run and the combination of the mean and standard deviations are then used to calculate a stability criterion to detect the number of clusters, which is based on the intuition that the correct cluster count yields the lowest variation of QC values:

$$SC_k = \frac{mean(QC)}{stdev(QC)} \quad (5)$$

Starting with two clusters the number of clusters is incremented until the stability criterion starts to decline. For the cluster number with the highest stability criterion the run with the highest quality criterion is selected as final clustering solution. The result of the sense induction processing is a list of centroids for the identified clusters.

2.4 Sense Assignment

The final processing step is to assign an instance of an ambiguous word to one of the pre-calculated senses. The sentence with the target word is processed exactly like the training sentences to generate a set of features. Finally the word is assigned to the sense cluster with the maximum relatedness.

3 System Configurations & Results

Our system can be configured to use a combination of feature sets for the word sense induction and discrimination calculations: a) *KCDC-GD*: Grammatical dependency features, b) *KCDC-PT*: Phrase terms features, c) *KCDC-PC*: Expanded phrase term features, d) *KCDC-PCGD*: All training sentences are first processed by using the expanded phrase term features and then by using the grammatical dependency features with an additional feature that encodes the cluster id found by the phrase features.

In the evaluation we also submitted multiple runs of the same configuration[1] to assess the influence of the random initialization of the clustering algorithm. Judging from the results the random seeding has no pronounced impact and it influence should decrease when the number of clustering runs for each cluster number is increased.

All configurations found on average about 3 senses for target words in the test set (2.8 for verbs, 3.3 for nouns), with exception of the *KCDC-PT* configuration which identified only 1.5 senses on average. In the gold standard the number of senses for verbs is 3.12 and for nouns 4.46, which shows that the stability criterion tends to underestimate the number of senses slightly.

To compare the performance of the different configurations, one can use the average rank within the evaluation result lists. Judging from the

[1]labeled KCDC-GD-2, KCDC-GDC for configuration 'a' and KCDC-PC-2 for the configuration 'c'

rankings, the configurations that utilize the grammatical dependencies and the expanded phrase terms provide similar performance. The configuration that takes the phrase terms directly as features comes in last, which is expected due to the sparse nature of the feature representation and the low number of detected senses.

Comparing the performance of our system with the two baselines shows that our system did outperform the random baseline in all evaluation runs and the most frequent baseline (MFS) in all runs with the exception of the F-Score based unsupervised evaluation, where the MFS baseline has not been beaten by any system. Although none of our submitted configurations was ranked first in any of the evaluations, their ranking was still better than average, with the exception of the *KCDC-PT* configuration.

Another observation that can be made is the difference in performance between nouns and verbs. Our system, especially the grammatical dependency based configurations, is tailored towards verbs. Therefore the better performance of verbs in the evaluation is in line with the expectations.

When looking at the results of the individual target words one can notice that for a set of words the quality of the sense detection is above average. For 16 of the 100 words a V-Measure of more than 30% in at least one configuration was achieved (average: 7.8%)[2]. This can be seen as indicator that our selection of features is effective for a specific group of words. For the remaining words an according feature set has to be developed in future work.

4 Conclusion

For the SemEval 2010 word sense induction and discrimination task we have tried to build a system that uses a minimal amount of information while still providing a competitive performance. This system contains a parser component to analyze the phrase structure of a sentence and the grammatical dependencies between words. The extracted features are then clustered to detect the senses of ambiguous words. In the evaluation runs our system did demonstrate a satisfying performance for a number of words.

The design of our system offers a wide range of possible enhancements. For example the integration of preposition disambiguation and noun-phrase co-reference resolution could help to further improve the word sense discrimination effectiveness.

[2]The best performing target words are: `root.v`, `presume.v`, `figure.v`, `weigh.v`, `cheat.v`

Acknowledgments

The Know-Center is funded within the Austrian COMET Program - Competence Centers for Excellent Technologies - under the auspices of the Austrian Federal Ministry of Transport, Innovation and Technology, the Austrian Federal Ministry of Economy, Family and Youth and by the State of Styria. COMET is managed by the Austrian Research Promotion Agency FFG. Results are partially funded by the EUROSTARS project 4811 MAKIN'IT.

References

D. Arthur and S. Vassilvitskii. 2007. k-means++: The advantages of careful seeding. In *Proceedings of the eighteenth annual ACM-SIAM symposium on Discrete algorithms*, page 10271035. Society for Industrial and Applied Mathematics Philadelphia, PA, USA.

Ping Chen, Wei Ding, Chris Bowes, and David Brown. 2009. A fully unsupervised word sense disambiguation method using dependency knowledge. *Human Language Technology Conference*.

M Daszykowski, B Walczak, and D L Massart. 2002. On the optimal partitioning of data with K-means, growing K-means, neural gas, and growing neural gas. *Journal of chemical information and computer sciences*, 42(6):1378–89.

M.C. de Marneffe, B. MacCartney, and C.D. Manning. 2006. Generating typed dependency parses from phrase structure parses. In *LREC 2006*.

Dan Klein and Christopher D. Manning. 2003. Accurate unlexicalized parsing. *Proceedings of the 41st Annual Meeting on Association for Computational Linguistics - ACL '03*, pages 423–430.

Suresh Manandhar, Ioannis P. Klapaftis, Dmitriy Dligach, and Sameer S. Pradhan. 2010. SemEval-2010 Task 14: Word Sense Induction & Disambiguation. In *Proceedings of SemEval-2*, Uppsala, Sweden, ACL.

Zheng-yu Niu, Dong-hong Ji, and Chew-lim Tan. 2007. I2R: Three Systems for Word Sense Discrimination, Chinese Word Sense Disambiguation, and English Word Sense Disambiguation. In *Proceedings of the 4th International Workshop on Semantic Evaluations*. ACL.

T. Pedersen. 2007. Umnd2: Senseclusters applied to the sense induction task of senseval-4. In *Proceedings of the 4th International Workshop on Semantic Evaluations*. ACL.

UoY: Graphs of Unambiguous Vertices for Word Sense Induction and Disambiguation

Ioannis Korkontzelos, Suresh Manandhar
Department of Computer Science
The University of York
Heslington, York, YO10 5NG, UK
{johnkork, suresh}@cs.york.ac.uk

Abstract

This paper presents an unsupervised graph-based method for automatic word sense induction and disambiguation. The innovative part of our method is the assignment of either a word or a word pair to each vertex of the constructed graph. Word senses are induced by clustering the constructed graph. In the disambiguation stage, each induced cluster is scored according to the number of its vertices found in the context of the target word. Our system participated in SemEval-2010 word sense induction and disambiguation task.

1 Introduction

There exists significant evidence that word sense disambiguation is important for a variety of natural language processing tasks: machine translation, information retrieval, grammatical analysis, speech and text processing (Veronis, 2004). However, the "fixed-list" of senses paradigm, where the senses of a target word is a closed list of definitions coming from a standard dictionary (Agirre et al., 2006), was long ago abandoned. The reason is that sense lists, such as WordNet (Miller, 1995), miss many senses, especially domain-specific ones (Pantel and Lin, 2002). The missing concepts are not recognised. Moreover, senses cannot be easily related to their use in context.

Word sense induction methods can be divided into vector-space models and graph based ones. In a vector-space model, each context of a target word is represented as a feature vector, e.g. frequency of cooccurring words (Katz and Giesbrecht, 2006). Context vectors are clustered and the resulting clusters represent the induced senses.

Recently, graph-based methods have been employed for word sense induction (Agirre and Soroa, 2007). Typically, graph-based methods represent each context word of the target word as a vertex. Two vertices are connected via an edge if they cooccur in one or more instances. Once the cooccurrence graph has been constructed, different graph clustering algorithms are applied to partition the graph. Each cluster (partition) consists of a set of words that are semantically related to the particular sense (Veronis, 2004). The potential advantage of graph-based methods is that they can combine both local and global cooccurrence information (Agirre et al., 2006).

Klapaftis and Manandhar (2008) presented a graph-based approach that represents pairs of words as vertices instead of single words. They claimed that single words might appear with more than one senses of the target word, while they hypothesize that a pair of words is unambiguous. Hard-clustering the graph will potentially identify less conflating senses of the target word.

In this paper, we relax the above hypothesis because in some cases a single word is unambiguous. We present a method that generates two-word vertices only when a single word vertex is unambiguous. If the word is judged as unambiguous, then it is represented as a single-word vertex. Otherwise, it is represented as a pair-of-words vertex.

The approach of Klapaftis and Manandhar (2008) achieved good results in both evaluation settings of the SemEval-2007 task. A test instance is disambiguated towards one of the induced senses if one or more pairs of words representing that sense cooccur in the test instance. This creates a sparsity problem, because a cooccurrence of two words is generally less likely than the occurrence of a single word. We expect our approach to address the data sparsity problem without conflating the induced senses.

2 Word Sense Induction

In this section we present our word sense induction and disambiguation algorithms. Figure

Proceedings of the 5th International Workshop on Semantic Evaluation, ACL 2010, pages 355–358,
Uppsala, Sweden, 15-16 July 2010.

1 shows an example showing how the sense induction algorithm works: The left side of part I shows the context nouns of four snippets containing the target noun “chip”. The most relevant of these nouns are represented as single word vertices (part II). Note that “customer” was not judged to be significantly relevant. In addition, the system introduced several vertices representing pairs of nouns. For example, note the vertex “company_potato”. The set of sentences containing the context word “company” was judged as very different from the set of sentences containing “company” and “potato”. Thus, our system hypothesizes that probably “company” and “company_potato” are relevant to different senses of “chip”, and allows them to be clustered accordingly. Vertices whose content nouns or pairs of nouns cooccur in some snippet are connected with an edge (part III and right side of part I). Edge weights depend upon the conditional probabilities of the occurrence frequencies of the vertex contents in a large corpus, e.g. $w_{2,6}$ in part III. Hard-clustering the graph produces the induced senses of “chip”: (a) potato crisp, and (b) microchip.

In the following subsections, the system is described in detail. Figure 2 shows a block diagram overview of the sense induction system. It consists of three main components: (a) corpus preprocessing, (b) graph construction, and (c) clustering.

In a number of different stages, the system uses a reference corpus to count occurrences of word or word pairs. It is chosen to be large because frequencies of words in a large corpus are more significant statistically. Ideally we would use the web or another large repository, but for the purposes of the SemEval-2010 task we used the union of all snippets of all target words.

2.1 Corpus Preprocessing

Corpus preprocessing aims to capture words that are contextually related to the target word. Initially, all snippets[1] that contain the target word are lemmatised and *PoS* tagged using the *GENIA* tagger[2]. Words that occur in a stoplist are filtered out. Instead of using all words as context, only nouns are kept, since they are more discriminative than verbs, adverbs and adjectives, that appear in a variety of different contexts.

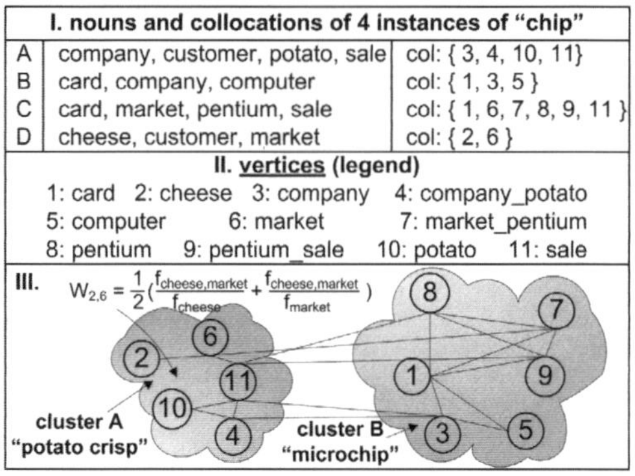

Figure 1: An example showing how the proposed word sense induction system works.

Nouns that occur infrequently in the reference corpus are removed (parameter P_1). Then, *log-likelihood ratio* (LL) (Dunning, 1993) is employed to compare the distribution of each noun to its distribution in reference corpus. The null hypothesis is that the two distributions are similar. If this is true, LL is small value and the corresponding noun is removed (parameter P_2). We also filter out nouns that are more indicative in the reference corpus than in the target word corpus; i.e. the nouns whose relative frequency in the former is larger than in the latter. At the end of this stage, each snippet is a list of lemmatised nouns contextually related to the target word.

2.2 Constructing the Graph

All nouns appearing in the list of the previous stage output are represented as graph vertices. Moreover, some vertices representing pairs of nouns are added. Each noun within a snippet is combined with every other, generating $\binom{n}{2}$ pairs. Log-likelihood filtering with respect to the reference corpus is used to filter out unimportant pairs.

Thereafter, we aim to keep only pairs that might refer to a different sense of the target word than their component nouns. For each pair we construct a vector containing the snippet IDs in which they occur. Similarly we construct a vector for each component noun. We discard a pair if its vector is very similar to both the vectors of its component nouns, otherwise we represent it as a vertex pair. Dice coefficient was used as a similarity measure and parameter P_4 as threshold value.

Edges are drawn based on cooccurrence of the corresponding vertices contents in one or more snippets. Edges whose respective vertices contents are infrequent are rejected. The weight ap-

[1] We refer to instances of the target word as snippets, since they can be either sentences or paragraphs.

[2] www-tsujii.is.s.u-tokyo.ac.jp/GENIA/tagger

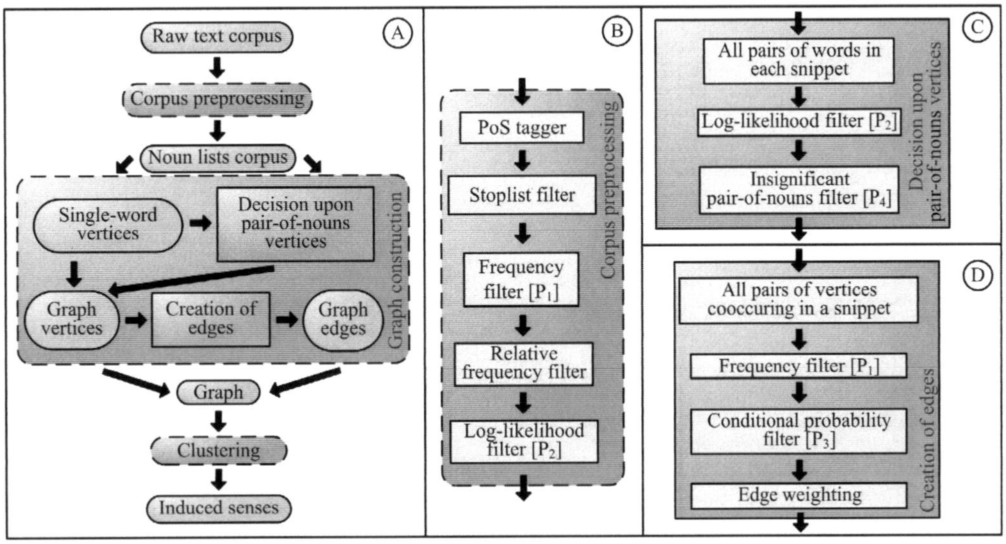

Figure 2: A: Block diagram presenting the system overview. B, C, D: Block diagrams further analysing the structure of complex components of A. Parameter names appear within square brackets.

plied to each edge is the maximum of the conditional probabilities of the corresponding vertices contents (e.g. $w_{2,6}$, part III, figure 1). Low weight edges are filtered out (parameter P_3).

2.3 Clustering the Graph

Chinese Whispers (CW) (Biemann, 2006) was used to cluster the graph. *CW* is a randomised graph-clustering algorithm, time-linear to the number of edges. The number of clusters it produces is automatically inferred. Evaluation has shown that *CW* suits well in sense induction applications, where class distributions are often highly skewed. In our experiments, *CW* produced less clusters using a constant mutation rate (5%).

To further reduce the number of induced clusters, we applied a post-processing stage, which exploits the *one sense per collocation* property (Yarowsky, 1995). For each cluster l_i, we generated the set S_i of all snippets that contain at least one vertex content of l_i. Then, any clusters l_a and l_b were merged if $S_a \subseteq S_b$ or $S_a \supseteq S_b$.

3 Word Sense Disambiguation

The induced senses are used to sense-tag each test instance of the target word (snippet). Given a snippet, each induced cluster is assigned a score equal to the number of its vertex contents (single or pairs of words) occurring in the snippet. The instance is assigned to the sense with the highest score or with equal weights to all highest scoring senses.

4 Tuning parameter and inducing senses

The algorithm depends upon 4 parameters: P_1 thresholds frequencies and P_3 collocation weights. P_2 is the LL threshold and P_4 the similarity threshold for discarding pair-of-nouns vertices.

We chose $P_1 \in \{5, 10, 15\}$, $P_2 \in \{2, 3, 4, 5, 10, 15, 25, 35\}$, $P_3 \in \{0.2, 0.3, 0.4\}$ and $P_4 \in \{0.2, 0.4, 0.6, 0.8\}$. The parameter tuning was done using the trial data of the SemEval-2010 task and on the noun data of corresponding SemEval-2007 task. Parameters were tuned by choosing the maximum supervised recall. For both data sets, the chosen parameter values were $P_1 \sim 10$, $P_3 \sim 0.4$ and $P_4 \sim 0.8$. Due to the size difference of the datasets, for the Semeval-2010 trial data $P_2 \sim 3$, while for the SemEval-2007 noun data $P_2 \sim 10$. The latter was adopted because the size of training data was announced to be large. We induced senses on the training data and then disambiguated the test data instances.

5 Evaluation results

Three different measures, V-Measure, F-Score, and supervised recall on word sense disambiguation task, were used for evaluation. V-Measure and F-Score are unsupervised. Supervised recall was measured on two different data splits. Table 1 shows the performance of our system, *UoY*, for all measures and in comparison with the best, worst and average performing system and the random and most frequent sense (MFS) baselines. Results are shown for all words, and nouns and verbs only.

	System	V-Msr	F-Sc	S-R_{80}	S-R_{60}
All	**UoY**	15.70	49.76	62.44	61.96
	Best	16.20	63.31	62.44	61.96
	Worst	0.00	16.10	18.72	18.91
	Average	6.36	48.72	54.95	54.27
	MFS	0.00	63.40	58.67	58.25
	Random	4.40	31.92	57.25	56.52
Nouns	**UoY**	20.60	38.23	59.43	58.62
	Best	20.60	57.10	59.43	58.62
	Average	7.08	44.42	47.85	46.90
	Worst	0.00	15.80	1.55	1.52
	MFS	0.00	57.00	53.22	52.45
	Random	4.20	30.40	51.45	50.21
Verbs	**UoY**	8.50	66.55	66.82	66.82
	Best	15.60	72.40	69.06	68.59
	Average	5.95	54.23	65.25	65.00
	Worst	0.10	16.40	43.76	44.23
	MFS	0.00	72.70	66.63	66.70
	Random	4.64	34.10	65.69	65.73

Table 1: Summary of results (%). V-Msr: V-Measure, F-Sc: F-Score, S-R_X: Supervised recall under data split: X% training, (100-X)% test

Table 2 shows the ranks of *UoY* for all evaluation categories. Our system was generally very highly ranked. It outperformed the random baseline in all cases and the MFS baseline in measures but F-Score. No participant system managed to achive higher F-Score than the MFS baseline.

The main disadvantage of the system seems to be the large number of induced senses. The reasons are data sparcity and tuning on nouns, that might have led to parameters that induce more senses. However, the system performs best among systems that produce comparable numbers of clusters. Table 3 shows the number of senses of *UoY* and the gold-standard. *UoY* produces significantly more senses than the gold-standard, especially for nouns, while for verbs figures are similar.

The system achieves low F-Scores, because this measure favours fewer induced senses. Moreover, we observe that most scores are lower for verbs than nouns. This is probably because parameters are tuned on nouns and because in general nouns appear with more senses than verbs, allowing our system to adapt better. As an overall conclusion, each evaluation measure is more or less biased towards small or large numbers of induced senses.

6 Conclusion

We presented a graph-based approach for word sense induction and disambiguation. Our approach represents as a graph vertex an unambiguous unit: (a) a single word, if it is judged as unambiguous, or (b) a pair of words, otherwise. Graph edges model the cooccurrences of the content of

	V-Msr	F-Sc	S-R_{80}	S-R_{60}
All	2	15	1	1
Nouns|Verbs	1|3	18|6	1|16	1|15

Table 2: Ranks of *UoY* (out of 26 systems)

	All	Nouns	Verbs
Gold-standard	3.79	4.46	3.12
UoY	11.54	17.32	5.76

Table 3: Number of senses

the vertices that they join. Hard-clustering the graph induces a set of senses. To disambiguate a test instance, we assign it to the induced sense whose vertices contents occur mostly in the instance. Results show that our system achieves very high recall and V-measure performance, higher than both baselines. It achieves low F-Scores due to the large number of induced senses.

References

E. Agirre and A. Soroa. 2007. Semeval-2007 task 02: Evaluating word sense induction and discrimination systems. In *proceedings of SemEval-2007*, Czech Republic. ACL.

E. Agirre, D. Martinez, O. Lopez de Lacalle, and A. Soroa. 2006. Two graph-based algorithms for state-of-the-art wsd. In *proceedings of EMNLP*, Sydney, Australia. ACL.

C. Biemann. 2006. Chinese whispers - an efficient graph clustering algorithm and its application to natural language processing problems. In *proceedings of TextGraphs*, New York City. ACL.

T. Dunning. 1993. Accurate methods for the statistics of surprise and coincidence. *Computational Linguistics*, 19(1):61–74.

G. Katz and E. Giesbrecht. 2006. Automatic identification of non-compositional multi-word expressions using latent semantic analysis. In *proceedings of the ACL workshop on Multi-Word Expressions*, Sydney, Australia. ACL.

I. Klapaftis and S. Manandhar. 2008. Word sense induction using graphs of collocations. In *proceedings of ECAI-2008*, Patras, Greece.

G. Miller. 1995. Wordnet: a lexical database for english. *Communications of the ACM*, 38(11):39–41.

P. Pantel and D. Lin. 2002. Discovering word senses from text. In *proceedings of KDD-2002*, New York, NY, USA. ACM Press.

J. Veronis. 2004. Hyperlex: lexical cartography for information retrieval. *Computer Speech & Language*, 18(3):223–252, July.

D. Yarowsky. 1995. Unsupervised word sense disambiguation rivaling supervised methods. In *proceedings of ACL*, Cambridge, MA, USA. ACL.

HERMIT: Flexible Clustering for the SemEval-2 WSI Task

David Jurgens
University of California, Los Angeles
Los Angeles, California, USA
jurgens@cs.ucla.edu

Keith Stevens
University of California, Los Angeles
Los Angeles, California, USA
kstevens@cs.ucla.edu

Abstract

A single word may have multiple unspecified meanings in a corpus. Word sense induction aims to discover these different meanings through word use, and knowledge-lean algorithms attempt this without using external lexical resources. We propose a new method for identifying the different senses that uses a flexible clustering strategy to automatically determine the number of senses, rather than predefining it. We demonstrate the effectiveness using the SemEval-2 WSI task, achieving competitive scores on both the V-Measure and Recall metrics, depending on the parameter configuration.

1 Introduction

The Word Sense Induction task of SemEval 2010 compares several sense induction and discrimination systems that are trained over a common corpus. Systems are provided with an unlabeled training corpus consisting of 879,807 contexts for 100 polysemous words, with 50 nouns and 50 verbs. Each context consists of several sentences that use a single sense of a target word, where at least one sentence contains the word. Systems must use the training corpus to induce sense representations for the many word senses and then use those representations to produce sense labels for the same 100 words in unseen contexts from a testing corpus.

We perform this task by utilizing a distributional word space formed using dimensionality reduction and a hybrid clustering method. Our model is highly scalable; the dimensionality of the word space is reduced immediately through a process based on random projections. In addition, an online part of our clustering algorithm maintains only a centroid that describes an induced word sense, instead of all observed contexts, which lets the model scale to much larger corpora than those used in the SemEval-2 WSI task.

2 The Word Sense Induction Model

We perform word sense induction by modeling individual contexts in a high dimensional word space. Word senses are induced by finding contexts which are similar and therefore likely to use the same sense of the target word. We use a hybrid clustering method to group similar contexts.

2.1 Modeling Context

For a word, each of its contexts are represented by the words with which it co-occurs. We approximate this high dimensional co-occurrence space with the Random Indexing (RI) word space model (Kanerva et al., 2000). RI represents the occurrence of a word with an *index vector*, rather than a set of dimensions. An index vector is a fixed, sparse vector that is orthogonal to all other words' index vectors with a high probability; the total number of dimensions in the model is fixed at a small value, e.g. 5,000. Orthogonality is obtained by setting a small percentage of the vector's values to ± 1 and setting the rest to 0.

A context is represented by summing the index vectors corresponding to the n words occurring to the left and right of the polysemous word. Each occurrence of the polysemous word in the entire corpus is treated as a separate context. Contexts are represented by a compact first-order occurrence vector; using index vectors to represent the occurrences avoids the computational overhead of other dimensional reduction techniques such as the SVD.

2.2 Identifying Related Contexts

Clustering separates similar context vectors into dissimilar clusters that represent the distinct senses of a word. We use an efficient hybrid of online K-Means and Hierarchical Agglomerative

Proceedings of the 5th International Workshop on Semantic Evaluation, ACL 2010, pages 359–362,
Uppsala, Sweden, 15-16 July 2010. ©2010 Association for Computational Linguistics

Clustering (HAC) with a threshold. The threshold allows for the final number of clusters to be determined by data similarity instead of having to specify the number of clusters.

The set of context vectors for a word are clustered using K-Means, which assigns a context to the most similar cluster centroid. If the nearest centroid has a similarity less than the *cluster threshold* and there are not K clusters, the context forms a new cluster. We define the similarity between contexts vectors as the cosine similarity.

Once the corpus has been processed, clusters are repeatedly merged using HAC with the average link criteria, following (Pedersen and Bruce, 1997). Average link clustering defines cluster similarity as the mean cosine similarity of the pairwise similarity of all data points from each cluster. Cluster merging stops when the two most similar clusters have a similarity less than the cluster threshold. Reaching a similarity lower than the cluster threshold signifies that each cluster represents a distinct word sense.

2.3 Applying Sense Labels

Before training and evaluating our model, all occurrences of the 100 polysemous words were stemmed in the corpora. Stemming was required due to a polysemous word being used in multiple lexical forms, e.g. plural, in the corpora. By stemming, we avoid the need to combine contexts for each of the distinct word forms during clustering.

After training our WSI model on the training corpus, we process the test corpus and label the context for each polysemous word with an induced sense. Each test context is labeled with the name of the cluster whose centroid has the highest cosine similarity to the context vector. We represent the test contexts in the same method used for training; index vectors are re-used from training.

3 Evaluation and Results

The WSI task evaluated the submitted solutions with two methods of experimentation: an unsupervised method and a supervised method. The unsupervised method is measured according to the V-Measure and the F-Score. The supervised method is measured using recall.

3.1 Scoring

The first measure used is the V-Measure (Rosenberg and Hirschberg, 2007), which compares the clusters of target contexts to word classes. This measure rates the homogeneity and completeness of a clustering solution. Solutions that have word clusters formed from one word class are homogeneous; completeness measures the degree to which a word class is composed of target contexts allocated to a single cluster.

The second measure, the F-Score, is an extension from information retrieval and provides a contrasting evaluation metric by using a different interpretation of homogeneity and completeness. For the F-Score, the precision and recall of all possible context pairs are measured, where a word class has the expected context pairs and a provided solution contains some word pairs that are correct and others that are unexpected. The F-Score tends to discount smaller clusters and clusters that cannot be assigned to a word class (Manandhar et al., 2010).

3.2 Parameter Tuning

Previous WSI evaluations provided a test corpus, a set of golden sense labels, and a scoring mechanism, which allowed models to do parameter tuning prior to providing a set of sense labels. The SemEval 2010 task provided a trial corpus that contains contexts for four verbs that are not in the evaluation corpus, which can be used for training and testing. The trial corpus also came with a set of golden sense assignments. No golden standard was provided for the training or test corpora, which limited any parameter tuning.

HERMIT exposes three parameters: cluster threshold, the maximum number of clusters and the window size for a context. An initial analysis from the trial data showed that the window size most affected the scores; small window sizes resulted in higher V-Measure scores, while larger window sizes maximized the F-Score. Because contexts are represented using only first-order features, a smaller window size should have less overlap, which potentially results in a higher number of clusters. We opted to maximize the V-Measure score by using a window size of ± 1.

Due to the limited number of training instances, our precursory analysis with the trial data did not show significant differences for the remaining two parameters; we arbitrarily selected a clustering threshold of **.15** and a maximum of **15** clusters per word without any parameter tuning.

After the release of the testing key, we performed a post-hoc analysis to evaluate the effects of parameter tuning on the scores. We include two alternative parameter configurations that were optimized for the F-Score (HERMIT-F) and the supervised evaluations (HERMIT-S). The HERMIT-F variation used a threshold of 0.85 and a window size of ±10 words. The HERMIT-S variation used a threshold of 0.85 and a window size of ±1 words. We did not vary the maximum number of clusters, which was set at 15.

For each evaluation, we provide the scores of seven systems: the three HERMIT configurations, the highest and lowest scoring submitted systems, the Most Frequent Sense (MFS) baseline, and a Random baseline provided by the evaluation team. We provide the scores for each experiment when evaluating all words, nouns, and verbs. We also include the system's rank relative to all submitted systems and the average number of senses generated for each system; our alternative HERMIT configurations are given no rank.

3.3 Unsupervised Evaluation

System	All	Nouns	Verbs	Rank	Senses
HERMIT-S	16.2	16.7	15.3		10.83
HERMIT	16.1	16.7	15.6	1	10.78
Random	4.4	4.6	4.1	18	4.00
HERMIT-F	0.015	0.008	0.025		1.54
MFS	0.0	0.0	0.0	27	1.00
LOW	0.0	0.0	0.1	28	1.01

Table 1: V-Measure for the unsupervised evaluation

System	All	Nouns	Verbs	Rank	Senses
MFS	63.4	57.0	72.7	1	1.00
HIGH	63.3	57.0	72.4	2	1.02
HERMIT-F	62.1	56.7	69.9		1.54
Random	31.9	30.4	34.1	25	4.00
HERMIT	26.7	30.1	24.4	27	10.78
HERMIT-S	26.5	23.9	30.3		10.83
LOW	16.1	15.8	16.4	28	9.71

Table 2: F-Scores for the unsupervised evaluation

The unsupervised evaluation considers a golden sense labeling to be word classes and a set of induced word senses as clusters of target contexts (Manandhar et al., 2010). Tables 1 and 2 display the results for the unsupervised evaluation when measured according to the V-Measure and the F-Score, respectively. Our system provides the best V-Measure of all submitted systems for this evaluation. This is in part due to the average number of senses our system generated (10.78), which favors more homogenous clusters. Conversely, this configuration does poorly when measured by F-Score, which tends to favor systems that generate fewer senses per word.

When configured for the F-Score, HERMIT-F performs well; this configuration would have ranked third for the F-Score if it had been submitted. However, its performance is also due to the relatively few senses per word it generates, 1.54. The inverse performance of both optimized configurations is reflective of the contrasting nature of the two performance measures.

3.4 Supervised Evaluation

System	All	Noun	Verb	Rank
HIGH	62.44	59.43	66.82	1
MFS	58.67	53.22	66.620	15
HERMIT-S	58.48	54.18	64.78	
HERMIT	58.34	53.56	65.30	17
Random	57.25	51.45	65.69	19
HERMIT-F	56.44	53.00	61.46	
LOW	18.72	1.55	43.76	28

Table 3: Supervised recall for the 80/20 split

System	All	Noun	Verb	Rank
HIGH	61.96	58.62	66.82	1
MFS	58.25	52.45	67.11	12
HERMIT	57.27	52.53	64.16	18
HERMIT-S	57.10	52.76	63.46	
Random	56.52	50.21	65.73	20
HERMIT-F	56.18	52.26	61.88	
LOW	18.91	1.52	44.23	28

Table 4: Supervised recall for the 60/40 split

The supervised evaluation simulates a supervised Word Sense Disambiguation (WSD) task. The induced sense labels for the test corpus are split such that the first set is used for mapping induced senses to golden senses and the remaining sense labels are treated as sense labels provided by a WSD system, which allows for evaluation. Five splits are done at random to avoid any biases created due to the separation of the mapping corpus and the evaluation corpus; the resulting score for this task is the average recall over the five divisions. Two sets of splits were used for evaluation: one with 80% of the senses as the mapping portion and 20% as the evaluation portion and one with 60% as the mapping portion corpus and 40% for evaluation.

The results for the 80/20 split and 60/40 split are displayed in tables 3 and 4, respectively. In both supervised evaluations, our submitted system

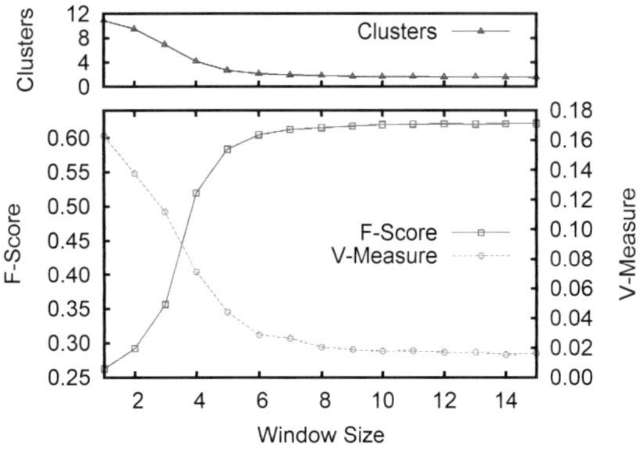

Figure 1: A comparison for F-Score and V-Measure for different window sizes. Scores are an average using thresholds of 0.15, 0.55 and 0.75.

does moderately well. In both cases it outperforms the Random baseline and does almost as well as the MFS baseline. The submitted system outperforms the Random baseline and approaches the MFS baseline for the 80/20 split. The HERMIT-S version, which is optimized for this task, provides similar results.

4 Discussion

The HERMIT system is easily configured to achieve close to state of the art performance for either evaluation measure on the unsupervised benchmark. This reconfigurability allows the algorithm to be tuned for producing a few coarse senses of a word, or many finer-grained senses.

We further investigated the performance with respect to the window size parameter on both measures. Since each score can be effectively optimized individually, we considered whether both scores could be maximized concurrently. Figure 1 presents the impact of the window size on both measures using an average of three threshold parameter configurations.

The analysis of both measures indicates that reasonable performance can be obtained from using a slightly larger context window. For example, a window size of 4 has an average F-Score of 52.4 and V-Measure of 7.1. Although this configuration produces scores lower than the optimized versions, its performance would have ranked 12th according to V-Measure and 15th for F-Score. These scores are consistent with the median performance of the submitted systems and offer a middle ground should a HERMIT user want a compromise between many fine-grained word senses and a few coarse-grained word senses.

5 Conclusion

We have shown that our model is a highly flexible and tunable Word Sense Induction model. Depending on the task, it can be optimized to generate a set of word senses that range from being broad and representative to highly refined. Furthermore, we demonstrated a balanced performance setting for both measures for when parameter tuning is not possible. The model we submitted and presented is only one possible configuration available, and in the future we will be exploring the effect of other context features, such as syntactic structure in the form of word ordering (Sahlgren et al., 2008) or dependency parse trees, (Padó and Lapata, 2007), and other clustering algorithms. Last, this model is provided as part of the S-Space Package (Jurgens and Stevens, 2010), an open source toolkit for word space algorithms.

References

David Jurgens and Keith Stevens. 2010. The S-Space Package: An Open Source Package for Word Space Models. In *Proceedings of the ACL 2010 System Deonstrations*.

Pentti Kanerva, Jan Kristoferson, and Anders Holst. 2000. Random indexing of text samples for latent semantic analysis. In L. R. Gleitman and A. K. Josh, editors, *Proceedings of the 22nd Annual Conference of the Cognitive Science Society*, page 1036.

Suresh Manandhar, Ioannis P. Klapaftis, Dmitriy Dligach, and Sameer S. Pradhan. 2010. SemEval-2010 Task 14: Word Sense Induction & Disambiguation. In *Proceedings of SemEval-2*.

Sebastian Padó and Mirella Lapata. 2007. Dependency-Based Construction of Semantic Space Models. *Computational Linguistics*, 33(2):161–199.

Ted Pedersen and Rebecca Bruce. 1997. Distinguishing word senses in untagged text. In *Proceedings of the Second Conference on Empirical Methods in Natural Language Processing*, pages 197–207.

Andrew Rosenberg and Julia Hirschberg. 2007. V-Measure: A Conditional Entropy-Based External Cluster Evaluation Measure. In *Proceedings of the 2007 Joint Conference on Empirical Methods in Natural Language Processing and Computational Natural Language Learning (EMNLP-CoNLL)*. ACL.

Magnus Sahlgren, Anders Holst, and Pentti Kanerva. 2008. Permutations as a means to encode order in word space. In *Proceedings of the 30th Annual Meeting of the Cognitive Science Society (CogSci'08)*.

Duluth-WSI: SenseClusters Applied to the Sense Induction Task of SemEval-2

Ted Pedersen
Department of Computer Science
University of Minnesota, Duluth
Duluth, MN 55812
tpederse@d.umn.edu
http://senseclusters.sourceforge.net

Abstract

The Duluth-WSI systems in SemEval-2 built word co–occurrence matrices from the task test data to create a second order co–occurrence representation of those test instances. The senses of words were induced by clustering these instances, where the number of clusters was automatically predicted. The Duluth-Mix system was a variation of WSI that used the combination of training and test data to create the co-occurrence matrix. The Duluth-R system was a series of random baselines.

1 Introduction

The Duluth systems in the sense induction task of SemEval-2 (Manandhar et al., 2010) were based on SenseClusters (v1.01), a freely available open source software package which relies on the premise that words with similar meanings will occur in similar contexts (Purandare and Pedersen, 2004). The data for the sense induction task included 100 ambiguous words made up of 50 nouns and 50 verbs. There were a total of 8,915 test instances and 879,807 training instances provided. Note that neither the training nor the test data was sense tagged. The training data was made available as a resource for participants, with the understanding that system evaluation would be done on the test instances only. Thc organizers held back a gold standard annotation of the test data that was only used for evaluation.

Five Duluth-WSI systems participated in this task, six Duluth-Mix systems, and five Duluth Random systems. The WSI and Mix systems almost always represented the test instances using second order co–occurrences, where each word in a test instance is replaced by a vector that shows the words with which it co-occurs. The word vectors that make up a test instance are averaged together to make up a new representation for that instance. All the test instances for a word are clustered, and the number of senses is automatically predicted by either the PK2 measure or Adapted Gap Statistic (Pedersen and Kulkarni, 2006).

In the Duluth systems the co-occurrence matrices are either based on order-dependent bigrams or unordered pairs of words, both of which can be separated by up to some given number of intervening words. Bigrams are used to preserve distinctions between collocations such as *cat house* and *house cat*, whereas co–occurrences do not consider order and would treat these two as being equivalent.

2 Duluth-WSI systems

The Duluth-WSI systems build co-occurrence matrices from the test data by identifying bigrams or co–occurrences that occur with up to eight intermediate words between them in instances of ambiguous nouns, and up to 23 intermediate words for the verbs. Any bigram (bi) or co–occurrence (co) that occurs more than 5 times with up to the allowed number of intervening words and has statistical significance of 0.95 or above according to the left-sided Fisher's exact test was selected (Pedersen et al., 1996). Some of the WSI systems reduce the co–occurrence matrix to 300 dimensions using Singular Value Decomposition (SVD).

The resulting co-occurrence matrix was used to create second order co–occurrence vectors to represent the test instances, which were clustered using the method of repeated bisections (rb), where similarity was measured using the cosine. Table 1 summarizes the distinctions between the various Duluth-WSI systems.

3 Duluth-Mix systems

The Duluth-Mix systems used the combination of the test and training data to identify features to represent the test instances. The goal of this combi-

Proceedings of the 5th International Workshop on Semantic Evaluation, ACL 2010, pages 363–366,
Uppsala, Sweden, 15-16 July 2010.

Table 1: Duluth-WSI Distinctions

name	options
Duluth-WSI	bigrams, no SVD, PK2
Duluth-WSI-Gap	bigrams, no SVD, Gap
Duluth-WSI-SVD	bigrams, SVD, PK2
Duluth-WSI-Co	co-occur, no SVD, PK2
Duluth-WSI-Co-Gap	co-occur, no SVD, Gap

nation was to increase the amount of data that was available for feature identification. Since there was a larger amount of data, some parameter settings as used in Duluth-WSI were reduced.

For example, the Duluth-Mix-PK2 and Duluth-Mix-Gap are identical to the Duluth-WSI and Duluth-WSI-Gap systems, except that they limit both nouns and verbs to 8 intervening words. Duluth-Mix-Narrow-PK2 and Duluth-Mix-Narrow-Gap are identical to Duluth-Mix-PK2 and Duluth-Mix-Gap except that bigrams and co–occurrences must be made up of adjacent words, with no intermediate words allowed.

Duluth-Mix-Uni-PK2 and Duluth-Mix-Uni-Gap are unique among the Duluth systems in that they do not use second order co-occurrences, but instead rely on first order co-occurrences. These are simply individual words (unigrams) that occur more than 5 times in the combined test and training data. These features are used to generate co-occurrence vectors for the test instances which are then clustered (this is very similar to a bag of words model).

4 Duluth-Random systems

Duluth-R12, Duluth-R13, Duluth-R15, and Duluth-R110 provide random baselines. R12 randomly assigns each instance to one of two senses, R13 to one of three, R15 to one of five, and R110 to one of ten senses. Random numbers are generated in the given range with equal probability, so the distribution of assigned senses is balanced.

5 Discussion

The evaluation of unsupervised sense discrimination and induction systems is still not standardized, so an important part of any exercise like SemEval-2 is to scrutinize the evaluation measures used in order to determine to what degree they are providing a useful and reasonable way of evaluating system results.

5.1 Evaluation Measures

Each participating system was scored by three different evaluation methods: the V-measure (Rosenberg and Hirschberg, 2007), the supervised recall measure (Agirre and Soroa, 2007), and the paired F-score (Artiles et al., 2009). The results of the evaluation are in some sense confusing - a system that ranks near the top according to one measure may rank at the bottom or middle of another. There was not any single system that did well according to all of the different measures. The situation is so extreme that in some cases a system would perform near the top in one measure, and then below random baselines in another. These stark differences suggest a real need for continued development of other methods for evaluating unsupervised sense induction.

One minimum expectation of an evaluation measure is that it should expose and identify random baselines by giving them low scores that clearly distinguish them from actual participating systems. The scores of all the evaluation measures used in this task when applied to different random baseline systems are summarized in Table 2. These include a number of post-evaluation random clustering systems, which are referred to as post-R1k, where k is the number of random clusters.

5.1.1 V-measure

The V-measure appears to be quite easily mislead by random baselines. As evidence of that, the Duluth-R (random) systems got increasingly better scores the more random they became, and in fact the post-evaluation random systems reached levels of performance better than any of the participating systems. Table 2 shows that the V-measure continues to improve (rather dramatically) as randomness increases.

The average number of senses in the gold standard data for all 100 words was 3.79. The official random baseline assigned one of four random senses to each instance of a word, and achieved a V-measure of 4.40. Duluth-R15 improved the V-measure to 5.30 by assigning one of five random senses, and Duluth-R110 improved it again to 8.60 by assigning one of ten random senses. The more random the result, the better the score. In fact Duluth-R110 placed sixth in the sense induction task according to the V-measure. In post-evaluation experiments a number of additional random baselines were explored, where instances were assigned senses randomly from 20, 33, and 50 possible values per word. The V-measures for these random systems were 13.9, 18.7, and 23.2 respectively, where the latter two were better than the first place participating system (which scored 16.2). In a post-evaluation experiment, the task organizers found that assigning one sense per instance resulted in a V–measure of 31.7.

5.1.2 Supervised Recall

The supervised recall measure takes the sense induction results (on the 8,915 test instances) as submitted by a participating system and splits that into a training and test portion for supervised learning. The recall attained on the test split by a classifier learned on the training split becomes the measure of the unsupervised system. Two different splits were used, with 80% or 60% of the test instances for training, and the remainder for testing.

This evaluation method was also used in SemEval-1, where (Pedersen, 2007) noted that it seemed to compress the results of all the systems into a narrow band that converged around the Most Frequent Sense result. The same appears to have happened in 2010. The supervised recall of the Most Frequent Sense baseline (MFS) is 58 or .59 (depending on the split), and the majority of participating systems (and even some of the random baselines) fall in a range of scores from .56 to .62 (a band of .06). This blurs distinctions among participating systems with each other and with random baselines.

The number of senses actually assigned by the classifier learned from the training split to the instances in the test split is quite small, regardless of the number of senses discovered by the participating system. There were *at most* 2.06 senses identified per word based on the 80-20 split, and *at most* 2.27 senses per word based on the 60-40 split. For most systems, regardless of their underlying methodology, the number of senses the classifier actually assigns is approximately 1.5 per word. This shows that the supervised learning algorithm that underlies this evaluation method gravitates towards a very small number of senses and therefore tends to converge on the MFS baseline. This could be caused by noise in the induced senses, a small number of examples in the training split for a sense, or it may be that the supervised recall measure is making different distinctions than are found by the unsupervised sense induction method it seeks to evaluate.

Table 2: Evaluation of Random Systems

name	k	V	F	60-40	80-20
MFS	1	0.0	**63.4**	**58.3**	**58.7**
Duluth-R12	2	2.3	47.8	57.7	58.5
Duluth-R13	3	3.6	38.4	57.6	58.0
Random	4	4.4	31.9	56.5	57.3
Duluth-R15	5	5.3	27.6	56.5	56.8
Duluth-R110	10	8.6	16.1	53.6	54.8
post-R120	20	13.9	7.5	46.2	48.6
post-R133	33	18.7	4.0	38.3	42.5
post-R150	50	**23.2**	2.3	30.0	34.2

5.1.3 Paired F-score

The paired F-score was the only evaluation measure that seemed able to identify and expose random baselines. Duluth-R110 was by far the most random of the officially participating systems, and it was by far the lowest ranked system according to the paired F-score, which assigned it a score of 16.1. All the Duluth-R systems ranked relatively low (20th or below). When presented with the 20, 33, and 50 random sense post–evaluation systems, the F-score assigned those scores of 7.46, 4.00, and 2.33, which placed them far below any of the other systems.

However, the paired F-score also showed that the Most Frequent Sense baseline outperformed all of the participating systems. The systems that scored close to the MFS tended to predict very small numbers of senses, and so were in effect acting much like the MFS baseline themselves. The F-score is not bounded by MFS and in fact it is possible (theoretically) to reach a score of 1.00 with a perfect assignment of instances to senses. The lesson learned in this task is that it would have been more effective to simply assume that there was just one sense per word, rather than using the senses induced by participating systems. While this may be a frustrating conclusion, in fact it is a reasonable observation given that in many domains a single sense for a given word can tend to dominate.

5.2 Duluth-WSI and Duluth-Mix Results

The Duluth-WSI systems used the test data to build co-occurrence matrices, while the Duluth-

Mix systems used both the training and test data. Within those frameworks bigrams or co–occurrences were used to represent features, the number of senses was automatically discovered with the PK2 measure or the Adapted Gap Statistic, and SVD was optionally used to reduce the dimensionality of the resulting matrix. Previous studies using SenseClusters have noted that the Adapted Gap Statistic tends to find a relatively small number of clusters, and that SVD typically does not help to improve results of unsupervised sense induction. These findings were again confirmed in this task.

Mixing together all of the training and test data for building the co–occurrence matrices was no more effective than just using the test data. However, the Duluth-Mix systems did not finish before the end of the evaluation period. The Duluth-Mix-Narrow-Gap and PK2 systems were able to finish 8,211 of the 8,915 test instances (92%), the Duluth-Mix-Gap and PK2 systems completed 7,417 instances (83%), and Duluth-Mix-Uni-PK2 and Gap systems completed 2,682 of these instances (30%). While these are partial results they seem sufficient to support this conclusion.

To be usable in practical settings, an unsupervised sense induction system should discover the number of senses accurately and automatically. Duluth-WSI and Duluth-WSI-SVD were very successful in that regard, and predicted 4.15 senses on average per word (with the PK2 measure) while the actual number of senses was 3.79.

The Duluth-WSI systems are direct descendents of UMND2 which participated in SemEval-1 (Pedersen, 2007), where Duluth-WSI-Gap is the closest relative. However, UMND2 used Pointwise Mutual Information (PMI) rather than Fisher's left sided test, and it performed clustering with k-means rather than the method of repeated bisections. Both UMND2 and Duluth-WSI-Gap used the Adapted Gap Statistic, and interestingly enough both discovered approximately 1.4 senses on average per word.

6 Conclusion

The SemEval-2 sense induction task was an opportunity to compare participating systems with each other, and also to analyze evaluation measures. At the very least, an evaluation measure should penalize random results in a fairly significant way. This task showed that the paired F-score is able to identify and expose random baselines, and that it drives them far down the rankings and places them well below participating systems. This seems preferable to the V-measure, which tends to rank random systems above all others, and to supervised recall, which provides little or no separation between random baselines and participating systems.

References

E. Agirre and A. Soroa. 2007. SemEval-2007 Task 02: Evaluating word sense induction and discrimination systems. In *Proceedings of the Fourth International Workshop on Semantic Evaluations (SemEval-2007)*, pages 7–12, Prague, Czech Republic, June.

J. Artiles, E. Amigó, and J. Gonzalo. 2009. The role of named entities in Web People Search. In *Proceedings of the 2009 Conference on Empirical Methods in Natural Language Processing*, pages 534–542, Singapore, August.

S. Manandhar, I. Klapaftis, D. Dligach, and S. Pradhan. 2010. SemEval-2010 Task 14: Word sense induction and disambiguation. In *Proceedings of the SemEval 2010 Workshop : the 5th International Workshop on Semantic Evaluations*, Uppsala, Sweden, July.

T. Pedersen and A. Kulkarni. 2006. Automatic cluster stopping with criterion functions and the gap statistic. In *Proceedings of the Demonstration Session of the Human Language Technology Conference and the Sixth Annual Meeting of the North American Chapter of the Association for Computational Linguistics*, pages 276–279, New York City, June.

T. Pedersen, M. Kayaalp, and R. Bruce. 1996. Significant lexical relationships. In *Proceedings of the Thirteenth National Conference on Artificial Intelligence*, pages 455–460, Portland, OR, August.

T. Pedersen. 2007. UMND2 : SenseClusters applied to the sense induction task of Senseval-4. In *Proceedings of the Fourth International Workshop on Semantic Evaluations (SemEval-2007)*, pages 394–397, Prague, Czech Republic, June.

A. Purandare and T. Pedersen. 2004. Word sense discrimination by clustering contexts in vector and similarity spaces. In *Proceedings of the Conference on Computational Natural Language Learning*, pages 41–48, Boston, MA.

A. Rosenberg and J. Hirschberg. 2007. V-measure: A conditional entropy-based external cluster evaluation measure. In *Proceedings of the 2007 Joint Conference on Empirical Methods in Natural Language Processing and Computational Natural Language Learning*, pages 410–420, Prague, Czech Republic, June.

KSU KDD: Word Sense Induction by Clustering in Topic Space

Wesam Elshamy, Doina Caragea, William H. Hsu
Kansas State University
{welshamy, dcaragea, bhsu}@ksu.edu

Abstract

We describe our language-independent unsupervised word sense induction system. This system only uses topic features to cluster different word senses in their global context topic space. Using unlabeled data, this system trains a latent Dirichlet allocation (LDA) topic model then uses it to infer the topics distribution of the test instances. By clustering these topics distributions in their topic space we cluster them into different senses. Our hypothesis is that closeness in topic space reflects similarity between different word senses. This system participated in SemEval-2 word sense induction and disambiguation task and achieved the second highest V-measure score among all other systems.

1 Introduction

Ambiguity of meaning is inherent in natural language because the deliverer of words tries to minimize the size of the vocabulary set he uses. Therefore, a sizable portion of this vocabulary is polysemous and the intended meaning of such words can be encoded in their context.

Due to the knowledge acquisition bottleneck problem and scarcity in training data (Cai et al., 2007), unsupervised corpus based approaches could be favored over supervised ones in word sense disambiguation (WSD) tasks.

Similar efforts in this area include work by Cai et al. (Cai et al., 2007) in which they use latent Dirichlet allocation (LDA) topic models to extract the global context topic and use it as a feature along other baseline features. Another technique uses clustering based approach with WordNet as an external resource for disambiguation without relying on training data (Anaya-Sánchez et al., 2007).

To disambiguate a polysemous word in a text document, we use the document topic distribution to represent its context. A document topic distribution is the probabilistic distribution of a document over a set of topics. The assumption is that: given two word senses and the topic distribution of their context, the closeness between these two topic distributions in their topic space is an indication of the similarity between those two senses.

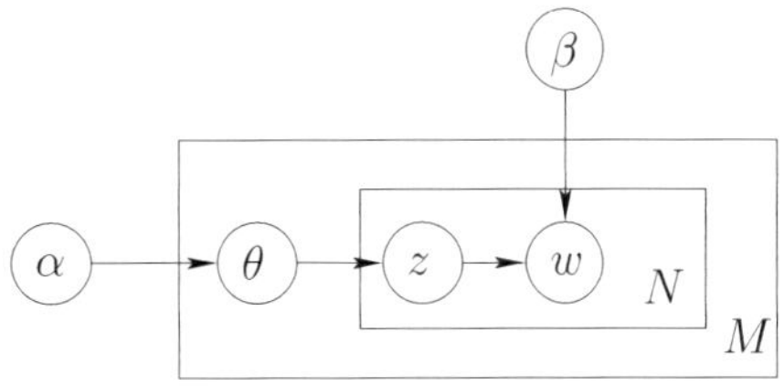

Figure 1: A graphical model for LDA

Our motivation behind building this system was the observation that the context of a polysemous word helps determining its sense to some degree. In our word sense induction (WSI) system, we use LDA to create a topic model for the given corpus and use it to infer the topic distribution of the documents containing the ambiguous words.

This paper describes our WSI system which participated in SemEval-2 word sense induction and disambiguation task (Manandhar et al., 2010).

2 Latent Dirichlet allocation

LDA is a probabilistic model for a collection of discrete data (Blei et al., 2003). It can be graphically represented as shown in Figure 1 as a three level hierarchical Bayesian model. In this model, the corpus consists of M documents, each is a multinomial distribution over K topics, which are in turn multinomial distributions over words.

To generate a document d using this probabilistic model, a distribution over topics θ_d is generated using a Dirichlet prior with parameter α. Then, for each of the N_d words w_{dn} in the document, a topic z_{dn} is drawn from a multinomial distribution with the parameter θ_d. Then, a word w_{dn} is drawn from that topic's distribution over words, given $\beta_{ij} = p(w = i|z = j)$. Where β_{ij} is the probability of choosing word i given topic j.

3 System description

We wanted to examine the trade-off between simplicity, cost and performance by building a simple

Proceedings of the 5th International Workshop on Semantic Evaluation, ACL 2010, pages 367–370,
Uppsala, Sweden, 15-16 July 2010.

language-independent, totally unsupervised, computationally cheap system and compare its performance to other WSI systems participating in the SemEval-2 WSI task (Manandhar et al., 2010). We expect a degradation in precision of our simple approach as the granularity of senses becomes finer; This is due to the degrading sensitivity in mapping between the topics space and the senses space. We note that our simple approach will fail if multiple senses of the same word appear in the same document; Since these senses will be represented by the same topic distribution of the document, they will be clustered in the same cluster.

Our system is a language-independent system. The used LDA topic model has no knowledge of the training or testing corpus language. Unlike most other WSI and WSD systems, it doesn't make use of part of speech (POS) features which are language dependent and require POS annotated training data. The only features used are the topics distribution of bag-of-words containing the ambiguous word.

First, for each target polysemous word *wp* (noun or verb), we train a MALLET[1] parallel topic model implementation of LDA on all the training instances of that word. Then we use the trained topic model to infer the topics distribution θ_l for each of the test instances of that word. For a K-topics topic model, each topics distribution can be represented as a point in a K-dimensional topic space. These points can be clustered into C different clusters, each representing a word sense. We used MALLET's K-means clustering algorithm with cosine similarity to measure the distance between different topic distributions in the topic space.

4 Evaluation measures

We use the same unsupervised evaluation measures used in SemEval-2 (Manandhar and Klapaftis, 2009). These measures do not require descriptive

The V-measure is used for unsupervised evaluation. It is the harmonic mean of the *homogeneity* and *completeness*. Homogeneity is a measure of the degree that each formed cluster consists of data points that belong to a single gold standard (GS) class as defined below.

$$homogeneity = 1 - \frac{H(GS|C)}{H(GS)} \quad (1)$$

$$H(GS) = -\sum_{i=1}^{|GS|} \frac{\sum_{j=1}^{|C|} a_{ij}}{N} \log \frac{\sum_{j=1}^{|C|} a_{ij}}{N} \quad (2)$$

$$H(GS|C) = -\sum_{j=1}^{|C|} \sum_{i=1}^{|GS|} \frac{a_{ij}}{N} \log \frac{a_{ij}}{\sum_{k=1}^{|GS|} a_{kj}} \quad (3)$$

[1]http://mallet.cs.umass.edu

Table 1: Effect of varying the number of topics K on performance

K	10	50	200	400	500
V-measure	5.1	5.8	7.2	8.4	8.1
F-score	8.6	32.0	53.9	63.9	64.2

Where $H()$ is an entropy function, $|C|$ and $|GS|$ refer to cluster and class sizes, respectively. N is the number of data points, a_{ij} are data points of class GS_i that belong to cluster C_j.

On the other hand, completeness measures the degree that each class consists of data points that belong to a single cluster. It is defined as follows.

$$completeness = 1 - \frac{H(C|GS)}{H(C)} \quad (4)$$

$$H(C) = -\sum_{j=1}^{|C|} \frac{\sum_{i=1}^{|GS|} a_{ij}}{N} \log \frac{\sum_{i=1}^{|GS|} a_{ij}}{N} \quad (5)$$

$$H(C|GS) = -\sum_{i=1}^{|GS|} \sum_{j=1}^{|C|} \frac{a_{ij}}{N} \log \frac{a_{ij}}{\sum_{k=1}^{|C|} a_{ik}} \quad (6)$$

Homogeneity and completeness can be seen as entropy based measures of precision and recall, respectively. The V-measure has a range of 0 (worst performance) to 1, inclusive.

The other evaluation measure is the F-score, which is the harmonic mean of precision and recall. It has a range of 0 to 1 (best performance), inclusive.

5 Experiments and results

The WSI system described earlier was tested on SemEval-1 WSI task (task 2) data (65 verbs, 35 nouns), and participated in the same task in SemEval-2 (task 14) (50 verbs, 50 nouns). The sense induction process was the same in both cases.

Before running our main experiments, we wanted to see how the number of topics K used in the topic model could affect the performance of our system. We tested our WSI system on SemEval-1 data using different K values as shown in Table 1. We found that the V-measure and F-score values increase with increasing K, as more dimensions are added to the topic space, the different senses in this K-dimensional space unfold. This trend stops at a value of $K = 400$ in a sign to the limited vocabulary of the training data. This K value is used in all other experiments.

Next, we evaluated the performance of our system on SemEval-1 WSI task data. Since no training data was provided for this task, we used an unannotated version of the test instances to create the LDA topic model. For each target word (verb or noun), we trained the topic model on its given test

Table 2: V-measure and F-score on SemEval-1

	All	Verbs	Nouns
V-measure	8.4	8.0	8.7
F-score	63.9	56.8	69.0

Table 3: V-measure and F-score on SemEval-2

	All	Verbs	Nouns
V-measure	15.7	12.4	18.0
F-score	36.9	54.7	24.6

instances. Then we used the generated model's inferencer to find the topics distribution of each one of them. These distributions are then clustered in the topic space using the K-means algorithm and the cosine similarity measure was used to evaluate the distances between these distributions. The results of this experiment are shown in Table 2.

Our WSI system took part in the main SemEval-2 WSI task (task 14). In the unsupervised evaluation, our system had the second highest V-measure value of 15.7 for all words[2]. A break down of the obtained V-measure and F-scores is shown in Table 3.

To analyze the performance of the system, we examined the clustering of the target noun word "*promotion*" to different senses by our system. We compared it to the GS classes of this word in the answer key provided by the task organizers. For a more objective comparison, we ran the K-means clustering algorithm with K equal to the number of GS classes. Even though the number of formed clusters affects the performance of the system, we assume that the number of senses is known in this analysis. We focus on the ability of the algorithm to cluster similar senses together. A graphical comparison is given in Figure 2.

The target noun word "promotion" has 27 instances and four senses. The lower four rectangles in Figure 2 represent the four different GS classes, and the upper four rectangles represent the four clusters created by our system. Three of the four instances representing a *job* "promotion" (○) were clustered together, but the fourth one was clustered in a different class due to terms like "driving," "troops," and "hostile" in its context. The offer sense of "promotion" (▽) was mainly split between two clusters, cluster 2 which most of its instances has mentions of numbers and monetary units, and cluster 4 which describes business and labor from an employee's eye.

The 13 instances of the third class which carry the sense *encourage* of the word promotion (□) are distributed among the four different clusters de-

[2] A complete evaluation of all participating systems is available online at: http://www.cs.york.ac.uk/semeval2010_WSI/task_14_ranking.html

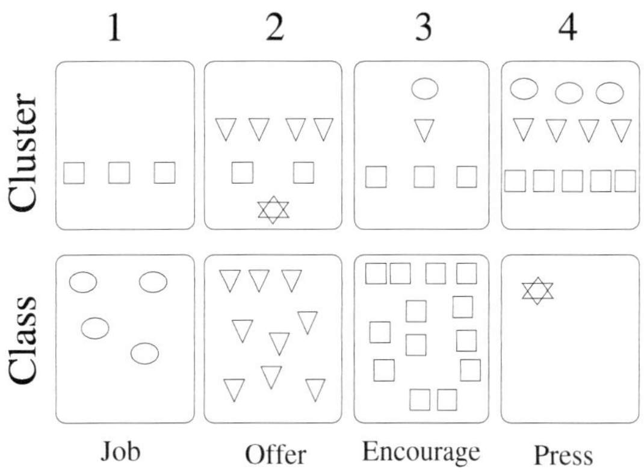

Figure 2: Analysis of sense clustering

pending on other topic words that classified them as either belonging to cluster 4 (encouragement in business), cluster 3 (encouragement in conflict or war context), cluster 2 (numbers and money context), or cluster 1 (otherwise). We can see that the topic model is unable to detect and extract topic words for the "encourage" sense of the word. Finally, due to the lack of enough training instances of the sense of a promotional issue of a newspaper (✡), the topic model inferencer clustered it in the numbers and monetary cluster because it was rich in numbers.

6 Conclusion

Clustering the topics distributions of the global context of polysemous words in the topic space to induce their sense is cheap as it does not require any annotated data and is language-independent.

Even though the clustering produced by our system did not fully conform with the set of senses given by the GS classes, it can be seen from the analyzed example given earlier that our clustering carried some different senses. In one case, a GS sense was not captured by the topic model, and instead, other cues from its instances context were used to cluster them accordingly. The induced clustering had some noise though.

This simple WSI approach can be used for cheap sense induction or for languages for which no POS tagger has been created yet. This system which had the second highest V-measure score in SemEval-2 WSI task achieves a good trade-off between performance and cost.

References

Henry Anaya-Sánchez, Aurora Pons-Porrata, and Rafael Berlanga-Llavori. 2007. Tkb-uo: Using sense clustering for wsd. In *Proceedings of the Fourth International Workshop on Semantic Evaluations (SemEval-2007)*, pages 322–325,

Prague, Czech Republic, June. Association for Computational Linguistics.

David M. Blei, Andrew Y. Ng, and Michael I. Jordan. 2003. Latent dirichlet allocation. *J. Mach. Learn. Res.*, 3:993–1022.

Junfu Cai, Wee Sun Lee, and Yee Whye Teh. 2007. Improving word sense disambiguation using topic features. In *Proceedings of the 2007 Joint Conference on Empirical Methods in Natural Language Processing and Computational Natural Language Learning (EMNLP-CoNLL)*, pages 1015–1023, Prague, Czech Republic, June. Association for Computational Linguistics.

Suresh Manandhar and Ioannis P. Klapaftis. 2009. Semeval-2010 task 14: evaluation setting for word sense induction & disambiguation systems. In *DEW '09: Proceedings of the Workshop on Semantic Evaluations: Recent Achievements and Future Directions*, pages 117–122, Morristown, NJ, USA. Association for Computational Linguistics.

Suresh Manandhar, Ioannis P. Klapaftis, Dmitriy Dligach, and Sameer S. Pradhan. 2010. Semeval-2010 task 14: Word sense induction & disambiguation. In *Proceedings of SemEval-2*, Uppsala, Sweden. ACL.

PengYuan@PKU: Extracting Infrequent Sense Instance with the Same N-gram Pattern for the SemEval-2010 Task 15

Peng-Yuan Liu[1] Shui Liu[2] Shi-Wen Yu[1] Tie-Jun Zhao[2]
[1]Institute of Computational Linguistics, Peking University, Beijing, China
[2]Department of Computer Science, Harbin Institute of Technology, Harbin, China
{liupengyuan,yusw}@pku.edu.cn,{tjzhao,liushui}@mtlab.hit.edu.cn

Abstract

This paper describes our infrequent sense identification system participating in the SemEval-2010 task 15 on Infrequent Sense Identification for Mandarin Text to Speech Systems. The core system is a supervised system based on the ensembles of Naïve Bayesian classifiers. In order to solve the problem of unbalanced sense distribution, we intentionally extract only instances of infrequent sense with the same N-gram pattern as the complemental training data from an untagged Chinese corpus – People's Daily of the year 2001. At the same time, we adjusted the prior probability to adapt to the distribution of the test data and tuned the smoothness coefficient to take the data sparseness into account. Official result shows that, our system ranked the first with the best Macro Accuracy 0.952. We briefly describe this system, its configuration options and the features used for this task and present some discussion of the results.

1 Introduction

We participated in the SemEval-2010 task 15 on Infrequent Sense Identification for Mandarin Text to Speech Systems. This task required systems to disambiguating the homograph word, a word that has the same POS (part of speech) but different pronunciation. In this case, we still considered it as a WSD (word sense disambiguation) problem, but it is a little different from WSD. In this task, two or more senses of the same word may correspond to one pronunciation. That is, the sense granularity is coarser than traditional WSD.

The challenge of this task is the much skewed distribution in real text: the most frequent pronunciation accounts for usually over 80%. In fact, in the training data provided by the organizer , we found that the sense distribution of some words are distinctly unbalanced. For each of these words, there are fewer than ten instances of one sense whereas the dominant sense instances are hundreds or more. At the same time, according to the task description on the task 15 of SemEval-2010(http://semeval2.fbk.eu/semeval2.php?location=tasks), the test dataset of this task is intentionally divided into the infrequent pronunciation instances and the frequent ones by half and half. Apparently, if we use traditional methods and only the provided training dataset to train whatever classifier, it is very likely that we will get an disambiguation result that all (at least the overwhelming number) the test instances of these words would be labeled with the most frequent pronunciation (sense) tag. Then our system is meaningless for the target of the task is focused on the performance of identifying the infrequent sense.

In order to solve the problem of the unbalanced sense distribution in the training data and the fairly balanced sense distribution in the test data, we designed our PengYuan@PKU system, which attempts to extract infrequent sense instances only and adjust the prior probability so as to counteract the problem as far as possible. The core system is a supervised system based on the ensembles of Naïve Bayesian classifiers. The complemental training data is extracted from an untagged Chinese corpus – People's Daily of the year 2001 automatically. Besides the motivation of investigating the function of our method of compensating infrequent sense instances, we are also interested in the role where the smoothness plays when it encounters with such a data sparseness here.

In section 2, we will describe our system that includes the core classifier, its configuration options and features. In section 3, we will show the official results of this task and present some analyses and discussions. Section 4 is related

Proceedings of the 5th International Workshop on Semantic Evaluation, ACL 2010, pages 371–374,
Uppsala, Sweden, 15-16 July 2010.

works. The conclusion and future work are in section 5.

2 System Description

2.1 Naïve Bayesian Classifier and Features

For a naïve Bayesian classifier, the joint probability of observing a certain combination of context features with a particular sense is expressed as:

$$p(F_1, F_2, ..., F_n, S) = p(S)\prod_{i=1}^{n} p(F_i \mid S) \qquad (1)$$

In equation (1), (F_1, F_2,..., F_n) is feature variables, S is classification variable and $p(S)$ is the prior probability of classification variable. Any parameter that has a value of zero indicates that the associated word never occurs with the specified sense value. These zero values are smoothed by additive smoothing method as expressed below:

$$P(F_i \mid S_k) = \frac{C(F_i, S_k) + \lambda}{C(S_k) + N}, \quad \lambda \in (0,1) \qquad (2)$$

In equation (2), λ is the smoothness variable. $C(S_k)$ is the times of instances with S_k label. $C(F_i,S_k)$ is the concurrences times of F_i and S_k. N is the times of total words in the corpus.

The features and their weights of context used in one single Naïve Bayesian classifier are described in Table 1.

Features	Description	weights
$w_{-i}...w_i$	Content words appearing within the window of $\pm i$ words on each side of the target word	1
w_j/j $j\in[-3,3]$	Word forms and their position information of the words at fixed positions from the target word.	3
$w_{k-1}w_k$ $k\in(-i,i]$	word bigrams appearing within the window of $\pm i$	1 when i>3, else 3
$P_{k-1}P_k$ $k\in(-i,i]$	POS bigrams appearing within the window of $\pm i$	1

Table 1: Features and their weights used in one Naïve Bayesian classifier

2.2 Ensembles the Naïve Bayesian Classifiers

The ensemble strategy of our system is like Pederson (2000). The windows of context have seven different sizes (i): 3, 5, 7, 9, 11, 13 and 15 words. The first step in the ensemble approach is to train a separate Naïve Bayesian classifier for each of the seven window sizes.

Each of the seven member classifiers votes for the most probable sense given the particular context represented by that classifier; the ensemble disambiguates by assigning the sense that receives the majority of the votes.

2.3 Infrequent Sense Instances Acquisition

N-gram		Increasing Instances Number	
3-gram	(-1,1)	246	1026(9135)
	(-2,0)	229	
	(0,2)	551	
2-gram	(-1,0)	1123	2967(9135)
	(0,1)	1844	

Table 2: The overview of the training data before and after the extracting stage

Target Words	Sense Distribution					
	Before (O)		After			
			(O+E3)		(O+E2)	
背	128	51	128	66	128	262[1]
车	503	83	503	83	503	194
澄清	168	13	168	16	168	23
冲	175	10	175	27	175	88
当	487	42	487	63	487	267
合计	134	44	134	44	134	49
见长	125	11	125	11	125	12
看	2020	8	2020	12	2020	25
落	300	3	300	6	300	32
没	268	3	268	4	268	45
上	1625	41	1625	346	1625	1625
系	144	13	144	15	144	33
兄弟	136	8	136	9	136	16
应	1666	253	1666	847	1666	1567
攒	142	17	142	17	142	17
转	438	76	438	136	438	414

Table 3: The sense distributions of the training data before and after the extracting stage

Our system uses a special heuristic rule to extract the sense labeled infrequent sense instances automatically. The heuristic rule assumes that *one sense per N-gram* which we testified initially through investigating a Chinese sense-tagged corpus STC (Wu et al., 2006). Our assumption is inspired by the celebrated *one sense per collocation* supposition (Yarowsky, 1993). STC is an ongoing project of building a sense-tagged

[1] We intentionally control the sense distribution of word ("背") and change it from approximately 2.5:1 to 1:2 so as to investigate the influence.

corpus which contained the sense-tagged 1, 2 and 3 months of People's Daily of the year 2000. According to our investigation, to any target multi-sense word, given a specific N-gram (N>1) including the target word, we will expect to see the same label that range from 88.6% to 99.2% of the time on average. So, based on the training data, we can extract instance with the same N - gram pattern from the untagged Chinese corpus and we assume if the N-gram is the same then the sense-label is the same.

For all the 16 multiple-sense target words in the training data of task 15, we found the N-gram of infrequence sense instances and extracted[2] the instances with the same N-gram from People's Daily of the year 2001(about 116M bytes). We extracted as many as possible until the total number of them is equal to the dominant sense instance number. We appointed the same N-gram instances the same sense tag and (merge?) it into the original training corpus. Table 2 and 3 show the overview and the sense distribution of the training data before and after the extracting stage. Number 9135 in brackets of Table 2 is the instance number of original training corpus. O, O+E3, O+E2 in Table 3 mean original training data, original training data plus extracted 3-gram instances and original training data plus extracted 2-gram instances respectively. Limited to the scale of the corpus, the unbalance sense distribution of some words does not improve much.

2.4 Other Configuration Options

Systems	Training Data	$p(S)$	λ
_3.001	O+E3	0.5	0.001
_3.1	O+E3	0.5	0.1
_2.001	O+E2	0.5	0.001
_2.1	O+E2	0.5	0.1

Table 4: The system configuration

To formula (1), we tune the prior probability of classification variable $p(S)$ as a constant to match the sense distribution of test data. Considering the data sparseness as there may have been in the test stage, to formula (2), we set 2 kinds of λ to investigate the effect of smoothness.

In total, we develop four systems based on various configuration options. They are showed in Table 4.

[2] In order to guarantee the extracted instances are not duplicated in the training data or in the test data in case, our system filters the repeated instances automatically if they are already in the original training or test dataset.

3 Results and Discussions

3.1 Official Results

System ID	Micro Accuracy	Macro Accuracy	Rank
_3.001	0.974	0.952	1/9
_3.1	0.965	0.942	2/9
_2.001	0.965	0.941	3/9
_2.1	0.965	0.942	2/9
Baseline	0.924	0.895	

Table 5: Official results 1 of PengYuan@PKU

Words	Precision				
	_3.001	_3.1	_2.001	_2.1	baseline
背	**0.844**	0.789	0.789	0.789	0.711
车	**0.976**	0.962	0.969	0.962	0.863
澄清	**0.901**	**0.901**	**0.901**	**0.901**	0.901
冲	0.978	**0.989**	0.978	**0.989**	0.957
当	**0.925**	0.853	0.864	0.853	0.925
合计	**0.956**	0.944	**0.956**	0.944	0.700
见长	**0.971**	0.956	0.956	0.956	0.956
看	**0.998**	0.997	0.997	0.997	0.996
落	**0.987**	0.974	0.974	0.974	0.987
没	0.956	0.963	**0.971**	0.963	0.956
上	**0.983**	0.975	0.969	0.975	0.978
系	0.924	**0.949**	0.937	**0.949**	0.886
兄弟	**0.986**	**0.986**	**0.986**	**0.986**	0.959
应	0.986	**0.989**	**0.989**	**0.989**	0.869
攒	0.875	**0.900**	0.875	**0.900**	0.838
转	**0.981**	0.946	0.953	0.946	0.844

Table 6: Official results 2 of PengYuan@PKU

Macro Accuracy is the average disambiguation precision of each target word. Micro Accuracy is the disambiguation precision of total instances of all words. For task 15 whose instance distribution of the target words is very unbalanced in the test dataset, Macro Accuracy maybe a better evaluation indicator. Our systems achieved from 1st to 4th position (ranked by Macro Accuracy) out of all nine systems that participated in this task. Our best system is PengYuan@PKU_3.001 which uses original training data plus extracted 3-gram instances as our training data, $P(S)$ is tuned to 0.5 and λ is equal to 0.001.

3.2 Discussions

From the official result in Table 5 and Table 6 we can see, for this task, our classifier and strategy of extracting infrequency instances is effective. Basically, for each target word, the performances of our systems are superior to the baseline.

From Table 6, we also see the performances of our systems are influenced by different λ and different instance extracting patterns. Comparatively smaller probability λ of nonoccurrence features is better. Using the Extracting 3-gram instances is better than that of using 2-gram. (By using the 3-gram method of extracting instances, we obtain a better result than that of 2-gram.)

Our original idea for the system is two-folds. On one hand, we consider the relieving of data sparseness through more instances extracted by 2-gram pattern can achieve a better performance than that of 3-gram pattern, though the instances extracted through 2-gram pattern induce more noise. On the other hand, we assume that the performance would be better if we had given a larger probability of nonoccurrence features, for this strategy favors more infrequent sense instances. However the unbalance of sense distribution in the real test data as is shown in Table 5 went beyond our expectation. It is very hard for us to evaluate our system from the viewpoint of smoothness and instance sense distribution.

4 Related Work

To our knowledge, the methods of auto-acquiring sense-labeled instances include using parallel corpora like Gale et al. (1992) and Ng et al. (2003), extracting by monosemous relative of WordNet like Leacock et al. (1998), Mihalcea and Moldovan (1999), Agirre and Martínez (2004), Martínez et al. (2006) and PengYuan et al. (2008). The method proposed by Mihalcea and Moldovan (2000) is also an effective way.

5 Conclusion and Future Work

We participated in the SemEval-2010 task 15 on Infrequent Sense Identification for Mandarin Text to Speech Systems. Official results show our system which extract infrequent sense instances is effective.

For the future studies, we will focus on how to identify the infrequent sense instances effectively based on the plan to change the proposition between dominant sense and infrequent sense step by step.

Acknowledgments

This work was supported by the project of National Natural Science Foundation of China (No.60903063) and China Postdoctoral Science Foundation funded project (No.20090450007).

References

Claudia Leacock, Martin Chodorow and George A. Miller, Using Corpus Statistics and WordNet Relations for Sense Identification. *Computational Linguistics*, 1998, 24(1):147~166

David Mart'inez, Eneko Agirre and Xinglong Wang. Word relatives in context for word sense disambiguation. *Proceedings of the 2006 Australasian Language Technology Workshop (ALTW2006)*, 2006:42~50

David Yarowsky. 1993. One sense per collocation. *Proceedings of the ARPA Workshop on Human Language Technology.*

Eneko Agirre and David Mart'inez. Unsupervised WSD based on automatically retrieved examples: The importance of bias. *Proceedings of the International Conference on Empirical Methods in Natural Language Processing, EMNLP*, 2004:25~32

Hwee Tou Ng, Bin Wang, Yee Seng Chan. Exploiting Parallel Texts for Word Sense Disambiguation: An Empirical Study. *Proceeding of the 41st ACL*, 455-462, Sappora, Japan.

Liu Peng-yuan Zhao Tie-jun Yang Mu-yun Li Zhuang. 2008. Unsupervised Translation Disambiguation Based on Equivalent PseudoTranslation Model. *Journal of Electronics & Information Technology.* 30(7):1690-1695.

Rada Mihalcea and Dan I. Moldovan. 1999. An automatic method for generating sense tagged corpora. *Proceedings of AAAI-99*, Orlando, FL, July, pages 461–466.

Rada Mihalcea and Dan .I. Moldovan. 2000. An iterative approach to word sense disambiguation. *Proceedings of FLAIRS-2000*, pages 219–223, Orlando, FL, May.

Ted. Pedersen. 2000. A Simple Approach to Building Ensembles of Naïve Bayesian Classifiers for Word Sense Disambiguation. *Proceedings of the First Annual Meeting of the North American Chapter of the Association for Computational Linguistics*, pages 63-69, Seattle, WA, May.

Yunfang Wu, Peng Jin, Yangsen Zhang, and Shiwen Yu. 2006. A Chinese corpus with word sense annotation. *Proceedings of ICCPOL-2006.*

William A. Gale, Kenneth W. Church and David Yarowsky. A method for disambiguating word senses in a large corpus. *Computers and the Humanities*, 26(2):415-539

RALI: Automatic weighting of text window distances

Bernard Brosseau-Villeneuve*#, Noriko Kando#, Jian-Yun Nie*
* Université de Montréal, Email: {brosseab, nie}@iro.umontreal.ca
# National Institute of Informatics, Email: {bbrosseau, kando}@nii.ac.jp

Abstract

Systems using text windows to model word contexts have mostly been using fixed-sized windows and uniform weights. The window size is often selected by trial and error to maximize task results. We propose a non-supervised method for selecting weights for each window distance, effectively removing the need to limit window sizes, by maximizing the mutual generation of two sets of samples of the same word. Experiments on Semeval Word Sense Disambiguation tasks showed considerable improvements.

1 Introduction

The meaning of a word can be defined by the words that accompany it in the text. This is the principle often used in previous studies on Word Sense Disambiguation (WSD) (Ide and Véronis, 1998; Navigli, 2009). In general, the accompanying words form a context vector of the target word, or a probability distribution of the context words. For example, under the unigram bag-of-word assumption, this means building $p(x|t) = \frac{count(x,t)}{\sum_{x'} count(x',t)}$, where $count(x,t)$ is the count of co-occurrences of word x with the target word t under a certain criterion. In most studies, x and t should co-occur within a window of up to k words or sentences. The bounds are usually selected as to maximize system performance. Occurrences inside the window usually weight the same without regard to their position. This is counterintuitive. Indeed, a word closer to the target word usually has a greater semantic constraint on the target word than a more distant word. Some studies have also proposed decaying factors to decrease the importance of more distant words in the context vector. However, the decaying functions are defined manually. It is unclear that the functions defined can capture the true impact of the context words on the target word. In this paper, we propose an unsupervised method to automatically learn the optimal weight of a word according to its distance to the target word. The general idea used to determine such weight is that, if we randomly determine two sets of texts containing the target word, the resulting probability distributions for its context words in the two sets should be similar. Therefore, the weights of context words at different distance are determined so as to maximize the mutual generation probabilities of two sets of samples. Experimentation on Semeval-2007 English and Semeval-2010 Japanese lexical sample task data shows that improvements can automatically be attained on simple Naive Bayes (NB) systems in comparison to the best manually selected fixed window system.

The remainder of this paper is organized as follows: example uses of text windows and related work are presented in Section 2. Our method is presented in Section 3. In Section 4 and 5, we show experimental results on English and Japanese WSD. We conclude in Section 6 with discussion and further possible extensions.

2 Uses of text windows

Modeling the distribution of words around one target word has many uses. For instance, the Xu&Croft co-occurrence-based stemmer (Xu and Croft, 1998) uses window co-occurrence statistics to calculate the best equivalence classes for a group of word forms. They suggest using windows of up to 100 words. Another example can be found in WSD systems, where a shorter window is preferred. In Semeval-2007, top performing systems on WSD tasks, such as NUS-ML (Cai et al., 2007), made use of bag-of-word features around the target word. In this case, they found that the best results can be achieved using a window size of 3.

Proceedings of the 5th International Workshop on Semantic Evaluation, ACL 2010, pages 375–378,
Uppsala, Sweden, 15-16 July 2010.

Both these systems limit the size of their windows for different purposes. The former aims to model the topic of the documents containing the word rather than the word's meaning. The latter limits the size because bag-of-word features further from the target word would not be sufficiently related to its meaning (Ide and Véronis, 1998). We see that because of sparsity issues, there is a compromise between taking few, highly related words, or taking several, lower quality words.

In most current systems, all words in a window are given equal weight, but we can easily understand that the occurrences of words should generally count less as they become farther; they form a long tail that we should use. Previous work proposed using non-linear functions of the distance to model the relation between two words. For instance, improvements can be obtained by using an exponential function (Gao et al., 2002). Yet, there is no evidence that the exponential – with its manually selected parameter – is the best function.

3 Computing weights for distances

In this section, we present our method for choosing how much a word should count according to its distance to the target word. First, for some definitions, let $\mathcal{C}$ be a corpus, W a set of text windows, $c_{W,i,x}$ the count of occurrences of word x at distance i in W, $c_{W,i}$ the sum of these counts, and α_i the weight put on one word at distance i. Then,

$$P_{ML,W}(x) = \frac{\sum_i \alpha_i c_{W,i,x}}{\sum_i \alpha_i c_{W,i}} \quad (1)$$

is the maximum likelihood estimator for x. To counter the zero-probability problem, we apply Dirichlet smoothing with the collection language model as a prior:

$$P_{Dir,W}(x) = \frac{\sum_i \alpha_i c_{W,i,x} + \mu_W P(x|\mathcal{C})}{\sum_i \alpha_i c_{W,i} + \mu_W} \quad (2)$$

The pseudo-count μ_W is found by using Newton's method via leave-one-out estimation. We follow the procedure shown in (Zhai and Lafferty, 2002), but since occurrences have different weights, the log-likelihood is changed to

$$\mathcal{L}_{-1}(\mu|W,\mathcal{C}) = \quad (3)$$
$$\sum_i \sum_{x \in V} \alpha_i c_{W,i,x} \log \frac{\alpha_i c_{W,i,x} - \alpha_i + \mu P(x|\mathcal{C})}{\sum_j \alpha_j c_{W,j} - \alpha_i + \mu}$$

To find the best weights for our model we propose the following:

- Let T be the set of all windows containing the target word. We randomly split this set into two sets A and B.
- We want to find $\alpha^\star$ that maximizes the mutual generation of the two sets, by minimizing their cross-entropy:

$$l(\alpha) = H(P_{ML,A}, P_{Dir,B}) + H(P_{ML,B}, P_{Dir,A}) \quad (4)$$

In other words, we want α_i to represent how much an occurrence at distance i models the context better than the collection language model, whose counts are controlled by the Dirichlet pseudo-count. We hypothesize that target words occurs in limited contexts, and as we get farther from them, the possibilities become greater, resulting in sparse and less related counts.

3.1 Gradient descent

We propose a simple gradient descent minimizing (4) over α. For the following experiments, we used one single curve for all words in a task. We used the mini-batch type of gradient descent: the gradients of a fixed amount of target words are summed, a gradient step is done, and the proces is repeated while cycling the data. The starting state was with all α_i to one, the batch size of 50 and a learning rate of 1. We notice that as the algorithm progress, weights on close distances increase and the farthest decrease. As further distances contribute less and less, middle distances start to decay more and more, until at some point, all distances but the closest start to decrease, heading towards a degenerate solution. We therefore suggest using the observation of several consecutive decreases of all except α_1 as an end criterion. We used 10 consecutive steps for our experiments.

4 Experiments on Semeval-2007 English Lexical Sample

The Semeval workshop holds WSD tasks such as the English Lexical Sample (ELS) (Pradhan et al., 2007). It consists of a selected set of polysemous words, contained within passages where a sense taken from a sense inventory is manually annotated. The task is to create supervised classifiers maximizing accuracy on test data.

Since there are only 50 words and instances are few, we judged there was not enough data to compute weights. Instead, we used the AP Newswire corpus of the TREC collection (CD 1 & 2). Words were stemmed with the Porter stemmer and text windows were grouped for all words. For simplicity and efficiency, windows to the right and to the left were considered independent, and we only kept words with between 30 and 1000 windows. Also, only windows with a size of 100, which was considered big enough without any doubt, were kept. A stop list of the top 10 frequent words was used, but place holders were left in the windows to preserve the distances. Multiple consecutive stop words (ex: "of the") were merged, and the target word, being the same for all samples of a set, was ignored. This results in 32,650 sets containing 5,870,604 windows. In Figure 1, we can see the resulting weight curve.

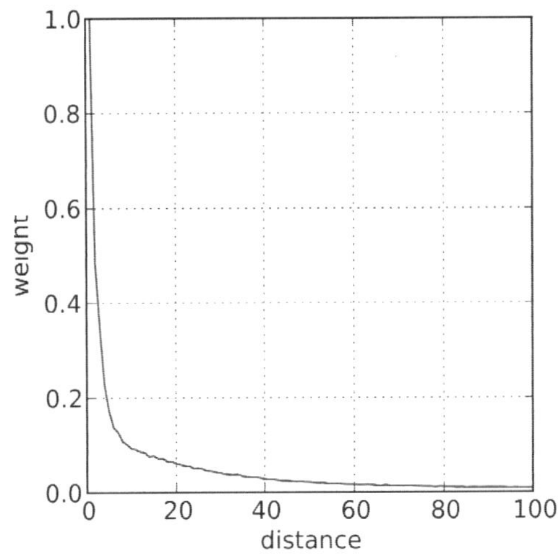

Figure 1: Weight curve for AP Newswire

Since the curve converges, words over the 100th distance were assigned the minimum weight found in the curve. From this we constructed NB models whose class priors used an absolute discounting of 0.5. The collection language model used the concatenation of the AP collection and the Semeval data. As the unstemmed target word is an important feature it was added to the models. It's weight was chosen to be 0.7 by maximizing accuracy on one-held-out cross-validation of the training data. The results are listed in Table 1.

System	Cross-Val (%)	Test set (%)
Prior only	78.66	77.76
Best uniform	85.48	83.28
RALI-2	88.23	86.45

Table 1: WSD accuracy on Semeval-2007 ELC

We used two baselines: most frequent sense (prior only), and the best uniform (except target word) fixed size window found from extensive search on the training data. The best settings were a window of size 4, with a weight of 4.4 on the target word and a Laplace smoothing of 2.9. The improvements seen using our system are substantial, beating most of the systems originally proposed for the task (Pradhan et al., 2007). Out of 15 systems, the best results had accuracies of 89.1*, 89.1*, 88.7, 86.9 and 86.4 (* indicates post-competition submissions). Notice that most were using Support Vector Machine (SVM) with bag-of-word features in a very small window, local collocations and POS tags. In our future work, we will investigate the applications of SVM with our new term weighting scheme.

5 Experiments on Semeval-2010 Japanese WSD

The Semeval-2010 Japanese WSD task (Okumura et al., 2010) consists of 50 polysemous words for which examples were taken from the BCCWJ tagged corpus. It was manually segmented, tagged, and annotated with senses taken from the Iwanami Kokugo dictionary. The task is identical to the ELS of the previous experiment.

Since the data was again insufficient to compute curves, we used the Mainichi-2005 corpus of NTCIR-8. We tried to reproduce the same kind of segmentation as the training data by using the Chasen parser with UniDic. For the corpus and Semeval data, conjugations (setsuzoku-to, jodô-shi, etc.), particles (all jo-shi), symbols (blanks, kigô, etc.), and numbers were stripped. When a base-form reading was present (for verbs and adjectives), the token was replaced by the Kanjis (chinese characters) in the word writing concatenated with the base-form reading. This treatment is somewhat equivalent to the stemming+stop list of the ELS tasks. The resulting curve can be seen in Figure 2.

The NB models are the same as in the previous experiments. Target words were again added the same way as in the ELS task. The best fixed window model was found to have a window size of 1 with a target word weight of 0.6 and used manual Dirichlet smoothing with a pseudo-count of 110. We submited two systems with the following settings: RALI-1 used manual Dirichlet smoothing and 0.9 for the target word. RALI-2 used auto-

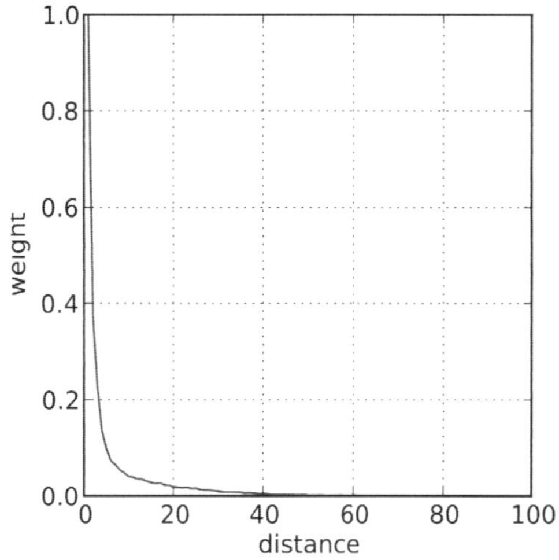

Figure 2: Weight curve for Mainichi Shinbun 2005

matic Dirichlet smoothing and 1.7 for the target word weight. Results are listed in Table 2.

System	Cross-Val (%)	Test set (%)
prior only	75.23	68.96
Best uniform	82.29	76.12
RALI-1	82.77	75.92
RALI-2	83.05	76.36

Table 2: WSD accuracy on Semeval-2010 JWSD

As we can see, the results are not significantly different from the best uniform model. This may be due to differences in the segmentation parameters of our external corpus. Another reason could be that the systems use almost the same weights: the best fixed window had size 1, and the Japanese curve is steeper than the English one.

This steeper curve can be explained by the grammatical structure of the Japanese language. While English can be considered a Subject-Verb-Complement language, Japanese is considered Subject-Complement-Verb. Verbs are mostly found at the end of the sentence, far from their subject, and vice versa. The window distance is therefore less useful in Japanese than in English since it has more non-local dependencies. These results show that the curves work as expected even in different languages.

6 Conclusions

This paper proposed an unsupervised method for finding weights for counts in text windows according to their distance to the target word. Results from the Semeval-2007 English lexical sample showed a substantial improvement in precision. Yet, as we have seen with the Japanese task, window distance is not always a good indicator of word relatedness. Fortunately, we can easily imagine extensions to the current scheme that bins word counts by factors other than word distance. For instance, we could also bin counts by parsing tree distance, sentence distance or POS-tags.

Acknowledgments

The authors would like to thank Florian Boudin and Satoko Fujisawa for helpful comments on this work. This work is partially supported by Japanese MEXT Grant-in-Aid for Scientific Research on Info-plosion (#21013046) and the Japanese MEXT Research Student Scholarship program.

References

Jun Fu Cai, Wee Sun Lee, and Yee Whye Teh. 2007. Nus-ml: improving word sense disambiguation using topic features. In *SemEval '07 Proceedings*, pages 249–252, Morristown, NJ, USA. Association for Computational Linguistics.

Jianfeng Gao, Ming Zhou, Jian-Yun Nie, Hongzhao He, and Weijun Chen. 2002. Resolving query translation ambiguity using a decaying co-occurrence model and syntactic dependence relations. In *SIGIR '02 Proceedings*, pages 183–190, New York, NY, USA. ACM.

Nancy Ide and Jean Véronis. 1998. Introduction to the special issue on word sense disambiguation: the state of the art. *Comput. Linguist.*, 24(1):2–40.

Roberto Navigli. 2009. Word sense disambiguation: A survey. *ACM Comput. Surv.*, 41(2):1–69.

Manabu Okumura, Kiyoaki Shirai, Kanako Komiya, and Hikaru Yokono. 2010. Semeval-2010 task: Japanese wsd. In *SemEval '10 Proceedings*. Association for Computational Linguistics.

Sameer S. Pradhan, Edward Loper, Dmitriy Dligach, and Martha Palmer. 2007. Semeval-2007 task 17: English lexical sample, srl and all words. In *SemEval '07 Proceedings*, pages 87–92, Morristown, NJ, USA. Association for Computational Linguistics.

Jinxi Xu and W. Bruce Croft. 1998. Corpus-based stemming using cooccurrence of word variants. *ACM Trans. Inf. Syst.*, 16(1):61–81.

ChengXiang Zhai and John Lafferty. 2002. Two-stage language models for information retrieval. In *SIGIR '02 Proceedings*, pages 49–56, New York, NY, USA. ACM.

JAIST: Clustering and Classification based Approaches for Japanese WSD

Kiyoaki Shirai **Makoto Nakamura**
Japan Advanced Institute of Science and Technology
{kshirai,mnakamur}@jaist.ac.jp

Abstract

This paper reports about our three participating systems in SemEval-2 Japanese WSD task. The first one is a clustering based method, which chooses a sense for, not individual instances, but automatically constructed clusters of instances. The second one is a classification method, which is an ordinary SVM classifier with simple domain adaptation techniques. The last is an ensemble of these two systems. Results of the formal run shows the second system is the best. Its precision is 0.7476.

1 Introduction

This paper reports about our systems in SemEval-2 Japanese Word Sense Disambiguation (WSD) task (Okumura et al., 2010). This task is a lexical sample task for Japanese WSD and has the following two characteristics. First, a balanced word-sense tagged corpus is used for the task. Since it consists of sub-corpora of several domains or genres, domain adaptation might be required. Second, the task takes into account not only the instances having a sense in the given set but also the instances having a sense not found in the set (called 'new sense'). Participants are required to identify new senses of words in this task.

The second characteristics of the task is mainly considered in our system. A clustering based approach is investigated to identify new senses. Our system first constructs a set of clusters of given word instances using unsupervised clustering techniques. This is motivated by the fact that the new sense is not defined in the dictionary, and sense induction without referring to the dictionary would be required. Clusters obtained would be sets of instances having the same sense, and some of them would be new sense instances. Then each cluster is judged whether instances in it have a new sense or not. An ordinary classification-based approach is also considered. That is, WSD classifiers are trained by a supervised learning algorithm. Furthermore, simple techniques considering genres of sub-corpora are incorporated into both our clustering and classification based systems.

The paper continues as follows, Section 2 describes our three participating systems, JAIST-1, JAIST-2 and JAIST-3. The results of these systems are reported and discussed in Section 3. Finally we conclude the paper in Section 4.

2 Systems

2.1 JAIST-1: Clustering based WSD System

JAIST-1 was developed by a clustering based method. The overview of the system is shown in Figure 1. It consists of two procedures: (A) clusters of word instances are constructed so that the instances of the same sense are merged, (B) then similarity between a cluster and a sense in a dictionary is measured in order to determine senses of instances in each cluster.

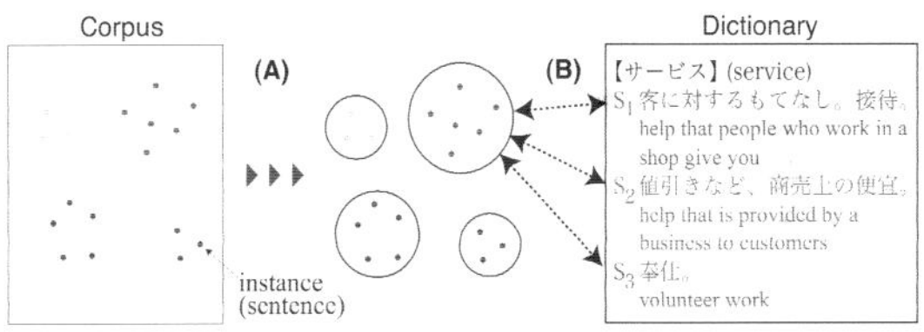

Figure 1: Overview of JAIST-1

2.1.1 Clustering of Word Instances

As previous work applying clustering techniques for sense induction (Schütze, 1998; Agirre and Soroa, 2007), each instance is represented by a feature vector. In JAIST-1, the following 4 vectors are used for clustering.

Collocation Vector This vector reflects collocation including the target instance. Words or POSs appearing just before and after the target instance are used as features, i.e. they correspond to one dimension in the vector. The weight of each feature is 1 if the feature exists for the instance, or 0 if not.

Context Vector The vector reflects words in the context of the target instance. All content words appearing in the context are used as features. The window size of the context is set to 50. Furthermore, related words are also used as features to en-

Proceedings of the 5th International Workshop on Semantic Evaluation, ACL 2010, pages 379–382,
Uppsala, Sweden, 15-16 July 2010.

rich the information in the vector. Related words are defined as follows: first topics of texts are automatically derived by Latent Dirichlet Allocation (LDA) (Blei et al., 2003), then words which are the most closely associated with each topic are formed into a 'related word set'. If one word in a related word set appears in the context, other words in that set also have a positive weight in the vector. More concretely, the weight of each feature is determined to be 1 if the word appears in the context or 0.5 if the word does not appear but is in the related word set.

Association Vector Similarly to context vector, this reflects words in the context of the target instance, but data sparseness is alleviated in a different manner. In advance, the co-occurrence matrix A is constructed from a corpus. Each row and column in A corresponds to one of the most frequent 10,000 content words. Each element $a_{i,j}$ in the matrix is $P(w_i|w_j)$, conditional probability representing how likely it is that two words w_i and w_j will occur in the same document. Now j-th column in A can be regarded as the co-occurrence vector of w_j, $\vec{o}(w_j)$. Association vector is a normalized vector of sum of $\vec{o}(w_j)$ for all words in the context.

Topic Vector Unlike other vectors, this vector reflects topics of texts. The topics z_j automatically derived by PLSI (Probabilistic Latent Semantic Indexing) are used as features. The weight for z_j in the vector is $P(z_j|d_i)$ estimated by Folding-in algorithm (Hofmann, 1999), where d_i is the document containing the instance. Topic vector is motivated by the well-known fact that word senses are highly associated with the topics of documents.

Target instances are clustered by the agglomerative clustering algorithm. Similarities between instances are calculated by cosine measure of vectors. Furthermore, pairs of instances in different genre sub-corpora are treated as 'cannot-link', so that they will not be merged into the same cluster. Clustering procedure is stopped when the number of instances in a cluster become more than a threshold N_c. N_c is set to 5 in the participating system.

The clustering is performed 4 times using 4 different feature vectors. Then the best one is chosen from the 4 sets of clusters obtained. A set of cluster C (=$\{C_i\}$) is evaluated by $E(C)$

$$E(C) = \textstyle\sum_i coh(C_i) \tag{1}$$

where 'cohesiveness' $coh(C_i)$ for each cluster C_i is defined by (2).

$$\begin{aligned} coh(C_i) &= \frac{1}{|C_i|}\sum_{j=1}^{|C_i|} rel\text{-}sim(\vec{v}_{ij}, \vec{g}_i) \\ &= \frac{1}{|C_i|}\sum_{j=1}^{|C_i|} \frac{sim(\vec{v}_{ij}, \vec{g}_i)}{\max_j sim(\vec{v}_{ij}, \vec{g}_i)} \end{aligned} \tag{2}$$

$\vec{v}_{ij}$ is an instance vector in the cluster C_i, while $\vec{g}_i$ is an average vector of C_i. $rel\text{-}sim(\vec{v}_{ij}, \vec{g}_i)$ means the relative similarity between the instance vector and average vector. Intuitively, $coh(C_i)$ evaluates how likely instances in the cluster are similar each other. C such that $E(C)$ is maximum is chosen as the final set of clusters.

2.1.2 Similarity between Clusters and Senses

After clustering, similarity between a cluster C_i and a sense S_j in the dictionary, $sim(C_i, S_j)$, is calculated for WSD. C_i and S_j are represented by cluster vector $\vec{c_i}$ and sense vector $\vec{s_j}$, respectively. Then cosine measure between these two vectors is calculated as $sim(C_i, S_j)$.

The cluster vector $\vec{c_i}$ is defined as (3):

$$\vec{c_i} = \frac{1}{N}\sum_{e_{ik}\in C_i}\sum_{t_l \in e_{ik}} \vec{o}(t_l) \tag{3}$$

In (3), e_{ik} stands for an instance in the cluster C_i, t_l words appearing in the context of e_{ik}, $\vec{o}(t_l)$ co-occurrence vector of t_l (similar one used in association vector), and N the constant for normalization. So $\vec{c_i}$ is similar to association vector, but the co-occurrence vectors of words in the contexts of all instances in the cluster are summed.

The sense vector $\vec{s_j}$ is defined as in (4).

$$\vec{s_j} = \frac{1}{N}\left(\sum_{t_k \in D_j} \vec{o}(t_k) + \sum_{t_l \in E_j} w_e \cdot \vec{o}(t_l)\right) \tag{4}$$

D_j stands for definition sentences of the sense S_j in the Japanese dictionary Iwanami Kokugo Jiten (the sense inventory in this task), while E_j a set of example sentences of S_j. Here E_j includes both example sentences from the dictionary and ones excerpted from a sense-tagged corpus, the training data of this task. w_e is the parameter putting more weight on words in example sentences than in definition sentences. We set $w_e = 2.0$ through the preliminary investigation.

Based on $sim(C_i, S_j)$, the system judges whether the cluster is a collection of new sense instances. Suppose that $MaxSim_i$ is $\max_j sim(C_i, S_j)$, the maximum similarity between the cluster and the sense. If $MaxSim_i$ is small, the cluster C_i is not similar to any defined senses, so instances in C_i could have a new sense. The system regards that the sense of instances in C_i is new when $MaxSim_i$ is less than a threshold T_{ns}. Otherwise, it regards the sense of instances in C_i as the most similar sense, S_j such that $j = \arg\max_j sim(C_i, S_j)$.

The threshold T_{ns} for each target word is determined as follows. First the training data is equally subdivided into two halves, the development data D_{dev} and the training data D_{tr}. Next, JAIST-1 is run for instances in D_{dev}, while example sentences in D_{tr} are used as E_j in (4) when sense vectors are constructed. For words where new sense instances exist in D_{dev}, T_{ns} is optimized for the accuracy of new sense detection. For words where no new sense instances are found in D_{dev}, T_{ns} is determined by the minimum of $MaxSim_i$ as follows:

$$T_{ns} = (\min_i MaxSim_i) \times \gamma \qquad (5)$$

Since even the cluster of which $MaxSim_i$ is minimum represents not a new but a defined sense, the minimum of $MaxSim_i$ is decreased by γ. To determine γ, the ratios

$$\frac{MaxSim_i \text{ of clusters of new senses}}{MaxSim_i \text{ of clusters of defined senses}} \qquad (6)$$

are investigated for 5 words[1]. Since we found the ratios are more than 0.95, we set γ to 0.95.

2.2 JAIST-2: SVM Classifier with Simple Domain Adaptation

Our second system JAIST-2 is the classification based method. It is a WSD classifier trained by Support Vector Machine (SVM). SVM is widely used for various NLP tasks including Japanese WSD (Shirai and Tamagaki, 2004). In this system, new sense is treated as one of the sense classes. Thus it would never choose "new sense" for any instances when no new sense instance is found in the training data. We used the LIBSVM package[2] to train the SVM classifiers. Linear kernel is used with default parameters.

The following conventional features of WSD are used for training the SVM classifiers.

- $W(0), W(-1), W(-2), W(+1), W(+2)$
  $P(-1), P(-2), P(+1), P(+2)$

  Words and their POSs appearing before or after a target instance. A number in parentheses indicates the position of a word from a target instance. $W(0)$ means a target instance itself.

- $W(-2)\&W(-1)$, $W(+1)\&W(+2)$, $W(-1)\&W(+1)$
  $P(-2)\&P(-1)$, $P(+1)\&P(+2)$, $P(-1)\&P(+1)$

  Pairs of words (or their POSs) near a target instance.

- Base form of content words appearing in the context (bag-of-words).

The data used in this task is a set of documents with 4 different genre codes: OC (Web page), OW (white paper), PB (book) and PN (newspaper). The training data consists of documents of 3 genres OW, PB and PN, while the test data contains all 4 genres. Considering domain adaptation, each feature f_i is represented as $f_i + g$ when SVM classifiers are trained. g is one of the genre codes $\{OW, PB, PN\}$ if f_i is derived from the documents of only one genre g in the training data, otherwise g is 'multi'. For instances in the test data, only features $f_i + g_t$ and $f_i + multi$ are used, where g_t is the genre code of the document of the target instance. If g_t is OC (which is not included in the training data), however, all features are used. The above method aims at distinguishing genre intrinsic features and improving the WSD performance by excluding features which might be associated with different genres.

2.3 JAIST-3: Ensemble of Two Systems

The third system combines clustering based method (JAIST-1) and classification based method (JAIST-2). The basic idea is that JAIST-1 be used only for reliable clusters, otherwise JAIST-2 is used. Here 'reliable cluster' means a cluster such that $MaxSim_i$ is high. The greater the similarity between the cluster and the sense is, the more likely the chosen sense is correct. Furthermore, JAIST-1 is used for new sense detection. The detailed procedure in JAIST-3 is:

1. If JAIST-1 judges a cluster to be a collection of new sense instances, output 'new sense' for instances in that cluster.

2. For instances in the top N_{cl} clusters of $MaxSim_i$, output senses chosen by JAIST-1.

3. Otherwise output senses chosen by JAIST-2.

[1] Among 50 target words in this task, there exist new sense instances of only 'kanou'(possibility) in D_{dev}. So we checked 4 more words, other than target words.

[2] http://www.csie.ntu.edu.tw/~cjlin/libsvm/

For the optimization of N_{cl}, D_{dev} and D_{tr}, each is a half of the training data described in Subsection 2.1, are used. D_{tr} is used for training SVM classifiers (JAIST-2). Then N_{cl} is determined so that the precision of WSD on D_{dev} is optimized. In the participating system, N_{cl} is set to 1.

3 Evaluation

Table 1 shows the results of our participating systems and the baseline system MFS, which always selects the most frequent sense in the training data. The column WSD reveals the precision (P) of word sense disambiguation, while the column NSD shows accuracy (A), precision (P) and recall (R) of new sense detection.

Table 1: Results

	WSD	NSD		
	P	A	P	R
MFS	0.6896	0.9844	0	0
JAIST-1	0.6864	0.9512	0.0337	0.0769
JAIST-2	0.7476	0.9872	1	0.1795
JAIST-3	0.7208	0.9532	0.0851	0.2051

JAIST-1 is the clustering based method. Performance of the clustering is also evaluated: Purity was 0.9636, Inverse-Purity 0.1336 and F-measure 0.2333. Although this system was designed for new sense detection, it seems not to work well. It could correctly find only three new sense instances. The main reason is that there were few instances of the new sense in the test data. Among 2,500 instances (50 instances of each word, for 50 target word), only 39 instances had the new sense. Our system supposes that considerable number of new sense instances exist in the corpus, and tries to gather them into clusters. However, JAIST-1 was able to construct only one cluster containing multiple new sense instances. The proposed method is inadequate for new sense detection when the number of new sense instances is quite small.

For domain adaptation, features which are intrinsic to different genres were excluded for test instances in JAIST-2. When we trained the system using all features, its precision was 0.7516, which is higher than that of JAIST-2. Thus our method does not work at all. This might be caused by removing features that were derived from different genre sub-corpora, but effective for WSD. More sophisticated ways to remove ineffective features would be required.

JAIST-3 is the ensemble of JAIST-1 and JAIST-2. Although a little improvement is found by combining two different systems in our preliminary experiments, however, the performance of JAIST-3 was worse than JAIST-2 because of the low performance of JAIST-1. We compared WSD precision of three systems for 50 individual target words, and found that JAIST-2 is almost always the best. The only exceptional case was the target word 'ookii'(big). For this adjective, the precision of JAIST-1, JAIST-2 and JAIST-3 were 0.74, 0.16 and 0.18, respectively. The precision of SVM classifiers (JAIST-2) is quite bad because of the difference of text genres. All 50 test instances of this word were excerpted from Web sub-corpus, which was not included in the training data. Furthermore, word sense distributions of test and training data were totally different. JAIST-1 works better in such a case. Thus clustering based method might be an alternative method for WSD when sense distribution in the test data is far from the training data.

4 Conclusion

The paper reports the participating systems in SemEval-2 Japanese WSD task. Clustering based method was designed for new sense detection, however, it was ineffective when there were few new sense instances. In future, we would like to examine the performance of our method when it is applied to a corpus including more new senses.

References

Eneko Agirre and Aitor Soroa. 2007. Semeval-2007 task 02: Evaluating word sense induction and discrimination systems. In *Proceedings of the 4th International Workshop on Semantic Evaluations*, pages 7–12.

David M. Blei, Andrew Y. Ng, and Michael I. Jordan. 2003. Latent dirichlet allocation. *Journal of Machine Learning Research*, 3:993–1022.

Thomas Hofmann. 1999. Probabilistic latent semantic indexing. In *Proceedings of the SIGIR*, pages 50–57.

Manabu Okumura, Kiyoaki Shirai, Kanako Komiya, and Hikaru Yokono. 2010. Semeval-2010 task: Japanese WSD. In *Proceedings of the SemEval-2010: 5th International Workshop on Semantic Evaluations*.

Hinrich Schütze. 1998. Automatic word sense discrimination. *Computational Linguistics*, 24(1):97–123.

Kiyoaki Shirai and Takayuki Tamagaki. 2004. Word sense disambiguation using heterogeneous language resources. In *Proceedings of the First IJCNLP*, pages 614–619.

MSS: Investigating the Effectiveness of Domain Combinations and Topic Features for Word Sense Disambiguation

Sanae Fujita Kevin Duh Akinori Fujino Hirotoshi Taira Hiroyuki Shindo
NTT Communication Science Laboratories
{sanae, kevinduh, taira, a.fujino, shindo}@cslab.kecl.ntt.co.jp

Abstract

We participated in the SemEval-2010 Japanese Word Sense Disambiguation (WSD) task (Task 16) and focused on the following: (1) investigating domain differences, (2) incorporating topic features, and (3) predicting new unknown senses. We experimented with Support Vector Machines (SVM) and Maximum Entropy (MEM) classifiers. We achieved 80.1% accuracy in our experiments.

1 Introduction

We participated in the SemEval-2010 Japanese Word Sense Disambiguation (WSD) task (Task 16 (Okumura et al., 2010)), which has two new characteristics: (1) Both training and test data across 3 or 4 domains. The training data include books or magazines (called **PB**), newspaper articles (**PN**), and white papers (**OW**). The test data also include documents from a Q&A site on the WWW (**OC**); (2) Test data include new senses (called **X**) that are not defined in dictionary.

There is much previous research on WSD. In the case of Japanese, unsupervised approaches such as extended Lesk have performed well (Baldwin et al., 2010), although they are outperformed by supervised approaches (Tanaka et al., 2007; Murata et al., 2003). Therefore, we selected a supervised approach and constructed Support Vector Machines (SVM) and Maximum Entropy (MEM) classifiers using common features and topic features. We performed extensive experiments to investigate the best combinations of domains for training.

We describe the data in Section 2, and our system in Section 3. Then in Section 4, we show the results and provide some discussion.

2 Data Description

2.1 Given Data

We show an example of Iwanami Kokugo Jiten (Nishio et al., 1994), which is a dictionary used as a sense inventory. As shown in Figure 1, each entry has POS information and definition sentences including example sentences.

We show an example of the given training data in (1). The given data are morphologically analyzed and partly tagged with Iwanami's sense IDs, such as "37713-0-0-1-1" in (1).

(1) <mor pos="動詞-一般" rd="トッ" bfm="トル" sense="37713-0-0-1-1" >取っ</mor>

This task includes 50 target words that were split into 219 senses in Iwanami; among them, 143 senses including two **X**s that were not defined in Iwanami, appear in the training data. In the test data, 150 senses including eight **X**s appear. The training and test data share 135 senses including two **X**s; that is, 15 senses including six **X**s in the test data are unseen in the training data.

2.2 Data Pre-processing

We performed two preliminary pre-processing steps. First, we restored the base forms because the given training and test data have no information about the base forms. (1) shows an example of the original morphological data, and then we added the base form (lemma), as shown in (2).

(2) <mor pos="動詞-一般" rd="トッ" bfm="トル" sense="37713-0-0-1-1" lemma="取る">取っ</mor>

Secondly, we extracted example sentences from Iwanami, which is used as a sense inventory. To compensate for the lack of training data, we analyzed examples with a morphological analyzer, Mecab[1] UniDic version, because the training and test data were tagged with POS based on UniDic.

[1] http://mecab.sourceforge.net/

Proceedings of the 5th International Workshop on Semantic Evaluation, ACL 2010, pages 383–386,
Uppsala, Sweden, 15-16 July 2010.

HEADWORD	とる【取る・採る・執る・捕る】*take* (五他 Transitive Verb)	
37713-0-0-1-0	<1>	置いてあったものなどを手に持つ。 to get something left into one's hand
37713-0-0-1-1	<ア>	手で握り持つ。「手を-って導く」 take and hold by hand. "to lead someone by the hand"

Figure 1: Simplified Entry for Iwanami Kokugo Jiten: とる *take*

For example, from the entry for とる *take*, as shown in Figure 1, we extracted an example sentence and morphologically analyzed it, as shown in (3)[2], for the second sense, 37713-0-0-1-1. In (3), the underlined part is the headword and is tagged with 37713-0-0-1-1.

(3) 手 を 取っ て 導く
hand ACC *take and lead*
"(I) take someone's hand and lead him/her"

3 System Description

3.1 Features

In this section, we describe the features we generated.

3.1.1 Baseline Features

For each target word w, we used the surface form, the base form, the POS tag, and the top POS categories, such as nouns, verbs, and adjectives of w. Here the target is the ith word, so we also used the same information of $i-2$, $i-1$, $i+1$, and $i+2$th words. We used bigrams, trigrams, and skip-bigrams back and forth within three words. We refer to the model that uses these baseline features as bl.

3.1.2 Bag-of-Words

For each target word w, we got all base forms of the content words within the same document or within the same article for newspapers (**PN**). We refer to the model that uses these baseline features as bow.

3.1.3 Topic Features

In the SemEval-2007 English WSD tasks, a system incorporating topic features achieved the highest accuracy (Cai et al., 2007). Inspired by (Cai et al., 2007), we also used topic features.

Their approach uses Bayesian topic models (Latent Dirichlet Allocation: LDA) to infer topics in an unsupervised fashion. Then the inferred topics are added as features to reduce the sparsity problem with word-only features.

In our proposed approach, we use the inferred topics to find "related'" words and directly add these word counts to the bag-of-words representation.

We applied gibbslda++[3] to the training and test data to obtain multiple topic classification per document or article for newspapers (**PN**). We used the document or article topics for newspapers (**PN**) including the target word. We refer to the model that uses these topic features as tpX, where X is the number of topics and tpdistX with the topics weighted by distributions. In particular, the topic distribution of each document/article is inferred by the LDA topic model using standard Gibbs sampling.

We also add the most typical words in the topic as a bag-of-words. For example, one topic might include 市 *city*, 東京 *Tokyo*, 線 *train line*, 区 *ward* and so on. A second topic might include 解剖 *dissection*, 後 *after*, 医学 *medicine*, 墓 *grave* and so on. If a document is inferred to contain the first topic, then the words (市 *city*, 東京 *Tokyo*, 線 *train line*, ...) are added to the bag-of-words feature. We refer to these features as twdY, including the most typical Y words as bag-of-words.

3.2 Investigation between Domains

In preliminary experiments, we used both SVM[4] and MEM (Nigam et al., 1999), with optimization method L-BFGS (Liu and Nocedal, 1989) to train the WSD model.

First, we investigated the effect between domains (**PN**, **PB**, and **OW**). For training data, we selected words that occur in more than 50 sentences, separated the training data by domain, and tested different domain combinations.

Table 1 shows the SVM results of the domain combinations. For Table 1, we did a 5-fold cross validation for the self domain and for comparison

[2] We use ACC as an abbreviation of accusative postposition.

[3] http://gibbslda.sourceforge.net/

[4] http://www.csie.ntu.edu.tw/~cjlin/libsvm/

Table 1: Investigation of Domain Combinations on Training data (features: bl + bow, SVM)

Target Words 77, No. of Instances > 50			
Domain	Acc.(%)	Diff.	Comment
PN	78.7	-	63 words,
PN +OW	79.25	0.55	1094 instances
PN +PB	79.43	**0.73**	
PN +ALL	79.34	0.64	
PB	79.29	-	75 words,
PB +PN	78.85	-0.45	2463 instances
PB +OW	78.56	-0.73	
PB +ALL	78.4	**-0.89**	
OW	87.91	-	42 words,
OW +PN	89.05	**1.14**	703 instances
OW +PB	88.34	0.43	
OW +ALL	89.05	**1.14**	

with the results after adding the other domain data. In Table 1, Diff. shows the differences to the self domain.

As shown in Table 1, for **PN** and **OW**, using other domains improved the results, but for **PB**, other domains degraded the results. So we decided to select the domains for each target word.

In the formal run, for each pair of domain and target words, we selected the combination of domain and dictionary examples that got the best cross-validation result in the training data. Note that in the case of no training data for the test data domain, for example, since no **OC**s have training data, we used all training data and dictionary examples.

We show the number of selected domain combinations for each target domain in Table 2. Because the distribution of target words is very unbalanced in domains, not all types of target words appear in every domain, as shown in Table 2.

3.3 Method for Predicting New Senses

We also tried to predict new senses (**X**) that didn't appear in the training data by calculating the entropy for each target given in the MEM. We assumed that high entropy (when the probabilities of classes are uniformly dispersed) was indicative of **X**; i.e., if [entropy > threshold] => predict **X**; else => predict with MEM's output sense tag.

Note that we used the words that were tagged with **X**s in the training data, except for the target words. We compared the entropies of **X** and not **X** of the words and heuristically tuned the threshold based on the differences among entropies. Our three official submissions correspond to different thresholds.

Table 2: Used Domain Combinations

Used Domain	MEM No.	MEM (%)	SVM No.	SVM (%)
Target: **PB** (48 types of target words)				
ALL +EX	26	54.2	23	47.9
ALL	4	8.3	6	12.5
PB	11	22.9	8	16.7
PB +EX	1	2.1	1	2.1
PB +OW	1	2.1	3	6.3
PB +PN	5	10.4	7	14.6
Target: **PN** (46 types of target words)				
ALL +EX	30	65.2	30	65.2
ALL	4	8.7	4	8.7
PN	4	8.7	1	2.2
PN +EX	0	0	1	2.2
PN +OW	2	4.3	2	4.3
PN +PB	6	13	8	17.4
Target: **OW** (16 types of target words)				
ALL +EX	5	31.3	5	31.3
ALL	2	12.5	1	6.3
OW	6	37.5	3	18.8
OW +PB	3	18.8	3	18.8
OW +PN	0	0	4	25.0
Target: **OC** (46 types of target words)				
ALL +EX	46	100	46	100

4 Results and Discussions

Our cross-validation experiments on the training set showed that selecting data by domain combinations works well, but unfortunately this failed to achieve optimal results on the formal run. In this section, we show the results using all of the training data with no domain selections (also after fixing some bugs).

Table 3 shows the results for the combination of features on the test data. MEM greatly outperformed SVM. Its effective features are also quite different. In the case of MEM, baseline features (bl) almost gave the best result, and the topic features improved the accuracy, especially when divided into 200 topics. But for SVM, the topic features are not so effective, and the bag-of-words features improved accuracy.

For MEM with bl +tp200, which produced the best result, the following are the best words: 外 *outside* (accuracy is 100%), 経済 *economy* (98%), 考える *think* (98%), 大きい *big* (98%), and 文化 *culture* (98%). On the other hand, the following are the worst words: 取る *take* (36%), 良い *good* (48%), 上げる *raise* (48%), 出す *put out* (50%), and 立つ *stand up* (54%).

In Table 4, we show the results for each POS (bl +tp200, MEM). The results for the verbs are comparably lower than the others. In future work, we will consider adding syntactic features that may improve the results.

Table 3: Comparisons among Features and Test data

TYPE	Precision (%)		
	MEM	SVM	Explain
Base Line	68.96	68.96	Most Frequent Sense
bl	**79.3**	69.6	Base Line Features
bl +bow	77.0	**70.8**	+ Bag-of-Words (BOW)
bl +bow +tp100	76.4	70.7	+BOW + Topics (100)
bl +bow +tp200	77.0	70.7	+BOW + Topics (200)
bl +bow +tp300	77.4	70.7	+BOW + Topics (300)
bl +bow +tp400	76.8	70.7	+BOW + Topics (400)
bl +bow +tpdist300	77.0	70.8	+BOW + Topics (300)*distribution
bl +bow +tp300 +twd100	76.2	70.8	+ Topics (300) with 100 topic words
bl +bow +tp300 +twd200	76.0	70.8	+ Topics (300) with 200 topic words
bl +bow +tp300 +twd300	75.9	70.8	+ Topics (300) with 300 topic words
without bow			
bl +tp100	79.3	69.6	+ Topics (100)
bl +tp200	**80.1**	69.6	+ Topics (200)
bl +tp300	**79.6**	69.6	+ Topics (300)
bl +tp400	**79.6**	69.6	+ Topics (400)
bl +tpdist100	79.3	69.6	+ Topics (100)*distribution
bl +tpdist200	79.3	69.6	+ Topics (200)*distribution
bl +tpdist300	79.3	69.6	+ Topics (300)*distribution
bl +tp200 +twd100	74.6	69.6	+ Topics (200) with 100 topic words
bl +tp300 +twd10	74.4	69.4	+ Topics (300) with 10 topic words
bl +tp300 +twd20	75.2	69.3	+ Topics (300) with 20 topic words
bl +tp300 +twd50	74.8	69.2	+ Topics (300) with 50 topic words
bl +tp300 +twd200	74.6	69.6	+ Topics (300) with 200 topic words
bl +tp300 +twd300	75.0	69.6	+ Topics (300) with 300 topic words
bl +tp400 +twd100	74.1	69.6	+ Topics (400) with 100 topic words
bl+tpdist100 +twd20	79.3	69.6	+ Topics (100)*distribution with 20 topic words
bl+tpdist200 +twd20	79.3	69.6	+ Topics (200)*distribution with 20 topic words
bl+tpdist400 +twd20	79.3	69.6	+ Topics (400)*distribution with 20 topic words

Table 4: Results for each POS (bl +tp200, MEM)

POS	No. of Types	Acc. (%)
Nouns	22	85.5
Adjectives	5	79.2
Transitive Verbs	15	76.9
Intransitive Verbs	8	71.8
Total	50	80.1

In the formal run, we selected training data for each pair of domain and target words and used entropy to predict new unknown senses. Although these two methods worked well in our cross-validation experiments, they did not perform well for the test data, probably due to domain mismatch.

Finally, we also experimented with SVM and MEM, and MEM gave better results.

References

Timothy Baldwin, Su Nam Kim, Francis Bond, Sanae Fujita, David Martinez, and Takaaki Tanaka. 2010. A Reexamination of MRD-based Word Sense Disambiguation. *Transactions on Asian Language Information Process, Association for Computing Machinery (ACM)*, 9(4):1–21.

Jun Fu Cai, Wee Sun Lee, and YW Teh. 2007. Improving Word Sense Disambiguation using Topic Features. In *Proceedings of EMNLP-CoNLL-2007*, pp. 1015–1023.

Dong C. Liu and Jorge Nocedal. 1989. On the Limited Memory BFGS Method for Large Scale Optimization. *Math. Programming*, 45(3, (Ser. B)):503–528.

Masaaki Murata, Masao Utiyama, Kiyotaka Uchimoto, Qing Ma, and Hitoshi Isahara. 2003. CRL at Japanese dictionary-based task of SENSEVAL-2. *Journal of Natural Language Processing*, 10(3):115–143. (in Japanese).

Kamal Nigam, John Lafferty, and Andrew McCallum. 1999. Using Maximum Entropy for Text Classification. In *IJCAI-99 Workshop on Machine Learning for Information Filtering*, pp. 61–67.

Minoru Nishio, Etsutaro Iwabuchi, and Shizuo Mizutani. 1994. *Iwanami Kokugo Jiten Dai Go Han [Iwanami Japanese Dictionary Edition 5]*. Iwanami Shoten, Tokyo. (in Japanese).

Manabu Okumura, Kiyoaki Shirai, Kanako Komiya, and Hikaru Yokono. 2010. SemEval-2010 Task: Japanese WSD. In *SemEval-2: Evaluation Exercises on Semantic Evaluation.*

Takaaki Tanaka, Francis Bond, Timothy Baldwin, Sanae Fujita, and Chikara Hashimoto. 2007. Word Sense Disambiguation Incorporating Lexical and Structural Semantic Information. In *Proceedings of EMNLP-CoNLL-2007*, pp. 477–485.

IIITH: Domain Specific Word Sense Disambiguation

Siva Reddy
IIIT Hyderabad
India
gvsreddy@students.iiit.ac.in

Abhilash Inumella
IIIT Hyderabad
India
abhilashi@students.iiit.ac.in

Diana McCarthy
Lexical Computing Ltd.
United Kingdom
diana@dianamccarthy.co.uk

Mark Stevenson
University of Sheffield
United Kingdom
m.stevenson@dcs.shef.ac.uk

Abstract

We describe two systems that participated in SemEval-2010 task 17 (All-words Word Sense Disambiguation on a Specific Domain) and were ranked in the third and fourth positions in the formal evaluation. Domain adaptation techniques using the background documents released in the task were used to assign ranking scores to the words and their senses. The test data was disambiguated using the Personalized PageRank algorithm which was applied to a graph constructed from the whole of WordNet in which nodes are initialized with ranking scores of words and their senses. In the competition, our systems achieved comparable accuracy of 53.4 and 52.2, which outperforms the most frequent sense baseline (50.5).

1 Introduction

The senses in WordNet are ordered according to their frequency in a manually tagged corpus, SemCor (Miller et al., 1993). Senses that do not occur in SemCor are ordered arbitrarily after those senses of the word that have occurred. It is known from the results of SENSEVAL2 (Cotton et al., 2001) and SENSEVAL3 (Mihalcea and Edmonds, 2004) that first sense heuristic outperforms many WSD systems (see McCarthy et al. (2007)). The first sense baseline's strong performance is due to the skewed frequency distribution of word senses. WordNet sense distributions based on SemCor are clearly useful, however in a given domain these distributions may not hold true. For example, the first sense for "bank" in WordNet refers to "sloping land beside a body of river" and the second to "financial institution", but in the domain of "finance" the "financial institution" sense would be expected to be more likely than the "sloping land beside a body of river" sense. Unfortunately, it is not feasible to produce large manually sense-annotated corpora for every domain of interest. McCarthy et al. (2004) propose a method to predict sense distributions from raw corpora and use this as a first sense heuristic for tagging text with the predominant sense. Rather than assigning predominant sense in every case, our approach aims to use these sense distributions collected from domain specific corpora as a knowledge source and combine this with information from the context.

Our approach focuses on the strong influence of domain for WSD (Buitelaar et al., 2006) and the benefits of focusing on words salient to the domain (Koeling et al., 2005). Words are assigned a ranking score based on its keyness (salience) in the given domain. We use these word scores as another knowledge source.

Graph based methods have been shown to produce state-of-the-art performance for unsupervised word sense disambiguation (Agirre and Soroa, 2009; Sinha and Mihalcea, 2007). These approaches use well-known graph-based techniques to find and exploit the structural properties of the graph underlying a particular lexical knowledge base (LKB), such as WordNet. These graph-based algorithms are appealing because they take into account information drawn from the entire graph as well as from the given context, making them superior to other approaches that rely only on local information individually derived for each word.

Our approach uses the Personalized PageRank algorithm (Agirre and Soroa, 2009) over a graph

Proceedings of the 5th International Workshop on Semantic Evaluation, ACL 2010, pages 387–391,
Uppsala, Sweden, 15-16 July 2010.

representing WordNet to disambiguate ambiguous words by taking their context into consideration. We also combine domain-specific information from the knowledge sources, like sense distribution scores and keyword ranking scores, into the graph thus personalizing the graph for the given domain.

In section 2, we describe domain sense ranking. Domain keyword ranking is described in Section 3. Graph construction and personalized page rank are described in Section 4. Evaluation results over the SemEval data are provided in Section 5.

2 Domain Sense Ranking

McCarthy et al. (2004) propose a method for finding predominant senses from raw text. The method uses a thesaurus acquired from automatically parsed text based on the method described by Lin (1998). This provides the top k nearest neighbours for each target word w, along with the distributional similarity score between the target word and each neighbour. The senses of a word w are each assigned a score by summing over the distributional similarity scores of its neighbours. These are weighted by a semantic similarity score (using WordNet Similarity score (Pedersen et al., 2004) between the sense of w and the sense of the neighbour that maximizes the semantic similarity score.

More formally, let $N_w = \{n_1, n_2, \ldots n_k\}$ be the ordered set of the top k scoring neighbours of w from the thesaurus with associated distributional similarity scores $\{dss(w, n_1), dss(w, n_2), \ldots dss(w, n_k)\}$. Let $senses(w)$ be the set of senses of w. For each sense of w ($ws_i \in senses(w)$) a ranking score is obtained by summing over the $dss(w, n_j)$ of each neighbour ($n_j \in N_w$) multiplied by a weight. This weight is the WordNet similarity score ($wnss$) between the target sense (ws_i) and the sense of n_j ($ns_x \in senses(n_j)$) that maximizes this score, divided by the sum of all such WordNet similarity scores for $senses(w)$ and n_j. Each sense $ws_i \in senses(w)$ is given a sense ranking score $srs(ws_i)$ using

$$srs(ws_i) = \sum_{n_j \epsilon N_w} dss(w, n_j) \times \frac{wnss(ws_i, n_j)}{\sum_{ws_i \epsilon senses(w)} wnss(ws_i, n_j)}$$

where $wnss(ws_i, n_j) =$

$$max_{ns_x \in senses(n_j)}(wnss(ws_i, ns_x))$$

Since this approach requires only raw text, sense rankings for a particular domain can be generated by simply training the algorithm using a corpus representing that domain. We used the background documents provided to the participants in this task as a domain specific corpus. In general, a domain specific corpus can be obtained using domain-specific keywords (Kilgarriff et al., 2010). A thesaurus is acquired from automatically parsed background documents using the Stanford Parser (Klein and Manning, 2003). We used $k = 5$ to built the thesaurus. As we increased k we found the number of non-domain specific words occurring in the thesaurus increased and negatively affected the sense distributions. To counter this, one of our systems IIITH2 used a slightly modified ranking score by multiplying the effect of each neighbour with its domain keyword ranking score. The modified sense ranking $msrs(ws_j)$ score of sense ws_i is

$$msrs(ws_i) = \sum_{n_j \epsilon N_w} dss(w, n_j) \times \frac{wnss(ws_i, n_j)}{\sum_{ws_i \epsilon senses(w)} wnss(ws_i, n_j)} \times krs(n_j)$$

where $krs(n_j)$ is the keyword ranking score of the neighbour n_j in the domain specific corpus. In the next section we describe the way in which we compute $krs(n_j)$.

WordNet::Similarity::lesk (Pedersen et al., 2004) was used to compute word similarity wnss. IIITH1 and IIITH2 systems differ in the way senses are ranked. IIITH1 uses $srs(ws_j)$ whereas IIITH2 system uses $msrs(ws_j)$ for computing sense ranking scores in the given domain.

3 Domain Keyword Ranking

We extracted keywords in the domain by comparing the frequency lists of domain corpora (background documents) and a very large general corpus, ukWaC (Ferraresi et al., 2008), using the method described by Rayson and Garside (2000). For each word in the frequency list of the domain corpora, words(domain), we calculated the log-likelihood (LL) statistic as described in Rayson and Garside (2000). We then normalized LL to compute keyword ranking score $krs(w)$ of word w $words(domain)$ using

$$krs(w) = \frac{LL(w)}{\sum\limits_{w_i \in words(domain)} LL(w_i)}$$

The above score represents the keyness of the word in the given domain. Top ten keywords (in descending order of krs) in the corpora provided for this task are *species, biodiversity, life, habitat, natura*[1], *EU, forest, conservation, years, amp*[2].

4 Personalized PageRank

Our approach uses the Personalized PageRank algorithm (Agirre and Soroa, 2009) with WordNet as the lexical knowledge base (LKB) to perform WSD. WordNet is converted to a graph by representing each synset as a node (synset node) and the relationships in WordNet (hypernymy, hyponymy etc.) as edges between synset nodes. The graph is initialized by adding a node (word node) for each context word of the target word (including itself) thus creating a context dependent graph (personalized graph). The popular PageRank (Page et al., 1999) algorithm is employed to analyze this personalized graph (thus the algorithm is referred as personalized PageRank algorithm) and the sense for each disambiguous word is chosen by choosing the synset node which gets the highest weight after a certain number of iterations of PageRank algorithm.

We capture domain information in the personalized graph by using sense ranking scores and keyword ranking scores of the domain to assign initial weights to the word nodes and their edges (word-synset edge). This way we personalize the graph for the given domain.

4.1 Graph Initialization Methods

We experimented with different ways of initializing the graph, described below, which are designed to capture domain specific information.

Personalized Page rank (PPR): In this method, the graph is initialized by allocating equal probability mass to all the word nodes in the context including the target word itself, thus making the graph context sensitive. This does not include domain specific information.

Keyword Ranking scores with PPR (KRS + PPR): This is same as PPR except that context words are initialized with krs.

Sense Ranking scores with PPR (SRS + PPR): Edges connecting words and their synsets are assigned weights equal to srs. The initialization of word nodes is same as in PPR.

KRS + SRS + PPR: Word nodes are initialized with krs and edges are assigned weights equal to srs.

In addition to the above methods of unsupervised graph initialization, we also initialized the graph in a *semi-supervised* manner. WordNet (version 1.7 and above) have a field *tag_cnt* for each synset (in the file *index.sense*) which represents the number of times the synset is tagged in various semantic concordance texts. We used this information, *concordance score* (cs) of each synset, with the above methods of graph initialization as described below.

Concordance scores with PPR (CS + PPR): The graph initialization is similar to PPR initialization additionally with concordance score of synsets on the edges joining words and their synsets.

CS + KRS + PPR: The initialization graph of KRS + PPR is further initialized by assigning concordance scores to the edges connecting words and their synsets.

CS + SRS + PPR: Edges connecting words and their synsets are assigned weights equal to sum of the concordance scores and sense ranking scores i.e. $cs + srs$. The initialization of word nodes is same as in PPR.

CS + KRS + SRS + PPR: Word nodes are initialized with krs and edges are assigned weights equal to $cs + srs$.

PageRank was applied to all the above graphs to disambiguate a target word.

4.2 Experimental details of PageRank

Tool: We used UKB tool[3] (Agirre and Soroa, 2009) which provides an implementation of personalized PageRank. We modified it to incorporate our methods of graph initialization. The LKB used in our experiments is WordNet3.0 + Gloss which is provided in the tool. More details of the tools used can be found in the Appendix.

Normalizations: Sense ranking scores (srs) and keyword ranking scores (krs) have diverse ranges. We found srs generally in the range between 0 to

[1] In background documents this word occurs in reports describing Natura 2000 networking programme.

[2] This new word *"amp"* is created by our programs while extracting body text from background documents. The HTML code *"&"* which represents the symbol *"&"* is converted into this word.

[3] `http://ixa2.si.ehu.es/ukb/`

	Precision	Recall
Unsupervised Graph Initialization		
PPR	37.3	36.8
KRS + PPR	38.1	37.6
SRS + PPR	48.4	47.8
KRS + SRS + PPR	48.0	47.4
Semi-supervised Graph Initialization		
CS + PPR	50.2	49.6
CS + KRS + PPR	50.1	49.5
* CS + SRS + PPR	53.4	52.8
CS + KRS + SRS + PPR	**53.6**	**52.9**
Others		
1^{st}sense	50.5	50.5
PSH	49.8	43.2

Table 1: Evaluation results on English test data of SemEval-2010 Task-17. * represents the system which we submitted to SemEval and is ranked 3rd in public evaluation.

1 and krs in the range 0 to 0.02. Since these scores are used to assign initial weights in the graph, these ranges are scaled to fall in a common range of [0, 100]. Using any other scaling method should not effect the performance much since PageRank (and UKB tool) has its own internal mechanisms to normalize the weights.

5 Evaluation Results

Test data released for this task is disambiguated using IIITH1 and IIITH2 systems. As described in Section 2, IIITH1 and IIITH2 systems differ in the way the sense ranking scores are computed. Here we project only the results of IIITH1 since IIITH1 performed slightly better than IIITH2 in all the above settings. Results of 1st*sense* system provided by the organizers which assigns first sense computed from the annotations in hand-labeled corpora is also presented. Additionally, we also present the results of Predominant Sense Heuristic (PSH) which assigns every word w with the sense ws_j ($ws_j \in senses(w)$) which has the highest value of $srs(ws_j)$ computed in Section 2 similar to (McCarthy et al., 2004).

Table 1 presents the evaluation results. We used TreeTagger [4] to Part of Speech tag the test data. POS information was used to discard irrelevant senses. Due to POS tagging errors, our precision values were not equal to recall values. In the competition, we submitted IIITH1 and IIITH2 systems with CS + SRS + PPR graph initialization. IIITH1 and IIIH2 gave performances of 53.4 % and 52.2 % precision respectively. In our later experiments, we found CS + KRS + SRS + PPR has given the best performance of 53.6 % precision.

From the results, it can be seen when srs information is incorporated in the graph, precision improved by 11.1% compared to PPR in unsupervised graph initialization and by 3.19% compared to CS + PPR in semi-supervised graph initialization. Also little improvements are seen when krs information is added. This shows that domain specific information like sense ranking scores and keyword ranking scores play a major role in domain specific WSD.

The difference between the results in unsupervised and semi-supervised graph initializations may be attributed to the additional information the semi-supervised graph is having i.e. the sense distribution knowledge of non-domain specific words (common words).

6 Conclusion

This paper proposes a method for domain specific WSD. Our method is based on a graph-based algorithm (Personalized Page Rank) which is modified to include information representing the domain (sense ranking and key word ranking scores). Experiments show that exploiting this domain specific information within the graph based methods produces better results than when this information is used individually.

[4] http://www.ims.uni-stuttgart.de/projekte/corplex/TreeTagger/

Acknowledgements

The authors are grateful to Ted Pedersen for his helpful advice on the WordNet Similarity Package. We also thank Rajeev Sangal for supporting the authors Siva Reddy and Abhilash Inumella.

References

Eneko Agirre and Aitor Soroa. 2009. Personalizing pagerank for word sense disambiguation. In *EACL '09: Proceedings of the 12th Conference of the European Chapter of the Association for Computational Linguistics*, pages 33–41, Morristown, NJ, USA. Association for Computational Linguistics.

Paul Buitelaar, Bernardo Magnini, Carlo Strapparava, and Piek Vossen. 2006. Domain-specific wsd. In *Word Sense Disambiguation. Algorithms and Applications, Editors: Eneko Agirre and Philip Edmonds*. Springer.

Scott Cotton, Phil Edmonds, Adam Kilgarriff, and Martha Palmer. 2001. Senseval-2. `http://www.sle.sharp.co.uk/senseval2`.

A. Ferraresi, E. Zanchetta, M. Baroni, and S. Bernardini. 2008. Introducing and evaluating ukwac, a very large web-derived corpus of english. In *Proceed-ings of the WAC4 Workshop at LREC 2008*, Marrakesh, Morocco.

Adam Kilgarriff, Siva Reddy, Jan Pomikálek, and Avinesh PVS. 2010. A corpus factory for many languages. In *LREC 2010*, Malta.

Dan Klein and Christopher D. Manning. 2003. Accurate unlexicalized parsing. In *ACL '03: Proceedings of the 41st Annual Meeting on Association for Computational Linguistics*, pages 423–430, Morristown, NJ, USA. Association for Computational Linguistics.

Rob Koeling, Diana McCarthy, and John Carroll. 2005. Domain-specific sense distributions and predominant sense acquisition. In *HLT '05: Proceedings of the conference on Human Language Technology and Empirical Methods in Natural Language Processing*, pages 419–426, Morristown, NJ, USA. Association for Computational Linguistics.

Dekang Lin. 1998. Automatic retrieval and clustering of similar words. In *Proceedings of the 17th international conference on Computational linguistics*, pages 768–774, Morristown, NJ, USA. Association for Computational Linguistics.

Diana McCarthy, Rob Koeling, Julie Weeds, and John Carroll. 2004. Finding predominant word senses in untagged text. In *ACL '04: Proceedings of the 42nd Annual Meeting on Association for Computational Linguistics*, page 279, Morristown, NJ, USA. Association for Computational Linguistics.

Diana McCarthy, Rob Koeling, Julie Weeds, and John Carroll. 2007. Unsupervised acquisition of predominant word senses. *Computational Linguistics*, 33(4):553–590.

Rada Mihalcea and Phil Edmonds, editors. 2004. *Proceedings Senseval-3 3rd International Workshop on Evaluating Word Sense Disambiguation Systems*. ACL, Barcelona, Spain.

George A. Miller, Claudia Leacock, Randee Tengi, and Ross T. Bunker. 1993. A semantic concordance. In *Proceedings of the ARPA Workshop on Human Language Technology*, pages 303–308. Morgan Kaufman.

Lawrence Page, Sergey Brin, Rajeev Motwani, and Terry Winograd. 1999. The pagerank citation ranking: Bringing order to the web. Technical Report 1999-66, Stanford InfoLab, November.

Ted Pedersen, Siddharth Patwardhan, and Jason Michelizzi. 2004. Wordnet::similarity: measuring the relatedness of concepts. In *HLT-NAACL '04: Demonstration Papers at HLT-NAACL 2004 on XX*, pages 38–41, Morristown, NJ, USA. Association for Computational Linguistics.

Paul Rayson and Roger Garside. 2000. Comparing corpora using frequency profiling. In *Proceedings of the workshop on Comparing corpora*, pages 1–6, Morristown, NJ, USA. Association for Computational Linguistics.

Ravi Sinha and Rada Mihalcea. 2007. Unsupervised graph-basedword sense disambiguation using measures of word semantic similarity. In *ICSC '07: Proceedings of the International Conference on Semantic Computing*, pages 363–369, Washington, DC, USA. IEEE Computer Society.

Appendix

Domain Specific Thesaurus, Sense Ranking Scores and Keyword Ranking Scores are accessible at

`http://web.iiit.ac.in/~gvsreddy/SemEval2010/`

Tools Used:

- UKB is used with options *–ppr –dict_weight*. Dictionary files which UKB uses are automatically generated using sense ranking scores *srs*.
- Background document words are canonicalized using KSTEM, a morphological analyzer
- The Stanford Parser is used to parse background documents to build thesaurus
- Test data is part of speech tagged using TreeTagger.

UCF-WS: Domain Word Sense Disambiguation using Web Selectors

Hansen A. Schwartz and Fernando Gomez
School of Electrical Engineering and Computer Science
University of Central Florida
Orlando, FL 32816
{hschwartz,gomez}@cs.ucf.edu

Abstract

This paper studies the application of the Web Selectors word sense disambiguation system on a specific domain. The system was primarily applied without any domain tuning, but the incorporation of domain predominant sense information was explored. Results indicated that the system performs relatively the same with domain predominant sense information as without, scoring well above a random baseline, but still 5 percentage points below results of using the first sense.

1 Introduction

We explore the use of the Web Selectors word sense disambiguation system for disambiguating nouns and verbs of a domain text. Our method to acquire selectors from the Web for WSD was first described in (Schwartz and Gomez, 2008). The system is extended for the all-words domain task by including part of speech tags from the Stanford Parser (Klein and Manning, 2003). Additionally, a domain adaptation technique of using domain predominant senses (Koeling et al., 2005) is explored, but our primary goal is concerned with evaluating the performance of the existing Web Selectors system on domain text.

In previous studies, the Web Selectors system was applied to text of a general domain. However, the system was not directly tuned for the general domain. The system may perform just as strong for domain WSD since the selectors, which are the core of disambiguation, can come from any domain present on the Web. In this paper, we study the application of the Web Selectors WSD algorithm to an all-words task on a specific domain, the SemEval 2010: Task 17 (Agirre et al., 2010).

2 Web Selectors

Selectors are words which take the place of a given target word within its local context (Lin, 1997). In the case of acquiring selectors from the Web, we search with the text of local context (Schwartz and Gomez, 2008). For example, if one was searching for selectors of 'channel' in the sentence, "The navigation channel undergoes major shifts from north to south banks", then a search query would be:

*The navigation * undergoes major shifts from north to south banks* .

where * represents a wildcard to match every selector. The query is shortened to produce more results until at least 300 selectors are acquired or the query is less than 6 words. The process of acquiring selectors repeats for every content word of the sentence. Example selectors that might be returned for 'channel' include 'route', 'pathway', and 'passage'.

Selectors serve for the system to essentially learn the areas or concepts of WordNet that the sense of a word should be similar or related. The target noun or verb is disambiguated by comparing its senses with all selectors for itself (*target selectors*), as well as with *context selectors* for other nouns, verbs, adjective, adverbs, proper nouns, and pronouns in the sentence. Figure 1 shows the overall process undertaken to rank the senses of an ambiguous word. A *similarity* measure is used when comparing with *target selectors* and a *relatedness* measure is used when comparing with *context selectors*. Referring to our previous example, the senses of 'channel' are compared to its own (*target*) selectors via *similarity* measures, while relatedness measures are used for the *context selectors*: noun selectors of 'navigation', 'shifts', 'north', 'south', and 'banks'; the verb selectors of

Proceedings of the 5th International Workshop on Semantic Evaluation, ACL 2010, pages 392–395,
Uppsala, Sweden, 15-16 July 2010. ©2010 Association for Computational Linguistics

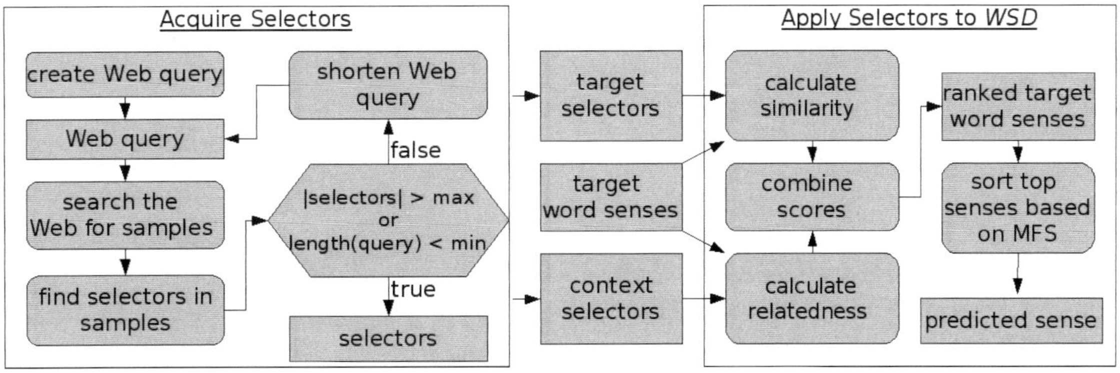

Figure 1: The overall process undertaken to disambiguate a word using Web selectors.

'undergoes'; plus the adjective selectors of 'major'. Adverbs, proper nouns, and pronouns are not present in the sentence, and so no selectors from those parts of speech are considered.

For this study, we implemented the Web Selectors system that was presented in (Schwartz and Gomez, 2009). This generalized version of the system may annotate verbs in addition to nouns, and it includes the previously unused context selectors of adverbs. We used the path-based similarity measure of (Jiang and Conrath, 1997) for *target selectors*, and the gloss-based relatedness measure of (Banerjee and Pedersen, 2002) for *context selectors*.

The incorporation of a part of speech tagger was a necessary addition to the existing system. Previous evaluations of Web Selectors relied on the testing corpus to provide part of speech (POS) tags for content words. In the case of SemEval-2010 Task 17, words were only marked as targets, but their POS was not included. We used the POS tags from the Stanford Parser (Klein and Manning, 2003). We chose this system since the dependency relationship output was also useful for our domain adaptation (described in section 2.1). A modification was made to the POS tags given the knowledge that the testing corpus only included nouns and verbs as targets. Any target that was not initially tagged as a noun or verb was reassigned as a noun, if the word existed as a noun in WordNet (Miller et al., 1993), or as a verb if not.

2.1 Domain Adaptation

Overall, the Web Selectors system is not explicitly tuned to the general domain. Selectors themselves can be from any domain. However, sense tagged data may be used indirectly within the system. First, the similarity and relatedness measures used in the system may rely on SemCor data (Miller et al., 1994). Also, the system breaks ties by choosing the most frequent sense according to WordNet frequency data (based on SemCor). These two aspects of the system can be seen as tuned to the general domain, and thus, they are likely aspects of the system for adaptation to a specific domain.

For this work, we focused on domain-adapting the tie breaker aspect of the Web Selectors system. The system defines a tie occurring when multiple sense choices are scored within 5% of the top sense choice. In order to break the tie, the system normally chooses the most frequent sense among the tied senses. However, it would be ideal to break the tie by choosing the most prevalent sense over the testing domain. Because sense tagged domain data is not typically available, Koeling et al. (2005) presented the idea of estimating the most frequent sense of a domain by calculating sense prevalence scores from unannotated domain text.

Several steps are taken to calculate the prevalence scores. First, a dependency database is created, listing the frequencies that each dependency relationship appears. In our case, we used the Stanford Parser (Klein and Manning, 2003) on the background data provided by the task organizers. From the dependency database, a thesaurus is created based on the method of (Lin, 1998). In our approach, we considered the following relationships from the dependency database:

subject *(agent, csubj, subjpass, nsubj, nsubjpass, xsubj)*

direct object *(dobj)*

indirect object *(iobj)*

adjective modifier (*amod*)

noun modifier (*nn*)

prepositional modifier (any preposition, excluding *prep_of* and *prep_for*)

(typed dependency names listed in parenthesis)

Finally, a prevalence score is calculated for each sense of a noun or verb by finding the similarity between it and the top 50 most similar words according to the automatically created thesaurus. As Koeling et al. did, we use the similarity measure of (Jiang and Conrath, 1997).

3 Results and Discussion

The results of our system are given in Table 1. The first set of results (**WS**) was a standard run of the system without any domain adaptation, while the second set (**WS**$_{dom}$) was from a run including the domain prevalence scores in order to break ties. The results show our domain adaptation technique did not lead to improved results. Overall, **WS** results came in ranked thirteenth among twenty-nine participating system results.

We found that using the prevalence scores alone to pick a sense (i.e. the 'predominant sense') resulted in an F score of 0.514 (***PS*** in Table 1). Koeling et al. (2005) found the predominant sense to perform significantly better than the first sense baseline (*1sense*: equivalent to most frequent sense for the English WordNet) on specific domains (32% error reduction on a finance domain, and 62% error reduction on a sports domain). Interestingly, there was no significant error reduction over the *1sense* for this task, implying either that the domain was more difficult to adapt to or that our implementation of the predominant sense algorithm was not as strong as that use by Koeling et al. In any case, this lack of significant error reduction over the *1sense* may explain why our **WS**$_{dom}$ results were not stronger than the **WS** results. In **WS**$_{dom}$, prevalence scores were used instead of *1sense* to break ties.

We computed a few figures to gain more insights on the system's handling of domain data. Noun precision was 0.446 while verb precision was 0.449. It was unexpected for verb disambiguation results to be as strong as nouns because a previous study using Web Selectors found noun sense disambiguation clearly stronger than verb sense disambiguation on a coarse-grained corpus

	P	**R**	**F**	**P**$_n$	**P**$_v$
rand	0.23	0.23	0.23		
1sense	0.505	0.505	0.505		
WS	0.447	0.441	0.444	.446	.449
WS$_{dom}$	0.440	0.434	0.437	.441	.438
PS	0.514	0.514	0.514	.53	.44

Table 1: (**P**)recision, (**R**)ecall, and (**F**)-score of various runs of the system on the Task 17 data. **P**$_n$ and **P**$_v$ correspond to precision results broken down by nouns and verbs.

	P$_{en1}$	**P**$_{en2}$	**P**$_{en3}$
WS	0.377	0.420	0.558
WS$_{dom}$	0.384	0.415	0.531

Table 2: Precision scores based on the three documents of the English testing corpora ('en1', 'en2', and 'en3').

(Schwartz and Gomez, 2009). Ideally, our results for noun disambiguation would have been stronger than the the *1sense* and *PS* results. In order to determine the effect of the POS tagger (parser in this case) on the error, we determined 1.6% of the error was due to the wrong POS tag at (0.9% of all instances). Lastly, Table 2 shows the precision scores for each of the three documents from which the English testing corpus was created. Without understanding the differences between the testing documents it is difficult to explain why the precision varies, but the figures may be useful for comparisons by others.

Several aspects of the test data were unexpected for our system. Some proper nouns were considered as target words. Our system was not originally intended to annotate proper nouns, but we were able to adjust it to treat them simply as nouns. To be sure this treatment was appropriate, we also submitted results where proper nouns were excluded, and got a precision of 0.437 and recall of 0.392. One would expect the precision to increase at the expense of recall if the proper nouns were more problematic for the system than other instances. This was not the case, and we conclude our handling of proper nouns was appropriate.

Unfortunately, another unexpected aspect of the data was not handled correctly by our system. Our system only considered senses from one form of the target word according to WordNet, while the key included multiple forms of a word. For example, the key indicated *low_tide-1* was the answer to an instance where our system had only considered senses of 'tide'. We determined that for 10.2% of the instances that were incorrect in our **WS** results we did not even consider the correct sense as a possible prediction due to using an inventory from only one form of the word. Since this issue mostly applied to nouns it may explain the observation that the noun disambiguation performance was not better than the verb disambiguation performance as was expected.

4 Conclusion

In this paper we examined the application of the Web Selectors WSD system to the SemEval-2010 Task 17: All-words WSD on a Specific Domain. A primary goal was to apply the pre-existing system with minimal changes. To do this we incorporated automatic part of speech tags, which we found only had a small impact on the error (incorrectly tagged 0.9% of all target instances). Overall, the results showed the system to perform below the *1sense* baseline for both nouns and verbs. This is a lower relative performance than past studies which found the disambiguation performance above the *1sense* for nouns. One reason for the lower noun performance is that for 10.2 % of our errors, the system did not consider the correct sense choice as a possibility. Future versions of the system will need to expand the sense inventory to include other forms of a word (example: 'low_tide' when disambiguating 'tide').

Toward domain adaptation, we ran an experiment in which one aspect of our system was tuned to the domain by using domain prevalence scores (or 'predominant senses'). We found no improvement from using this adaptation technique, but we also discovered that results entirely based on predictions of the domain predominant senses were only minimally superior to *1sense* (F-score of 0.514 versus 0.505 for *1sense*). Thus, future studies will examine better implementation of the predominant sense algorithm, as well as explore other complimentary techniques for domain adaptation: customizing similarity measures for the domain, or restricting areas of WordNet as sense choices based on the domain.

Acknowledgement

This research was supported by the NASA Engineering and Safety Center under Grant/Cooperative Agreement NNX08AJ98A.

References

Eneko Agirre, Oier Lopez de Lacalle, Christiane Fellbaum, Shu kai Hsieh, Maurizio Tesconi, Monica Monachini, Piek Vossen, and Roxanne Segers. 2010. Semeval-2010 task 17: All-words word sense disambiguation on a specific domain. In *Proceedings of SemEval-2010*. Association for Computational Linguistics.

Satanjeev Banerjee and Ted Pedersen. 2002. An adapted lesk algorithm for word sense disambiguation using wordnet. In *Proceedings of the Third International Conference on Intelligent Text Processing and Computational Linguistics*, Mexico City, Mexico.

Jay J. Jiang and David W. Conrath. 1997. Semantic similarity on corpus statistics and lexical taxonomy. In *Proceedings of ROCLING X*, Taiwan.

Dan Klein and Christopher D. Manning. 2003. Fast exact inference with a factored model for natural language parsing. In *In Advances in Neural Information Processing Systems 15*, pages 3–10.

Rob Koeling, Diana McCarthy, and John Carroll. 2005. Domain-specific sense distributions and predominant sense acquisition. In *Proceedings of the conference on Human Language Technology and Experimental Methods in NLP*, pages 419–426, Morristown, NJ, USA.

Dekang Lin. 1997. Using syntactic dependency as local context to resolve word sense ambiguity. In *Proceedings of the 35th annual meeting on Association for Computational Linguistics*, pages 64–71.

Dekang Lin. 1998. Automatic retrieval and clustering of similar words. In *Proceedings of COLING-ACL 98*, pages 768–774, Montreal, Canada. Morgan Kaufmann.

George Miller, R. Beckwith, Christiane Fellbaum, D. Gross, and K. Miller. 1993. Five papers on wordnet. Technical report, Princeton University.

George A. Miller, Martin Chodorow, Shari L, Claudia Leacock, and Robert G. Thomas. 1994. Using a semantic concordance for sense identification. In *In Proc. of ARPA Human Language Technology Workshop*.

Hansen A. Schwartz and Fernando Gomez. 2008. Acquiring knowledge from the web to be used as selectors for noun sense disambiguation. In *CoNLL 2008: Proceedings of the Twelfth Conference on Computational Natural Language Learning*, pages 105–112, Manchester, England, August.

Hansen A. Schwartz and Fernando Gomez. 2009. Using web selectors for the disambiguation of all words. In *Proceedings of the NAACL-2009 Workshop on Semantic Evaluations: Recent Achievements and Future Directions*, pages 28–36, Boulder, Colorado, June.

TreeMatch: A Fully Unsupervised WSD System Using Dependency Knowledge on a Specific Domain

Andrew Tran **Chris Bowes** **David Brown** **Ping Chen**
University of Houston-Downtown

Max Choly **Wei Ding**
University of Massachusetts-Boston

Abstract

Word sense disambiguation (WSD) is one of the main challenges in Computational Linguistics. TreeMatch is a WSD system originally developed using data from SemEval 2007 Task 7 (Coarse-grained English All-words Task) that has been adapted for use in SemEval 2010 Task 17 (All-words Word Sense Disambiguation on a Specific Domain). The system is based on a fully unsupervised method using dependency knowledge drawn from a domain specific knowledge base that was built for this task. When evaluated on the task, the system precision performs above the First Sense Baseline.

1 Introduction

There are many words within natural languages that can have multiple meanings or senses depending on its usage. These words are called homographs. Word sense disambiguation is the process of determining which sense of a homograph is correct in a given context. Most WSD systems use supervised methods to identify senses and tend to achieve the best results. However, supervised systems rely on manually annotated training corpora. Availability of manually tagged corpora is limited and generating these corpora is costly and time consuming. With our TreeMatch system, we use a fully unsupervised domain-independent method that only requires a dictionary (WordNet, Fallbaum, 1998.) and unannotated text as input (Chen et.al, 2009).

WSD systems trained on general corpora tend to perform worse when disambiguating words from a document on a specific domain. The SemEval 2010 WSD-domain task (Agirre et. al., 2010) addresses this issue by testing participant systems on documents from the environment domain. The environment domain specific corpus for this task
was built from documents contributed by the European Centre for Nature Conservation (ECNC) and the World Wildlife Fund (WWF). We adapted our existing TreeMatch system from running on a general context knowledge base to one targeted at the environment domain.

This paper is organized as follows. Section 2 will detail the construction of the knowledge base. In Section 3 the WSD algorithm will be explained. The construction procedure and WSD algorithm described in these two sections are similar to the procedure presented in our NAACL 2009 paper (Chen et.al, 2009). In Section 4 we present our experiments and results, and Section 5 discusses related work on WSD. Section 6 finishes the paper with conclusions.

2 Context Knowledge Acquisition and Representation

Figure 1 shows an overview of our context knowledge acquisition process. The collected knowledge is saved in a local knowledge base. Here are some details about each step.

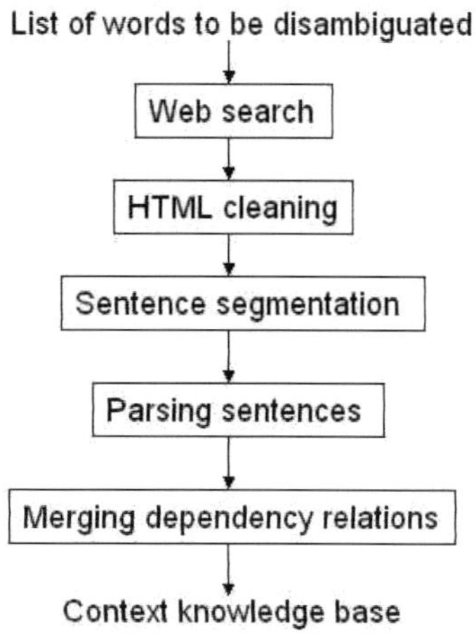

Figure 1: Context Knowledge Acquisition and Representation Process

2.1 Corpus Building Through Web Search

The goal of this step is to collect as many valid sample sentences as possible that contain instances of the target word. Preferably these instances are also diverse enough to contain all the different glosses of a word.

Proceedings of the 5th International Workshop on Semantic Evaluation, ACL 2010, pages 396–401,
Uppsala, Sweden, 15-16 July 2010. ©2010 Association for Computational Linguistics

The World Wide Web is a boundless source of textual information that can be utilized for corpus building. This huge dynamic text collection represents a wide cross section of writing backgrounds that may not be represented in other corpora and may be able to better represent common human knowledge.

However, because the content on the internet is not necessarily checked for grammatical or factual accuracy, concerns may arise about the use of a corpus built from it. The quality of context knowledge will be affected by sentences of poor linguistic and poor word usage but from our experience these kind of errors are negligible when weighted against the staggering volume of valid content also retrieved.

To start the acquisition process, words that are candidates for disambiguation are compiled and saved in a text file as seeds for search queries. Each single word is submitted to a Web search engine as a query. Several search engines provide API's for research communities to automatically retrieve large number of Web pages. In our experiments we used MSN Bing! API (Bing!, 2010) to retrieve up to 1,000 Web pages and PDF documents for each to-be-disambiguated word. Collected Web pages are cleaned first, e.g., control characters and HTML tags are removed. Then sentences are segmented simply based on punctuation (e.g., ?, !, .). PDF files undergo a similar cleaning process, except that they are converted from PDF to HMTL beforehand. Sentences that contain the instances of a specific word are extracted and saved into a local repository.

2.2 Parsing

After the sentences have been cleaned and segmented they are sent to the dependency parser Minipar (Lin, 1998). After parsing, sentences are converted to parsing trees and saved into files. The files contain the weights of all connections between all words existing within the knowledge base. Parsing tends to take the most time in the entire WSD process. Depending on the initial size of the corpus, parsing can take weeks. The long parsing time can be attributed to Minipar's execution through system calls and also to the lack of multithreading used. However, we only need to parse the corpus once to construct the knowledge base. Any further parsing is only done on the input sentences from the words to-be-disambiguated, and the glosses of those words.

2.3 Merging dependency relations

After parsing, dependency relations from different sentences are merged and saved in a context knowledge base. The merging process is straightforward. A dependency relation includes one head word/node and one dependent word/node. Nodes from different dependency relations are merged into one as long as they represent the same word. An example is shown in Figure 2, which merges the following two sentences:

"Computer programmers write software."

"Many companies hire computer programmers."

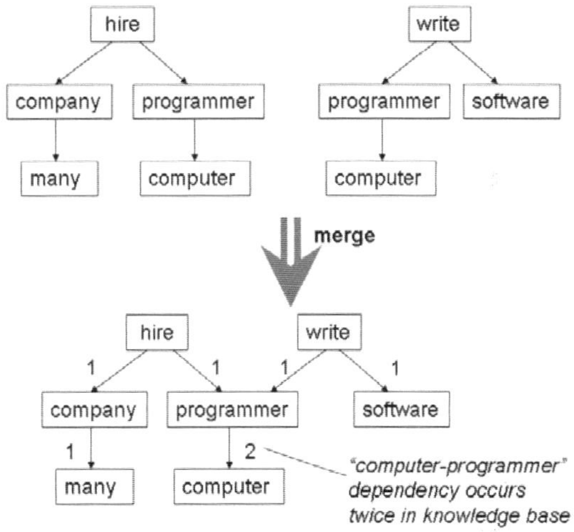

Figure 2: Merging two parsing trees. The number beside each edge is the number of occurrences of this dependency relation existing in the context knowledge base.

In a dependency relation "word1 -> word2", word1 is the head word, and word2 is the dependent word. After merging dependency relations, we will obtain a weighted directed graph with a word as a node, a dependency relation as an edge, and the number of occurrences of dependency relation as weight of an edge. This weight indicates the strength of semantic relevancy of head word and dependent word. This graph will be used in the following WSD process as our context knowledge base. As a fully automatic knowledge acquisition process, it is inevitable to include erroneous dependency relations in the knowledge base. However, since in a large text collection valid dependency relations tend to repeat far more times than invalid ones, these erroneous edges only have minimal impact on the disambiguation quality as shown in our evaluation results.

3 WSD Algorithm

Our WSD approach is based on the following insight:

If a word is semantically coherent with its context, then at least one sense of this word is semantically coherent with its context.

Assuming that the documents given are semantically coherent, if we replace a targeted to-be-disambiguated word with its glosses one by one, eventually one of the glosses will have semantic coherence within the context of its sentence. From that idea we can show the overview of our WSD procedure in Figure 3. For a given to-be-disambiguated word, its glosses from WordNet are parsed one by one along with the original sentence of the target word. The semantic coherency between the parse tree of each individual gloss and the parse tree of the original sentence are compared one by one to determine which sense is the most relevant.

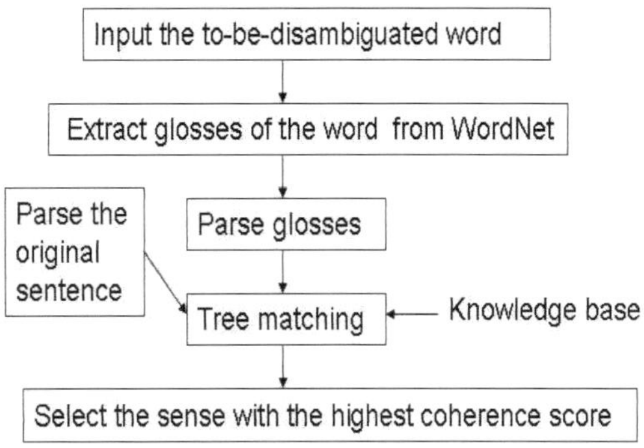

Figure 3: WSD Procedure

To measure the semantic coherence we use the following hypotheses (assume *word*1 is the to-be-disambiguated word):

- If in a sentence $word_1$ is dependent on $word_2$, and we denote the gloss of the correct sense of $word_1$ as g_{1i}, then g_{1i} contains the most semantically coherent words that are dependent on $word_2$;
- If in a sentence a set of words DEP_1 are dependent on $word_1$, and we denote the gloss of the correct sense of $word_1$ as g_{1i}, then g_{1i} contains the most semantically coherent words that DEP_1 are dependent on.

These hypotheses are used for the functions in Figure 4. The TreeMatching function uses what we call dependency matching to ascertain the correct sense of the to-be-disambiguated word. NodeMatching function is an extension from Lesk algorithm (Lesk, 1986).

Input: Glosses from WordNet;
***S*: the to-be-disambiguated sentence;**
***G*: the knowledge base generated in Section 2;**

1. Input a sentence S, $W = \{w|\ w$'s part of speech is noun, verb, adjective, or adverb, $w \in S\}$;
2. Parse S with a dependency parser, generate parsing tree T_S;
3. For each $w \in W$ {
4. Input all w's glosses from WordNet;
5. For each gloss w_i {
6. Parse w_i, get a parsing tree T_{wi};
7. score_d = TreeMatching(T_S, T_{wi});
   Score_n = NodeMatching(T_S, T_{wi});
   }
8. If the highest score_d and Score_n indicate the sense, choose this sense;
9. Otherwise, choose the first sense.
10. }

TreeMatching(T_S, T_{wi})

11. For each node $n_{Si} \in T_S$ {
12. Assign weight $w_{Si} = \frac{1}{lsi}$, l_{Si} is the length between n_{Si} and w_i in T_S;
13. }
14. For each node $n_{wi} \in T_{wi}$ {
15. Load its dependent words D_{wi} from G;
16. Assign weight $w_{wi} = \frac{1}{lwi}$, l_{wi} is the level number of n_{wi} in T_{wi};
17. For each n_{Sj} {
18. If $n_{Sj} \in D_{wi}$
19. calculate connection strength s_{ji} between n_{Sj} and n_{wi};
20. score = score + $w_{Si} \times w_{wi} \times s_{ji}$;
21. }
    }
22. Return score;

NodeMatching (T_S, T_{wi})

23. For each node $n_{Si} \in T_S$ {
24. Assign weight $w_{wi} = \frac{1}{lwi}$, l_{wi} is the level number of n_{wi} in T_{wi};
25. For each n_{Sj} {
28. If $n_{Si} == w_{wi}$
29. score = score + $w_{Si} \times w_{wi}$
    }
    }

Figure 4: WSD Algorithm

4 Experiment

The WSD-domain task for SemEval 2010 focused on the environment domain. To prepare for the tests, we constructed a new domain specific knowledge base.

System	Precision	Recall
1sense	0.505	0.505
TreeMatch-1	0.506	0.493
TreeMatch-2	0.504	0.491
TreeMatch-3	0.492	0.479
Random	0.23	0.23

Table 1: Fine-Grained SemEval 2010 Task 17 Disambiguation Scores

Since we knew the task's domain specific corpus would be derived from ECNC and WWF materials, we produced our query list from the same source. A web crawl starting from both the ECNC and WWF main web pages was performed that retrieved 772 PDF documents. Any words that were in the PDFs and also had more than one gloss in WordNet were retained for Bing! search queries to start the acquisition process as described in section 2. 10779 unique words were obtained in this manner.

Using the 10779 unique words for search queries, the web page and PDF retrieval step took 35 days, collecting over 3 TB of raw html and PDF files, and the cleaning and sentence extraction step took 2 days, reducing it down to 3 GB of relevant sentences, while running on 5 machines. Parsing took 26 days and merging took 6 days on 9 machines. From the parse trees we obtained 2202295 total nodes with an average of 87 connections and 13 dependents per node.

Each machine was a 2.66 GHz dual core PC with 2 GB of memory with a total of 10 machines used throughout the process.

There were 3 test documents provided by the task organizers with about 6000 total words and 1398 to-be-disambiguated words. Disambiguation of the target words took 1.5 hours for each complete run. Each run used the same WSD procedure with different parameters.

The overall disambiguation results are shown in Table 1. The precision of our best submission edged out the First Sense Baseline (1sense) baseline by .001 and is ahead of the Random selection baseline by .276.

The recall of our submissions is lower than the precision because of our reliance on Minipar for the part of speech and lemma information of the target words. Sometimes Minipar would give an incorrect lemma which at times cannot be found in WordNet and thus our system would not attempt to disambiguate the words. Previous tasks provided the lemma and part of speech for target words so we were able to bypass that step.

5 Related work

Generally WSD techniques can be divided into four categories (Agirre, 2006),

- Dictionary and knowledge based methods. These methods use lexical knowledge bases (LKB) such as dictionaries and thesauri, and extract knowledge from word definitions (Lesk, 1986) and relations among words/senses. Recently, several graph-based WSD methods were proposed. In these approaches, first a graph is built with senses as nodes and relations among words/senses (e.g., synonymy, antonymy) as edges, and the relations are usually acquired from a LKB (e.g., Wordnet). Then a ranking algorithm is conducted over the graph, and senses ranked the highest are assigned to the corresponding words. Different relations and ranking algorithms were experimented with these methods, such as TexRank algorithm (Mihalcea, 2005), personalized PageRank algorithm (Agirre, 2009), a two-stage searching algorithm (Navigli, 2007), Structural Semantic Interconnections algorithm (Navigli, 2005), centrality algorithms (Sinha, 2009).
- Supervised methods. A supervised method includes a training phase and a testing phase. In the training phase, a sense-annotated training corpus is required, from which syntactic and semantic features are extracted to build a classifier using machine learning techniques, such as Support Vector Machine (Novisch, 2007). In the following testing phase, the classifier picks the best sense for a word based on its surrounding words (Mihalcea, 2002). Currently supervised methods achieved the best disambiguation quality (about 80% in precision and recall for coarse-grained WSD in the most recent WSD evaluation conference SemEval 2007 (Novisch, 2007). Nevertheless, since training corpora are manually annotated and expensive, supervised methods are often brittle due to data scarcity, and it is impractical to manually annotate huge number of words existing in a natural language.
- Semi-supervised methods. To overcome the knowledge acquisition bottleneck suffered in supervised methods, semi-supervised methods make use of a small annotated corpus as seed data in a bootstrapping process (Hearst, 1991) (Yarowsky, 1995). A

word-aligned bilingual corpus can also serve as seed data (Zhong, 2009).

- Unsupervised methods. These methods acquire knowledge from unannotated raw text, and induce senses using similarity measures (Lin, 1997). Unsupervised methods overcome the problem of knowledge acquisition bottleneck, but none of existing methods can outperform the most frequent sense baseline, which makes them not useful at all in practice. The best unsupervised systems only achieved about 70% in precision and 50% in recall in the SemEval 2007 (Navigli, 2007). One recent study utilized automatically acquired dependency knowledge and achieved 73% in precision and recall (Chen, 2009), which is still below the most-frequent-sense baseline (78.89% in precision and recall in the SemEval 2007 Task 07).

Additionally there exist some "meta-disambiguation" methods that ensemble multiple disambiguation algorithms following the ideas of bagging or boosting in supervised learning (Brody, 2006).

6 Conclusion

This paper has described a WSD system which has been adapted for use in a specific domain for SemEval 2010 Task 17: All-Words Word Sense Disambiguation on a Specific Domain. Our system has shown that domain adaptation can be handled by unsupervised systems without the brittleness of supervised methods by utilizing readily available unannotated text from internet sources and still achieve viable results.

Acknowledgments

This work is partially funded by National Science Foundation grants CNS 0851984 and DHS #2009-ST-061-C10001.

References

E. Agirre, Philip Edmonds, editors. *Word Sense Disambiguation: Algorithms and Applications*, Springer. 2006.

E. Agirre, O. Lopez de Lacalle, C. Fellbaum, S. Hsieh, M. Tesconi, P. Vossen, and R. Segers. SemEval-2010 Task 17: All-words Word Sense Disambiguation on a Specific Domain. In *Proceedings of the 5th International Workshop on Semantic Evaluations*(SemEval-2010), Association for Computational Linguistics, Uppsala, Sweden. 2010.

E. Agirre, A. Soroa. Personalizing pagerank for word sense disambiguation. *In Proceedings of the 12th conference of the European chapter of the Association for Computational Linguistics* (EACL-2009).

Bing! API, available at msdn.microsoft.com

A. Brody, R. Navigli, M. Lapata, *Ensemble Methods For Unsupervised WSD*, COLING-ACL, 2006

P. Chen, W. Ding, C. Bowes, D. Brown. 2009. A Fully Unsupervised Word Sense Disambiguation Method and Its Evaluation on Coarse-grained All-words Task, NAACL 2009.

C. Fellbaum. 1998. WordNet: An Electronic Lexical Database, MIT press, 1998

M. Hearst. Noun Homograph Disambiguation Using Local Context in Large Text Corpora. *Proc. 7th Annual Conference of the Univ. of Waterloo Center for the New OED and Text Research*, Oxford. 1991.

M. Lesk. 1986. Automatic sense disambiguation using machine readable dictionaries: how to tell a pine cone from an ice cream cone. *In Proceedings of the 5th Annual international Conference on Systems Documentation* (Toronto, Ontario, Canada). V. DeBuys, Ed. SIGDOC '86.

D. Lin. Using syntactic dependency as local context to resolve word sense ambiguity. *In Proceedings of the 35th Annual Meeting of the Association For Computational Linguistics and Eighth Conference of the European Chapter of the Association For Computational Linguistics*. 1997.

D. Lin. 1998. Dependency-based evaluation of minipar. In *Proceedings of the LREC Workshop on the Evaluation of Parsing Systems*, pages 234–241, Granada, Spain.

R. Mihalcea. Unsupervised Large-Vocabulary Word Sense Disambiguation with Graph-based Algorithms for Sequence Data Labeling, in *Proceedings of the Joint Conference on Human Language Technology Empirical Methods in Natural Language Processing* (HLT/EMNLP), Vancouver, October, 2005.

R. Mihalcea. Instance based learning with automatic feature selection applied to word sense disambiguation. In *Proceedings of the 19th International Conference on Computational linguistics*. 2002.

R. Navigli, Mirella Lapata. *Graph Connectivity Measures for Unsupervised Word Sense Disambiguation*. IJCAI 2007

R. Navigli, Paola Velardi. Structural semantic interconnections: a knowledge-based approach to word sense disambiguation. *IEEE Transactions on Pattern Analysis and Machine Intelligence* (PAMI), 27(7):1063-1074. 2005.

A. Novischi, Muirathnam Srikanth, and Andrew Bennett. Lcc-wsd: System description for English coarse grained all words task at semeval 2007. *Proceedings of the Fourth International Workshop on Semantic Evaluations* (SemEval-2007), pages 223--226, Prague, Czech Republic. 2007.

R. Sinha, Rada Mihalcea. Unsupervised Graph-based Word Sense Disambiguation, in "Current Issues in Linguistic Theory: Recent Advances in Natural Language Processing", Editors Nicolas Nicolov and Ruslan Mitkov, John Benjamins, 2009.

D. Yarowsky. Unsupervised word sense disambiguation rivaling supervised methods. In *Proceedings of the 33rd Annual Meeting on Association For Computational Linguistics*, Cambridge, Massachusetts, 1995.

Z. Zhong, Hwee Tou Ng. Word Sense Disambiguation for All Words without Hard Labor. *In Proceeding of the Twenty-first International Joint Conference on Artificial Intelligence.* 2009.

GPLSI-IXA: Using Semantic Classes to Acquire Monosemous Training Examples from Domain Texts

Rubén Izquierdo & Armando Suárez
GPLSI Group
University of Alicante. Spain
{ruben,armando}@dlsi.ua.es

German Rigau
IXA NLP Group.
EHU. Donostia, Spain
german.rigau@ehu.es

Abstract

This paper summarizes our participation in task #17 of SemEval–2 (All–words WSD on a specific domain) using a supervised class-based Word Sense Disambiguation system. Basically, we use Support Vector Machines (SVM) as learning algorithm and a set of simple features to build three different models. Each model considers a different training corpus: SemCor (SC), examples from monosemous words extracted automatically from background data (BG), and both SC and BG (SCBG). Our system explodes the monosemous words appearing as members of a particular WordNet semantic class to automatically acquire class-based annotated examples from the domain text. We use the class-based examples gathered from the domain corpus to adapt our traditional system trained on SemCor. The evaluation reveal that the best results are achieved training with SemCor and the background examples from monosemous words, obtaining results above the first sense baseline and the fifth best position in the competition rank.

1 Introduction

As empirically demonstrated by the last SensEval and SemEval exercises, assigning the appropriate meaning to words in context has resisted all attempts to be successfully addressed. In fact, supervised word-based WSD systems are very dependent of the corpora used for training and testing the system (Escudero et al., 2000). One possible reason could be the use of inappropriate level of abstraction.

Most supervised systems simply model each polysemous word as a classification problem where each class corresponds to a particular synset of the word. But, WordNet (WN) has been widely criticized for being a sense repository that often provides too fine–grained sense distinctions for higher level applications like Machine Translation or Question & Answering. In fact, WSD at this level of granularity has resisted all attempts of inferring robust broad-coverage models. It seems that many word–sense distinctions are too subtle to be captured by automatic systems with the current small volumes of word–sense annotated examples.

Thus, some research has been focused on deriving different word-sense groupings to overcome the fine–grained distinctions of WN (Hearst and Schütze, 1993), (Peters et al., 1998), (Mihalcea and Moldovan, 2001), (Agirre and LopezDeLaCalle, 2003), (Navigli, 2006) and (Snow et al., 2007). That is, they provide methods for grouping senses of the same **word**, thus producing coarser word sense groupings for better disambiguation.

In contrast, some research have been focused on using predefined sets of sense-groupings for learning class-based classifiers for WSD (Segond et al., 1997), (Ciaramita and Johnson, 2003), (Villarejo et al., 2005), (Curran, 2005), (Kohomban and Lee, 2005) and (Ciaramita and Altun, 2006). That is, grouping senses of different words into the same explicit and comprehensive semantic class. Most of the later approaches used the original Lexicographical Files of WN (more recently called SuperSenses) as very coarse–grained sense distinctions.

We suspect that selecting the appropriate level of abstraction could be on between both levels. Thus, we use the semantic classes modeled by the **Basic Level Concepts**[1] (BLC) (Izquierdo et al., 2007). Our previous research using BLC empirically demonstrated that this automatically derived

[1] http://adimen.si.ehu.es/web/BLC

Proceedings of the 5th International Workshop on Semantic Evaluation, ACL 2010, pages 402–406,
Uppsala, Sweden, 15-16 July 2010.

set of meanings groups senses into an adequate level of abstraction in order to perform class-based Word Sense Disambiguation (WSD) (Izquierdo et al., 2009). Now, we also show that class-based WSD allows to successfully incorporate monosemous examples from the domain text. In fact, the robustness of our class-based WSD approach is shown by our system that just uses the SemCor examples (SC). It performs without any kind of domain adaptation as the Most Frequent Sense (MFS) baseline.

This paper describes our participation in SemEval-2010 Task 17 (Agirre et al., 2010). In section 2 semantic classes used and selection algorithm used to obtain them automatically from WordNet are described. In section 3 the technique employed to extract monosemous examples from background data is described. Section 4 explains the general approach of our system, and the experiments designed, and finally, in section 5, the results and some analysis are shown.

2 Semantic Classes

The set of semantic classes used in this work are the **Basic Level Concepts**[2] (BLC) (Izquierdo et al., 2007). These concepts are small sets of meanings representing the whole nominal and verbal part of WN. BLC can be obtained by a very simple method that uses basic structural WordNet properties. In fact, the algorithm only considers the relative number of relations of each synset along the hypernymy chain. The process follows a bottom-up approach using the chain of hypernymy relations. For each synset in WN, the process selects as its BLC the first local maximum according to the relative number of relations. The local maximum is the synset in the hypernymy chain having more relations than its immediate hyponym and immediate hypernym. For synsets having multiple hypernyms, the path having the local maximum with higher number of relations is selected. Usually, this process finishes having a number of preliminary BLC. Figure 1 shows an example of selection of a BLC. The figure represents the hypernymy hierarchy of WordNet, with circles representing synsets, and links between them representing hypernym relations. The algorithm selects the D synset as BLC for J, due to D is the first maximum in the hypernymy chain, according to the number of relations (F has 2 hyponyms, D has 3, and A has 2, so D is the first maximum).

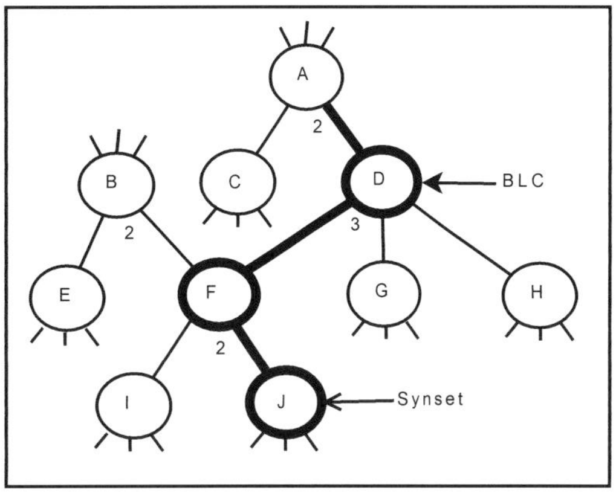

Figure 1: Example of BLC selection

Obviously, while ascending through this chain, more synsets are subsumed by each concept. The process finishes checking if the number of concepts subsumed by the preliminary list of BLC is higher than a certain threshold. For those BLC not representing enough concepts according to the threshold, the process selects the next local maximum following the hypernymy hierarchy. Thus, depending on the type of relations considered to be counted and the threshold established, different sets of BLC can be easily obtained for each WN version.

We have selected the set which considers WN version 3.0, the total number of relations per synset, and a minimum threshold of 20 concepts to filter out not representative BLC (BLC–20). This set has shown to reach good performance on previous SensEval and SemEval exercices (Izquierdo et al., 2009). There are 649 different BLC for nouns on WordNet 3.0, and 616 for verbs. Table 2 shows the three most frequent BLC per POS, with the number of synsets subsumed by each concept, and its WordNet gloss.

3 Using Monosemous Examples from the Domain

We did not applied any kind of specific domain adaptation technique to our class-based supervised system. In order to adapt our supervised system to the environmental domain we only increased the training data with new examples of the domain. To acquire these examples, we used the environmental domain background documents provided by the organizers. Specifically, we used the 122 back-

[2]http://adimen.si.ehu.es/web/BLC

PoS	Num.	BLC	Gloss
Nouns	4.792	person.n.01	a human being
	1.935	activity.n.01	any specific behavior
	1.846	act.n.02	something that people do or cause to happen
Verbs	1.541	change.v.01	cause to change; make different; cause a transformation
	1.085	change.v.02	undergo a change; become different in essence; losing one's or its original nature
	519	move.v.02	cause to move or shift into a new position or place, both in a concrete and in an abstract sense

Table 1: Most frequent BLC–20 semantic classes on WordNet 3.0

ground documents[3]. TreeTagger has been used to preprocess the documents, performing PoS tagging and lemmatization. Since the background documents are not semantically annotated, and our supervised system needs labeled data, we have selected only the monosemous words occurring in the documents. In this way, we have obtained automatically a large set of examples annotated with BLC. Table 3 presents the total number of training examples extracted from SemCor (SC) and from the background documents (BG). As expected, by this method a large number of monosemous examples can be obtained for nouns and verbs. Also as expected, verbs are much less productive than nouns. However, all these background examples correspond to a reduced set of 7,646 monosemous words.

	Nouns	Verbs	N+V
SC	87.978	48.267	136.245
BG	193.536	10.821	204.357
Total	*281.514*	*59.088*	*340.602*

Table 2: Number of training examples

Table 3 lists the ten most frequent monosemous nouns and verbs occurring in the background documents. Note that all these examples are monosemous according to BLC–20 semantic classes.

	Nouns		Verbs	
	Lemma	# ex.	Lemma	# ex.
1	biodiversity	7.476	monitor	788
2	habitat	7.206	achieve	784
3	specie	7.067	target	484
4	climate	3.539	select	345
5	european	2.818	enable	334
6	ecosystem	2.669	seem	287
7	river	2.420	pine	281
8	grassland	2.303	evaluate	246
9	datum	2.276	explore	200
10	directive	2.197	believe	172

Table 3: Most frequent monosemic words in BG

[3]We used the documents contained on the trial data and the background.

4 System Overview

Our system applies a supervised machine learning approach. We apply a feature extractor to represent the training examples of the examples acquired from SemCor and the background documents. Then, a machine learning engine uses the annotated examples to train a set of classifiers. Support Vector Machines (SVM) have been proven to be robust and very competitive in many NLP tasks, and in WSD in particular (Màrquez et al., 2006). We used the SVM-Light implementation[4] (Joachims, 1998).

We create a classifier for each semantic class. This approach has several advantages compared to word–based approach. The training data per classifier is increased (we can use examples of different target words for a single classifier, whenever all examples belong to the same semantic class), the polysemy is reduced (some different word senses can be collapsed into the same semantic class), and, finally, semantic classes provide higher levels of abstraction.

For each polysemous word occurring in the test corpus, we obtain its potential BLC–20 classes. Then, we only apply the classifiers corresponding to the BLC-20 classes of the polysemous word. Finally, our system simply selects the BLC–20 class with the greater prediction.

In order to obtain the correct WordNet 3.0 synset required by the task, we apply a simple heuristic that has shown to be robust and accurate (Kohomban and Lee, 2005). Our classifiers obtain first the semantic class, and then, the synset of the first WordNet sense that fits with the semantic class is assigned to the word.

We selected a simple feature set widely used in many WSD systems. In particular, we use a window of five tokens around the target word to extract word forms, lemmas; bigrams and trigrams of word forms and lemmas; trigrams of PoS tags,

[4]`http://svmlight.joachims.org`

and also the most frequent BLC–20 semantic class of the target word in the training corpus.

Our system is fully described in (Izquierdo et al., 2009). The novelty introduced here is the use of semantic classes to obtain monosemous examples from the domain corpus.

Following the same framework (BLC–20 semantic architecture and basic set of features) we designed three runs, each one using a different training corpus.

- SC: only training examples extracted from SemCor
- BG: only monosemous examples extracted from the background data
- SCBG: training examples extracted from SemCor and monosemous background data

The first run shows the behavior of a supervised system trained on a general corpus, and tested in a specific domain. The second one analyzes the contribution of the monosemous examples extracted from the background data. Finally, the third run studies the robustness of the approach when combining the training examples from SemCor and from the background.

5 Results and Discussion

A total of 29 runs has been submitted for the English All–words WSD on a Specific Domain. Table 5 shows the ranking results of our three runs with respect to the other participants. The figures for the first sense (*1sense*) and random sense (*Random*) baselines are included.

In general, the results obtained are not very high. The best system only achieves a precision of 0.570, and the first sense baseline reaches a precision of 0.505. This shows that the task is hard to solve, and the domain adaptation of WSD systems is not an easy task.

Interestingly, our worst result is obtained by the system using only the monosemous background examples (BG). This system ranks 23th with a Precision and Recall of 0.380 (0.385 for nouns and 0.366 for verbs). The system using only SemCor (SC) ranks 6th with Precision and Recall of 0.505 (0.527 for nouns and 0.443 for verbs). This is also the performance of the first sense baseline. As expected, the best result of our three runs is obtained when combining the examples from SemCor and the background (SCBG). This supervised system obtains the 5th position with a Precision and Recall of 0.513 (0.534 for nouns, 0.454 for verbs) which is slightly above the baseline.

Rank	Precision	Recall
1	0.570	0.555
2	0.554	0.540
3	0.534	0.528
4	0.522	0.516
(SCBG) 5	**0.513**	**0.513**
1sense	*0.505*	*0.505*
(SC) 6	**0.505**	**0.505**
7	0.512	0.495
8	0.506	0.493
9	0.504	0.491
10	0.481	0.481
11	0.492	0.479
12	0.461	0.460
13	0.447	0.441
14	0.436	0.435
15	0.440	0.434
16	0.496	0.433
17	0.498	0.432
18	0.433	0.431
19	0.426	0.425
20	0.424	0.422
21	0.437	0.392
22	0.384	0.384
(BG) 23	**0.380**	**0.380**
24	0.381	0.356
25	0.351	0.350
26	0.370	0.345
27	0.328	0.322
28	0.321	0.315
29	0.312	0.303
Random	*0.230*	*0.230*

Table 4: Results of task#17

Possibly, the reason of low performance of the BG system is the high correlation between the features of the target word and its semantic class. In this case, these features correspond to the monosemous word while when testing corresponds to the target word. However, it also seems that class-based systems are robust enough to incorporate large sets of monosemous examples from the domain text. In fact, to our knowledge, this is the first time that a supervised WSD algorithm have been successfully adapted to an specific domain. Furthermore, our system trained only on SemCor also achieves a good performance, reaching the first sense baseline, showing that class-based WSD approaches seem to be robust to domain variations.

Acknowledgments

This paper has been supported by the European Union under the project KYOTO (FP7 ICT-211423), the Valencian Region Government under PROMETEO project for excellence groups and the Spanish Government under the projects

KNOW2 (TIN2009-14715-C04-04) and TEXT-MESS-2 (TIN2009-13391-C04-04).

References

E. Agirre and O. LopezDeLaCalle. 2003. Clustering wordnet word senses. In *Proceedings of RANLP'03*, Borovets, Bulgaria.

Eneko Agirre, Oier Lopez de Lacalle, Christiane Fellbaum, Shu kai Hsieh, Maurizio Tesconi, Monica Monachini, Piek Vossen, and Roxanne Segers. 2010. Semeval-2010 task 17: All-words word sense disambiguation on a specific domain. In *Proceedings of the 5th International Workshop on Semantic Evaluations (SemEval-2010), Association for Computational Linguistics.*

M. Ciaramita and Y. Altun. 2006. Broad-coverage sense disambiguation and information extraction with a supersense sequence tagger. In *Proceedings of the Conference on Empirical Methods in Natural Language Processing (EMNLP'06)*, pages 594–602, Sydney, Australia. ACL.

M. Ciaramita and M. Johnson. 2003. Supersense tagging of unknown nouns in wordnet. In *Proceedings of the Conference on Empirical methods in natural language processing (EMNLP'03)*, pages 168–175. ACL.

J. Curran. 2005. Supersense tagging of unknown nouns using semantic similarity. In *Proceedings of the 43rd Annual Meeting on Association for Computational Linguistics (ACL'05)*, pages 26–33. ACL.

G. Escudero, L. Màrquez, and G. Rigau. 2000. An Empirical Study of the Domain Dependence of Supervised Word Sense Disambiguation Systems. In *Proceedings of the joint SIGDAT Conference on Empirical Methods in Natural Language Processing and Very Large Corpora, EMNLP/VLC*, Hong Kong, China.

M. Hearst and H. Schütze. 1993. Customizing a lexicon to better suit a computational task. In *Proceedingns of the ACL SIGLEX Workshop on Lexical Acquisition*, Stuttgart, Germany.

R. Izquierdo, A. Suarez, and G. Rigau. 2007. Exploring the automatic selection of basic level concepts. In Galia Angelova et al., editor, *International Conference Recent Advances in Natural Language Processing*, pages 298–302, Borovets, Bulgaria.

Rubén Izquierdo, Armando Suárez, and German Rigau. 2009. An empirical study on class-based word sense disambiguation. In *Proceedings of the 12th Conference of the European Chapter of the ACL (EACL 2009)*, pages 389–397, Athens, Greece, March. Association for Computational Linguistics.

T. Joachims. 1998. Text categorization with support vector machines: learning with many relevant features. In Claire Nédellec and Céline Rouveirol, editors, *Proceedings of ECML-98, 10th European Conference on Machine Learning*, pages 137–142, Chemnitz, DE. Springer Verlag, Heidelberg, DE.

Upali S. Kohomban and Wee Sun Lee. 2005. Learning semantic classes for word sense disambiguation. In *ACL '05: Proceedings of the 43rd Annual Meeting on Association for Computational Linguistics*, pages 34–41, Morristown, NJ, USA. Association for Computational Linguistics.

Ll. Màrquez, G. Escudero, D. Martínez, and G. Rigau. 2006. Supervised corpus-based methods for wsd. In *E. Agirre and P. Edmonds (Eds.) Word Sense Disambiguation: Algorithms and applications.*, volume 33 of *Text, Speech and Language Technology*. Springer.

R. Mihalcea and D. Moldovan. 2001. Automatic generation of coarse grained wordnet. In *Proceding of the NAACL workshop on WordNet and Other Lexical Resources: Applications, Extensions and Customizations*, Pittsburg, USA.

R. Navigli. 2006. Meaningful clustering of senses helps boost word sense disambiguation performance. In *ACL-44: Proceedings of the 21st International Conference on Computational Linguistics and the 44th annual meeting of the Association for Computational Linguistics*, pages 105–112, Morristown, NJ, USA. Association for Computational Linguistics.

W. Peters, I. Peters, and P. Vossen. 1998. Automatic sense clustering in eurowordnet. In *First International Conference on Language Resources and Evaluation (LREC'98)*, Granada, Spain.

F. Segond, A. Schiller, G. Greffenstette, and J. Chanod. 1997. An experiment in semantic tagging using hidden markov model tagging. In *ACL Workshop on Automatic Information Extraction and Building of Lexical Semantic Resources for NLP Applications*, pages 78–81. ACL, New Brunswick, New Jersey.

R. Snow, Prakash S., Jurafsky D., and Ng A. 2007. Learning to merge word senses. In *Proceedings of Joint Conference on Empirical Methods in Natural Language Processing and Computational Natural Language Learning (EMNLP-CoNLL)*, pages 1005–1014.

L. Villarejo, L. Màrquez, and G. Rigau. 2005. Exploring the construction of semantic class classifiers for wsd. In *Proceedings of the 21th Annual Meeting of Sociedad Espaola para el Procesamiento del Lenguaje Natural SEPLN'05*, pages 195–202, Granada, Spain, September. ISSN 1136-5948.

HIT-CIR: An Unsupervised WSD System Based on Domain Most Frequent Sense Estimation

Yuhang Guo, Wanxiang Che, Wei He, Ting Liu, Sheng Li
Harbin Institute of Technolgy
Harbin, Heilongjiang, PRC
yhguo@ir.hit.edu.cn

Abstract

This paper presents an unsupervised system for all-word domain specific word sense disambiguation task. This system tags target word with the most frequent sense which is estimated using a thesaurus and the word distribution information in the domain. The thesaurus is automatically constructed from bilingual parallel corpus using paraphrase technique. The recall of this system is 43.5% on SemEval-2 task 17 English data set.

1 Introduction

Tagging polysemous word with its most frequent sense (MFS) is a popular back-off heuristic in word sense disambiguation (WSD) systems when the training data is inadequate. In past evaluations, MFS from WordNet performed even better than most of the unsupervised systems (Snyder and Palmer, 2004; Navigli et al., 2007).

MFS is usually obtained from a large scale sense tagged corpus, such as SemCor (Miller et al., 1994). However, some polysemous words have different MFS in different domains. For example, in the Koeling et al. (2005) corpus, target word *coach* means *"manager"* mostly in the SPORTS domain but means *"bus"* mostly in the FINANCE domain. So when the MFS is applied to specific domains, it needs to be re-estimated.

McCarthy et al. (2007) proposed an unsupervised predominant word sense acquisition method which obtains domain specific MFS without sense tagged corpus. In their method, a thesaurus, in which words are connected with their distributional similarity, is constructed from the domain raw text. Word senses are ranked by their prevalence score which is calculated using the thesaurus and the sense inventory.

In this paper, we propose another way to construct the thesaurus. We use statistical machine

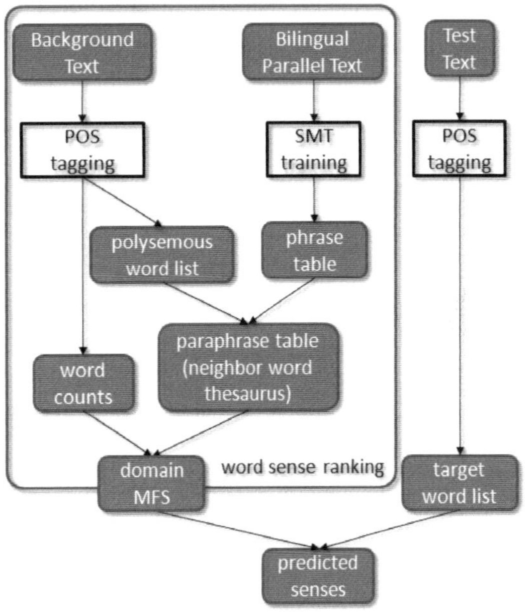

Figure 1: The architecture of HIT-CIR

translation (SMT) techniques to extract paraphrase pairs from bilingual parallel text. In this way, we avoid calculating similarities between every pair of words and could find semantic similar words or compounds which have dissimilar distributions.

Our system is comprised of two parts: the word sense ranking part and the word sense tagging part. Senses are ranked according to their prevalence score in the target domain, and the predominant sense is used to tag the occurrences of the target word in the test data. The architecture of this system is shown in Figure 1.

The word sense ranking part includes following steps.

1. Tag the POS of the background text, count the word frequency in each POS, and get the polysemous word list of the POS.

2. Using SMT techniques to extract phrase table

Proceedings of the 5th International Workshop on Semantic Evaluation, ACL 2010, pages 407–410,
Uppsala, Sweden, 15-16 July 2010.

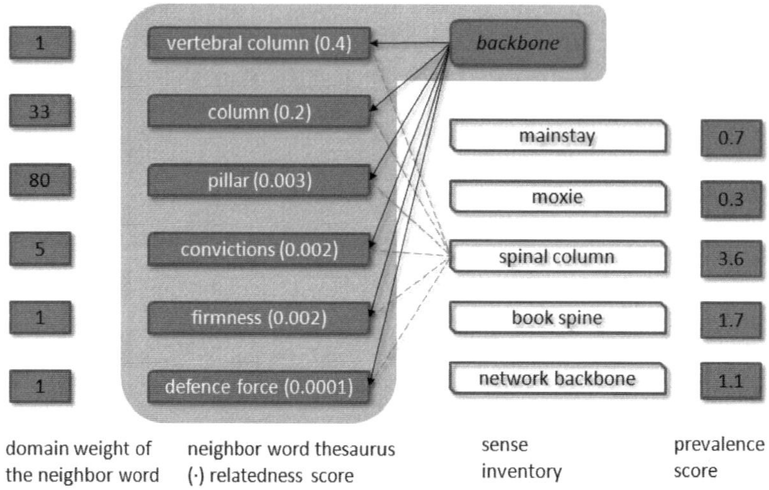

Figure 2: Word sense ranking for the noun *backbone*

from the bilingual corpus. Extract the paraphrases (called as neighbor words) with the phrase table for each word in the polysemous word list.

3. Calculate the prevalence score of each sense of the target words, rank the senses with the score and obtain the predominant sense.

We applied our system on the English data set of SemEval-2 specific domain WSD task. This task is an all word WSD task in the environmental domain. We employed the domain background raw text provided by the task organizer as well as the English WordNet 3.0 (Fellbaum, 1998) and the English-Spanish parallel corpus from Europarl (Koehn, 2005).

This paper is organized as follows. Section 2 introduces how to rank word senses. Section 3 presents how to obtain the most related words of the target words. We describe the system settings in Section 4 and offer some discussions in Section 5.

2 Word Sense Ranking

In our method, word senses are ranked according to their prevalence score in the specific domain. According to the assumption of McCarthy et al. (2007), the prevalence score is affected by the following two factors: (1) The relatedness score between a given sense of the target word and the target word's neighbor word. (2) The similarity between the target word and its neighbor word. In addition, we add another factor, (3) the importance of the neighbor word in the specific domain. In this paper, "neighbor words" means the words which are most semantically similar to the target word.

Figure 2 illustrates the word sense ranking process of noun *backbone*. The contribution of a neighbor word to a given word sense is measured by the similarity between them and weighted by the importance of the neighbor word in the target domain and the relatedness between the neighbor word and the target word. Sum up the contributions of each neighbor words, and we get the prevalence score of the word sense.

Formally, the prevalence score of sense s_i of a target word w is assigned as follows:

$$ps(w, s_i) = \sum_{n_j \in N_w} rs(w, n_j) \times ns(s_i, n_j) \times dw(n_j) \quad (1)$$

where

$$ns(s_i, n_j) = \frac{sss(s_i, n_j)}{\sum_{s_{i'} \in senses(w)} sss(s_{i'}, n_j)}, \quad (2)$$

$$sss(s_i, n_j) = max_{s_x \in senses(n_j)} sss'(s_i, s_x). \quad (3)$$

$rs(w, n_j)$ is the relatedness score between w and a neighbor word n_j. $N_w = \{n_1, n_2, \ldots, n_k\}$ is the top k relatedness score neighbor word set. $ns(s_i, n_j)$ is the normalized form of the sense similarity score between sense s_i and the neighbor word n_j (i.e. $sss(s_i, n_j)$). We define this score with the maximum WordNet similarity score between s_i and the senses of n_j (i.e. $sss'(s_i, n_j)$). In our system, lesk algorithm is used to measure the sense similarity score between word senses.

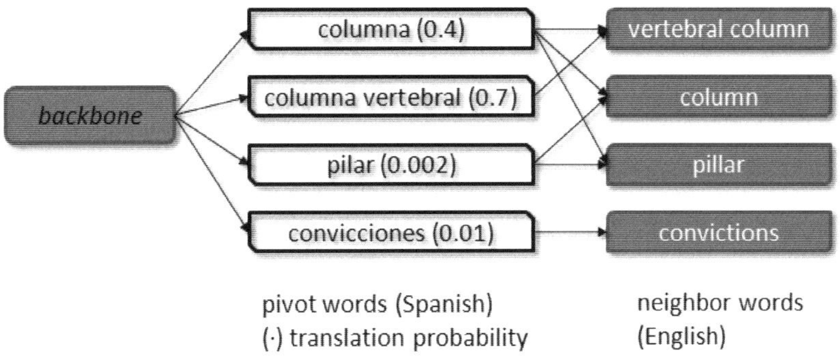

Figure 3: Finding the neighbor words of noun *backbone*

The similarity of this algorithm is the count of the number of overlap words in the gloss or the definition of the senses (Banerjee and Pedersen, 2002). The domain importance weight $dw(n_j)$ is assigned with the count of n_j in the domain background corpus. For the neighbor word that does not occur in the domain background text, we use the *add-one* strategy. We will describe how to obtain n_j and rs in Section 3.

3 Thesaurus Construction

The neighbor words of the target word as well as the relatedness score are obtained by extracting paraphrases from bilingual parallel texts. When a word is translated from source language to target language and then translated back to the source language, the final translation may have the same meaning to the original word but with different expressions (e.g. different word or compound). The translation in the same language could be viewed as a paraphrase term or, at least, related term of the original word.

For example, in Figure 3, English noun *backbone* can be translated to *columna*, *columna vertebral*, *pilar* and *convicciones* etc. in Spanish, and these words also have other relevant translations in English, such as *vertebral column*, *column*, *pillar* and *convictions* etc., which are semantically related to the target word *backbone*.

We use a statistical machine translation system to calculate the translation probability from English to another language (called as pivot language) as well as the translation probability from that language to English. By multiplying these two probabilities, we get a paraphrase probability. This method was defined in (Bannard and Callison-Burch, 2005).

In our system, we choose the top k paraphrases as the neighbor words of the target word, which have the highest paraphrase probability. Note that there are two directions of the paraphrase, from target word to its neighbor word and from the neighbor word to the target word. We choose the paraphrase score of the former direction as the relatedness score (rs). Because the higher of the score in this direction, the target word is more likely paraphrased to that neighbor word, and hence the prevalence of the relevant target word sense will be higher than other senses. Formally, the relatedness score is given by

$$rs(w, n_j) = \sum_f p(f|w)p(n_j|f), \qquad (4)$$

where f is the pivot language word.

We use the English-Spanish parallel text from Europarl (Koehn, 2005). We choose Spanish as the pivot language because in the both directions the BLEU score of the translation between English and Spanish is relatively higher than other English and other languages (Koehn, 2005).

4 Data set and System Settings

The organizers of the SemEval-2 specific domain WSD task provide no training data but raw background data in the environmental domain. The English background data is obtained from the official web site of World Wide Fund (WWF), European Centre for Nature Conservation (ECNC), European Commission and the United Nations Economic Commission for Europe (UNECE). The size of the raw text is around 15.5MB after simple text cleaning. The test data is from WWF and ECNC, and contains 1398 occurrence of 436 target words.

For the implementation, we used bpos (Shen et al., 2007) for the POS tagging. The maximum number of the neighbor word of each target word k was set to 50. We employed Giza++[1] and Moses[2] to get the phrase table from the bilingual parallel corpus. The WordNet::Similarity package[3] was applied for the implement of the lesk word sense similarity algorithm.

For the target word that is not in the polysemous word list, we use the MFS from WordNet as the back-off method.

5 Discussion and Future Work

The recall of our system is 43.5%, which is lower than that of the MFS baseline, 50.5% (Agirre et al., 2010). The baseline uses the most frequent sense from the SemCor corpus (i.e. the MFS of WordNet). This means that for some target words, the MFS from SemCor is better than the domain MFS we estimated in the environmental domain. In the future, we will analysis errors in detail to find the effects of the domain on the MFS.

For the domain specific task, it is better to use parallel text in the domain of the test data in our method. However, we didn't find any available parallel text in the environmental domain yet. In the future, we will try some parallel corpus acquisition techniques to obtain relevant corpus for environmental domain for our method.

Acknowledgments

This work was supported by National Natural Science Foundation of China (NSFC) via grant 60803093, 60975055, the "863" National High-Tech Research and Development of China via grant 2008AA01Z144, and Natural Scientific Research Innovation Foundation in Harbin Institute of Technology (HIT.NSRIF.2009069).

References

Eneko Agirre, Oier Lopez de Lacalle, Christiane Fellbaum, Shu kai Hsieh, Maurizio Tesconi, Monica Monachini, Piek Vossen, and Roxanne Segers. 2010. Semeval-2010 task 17: All-words word sense disambiguation on a specific domain. In *Proceedings of the 5th International Workshop on Semantic Evaluations (SemEval-2010), Association for Computational Linguistics.*

Satanjeev Banerjee and Ted Pedersen. 2002. An adapted lesk algorithm for word sense disambiguation using wordnet. In *CICLing '02: Proceedings of the Third International Conference on Computational Linguistics and Intelligent Text Processing*, pages 136–145, London, UK. Springer-Verlag.

Colin Bannard and Chris Callison-Burch. 2005. Paraphrasing with bilingual parallel corpora. In *ACL '05: Proceedings of the 43rd Annual Meeting on Association for Computational Linguistics*, pages 597–604, Morristown, NJ, USA. Association for Computational Linguistics.

Christiane Fellbaum. 1998. *WordNet: An Electronic Lexical Database*. MIT Press.

Philipp Koehn. 2005. Europarl: A parallel corpus for statistical machine translation. In *The Tenth Machine Translation Summit*, Phuket, Thailand.

Rob Koeling, Diana McCarthy, and John Carroll. 2005. Domain-specific sense distributions and predominant sense acquisition. In *Proceedings of Human Language Technology Conference and Conference on Empirical Methods in Natural Language Processing*, pages 419–426, Vancouver, British Columbia, Canada, October. Association for Computational Linguistics.

Diana McCarthy, Rob Koeling, Julie Weeds, and John Carroll. 2007. Unsupervised acquisition of predominant word senses. *Computational Linguistics*, 33(4):553–590, December.

G. A. Miller, C. Leacock, R. Tengi, and R. Bunker. 1994. A semantic concordance. In *Proc. ARPA Human Language Technology Workshop '93*, pages 303–308, Princeton, NJ, March. distributed as *Human Language Technology* by San Mateo, CA: Morgan Kaufmann Publishers.

Roberto Navigli, Kenneth C. Litkowski, and Orin Hargraves. 2007. Semeval-2007 task 07: Coarse-grained english all-words task. In *Proceedings of the Fourth International Workshop on Semantic Evaluations (SemEval-2007)*, pages 30–35, Prague, Czech Republic, June. Association for Computational Linguistics.

Libin Shen, Giorgio Satta, and Aravind Joshi. 2007. Guided learning for bidirectional sequence classification. In *Proceedings of the 45th Annual Meeting of the Association of Computational Linguistics*, pages 760–767, Prague, Czech Republic, June. Association for Computational Linguistics.

Benjamin Snyder and Martha Palmer. 2004. The english all-words task. In Rada Mihalcea and Phil Edmonds, editors, *Senseval-3: Third International Workshop on the Evaluation of Systems for the Semantic Analysis of Text*, pages 41–43, Barcelona, Spain, July. Association for Computational Linguistics.

[1] http://www.fjoch.com/GIZA++.html

[2] http://www.statmt.org/moses/

[3] http://wn-similarity.sourceforge.net/

RACAI: Unsupervised WSD experiments @ SemEval-2, Task #17

Radu Ion
Institute for AI, Romanian Academy
13, Calea 13 Septembrie, Bucharest
050711, Romania
radu@racai.ro

Dan Ştefănescu
Institute for AI, Romanian Academy
13, Calea 13 Septembrie, Bucharest
050711, Romania
danstef@racai.ro

Abstract

This paper documents the participation of the Research Institute for Artificial Intelligence of the Romanian Academy (RACAI) to the Task 17 – All-words Word Sense Disambiguation on a Specific Domain, of the SemEval-2 competition. We describe three unsupervised WSD systems that make extensive use of the Princeton WordNet (WN) structure and WordNet Domains in order to perform the disambiguation. The best of them has been ranked the 12th by the task organizers out of 29 judged runs.

1 Introduction

Referring to the last SemEval (SemEval-1, (Agirre et al., 2007a)) and to our recent work (Ion and Ştefănescu, 2009), unsupervised Word Sense Disambiguation (WSD) is still at the bottom of WSD systems ranking with a significant loss in performance when compared to supervised approaches. With Task #17 @ SemEval-2, this observation is (probably [1]) reinforced but another issue is re-brought to light: the difficulty of supervised WSD systems to adapt to a given domain (Agirre et al., 2009). With general scores lower with at least 3% than 3 years ago in Task #17 @ SemEval-1 which was a supposedly harder task (general, no particular domain WSD was required for all words), we observe that supervised WSD is certainly more difficult to implement in a real world application.

Our unsupervised WSD approach benefited from the specification of this year's Task #17 which was a domain-limited WSD, meaning that the disambiguation would be applied to content words drawn from a specific domain: the surrounding environment. We worked under the assumption that a term of the given domain would have the same meaning with all its occurrences throughout the text. This hypothesis has been put forth by Yarowsky (1993) as the "one sense per discourse" hypothesis (OSPD for short).

The task organizers offered a set of background documents with no sense annotations to the competitors who want to train/tune their systems using data from the same domain as the official test set. Working with the OSPD hypothesis, we set off to construct/test domain specific WSD models from/on this corpus using the WordNet Domains (Bentivogli et al., 2004). For testing purposes, we have constructed an in-house gold standard from this corpus that comprises of 1601 occurrences of 204 terms of the "surrounding environment" domain that have been automatically extracted with the highest confidence. We have observed that our gold standard (which has been independently annotated by 3 annotators but on non-overlapping sections which led to having no inter-annotator agreement scores) obeys the OSPD hypothesis which we think that is appropriate to domain-limited WSD.

In what follows, we will briefly acknowledge the usage of WordNet Domains in WSD, we will then describe the construction of the corpus of the background documents including here the creation of an in-house gold standard, we will then briefly describe our three WSD algorithms and finally we will conclude with a discussion on the ranking of our runs among the 29 evaluated by the task organizers.

2 Related Work

WordNet Domains is a hierarchy of labels that have been assigned to WN synsets in a one to (possible) many relationship (but the frequent case is a single WN domain for a synset). A domain is the name of an area of knowledge that is recognized as unitary (Bentivogli et al., 2004).

[1] At the time of the writing we only know the systems ranking without the supervised/unsupervised distinction.

Proceedings of the 5th International Workshop on Semantic Evaluation, ACL 2010, pages 411–416,
Uppsala, Sweden, 15-16 July 2010.

Thus labels such as "*architecture*", "*sport*" or "*medicine*" are mapped onto synsets like "*arch(4)*-noun", "*playing(2)*-noun" or "*chronic(1)*-adjective" because of the fact that the respective concept evokes the domain.

WordNet Domains have been used in various ways to perform WSD. The main usage of this mapping is that the domains naturally create a clustering of the WN senses of a literal thus offering a sense inventory that is much coarser than the fine sense distinctions of WN. For instance, senses 1 ("*a flat-bottomed motor vehicle that can travel on land or water*") and 2 ("*an airplane designed to take off and land on water*") of the noun "*amphibian*" are both mapped to the domain "*transport*" but the 3rd sense of the same noun is mapped onto the domains "*animals/biology*" being the "*cold-blooded vertebrate typically living on land but breeding in water; aquatic larvae undergo metamorphosis into adult form*" (definitions from version 2.0 of the WN).

Vázquez et al. (2004) use WordNet Domains to derive a new resource they call the Relevant Domains in which, using WordNet glosses, they extract the most representative words for a given domain. Thus, for a word w and a domain d, the Association Ratio formula between w and d is

$$\mathrm{AR}(w,d) = \mathrm{P}(w \mid d) \cdot \log_2 \frac{\mathrm{P}(w \mid d)}{\mathrm{P}(w)}$$

in which, for each synset its gloss has been POS tagged and lemmatized. The probabilities are computed counting pairs $\langle w,d \rangle$ in glosses (each gloss has an associated d domain via its synset).

Using the Relevant Domains, the WSD procedure for a given word w in its context C (a 100 words window centered in w), computes a similarity measure between two vectors of AR scores: the first vector is the vector of AR scores of the sentence in which w appears and the other is the vector of domain scores computed for the gloss of a sense of w (both vectors are normalized such that they contain the same domains). The highest similarity gives the sense of w that is closest to the domain vector of C. With this method, Vázquez et al. obtain a precision of 0.54 and a recall of 0.43 at the SensEval-2, English All-Words Task placing them in the 10th position out of 22 systems where the best one (a supervised system) achieved a 0.69 precision and an equal recall.

Another approach to WSD using the WordNet Domains is that of Magnini et al. (2002). The method is remarkably similar to the previous one in that the description of the vectors and the selection of the assigned sense is the same. What differs, is the weights that are assigned to each domain in the vector. Magnini et al. distinguish between text vectors (C vectors in the previous presentation) and sense vectors. Text (or context) vector weights are computed comparing domain frequency in the context with the domain frequency over the entire corpus (see Magnini et al. (2002) for details). Sense vectors are derived from sense-annotated data which qualifies this method as a supervised one. The results that have been reported at the same task the previous algorithm participated (SensEval-2, English All-Words Task), are: precision 0.748 and recall 0.357 (12th place).

Both the methods presented here are very simple and easy to adapt to different domains. One of our methods (RACAI-1, see below) is even simpler (because it makes the OSPD simplifying assumption) and performs with approximately the same accuracy as any of these methods judging by the rank of the system and the total number of participants.

3 Using the Background Documents collection

Task #17 organizers have offered a set of background documents for training/tuning/testing purposes. The corpus consists of 124 files from the "surrounding environment" domain that have been collected in the framework of the Kyoto Project (http://www.kyoto-project.eu/).

First, we have assembled the files into a single corpus in order to be able to apply some cleaning procedures. These procedures involved the removal of the paragraphs in which the proportion of letters (Perl character class "`[A-Za-z_-]`") was less than 0.8 because the text contained a lot of noise in form of lines of numbers and other symbols which probably belonged to tables. The next stage was to have the corpus POS-tagged, lemmatized and chunked using the TTL web service (Tufiş et al., 2008). The resulting file is an XML encoded corpus which contains 136456 sentences with 2654446 tokens out of which 348896 are punctuation tokens.

In order to test our domain constrained WSD algorithms, we decided to construct a test set with the same dimension as the official test set of about 2000 occurrences of content words specific to the "surrounding environment" domain. In doing this, we have employed a simple term extraction algorithm which considers that terms, as opposed to words that are not domain specific, are not evenly distributed throughout the corpus. To formalize this, the corpus is a vector of lemmas $C = [l_1, l_2, \ldots, l_N]$ and for each unique lemma $l_j, 1 \le j \le N$, we compute the mean of the absolute differences of its indexes in C as

$$\mu = \frac{\sum_{1 \le j < k \le N} |j - k|}{f(l_j) - 1}, l_j = l_k \wedge \forall m, j < m < k, l_j \ne l_m$$

where $f(l_j)$ is the frequency of l_j in C. We also compute the standard deviation of these differences from the mean as

$$\sigma = \sqrt{\frac{\sum_{1 \le j < k \le N} (|j - k| - \mu)^2}{f(l_j) - 2}}$$

in the same conditions as above.

With the mean and standard deviation of indexes differences of a content word lemma computed, we construct a list of all content word lemmas that is sorted in descending order by the quantity σ / μ which we take as a measure of the evenness of a content word lemma distribution. Thus, lemmas that are in the top of this list are likely to be terms of the domain of the corpus (in our case, the "surrounding environment" domain). Table 1 contains the first 20 automatically extracted terms along with their term score.

Having the list of terms of our domain, we have selected the first *ambiguous* 210 (which have more than 1 sense in WN) and constructed a test set in which each term has (at least) 10 occurrences in order to obtain a test corpus with at least 2000 occurrences of the terms of the "surrounding environment" domain. A large part of these occurrences have been independently sense-annotated by 3 annotators which worked on disjoint sets of terms (70 terms each) in order to finish as soon as possible. In the end we managed to annotate 1601 occurrences corresponding to 204 terms.

When the gold standard for the test set was ready, we checked to see if the OSPD hypothesis holds. In order to determine if it does, we computed the average number of annotated different senses per term which is 1.36. In addition, considering the fact that out of 204 annotated terms, 145 are annotated with a single sense, we may state that in this case, the OSPD hypothesis holds.

Term	Score	Term	Score
gibbon	15.89	Oceanica	9.41
fleet	13.91	orangutan	9.19
sub-region	13.01	laurel	9.08
Amazon	12.41	coral	9.06
roundwood	12.26	polar	9.05
biocapacity	12.23	wrasse	8.80
footprint	11.68	reef	8.78
deen	11.45	snapper	8.67
dune	10.57	biofuel	8.53
grouper	9.67	vessel	8.35

Table 1: The first 20 automatically extracted terms of the "surrounding environment" domain

4 The Description of the Systems

Since we are committed to assign a unique sense per word in the test set, we might as well try to automatically induce a *WSD model* from the background corpus in which, for each lemma along with its POS tag that also exists in WN, a single sense is listed that is derived from the corpus. Then, for any test set of the same domain, the algorithm would give the sense from the WSD model to any of the occurrences of the lemma.

What we actually did, was to find a list of most frequent 2 WN domains (frequency count extracted from the *whole corpus*) for each lemma with its POS tag, and using these, to list all senses of the lemma that are mapped onto these 2 domains (thus obtaining a reduction of the average number of senses per word). The steps of the algorithm for the creation of the WSD model are:

1. in the given corpus, for each lemma *l* and its POS-tag *p* normalized to WN POS notation ("n" for nouns, "v" for verbs, "a" for adjectives and "b" for adverbs), for each of its senses from WN, increase by 1 each frequency of each mapped domain;
2. for each lemma *l* with its POS-tag *p*, retain only those senses that map onto the most frequent 2 domains as determined by the frequency list from the first step.

Using our 2.65M words background corpus to build such a model (Table 2 contains a sample), we have obtained a decrease in average ambiguity degree (the average number of senses per content word lemma) from 2.43 to 2.14. If we set a threshold of at least 1 for the term score of the lemmas to be included into the WSD model (which selects 12062 lemmas, meaning about 1/3 of all unique lemmas in the corpus), we obtain the same reduction thus contradicting our hypothesis that the average ambiguity degree of terms would be reduced more than the average ambiguity degree of all words in the corpus. This result might be due to the fact that the "*factotum*" domain is very frequent (much more frequent than any of the other domains).

Lemma	POS:Total no. of WN senses	First 2 selected domains	Selected senses
fish	n:2	animals,biology	1
Arctic	n:1	geography	1
coral	n:4	chemistry,animals	2,3,4

Table 2: A sample of the WSD model built from the background corpus

In what follows, we will present our 3 systems that use WSD models derived from the test sets (both the in-house and the official ones). In the Results section we will explain this choice.

4.1 RACAI-1: WordNet Domains-driven, Most Frequent Sense

The first system, as its name suggests, is very simple: using the WSD model, it chooses the most frequent sense (MFS) of the lemma l with POS p according to WN (that is, the lowest numbered sense from the list of senses the lemma has in the WSD model).

Trying this method on our in-house developed test set, we obtain encouraging results: the overall accuracy (precision is equal with the recall because all test set occurrences are tried) is at least 4% over the general MFS baseline (sense no. 1 in all cases). The Results section gives details.

4.2 RACAI-2: The Lexical Chains Selection

With this system, we have tried to select only one sense (not necessarily the most frequent one) of lemma l with POS p from the WSD model. The selection procedure is based on lexical chains computation between senses of the target word (the word to be disambiguated) and the content words in its sentence in a manner that will be explained below.

We have used the lexical chains description and computation method described in (Ion and Ştefănescu, 2009). To reiterate, a lexical chain is not simply a set of topically related words but becomes a path of synsets in the WordNet hierarchy. The lexical chain procedure is a function of two WN synsets, LXC(s_1, s_2), that returns a semantic relation path that one can follow to reach s_2 from s_1. On the path from s_2 to s_1 there are k synsets ($k \geq 0$) and between 2 adjacent synsets there is a WN semantic relation. Each lexical chain can be assigned a certain score that we interpret as a measure of the semantic similarity (SS) between s_1 and s_2 (see (Ion and Ştefănescu, 2009) and (Moldovan and Novischi, 2002) for more details). Thus, the higher the value of SS(s_1, s_2), the higher the semantic similarity between s_1 and s_2.

We have observed that using RACAI-1 on our in-house test set but allowing it to select the most frequent **2** senses of lemma l with POS p from the WSD model, we obtain a whopping **82% accuracy**. With this observation, we tried to program RACAI-2 to make a binary selection from the first 2 most frequent senses of lemma l with POS p from the WSD model in order to approach the 82% percent accuracy limit which would have been a very good result. The algorithm is as follows: for a lemma l with POS p and a lemma l_c with POS p_c from the context (sentence) of l, compute the best lexical chain between any of the first 2 senses of l and any of the first 2 senses of l_c according to the WSD model. If the first 2 senses of l are a and b and the first 2 senses of l_c are x and y and the best lexical chain score has been found between a and y for instance, then credit sense a of l with SS(a, y). Sum over all l_c from the context of l and select that sense of l which has a maximum semantic similarity with the context.

4.3 RACAI-3: Interpretation-based Sense Assignment

This system tries to generate all the possible sense assignments (called interpretations) to the lemmas in a sentence. Thus, in principle, for each content word lemma, all its WN senses are considered thus generating an exponential explosion of the sense assignments that can be attributed to a sentence. If we have N content word lemmas which have k senses on average, we obtain a search space of k^N interpretations which have to be scored.

Using the observation mentioned above that the first 2 senses of a lemma according to the WSD model yields a performance of 82%, brings the search space to 2^N but for a large N, it is still too big.

The solution we adopted (besides considering the first 2 senses from the WSD model) consists in segmenting the input sentence in M independent segments of 10 content word lemmas each, which will be processed independently, yielding a search space of at most $M \cdot 2^{10}$ of smaller interpretations. The best interpretation per each segment would thus be a part of the best interpretation of the sentence. Next, we describe how we score an interpretation.

For each sense *s* of a lemma *l* with POS *p* (from the first 2 senses of *l* listed in the WSD model) we compute an associated set of content words (lemmas) from the following sources:

- all content word lemmas extracted from the sense *s* corresponding gloss (disregarding the auxiliary verbs);
- all literals of the synset in which lemma *l* with sense *s* exists;
- all literals of the synsets that are linked with the synset *l*(*s*) by a relation of the following type: *hypernym*, *near_antonym*, *eng_derivative*, *hyponym*, *meronym*, *holonym*, *similar_to*, *derived*;
- all content word lemmas extracted from the glosses corresponding to synsets that are linked with the *l*(*s*) synset by a relation of the following type: *hypernym*, *eng_derivative*, *similar_to*, *derived*;

With this feature set V of a sense *s* belonging to lemma *l* with POS *p*, for a given interpretation (a specific assignment of senses to each lemma in a segment), its score S (initially 0) is computed iteratively (for two adjacent position *i* and *i* + 1 in the segment) as

$$S \leftarrow S + |V_i \cap V_{i+1}|, \quad V_{i+1} \leftarrow V_i \cup V_{i+1}$$

where the |X| function is the cardinality function on the set X and ← is the assignment operator.

5 Results

In order to run our WSD algorithms, we had to extract WSD models. We tested the accuracy of the disambiguation (onto the in-house developed gold standard) with RACAI-1 and RACAI-2 systems (RACAI-3 was not ready at that time) with models extracted **a)** from the whole background corpus and **b)** from the in-house developed test set (named here the RACAI test set, see section 3). The results are reported in Table 3 along with RACAI-1 system returning the first 2 senses of a lemma from the WSD model and the general MFS baseline.

As we can see, the results with the WSD model extracted from the test set are marginally better than the other results. This was the reason for which we chose to extract the WSD model from the official test set as opposed to using the WSD model extracted from the background corpus.

	RACAI Test Set	**Background Corpus**
RACAI-1	0.647	0.644
RACAI-1 (2 senses)	0.825	0.811
RACAI-2	0.591	0.582
MFS (sense no. 1)	0.602	0.602

Table 3: RACAI systems results (accuracy) on the RACAI test set

However, we did not research the possibility of adding the official test set to either the RACAI test set or the background corpus and extract WSD models from there.

The official test set (named the SEMEVAL test set here) contains 1398 occurrences of content words for disambiguation, out of which 366 are occurrences of verbs and 1032 are occurrences of nouns. These occurrences correspond to 428 lemmas. Inspecting these lemmas, we have found that there are many of them which are not domain specific (in our case, specific to the "surrounding environment" domain). For instance, the verb to "*be*" is at the top of the list with 99 occurrences. It is followed by the noun "*index*" with 32 occurrences and by the noun "*network*" with 22 occurrences. With fewer occurrences follow "*use*", "*include*", "*show*", "*provide*", "*part*" and so on. Of course, the SEMEVAL test set includes proper terms of the designated domain such as "*area*" (61 occurrences), "*species*" (58 occurrences), "*nature*" (31 occurrences), "*ocean*", "*sea*", "*water*", "*planet*", etc.

Table 4 lists our official results on the SEMEVAL test set.

	Precision	**Recall**	**Rank**
RACAI-1	0.461	0.46	#12
RACAI-2	0.351	0.35	#25
RACAI-3	0.433	0.431	#18
MFS	0.505	0.505	#6

Table 4: RACAI systems results (accuracy) on the SEMEVAL test set

Precision is not equal to recall because of the fact that our POS tagger found two occurrences of the verb to "*be*" as auxiliaries which were ignored. The column Rank indicates the place our systems have in a 29 run ranking of all systems that participated in Task 17 – All-words Word Sense Disambiguation on a Specific Domain, of the SemEval-2 competition which was won by a system that achieved a precision of 0.57 and a recall of 0.555.

The differences with the runs on the RACAI test set are significant but this can be explained by the fact that our WordNet Domains WSD method cannot cope with general (domain independent) WSD requirements in which the "one sense per discourse" hypothesis does not necessarily hold.

6 Conclusions

Regarding the 3 systems that we entered in the Task #17 @ SemEval-2, we think that the lexical chains algorithm (RACAI-2) is the most promising even if it scored the lowest of the three. We attribute its poor performances to the lexical chains computation, especially to the weights of the WN semantic relations that make up a chain. Also, we will extend our research regarding the correctness of lexical chains (the degree to which a human judge will appreciate as correct or evocative or as common knowledge a semantic path between two synsets).

We also want to check if our three systems make the same mistakes or not in order to devise a way in which we can combine their outputs.

RACAI is at the second participation in the SemEval series of WSD competitions. We are committed to improving the unsupervised WSD technology which, we think, is more easily adaptable and usable in real world applications. We hope that SemEval-3 will reveal significant improvements in this direction.

Acknowledgments
The work reported here was supported by the Romanian Ministry of Education and Research through the STAR project (no. 742/19.01.2009).

References

Eneko Agirre, Lluís Màrquez and Richard Wicentowski, Eds., 2007. *Proceedings of Semeval-2007 Workshop*. Prague, Czech Republic: Association for Computational Linguistics, 2007.

Eneko Agirre, Oier Lopez de Lacalle, Christiane Fellbaum, Andrea Marchetti, Antonio Toral, Piek Vossen. 2009. *SemEval-2010 Task 17: All-words Word Sense Disambiguation on a Specific Domain*. In Proceedings of NAACL workshop on Semantic Evaluations (SEW-2009). Boulder,Colorado, 2009.

Luisa Bentivogli, Pamela Forner, Bernardo Magnini and Emanuele Pianta. 2004. *Revising WordNet Domains Hierarchy: Semantics, Coverage, and Balancing*. In COLING 2004 Workshop on "Multilingual Linguistic Resources", Geneva, Switzerland, August 28, 2004, pp. 101-108.

Radu Ion and Dan Ştefănescu. 2009. Unsupervised Word Sense Disambiguation with Lexical Chains and Graph-based Context Formalization. In Zygmunt Vetulani, editor, Proceedings of the 4th Language and Technology Conference: Human Language Technologies as a Challenge for Computer Science and Linguistics, pages 190–194, Poznań, Poland, November 6–8 2009. Wydawnictwo Poznańskie Sp.

Bernardo Magnini, Carlo Strapparava, Giovanni Pezzulo, Alfio Gliozzo. 2002. *The role of domain information in Word Sense Disambiguation*. Natural Language Engineering, 8(4), 359—373, December 2002.

Dan Moldovan and Adrian Novischi. 2002. *Lexical chains for question answering*. In Proceedings of the 19th International Conference on Computational Linguistics, August 24 – September 01, 2002, Taipei, Taiwan, pp. 1—7.

Dan Tufiş, Radu Ion, Alexandru Ceauşu and Dan Ştefănescu. 2008. *RACAI's Linguistic Web Services*. In Proceedings of the 6th Language Resources and Evaluation Conference – LREC 2008, Marrakech, Morocco, May 2008. ELRA – European Language Ressources Association. ISBN 2-9517408-4-0.

Sonia Vázquez, Andrés Montoyo and German Rigau. 2004. *Using Relevant Domains Resource for Word Sense Disambiguation*. In Proceedings of the International Conference on Artificial Intelligence (IC-AI'04), Las Vegas, Nevada, 2004.

David Yarowsky. 1993. *One sense per collocation*. In ARPA Human Language Technology Workshop, pp. 266–271, Princeton, NJ, 1993.

Kyoto: An Integrated System for Specific Domain WSD

Aitor Soroa, Eneko Agirre, Oier Lopez de Lacalle
University of the Basque Country
a.soroa@ehu.es

Monica Monachini
Istituto di Linguistica Computazionale
monica.monachini@ilc.cnr.it

Jessie Lo, Shu-Kai Hsieh
National Taiwan Normal University
shukai@ntnu.edu.tw

Wauter Bosma, Piek Vossen
Vrije Universiteit
{p.vossen,w.bosma}@let.vu.nl

Abstract

This document describes the preliminary release of the integrated Kyoto system for specific domain WSD. The system uses concept miners (Tybots) to extract domain-related terms and produces a domain-related thesaurus, followed by knowledge-based WSD based on wordnet graphs (UKB). The resulting system can be applied to any language with a lexical knowledge base, and is based on publicly available software and resources. Our participation in Semeval task #17 focused on producing running systems for all languages in the task, and we attained good results in all except Chinese. Due to the pressure of the time-constraints in the competition, the system is still under development, and we expect results to improve in the near future.

1 Introduction

In this paper we describe the participation of the integrated Kyoto system on the "SemEval-2010 task #17: All-words Word Sense Disambiguation on a Specific Domain" task (Agirre et al., 2010). The goal of our participation was to evaluate the preliminary release of the integrated system for specific domain WSD developed for the Kyoto project[1]. Besides, we wanted to test the performance of our domain specific WSD system (Agirre et al., 2009) on this test set, and to integrate the thesaurus construction software (Tybots) developed for the project. The system can be run for any language and domain if provided with a lexical knowledge base and some background documents on the domain.

We will first present the components of our system, followed by the experimental design and the results. Finally, the conclusions are presented.

[1] http://www.kyoto-project.eu

2 The Kyoto System for Domain Specific WSD

We will present in turn UKB, the Tybots, and the lexical knowledge-bases used.

2.1 UKB

UKB is a knowledge-based unsupervised WSD system which exploits the structure of an underlying Language Knowledge Base (LKB) and finds the most relevant concepts given an input context (Agirre and Soroa, 2009). UKB starts by taking the LKB as a graph of concepts $G = (V, E)$ with a set of vertices V derived from LKB concepts and a set of edges E representing relations among them. Giving an input context, UKB applies the so called *Personalized PageRank* (Haveliwala, 2002) over it to obtain the most representative senses for the context.

PageRank (Brin and Page, 1998) is a method for scoring the vertices V of a graph according to each node's structural importance. The algorithm can be viewed as random walk process that postulate the existence of a particle that randomly traverses the graph, but at any time may jump to a new vertex with a given *damping factor* (also called *teleport probability*). After PageRank calculation, the final weight of node i represents the proportion of time that a random particle spends visiting node i after a sufficiently long time. In standard PageRank, the teleport vector is chosen uniformly, whereas for Personalized PageRank it is chosen from a nonuniform distribution of nodes, specified by a *teleport vector*.

UKB concentrates the initial probability mass of the teleport vector in the words occurring in the context of the target word, causing all random jumps on the walk to return to these words and thus assigning a higher rank to the senses linked to these words. Moreover, the high rank of the words

Proceedings of the 5th International Workshop on Semantic Evaluation, ACL 2010, pages 417–420,
Uppsala, Sweden, 15-16 July 2010.

spreads through the links in the graph and make all the nodes in its vicinity also receive high ranks. Given a target word, the system checks which is the relative ranking of its senses, and the WSD system would output the one ranking highest.

UKB is very flexible and can be use to perform WSD on different settings, depending on the context used for disambiguating a word instance. In this paper we use it to perform general and domain specific WSD, as shown in section 3. PageRank is calculated by applying an iterative algorithm until convergence below a given threshold is achieved. Following usual practice, we used a damping value of 0.85 and set the threshold value at 0.001. We did not optimize these parameters.

2.2 Tybots

Tybots (Term Yielding Robots) are text mining software that mine domain terms from corpus (e.g. web pages), organizing them in a hierarchical structure, connecting them to wordnets and ontologies to create a semantic model for the domain (Bosma and Vossen, 2010). The software is freely available using Subversion [2]. Tybots try to establish a view on the terminology of the domain which is as complete as possible, discovering relations between terms and ranking terms by domain relevance.

Preceding term extraction, we perform tokenization, part-of-speech tagging and lemmatization, which is stored in Kyoto Annotation Format (KAF) (Bosma et al., 2009). Tybots work through KAF documents, acquire domain relevant terms based on the syntactic features, gather cooccurrence statistics to decide which terms are significant in the domain and produce a thesaurus with sets of related words. Section 3.3 describes the specific settings that we used.

2.3 Lexical Knowledge bases

We used the following wordnets, as suggested by the organizers:

WN30g: English WordNet 3.0 with gloss relations (Fellbaum, 1998).

Dutch: The Dutch LKB is part of the Cornetto database version 1.3 (Vossen et al., 2008). The Cornetto database can be obtained from the Dutch/Flanders Taalunie[3]. Cornetto comprises taxonomic relations and equivalence relations from both WordNet 2.0 and 3.0. Cornetto concepts are mapped to English WordNet 3.0.

Italian: Italwordnet (Roventini et al., 2003) was created in the framework of the EuroWordNet, employs the same set of semantic relations used in EuroWordNet, and includes links to WordNet 3.0 synsets.

Chinese: The Chinese WordNet (Version 1.6) is now partially open to the public[4] (Tsai et al., 2001). The Chinese WordNet is also mapped to WordNet 3.0.

	#entries	#synsets	#rels.	#WN30g
	Monolingual			
Chinese	8,186	14,243	20,433	20,584
Dutch	83,812	70,024	224,493	83,669
Italian	46,724	49,513	65,567	52,524
WN30g	147,306	117,522	525,351	n/a
	Bilingual			
Chinese-eng	8,186	141,561	566,368	
Dutch-eng	83,812	188,511	833,513	
Italian-eng	46,724	167,094	643,442	

Table 1: Wordnets and their sizes (entries, synsets, relations and links to WN30g).

Table 1 shows the sizes of the graphs created using each LKB as a source. The upper part shows the number of lexical entries, synsets and relations of each LKB. It also depicts the number of links to English WordNet 3.0 synsets.

In addition, we also created bilingual graphs for Dutch, Italian and Chinese, comprising the original monolingual LKB, the links to WordNet 3.0 and WordNet 3.0 itself. We expected this richer graphs to perform better performance. The sizes of the bilingual graphs are shown in the lower side of Table 1.

3 Experimental setting

All test documents were lemmatized and PoS-tagged using the linguistic processors available within the Kyoto project. In this section we describe the submitted runs.

3.1 UKB parameters

We use UKB with the default parameters. In particular, we don't use dictionary weights, which in the case of English come from annotated corpora. This is done in order to make the system fully unsupervised. It's also worth mentioning that in the default setting parts of speech were not used.

[2] http://kyoto.let.vu.nl/svn/kyoto/trunk

[3] http://www.inl.nl/nl/lexica/780

[4] http://cwn.ling.sinica.edu.tw

RANK	RUN	P	R	R-NOUN	R-VERB
		Chinese			
-	*1sense*	0.562	0.562	0.589	0.518
1	*Best*	0.559	0.559	-	-
-	*Random*	0.321	0.321	0.326	0.312
4	kyoto-3	0.322	0.296	0.257	0.360
3	kyoto-2	0.342	0.285	0.251	0.342
5	kyoto-1	0.310	0.258	0.256	0.261
		Dutch			
1	kyoto-3	0.526	0.526	0.575	0.450
2	kyoto-2	0.519	0.519	0.561	0.454
-	*1sense*	0.480	0.480	0.600	0.291
3	kyoto-1	0.465	0.465	0.505	0.403
-	*Random*	0.328	0.328	0.350	0.293
		English			
1	*Best*	0.570	0.555	-	-
-	*1sense*	0.505	0.505	0.519	0.454
10	kyoto-2	0.481	0.481	0.487	0.462
22	kyoto-1	0.384	0.384	0.382	0.391
-	*Random*	0.232	0.232	0.253	0.172
		Italian			
1	kyoto-3	0.529	0.529	0.530	0.528
2	kyoto-2	0.521	0.521	0.522	0.519
3	kyoto-1	0.496	0.496	0.507	0.468
-	*1sense*	0.462	0.462	0.472	0.437
-	*Random*	0.294	0.294	0.308	0.257

Table 2: Overall results of our runs, including precision (P) and recall (R), overall and for each PoS. We include the First Sense (1sense) and random baselines, as well as the best run, as provided by the organizers.

3.2 Run1: UKB using context

The first run is an application of the UKB tool in the standard setting, as described in (Agirre and Soroa, 2009). Given the input text, we split it in sentences, and we disambiguate each sentence at a time. We extract the lemmas which have an entry in the LKB and then apply Personalized PageRank over all of them, obtaining a score for every concept of the LKB. To disambiguate the words in the sentence we just choose its associated concept (sense) with maximum score.

In our experiments we build a context of at least 20 content words for each sentence to be disambiguated, taking the sentences immediately before when necessary. UKB allows two main methods of disambiguation, namely *ppr* and *ppr_w2w*. We used the latter method, as it has been shown to perform best.

In this setting we used the monolingual graphs for each language (cf. section 2.3). Note that in this run there is no domain adaptation, it thus serves us as a baseline for assessing the benefits of applying domain adaptation techniques.

3.3 Run2: UKB using related words

Instead of disambiguating words using their context of occurrence, we follow the method described in (Agirre et al., 2009). The idea is to first obtain a list of related words for each of the target words, as collected from a domain corpus. On a second step each target word is disambiguated using the N most related words as context (see below). For instance, in order to disambiguate the word *environment*, we would not take into account the context of occurrence (as in Section 3.2), but we would use the list of most related words in the thesaurus (e.g. *"biodiversity, agriculture, ecosystem, nature, life, climate, . . ."*). Using UKB over these contexts we obtain the most predominant sense for each target word in the domain(McCarthy et al., 2007), which is used to label all occurrences of the target word in the test dataset.

In order to build the thesaurus with the lists of related words, we used Tybots (c.f. section 2.2), one for each corpus of the evaluation dataset, i.e. Chinese, Dutch, English, and Italian. We used the background documents provided by the organizers, which we processed using the linguistic processors of the project to obtain the documents in KAF. We used the Tybots with the following settings. We discarded co-occurring words with frequencies below 10[5]. Distributional similarity was computed using (Lin, 1998). Finally, we used up to 50 related words for each target word.

As in run1, we used the monolingual graphs for the LKBs in each language.

3.4 Run3: UKB using related words and bilingual graphs

The third run is exactly the same as run2, except that we used bilingual graphs instead of monolingual ones for all languages other than English (cf. section 2.3). There is no run3 for English.

4 Results

Table 2 shows the results of our system on the different languages. We will analyze different aspects of the results in turn.

Domain adaptation: Using Personalized Pagerank over related words (run2 and run3) consistently outperforms the standard setting (run1) in all languages. This result is consistent with

[5]In the case of Dutch we did not use any threshold due to the small size of the background corpus.

our previous work on English (Agirre et al., 2009), and shows that domain adaptation works for knowledge-based systems.

Monolingual vs. Bilingual graphs: As expected, we obtained better results using the bilingual graphs (run3) than with monolingual graphs (run2), showing that the English WordNet has a richer set of relations, and that those relations can be successfully ported to other languages. This confirms that aligning different wordnets at the synset level is highly beneficial.

Overall results: the results of our runs are highly satisfactory. In two languages (Dutch and Italian) our best runs perform better than the first sense baseline, which is typically hard to beat for knowledge-based systems. In English, our system performs close but below the first sense baseline, and in Chinese our method performed below the random baseline.

The poor results obtained for Chinese can be due the LKB topology; an analysis over the graph shows that it is formed by a large number of small components, unrelated with each other. This 'flat' structure heavily penalizes the graph based method, which is many times unable to discriminate among the concepts of a word. We are currently inspecting the results, and we don't discard bugs, due to the preliminary status of our software. In particular, we need to re-examine the output of the Tybot for Chinese.

5 Conclusions

This paper describes the results of the preliminary release of he integrated Kyoto system for domain specific WSD. It comprises Tybots to construct a domain-related thesaurus, and UKB for knowledge-based WSD based on wordnet graphs. We applied our system to all languages in the dataset, obtaining good results. In fact, our system can be applied to any language with a lexical knowledge base, and is based on publicly available software and resources. We used the wordnets and background texts provided by the organizers of the task.

Our results show that we were succesful in adapting our system to the domain, as we managed to beat the first sense baseline in two languages. Our results also show that adding the English WordNet to the other language wordnets via the available links is beneficial.

Our participation focused on producing running systems for all languages in the task, and we attained good results in all except Chinese. Due to the pressure and the time-constraints in the competition, the system is still under development. We are currently revising our system for bugs and finetuning it.

Acknowledgments

This work task is partially funded by the European Commission (KYOTO ICT-2007-211423), the Spanish Research Department (KNOW-2 TIN2009-14715-C04-01) and the Basque Government (BERBATEK IE09-262).

References

E. Agirre and A. Soroa. 2009. Personalizing pagerank for word sense disambiguation. In *Proceedings of EACL09*, pages 33–41. Association for Computational Linguistics.

E. Agirre, O. López de Lacalle, and A. Soroa. 2009. Knowledge-based wsd on specific domains: Performing better than generic supervised wsd. In *Proceedigns of IJ-CAI. pp. 1501-1506."*.

E. Agirre, O. López de Lacalle, C. Fellbaum, S.K. Hsieh, M. Tesconi, M. Monachini, P. Vossen, and R. Segers. 2010. Semeval-2010 task 17: All-words word sense disambiguation on a specific domain. In *Same volume*.

W. E. Bosma and P. Vossen. 2010. Bootstrapping language neutral term extraction. In *Proceedings of LREC2010*, May.

W. E. Bosma, P. Vossen, A. Soroa, G. Rigau, M. Tesconi, A. Marchetti, M. Monachini, and C. Aliprandi. 2009. KAF: a generic semantic annotation format. In *Proceedings of the GL2009 Workshop on Semantic Annotation*.

S. Brin and L. Page. 1998. The anatomy of a large-scale hypertextual web search engine. *Computer Networks and ISDN Systems*, 30(1-7).

C. Fellbaum. 1998. *WordNet: An Electronical Lexical Database*. The MIT Press, Cambridge, MA.

T. H. Haveliwala. 2002. Topic-sensitive pagerank. In *WWW '02: Proceedings of the 11th international conference on WWW*, pages 517–526, New York, NY, USA. ACM.

D. Lin. 1998. Automatic retrieval and clustering of similar words. In *Proceedings of ACL98*, Montreal, Canada.

D. McCarthy, R. Koeling, J. Weeds, and J. Carroll. 2007. Unsupervised acquisition of predominant word senses. *Computational Linguistics*, 33(4).

A. Roventini, A. Alonge, F. Bertagna, N. Calzolari, J. Cancila, C. Girardi, B. Magnini, R. Marinelli, M. Speranza, and A. Zampolli. 2003. Italwordnet: building a large semantic database for the automatic treatment of Italian. *Linguistica Computazionale, Special Issue (XVIII-XIX)*, pages 745–791.

B.S. Tsai, C.R. Huang, S.c. Tseng, J.Y. Lin, K.J. Chen, and Y.S. Chuang. 2001. Definition and tests for lexical semantic relations in Chinese. In *Proceedings CLSW 2001*.

P. Vossen, I. Maks, R. Segers, H. van der Vliet, and H. van Zutphen. 2008. The cornetto database: the architecture and alignment issues. In *Proceedings GWC 2008*, pages 485–506.

CFILT: Resource Conscious Approaches for All-Words Domain Specific WSD

Anup Kulkarni **Mitesh M. Khapra** **Saurabh Sohoney** **Pushpak Bhattacharyya**
Department of Computer Science and Engineering,
Indian Institute of Technology Bombay,
Powai, Mumbai 400076,
India
{anup,miteshk,saurabhsohoney,pb}@cse.iitb.ac.in

Abstract

We describe two approaches for *All-words Word Sense Disambiguation on a Specific Domain*. The first approach is a knowledge based approach which extracts domain-specific largest connected components from the Wordnet graph by exploiting the semantic relations between all candidate synsets appearing in a domain-specific untagged corpus. Given a test word, disambiguation is performed by considering only those candidate synsets that belong to the *top-k* largest connected components.

The second approach is a weakly supervised approach which relies on the "*One Sense Per Domain*" heuristic and uses a few hand labeled examples for the most frequently appearing words in the target domain. Once the most frequent words have been disambiguated they can provide strong clues for disambiguating other words in the sentence using an iterative disambiguation algorithm. Our weakly supervised system gave the **best performance** across all systems that participated in the task even when it used as few as 100 hand labeled examples from the target domain.

1 Introduction

Domain specific WSD exhibits high level of accuracy even for the all-words scenario (Khapra et al., 2010) - provided training and testing are on the same domain. However, the effort of creating the training corpus - annotated sense marked corpora - for every domain of interest has always been a matter of concern. Therefore, attempts have been made to develop unsupervised (McCarthy et al., 2007; Koeling et al., 2005) and knowledge based techniques (Agirre et al., 2009) for WSD which do not need sense marked corpora. However, such approaches have not proved effective, since they typically do not perform better than the Wordnet first sense baseline accuracy in the all-words scenario.

Motivated by the desire to develop *annotation-lean* all-words domain specific techniques for WSD we propose two resource conscious approaches. The first approach is a knowledge based approach which focuses on retaining only domain specific synsets in the Wordnet using a two step pruning process. In the first step, the Wordnet graph is restricted to only those synsets which contain words appearing in an untagged domain-specific corpus. In the second step, the graph is pruned further by retaining only the largest connected components of the pruned graph. Each target word in a given sentence is then disambiguated using an iterative disambiguation process by considering only those candidate synsets which appear in the *top-k* largest connected components. Our knowledge based approach performed better than current state of the art knowledge based approach (Agirre et al., 2009). Also, the precision was better than the Wordnet first sense baseline even though the F-score was slightly lower than the baseline.

The second approach is a weakly supervised approach which uses a few hand labeled examples for the most frequent words in the target domain in addition to the publicly available mixed-domain SemCor (Miller et al., 1993) corpus. The underlying assumption is that words exhibit *"One Sense Per Domain"* phenomenon and hence even as few as 5 training examples per word would be sufficient to identify the predominant sense of the most frequent words in the target domain. Further, once the most frequent words have been disambiguated using the predominant sense, they can provide strong clues for disambiguating other words in the

Proceedings of the 5th International Workshop on Semantic Evaluation, ACL 2010, pages 421–426,
Uppsala, Sweden, 15-16 July 2010.

sentence. Our weakly supervised system gave the **best performance** across all systems that participated in the task even when it used **as few as 100 hand labeled examples from the target domain**.

The remainder of this paper is organized as follows. In section 2 we describe related work on domain-specific WSD. In section 3 we discuss an Iterative Word Sense Disambiguation algorithm which lies at the heart of both our approaches. In section 4 we describe our knowledge based approach. In section 5 we describe our weakly supervised approach. In section 6 we present results and discussions followed by conclusion in section 7.

2 Related Work

There are two important lines of work for domain specific WSD. The first focuses on target word specific WSD where the results are reported on a handful of target words (41-191 words) on three lexical sample datasets, *viz.*, DSO corpus (Ng and Lee, 1996), MEDLINE corpus (Weeber et al., 2001) and the corpus of Koeling et al. (2005). The second focuses on all-words domain specific WSD where the results are reported on large annotated corpora from two domains, *viz.*, TOURISM and HEALTH (Khapra et al., 2010).

In the target word setting, it has been shown that unsupervised methods (McCarthy et al., 2007) and knowledge based methods (Agirre et al., 2009) can do better than wordnet first sense baseline and in some cases can also outperform supervised approaches. However, since these systems have been tested only for certain target words, the question of their utility in all words WSD it still open .

In the all words setting, Khapra et al. (2010) have shown significant improvements over the wordnet first sense baseline using a fully supervised approach. However, the need for sense annotated corpus in the domain of interest is a matter of concern and provides motivation for adapting their approach to annotation scarce scenarios. Here, we take inspiration from the target-word specific results reported by Chan and Ng (2007) where by using just 30% of the target data they obtained the same performance as that obtained by using the entire target data.

We take the fully supervised approach of (Khapra et al., 2010) and convert it to a weakly supervised approach by using only a handful of hand labeled examples for the most frequent words appearing in the target domain. For the remaining words we use the sense distributions learnt from SemCor (Miller et al., 1993) which is a publicly available mixed domain corpus. Our approach is thus based on the *"annotate-little from the target domain"* paradigm and does better than all the systems that participated in the shared task.

Even our knowledge based approach does better than current state of the art knowledge based approaches (Agirre et al., 2009). Here, we use an untagged corpus to prune the Wordnet graph thereby reducing the number of candidate synsets for each target word. To the best of our knowledge such an approach has not been tried earlier.

3 Iterative Word Sense Disambiguation

The Iterative Word Sense Disambiguation (IWSD) algorithm proposed by Khapra et al. (2010) lies at the heart of both our approaches. They use a scoring function which combines corpus based parameters (such as, sense distributions and corpus co-occurrence) and Wordnet based parameters (such as, semantic similarity, conceptual distance, *etc.*) for ranking the candidates synsets of a word. The algorithm is iterative in nature and involves the following steps:

- Tag all monosemous words in the sentence.
- Iteratively disambiguate the remaining words in the sentence in increasing order of their degree of polysemy.
- At each stage rank the candidate senses of a word using the scoring function of Equation (1).

$$S^* = \arg\max_i(\theta_i V_i + \sum_{j \in J} W_{ij} * V_i * V_j) \qquad (1)$$

where,

$$\begin{aligned} i &\in \mathit{Candidate\ Synsets} \\ J &= \mathit{Set\ of\ disambiguated\ words} \\ \theta_i &= BelongingnessToDominantConcept(S_i) \\ V_i &= P(S_i|word) \\ W_{ij} &= CorpusCooccurrence(S_i, S_j) \\ &\quad * 1/WNConceptualDistance(S_i, S_j) \\ &\quad * 1/WNSemanticGraphDistance(S_i, S_j) \end{aligned}$$

The scoring function as given above cleanly separates the self-merit of a synset ($P(S_i|word)$)

as learnt from a tagged corpus and its interaction-merit in the form of corpus co-occurrence, conceptual distance, and wordnet-based semantic distance with the senses of other words in the sentence. The scoring function can thus be easily adapted depending upon the amount of information available. For example, in the weakly supervised setting, $P(S_i|word)$ will be available for some words for which either manually hand labeled training data from environment domain is used or which appear in the SemCor corpus. For such words, all the parameters in Equation (1) will be used for scoring the candidate synsets and for remaining words only the interaction parameters will be used. Similarly, in the knowledge based setting, $P(S_i|word)$ will never be available and hence only the wordnet based interaction parameters (*i.e.*, $WNConceptualDistance(S_i, S_j)$ *and* $WNSemanticGraphDistance(S_i, S_j)$) will be used for scoring the pruned list of candidate synsets. Please refer to (Khapra et al., 2010) for the details of how each parameter is calculated.

4 Knowledge-Based WSD using Graph Pruning

Wordnet can be viewed as a graph where synsets act as nodes and the semantic relations between them act as edges. It should be easy to see that given a domain-specific corpus, synsets from some portions of this graph would be more likely to occur than synsets from other portions. For example, given a corpus from the HEALTH domain one might expect synsets belonging to the sub-trees of *"doctor", "medicine", "disease"* to appear more frequently than the synsets belonging to the sub-tree of *"politics"*. Such dominance exhibited by different components can be harnessed for domain-specific WSD and is the motivation for our work.

The crux of the approach is to identify such domain specific components using a two step pruning process as described below:

Step 1: First, we use an untagged corpus from the environment domain to identify the unique words appearing in the domain. Note that, by unique words we mean all content words which appear at least once in the environment corpus (these words may or may not appear in a general mixed domain corpus). This untagged corpus containing 15 documents (22K words) was downloaded from the websites of WWF[1] and ECNC[2] and contained articles on *Climate Change, Deforestation, Species Extinction, Marine Life and Ecology*. Once the unique words appearing in this environment-specific corpus are identified, we restrict the Wordnet graph to only those synsets which contain one or more of these unique words as members. This step thus eliminates all spurious synsets which are not related to the environment domain.

Step 2: In the second step, we perform a *Breadth-First-Search* on the pruned graph to identify the connected components of the graph. While traversing the graph we consider only those edges which correspond to the *hypernymy-hyponymy* relation and ignore all other semantic relations as we observed that such relations add noise to the components. The *top*-5 largest components thus identified were considered to be environment-specific components. A subset of synsets appearing in one such sample component is listed in Table 1.

Each target word in a given sentence is then disambiguated using the IWSD algorithm described in section 3. However, now the $\arg\max$ of Equation (1) is computed only over those candidate synsets which belong to the *top*-5 largest components and all other candidate synsets are ignored. The suggested pruning technique is indeed very harsh and as a result there are many words for which none of their candidate synsets belong to these *top*-5 largest components. These are typically domain-invariant words for which pruning does not make sense as the synsets of such generic words do not belong to domain-specific components of the Wordnet graph. In such cases, we consider all the candidate synsets of these words while computing the $\arg\max$ of Equation (1).

5 Weakly Supervised WSD

Words are known to exhibit *"One Sense Per Domain"*. For example, in the HEALTH domain the word *cancer* will invariably occur in the *disease* sense and almost never in the sense of *a zodiac sign*. This is especially true for the most frequently appearing nouns in the domain as these are typically domain specific nouns. For example, nouns such as *farmer, species, population, conservation, nature, etc.* appear very frequently in the environment domain and exhibit a clear predominant

[1]http://www.wwf.org
[2]http://www.ecnc.org

{**safety**} - NOUN - the state of being certain that adverse effects will not be caused by some agent under defined conditions; "insure the safety of the children"; "the reciprocal of safety is risk"
{**preservation, saving**} - NOUN - the activity of protecting something from loss or danger
{**environment**} - NOUN - the totality of surrounding conditions; "he longed for the comfortable environment of his living room"
{**animation, life, living, aliveness**} - NOUN - the condition of living or the state of being alive; "while there's life there's hope"; "life depends on many chemical and physical processes"
{**renovation, restoration, refurbishment**} - NOUN - the state of being restored to its former good condition; "the inn was a renovation of a Colonial house"
{**ecology**} - NOUN - the environment as it relates to living organisms; "it changed the ecology of the island"
{**development**} - NOUN - a state in which things are improving; the result of developing (as in the early part of a game of chess); "after he saw the latest development he changed his mind and became a supporter"; "in chess your should take care of your development before moving your queen"
{**survival, endurance**} - NOUN - a state of surviving; remaining alive
... ...
... ...

Table 1: Environment specific component identified after pruning

sense in the domain. As a result as few as 5 hand labeled examples per noun are sufficient for finding the predominant sense of these nouns. Further, once these most frequently occurring nouns have been disambiguated they can help in disambiguating other words in the sentence by contributing to the interaction-merit of Equation (1) (note that in Equation (1), J = *Set of disambiguated words*).

Based on the above intuition, we slightly modified the IWSD algorithm and converted it to a weakly supervised algorithm. The original algorithm as described in section 3 uses monosemous words as seed input (refer to the first step of the algorithm). Instead, we use the most frequently appearing nouns as the seed input. These nouns are disambiguated using their pre-dominant sense as calculated from the hand labeled examples. Our weakly supervised IWSD algorithm can thus be summarized as follows

- If a word w in a test sentence belongs to the list of most frequently appearing domain-specific nouns then disambiguate it first using its self-merit (*i.e.,* $P(S_i|word)$) as learnt from the hand labeled examples.
- Iteratively disambiguate the remaining words in the sentence in increasing order of their degree of polysemy.
- While disambiguating the remaining words rank the candidate senses of a word using the self-merit learnt from SemCor and the interaction-merit based on previously disambiguated words.

The most frequent words and the corresponding examples to be hand labeled are extracted from the same 15 documents (22K words) as described in section 4.

6 Results

We report the performance of our systems in the SEMEVAL task on *All-words Word Sense Disambiguation on a Specific Domain* (Agirre et al., 2010). The task involved sense tagging 1398 nouns and verbs from 3 documents extracted from the environment domain. We submitted one run for the knowledge based system and 2 runs for the weakly supervised system. For the weakly supervised system, in one run we used 5 training examples each for the 80 most frequently appearing nouns in the domain and in the second run we used 5 training examples each for the 200 most frequently appearing nouns. Both our submissions in the weakly supervised setting performed better than all other systems that participated in the shared task. Post-submission we even experimented with using 5 training examples each for **as few as 20 most frequent nouns** and even in this case we found that our weakly supervised system **performed better than all other systems** that participated in the shared task.

The precision of our knowledge based system was slightly better than the most frequent sense (MFS) baseline reported by the task organizers but the recall was slightly lower than the baseline. Also, our approach does better than the current state of the art knowledge based approach (Personalized Page Rank approach of Agirre et al. (2009)).

All results are summarized in Table 2. The following guide specifies the systems reported:

- ***WS-k:*** Weakly supervised approach using 5 training examples for the *k* most frequently appearing nouns in the environment domain.
- ***KB:*** Knowledge based approach using graph based pruning.
- ***PPR:*** Personalized PageRank approach of Agirre et al. (2009).
- ***MFS:*** Most Frequent Sense baseline provided by the task organizers.
- ***Random:*** Random baseline provided by the task organizers.

System	Precision	Recall	Rank in shared task
WS-200	0.570	0.555	1
WS-80	0.554	0.540	2
WS-20	0.548	0.535	3 (Post submission)
KB	0.512	0.495	7
PPR	0.373	0.368	24 (Post submission)
MFS	0.505	0.505	6
Random	0.23	0.23	30

Table 2: The performance of our systems in the shared task

In Table 3 we provide the results of WS-200 for each POS category. As expected, the results for nouns are much better than those for verbs mainly because nouns are more likely to stick to the "One sense per domain" property than verbs.

Category	Precision	Recall
Verbs	45.37	42.89
Nouns	59.64	59.01

Table 3: The performance of WS-200 on each POS category

7 Conclusion

We presented two resource conscious approaches for *All-words Word Sense Disambiguation on a Specific Domain*. The first approach is a knowledge based approach which retains only domain specific synsets from the Wordnet by using a two step pruning process. This approach does better than the current state of the art knowledge based approaches although its performance is slightly lower than the Most Frequent Sense baseline. The second approach which is a weakly supervised approach based on the *"annotate-little from the target domain"* paradigm performed better than all systems that participated in the task even when it used as few as 100 hand labeled examples from the target domain. This approach establishes the veracity of the *"One sense per domain"* phenomenon by showing that even as few as five examples per word are sufficient for predicting the predominant sense of a word.

Acknowledgments

We would like to thank Siva Reddy and Abhilash Inumella (from IIIT Hyderabad, India) for providing us the results of Personalized PageRank (PPR) for comparison.

References

Eneko Agirre, Oier Lopez De Lacalle, and Aitor Soroa. 2009. Knowledge-based wsd on specific domains: Performing better than generic supervised wsd.

Eneko Agirre, Oier Lopez de Lacalle, Christiane Fellbaum, Shu kai Hsieh, Maurizio Tesconi, Monica Monachini, Piek Vossen, and Roxanne Segers. 2010. Semeval-2010 task 17: All-words word sense disambiguation on a specific domain.

Yee Seng Chan and Hwee Tou Ng. 2007. Domain adaptation with active learning for word sense disambiguation. In *In Proceedings of the 45th Annual Meeting of the Association of Computational Linguistics*, pages 49–56.

Mitesh Khapra, Sapan Shah, Piyush Kedia, and Pushpak Bhattacharyya. 2010. Domain-specific word sense disambiguation combining corpus based and wordnet based parameters. In *5th International Conference on Global Wordnet (GWC2010)*.

Rob Koeling, Diana McCarthy, and John Carroll. 2005. Domain-specific sense distributions and predominant sense acquisition. In *HLT '05: Proceedings of the conference on Human Language Technology and Empirical Methods in Natural Language Processing*, pages 419–426, Morristown, NJ, USA. Association for Computational Linguistics.

Diana McCarthy, Rob Koeling, Julie Weeds, and John Carroll. 2007. Unsupervised acquisition of predominant word senses. *Comput. Linguist.*, 33(4):553–590.

George A. Miller, Claudia Leacock, Randee Tengi, and Ross T. Bunker. 1993. A semantic concordance. In *HLT '93: Proceedings of the workshop on Human Language Technology*, pages 303–308, Morristown, NJ, USA. Association for Computational Linguistics.

Hwee Tou Ng and Hian Beng Lee. 1996. Integrating multiple knowledge sources to disambiguate word senses: An exemplar-based approach. In *In Proceedings of the 34th Annual Meeting of the Association for Computational Linguistics (ACL)*, pages 40–47.

Marc Weeber, James G. Mork, and Alan R. Aronson. 2001. Developing a test collection for biomedical word sense disambiguation. In *In Proceedings of the American Medical Informatics Association Annual Symposium (AMIA 2001)*, pages 746–750.

UMCC-DLSI: Integrative resource for disambiguation task

Yoan Gutiérrez and **Antonio Fernández**
DI, University of Matanzas
Autopista a Varadero km $3^{1/2}$
Matanzas, Cuba
yoan.gutierrez,antonio.fernandez@umcc.cu

Andrés Montoyo and **Sonia Vázquez**
DLSI, University of Alicante
Carretera de San Vicente S/N
Alicante, Spain
montoyo,svazquez@dlsi.ua.es

Abstract

This paper describes the UMCC-DLSI system in SemEval-2010 task number 17 (All-words Word Sense Disambiguation on Specific Domain). The main purpose of this work is to evaluate and compare our computational resource of WordNet's mappings using 3 different methods: Relevant Semantic Tree, Relevant Semantic Tree 2 and an Adaptation of k-clique's Technique. Our proposal is a non-supervised and knowledge-based system that uses Domains Ontology and SUMO.

1 Introduction

Ambiguity is the task of building up multiple alternative linguistic structures for a single input (Kozareva et al., 2007). Word Sense Disambiguation (WSD) is a key enabling-technology that automatically chooses the intended sense of a word in context. In this task, one of the most used lexical data base is WordNet (WN) (Fellbaum, 1998). WN is an online lexical reference system whose design is inspired by current psycholinguistic theories of human lexical memory. Due to the great popularity of WN in Natural Language Processing (NLP), several authors (Magnini and Cavaglia, 2000), (Niles and Pease, 2001), (Niles and Pease, 2003), (Valitutti, 2004) have proposed to incorporate to the semantic net of WN, some taxonomies that characterize, in one or several concepts, the senses of each word. In spite of the fact that there have been developed a lot of WordNet's mappings, there isn't one unique resource to integrate all of them in a single system approach. To solve this need we have developed a resource that joins WN[1], the SUMO Ontology[2], WordNet Domains[3] and WordNet Affect[4]. Our purpose is to test the advantages of having all the resources together for the resolution of the WSD task.

The rest of the paper is organized as follows. In Section 2 we describe the architecture of the integrative resource. Our approach is shown in Section 3. Next section presents the obtained results and a discussion. And finally the conclusions in Section 5.

2 Background and techniques

2.1 Architecture of the integrative resource

Our integrative model takes WN 1.6 as nucleus and links to it the SUMO resource. Moreover, WordNet Domains 2.0 (WND) and WordNet Affect 1.1 (WNAffects) are also integrated but mapped instead to WN 2.0. From the model showed in Figure 1, a computational resource has been built in order to integrate the mappings above mentioned.

The model integrator's proposal provides a software that incorporates bookstores of programming classes, capable to navigate inside the semantic graph and to apply any type of possible algorithm to a net. The software architecture allows to update WN's version.

In order to maintain the compatibility with other resources mapped to WN, we have decided to use WN 1.6 version. However, the results can be offered in anyone of WN's versions.

[1] http://www.cogsci.princeton.edu/ wn/
[2] http://suo.ieee.org
[3] http://wndomains.fbk.eu/
[4] http://wndomains.fbk.eu/wnaffect.html

Proceedings of the 5th International Workshop on Semantic Evaluation, ACL 2010, pages 427–432,
Uppsala, Sweden, 15-16 July 2010.

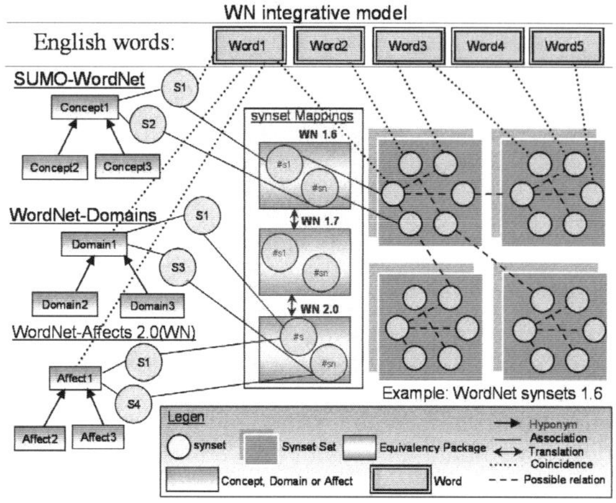

Figure 1: WordNet integrative model

2.2 The k-clique's Technique

Formally, a clique is the maximum number of actors who have all possible ties presented among themselves. A "Maximal complete sub-graph" is such a grouping, expanded to include as many actors as possible.

"A k-clique is a subset of vertices C such that, for every $i, j \in C$, the distance $d(i,j)_k$. The 1-clique is identical to a clique, because the distance between the vertices is one edge. The 2-clique is the maximal complete sub-graph with a path length of one or two edges". (Cavique et al., 2009)

3 The Proposal

Our proposal consists in accomplishing three runs with different algorithms. Both first utilize the domain's vectors; the third method utilizes k-cliques' techniques.

This work is divided in several stages:

1. Pre-processing of the corpus (lemmatization with Freeling) (Atserias et al., 2006).

2. Context selection (For the first (3.1), and the third (3.3) run the context window was constituted by the sentence that contains the word to disambiguate; in the second run the context window was constituted by the sentence that contains the word to disambiguate, the previous sentence and the next one).

3. Obtaining the domain vector, this vector is used in first and the second runs (when the lemma of the words in the analyzed sentence is obtained, the integrative resource of WordNet's Mappings is used to get the respective senses from each lemma).

4. Obtaining the all resource vector: SUMO, Affects, and Domain resource. This is only for the third run (3.3).

5. Relevant Semantic Tree construction (Addition of concepts parents to the vectors. For the first (3.1) and second (3.2) runs only Domain resource is used; for the third (3.3) run all the resources are used).

6. Selection of the correct senses (the first and the second runs use the same way to do the selection; the third run is different. We make an exception: For the verb "be" we select the sense with the higher frequency according to Freeling.

3.1 Relevant Semantic Tree

With this proposal we measure how much a concept is correlated to the sentence, similar to Reuters Vector (Magnini et al., 2002), but with a different equation. This proposal has a partial similarity with the Conceptual Density (Agirre and Rigau, 1996) and DRelevant (Vázquez et al., 2004) to get the concepts from a hierarchy that they associate with the sentence.

In order to determine the Association Ratio (RA) of a domain in relation to the sentence, the Equation 1 is used.

$$RA(D, f) = \sum_{i=1}^{n} RA(D, f_i) \quad (1)$$

where:

$$RA(D, w) = P(D, w) * \log_2 \frac{P(D, w)}{P(D)} \quad (2)$$

f: is a set of words w.

f_i: is a i-th word of the phrase f.

$P(D, w)$: is joint probability distribution.

$P(D)$: is marginal probability.

From now, vectors are created using the Senseval-2's corpus. Next, we show an example:

For the phrase: "But it is unfair to dump on teachers as distinct from the educational establishment".

By means of the process *Pres-processing* analyzed in previous stage 1 we get the lemma and the following vector.

Phrase [unfair; dump; teacher, distinct, educational; establishment]

Each lemma is looked for in WordNet's integrative resource of mappings and it is correlated with concepts of WND.

Vector	
RA	**Domains**
0.9	Pedagogy
0.9	Administration
0.36	Buildings
0.36	Politics
0.36	Environment
0.36	Commerce
0.36	Quality
0.36	Psychoanalysis
0.36	Economy

Table 1: Initial Domain Vector

After obtaining the Initial Domain Vector we apply the Equation 3 in order to build the Relevant Semantic Tree related to the phrase.

$$DN(CI, Df) = RA\_CI - \frac{MP(CI, Df)}{TD} \quad (3)$$

Where DN: is a normalized distance

CI: is the Initial Concept which you want to add the ancestors.

Df: is Parent Domain.

RA_CI: is a Association Ratio of the child Concept.

TD: is Depth of the hierarchic tree of the resource to use.

MP: is Minimal Path.

Applying the Equation 3 the algorithm to decide which parent domain will be added to the vector is shown here:

if $(DN(CI, Df) > 0)$
{
if (Df not exist)
  Df is added to the vector with DN value;
else
  Df value = Df value + DN;
}

As a result the Table 2 is obtained.

This vector represents the Domain tree associated to the phrase.

After the Relevant Semantic Tree is obtained, the Domain Factotum is eliminated from the tree. Due to the large amount of WordNet synsets,

Vector	
RA	**Domains**
1.63	Social_Science
0.9	Administration
0.9	Pedagogy
0.8	RootDomain
0.36	Psychoanalysis
0.36	Economy
0.36	Quality
0.36	Politics
0.36	Buildings
0.36	Commerce
0.36	Environment
0.11	Factotum
0.11	Psychology
0.11	Architecture
0.11	Pure_Science

Table 2: Final Domain Vector

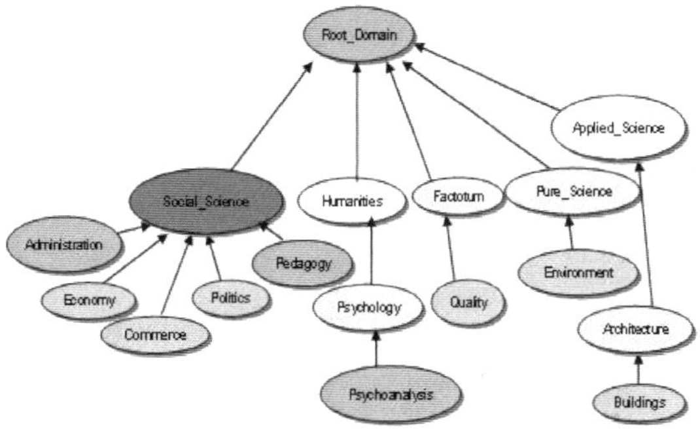

Figure 2: Relevant semantic tree

that do not belong to a specific domain, but rather they can appear in almost all of them, the Factotum domain has been created. It basically includes two types of synsets: Generic synsets, which are hard to classify in a particular domain; and Stop Senses synsets which appear frequently in different contexts, such as numbers, week days, colors, etc. (Magnini and Cavaglia, 2000), (Magnini et al., 2002). Words that contain this synsets are frequently in the phrases, therefore the senses associated to this domain are not selected.

After processing the patterns that characterize the sentence, the following stage is to determine the correct senses, so that the next steps ensue:

1. Senses that do not coincide with the grammatical category of Freeling are removed.

2. For each word to disambiguate all candidate senses are obtained. Of each sense the relevant vector are obtained using the Equation 4, and according to the previous Equation 3 parent concepts are added.

$$RA(D, s) = P(D, s) * \log_2 \frac{P(D, s)}{P(D)} \quad (4)$$

   where s: is a sense of word.

   $P(D, s)$: is joint probability distribution between Domain concept D and the sense s.

   $P(D)$: is marginal probability of the Domain concept.

3. The one that accumulates the bigger value of relevance is assigned as correct sense. The following process is applied:

   For each coincidence of the elements in the senses' domain vector with the domain vector of the sentence, the RA value of the analyzed elements is accumulated. The process is described in the Equation 5.

$$AC(s, VRA) = \frac{\sum_k VRA[Vs^k]}{\sum_{i=1} VRA_i} \quad (5)$$

   where AC: The RA value accumulated for the analyzed elements.

   VRA: Vector of relevant domains of the sentence with the format: VRA [domain — value RA].

   Vs: Vector of relevant domain of the sense with the format: Vs [domain].

   Vs_k: Is a k-th domain of the vector Vs.

   $VRA[Vs^k]$: Represents the value of RA assigned to the domain Vs^k for the value VRA.

   The $\sum_{i=1} VRA_i$ term normalizes the result.

3.2 Relevant Semantic Tree 2

This run is the same as the first one with a little difference, the context window is constituted by the sentence that contains the word to disambiguate, the previous sentence and the next one.

3.3 Adaptation of k-clique's technique to the WSD

They are applied, of the section 3, the steps from the 1 to the 5, where the semantic trees of concepts are obtained.

Then they are already obtained for all the words of the context, all the senses discriminated according to Freeling (Atserias et al., 2006).

Then a sentence's net of knowledge is built by means of minimal paths among each sense and each concept at trees. Next the k-clique's technique is applied to the net of knowledge to obtain cohesive subsets of nodes.

To obtain the correct sense of each word it is looked, as proposed sense, the sense belonging to the subset containing more quantities of nodes and if it has more than a sense for the same word, the more frequent sense is chosen according to Freeling.

4 Results and Discussion

The conducted experiments measure the influence of the aforementioned resources in the disambiguation task. We have evaluated them individually and as a whole. In the Table 3 it is represented each one of the inclusions and combinations experimented with the Relevant Semantic Tree method.

Resources	Precision	Recall	Attempted
WNAffect	0.242	0.237	97.78%
SUMO	0.267	0.261	98.5%
WND	0.328	0.322	98.14%
WND & SUMO	0.308	0.301	97.78%
WND & SUMO & WNAffect	0.308	0.301	97.78%

Table 3: Evaluation of integrated resources

As it can be observed, in the evaluation for specific domain corpus the best results are reached when only domain resource is used. But this is not a conclusion about the resources inclusion because the use of this method for global domain, for example with the task English All words from Senseval-2 (Agirre et al., 2010), the experiment adding all the resources showed good results. This is due to the fact that the global domain includes information of different contexts, exactly what is representing in the mentioned resources. For this reason, in the experiment with global domain and the inclusion of all the resource obtained better results than using this method with specific domain, 42% of recall and 45% of precision (Gutiérrez, 2010).

For example, with the k-clique's technique, utilizing the English All word task from Senseval-2´s corpus, the results for the test with global dominion were: with single domain inclusion 40 % of precision and recall; but with the three resources 41.7 % for both measures.

Table 4 shows the obtained results for the test data set. The average performance of our system is 32% and we ranked on 27-th position from 27 participating systems. Although, we have used different sources of information and various approximations, in the future we have to surmount a number of obstacles.

One of the limitations comes from the usage of the POS-tagger Freeling which introduces some errors in the grammatical discrimination. Representing a loss of 3.7% in the precision of our system.

The base of knowledge utilized in the task was WordNet 1.6; but the competition demanded the results with WordNet 3.0. In order to achieve this we utilized mappings among versions where 119 of 1398 resulting senses emitted by Semeval-2 were did not found. This represents an 8.5%.

In our proposal, the sense belonging to the Factotum Domain was eliminated, what disabled that the senses linked to this domain went candidates to be recovered. 777 senses of 1398 annotated like correct for Semeval-2 belong to domain Factotum, what represents that the 66% were not recovered by our system. Considering the senses that are not correlated to Factotum, that is, that correlate to another domains, we are speaking about 621 senses to define; The system would emit results of a 72,4%. Senses selected correctly were 450, representing a 32%. However, 189 kept on like second candidates to be elected. This represents a 13.5%. If a technique of more precise decision takes effect, the results of the system could be increased largely.

5 Conclusion and future works

For our participation in the Semeval-2 task 17 (All-words Word Sense Disambiguation on Specific Domain), we presented three methods for disambiguation approach which uses an integrative resource of WordNet mappings. We conducted an experimental study with the trail data set, according to which the Relevant Semantic Tree reaches the best performance. Our current approach can be improved with the incorporation of more granularities in the hierarchy of WordNet Domains. Because it was demonstrated that to define correct senses associated to specific domains an improvement of 72.4% is obtained. At this moment, only domain information is used in our first and second method. Besides was demonstrated for specific domains, the inclusion of several resources worsened the results with the first and second proposal method, the third one has been not experimented yet. Despite the fact that we have knowledge of SUMO, WordNet-Affect and WordNet Domain in our third method we still not obtain a relevant result.

It would be convenient to enrich our resource with other resources like Frame-Net, Concept-Net or others with the objective of characterizing even more the senses of the words.

Methods	Precision	Recall	Attempted
Relevant Domains Tree	0.328	0.322	98.14%
Relevant Semantic Tree 2	0.321	0.315	98.14%
Relevant Cliques	0.312	0.303	97.35%

Table 4: Evaluation results

Acknowledgments

This paper has been supported partially by Ministerio de Ciencia e Innovación - Spanish Government (grant no. TIN2009-13391-C04-01), and Conselleria d'Educació - Generalitat Valenciana (grant no. PROMETEO/2009/119 and ACOMP/2010/288).

References

Eneko Agirre and German Rigau. 1996. Word sense disambiguation using conceptual density. In *Proceedings of the 16th International Conference on Computational Linguistic (COLING'96)*, Copenhagen, Denmark.

Eneko Agirre, Oier Lopez de Lacalle, Christiane Fellbaum, Shu-kai Hsieh, Maurizio Tesconi, Monica

Monachini, Piek Vossen, and Roxanne Segers. 2010. Semeval-2010 task 17: All-words word sense disambiguation on a specific domain. In *Proceedings of the 5th International Workshop on Semantic Evaluations (SemEval-2010), Association for Computational Linguistics.*

Jordi Atserias, Bernardino Casas, Elisabet Comelles, Meritxell González, Lluís Padró, and Muntsa Padró. 2006. Freeling 1.3: Syntactic and semantic services in an open-source nlp library. In *Proceedings of the fifth international conference on Language Resources and Evaluation (LREC 2006), ELRA.*

Luís Cavique, Armando B. Mendes, and Jorge M. Santos. 2009. An algorithm to discover the k-clique cover in networks. In *EPIA '09: Proceedings of the 14th Portuguese Conference on Artificial Intelligence*, pages 363–373, Berlin, Heidelberg. Springer-Verlag.

Christiane Fellbaum. 1998. *WordNet: An Electronic Lexical Database.* The MIT Press.

Yoan Gutiérrez. 2010. Resolución de ambiguedad semántica mediante el uso de vectores de conceptos relevantes.

Zornitsa Kozareva, Sonia Vázquez, and Andrés Montoyo. 2007. Ua-zsa: Web page clustering on the basis of name disambiguation. In *Semeval I. 4th International Wordshop on Semantic Evaluations.*

Bernardo Magnini and Gabriela Cavaglia. 2000. Integrating subject field codes into wordnet. In *Proceedings of Third International Conference on Language Resources and Evaluation (LREC-2000).*

Bernardo Magnini, Carlo Strapparava, Giovanni Pezzulo, and Alfio Gliozzo. 2002. Comparing ontology-based and corpus-based domain annotations in wordnet. In *Proceedings of the First International WordNet Conference*, pages 146–154.

Ian Niles and Adam Pease. 2001. Towards a standard upper ontology. In *FOIS*, pages 2–9.

Ian Niles and Adam Pease. 2003. Linking lexicons and ontologies: Mapping wordnet to the suggested upper merged ontology. In *IKE*, pages 412–416.

Ro Valitutti. 2004. Wordnet-affect: an affective extension of wordnet. In *Proceedings of the 4th International Conference on Language Resources and Evaluation*, pages 1083–1086.

Sonia Vázquez, Andrés Montoyo, and German Rigau. 2004. Using relevant domains resource for word sense disambiguation. In *IC-AI*, pages 784–789.

HR-WSD: System Description for All-words Word Sense Disambiguation on a Specific Domain at SemEval-2010

Meng-Hsien Shih
National Taipei University of Technology
Taipei, Taiwan, ROC.
simon.xian@gmail.com

Abstract

The document describes the knowledge-based Domain-WSD system using heuristic rules (knowledge-base). This HR-WSD system delivered the best performance (55.9%) among all Chinese systems in SemEval-2010 Task 17: All-words WSD on a specific domain.

1 Introduction

Word Sense Disambiguation (WSD) is essential for language understanding systems such as information retrieval, summarization, and machine translation systems (Dagan and Itai, 1994; Schutze and Pedersen, 1995; Ng and Zelle, 1997). In particular due to the rapid development of other issues in computational linguistics, WSD has been considered the next important task to be solved. Among various WSD tasks, the lexical sample task can achieve a precision rate more than 70% in Chinese, so can the all-words task in English, but currently no Chinese all-words WSD system is available. This study proposes an all-words WSD system conducted on a specific domain which can achieve a 55.9% precision rate.

This system makes use of certain characteristics of WordNet. First, the sense inventory in Chinese WordNet is ordered by the "prototypicality" of the words. In other words, the first sense of a word with multiple senses will be the prototype meaning of that word. In addition to semantic relations and sense definitions, Chinese WordNet also includes sense axes which indicate the relations between Chinese senses and corresponding English senses.

2 Proposed Approach

Two heuristic rules are devised to characterize domain texts: In a domain text, domain senses are more likely to occur in words if they have one (Heuristic Rule 1); on the other hand, for words with no domain senses, the most generic usages (prototype senses) are more likely to be adopted (Heuristic Rule 2). Therefore, as proposed by Li et al.(1995) for the WordNet-based domain-independent texts WSD task, two heuristic rules (HR) are taken into consideration in the domain WSD test:

for all senses s_k of w **do**
  if w has domain sense
    choose domain sense s_k
  else
    choose prototype sense s_1
end

Figure 1: Heuristic Rules based WSD

Besides, sense definitions from WordNet were also tested with simplified Lesk algorithm (Lesk, 1986; Kilgarriff and Rosenzweig, 2000) in another experiment to examine the effect of considering sense definitions in domain WSD:

for all senses s_k of w **do**
  if w has domain sense
    choose domain sense s_k
  elseif D_k overlaps with C:
    choose sense s_k with D_k
    that overlaps the most
  else:
    choose prototype sense s_1
end

Figure 2: HR with simplified Lesk Algorithm. D_k is the set of content words occurring in the dictionary definition of sense s_k. C is the set of content words in the context.

Proceedings of the 5th International Workshop on Semantic Evaluation, ACL 2010, pages 433–435,
Uppsala, Sweden, 15-16 July 2010.

3 Procedures

Before the test only preprocessing including segmentation and parts of speech tagging will be applied to the target texts, in order to eliminate those senses of the same word form in other parts of speech; the background documents provided by SemEval-2010 are not used for training since this is not a supervised system. According to Wang (2002), with preprocessing of PoS tagging alone, 20% of word sense ambiguity can be distinguished.

Since the current number of semantic relations in Chinese WordNet is still less than that in English WordNet (PWN), to detect domain senses, the sense axes in Chinese WordNet are exploited. By seeding with English words such as "environment" and "ecology," all English words related to these seed words can be captured with the help of the semantic relations in Princeton WordNet. By mapping these environment-related English words to Chinese words with any kind of semantic relations in the sense axes, the corresponding Chinese domain senses can be identified.

Therefore, the HR-WSD system will first consider any domain senses for the words to be disambiguated; if there is no such sense, the prototype sense will be adopted. Another test where sense definitions from WordNet are considered to facilitate HR-based disambiguation was also conducted.

4 Evaluation

The results were evaluated according to three manually tagged documents in SemEval-2010 Task 17: All-words WSD on a Specific domain (Agirre et al., 2010). The most frequent sense baseline (MFS) refers to the first sense in WordNet lexical markup framework (In Chinese WordNet senses are ordered according to annotations in hand-labelled corpora). In these tagged domain texts, only nouns and verbs (two major types of content words) as a single word are disambiguated. Therefore, in this system only these two kinds of words will be tagged with senses. Adjectives, adverbs, or words in multiple forms (e.g., idioms and phrases) are not considered, in order to simplify the test and observe the results more clearly.

5 Results

By observing that the HR-WSD system* (Rank 1) outperformed other systems and was closest to the MFS performance we can infer that Heuristic Rule 2 works. However, since this system performance is still worse than MFS, it may indicate that Heuristic Rule 1 does not work well, or even decreases the system performance, so the mechanism to detect domain senses needs to be refined. Besides, the inclusion of simplified Lesk algorithm** did not perform better than the original HR-WSD system, further investigation such as more fine-grained definition can be expected.

Rank	Precision	Recall
MFS	0.562	0.562
1*	0.559	0.559
2**	0.517	0.517
3	0.342	0.285
4	0.322	0.296
Random	0.32	0.32
5	0.310	0.258

Table 1: Results.

6 Discussion and Future Development

Although PoS tagging may help filter out senses from other parts of speech of the same word form, incorrect PoS tagging will lead to incorrect sense tagging, which did happen in the HR-WSD system, in particular when there is more than one possible PoS tag for the word. For instance, 'nuan-hua' in 'quan-qiu nuan-hua' (global warming) is manually tagged with a verbal sense in the answer key from SemEval-2010, but tagged as a noun in the pre-processing stage of the HR-WSD system. The difference between manual tagged texts and automatic tagged texts should be examined, or consider allowing more than one PoS tag for a word, or even no PoS pre-processing at all.

To disambiguate with the help of gloss definition, gloss words of the polysemous word must have direct overlapping with that of its context word, which does not always occur. To solve this problem, we may expand gloss words to related words such as hyponyms, hypernyms, meronyms, or the gloss definition of the current gloss words.

Apart from nouns and verbs, if function words and other kinds of content words such as adjectives and adverbs are to be disambiguated, the performance of the current WSD system needs to be re-examined.

As mentioned in the beginning, WSD is an essential part in language understanding systems.

With this Chinese WSD program, information retrieval, summarization, or machine translation tasks would be more plausible. The proposed heuristic rules may also work for other languages with similar WordNet resources. Besides, this system was currently tested on three texts from the environment domain only. It can be expected that this Chinese WSD can work on texts of other domains.

References

Adam Kilgarriff and Joseph Rosenzweig. 2000. Framework and results for English SENSEVAL. *Computers and the Humanities*,34:15–48.

Eneko Agirre, Oier Lopez de Lacalle, Christiane Fellbaum, Shu-kai Hsieh, Maurizio Tesconi, Monica Monachini, Piek Vossen and Roxanne Segers. 2010. SemEval-2010 Task 17: All-words Word Sense Disambiguation on a Specific Domain. *In Proceedings of the 5th International Workshop on Semantic Evaluations (SemEval-2010), Association for Computational Linguistics, Uppsala, Sweden..*

Hinrich Schutze and Jan O. Pedersen. 1995. Information Retrieval Based on Word Senses. *In Proceedings of the ACM Special Interest Group on Information Retrieval.*

Hui Wang. 2002. A Study on Noun Sense Disambiguation Based on Syntagmatic Features. *International Journal of Computational Linguistics and Chinese Language Processing*,7(2):77–88.

Hwee Tou Ng and John Zelle. 1997. Corpus-Based Approaches to Semantic Interpretation in Natural Language Processing. *AI magazine*,18(4):45–64.

Ido Dagan and Alon Itai. 1994. Word-Sense Disambiguation Using a Second-Language Monolingual Corpus. *Computational Linguistics*,20(4):563–596.

Michael Lesk. 1986. Automatic sense disambiguation using machine readable dictionaries: How to tell a pine from a ice cream cone. *In Proceedings of the 5th International Conference on Systems Documentation, Toronto, CA, pp. 24–26..*

Xiaobin Li, Stan Szpakowicz, and Stan Matwin. 1995. A WordNet-based Algorithm for Word Sense Disambiguation. *The 14th International Joint Conference on Artificial Intelligence.*

Twitter Based System: Using Twitter for Disambiguating Sentiment Ambiguous Adjectives

Alexander Pak, Patrick Paroubek
Université de Paris-Sud,
Laboratoire LIMSI-CNRS, Bâtiment 508,
F-91405 Orsay Cedex, France
alexpak@limsi.fr, pap@limsi.fr

Abstract

In this paper, we describe our system which participated in the SemEval 2010 task of disambiguating sentiment ambiguous adjectives for Chinese. Our system uses text messages from Twitter, a popular microblogging platform, for building a dataset of emotional texts. Using the built dataset, the system classifies the meaning of adjectives into positive or negative sentiment polarity according to the given context. Our approach is fully automatic. It does not require any additional hand-built language resources and it is language independent.

1 Introduction

The dataset of the SemEval task (Wu and Jin, 2010) consists of short texts in Chinese containing target adjectives whose sentiments need to be disambiguated in the given contexts. Those adjectives are: 大 big, 小 small, 多 many, 少 few, 高 high, 低 low, 厚 thick, 薄 thin, 深 deep, shallow, 重 heavy, light, 巨大 huge, 重大 grave.

Disambiguating sentiment ambiguous adjectives is a challenging task for NLP. Previous studies were mostly focused on word sense disambiguation rather than sentiment disambiguation. Although both problems look similar, the latter is more challenging in our opinion because impregnated with more subjectivity. In order to solve the task, one has to deal not only with the semantics of the context, but also with the psychological aspects of human perception of emotions from the written text.

In our approach, we use Twitter[1] microblogging platform to retrieve emotional messages and form two sets of texts: messages with positive emotions and those with negative ones (Pak and Paroubek, 2010). We use emoticons[2] as indicators of an emotion (Read, 2005) to automatically classify texts into positive or negative sets. The reason we use Twitter is because it allows us to collect the data with minimal supervision efforts. It provides an API[3] which makes the data retrieval process much more easier then Web based search or other resources.

After the dataset of emotional texts has been obtained, we build a classifier based on n-grams Naïve Bayes approach. We tested two approaches to build a sentiment classifier:

1. In the first one, we collected Chinese texts from Twitter and used them to train a classifier to annotate the test dataset.

2. In the second one, we used machine translator to translate the dataset from Chinese to English and annotated it using collected English texts from Twitter as the training data.

We have made the second approach because we were able to collect much more of English texts from Twitter than Chinese ones and we wanted to test the impact of machine translation on the performance of our classifier. We have experimented with Google Translate and Yahoo Babelfish[4]. Google Translate yielded better results.

2 Related work

In (Yang et al., 2007), the authors use web-blogs to construct a corpora for sentiment analysis and use emotion icons assigned to blog posts as indicators of users' mood. The authors applied SVM and CRF learners to classify sentiments at the sentence level and then investigated several strategies to determine the overall sentiment of the document. As

[1] http://twitter.com

[2] An emoticon is a textual representation of an author's emotion often used in Internet blogs and textual chats

[3] http://dev.twitter.com/doc/get/search

[4] http://babelfish.yahoo.com/

Proceedings of the 5th International Workshop on Semantic Evaluation, ACL 2010, pages 436–439,
Uppsala, Sweden, 15-16 July 2010. ©2010 Association for Computational Linguistics

the result, the winning strategy is defined by considering the sentiment of the last sentence of the document as the sentiment at the document level.

J. Read in (Read, 2005) used emoticons such as ":-)" and ":-(" to form a training set for the sentiment classification. For this purpose, the author collected texts containing emoticons from Usenet newsgroups. The dataset was divided into "positive" (texts with happy emoticons) and "negative" (texts with sad or angry emoticons) samples. Emoticons-trained classifiers: SVM and Naïve Bayes, were able to obtain up to 70% accuracy on the test set.

In (Go et al., 2009), authors used Twitter to collect training data and then to perform a sentiment search. The approach is similar to the one in (Read, 2005). The authors construct corpora by using emoticons to obtain "positive" and "negative" samples, and then use various classifiers. The best result was obtained by the Naïve Bayes classifier with a mutual information measure for feature selection. The authors were able to obtain up to 84% of accuracy on their test set. However, the method showed a bad performance with three classes ("negative", "positive" and "neutral").

In our system, we use a similar idea as in (Go et al., 2009), however, we improve it by using a combination of unigrams, bigrams and trigrams ((Go et al., 2009) used only unigrams). We also handle negations by attaching a negation particle to adjacent words when forming ngrams.

3 Our method

3.1 Corpus collection

Using Twitter API we collected a corpus of text posts and formed a dataset of two classes: positive sentiments and negative sentiments. We queried Twitter for two types of emoticons considering eastern and western types of emoticons[5]:

- Happy emoticons: :-), :), ^_^, ^o^, etc.
- Sad emoticons: :-(, :(, T_T, ;_;, etc.

We were able to obtain 10,000 Twitter posts in Chinese, and 300,000 posts in English evenly split between negative and positive classes.

The collected texts were processed as follows to obtain a set of n-grams:

1. Filtering – we remove URL links (e.g. http://example.com), Twitter user names (e.g. @alex – with symbol @ indicating a user name), Twitter special words (such as "RT"[6]), and emoticons.

2. Tokenization – we segment text by splitting it by spaces and punctuation marks, and form a bag of words. For English, we kept short forms as a single word: "don't", "I'll", "she'd".

3. Stopwords removal – in English, texts we removed articles ("a", "an", "the") from the bag of words.

4. N-grams construction – we make a set of n-grams out of consecutive words.

A negation particle is attached to a word which precedes it and follows it. For example, a sentence "I do not like fish" will form three bigrams: "I do+not", "do+not like", "not+like fish". Such a procedure improves the accuracy of the classification since the negation plays a special role in opinion and sentiment expression (Wilson et al., 2005). In English, we used negative particles 'no' and 'not'. In Chinese, we used the following particles:

1. 不 – is not + noun

2. 未 – does not + verb, will not + verb

3. 莫 (別) – do not (imperative)

4. 無 (沒有) – does not have

3.2 Classifier

We build a sentiment classifier using the multinomial Naïve Bayes classifier which is based on Bayes' theorem.

$$P(s|M) = \frac{P(s) \cdot P(M|s)}{P(M)} \quad (1)$$

where s is a sentiment, M is a text. We assume that a target adjective has the same sentiment polarity as the whole text, because in general the lengths of the given texts are small.

Since we have sets of equal number of positive and negative messages, we simplify the equation:

$$P(s|M) = \frac{P(M|s)}{P(M)} \quad (2)$$

[5] http://en.wikipedia.org/wiki/Emoticon#Asian_style

[6] An abbreviation for retweet, which means citation or reposting of a message

$$P(s|M) \sim P(M|s) \quad (3)$$

We train Bayes classifiers which use a presence of an n-grams as a binary feature. We have experimented with unigrams, bigrams, and trigrams. Pang et al. (Pang et al., 2002) reported that unigrams outperform bigrams when doing sentiment classification of movie reviews, but Dave et al. (Dave et al., 2003) have obtained contrary results: bigrams and trigrams worked better for the product-review polarity classification. We tried to determine the best settings for our microblogging data. On the one hand high-order n-grams, such as trigrams, should capture patterns of sentiments expressions better. On the other hand, unigrams should provide a good coverage of the data. Therefore we combine three classifiers that are based on different n-gram orders (unigrams, bigrams and trigrams). We make an assumption of conditional independence of n-gram for the calculation simplicity:

$$P(s|M) \sim P(G1|s) \cdot P(G2|s) \cdot P(G3|s) \quad (4)$$

where $G1$ is a set of unigrams representing the message, $G2$ is a set of bigrams, and $G3$ is a set of trigrams. We assume that n-grams are conditionally independent:

$$P(Gn|s) = \prod_{g \in Gn} P(g|s) \quad (5)$$

Where Gn is a set of n-grams of order n.

$$P(s|M) \sim \prod_{g \in G1} P(g|s) \cdot \prod_{g \in G2} P(g|s) \cdot \prod_{g \in G3} P(g|s) \quad (6)$$

Finally, we calculate a log-likelihood of each sentiment:

$$L(s|M) = \sum_{g \in G1} log(P(g|s)) + \sum_{g \in G2} log(P(g|s)) + \sum_{g \in G3} log(P(g|s)) \quad (7)$$

In order to improve the accuracy, we changed the size of the context window, i.e. the number of words before and after the target adjective used for classification.

4 Experiments and Results

In our experiments, we used two datasets: a trial dataset containing 100 sentences in Chinese and a test dataset with 2917 sentences. Both datasets were provided by the task organizers. Micro and macro accuracy were chosen as the evaluation metrics.

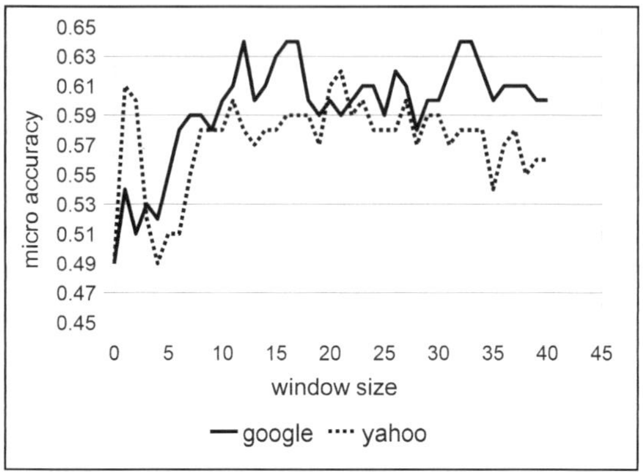

Figure 1: Micro accuracy when using Google Translate and Yahoo Babelfish

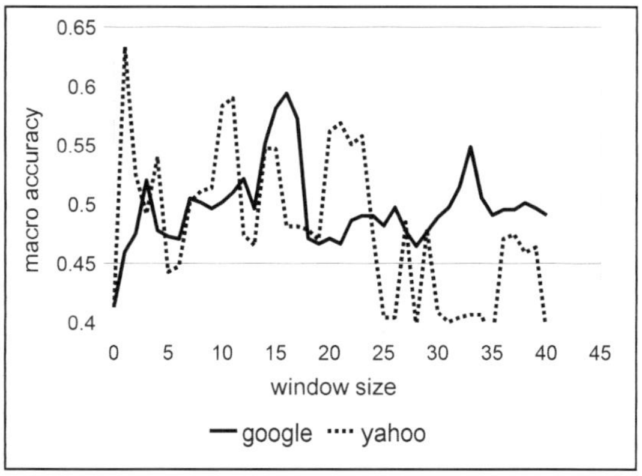

Figure 2: Macro accuracy when using Google Translate and Yahoo Babelfish

First, we compared the performance of our method when using Google Translate and Yahoo Babelfish for translating the trial dataset. The results for micro and macro accuracy are shown in Graphs 1 and 2 respectively. The x-axis represents a context window-size, equal to a number of words on both sides of the target adjective. The y-axis shows accuracy values. From the graphs we see that Google Translate provides better results, therefore it was chosen when annotating the test dataset.

Next, we studied the impact of the context window size on micro and macro accuracy. The impact of the size of the context window on the accuracy of the classifier trained on Chinese texts is depicted in Graph 3 and for the classifier trained on English texts with translated test dataset

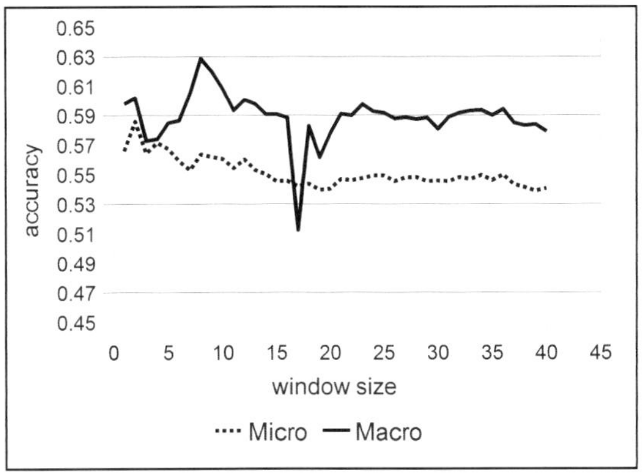

Figure 3: Micro and macro accuracy for the first approach (training on Chinese texts)

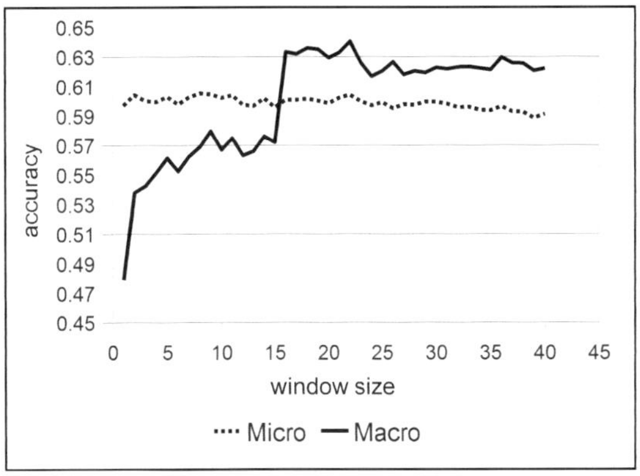

Figure 4: Micro and macro accuracy for the second approach (training on English texts which have been machine translated)

in Graph 4.

The second approach achieves better results. We were able to obtain 64% of macro and 61% of micro accuracy when using the second approach but only 63% of macro and 61% of micro accuracy when using the first approach.

Another observation from the graphs is that Chinese requires a smaller size of a context window to obtain the best performance. For the first approach, a window size of 8 words gave the best macro accuracy. For the second approach, we obtained the highest accuracy with a window size of 22 words.

5 Conclusion

In this paper, we have described our system for disambiguating sentiments of adjectives in Chinese texts. Our Naïve Bayes approach uses information automatically extracted from Twitter microblogs using emoticons. The techniques used in our approach can be applied to any other language. Our system is fully automate and does not utilize any hand-built lexicon. We were able to achieve up to 64% of macro and 61% of micro accuracy at the SemEval 2010 task

For the future work, we would like to collect more Chinese texts from Twitter or similar microblogging platforms. We think that increasing the training dataset will improve much the accuracy of the sentiment disambiguation.

References

Kushal Dave, Steve Lawrence, and David M. Pennock. 2003. Mining the peanut gallery: opinion extraction and semantic classification of product reviews. In *WWW '03: Proceedings of the 12th international conference on World Wide Web*, pages 519–528, New York, NY, USA. ACM.

Alec Go, Lei Huang, and Richa Bhayani. 2009. Twitter sentiment analysis. Final Projects from CS224N for Spring 2008/2009 at The Stanford Natural Language Processing Group.

Alexander Pak and Patrick Paroubek. 2010. Twitter as a corpus for sentiment analysis and opinion mining. In *Proceedings of LREC 2010*.

Bo Pang, Lillian Lee, and Shivakumar Vaithyanathan. 2002. Thumbs up? sentiment classification using machine learning techniques. In *Proceedings of the Conference on Empirical Methods in Natural Language Processing (EMNLP)*, pages 79–86.

Jonathon Read. 2005. Using emoticons to reduce dependency in machine learning techniques for sentiment classification. In *Proceedings of the ACL Student Research Workshop*, pages 43–48.

Theresa Wilson, Janyce Wiebe, and Paul Hoffmann. 2005. Recognizing contextual polarity in phrase-level sentiment analysis. In *HLT '05: Proceedings of the conference on Human Language Technology and Empirical Methods in Natural Language Processing*, pages 347–354, Morristown, NJ, USA. Association for Computational Linguistics.

Yunfang Wu and Peng Jin. 2010. Semeval-2010 task 18: Disambiguating sentiment ambiguous adjectives. In *SemEval 2010: Proceedings of International Workshop of Semantic Evaluations*.

Changhua Yang, Kevin Hsin-Yih Lin, and Hsin-Hsi Chen. 2007. Emotion classification using web blog corpora. In *WI '07: Proceedings of the IEEE/WIC/ACM International Conference on Web Intelligence*, pages 275–278, Washington, DC, USA. IEEE Computer Society.

YSC-DSAA: An Approach to Disambiguate Sentiment Ambiguous Adjectives Based On SAAOL

Shi-Cai Yang
Ningbo University of Technology
Ningbo, Zhejiang, China
nbcysc@126.com

Mei-Juan Liu
Zhejiang Ocean University
Zhoushan, Zhejiang, China
azalea1212@126.com

Abstract

In this paper, we describe the system we developed for the SemEval-2010 task of disambiguating sentiment ambiguous adjectives (hereinafter referred to SAA). Our system created a new word library named SAA-Oriented Library consisting of positive words, negative words, negative words related to SAA, positive words related to SAA, and inverse words, etc. Based on the syntactic parsing, we analyzed the relationship between SAA and the keywords and handled other special processes by extracting such words in the relevant sentences to disambiguate sentiment ambiguous adjectives. Our micro average accuracy is 0.942, which puts our system in the first place.

1 Introduction

We participated in disambiguating sentiment ambiguous adjectives task of SemEval-2010(Wu and Jin, 2010).

Together 14 sentiment ambiguous adjectives are chosen by the task organizers, which are all high-frequency words in Mandarin Chinese. They are: 大|big, 小|small, 多|many, 少|few, 高|high, 低|low, 厚|thick, 薄|thin, 深|deep, 浅|shallow, 重|heavy, 轻|light, 巨大|huge, 重大|grave. These adjectives are neutral out of context, but when they co-occur with some target nouns, positive or negative emotion will be evoked. The task is designed to automatically determine the semantic orientation of these sentiment ambiguous adjectives within context: positive or negative (Wu and Jin, 2010). For instance, "价格高|the price is high" indicates negative meaning, while "质量高|the quality is high" has positive connotation.

Considering the grammar system of contemporary Chinese, a word is one of the most basic linguistic granularities consisting of a sentence. Therefore, as for the sentiment classification of a sentence, the sentiment tendency of a sentence can be identified on the basis of that of a word. Wiebe et al. (2004) proposed that whether a sentence is subjective or objective should be discriminated according to the adjectives in it. On the basis of *General Inquirer Dictionary, A Learner's Dictionary of Positive and Negative Words, HowNet , A Dictionary of Positive Words and A Dictionary of Negative Words* etc., Wang et al.(2009) built a word library for Chinese sentiment words to discriminate the sentiment category of a sentence using the weighted linear combination method.

Unlike the previous researches which have not taken SAA into consideration specially in discriminating the sentiment tendency of a sentence, in the SemEval-2010 task of disambiguating sentiment ambiguous adjectives, systems have to predict the sentiment tendency of these fourteen adjectives within specific context.

From the view of linguistics, first we developed a SAA–oriented keyword library, then analyzed the relationship between the keywords in the clauses and SAA, and classified its positive or negative meaning of SAA by extracting the clauses related to SAA in the sentence.

2 SAAOL

We create a SAA-oriented library marked as SAAOL which is made up of positive and negative words irrelevant to context, negative words related to SAA (NSAA), positive words related to SAA (PSAA), and inverse words. The above five categories of words are called keywords for short in the paper.

Positive and negative words irrelevant to context refer to the traditional positive or negative words which are gathered from *The Dictionary*

Proceedings of the 5th International Workshop on Semantic Evaluation, ACL 2010, pages 440–443,
Uppsala, Sweden, 15-16 July 2010. ©2010 Association for Computational Linguistics

of Positive Words(Shi, 2005), *The Dictionary of Negative Words*(Yang, 2005), HowNet [1] and other network resources, such as Terms of Adverse Drug Reaction, Codes of Diseases and Symptoms, etc.

Distinguishing from the traditional positive and negative words, NSAA and PSAA in our SAAOL refer to those positive and negative words which are related to SAA, yet not classified into the positive and negative words irrelevant to context mentioned above.

We divide SAA into two categories: A category and B category listed in Table 1.

A category	B category
大|big	小|small
多|many	少|few
高|high	低|low
厚|thick	薄|thin
深|deep	浅|shallow
重|heavy	轻|light
巨大|huge	
重大|grave	

Table 1: SAA Classification Table

We identify whether a word belongs to NSAA or not on the following principle: any words when used with A category are negative; conversely, when used with B category, they are positive.

For example, in the following clauses,

"油价很高|oil prices are high",

"责任重大|the responsibility is important",

"任务很重| the task is very heavy",

"工作量很大|the workload is very large",

"油价|oil prices", "责任|responsibility", "任务|task", "工作量|workload" are NSAA.

Correspondingly, we identify whether a word belongs to PSAA or not on the following principle: any words when used with A category are positive; however, when used with B category, they are negative.

In the clauses,

"粮食很多| much food",

"效率极低| efficiency is extremely low",

"存款利率高|interest rate on deposit is high", "粮食| food", "效率| efficiency", "存款利率|interest rate on deposit" are PSAA.

In general, when two negative words are used together, the sentiment tendency that they show is negative. For instances, "糖尿病发病率|incidence of diabetes", "病毒感染|virus infection", "战争破坏|destruction of wars". However, in certain cases, some words play a part in eliminating negative meaning when used with negative words, for example, "反|anti-", "抑制|restrain", "避免|avoid", "抗|resist", "降低|reduce", "降幅|fall", "减少|decrease", "控制|control", "成本|cost", "反对|oppose", "下调|decrease", "非|non-", "不|not". These special words are called inverse words in our SAAOL.

In the following instances, "减轻伤害|reduce the injury", "抑制通胀| curb inflation", "反战|anti-war", the words "伤害|injury", "抑制| inflation", and "战争|war" themselves are all negative. When used with the inverse words"减轻|reduce ", "抑制| curb", "反|anti-", they express positive meaning instead.

On the basis of the above collected word library, we discriminate manually the positive and negative meaning, PSAA, NSAA, and inverse words in 50,000 Chinese words according to *Richard Xiao's Top 50,000 Chinese Word Frequency List*, which collects the frequency of the top 50000 Chinese words covered in the just published frequency dictionary of Mandarin Chinese based on a balanced corpus of ca. 50 million words. The list is available at `http://www.lancs.ac.uk/fass/projects/corpus/data/top50000_Chinese_words.zip`.

Based on HowNet lexical semantic similarity computing(Liu, 2002), Yang and Wu(2009) selected the new positive and negative bench-mark words to identify the sentiment tendency by adopting the improved benchmark words and the modified method of computing similarity between words and benchmark words. Their accuracy rate arrived at 98.94%.

In light of the errors of manual calibration, we extended the keywords in SAAOL by applying Yang and Wu's (2009) method and added synonymic and antonymous words in it. Eventually we proofread and revised manually the new extended keywords.

3 Our method

According to the structural characteristics of the sentence, the sentence can be divided into simple sentences and complex sentences. A simple sentence consists of a single clause which contains a subject and a predicate and stands alone as its own sentence. However, a complex sentence is the one which is linked by conjunctions or con-

[1] http://www.keenage.com.

sists of at least two or more clauses without any conjunctions in it.

A complicated sentence in structure is divided into several clauses in accordance with punctuations, such as a full stop, or a exclamatory mark, or a comma, or a semicolon, etc. We analyze the syntax of the clause by extracting the clause including SAA and the adjacent one. We extract SAAOL keywords in the selected clauses, and then analyze the grammatical relationship between the keywords and SAA.

Wang et al's research of extraction technology based on the dependency relation of Chinese sentimental elements indicated that the dependency analyzer designed by Stanford University had not showed a high rate of accuracy. And the wrong dependency relation will interfere with the subsequent parsing process seriously (Wang, et al., 2009).

Taking the above factors into consideration, we have not analyzed the dependency relation at present. Through studying abundant instances, we specialize in the structural relationship between the keywords and SAA to extract the relation patterns which have a higher occurrence frequency. In the meantime, inverse words are processed particularly. Eventually we supplemented modification of the inaccuracy of automatic segmented words and some special adverbs, such as 偏| prejudiced, 过|excessive, 太|too.

To sum up, based on the word library SAAOL and structural analysis, SAA classification procedures are as follows:

- Step 1 Extract unidentified clauses including SAA;
- Step 2 Extract the keywords in SAAOL from the clause;
- Step 3 Label the sentiment tendency of each sentiment word by using SAAOL;
- Step 4 Discriminate the positive or negative meaning of a sentence in accordance with the different relationships. If there are no keywords in the sentence, perform step 5; otherwise, discrimination is over.
- Step 5 Extract the clauses next to SAA, and identify them according to Steps 2-4. If there are no extractable clauses, mark them as SAA which will be recognized. A is for the positives, and B for the negatives.

4 Evaluation

In disambiguating sentiment ambiguous adjectives task of SemEval-2010, there are 2917 instances in test data for 14 Chinese sentiment ambiguous adjectives. According to the official result of the task, our micro average accuracy is 0.942, which puts our system in the first position among the participants.

Depending upon the answers from organizers of the task, we notice that errors occur mainly in the following cases.

Firstly, there is a key word related to SAA, but it has no such key word in our SAAOL.

For instance,

为什么我的电脑上 pf 使用率很<head>高</head>啊 | Why is the usage rate of pf so high in my computer?

"pf 使用率|The usage rate of pf" should be NSAA, but it does not exist in our SAAOL.

Secondly, the sentence itself is too complicated to be analyzed effectively in our system so far.

Thirdly, as the imperfection of SAAOL itself, there are some inevitable mistakes in it.

For instance,

这位跳水运动员的动作难度很<head>大</head> | The diver's feat is extremely difficult.

It is generally known that if the bigger the difficulty of the dive is, the better the diver's performance will be, both of which are of proportional relation. However, generally speaking, the degree of difficulty is negative. For this reason, we made a mistake in such instance.

5 Conclusions

In this paper, we describe the approach taken by our systems which participated in the disambiguating sentiment ambiguous adjectives task of SemEval-2010.

We created a new word library named SAAOL. Through gathering words from relative dictionaries, HowNet, and other network resources, we discriminated manually the positive and negative meaning, PSAA, NSAA, and inverse words in 50,000 Chinese words according to *Richard Xiao's Top 50,000 Chinese Word Frequency List*. And then we extended the keywords in SAAOL by applying Yang's (2009) method and added synonymic and antonymous words in it. Eventually the new extended keywords were proofread and revised manually.

Based on SAAOL and structural analysis, we describe a procedure to disambiguate sentiment ambiguous adjectives. Evaluation results show that this approach achieves good performance in the task.

References

Qun Liu, JianSu Li. 2002. Calculation of semantic similarity of words based on the HowNet. *The Third Chinese Lexical Semantics Workshop.* Tai Bei.

Jilin Shi, Yinggui Zhu. 2005. *A Dictionary of Positive Words.* Lexicographical Publishing House, Chengdu, Sichuan.

Su Ge Wang, An Na Yang, De Yu Li. 2009. Research on sentence sentiment classification based on Chinese sentiment word table. *Computer Engineering and Applications*, 45(24):153-155.

Qian Wang, TingTing He, et al. 2009. Research on dependency Tree-Based Chinese sentimental elements extraction, *Advances of Computational Linguistics in China,* 624-629.

Janyce Wiebe, Theresa Wilson, et al. 2004. Learning subjective language. *Computational Linguistics*, 30(3): 277-308.

Yunfang Wu, Peng Jin. SemEval-2010 task 18: Disambiguating sentiment ambiguous adjectives.

Yu bing Yang, Xian wei Wu. Improved lexical semantic tendentiousness recognition computing. 2009. *Computer Engineering and Applications,* 45(21): 91-93.

Ling Yang, Yinggui Zhu. 2005. *A Dictionary of Negative Words.* Lexicographical Publishing House, Chengdu, Sichuan.

OpAL: Applying Opinion Mining Techniques for the Disambiguation of Sentiment Ambiguous Adjectives in SemEval-2 Task 18

Alexandra Balahur
University of Alicante
Department of Software and
Computing Systems
abalahur@dlsi.ua.es

Andrés Montoyo
University of Alicante
Department of Software and
Computing Systems
montoyo@dlsi.ua.es

Abstract

The task of extracting the opinion expressed in text is challenging due to different reasons. One of them is that the same word (in particular, adjectives) can have different polarities depending on the context. This paper presents the experiments carried out by the OpAL team for the participation in the SemEval 2010 Task 18 – *Disambiguation of Sentiment Ambiguous Adjectives*. Our approach is based on three different strategies: a) the evaluation of the polarity of the whole context using an opinion mining system; b) the assessment of the polarity of the local context, given by the combinations between the closest nouns and the adjective to be classified; c) rules aiming at refining the local semantics through the spotting of modifiers. The final decision for classification is taken according to the output of the majority of these three approaches. The method used yielded good results, the OpAL system run ranking fifth among 16 in micro accuracy and sixth in macro accuracy.

1 Credits

This research has been supported by Ministerio de Ciencia e Innovación - Spanish Government (grant no. TIN2009-13391-C04-01), and Conselleria d'Educación-Generalitat Valenciana (grant no. PROMETEO/2009/119 and ACOMP/2010/288).

2 Introduction

Recent years have marked the beginning and expansion of the Social Web, in which people freely express and respond to opinion on a whole variety of topics. Moreover, at the time of taking a decision, more and more people search for information and opinions expressed on the Web on their matter of interest and base their final decision on the information found (Pang and Lee, 2008). Nevertheless, the high quantity of data that has to be analysed imposed the development of specialized Natural Language Processing (NLP) systems that automatically extract, classify and summarize the opinions available on the web on different topics. Research in this field, of *opinion mining* (sentiment analysis), has addressed the problem of extracting and classifying opinions from different perspectives and at different levels, depending on various factors. While determining the overall opinion on a movie is sufficient for taking the decision to watch it or not, when buying a product, people are interested in the individual opinions on the different product characteristics. Especially in this context, opinion mining systems are confronted with a difficult problem: the fact that the adjectives used to express opinion have different polarities depending on the characteristic they are mentioned with. For example, "high price" is negative, while "high resolution" is positive. Therefore, specialized methods have to be employed to correctly determine the contextual polarity of such words and thus accurately assign polarity to the opinion.

This is the aim of the SemEval 2010 Task 18 – Disambiguation of Sentiment Ambiguous Adjectives (Wu and Jin, 2010). In the following sections, we first present state-of-the art approaches towards polarity classification of opinions, subsequently describing our approach in the SemEval task. Finally, we present the results we obtained in the evaluation and our plans for future work.

Proceedings of the 5th International Workshop on Semantic Evaluation, ACL 2010, pages 444–447,
Uppsala, Sweden, 15-16 July 2010. ©2010 Association for Computational Linguistics

3 State of the Art

Subjectivity analysis is defined by (Wiebe, 1994) as the "linguistic expression of somebody's opinions, sentiments, emotions, evaluations, beliefs and speculations". *Sentiment analysis*, on the other hand, is defined as the task of extracting, from a text, the opinion expressed on an object (product, person, topic etc.) and classifying it as positive, negative or neutral. The task of sentiment analysis, considered a step further to subjectivity analysis, is more complex than the latter, because it involves an extra step: the classification of the retrieved opinion words according to their polarity. There are a series of techniques that were used to obtain lexicons of subjective words – e.g. the Opinion Finder lexicon (Wilson et al., 2005) and opinion words with associated polarity. (Hu and Liu, 2004) start with a set of seed adjectives ("good" and "bad") and apply synonymy and antonymy relations in WordNet. A similar approach was used in building WordNet Affect (Strapparava and Valitutti, 2004), starting from a larger set of seed affective words, classified according to the six basic categories of emotion (joy, sadness, fear, surprise, anger and disgust) and expanding the lexicon using paths in WordNet. Another related method was used in the creation of SentiWordNet (Esuli and Sebastiani, 2005), using a set of seed words whose polarity was known and expanded using gloss similarity. The collection of appraisal terms in (Whitelaw et al., 2005), the terms also have polarity assigned. MicroWNOp (Cerini et al., 2007), another lexicon containing opinion words with their associated polarity, was built on the basis of a set of terms extracted from the General Inquirer lexicon and subsequently adding all the synsets in WordNet where these words appear. Other methods built sentiment lexicons using the local context of words. (Pang et al., 2002) built a lexicon of sentiment words with associated polarity value, starting with a set of classified seed adjectives and using conjunctions ("and") disjunctions ("or", "but") to deduce orientation of new words in a corpus. (Turney, 2002) classifies words according to their polarity on the basis of the idea that terms with similar orientation tend to co-occur in documents. Thus, the author computes the Pointwise Mutual Information score between seed words and new words on the basis of the number of AltaVista hits returned when querying the seed word and the word to be classified with the "NEAR" operator. In our work in (Balahur and Montoyo, 2008a), we compute the polarity of new words using "polarity anchors" (words whose polarity is known beforehand) and Normalized Google Distance (Cilibrasi and Vitanyi, 2006) scores. Another approach that uses the polarity of the local context for computing word polarity is (Popescu and Etzioni, 2005), who use a weighting function of the words around the context to be classified.

4 The OpAL system at SemEval 2010 Task 18

In the SemEval 2010 Task 18, the participants were given a set of contexts in Chinese, in which 14 dynamic sentiment ambiguous adjectives are selected. They are: 大|big, 小|small, 多|many, 少|few, 高|high, 低|low, 厚|thick, 薄|thin, 深|deep, 浅|shallow, 重|heavy, 轻|light, 巨大|huge, 重大|grave. The task was to automatically classify the polarity of these adjectives, i.e. to detect whether their sense in the context is positive or negative. The contexts were given in two forms: as plain text, in which the adjective to be classified was marked; in the second for, the text was tokenized and the tokens were tagged with part of speech (POS). There was no training set provided.

Our approach uses a set of opinion mining resources and an opinion mining system that is implemented to work for English. This is why, the first step we took in our approach was to translate the given contexts into English using the Google Translator1. In order to perform this task, we first split the initial file into 10 smaller files, using a specialized program – GSplit32. The OpAL adjective polarity disambiguation system combines supervised methods with unsupervised ones. In order to judge the polarity of the adjectives, it uses three types of judgments. The first one is the general polarity of the context, determined by our in-house opinion mining system - based on SVM machine learning on the NTCIR data and the EmotiBlog (Boldrini et al., 2009) annotations and different subjectivity, opinion and emotion lexica (Opinion Finder, MicroWordNet Opinion, General Inquirer, WordNet Affect, emotion triggers (Balahur and Montoyo, 2008b). The second one is the local polarity, given by the highest number of results obtained when issuing queries containing the closest noun with the adjective to be disambiguated followed by the conjunction "AND" and a predefined set of 6 adjectives whose polarity is non-

[1] http://translate.google.com/
[2] www.gdgsoft.com/gsplit/

ambiguous – 3 positive - "positive", "beautiful", "good" and 3 negative – "negative", "ugly", "bad". An example of such queries is "price high and good". The third component is made up of rules, depending on the presence of specific modifiers in a window of 4 words before the adjective. The final verdict is given based on the vote given by the majority of the three components, explained in detail in the next sections:

4.1 The OpAL opinion mining component

First, we process each context using Minipar[3]. We compute, for each word in a sentence, a series of features, computed from the NTCIR 7 data and the EmotiBlog annotations. These words are used to compute vectors of features for each of the individual contexts:

- the part of speech (POS)
- opinionatedness/intensity - if the word is annotated as opinion word, its polarity, i.e. 1 and -1 if the word is positive or negative, respectively and 0 if it is not an opinion word, its intensity (1, 2 or 3) and 0 if it is not a subjective word
- syntactic relatedness with other opinion word – if it is directly dependent of an opinion word or modifier (0 or 1), plus the polarity/intensity and emotion of this word (0 for all the components otherwise)
- role in 2-word, 3-word, 4-word and sentence annotations: opinionatedness, intensity and emotion of the other words contained in the annotation, direct dependency relations with them if they exist and 0 otherwise.

We add to the opinion words annotated in EmotiBlog the list of opinion words found in the Opinion Finder, Opinion Finder, MicroWordNet Opinion, General Inquirer, WordNet Affect, emotion triggers lexical resources. We train the model using the SVM SMO implementation in Weka4.

4.2 Assessing local polarity using Google queries

This approach aimed at determining the polarity of the context immediately surrounding the adjective to be classified. To that aim, we constructed queries using the noun found before the adjective in the context given, and issued six different queries on Google, together with six predefined adjectives whose polarity is known (3 positive - "positive", "beautiful", "good" and 3 negative – "negative", "ugly", "bad"). The form of the queries was "noun+adjective+AND+predefined adjective". The local polarity was considered as the one for which the query issued the highest number of total results (total number of results for the 3 queries corresponding to the positive adjectives or to the negative adjectives, respectively).

4.3 Modifier rules for contextual polarity

This rule accounts for the original, most frequently used polarity of the given adjectives (e.g. *high* is *positive*, *low* is *negative)*. For each of them, we define its default polarity. Subsequently, we determine whether in the window of 4 words around the adjective there are any modifiers (valence shifters). If this is the case, and they have an opposite value of polarity, the adjective is assigned a polarity value opposite from its default one (e.g. *too high* is *negative)*. We employ a list of 82 positive and 87 negative valence shifters.

5 Evaluation

Table 1 and Table 2 present the results obtained by the OpAL system in the SemEval 2010 Task 18 competition. The system ranked fifth, with a Micro accuracy of 0.76037 and sixth, with a Macro accuracy of 0.7037.

System name	Micro accuracy
98-35_result	0.942064
437-381_HITSZ_CITYU_Task18_Run1.key	0.936236
437-380_HITSZ_CITYU_Task18_Run2.key	0.93315
53-211_dsaa	0.880699
186-325_OpAL_results.txt	0.76037
291-389_submission4.txt	0.724717
291-388_submission3.txt	0.715461
437-382_HITSZ_CITYU_Task18_Run3	0.665752

Table 1: Results - top 8 runs (micro accuracy)

System name	Macro accuracy
437-380_HITSZ_CITYU_Task18_Run2.key	0.957881
437-381_HITSZ_CITYU_Task18_Run1.key	0.953238
98-35_result	0.929308
53-211_dsaa	0.861964

[3] http://webdocs.cs.ualberta.ca/~lindek/minipar.htm
[4] http://www.cs.waikato.ac.nz/ml/weka/

291-388_submission3.txt	0.755387
186-325_OpAL_results.txt	0.703777
291-389_submission4.txt	0.698037
460383_New_Task18_ Chinese_test_pos_QiuLikun_R.rar	0.695448

Table 2: Results – top 8 runs (macro accuracy)

Since the gold standard was not provided, we were not able to perform an exhaustive analysis of the errors. However, from a random inspection of the system results, we could see that a large number of errors was due to the translation – through which modifiers are placed far from the word they determine or the words are not translated with their best equivalent.

6 Conclusions and future work

In this article we presented our approach towards the disambiguation of polarity ambiguous adjectives depending on the context in which they appear. The OpAL system's run was based on three subcomponents working in English – one assessing the overall polarity of the context using an opinion mining system, the second assessing the local polarity using Google queries formed by expressions containing the noun present in the context before the adjective to be classified and the third one evaluating contextual polarity based on the adjective's default value and the modifiers around it. The final output is based on the vote given by the majority of the three components. The approach had a good performance, the OpAL system run ranking fifth among 16 runs. Future work includes the separate evaluation of the three components and their combination in a unique approach, using machine learning, as well as a thorough assessment of errors that are due to translation.

References

Balahur, A. and Montoyo, A. 2008a. *A feature-driven approach to opinion mining and classification.* In Proceedings of the NLPKE 2008.

Balahur, A. and Montoyo, A. 2008b. *Applying a culture dependent emotion triggers database for text valence and emotion classification.* Procesamiento del Lenguaje Natural, 40(40).

Boldrini, E., Balahur, A., Martínez-Barco, P., and Montoyo, A. 2009. *EmotiBlog: an annotation scheme for emotion detection and analysis in non-traditional textual genres.* In Proceedings of the 5th International Conference on Data Mining (DMIN 2009).

Cerini, S., Compagnoni, V., Demontis, A., Formentelli, M., and Gandini, G. 2007. *Micro-WNOp: A gold standard for the evaluation of automatically compiled lexical resources for opinion mining.*

Cilibrasi, D. and Vitanyi, P. 2006. *Automatic Meaning Discovery Using Google.* IEEE Journal of Transactions on Knowledge and Data Engineering.

Esuli, A. and Sebastiani, F. 2006. *SentiWordNet: a publicly available resource for opinion mining.* In Proceedings of the 6th International Conference on Language Resources and Evaluation.

Hu, M. and Liu, B. 2004. *Mining Opinion Features in Customer Reviews.* In Proceedings of Nineteenth National Conference on Artificial Intellgience AAAI-2004.

Pang, B. and Lee, L. 2008. *Opinion mining and sentiment analysis.* Foundations and Trends in Information Retrieval 2(1-2), pp. 1–135, 2008

Pang, B., Lee, L., and Vaithyanathan, S. 2002. *Thumbs up? Sentiment classification using machine learning techniques.* In Proceedings of EMNLP-02, the Conference on Empirical Methods in Natural Language Processing.

Popescu, A. M. and Etzioni, O. 2005. *Extracting product features and opinions from reviews.* In In Proceedings of HLTEMNLP 2005.

Stone, P., Dumphy, D. C., Smith, M. S., and Ogilvie, D. M. 1966. *The General Inquirer: A Computer Approach to Content Analysis.* The MIT Press.

Strapparava, C. and Valitutti, A. 2004.*WordNet-Affect: an affective extension of WordNet.* In Proceedings of the 4th International Conference on Language Resources and Evaluation (LREC 2004).

Turney, P. 2002. *Thumbs up or thumbs down? Semantic orientation applied to unsupervised classification of reviews.* In Proceedings 40th Annual Meeting of the Association for Computational Linguistics.

Whitelaw, C., Garg, N., and Argamon, S. 2005. *Using appraisal groups for sentiment analysis.* In Proceedings of the CIKM 2005.

Wiebe, J. (1994). *Tracking point of view in narrative.* Computational Linguistics, 20.

Wilson, T., Wiebe, J., and Hoffmann, P. 2005. *Recognizing contextual polarity in phrase-level sentiment analysis.* In Proceedings of HLT-EMNLP 2005.

Wu, Y., Jin, P. 2010. *SemEval-2010 Task 18: Disambiguating Sentiment Ambiguous Adjectives.* In Proceedings of the SemEval 2010 Workshop, ACL 2010.

HITSZ_CITYU: Combine Collocation, Context Words and Neighboring Sentence Sentiment in Sentiment Adjectives Disambiguation

Ruifeng Xu[1,2], **Jun Xu**[1]
[1]Harbin Institute of Technology, Shenzhen Campus, China
xuruifeng@hitsz.edu.cn
hit.xujun@gmail.com

Chunyu Kit[2]
[2]City University of Hong Kong, Hong Kong
ctckit@cityu.edu.hk

Abstract

This paper presents the HIT_CITYU systems in Semeval-2 Task 18, namely, disambiguating sentiment ambiguous adjectives. The baseline system (HITSZ_CITYU_3) incorporates bi-gram and n-gram collocations of sentiment adjectives, and other context words as features in a one-class Support Vector Machine (SVM) classifier. To enhance the baseline system, collocation set expansion and characteristics learning based on word similarity and semi-supervised learning are investigated, respectively. The final system (HITSZ_CITYU_1/2) combines collocations, context words and neighboring sentence sentiment in a two-class SVM classifier to determine the polarity of sentiment adjectives. The final systems achieved 0.957 and 0.953 (ranked 1st and 2nd) macro accuracy, and 0.936 and 0.933 (ranked 2nd and 3rd) micro accuracy, respectively.

1 Introduction

Sentiment analysis is always puzzled by the context-dependent sentiment words that one word brings positive, neutral or negative meanings in different contexts. Hatzivassiloglou and Mckeown (1997) predicated the polarity of adjectives by using the pairs of adjectives linked by consecutive or negation conjunctions. Turney and Littman (2003) determined the polarity of sentiment words by estimating the point-wise mutual information between sentiment words and a set of seed words with strong polarity. Andreevskaia and Bergler (2006) used a Sentiment Tag Extraction Program to extract sentiment-bearing adjectives from WordNet. Esuli and Sebasian (2006) studied the context-dependent sentiment words in WordNet but ignored the instances in real context. Wu et al. (2008) applied collocation plus a SVM classifier in Chinese sentiment adjectives disambiguation. Xu et al. (2008) proposed a semi-supervised learning algorithm to learn new sentiment word and their context-dependent characteristics.

Semeval-2 Task 18 is designed to provide a common framework and dataset for evaluating the disambiguation techniques for Chinese sentiment adjectives. The HITSZ_CITYU group submitted three runs corresponding to one baseline system and one improved systems (two runs). The baseline system (HITSZ_CITYU_3) is based on collocations between sentiment words and their targets as well as their context words. For the ambiguous adjectives, 412 positive and 191 negative collocations are built from a 100-million-word corpus as the seed collocation set. Using the context words of seed collocations as features, a one-class SVM classifier is trained in the baseline system. Using HowNet-based word similarity as clue, the seed collocations are expanded to improve the coverage of collocation-based technique. Furthermore, a semi-supervised learning algorithm is developed to learn new collocations between sentiment words and their targets from raw corpus. Finally, the inner sentence features, such as collocations and context words, and the inter sentence features, i.e. neighboring sentence sentiments, are incorporated to determine the polarity of ambiguous adjectives. The improved systems (HITSZ_CITYU_1/2) achieved 0.957 and 0.953 macro accuracy (ranked 1st and 2nd) and 0.936 and 0.933 micro accuracy (ranked 2nd and 3rd), respectively. This result shows that collocation, context-words and neighboring sentence sentiment are effective in sentiment adjectives disambiguation.

The rest of this paper is organized as follows. Section 2 presents the collocation extraction subsystem based on lexical statistics. Section 3

Proceedings of the 5th International Workshop on Semantic Evaluation, ACL 2010, pages 448–451,
Uppsala, Sweden, 15-16 July 2010.

presents the baseline system and Section 4 presents the improved systems. The experiment results are given in Section 5 and finally, Section 6 concludes.

2 Collocation Extraction

A lexical statistics-based collocation extraction subsystem is developed to identify both the bi-gram and n-gram collocations of sentiment adjectives. This subsystem is based on our previous research on Chinese collocation extraction. It recognizes the co-occurring words of a headword as collocations which have co-occurrence frequency significance among all co-occurring words and co-occurrence position significance among all co-occurring positions.

For a sentiment adjective, noted as w_{head}, any word within the [-5,+5] context window is a co-word, denoted as w_{co-i} for $1 \leq i \leq k$, where k is the total number of different co-words of w_{head}.

BI-Strength(w_{head},w_{co-i}) between a head word w_{head} and a co-word w_{co-i} ($i=1$, *to* k) is designed to measure the co-occurrence frequency significance as follows:

$$BI-Strength(w_{head}, w_{co-i}) = 0.5 \cdot \frac{f(w_{head} w_{co-i}) - \overline{f(w_{head})}}{f_{\max}(w_{head}) - f_{\min}(w_{head})} + 0.5 \cdot \frac{f(w_{head} w_{co-i}) - \overline{f(w_{co-i})}}{f_{\max}(w_{co-i}) - f_{\min}(w_{co-i})} \quad (1)$$

where, $f_{max}(w_{head})$, $f_{min}(w_{head})$ and $\overline{f(w_{head})}$ are the highest, lowest and average co-occurrence frequencies among all the co-words of w_{head}, respectively; $f_{max}(w_{co-i})$, $f_{min}(w_{coi})$ and $\overline{f(w_{co-i})}$ are respectively the highest, lowest and average co-occurrence frequencies of the co-words for w_{co-i}. The value of *BI-Strength*(w_{head} w_{co-j}) ranges from -1 to 1, and a larger value means a stronger association. Suppose $f(w_{head}, w_{co-i}, m)$ is the frequency that w_{co-i} co-occurs with w_{head} at position m($-5<=m<=5$). The *BI-Spread*(w_{head},w_{co-i}) is designed to characterizes the significance that w_{co-i} around w_{head} at neighbouring places as follows:

$$BI-Spread(w_{head}, w_{co-i}) = \frac{\sum_{m=-5}^{5} | f(w_{head}, w_{co-i}, m) - \overline{f(w_{head}, w_{co-i})} |}{\sum_{m=-5}^{5} f(w_{head}, w_{co-i}, m)} \quad (2)$$

where, $\overline{f(w_{head}, w_{co-i})}$, $f_{max}(w_{head}, w_{co-i})$, and f_{min} ($w_{hea,d} w_{co-i}$) are the average, highest, and lowest co-occurrence frequencies among all 10 positions, respectively. The value of *BI-Spread*(w_{head}, w_{co-i}) ranges from 0 to 1. A larger value means that w_{head} and w_{co-i} tend to co-occur in one or two positions.

The word pairs satisfying, (1) *BI-Strength*(w_{head} w_{co-j})>K_0 and (2) *BI-Spread*(w_{head}, w_{co-i})>U0, are extracted as bi-gram collocations, where K_0 and U_0 are empirical threshold.

Based on the extracted bi-gram collocations, the appearance of each co-word in each position around w_{head} is analyzed. For each of the possible relative distances from w_{head}, only words occupying the position with a probability greater than a given threshold T are kept. Finally, the adjacent words satisfying the threshold requirement are combined as n-gram collocations.

3 The Baseline System

The baseline system incorporates collocation and context words as features in a one-class SVM classifier. It consists of two steps:

STEP 1: To match a test instance containing seed collocation set. If the instance cannot be matched by any collocations, go to **STEP 2**.

STEP 2: Use a trained classifier to indentify the sentiment of the word.

The collocations of 14 testing sentiment adjectives are extracted from a 100-million-word corpus. Collocations with obvious and consistent sentiment are manually identified. 412 positive and 191 negative collocations are established as the seed collocation set.

We think that the polarity of a word can be determined by exploiting the association of its co-occurring words in sentence. We assume that, the two instances of an ambiguous sentiment adjectives that have similar neighboring nouns may have the same polarity. Gamon and Aue (2005) made an assumption to label sentiment terms.

We extract 13,859 sentences containing collocations between negative adjective and targets in seed collocation set or collocations between ambiguous adjective and negative modifier (such as 过于 *too*) as the training data. These sentences are assume negative. A single-class classifier is then trained to recognize negative sentences. Three types of features are used:

(1) Context features include bag of words within context in window of [-5, +5]
(2) Collocation features contain bi-grams in window [-5,+5]
(3) Collocation features contain n-grams in window [-5,+5]

In our research, SVM with linear kernel is employed and the open source SVM package – LIBSVM is selected for the implementation.

4 The Improved System

The preliminary experiment shows that the baseline system is not satisfactory, especially the coverage is low. It is observed that the seed collocation set covers 17.54% of sentences containing the ambiguous adjectives while the collocations between adjective and negative modifier covers only 11.28%. Therefore, we expand the sentiment adjective-target collocation set based on word similarity and a semi-supervised learning algorithm orderly. We then incorporate both inner-sentence features (collocations, context words, etc.) and inter-sentence features in the improved systems for sentiment adjectives disambiguation.

4.1 Collocation Set Expansion based on Word Similarity

First, we expand the seed collocation set on the target side. The words strongly similar to known targets are identified by using a word similarity calculation package, provided by HowNet (a Chinese thesaurus). Once these words co-occur with adjective within a context window more often than a threshold, they are appended to seed collocation set. For example, "低-技能(*low capacity*)" is expanded from a seed collocation "低-能力 (*low capacity*)".

Second, we manually identify the words having the same "trend" as the testing adjectives. For example, "上升 *increase*" is selected as a same-trend word of "高 *high*". The collocations of "上升" are extracted from corpus. Its collocated targets with confident and consistent sentiment are appended to the sentiment collocation set of "高" if they co-occurred with "高" more than a threshold. In this way, some low-frequency sentiment collocation can be obtained.

4.2 Semi-supervised Learning of Sentiment Collocations

A semi-supervised learning algorithm is developed to further expand the collocation seed set, which is described as follows. (It is revised based on our previous research (Xu et al. 2008). The basic assumption here is that, the sentiment of a sentence having ambiguous adjectives can be estimated based on the sentiment of its neighboring sentences.

Input: Raw training corpus, labeled as S_u,

Step 1. The sentences holding strong polarities are recognized from S_u which satisfies any two of following requirements, (1) contains known context-free sentiment word (CFSW); (2) contains more than three known context-dependent sentiment words (CDSW); (3) contains collocations between degree adverbs and known CDSWs; (4) contains collocations between degree adverbs and opinion operators (the verbs indicate a opinion operation, such as 称赞 *praise*); (5) contains known opinion indicator and known CDSWs.

Step 2. Identify the strong non-opinionated sentences in S_u. The sentences satisfying all of following four conditions are recognized as non-opinionated ones, (1) have no known sentiment words; (2) have no known opinion operators; (3) have no known degree adverbs and (4) have no known opinion indicators.

Step 3. Identify the opinion indicators in the rest sentences. Determine their polarities if possible and mark the conjunction (e.g.和 *and*) or negation relationship (e.g.但 but) in the sentences.

Step 4. Match the CFSWs and known CDSWs in S_u. The polarities of CFSWs are assigned based on sentiment lexicon.

Step 5. If a CDSW occurs in a sentence with certain orientations which is determined by the opinion indicators, its polarity is assigned as the value suggested. If a CDSW co-occur with a seed collocated target, it polarity is assigned according to the seed sentiment collocation set. Otherwise, if a CDSW co-occur with a CFSW in the same sentence, or the neighboring continual or compound sentence, the polarity of CDSW is assigned as the same as CFSW, or the reversed polarity if a negation indicator is detected.

Step 6. Update the polarity scores of CDSWs in the target set by using the cases where the polarity is determined in Step 5.

Step 7. Determine the polarities of CDSWs in the undetermined sentences. Suppose S_i is a sentence and the polarity scores of all its CFSWs and CDSWs are known, its polarity, labeled as $Plo(S_i)$, is estimated by using the polarity scores of all of the opinion words in this sentence, viz.:

$$Plo(Si) = \sum \begin{matrix} P\_pos(CFSW) - P\_neg(CFSW) \\ + P\_pos(CDSW) - P\_neg(CDSW) \end{matrix} \quad (3)$$

A large value (>0) of $Plo(s_i)$ implies that s_i tends to be positive, and vice versa.

Step 8. If the sentence polarity cannot be determined by its components, we use the polarity of its neighboring sentences s_{j-1} and s_{j+1}, labeled as $Plo(s_{j-1})$ and $Plo(s_{j+1})$, respectively, to help determine $Plo(s_j)$, viz.:

$$Plo(s_j) = 0.5 \cdot Plo(s_{j-1}) + Plo*(s_j) + 0.5 \cdot Plo(s_{j+1}) \quad (4)$$

where, $Plo*(s_j)$ is the polarity score of S_j (Following Equation 3) but ignore the contribution of testing adjectives while 0.5 are empirical weights.

Step 9. After all of the polarities of known CDSWs in the training data are determined, update the collocation set by identifying co-occurred pairs with consistent sentiment.
Step 10. Repeat Step 5 to Step 9 to re-estimate the sentiment of CDSWs and expand the collocation set, until the collocation set converge.

In this way, the seed collocation set is further expanded and their sentiment characteristics are obtained.

4.3 Sentiment Adjectives Classifier

We incorporate the following 8 groups of features in a linear-kernel two-class SVM classifier to classify the sentences with sentiment adjectives into positive or negative:

(1) The presence of known positive/negative opinion indicator and opinion operator
(2) The presence of known positive/negative CFSW
(3) The presence of known positive/negative CDSW(exclude the testing adjectives)
(4) The presence of known positive/negative adjective-target bi-gram collocations
(5) The presence of known positive/negative adjective-target n-gram collocations
(6) The coverage of context words surrounding the adjectives in the context words in training positive/negative sentences
(7) The sentiment of -1 sentence
(8) The sentiment of +1 sentence

The classifier is trained by using the sentences with determined sentiment which is obtained in the semi-supervised learning stage.

5 Evaluations and Conclusion

The ACL-SEMEVAL task 18 testing dataset contains 14 ambiguous adjectives and 2,917 instances. HITSZ_CITYU group submitted three runs. Run-1 and Run-2 are two runs corresponding to the improved system and Run-3 is the baseline system. The achieved performances are listed in Table 1.

Run ID	Marco Accuracy	Micro Accuracy
1	0.953	0.936
2	0.957	0.933
3(baseline)	0.629	0.665

Table 1: Performance of HITSZ_CITYU Runs

It is observed that the improved systems achieve promising results which is obviously higher than the baseline. They are ranked 1st and 2nd in Macro Accuracy evaluation and 2nd and 3rd in Micro Accuracy evaluation among 16 submitted runs, respectively.

6 Conclusion

In this paper, we proposed similarity-based and semi-supervised based methods to expand the adjective-target seed collocation set. Meanwhile, we incorporate both inner-sentence (collocations and context words) and inter-sentence features in a two-class SVM classifier for the disambiguation of sentiment adjectives. The achieved promising results show the effectiveness of collocation features, context words features and sentiment of neighboring sentences. Furthermore, we found that the neighboring sentence sentiments are important features for the disambiguation of sentiment ambiguous adjectives, which is obviously different from the traditional word sense disambiguation that emphasize the inner-sentence features.

References

Andreevskaia, A. and Bergler, S. 2006. Mining WordNet for fuzzy sentiment: Sentiment tag extraction from WordNet glosses. In *Proceedings of EACL 2006*, pp. 209-216

Esuli, A. and Sebastian, F. 2006. SENTIWORDNET: A publicly available lexical resource for opinion mining. In *Proceeding of LREC 2006*, pp. 417-422.

Hatzivassiloglou, V. and McKeown, K. R. 1997. Predicting the semantic orientation of adjectives. In *Proceeding of ACL 1997,* pp.174-181

Michael Gamon and Anthony Aue. 2005. Automatic identification of sentiment vocabulary: Exploiting low association with known sentiment terms. In *Proceedings of the ACL05 Workshop on Feature Engineering for Machine Learning in Natural Language Processing*, pp.57-64

Ruifeng Xu, Kam-Fai Wong et al. 2008. Learning Knowledge from Relevant Webpage for Opinion Analysis, in *Proceedings of 2008 IEEE / WIC / ACM Int. Conf. Web Intelligence*, pp. 307-313

Turney, P. D. and Littman, M. L. 2003. Measuring praise and criticism: Inference of semantic orientation from association. ACM Transactions on Information Systems, vol. 21, no. 4, pp.315-346

Yunfang Wu, Miao Wang and Peng Jin. 2008. Disambiguating sentiment ambiguous adjectives, In *Proceedings of Int. Conf. on Natural Language Processing and Knowledge Engineering 2008*, pp. 1-8

Author Index